Scotland

THE ROUGH GUIDE

There are more than eighty Rough Guide titles covering
destinations from Amsterdam to Zimbabwe

Forthcoming titles include
China • Corfu • Jamaica • New Zealand • South Africa
Southwest USA • Vienna

Rough Guide Reference Series
Classical Music • The Internet • Jazz • Opera • Rock Music • World Music

Rough Guide Phrasebooks
Czech • French • German • Greek • Indonesian • Italian • Mandarin Chinese
Mexican Spanish • Polish • Portuguese • Spanish • Thai • Turkish

Rough Guides on the Internet
http://www.roughguides.com/
http://www.hotwired.com/rough

Rough Guide Credits

Text editor:	Catherine McHale
Series editor:	Mark Ellingham
Editorial:	Martin Dunford, Jonathan Buckley, Samantha Cook, Jo Mead, Alison Cowan, Amanda Tomlin, Lemisse Al-Hafidh, Vivienne Heller, Paul Gray, Alan Spicer (Online UK), Andrew Rosenberg (Online US)
Production:	Susanne Hillen, Andy Hilliard, Melissa Flack, Judy Pang, Link Hall, Nicola Williamson, David Callier, Helen Ostick
Finance:	John Fisher, Celia Crowley, Catherine Gillespie
Marketing and Publicity:	Richard Trillo, Simon Carloss (UK), Jean-Marie Kelly, Jeff Kaye (US)
Administration:	Tania Hummel

Acknowledgements

Caledonian MacBrayne ferries; Historic Scotland; the National Trust for Scotland; the Scottish Tourist Board, and everyone at the regional tourist boards; the Scottish Youth Hostel Association and all the hostels throughout Scotland – in particular, the Glasgow, Torridon, Lanark, Ullapool, Loch Ness, Eglinton, Pitlochry, Perth, Melrose, Armadale and Islay hostels for providing lots of useful information. Thanks also to Gareth Nash for proofreading; to Judy Pang for typesetting; to Melissa Flack and David Callier for the maps.

The authors would like to thank: André Klein (Kylesku); Ewen Denney (Edinburgh); Mrs A Cameron (Dingwall); Michael Lavelle and Chrissy Boyd (Ullapool); Christopher Thornton of the National Trust for Scotland; Stuart Maclean of Historic Scotland; SYHA wardens and assistants across the Highlands, especially Durness, Ullapool, Torridon, Loch Ness and Carn Deag for their advice and hospitality; Mr & Mrs M Haycox (Cromarty); the helpful staff of the Highlands regional tourist offices; Polyanna Chapman (Aberdeen); Orkney Tourist Board; Shetland Islands Tourism; Brian Smith at Shetland Archives; Tracy Bonham; George Hay; Kevin Bruce and all at Nether Newbigging; Janet McLaren and Fiona Martin at Grampian; Highlands and Aberdeen Tourism; Toni MacPherson at Dundee Tourism; Cathy, for her patience; Dan Smith; Gordon McCulloch of the Edinburgh Tourist Board; Ian Drum.

Finally, thanks to the following readers who have written in with their comments, information and suggestions: Alan Baker, Nicole Brüggemann, Susan Buck, Roger Butler, Mrs A Cameron, Christine & Malcolm Clark, Nancy O'DeMille, Anthony Duffy, Sean Dawson, Dr Osman Durrani, D W Emslie, Myfanwy Ford, Maurice Frank, Olaf Furniss, Brenda Gamlin, May Glendenning, Broderick Haldane, Andy & Sabina Holt-Brooke, Helene Hubers, John & Diane Jackson, Philip Le Vesconte, Marjory McCleery, Patrick Marks, Prof S Medlik, Robyn Moore, Helen Mycroft, Damain O'Brien, Chris Rix, Lynee Sinclair, Richard Smith, Catherine Spence, Gary Spinks, Gary Willis, Keith Wilson, Richard & Judith Winwood, Catherine Zawadski.

This second edition published in 1996 by Rough Guides Ltd, 1 Mercer Street, London WC2H 9QJ.

Reprinted in July 1996 and February 1997.

Distributed by the Penguin Group:
Penguin Books Ltd, 27 Wrights Lane, London W8 5TZ
Penguin Books USA Inc., 375 Hudson Street, New York 10014, USA
Penguin Books Australia Ltd, 487 Maroondah Highway, PO Box 257, Ringwood, Victoria 3134, Australia Penguin Books Canada Ltd, 10 Alcorn Avenue, Toronto, Ontario M4V 1E4, Canada
Penguin Books (NZ) Ltd, 182–190 Wairau Road, Auckland 10, New Zealand

Typeset in Linotron Univers and Century Old Style to an original design by Andrew Oliver.

Printed in the UK by Cox & Wyman Ltd, Reading, Berks.
Illustrations in Part One and Part Three by Ed Briant.
Basics and Contexts illustrations by Henry Iles.

Mapping is based upon the Ordnance Survey maps with the permission of the Controller of Her Majesty's Stationery Office, © Crown copyright.

© Rough Guides 1994, 1996

576pp. Includes index

A catalogue record for this book is available from the British Library.

ISBN 1-85828-166-0

Scotland

THE ROUGH GUIDE

Written and researched by
**Dave Abram, Donald Greig, Alastair Hamilton,
Rob Humphreys, Phil Lee, Gordon McLachlan,
Mike Parker, Sophie Pragnell, Helena Smith,
Tania Smith and Julian Ward**

Additional contributions by
Hamish Brown, Colin Irwin, Alan McIntosh, Sally Roy,
James D Scarlett and Mark Whatmore

THE ROUGH GUIDES

LIST OF MAPS

Scotland	vi	Oban	267
Chapter divisions of this guide	1	Mull	271
The Edinburgh area	47	Kilmartin	282
Edinburgh	50	Arran	289
Royal Mile	62	Islay	293
Southern Scotland	108	Skye and the Western Isles	299
Dumfries	136	Skye and the Small Isles	301
Ayr	150	Lewis and Harris	316
Glasgow and the Clyde	158	Unist, Benbecula and Barra	329
Glasgow	164	Northeast Scotland	334
The Greater Glasgow area	181	Dundee	339
Central Scotland	202	Aberdeen	360
Stirling	207	The Highlands	392
St Andrews	235	Inverness	397
Perth	243	Orkney Islands	464
Argyll	256	Shetland Islands	485

MAP SYMBOLS

═══ Motorway		♟	Museum
══ Main road		⚔	Battlefield
── Minor road		⚑	Campsite
▬▬ Railway		▲	Mountain peak
── Ferry route		↯	Waterfall
── Waterway		ⓘ	Tourist Office
▬▪▬ National border		⊠	Post Office
─── Chapter division boundary		⊠	Gate
─── Wall		■	Building
✈ Airport		⊞	Church
🏛 Stately home		⁺₊⁺	Cemetery
♜ Castle			Park
⌂ Abbey			Forest
∴ Ruins			Beach

CONTENTS

Introduction vii

PART ONE   BASICS   1

Getting There from England, Ireland and Europe 3
Getting There from North America 7
Getting There from Australia and New Zealand 11
Visas, Customs Regulations and Tax 14
Money, Banks and Costs 15
Insurance, Health and Emergencies 16
Information and Maps 19
Getting Around 21
Accommodation 27

Food and Drink 29
Post and Phones 32
Opening Hours and Holidays 33
Sights, Museums and Monuments 34
The Media 35
Annual Events 36
Sport and Outdoor Pursuits 38
Travellers with Disabilities 41
Directory 42

PART TWO   THE GUIDE   45

- 1 EDINBURGH 47
- 2 SOUTHERN SCOTLAND 107
- 3 GLASGOW AND THE CLYDE 157
- 4 CENTRAL SCOTLAND 201
- 5 ARGYLL 256
- 6 SKYE AND THE WESTERN ISLES 298
- 7 NORTHEAST SCOTLAND 333
- 8 THE HIGHLANDS 344
- 9 ORKNEY AND SHETLAND 461

PART THREE   CONTEXTS   511

The Historical Framework 513
The Wildlife of Scotland 527
The Architecture of Scotland 532
The Music of Scotland 539

Books 544
Language 551
A Scottish Glossary 555

Index 556

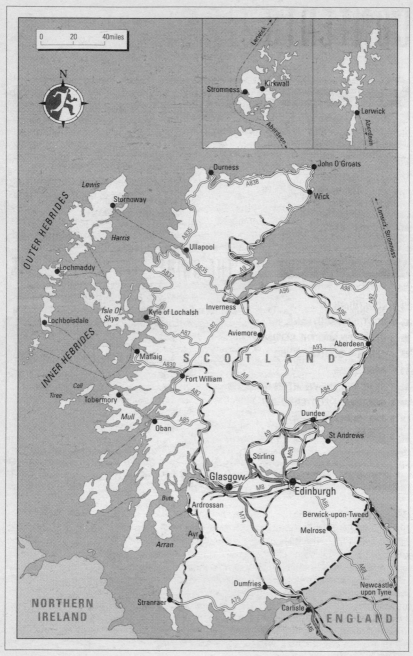

INTRODUCTION

Scotland is, quite simply, despite an abysmal climate, a wonderfully rewarding and diverse place to travel. The main urban centres of Edinburgh and
Glasgow are two of Britain's most complex and intriguing cities, perfectly
complementing each other and only 30 miles apart; and the countryside
more than lives up to all the praise that has been heaped upon it – whether you're
visiting the wooded dales that weave across the south of the country, touring the
supremely remote lochs, glens and mountains of the Highlands, or hopping the
sea-battered islands that arc around its west and north coasts.

For centuries Scotland was a divided nation, with Gaelic-speaking, cattle-raising
clans concentrated to the north and west, and English-speaking Scots, distinguished by their Norman-style feudal loyalties and allegiances, dominant to the
south and east. These two linguistically distinct Scotlands developed on separate
lines, their mutually antagonistic populations creating the first of several overlapping sources of national tension. After the Reformation, religion became another
flashpoint, not just between Catholic and Protestant, but amongst a host of reform-
ist sects, and, later still, industrialization divided the rural from the urban, generating the class-conscious, socialist-minded cities of central and eastern Scotland.

In the background there has always been Scotland's problematic relationship
with England. In 1707, the Act of Union united the English and Scottish parliaments, ending centuries of political strife, and shortly afterwards, in 1745, the failure of Bonnie Prince Charlie's Jacobite rebellion gave the English and their
Scottish allies the opportunity to bring the Gaels to heel. However, the union only
partly integrated the two nations, and Scotland's relationship with its more powerful neighbour remains an anomalous one. Although they retain a separate legal
and educational system, the Scots have no regional assembly, few autonomous
powers, and are effectively governed from London. Since 1979, English voters
have kept the Conservative Party in power, while the huge majority of Scots have
consistently favoured the opposition – the Liberal Democrats in the Highlands
and islands, and the Labour Party in the cities. This has fuelled renewed ill-will
towards the union, with many Scots feeling resentful and disenfranchized. The
attitude in England, meanwhile, is one that is ready to recognize – indeed patron-
ize – the harmless symbols of Scottish nationhood), while being very reluctant to
hand over any real power or independence to the Scottish people.

Where to go

If you're short of time, you can still sample a little of everything, beginning with
either – or both – of the country's great cities, Glasgow and Edinburgh, before
moving on up the west coast, where stunning land and seascapes are studded
with reminders of Scotland's long and fractious history.

Travelling around mainland Scotland is comparatively easy: the road network
reaches almost every corner of the country, the trains serve the major towns and
an extensive bus system links all but the most remote villages. Hikers are well
served, too: all of the country's parks and most of the wilderness areas are criss-
crossed by popular walking trails. Without your own transport, it's more difficult to
move around the islands, where, especially on the Western Isles, bus services

deteriorate and are often impossible to coordinate with ferry sailing times. Almost all of the ferries are operated by *Caledonian MacBrayne*, who provide a splendidly punctual and efficient service, along with various island-hopping discount tickets to reduce the substantial costs of ferry travel. Reasonably priced accommodation is available almost everywhere, at its least expensive (and sometimes grimmest) in the youth hostels, and more popularly in hundreds of family-run B&Bs.

The majority of visitors begin their tour of Scotland in the capital, **Edinburgh**, a handsome and ancient town famous for its magnificent castle and the Palace of Holyroodhouse, as well as for the excellence of its museums – not to mention the **Edinburgh International Festival**, a world-acclaimed arts shindig held for three weeks, in August and early September. From here it's just a short journey west to the capital's rival, lively **Glasgow**, a sprawling industrial metropolis that was once the second city of the British Empire. In recent years, though its industrial base remains in decline, Glasgow has done much to improve its image, aided in particular by the impressive architectural legacy of its late eighteenth- and nineteenth-century heyday.

Southern Scotland, often underrated, features some of the country's finest scenery, especially among the elevated river valleys surrounding **Moffat** and in the forests and flat-peaked hills of the **Galloway Forest Park**, close to the **Solway coast**. Away to the east lie the better-known ruins of the four medieval Border abbeys of Melrose, Dryburgh, Jedburgh and Kelso. **Jedburgh** is the pick of the bunch, but the trim town of **Melrose**, tucked into the one of the prettiest parts of the valley of the River Tweed, is the best peg on which to hang your visit, especially as it's close to **Abbotsford**, the intriguing, treasure-crammed mansion of Sir Walter Scott.

To the north of Edinburgh, across the Firth of Forth, **Central Scotland's** varied landscape embraces deep and shadowy glens, jagged-edged mountains and the well-walked hills of the **Trossachs**. It's here you'll find the impressive remains of **Stirling** castle and, on the coast, prosperous **St Andrews**, home of golf. **Northeast Scotland** may seem at first to have less to offer, but you could consider following the **Speyside** malt whisky trail, or taking a walk in the tranquil and majestic valleys of the **Angus glens**, or making a visit to oil-rich **Aberdeen**, the nation's third largest city, or **Deeside**, home to Queen Victoria's "dear paradise", Balmoral.

Most visitors move on from the central belt to **Argyll**, a sparsely populated territory of sea lochs and mountains. Mainland Argyll points out towards the southernmost reaches of the **Hebrides**, the long chain of rocky islands necklacing Scotland's Atlantic shoreline. **Bute** and **Arran**, with its striking granite peaks, are reached by ferry from Ardrossan in Ayrshire. From Oban you can reach the gorgeous scenery of **Mull**, and the quieter islands of **Islay** and **Jura**, wonderful places for a walking holiday.

Up along the coast, reached by boat from Mallaig or Kyleakin, is **Skye**, the most visited of the Hebrides, made famous by the exploits of Flora MacDonald, who smuggled Bonnie Prince Charlie "over the sea to Skye" after his defeat at the Battle of Culloden. The harsh rocky promontories that make up the bulk of the island are serrated by scores of deep sea lochs, together creating some of the western coast's fiercest scenery. The island also boasts the snow-tipped **Cuillins**, whose clustered summits offer perhaps the most challenging climbing in the country, and the bizarre rock formations of the Quiraing ridge on the **Trotternish peninsula**. The only settlement of any size is **Portree**, draped around the cliffs of a narrow bay, but many visitors prefer to explore the isolated hotels, B&Bs and youth hostels scattered across the island.

From Uig, on the west coast of Skye, and from Oban and Ullapool, there are frequent boats across to the **Western Isles**, an elongated archipelago extending south from the single island of **Lewis and Harris**, to the uninhabited islets below **Barra**. The Isles are some of the last bastions of the Gaelic language, and you'll find many road signs in Gaelic only. Of the islands, Lewis is distinguished by the prehistoric standing stones of **Callanish**, one of the best-preserved monuments of its type in Europe, while North Harris possesses a remarkably hostile landscape of forbidingly bare mountains giving way to the wide sandy beaches and lunar-like hills of South Harris.

Back on the mainland, the **Highlands**, whose multitude of mountains, sea cliffs, glens and lochs cover the northern two-thirds of the country, is probably the region most commonly associated with Scotland. Its great popularity belies its stark remoteness, despite a number of internationally known sights, not least **Loch Ness**, midway along the Great Glen and home to the eponymous monster. **Inverness**, near the site of the **Battle of Culloden**, is an obvious base for exploring the region, although **Fort William**, at the opposite end of the Great Glen close by **Ben Nevis**, Scotland's highest peak, is a possible alternative, especially if you're heading west.

In the far north, boats leave for the cluster of islands that make up the agricultural **Orkney Islands**, whose main town, **Kirkwall**, crowds round its magnificent medieval cathedral. Further north, 200 miles north of Aberdeen, are the much more rugged **Shetland Islands**, where the bustling and historic harbour at **Lerwick** shelters craft from every corner of the North Atlantic. Orkney and Shetland, both with a rich Norse heritage, differ not only from each other, but also quite distinctly, in dialect and culture, from mainland Scotland. These farflung, sea- and wind-buffeted islands, offer some of the country's wildest scenery, finest bird-watching and stunning archeological remains.

When to go

The pressure systems rolling in off the Atlantic pretty much control Scotland's volatile **climate**, especially on the west coast, where a bright, sunny morning can soon turn into a wet and windy afternoon. The west coast is appreciably wetter than the rest of the country, but milder in winter, due to the moderating influence of the Gulf Stream. There's no way of predicting when the fine weather will arrive, though spring and early autumn have proved good bets in recent years: you just have to trust your luck and be well prepared, even in high summer. Always pack warm and waterproof clothing – and an umbrella.

SCOTLAND'S CLIMATE

Average daily maximum temperatures in °C and monthly rainfall in mm

	Jan	Feb	March	April	May	June	July	Aug	Sept	Oct	Nov	Dec
Dumfries												
°C	5.6	6.0	8.2	11.2	14.4	17.3	18.3	18.1	15.9	12.9	8.6	6.8
mm	103	72	66	55	71	63	77	93	104	106	109	104
Edinburgh												
°C	6.2	6.4	8.5	11.2	14.2	17.1	18.4	18.2	16.3	13.3	9	7.1
mm	47	39	39	38	49	45	69	73	57	56	58	56
Fort William												
°C	6.3	6.7	8.6	11.2	14.5	16.6	17.2	17.3	15.4	12.8	8.8	7.3
mm	200	132	152	111	103	124	137	150	199	215	220	238
Lerwick												
°C	5.1	4.9	6	7.8	10	12.5	13.7	14	12.5	10.3	7.4	6
mm	127	93	93	72	64	64	67	78	113	119	140	147
Perth												
°C	5.7	6	8.4	11.8	14.9	18	19.1	18.6	16.2	12.9	8.5	6.6
mm	70	52	47	43	57	51	67	72	63	65	69	82
Tiree												
°C	7.2	7	8.3	10.3	12.7	14.8	15.8	16.1	14.7	12.6	9.6	8.2
mm	120	71	77	60	56	66	79	83	123	125	123	123
Wick												
°C	5.6	5.7	7.3	9.3	11.3	14.2	15.4	15.4	14.1	11.8	8.2	6.5
mm	81	58	55	45	47	49	61	74	68	73	90	82

HELP US UPDATE

We've endeavoured to make this guide as up-to-date as possible, but it's inevitable that some of the information will become inaccurate between now and the preparation of the next edition. Readers' updates and suggestions are very welcome – please mark letters "Scotland Update" and send them to:

Rough Guides, 1 Mercer Street, London WC2H 9QJ,
or Rough Guides, 375 Hudson Street, 9th Floor, New York, NY 10014.

PART ONE

THE

BASICS

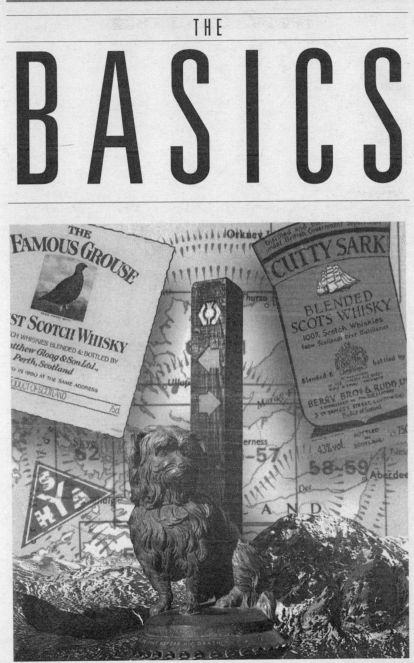

GETTING THERE FROM ENGLAND, IRELAND & EUROPE

Crossing the border from England into Scotland is straightforward, with train and bus services forming part of the British national network. Flights are another option, though fares tend to be high. If you're driving from the south the two main routes run up the east of England via the A1 and up the west side of the country using the M6 and the A74; only the latter offers at least dual carriageway driving the whole way. It takes the best part of a day to reach Edinburgh or Glasgow by car; although it is possible, if you drive flat out and encounter no road-work delays, to get to either city in around 8 hours. If you'd prefer a slower, more scenic route, take the A68 up through eastern England and over the border at Carter Bar (this route adds a couple of hours to the journey time).

FLIGHTS

You can fly to Scotland's **main airports** – Edinburgh, Glasgow and Aberdeen – in an hour or so from all three London airports as well as from various English provincial airports and from Ireland. There's usually a confusingly wide array of fares. The **best deals** are special-offer tickets sold within 7 days of departure – it's pot luck as to whether any flight has these bargain fares, but certainly worth a phone call. No refund is payable in the event of cancellation, and your stay must cover at least one Saturday.

The next cheapest seats are **Apex** tickets, available on all flights, at about half the price of a full-price economy class scheduled ticket. The full amount for Apex must be paid at least 2 weeks before departure, and only 50 percent of the price will be returned if the booking is cancelled. It's also worth checking fares through a specialist agency such as *Campus Travel* or *STA Travel*, as they may be able to offer special deals – again, we've listed addresses overleaf.

There are flights almost hourly to Edinburgh and Glasgow from **London**, and about 8 or so daily to Aberdeen. As a broad guide to what you're likely to pay, reckon on around £80 for the cheapest fare from London to Edinburgh or Glasgow on *British Airways*, *British Midland* or *Air UK*, around £100 for an Apex on this same route and up to £200 or more for the full fare. See below for the full picture on airlines and routes.

Flights from other parts of Britain are less frequent but similarly pricey. About 7 or 8 flights a day leave **Birmingham** for Edinburgh, Glasgow and Aberdeen – the cheapest return fares to all three with *British Airways* hover around £100. From the south of England, *Manx Airlines* offer flights from **Southampton** to Edinburgh or Glasgow for an Apex fare of around £150.

Coming from **Dublin** by air, there are 5 flights a day to Edinburgh and Glasgow – the Apex fare to both on *Aer Lingus* is around IR£80, while an ordinary return might be 3 times that amount. From **Belfast** things work out even cheaper. *British Airways* has 8 flights a day to Glasgow and about 3 to Edinburgh; the Apex fare is around £60. See overleaf for full details of airlines and their routes.

TRAINS

Glasgow and Edinburgh are both served by frequent direct **InterCity** services from **London**, and easily reached from other main English towns and cities, though you may have to change trains en route. Ordinary standard-class **fares** are high, and first class costs an extra 33 percent, but in many cases you can take advantage of 5 types of reduced-fare ticket (see p.5), all of which come with their own restrictions and conditions. On Sundays, on many long-distance services, you

AIRLINE ADDRESSES AND ROUTES FROM ENGLAND, IRELAND AND EUROPE

Aer Lingus
Dublin Airport,
Dublin, Eire ☎01/844 4777
Dublin to Edinburgh and Glasgow.

Air France
119 Champs-Élysées, Paris ☎44.35.61.61
Paris to Edinburgh.

Air UK
Stansted House, Stansted Airport,
Stansted, Essex ☎0345/666777
London to Edinburgh, Glasgow and Aberdeen.
Humberside to Aberdeen.
Norwich to Edinburgh.
Amsterdam to Edinburgh, Glasgow and Aberdeen.
Stavanger to Aberdeen.

British Airways
156 Regent St, London ☎0345/222111
London to Edinburgh, Glasgow and Aberdeen.
Manchester to Aberdeen.
Birmingham to Edinburgh, Glasgow and Aberdeen.
Bristol to Edinburgh, Glasgow and Aberdeen.
Belfast to Glasgow and Edinburgh.

British Airways Express (Loganair)
Glasgow Airport ☎0141/889 1311
Flights within Scotland only.

British Midland
Donington Hall,
Castle Donington,
Derby ☎0345/554554
London to Edinburgh and Glasgow.
East Midlands to Glasgow and Edinburgh.
Paris to Edinburgh via London and Glasgow direct.

Business Air
Kirkhill Business House,
Howmoss Drive, Dyce, Aberdeen ☎0500/340146
East Midlands to Edinburgh and Aberdeen.
Esbjerg to Aberdeen.
Manchester to Edinburgh, Glasgow, Aberdeen
and Dundee.

Icelandair
Reykjavik Airport, Reykjavik ☎91/5050300
Reykjavik to Glasgow.

Lufthansa
Hauptbahnhof 2,
60329 Frankfurt-am-Main ☎069/25525
Frankfurt to Edinburgh and Glasgow via
Manchester.

Manx Airlines
Ronaldsway Airport
Ballasalla, Isle of Man ☎0345/256256
Isle of Man to Glasgow.
Southampton to Glasgow and Edinburgh.

Ryanair
Barkat House, 116–118 Finchley Road
London ☎0171/435 7101
London to Glasgow

Sabena
Hotel Carrefour de l'Europe
Brussels ☎02/723 2323
Brussels to Edinburgh and Glasgow.

SAS
Resebutik Stureplan 8, Stockholm ☎08/797 4175
Stavanger to Aberdeen.

FLIGHT AGENTS IN BRITAIN

Campus Travel
52 Grosvenor Gdns, London SW1 ☎0171/730 3402
Also many branches around the country.

Council Travel
28A Poland St, London W1 ☎0171/287 3337
Flights and student discounts.

Destination Group
41–45 Goswell Rd, London EC1 ☎0171/253 9000
Good discount fares.

STA Travel
86 Old Brompton Rd, London SW7 ☎0171/937 9921
Offices nationwide.

Trailfinders
42–50 Earls Court Rd,
London W8 6FT ☎0171/938 3366
Many branches nationwide.

Travel Bug
597 Cheetham Hill Rd,
Manchester M8 5EJ ☎0161/721 4000
Large range of discounted tickets.

Union Travel
93 Piccadilly, London W1 ☎0171/493 4343
Competitive airfares.

can convert your standard-class ticket to a first-class one by paying a £5 supplement — well worth it if you're facing a 6-hour journey on a popular route.

Journey times from London can be as little as 4hr 30min to Edinburgh and 5hr to Glasgow; from Manchester reckon on around 2hr 30min to Edinburgh and 3hr to Glasgow. From either of these two points allow another 2hr 30min to Aberdeen and 3hr 30min to Inverness. These cities are all served by overnight **sleeper trains**, reservations for which cost an additional £25 and can be made at any mainline train station.

Eurostar (☎01233/617575; Paris/Lille ☎45.82.50.50; Brussels ☎02/224 8856) now operates frequent train services through the Channel Tunnel to London from Lille (2hr), Paris (3hr) and Brussels (3hr 15min); you then change trains for the onward journey. If you are driving from mainland Europe, you might want to take the frequent train service — *Le Shuttle* — that carries you and your car from Calais to Folkestone in 35 minutes. For information on journey times and fares, call Calais ☎21.00.61.00 or Folkestone ☎0990/353535.

TICKETS AND PASSES

In decreasing order of cost, **Savers** are return tickets that can be used on all trains on Saturdays, Sundays and public holidays, on most weekday trains outside rush hour for the outward journey and all trains for the return leg. If you buy a return ticket at any station outside the rush hour, you'll routinely be issued with a Saver. **SuperSavers**, cheaper still, cannot be used on Fridays nor on a dozen other specified days of the year, and are not valid for any peak-hour service to or from London. Saver and SuperSaver tickets are valid for a month (outward travel has to be within 2 days of the date on the ticket), and can be used on London Underground if your journey involves crossing from one London station to another. **Apex** tickets are issued in limited numbers on certain *InterCity* journeys of 150 miles or more, and have to be booked at least 7 days before travelling; a seat reservation is included with the ticket. The rock-bottom **SuperApex** tickets have to be booked at least 14 days in advance, and are available in limited numbers on *InterCity* services from London to Edinburgh, Glasgow and Motherwell. **Children** aged 5–15

pay half the adult fare on most journeys — but there are no discounts on Apex and SuperApex tickets. Under-5s travel free.

To take the London–Edinburgh service as an example, an ordinary single fare costs £65, which is more than the majority of the reduced return fares: a Saver return costs £72, a SuperSaver £60, an Apex costs £46, and a SuperApex just £34. For all these tickets you should book as far in advance as you possibly can — many Apex and SuperApex are sold out weeks before the travel date.

Three discount **passes**, all valid for a year, are available in Britain to nationals and foreign visitors alike. The **Young Person's Railcard** costs £16 and gives 33 percent reductions on all standard, Saver and SuperSaver fares to full-time students studying in Britain and anyone who is between 16 and 24 years of age. A **Senior Citizens' Railcard**, also £16 and offering 30 percent reductions, is available to all those aged 60 or over. For both passes you'll need to show proof of age (for foreign visitors your passport is preferred) and provide two passport-size photographs. Foreign students will need to show proof of full-time study in Britain. Another option is the **Family Railcard**, which costs £20 and gives a variety of discounts from 20 to 33 percent for up to 4 adults, travelling with children (visitors will need to show their passports). Even more enticingly, it allows up to 4 children aged 5–15 to travel anywhere in the country for a flat fare of £2 each (which includes a seat reservation). If all your children are under 5, you must buy at least one £2 fare to qualify for the discount.

For those under 26 (and resident in a European country for at least 6 months), **InterRail** passes may be a cost-effective way to travel if Scotland is part of a longer European trip. They offer discounts on UK train travel, on cross-Channel ferries and *Eurostar* (check with a travel agent or at a main train station for any discounts on other ferry routes). There are two types of pass: the **InterRail "All-zone"** (£249 for a month), and the **InterRail Zonal** (price varies according to the number of zones you want to travel in and the duration of your trip). For those over 26, the **InterRail 26 Plus** pass (£269 for a month or £209 for 15 days) covers all of Europe except France, Belgium, Switzerland, Spain, Italy and Portugal. Remember that no InterRail pass is valid in the country of purchase.

BUSES

Inter-town **bus** services (known as **coaches** in Scotland and the rest of Britain) duplicate many train routes, often at half the price or less. The frequency of service is often comparable to the train, and in some instances the difference in journey time isn't great enough to be a deciding factor; buses are also reasonably comfortable, and on longer routes often have drinks and sandwiches available on board. Two of the main operators between England and Scotland are *National Express* (☎0990/808080) and its subsidiary company *Scottish Citylink Coaches* (☎0990/898989). They both offer the same reduced rates to children (33 percent); if you're a student, under 25 or a senior citizen you have to buy a one-year pass for £7 to get this discount — you are only required to show proof of age if you're a British national or foreign visitor. Foreign travellers can also purchase a **Tourist Trail Pass**, which offers unlimited travel on the *National Express* and *Scottish CityLink* routes, costing £90 for any 8 days within 16 for students and under-23s, £119 for others; unlimited travel on any 15 days within 30 costs £145 and £179 respectively.

Direct buses run from **London**, **Birmingham**, **Manchester** and **Newcastle** to **Edinburgh**, **Glasgow, Aberdeen and Inverness**. Tickets are widely available from bus stations and hundreds of agents throughout England. Typical fares from London to Glasgow and Edinburgh — journeys of around 7hr 30min — cost £25 return, while to Aberdeen or Inverness the journey takes around 12 hours and the ticket costs about £47.50 return. There's a 25 percent **discount** on bookings made 7 days in advance.

FERRIES

The only way to get to the Scottish mainland direct by ferry **from Europe** is on the *P&O Scottish Ferries* service from **Bergen** in Norway to **Aberdeen** via **Lerwick** on Shetland, but the service only runs from June to August (1 weekly). The journey to Lerwick takes 12 hours, with a single fare of £55. From there it's another 14 hours and £35 on to Aberdeen. If you want to take your car on either journey, add another £50 or so.

There's a greater choice of ferry services from Europe to ports in England, the most convenient of which are those to Newcastle or Hull in the northeast, from where it's an easy 2-hour drive across the border into Scotland. *North Sea Ferries* sail daily to Hull from **Rotterdam** and **Zeebrugge**; both crossings take about 14 hours and, for 2 people with a small car, cost from around £130 single, depending on season and sailing times. From **Scandinavia**, *Color Line* sail to **Newcastle** from Bergen and/or Stavanger 1–3 times a week; the journey takes 20–27 hours depending on whether it's direct or not.

From June to mid-September, *Scandinavian Seaways* run one service a week from Gothenburg in Sweden to Newcastle, and from Easter to October they run a more or less daily service from Esbjerg in Denmark to Newcastle. The former takes about 24 hours and costs £240–380 single for a car and 2 adults; the latter 20 hours, from £170–300 single. From Easter to October there's also the **Hamburg** to Newcastle service, which runs 4 times a week, takes

---

FERRY COMPANIES IN SCOTLAND

Color Line ☎0191/296 1313.

North Sea Ferries ☎01482/377177.

P&O European Ferries ☎01581/200276.

P&O Scottish Ferries ☎01224/572615.

Scandinavian Seaways ☎0191/293 6262.

Stena Sealink ☎01776/702262.

FERRY COMPANIES IN EUROPE

Color Line Oslo ☎22.94.44.00.

Hoverspeed Belfast ☎0345/523523; Calais ☎21.46.14.14.

North Sea Ferries Rotterdam ☎01819/55 500; Zeebrugge ☎50.54.34.11.

P&O European Ferries Calais ☎21.46.04.40; Larne ☎01574/274321.

Scandinavian Seaways Amsterdam ☎20/611 6615; Esbjerg ☎75 121700; Gothenburg ☎31/650 600; Hamburg ☎40/389 0371.

Stena Sealink Calais ☎21.96.70.70; Larne ☎01574/273616.

just under 24 hours and costs £180–275 single. From mid-May to mid-September, 3 or 4 sailings a week leave **Amsterdam** for Newcastle, taking around 17 hours and costing £180–210 single.

A further alternative is to take one of the very frequent ferries to England from the **French ports**; there's more choice of sailings this way, though the drive up to Scotland from the south coast can easily take a full day. There are regular crossings with *Hoverspeed*, *Stena Sealink* and *P&O* from Calais to Dover, the shortest route, for which the lowest fare for a small car and 2 adults is £90–130 single. For full details of ferry routes and prices call the ferry companies direct.

From **Ireland** ferries run from **Larne** in Northern Ireland to **Stranraer** and **Cairnryan**. *Stena Sealink* and *P&O European Ferries* both have several crossings daily, taking 2hr 15min – reckon on £230–290 return for a small car and 2 people with *Stena* and £220–260 return with *P&O* to Cairnryan. **Hoverspeed** run Seacat catamarans daily from **Belfast** to Stranraer, taking just 1hr 30min, and costing between £180–280 return, depending on the season and sailing times. All ferry companies from Ireland also offer much cheaper 5-day return fares. For more details, call for a brochure from the companies.

GETTING THERE FROM NORTH AMERICA

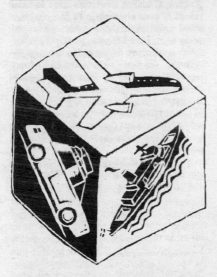

cross the Atlantic overnight, reaching Britain the next morning, although a few flights from the East Coast leave early in the morning, landing late the same evening, just as everything is shutting down.

Of Scottish cities, only one – **Glasgow** – is reachable **nonstop** from North America. However, nonstop flights are not specified by the airlines, and cost the same as direct flights (which involve a brief stop in another city), so always check availability. You're more likely to fly direct to Glasgow, probably, via London. Direct flights to Edinburgh tend to route through London or Dublin; to get to Aberdeen or Inverness you'll have to change planes and hop on a *British Airways* shuttle from London. *British Airways Express* (also known as *Loganair*) flies to the Scottish islands mainly from Glasgow or Edinburgh. See p.4 for the full picture on flying to Scotland from other parts of Britain.

Travelling to Scotland from North America, your choice of arrival point will depend largely on whether your itinerary also includes England. If it does, you'll almost certainly stand to save on the airfare by flying into London and making your way up to Scotland from there.

Figure on 6hr 30min flying time from New York to any of the British airports, 11hr 30min from the West Coast. Most eastbound flights

SHOPPING FOR TICKETS

If you're flying direct to Scotland, barring special offers, the cheapest fare is usually an **Apex** (Advance Purchase Excursion) ticket through a travel agent or from the airline. Apex tickets carry certain restrictions: you have to book – and pay – at least 21 days before departure, spend at least 7 days abroad (maximum stay 3 months), and you tend to get penalized if you change your schedule. There are also winter **SuperApex** tickets, sometimes known as "Eurosavers" – slightly less expensive than an ordinary Apex, but limiting your stay to between 7 and 21 days. Some airlines also issue **Special Apex** tickets to those under 24, often extending the maximum stay to a year. Many airlines offer youth or student fares to under-25s; a passport or driving licence are sufficient proof of age, though these tickets are subject to availability and can have eccentric booking conditions. It's worth remembering that most cheap return fares involve spending at least one Saturday night away and that many will only give a percentage refund if you need to cancel or alter your journey, so make sure you check the restrictions carefully before buying a ticket. Any local travel agent should be able to access up-to-the-minute fares, although in practice they may not have time to research all the possibilities – you might want to call the airlines directly.

Although flights to Scotland are seldom discounted, it's still worth shopping around – and definitely so if you're flying into London; check with the specialist travel companies listed opposite or in the Sunday newspaper travel sections. **Discounted fares** (usually only for direct or stopover flights) are available from **specialist flight agents** – either **consolidators**, who buy up large blocks of tickets from the airlines, and sell them at a discount, or **discount agents**, who wheel and deal in blocks of tickets offloaded by the airlines, and often offer, in particular, special student and youth fares, and a range of other travel-related services such as travel insurance, rail passes, youth and student ID cards, car rentals and tours. Some agencies specialize in **charter flights**, which may be cheaper than any scheduled flight deal, but again there's a trade-off: departure dates are fixed and withdrawal penalties are high (check the refund policy). **Discount travel clubs** are another option for those who travel a lot – most charge an annual membership fee, which may be worth it for discounts on air tickets, car rental and the like.

Be advised also that the pool of travel companies is swimming with sharks – exercise caution with any outfit that sounds shifty or impermanent, and *never* deal with a company that demands cash up front or refuses to accept payment by credit card.

Regardless of where you buy your ticket, the **fare** will depend on season. Fares to Britain are highest from around early June to mid-September, when everyone wants to travel; they drop during the "shoulder" seasons, mid-September to early November and mid-April to early June, and you'll get the best deals during the low season, November through to April (excluding Christmas). The Christmas–New Year holiday period is a thing unto itself – if you want to travel at this time, book at least 2 or 3 months ahead, and be prepared for fares even higher than those in summer.

Fares quoted below are based on the typical Apex fares in low season, exclusive of tax (figure on $40–60), and travelling midweek; flying on weekends ordinarily adds $20–60. In America, peak-season prices are likely to run $150–200 higher; in Canada, CAN$300–400.

FLIGHTS FROM THE USA

Glasgow, Edinburgh and London are "**common rated**" by most airlines that fly to these cities, which means that the Apex fares are the same. However, it's much harder to find discounted fares to Scotland (consolidators and discount agents tend to deal only in high-volume destinations), and there are far fewer direct flights to Glasgow and Edinburgh than there are to London. If you fly to London on a discounted ticket, expect to pay $100–150 each way for an onward flight. As you are unlikely to get a discount equivalent to the onward fare, a direct flight is usually the cheapest option.

You can fly **nonstop** from the two **Eastern US** "gateway" cities of New York (*British Airways*) and Chicago (*American Airlines*) **to Glasgow**. Low-season, midweek Apex fares from New York come in at about $400–500; from Chicago figure on around $575. Other direct flights to Glasgow include: $500 from Boston; $520 from Washington DC or Atlanta; $575 from Miami; and around $600 from St Louis, Denver, Dallas-Fort Worth and Houston. From the **West Coast USA** you can fly direct from San Francisco and Los Angeles to Glasgow for around $600.

British Airways offers the greatest selection of onward connections from London to Scotland (see p.4). *Aer Lingus* also serves Edinburgh, and *United* can ticket you straight through to several Scottish destinations on *British Midland*. Flying to **Manchester** in the north of England is another possibility, though this isn't any cheaper than the direct Apex fare to Glasgow.

NORTH AMERICAN AIRLINES AND ROUTES

Only nonstop routes are listed, but many other routings are possible via these "gateway" cities.

Aer Lingus ☎1-800/223-6537
Boston and New York to Dublin or Shannon.

Air Canada dial directory inquiries ☎1-800/555-1212) for local toll-free number
Toronto to Glasgow, London and Manchester.
Montréal to Glasgow and London.
Halifax and Vancouver to London.

Air India ☎212/751-6200
New York and Toronto to London.

American Airlines ☎1-800/433-7300
Chicago to Glasgow, London, Manchester and Birmingham.
New York to London and Manchester.
Boston, Dallas-Fort Worth, Los Angeles, Miami, Nashville and Raleigh-Durham to London.

British Airways ☎1-800/247-9297
New York to Glasgow, London, Manchester and Birmingham.
From all the other major gateways and many other US cities. Connections to Glasgow, Edinburgh, Aberdeen, Inverness, Orkney (Kirkwall), Shetland (Lerwick) and Stornoway.

Canadian Airlines ☎1-800/665-1177
Calgary, Edmonton and Toronto to London.

Continental Airlines ☎1-800/231-0856
Newark to London and Manchester.
Houston to London.

Delta Airlines ☎1-800/241-4141
Atlanta to London and Manchester.
Boston, Cincinnati, Los Angeles, Miami, Newark, New York, Orlando and San Francisco to London.

Kuwait Airways ☎1 800/458-9248
New York to London.

Northwest Airlines ☎1-800/225-2525
Boston, Detroit and Minneapolis to London.

TWA ☎1-800/221-2000
St Louis to London.

United Airlines ☎1-800/538-2929
Chicago, Los Angeles, Newark, New York, San Francisco and Washington DC to London (with many other onward connections possible through a cooperative agreement with British Midland).

Virgin Atlantic Airways ☎1-800/862-8621
Boston, Los Angeles, Miami, Newark, New York, Orlando and San Francisco to London (with onward connections to Edinburgh with British Midland).

DISCOUNT TRAVEL AGENTS, CONSOLIDATORS AND TRAVEL CLUBS IN NORTH AMERICA

Air Brokers International, 323 Geary St, Suite 411, San Francisco, CA 94102 (☎1-800/883-3273). *Consolidator.*

Council Travel, 205 E 42nd St, New York, NY 10017 (☎1-800/743-1823), and branches in many other US cities. *Youth/student travel organization. A sister company,* **Council Charter** (☎1-800/223-7402), *specializes in charter flights*

Educational Travel Center, 438 N Frances St, Madison, WI 53703 (☎1-800/747-5551). *Student/youth discount agent.*

Last Minute Travel Club, 132 Brookline Ave, Boston, MA 02215 (☎1800/LAST MIN). *Travel club specializing in standby deals.*

New Frontiers/Nouvelles Frontières, 12 E 33rd St, New York, NY 10016 (☎1-800/366 6387); 1001 Sherbrook East, Suite 720, Montréal, H2L 1L3 (☎514/526 8444); and other branches in LA, San Francisco and Québec City. *French discount travel firm.*

Preferred Traveler's Club, 4501 Forbes Blvd, Lanham, MD 20706 (☎1-800/444 9800). *Discount travel club.*

STA Travel, 48 E 11th St, New York, NY 10003 (☎1-800/777 0112), and other branches in the Los Angeles, San Francisco and Boston areas. *Worldwide specialist in independent travel.*

TFI Tours International, 34 W 32nd St, New York, NY 10001 (☎1 800/745 8000), and other offices in Las Vegas and Miami. *Consolidator.*

Travac, 989 6th Ave, New York NY 10018 (☎1-800/872 8800). *Consolidator and charter broker.*

Travel Avenue, 10 S Riverside, Suite 1404, Chicago, IL 60606 (☎1-800/333 3335). *Discount travel agent.*

Travel CUTS, 187 College St, Toronto, ON M5T 1P7 (☎416/979 2406), and other branches all over Canada. *Student travel organization.*

Travelers Advantage, 3033 S Parker Rd, Suite 900, Aurora, CO 80014 (☎1-800/548 1116). *Discount travel club.*

UniTravel, 1177 N Warson Rd, St Louis, MO 63132 (☎1-800/325 2222). *Consolidator.*

Worldtek Travel, 111 Water St, New Haven, CT 06511 (☎1-800/243 1723). *Discount travel agency.*

If Scotland is only one stop on a longer journey, you might want to consider buying a **Round The World (RTW)** ticket. Some travel agents can sell you an "off-the-shelf" RTW ticket that will have you touching down in about half a dozen cities (London is easily arranged, but a Scottish connection will probably have to be added on separately). Others will have to assemble one for you, which can be more tailored to your needs but is apt to be more expensive. Figure on $1400 ($1600 in summer) for a RTW ticket including London.

FLIGHTS FROM CANADA

Air Canada flies **nonstop** to **Glasgow** from its "gateway" cities of Toronto and Montréal; low-season midweek Apex fares start at CAN$750. From Vancouver you can fly direct for CAN$900.

You won't necessarily save any money by flying direct to **London**, although you will have a greater choice of carriers, and it's certainly a good idea if you're coming from any other Canadian city. The best deals are out of Toronto and Montréal, where competition drives low season midweek fares as low as CAN$650, flights from Ottawa and Halifax will probably cost only slightly more. From Edmonton and Calgary, fares start at CAN$950, from Vancouver around CAN$900.

British Airways offers the greatest selection of onward connections to Scotland (see box); expect to pay $100–150 each way. You can also pick up direct flights from many Canadian cities to **Manchester** or **Birmingham** (usually via London), often at no extra cost over the fare to London. For round-the-world tickets see above.

PACKAGES AND INCLUSIVE TOURS

Although you may want to see Scotland at your own speed, you shouldn't dismiss out of hand the idea of a **package deal**. Many agents and airlines put together very flexible deals, sometimes amounting to no more than a flight plus car or train pass and accommodation, which can actually work out better value than the same arrangements made on arrival – especially fly-drive deals, as car rental is expensive in Britain.

There are many tour operators that specialize in travel to Scotland. Most can do packages of the standard highlights, and many also organize **walking or cycling** trips through the countryside, with any number of theme tours based around Scotland's literary heritage, history, pubs, gardens, golf – you name it. A few possibilities are listed in the box opposite, and a travel agent will be able to point out others (remember, bookings made through travel agents cost no more than going through the tour operator). For a full listing, contact the Scottish Tourist Board (see p.19). Be sure to examine the fine print of any deal, and make sure the operator is a member of the United States Tour Operator Association (USTOA) or approved by the American Society of Travel Agents (ASTA).

TRAIN PASSES FOR NORTH AMERICANS

Eurail Pass is not likely to pay for itself if you're planning to stick to Scotland. The pass, which must be purchased before arrival in Europe, allows unlimited free train travel in Scotland and 16 other countries including: England, Denmark, Finland, France, Germany, Greece, Ireland (Rep.), Italy, Netherlands, Norway, Portugal, Spain.

The **Eurail Youthpass** (for under-26s) costs US$398 for 15 days, $578 for a month or $768 for 2 months; if you're 26 or over you'll have to buy a first-class pass, available in 15-day ($498), 21-day ($648), 1-month ($798), 2-month ($1098) and 3-month ($1398) increments. You stand a better chance of getting your money's worth out of a **Eurail Flexipass**, which is good for a certain number of travel days in a 2-month period. This, too, comes in under-26/first-class versions: 5 days cost $255/$348; 10 days, $398/$560; and 15 days, $540/$740. A further alternative is to attempt to buy an **InterRail Pass** in Europe (see "Getting There from England, Ireland and Europe") – most agents don't check residential qualifications, but once you're in Europe it'll be too late to buy a Eurail Pass if you have problems. You can purchase Eurail passes from one of the agents listed on p.9 and in "Getting Around" on p.21.

NORTH AMERICAN TOUR OPERATORS TO SCOTLAND

BCT ☎1-800/473-1210
Walking trips in the Highlands and Borders.

British Travel International ☎1-800/327-6097
Agent for all independent arrangements: air tickets, rail and bus passes, hotels, and a comprehensive vacation rental homes and B&B reservation service.

English Lakeland Ramblers ☎1-800/724-8801
Walking tours in the Highlands.

Especially Britain ☎1-800/869-0538
Fly-drives and independent rail tours built around B&Bs, country houses and castle stays.

Hostelling International USA ☎202/783-6161;
CAN ☎613/237 7884
or ☎1-800/663 5777
Affiliated with the Scottish Youth Hostels Association; organizes walking, cycling and general youth tours.

Journeys Through Scotland ☎1-800/828-7583
Customized sightseeing and golf tours.

Lynott Tours ☎1-800/221-2474
Special-interest tours, hotel and castle stays, self-drives.

Mountain Travel/Sobek ☎1-800/227-2384
Hiking and cycling tours.

Renaissance Travel ☎1-800/43-SCOTS
Scottish specialist.

Scottish Connections ☎617/770-4172
Scotland tours.

Sterling Tours ☎1-800/727-4359
Scottish specialist offering a variety of independent itineraries, some packages.

GETTING THERE FROM AUSTRALIA & NEW ZEALAND

There are very few direct flights to Scotland from Australia and New Zealand, and mostly you will have to route through London and then travel north. There is no price differ-ence between the major airlines as fares from both Australia and New Zealand are "common rated", but they do vary significantly with the seasons. For most major airlines, low season is October to mid-November and mid-January to February 28, mid season is from Dec 24 to mid-January, and high from mid-May to August 31 and December 11 23. The prices quoted below, unless otherwise stated, are the low-season fares published by the airlines (there's no variation in price during the week). On top of a low-season fare you can expect to pay between A/NZ$200 and $400 in mid-season and A/NZ$500 and $700 in high season. The published fares are the maximum you are likely to pay; however, special "on spec" offers (of up to 20 percent) are available throughout the year from many of the major carriers. Contact a travel agent for the latest information on limited special deals, as changes are made constantly throughout the year. On top of this individual travel agents offer further reductions of up to 10 percent, and for students and under-26s, 20 percent. So you can usually expect to pay around A\$500/NZ\$600 less than the published fares in all seasons.

Japanese Airlines are the only carriers to fly daily from **Sydney** and several times weekly from Brisbane, Cairns and **Auckland** to **Edinburgh** with an overnight stopover in either Tokyo or Osaka and a connecting flight from London Heathrow with *British Midland*. From Australia, the low-season fare is A\$2800; from New Zealand, NZ\$3100.

AIRLINES IN AUSTRALIA

Aeroflot, 388 George St, Syndey (☎02/233 7148); 142 Great North Rd, Auckland (☎09/378 0157).

Air New Zealand, 5 Elizabeth St, Sydney (☎02/9223 4666); corner of Customs and Queen streets, Auckland (☎09/366 2424).

Britannia Airways, 263 Alfred St, North Sydney (☎02/9251 1299); no NZ office.

British Airways, 64 Castlereagh St, Sydney (☎02/9258 3300); Dilworth Building, corner of Queen and Customs streets, Auckland (☎09/367 7500)

Canadian Airlines 30 Castlereagh St, Sydney (☎02/9299 7843); Floor 15 Jetset Centre, 44 Emily Place, Auckland (☎ 09/309 3620).

Garuda Airlines, 175 Clarence St, Sydney (☎02/9262 2011); WestPac Tower Bldg, 10th Floor, 120 Albert St, Auckland (☎09/366 1855).

Japanese Airlines, 17 Blight St, Sydney (☎02/9233 4500); no NZ office.

KLM 5 Elizabeth St, Sydney (☎02/9231 6333 or 1800/222747); no NZ office.

Korean Air, 36 Carrington St, Sydney (☎02/262 6000); 7–9 Falcon St, Parnell, Auckland (☎09/307 3687).

Malaysian Airways, 11th Floor, Amex Tower 388, George St, Sydney (☎02/9231 5066); 12th Floor, Swanson Centre, 12–26 Swanson St, Auckland (☎09/373 2741).

Philippine Airlines, 49 York St, Sydney (☎02/262 3333; toll-free ☎1-800/112 458).

Qantas, Qantas International Centre, International Square, Jamison St, Sydney (☎02/ 9236 3636); Quantas House, 154 Queen St, Auckland (☎09/303 2506).

Thai International Airways, 75–77 Pitt St, Sydney (☎02/9844 0999 or 1800/221320); Kensington Swan Bldg, 22 Fanshawe St, Auckland (☎09/377 0268).

United Airlines,10 Barrack St, Sydney (☎02/ 9237/8888); 7 City Rd, Auckland (☎09/307 9500).

DISCOUNT AGENTS IN AUSTRALASIA

Accent on Travel, 545 Queen St, Brisbane (☎07/ 3832 1777).

Adventure World, 73 Walker St, North Sydney (☎02/956 7766); 8 Victoria Ave, Perth (☎09/221 2300; ☎08/9221 2300 from Sept 1997).

Anywhere Travel, 345 Anzac Parade, Kingsford, Sydney (☎02/663 0411).

Brisbane Discount Travel, 360 Queen St, Brisbane (☎07/3229 9211).

Budget Travel, PO Box 505, Auckland (☎09/309 4313).

Discount Travel Specialists, Shop 53, Forrest Chase, Perth (☎09/221 1400; ☎08/9221 1400 from Sept 1997).

Flight Centres, *Australia* Circular Quay, Sydney (☎02/9241 2422); Bourke St, Melbourne (☎03/ 9650 2899); plus branches nationwide. *New Zealand* National Bank Towers, 205–225 Queen St, Auckland (☎09/309 6171); Shop 1M, National Mutual Arcade, 152 Hereford St, Christchurch (☎09/379 7145); 50–52 Willis St, Wellington (☎04/472 8101); plus branches nationwide.

Passport Travel, 320b Glenfarrie Rd, Malvern, Melbourne (☎03/9824 7183).

STA, *Australia* 732 Harris St, Sydney (☎02/9212 1255 or 9281 9866); CAE Shop, 256 Flinders St, Melbourne (☎03/9347 4711); other offices in Townsville, Cairns and state capitals. *New Zealand* Traveller's Centre, 10 High St, Auckland (☎09/309 4058); 233 Cuba St, Wellington (☎04/ 385 0561); 223 High St, Christchurch (☎03/379 9098); other offices in Dunedin, Palmerston North and Hamilton.

STS Travel, 10 High St, Auckland (☎09/309 9995); 233 Cuba St, Wellington (☎04/385 0561); 223 High St, Christchurch (☎03/379 9098).

Topdeck Travel, 45 Grenfell St, Adelaide (☎08/ 8410 1110).

Tymtro Travel, Suite G12, Wallaceway Shopping Centre, Chatswood, Sydney (☎02/411 1222).

SPECIALIST AGENTS

Adventure Specialists, 1st Floor, 69 Liverpool St, Sydney (☎02/9261 2927). *Walking and cycling holidays.*

Explore Holidays, corner of Marsden and Pennent Hills roads, Carlingford, Sydney (☎02/872 6222). *Accommodation and walking holiday agent.*

Destination Adventure, 2nd Floor, Premier Building, corner of Queen and Durham streets, East Auckland (☎09/309 0464). *Agents for Peregrine Adventures.*

Peregrine Adventures, 258 Lonsdale St, Melbourne (☎03/9663 8611). *Exploration holidays involving cycling or canoeing.*

Wiltrans/ Maupintour, Level 10, 189 Kent St, Sydney (☎02/255 0899). *Escorted historic tours.*

YHA Travel Centre, 205 King St, Melbourne (☎03/9670 9611); 36 Customs House, Auckland (☎09/379 4224). *Budget accommodation throughout Britain for YHA members.*

The majority of routes and the cheapest fares from Australia are **via Asia** with *Garuda, Philippine, Aeroflot, Britannia, Malaysian Airways* and *KLM*. Daily direct flights connect **London** with Melbourne, Sydney, Brisbane and Perth, with no great difference in the fares. The lowest priced direct flights are with: *Garuda*, which flies to Gatwick (via Jakarta or Denpasar) several times a week from the east coast for A\$1550 (discounted; low season), and *Philippine*, which flies twice weekly from Sydney to Heathrow (via Manilla and Frankfurt) for A\$1499 (discounted; low season), Darwin and Cairns for A\$1450 (discounted; low season). Most flights, however, require a stopover in the carrier's hub city; prices are much the same as for direct flights. *United* and *Air New Zealand* fly several times a week from Sydney and Melbourne **via US cities** (LA or either New York, Washington or Chicago) for around A\$2300 in low season, and *Canadian Airlines* daily to Heathrow via Toronto or Vancouver for around A\$2500.

Britannia Airways have several direct **charter** flights per month (via Singapore and Abu Dhabi) to Gatwick and **Manchester** during their charter season (Nov–March). Fares from the east and west coasts are all A\$1199 in low season.

In **New Zealand**, you can expect to pay around NZ\$2400 from Auckland in low season – add at least NZ\$350 for flights from Christchurch. *British Airways* (via LA) and *Qantas* (via Asia) fly direct from Auckland to London Heathrow several times per week. Stopover flights are with *JAL, Thai* and *Korean Air*, who all offer good deals of around NZ\$1999. *Air New Zealand* flies from Auckland to Heathrow via LA once a week (NZ\$2400). *United Airlines* also offer US stopover flights (LA and Chicago) from Auckland. *Britannia* runs **charter** flights (Nov–March) from Auckland to Gatwick several times a month (once a month to Manchester) for NZ\$1415 in low season.

The **add-on cost** to either Glasgow or Edinburgh will be anything between A\$200 and A\$300 (NZ\$250–350) depending on the season, so you might want to consider travelling on by bus or train from London.

Numerous **discount agents** (see box) can supply these and other low-price tickets. One of the most reliable operators is *STA*, who can also advise on **visa regulations** for Australian and New Zealand citizens – and for a fee will do all the paperwork for you.

For extended trips, **Round the World** (RTW) tickets, valid for up to a year, are a good option. Six free stopovers are usually offered by participating airlines with additional stopovers around A/NZ\$100. Many routes include London but for Scotland you'll need to to find an airline whose routes allow either backtracking or side trips. Fares start from A\$2399/NZ\$2599.

A further alternative, if Scotland is part of a wider European trip, is to attempt to buy an **InterRail Pass** once you are in Europe (see "Getting There from England, Ireland and Europe") – most agents don't check residential qualifications.

VISAS, CUSTOMS REGULATIONS AND TAX

Citizens of all the countries of Europe – except Albania, Bulgaria, Romania and all states of the former Soviet Union (except the Baltic states) – can enter Britain with just a passport, generally for up to 3 months. For US, Canadian, Australian and New Zealand citizens, it's up to 6 months. Citizens of all other nationalities require a visa, obtainable from the British Consular office in the country of application. All overseas consulates in Scotland are detailed in the listings sections for Edinburgh and Glasgow.

For **longer stays**, North American citizens can apply to the British Embassy (see box below). Full-time, bona fide college students can get temporary work or study permits through the **Council on International Education Exchange** (CIEE), 205 E 42nd St, New York, NY 10017 (☎212/661-1414). Work permits cost $160 to arrange and are good for 6 months; CIEE will give you leads, but it's up to you to find the work. If **Australian and New Zealand** citizens want

to extend their stay, they can apply to the British High Commission (see box below) for an Entry Clearance Certificate. If between 17 and 26, you can try for a 2-year Working Holiday-Maker Entry Certificate.

Travellers coming into Britain directly from another **EU** country do not have to make a declaration to customs at their place of entry and can effectively bring almost as much wine or beer across the Channel as they like. However, there are still strict restrictions – details of which are prominently displayed in all duty free outlets – on tax- or duty-free goods, so you can't invest in a stockpile of cheap cigarettes, wherever you're coming from.

There are **import restrictions** on a variety of articles and substances, from firearms to furs derived from endangered species, none of which should bother the average tourist. However, if you need any clarification on British import regulations, contact HM Customs and Excise, Dorset House, Stamford St, London SE1 9PJ (☎0171/928 3344). You cannot bring pets into Britain on holiday, as tight quarantine restrictions apply to animals brought over from overseas (except Northern and Southern Ireland).

Many goods in Britain, with the chief exceptions of books and food, are subject to **Value Added Tax** (VAT), which currently increases the cost of an item by 17.5 percent. Visitors from non-EU countries can save a lot of money through the Retail Export Scheme, which allows a refund of VAT on goods to be taken out of the country – though savings will usually be minimal, if anything, for EU nationals, because of their own VAT rates. Note that not all shops participate in this scheme – those doing so display a sign to this effect – and that you cannot reclaim VAT charged on hotel bills or other services.

BRITISH EMBASSIES ABROAD

Australia (High Commission) Commonwealth Ave, Yarralumla, Canberra, ACT 2600 (☎06/6257-1982).

Canada (High Commission) 80 Elgin St, Ottawa, ON K1P 5K7 (☎613/237-1303).

Ireland 31–33 Merrion Rd, Dublin 4 (☎01/269 5211).

Netherlands Koningslaan 44, Amsterdam (☎676 43 43).

New Zealand (High Commission) 44 Hill St, Wellington (☎04/495-0889).

USA 3100 Massachusetts Ave NW, Washington, DC 20008 (☎202/462-1340).

MONEY, BANKS AND COSTS

The basic unit of currency in Britain is the **pound sterling (£)**, divided into 100 pence (p). Coins come in denominations of 1p, 2p, 5p, 10p, 20p, 50p and £1 – there's a rare £2 coin in circulation as well. *Bank of England* and Northern Ireland banknotes are legal tender in Scotland; in addition the *Bank of Scotland*, the *Royal Bank of Scotland* and the *Clydesdale Bank* issue their own banknotes in denominations of £1, £5, £10, £20, £50 and £100 – legal tender in the rest of Britain, no matter what shopkeepers south of the border might say. Shopkeepers will carefully scrutinize any £20 or £50 notes, as forgeries are widespread, and you'd be well advised to do the same. The quickest test is to hold the note up to the light to make sure there's a thin wire filament running from top to bottom; this is by no means foolproof, but it will catch most fakes.

CARRYING MONEY

There are no exchange controls in Britain, so you can bring in as much money as you like. The easiest and safest way to carry your money is in travellers' cheques, available for a small commission (usually 1 percent) from any major bank. The most commonly accepted travellers' cheques are *American Express*, followed by *Visa* and *Thomas Cook* – most cheques issued by banks will be one of these brands. You'll usually pay commission again when you cash each cheque, normally

another 1 percent or so, or a flat rate, though no commission is payable on Amex cheques exchanged at Amex branches. Make sure to keep a record of the cheques as you cash them, so that you'll be able to get the value of all uncashed cheques refunded immediately if you lose them.

Most hotels, shops and restaurants in Scotland accept the major **credit cards** – *Access/MasterCard, Visa, American Express* and *Diners Club* – although they're less useful in rural areas; smaller establishments all over the country, such as B&Bs, will often accept cash only. You can get cash advances from selected banks and bureaux de change on credit cards, though there will invariably be a minimum amount you can draw.

If you have a PIN, *Visa* and *Access/Mastercard* can also be used at *Bank of Scotland* and *Royal Bank of Scotland* cashpoint machines. *Bank of Scotland* and *Royal Bank of Scotland* cashpoints also take *Lloyds* and *Barclays* cashcards, while *Clydesdale* take *Midland* and *National Westminster.*

BANKING HOURS

In every sizeable town in Scotland, and, surprisingly, in some small places, you'll find a branch of at least one of the big High-Street banks: *Bank of Scotland, Royal Bank of Scotland, Clydesdale* and *TSB Scotland.* However, on some islands, and in remoter parts, you may find there is only a mobile bank that runs to a timetable, usually available from the local post office. Basic **opening hours** are Monday to Friday 9.15am until 4 or 4.45pm, though all are open until 5.45pm on Thursdays. Almost everywhere, banks are the best places in which to **change money and cheques**; outside banking hours you'll have to use a **bureau de change**, widely found in most city centres, often at train stations or airports. Avoid changing money or cheques in hotels, where the rates are normally very poor.

EMERGENCIES

If, as a foreign visitor, you run out of money or there is some kind of emergency, the quickest way to get **money sent out** is to contact your bank at home and have them wire the cash to the nearest bank. You can do the same thing through *Thomas Cook* or *American Express* if there is a branch nearby. Americans and Canadians can also have cash sent out through *Western Union* (information in UK ☎0800/833833) to a nearby bank or post office. Make sure you know when it's likely to arrive, since you won't be notified by the receiving office. Remember, too, that you'll need some form of identification when you pick up the money.

COSTS

Scotland has become an expensive place to visit, although in general it is marginally less pricy than England. The minimum expenditure, if you're camping, hitching a lot of the time and preparing most of your own food, would be in the region of £20 a day, rising to around £30 a day using the hostelling network, some public transport and grabbing the odd meal. Couples staying at budget B&Bs, eating at unpretentious restaurants and visiting a fair number of tourist attractions are looking at around £45 each per day; if you're renting a car, staying in comfortable B&Bs or hotels and eating well, you should reckon on at least £70 a day per person. Single travellers should budget on spending around 60 percent of what a couple would spend (single rooms cost more than half a double). If you're visiting **Edinburgh**, which can get pricy, allow at least an extra £10 or so a day to get full pleasure out of the place.

YOUTH AND STUDENT DISCOUNTS

Various offical youth/student ID cards are widely available and most will soon pay for themselves in savings.

Full-time students are eligible for the **International Student ID Card** (ISIC), which entitles the bearer to special fares on local transport, and discounts at museums, theatres and other attractions. For Americans there's also a health benefit, providing up to US$3000 in emergency medical coverage and US$100 a day for 60 days in the hospital, plus a 24-hour hotline to call in the event of a medical, legal or financial emergency. The card, which costs US$16 for Americans, CAN$15 for Canadians and A$10 for Australians, is available from branches of *Council Travel, STA* and *Travel CUTS* (see p.9 and p.12 for addresses).

You only have to be 25 or younger to qualify for the **Go-25 Card**, which costs the same as the ISIC and carries the same benefits. It can be purchased through *Council Travel* in the US and around the world, *Hostelling International* in Canada (see "Accommodation") and *STA* in Australia.

INSURANCE, HEALTH AND EMERGENCIES

Wherever you're travelling from, it's a good idea to have some kind of travel insurance, which covers you for loss of possessions and money too, as well as the cost of all medical and dental treatment. If you're travelling to Scotland from elsewhere in Britain, you may well be covered by your domestic insurance policies.

If you do need extra cover, in **Britain and Ireland**, travel insurance schemes (from around £23 a month) are sold by almost every travel agent or bank, and by specialist insurance companies. *Endsleigh* is about the cheapest British insurer, offering a month's travel cover for around £12. Its policies are available from most youth/student travel specialists or direct from its main Scottish offices at 7–9 Shandwick Place, Edinburgh (☎0131/228 4878) and 178 Hope St, Glasgow (☎0141/332 5252). In London it's based at 97–107 Southampton Row (☎0171/436 4451). Whatever your policy, if you have anything stolen, get a copy of the police report of the incident, as this is essential to substantiate your claim.

NORTH AMERICAN COVER

In the **US and Canada** you should also check the insurance policies you already have carefully before taking out a new one. You may discover that you're covered already for medical and other losses while abroad. Canadians especially are usually covered by their provincial health plans. Holders of official student/youth cards (see above) are entitled to accident cover and hospital in-patient benefits. Students may also find their health coverage extends during vacations, and many bank and charge accounts (particularly *American Express*) include some form of travel cover; insurance is also sometimes included if you pay for your trip with a credit card.

(*UTAG*), 122 Walker St, North Sydney (☎02/956 8399); *Australian Federation of Travel Agents Ltd.* (*AFTA*), 144 Pacific Highway, North Sydney (☎02/956 4800); *Ready Plan*, 141 Walker St, Dunenong (☎005/312345); and 10th Floor, 63 Albert St, Auckland (☎09/379 3208). A typical insurance policy for the UK will cost A$161/NZ$180 for a month and A$226/NZ$254 for 2 months.

HEALTH

No vaccinations are required for entry into Britain. Citizens of all **EU** countries are entitled to free medical treatment at National Health Service hospitals on production of an **E111** form (available from post offices, DSS offices or travel agents); you can just show your passport, but will have to pay on the spot and claim the money back later. Citizens of other countries will be charged for all medical services except those

---

TRAVEL INSURANCE COMPANIES IN NORTH AMERICA

Access America, PO Box 90310, Richmond, VA 23230 (☎1-800/284-8300).

Carefree Travel Insurance, PO Box 310, 120 Mineola Blvd, Mineola, NY 11501 (☎1-800/323-3149).

International Student Insurance Service (**ISIS**) – sold by *STA Travel*, which has several branches in the US (head office is 48 E 11th St, New York, NY 10003; ☎1-800/777-0112)

Travel Assistance International, 1133 15th St NW, Suite 400, Washington, DC 20005 (☎1-800/821-2828).

Travel Guard, 1145 Clark St, Stevens Point, WI 54481 (☎1-800/826-1300).

Travel Insurance Services, 2930 Camino Diablo, Suite 300, Walnut Creek, CA 94596 (☎1-800/937-1387).

If you do want a specific travel insurance policy, there are numerous ones from which to choose. The best deals are usually through student/youth travel agencies – ISIS policies, for example, cost $48–69 for 15 days (depending on cover); $80–105 for a month, $149–207 for 2 months, on up to $510–700 for a year. If you are planning to do any "dangerous sports" (skiing, climbing, etc.), be sure to ask whether these activities are covered; some policies add a hefty surcharge. One thing to bear in mind is that none of the currently available policies covers theft; they only cover loss while in the custody of an identifiable person – though even then you must make a report to the police and get their written statement.

AUSTRALASIAN COVER

In **Australia and New Zealand**, travel insurance is offered by airlines and travel agent groups such as *United Travel Agent Group*

administered by accident and emergency units at National Health Service hospitals. Thus a **US** citizen who has been hit by a car would not be charged if the injuries simply required stitching and setting in the emergency unit, but would if admission to a hospital ward were necessary. Health insurance is therefore extremely advisable for all non-EU nationals. In **Australia**, Medicare has a reciprocal healthcare arrangement with Britain.

Pharmacists can dispense only a limited range of drugs without a doctor's prescription. Most are open standard shop hours, though in large towns some may close as late as 10pm – local newspapers carry lists of late-opening pharmacies. **Doctors' surgeries** tend to be open from about 9am to noon and then for a couple of hours in the evening; outside surgery hours, you can turn up at the casualty department of the local hospital for complaints that require immedi-

THE MIDGE

Despite being around a millimetre long, and enjoying a life-span on the wing of just a few weeks, the **midge** (*culicoides*) – a tiny biting fly prevalent in the Highlands (mainly the west coast) and islands – is considered to be second only to the weather as the major deterrent to tourism in Scotland. Over 30 varieties of midge exist here, though only half of these actually bite humans. Ninety percent of all midge bites are down to the female *culicoides impunctatus* or Highland midge (the male does not bite). To some, these persistent creatures are merely a nuisance; others have a violent allergic reaction when bitten. The easiest way to avoid midges is to visit in the winter, since they only appear between April and October; less drastic deter-rents include smoke and noise – wind, direct sunlight, heavy rain and drought also discourage them. Basically, midges love still, damp, overcast or shady conditions and are at their meanest around sunrise and sunset. You'll soon notice if they're near; cover up arms and legs and try and avoid wearing dark colours, which attract them. Various repellents are worth a try, among them *Autan* and *Jungle Formula*, widely available from pharmacists, and the herbal remedy citronella. An alternative to repellents for protecting your face, especially if you are walking or camping, is the midge net, which you secure by tucking under your hat. Although they appear ridiculous at first, midge nets are commonplace and extremely useful.

ate attention – unless it's an emergency, in which case ring for an ambulance, ☎999.

THE POLICE

For the most part the Scottish **police** continue to be approachable and helpful to visitors. If you're lost in a major town, asking a police officer is generally the quickest way to get help – alternatively, you could ask a **traffic warden**, a much maligned species of law-enforcer responsible for parking restrictions and other vehicle-related matters. They're distinguishable by their flat caps with a yellow band, and by the fact that they are generally armed with a book of parking-fine tickets; police officers on street duty wear a peaked flat hat with a black and white chequered band, and are generally armed with a truncheon (baton).

As with any country, Scotland's major towns have their danger spots, but these tend to be inner-city housing estates where no tourist has any reason to be. The chief risk on the streets is pickpocketing, so carry only as much money as you need, and keep all bags and pockets fastened. Should you have anything stolen or be involved in some incident that requires reporting, go to the local police station (addresses in the major cities are listed in the *Guide*); the ☎999 number should only be used in emergencies.

EMERGENCIES

For Police, Fire Brigade, Ambulance and, in certain areas, Mountain Rescue or Coastguard, dial ☎999.

INFORMATION AND MAPS

If you want to do a bit of research before arriving in Scotland, you should contact the British Tourist Authority (BTA) in your country or write direct to the main office of the Scottish Tourist Board (STB), marking your letter Information Department – the addresses are given below. The BTA and the STB will send you a wealth of free

SCOTTISH TOURIST BOARD OFFICES

Scotland: 23 Ravelston Terrace, Edinburgh EH4 3EU (☎0131/332 2433).

England: 19 Cockspur St, London SW1 5BL (☎0171/930 8661 or 8662 or 8663).

BRITISH TOURIST AUTHORITY OFFICES

Australia 210 Clarence St, 4th Floor, Sydney, NSW 2000 (☎02/9267 4555 or toll-free 1 902/261603).

Canada 111 Avenue Rd, Suite 450, Toronto, Ontario M5R 3J8 (☎416/961-8124).

Ireland 18–19 College Green, Dublin 2 (☎1/670 8000).

New Zealand Suite 305, 3rd Floor, Dilworth Building, corner of Customs and Queen streets, Auckland (☎09/303 1805).

USA 551 5th Ave, Suite 701, New York, NY 10176 (☎1-800/Go Britain or ☎212/986-2200).

625 N Michigan Ave, Suite 1510, Chicago, IL (walk-in service only).

AREA TOURIST BOARDS IN SCOTLAND

Scotland's regional tourist boards have been reorganized several times in the last few years, most recently in April 1995, when 31 unwieldy areas were merged into just 14. At the time of going to press, the exact location of each of the head offices had yet to be decided, so the contact addresses and phone numbers given below are only provisional.

Aberdeen & Grampian Tourist Board, Migvie House, North Silver St, Aberdeen AB1 1RJ (☎01224/632727).

Angus & City of Dundee Tourist Board, 4 City Square, Dundee DD1 3BA (☎01382/227723).

Argyll, the Isles, Loch Lomond, Stirling & Trossachs Tourist Board, 41 Dumbarton Rd, Stirling FK8 2QQ (☎01786/475019).

Ayrshire & Arran Tourist Board, Burns House, Burns Statue Square, Ayr KA7 1UT (☎01292/288688).

Dumfries and Galloway Tourist Board, Campbell House, Bankend Rd, Dumfries DG1 4TH (☎01387/253862).

Edinburgh & Lothians Tourist Board, 4 Rothesay Terrace, Edinburgh EH3 7RY (☎0131/557 1700).

Glasgow & Clyde Valley Tourist Board, 39 St Vincent Place, Glasgow G1 2ER (☎0141/204 4400).

Highlands of Scotland Tourist Board, Beechwood Park North, Inverness IV2 3ED (☎01463/223512).

Kingdom of Fife Tourist Board, Huntsman's House, 33 Cadham Centre, Glenrothes KY7 6RU (☎01334/472021).

Orkney Tourist Board, 6 Broad St, Kirkwall, Orkney KW15 1DH (☎01856/872856).

Perthshire Tourist Board, 45 High St, Perth PH1 5TJ (☎01738/627958).

Scottish Borders Tourist Board, 70 High St, Selkirk TD7 4DD (☎01835/863435).

Shetland Island Tourism, Market Cross, Lerwick, Shetland ZE1 0LU (☎01595/693434).

Western Isles Tourist Board, 26 Cromwell St, Stornoway, Isle of Lewis HS1 2DD (☎01851/703088).

literature, some of it just rosy-tinted advertising copy, but much of it extremely useful – especially the maps, city guides and event calendars. If you want more hard facts on a particular area, you should approach the area tourist boards, which are listed overleaf. Some are extremely helpful, others give the impression of being harassed to breaking point by years of understaffing, but all of them will have a few leaflets worth scanning before you set out.

Tourist offices (sometimes called Tourist Information Centres) exist in virtually every Scottish town – you'll find their phone numbers and opening hours in the relevant sections of the *Guide*. The average opening hours are much the same as standard shop hours, with the difference

that in summer they'll often be open on a Sunday and for a couple of hours after the shops have closed on weekdays; opening hours are generally shorter in winter, and in more remote areas the office may well be closed for the season. All centres offer information on accommodation (and can usually book rooms – see "Accommodation"), local public transport, attractions and restaurants as well as town and regional maps. In many cases their services are free, but a growing number of offices make a small charge for an accommodation list or a town guide with an accompanying street plan.

MAPS

Most bookshops will have a good selection of maps of Scotland and Britain in general, but see

---

MAP OUTLETS

IN THE UK

Edinburgh, *HMSO Books*, 71 Lothian Rd, EH3 9AZ (☎0131/228 4181).

Glasgow, *John Smith and Sons*, 57–61 St Vincent St, G2 5TB (☎041/221 7472).

London, *Daunt Books*, 83 Marylebone High St, W1 (☎0171/224 2295); *National Map Centre*, 22–24 Caxton St, SW1 (☎0171/222 4945); *Stanfords*, 12–14 Long Acre, WC2 (☎0171/836 1321); *The Travellers Bookshop*, 25 Cecil Court, WC2 (☎0171/836 9132).

Maps by **mail or phone** order are available from *Stanfords*. ☎0171/836 1321.

IN NORTH AMERICA

Chicago, *Rand McNally*, 444 North Michigan Ave, IL 60611 (☎312/321-1751).

Los Angeles, *Map Link Inc*, 25 E Mason St, Santa Barbara, CA 93101 (☎805/965-4402)

Montréal, *Ulysses Travel Bookshop*, 4176 St-Denis (☎514/289-0993).

New York, *British Travel Bookshop*, 551 5th Ave, NY 10176 (☎ 212/490-6688), mail order through *BritRail Travel* ☎ 800/677-8585); *The Complete Traveler Bookstore*, 199 Madison Ave, NY 10016 (☎212/685-9007); *Rand McNally*, 150 E 52nd St, NY 10022 (☎212/758-7488); *Traveler's Bookstore*, 22 W 52nd St, NY 10019 (☎212/664-0995).

San Francisco, *The Complete Traveler Bookstore*, 3207 Filmore St, CA 92123 (☎415/923-1511); *Rand McNally*, 595 Market St, CA 94105

(☎415/777-3131); *Phileas Fogg's Books & Maps*, 87 Stanford Shopping Centre, Palo Alto, CA 94304 (☎800/233-FOGG in California; ☎1-800/533-FOGG elsewhere).

Seattle, *Elliot Bay Book Company*, 101 South Main St, WA 98104 (☎206/624-6600).

Toronto, *Open Air Books and Maps*, 25 Toronto St, M5R 2C1 (☎416/363-0719).

Vancouver, *World Wide Books and Maps*, 1247 Granville St (☎604/687-3320).

Washington DC, *Rand McNally*, 1201 Connecticut Ave NW, Washington, DC 20036 (☎202/223-6751).

Rand McNally now have 24 stores nationwide. For details of your local branch, and direct-mail maps call ☎1-800/333-0136 ext 2111.

IN AUSTRALIA AND NEW ZEALAND

Adelaide, *The Map Shop*, 16a Peel St, Adelaide, SA 5000 (☎08/8231 2033).

Auckland, *Speciality Maps*, 58 Albert St, City, Auckland (☎09/307 2217).

Brisbane, *Hema*, 239 George St, Brisbane, QLD 4000 (☎07/3221 4330).

Melbourne, *Bowyangs*, 372 Little Bourke St, Melbourne, VIC 3000 (☎03/9670 4383).

Perth, *Perth Map Centre*, 891 Hay St, Perth, WA 6000 (☎09/322 5733; ☎08/9322 5733 from Sept 1997).

Sydney, *Travel Bookshop*, 20 Bridge St, Sydney, NSW 2000 (☎02/9241 3554).

the box below for a list of travel specialists. Of the many North American outlets, the *British Travel Bookshop* in New York, in particular, stocks a phenomenal array. *Rand McNally Map and Travel* is also a good bet.

Virtually every service station in Scotland stocks one or more of the big **road atlases**. The best of these are the large-format ones produced by the *AA, RAC, Collins* and *Ordnance Survey*, which cover all of Britain at around 3miles:1in and include larger-scale plans of major towns. You could also invest in the excellent **fold-out maps** published by *Michelin* and *Bartholomew*, the latter includes clear town plans of the major cities. Another option is the official tourist map series published by Estate Publications, perfect if you're driving or cycling round one particular region since it marks all the major tourist sights as well as youth hostels and campsites.

If you're after more detail, the most comprehensive **maps** of Scotland are produced by the **Ordnance Survey** series – renowned for its accuracy and clarity. The 204 maps in their 1:50,000 (a little over 1mile:1in) *Landranger* series cover the whole of Britain and show enough detail to be useful for most walkers. Their more detailed 1:25,000 *Pathfinder* series, which also covers the whole of Britain, is invaluable for serious hiking. For many of the walks in this guide, the use of *Ordnance Survey* maps is strongly recommended (see p.39). The full *Ordnance Survey* range is only available at a few big-city stores, although in any walking district of Scotland you'll find the relevant maps in local shops or tourist offices.

GETTING AROUND

As you'd expect, the efficiency of Scotland's train and bus services is largely dictated by geography and population density. The majority of Scots live in the central belt, which spreads from Glasgow in the west to Edinburgh, virtually on the east coast. Public transport here is efficient and most places are easily accessible by train and bus. To the south and north it can be a different story; off the main routes public transport services are few and far between, particularly in more remote regions such as the Highlands, although with careful planning practically everywhere is reachable and you'll have no trouble getting to the main tourist destinations. In most parts of Scotland, especially if you take the scenic back roads, the low level of traffic makes driving wonderfully unstressful.

TRAINS

Always something of a national joke, recent government policies have led to a severe decline in **rail services** all over Britain, and Scotland is no exception. For the time being **ScotRail**, runs the majority of train services, reaching all the major towns, sometimes on lines rated as among the great scenic routes of the world. For a **rundown of the different fares available**, see "Getting There from England, Ireland and Europe".

You can buy tickets for *ScotRail* trains at stations or from major travel agents. For busy

TRAIN INFORMATION AND BOOKING IN SCOTLAND

The following numbers will give train information and take credit-card bookings for the *ScotRail* network. Local and mainline information is also available from all manned Scottish stations (see *Yellow Pages* for telephone numbers).

Edinburgh	☎0131/556 2451.
Glasgow	☎0141/204 2844.
Aberdeen	☎01224/594222.
Inverness	☎01463/238924.

long-distance **InterCity** routes, it's advisable to **reserve** a seat. Seat reservations to Edinburgh, Glasgow, Aberdeen or Inverness are included in the price of the ticket if you book in advance. The ticket offices at many rural and commuter stations are closed at weekends; in these instances there's sometimes a vending machine on the platform. If the machines aren't working, you can buy your ticket on board, but if you've embarked at a station that does have a machine and you haven't bought a ticket, there's a spot fine of £10.

ScotRail offer a number of **travel cards** and **special tickets** that are available to British nationals and foreign visitors alike. The *Freedom of Scotland Travelpass* gives unlimited train travel and is valid on all *CalMac* west coast ferry links (see ferry information on p.24) as well as offering 33 percent reductions on many buses and on some *P&O* Orkney and Shetland ferries. It costs £99 for 8 consecutive days, £139 for 15 days, or £110 for 8 out of 15 days, and comes complete with timetables and a card allowing discounts at tourist attractions, shops and restaurants throughout Scotland. The *ScotRail Rover* is perhaps the most flexible option, allowing unlimited travel on *ScotRail* for varying periods; prices range from £60 for 4 days out of 8 consecutive days travel to £115 for 12 out of 15 days. *ScotRail* also do 3 other regional *Rover* passes: the *West Highland* (covering the area from Glasgow to Fort William) which costs £39 for 4 out of 8 days; the *North Highland,* which for the same price is valid

on all lines from Thurso to Aberdeen; and the *Festival Cities*, which includes routes from Glasgow to Edinburgh and Stirling, and costs £21 (3 out of 7 days).

For **North American visitors** who anticipate covering a lot of ground around Britain, a rail pass is a wise investment. The standard **BritRail Pass**, available from *BritRail Travel International* (see above), gives unlimited travel in England, Scotland and Wales for 8 days (US$230), 15 days ($355), 22 days ($445) or a month ($520). The **BritRail Flexipass** is good for travel on 4 days out of a month ($195), 8 days out of a month ($275), or 15 days out of a month ($405). Note that with both these passes there are discounts for those under 26 (*BritRail Youth* passes) or over 60 (*BritRail Senior* passes), and the *Flexipass* has a special 15 days out of 2 months rate for under-26s ($319).

For **Australians** and **New Zealanders**, these passes are available from branches of *Thomas Cook*. The *BritRail Pass* costs for 8 days A$280/NZ$310, for 15 A$395/NZ$440, for 22 A$525/NZ$590, for a month A$575/NZ640; and the *BritRail Flexipass*, A$240/NZ$265 for 4 days out of a month, A$345/NZ$385 for 8 days and A$500/NZ$555 for 15 days.

For information on the **Eurail** pass see "Getting There from North America". Three passes are available only in **Britain** itself, all valid for a year; for details of these and **InterRail** passes see "Getting There from England, Ireland and Europe".

BUSES

Travelling around Scotland by bus may take a little longer than using the train, but works out considerably cheaper. There's a plethora of regional companies, but by far the biggest national operators are *Scottish Citylink* (☎0990/898989), a subsidiary company of *National Express*. With the price of train travel becoming exorbitant, their services are so popular that for busy routes and on any route at weekends and during holidays it's a very good idea to buy a "reserved-journey ticket", which guarantees you a seat.

Foreign travellers can purchase a **Tourist Trail Pass**, which offers unlimited travel on the *National Express* network: on any 8 days within 16 it costs £90 for students and under-23s, £119 for others; on any 15 days within 30 £145 and £179 respectively. In England you can obtain both from major travel agents, at Gatwick and Heathrow airports and at the British Travel Centre, 12 Regent St, London W1 (walk-in service only). In Scotland outlets include St Andrew Square Bus Station, Edinburgh, and Buchanan Bus Station, Glasgow, as well as other local bus stations. In **North America** these passes are available for the dollar equivalent through specialist tour operators (see p.11) or direct from *British Travel International*, PO Box 299, Elkton, VA 22827 (☎1-800/327-6097). In **Australia** and **New Zealand**, the passes are available from *Thomas Cook*. For details of other discount passes only available in Britain itself see "Getting There from England, Ireland and Europe".

Local bus services are run by a bewildering array of companies, and it's increasingly the case that private companies duplicate the busiest routes in an attempt to undercut the commercial opposition, leaving the remoter spots neglected. As a general rule, the further away from urban areas you get, the less frequent and more expensive bus services become.

Those rural areas not covered by other forms of public transport are served by the **postbus** network, which operates 140 minibuses carrying mail and about 8 fare-paying passengers. They set off in the morning – usually around 8am from the main post office and collect mail (or deliver it) from/to the nether regions. It's an extremely cheap way to travel, costing about £2 or so for every 20 miles, and can be a convenient way of getting to hidden-away B&Bs, although often excruciatingly slow. You can get a booklet of routes and timetables from the *Royal Mail Public Relations Unit*, 102 West Port, Edinburgh EH3 9HS (☎0131/228 7407).

If you're **backpacking**, it's worth investigating a small outfit called *Go Blue Banana*, whose minibus calls at Edinburgh, Perth, Aviemore, Inverness, Skye, Fort William, Glencoe, Oban and Loch Lomond every 2 days except Monday, stopping at independent hostels en route. You can hop on and off wherever you like, and a ticket, for one circuit but with no time limit, costs £65. Further details are available from their office at Room 8, North Bridge House, 28 North Bridge, Edinburgh EH1 1QR (☎0131/220 6869).

DRIVING AND HITCHING

If you want to cover a lot of the country in a short time, or just want more flexibility, you'll need your own transport. In order to **drive** in Scotland you must have a current driving licence; foreign

nationals will need to supplement this with an international driving permit available from national motoring organizations for a small fee. If you're bringing your own car into the country you should also carry your vehicle registration or ownership document at all times. Furthermore, you must be adequately insured, so be sure to check your existing policy.

Scotland remains one of the few countries in the world where you drive on the left, a situation that can lead to a few tense days of acclimatization for many overseas drivers. **Speed limits** are 30–40mph (50–65kmph) in built-up areas, 70mph (110kmph) on motorways and dual carriageways and 60mph (100kmph) on most other roads. As a rule, assume that in any area with street lighting the speed limit is 30mph (50kmph) unless stated otherwise. Out in the remoter regions, many roads are still **single-track**, with passing places – these should also be used to enable cars to overtake you. In the Highlands, the roads are littered with sheep who are entirely oblivious to cars, so slow down and edge your way past – should you kill one, it is your duty to inform the local farmer.

The 3 major motoring organizations, the *Automobile Association* (*AA*), the *Royal Automobile Club* (*RAC*) and *National Breakdown*, all operate 24-hour emergency **breakdown** services. The *AA* and *RAC* also provide many other motoring services, including a reciprocal arrangement for free assistance through many overseas motoring organizations – check the situation with yours before setting out. On motorways the *AA* and *RAC* can be called from roadside booths; elsewhere ring ☎0000/887766 for the *AA*, ☎0800/828282 for the *RAC* and ☎0800/400600 for *National Breakdown* – though in remote areas, particularly in the Highlands, you may have a long wait for assistance. You can ring these emergency numbers even if you are not a member of the respective organization, although a substantial fee will be charged.

Like the rest of Britain, it's inadvisable for anyone travelling alone to **hitch** in Scotland, even in the central region where there's a good motorway network and a lot of traffic. Things are less problematic in remote areas, especially in the Highlands, where there's a long tradition of giving lifts, but locals clearly have priority, and you may have to wait a long time before you're picked up.

CAR AND MOTORBIKE RENTAL

Car rental in Scotland is expensive, and, especially if you're travelling from North America, you'll probably find it cheaper to arrange things in advance through one of the multinational chains. If you do rent a car, the least you can expect to pay is around £130 a week – the rate for a small hatchback from *Holiday Autos*, the most competitive rental agency; reckon on paying £40 per day direct from one of the multinationals, £5 or so less at a local firm. Most companies prefer you to pay with a credit card, otherwise you may have to leave a deposit of at least £100. There are very few automatics at the lower end of the price scale – if you want one, you should book well ahead. To rent a car you need to show your driving licence; few companies will rent to drivers with less than a year's experience and most will only rent to people between 21 and 70 years of age.

Motorbike rental is ludicrously expensive, at around £45 a day/£200 a week for a 500cc machine, and around £80/£300 for a one-litre tourer, including everything from insurance, helmets and luggage.

FERRIES

Scotland has 130 inhabited islands, and ferries play an important part in travelling around the country. Most ferries carry cars and vans, for which advance reservations can be made – highly advisable, particularly during the busy summer season (April–Oct). Of the major operators, *Caledonian MacBrayne* (abbreviated by most

---

MOTORING ORGANIZATIONS

American Automobile Association (AAA), 4100 E Arkanas Ave, Denver, CO 80222 (☎1-800/ 222-4357). *Most member services apply only in the US and Canada, but the AAA can refer members to Britain's AA, and also provide international drivers' licenses.*

Australian Automobile Association, 212 Northbourne Ave, Canberra ACT 2601 (☎61/6247 7311).

Automobile Association, Fanum House, Basingstoke, Hants RG21 2EA (☎01256/20123).

Canadian Automobile Association (CAA)
Each region has its own club – check the phone book for local address and phone number. Benefits are comparable to the AAA's.

New Zealand Automobile Association, PO Box 1794, Wellington (☎64/473 8738).

Royal Automobile Club, PO Box 100, RAC House, Bartlett St, S Croydon CR2 6XZ (☎0181/ 686 0088).

CAR RENTAL FIRMS

IN BRITAIN

Avis ☎0131/337 6363.

Budget ☎0131/334 7740.

Eurodollar ☎0131/556 0565.

Europcar ☎0131/661 252.

Hertz ☎0131/556 8311.

Holiday Autos ☎0171/491 1111.

Mitchell Self Drive ☎0131/229 5384.

IN NORTH AMERICA

Alamo domestic ☎1-800/354-2322; international ☎1-800/522-9696.

Avis domestic ☎1-800/331-1212; international ☎1-800/331-1084.

Budget ☎1-800/527-0700.

Europe By Car ☎1-800/223-1516.

Hertz domestic ☎1-800/654-3131; international ☎1-800/654-3001; in Canada ☎1-800/263-0600.

Holiday Autos ☎1-800/422-7737.

National Car Rental ☎1-800/CAR-RENT.

IN AUSTRALIA

Avis ☎1800/22 5533.

Budget ☎13 2848.

Hertz ☎13 1918.

Renault Eurodrive ☎02/9299 3344.

IN NEW ZEALAND

Avis ☎09/525 1982.

Budget ☎09/309 6737.

Fly and Drive Holidays ☎09/366 0759.

Hertz ☎09/309 0989.

FERRY OFFICES AND INFORMATION IN SCOTLAND

Caledonian MacBrayne Ltd, The Ferry Terminal, Gourock, Renfrewshire PA19 1QP (☎01475/650100).

Orkney Islands Shipping Co Ltd, Head Office, 4 Ayre Rd, Kirkwall KW15 1QX (☎01856/872044).

P&O Scottish Ferries, PO Box 5, Jamieson's Quay, Aberdeen AB9 8DL (☎01224/572615).

Western Ferries (Clyde) Ltd, 16 Woodside Crescent, Glasgow G3 7UT (☎0141/332 9766).

people and throughout this book to *CalMac*) covers the majority of routes.

CalMac have a virtual monopoly on services on the River Clyde and those to the Inner and Outer Hebrides, sailing to 23 islands altogether. They aren't cheap, but they do have two types of **reduced fare pass**, the *Island Hopscotch* and the *Island Rover*. The *Hopscotch* covers a range of economy fares for cars and passengers on 23 pre-planned routes which are valid for 3 months from the date of the first journey. There are 2 types of *Island Rover*, for 8 and 15 consecutive days, which offer unlimited travel on *CalMac* ferries, though you must inform them of your exact itinerary in advance and fares will be costed accordingly. Schedules vary and are highly complicated, but you can get details from the address below.

P&O Scottish Ferries sail to Orkney and Shetland from Aberdeen and Scrabster (Thurso). To Shetland from Aberdeen takes 14hr and costs about £50 for a foot passenger, plus £120 or so for a car; to Orkney takes 8hr and costs £36.50,

plus £100 or so for a car; Scrabster to Orkney takes 1hr 50min, which costs £13.50 or so, plus a further £50 or so for a car. For both routes you should book if you are taking a vehicle. *P&O* offer no passes.

In addition, *Western Ferries* operate between Gourock and Dunoon on the mainland to the islands of Islay and Jura. The various Orkney islands are linked by the services run by the *Orkney Islands Shipping Co Ltd*. Numerous small operators round the Scottish coast run day-excursion trips; their phone numbers are listed in the relevant chapters in the *Guide*.

It is possible to book ferry tickets in advance in **North America**, if you're organized enough to know exactly when you'll be making the crossing. For sailings to/from France, Belguim or the Netherlands, contact *BritRail Travel International* (☎1-800/677-8585) or *Scots American* (☎1-201/768-1187); to/from Scandinavia, contact *Bergen Line* (☎1-800/323-7436) or *Scandinavian Seaways* (☎1-800/533-3755); and to/from Ireland, try *Lynott Tours* (☎1-800/221 2474). In **Australia** and **New Zealand**, you can book ferry tickets in advance at branches of *Thomas Cook*.

INTERNAL FLIGHTS

Scotland has 17 internal airports, many of them on the islands and useful if you are short on time. Flights between the Islands are mainly operated by *British Airways Express* (also known as *Loganair*; ☎0141/889 1311), with *British Airways* (☎0345/222111) flying between Edinburgh, Glasgow, Aberdeen and Inverness and to some of the main islands. Airports are listed below; call them direct for further details.

AIRPORTS IN SCOTLAND

Aberdeen ☎01224/722331.	**Islay** ☎01496/302361.
Barra Northbay ☎018715/890283.	**Kirkwall** ☎01856/872421.
Benbecula ☎01870/602051.	**Stornoway** ☎01851/702256.
Campbeltown ☎01586/552571.	**Sumburgh** ☎01950/460654.
Dundee ☎01382/643242.	**Tingwall** ☎01595/840306.
Edinburgh ☎0131/333 1000.	**Tiree** ☎018792/220456.
Fair Isle ☎013512/760224.	**Unst** ☎01957/711404.
Glasgow ☎0141/887 1111.	**Wick** ☎01955/602215.
Inverness ☎01463/232471.	

ACCOMMODATION

The prevalence of bed and breakfast (B&B) and youth hostels in Scotland ensures that budget accommodation is easy to come by. There are also scores of upmarket hotels, ranging from bland business-oriented places in the centres of the big towns to plush converted country mansions and ancient castles. Most tourist offices will book all kinds of accommodation for you when you arrive, although usually there is a fee for this service, which varies considerably. In some areas you will pay a deposit that's deducted from your first night's bill (usually 10 percent), in others the office will take a percentage or flat-rate commission – on average around £3 – and occasionally it's free. Another useful service operated by the majority of tourist offices is the *Book-a-bed-ahead* service, which locates accommodation in your next port of call. This will cost at least £2.50.

HOTELS AND B&Bs

The STB operates a nationwide system for grading **hotels, guest houses and B&Bs**, which is updated annually – although by no means everyone participates, and you shouldn't assume that any one particular B&B is no good if it's ungraded. There are so many of these establishments in Scotland that the grading inspectors can't possibly keep track of them all, and in the rural backwaters some of the most enjoyable accommodation is to be found in welcoming and beautifully set houses whose facilities may technically fall short of official standards. Everything in this scheme is graded into 4 categories: Approved, Commended, Highly Commended and Deluxe. Within these, one to five Crowns are awarded for "facilities" which theoretically cover the condition of buildings and grounds, the quality of the food and general comfort as well as the warmth of welcome and the efficiency and friendliness shown by the staff. It's probably also worth using the the grades supplied by the *AA* and the *RAC* as they independently combine evaluation of facilities with a degree of subjective judgement. Though there's not a hard and fast correlation between standards and price, you'll probably be paying in the region of £40 per night for a double room at a 1-star hotel (breakfast included), rising to around £70 in a 3-star, and from around £120 for a 5-star. In some larger towns and cities you'll find that the big hotels often offer cut-price deals at the weekend to fill the rooms vacated by the week's business trade, but these places tend to be soulless multinational chain operations. If you can afford it, stay in a refurbished old building – many towns have atmospheric coaching inns and such like, while out in the countryside you'll find converted mansions and castles, often with brilliant restaurants attached.

ACCOMMODATION PRICE CODES

Throughout this book, accommodation **prices** have been graded with the numbers below, according to the cost of the least expensive double room in high season. Although costs will rise slightly overall with the life of this edition, the relative comparisons should remain valid. The bulk of the recommendations will fall in categories ② to ⑥; those in the highest categories are limited to places that are especially attractive. Bear in mind that many of the swanky hotels often slash their tariffs at the weekend when the business types have gone home, and that many of the cheaper places will also have more expensive rooms. Note that in our accommodation listings price codes are not given for youth hostels – they all come into the lower end of the ① category.

① under £20	④ £40–50	⑦ £70–80
② £20–30	⑤ £50–60	⑧ £80–100
③ £30–40	⑥ £60–70	⑨ over £100

At the lower end of the scale, hotels merge almost imperceptibly into **B&Bs** – often known as **guest houses** in resorts and other tourist towns. These range from ordinary private houses with a couple of bedrooms set aside for paying guests and a dining room for the consumption of a rudimentary breakfast, to rooms as well furnished as those in hotels costing twice as much, with delicious home-prepared breakfasts, and an informal hospitality that a larger place couldn't match. B&Bs are also graded by the STB, the *AA* and the *RAC*. As a guideline to costs, it's easy to find a grade 1 STB place for under £30 per night a double; grade 4 places go for around £80. As many B&Bs, even the pricier ones, have a very small number of rooms, you should certainly book a place as far in advance as possible.

Another important point to remember in rural Scotland is that many B&Bs as well as hotels, are only open for the summer season, roughly from Easter to October. You'll always find somewhere to stay outside this period, but the choice may be pretty limited.

YOUTH HOSTELS

The network of the **Scottish Youth Hostels Association (SYHA)** consists of some 80 properties, usually offering bunk-bed accommodation in single-sex dormitories or smaller rooms. A few of these places are spartan establishments of the

---

SYHA OFFICES

Aberdeen 11 Ashvale Place, AB1 6QD (☎01224/588156).

Ayr Craigweil House, Craigweil Rd, KA7 BJ (no phone).

Dundee 86 Bell St, DD1 1JG (☎01382/322150).

Edinburgh 161 Warrender Park Rd, EH9 1EQ (☎0131/229 8660).

Glasgow 12 Renfield St, G2 5AL (☎0141/226 3976).

Stirling 7 Glebe Crescent, FK8 2JA (☎01786/451181).

---

sort traditionally associated with the wholesome, fresh-air ethic of the early hostels, but most have moved well away from this and are beginning to offer private facilities with no curfew.

All the youth hostels referred to in the *Guide* are official SYHA properties unless stated otherwise. For Scottish residents, membership – which includes membership of the hostelling associations in the 60 countries affiliated to the **International Youth Hostels Association (IYHF)** – costs £2.50 per year for under-18s, £6 for others, and can be obtained either by writing to or visiting the SYHA offices listed overleaf, or in person at most SYHA hostels. Visitors from elsewhere in Britain and foreign nationals who wish to join the IYHF can do so at the SYHA offices or most Scottish youth hostels for a £9 fee. Youth hostel members are allowed half-price entry to National Trust for Scotland properties (see p.34).

At any time of the year, particularly in the Grade 1 youth hostels, it's best to **book your place** well in advance, and it's essential at Easter, Christmas and between May and August. You can book by post or telephone; in both cases your bed will be held until 6pm on the day of arrival. Some hostels, particularly in the Highlands, are closed for the whole of the winter except for the Christmas and New Year period. Even if you haven't booked, always phone ahead – we've given phone numbers in the *Guide*. Most hostels are closed from 10am to 5pm with an 11.30pm curfew, but some are open all day. Length of stay is normally unlimited. It's worth getting a copy of the *SYHA Handbook*, which clarifies the intricacies of the system, and lists every hostel in the association; it's available from the address below.

SYHA GRADES AND COSTS

All SYHA hostels are **graded** to indicate their level of facilities. **Grade 1** hostels, which cost £6.75–7.55 (£5.70–6.20 for 5–17 year olds), are the top of the range, including free hot showers, and, occasionally, extended opening hours. At **Grade 2** hostels – the most common – the rate is £5.25 per night (£4.30), and hot showers are usually available for a small fee. **Grade 3** (£4/£3.30) places are the simplest, with limited facilities. However, in Stirling, Glasgow and Edinburgh (except Bruntsfield) the hostels (all Grade 1) cost slightly more (£10.15/£8.75). We've given the grades for each hostel in the guide.

Over most of Scotland students aged 18–25 can get a £1 reduction on admission prices on production of a valid student card. The cost of hostel **meals**, where available, is low: breakfast is around £2.50, and evening meals start at around £4. Nearly all hostels have kitchen facilities, for those who prefer self-catering.

YOUTH HOSTEL ASSOCIATIONS

Australia *Australian Youth Hostels Association*, Level 3, 10 Mallett St, Camperdown, NSW (☎02/565 1325).

Canada *Hostelling International-Canadian Hostelling Association*, Room 400, 205 Catherine St, Ottawa, ON K2P 1C3 (☎613/237-7884 or ☎1-800/663-5777). *Annual membership for adults $25, children under 18 free when accompanied by parents; 2-year memberships cost £35.*

England and Wales *Youth Hostel Association* (*YHA*), Trevelyan House, 8 St Stephen's Hill, St Albans, Herts AL1 2DY (☎017278/45047). London information office: 14 Southampton St, London WC2E 7HY (☎0171/836 1036). *There are 15 other YHA city locations throughout England.*

Ireland *An Óige*, 61 Mountjoy St, Dublin 7 (☎01/830 4555).

New Zealand *Youth Hostels Association of New Zealand*, PO Box 436, Christchurch 1 (☎03/799970).

Northern Ireland *Youth Hostel Association of Northern Ireland*, 22 Donegal Rd, Belfast, BT12 5JN (☎01232/324733).

Scotland *Scottish Youth Hostel Association*, 7 Glebe Crescent, Stirling, FK8 2JA (☎01786/451181).

USA *Hostelling International-American Youth Hostels (HI-AYH)*, 773 15th St NW, Suite 840, PO Box 37613, Washington, DC 200013 (☎202/783-6161). *Annual membership for adults $25, youths (under 19) $10, seniors (55 or over) $15, families $35.*

Allied to the SYHA, the **Gatliff Hebridean Hostels Trust** is a charitable organization that rents out very simple croft accommodation in the Hebridean Islands. Accommodation is very basic, almost primitive, but the settings are spectacular. These places are ungraded, and many have no phones. There's also the **Independent Backpackers Hostels Association,** an association of 37 independent hostels, mainly situated in the Highlands and islands, though including 3 in Edinburgh. These are mostly family-run places with no membership and no curfew, and most are open all year. Housed in buildings ranging from crofthouses to converted churches, they all have dormitories, hot showers, common rooms and self-catering kitchens, while many organize a range of outdoor activities. Prices hover around £7 per person per night. A brochure listing all the properties is available from *The Independent Backpackers Hostels Scotland*, c/o The Loch Ness Backpackers Lodge, Leiston, Drumnadrochit, Inverness-shire IV3 6UT (☎01456/450807).

CAMPING, CARAVANNING AND SELF-CATERING

There are hundreds of **campsites** in Scotland, most of which are open from April to October. The most expensive sites, which charge about £8 to pitch a tent, are usually well equipped with shops, a restaurant, a bar and occasionally sports facilities. At the other end of the scale, farmers sometimes offer pitches on their land for as little as £2 per night. The *AA* list and grade campsites in their publication *Camping and Caravanning in Britain and Ireland*, and the area tourist boards can all supply lists of their recommended sites.

In the most popular parts of rural Scotland – especially in the Highlands and the islands – tents have to share space with **caravans**. The great majority are permanently moored at their sites, where they are rented out for **self-catering** holidays, and the ranks of nose-to-tail trailers in the vicinity of some of Scotland's finest scenery might make you think that half the population of Britain shacks up in a caravan for the midsummer break. You may prefer more robust self-catering accommodation, and there are thousands of STB-approved properties for rent by the week, ranging from city penthouses to secluded cottages. The least you can expect to pay for 4-berth self-catering accommodation in summer would be around £150 per week, but for something special – such as a well-sited coastal cottage – you should budget for twice that amount.

Another cheap self-catering option, especially if you're staying a week or more, is **campus accommodation.** Many Scottish universities open their halls of residence to overseas visitors during the summer break, and rooms vary from tiny single rooms in long, lonely corridors, to relatively comfortable places in small shared apartments. The *British Universities Accommodation Consortium* (*BUAC*) have full details: contact them at PO Box 1274, University Park, Nottingham NG7 2RD (☎0115/950 4571).

For **North Americans** planning to do a lot of camping, an **international camping carnet** is a sound investment, available from home motoring organizations, or from *Family Campers and RVers* (*FCRV*), 4804 Transit Rd, Building 2, Depew, NY 14043 (☎1-800/245-9755) in the US; in Canada, 51 W 22nd St, Hamilton, Ontario LC9 4N5 (☎1-800/245-9755). The carnet is good for discounts at member sites and serves as useful identification. *FCRV* annual membership costs $20, and the carnet an additional $10.

FOOD AND DRINK

Though the Scots still tend to regard eating as a necessity rather than the focal point of the day, the quality of Scottish food has improved by leaps and bounds in recent years. Scots produce – superb meat, fish and game, a wide range of dairy products, the best soft fruit in Europe and a bewildering variety of traditional baked goodies – is of outstanding quality and has to some extent been rediscovered of late; bear in mind, too, that in the larger cities, the presence of various immigrant communities has led to a fine array of ethnic restaurants.

FOOD AND DRINK

In many hotels and B&Bs you'll be offered a **Scottish breakfast**; similar to its English counterpart of sausage, bacon and egg but with the addition of porridge – properly made with genuine oatmeal and traditionally eaten with salt rather than sugar, though the latter is always on offer. You may also be served kippers or Arbroath smokies (delicately smoked haddock with butter), or a large piece of haddock eaten with a poached egg on top. Oatcakes (plain, slightly salty biscuits) and a "buttery" – a butter-enriched bread related to the French croissant – will often feature. Scotland's staple drink, like England's, is **tea**, drunk strong and with milk, though **coffee** is just as readily served everywhere.

The quintessential Scots dish is **haggis**, a sheep's stomach bag stuffed with spiced liver, offal, oatmeal and onion and traditionally eaten with bashed neeps (mashed turnips) and chappit tatties (mashed potatoes). The humble haggis has become rather trendy in recent years, and you can even, in the big cities, get an occasional vegetarian version. Other staples include steak and kidney pie and shepherd's pie (minced beef covered with mashed potato and baked), as well as **stovies**, a tasty mash of onion and fried potato heated up with minced beef. In this cold climate home-made soup is generally welcome; try **Scots broth**, made with combinations of lentil, split pea, mutton stock or vegetables and barley.

Scots **beef** is delicious, especially the Aberdeen Angus breed; menus will specify if your steak falls into that fine category. **Venison**, the meat of the red deer, also features large – low in cholesterol and very tasty, it's served roasted or in casseroles, often flavoured with juniper or with a whisky sauce. If you like **game** and can afford it, splash out on grouse, the most highly prized of all game birds, strong, dark and succulent, best eaten with bread sauce. Pheasant is also worth a try; less rich than other game, more like a particularly tasty chicken – you can eat it stuffed with oatmeal or with a mealie pudding, a kind of vegetarian black pudding made from onion, oatmeal and spices.

Scotland has a huge variety of fresh **fish** to choose from. In the coastal towns, prawns, oysters, crab and scallops are always available, while inland salmon is a must, especially the more delicately flavoured wild salmon – though this will always cost more than the farmed variety. Both are served either hot with melted butter, small new potatoes and a creamy Hollandaise sauce, or cold in a salad. Trout is also farmed in Scotland, often fried in oatmeal and eaten with bacon. Look out especially for the wild brown trout, whose firm pink flesh is nearly as good as salmon.

Puddings, often smothered in butterscotch sauce or syrup, are taken very seriously in Scotland. One traditional favourite is Cranachan, made with toasted oatmeal steeped in whisky and folded into whipped cream flavoured with fresh raspberries; on the same lines, Atholl Brose, related to the English syllabub, is made with oatmeal, whisky and cream. For the ultimate dessert decadence try the clootie dumpling, a sweet, stodgy fruit pudding soaked in a cloth for hours. If it all sounds a bit rich you might prefer the black bun, a peppery fruit cake encased in a thin pastry and traditionally eaten at New Year, or the many homemade shortbreads – far superior to the commercial varieties. One Scottish institution that satisfies the Scots sweet tooth is the **high tea**, consisting of a cooked main course and a plethora of cakes, washed down with tea or coffee and eaten between about 5 and 6.30pm.

As for **fast food**, fish and chips is as popular in Scotland as in England and "**chippies**" abound, serving battered fish (invariably known as a "fish supper" even if eaten at lunchtime), haggis, and oatmeal-based numbers such as black and mealie puddings. For alternative fast food in the major towns there are all the usual **pizza** and **burger** outlets, and the more recent **baked potato** shops.

WHERE TO EAT

For **budget food** in Scotland you'll find hordes of **cafés** – which range from the most basic "greasy spoons" to vaguely French-style **brasseries**, where you can have anything from a glass of wine to a cup of coffee, as well as a simple meal. Many provincial towns have **tearooms** of sorts, where you can sample Scottish baking. Some of the cheapest places to eat in Scotland are the **pubs,** many of which serve food all day – indeed, in the smallest villages these might be your only options.

The ranks of Scottish **gastronomic restaurants** grow with each passing year, with cordon bleu chefs producing high-class dishes with a Scottish slant that certainly rival their English and European counterparts. Outside Edinburgh and Glasgow many of these are found in hotels but are happy to serve non-residents, though you could easily land up paying £25–50 a head.

In central Scotland, particularly in Edinburgh and Glasgow, the **Indian** and **Chinese** communities ensure there is a good choice of restaurants, offering quality meals at fair prices. Some of the **French** restaurants in Edinburgh are excellent, and Scotland's large **Italian** community means there are numerous good trattorias. On the whole, though, you won't find the range of choice that exists south of the border, and outside the big cities **vegetarians** are still looked on somewhat askance, though the *Taste of Scotland* members do their best to remedy this.

The restaurant listings in the *Guide* include a mix of high-quality and budget establishments. As a general rule on **costs**, if we call a place inexpensive, you can expect to pay under £10 a head, without drinks; moderate means it will cost between £10 and £20; expensive from £20 to £30; and very expensive over £30.

DRINK

Like the rest of Britain, Scottish **pubs**, which originated as travellers' hostelries and coaching inns, are *the* great social institution, and the pub crawl, a drunken trawl through as many pubs as possible in one night, is a national pastime. The focal points of any community, the local British pub can vary from oak-beamed and ingle-nooked inns with heaps of atmosphere, open fires and polished brass fittings, to blaring, noisy theme pubs, lined wall-to-wall with juke boxes and pinball machines. Most pubs are owned by large breweries who favour their own cask-conditioned real ales served from the distinctive Scottish tall font (for more on types of beer, see below). Many of them, especially outside the big cities, are no-nonsense spit-and-sawdust public bars with an almost exclusively male clientele, making some visitors, especially women, feel highly uncomfortable. However, there are plenty of places that can be as welcoming as the full name, "public house", suggests, along with – in Edinburgh and Glasgow at least – a rash of upbeat, trendy café-bars favoured by a young, pre-clubbing set.

Scotland was ahead of England in changing to all-day **opening hours** and pubs are generally open from Monday to Saturday 11am–11pm, with "last orders" called by the bar staff about 15 minutes before closing time. On Sunday the hours are reduced; many pubs are closed in the afternoon and last orders are called at 10.30pm. In general, you have to be 16 to enter a pub unaccompanied, though some places have special family rooms for people with children, and beer gardens where younger kids can run free. The legal drinking age is 18.

BEER

Beer is the staple drink in Scotland's pubs, the indigenous variety a thick, dark **ale** with a full head served in pints or half-pints at room temperature, much like the English bitter (in Scotland known as **heavy**). Scottish beers are graded by the shilling: a system used since the 1870s and indicating the level of potency – the higher the shilling mark, the stronger, or "heavier" the beer. A pint costs anything from £1.20 to £2, depending on the brew and the locale of the pub.

Scotland's biggest name breweries are *McEwan's* and *Younger's*, part of the mighty *Scottish and Newcastle* group, and *Tennents*, owned by the English firm *Bass*. The beers produced by these companies tend to be heavier, smoother and stronger than their English equivalents, especially *McEwan's Export*, a mass-produced, highly potent brew, and *Tennents' Fowler's Wee Heavy*, a famously tasty smooth

ale. *Younger's Tartan*, though less flavoursome, is Scotland's biggest seller.

However, if you really want to discover how good Scottish beer, once renowned throughout the world for its strength, can be, look out for the products of the small **local breweries** scattered throughout Scotland. Edinburgh's *Caledonian Brewery* makes nine good cask beers, operating from Victorian premises that preserve much of their original equipment, including the only direct-fired coppers left in Britain. Others to look out for are *Bellhaven*, a brewery near Edinburgh whose 80-shilling *Export* is a typical Scottish ale; *Maclays*, a hoppy, lightish ale brewed in Alloa; and *Traquair*, in the Borders, which does a wonderfully smooth *House Ale*. The dry, fruity *Alice Ale*, brewed in Inverness, and the *Orkney Brewery's Raven Ale* could be life-savers in the north, where good beer is hard to come by.

Blond pilsner beers, or **lagers**, are served all over Scotland, along with European and American bottled varieties, but the major Scottish brews have little to fear from these pale and often tasteless competitors. **Wines** sold in pubs are generally appalling – strange in view of the excellent selection sold in off-licences and supermarkets.

WHISKY

Scotland's national drink is **whisky** – *uisge beatha*, the "water of life" in Gaelic – traditionally drunk in pubs with a half-pint of beer on the side, a combination known as a "nip and a hauf".

Whisky has been produced in Scotland since the fifteenth century, and really took off in popularity after the 1780 tax on claret made wine too expensive for most people. The taxman soon caught up with illicit whisky distilling and drove the stills underground, and today many malt distilleries operate on the site of simple cottages that once distilled the stuff illegally. In 1823 Parliament revised its Excise Laws, in the process legalizing whisky production, and today the drink is Scotland's chief export. There are two types of whisky: **single malt**, made from malted barley, and **grain whisky**, which, relatively cheap to produce, is made from maize and a small amount of malted barley in a continuous still. **Blended**, which accounts for more than 90 percent of all sales, is as the name suggests, a blend of the two types.

Grain whisky forms about 70 percent of the average bottle of blended whisky, but the distinctive flavour of the different blends comes from the malt whisky which is added to the grain in different quantities. The more expensive the blend, the higher proportion of skilfully chosen and aged malts that have gone into it. Among many brand names, *Johnnie Walker, Bells, Teachers* and *The Famous Grouse* are some of the most widely available. All have a similar flavour, and are often drunk with mixers such as lemonade or mineral water.

Despite the dominance of the blended whiskies, **single malt whiskies** are infinitely superior, and best drunk neat to appreciate their distinctive flavours. Malt whisky is made by soaking barley in water for 2 or 3 days until it swells, after which it is left to germinate for up to 12 days, allowing the starch in the barley seed to become soluble. The malted barley is dried and peated, mashed with hot water and fermented with yeast to convert the sugar into crude alco-

hol, which is then twice distilled and the vapours condensed as a spirit, aged for a minimum of three years in oak casks. Single malts vary enormously depending on the peat used for drying, the water used for mashing, and the type of oak cask used in the maturing process, but they fall into 4 distinct groups – Highland, Lowland, Campbeltown and Islay, with the majority falling into the Highland category and being produced largely on Speyside. You can get the best-known blends – among them *Glenlivet, Glenmorangie, MacAllan, Talisker, Laphroaig, Highland Park* and *Glenfiddich*, the top seller – in most of the pubs.

Most distilleries have a highly developed nose for PR and offer free tours that range from slick and streamlined to small and friendly. All of them offer visitors a "wee dram" as a finale, and you can buy bottles of the stuff – though prices are no lower at source than in the shops. See *Argyll* and *Northeast Scotland* for more on whisky.

POST AND PHONES

Virtually all post offices are open Mon–Fri 9am–5.30pm, Sat 9am–12.30 or 1pm; in small communities you'll find sub-post offices operating out of a shop, open the same hours, even if the shop itself is open for longer. Stamps can be bought at post office counters, from vending machines outside, or from an increasing number of newsagents, usually in books of four or ten. **A first-class letter to anywhere in the British Isles currently costs 25p and should – in theory – arrive the next day; second-class letters cost 19p, and take from 2 to 4 days. Airmail letters of less than 20g (0.7oz) to EU countries also cost 25p, to non-EU European countries 30p and elsewhere overseas from 41p. Pre-stamped aerogrammes conforming to overseas airmail weight limits of under 10g can be bought for 39p from post offices only.**

Public **payphones** are operated by *British Telecom* (*BT*) and, in towns, at least, are widespread. Many *BT* payphones take all coins from 10p upwards, although an increasing proportion of *BT*'s payphones only accept **phonecards**, available from post offices and

OPERATOR SERVICES AND PHONE CODES
Operator ☎100.
Directory assistance ☎192.
Overseas directory assistance ☎153.
International operator ☎155.

INTERNATIONAL CALLS

To call **overseas from Scotland** dial ☎00, then the appropriate country code and finally the number, including the local code minus any initial zero. Country codes include:

USA and Canada ☎1

Ireland ☎353

Australia ☎61

New Zealand ☎64.

To **telephone Scotland** from overseas it's ☎011 from the US and Canada, ☎0011 from Australia and ☎00 from New Zealand, followed in all cases by 44, then the area code minus its initial zero, and finally the number.

newsagents which display *BT's* green logo. These cards come in denominations of £1, £2, £4, £5 and £10; some *BT* phones accept credit cards too.

Inland calls are cheapest between 6pm and 8am. **Reduced rate periods** for most **international calls** are 8pm–8am from Monday to Friday and all day on Saturday and Sunday, though for Australia and New Zealand it's midnight–7am and 2.30–7.30pm daily. Any number that begins ☎0800 is free.

Throughout the *Guide*, telephone numbers are prefixed by the area code, except in the case of the big cities, when the area code is indicated once only, in a shaded box.

OPENING HOURS AND HOLIDAYS

General shop hours are Mon–Sat 9am–5.30 or 6pm, although shops are increasingly opening on Sunday and late-night in the larger towns, with Thursday or Friday the favoured evenings. The big supermarkets also tend to stay open until 8pm or 9pm from Monday to Saturday, as do many of the stores in the shopping complexes that are springing up on the outskirts of many major towns. Many provincial towns still retain an "early closing day" when shops close at 1pm – Wednesday is the favourite.

Unlike in England, Scotland's "**bank holidays**" mean just that: they are literally days when the banks are closed rather than general

public holidays, and they vary from year to year. They include January 2, the Friday before Easter, the first and last Monday in May, the first Monday in August, St Andrew's Day (November 30), Christmas Day (December 25) and Boxing Day (December 26).

New Year's Day, January 1, is the only fixed **public holiday**, but all Scottish towns and cities have a one-day holiday in both spring and autumn – dates vary from place to place but normally fall on a Monday. If you want to know the exact dates, you can get a booklet detailing them from *Glasgow Chamber of Commerce*, 30 George Square, Glasgow G2 1EQ.

SIGHTS, MUSEUMS AND MONUMENTS

Apart from the really big museums, and a number of attractions high on the tourist trail, Scotland's tourist season runs from Easter to October and outside this period many indoor attractions are shut – though ruins, parks and gardens are normally accessible year-round. We've given full details of opening hours and admission charges in the *Guide*.

Many of Scotland's most treasured sights – from castles and country houses to islands, gardens and tracts of protected landscape – come under the control of the privately run **National Trust for Scotland**, 5 Charlotte Square, Edinburgh EH2 4DU (☎0131/226 5922), or the state-run **Historic Scotland**, Longmore House, Salisbury Place, Edinburgh EH9 15H (☎0131/668 8600), shown respectively as the "NTS" or "HS" in the *Guide*. Both organizations charge an entry fee for most places, and these can be quite high, especially for the more grandiose NTS estates. If you think you'll be visiting more than half a dozen owned by the NTS, or more than a dozen owned by HS, it's worth taking **annual membership** (NTS £24, family £40; HS £17, family £35), which allows free entry to their properties.

In addition, both the NTS and HS offer short-term passes that give discounts on admission prices. The **National Trust Touring Pass**, which costs £9 for an adult and £20 for a family, is valid for 7 days and gives free admission to all NTS properties. The HS **Scottish Explorer** 7-day ticket allows free entry to 70 monuments, castles and other properties and costs £11 or £23 for a family; a 2-week equivalent is £18/£35. **Members of the IYHF** (see p.27) are automatically eligible for half-price entry into all NTS properties.

A lot of Scottish **stately homes** remain in the hands of the landed gentry, who tend to charge in the region of £5 for admission to edited highlights of their domain. Many other old buildings, albeit rarely the most momentous structures, are owned by local authorities, and admission is often cheaper, sometimes free. Municipal art galleries and museums are usually free, as are most of the **state-owned museums**, although "voluntary" donations are normally solicited.

The majority of fee-charging attractions in Scotland have 25–50 percent **reductions** for senior citizens, the unemployed, full-time students and children under 16, with under-5s being admitted free almost everywhere. Proof of age will be required in most cases. The entry charges given in the *Guide* are the full adult charges.

North Americans can buy the *Scottish Explorer* and *National Trust Touring* passes at a travel agent or directly from *Especially Britain* (see under "Getting There from North America"). A further option, only open to overseas visitors, is the **Great British Heritage Pass**, which gives free admission to some 600 sites throughout Britain, many of which are not run by the NTS or HS. Costing under $50 for 7 days, around $60 for 15 days and $80 for a month, it can be purchased through most travel agents, *British Airways* offices or the British Travel Centre, 22 Regent St, London W1 (walk-in service only).

THE MEDIA

The principal **British daily newspapers** are all available in Scotland, often in a specific Scottish edition. The tabloids are as popular as in England – among them Rupert Murdoch's sex-and-scandal *Sun*, the self-consciously ridiculous *Daily Sport*, and the vaguely left-wing *Mirror*, the only tabloid that manages anything approximating an antidote to the *Sun's* reactionary politics. The "quality" end of the market is cornered by the Murdoch-owned *Times*, the staunchly Conservative *Daily Telegraph*, the *Independent*, which strives worthily to live up to its name, and the *Guardian*, which inhabits a niche marginally left of centre.

The **Scottish press**, in the main rather staid and parochial, produces 2 major serious daily newspapers, the liberal-left *Scotsman* and the slightly less-so *Herald*, published in Edinburgh and Glasgow respectively. Scotland's biggest selling daily paper, though, is the downmarket *Daily Record*, from the same group as the *Daily Mirror*. The provincial daily press is probably more widely read than its English counterpart, with Aberdeen's *Press and Journal*, Dundee's fiercely parochial *Courier and Advertiser* and the *Inverness Courier* enjoying the largest regional circulations. For an insight into life in the Highlands and islands, the weekly *Oban Times* is a must, the *Stornoway Gazette* is the only weekly printed in the Western Isles. The *West Highland Free Press*, printed on Skye, is a more radical, campaigning weekly. All carry articles in Gaelic as well as English.

Many national **Sunday newspapers** have a Scottish section north of the border, but Scotland's own Sunday "heavy" is the wholly serious and somewhat dull *Scotland on Sunday*. Far more fun is the anachronistic *Sunday Post*, published by Dundee's mighty Thomson and Legg publishing group and read by over half of the population. It's a wholesome paper, uniquely Scottish, and has changed little since the 1950s, since when its 2 long-running cartoon strips, *Oor Wullie* and *The Broons*, have acquired something of a cult status.

When it comes to **specialist periodicals**, the best-selling weekly news magazine is the dry, scholarly *Economist*. The earnest socialist alternative, the *New Statesman and New Society*, has so few readers that it's stuck with the nickname "The Staggers", while the satirical bi-weekly *Private Eye* is a much-loved institution that prides itself on printing the stories the rest of the press won't

touch, and on surviving the consequent stream of libel suits. Scottish **monthlies** include the *Scottish Field*, a low-brow version of England's *Tatler*, covering the interests and pursuits of the landed gentry, and the widely read *Scots Magazine*, an old-fashioned middle-of-the-road publication which promotes family values, a stiff upper lip and lots of good fresh air. *USA Today* is the most widely available **North American paper**, though only the larger newsagents will stock it; you can also find *Time* and *Newsweek* in quality bookstores and newsagents. For visitors to Glasgow and Edinburgh, the fortnightly **listings magazine** *The List* is a must, covering all events in both cities.

TELEVISION AND RADIO

In Scotland there are 4 main **television channels**, the state-owned BBC1 and 2, and the independent commercial channels, ITV and Channel Four. Though assailed by government critics of late, the **BBC** is just about maintaining its worldwide reputation for in-house quality productions, ranging from expensive costume dramas to intelligent documentaries – split between the avowedly mainstream BBC1 and the more rarefied fare of BBC2. The populist STV, Grampian and Border companies together form the **ITV** network in Scotland, complemented by the more eclectic and less mainstream broadcasting of the partly subsidized **Channel Four**. Rupert Murdoch's multi-channel BSkyB has a monopoly of the satellite business, presenting a blend of movies, news, sport, re-runs and overseas soaps, and **cable** TV companies are beginning to appear in Scotland. But for the time being the old terrestrial stations still attract the majority of viewers.

Market forces are eating away too at the BBC's **radio** network, which has 5 stations catering for a range of tastes: Radio One, almost exclusively mainstream pop music; Radio Two, MOR music; Radio Three, predominantly classical music; Radio Four, a blend of current affairs, arts and drama; and Radio Five Live, the newest station, a mix of sport and news. Radio One has rivals in the form of commercial radio all over Scotland – most stations are far less raucous and teen-targeted than their English equivalents – while Classic FM has lured people away from Radio Three, by offering a less earnest approach to its subject. The BBC also operates several regional Scottish stations, presenting a worthy mix of local news and chart hits.

ANNUAL EVENTS

Scotland offers a huge range of annual events, reflecting contemporary culture and heritage as well as its world-renowned tartan image. Many tourists will want to home straight in on bagpipes, ceilidhs and Highland Games, but it's worth bearing in mind that there's more to Scotland than this: numerous regional celebrations perpetuate ancient customs and accentuate the differences between Scotland and England, while the Edinburgh Festival and Glasgow's Mayfest are arts festivals on an international scale. Scotland's sporting events range from Highland Games, International Rugby and golf championships to homegrown pastimes such as curling – an activity that can be loosely described as bowls on ice, which originated in Scotland nearly five hundred years ago and is now played all over the world – and shinty, a simple form of hockey. Soccer is the national game, and weekly league matches are held from August to May.

It's important to bear in mind that a few of the smaller, more obscure events, particularly those with a pagan bent, are in no way created for tourists, and indeed do not always welcome the

EVENTS CALENDAR

December 31 and January 1: Hogmanay and Ne'er Day. More important to the Scots than Christmas. Festivities revolve around the "first-footing", when at midnight crowds of revellers troop into neighbours' houses bearing gifts. Traditionally the first foot should be a dark-haired stranger carrying coal and salt (so the house won't lack for warmth or food), and a bottle of whisky (for obvious reasons).

December 31: Flambeaux procession at Comrie. Locals parade through the streets carrying flaming torches to welcome New Year.

January 1: Stonehaven fireball ceremony. Locals swing fireballs on long sticks to welcome New Year and ward off evil spirits.

January 1: Kirkwall Boy's and Men's Ba' Games, Orkney. Mass, drunken football game through the streets of the town, with the castle and the harbour the respective goals – as a grand finale the players jump into the harbour.

January 11: Burning of the Clavie, Burghead, Moray. Burning tar barrel is carried through the town and then rolled down Doorie Hill. Charred fragments of the Clavie offer protection against the evil eye.

Last Tuesday in January: Up-Helly-Aa, Lerwick, Shetland. Norse fire festival culminating in the burning of a specially built Viking longship. Visitors will need an invite from one of the locals; or you can buy a ticket for the Town Hall celebrations; see p.490.

End of January: Burns Night. Burns suppers all over Scotland. Dinners held to commemorate Scotland's greatest poet; haggis, whisky and lots of poetry recital.

February: Scottish Curling Championship held in a different (indoor) venue each year.

February: Aberdeen Angus Bull Sales at Perth.

February: Scotland v. England Rugby Union.

March 1: Whuppity Scourie at Lanark. Local children race round the church beating each other with home-made paper weapons as they go: a representation (it's thought) of the chasing away of winter or the warding off of evil spirits.

March: Scotland v. France Rugby Union.

March: Edinburgh Folk Festival.

April: Scottish Grand National at Ayr; not quite as testing as the English equivalent steeplechase but an important event on the Scottish racing calendar.

April: Rugby 7s (7-a-side rugby tournament) in full swing all over the Borders.

April: Kate Kennedy procession at St Andrews. An exclusively male university tradition in honour of distinguished figures in the town and university's history. The role of Kate, niece of the founder of the university, and mythologized as a great beauty, is always played by a first-year student.

April: Shetland Folk Festival.

May 1: Beltane Fire festival on Calton Hill in Edinburgh.

May: Mayfest; Glasgow's recent and very successful answer to the Edinburgh Festival.

May: Scottish FA Cup Final in Glasgow.

Late May: Atholl Highlanders Parade at Blair Castle, Perthshire; the annual parade and inspection of Britain's last private army by their colonel-in-chief, the Duke of Atholl.

Late May: Scottish Hebridean Islands Peak Race; the biggest combined sailing and fell running competition in the world.

June–August: Riding of the Marches in the border towns of Hawick, Selkirk, Annan, Dumfries, Duns, Peebles, Jedburgh, Langholm and Lauder. The Rides originated to check the boundaries of common land owned by the town and also to commemorate warfare between the Scots and the English. Nowadays individual Ridings have their own special ceremonies, though they all start with a parade of pipes and brass bands.

June: Shinty Camanachd Cup Final, usually in Inverness. Finals of the intensely competitive games between the northern towns who play Scotland's own stick-and-ball game.

June: Royal Highland Agricultural Show, Ingliston, near Edinburgh. Scotland's biggest and best.

June: Highland Games at Campbeltown, Aberdeen and Grantown-on-Spey.

July: Scottish Open Golf Championship held at a different venue annually.

July: Glasgow International Folk Festival.

July: Highland Games at Caithness, Elgin, Glengarry, North Uist, Inverness, Inveraray, Mull, Lewis, Durness, Lochaber, Dufftown, Halkirk.

August: Edinburgh International Festival and Fringe. One of the world's great arts jamborees, detailed in full on p.90.

August: Edinburgh Military Tattoo held on the Castle esplanade; massed pipe bands and drums by floodlight.

August: World Pipe Band Championship at Glasgow.

August: International Horse Trials at Blair Atholl.

August: Horse festival on South Ronaldsay in Orkney. Small children dress as horses and drag decorative wooden ploughs along the beach in a competition to turn the straightest furrows.

August: Northern Meeting Piping Championships at Inverness.

August: Highland Games at Dunoon (Cowal), Mallaig, Skye, Dornoch, Aboyne, Strathpeffer, Assynt, Bute, Glenfinnan, Argyllshire, Glenurquhart and Invergordon.

September: Highland Games at Braemar.

September: Ben Nevis Race for amateurs to the top of the highest mountain in Scotland and back again.

October: The National Mod. Competitive festival of all aspects of Gaelic performing arts, held in varying venues.

October: Glenfiddich Piping Championships at Blair Atholl for the world's top 10 solo pipers.

November: St Andrew's Day celebrations at St Andrews.

---

casual visitor. If in doubt, check at the local tourist office. The STB publishes a weighty and complete list of Scottish events annually in December: it's free and you can get it from area tourist offices or direct from their headquarters.

HIGHLAND GAMES

Despite their name, **Highland Games** are held all over Scotland, from May until mid-September: they vary in size and differ in the range of events they offer, and although the most famous are at Oban, Cowal and especially Braemar, often the smaller ones are more fun. They probably originated in the fourteenth century as a means of recruiting the best fighting men for the clan chiefs, and were popularized by Queen Victoria to encourage the traditional dress, music, games and dance of the Highlands; various royals still attend the Games at Braemar. The most distinctive events are known as the **"heavies"** – tossing the caber, putting the stone, and tossing the weight over the bar – all of which require prodigious strength and skill. Tossing the caber is the most spectacular, when the athlete must run carrying an entire tree trunk and attempt to heave it end over end in a perfect, elegant throw. Just as important as the sporting events are the **piping competitions** – for individuals and bands – and **dancing competitions,** where you'll see girls as young as three years old tripping the quick, intricate steps of such traditional dances as the Highland Fling.

The list above includes some of the better-known Games; for the smaller, local games, check at individual tourst offices.

SPORT AND OUTDOOR PURSUITS

Many visitors bypass Scotland's main cities and come purely for the beautiful scenery. There are vast tracts of land where you'll never see a soul, ideal walking for even the toughest hiker, and spectacular mountains on which some of the world's great mountaineers have cut their teeth and which in winter provide great skiing. For more sedate walkers, numerous marked trails range from hour-long ambles to coast-to-coast treks. The coast, lochs and rivers give opportunities for fishing as well as sailing and numerous water sports, and there are plenty of fine beaches for less structured fresh-air activities or just slobbing around. Scotland is also known as the "home of golf": it's cheaper here and there are proportionally more courses than anywhere else in the world. For specific details on where to go to watch or participate in any of the following activities, contact the Scottish Sports Council, Caledonian House, South Gyle, Edinburgh EH12 9DG (☎ 0131/317 7200).

CLIMBING AND WALKING

The whole of Scotland offers good opportunities for gentle hillwalking, from the smooth, grassy hills and moors of the **Southern Uplands** to the wild and rugged country of the northwest. Scotland has 3 **Long Distance Footpaths** (LDPs) which will take days to walk, though you can, of course, just do part of them. The **Southern Upland Way** crosses Scotland from coast to coast in the south, and is the longest at 212 miles. The best-known is the **West Highland Way**, a 95-mile hike from Glasgow to Fort William via Loch Lomond and Glen Coe. The gentler **Speyside Way**, in Aberdeenshire, is a mere 30 miles. The green signposts of the Scottish Rights of Way Society point to these and many other cross-country routes; while in

---

SAFETY IN THE SCOTTISH HILLS

Scottish mountains are not high, but, due to rapid weather changes, they are potentially extremely dangerous and should be treated with respect. Every year, in every season, climbers and hill walkers die on Scottish mountains. If the weather looks as if it's closing in, *get down fast*. It is essential that you are properly equipped – even for what appears to be an easy expedition in apparently settled weather – with proper warm and waterproof layered clothing, supportive footwear and adequate maps, a compass (which you should know how to use) and food. Always leave word of your route and what time you expect to return; and remember to contact the person again to let them know that you are back.

USEFUL ADDRESSES FOR WALKING

Cordee (Book Distributors), 3a de Montefort St, Leicester LE1 7HD (☎0116/254 3579). *Produces extensive book lists and distributes all* SMC *publications.*

John Muir Trust, Freepost, Musselburgh, Midlothian EH21 7BR (☎0131/665 0596).

Mountaineering Council of Scotland, 71 King St (IR), Crieff, Perthshire PH7 3HB (☎01746/654962). *The representative body for all mountain activities.*

National Trust for Scotland, 5 Charlotte Square, Edinburgh EH2 4DU (☎0131/226 5922).

Scottish Rights of Way Society, John Cotton Business Centre, 10–12 Sunnyside, Edinburgh EH7 5RA (☎0131/652 2937) .

Scottish Youth Hostel Association, 7 Glebe Crescent, Stirling FK8 2JA (☎01786/451181).

the wilder parts the accepted freedom to roam allows extensive mountain walking, rock climbing, orienteering and allied activities.

Scotland's main climbing areas are in the **Highlands**, which boast many challenging peaks as well as great hill walks. There are 279 mountains over 3000ft (914m) in Scotland, known as **Munros** after the man who first classified them; many walkers "collect" them, and it's possible to chalk up several in a day. Serious climbers will probably head for **Glen Coe** or **Torridan** which offer difficult routes in spectacular surroundings. These and some of the other finest Highland areas (Lawers, Kintail, West Affric) are in the ownership of the National Trust for Scotland, while Blaven and Ladhar Bheinn (Knoydart) are John Muir Trust properties; both allow year-round access. Elsewhere there may be restricted access during lambing (dogs are particularly unwelcome during April and May) and deer-stalking seasons (mid-August to the third week in October). The booklet *Heading for the Scottish Hills* (published by the *Scottish Mountaineering Club* or *SMC*) provides such information on all areas.

Numerous short walks, from accessible towns and villages, and several major walks are covered in the *Guide*. However, you should only use these notes as general outlines and always in conjunction with a good map. Where possible we have given details of the best maps to use – in most cases one of the *Ordnance Survey* (*OS*) series (see p.21). You should never attempt walks beyond your abilities and always follow the guidelines in the box above. Other useful sources for information on walks are listed in the box above. If you decide to follow one of the walks and haven't got a map with you, head

for the nearest tourist office who will usually supply *OS* and other local maps, safety advice and guidebooks/leaflets, as will shops in most areas. Among the many **guidebooks** available for serious walking and climbing, the *SMC*'s series of *District Guides* offer blow-by-blow accounts of climbs written by professional mountaineers – for other good walking guides see the "Books" section of *Contexts*.

CYCLING

Despite the recent boom in the sale of mountain bikes, **cyclists** are treated with notorious neglect by many motorized road users and by the people who plan the country's traffic systems. Very few of Scotland's towns have proper cycle routes, but if you're hellbent on tackling the congestion, pollution and aggression of city traffic, get a **helmet** and a secure **lock** – cycle theft in Scotland is an organized and highly effective racket. The rural backroads are infinitely more enjoyable, particularly in the gentle landscape of the south of the country, whose generally amiable gradients and decent density of pubs and B&Bs make it a perfect area for cycle touring. Your main problem out in the countryside will be finding any spare parts – only inner tubes and tyres are easy to find.

Cycling is popular in the highland walking areas, but cyclists should remember to keep to rights of way and to pass walkers at considerate speeds. Footpaths, unless otherwise marked, are for pedestrian use only.

Transporting your **bike** by train is a good way of getting to the interesting parts of Scotland without a lot of stressful pedalling. Bikes are not allowed on InterCity express trains, but on other inter-town routes are carried at £3 per journey.

Bike rental is available at shops in most large towns and many tourist centres, but the specimens on offer are often pretty derelict – all right for a brief spin, but not for any serious touring. Expect to pay in the region of £8–10 per day, £40–60 per week.

Britain's biggest **cycling organization** is the *Cycle Touring Club* or *CTC* (Cotterell House, 69 Meadrow, Godalming, Surrey, GU7 3HS; ☎01483/417217), which supplies members with touring and technical advice as well as insurance. A recommended country-wide guide is its *Route Guide to Cycling in Britain and Ireland*, a third of which covers Scotland .

GOLF

There are over 400 **golf courses** in Scotland, where the game is less elitist, cheaper and more accessible than anywhere else in the world. The game as it's known today took shape in the sixteenth century on the dunes of Scotland's east coast, and today you'll find some of the oldest courses in the world on these early coastal sites, known as "links". If you want a round of golf, it's often possible just to turn up and play, though it's sensible to phone ahead and book, and essential for the championship courses (see below).

Public courses are owned by the local council, while **private** courses belong to a club. You can play on both – occasionally the private courses require that you be a member of another club, and the odd one asks for introductions from a member, but these rules are often waived for overseas visitors and all you need to do is pay a one-off fee. The cost of one round will set you back between around £5 for small, 9-hole courses, up to more than £20 for 18 holes. Simply pay as you enter and play. In remote areas the courses are sometimes unmanned – just put the admission fee into the honour box. Most courses have **resident professionals** who give lessons, and some rent equipment at reasonable rates. Renting a caddy car will add an extra few pounds depending on the swankiness of the course.

Scotland's **championship** courses, which often host the British Open tournament, are renowned for their immaculately kept greens and challenging holes, and though they're favoured by serious players, anybody with a valid handicap certificate can enjoy them. **St** Andrews (☎01334/475757) is *the* destination for golfers: it's the home of the *Royal and Ancient Golf Club*, the worldwide controlling body that regulates the rules of the game. Of its 5 courses, the best known is the Old Course, a particularly intriguing ground with 11 enormous greens and the world-famous "Road Hole". If you want to play, there's no introduction needed, but you'll need to book months in advance and have a handicap certificate – handicap limits are 24 for men and 36 for women. You could also enter your name for the daily right-to-play lottery – contact the club before 2pm on the day you'd like to play. One of the easiest championship courses to get into is *Carnoustie*, in Angus (☎01241/853249), though you should still try to book as far ahead as possible. No handicap certificate is required for play here before 1.30pm on Saturday and 11am on Sunday. Other championship courses include *Gleneagles* in Perthshire (☎0176/663543); *Royal Dornoch* in Sutherland (☎01862/810219); and *Turnberry* in Ayrshire (☎01655/331000). A round of golf at any of these will set you back at least £20, double that if you rent a human caddy – and you'll be expected to tip over and above that. Near Edinburgh, *Muirfield*, considered by professional players to be one of the most testing grounds in the world, is also one of the most elitist – women can only play if accompanied by a man and aren't allowed into the clubhouse.

BEACHES

Scotland is ringed by fine beaches and bays, most of them clean and many of them deserted even in high summer – perhaps hardly surprising given the bracing winds and icy water. Few people come to Scotland for a beach holiday, but it's worth sampling one or two, even if you never shed as much as a sweater. A rash of slightly melancholy seaside towns lies within easy reach of Glasgow, while on the east coast, the relatively low cliffs and miles of sandy beaches are ideal for walking. Bizarrely enough, given the low temperature of the water, the beaches in the northeast are beginning to figure on surfers' itineraries, attracting enthusiasts from all over Europe. Perhaps the most beautiful beaches of all are to be found on Scotland's islands: endless, isolated stretches that on a sunny day can be the epitome of the Scottish Hebridean dream.

SCOTLAND'S DIRTY BEACHES

This is a list of Scottish beaches where the shore and bathing waters **failed to meet EU standards** in 1994; an asterisk denotes places that failed for the previous 2 years as well. The government pledged to bring all beaches up to minimum EU standards by the end of 1995 – great strides have been made, but at the time of going to press this looked unlikely.

Northeast	Tayport*	Portobello*
Aberdour Harbour	Westhaven	Prestwick*
Broughty Ferry		Saltcoats*
Bruntisland	**Southern Scotland**	Sandyhills
Cruden Bay	Annan*	Stranraer
Kinghorn	Ayr*	Turnberry*
Kirkcaldy Linktown	Drummore	
Leven East	Girvan	
Lower Largo	Irvine*	
St Andrews East	Powfoot*	

TRAVELLERS WITH DISABILITIES

Scotland has numerous specialist tour operators catering for physically handicapped travellers, and the number of non-specialist operators who welcome clients with disabilities is increasing. For more information on these operators, you should get in touch with *Disability Scotland*, Princes House, 5 Shandwick Place, Edinburgh EH2 4RG (☎0131/229 8632). It has a comprehensive computer database covering all aspects of disabled holidays in Scotland, publishes a full directory, and is happy to deal with queries; also see the box below for other useful organizations in Britain.

Should you go it alone, you'll find that Scottish attitudes towards travellers with disabilities are often begrudging, and years behind advances towards independence made in North America and Australia. Access to theatres, cinemas and other public places has improved recently, but **public transport** companies rarely make any effort to help disabled people, though some *BritRail InterCity* services now accommodate wheelchair users in comfort.

Wheelchair users and blind or partially sighted people are automatically given 30–50 percent reductions on train fares, and people with other disabilities are eligible for the **Disabled Persons Railcard** (£14 per year), which gives a third off most tickets. There are no bus discounts for the disabled, and of the major **car rental** firms only *Hertz* offer models with hand controls at the same rate as conventional vehicles, and even these are in the more expensive categories. **Accommodation** is the same story, with modified suites for people with disabilities available only at higher-priced establishments and perhaps the odd B&B.

Useful **publications** include *RADAR*'s annually updated *Holidays in the British Isles; A Guide For Disabled People*. Two other publications to look out for are *The World Wheelchair Traveller* by Susan Abbott and Mary Ann Tyrrell (AA Publications), which includes basic hints and advice, and our own *Nothing Ventured/Able to Travel: Disabled People Travel the World* by Alison Walsh (Rough Guides), which has practical advice and inspiring accounts of disabled travel worldwide.

CONTACTS FOR TRAVELLERS WITH DISABILITIES

IN BRITAIN

Holiday Care Service, 2nd floor, Imperial Building, Victoria Rd, Horley, Surrey RH6 9HW (☎01293/774535). *Information on all aspects of travel.*

Mobility International, 228 Borough High St, London SE1 1JX (☎0171/403 5688). *Puts out a quarterly newsletter that keeps up-to-date with developments in disabled travel.*

Royal Association for Disability and Rehabilitation (RADAR), 250 City Rd, London EC1V 8AF (☎0171/250 3222). *All kinds of information and advice.*

IN NORTH AMERICA

Directions Unlimited, 720 N Bedford Rd, Bedford Hills, NY 10507 (☎1-800/533-5343). *Tour operator specializing in custom tours for people with disabilities.*

Jewish Rehabilitation Hospital, 3205 Place Alton Goldbloom, Montréal, PQ H7V 1R2 (☎514/688-9550, ext 226). *Guidebooks and travel information.*

Mobility International USA, PO Box 10767, Eugene, OR 97440 (Voice and TDD: ☎503/343-1284). *Information and referral services, access guides, tours and exchange programs. Annual membership $20 (includes quarterly newsletter).*

Society for the Advancement of Travel for the Handicapped (SATH), 347 5th Ave, New York, NY 10016 (☎212/4470-7284). *Non-profit travel-industry referral service that passes queries on to its members as appropriate; allow plenty of time for a response.*

Travel Information Service, Moss Rehabilitation Hospital, 1200 W Tabor Rd, Philadelphia, PA 19141 (☎215/456-9600). *Telephone information and referral service.*

Twin Peaks Press, Box 129, Vancouver, WA 98666; ☎206/694 2462 or 1-800/637-2256). *Publisher of the* Directory of Travel Agencies for the Disabled *($19.95), listing more than 370 agencies worldwide;* Travel for the Disabled *($14.95); the* Directory of Accessible Van Rentals *and* Wheelchair Vagabond *($9.95), loaded with personal tips.*

IN AUSTRALASIA

ACROD, PO Box 60, Curtin, ACT 2605 (☎06/682 4333). *Compiles lists of organizations, accommodation, travel agencies and tour operators.*

Barrier Free Travel, 36 Wheatley St, North Bellingen, NSW 2454 (☎066/551733; ☎02/6655 1733 from April 1998). *Fee-based travel access information service.*

Disabled Persons Assembly, PO Box 10, 138 The Terrace, Wellington (☎04/472 2626).

DIRECTORY

Electricity In Britain the current is 240V AC. North American appliances need a transformer and adaptor; Australasian appliances need only an adaptor.

Gaelic In some areas of Scotland, particularly in the Highlands and islands, road signs are bilingual English/Gaelic. In the *Guide*, the Gaelic translation is given – in italics and parentheses – the first time any village or island is mentioned, after which the English name is used. The main exception to this rule is in the Western Isles, where signposting is exclusively in Gaelic – we've reflected this in the main text by giving the Gaelic first, and putting the English in parentheses. Thereafter we've used the Gaelic, except for the islands and ferry ports which are more familiar in the English, as they appear on *CalMac* timetables.

Laundry Coin-operated laundries are found in nearly all Scottish cities and some towns, and are open about twelve hours a day from Monday to Friday, less on weekends. A wash followed by a spin or tumble dry costs about £2; a "service wash" (your laundry done for you in a few hours) costs about £1 extra.

Public toilets Found at all train and bus stations and signposted on town high streets: a fee of 10p or 20p is usually charged.

Smoking Although many Scots still smoke, the last decade has seen a dramatic change in attitudes towards smoking and a significant reduction in the consumption of cigarettes. Smoking is now outlawed from just about all public buildings and on public transport, and many restaurants and hotels have become totally non-smoking. Smokers are advised, when booking a table or a room, to check their vice is tolerated there.

Time Greenwich Mean Time (GMT) is in force from late October to late March, after which the clocks go forward an hour for British Summer Time (BST). GMT is five hours ahead of the US Eastern Standard Time and ten hours behind Australian Eastern Standard Time.

Tipping and service charges In restaurants a service charge is usually included in the bill; if it isn't, you should leave a tip of 10–15 percent or so. Some restaurants are in the habit of leaving the total box blank on credit-card counterfoils, to encourage customers to add another few percent on top of the service charge. There's no need to, and if you're paying by credit card, check that the total box is filled in before you sign. Taxi drivers expect a tip in the region of 10 percent. You do not have to tip bar staff.

Videos Visitors from North America planning to use their video cameras in Britain should note that Betamax video cassettes are less easy to obtain in Scotland, where VHS is the commonly used format, so bring a supply with you.

PART TWO

THE

GUIDE

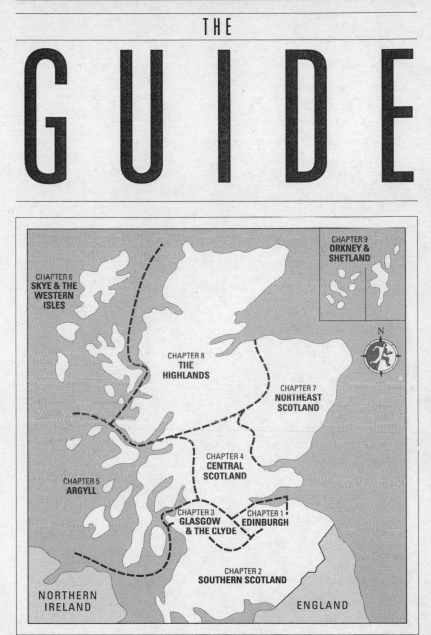

CHAPTER ONE

EDINBURGH

Well-heeled **EDINBURGH**, the showcase capital of Scotland, is a cosmopolitan and cultured city. Its setting is undeniably striking; perched on a series of extinct volcanoes and rocky crags which intrude on the generally flat landscape of the Lothians, with the sheltered shoreline of the

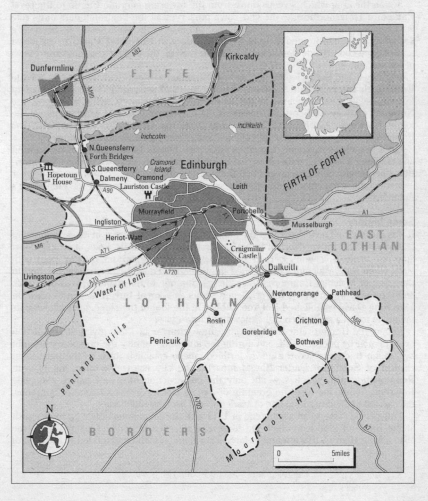

Firth of Forth to the north. "My own Romantic town", Sir Walter Scott called it, although it was another native author, Robert Louis Stevenson, who perhaps best captured the feel of his "precipitous city", declaring that "No situation could be more commanding for the head of a kingdom; none better chosen for noble prospects."

The centre has two distinct parts. North of the **Castle Rock**, the dignified, Grecian-style **New Town** was immaculately laid out during the Age of Reason, after the announcement of a plan to improve conditions in the city. The **Old Town**, on the other hand, with its tortuous alleys and tightly packed closes, is unrelentingly medieval, associated in popular imagination with its underworld lore of the schizophrenic Deacon Brodie, inspiration for Stevenson's *Dr Jekyll and Mr Hyde*, and the body snatchers Burke and Hare. Edinburgh earned its nickname of "Auld Reekie" for the smog and smell generated by the Old Town, which for centuries swam in sewage tipped out of the windows of cramped tenements.

Set on the crag which sweeps down from the towering fairytale **Castle** to the royal **Palace of Holyroodhouse**, the Old Town preserves all the key reminders of its role as a capital, while, in contrast, a tantalizing glimpse of the wild beauty of Scotland's scenery can be had immediately beyond the palace in **Holyrood Park**, an extensive area of open countryside dominated by **Arthur's Seat**, the largest and most impressive of the volcanoes.

In August and early September, around a million visitors flock to the city for the **Edinburgh International Festival**, in fact a series of separate festivals that make up the largest arts extravaganza in the world. Among the city's many museums, the **National Gallery of Scotland** boasts as choice an array of Old Masters as can be found anywhere; its offshoot, the **Scottish National Gallery of Modern Art**, has Britain's oldest specialist collection of twentieth-century painting and sculpture.

On a less elevated theme, the city's distinctive howffs (pubs), allied to its brewing and distilling traditions, make it a great **drinking** city. The presence of three **universities**, plus several colleges, means that there is a youthful presence for most of the year – a welcome corrective to the stuffiness which is often regarded as Edinburgh's Achilles heel.

Some history

It was during the **Dark Ages** that the name of Edinburgh – at least in its early forms of Dunedin or Din Eidyn ("fort of Eidyn") – first appeared. Castle Rock, a strategic fort atop one of the volcanoes, served as the nation's **southernmost border post** until 1018, when King Malcolm I established the River Tweed as the permanent frontier. In the reign of Malcolm Canmore the castle became one of the main seats of the court; and the town, which was given privileged status as a **royal burgh**, began to grow. In 1128 King David established Holyrood Abbey at the foot of the slope, later allowing its monks to found a separate burgh, known as **Canongate**.

Robert the Bruce granted Edinburgh a **new charter** in 1234, giving it jurisdiction over the nearby port of **Leith**, and during the following century the prosperity brought by foreign trade enabled the newly fortified city to establish itself as the permanent **capital of Scotland**. Under King James IV, the city enjoyed a short but brilliant **Renaissance era**, which saw not only the construction of a new palace alongside Holyrood Abbey, but also the granting of a royal charter to the College of Surgeons, the earliest in the city's long line of academic and professional bodies.

This period came to an abrupt end in 1513 with the calamitous defeat by the English at the Battle of Flodden, which led to several decades of political instability. In the 1540s, King Henry VIII's attempt to force a royal union with Scotland led to the sack of

The telephone code for Edinburgh is ☎0131.

Edinburgh, prompting the Scots to turn to France: French troops arrived to defend the city, while the young queen Mary was despatched to Paris as the promised bride of the Dauphin. While the French occupiers succeeded in removing the English threat, they themselves antagonized the locals, who had become increasingly sympathetic to the ideals of the **Reformation**. When the radical preacher John Knox returned from exile in 1555, he quickly won over the city to his Calvinist message.

James VI's rule saw the foundation of the University of Edinburgh in 1582, but following the **Union of the Crowns** in 1603, the city was totally upstaged by London: although James promised to visit every three years, it was not until 1617 that he made his one and only return trip. In 1633 Charles I visited Edinburgh for his coronation, but soon afterwards precipitated a crisis by introducing episcopacy to the Church of Scotland, in the process making Edinburgh a bishopric for the first time. Fifty years of religious turmoil followed, culminating in the triumph of **presbyterianism**. Despite these vicissitudes, Edinburgh expanded throughout the seventeenth century and, constrained by its walls, was forced to build both upwards and inwards.

The **Union of the Parliaments** of 1707 dealt a further blow to Edinburgh's political prestige, though the guaranteed preservation of the national church and the legal and educational systems ensured that it was never relegated to a purely provincial role. On the contrary, it was in the second half of the eighteenth century that Edinburgh achieved the height of its intellectual influence, led by an outstanding group, including David Hume and Adam Smith. Around the same time, the city began to expand beyond its medieval boundaries, laying out a **New Town**, a masterpiece of the Neoclassical style.

Industrialization affected Edinburgh less than any other major city in the nation, and it never lost its white-collar character. Nevertheless, the city underwent an enormous **urban expansion** in the course of the century, annexing, among many other small burghs, the large port of Leith.

In 1947 Edinburgh was chosen to host the great **International Festival** which served as a symbol of the new peaceful European order; despite some hiccups, it has flourished ever since, in the process helping to make tourism a mainstay of the local economy. In 1975 the city carried out another territorial expansion, moving its boundaries westwards as far as the old burgh of South Queensferry and the Forth Bridges. Four years later, the inconclusive referendum on Scottish devolution robbed Edinburgh of the chance of reviving its role as a governmental capital; and Glasgow, previously the poor relation, began to overtake the city as a cultural centre. The keen rivalry between the two cities was most recently manifested in a hard-fought campaign, won by Glasgow, for the title of City of Architecture 1999. Despite these blows, however, Edinburgh remains a fascinating and complex place, whose character typifies that of a nation that has maintained its essential autonomy despite nearly three centuries of full political union with England.

Orientation

Although Edinburgh occupies a large area relative to its population – less than half a million people – most places worth visiting lie within the compact city centre, which is easily explored on foot. This is divided clearly and unequivocally between the maze-like **Old Town**, which lies on and around the crag linking the Castle and the Palace, and the **New Town**, laid out in a symmetrical pattern on the undulating ground to the north. It's also worth venturing into the **outskirts**, which range from residential inner suburbs to formerly separate villages that still retain their own distinctive identities.

Orientation in Edinburgh is straightforward, particularly as most public transport services terminate on or near **Princes Street**, the city's main thoroughfare, which lies

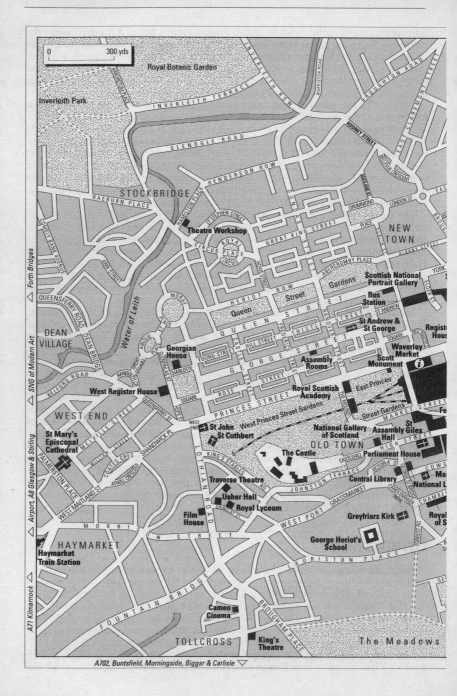

0   300 yds

Royal Botanic Garden

Inverleith Park

INVERLEITH TERRACE

GLENOGLE ROAD

HENDERSON ROW

STOCKBRIDGE

RAEBURN PLACE

RODNEY STREET

NEW TOWN

Theatre Workshop

ROYAL CIRCUS PLACE

GREAT KING STREET

Scottish National Portrait Gallery

Gardens

Bus Station

Queen Street

St Andrew & St George

Georgian House

Assembly Rooms

Waverley Market

Scott Monument

West Register House

GEORGE STREET

ROSE STREET

Royal Scottish Academy

East Princes

PRINCES STREET

West Princes Street Gardens

Street Gardens

WEST END

St John
St Cuthbert

National Gallery of Scotland

Assembly Giles Hall

St Mary's Episcopal Cathedral

The Castle

OLD TOWN

Parliament House

Traverse Theatre

Central Library

Usher Hall

Royal Lyceum

GRASSMARKET

WEST PORT

Greyfriars Kirk

Film House

HAYMARKET

George Heriot's School

Haymarket Train Station

LAURISTON PLACE

Cameo Cinema

TOLLCROSS

King's Theatre

The Meadows

DEAN VILLAGE

Water of Leith

Forth Bridges

SNG of Modern Art

Airport, A8 Glasgow & Stirling

A71 Kilmarnock

A702, Bruntsfield, Morningside, Biggar & Carlisle

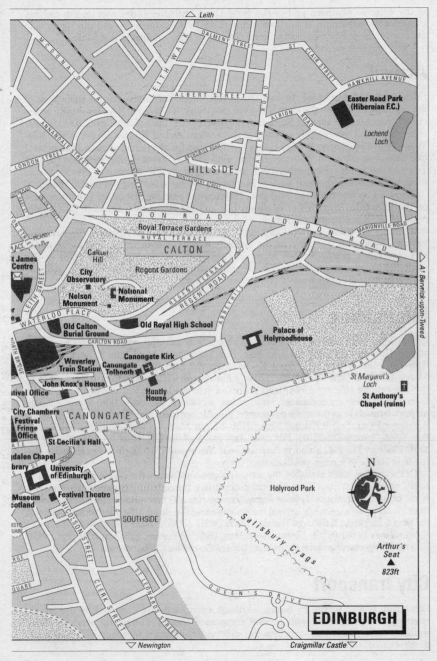

△ Leith

DALMENY STREET

ALBERT STREET

HAWKHILL AVENUE

Easter Road Park
(Hibernian F.C.)

Lochend
Loch

HILLSIDE

LONDON ROAD

LONDON ROAD

MARIONVILLE ROAD

Royal Terrace Gardens

ROYAL TERRACE

CALTON

Calton
Hill

Regent Gardens

City
Observatory

National
Monument

Nelson
Monument

St James
Centre

Waterloo Place

Old Calton
Burial Ground

Old Royal High School

CARLTON ROAD

Palace of
Holyroodhouse

St Margaret's
Loch

St Anthony's
Chapel (ruins)

Waverley
Train Station

Canongate Kirk

Canongate
Tolbooth

John Knox's House

Huntly
House

Festival Office

City Chambers

Festival
Fringe
Office

CANONGATE

St Cecilia's Hall

Magdalen Chapel
Library

University
of Edinburgh

Museum
Scotland

Festival Theatre

SOUTHSIDE

Holyrood Park

N

Salisbury Crags

Arthur's
Seat

823ft

CLERK STREET

ST LEONARD'S STREET

QUEEN'S DRIVE

EDINBURGH

▽ Newington

Craigmillar Castle ▽

△ A1 Berwick-upon-Tweed

at the extreme southern end of the New Town, with the Old Town on the heights immediately to the rear. If you want to travel out to the suburbs, or are staying outside the centre, the public transport system, although a little confusing, is reliable.

Arrival

Edinburgh International Airport (☎333 1000) is at Turnhouse, seven miles west of the city centre, close to the start of the M8 motorway to Glasgow. Regular shuttle buses (£3.20) connect to **Waverley Station** in the town centre; taxis charge around £11 for the same journey. Conveniently situated at the eastern end of Princes Street in the New Town, Waverley Station (☎556 2451) is the terminus for all mainline **trains**. The central exit takes you out on to Waverley Bridge, with Princes Street to the north and the Old Town to the south. The northern exit leads straight up the stairway to Princes Street itself, while the southern exit leads to Market Street, the outer fringe of the Old Town.

There's a second mainline train stop, **Haymarket Station**, just under two miles west on the lines from Waverley to Glasgow, Fife and the Highlands, although this is only really of use if you're staying nearby.

The **bus terminal** for local and inter-city services is on **St Andrew Square**, two minutes' walk from Waverley, on the opposite side of Princes Street. One of the major bus companies, *SMT* (*Scottish Midland Transport*), has a shop (☎558 1616) at the southeastern corner of the station, where timetables are kept and tickets sold for several of the confusing array of private bus operators.

Information

Edinburgh's main **tourist office** is at 3 Princes St beside the northern entrance to the station (July & Aug Mon–Sat 9am–8pm, Sun 11am–8pm; May, June & Sept Mon–Sat 9am–7pm, Sun 11am–7pm; April & Oct Mon–Sat 9am–6pm, Sun 11am–6pm; Nov–March Mon–Sat 9am–6pm; ☎557 1700). Although inevitably flustered at the height of the season, it's efficiently run, with scores of free leaflets; when the office is closed, there's a 24-hour computerized information service at the door. The much smaller **airport branch** is in the main concourse, directly opposite Gate 5 (April–Oct Mon–Sat 8.30am–9.30pm, Sun 9.30am–9.30pm; Nov–March Mon–Fri 9am–6pm, Sat 9am–1pm, Sun 10am–2pm; ☎333 2167). For up-to-date maps of the city head for *Map Centre*, 51 York Place (☎557 3011), and to *International Newsagent*, 351 High St (☎225 4827), for the best choice of foreign publications.

Of the guided tours available, the most recommendable are the *Guide Friday* open-top buses, which depart from Waverley Station and cruise through the city streets, allowing you to get on and off at leisure. *Lothian Region Transport* (*LRT*) has various coach tours leaving from Waverley Bridge, while several companies along the Royal Mile offer walking tours of the street, including *Edinburgh Walking Tours* (☎557 4700), *Mercat Tours* (☎661 4541) and *Robin's Tours* (☎661 0125). *Glenair Helicopters*, Old Fire Station, Edinburgh Airport (☎339 2321), offer spectacular aerial sightseeing trips of the city for £35 per person.

City transport

Edinburgh is well served by **buses**, although even locals are confused by the consequences of deregulation, with several companies offering competing services along similar routes. Each bus stop lists the different companies together with the route numbers that stop there.

Most useful are the maroon buses operated by *Lothian Regional Transport* (*LRT*); all buses referred to in the text are run by them unless stated otherwise. Timetables and passes (a good investment is the £9 pass for a week's unlimited travel, Sun–Sat, especially if you're staying far out, or want to explore the suburbs; passport photo needed) are available from the ticket centre at 31 Waverley Bridge (☎225 8616) or its headquarters at 14 Queen St (☎220 4111). You can, of course, buy tickets from the driver, for which you'll need exact change.

The green buses run by *Eastern Scottish* and the green and yellow buses of *Lowland Scottish* link the capital with outlying towns and villages. Most services depart from and terminate at the St Andrew Square bus station.

The city is well endowed with taxi ranks, especially around Waverley Bridge. Costs start at about 90p for the first 340 yards and 20p for each additional 240 yards. The phone numbers of the main local cab companies are: *Capital Castle Cabs* (☎228 2555), *Central Taxis* (☎229 2468) and *City Cabs* (☎228 1211).

It is emphatically *not* a good idea to take a **car** into central Edinburgh: despite the presence of several expensive multi-storey car parks, looking for somewhere to leave the car often involves long, fruitless searches. Bus lanes must be left clear during rush hours, and cars parked on yellow lines are regularly clamped or towed away, with a retrieval fee of £120. Most ticket and parking meter regulations cease at 5.30pm Monday to Friday, and at 1.30pm on Saturday.

Edinburgh is a reasonably cycle-friendly city – although hilly – with several **cycle paths**. The local cycling action group, *Spokes* (☎313 2114), publishes an excellent cycle map of the city. For rental, try *Central Cycles*, 13 Lochrin Place (☎228 6333), or *Sandy Gilchrist Cycles*, 1 Cadzow Place (☎652 1760).

Accommodation

As befits its status as a top tourist city, Edinburgh has a larger and wider choice of **accommodation** than any other place in Britain outside London. The greatest number of places to stay can be found in the streets immediately north of Haymarket Station, Royal Terrace and the lower reaches of the New Town, and to the south, the inner suburbs of Bruntsfield and Newington, where numerous hotels and guest houses line the major roads into the city from England.

In addition to Edinburgh's **hotels**, hundreds of **private houses** offer B&B deals at low rates, but in order to protect the guest house trade from excessive competition,

---

ACCOMMODATION PRICE CODES

Throughout this book, accommodation **prices** have been graded with the numbers below, according to the cost of the least expensive double room in high season. Although costs will rise slightly overall with the life of this edition, the relative comparisons should remain valid. The bulk of the recommendations will fall in categories ③ to ⑤; those in the highest categories are limited to places that are especially attractive. Edinburgh will inevitably be more expensive than equivalent accommodation in the countryside or small towns, and a number of places will have a big mark-up for the three weeks of the Festival. Also bear in mind that many of the swanky hotels often slash their tariffs at the weekend when the business types have gone home, and that many of the cheaper places will also have more expensive rooms. Note that in our accommodation listings price codes are not given for youth hostels and campsites – they all come into the lower end of the ① category.

① under £20	④ £40–50	⑦ £70–80
② £20–30	⑤ £50–60	⑧ £80–100
③ £30–40	⑥ £60–70	⑨ over £100

they are only open between Easter and October. There is also a decent choice of both official and private **hostels**, and four **campsites** attached to caravan parks. Surprisingly, the wide range of **campus accommodation** is neither as cheap nor as convenient as might be expected. **Self-catering** is an alternative, extremely cost-effective for groups intending to stay a week or more, with some exceptionally enticing addresses available for let.

Advance reservations are very strongly recommended during the Festival: turning up on spec entails accepting whatever is left (which is unlikely to be good value) or else commuting from the suburbs. The **tourist office** (see previous page) sends out accommodation lists for free, and can reserve any type of accommodation in advance for a non-refundable £3 fee: call in personally when you arrive or write in advance to Edinburgh Marketing Central Reservations Department, 3 Princes St, Edinburgh EH2 2QP (☎557 9655), stating requirements. In Waverley Station the *Edinburgh Hotel and Guest House Association* runs an agency (Mon–Sat 7am–10pm, Sun 8am–10pm; ☎556 0030) which makes no charge for bookings with any of its members.

Hotels

Although considerably more expensive than the guest houses, Edinburgh's **hotels** are generally of a high standard and cover a wide range of tastes, from the hub of New Town elegance to quieter retreats out of the centre.

New Town

Ailsa Craig Hotel, 24 Royal Terrace (☎556 6055). One of a clutch of good hotels on this elegant Georgian street overlooking a park. ⑤.

Albany Hotel, 39–43 Albany St (☎556 0397). Georgian listed building with many period features and comfortable rooms in a quiet street a couple of minutes' walk south of the bus station. ⑧.

Argus Hotel, 14 Coates Gardens (☎337 6159). Smallish rooms in a low-key hotel close to Haymarket Station. ⑤.

Channings, South Learmonth Gardens (☎315 2226). Five elegant town houses joined together for this very comfortable, but somewhat bland, hotel. ⑨.

Claymore Hotel, 6 Royal Terrace (☎556 2693). Small, family-run hotel on one of the city's most desirable streets. ⑤.

Clifton Private Hotel, 1 Clifton Terrace (☎337 1002). Another family-run hotel, in roomy Victorian town house directly opposite Haymarket Station. ⑤.

Grosvenor Hotel, Grosvenor St (☎226 6001). Chain hotel retaining its old character; in the West End, just across from Haymarket Station. ⑦.

Halcyon Hotel, 8 Royal Terrace (☎556 1032). A very reasonably priced unpretentious hotel, considering the location. ⑥.

Howard Hotel, 32–36 Great King St (☎557 3500). Top of the range (£180 a night) elegant townhouse hotel. Lavishly decorated and serving excellent food. ⑨.

Old Waverley Hotel, 43 Princes St (☎556 4648). Large, recently refurbished, grand hotel in ideal location, right across from Waverley Station and with sweeping city views. Good restaurant, *Cranston's*, serving mainly Scottish dishes, with several vegetarian options. ⑨.

Osbourne Hotel, 53–59 York Place (☎556 1012). Behind the bus station; small rooms and a bit dingy but excellent location. ⑦.

Ritz Hotel, 14–18 Grosvenor St (☎337 4315). Posh 5-storey hotel close to Haymarket Station. Some rooms feature antique 4-poster beds.⑦.

Rothesay Hotel, 8 Rothesay Place (☎225 4125). Quiet West End hotel in a Georgian terrace close to St Mary's Cathedral; bright high-ceilinged rooms. ⑦.

Roxburghe Hotel, 38 Charlotte Square (☎225 3921). Characterful traditional hotel, right on the corner of Edinburgh's most beautiful square; food is good but unimaginative. ⑧.

Royal British Hotel, 20 Princes St (☎556 4901). Swanky hotel with a prime location on Edinburgh's main street, offering stunning views. ⑨.

Royal Terrace Hotel, 18 Royal Terrace (☎557 3222). On one of the city's handsomest Georgian streets, part of the eastern extension to the New Town. Has its own landscaped gardens, plus a leisure club with bathing pool. Popular with tour groups. ⑨.

Leith and Inverleith

Malmaison, 1 Tower Place (☎555 6868). New and instantly popular Leith hotel on the harbour: each room has its own highly distinctive decoration. ⑦.

Merith House Hotel, 2 Leith Links (☎554 5045). Busy and often used for functions; overlooking Leith Links, about 2 miles from the centre. ④.

South of the centre

Allison House Hotel, 15–17 Mayfield Gardens (☎667 8049). Popular, well-run and recently expanded hotel with "honesty" bar – guests serve themselves and pay on departure. ⑤.

Arthur's View Hotel, 10 Mayfield Gardens (☎667 3468) Pleasant, friendly hotel in convenient southside location. ⑦.

Braid Hills Hotel, 134 Braid Rd (☎447 8888). Old-fashioned, Baronial-style hotel in a residential area up in the hilly southern outskirts, with fine views (10-min drive from the city). ⑧.

Bruntsfield Hotel, 69–74 Bruntsfield Place (☎229 1393). Comfortable, peaceful large hotel overlooking Bruntsfield Park, a mile south of Princes St. ⑨.

Donmaree Hotel, 21 Mayfield Gardens (☎667 3641). Victorian mansion on the south side of the city, well known for its restaurant specializing in traditional Scottish food. ⑦.

Prestonfield House Hotel, Priestfield Rd (☎668 3346). Edinburgh's most eccentric hotel, a seventeenth-century mansion with opulent interiors set in its own park below Arthur's Seat. Just 5 rooms, only 2 of which have private facilities – historical values have not been sacrificed to modern comforts. Must book well in advance. ⑨.

Teviotdale House Hotel, 53 Grange Loan (☎667 4376). Peaceful non-smoking hotel, offering luxurious standards at moderate prices. Particularly renowned for the huge home-cooked Scottish breakfasts. ⑤.

Thrums Private Hotel, 14–15 Minto St (☎667 5545). Excellent hotel in large Georgian house with equally classy restaurant. ⑥.

West of the centre

Ellersly Country House Hotel, 4 Ellersly Rd (☎337 6888). Edwardian country mansion set in walled garden in quiet suburban Corstorphine, between the city centre and the airport. Predominantly business clientele. ⑨.

Norton House Hotel, Ingliston (☎333 1275). Country house owned by the Virgin group with spacious rooms and conservatory restaurant, set in extensive parkland a mile from the airport. ⑨.

Guest houses

Edinburgh's innumerable **guest houses** are excellent value for money and far more personal places to stay than the larger city hotels.

New Town

Dickie Guest House, 22 E Claremont St (☎556 4032). Friendly B&B in a Victorian town house on the eastern edge of the New Town. ④.

Drummond House, 17 Drummond Place (☎557 9189). Just 3 rooms in this luxurious, guest house in the heart of the New Town, an attractive alternative to the large hotels. ⑦.

Galloway Guest House, 22 Dean Park Crescent (☎332 3672). Friendly, family-run place in elegant Stockbridge, within walking distance of the centre. ④.

Marrakech Guest House, 30 London St (☎556 4444). Small rooms in a residential street just a few minutes' walk south of the bus station. Superb Moroccan restaurant in the basement. ④.

St Bernard's Guest House, 22 St Bernard's Crescent (☎332 2339). Well located in Georgian Stockbridge, with tasteful pink rooms. ⑤.

Sibbet House, 26 Northumberland St (☎556 1078). Small, sumptuous family guest house, where British sang-froid is challenged by a communal breakfast table, an occasion regularly enlivened by the host's bagpipe playing. ⑦.

Six St Mary's Place, Raeburn Place (☎332 8965). Collectively run, "alternative" guest house; has a no smoking policy, and offers excellent home-cooked vegetarian meals. ⑤.

Stuart House, 12 E Claremont St (☎557 9030). Homely, bright refurbished Georgian house in eastern New Town, a few minutes' walk from the bus station; no smoking. ⑥.

South of the centre

Arrandale House, 28 Mayfield Gardens (☎667 6029). Good-value option among a large clutch of guest houses in Mayfield, a residential quarter about a mile from the centre. ④.

International Guest House, 37 Mayfield Gardens (☎667 2511). One of the best of the Mayfield guest houses, with comfortable, well-equipped rooms. ⑤.

Ravensneuk Guest House, 11 Blacket Ave (☎667 5347). Good-value rooms set in a quiet conservation area, close to the Royal Commonwealth Pool and Holyrood Park. ④.

Town House, 65 Gilmore Place (☎229 1985). Small but friendly Victorian guesthouse close to the King's Theatre; no smoking. ⑤.

Leith and Inverleith

A-Haven Guest House, 180 Ferry Rd (☎554 6559). Exceptionally friendly place; among the best of a number of guest houses on one of Edinburgh's main east–west arteries. ④.

Ashlyn Guest House, 42 Inverleith Row (☎552 2954). Right by the Botanical Gardens, and within walking distance of the centre. Non-smoking. ④.

Bonnington Guest House, 202 Ferry Rd (☎554 7610). Comfortable, friendly guest house pleasantly sited just by the park. ⑤.

Ravensdown Guest House, 248 Ferry Rd (☎552 5438). Another place on Ferry Rd, with fine panoramic view across Inverleith playing fields to the city centre. ④.

Sheridan Guest House, 1 Bonnington Terrace (☎554 4107). Comfortable guest house in elegant Victorian terrace. ④.

East of the centre

Daisy Park Guest House, 41 Abercorn Terrace (☎669 2503). Relaxed atmosphere in this guest house opposite the Daisy Park and close to the sea. ④.

Devon House Guest House, 2 Pittville St (☎669 6067). Pleasant rooms, 2 minutes from the shore. ③.

Joppa Turrets Guest House, 1 Lower Joppa (☎669 5806). The place to come if you want an Edinburgh holiday by the sea: a quiet establishment right by the beach in Joppa, 5 miles east of the centre (close to bus routes #15, #26 and #86). ③.

Self-catering apartments

Cramond Village, Riverside, Cramond (☎312 6555). For those seeking a tranquil holiday, 6 luxury apartments, approximately 25 minutes' drive from the city. Four 2-person apartments for £250 per week; one 6-person, £350.

National Trust for Scotland, 5 Charlotte Square (☎243 9331). Has a 2-room apartment in Gladstone's Land (the finest house on the Royal Mile) available for rent. Minimum period one week; open March–Oct only. Sleeps 2; costs from £190 per week.

No 5 Self Catering Apartments, 5 Abercorn Terrace (☎669 1044). These Georgian houses in Portobello have apartments for 3 people for £150–300 per week; for 2, £115–200; single units, £80–950; reduced rates for longer stays.

Rosslyn Castle, Roslin, Midlothian (☎01628/825925). A fifteenth-century castle dramatically sited on a rock high above the River Esk and just 5 minutes' walk from Rosslyn Chapel (7 miles from city centre). Sleeps up to 7 people; £606–1,010 per week.

Royal Mile Enterprises, c/o Vivien Andersen, 3 Doune Terrace (☎225 7189). Two apartments for rent in a historical tenement on the Royal Mile. Minimum stay 3 nights; open all year. Sleeps 2–4; £250–400 per week.

West End Apartments, c/o Brian Matheson, 2 Learmonth Terrace (☎332 0717 or ☎225 7900). Five apartments in West End town house. Minimum let 2 nights; open all year. Sleeps 2–6; £150–500 per week.

Campus accommodation

Heriot-Watt University Riccarton Campus, Currie (☎449 5111 ext. 3113). Rather inconveniently sited at the extreme western fringe of the city, but open all year. ⑤.

Jewel and Esk Valley College, 24 Milton Rd E (☎657 7523). Again the location, about 5 miles east of the centre, is not ideal, but is served directly by bus #44 and lies just beyond the terminus of bus #5. Open all year, except Dec. ④.

Napier University, 219 Colinton Rd (☎445 4621; minimum stay 2 months). Reasonable location in the southern inner suburbs, but open Easter and July to mid-Sept only. ③.

University of Edinburgh Pollock Halls of Residence, 18 Holyrood Park Rd (☎667 1971). Unquestionably the best setting of any of the campuses, right beside the Royal Commonwealth Pool and Holyrood Park. Open Easter and late June to mid-Sept only. ⑤.

Youth Hostels

Belford Youth Hostel, 6–8 Douglas Gardens (☎225 6209). Housed in a converted Arts and Crafts church just west of the centre, close to the Dean Village. Open all year; dorm beds and doubles.

Bruntsfield Hostel, 7 Bruntsfield Crescent (☎447 2994; Grade 1). Strictly run SYHA youth hostel, overlooking Bruntsfield Links a mile south of Princes St; take bus #11, #15 or #16. 2am curfew; closed Jan.

Christian Alliance Female Residence, 14 Coates Crescent (☎225 3608). Clean, women-only hostel in an excellent West End location. No kitchen. Dorm beds and singles. Midnight curfew, extended to 1.30am during the Festival.

Cowgate Tourist Hostel, 112 Cowgate (☎226 2153). Basic, excellent-value accommodation, in small apartments with kitchens, in the heart of the Old Town. Laundry facilities. July–Sept only; no curfew.

Edinburgh Central Youth Hostel, College Wynd (Grade 1). Lively SYHA hostel open July–Aug only. Advance bookings through Edinburgh District Office, 161 Warrender Park Rd, Edinburgh EH9 1EQ (☎229 8660).

Eglington Hostel, 18 Eglington Crescent (☎337 1120; Grade 1). SYHA hostel west of the centre, near Haymarket Station; easier going than its Bruntsfield counterpart. 2am curfew, closed Dec.

High Street Hostel, 8 Blackfriars St (☎557 3984). Privately run venture with room for 130 people, just off the Royal Mile. Slightly cramped, but its lively atmosphere makes up for it. Open 24hr, all year.

Princes Street Hostel, 5 W Register St (☎556 6894). Recently converted guesthouse, with 2 dorms and 2 double rooms. Great central location.

Campsites

Little France Caravan Site, 219 Old Dalkeith Rd (☎666 2326). Three miles south of the centre, reached by bus #33, #82 or #89 from Princes St. April–Sept.

Mortonhall Caravan Park, 38 Mortonhall Gate, Frogston Rd E (☎664 1533). A good site, 5 miles out, near the Braid Hills; take bus #11 from Princes St. March–Oct.

Silverknowes Caravan Site, Marine Drive, Silverknowes (☎312 6874). Pleasant campsite, popular with backpackers, close to the shore in the western suburbs, a 20-minute ride from the centre by bus #14. April–Sept.

Slatebairns Caravan Club Site, Roslin, Midlothian (☎440 2192). Caravans and tents welcome at this attractive countryside site 7 miles from the city centre (bus #87a). Good facilities; open Easter to October 1.

The Old Town

The **OLD TOWN**, although only about a mile long and 300 yards wide, represents the total extent of the twin burghs of Edinburgh and Canongate for the first 650 years of their existence, and its general appearance and character remain indubitably medieval. Containing as it does the majority of the city's most famous tourist sights, it makes by far the best starting-point for your explorations. **The Old Town Information Centre** (late April–May Thurs–Sun 10am–5pm; June–Sept daily 10am–7pm; ☎220 1637) in the Tron Kirk (see p.66) has displays on the history of the Old Town, as well as a wealth of practical information.

In addition to the obvious goals of the **Castle**, the **Palace of Holyroodhouse** and **Holyrood Abbey**, there are scores of historic monuments along the length of the **Royal Mile** linking the two. Inevitably, much of the Old Town is sacrificed to hard-sell tourism, and can be uncomfortably crowded throughout the summer, especially during the Festival. A welcome antidote, and a reminder that the Old Town is by no means fossilized for the benefit of tourists, is provided by the area to the south, notably Chambers Street, location of the **Royal Museum of Scotland** and the **University of Edinburgh**.

While it's possible to cover the highlights of the Old Town in the course of a single day, a detailed visit requires several times as long. No matter how pressed you are, make sure to spare time for the wonderfully varied scenery and breathtaking vantage points of **Holyrood Park**, an extensive tract of open countryside on its eastern edge.

The Castle

The history of Edinburgh, and indeed of Scotland, is indissolubly bound up with its **Castle** (April–Sept daily 9.30am–6pm; Oct–March 9.30am–5pm; £5.50) that dominates the city from its lofty seat atop an extinct volcanic rock. It requires no great imaginative feat to comprehend the strategic importance that underpinned the Castle's, and hence Edinburgh's, pre-eminence within Scotland: in the dramatic view from Princes Street (perhaps most impressive under the clear, bright skies of spring), the north side rears high above an almost sheer rockface; the southern side is equally formidable, the western, where the rock rises in terraces, only marginally less so. Would-be attackers, like modern tourists, were forced to approach the Castle from the crag to the east on which the Royal Mile runs down to Holyrood.

The Castle's many disparate styles reflect its many changes in usage, as well as advances in military architecture: the oldest surviving part, St Margaret's Chapel, is from the twelfth century, while the most recent additions date back to the 1920s. Nothing remains from its period as a seat of the Scottish court in the reign of Malcolm Canmore; indeed, having been lost to (and subsequently recaptured from) the English on several occasions, the defences were dismantled by the Scots themselves in 1313, and only rebuilt in 1356 when the return of King David II from captivity introduced a modicum of political stability. Thereafter, it gradually developed into Scotland's premier castle, with the dual function of fortress and royal palace. It last saw action in 1745, when the Young Pretender's forces, fresh from their victory at Prestonpans, made a half-hearted attempt to storm it. Subsequently, advances in weapon technology diminished its importance, but under the influence of the Romantic movement it came to be seen as a great national monument. A grandiose "improvement" scheme, which would have transformed it into a bloated nineteenth-century vision of the Middle Ages, was considered, but, perhaps fortunately, only a few elements of it were actually built.

Though you can easily take in the views and wander round the Castle yourself, you might like to join one of the somewhat overheated **guided tours** offered by kilted locals, furiously hamming up a thick Scottish brogue as they talk of war, boiling oil and the roar of the cannon.

The Esplanade

The Castle is entered via the **Esplanade**, a parade ground laid out in the eighteenth century and enclosed a century later by ornamental walls, the southern one of which commands fine views towards the Pentland Hills. Each evening during the Festival (see p.90), the Esplanade is the setting for the city's most shameless and spectacular demonstration of tourist kitsch, the Edinburgh Military Tattoo. An unfortunate side-effect of this is that the skyline is disfigured for virtually the entire summer by the grandstands needed to accommodate the spectators.

Dotted around are several military monuments, including an equestrian **statue of Field Marshal Earl Haig**, the controversial Edinburgh-born commander of the British forces in World War I, whose trench warfare strategy of sending men "over the top" led to previously unimaginable casualties.

The lower defences

The **Gatehouse** to the Castle is a Romantic-style addition of the 1880s, complete with the last drawbridge ever built in Scotland. It was later adorned with appropriately heroic-looking statues of Sir William Wallace and Robert the Bruce.

Rearing up behind is the most distinctive and impressive feature of the Castle's silhouette, the sixteenth-century **Half Moon Battery**, which marks the outer limit of the actual defences. Continuing uphill, you pass through the **Portcullis Gate**, a hand-some Renaissance gateway of the same period, marred by the addition of a nineteenth-century upper storey equipped with anachronistic arrow slits rather than gunholes.

Beyond is the six-gun **Argyle Battery**, built in the eighteenth century by Major-General Wade, whose network of military roads and bridges still forms an essential part of the transport infrastructure of the Highlands. Further west is **Mill's Mount Battery**, setting every weekday for a well-known Edinburgh ritual, the firing of the one o'clock gun – originally designed for the benefit of ships in the Firth of Forth, now used as a time signal by city centre office workers. Both batteries offer wonderful panoramic views over Princes Street and the New Town to the coastal towns and hills of Fife across the Forth.

Up the tortuously sloping road, the **Governor's House** is a 1740s mansion whose harled masonry and crow-stepped gables are archetypal features of vernacular Scottish architecture. It now serves as the officers' mess for members of the garrison, while the Governor himself lives in the northern side wing. Behind stands the largest single construction in the Castle complex, the **New Barracks**, built in the 1790s in an austere Neoclassical style. The road then snakes round towards the enclosed citadel at the uppermost point of Castle Rock, entered via the seventeenth-century **Foog's Gate**.

St Margaret's Chapel

At the eastern end of the citadel, **St Margaret's Chapel** is the oldest surviving build-ing in the Castle, and probably also in Edinburgh itself. Used as a powder magazine for 300 years, this tiny Norman church was rediscovered in 1845 and was eventually reded-icated in 1934, after sympathetic restoration. Externally, it is plain and severe, but the interior preserves an elaborate zigzag archway dividing the nave from the sanctuary. Although once believed to have been built by the saint herself, and mooted as the site of her death in 1093, its architectural style suggests that it actually dates from about 30 years later, and was thus probably built by King David I as a memorial to his mother.

The battlements in front of the chapel offer the best of all the Castle's panoramic views. They are interrupted by the **Lang Stairs**, which provide an alternative means of access from the Argyle Battery via the side of the Portcullis Gate. Just below the battlements there's a small **cemetery**, the last resting place of the **soldiers' pets**: it is kept in immaculate condition, particularly when contrasted with the delapidated state of some of the city's public cemeteries. Continuing eastwards, you skirt the top of the Forewall and Half Moon Batteries, passing the 110ft-deep **Castle Well** en route to **Crown Square**, the highest, most secure and most important section of the entire complex.

The Palace

The eastern side of Crown Square is occupied by the **Palace**, a surprisingly unassuming edifice built round an octagonal stair turret heightened last century to bear the Castle's main flagpole. Begun in the 1430s, the Palace's present Renaissance appearance is thanks to King James IV, though it was remodelled for Mary, Queen of Scots and her consort Henry, Lord Darnley, whose entwined initials (MAH), together with the date 1566, can be seen above one of the doorways. This gives access to a few historic rooms, the most interesting of which is the tiny panelled bedchamber at the extreme southeastern corner, where Mary gave birth to James VI. Along with the rest of the Palace, the room was remodelled for James' triumphant homecoming in 1617, though this was to be the last time it served as a royal residence.

Another section of the Palace has recently been refurbished with a detailed audio-visual presentation on the **Honours of Scotland**, the originals of which are housed in the Crown Room at the very end of the display. These magnificent crown jewels – the only pre-Restoration set in the United Kingdom – serve as one of the most potent images of Scotland's nationhood. They were last used for the Scottish-only coronation of Charles II in 1651, an event which provoked the wrath of Oliver Cromwell, who made exhaustive attempts to have the jewels melted down. Having narrowly escaped his clutches by being smuggled out of the Castle and hidden in a rural church, the jewels later served as symbols of the absent monarch at sittings of the Scottish parliament before being locked away in a chest following the Union of 1707. For over a century they were out of sight and eventually presumed lost, before being rediscovered in 1818 as a result of a search initiated by Sir Walter Scott.

Of the three pieces comprising the Honours, the oldest is the **sceptre**, which bears statuettes of the Virgin and Child, St James and St Andrew, rounded off by a polished globe of rock crystal: it was given to James IV in 1494 by Pope Alexander VI, and refashioned by Scottish craftsmen for James V. Even finer is the **sword**, a swaggering Italian High Renaissance masterpiece by the silversmith Domenico da Sutri, presented to James IV by the great artistic patron Pope Julius II. Both the hilt and the scabbard are engraved with Julius' personal emblem, showing the oak tree and its acorns, the symbols of the Risen Christ, together with dolphins, symbols of the Church. The jewel-encrusted **crown**, made for James V by the Scottish goldsmith James Mosman, incorporates the gold circlet worn by Robert the Bruce and is surmounted by an enamelled orb and cross.

Around Crown Square

The south side of Crown Square is occupied by the **Great Hall**, built under James IV as a venue for banquets and other ceremonial occasions. Until 1639 the meeting place of the Scottish Parliament, it later underwent the indignity of conversion and subdivision, firstly into a barracks, then a hospital. During this time, its hammer-beam roof – the earliest of three in the Old Town – was hidden from view. It was restored towards the end of the last century, when the hall was decked out in the full-blown Romantic manner.

On the west side of the square, the eighteenth-century **Queen Anne Barracks** house part of the **Scottish United Services Museum**, with displays on each of the different Scottish military regiments, plus the navy and air force. Note the model of the ship *The Great George*, made by French prisoners incarcerated in the Castle during the eighteenth and early nineteenth centuries.

In 1755, the castle church of St Mary on the north side of the square was replaced by a barracks, which in turn was skilfully converted into the quietly reverential **Scottish National War Memorial** in honour of the 150,000 Scots who fell in World War I.

The rest of the complex

From Crown Square, you can descend to the **Vaults**, a series of cavernous chambers erected by order of James IV to provide an even surface for the showpiece buildings above. They were later used as a prison for captured foreign nationals, who have bequeathed a rich legacy of graffiti. One of the rooms houses the famous fifteenth-century siege gun, **Mons Meg**, which could fire a 500-pound stone nearly two miles. A seventeenth-century visitor, the London poet, John Taylor, commented: "It is so great within, that it was told me that a child was once gotten there". In 1736, Mons Meg was taken to the Tower of London where it stayed till Sir Walter Scott persuaded George IV, on the occasion of his 1822 state visit to Scotland, to return it.

Directly opposite the entrance to the Vaults is the **Military Prison**, built in 1842, when the design and function of jails was a major topic of public debate. The cells, though designed for solitary confinement, are less forbidding than might be expected. Finally, beyond the Governor's House, and overlooking the two-tier western defences, the late nineteenth-century **Hospital** is a continuation of the Scottish United Services Museum.

The Royal Mile

The **Royal Mile**, the name given to the ridge linking the Castle with Holyrood, was described by Daniel Defoe, in 1724, as "the largest, longest and finest street for Buildings and Number of Inhabitants, not in Bretain only, but in the World". Almost exactly a mile in length, it is divided into four separate streets – Castlehill, Lawnmarket, High Street and Canongate. From these, branching out in a herringbone pattern, a series of tightly packed closes and steep lanes are entered via archways known as pends. After the construction of the New Town, the Royal Mile degenerated into a notorious slum, but has since shaken off that reputation, becoming once again a highly desirable place to live. Although marred somewhat by rather too many over-priced shops, it is still among the most evocative parts of the city, and one that particularly rewards detailed exploration.

Castlehill

The narrow uppermost stretch of the Royal Mile is known as **Castlehill**. On the side facing the Esplanade the pretty Art Nouveau **Witches' Fountain** commemorates the 300 or more women burned at the spot on charges of sorcery, the last of whom died in 1722. Rising up behind is the picturesque **Ramsay Gardens**, centring on the octagonal **Goose Pie House**, home of the eighteenth-century poet Allan Ramsay, author of *The Gentle Shepherd* and father of the better-known portrait painter of the same name. The rest dates from the 1890s and was the brainchild of Patrick Geddes, a pioneer of the modern town-planning movement, who created these desirable apartments in an attempt to regenerate the Old Town.

At the top of the southern side of Castlehill, the so-called **Cannonball House** takes its name from the cannonball embedded in its masonry, which according to legend was the result of a poorly targeted shot fired by the Castle garrison at Bonnie Prince Charlie's encampment at Holyrood. The truth is far more prosaic: the ball marks the gravitation height of the city's first piped water supply. Alongside, the **Scotch Whisky**

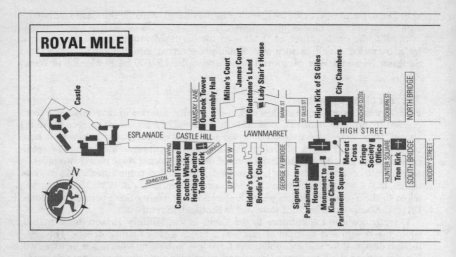

Heritage Centre (daily 10am–5.30pm, extended opening in high summer; £3.80) gives the lowdown on all aspects of Scotland's national beverage, featuring a gimmicky ride in a "barrel" through a series of uninspiring historical tableaux, plus a film on aspects of production and blending. It's worth popping into the shop, whose stock gives an idea of the sheer range and diversity of the drink, with dozens of different brands on sale.

Across the road, the **Outlook Tower** (April–Oct Mon–Fri 9.30am–6pm, Sat & Sun 10am–6pm, Nov–March 10am–5pm; £3.20) has been one of Edinburgh's top tourist attractions since 1853, when the original seventeenth-century tenement was equipped with a **camera obscura**. It makes a good introduction to the city: actual moving images are beamed on to a white table, accompanied by live running commentary. For the best views visit when dark, or at noon when there are fewer shadows. The viewing balcony is one of Edinburgh's best vantage points, and there are exhibitions on pinhole photography, holography, Victorian photographs of the city, and topographic paintings made between 1780 and 1860.

A few steps further on is the **Assembly Hall**, meeting place of the annual General Assembly of the Church of Scotland, and, during the Festival, an extraordinarily effective venue for large-scale drama, normally staging the most ambitious event on the programme. It was built in 1859 for the breakaway Free Church; the established church previously met at the **Tolbooth Kirk** across the road. Stunningly sited at the foot of Castlehill, the Kirk is one of the most distinctive features of the Edinburgh skyline, thanks to its majestic spire, the highest in the city; sadly, it has lain disused since vacated by its Gaelic-speaking congregation in 1981, though it is hoped that, with the help of the Millennium Fund (a government fund for special projects to mark the new millennium), it will be converted for use as a centre for the Edinburgh Festival, incorporating ticket sales, press facilities and a Festival Club. The church's superb neo-Gothic detailing is due to Augustus Pugin, co-architect of the Houses of Parliament in London.

Lawnmarket

Below the Tolbooth Kirk, the Royal Mile opens out into the much broader expanse of **Lawnmarket**, which, as its name suggests, was once a marketplace. At its northern end is the entry to **Milne's Court**, whose excellently restored tenements now serve as student residences, and immediately beyond, **James Court**, one of Edinburgh's most

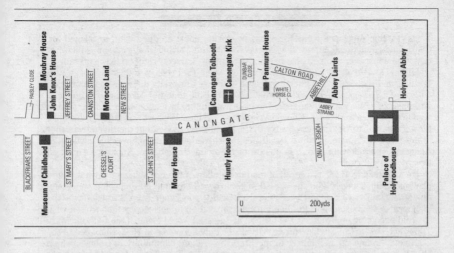

fashionable addresses prior to the advent of the New Town, with David Hume and James Boswell among those who lived there.

Back on Lawnmarket itself, **Gladstone's Land** (April–Oct Mon–Sat 10am–5pm, Sun 2–5pm; July–Aug also Thurs until 8pm; £2.50) takes its name from the merchant Thomas Gledstane (sic), who in 1617 acquired a modest dwelling on the site, transforming it into a magnificent six-storey mansion. The Gledstane family are thought to have occupied the third floor, renting out the rest to merchants, in the style of tenement occupation still widespread in the city today. The arcaded ground floor, the only authentic example left of what was once a common feature of Royal Mile houses, has been restored to illustrate its early function as a shopping booth. Several other rooms have been kitted out in authentic period style to give an impression of the lifestyle of a well-to-do household of the late seventeenth century; the Painted Chamber, with its decorated wooden ceiling and wall friezes, is particularly impressive. You can also stay here (see p.56).

A few paces further on, steps lead down to Lady Stair's Close, in which stands **Lady Stair's House** (June–Sept Mon–Sat 10am–6pm; Oct–May Mon–Sat 10am–5pm; Sun 2–5pm during the Festival only; free), another fine seventeenth-century residence, albeit one subject to a considerable amount of Victorian refurbishment. It now serves as Edinburgh's literary museum, featuring a collection of personal mementoes (among them locks of hair and walking sticks) of the three lions of Scottish literature – Robert Burns, Sir Walter Scott and Robert Louis Stevenson.

On the south side of Lawnmarket is **Riddle's Court**, actually a double courtyard, each with its own pend. Further down the street, **Brodie's Close** is named after the father of one of Edinburgh's most morbid characters, Deacon William Brodie, burglar by night, apparent pillar of society by day. Following his eventual capture, he managed to escape to Holland, but was betrayed, brought back to Edinburgh and hanged in 1788 on gallows of his own design. His ruse of trying to cheat death by secretly wearing an iron collar under his shirt failed to save him.

The High Kirk of St Giles

Across George IV Bridge, the **High Kirk of St Giles** (Mon–Sat 9am–5pm, extended opening in summer) closes off Parliament Square from High Street. The sole parish

JOHN KNOX

The Protestant reformer **John Knox** has been alternately credited with, or blamed for, the distinctive national culture that emerged from the Calvinist Reformation, which has cast its shadow over Scottish history and the Scottish character right up to the present.

Little is known about Knox's early years: he was born between 1505 and 1514 in East Lothian, and trained for the priesthood at St Andrews University under John Major (sic), author of a *History of Great Britain* that advocated the union of Scotland and England. Ordained in 1540, Knox then served as a private tutor, in league with Scotland's first significant Protestant leader, **George Wishart** – and after Wishart was burnt at the stake for heresy in 1546, became involved with the group who carried out the revenge murder of the Scottish Primate, Cardinal David Beaton, subsequently taking over his castle in St Andrews. The following year, this was captured by the French, and Knox was carted off to work as a galley slave.

He was freed in 1548, as a result of the intervention of the English, who invited him to play an evangelizing role in the spread of their own Reformation. Following successful ministries in Berwick-upon-Tweed and Newcastle-upon-Tyne, Knox turned down the bishopric of Rochester, less from an intrinsic opposition to episcopacy than from a wish to avoid becoming embroiled in the turmoil he guessed would ensue if the Catholic Mary Tudor acceded to the English throne. When this duly happened in 1553, Knox fled to the Continent, ending up as minister to the English-speaking community in Geneva, which was then in the grip of the theocratic government of the Frenchman **Jean Calvin**. Knox was quickly won over to his radical version of Protestantism, declaring Geneva to be "the most perfect school of Christ since the days of the Apostles".

In exile, Knox was much preoccupied with the question of the influence wielded by political rulers, believing that the future of the Reformation in Europe was at risk because of the opposition of a few powerful sovereigns. This prompted him to write his most infamous treatise, *The First Blast of the Trumpet against the Monstruous Regiment of Women*, a specific attack on the three Catholic women then ruling Scotland, England and France, which has made his name synonymous with misogyny ever since.

When Knox was allowed to return to Scotland in 1555, he took over as spiritual leader of the Reformation, becoming minister of St Giles in Edinburgh, where he established a reputation as a charismatic preacher. However, the establishment of Protestantism as the official religion of Scotland in 1560 was dependent on the forging of an alliance with Elizabeth I, which Knox himself rigorously championed: the swift deployment of English troops against the French garrison in Edinburgh dealt a fatal blow to Franco-Spanish hopes of re-establishing Catholicism in both Scotland and England. Although the return of Mary, Queen of Scots the following year placed a Catholic monarch on the Scottish throne, reputedly Knox was always able to retain the upper hand in his famous disputes with her.

Before his death in 1572, Knox began mapping out the organization of the Scots Kirk, sweeping away all vestiges of episcopal control and giving laymen a role of unprecedented importance. He also proposed a nationwide education system, to be compulsory for the very young, and free for the poor; though lack of funds meant this could not be implemented in full. His final legacy was the posthumously published *History of the Reformation of Religion in the Realm of Scotland*, a justification of his life's work.

For all his considerable influence, Knox was not responsible for many of the features which have created the popular image of Scottish presbyterianism – and of Knox himself – as austere and joyless. A man of refined cultural tastes, he did not encourage the iconoclasm that destroyed so many of Scotland's churches and works of art: indeed, much of this was carried out by English hands. Nor did he promote the unbending Sabbatarianism, the obsessive work ethic or even the inflexible view of the doctrine of predestination favoured by his far more fanatical successors. Ironically, though, by fostering an irrevocable rift in the "Auld Alliance" with France, he did do more than anyone else to ensure that Scotland's future was to be linked irrevocably with that of England.

church of medieval Edinburgh and where John Knox (see box opposite) launched and directed the Scottish Reformation, the Kirk is almost invariably referred to as a cathedral, although it has only been the seat of a bishop on two brief and unhappy occasions in the seventeenth century. According to one of the city's best-known legends, the attempt in 1637 to introduce the English prayer book, and thus episcopal government, so incensed a humble stallholder named Jenny Geddes that she hurled her stool at the preacher, prompting the rest of the congregation to chase the offending clergy out of the building. A tablet in the north aisle marks the spot from where she let rip.

In the early nineteenth century, St Giles received a much-needed but over-drastic restoration, covering most of the Gothic exterior with a smooth stone coating that gives it a certain Georgian dignity while sacrificing its medieval character almost completely. The only part to survive this treatment is the late fifteenth-century tower, whose resplendent crown spire is formed by eight flying buttresses. The **interior** has survived in much better shape. Especially notable are the four massive piers supporting the tower, which date back, at least in part, to the church's Norman predecessor. In the nineteenth century, St Giles was adorned with a whole series of funerary monuments in order to give it the character of a national pantheon on the model of Westminster Abbey. It was also equipped with several Pre-Raphaelite stained-glass windows. The best of these, designed by Edward Burne-Jones and William Morris, showing Old Testament prophets and the Israelites crossing the River Jordan, can be seen on the facade wall of the **north aisle**. Alongside is the great **west window**, which was dedicated to Robbie Burns in 1985 causing enormous controversy – as a hardened drinker and womanizer, the national bard was far from being an upholder of accepted Presbyterian values.

At the southeastern corner of St Giles, with its own separate entrance on Parliament Square, the **Thistle Chapel** was built by Sir Robert Lorimer in 1911 as the private chapel of the 16 knights of the Most Noble Order of the Thistle. Self-consciously derivative of St George's Chapel in Windsor, it's an exquisite piece of craftsmanship, with an elaborate ribbed vault, huge drooping bosses, and extravagantly ornate stalls.

Parliament Square

The rest of **Parliament Square** is dominated by the continuous Neoclassical facades of the **Law Courts**, originally planned by Robert Adam (1728–1792), one of four brothers in a family of architects (their father William Adam designed Hopetoun House; see p.88) whose work helped give the New Town much of its grace and elegance. Because of a shortage of funds, the present exteriors were built to designs by Robert Reid (1776–1856), the designer of the northern part of New Town, who faithfully quoted from Adam's architectural vocabulary without matching his flair. Mentor of William Playfair (see p.72), another architect, William Stark was flamboyant with design, and his **Signet Library**, which occupies the west side of the square, is one of the most beautiful interiors in Edinburgh – its sumptuous colonnaded hall a perfect embodiment of the ideals of the Age of Reason. Unfortunately it can only be seen by prior written application, except on very occasional open days.

Around the corner, facing the southern side of St Giles, is **Parliament House**, built in the 1630s for the Scottish Parliament, a role it maintained until the Union, when it passed into the hands of the legal fraternity. Today it is readily accessible during the week, used by lawyers and their clients for hushed conferrals in between court sittings. Inside, the most notable feature is the extravagant hammerbeam roof, and the delicately carved stone corbels from which it springs: in addition to some vicious grotesques, they include accurate depictions of several castles, including Edinburgh.

Outside on the square, an imposing equestrian **monument to King Charles II** depicts him in fetching Roman garb. Set in the pavement beside a bloated memorial to the fifth Duke of Buccleuch, a brickwork pattern known as the **Heart of Midlothian**, immortalized in Scott's novel of the same name, marks the site of the demolished Tolbooth. Passers-by traditionally spit on it for luck. Public proclamations have traditionally been read from the **Mercat Cross** at the back of St Giles. The present structure, adorned with coats-of-arms and topped by a sculpture of a unicorn, looks venerable enough, but most of it is little more than a hundred years old, a gift to the city from nineteenth-century prime minister, William Ewart Gladstone.

High Street: the western block

The third section of the Royal Mile proper is known as **High Street**, and occupies two blocks on either side of the intersection between North Bridge and South Bridge. Directly opposite the Mercat Cross, the U-shaped **City Chambers** were designed by John Adam, brother of Robert, as the Royal Exchange. Local traders never warmed to the exchange, however, so the town council established its headquarters there instead. Beneath the City Chambers lies **Mary King's Close**, one of Edinburgh's most unusual attractions. Built in the early sixteenth century, it was closed off for many years after the devastation of the 1645 plague, before being entirely covered up by the chambers in 1753. The guide spices up an already interesting tale with florid stories of ghosts and headless dogs. For many years tours of the close were occasional and sporadic; however, during the 1995 Festival, regular tours were successfully held and it's hoped these will continue (check with True North Events on ☎220 2056). A little further down the street is **Anchor Close**, site of the printing works of William Smellie, who published the first ever edition of the *Encyclopaedia Britannica* there in 1768.

Across the road is the **Tron Kirk**, best known as the favourite rendezvous for hardy Hogmanay revellers. The church was built in the 1630s to accommodate the Presbyterian congregation ejected from St Giles when the latter became the seat of a bishop; the spire is an 1820s replacement for one destroyed by fire. The Tron remained in use as a church until 1952. It was then closed for 40 years before reopening in as the **Old Town Information Centre** (see p.58). Excavations within the church have revealed sections of an old close, Marlin's Wynd, which ran from High Street down to the Cowgate.

High Street: the eastern block

Beyond the intersection of North Bridge and South Bridge back on the northern side of High Street, is **Paisley Close**, above whose entrance is a bust of a youth with the inscription "Heave awa' chaps, I'm no' dead yet", uttered in 1861 by a boy trapped by rubble following the collapse of a tenement in the close, and who was subsequently dug out by rescue workers.

In Chalmers Close, just to the west, **Trinity Apse** is a poignant reminder of the fifteenth-century Holy Trinity Collegiate Church, formerly one of Edinburgh's most outstanding buildings, but demolished in 1848 to make way for an extension to Waverley Station. The stones were carefully numbered and stored on Calton Hill so that it could be reassembled at a later date, but many were pilfered before sufficient funds became available, and only the apse could be reconstructed on this new site. A few years ago, it was transformed into a **Brass Rubbing Centre** (June–Sept Mon–Sat 10am–6pm; Oct–May Mon–Sat 10am–5pm; Sun 2–5pm during the Festival only; free), where you can rub your own impressions from Pictish crosses for around 40p.

The noisy **Museum of Childhood** (same times as the Brass Rubbing Centre; free) was, oddly enough, founded by an eccentric local councillor who disliked children. Although he claimed that the museum was a serious social archive for adults, and dedicated it to King Herod, it has always attracted swarms of kids, who delight in the dolls' houses, teddy bears, train sets, marionettes, and hosts of other paraphernalia.

Almost directly opposite is what's thought to be the city's oldest surviving dwelling, the early sixteenth-century **Moubray House** (closed to the public). The uses of the four-storied house have included tavern, bookshop and even, towards the end of the nineteenth century, temperance hotel. It also served as Daniel Defoe's office during his stay as an English government representative in 1707. Next door lies the picturesque **John Knox's House** (Mon–Sat 10am–4.30pm; £1.30), built some 30 years later. With its outside stairway, Biblical motto, and sundial adorned with a statue of Moses, it gives a good impression of how the Royal Mile must have once looked. Whether or not it was ever really the home of Knox is debatable: he may have moved here for safety at the height of the religious troubles. The house did, however, once belong to goldsmith James Mosman, son of the designer of the Scottish crown, who was executed for his dogged loyalty to Knox's *bête noire*, Mary, Queen of Scots. The rather bare interiors, which give a good idea of the labyrinthine layout of Old Town houses, display explanatory material on Knox's life and career.

Canongate

For over 700 years, the district through which Canongate runs was a burgh in its own right, officially separate from the capital. In recent decades, it has been the subject of some of the most ambitious restoration programmes in the Old Town, two notable examples of which can be seen at the top of the street. On the south side is the residential **Chessel's Court**, a mid-eighteenth-century development with fanciful Rococo chimneys; formerly the site of the Excise Office, scene of the robbery that led to the arrest and execution of Deacon Brodie. Over the road the **Morocco Land** is a reasonably faithful reproduction of an old tenement, incorporating the original bust of a Moor from which its name derived.

Dominated by a turreted steeple, the late sixteenth-century **Canongate Tolbooth** (June–Sept Mon–Sat 10am–6pm; Oct–May 10am–5pm, Sun 2–5pm during the Festival only; free), a little further down the north side of the street, has served both as the headquarters of the burgh administration and as a prison, and now houses **The People's Story**, a lively museum devoted to the everyday life and work of Edinburgh people down the centuries, with sounds and tableaux on various aspects of city living – including a typical Edinburgh pub. Next door, **Canongate Kirk** was built in the 1680s to house the congregation expelled from Holyrood Abbey when the latter was commandeered by James VII (James II in England) to serve as the chapel for the Order of the Thistle. It's a curiously archaic design, still Renaissance in outline, and built to a cruciform plan wholly at odds with the ideals and requirements of Protestant worship. Its churchyard, one of the city's most exclusive cemeteries, commands a superb view across to Calton Hill. Among those buried here are Adam Smith, Mrs Agnes McLehose (better known as Robert Burns' "Clarinda") and Robert Fergusson, regarded by some as Edinburgh's greatest poet, despite his death at the age of 24; his headstone was donated by Burns, a fervent admirer, who also wrote the inscription.

Opposite the church, the local history museum in **Huntly House** (June–Sept Mon–Sat 10am–6pm; Oct–May Mon–Sat 10am–5pm, Sun 2–5pm during the Festival only; free) includes a quirky array of old shop signs, some dating back to the eighteenth century, as well as displays on indigenous industries such as glass, silver, pottery and clockmaking, and on the dubious military career of Earl Haig. Also on view is the original version of the National Covenant of 1638; modern science has failed to resolve whether or not some of the signatories signed with their own blood, as tradition has it.

Among the several fine seventeenth-century mansions on the easternmost stretch of Canongate, **Panmure House** was for a time the home of Adam Smith, father of the science of political economy and unwitting guru of latter-day Conservatism. At the very foot of the street, the entrance to the residential **White Horse Close** was once the site of the inn from where stagecoaches began the journey to London.

Stridently quaint, it drips with all the most characteristic features of Scottish vernacular architecture, crow-stepped gables, dormer windows, overhanging upper storeys and curving outside stairways.

Holyrood

At the foot of Canongate lies **Holyrood**, Edinburgh's royal quarter, the **legend** of whose foundation in 1128 is described in a fifteenth-century manuscript which is still kept there. The story goes that King David I, son of Malcolm Canmore and St Margaret, went out hunting one day and was suddenly confronted by a stag who threw him from his horse and seemed ready to gore him. In desperation, the king tried to protect himself by grasping its antlers, but instead found himself holding a crucifix, whereupon the animal ran off. In a dream that night, he heard a voice commanding him to "make a house for Canons devoted to the Cross"; he duly obeyed, naming the abbey Holyrood (rood being an alternative name for a cross). More likely, however, is that David, the most pious of all Scotland's monarchs, simply acquired a relic of the True Cross and decided to build a suitable home for it.

Holyrood soon became a favoured **royal residence**, its situation in a secluded valley making it far more agreeable than the draughty Castle. At first, monarchs lodged in the monastic guest house, for which a wing for the exclusive use of the court was constructed during the reign of James II. This was transformed into a full-blown palace for James IV, which in turn was replaced by a much larger building for Charles II, although he never actually lived there. Indeed, it was something of a white elephant until Queen Victoria started making regular trips to her northern kingdom, a custom that has been maintained by her successors.

The precincts

On the north side of **Abbey Strand**, which forms a sort of processional way linking Canongate with Holyrood, Abbey Lairds is a four-storey sixteenth-century mansion which once served as a home for aristocratic debtors and is now occupied by royal flunkeys during the summer seat of the court.

Legend has it that Mary, Queen of Scots used to bathe in sweet white wine in the curious little turreted structure nearby known as **Queen Mary's Bath House**; it is more likely, however, that it was either a summer pavilion or a dovecot. Its architecture is mirrored in the **Croft an Righ**, a picturesque L-shaped house in a quiet, generally overlooked corner beside the eastern wall of the complex.

The Palace of Holyroodhouse

In its present form, the **Palace of Holyroodhouse** (April–Oct Mon–Sat 9.30am–5.15pm, Sun 10am–4.30pm; Nov–March daily 9.30am–3.45pm; £5) is largely a seventeenth-century creation, planned for Charles II. However, the tower house of the old palace was skilfully incorporated to form the northwestern block, with a virtual mirror image of it erected as a counterbalance at the other end. The three-storey **courtyard** is

---

ADMISSION TO HOLYROOD

Following reorganization, there are no longer guided tours to Holyrood. Visitors are free to move at their own pace and can consult the knowledgeable attendants on hand in each room. It is worth remembering that Holyrood is still a working Palace, so the buildings are closed to the public for long periods during state functions; you won't be able to visit for a fortnight in the middle of May, and during the annual royal visit which takes place in the last two weeks of June and the first in July.

an early exercise in Palladian style, exhibiting a punctiliously accurate knowledge of the main Classical orders to create a sense of absolute harmony and unity.

Inside, the **State Apartments**, as Charles II's palace is known, are decked out with oak panelling, tapestries, portraits and decorative paintings, all overshadowed by the magnificent white stucco **ceilings**, especially in the Morning Drawing Room. The most eye-catching chamber, however, is the **Great Gallery**, which takes up the entire first floor of the northern wing. During the 1745 sojourn of the Young Pretender this was the setting for a banquet, described in detail in Scott's novel *Waverley*, and it is still used for big ceremonial occasions. Along the walls are 89 portraits commissioned from the seventeenth-century Dutch artist Jacob de Wet to illustrate the royal lineage of Scotland from its mythical origins in the fourth century BC; the result is unintentionally hilarious, as it is clear that the artist's imagination was taxed to bursting point by the need to paint so many different facial types without having an inkling as to what the subjects actually looked like. In the adjacent **King's Closet**, de Wet's *The Finding of Moses* provides a Biblical link to the portraits, the Scottish royal family claiming descent from Scota, the Egyptian pharaoh's daughter who discovered Moses in the bullrushes.

The oldest parts of the palace, the **Historical Apartments**, are mainly of note for their associations with Mary, Queen of Scots and in particular for the brutal murder, organized by her husband, Lord Darnley, of her private secretary, David Rizzio, who was stabbed 56 times and dragged from the small closet, through the Queen's Bedchamber, and into the Outer Chamber. Until a few years ago, visitors were shown apparently indelible bloodstains on the floor of the latter, but these are now admitted to be fakes, and have been covered up. A display cabinet in the same room shows some pieces of **needlework** woven by the deposed queen while in English captivity; another case has an outstanding **miniature portrait** of her by the French court painter, François Clouet.

Holyrood Abbey

In the grounds of the Palace are the wonderfully evocative ruins of **Holyrood Abbey**. Of King David's original Norman church, the only surviving fragment is a doorway in the far southeastern corner. Most of the remainder dates from a late twelfth- and early thirteenth-century rebuilding in the Early Gothic style.

The surviving parts of the **west front**, including one of the twin towers and the elaborately carved entrance portal, show how resplendent the abbey must once have been. Unfortunately, its sacking by the English in 1547, followed by the demolition of the transept and chancel during the Reformation, all but destroyed the building. Charles I attempted to restore some semblance of unity by ordering the erection of the great east window and a new stone roof, but the latter collapsed in 1768, causing grievous damage to the rest of the structure. By this time, the Canongate congregation had another place of worship, and schemes to rebuild the abbey were abandoned.

Holyrood Park

Holyrood Park – or **Queen's Park** – a natural wilderness in the very heart of the modern city, is unquestionably one of Edinburgh's main assets, as locals (though relatively few tourists) readily appreciate. Packed into an area no more than five miles in diameter is an amazing variety of landscapes – mountains, crags, moorland, marshes, glens, lochs and fields – representing something of a microcosm of Scotland's scenery. The **Queen's Drive** circumnavigates the park, enabling many of its features to be seen by car, though you really need to stroll around to appreciate it fully.

Opposite the southern gates of the Palace a pathway, nicknamed the Radical Road, traverses the ridge immediately below the **Salisbury Crags**, one of the main features of the Edinburgh skyline. Even though there is no path, you can walk along the top of the basalt crags, from where there are excellent views of the Palace of Holyroodhouse and Holyrood Abbey.

Following Queen's Drive in the other direction, you arrive at **St Margaret's Loch**, a nineteenth-century man-made pond, above which stand the scanty ruins of **St Anthony's Chapel**, another fine vantage point. From here, the road's loop is one-way only, ascending to **Dunsapie Loch**, again an artificial stretch of water, which makes an excellent foil to the eponymous crag behind.

This is the usual starting-point for the ascent of **Arthur's Seat**, a majestic extinct volcano rising 823ft above sea level. The seat is Edinburgh's single most prominent landmark, resembling a huge crouched lion when seen from the west. The climb from Dunsapie, up a grassy slope, followed by a rocky path near the summit, is considerably less arduous than it looks, and is a fairly straightforward 20-minute walk, though there are several other, somewhat longer and more taxing ways up from other points in the park. The views from the top are all you'd expect, covering the entire city and much of the Firth of Forth; on a clear day, you can even see the southernmost mountains of the Highlands. The composer, Felix Mendelssohn, climbed Arthur's Seat in July 1829, noting: "It is beautiful here! In the evening a cool breeze is wafted from the sea, and then all objects appear clearly and sharply defined against the gray sky; the lights from the windows glitter brilliantly." As there is little reason to associate it with the British king of the Holy Grail legends, there's no satisfactory story to explain the name.

Queen's Drive circles round to the foot of Salisbury Crags, from where the feline appearance of Arthur's Seat is particularly marked. The road then makes a sharp switchback, passing beneath **Samson's Ribs**, a group of basalt pillars strikingly reminiscent of the Hebridean island of Staffa (see *Argyll*). It continues on to **Duddingston Loch**, the only natural stretch of water in the park, now a bird sanctuary. Perched above it, just outside the park boundary, **Duddingston Kirk** dates back in part to the twelfth century and serves as the focus of one of the most unspoiled old villages within modern Edinburgh.

The rest of the Old Town

Although most visitors to the Old Town understandably concentrate on the Royal Mile, the area has many other intriguing corners, none of which has so much as a hint of commercialism.

Cowgate

Immediately south of the Royal Mile, and following a roughly parallel course from the Lawnmarket to St Mary's Street, is **Cowgate**. One of Edinburgh's oldest surviving streets, it was also formerly one of the city's most prestigious addresses. However, the construction of the great **viaducts** linking the Old and New Towns entombed it below street level, condemning it to decay and neglect; and leading the nineteenth-century writer, Alexander Smith, to declare that "the condition of the inhabitants is as little known to respectable Edinburgh as are the habits of moles, earthworms, and the mining population". In the last decade or so Cowgate has experienced something of a revival, though few tourists venture here and the contrast with the neighbouring Royal Mile remains stark.

At the corner with Niddry Street, which runs down from the eastern block of High Street, the unprepossessing **St Cecilia's Hall** (Wed & Sat 2–5pm; £1) was built in the 1760s for the Musical Society of Edinburgh. Inside, Scotland's oldest and most beautiful concert room, oval in shape and set under a shallow dome, makes a perfect venue for concerts of Baroque and early music, held during the Festival and occasionally at other times of the year.

Towards the western end of Cowgate stands the **Magdalen Chapel**, a sixteenth-century almshouse under the jurisdiction of the Incorporation of Hammermen, a guild to which most Edinburgh workers, other than goldsmiths, belonged. A few years later, as one of the focal points of the Reformation, it was probably the setting for the first-ever General Assembly of the Church of Scotland. The Hammermen added a handsome tower and steeple in the 1620s, and later transformed the chapel into their guildhall, which was suitably adorned with fine ironwork. However, the main feature of the interior is the only significant pre-Reformation stained glass in Scotland still in its original location. That it escaped the iconoclasts is probably due to the fact that it is purely heraldic.

Grassmarket and George IV Bridge

At its western end, Cowgate opens out into **Grassmarket**, which has played an important role in the murkier aspects of Edinburgh's turbulent history. The public gallows were located here, and it was the scene of numerous riots and other disturbances down the centuries. It was here, in 1736, that Captain Porteous was lynched after he had ordered shots to be fired at the crowd watching a public execution. The notorious duo William Burke and William Hare had their lair in a now-vanished close just off the western end of Grassmarket, luring to it victims whom they murdered with the intention of selling their bodies to the eminent physician Robert Knox. Eventually, Hare betrayed his partner, who was duly executed in 1829, and Knox's career was finished off as a result. Today, Grassmarket can still be seamy, though the cluster of busy bars and restaurants along its northern side are evidence of a serious attempt to clean up its image.

At the northeastern corner of Grassmarket are five old tenements of the old **West Bow**, which formerly zigzagged up to the Royal Mile. The rest of this was replaced in the 1840s by the curving **Victoria Street**, an unusual two-tier thoroughfare, with arcaded shops below, and a pedestrian terrace above. This sweeps up to **George IV Bridge** and the **National Library of Scotland** which holds a rich collection of illuminated manuscripts, early printed books, historical documents, and the letters and papers of prominent Scottish literary figures, displayed in regularly changing thematic exhibitions (usually Mon–Sat 10am–5pm, Sun 2–5pm; free).

Greyfriars and around

The **statue of Greyfriars Bobby** at the southwestern corner of **George IV Bridge** must rank as Edinburgh's most sentimental tourist attraction. Bobby was a Skye terrier acquired as a working dog by a police constable named John Gray. When the latter died in 1858, Bobby began a vigil on his grave which he maintained until he died fourteen years later. In the process, he became an Edinburgh celebrity, fed and cared for by locals who gave him a special collar (now in the Huntly House Museum; see p.67) to prevent him being impounded as a stray. His statue, originally a fountain, was modelled from life, and erected soon after his death; his story has gained international renown, thanks to a spate of cloying books and tear-jerking movies.

The grave Bobby mourned over is in the **Greyfriars Kirkyard**, which among its clutter of grandiose seventeenth- and eighteenth-century funerary monuments boasts the striking mausoleum of the Adam family of architects. Greyfriars is particularly associated with the long struggle to establish presbyterianism in Scotland: in 1638, it was the setting for the signing of the National Covenant, while in 1679 some 1200 Covenanters were imprisoned in the enclosure at the southwestern end of the yard. Set against the northern wall is the Martyrs' Monument, a defiantly worded memorial commemorating all those who died in pursuit of the eventual victory.

The graveyard rather overshadows **Greyfriars Kirk** itself, completed in 1620 as the first new church in Edinburgh since the Reformation. It's a real oddball in both layout and design, having a nave and aisles but no chancel, and adopting the anachronistic architectural language of the friary that preceded it, complete with medieval-looking windows, arches and buttresses.

At the western end of Greyfriars Kirkyard is one of the most significant surviving portions of the **Flodden Wall**, the city fortifications erected in the wake of Scotland's disastrous military defeat of 1513. When open, the gateway beyond offers a short cut to **George Heriot's Hospital**, otherwise approached from Lauriston Place to the south. Founded as a home for poor boys by "Jinglin Geordie" Heriot, James VI's goldsmith, it is now one of Edinburgh's most prestigious fee-paying schools; although you can't go inside, you can wander round the quadrangle, whose array of towers, turrets, chimneys, carved doorways and traceried windows is one of the finest achievements of the Scottish Renaissance.

The Royal Museum of Scotland

On the south side of Chambers Street, which runs east from Greyfriars Bobby, stands the **Royal Museum of Scotland** (Mon–Sat 10am–5pm, Sun noon–5pm; free), a dignified Venetian-style palace with a cast-iron interior modelled on that of the Crystal Palace in London. Intended as Scotland's answer to the museum complex in London's South Kensington, it contains an extraordinarily eclectic range of exhibits; the scope will be broader still after the completion of an annexe in 1998.

The **sculpture** in the lofty entrance hall begins with a superb Assyrian relief from the royal palace at Nimrud, and ranges via Classical Greece, Rome and Nubia to Buddhas from Japan and Burma and a totem pole from British Columbia. Also on the ground floor are collections of stuffed animals and birds, and a predominantly hands-on **technology** section featuring classic pieces of machinery of the Industrial Revolution. These include a double-action beam engine designed by James Watt in 1786; the *Wylam Dilly* of 1813, twin of the *Puffing Billy*; and the 1896 *Hawk Glider*, the earliest British flying machine. The 1862 watermill from Manchester is claimed to be the largest object in any museum in Britain. Upstairs there's a fine array of Egyptian mummies, ceramics from ancient Greece to the present day, costumes, jewellery, natural history displays and a splendid selection of European decorative art ranging from early medieval liturgical objects via Limoges enamels and sixteenth-century German woodcarving to stunning **French silverware** made during the reign of Louis XIV. Finally, on the top floor, you'll come to a distinguished collection of historic scientific instruments, a small selection of arms and armour, plus sections on geology, fossils, ethnology, and the arts of Islam, Japan and China.

The University of Edinburgh

Immediately alongside the Royal Museum is the earliest surviving part of the **University of Edinburgh**, variously referred to as Old College or Old Quad, although nowadays it houses only a few university departments; the main campus colonizes the streets and squares to the south.

The Old College was designed by Robert Adam, but built after his death in a considerably modified form by William Playfair (1789–1857), one of Edinburgh's greatest architects. Playfair built just one of Adam's two quadrangles (the dome was not added until 1879) and his magnificent Upper Library is now mostly used for ceremonial occasions. The **Talbot Rice Art Gallery** (Tue–Sat 10am–5pm; free), housed in the Old College, includes many splendid seventeenth-century works from the Low Countries, with Teniers, Steen and van de Velde well represented. There are also some outstanding bronzes, notably the *Anatomical Horse* by an unknown Italian sculptor of the High Renaissance, and *Cain Killing Abel* by the Dutch Mannerist Adrian de Vries.

The New Town

The **NEW TOWN**, itself well over 200 years old, stands in total contrast to the Old Town: the layout is symmetrical, the streets broad and straight, and most of the buildings are Neoclassical. Originally intended to be residential, the entire area, right down to the names of its streets, is something of a celebration of the Union, which was then generally regarded as a proud development in Scotland's history. Today the New Town is the bustling hub of the city's professional, commercial and business life, dominated by shops, banks and offices.

The existence of the New Town is chiefly due to the vision of **George Drummond**, who made schemes for the expansion of the city soon after becoming Lord Provost in 1725. However, it was not until 1759, when the Nor' Loch below the Castle was drained, that work began. The North Bridge, linking the Old Town with the port of Leith, was built between 1763 and 1772 and, in 1766, following a public competition, a plan for the New Town by a 22-year-old architect, **James Craig**, was chosen. Its gridiron pattern was perfectly matched to the site: the central George Street, flanked by showpiece squares, was laid out along the main ridge, with the parallel Princes Street and Queen Street on either side below, with two smaller streets, Thistle Street and Rose Street in between the three major thoroughfares to provide coach houses, artisans' dwellings and shops. Princes and Queen streets were built up on one side only, so as not to block the spectacular views of the Old Town and Fife. Architects were accordingly afforded a wonderful opportunity to play with vistas and spatial relationships, particularly well exploited by Robert Adam, who contributed extensively to the later phases of the work. The First New Town, as the area covered by Craig's plan came to be known, received a whole series of extensions in the first few decades of the nineteenth century, all carefully in harmony with the Neoclassical idiom.

In many ways, the layout of the New Town is its own most remarkable sight, an extraordinary grouping of squares, circuses, terraces, crescents and parks with a few set pieces such as **Register House**, the north frontage of **Charlotte Square** and the assemblage of curiosities on and around **Calton Hill**. However, it also contains an assortment of Victorian additions, notably the **Scott Monument**, as well as three of the city's most important public collections – the **National Gallery of Scotland**, the combined **Scottish National Portrait Gallery** and **Museum of Antiquities** and the **Scottish National Gallery of Modern Art**.

Princes Street

Although only allocated a subsidiary role in the original plan of the New Town, **Princes Street** had developed into Edinburgh's principal thoroughfare by the middle of the last century, a role it has retained ever since. Its unobstructed views across to the Castle and the Old Town are undeniably magnificent. Indeed, without the views, Princes Street would lose much of its appeal; its northern side, dominated by ugly department stores, is almost always crowded with shoppers, and few of the original eighteenth-century buildings remain.

It was the coming of the railway, which follows a parallel course to the south, that ensured Princes Street's rise to prominence. The tracks are well concealed at the far end of the sunken **gardens** that replaced the Nor' Loch, which provide ample space to relax or picnic during the summer. Thomas De Quincey (1785–1859), author of the classic account of drug addiciton, *Confessions of an Opium Eater* (published in 1821), spent the last 30 years of his life in Edinburgh and is buried in the graveyard of St Cuthbert's Church, beneath the castle at the western end of the gardens.

The East End

Register House (Mon–Fri 10am–4pm; free), Princes Street's most distinguished building, is at its extreme northeastern corner, framing the perspective down North Bridge, and providing a good visual link between the Old and New Towns. Unfortunately, the majesty of the setting is marred by the **St James Centre** to the rear, a covered shopping arcade now regarded as the city's worst-ever planning blunder. Register House was designed in the 1770s by Robert Adam to hold Scotland's historic records, a function it has maintained ever since. Its exterior is a model of restrained Neoclassicism; the interior, centred on a glorious Roman rotunda, has a dome lavishly decorated with plasterwork and antique-style medallions.

Opposite is one of the few buildings on the south side of Princes Street, the **North British Hotel** or "NB" as it is popularly known, despite its re-designation as *The Balmoral* in a gesture of political correctness by its owners: North Britain was an alternative name for Scotland throughout the eighteenth and nineteenth centuries, but has been regarded by Scots as an affront ever since. Among the most luxurious hotels in the city, it has always been associated with the railway, and the timepiece on its bulky clock tower is always kept two minutes fast in order to encourage passengers to hurry to catch their trains. Alongside the hotel, the **Waverley Market** is a sensitive modern redevelopment that carefully avoided repeating the mistakes of the St James Centre. Its roof makes an excellent open-air piazza, a favourite haunt of street theatre groups and other performing artists during the Festival.

The Scott Monument and the Royal Scottish Academy

Facing the Victorian shopping emporium *Jenners*, and set within East Princes Street Gardens, the 200ft-high **Scott Monument** was erected by public subscription in memory of the writer within a few years of his death. The largest monument in the world to a man of letters, its magisterial, spire-like design is due to George Meikle Kemp, a carpenter and joiner whose only building this is; while it was still under construction, he stumbled into a canal one foggy evening and drowned. The architecture is closely modelled on Scott's beloved Melrose Abbey (see p.119), while the rich sculptural decoration shows sixteen Scottish writers and 64 characters from the *Waverley* novels. Underneath the archway is a **statue** of Scott with his deerhound Maida, carved from a 30-ton block of Carrara marble.

The monument's blackened condition is a pity, and it was recently hidden under shrouds for two years while studies were carried out as to the possibility of cleaning it by sandblasting, a technique successfully applied on many of Edinburgh's other historic buildings. This exercise divided professional opinion, some believing the monument to be too slender to stand up to the treatment. Eventually, it was decided that cleaning would not go ahead. The monument is undergoing extensive repair work, and is due to reopen in 1996.

The Princes Street Gardens are bisected by the **Mound**, which provides a road link between the Old and New Towns. Its name is an accurate description: it was formed in the 1780s by dumping piles of earth brought from the New Town's building plots. At the foot of the mound, Playfair's **Royal Scottish Academy** (Mon–Sat 10am–5pm, Sun 2–5pm; price varies) is a Grecian-style Doric temple used for temporary exhibitions, culminating during the Festival in a big international show, or a display of otherwise unseen Scottish art from the National Galleries. A few years back, the Academy was bequeathed the Borthwick-Norton collection of around 30 Old Masters, but at the time of writing legal complications meant that only four of these had been received – a pair of portraits by Gainsborough and single examples of Rubens and the rare Dutch landscape master Hercules Seghers, much admired by Rembrandt.

The National Gallery of Scotland

To the rear of the Royal Scottish Academy the **National Gallery of Scotland** (Mon–Sat 10am–5pm, Sun 2–5pm; free) is another Playfair construction, built in the 1840s and now housing a choice display of Old Masters, many of which belong to the Duke of Sutherland. The knowledgeable staff now wear tartan trousers, one of a series of innovations introduced by the flamboyant English director, Timothy Clifford. A few years ago, and more controversially, the original Playfair rooms on the ground floor were restored to their 1840s appearance, with the pictures hung closely together, often on two levels, and intermingled with sculptures and *objets d'art* to produce a deliberately cluttered effect (some lesser works, which would otherwise languish in the vaults, are a good 15ft up). Two small late-nineteenth-century works in Room 12 – one anonymous, the other by A E Moffat – show the gallery as it was, with paintings stacked up even higher than at present.

Though individual works are frequently rearranged, the layout is broadly chronological, starting in the upper rooms above the entrance, and continuing clockwise around the ground floor. The upper part of the rear extension is devoted to smaller panels of the eighteenth and nineteenth centuries, while the basement contains the majority of the Scottish collection.

EARLY NETHERLANDISH AND GERMAN WORKS

Among the gallery's most valuable treasures are the *Trinity Panels*, the remaining parts of the only surviving pre-Reformation altarpiece made for a Scottish church. Painted by **Hugo van der Goes** in the mid-fifteenth century, they were commissioned for the Holy Trinity Collegiate Church by its provost Edward Bonkil, who appears in company of organ-playing angels in the finest and best preserved of the four panels. On the reverse sides are portraits of James III, his son (the future James IV) and Queen Margaret of Denmark. Their feebly characterized heads, which stand in jarring contrast to the superlative figures of the patron saints accompanying them, were modelled from life by an unknown local painter after the altar had been shipped to Edinburgh.

Of the later Netherlandish works, **Gerard David** is represented by the touchingly anecdotal *Three Legends of St Nicholas*, while the *Portrait of a Notary* by **Quentin Massys** is an excellent early example of Northern European assimilation of the forms and techniques of the Italian Renaissance. Many of his German contemporaries developed their own variations on this style, among them **Cranach**, by whom there is a splendidly erotic *Venus and Cupid*, and **Holbein**, whose *Allegory of the Old and New Testaments* is a Protestant tract painted for an English patron.

ITALIAN RENAISSANCE WORKS

The Italian section includes a wonderful array of **Renaissance** masterpieces. Of these, *The Virgin Adoring the Child* is a beautiful composition set against a ruined architectural background shown in strict perspective: although known to have been painted in the workshop of the great Florentine sculptor **Andrea del Verrocchio**, its authorship remains a mystery. Equally graceful are the three works by **Raphael**, particularly *The Bridgewater Madonna* and the tondo of *The Holy Family with a Palm Tree*, whose striking luminosity has been revealed after recent restoration.

Of the four mythological scenes by **Titian**, the sensuous *Three Ages of Man*, an allegory of childhood, adulthood and old age, is one of the most accomplished compositions of his early period, while the later *Venus Anadyomene* ranks among the great nudes of Western art, notwithstanding its rough state of preservation. The companion pair of *Diana and Acteon* and *Diana and Calisto*, painted for Philip II of Spain, show the almost impressionistic freedom of his late style. **Bassano**'s truly regal *Adoration of the Kings*, a dramatic altarpiece of *The Descent from the Cross* by **Tintoretto**, and several other works by **Veronese** complete a fine Venetian collection.

SEVENTEENTH-CENTURY SOUTHERN EUROPEAN WORKS

Among the seventeenth-century works is the gallery's most important sculpture, **Bernini**'s *Bust of Monsignor Carlo Antonio dal Pozzo*. **El Greco**'s *A Fable*, painted during his early years in Italy, is a mysterious subject whose exact meaning is unclear, while *The Saviour of the World* is a typically intense, visionary image from his mature years in Spain. Indigenous Spanish art is represented by **Velázquez**'s *An Old Woman Cooking Eggs*, an astonishingly assured work for a lad of nineteen, and by **Zurbaran**'s *The Immaculate Conception*, part of his ambitious decorative scheme of the Carthusian monastery in Jerez. There are two small copper panels by the short-lived but enormously influential Rome-based German painter **Adam Elsheimer**; of these, *Il Contento*, showing Jupiter's descent to earth to punish the ungodly, is a *tour de force* of technical precision.

The series of *The Seven Sacraments* by **Poussin** are displayed in their own room, whose floor and central octagaonal seat repeat, albeit loosely, some of the motifs in the paintings. Based on the artist's own extensive research into Biblical times, the set marks the first attempt to portray scenes from the life of Jesus and the early Christians in an authentic manner, rather than one overlaid by artistic conventions. The result is profoundly touching, with a myriad of imaginative and subtle details. Poussin's younger contemporary **Claude**, who likewise left France to live in Rome, is represented by his largest canvas, *Landscape with Apollo, the Muses and a River God*, which radiates his characteristically idealized vision of Classical antiquity.

SEVENTEENTH-CENTURY FLEMISH AND DUTCH WORKS

Rubens' *The Feast of Herod* is an archetypal example of his grand manner, in which the gory subject matter is overshadowed by the lively depiction of the delights of the table; the painting's rich colours have been revived by recent restoration. Like all his large works, it was executed with extensive studio assistance, whereas the three small *modellos*, including the highly finished *Adoration of the Shepherds*, are all from his own hand. The trio of large upright canvases by **Van Dyck** date from his early Genoese period; of these, *The Lomellini Family* shows his mastery at creating a definitive dynastic image.

Among the four canvases by **Rembrandt** is a poignant *Self-Portrait aged 51*, and the ripely suggestive *Woman in Bed*, which probably represents the Biblical figure of Sarah on her wedding night, waiting for her husband Tobias to put the devil to flight. *Christ in the House of Martha and Mary* is the largest and probably the earliest of the 30 or so surviving paintings of **Vermeer**; as the only one with a religious subject, it inspired a notorious series of forgeries by Han van Meegeren. By **Hals** are a typical pair of portraits plus a brilliant caricature, *Verdonck*. There's also an excellent cross section of the specialist Dutch painters of the age, highlights being the mischievous *School for Boys and Girls* by **Jan Steen**, and the strangely haunting *Interior of the Church of St Bavo in Haarlem* by **Pieter Saenredam**, one of the gallery's most expensive purchases.

EUROPEAN WORKS OF THE EIGHTEENTH AND NINETEENTH CENTURIES

Of the large-scale eighteenth-century works, **Tiepolo**'s *The Finding of Moses*, a gloriously bravura fantasy (the Pharoah's daughter and her attendants appear in sixteenth-century garb), stands out; despite its enormous size, it has lost a sizeable portion from the right-hand side. Other decorative compositions of the same period are **Goya**'s *The Doctor*, a cartoon for a tapestry design, and the three large upright pastoral scenes by **Boucher**. However, the gems of the French section are the smaller panels, in particular **Watteau**'s *Fêtes Vénitiennes*, an effervescent Rococo idyll, and **Chardin**'s *Vase of Flowers*, a copybook example of still-life painting. One of the gallery's most recent major purchases is Canova's 1817 statue *The Three Graces* – saved at the last minute from the hands of the J Paul Getty Museum in California.

There's also a superb group of Impressionist and Post-Impressionist masterpieces, including a particularly good cross section of the works of **Degas**, not least his seminal *Portrait of Diego Martelli*, depicting the Florentine critic who was one of the most fervent early champions of the movement; three outstanding examples of **Gauguin**, set respectively in Brittany, Martinique and Tahiti; and **Cezanne**'s *The Tall Trees* – a clear forerunner of modern Abstraction.

ENGLISH AND AMERICAN WORKS

Surprisingly, the gallery has relatively few English paintings, but those here are impressive. **Hogarth**'s *Sarah Malcolm*, painted in Newgate Prison the day the murderess was executed, once belonged to Horace Walpole, who also commissioned **Reynolds' *The Ladies Waldegrave***, a group portrait of his three great-nieces. **Gainsborough**'s *The Honourable Mrs Graham* is one of his most memorable society portraits, while **Constable** himself described *Dedham Vale* as being "perhaps my best". There are two prime Roman views by **Turner**, by whom the gallery owns a wonderful array of watercolours, faithfully displayed each January, when the light is at its weakest.

Even more unexpected than the scarcity of English works is the presence of some exceptional American canvases: **Benjamin West**'s Romantic fantasy, *King Alexander III Rescued from a Stag*; **John Singer Sargent**'s virtuosic *Lady Agnew of Lochnaw*; and **Frederic Edwin Church**'s *View of Niagara Falls from the American Side*. The latter, having been kept in store for decades, was put back on display when the "rediscovery" of the artist in the late 1970s prompted astronomical bids from American museums keen to acquire the only work by the artist owned by a European gallery.

SCOTTISH WORKS

On the face of it, the gallery's Scottish collection, which shows the entire gamut of Scottish painting from seventeenth-century portraiture to the Arts and Crafts movement, is something of an anticlimax. There are, however, some important works displayed within a broad European context; **Gavin Hamilton**'s *Achilles Mourning the Death of Patrocolus*, for example, painted in Rome, is an unquestionably arresting image. **Allan Ramsay**, who became court painter to George III, is represented by his intimate *The Artist's Second Wife* and *Jean-Jacques Rousseau*, in which the philosopher is shown in Armenian costume.

Of **Sir Henry Raeburn**'s large portraits note the swaggering masculinity of *Sir John Sinclair* or *Colonel Alistair MacDonell of Glengarry*, both of whom are shown in full Highland dress. Raeburn's technical mastery was equally sure when working on a small scale, as shown in one of the gallery's most popular pictures, *The Rev Robert Walker Skating on Duddingston Loch*.

Other Scottish painters represented include the versatile **Sir David Wilkie**, whose huge history painting, *Sir David Baird Discovering the Body of Sultaun Tippo Saib*, is in marked contrast to the early documentary and genre scenes displayed in the basement, and **Alexander Nasmyth**, whose tendency to gild the lily can be seen in his *View of Tantallon Castle and the Bass Rock*, where the dramatic scenery is further spiced up by the inclusion of a shipwreck.

George Street

Just north and parallel to Princes Street is **George Street**, the city's chief financial thoroughfare and the least prepossessing of the main streets of the First New Town, built up on both sides with a preponderance of unsympathetic development. At its eastern end is **St Andrew Square**, in the middle of which is the Melville Monument, a statue of Lord Melville, Pitt the Younger's Navy Treasurer. On the eastern side of the square stands a handsome eighteenth-century town mansion, designed by Sir William Chambers. Headquarters of the Royal Bank of Scotland since 1825, the palatial mid-nineteenth-century banking hall is a symbol of the success of the New Town. On the south side of the street, the oval-shaped church of **St Andrew** (now known as St Andrew and St George) is chiefly famous as the scene of the 1843 Disruption led by Thomas Chalmers, which split the Church of Scotland in two. Famous visitors to George Street have included Percy Bysshe Shelley, who stayed at no. 60 with the 16-year-old Harriet Westbrook during the summer of 1811, and Charles Dickens who gave a number of readings of his works in the Assembly Rooms in the 1840s and 50s.

At the western end of of the street, **Charlotte Square** was designed by Robert Adam in 1791, a year before his death. For the most part, his plans were faithfully implemented, an exception being the domed and porticoed church of St George, which was simplified on grounds of expense. Its interior was gutted in the 1960s and refurbished as **West Register House**; like its counterpart at the opposite end of Princes Street, it features changing documentary exhibitions (Mon–Fri 10am–4pm; free).

The **north side** of the square has deservedly become the most exclusive address in the city. No. 6 is the official residence of the Secretary of State for Scotland, while the upper storeys of no. 7 are the home of the Moderator of the General Assembly, the annually elected leader of the Church of Scotland. Restored by the NTS, the lower floors are open to the public under the name of the **Georgian House** (April–Oct Mon–Sat 10am–5pm, Sun 2–5pm; £3.50), whose contents give a good idea of what the house must have looked like during the period of the first owner, the head of the clan Lamont. The rooms are decked out in period furniture, including a working barrel organ which plays a selection of Scottish airs, and hung with fine paintings, including portraits by Ramsay and Raeburn, seventeenth-century Dutch cabinet pictures, and a beautiful *Marriage of the Virgin* by El Greco's teacher, the Italian miniaturist Giulio Clovio. In the basement are the original wine cellar, lined with roughly made bins, and a kitchen, complete with an open fire for roasting, and a separate oven for baking; video reconstructions of life below and above stairs are shown in a nearby room.

Queen Street

Queen Street, the last of the three main streets of the First New Town, is bordered to the north by gardens, and commands sweeping views across to Fife. Much the best preserved of the area's three main streets, its main attraction is its excellent gallery-cum-museum.

The Scottish National Portrait Gallery and Museum of Antiquities

At the far eastern end of Queen Street is the **Scottish National Portrait Gallery**, which shares its premises with the **Museum of Antiquities** (Mon–Sat 10am–5pm, Sun 2–5pm; free). The gallery building is itself a fascinating period piece, its red sandstone exterior, modelled on the Doge's Palace in Venice, encrusted with statues of famous Scots – a theme taken up in the entrance hall, which has a mosaic-like frieze procession by William Hole of great figures from Scotland's past, with heroic murals by the same artist of stirring episodes from the nation's history adorning the balcony above.

THE STEWART EXHIBITION

On the ground floor of the western wing an exhibition on the **Stewart dynasty** traces the history of the family from its origins as stewards (hence the name) to medieval royalty, via its zenith under James VI, who engineered the union with England, to its final demise under Bonnie Prince Charlie.

From the early periods, look out for two superb artefacts from the reign of Robert the Bruce, the **Kames Brooch** and the **Bute Mazer** (a large wooden bowl). An excellent collection of Mary, Queen of Scots memorabilia includes her **Penicuik Jewels** and a portrait by Rowland Lockey. The reign of Charles I is represented by several outstanding paintings by Flemish artists including **Daniel Mytens** and **Alexander Keirinocx**, and there are fine official portraits of the later Stewart monarchs and members of their entourage. Mementoes of the Young Pretender include the ornate backsword and silver-mounted shield with which he fought at Culloden, and a Rococo **canteen** he left abandoned on the battlefield.

THE PORTRAIT GALLERY

The floors above the Stewart exhibition are devoted to portraits, accompanied by potted biographies, of famous Scots – a definition stretched to include anyone with the slightest Scottish connection. From the seventeenth century, there's an excellent Van Dyck portrait of Charles Seton, second Earl of Dunfermline, and the tartan-clad Lord Mungo Murray, who died in the disastrous attempt to establish a Scottish colony in Panama. Eighteenth-century highlights include portraits of the philosopher-historian David Hume by Allan Ramsay, and the bard Robert Burns by his friend Alexander Nasmyth, and a varied group by Raeburn: subjects include Sir Walter Scott, the fiddler Niel Gow, and the artist himself. The star portrait from the nineteenth century is that of physician Sir Alexander Morison by his patient, the mad painter **Richard Dadd** – Edinburgh's fishing port of Newhaven is in the background. Twentieth-century portraits include a very angular Alec Douglas-Home, briefly prime minister in the 1960s, the stern figure of union leader Mick McGahey, soccer star Danny McGrain (in a kilt) and film-maker Bill Forsyth.

THE MUSEUM OF ANTIQUITIES

Ranged across three levels, objects in the Museum of Antiquities are displayed in a splendidly eclectic manner. The ground floor is, in the main, devoted to **Dark Age sculpture**, giving convincing proof of the vitality of artistic life among the tribes who later combined to form the Scottish kingdom: look out for the eighth-century Birsay Stone from Orkney, with its carvings of warriors; the ninth-century Hilton of Cadboll Stone from Easter Ross, whose main scene shows a woman riding side-saddle, and the twelfth-century **walrus ivory chessmen** from the island of Lewis. You can also see the **Deskford Carnyx**, a swine's head in brass which formed part of a Celtic war trumpet, and the so-called **Maiden**, Edinburgh's public guillotine from 1564 to 1710.

On the first floor, the **prehistoric and Viking collection** features excavations from a variety of sites beginning with the Neolithic settlement of Skara Brae in the Orkneys. Most of the artefacts are of specialist appeal only, but the Bronze Age Torrs Chamfrein, a war mask or drinking horn from around 200 BC, and the Hunterston Brooch, an intricate piece of Viking jewellery, are eye-catching. Most striking of of all is the eighth-century St Ninian's Isle Treasure from the Shetlands, an ornamental set of Pictish silverware. The top floor is devoted to **Roman antiquities**, the most important of which are a milestone found at Ingliston, near the site of Edinburgh Airport; and the Traprain Treasure, a hoard of fourth- and fifth-century silver buried at Traprain Law near Haddington.

Calton

Of the various extensions to the New Town, the most intriguing is **Calton**, which branches out from the eastern end of Princes Street and encircles a volcanic hill. For years the centre of a thriving **gay** scene (see p.101), it is an area of extraordinary show-piece architecture, all dating from the time of the Napoleonic Wars or just after, and intended as an ostentatious celebration of the British victory. While the predominantly Grecian architecture led to Calton being regarded as a Georgian Acropolis, it is, in fact, more of a shrine to local heroes.

Waterloo Place forms a ceremonial way from Princes Street to Calton Hill. On its southern side is the sombre **Old Calton Burial Ground**, in which you can see Robert

Adam's plain, cylindrical memorial to David Hume and a monument, complete with a statue of Abraham Lincoln, to the Scots who died in the American Civil War. Hard up against the cemetery's eastern wall, perched above a sheer rockface, is a picturesque castellated building which many visitors arriving at Waverley Station below imagine to be Edinburgh Castle itself. In fact, it's the only surviving part of the **Calton Gaol**, once Edinburgh's main prison.

Further on, set majestically in a confined site below Calton Hill, is one of Edinburgh's greatest buildings, the Grecian Old **Royal High School**. Previously in the Old Town, the new site for Edinburgh's oldest school – *alma mater* to, among others, Robert Adam, Walter Scott and Alexander Graham Bell – was built by Thomas Hamilton, himself an old boy. Earmarked in the 1970s as the home of the planned Scottish Assembly, the building has remained empty for years, a symbol of the thwarted nationalist aspirations. It has recently been sold to Edinburgh District Council, who have designated it New Parliament House. Across the road, Hamilton also built the **Burns Monument**, a circular Corinthian temple modelled on the Monument to Lysicrates in Athens, as a memorial to the national bard.

Robert Louis Stevenson reckoned that **Calton Hill** was the best place to view Edinburgh: "since you can see the Castle, which you lose from the Castle, and Arthur's Seat, which you cannot see from Arthur's Seat." Though the panoramas from ground level are spectacular enough, those from the top of the **Nelson Monument** (April–Sept Mon 1–6pm, Tues–Sat 10am–6pm; Oct–March Mon–Sat 10am–3pm; £1) are even better. Begun just two years after Nelson's death at Trafalgar, this is one of Edinburgh's oddest buildings, resembling a gigantic spy-glass.

Alongside, the **National Monument** was begun in 1822 by Playfair to plans by the English architect Charles Cockerell. Had it been completed, it would have been a reasonably accurate replica of the Parthenon, but funds ran out with only twelve columns built. Various later schemes to finish it similarly foundered, earning it the nickname "Edinburgh's Disgrace". At the opposite side of the hill, the grandeur of Playfair's Classical **Monument to Dougald Stewart** seems totally disproportionate to the stature of the man it commemorates: a now-forgotten Professor of Philosophy at the University.

Playfair also built the **City Observatory** for his uncle, the mathematician and astronomer John Playfair, whom he honoured in the cenotaph outside. Because of pollution and the advent of street lighting, which impaired views of the stars, the observatory proper had to be relocated to Blackford Hill before the end of the century, though the equipment here continues to be used by students. The small domed pavilion at the northeastern corner, an addition of the 1890s, now houses the **Edinburgh Experience** (July & Aug daily 10.30am–5pm; April–June, Sept & Oct Mon–Fri 2–5pm, Sat & Sun 10.30am–5pm; £2), a 20-minute 3-D show on the city's history viewed through special glasses. At the opposite end of the complex is the **Old Observatory**, one of the few surviving buildings by James Craig, designer of the New Town.

Elsewhere in the New Town

The **Northern New Town** was the earliest extension to the First New Town, begun in 1801, and today roughly covers the area north of Queen Street between India Street to the west and Broughton Street to the east and as far as Fettes Row to the north. This has survived in far better shape than its predecessor: with the exception of one street, almost all of it is intact, and it has managed to preserve its predominantly residential character. One of the area's most intriguing buildings is the Neo-Norman **Mansfield Place Church**, on the corner of Broughton and East London streets, designed in the late nineteenth century for the strange, now defunct Catholic Apostolic sect. Having lain redundant and neglected for three decades, it has suddenly acquired cult status, its preservation the current obsession of local conservation groups. The chief reason for this is its cycle of **murals** by the Dublin-born **Phoebe Traquair**, a leading light in the Scottish Arts and Crafts movement. She laboured for eight years on this decorative scheme, which has all the freshness and luminosity of a medieval manuscript, but desperately needs a thorough restoration to avert its already alarming decay. Interest in the murals was revived in 1993 when the church was opened to the public for the summer. In the future, funding permitting, the Mansfield Traquair Trust (☎557 1662) hopes to restore the murals and turn the church into a civic and arts centre.

Dean Village and Stockbridge

Work began on the western end of the New Town in 1822, in a small area of land north of Charlotte Square and west of George Street. Instead of the straight lines of the earlier sections, there were now the gracious curves of Randolph Crescent, Ainslie Place and the magnificent twelve-sided Moray Place, designed by the vainglorious James Gillespie Graham who described himself, with no authority to do so, as "architect in Scotland to the Prince Regent". Round the corner from Randolph Crescent, the four-arched **Dean Bridge**, a bravura feat of 1830s engineering by Thomas Telford, carries the main road high above Edinburgh's placid little river, the **Water of Leith**. Down to the left lies **Dean Village**, an old milling community that is one of central Edinburgh's most picturesque yet oddest corners, its atmosphere of terminal decay arrested by the conversion of some of the mills into designer flats. The riverside path into Stockbridge passes **St Bernard's Well**, a pump room covered by a mock Roman temple. Commissioned in 1788 by Lord Gardenstone to draw mineral waters from the Water of Leith, it has been recently restored, and is occasionally open (contact Water of Leith Conservation Trust; ☎445 7367).

Stockbridge, which straddles both sides of the Water of Leith on the other side of Dean Bridge, is another old village which has retained its distinctive identity, in spite of its absorption into the Georgian face of the New Town, and is particularly renowned for its antique shops and "alternative" outlets. The residential upper streets on the far side of the river were developed by Sir Henry Raeburn, who named the finest of them **Ann Street**, which after Charlotte Square is the most prestigious address in Edinburgh (writers Thomas de Quincey and J M Ballantyne were residents); alone among New Town streets, its houses each have a front garden.

The West End

The western extension to the New Town was the last part to be built, deviating from the area's overriding Neoclassicism with a number of Victorian additions. Because of this, the huge **St Mary's Episcopal Cathedral**, an addition of the 1870s, is less intrusive than it would otherwise be, its three spires forming an eminently satifying landmark for the far end of the city centre. The last major work of Sir George Gilbert Scott, the cathedral is built in imitation of the Early English Gothic style and was, at the time of its construction, the most ambitious church built in Britain since the Reformation.

The Scottish National Gallery of Modern Art

Set in spacious wooded grounds at the far northwestern fringe of the New Town, about ten minutes' walk from either the cathedral or Dean Village, the **Scottish National Gallery of Modern Art** (Mon–Sat 10am–5pm, Sun 2–5pm; free) was established in 1959 as the first collection in Britain devoted solely to twentieth-century painting and sculpture. The grounds serve as a sculpture park, featuring works by Jacob Epstein, Henry Moore, Barbara Hepworth and the Constructivist creations of the Edinburgh-born Eduardo Paolozzi. Inside, the display space is divided between temporary loan exhibitions and selections from the gallery's own holdings; the latter are arranged thematically, but are almost constantly moved around. What you get to see at any particular time is therefore a matter of chance, though the most important works are nearly always on view.

French painters are particularly well represented, beginning with **Bonnard**'s *Lane at Vernonnet* and **Vuillard**'s jewel-like *Two Seamstresses*, and by a few examples of the Fauves, notably **Matisse**'s *The Painting Lesson* and **Derain**'s dazzlingly brilliant *Collioure*; there's also a fine group of late canvases by **Leger**, notably *The Constructors*. Among some striking examples of German Expressionism are **Kirchner**'s *Japanese Theatre*, **Feininger**'s *Gelmeroda III*, and a wonderfully soulful wooden sculpture of a woman by **Barlach** entitled *The Terrible Year, 1937*. Highlights of the Surrealist section are **Magritte**'s haunting *Black Flag*, **Miró**'s seminal *Composition* and **Giacometti**'s contorted *Woman with her Throat Cut*, while Cubism is represented by **Picasso**'s *Soles* and **Braque**'s *Candlestick*.

Of works by Americans, **Roy Lichtenstein**'s *In the Car* is a fine example of his Pop-Art style, while **Duane Hanson**'s fibre-glass *Tourists* is typically cruel. English artists on show include Sickert, Nicholson, Spencer, Freud and Hockney, but, as you'd expect, considerably more space is allocated to Scottish artists. Of particular note are the so-called Colourists – **S J Peploe, J D Fergusson, Francis Cadell** and **George Leslie Hunter** – whose works are attracting fancy prices on the art market, as well as ever-growing posthumous critical acclaim. Although they did not form a recognizable school, they all worked in France and displayed considerable French influence in their warm, bright palettes. The gallery also shows works by many contemporary Scots, among them **John Bellany**, a portraitist of striking originality, and the poet-artist-gardener **Ian Hamilton Finlay**.

The Suburbs

Edinburgh's principal sights are by no means confined to the city centre: indeed, at least three of its most popular tourist draws – the **Royal Botanic Garden**, the **Zoo** and the **Royal Observatory** – are out in the suburbs. Other major attractions in the outskirts include **Craigmillar Castle** and the southern hill ranges, the **Braids** and the **Pentlands**. Additionally, there are several districts with their own very distinct identity, among them the academic enclave of the **Southside**, the seaside resort of **Portobello** and the port of **Leith**.

The Royal Botanic Garden

Just beyond the northern boundaries of the New Town, with entrances on Inverleith Row and Arboretum Place, is the 70-acre site of the **Royal Botanic Garden** (daily May–Aug 10am–8pm; March, April, Sept & Oct 10am–6pm; Nov–Feb 10am–4pm; free), particularly renowned for the **rhododendrons,** which blaze out in a glorious patchwork of colours in April and May. In the heart of the grounds a group of hothouses designated the **Glasshouse Experience** (daily March–Oct 10am–5pm; Nov–Feb 10am–3.30pm; free, but £1.50 donation requested) display orchids, giant Amazonian water lilies, and a 200-year-old West Indian palm tree. The last-named is in the elegant glass-topped Palm House, built in the 1850s. Many of the most exotic plants were brought to Edinburgh by the aptly named George Forrest, who made seven expeditions to southwestern China between 1904 and 1932. A major Chinese-style garden has recently been added.

The Southwest

The area southwest of the Old Town was formerly known as **Portsburgh**, a theoretically separate burgh outside the city walls that was nonetheless a virtual fiefdom of Edinburgh. Since the 1880s and the construction of the **Royal Lyceum Theatre** on Grindlay Street, the area has gradually developed into something of a theatre district.

The **Museum of Fire** (Mon–Fri 9am–4.30pm; free) situated on Lauriston Place next to the Art School, records the history of the oldest municipal fire brigade in Britain, formed in 1824. It contains a small collection of well-preserved manual, horse-drawn and motorized fire appliances. At its southern edge, the open parkland areas of the **Meadows** and **Bruntsfield Links** mark the transition to Edinburgh's genteel Victorian villa suburbs. South of the Meadows, a plaque on the wall of Sciennes Hill House in Sciennes House Place records the only known meeting, in 1787, of Robert Burns and Sir Walter Scott. Prominent among the suburbs is **Morningside**, whose prim and proper outlook, accompanied by an appropriately plummy accent, was immortalized in Muriel Spark's *The Prime of Miss Jean Brodie*, and remains a favourite target for ridicule.

The Southside

The New Town was not the only mid-eighteenth-century expansion of Edinburgh: the city also spread in the opposite direction, creating a tenement suburb which became known as the **Southside**. Since the 1950s, this has developed into a lively academic quarter, having been progressively colonized by the overspill southwest of university buildings.

On Nicolson Street, the southern extension of South Bridge, is **Surgeons' Hall**, a handsome Ionic temple built by Playfair as the headquarters of the Royal College of Surgeons. Most of it is accessible to the public only one day a year, an exception being the museum (Mon–Fri 10am–4pm; free) which has intriguing, if somewhat specialist exhibits on the history of medicine. Across the street is the **Festival Theatre**, a refurbished music hall, which opened in 1994, giving the city a long-awaited venue capable of presenting the grandest opera.

Craigmillar Castle

Craigmillar Castle (April–Sept Mon–Sat 9.30am–6pm, Sun 2–6pm; Oct–March Mon–Wed & Sat 9.30am–4pm, Thurs 9.30am–noon, Sun 2–4pm; £1.50), where the murder of Lord Darnley, second husband of Mary, Queen of Scots was plotted, lies in a green belt five miles southeast of the centre. It's one of the best-preserved medieval fortresses in Scotland, marred only by the proximity of the ugly council housing scheme of Craigmillar, one of Edinburgh's most deprived districts.

The oldest part of the complex is the L-shaped **tower house**, which dates back to the early 1600s: it remains substantially intact, and the great hall, with its resplendent late Gothic chimneypiece, is in good enough shape to be rented out for functions. A few decades after Craigmillar's completion, the tower house was surrounded by a quadrangular wall with cylindrical corner towers pierced by some of the earliest surviving gunholes in Britain. The west range was remodelled as an aristocratic mansion in the mid-seventeenth century, but its owners abandoned the place a hundred years later, leaving it to decay into picturesque ruin.

The southern hills

The **hills** in Edinburgh's southern suburbs offer good, not overly demanding walking opportunities, with plenty of sweeping panoramic views. The **Royal Observatory** (April–Sept daily noon–5.30pm & 7–9pm Oct–March; daily 1–5pm & 7–9pm except Fri 1–9pm; £2) stands at the top of Blackford Hill, just a short walk south of Morningside, or by buses #40 or #41 direct from the centre. The visitor centre here seeks to explain the mysteries of the solar system by means of models, videos and space photographs, and you also get to see the two main telescopes, which are put into operation during the winter evenings, the best time for a visit.

Ordnance Survey Landranger map No.66.

Allow four hours for this walk. Exit the city on the A702 and look out for the *Flotterstone Inn* where there is a car park and small interpretive centre. A side road leads pleasantly up to Glencorse Reservoir, a lochan, then swings round it to go through a tight pass and on to Loganlee Reservoir, a quite remote area that feels far away from city life. The more energetic can strike up onto Turnhouse Hill and cross Carnethy Hill (576m) to come down to the Howe, at the loch's west end.

A path leads on through a short pass to come out on the far side of the Pentland range. Here the large expanse of Thriepmuir Reservoir stretches out in front of you; cross a bridge over a "neck" in the reservoir. The path heads inland for a while, but take the first right to return to the reservoir and then follow it along Harlaw Reservoir beyond.

Here cross the dam to pass a trim cottage and then turn left on the woodside track. When the track bears left take the path, right, which leads up towards the hills again. After about 220 yards be sure to take the left fork which leads up to the pass between Bell's Hill and Harbour Hill. The path runs down the burn to rejoin Glencorse Reservoir.

There are quite a number of books and special maps about the Pentlands; *25 Walks, Edinburgh and Lothian* (HMSO, 1995) is excellent.

At the foot of the hill, the bird sanctuary of Blackford Pond is the starting point for the **Hermitage of Braid** nature trail, a lovely shady path along the course of the Braid Burn. The castellated eighteenth-century mansion along the route, after which the trail is named, now serves as an information centre (Mon–Fri 11am–4pm, Sun 10am–6pm; café Sun only 11am–5.30pm). Immediately to the south are the **Braid Hills**, most of whose area is occupied by two golf courses, closed on alternate Sundays in order to allow access to walkers.

Further south are the **Pentland Hills**, a chain some eighteen miles long and five wide. The best entry point from within Edinburgh is **SWANSTON**, an unspoiled, highly exclusive hamlet of whitewashed thatched roof dwellings separated by almost a mile of farmland from the rest of the city. Robert Louis Stevenson (see overleaf) spent his boyhood summers in Swanston Cottage, the largest of the houses, immortalizing it in the novel *St Ives*. To get a taste of the scenery of the Pentlands, follow the marked hiking trail to the artificial ski slope of **Hillend** to the east; this traverses two summits and passes the remains of an Iron Age fort in addition to offering outstanding views over Edinburgh and Fife. The lazy way into the range is to take the **chair lift** from Hillend itself (Mon–Sat 9.30am–9pm, Sun 9.30am–7pm; £1.50), which is connected with the city centre by buses #4 and #15.

Portobello

Among Edinburgh's less expected assets is its **beach**, most of which falls within **PORTOBELLO**, once a lively **seaside resort** but now a forlorn kind of place, its funfairs and amusement arcades decidedly down-at-heel. Nonetheless, it retains a certain faded charm, and – on hot summer weekends at least – the promenade and the beach can be a mass of swimmers, sunbathers, surfers and pleasure boats. A walk along the promenade is a pleasure at any time of the year. Portobello is about three miles east of the centre of town, and can be reached on buses #15, #26, #42 or #86 .

Leith

For several hundred years **LEITH** was separate from Edinburgh. As Scotland's major east coast port, it played a key role in the nation's history, even serving as the seat of government for a time, and in 1833 finally became a burgh in its own right. In 1920, however, it was incorporated into the capital, and in the decades that followed, went into seemingly terminal decline: the population dropped dramatically, and much of its centre was ripped out, to be replaced by grim housing schemes.

The 1980s, however, saw an astonishing turnaround. Against all the odds, a couple of waterfront bistros proved enormously successful; competitors followed apace, and by the end of the decade the port had acquired what's arguably the best concentration of restaurants and pubs in Edinburgh. The surviving historic monuments were spruced up, and a host of housing developments built or restored, earning the town the sardonic nickname of "Leith-sur-Mer".

To reach Leith from the city centre, take one of the many buses going down Leith Walk, near the top end of which is a statue of Sherlock Holmes, whose creator, Sir Arthur Conan Doyle, was born nearby. Otherwise, it's a brisk walk of around 20 minutes plus, or you can travel on from Portobello by bus #12.

Around the port

While you're most likely to come to Leith for the bars and restaurants, the area itself warrants exploration; though the shipbuilding yards have gone, it remains an active port with a rough-edged character. Most of the showpiece Neoclassical buildings lie on or near **The Shore**, the tenement-lined road along the final stretch of the Water of Leith, just before it disgorges into the Firth of Forth. Note the former **Town Hall**, on the parallel Constitution Street, now the headquarters of the local constabulary, immortalized in the tongue twister, "The Leith police dismisseth us"; the Classical Trinity House on Kirkgate, built in 1816 and the massive Customs House on Commercial Street. To the west, set back from The Shore, is **Lamb's House**, a seventeenth-century mansion comparable to Gladstone's Land in the Old Town. Built as the home of the prosperous merchant Andro Lamb, it currently functions as an old people's day centre.

Leith Links is an area of predominantly flat parkland, just east of the police station. Documentary evidence suggests that The Links was a golf course in the fifteenth century, giving rise to Leith's claim to be regarded as the birthplace of the sport: in 1744 its first written rules were drawn up here, ten years before they were formalized in St Andrews.

To the west of Leith lies the village of **NEWHAVEN**, built by James IV, at the start of the sixteenth century, as an alternative shipbuilding centre to Leith: his massive warship, the *Michael*, capable of carrying 120 gunners, 300 mariners and 1,000 troops, and said to have used up all the trees in Fife, was built here. It has also been a ferry station and an important fishing centre, landing at the height of its success in the 1860s, some six million oysters a year. Today, although a few boats still operate from the harbour, the fish market is no more and the last of the colourfully dressed fish-wives long since retired. A variety of costumes and other memorabilia of the village's only industry can be found in the **Newhaven Heritage Museum** (daily noon–5pm; free), a fascinating collection staffed by enthusiastic members of local fishing families.

The Zoo

Edinburgh's **Zoo** (April–Sept Mon–Sat 9am–6pm, Sun 9.30am–6pm; Oct & March Mon–Sat 9am–5pm, Sun 9.30am–5pm, Nov–Feb Mon–Sat 9am–4.30pm, Sun 9.30am–4.30pm; £5.50) lies three miles west of Princes Street on an 80-acre site on the slopes of Corstorphine Hill (buses from town: #2, #26, #31, #36, #69, #85, #86). Here you can see 1500 animals, including a number of endangered species such as white rhinos, red pandas, pygmy hippos and Madagascar tree boas. However, its chief claim to fame is

ROBERT LOUIS STEVENSON

Though **Robert Louis Stevenson** (1850–94) is often dismissed in highbrow academic circles for his deceptively simple manner, he was undoubtedly one of the best-loved writers of his generation, and one whose travelogues, novels, short stories and essays remain enormously popular a century after his death.

Born in Edinburgh into a distinguished family of engineers, Stevenson was a sickly child, with a solitary childhood dominated by his governess Alison "Cummie" Cunningham, who regaled him with tales drawn from Calvinist folklore. Sent to the university to study engineering, Stevenson rebelled against his upbringing by spending much of his time in the low-life howffs and brothels of the city, and eventually switching to law. Although called to the bar in 1875, by then he had decided to channel his energies into literature: while still a student, he had already made his mark as an **essayist**, and published in his lifetime over a hundred essays, ranging from lighthearted whimsy to trenchant political analysis. A set of topographical pieces about his native city was later collected together as *Edinburgh: Picturesque Notes*, which conjure up nicely its atmosphere, character and appearance – warts and all.

Stevenson's other early successes were two **travelogues**, *An Inland Voyage* and *Travels with a Donkey in the Cevennes*, kaleidoscopic jottings based on his journeys in France, where he went to escape Scotland's bad weather. It was there that he met Fanny Osbourne, an American ten years his senior, who was estranged from her husband and had two children in tow. His voyage to join her in San Francisco formed the basis for his most important factual work, *The Amateur Emigrant*, a vivid first-hand account of the great nineteenth-century European migration to the United States.

Having married the now-divorced Fanny, Stevenson began an elusive search for an agreeable climate that led to Switzerland, the French Riviera and the Scottish Highlands. He belatedly turned to the **novel**, achieving immediate acclaim in 1881 for *Treasure Island*, a highly moralistic adventure yarn that began as an entertainment for his stepson and future collaborator, Lloyd Osbourne. In 1886, his most famous **short story**, *Dr Jekyll and Mr Hyde*, despite its nominal London setting, offered a vivid evocation of Edinburgh's Old Town; an allegory of its dual personality of prosperity and squalour, and an analysis of its Calvinistic preoccupations with guilt and damnation. The same year saw the publication of the historical romance *Kidnapped*, an adventure novel which exemplified his view that literature should seek above all to entertain.

In 1887 Stevenson left Britain for good, travelling first to the United States where he began one of his most ambitious novels, *The Master of Ballantrae*. A year later, he set sail for the South Seas, and eventually settled in Samoa; his last works include a number of stories with a local setting, such as the grimly realistic *The Ebb Tide* and *The Beach of Falesà*. However, Scotland continued to be his main inspiration: he wrote *Catriona* as a sequel to *Kidnapped*, and was at work on two more novels with Scottish settings, *St Ives* and *Weir of Hermiston*, a dark story of father-son confrontation, at the time of his sudden death from a brain haemorrage in 1894. He was buried on the top of Mount Vaea overlooking the Pacific Ocean.

its crowd of penguins (the largest number in captivity anywhere in the world), a legacy of Leith's whaling trade in the South Atlantic. The penguin parade, which takes place daily at 2pm from April to September, and on sunny March and October days, has gained something of a cult status.

Lauriston Castle and Cramond

Lauriston Castle (40-min guided tours mid-June to mid-Sept Sat–Thurs 11am–5pm; April to mid-June & mid-Sept to Oct Sat–Thurs 11am–1pm & 2–5pm; Nov–March Sat & Sun 2–4pm; £2) is a country mansion set in its own parkland overlooking the Firth of Forth, about five miles west of the centre. The original sixteenth-century tower house forms the centrepiece of what is otherwise a neo-Jacobean structure, which in 1902 became the retirement home of a prosperous local cabinet-maker. He decked out the interior with his private collection of furniture and antiques, which include Flemish tapestries and ornaments made of blue john from Derbyshire. The castle can be reached from the city centre by bus #41.

One mile further west, **CRAMOND** is one of the city's most atmospheric – and poshest – old villages. The enduring image of Cramond is of step-gabled whitewashed houses rising uphill from the waterfront, though it also boasts the foundations of a Roman fort, a medieval bridge and tower house, and a church, inn and mansion, all from the seventeenth century. There are a number of interesting **short walks** in the area: across the causeway at low tide to the uninhabited, except for seabirds, **Cramond Island**; eastwards along the seafront towards the gasometers of **Granton** with sweeping views out to sea; upstream along the River Almond past former mills and their adjoining cottages towards the sixteenth-century **Old Cramond Brig**; and, after a short ferry crossing, through the Dalmeny estate to **Dalmeny House** (see below). Apart from the last one, which is just a little longer, these walks should take around an hour each.

Dalmeny

In 1975, Edinburgh's boundaries were extended to include a number of towns and villages which were formerly part of West Lothian. Among them is **DALMENY**, two miles west of Cramond and which can be reached directly from the city centre by bus (#43 *Scottish Eastern*) or train. Another option is to take the coastal path from Cramond, which passes through the estate of **Dalmeny House** (May–Sept Sun 1– 5.30pm, Mon & Tues noon–5.30pm; £3.50), the seat of the Earls of Rosebery. Built in 1815 by the English architect William Wilkins, it was the first stately home in Scotland in the neo-Gothic style, vividly evoking Tudor architecture in its picturesque turreted roofline, and in its fan vaults and hammerbeam ceilings. The family portraits include one of the fourth Earl (who commissioned the house) by Raeburn, and of the fifth Earl (the last British prime minister to govern from the House of Lords) by Millais; there are also likenesses of other famous society figures by Reynolds, Gainsborough and Lawrence. Among the furnishings are a set of tapestries made from cartoons by Goya, and the Rothschild Collection of eighteenth-century French furniture and *objets d'art*. There's also a fascinating collection of memorabilia of Napoleon Bonaparte – notably some items he used during his exile in St Helena – amassed by the fifth Earl, who wrote a biography of the French dictator.

Dalmeny **village** is a quiet community built around a spacious green. Its focal point is the mid-twelfth-century **St Cuthbert's Kirk**, a wonderful Norman church that has remained substantially intact. Although very weather-beaten, the south doorway is particularly notable for its illustrations of strange beasts. More vivaciously grotesque carvings can be seen inside on the chancel corbels and arch.

South Queensferry and around

Less than a mile of countryside separates Dalmeny from **SOUTH QUEENSFERRY**, a compact little town used by Saint Margaret as a crossing point for her frequent trips between her palaces in Edinburgh and Dunfermline. **High Street**, squeezed into the narrow gap between the sea shore and the hillside above, is lined by a picturesque array of old buildings, among them an unusual two-tiered row of shops, the roofs of the lower level serving as the walkway for the upper storey. The small **museum**, 53 High St (Mon & Thurs–Sat 10am–1pm & 2.15–5pm; Sun 2–5pm; free), contains relics of the town's history and the building of the two bridges.

Everything in South Queensferry is overshadowed, quite literally, by the two great bridges, each about a mile and a half in length, which traverse the Firth of Forth at its narrowest point. The cantilevered **Forth Rail Bridge**, built from 1883 to 1890 by Sir John Fowler and Benjamin Baker, ranks among the supreme achievements of Victorian engineering. Some 50,000 tons of steel were used in the construction of a design that manages to exude grace as well as might. Derived from American models, the suspension format chosen for the **Forth Road Bridge** makes a perfect complement to the older structure. Erected between 1958 and 1964, it finally killed off the 900-year-old ferry, and attracts such a heavy volume of traffic that plans are afoot to build yet another bridge. It's well worth walking across its footpath to Fife (see *Central Scotland*) for the tremendous views of the Rail Bridge.

Inchcolm

From South Queensferry's Hawes Pier, just west of the Rail Bridge, pleasure boats leave for a variety of cruises on the Forth (July to mid-Sept daily; Easter, May & June Sat & Sun; ☎331 4857; prices range from £3 to £7). Be sure to check in advance as sailings are always subject to cancellation in bad weather.

The most enticing destination is the island of **Inchcolm**, whose beautiful ruined **Abbey** was founded in 1123 by King Alexander I in gratitude for the hospitality he received from a hermit (whose cell survives at the northwestern corner of the island) when his ship was forced ashore in a storm. The best-preserved medieval monastic complex in Scotland, the abbey's surviving buildings date from the thirteenth to the fifteenth centuries, and include a splendid octagonal chapter house. Although the church is almost totally delapidated, its tower can be ascended for a great aerial view of the island, which is populated by a variety of nesting birds and a colony of grey seals.

Hopetoun House

Immediately beyond the western edge of South Queensferry, just over the West Lothian border, **Hopetoun House** (April–Oct daily 10am–5.30pm; £4 house & grounds, £2 grounds only) is one of Scotland's grandest stately homes. The original house was built at the turn of the eighteenth century for the first Earl of Hopetoun by Sir William Bruce, the architect of Holyroodhouse. A couple of decades later, William Adam carried out an enormous extension, engulfing the house in a curvaceous main facade and two projecting wings – superb examples of Roman Baroque pomp and swagger. The scale and lavishness of the Adam interiors, most of whose decoration was carried out after the architect's death by his sons, make for a stark contrast with the intimacy of those designed by Bruce. Particularly impressive are the Red and Yellow Drawing Rooms, with their splendid ceilings by the young Robert Adam. Among the house's furnishings are seventeenth-century tapestries, Meissen porcelain, and a distinguished collection of paintings, including portraits by Gainsborough, Ramsay and Raeburn. The grounds of Hopetoun House are also open with magnificent walks along the banks of the Forth and great opportunities for picnics.

Midlothian

Immediately south of Edinburgh lies the old county of **MIDLOTHIAN**, once called Edinburghshire. It's one of the hilliest parts of the Central Lowlands, with the Pentland chain running down its western side, and the Moorfoots defining its boundary with the

Borders to the south. Though predominantly rural, it contains a belt of former mining communities, which are struggling to come to terms with the recent decline of the industry. Such charms as it has are mostly low-key, with the exception of the riotously ornate chapel at **Roslin**.

Dalkeith and around

Despite its Victorian demeanour, **DALKEITH**, eight miles southeast of central Edinburgh – to which it is linked by very regular buses (#3, #30, #82) – grew up in the Middle Ages as a baronial burgh under the successive control of the Douglases and Buccleuchs. Today it's a bustling shopping centre, with an unusually broad High Street at its heart.

At the far end of the street is the entrance to **Dalkeith Country Park** (March–Oct daily 10am–6pm; £1.50), the estate of the Dukes of Buccleuch, whose seat, the early eighteenth-century **Dalkeith Palace**, can only be seen from the outside. You can, however, visit its one-time chapel, now the episcopalian parish church of **St Mary**, adorned inside with extremely rich furnishings. Further north, Robert Adam's **Montagu Bridge** straddles the River North Esk in a graceful arch; beyond are some derelict but once wonderfully grandiose garden follies.

A mile or so south of Dalkeith is **NEWTONGRANGE**, whose Lady Victoria Colliery is now open to the public as the **Scottish Mining Museum** (guided tours March–Oct daily 10am–4pm; £2), with a 1625ft-deep shaft, and a winding tower powered by Scotland's largest steam engine. A series of nostalgic tableaux depict everyday life in the community.

Roslin

The tranquil village of **ROSLIN** lies seven miles south of the centre of Edinburgh, from where it can be reached by bus #87a or by regular *Eastern Scottish* services from St Andrew Square. An otherwise nondescript place, the village does boast the richly decorated late Gothic **Rosslyn Chapel** (April–Oct Mon–Sat 10am–5pm, Sun noon–5pm; £2.25). Only the choir, Lady Chapel and part of the transepts were built of what was intended to be a huge collegiate church dedicated to St Matthew: construction halted soon after the founder's death in 1484, and the vestry added to the facade nearly 400 years later is the sole subsequent addition.

The outside of the chapel bristles with pinnacles, gargoyles, flying buttresses and canopies, while inside the foliage carving is particularly outstanding, with botanically accurate depictions of over a dozen different leaves and plants. Among them are cacti and Indian corn, providing fairly convincing evidence that the founder's grandfather, the daring sea adventurer Prince Henry of Orkney, did indeed, as legend has it, set foot in the New World a century before Columbus. The rich and subtle figurative sculptures have given Rosslyn the nickname of "a Bible in stone", though they're more allegorical than literal, with portrayals of the Dance of Death, the Seven Acts of Mercy and the Seven Deadly Sins.

The greatest and most original carving of all is the extraordinary knotted **Prentice Pillar** at the southeastern corner of the Lady Chapel. According to local legend, the pillar was made by an apprentice during the absence of the master mason, who killed him in a fit of jealousy on seeing the finished work. A tiny head of a man with a slashed forehead, set at the apex of the ceiling at the far northwestern corner of the building, is popularly supposed to represent the apprentice, his murderer the corresponding head at the opposite side. The entwined dragons at the foot are symbols of Satan, and were probably inspired by Norse mythology.

The **Edinburgh Festival**, now the largest arts festival in the world, first took place in August 1947. Driven by a desire for reconciliation and escape from post-war austerity, the Austrian conductor, Rudolf Bing, brought together a host of distinguished musicians from the war-ravaged countries of central Europe. The symbolic centrepiece of his vision was the emotional reunion of Bruno Walter, a Jewish refugee from Nazi tyranny, and the Vienna Philharmonic Orchestra. At the same time, eight theatrical groups, both Scottish and English, turned up in Edinburgh, uninvited, performing in an unlikely variety of local venues, thus establishing the Fringe. Today the festival attracts a million people to the city over three weeks (the last three in August, or the last fortnight and first week in September) and encompasses several separate festivals, each offering a wide variety of artists and events – everything is on show, from the highbrow to the controversial.

The legacy of Rudolf Bing's Glyndebourne connections ensured that, for many years, the official **Edinburgh International Festival** was dominated by opera. Although, in the 1980s, efforts were made to involve locals and provide a broader cultural mix of international theatre, dance and classical music, the official festival is still very much a high-brow event. The **programme** is published in April by the Edinburgh International Festival Society, 21 Market St, EH1 1BW (☎255 5756), bookings begin shortly afterwards.

For many years largely the domain of student revues – notable exceptions include Joan Littlewood's distinguished Theatre Workshop, with their early 1950s production of *The Other Animal*, about life in a concentration camp, and work by the great Spanish playwright, Lorca – the **Festival Fringe** began to really take off in the 1970s. Set up in 1951, the **Fringe Society** has grown from a small group to today's large-scale operation serving an annual influx of more than 500 acts – national theatre groups to student troupes – using around 200 venues. In spite of this expansion, the Fringe has remained loyal to the original open policy and there is still no vetting of performers. This means that the shows range from the inspired to the truly diabolical and ensures a highly competitive atmosphere, in which one bad review in a prominent publication means box-office disaster. Many unknowns rely on self-publicity, taking to the streets to perform highlights from their show, or pressing leaflets into the hands of every passer-by. Performances go on round the clock: if so inclined, you could sit through 20 shows in a day.

Over the years there has been a remarkable choice of both performers and venues: both Jean-Louis Barrault (star of 1945 movie *Les Enfants du Paradis*) and Richard Burton as Hamlet; Grace Kelly reading the works of early American poets; 65-year-old Marlene Dietrich in cabaret; *Macbeth* on Inchcolm Island in the Firth of Forth; and *2,001: A Space Odyssey* performed to an audience sitting in a Hillman Avenger. The 1980s saw the anarchic circus performers *Archaos*, whose publicity involved sawing up cars outside the Fringe office. Although now disbanded, their spirit lives on in a number of ever more shocking shows, including a recent troupe of naked lesbian trapeze artists.

Edinburgh fringe is also, of course, the place to witness the emergence of new **stars**; from actors Donald Pleasance and Penelope Keith in the 1950s, to the Beyond the Fringe comedy team of Alan Bennett, Jonathan Miller, Peter Cook and Dudley Moore in 1960; and, in the 1980s and 1990s, contemporary stars such as comedians Harry Enfield, Lee Evans and the late Bill Hicks, and actress Emma Thompson. The full programme is usually available in

Cafés and restaurants

You can eat well in Edinburgh at almost any price, choosing from a wide range of cuisines. Plenty of places specialize in **traditional Scottish cooking**, using fresh local produce, while the city's ethnic communities, despite their small size, have offered a lot to the **restaurant** scene, including some great **Italian** trattorias, and a host of excellent **Indian** restaurants serving regional dishes. In addition, the adapta-

June from the Festival Fringe Office, 180 High St, EH1 1QS (☎226 5257). Postal and telephone (☎226 5138) bookings can be made almost immediately afterwards.

The **Film Festival** also began at the same time as the main festival, making it the longest running Film Festival in the world. After a period in the doldrums, it has grown to its current position as a respected fixture on the international circuit, incorporating both mainstream and independent new releases and presenting a series of valuable retrospectives from Sam Fuller to Shohei Immamura. It also hosts interviews and discussions with film directors; in recent years visitors have included Kenneth Anger, the Coen brothers, Clint Eastwood and Steve Martin. A particular feature has been the high profile support given to Scottish film from Bill Douglas's austere and brilliant *Childhood* trilogy, through the lighter style of Bill Forsyth to the recent small budget hit, *Shallow Grave*. Tickets and information are available from the main venue, The Filmhouse, 88 Lothian Rd, EH3 9BZ (☎228 4051). The programme is usually ready by late June, when bookings start.

Meanwhile, other Festivals have emerged: the **Jazz Festival**, which has attracted the likes of Teddy Wilson and Benny Waters and stages a lively parade through the Grassmarket (programme available in July from the office at 116 Canongate, EH8 8DD; ☎557 1624); and the **Book Festival**, which evolved from existing meet-the-author sessions to become a biannual jamboree held in the douce setting of a marquee-covered Charlotte Square. Hundreds of established authors from throughout the English-speaking world come to take part in readings, lectures, panel discussions and audience question-and-answer sessions. For further information, contact the Scottish Book Centre, 137 Dundee St, EH11 1BG (☎228 5444). The **Television Festival** is largely an in-house event, surfacing in the public consciousness only briefly as the keynote speaker indulges in the sport of deriding the latest changes at the BBC.

Although officially a separate event, the **Edinburgh Military Tattoo**, held in a splendid setting on the Castle Esplanade, is very much part of the Festival scene and an unashamed display of the kilt and bagpipes view of Scottish culture. Pipes and drums form the kernel of the programme, with a lone piper towards the end; performing animals, gymnastic and dare-devil displays, plus at least one guest regiment from abroad provide variety. Information and tickets are available from the Tattoo Office, 22 Market St, EH1 1QB (☎225 1188).

Although dubbed by many as elitist and irrelevant to locals, the Festival seems as much a part of the fabric of Edinburgh as its Castle (one third of the tickets are sold to local people). Aside from providing a substantial boost to the city's economy, the Festival does stage two events which regularly bring in huge crowds of townspeople: Fringe Sunday, when Holyrood Park is taken over for a vast open-air party, and the massive firework display and free concert, held in Princes Street Gardens. And there are, of course, the annual Festival **rituals**: celebrity-spotting at the Assembly Rooms; newspaper gossip revolving around fears of imminent financial catastrophe for a major venue, if not the Festival itself; and the constant, raging debate about the strengths or otherwise of the Scottish element. Above all, though, there is a buzz to the city: the rumoured visit of a superstar, or even a soap star, the best and worst shows in towns, and the hot tips for the winners of the plethora of awards up for grabs, all become matters of supreme importance. By the Sunday following the end of the Festival, the performers have all departed: the winners to London for the various "Pick of the Fringe" seasons and the losers back home to dream of next year. The church halls and masonic lodges are locked up, the traders and hoteliers count their takings and the city streets are quiet once again.

For information on other festivals in the city see "Nightlife and entertainment".

tion of home-grown ingredients to classic Gallic recipes is something the city does particularly well, resulting in a whole group of fabulous **French** restaurants. **Vegetarians** and vegans are well catered for, and there are plenty of **fish** specialists – seafood fans should make some attempt to get out to **Leith**, whose waterside restaurants serve consistently good food.

Although the city has nothing approaching the **café** society of other European capitals, if you fancy a snack, a series of good establishments serves cakes and sandwiches.

In choosing a place to eat, bear in mind that most **pubs** (which are covered in the following section) serve food, and that many have a restaurant attached. Edinburgh has a fairly high turnover of restaurants – some of impeccable repute have bitten the dust in the past few years – so don't be surprised if one or two of the listings have closed by the time you read this.

Old Town

Wonderful cafés and most of the upmarket Scottish and French restaurants are concentrated in the atmospheric streets of the **Old Town**; with a wide range of other cuisines also on offer, including vegetarian.

Budget Food: cafés and diners

Café-Patisserie Florentin, 8–10 St Giles St (☎225 6267). French-style café off High St whose extended opening hours make it a popular late-night rendezvous. Open 7am–midnight, 2am at weekends.

Clarinda's, 69 Canongate (☎557 1888). Spruce olde-worlde café serving home-cooked breakfasts and light lunches.

Courthouse Café, Brodies Close (☎0860/902095). Calm retreat just off the Royal Mile, with newspapers to peruse and interesting, well-presented snacks and salads.

Edinburgh Fudge House, 197 Canongate (☎556 4172). Minimalist place serving snacks, sandwiches and cakes; notable for its huge range of delicious but pricy home-made fudges.

Elephant House, 21 George IV Bridge (☎225 6267). Attractive new café with a large selection of coffees, teas, sandwiches and cakes. Wonderful views of the castle. Open 8am–10pm.

Elephant's Sufficiency, 170 High St (☎220 0666). This bright, lively café near the Fringe Office serves a great selection of sandwiches and baked potatoes.

Lower Aisle, in the High Kirk of St Giles, High St (☎225 5147). Light lunches in the crypt. Popular with lawyers.

Netherbow Café, Netherbow Arts Centre, 43 High St (☎556 9579). Excellent wholefood snacks using produce from the café's own allotment.

Scottish

The Atrium, Cambridge St (☎228 8882) Award-winning and considered by many the city's best restaurant, with prices to match. Tables made from railway sleepers.

Creelers, 3 Hunter Square (☎220 4447). Excellent seafood restaurant priding itself on fresh produce brought in from a sister restaurant/fish shop on Arran. Lunch £7.50, supper £16.50.

Dubh Prais, 123b High St (☎557 5732). Basement restaurant offering innovative Scottish cuisine at affordable prices. Closed Sun & Mon.

Jacksons, 209 High St (☎225 1793). Upmarket meat restaurant which turns the humble haggis into haute cuisine. Set lunches are among Edinburgh's best bargains at around £6; dinners are nearer £20. Closed Sat & Sun lunch.

Stac Polly, 8a Grindlay St (☎229 5405). Emphasis on game, fish and meat. Special pre- and post-theatre dinners for around £14.

French

L'Auberge, 58 St Mary's St (☎556 5888). French nouvelle cuisine in a luxurious setting: a bit of a treat. Splurge on *Le Grand Menu Gourmand* at £30.

Chez Jules, 1 Craigs Close (☎225 7007). Classic French food in fine, no-frills establishment. New Town branch at 61 Frederick St (☎225 7983). Closed Sun.

Grain Store, 30 Victoria St (☎225 7635). Another reasonably priced, solid Old Town French restaurant.

Pierre Victoire, 10 Victoria St (☎225 1721); 38 Grassmarket (☎226 2442). Ever-expanding group offering unmistakably French and affordable meals. Like the service, the food can be erratic, but is normally superb. Very popular so book. Each branch closes either Sun or Mon.

Le Sept, Old Fishmarket Close (☎225 5428). Brasserie upstairs and à la carte restaurant downstairs. Walk in and (if necessary) wait for the brasserie, but book for the restaurant.

Italian

Cosmo, 58a N Castle St (☎226 6743). Straightforward, delicious Italian cuisine at long-established trattoria. Main courses start at around £10. Closed Sun & Mon.

Lazio, 95 Lothian Rd (☎229 7788). Pick of the family-run trattorias on this block. Moderately priced and particularly handy for a late-night meal after a show in the nearby theatre district. Closes 2am.

Indian

Spices, 110 W Bow (☎225 1028). A spin-off of the long-established *Kalpna* (in Southside), but geared towards carnivores. Innovative Indian cooking with a few African choices. All-you-can-eat buffet lunches for around a fiver. Closed Sun.

Suruchi, 14a Nicholson St (☎556 6583). Popular establishment introducing genuine South Indian cooking to Scotland for the first time. The emphasis is on rice and vegetables, with a few splendid poultry dishes. Inexpensive; set lunch about £5, and special pre-theatre menu around £12.

Chinese and Southeast Asian

Loon Fung, 32 Grindlay St (☎229 5757). Across the street from the Lyceum and the Usher Hall with a strong line in fresh fish. Moderately priced.

Singapore Sling, 503 Lawnmarket (☎226 2826). Real fire-in-the-stomach inexpensive Singaporean and Malaysian cuisine in modest surroundings just down from the castle.

Mexican

Viva Mexico, 10 Anchor Close (☎226 5145). Inexpensive restaurant, with plenty of choice for vegetarians, and bargain options at lunchtimes.

Vegetarian

Bann's Vegetarian Café, 5 Hunter Square (☎226 1122). Inexpensive café, ideally placed halfway up the Royal Mile. Reliable, frequently changing menu, with 2 courses from around £4. Daily 10am–11pm.

Black Bo's, 57 Blackfriars St (☎557 6136). Non-meat diner with earthy atmosphere, moderate prices and friendly service. Open after 11pm for drinks only. Closed Sun.

Henderson's at the Traverse, 10 Cambridge St (☎228 8003) *Henderson's* took over the Traverse café, situated in the basement of the Traverse Theatre in 1994. Small reliable menu and a discreet Morricone soundtrack in the background. Open till 8pm daily.

New Town

With everything from Swiss and North African to organic Scottish food, the **New Town** has a number of very good places to eat; prices are often cheaper than the Old Town too.

Budget Food: cafés and diners

Cyberia, 88 Hanover St (☎220 4403). Bright internet café with with a wide range of snacks and 15 computers (£3.50 per hour; e-mail: edinburgh@easynet.co.uk).

Laigh Kitchen, 117a Hanover St (☎225 1552). Long-established, homely New Town café with flagstone floor and cast-iron stoves. Good salads and soups, but best known for its wonderful home-baked scones and cakes.

Stac Polly, 29–33 Dublin St (☎556 2231). Very much a carnivore's eating place, with good game, fish and meat dishes.

Web 13, 13 Bread St (☎229 8883). "Anoraky" internet café with 11 computers (£2.50 per hour; e-mail: queries@web13.presence.co.uk), serving toasties and sandwiches.

Scottish

Martin's, 70 Rose St N Lane (☎225 3106). The emphasis is on organic, unfarmed ingredients – salmon, venison, unpasteurized cheeses – in this long-standing restaurant in an unlikely looking back street. Expensive, especially in the evenings, but worth it. Closed Sun & Mon.

French

Café St Honoré, 34 Thistle St Lane (☎226 2211). New Town brasserie serving good, inexpensive traditional French cooking, with fabulous pastries and coffee. Closed Sun.

La Cuisine d'Odile, French Institute, 13 Randolph Crescent (☎225 5685). Inexpensive and popular French home cooking in a West End basement. Lunch only. Closed Sun, Mon & throughout July.

Le Marché Noir, 2–4 Eyre Place (☎558 1608). Just off Dundas St. Adventurous Provençal menu, excellent wines and friendly hosts. Dinner about £25. Closed Sun.

Pierre Victoire, 8 Union St (☎557 8451); 17 Queensferry St (☎226 1890). Unmistakably French and affordable. Like the service, the food can be erratic, but is usually excellent. Popular so book. Each branch closes either Sun or Mon.

Italian

Giuliano's, 18–19 Union Place (☎556 6590). Raucous trattoria across from the Playhouse, much favoured for family and office nights out. Does its best to conjure up the full Italian atmosphere. Closes 2.30am.

Rafaelli, 10–11 Randolph Place (☎225 6060). Classy ristorante in backstreet setting, with prices to match. Closed Sun.

Vito's, 55a Frederick St (☎225 5052). Bustling, quality Italian cooking at mid-range prices with the emphasis on seafood. Closed Sun except during the Festival.

Swiss

Alp-Horn, 167 Rose St (☎225 4787). Fondues, air-dried meats and wonderful desserts in this handy little restaurant just off Charlotte Square. Good-value 2-course lunches. Closed Sun.

Spanish

Igg's, 15 Jeffrey St (☎557 8184). A Spanish-owned hybrid, offering tapas snacks and Mediterranean dishes, plus traditional Scottish food. Good lunchtime tapas for around a fiver. Closed Sun & Mon.

Parador, 26 William St (☎225 2973). A convincing West End mock-up of a Spanish bodega, with full restaurant menu as well as tapas. All-you-can-eat lunchtime buffet £6. Bar and tapas 2–6.30pm only.

Indian

Indian Cavalry Club, 3 Atholl Place (☎228 3282). Upmarket, but moderately priced West End Indian restaurant with a pseudo-Raj decor and mildly spiced food.

Chinese and Southeast Asian

Bamboo Garden, 57a Frederick St (☎225 2382). Many of Edinburgh's Chinese community gather in this inexpensive place for great *dim sum* on Sunday lunchtime. Get the waiter to explain the choices rather than rely on the limited English-language menu.

Buntoms, 9–13 Nelson St (☎557 4344). First Thai restaurant in Scotland, and still as good as any of its competitors.

North African

Marrakech, 30 London St (☎556 7293). Scotland's only Moroccan restaurant, very reasonably priced, dishing up superb and authentic *couscous*, and *tajine* plus a range of soups, superb fresh bread and pastries. Unlicensed, but you can take your own and there's no corkage charge.

Mexican

Tex Mex, 47 Hanover St (☎225 1796). Authentic, reasonably priced Mexican burritos and steaks.

Seafood

Café Royal Oyster Bar, 17a W Register St (☎556 4124). Splendidly ornate Victorian interior featured in *Chariots of Fire* – look out for the stained-glass windows showing sportsmen. Classic seafood dishes, including freshly caught oysters, served in a civilized, chatty atmosphere. Expensive – be prepared to pay at least £30 for a full meal.

Oyster Bar, 6a Queen St (☎226 2530); 2 Calton Rd, Carlton Hill (☎557 2925). Wood-panelled bars with moderately priced fresh oysters and a superb choice of cask; lively atmosphere.

Vegetarian

Henderson's, 94 Hanover St (☎225 2131). Self-service vegetarian basement restaurant, with adjacent bar. Freshly prepared hot dishes, plus a great choice of salads, soups, sweets and cheeses. An Edinburgh institution, so arrive early for lunch or be prepared to queue. Closed Sun.

The Northern New Town and Stockbridge

The **Northern New Town** and **Stockbridge** offer a decent choice of good eating places; especially convenient if you are here visiting the Modern Art Gallery.

Budget Food: cafés and diners

Bell's Diner, 7 St Stephen St (☎225 8116). Unpretentious little diner tucked away in Stockbridge. Good, inexpensive burgers, plus a wide choice of steaks and pancakes.

Scottish National Gallery of Modern Art Café, Belford Rd (☎332 8600). Far more than a standard refreshment stop for gallery visitors: many locals come here for lunch or a snack. Changing daily menu of salads, hot food and home baking. Second branch in the National Portrait Gallery building.

Terrace Café, in Royal Botanic Garden (☎552 0616). Superior spot offering stunning views of the city. Changing menu includes hot dishes, sandwiches and cakes.

Italian

San Marco, 107 St Mary's Place (☎332 1569). Family-run Stockbridge pasta and pizza joint with fun atmosphere. Good value.

Indian

Lancers, 5 Hamilton Place (☎332 3444). Afficionados rate the curries at this moderately priced restaurant as the best in Scotland. Primarily Bengali and Punjabi.

Chinese

Loon Fung. 2 Warriston Place (☎556 1781). Something of a trailblazer for Cantonese cuisine in Scotland, is near the eastern entrance to the Botanics.

Southside

The **Southside** has a wide range of interesting restaurants, among them some of the best and most popular in Edinburgh.

Budget Food: cafés and diners

Brattesani's, 85–87 Newington Rd (☎667 5808). Typical Italo-Scottish chippie, with choice of sit-down or carry-out meals. Daily 9.30am–midnight.

Buffalo Grill, 14 Chapel St (☎667 7427). Charcoal-grilled steaks are the speciality in this popular and busy diner facing the main university campus.

Nicolson's, 6a Nicolson St (☎557 4567). Spacious first-floor café opposite the Festival Theatre, with a varied daytime menu and evening à la carte for £12–15.

Queen's Hall Café, 89 Clerk St (☎668 2019). Well-prepared salads, vegetarian dishes, soups and puddings; some decent wines and beers in this Southside converted church.

Scottish

Howies, 75 St Leonard's St (☎668 2917). Smaller branch of Haymarket partner with brasserie-style Scottish cooking. BYOB. Closed Mon lunch.

Kelly's, 46b W Richmond St (☎668 3847). Enjoys virtual cult status among Edinburgh foodies, serving modern Scottish food and scrumptious desserts. Closed Mon lunch & Sun.

French

La Bonne Vie, 49 Causewayside (☎667 1110). Very popular French restaurant opened by David Wilson of *Peat Inn* (see p.239) fame. As yet unlicensed.

Indian

Annpurna, 45 St Patrick Square (☎662 1807). Authentic Gujarati and Southern Indian cuisine (so mainly vegetarian); excellent value.

Kalpna, 2 St Patrick Square (☎667 9890). Outstanding vegetarian restaurant, popular with students, serving authentic Gujarati dishes. On the southern continuation of Nicholson St. As much as you want lunchtime buffet for £4. Closed Sun.

Chinese and Southeast Asian

Good Year, 62 Ratcliffe Terrace (☎667 7532); 21 Argyle Place, south of the Meadows (☎229 4404). The much-loved *Chinese Home Cooking* is now under new management and part of a chain, though still offering the same excellent-value, wholesome food. BYOB; no corkage charge. The Leith branch has wonderful seafood.

North African

Phenecia, 55–57 W Nicolson St (☎662 4493). Rock-bottom prices at this basic food joint beside the main university campus. Mostly Tunisian but draws on a variety of Mediterranean cuisines.

Brasseries

Maxies, 32 W Nicolson St (☎667 0845). Large basement brasserie and wine bar with regular live music. Some vegetarian offerings. Popular with students and university staff. Closed Sun.

Vegetarian

Pierre Lapin, 32 W Nicolson St (☎668 4332). Drolly named vegetarian offshoot of the *Pierre Victoire* chain, offering superb-value set menus. Closed Sun.

Sue's Diner, 51–53 W Nicolson St (☎667 8673). Long-standing unlicensed café serving inventive soups, savouries and puddings, and a range of vegan food, to crowds of students.

Southwest of the Old Town

Handy for many of the city's theatres, there's a good sprinkling of restaurants **Southwest** of the Old Town, most notably some interesting Chinese options.

Scottish

Howies, 63 Dalry Rd (☎313 3334). Just beyond Haymarket, a brasserie-style variant of traditional Scottish cooking. Good-value lunch and dinner menus; renowned for its venison. BYOB. Closed Mon lunch.

French

La Bagatelle, 22a Brougham Place, Tollcross (☎229 0869). Fine French food in an authentic atmosphere. Closed Sun.

Indian

Shamiana, 14 Brougham Place, Tollcross (☎229 5578). Established, first-class North Indian and Kashmiri cuisine in a tasteful environment located midway between the Kings and Lyceum theatres. One of the more expensive restaurants in this category, but well worth it.

Chinese

Oriental Dining Centre, 8–14a Morrison St, Tollcross (☎221 1288). Three distinct restaurants, the most popular being the *Ho-Ho-Mei Noodle Shak*. Also contains the *Rainbow Arch Gourmet Restaurant* and *Henry's Dim Sum Cellar*.

Szechuan House, 12 Leamington Place (☎229 4655). Authentically fiery and inexpensive Szechuan cuisine in basic surroundings near the King's Theatre. Closed Sun.

Mexican

Viva Mexico, 50 E Fountainbridge, Tollcross (☎228 4005). Good, affordable meals and many vegetarian options and lunchtime bargains.

Leith

Now a fashionable place to eat, **Leith** is packed with high-quality restaurants and waterfront brasseries, and is particularly good for seafood.

French

Pierre Victoire, 5 Dock Place (☎555 6178). Usually good, affordable French food. Very popular so book.

The Vintner's Rooms, 87 Giles St (☎554 6767). Splendid restaurant in a seventeenth-century warehouse. The bar in the cellar has a sombre, candlelit ambience and a coal fire; the ornate Rococo dining room serves expertly prepared food, especially strong on fish and Gallic dishes, using ingredients of the highest quality. Expensive, but well worth it.

Italian

Caprice Pizzerama, 327 Leith Walk (☎554 1279). Enormous place, almost exactly halfway between Princes St and Leith. Specializes in giant pizzas baked in a wood-fired oven. Inexpensive.

Silvio's, 54 The Shore (☎553 3557). A variety of fresh pastas, excellent antipasto and fish dishes. Non-smoking.

Swiss

Denzlers, 121 Constitution St (☎554 3268). Although it has moved premises a few times over the years, this has consistently ranked among Scotland's most highly praised restaurants. The ever-innovative menu is constantly changing, and prices are surprisingly reasonable, with most main courses under £10. Closed Sun & Mon.

Indian

Raj, 89–91a Henderson St (☎553 3980). An excellent ethnic alternative to the waterfront brasseries. Moderately priced Bangladeshi and North Indian dishes; few vegetarian choices.

Chinese and Southeast Asian

Good Year, 40–42 Queen Charlotte St (☎555 6968). There's wonderful seafood at this branch of the much-loved *Chinese Home Cooking*, now under new management and part of a chain (other branches in Southside), though still offering the same excellent-value, wholesome food. BYOB; no corkage charge.

Yee Kiang, 42 Dalmeny St (☎554 5833). Homely little place, on a side street leading east off the middle of Leith Walk. Menu includes wonderful Pekinese specialities, notably duck. Closed Mon.

Seafood

Harry Ramsden's, 5 Newhaven Place (☎551 5566). Part of the Yorkshire chain, just west of Leith in Newhaven, offering substantial portions of fish and chips in attractive harbourside setting.

Oyster Bar, 10 Burgess St, Leith (☎554 6294); 6a Queen St, New Town (☎226 2530); 2 Calton Rd, Carlton Hill (☎557 2925); 28 W Maitland St, Haymarket (☎225 3861). Lively, wood-panelled bars with a superb choice of cask beers and moderately priced fresh oysters.

Brasseries

Malmaison Café Bar, 1 Tower Place (☎555 6969). Successful attempt to re-create the feel of a French café: not for those on a diet.

Ship on the Shore, 24–26 The Shore (☎555 0409). The homeliest and least expensive of the waterfront brasseries. Changing range of cask ales.

The Shore, 3 The Shore (☎553 5080). Bar/restaurant with good, moderately priced fish and decent wines. Great views at sunset, and live jazz and folk in the adjoining bar. Non–smoking. Closed Sun.

Skippers, 1a Dock Place (☎554 1018). Across the Water of Leith from The Shore, with a vaguely nautical atmosphere and a superb – if expensive – fish-oriented menu that changes according to what's fresh. Closed Sun.

Waterfront Wine Bar, 1c Dock Place (☎554 7427). Housed in the former lock-keeper's cottage with outdoor seating overlooking the waterfront, this popular wine bar/restaurant serves moderately priced fish dishes and good wines.

Pubs and bars

Many of Edinburgh's **pubs**, especially in the Old Town, have histories that stretch back centuries, while others, particularly in the New Town, are unaltered Victorian or Edwardian period pieces that rank among Edinburgh's most outstanding examples of interior design. Add in the plentiful supply of trendy modern bars, and there's a variety of styles and atmospheres to cater for all tastes. Many honest howffs stay open late, and during the Festival especially, it's no problem to find bars open till at least midnight.

Currently, Edinburgh has three **breweries**, including the giant Scottish and Newcastle (who produce *McEwan's* and *Younger's*). The small independent Caledonian Brewery uses old techniques and equipment to produce some of the best beers in Britain, and there's also the tiny Rose Street Brewery, which has its own pub.

Edinburgh's main drinking strip is the near-legendary **Rose Street**, a pedestrianized lane of minimal visual appeal tucked between Princes and George streets. The ultimate Edinburgh pub crawl is to drink a half-pint in each of its dozen or so establishments – plus the two in West Register Street, its eastern continuation. Most of the **student pubs** are in and around Grassmarket, with a further batch on the Southside, an area overlooked by most tourists. **Leith** has a nicely varied crop of bars, ranging from the roughest type of spit-and-sawdust places to polished pseudo-Victoriana, while two of the city's best and most characterful pubs are further west along the seafront in **Newhaven**.

The Old Town

Bank Bar, 1 South Bridge. Attractive conversion of a bank, with live jazz on Thurs & Sat.

Bannermans, 212 Cowgate. The best pub in the street, formerly a vintner's cellar, with a labyrinthine interior and good beer on tap. On weekdays, tasty veggie lunches at rock-bottom prices; breakfasts available at weekends 11am–4pm. Open till 1am Mon–Sat.

Bow Bar, 80 West Bow. Old wood-panelled bar that recently won an award as the best drinkers' pub in Britain. Choose from among nearly 150 whiskies, an almost equally wide range of other spirits, and a changing selection of first-rate Scottish and English cask beers.

BREWERY TOURS

If you fancy finding out a bit more about Scottish beers, *Scottish and Newcastle*'s *Fountain Brewery*, Fountainbridge (☎229 9377 ext. 3015), runs good tours (Mon–Thurs 10.15am & 2.15pm, Fri 10.15am only; £2.95). For the morning tours, you have to book directly with the brewery, for the afternoon tours, with the main tourist office. In summer, the *Caledonian Brewery*, Slateford Rd (☎337 1286), also runs regular tours: phone ahead to reserve a place.

Cellar No.1, 2 Chambers St. Lively stone-clad vault that doubles as a restaurant. Excellent wines by bottle or glass. Open until 1am.

Deacon Brodie's Tavern, 435 Lawnmarket. Named after the eighteenth-century city councillor who inspired Stevenson's Jekyll and Hyde, the pub is lined with murals that tell his life story. Busy bars on 2 floors; good lunches. Open until midnight.

Doric Tavern, 15 Market St. Favoured watering hole of journalists from the nearby *Scotsman* building. The downstairs *McGuffie's Tavern* is a traditional Edinburgh howff, while the upstairs restaurant is more of a brasserie-cum-wine bar.

Ensign Ewart, 521 Lawnmarket. Cosy, beamed bar with intimate alcoves. Being named after a hero of the Battle of Waterloo, and hung with military prints and paintings, it's appropriate that it's well patronized by members of the Castle garrison. Open until midnight.

Fiddlers Arms, 9–11 Grassmarket. Traditional bar serving excellent *McEwan's* 80 shilling. The walls are adorned with forlorn, stringless violins. Open Mon–Thurs till 11.30pm, Fri & Sat 1am.

Green Tree, 184 Cowgate. Popular student bar with occasional folk music and a walled beer garden.

Greyfriars Bobby, 34 Candlemaker Row. Long-established favourite with both students and tourists, named after the statue outside. Lunch available.

Hebrides Bar, 17 Market St. Home from home for Edinburgh's Highland community: ceilidh atmosphere with lots of jigs, strathspeys and reels but no tartan kitsch.

Jolly Judge, 7a James Court. Atmospheric bar in a close just down from the castle. Popular with tourists.

Last Drop, 74–78 Grassmarket. "Drop" refers to the Edinburgh gallows, which were located in front, and whose former presence is symbolized in the red paintwork of the exterior. Cheapish pub food, and, like its competitors in the same block, patronized mainly by students.

Malt Shovel, 11–15 Cockburn St. Dimly lit, comfortable bar with an excellent range of cask beers and single malt whiskies. Pub lunches. Open Sun–Wed 11am–midnight, Thurs–Sat 11am–12.30am.

Oddfellows, 14 Forrest Rd. Hip hangout for students and hard-up fashion victims. An amazing clutter of paraphernalia reflects the building's previous incarnation as a flea market.

Sandy Bell's, 25 Forrest Rd. A folk music institution, hosting regular impromptu sessions. Small but busy with an impressive selection of beers and whiskies.

The New Town

Abbotsford, 3 Rose St. Upscale pub whose original Victorian decor, complete with wood panelling and "island bar", is among the finest in the city. Good range of ales, including *Broughton Greenmantle*. Restaurant upstairs serves hearty Scottish food. Closed Sun.

Basement Bar, 10a Broughton St (☎557 0097). Packed out, especially at the weekends, with a pre-club crowd, the city's trendiest bar is efficiently run by young and enthusiastic Hawaiian shirted staff.

Café Royal, 17 W Register St. The pub part of this stylish Victorian restaurant, the *Circle Bar*, is worth a visit for its decor alone, notably the huge elliptical "island" counter and the tiled portraits of renowned inventors. Open until midnight Thurs–Sat.

Guildford Arms, 1–5 W Register St. Excellent selection of ales, reasonable food and a very mixed clientele in this splendidly Baroque bar.

Kenilworth, 152–154 Rose St. Attractive high-ceilinged pub dating from 1899; has something of a gay tradition, though this is declining. Good Alloa beers, especially the *Arrol*'s 70 shilling.

Milne's Bar, corner of Rose St & Hanover St. Cellar bar once beloved of Edinburgh's literati, earning the nickname "The Poets' Pub" courtesy of Hugh MacDiarmid et al. Good range of cask beers, including *McEwan's* 80 shilling. Open Mon–Sat until midnight, Sun 7–11pm.

Oxford Bar, 8 Young St. Traditional city bar, unpretentious and somewhat of a shrine for rugby fans and off-duty policemen. Good Scottish pub food: Forfar bridies and mutton pie.

Rose Street Brewery, 55 Rose St. Edinburgh's only micro-brewery, whose equipment can be inspected in the upstairs restaurant; the 2 beers made there are also on tap in the ground-floor bar.

Whigham's Wine Cellars, 13 Hope St. Basement wine bar with French wine and fresh oysters amid lots of stone flagging and catacomb-like booths. Closed Sun, otherwise open till midnight.

The Northern New Town and Stockbridge

Baillie Bar, 2 St Stephen St. Basement bar at corner of Edinburgh's most self-consciously bohemian street. English and Scottish ales, including some from the Caledonian Brewery.

Bert's Bar, 29 William St & 2–4 Raeburn Place. The former fills up with the office lunchtime crowd, the latter at night with Stockbridge yuppies. Both have excellent beer, good food and strive to be authentic, non-theme-oriented pubs.

Cumberland Bar, 1 Cumberland St. Highly popular bar with no juke box and a wide variety of ales.

Kay's Bar, 39 Jamaica St. Small, civilized one-time wine shop, warmed by a roaring log fire in winter. Fine cask ales. Closed Sun.

Mathers, 25 Broughton St. Relaxed, old-fashioned pub which attracts a mixed crowd. The best place in Edinburgh for stout, with *Guinness* and *Murphy's* on tap, as well as the local *Gillespie's*.

The Southside

Pear Tree House, 36 W Nicolson St. Fine bar in eighteenth-century house with courtyard, one of Edinburgh's very few beer gardens. Decent bar lunches; open until midnight Thurs–Sat.

Southsider, 3–5 W Richmond St. Genuine local pub with a superb range of draught and imported bottled beers.

Stewart's, 14 Drummond St. A Southside institution since the beginning of the century, and seemingly little changed since then; popular with lecturers and students.

Southwest of the Old Town

Bennets Bar, 8 Leven St, Tollcross. Edwardian pub with mahogany-set mirrors and Art Nouveau stained glass. Lunch daily except Sun. Packed in the evening, particularly when there's a show at the King's Theatre next door. Open until midnight Mon–Sat.

Blue Blazer, 2 Spittal St. Traditional Edinburgh howff with oak-clad bar and church pews. Closed Sun.

Braidwood's, 52 W Port. James Braidwood was the city's first firefighter, and this bar is based in an old Victorian fire station. Lunches recommended. Open until 1am.

Canny Man's (Volunteer Arms), 237 Morningside Rd, Morningside. Atmospheric pub/museum adorned with anything that can be hung on the walls or from the ceiling. Open until midnight Mon–Sat.

Leith

Bay Horse, 63 Henderson St. Elegant Edwardian bar with stained-glass windows and walls lined with black-and-white photographs of old Edinburgh and Leith.

Kings Wark, 36 The Shore. Real ale and good food in a restored eighteenth-century pub.

Malt and Hops, 45 The Shore. Real ale pub offering basic bar snacks.

Merman, 42 Bernard St. Intimate pub that dates back to 1775, and is still preserved in its original state with a blazing log fire. Specializes in high-quality cask beers.

Tattler, 23 Commercial St. Bar restaurant decked out in plush Victorian style. The award-winning bar meals are wonderful: high-quality Scottish food including fish, meat and poultry.

Newhaven

Starbank Inn, 64 Laverockbank Rd. Fine old stone-built pub overlooking the Forth with a high reputation for cask ales and bar food.

Ye Olde Peacock Inn, Lindsay Rd (☎552 8707). Serves cheap, homely food, including the best fish and chips in the city. Advance reservations are advisable for the main bar and restaurant; otherwise try for a table in the small lounge. Be sure to see the gallery of prints of the pioneering Hill and Adamson calotypes of Newhaven fishwives.

Elsewhere in the city

Athletic Arms (The Gravediggers), 1 Angle Park Terrace. Out in the western suburbs, near Tynecastle football ground and Murrayfield rugby stadium, the pub's nickname comes from the cemetery nearby. For decades, it has had the reputation of being Edinburgh's best pub for serious ale drinkers.

Caley Sample Room, 58 Angle Park Terrace. 1970s horror, *The Blue Lagoon*, has been reborn as showpiece pub for the cask ales of the nearby Caledonian Brewery.

Hawes Inn, Newhalls Rd, S Queensferry. Famous old whitewashed tavern virtually under the Forth Rail Bridge, immortalized by Stevenson in *Kidnapped*. Bar serves a wide range of food and drink; the rambling complex also includes a hotel and upmarket restaurant (☎319 1120).

Sheep Heid, 43 The Causeway, Duddingston. Eighteenth-century inn with family atmosphere, making an ideal refreshment stop at the end of a tramp through Holyrood Park. Decent home-cooked meals are available at the bar, more substantial meals in the upstairs restaurant (☎661 1020).

Nightlife and entertainment

Inevitably, Edinburgh's **nightlife** is at its best during the Festival (see p.90), which can make the other 49 weeks of the year seem like one long anti-climax. However, by any normal standards, rather than by the misleading yardstick of the Festival, the city has a lot to offer, especially in the realm of **performing arts** and **concerts**.

Nightclubs don't offer anything startlingly original, but they serve their purpose, hosting a changing selection of one-nighters. While you can normally hear **live jazz**, **folk** and **rock** every evening in one or other of the city's pubs, for the really big rock events, ad hoc venues – such as the Castle Esplanade, Meadowbank Stadium or the exhibition halls of the Royal Highland Show at Ingliston – are often used.

With an estimated homosexual population of around 15,000–20,000, Edinburgh has a dynamic **gay** culture, for years centred on the area Calton Hill and the top of Leith Walk (p.79). The first gay and lesbian centre appeared in Broughton Street in the 1970s. Since the start of the 1990s, more and more gay enterprises, especially cafés and nightclubs, have moved into this area, now dubbed the "Broughton triangle", and there is a constant stream of new places and old ones changing name. In our listings "mixed" refers to a gay/lesbian crowd.

The best way to find out **what's on** is to pick up a copy of *The List*, a fortnightly listings magazine covering both Edinburgh and Glasgow (£1.50). Alternatively, get hold of the *Edinburgh Evening News*, which appears daily except Sunday: its listings column gives details of performances in the city that day, hotels and bars included. **Tickets** and information on all events are available from the tourist office. Box offices of individual halls and theatres are likewise liberally supplied with promotional leaflets, and some are able to sell tickets for more than one venue.

Nightclubs

La Belle Angèle, 11 Hasties Close (☎225 2774). A rotating selection of Latin, soul, hip-hop and jazz.

The New Calton, 24 Calton Rd (☎228 3252). Popular nightclub with regular gay night on Sat.

The Cavendish, W Tollcross. Packed out roots, ragga and reggae night on Fri; "The Mambo" on Sat plays African and Latin rhythms.

Century 2000, 31 Lothian Rd (☎229 7670). Big dance-round-a-hangbag club, converted from a cinema. Open till 3am.

The Citrus, 40–42 Grindlay St (☎229 6697). Eighties indie music along with some funk and disco.

The Cooler, 15 Calton Rd (☎557 3073). Small, intimate sweaty club popular with up-and-coming indie bands. Also used for a variety of hip one-nighters specializing in house, funk and reggae.

Moray House Student Union, Holyrood Rd (☎556 5184). Popular Sat club nights ranging from 1970s funk to wistful indie.

Red Hot Pepper Club, 3 Semple St (☎229 7733) Large disco with mainstream music; students free. Open till 2am.

Rocking Horse, Cowgate (☎225 7733). Rock nights from heavy metal to goth-rock and grunge.

The Venue, 15 Calton Rd, (☎557 3073). Small, intimate sweaty club popular with up-and-coming indie bands. Also good for a variety of one-nighters specializing in house, funk and garage.

The Vaults, 15–17 Niddry St (☎556 0001). Currently the city's most popular night club, with the emphasis on the ever-burgeoning dance music scene.

Wide Awake Club, 11 Cowgate (☎226 2151). Popular with students. More mainstream rave than hardcore, plus chart music and soul/funk nights. Open till 4am.

Gay clubs and bars

Blue Moon Café/Over the Moon Brasserie, 1 Barony St & 36 Broughton St (☎556 2788). Burgers and salads, coffees and beer. Very mixed crowd. Open 9–1am. Champagne breakfast £4.95.

CC Bloom's, 23 Greenside Place (☎556 9331). Big dance floor, stonking rhythms. Mixed friendly crowd.

Eat Out, 60 Broughton St (☎556 0512). Newly opened café at the Edinburgh *Gay, Lesbian and Bisexual Centre*. Open 11am–1pm.

Kudos, 22 Greenside Place. For the smart young crowd. Mixed clientèle.

New Town Club Bar, 26 Dublin St (☎538 7775). Eclectic male crowd, high number of professionals: raunchy *Jailhouse* bar downstairs.

Picardy's, 2 Picardy Place (☎556 0499). Opened August 1995 with the *LADS* (*Leather and Denim Scotland*) bar in the basement.

Route 66, 6 Baxter's Place. Friendly and relaxed bar located in the heart of the "Broughton Triangle". Mostly male.

Live music pubs and venues

La Belle Angèle, 11 Hasties Close (☎225 2774). A home to both indie bands and Latin divas.

Café Royal, 17 W Register St (☎.556 4124). Regular folk nights upstairs in one of the city's most famous bars.

Cas Rock Café, 104 W Port (☎229 4341). A mixture of sedate folk during the week and raucous punky sounds at the weekends.

Negociants, 45–47 Lothian St (☎225 6313). Upstairs brasserie serves breakfast and lunch, plus Belgian fruit beers alongside more conventional booze. Downstairs bar hosts varied live bands. Popular with students. Open until 1am.

The Music Box, 9c Victoria St (☎225 2564). Good size and popular, used by visiting indie and local R & B bands.

Nobles Bar, 44a Constitution St, Leith (☎553 3873). A standard of the local jazz scene, featuring live sessions 6 days a week in lovely Victorian pub with leaded glass windows and horseshoe bar. All-day Sunday breakfasts.

EDINBURGH'S OTHER FESTIVALS

Quite apart from the Edinburgh Festival, the city is now promoting itself as a year-round festival city, beginning with a **Hogmanay Festival** (☎557 3990) which involves street parties, folk and rock concerts and drive-in cinema shows. The **Folk Festival** (☎556 3181) in April draws local and international performers, while the **Science Festival** (☎557 4296) in April incorporates hands-on children's events as well as numerous lectures on a vast array of subjects. There is a **Puppet and Animation Festival** (☎556 9579) in March, and a **Children's Festival** (☎554 6297) in May with readings, magicians et cetera. In the summer, a series of concerts (usually free), ranging from tea dances to World Music, is held in the **Ross Bandstand** in Princes Street Gardens. The *Caledonian Brewery*, 42 Slateford Rd, runs its own German-style **beer festival** in June; the **Edinburgh Traditional Beer Festival**, with real ales from all over Britain, is held at Meadowbank Sports Stadium in October.

The **Open Doors Day**, around mid-September, provides an opportunity to visit a number of noteworthy buildings, otherwise closed to the public. In recent years, these have included private homes in the New Town, disused churches and company offices. Contact the **Cockburn Association** (☎557 8686) for details. The **Filmhouse** (☎228 2688) also has a number of annual seasons of international cinema, notably French (in November) and Italian (April), and a gay season (June).

Platform 1, Rutland St (☎225 2433). Young, loud and fashionable venue with comfortable downstairs bar. Live music in the basement. Open till 2am.

The Queen's Hall, 37 Clerk St (☎668 3456). Housed in a former Southside church, with some pews still in place, hosting African, funk and rock bands, as well as smaller jazz, folk concerts and comedy nights with well-established comedians.

Tron Ceilidh House, 9 Hunter Square (☎220 1500). Busy huge complex of bars on different levels, with regular jazz and folk nights.

Theatre and comedy

Assembly Rooms, 54 George St (☎220 4348). Varied complex of small and large halls. Used all year, but really comes into its own during the Fringe, with large-scale drama productions and mainstream comedy.

Bedlam Theatre, 2a Forrest Rd (☎225 9893). Used predominantly by student groups and housed in a converted Victorian church.

Festival Theatre, Nicholson St (☎529 6000). Everything from the children's show *Singing Kettle* to Engelbert Humperdinck and *La Traviata*.

Gilded Balloon Theatre, 233 Cowgate (☎226 6550). Fringe festival comedy venue, noted for the Late 'n' Live (1–4am) slot which gives you the chance to see top comedians whose main show elsewhere may be booked out.

King's Theatre, 2 Leven St (☎229 1201). Stately Edwardian civic theatre that offers the most eclectic programme in the city: includes opera, ballet, Shakespeare, pantomime and comedy.

Netherbow Arts Centre, 43 High St (☎556 9579). Although the centre is run by the Church of Scotland, the emphasis in their adventurous year-round drama productions is more Scottish than religious.

Playhouse Theatre, 18–22 Greenside Place (☎557 2590). The most capacious theatre in Britain, formerly a cinema. Recently refurbished, now used for extended runs of popular musicals and occasional rock concerts.

Pleasance Theatre, 60 The Pleasance (☎556 6550). Fringe festival venue. Cobbled courtyard with stunning views across to Arthur's Seat and an array of auditoria used for a varied programme.

Royal Lyceum Theatre, 30 Grindlay St (☎229 9697). Fine Victorian civic theatre with compact auditorium. The city's leading year-round venue for mainstream drama.

St Bride's Centre, 10 Orwell Terrace (☎346 1405). Neo-Gothic church converted into an intimate stage that can be adapted for theatre in the round.

Theatre Workshop, 34 Hamilton Place (☎226 5425). Enticing programmes of international innovative theatre and performance art all year.

Traverse Theatre, 10 Cambridge St (☎228 1404). A byword in experimental theatrical circles, and unquestionably one of Britain's premier venues for new plays. Going from strength to strength in its new custom-built home beside the Usher Hall.

Concert halls

Queen's Hall, 89 Clerk St (☎668 2019). Converted Georgian church with a capacity of around 800, though many seats have little or no view of the platform. Home base of both the Scottish Chamber Orchestra and Scottish Ensemble, and much favoured by jazz, blues and folk groups. Also hosts established comedians during the Fringe.

Reid Concert Hall, Bristo Square (☎650 4367). Narrow, steeply pitched Victorian hall owned by the university.

St Cecilia's Hall, corner of Cowgate & Niddry St (☎650 2805). A Georgian treasure that is again university-owned and not used as frequently as it deserves to be.

Usher Hall, corner of Lothian Rd & Grindlay St (☎228 1155). Edinburgh's main civic concert hall, seating over 2500. Excellent for choral and symphony concerts, but less apt for solo vocalists. The upper circle seats are cheapest and have the best acoustics; avoid the back of the grand tier and the stalls, where the sound is muffled by the overhanging balconies.

Cinemas

Cameo, 38 Home St (☎228 4141). New arthouse releases and cult late nighters.

Dominion, 18 Newbattle Terrace (☎447 4771). Latest releases.

Filmhouse, 88 Lothian Rd (☎228 2688). Eclectic programme of independent, arthouse and classic films.

MGM, Lothian Rd (☎228 1638). Mainstream cinema.

Odeon, 7 Clerk St (☎667 7331). Five-screen cinema showing latest releases.

UCI, Kinnaird Park (☎669 0777). Multiplex in the southeast of the city.

Shopping

Despite the relentless advance of the big chains, central Edinburgh remains an enticing place for **shopping**, with many of its streets having their own distinctive character. **Princes Street**, though dominated by standard chain outlets, retains a number of independent emporia. At the eastern end is the **Waverley Market**, a glossy mall of specialist shops, while the middle section of **Rose Street** has a good array of small jewellers and trendy clothes shops. Along the **Royal Mile** there are several distinctly offbeat places among the tacky souvenir sellers, and in and around **Grassmarket** you'll find antique and arts and crafts shops plus some antiquarian booksellers. The main concentration of general, academic and remainder bookshops is in the area stretching from **South Bridge** to **George IV Bridge**. For antique shops the two best areas are **St Stephen Street** in Stockbridge and **Causewayside** in Southside.

Bagpipes *Bagpipe Centre*, 49 Blackfriars St (☎557 3090); *Clan Bagpipes*, 13a James Court, Lawnmarket (☎225 2415).

Books *Bauermeisters*, 19 George IV Bridge (☎226 5561) is a row of separate shops (general and academic, music and stationery, paperbacks). *James Thin*, 53–59 South Bridge (☎556 6743) and 57 George St (☎225 4495); the first is a huge, rambling general and academic shop; the second smaller and more genteel, with a good café. *Waterstones* are at 128 Princes St (☎226 2666), 13–14 Princes St (☎556 3034) and 83 George St (☎225 3436); all host regular literary events. There is a good selection of antiquarian bookshops in the city: *Peter Bell*, 68 West Port (☎229 0562); *Castle Books*, 204 Canongate (☎556 0624); *Tolbooth Books*, 175 Canongate (☎558 3411); *West Port Books*, 151 West Port (☎229 4431); also *McNaughton's Bookshop* 3a–4a Haddington Place, Leith Walk (☎556 5897). The best of the second-hand bookshops are: *Broughton Books*, 2A Broughton Place (☎557 8010); *Second Edition*, 9 Howard Place (☎556 9403).

Clothes (second-hand) *Anna's*, 2a Tarvit St (☎229 9126); *Wm. Armstrong*, 313 Cowgate (☎556 6521); *Flip*, 59–61 South Bridge (☎556 4966); *Herman Brown*, 2a East Fountainbridge; *Paddy Barass*, 15 Grassmarket (☎226 3087); *55 St Stephen Street* (no phone).

Haggis *Charles MacSween & Son*, 130 Bruntsfield Place (☎229 1216), has an international reputation. Also makes a tasty vegetarian alternative.

Maps *Carson Clark*, 173 Canongate (☎556 4710), has wonderful antique maps, charts and globes.

Records *Avalanche*, 17 West Nicholson St (☎668 2374) and 28 Lady Lawson St (☎228 1939); for Indie music *Fopp*, 55 Cockburn St (☎220 0133), has a pleasingly large selection of vinyl; *Ripping Records*, 91 South Bridge (☎226 7010), also a booking agent; *Vinyl Villians*, 5 Elm Row (☎558 1170) stocks second-hand records, tapes, and ephemera.

Tartan *Kinloch Anderson*, corner of Commercial St and Dock St, Leith (☎555 1390). *James Pringle Woollen Mill*, 70 Bangor Rd, Leith (☎553 5161), has an archive computer which tells you if you're entitled to wear a clan tartan, and will give full historic information. *Geoffrey (Tailor)*, 57–59 High St (☎557 0256) and *Celtic Craft Centre*, 101 High St (☎556 3228) are two of many similar places on the Royal Mile.

Tweed *Romanes and Paterson*, 62 Princes St (☎225 4966) has tweeds, tartans and woollens.

Whisky *Royal Mile Whiskies*, 379–381 High St (☎225 3383); *William Cadenhead*, 172 Canongate (☎556 5864).

Woollen goods *Bill Baber Knitwear*, 66 Grassmarket (☎225 3249) designs and makes the garments on the premises; *Ragamuffin*, 276 Canongate (☎557 6007) for Skye knitwear; *The Shetland Connection*, 491 Lawnmarket (☎225 3525) and *Simply Shetland*, 9 West Port (☎228 4578) for Shetland knitting wool, lace and cobweb.

Listings

Airlines *British Airways*, 32 Frederick St (☎0345 222111). Other carriers handled by *Servisair*, Edinburgh Airport (☎344 3111).

American Express, 139 Princes St (Mon–Fri 9am–5.30pm, Sat 9am–4pm; July–Sept also Sun 10am–4pm; ☎225 9179).

Banks *Bank of Scotland*, The Mound (head office), 38 St Andrew Square, 141 Princes St; *Barclays*, 1 St Andrew Square; *Clydesdale*, 29 George St; *Lloyds*, 113–115 George St; *Midland*, 76 Hanover St; *NatWest*, 80 George St; *Royal Bank of Scotland*, 42 St Andrew Square (head office), 14 George St, 142–144 Princes St, 31 North Bridge; *TSB*, 28 Hanover St.

Car rental *Arnold Clark*, Lochrin Place (☎228 4747); *Avis*, 100 Dalry Rd (☎337 6363); *Budget*, 111 Glasgow Rd (☎334 7740); *Carnies*, 46 Westfield Rd (☎346 4155); *Europcar*, 24 E London St (☎557 3456); *Hertz*, Waverley Station (☎557 5272); *Mitchells*, 32 Torphichen St (☎229 5384); *Thrifty Car Rental*, 24 Haymarket Terrace (☎313 1613).

Consulates *Australia*, 25 Bernard St (☎555 4500); *Belgium*, 19 Ainslie Place (☎226 6881); *Denmark*, 4 Royal Terrace (☎556 4043); *France*, 11 Randolph Crescent (☎225 7954); *Germany*, 16 Eglington Crescent (☎337 2323); *Italy*, 32 Melville St (☎226 3631); *Netherlands*, 53 George St (☎220 3226); *Norway*, 86 George St (☎226 5701); *Poland*, 2 Kinnear Rd (☎552 0301); *Spain*, 63 N Castle St (☎220 1843); *Sweden*, 6 St John's Place (☎554 6631); *Switzerland*, 66 Hanover Place (☎226 5660); *USA*, 3 Regent Terrace (☎556 8315).

Exchange *Thomas Cook*, 79a Princes St (Mon–Fri 9am–5.30pm, Sat 9am–5pm; ☎220 4039); currency exchange bureaux in the main tourist office (Mon–Sat 9am–8pm, Sun 10am–8pm) and in the accommodation office at Waverley Station (see "Arrival and Accommodation"). To change money after hours, try one of the swanky hotels – but expect to pay a hefty commission charge.

Football Edinburgh has two Scottish Premier Division teams, who are at home on alternate Saturdays. *Heart of Midlothian* (or *Hearts*) play at *Tynecastle Stadium*, Gorgie Rd, a couple of miles west of the centre; *Hibernian* (or *Hibs*) play at *Easter Road Stadium*, a similar distance east of the centre. Between them, the two clubs dominated Scottish football in the 1950s, but neither has won more than the odd trophy since, though one or the other periodically threatens to make a major breakthrough. Tickets from £10.

Gay and lesbian contacts *Gay Scotland*, 58a Broughton St (☎557 2625); *Gay Switchboard* (☎556 4049); *Lesbian Line* (☎557 0751).

Genealogical research *Scots Ancestry Research Society*, 29a Albany St (☎556 4220); *Scottish Geneaology Society*, 15 Victoria Terrace (☎220 3677); *Scottish Roots*, 57–59 High St (☎557 6550).

Golf Edinburgh is awash with fine golf courses, but most of them are private. The best public courses are the 2 on the *Braid Hills* (☎447 6666); others are *Carrick Knowe* (☎337 1096), *Craigentinny* (☎554 7501) and *Silverknowes* (☎336 3843).

Hospital 24hr casualty department at the *Royal Infirmary*, 1 Lauriston Place (☎229 2477).

Left luggage Lockers available at Waverley Station and St Andrew Square bus station.

Libraries *Central Library*, George IV Bridge (Mon–Fri 9am–9pm, Sat 9am–1pm; ☎225 5584). In addition to the usual departments, there's a separate Scottish section, plus an Edinburgh Room which is a mine of information on the city. *National Library of Scotland*, George IV Bridge (Mon–Fri 9.30am–8.30pm, Sat 9.30am–1pm; ☎226 4531) is for research purposes only, though there are no formalities at its *Map Room*, 33 Salisbury Place (Mon–Fri 9.30am–5pm, Sat 9.30am–1pm).

Motoring organizations *AA*, 18–22 Melville St (☎225 3301); *RAC*, 35 Kinnaird Park (657 3444).

Pharmacy *Boots*, 48 Shandwick Place (Mon–Sat 8.45am–9pm, Sun 11am–4pm; ☎225 6757).

Post office 2–4 Waterloo Place (Mon–Fri 9.30am–5.30pm, Sat 9.30am–12.30pm; ☎550 8232).

Rape crisis centre ☎556 9437.

Rugby Scotland's international fixtures are played at *Murrayfield Stadium*, a couple of miles west of the city centre. Casual visitors will find tickets very hard to come by.

Sports stadium *Meadowbank Sports Centre and Stadium*, 139 London Rd (☎661 5351), is Edinburgh's main venue for most spectator and participatory sports. Facilities include an athletics track, a velodrome, and indoor halls.

Swimming pools The city has one olympic-standard modern pool, *The Royal Commonwealth Pool*, 21 Dalkeith Rd (☎667 7277), and a number of considerably older pools: Glenogle Rd (☎343 6376); 10 Infirmary St (☎557 3973); 15 Bellfield St, Portobello (☎669 4077); 6 Thirlestane Rd (☎447 0052).

Travel agents *Campus Travel* (student and youth specialist), 53 Forrest Rd (☎225 6111) and 5 Nicolson Square (☎225 6111); *Edinburgh Travel Centre* (student and youth specialist), 196 Rose St (☎668 3303), 92 S Clerk St (☎667 9488) and 3 Bristo Square (☎668 2221).

travel details

Trains

Edinburgh to: Aberdeen (hourly; 2hr 40min); Aviemore (5 daily; 3hr); Birmingham (6 daily; 5hr 30min); Crewe (6 daily; 3hr 30min); Dundee (hourly; 1hr 45min); Fort William (change at Glasgow; 3 daily; 4hr 55min); Glasgow (38 daily; 50min); Inverness (4 direct; 3hr 50min); London (20 daily; 4 hr 30min); Manchester (4 daily direct; 4hr; 7 daily, change at Preston 4hr); Newcastle upon Tyne (19 daily; 1hr 30min); Oban (3 daily, change at Glasgow; 4hr 10min); Perth (6 daily; 1hr 15min); Stirling (every 30min; 45min); York (20 daily; 2hr 30min).

Buses

Edinburgh St Andrew Square bus station to: Aberdeen (13 daily; express 3hr, standard 3hr 50min); Birmingham (2 daily; 6hr 50min); Campbeltown (3 daily; 6hr); Dundee (14 daily; express 1hr 25min, standard 2hr); Fort William (3 daily; 5hr); Glasgow (44 daily; 1hr 10min); Inverness (11 daily; express 3hr, standard 4hr); London (2 daily; 7hr 50min); Newcastle upon Tyne (3 daily; 3hr 15min); Oban (3 daily; 5hr); Perth (14 daily; 1hr 20min); Pitlochry (11 daily; 2hr); York (1 daily; 5hr).

Flights

Edinburgh to: Birmingham (Mon–Fri 7 daily, Sat & Sun 4 daily; 1hr); Dundee (Mon–Fri 2 daily; 15min); Manchester (Mon–Fri 3 daily; 50min); London (Gatwick Mon–Fri 5 daily, Sat & Sun 3 daily; 1hr 15min; Heathrow Mon–Fri 20 daily Sat & Sun 15 daily; Stansted Mon–Fri 5 daily, Sat & Sun 2 daily).

CHAPTER TWO

SOUTHERN SCOTLAND

Although **southern Scotland** doesn't have the high tourist profile of other areas of the country, in many ways the region is at its very heart. Its inhabitants bore the brunt of long wars with the English, its farms have fed Scotland's cities since industrialization, and two of the country's literary icons, **Sir Walter Scott** and **Robbie Burns**, lived and died here. The main roads, the fast routes from northern England to Glasgow and Edinburgh, bypass the best of the region, but if you make an effort to get off the highways, there's plenty to see, from the ruins of medieval castles and abbeys to well-preserved market towns set within a wild, hilly countryside.

Geographically, southern Scotland is dominated by the **Southern Uplands** – a chain of bulging flat-peaked hills and weather-beaten moorland punctuated by narrow glens, fast-flowing rivers and blue-black lochs – extending south and west from an imaginary line drawn between Peebles and Jedburgh in central southern Scotland over to the Ayrshire coast. It's in the west, in **Galloway Forest Park**, that they are at their most dramatic, with peaks soaring over 2000ft, and criss-crossed by many popular **walking** trails.

North of the inhospitable Cheviot Hills, which straddle the border with England, a clutch of tiny towns in the **Tweed River Valley** – including delightful **Melrose** – form the nucleus of the Borders, inspiration for countless folkloric ballads telling of bloody battles with the English and clashes between the notorious warring families, the Border Reivers. East of **Kelso**, one of four abbeys founded on the Borders by the medieval Canmore kings, the Tweed Valley widens to form the Merse basin, an area of flat farmland that boasts a series of grand stately homes, principally **Floors Castle**, **Manderston**, **Paxton** and **Mellerstain House**. These feature the work of the Adam family – William, and two of his four sons, John and Robert, whose fine skills are also displayed at Ayr's **Culzean Castle**.

North of the Tweed, a narrow band of foothills – the **Pentland, Moorfoot** and **Lammermuir** ranges – forms the southern edge of the Central Lowlands. These Lowlands spread west beyond Edinburgh, but here they constitute the slender coastal plain of **East Lothian**, which rolls down towards a string of fine sandy beaches. Further east, the coastline becomes more rugged, its cliffs and rocky outcrops harbouring a series of ruined castles, and inland, the flatness of the terrain is interrupted by the occasional extinct volcano, inspiration for all sorts of ancient myths.

The gritty town of **Dumfries** is gateway to **southwest Scotland**, where on the marshy Solway coast you can visit charming **Kirkcudbright** and see the magnificent remains of **Caerlaverock Castle**. The **Ayrshire coast** also rewards a visit for its strong associations with Robert Burns, especially at Ayr and **Alloway**, the poet's birthplace, as well as for its pastoral coastline and sandy beaches.

There's a **train** line along both coasts, and a good **bus** service linking all the major towns and many of the villages. The region is also excellent **walking** country; for the ambitious hiker there's the **Southern Upland Way**, a 212-mile path stretching from Portpatrick on the west to Cockburnspath on the east coast. For the less dedicated, this is parcelled up into easy-to-handle sections – and all the major tourist offices have leaflets on the nearest stretch.

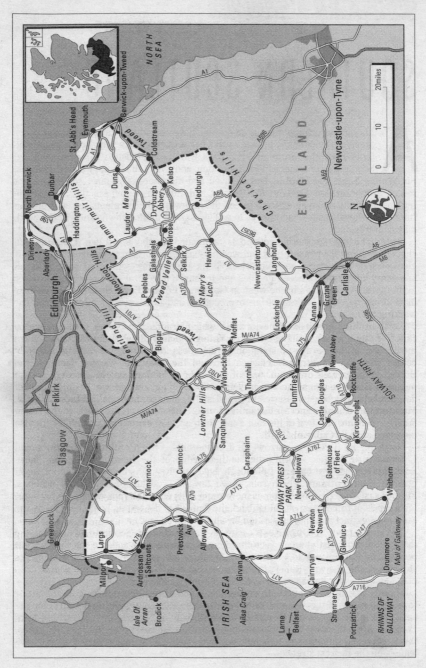

EAST LOTHIAN AND THE EASTERN BORDERS

East Lothian consists of the coastal strip and hinterland immediately east of Edinburgh. Its western reaches, around Musselburgh, are an easy day trip from the capital; the remainder takes a couple of overnight stays to explore. The prosperous market town of **Haddington** serves as a base for exploring the interior, whose bumpy farmland is bordered to the south by the Lammermuir Hills. But most people make a beeline for the shore, the 50 miles or so of coastline extending from **Aberlady** right round through the **Eastern Borders** to England's Berwick-upon-Tweed. There's something for most tastes here, from the sandy beaches and volcanic islets around the resort of **North Berwick** and neighbouring **Dirleton**, to the piercing cliffs of **St Abb's Head**, and a number of ruined medieval strongholds, the most dramatic at **Tantallon**. Inland, the **Lammermuir Hills** cross the boundary between East Lothian and the Borders to form the northern edge of the Merse, centring on modest **Duns**. Further south still, the busy Georgian town of **Kelso** is the key attraction of the **Lower Tweed Valley**.

Haddington and around

The East Lothian gentry keep a careful eye on **HADDINGTON**, their favourite country town. Its compact centre preserves an intriguing ensemble of seventeenth- to nineteenth-century architectural styles where everything of any interest has been labelled and plaqued. Yet the town's staid appearance belies an innovative past. During the early 1700s, Haddington became a byword for modernization as its merchants supplied the district's progressive landowners with all sorts of new-fangled equipment, stock and seed, and in only a few decades utterly transformed Lothian agriculture.

Haddington was also the birthplace of **John Knox**, the fiery sixteenth-century religious reformer who led the Protestant assault on Scotland's Catholic Church. He laid the foundations of the Presbyterian movement, but is mainly remembered for his two treatise of 1558 entitled *The First Blast of the Trumpet against the Monstruous Regiment of Women*: a specific attack on Mary of Guise, regent of Scotland; Mary, Queen of England; and Catherine de Medici. It didn't help him in his dealings with Queen Elizabeth I or Mary Stuart either (see p.64).

A thorough exploration of Haddington takes two or three hours. Afterwards, consider a visit to **Lennoxlove House**, one of the area's more accessible stately homes, or venture a few miles south to the hamlet of **Gifford**, on the edge of the Lammermuir Hills.

The Town

Haddington's centre is best approached from the west, where tree-trimmed **Court Street** ends suddenly with the soaring spire, stately stonework and dignified Venetian windows of the **Town House**, designed by William Adam in 1748. Close by, to the right and next door to a fine Italianate facade, the **Jane Welsh Carlyle House** (April–Sept Wed–Sat 2–5pm; £1) was the childhood home of the wife of essayist and historian Thomas Carlyle (see p.131). The dining room – the only part of the house open to the public – has been restored to its early nineteenth-century appearance and sports pictures of the influential personalities of the day. The lovely garden is pretty much as Jane would have known it too. Carrying straight on, **High Street** is distinguished by its pastel-painted gables and quaint pends, a tad prettier than those in neighbouring **Market Street**. Keep an eye open, however, for **Mitchell's Close** on Market Street, a recently restored seventeenth-century close with crow-stepped gables, rubble masonry and the narrowest of staircase towers.

Leaving the town centre to the east along High Street, it's a brief walk down Church Street – past the hooped arches of **Nungate Bridge** – to the hulking mass of **St Mary's Church** (daily 10am–4pm). Built close to the reedy River Tyne, the church dates from the fourteenth century, but it's a real hotch-potch of styles, the squat grey tower uneasy above clumsy buttressing and pinkish-ochre stone walls. Inside, on the **Lauderdale Aisle** a munificent tomb features the best of Elizabethan alabaster carving, moustached knights and their ruffed ladies lying beneath a finely ornamented canopy. In stark contrast, a plain slab nearby is inscribed with Thomas Carlyle's beautiful tribute to his wife, who died on April 21, 1866. Carlyle rounds the inscription off : "Suddenly snatched away from him, and the light of his life as if gone out". They had been married for 40 years.

Practicalities

Fast and frequent **buses** connect Haddington with Edinburgh, 15 miles to the west, and with North Berwick on the east coast. All services stop on High Street. There's no **tourist office**, but orientation is easy and *A Walk around Haddington* (£1), detailing every building of any conceivable consequence, is available from local newsagents.

If you decide to **stay** the night, there are several central **B&Bs**, including *Mrs Richards*, whose well-kept Georgian town house is at 19 Church St (☎01620/825663; ③), and the *Plough Tavern*, 11 Court St (☎01620/823326; ③). Alternatively, try the more pricy and luxurious *Brown's Hotel*, 1 West Rd (☎01620/822254; ⑧), which occupies a fine Regency town house. *Monks' Muir Caravan Park* (all year; ☎01620/860340), on the edge of town by the A1, also takes tents.

For **daytime snacks** and light lunches, *Simply Scrumptious*, next to the Town House, has an imaginative menu that outshines its main rival, the *Golden Grain* café, 13 High St. A third option is *Peter Potter*, attached to a craft shop at 10 The Sand, on the way to St Mary's. The best place for an **evening meal** is the *Waterside Bistro*, on the far side of Nungate Bridge; or try the *Brown's Hotel* restaurant, where you'll need to book.

Lennoxlove House and Gifford

One mile south of Haddington, **Lennoxlove House** (May–Sept Wed, Sat & Sun 2–5pm; £3), a sprawling pile incorporating a medieval tower house, boasts much of the fine and applied art collection of the Duke of Hamilton. The hour-long tour takes in the usual oligarchic trappings – portraits of the family and their allies, French furniture, fancy porcelain and damask wall hangings; more unusual is the death mask of Mary, Queen of Scots, in the Great Hall.

A further three miles south along the B6369 lies tiny **GIFFORD**, whose tidy, eighteenth-century estate cottages edge a trim whitewashed church. The Reverend John Witherspoon, a signatory of the American Declaration of Independence, was born in the adjacent manse in 1723. Several footpaths set out across the surrounding red-soiled farmland for the burns, laws and moors of the Lammermuir Hills. Longer trails connect with the Southern Upland Way (see p.115). Gifford has a brace of **hotels**: the garish *Goblin Ha'* (☎01620/810244; ⑤) and the more traditional *Tweeddale Arms* (☎01620/810240; ⑤).

The east coast to the Lammermuir Hills

Skirting the southern shore of the Firth of Forth before curving down along the North Sea coast, that 50-mile section of the **east coast** we've set apart from Edinburgh begins at **ABERLADY**, an elongated village just 16 miles from the capital. Aberlady served as Haddington's port until its river silted up in the sixteenth century, and the costly stained-glass windows of the honey-coloured stone medieval church act as a reminder of wealthier times. The salt marshes and sand dunes of the adjacent **Aberlady Bay Nature Reserve**, a bird-watchers' haven, mark the site of the old harbour. From the reserve, it's a couple of miles to the modern villas and hotels of **GULLANE**, a disappointing location for the famous shoreline links of **Muirfield Golf Course**.

Things improve two miles east of Gullane with the genteel hamlet of **DIRLETON**, where a pair of triangular greens are bordered by tastefully refurbished cottages with thriving gardens. **Dirleton Castle** (April–Sept Mon–Sat 9.30am–6pm, Sun 2–6pm; Oct–March Mon–Sat 9.30am–4pm, Sun 2–4pm; £1.70) has lovely gardens too, leading to a volcanic knoll crowned by the Cromwell-shattered ruins. Scrambling round the castle is fun, and if the weather's good, you can take the mile-long path from the village church to the sandy beach. Also near the beach, the *Yellowcraig Caravan Club Site* (April–Sept; ☎01620/850217) is the only budget place to **stay**; the splendid *Open Arms Hotel* opposite the castle (☎01620/850241; ⑨), on the other hand, has every luxury, including a fantastic restaurant serving moderate to expensive dinners from a varied and imaginative menu. Across the green, the *Castle Inn* (☎01620/850221; ④) falls somewhere in between.

North Berwick

NORTH BERWICK has an old-fashioned air, its guest houses and hotels extending along the shore in all their Victorian and Edwardian sobriety. Set within sight of two volcanic heaps – the **Bass Rock** and **North Berwick Law** – the resort's pair of wide and sandy **beaches** are the main attraction. These fall either side of a narrow headland harbour that's an extension of the short main street, Victoria Road, itself an extension of Quality Street.

Little now remains of the original medieval town, but the fragmentary ruins of the **Auld Kirk**, next to the harbour, bear witness to one of the most extraordinary events of sixteenth-century Scotland. In 1590, while **King James VI** spent the summer in Denmark wooing his prospective wife, Francis Stuart, **Earl of Bothwell**, was plotting against him. On hearing of the king's imminent return, Bothwell, a keen practitioner of the "black arts", summoned the witches of Lothian to meet the Devil in the Auld Kirk. Bothwell turned up disguised as the Devil and instructed his 200 acolytes to raise a storm that would shipwreck the king. To cast the spell, they opened a few graves and engaged in a little flagellation before kissing the bare buttocks of the "Devil" – reportedly "as cold as ice and as hard as iron" as it hung over the pulpit. Despite these shenanigans, the king returned safely – when rumours reached him of Bothwell's treachery he refused to believe them, and the earl went unpunished, possibly because James was reassured by his failure. After all, if the Devil himself was unable to harm him, he must surely be blessed by God, a belief the monarch was later to elaborate as the "Divine Right of Kings".

Bass Rock

Resembling a giant molar, the **Bass Rock** rises 350ft above the sea some three miles east of North Berwick. This massive chunk of basalt, formerly a prison, fortress and monastic retreat, is home to millions of nesting seabirds – among them razorbills, terns, puffins, guillemots, fulmars and gannets. Weather permitting, there are regular 90-minute **boat trips** round the island from North Berwick harbour (Easter to early Oct daily; £3.50), but only Fred Marr (daytime ☎01620/893863; evening ☎01620/892838) has landing rights: he charges £10 for an excursion that allows about four hours on the rock. It's not to everyone's taste – as William Dunbar, a fifteenth-century poet, described it:

> *The air was dirkit with the fowlis*
> *That cam with jammeris and with youlis*
> *With shrykking, shrieking, skyrmming scowlis*
> *And meikle noyis and showtes.*

North Berwick Law

The other volcanic monolith, 613ft-high **North Berwick Law**, is about an hour's walk from the beach (take Law Rd off High St and follow the signs). On a clear day, the views out across the Firth of Forth make the effort worthwhile, and at the top you can see the remains of a Napoleonic watchtower and an arch made from the jawbone of a whale.

Practicalities

It's ten minutes' walk east from North Berwick **train station**, with its frequent services from Edinburgh, to the town centre along Abbey Road, Westgate and High Street. **Buses** from Edinburgh stop on High Street and those from Haddington and Dunbar outside the **tourist office**, Quality St (mid-April to May Mon–Sat 9am–6pm; June–Sept Mon–Sat 9am–8pm, Sun 11am–6pm; Oct to mid-April Mon–Fri 9am–5pm; ☎01620/892197). Here you can buy town maps, and, for a £1 fee, arrange accommodation; particularly useful in the height of summer.

Several excellent **B&Bs** are open from April to September, including *Mrs Duns*, 20 Marmion Rd (☎01620/892066; ②) and *Mrs McQueen*, 5 W Bay Rd (☎01620/894576; ③). Out of season, try *Mrs Clelland*, 16 Marine Parade (☎01620/892879; ③); *Mrs Ralph*, 13 Westgate (☎01620/892782; ③); or *Mrs Gray*, 12 Marine Parade (☎01620/892884; ③). Alternatively, *Craigview*, 5 Beach Rd (☎01620/892257; ④) is a well-maintained **guest house**, and *Point Garry*, 20 W Bay Rd (April–Oct; ☎01620/892380; ⑦), an upmarket **hotel**. The nearest **campsite**, *Tantallon Rhodes Caravan Park* (April–Oct; ☎01620/893348), occupies a prime clifftop location a couple of miles east of the centre – take the Dunbar bus (Mon–Sat 6 daily, Sun 2 daily).

Several little cafés, such as the *Buttercup*, High St, sell cheap **food**, but for an evening meal, head for *Harding's*, 2 Station Rd, next to the train station (Wed–Sat only; ☎01620/894737), which serves good food and wine from a daily menu.

East of North Berwick

The melodramatic ruins of **Tantallon Castle** (April–Sept Mon–Sat 9.30am–6pm, Sun 2–6pm; Oct–March Mon–Wed & Sat 9.30am–4pm, Thurs 9.30am–noon, Sun 2–4pm; £2), three miles east of North Berwick, on the A198, stand on the precipitous cliffs facing the Bass Rock. This pinkish sandstone edifice, with its imposing cylindrical towers, protected the powerful "Red" Douglases, Earls of Angus, from their enemies for over 300 years. With a sheer drop down to the sea on three sides and a sequence of moats and ditches on the fourth, the castle's desolate invincibility is daunting, especially when the wind howls over the remaining battlements and the surf crashes on the rocks far below. In fact, the setting is more striking than the ruins: Cromwell's army savaged the castle in 1651 and only the impressive 50ft-high and 14ft-thick curtain wall has survived relatively intact. To reach Tantallon Castle from North Berwick, a 15-minute trip, take the Dunbar **bus** (Mon–Sat 6 daily, Sun 2 daily).

There's little to see at down-at-heel **DUNBAR**, 12 miles from North Berwick, though the wide High Street is graced by several grand old stone buildings and the double **harbour** remains a delightfully intricate affair of narrow channels, cobbled quays and roughened rocks, set beside the shattered remains of the once mighty castle. Incidentally, **John Muir**, the explorer and naturalist who created the United States national park system, was born in Dunbar, and his boyhood home, 126 High St, has been turned into a tiny **museum** (June–Sept Mon, Tues & Thurs–Sat 11am–1pm & 2–5.30pm, Sun 2–5.30pm, plus Wed in Aug; free).

Good **bus** and **train** connections mean there's no reason to get stuck here, but if you do the **tourist office**, 143 High St (mid-April to May Mon–Sat 9am–6pm; June–Sept Mon–Sat 9am–8pm, Sun 11am–6pm; Oct to mid-April Mon–Fri 9am–5pm; ☎01368/863353) will help with **accommodation**. Pleasant bay-windowed, *Overcliffe Guest House*, 11 Bayswell Park (☎01368/864004; ③), is just a short walk west from the castle. For food, try the *William Smith Coffee Shop*, High St, or *The Cromwell* pub and bistro beside the harbour.

St Abb's Head

Heading south from Dunbar, it's around seven miles to tiny Cockburnspath where the Southern Upland Way reaches its end about a mile from the coast – though there's now a five-mile extension which takes hikers from Cockburnspath square, underneath the A1 and down along the coast via Pease Bay, to **PENMANSHEIL**, back beside the A1. Nearby, the A1107 cuts off the main road for **ST ABBS**, a remote fishing village stuck onto the steepest of sea shores. Flanked by jagged cliffs, St Abbs has a dramatic setting, with a jangle of old fishermens' cottages tumbling down to the surf-battered harbour. The village is named after Ebba, a seventh century Northumbrian princess who struggled ashore here after being shipwrecked and, in the way of such things, promptly founded a nunnery. From the harbour, *St Abb's Marine Services* (☎01890/771412) operate sea angling, sub-aqua diving, birdwatching and regular sightseeing **boat trips** – all at reasonable prices. It's also an ideal base for visiting **St Abb's Head Nature Reserve**, reached from the tearoom and car park just half a mile back along the road. Owned by the NTS, this comprises 200 acres of wild and rugged coastline with sheer, seabird-encrusted cliffs rising 300ft above the water. The easy-to-follow walking trail ends at the lighthouse, a mile or so from the car park.

Twice daily the Edinburgh/Dunbar to Berwick-upon-Tweed **bus** passes through Coldringham on the A1107, where a **taxibus** service connects to St Abbs, a mile away down the B6438; connections are, however, only guaranteed for pre-booked passengers (Mon–Fri 9am–4pm; ☎01289/308719). Buses south from St Abbs to Eyemouth run hourly. There are just two places to **stay** in St Abbs, the excellent *Castle Rock Guest House*, Murrayfield (Easter–Oct; ☎01890/71298; ④): the Victorian manse whose spick-and-span bedrooms and gingerbread woodwork set out along the sea cliffs, and the **B&B** of *Wilma Wilson*, 7 Murrayfield (☎018907/71468; ②).

Coldringham itself is unremarkable, but a second minor road leaves here for the mile-long trip down to the coast at **COLDRINGHAM SANDS**. This pint-sized resort has a fine sandy beach and a **youth hostel** (April–Sept; ☎018907/71298; Grade 2). A large Victorian villa on a hill overlooking the sea shore, the hostel is popular with divers, walkers and birdwatchers alike. The B&B *Cul-Na-Sithe* (Feb–Nov; ☎01890/71565; ④) is nearby.

Eyemouth

Almost the entire 3500 population of **EYEMOUTH**, a few miles south of St Abbs, is dependent on the fishing industry. Consequently, the town's slender harbour is very much the focus of activity, its waters packed with deep sea and in-shore fleets and its quay strewn with tatters of old net, discarded fish and fish crates.

Eyemouth's tiny centre, to the west of the harbour, is drearily modern, despite the town's medieval foundation. But **The Eyemouth Museum**, in the Auld Kirk on the Market Place (April & May Mon–Sat 10am–5pm, Sun 2–4pm; June & Sept Mon–Sat 10am–5.30pm, Sun 2–4pm; July & Aug Mon–Sat 9.30am–6pm, Sun 1–5.30pm; Oct Mon–Sat 10am–12.30pm & 1.30–4.30pm; £1) is just about worth a visit for the **Eyemouth Tapestry**, a recent composition commemorating the east coast fishing disaster of 1881 when a freak storm destroyed most of the in-shore fleet: 129 local men were lost, a tragedy of extraordinary proportions for a place of this size. Nearby, along High Street, in the old **cemetery**, a stone memorial surmounted by a broken mast also pays tribute to the dead. Years before in 1849, the inhabitants had to raise the level of the cemetery by 6ft to cope with the victims of a cholera epidemic. However, the work was for nothing, as the site was soon abandoned (hence the lack of gravestones); but they did use the old tombstones to build the ghoulish **watch house** – a precaution against body-snatchers – which you can still see today.

The elegant **Gunsgreen House**, standing alone on the far side of the harbour, was designed by James Adam (one of the famous family of architects) in the 1750s. Despite its respectable appearance – in keeping with its present use by the golf club – the house was once used by smugglers, with secret passages and underground tunnels leading back into town. This illicit trade in tobacco and booze peaked in the late eighteenth century, with local fishermen using their knowledge of the coast to regularly outwit the excise.

In the unlikely event you'll want to **stay** overnight, the **tourist office**, also in the Auld Kirk (April–Oct same hours as the museum; ☎018907/50678) can recommend a small cache of **B&Bs**. Or you could try *Mrs Aitchison*, Coldringham Rd (April–Oct; ☎018907/50361; ③). Leaving town, regular **bus** services run north along the coast and south across the border to Berwick-upon-Tweed, eight miles away.

Duns

Heading inland from Eyemouth, the B6355 and then the A6105 cross the fertile farmland of the Merse to the little-visited market town of **DUNS**. Jim Clark, the farmer-turned-motor-racing ace, was born here and the **Jim Clark Room**, 44 Newtown St (Easter–Oct Mon–Sat 10am–1pm & 2–5pm, Sun 2–5pm; £1), celebrates a brilliant career that ended with his death on the track at Hockenheim in Germany in 1968. There's little else to do in Duns, but it's only a 20-minute walk to the top of **Duns Law** (take North Castle St and follow the signs). Most people make the trek up to the 714ft-high summit for the view, some to see the **Covenanters' Stone**, marking the spot where Alexander Leslie's army camped in 1639. Leslie assembled his troops on the Law to watch for Charles I's mercenaries, who had been sent north to crush the Covenanters. In the event, the royalist army faded away without even forcing a battle, and the king, by refusing to accept defeat, took one more step towards the Civil War.

Duns is well connected by **bus** to all the major settlements of the east Borders, so you don't have to stay the night. However, the town does have half a dozen **B&Bs**, such as the central *St Albans*, Clouds (☎01361/883285; ③). For a **drink** and a snack, try the *Whip and Saddle* pub in Market Square.

Manderston House

Manderston House (May–Sept Thurs & Sun 2–5.30pm; £4), two miles east of Duns on the A6105, is the very embodiment of Edwardian Britain. Between 1871 and 1905, the Miller family spent most of their herring and hemp fortune on turning their home into a prestigious country house, with no expense spared as architect John Kinross added entire suites of rooms in the Classical Revival style. It's certainly a staggering sight, from the intricate plasterwork ceilings to the inlaid marble floor in the hall and the extravagant silver staircase, the whole lot sumptuously furnished with trappings worthy of a new member of the aristocracy: James Miller married Eveline Curzon, the daughter of Lord Scarsdale, in 1893. When you've finished inside the house, stroll round the 50 acres or so of garden, noted for their rhododendrons and azaleas.

The Lammermuir Hills and Lauder

Leaving Duns to the north, it's about three miles to the edge of the **Lammermuir Hills**, a slender, east–west chain whose flat-topped summits and quiet streams are a favourite haunt of ramblers. The hills are criss-crossed with footpaths, some of which follow ancient carting and droving trails as they slice from north to south. In the other direction, tracking along the body of the Lammermuirs between Lauder in the west and Cockburnspath on the coast, is the Southern Upland Way. If you're keen to sample a portion, leave Duns on the A6112, turn left along the B6355 and then follow the minor road to Abbey St Bathans, a hamlet beside the Whiteadder Water, where a pretty and undemanding ten-mile stretch of the trail leads down to the sea. The tiny Abbey St Bathans **youth hostel** (☎01361/840245; Grade 2) is open all year. Alternatively, you could carry on up to East Lothian's Gifford (see p.111), some 20 miles from Duns on the other side of the Lammermuirs.

It is also easy to join the Southern Upland Way on the western edge of the Lammermuir Hills in **LAUDER**, a grey market town 20 miles west of Duns on the A68. Lauder's only attraction is **Thirlestane Castle** (May, June & Sept Mon, Wed, Thurs & Sun 2–5pm; July & Aug Mon–Fri & Sun 2–5pm; £3.50), an imposing pile on the eastern edge of town: the main entrance is half a mile south of Lauder, but pedestrians can take the signposted footpath from The Avenue, effectively the main square about halfway along High Street. Owned by the Maitland family since the sixteenth century, the castle has been refashioned and remodelled on several occasions, but its impressive reddish turrets and castellated towers appear as a cohesive whole nevertheless. The interior is disappointing, with little to see beyond the delicate plasterwork of the Restoration ceilings: most of the original furnishings were carted off to London in the 1840s to be replaced by inferior Victoriana.

The Lower Tweed Valley

Rising in the hills far to the west, the River Tweed snakes its way across the Borders until it reaches the North Sea at Berwick-upon-Tweed. The eastern reaches of the river, constituting the **Lower Tweed Valley**, run from Kelso to the coast and for the most part form the boundary between Scotland and England. This is a gentle, rural landscape of farmland and wooded river banks where the occasional military ruin, usually on the south side of the border, serves as a reminder of more violent days. For the English, the east Borders were the quickest land route to the centre of Scotland and time and again they launched themselves north destroying everything in their way. Indeed, the English turned Berwick-upon-Tweed into one of the most heavily guarded frontier towns in northern Europe, and the massive fortifications survive today. The region also witnessed one of the most devastating of medieval battles when the Scots, under James IV, were decimated at **Flodden Field** in 1513. The heavily armoured Scottish noblemen got stuck in the mud at the bottom of a hill near Branxton, south of the border near Coldstream, and their over-long pikes and lances were simply no match for the shorter and sturdier English halberds.

Nowadays, the Lower Tweed Valley has one town of note, **Kelso**, a busy agricultural centre distinguished by the Georgian elegance of its main square and its proximity Floors Castle (also Mellerstain House; see p.122). Perhaps surprisingly, Kelso is often visited for its abbey, even though the ruins of the colossal twelfth-century foundation, whose abbots claimed precedence over St Andrews, are scant indeed. Further downstream, close to Berwick-upon-Tweed, is the district's other main attraction, the Georgian **Paxton House**.

Paxton House

Built for Patrick Home in the middle of the eighteenth century, Paxton House (mid-April to Oct daily noon–5pm; £3.50), some five miles west of Berwick-upon-Tweed along the B6461, was the last act of a would-be matrimonial fiasco. Resident in Germany, the young Scot had been a great success at the court of Frederick the Great, even seducing the king's only daughter, Charlotte de Brandt. The affair became public and Home was forced to leave Berlin, but not before the lovers "plighted their troth". Back in Scotland, Home built Paxton for his putative bride, but she never appeared – much to Frederick's dynastic satisfaction.

The building, designed by John and James Adam, is a grand neo-Palladian mansion, with a carefully contrived facade focused on the main house, whose imposing centrepiece comprises temple-like columns rising two storeys to an equally impressive pediment. This geometrical simplicity is continued inside, where a particular highlight of the guided tour is the contrast between John and James' Rococo and their more famous brother Robert's Neoclassical plasterwork. Also on display is a stunning collection of Chippendale and Regency rosewood furniture. Finally, the expansive **Picture Gallery**, completed in the 1810s, blends aspects of earlier Neoclassicism into a more austere design, with most of the plasterwork moulded to look like masonry. The National Gallery of Scotland uses this room as an outstation, exhibiting part of its collection here (changes frequently; mostly lesser works).

The grounds (April–Oct 10am–sunset), 80 acres of mixed parkland and woodland abutting the Tweed, boast gentle footpaths and a brand new salmon-fishing museum.

Coldstream

Battered and bruised by traffic, tiny **COLDSTREAM** sits tight against the Tweed, its long High Street part of the trunk road linking Newcastle across the border and Edinburgh. The town's only claim to fame is its association with the **Coldstream Guards**. General George Monck billeted his Cromwellian soldiers here in the winter of 1659–60, just before they were persuaded to discard their parliamentary allegiance and march on London to restore Charles II to the throne. Monck's regiment was thereafter recognized as the "Coldstream Guards" and the general became the first Duke of Albemarle – a handsome payoff for his timely change of heart. Oddly enough, in the sort of detail beloved of military historians, the Coldstreamers still sport the crownless tunic buttons they first wore as part of Cromwell's Model Army. The regiment's deeds are recorded in the **Coldstream Museum** (Easter–Oct Mon–Sat 10am–5pm, Sun 2–5pm; £1), on the attractively old-fashioned (and traffic-free) Market Square, just off High Street. The huge obelisk at the east end of town is dedicated to an obscure nineteenth-century MP, a certain Charles Marjoribanks.

Practicalities

Coldstream's **tourist office**, about halfway down High St (April–June & Sept Mon–Sat 10am–5pm, Sun 10am–1pm; July & Aug Mon–Sat 10am–6pm, Sun 10am–2pm; Oct Mon–Sat 10am–12.30pm & 1.30–4.30pm; ☎01890/882607), has a comprehensive supply of brochures and booklets on the Borders as well as a brief list of local B&Bs. The best of these is the trimly kept *Atterdale*, just off Market Square at 1 Leet St (01890/883047; ②). The *Castle Hotel*, 11 High St, offers substantial and reasonably priced **meals**; for a **drink**, the *Besom Inn*, next to the tourist office, is a cosy pub decked out with all sorts of military mementos.

Kelso and around

Compact **KELSO**, at the confluence of the Tweed and Teviot, grew up in the shadow of its abbey, once the richest and most powerful in Southern Scotland. The abbey was founded in 1128 during the reign of King David (1124–53), whose policy of encouraging the monastic orders had little to do with spirituality. The bishops and monks David established here, as well as at Melrose, Jedburgh and Dryburgh, were the frontiersmen of his kingdom, helping to advance his authority in areas of doubtful allegiance. This began a long period of relative stability across the region which enabled its abbeys to flourish, until frequent raids by the English, who savaged Kelso three times in the early sixteenth century (in 1522, 1544 and 1545) brought ruin. The last assault – part of the "Rough Wooing" led by the Earl of Hertford when the Scots refused to ratify a marriage treaty between Henry VIII's son and the infant Mary Stuart – was the worst. Such was the extent of the devastation – compounded by the Reformation – that the surviving ruins of **Kelso Abbey** (April–Dec Mon–Sat daylight hours, Sun afternoons; Jan–March ask for key at the tourist office; free) are disappointing: a heavy central tower and supporting buttresses represent a scant memorial to the massive Romanesque original that took over 80 years to build. Just behind the abbey, notice the Old Parish Church, constructed in 1773 to an octagonal design that excited universal execration. "It is", wrote one contemporary, "a misshapen pile, the ugliest Parish Church in Scotland, but it is an excellent model for a circus."

From the abbey, it's a couple of minutes' walk along Bridge Street to **The Square**, a cobbled expanse where the columns and pediments of the **Town Hall** are flanked by a splendid ensemble of three-storey eighteenth- and nineteenth-century pastel buildings. Beyond the general air of elegance, though, there's little to actually see.

Kelso has one other diversion. Leaving The Square along Roxburgh Street, take the alley down to the **Cobby Riverside Walk**, where a brief stroll leads to Floors Castle. En route, but hidden from view by the islet in the middle of the river, is the spot where the Teviot meets the Tweed. This junction has long been famous for its salmon fishing, with permits booked years in advance irrespective of the cost: currently around £5000 per rod per week. Permits for fishing other (less expensive) reaches of the Tweed and Teviot are available from *Tweeside Fishing Tackle*, 36 Bridge St (☎01573/225306). Details of last-minute fishing lets are also on ☎0891/666412; fishing catches and prospects ☎0891/666410.

Floors Castle

There's nothing medieval about **Floors Castle** (May–Aug daily 10.30am–5.30pm; Sept Sun–Thurs 10.30am–5.30pm; Oct Wed & Sun 10.30am–4.30pm; £3.80), a vast castellated mansion overlooking the Tweed about a mile northwest of Kelso. The bulk of the building was designed by William Adam in the 1720s, and, picking through the Victorian modifications, much of the interior demonstrates his uncluttered style. Not that you'll see much of it: just ten rooms and a basement are open to the public. Highlights include Hendrick Danckert's splendid panorama of Horse Guards Parade in the entrance hall; the Brussels tapestries in the ante and drawing rooms; paintings by Augustus John and Henri Matisse in the Needle Room; and all sorts of snuff boxes and cigarette cases in the gallery.

Floors remain privately owned, the property of the tenth Duke of Roxburghe, whose arrogant features can be seen in a variety of portraits. The duke is a close friend of royalty: it was here, apparently, that Prince Andrew proposed to Sarah Ferguson in 1986.

Practicalities

With good connections to Coldstream in the east and Melrose and Jedburgh to the west, Kelso **bus station**, Roxburgh St, is a brief walk from The Square where you'll find the **tourist office** (April–June & Sept Mon–Sat 10am–5pm, Sun 10am–1pm; July & Aug Mon–Sat 9.30am–6.30pm, Sun 10.30–6pm; Oct Mon–Sat 10am–4.30pm, Sun 10am–1pm; ☎01573/223464).

The tourist office can provide you with a long list of **B&Bs**, three good choices being the convenient *Wester House*, 155 Roxburgh St (☎01573/224428; ③); the *Charlesfield*, a comfortable Victorian house a few minutes' walk north of The Square on Edenside Rd (☎01573/224583; ③); and, best of all, *Wooden* (May–Sept; 01573/224204; ④), an ivy-clad country house of 1824 that's set in its own grounds about half a mile east of Kelso on the B6350. If you ignore the modern extension, there's also one rather special **hotel**, *Ednam House*, on Bridge St, near The Square (☎01573/224168; ⑧), a splendid Georgian mansion, with antique furnishings and fittings, whose gardens abut the Tweed. Kirk Yetholm **youth hostel** (late March–Sept; ☎01573/420631; Grade 2) is on the edge of the Cheviot Hills about six miles southeast of town along the B6352. A bus service (3–6 daily; 20 min) runs from Kelso to the hostel, which is also at the north end of the Pennine Way, the long-distance walking route that travels the length of northern England. It's almost impossible to find anywhere to stay during Kelso's main **festivals**: the prestigious Border Union Dog Show in late June, the Border Union Agricultural Show in late July, the Kelso Rugby 7s in early September and the fascinating Ram Sales a week or so later.

For **food**, *Lombardi's Café*, on The Square, sells cheap snacks and meals, as does the *Queen's Head*, Bridge St, though the restaurant of the *Ednam House* hotel stands head and shoulders above the rest.

CENTRAL SOUTHERN SCOTLAND

Central Southern Scotland encompasses a rough rectangle of land sandwiched between the Cheviot Hills on the English border and the chain of foothills – the Pentland and Moorfoot ranges – to the south of Edinburgh. The region incorporates some of the finest stretches of the **Southern Uplands**, with bare, rounded peaks and heathery hills punctuated by dales.

Most of the roads stick assiduously to the dales, and the main problem is finding a route that avoids endless to and froing. Whichever way you're travelling, be sure to take in the section of the **Tweed Valley** stretching from **Melrose** (the best base for your explorations) to **Peebles**, where you'll find a string of attractions, from the ruins of **Dryburgh** and **Melrose Abbey** to the eccentricities of Sir Walter Scott's mansion at **Abbotsford** and the intriguing Jacobite past of **Traquair House**. The extensive medieval remains of the abbey at **Jedburgh**, just south, also merit a visit.

Along with industrialized Selkirk and Galashiels, these towns form the heart of the **Borders** region, whose turbulent history was, until the Act of Union, characterized by endless clan warfare and Reivers' raids. Consequently, the countryside is strewn with ruined castles and keeps, while each major town celebrates its agitated past in the **Common Ridings**, when locals – especially the "Callants", the young men – dress up in period costume and ride out to check the burgh boundaries. It's a boisterous business, as is the local love of **Rugby Union**, which reaches a crescendo with the **Melrose 7s** tournament in April.

The Southern Uplands assume a wild aspect in **Liddesdale**, southwest of Jedburgh, and along the **Yarrow Water** and **Moffat Water** connecting Selkirk with Moffat. Choose either of these two routes for the scenery, using the old spa town of **Moffat** as a base.

Travelling around the region by **bus** takes some forethought: pick up timetables from any tourist office and plan your connections closely – it's often difficult to cross between valleys. Some relief is, however, provided by the *Harrier Scenic Bus Service*, which threads its way between the more noteworthy towns from early July to September: again, the tourist office has schedules (see "Travel Details" at the end of the chapter).

Melrose

Tucked in between the Tweed and the Eildon Hills, minuscule **MELROSE** is the most beguiling of towns, its narrow streets trimmed by a harmonious ensemble of styles, from pretty little cottages and tweedy shops to high-standing Georgian and Victorian facades. At the foot of the town the pink- and ochre-tinted stone ruins of **Melrose Abbey** (April–Sept Mon–Sat 9.30am–6pm, Sun 2–6pm; Oct–March Mon–Sat 9.30am–4pm, Sun 2–4pm; £2.50) soar above their riverside surroundings. The abbey, founded in 1136 by David I, grew rich selling wool and hides to Flanders, but its prosperity was fragile: the English repeatedly razed Melrose, most viciously under Richard II in 1385 and the Earl of Hertford in 1545. Most of the present remains date from the intervening period, when extensive rebuilding abandoned the original austerity for an elaborate, Gothic style inspired by the abbeys of northern England.

The site is dominated by the **Abbey Church**, where the elegant window arches of the nave approach the **monk's choir**, whose grand piers are disfigured by the masonry of a later parish church. The adjacent **presbytery** is better preserved, its dignified lines illuminated by a magnificent perpendicular window pointing piously high into the sky, with the capitals of the surrounding columns sporting the most intricate of curly kale carving. Legend has it that the heart of Robert the Bruce was buried here beneath the window. Although this wasn't in accordance with his wishes: in 1329, the dying king told his friend, James Douglas, to carry his heart on a Crusade to the Holy Land in fulfilment of an old vow – "Seeing therefore, that my body cannot go to achieve what my heart desires, I will send my heart instead of my body, to accomplish my vow". Douglas tried his best, but was killed fighting the Moors in Spain – and Bruce's heart ended up in Melrose.

In the **south transept**, another fine fifteenth-century window sprouts yet more delicate, foliate tracery and the adjacent cornice is enlivened by angels playing musical intruments, though these figures are badly weathered. This kind of finely carved detail is repeated everywhere you look – and outside all sorts of **gargoyles** humour the majestic lines of the church from peculiar crouching beasts and moaning men to, most unusual of the lot, a pig playing the bagpipes on the roof on the south side of the nave.

The fragmentary ruins of the old monastic buildings edge the church and lead across to the **Commendator's House** (same times as the abbey), which displays a modest collection of ecclesiastical bric-a-brac in the house of the abbey's sixteenth-century lay administrators. Next door to the abbey in the opposite direction is the delightful **Priorwood Garden** (April–Dec Mon–Sat 10am–5.30pm, Sun 1.30–5.30pm; free), whose walled precincts, owned by the NTS, are given over to flowers that are suitable for drying – there's a dried flower shop too. Melrose's other museum, the **Trimontium Exhibition**, just off Market Square (April–Oct daily 10.30am–4.30pm; £1), is a modest affair, with dioramas, models and the odd archeological find outlining the three Roman occupations of the region.

Practicalities

Buses to Melrose stop in Market Square, a brief walk from both the abbey ruins and the adjacent **tourist office** (April, May & Oct Mon–Sat 10am–5pm, Sun 2–5pm; June Mon–Sat 10am–6pm, Sun 2–6pm; July & Aug Mon–Sat 9.30am–6.30pm, Sun 10.30am–6.30pm; Sept Mon–Sat 10am–6pm, Sun 2–6pm; ☎01896/822555).

Melrose has a clutch of **hotels**, including the smart and tidy *Burts Hotel*, on Market Square (☎01896/822285; ⑦); the neat, ten-bedroom *Bon Accord* (☎01896/822645; ⑧) just across the street; and the far less expensive – but rather humdrum – *Station Hotel* (☎01896/822038; ③), up the hill from Market Square. It's among Melrose's **B&Bs**, however, that you'll get the real flavour of the place, most notably at the easy-going and comfortable *Braidwood*, Buccleuch St (☎01896/822488; ③), just a stone's throw from the abbey, and the equally agreeable *Dunfermline House* (☎01896/822148; ③) opposite – advance booking is recommended at both during the summer. Other nearby options include *Little Fordel*, Abbey St (☎01896/822206; ④), and the basic *Orchard House*, High St (☎01896/822005; ③). The town also has a **youth hostel** (☎01896/822521; Grade 1), occupying a sprawling Victorian villa overlooking the abbey from beside the access road into the bypass. The *Gibson Caravan Park* (☎01896/822969), off High St, is a few minutes' walk west of the square.

Some of the B&Bs serve reasonably priced **dinner** on request. But if you venture forth *Marmion's Brasserie*, Buccleuch St, offers well-prepared meals from an imaginative menu. Alternatively, the formal *Melrose Station*, in the old train station above the

---

WALKING IN THE EILDON HILLS

Ordnance Survey Landranger map No.73

From the centre of Melrose, it's a vigorous three-mile walk to the top of the **Eildon Hills**, the triple-peaked volcanic pile rearing up behind the town. The tourist office sells a leaflet detailing the hike, which begins about 90 yards south of – and up the hill from – Market Square, along B6359 to Lilliesleaf. The path is signposted to the left and leads to the saddle between the North and Mid Hills. To the right of the saddle are **Mid Hill**, the highest summit at 1385ft, and further south **West Hill**; to the left **North Hill** is topped by the scant remains of an Iron Age Fort and a Roman signal station. The hills have been associated with all sorts of legends, beginning with their creation by the wizard-cum-alchemist Michael Scot. It was here that the mystic Thomas the Rhymer received the gift of prophecy from the Faery Queen, and Arthur and his Knights are reckoned to lie asleep deep within the hills, victims of a powerful spell. There are several routes back to town; one heading down from the northeast picks up a path to Newstead and you can return to Melrose by the river. Newstead is the site of the important Roman fort of Trimontium (Three Hills), whose remains are on display in Edinburgh's National Museum.

square, has a good range of daily specials featuring local produce. Back on Market Square, *Pyemont & Company* has good coffee and snacks; while the busy *Burts Hotel* has excellent bar meals, although their attitude to backpackers can be a bit snooty. No such restrictions exist at *Haldane's Fish & Chip Shop* (closed Wed), just off the square, or at the nearby *Ship Inn*, the liveliest pub in town, especially on Saturday afternoons when the Melrose Rugby Union team have played at home.

Around Melrose

Melrose makes a great base for exploring the middle reaches of the **Tweed Valley**. The rich, forested scenery inspired Sir Walter Scott, and the area's most outstanding attractions – the elegiac ruins of **Dryburgh Abbey** and lonely **Smailholm Tower**, not to mention Scott's purpose-built creation, **Abbotsford House** – bear his mark. Perhaps fortunately, Scott died before the textile boom industrialized parts of the Tweed Valley, turning his beloved **Selkirk** and **Galashiels** into mill towns. Allow time too for a visit to **Mellerstain House**, an example of the work of William and Robert Adam.

A comprehensive network of **bus** services connects Melrose with its surroundings and footpaths line much of the river's length. *Gala Cycles*, 58 High St, Galashiels (☎01896/757587), rents mountain **bikes**.

Dryburgh Abbey

Hidden away on a bend in the Tweed a few miles east of Melrose, the remains of **Dryburgh Abbey** (April–Sept Mon–Sat 9.30am–6pm, Sun 2–6pm; Oct–March Mon–Sat 9.30am–4pm, Sun 2–4pm; £2) occupy a superb position against a hilly backdrop, with ancient trees and wide lawns flattering the reddish hues of the stonework. The Premonstratensians, or White Canons, founded the abbey in the twelfth century, but they were never as successful – or apparently as devout – as their Cistercian neighbours in Melrose. Their chronicles detail interminable disputes about land and money – in one incident, a fourteenth-century canon called Marcus flattened the abbot with his fist. Later, the abbey attained its own folklore; Scott's *Minstrelsy* records the tale of a woman who lived in the vaults with a sprite called Fatlips. She only came out after dark to beg from her neighbours and was variously thought mad or demonic.

The abbey, demolished and rebuilt on several occasions, incorporates several architectural styles, beginning in the shattered **church** where the clumsy decoration of the main entrance contrasts with the spirited dog-tooth motif around the east processional doorway. The latter leads through to the **monastic buildings**, a two-storey ensemble that provides an insight into the lives of the monks. Bits and pieces of several rooms have survived, but the real highlight is the barrel-vaulted **chapterhouse**, complete with low stone benches, grouped windows and carved arcade. The room was used by the monks for the daily reading of a chapter from either the Bible or their rule book, and was, as they prospered, draped with expensive hangings.

Finally, back in the church, the battered north transept contains the grave of **Sir Walter Scott**; close by lies Field Marshal Haig, the World War I commander whose ineptitude cost thousands of soldiers' lives.

Practicalities

There are several ways to get to **Dryburgh** from Melrose: if you're **driving**, the clearly signposted, 15-minute scenic route proceeds east along the B6361, past Newstead, to the A68, where you should turn left and, soon after, take a right turn and follow the back roads to the abbey. On the way, you'll pass **Scott's View** overlooking the Tweed Valley, where the writer and friends often picnicked; the scene inspired Joseph

Turner's *Melrose 1831*, now on display in the National Gallery of Scotland (see p.75). Alternatively, you can also take the Jedburgh **bus** (Mon–Sat hourly, Sun 5 daily; 10min) as far as St Boswells. Walk north from the village back along the main road and take the third right down the mile-long lane that leads to the footbridge and Dryburgh. The only direct service is with the four-seater **postbus** (Mon–Fri 1 daily; 25min), but this doesn't make a return trip.

Dryburgh has just one **place to stay**, the commodious **Dryburgh Abbey Hotel** (☎01835/822261; ⑤), a sprawling red-sandstone building right next to the ruins.

Smailholm Tower

Driving is the only way to reach the fifteenth-century **Smailholm Tower** (April–Sept Mon–Sat 9.30am–6pm, Sun 2–6pm; £1.50), perched on a rocky outcrop a few miles east of Dryburgh via the B6404. A remote and evocative fastness recalling Reivers' raids and border skirmishes, the tower was designed to withstand sudden attack: the rough rubble walls average 6ft thick and both the entrance – once guarded by a heavy door plus an iron yett (gate) – and the windows are disproportionately small. These were necessary precautions. On both sides of the border clans were engaged in endless feuds, a violent history that stirred the imagination of a "wee, sick laddie" who was brought here to live in 1773. The boy was Walter Scott and his epic poem Marmion resounds to the clamour of Smailholm's ancient quarrels:

> [The forayers], *home returning, fill'd the hall*
> *With revel, wassel-rout, and brawl.*
> *Methought that still with trump and clang,*
> *The gateway's broken arches rang;*
> *Methought grim features, seam'd with scars,*
> *Glared through the window's rusty bars.*

Inside, ignore the inept costumed models and press on up to the roof, where two narrow **wall-walks**, jammed against the barrel-vaulted roof and the crow-stepped gables, provide panoramic views. On the north side the watchman's seat has also survived, stuck against the chimney stack for warmth and with a recess for a lantern.

Mellerstain House

Mellerstain House (May, June & Sept Wed, Fri & Sun 12.30–4.30pm; July & Aug daily except Sat 12.30–4.30pm; £3.50) is about four miles east of Smailholm via a series of signposted by-roads – and six miles northwest of Kelso along the A6089. The house represents the very best of the Adams' work: William designed the wings in 1725, and his son Robert the castellated centre 50 years later. Robert's love of columns, roundels and friezes culminates in a stunning sequence of plaster-moulded, pastel-shaded ceilings, from the looping symmetry of the library ceiling, adorned by medallion oil paintings of *Learning* and *Reading* on either side of *Minerva*, to the whimsical griffin and vase pattern in the drawing room. It takes about an hour to tour the house; afterwards you can wander the formal Edwardian gardens, which slope down towards the lake.

Abbotsford House

Abbotsford House (mid-March to Oct Mon–Sat 10am–5pm, Sun 2–5pm; £3) was designed to satisfy the Romantic inclinations of Sir Walter Scott, who lived here from 1812 until his death 20 years later. Built on the site of a farmhouse Scott bought and subsequently demolished, Abbotsford took 12 years to evolve with the fanciful turrets and castellations of the Scots Baronial exterior incorporating copies of medieval originals: thus the entrance porch imitates that of Linlithgow Palace and the screen wall in

SIR WALTER SCOTT

Walter Scott (1771–1832) was born in Edinburgh to a solidly bourgeois family whose roots were in Selkirkshire. As a child he was left lame by polio and his anxious parents sent him to recuperate at his grandfather's farm in Smailholm, where the boy's imagination was fired by his relatives' tales of derring-do, the violent history of the Borders retold amidst a rugged landscape that he spent long summer days exploring. Scott returned to Edinburgh to resume his education and take up a career in law, but his real interests remained elsewhere. Throughout the 1790s he transcribed hundreds of old Border ballads, publishing a three-volume collection entitled *Minstrelsy of the Scottish Borders* in 1802. An instant success, *Minstrelsy* was followed by Scott's own *Lay of the Last Minstrel*, a narrative poem whose strong story and rose-tinted regionalism proved very popular.

More poetry was to come, most successfully *Marmion* (1808) and *The Lady of the Lake* (1810), not to mention an eighteen-volume edition of the works of John Dryden and nineteen volumes of Jonathan Swift. However, despite having two paid jobs, one as the Sheriff-Depute of Selkirkshire, the other as clerk to the Court of Session in Edinburgh, his finances remained shaky. He had become a partner in a printing firm, which put him deeply into debt, not helped by the enormous sums he spent on his mansion, Abbotsford. From 1813, Scott was writing to pay the bills and thumped out a veritable flood of historical novels using his extensive knowledge of Scottish history and folklore. He produced his best work within the space of ten years: *Waverley* (1814), *The Antiquary* (1816), *Rob Roy* and the *The Heart of Midlothian* (both 1818) and, after he had exhausted his own country, two notable novels set in England, *Ivanhoe* (1819) and *Kenilworth* (1821). In 1824 he returned to Scottish tales with *Redgauntlet*, the last of his quality work.

A year later Scott's money problems reached crisis proportions after an economic crash bankrupted his printing business. Attempting to pay his creditors in full, he found the quality of his writing deteriorating with its increased speed and the effort broke his health. His last years were plagued by illness and in 1832 he died at Abbotsford and was buried within the ruins of Dryburgh Abbey.

Although Scott's interests were diverse, his historical novels mostly focused on the Jacobites, whose loyalty to the Stuarts had riven Scotland since the "Glorious Revolution" of 1688. That the nation was prepared to be entertained by such tales was essentially a matter of timing: by the 1700s it was clear the Jacobite cause was lost for good and Scotland, emerging from its isolated medievalism, had been firmly welded into the United Kingdom. Thus its turbulent history and independent spirit was safely in the past, and ripe for romancing – as shown by the arrival of King George IV in Edinburgh during 1822 decked out in Highland dress. Yet, for Sir Walter the romance was tinged with a genuine sense of loss. Loyal to the Hanoverians, he still grieved for Bonnie Prince Charlie; he welcomed a commercial Scotland but lamented the passing of feudal ties; and so his heroes are transitional, fighting men of action superseded by bourgeois figures searching for a clear identity.

Although today many of Scott's works are out of print, Edinburgh University Press has recently begun a long-term project to issue proper critical editions of the Waverley novels for the first time, correcting hitherto heavily corrupted texts and restoring passages and endings that had been altered – often drastically – by the original publishers. See "Books" in *Contexts* for details of books by Scott currently in print.

the garden echoes Melrose Abbey's cloister. Scott was proud of his creation, writing to a friend, "It is a kind of conundrum castle to be sure (which) pleases a fantastic person in style and manner".

Inside, visitors start in the wood-panelled **study**, with its small writing desk made of salvage from the Spanish Armada. The **library** boasts an extraordinary assortment of Scottish memorabilia, including Rob Roy's purse and *skene dhu* (knife), a lock of Bonnie Prince Charlie's hair and his *quaich* (drinking cup), Flora Macdonald's pocket book, the inlaid pearl crucifix that accompanied Mary, Queen of Scots to the scaffold, and even a piece of oatcake found in the pocket of a dead Highlander at Culloden. You can also see Henry Raeburn's famous portrait of Scott hanging in the **drawing room** and all sorts of weapons, notably Rob Roy's sword, dagger and gun, in the **armoury**. In the barbaric-looking **entrance hall**, hung with elk and wild cattle skulls, is a cast of the head of Robert the Bruce.

Abbotsford is sandwiched between the Tweed and the B6360, about three miles west of Melrose. The fast and frequent Melrose–Galashiels bus provides easy access: ask for the Tweedbank island on the A6091 and walk up the road from there, for about ten minutes.

Selkirk and around

Whichever way you're heading it's likely you'll pass through **SELKIRK**, an unremarkable textile town of high stone houses that spread along the hillside above the Ettrick Water about four miles south of Abbotsford. The **tourist office**, at the west end of High St, off Market Square (April–June & Sept Mon–Sat 10am–5pm, Sun 2–4pm; July & Aug Mon–Sat 10am–6.30pm, Sun 2–6pm; Oct Mon–Sat 10am–4.30pm, Sun 2–4pm; ☎01750/20054), is a good place to stock up with pamphlets and books. In the same building, **Halliwell's House Museum** (free) features an old-style hardware shop and an informative exhibit on the industrialization of the Tweed Valley, from the development of the first mills in the early nineteenth century to their slow decline after 1910. At the other end of High Street, the statue of **Mungo Park**, the renowned explorer born in Selkirkshire in 1771, displays two finely cast bas-reliefs depicting his exploits along the River Niger, which came to an end with his accidental drowning in 1805. The life-size figures of *Peace, War, Slavery* and *Home Life in the Niger* were added in 1913, after several petitions and newspaper editorials demanded that he be further commemorated.

Bowhill House

Three miles west of Selkirk on the A708, nineteenth-century **Bowhill House** (July daily 1–4.30pm; £4) is the property of the Duke of Buccleuch and Queensberry, a seriously wealthy man. Beyond the mansion's grand and extensive facade is an outstanding collection of French antiques and European paintings: in the **dining room**, for example, there are portraits by Reynolds and Gainsborough and a Canaletto cityscape, while the **drawing room** boasts Boulle furniture, Meissen tableware, paintings by Ruysdael, Leandro Bassano and Claude Lorraine, as well as two more family portraits by Reynolds. Look out also for the **Scott Room** – otherwise **the study** – which features another splendid portrait of Sir Walter by Henry Raeburn, and the **Monmouth Room**, commemorating James, Duke of Monmouth, the illegitimate son of Charles II, who married Anne of the Buccleuchs. After several years in exile, Monmouth returned to England when his father died in 1685, hoping to wrest the crown from James II. He was defeated at the battle of Sedgemoor in Somerset and subsequently sent to the scaffold: among other items, his execution shirt is on display.

The wooded hills of **Bowhill Country Park** (May to late Aug daily except Fri noon–5pm; £1), which adjoins the house, are criss-crossed by scenic footpaths and cycle trails. **Mountain bikes** can be rented from the visitor centre. Getting to Bowhill by **bus** is difficult: from July to late September, a weekly *Harrier Scenic Bus Service* leaves Selkirk (and Melrose) in the morning and returns in the afternoon; on weekdays there's also a bus from Selkirk in the early afternoon, but you'll have to walk back.

Aikwood Tower

Aikwood Tower (April to mid-Sept Tues, Thurs & Sun 2–5pm), four miles west of Selkirk on the B7009, is a recently restored fortified tower house whose stern rubble walls stand surrounded by the forests of the valley of the Ettrick Water. Inside, an exhibition explores the life and work of Sir Walter Scott's friend, **James Hogg**, otherwise the "Ettrick Shepherd". Born locally, in sheep-farming Ettrick Valley, self-taught Hogg was a poet of some contemporary renown who spent several years living among the Edinbrugh literary elite. Today he's largely forgotten and – if you read any of his work – this is not entirely surprising. Incidentally, Aikwood doubles as the home of Liberal politician David Steel.

The Tweed Valley: Galashiels to Peebles

There's a wide choice of routes on from Melrose; one of the more popular options is to travel 22 miles west along the **Tweed Valley** to the pleasant country town of Peebles. On the way, savour the wooded scenery and drop into **Traquair House**, just off the main road at tiny Innerleithen. Public transport is no problem: frequent buses along the valley are supplemented by the seasonal *Harrier Scenic Bus Service* (see p.156). Just west of Peebles, the River Tweed curves south towards Tweedsmuir, from where it's just a few miles further to Moffat (see p.132).

Galashiels and Traquair House

Four miles west of Melrose, it's probably best to avoid **GALASHIELS**, a workaday textile town spread along the valley of the Gala Water near its junction with the Tweed. You may, however, have to pass through the region's principal bus station, close to (and across the river from) the town centre. If you're delayed you could take a stroll along the main drag, High, then Bank, Street, whose eastern end is cheered by a melodramatic statue of a mounted Border Reiver. The long-demolished New Gala House, a mansion which stood at the top of the town, was taken over during World War II by an Edinburgh girls' school, St Trinnean's – Ronald Searle met two of the pupils in 1941, inspiration for the unruly school girls in his St Trinians' novels. Galashiels **tourist office**, 3 St John's St, is across the square from the statue (April, June & Sept Mon–Sat 10am–5pm, Sun 11am–2pm; July & Aug Mon–Sat 9.30am–6pm, Sun 11am–4pm; Oct Mon–Sat 10am–12.30pm & 1.30–4.30pm).

Traquair House

West of Galashiels, tiny **WALKERBURN** is home to the pint-sized **Museum of Woollen Textiles** (Mon–Sat 9am–5.30pm; April–Nov also Sun 11am–5pm; free). Some of the early wool and cloth patterns are of interest, but it won't be long before you're moving on. Peeping out from the trees a miles or so south of the main road at the nearby village of Innerleithen, **Traquair House** (mid-April to June & Sept daily 12.30–5.30pm; July & Aug daily 10.30am–5.30pm; £3.75) is the oldest continuously inhabited house in Scotland, with the present owners – the Maxwell Stuarts – living here since 1491. The first of the line, **James**, first Laird of Traquair, inherited an elementary fortified tower, which his powerful descendants gradually converted into a mansion, visited, it is said, by 27 monarchs including Mary, Queen of Scots. Persistently Catholic, the family paid for its principles: the fifth earl got two years in the Tower of London for his support of Bonnie Prince Charlie, Protestant mill workers repeatedly attacked their property, and by 1800 little remained of the family's once enormous estates – certainly not enough to fund any major rebuilding.

Consequently, Traquair's main appeal is in its ancient shape and structure. The whitewashed facade is strikingly handsome, with narrow windows and trim turrets surrounding the tiniest of front doors – an organic, homogeneous edifice that's a welcome change from other grandiose stately homes. Inside, the house has kept many of its oldest features. You can see original vaulted cellars, where locals once hid their cattle from raiders; the twisting main staircase as well as the earlier medieval version, later a secret escape route for persecuted Catholics; a carefully camouflaged priest's hole; and even a **priest's room** where a string of resident chaplains lived in hiding until the Catholic Emancipation Act freed things up in 1829. Of the furniture and fittings, the carved oak door at the foot of the stairs is outstanding, as are the Dutch *trompe l'oeil* in the **still room** and the bright-yellow four-poster of the **king's room**, with a bedspread allegedly embroidered by Mary, Queen of Scots. That said, it's not any particuluar piece that impresses, but rather the accumulation of family bygones that give a real insight into the family's revolving-door fortunes and eccentricities. In the **museum room** there are several fine examples of Jacobite or **Amen glass**, inscribed with pictures of the Bonnie Prince or verses in his honour; a handful of personal items thought to have been owned by Mary, Queen of Scots; and the cloak worn by the fourth earl during his dramatic escape from the Tower of London. Under sentence of death for his part in the Jacobite Rising of 1715, the earl was saved by his wife, Lady Winifred Herbert, who got his jailers drunk and smuggled him out disguised as a maid.

It's worth sparing time for the surrounding gardens where you'll find a maze, several craft workshops and a working brewery, whose fine products are on sale at the laid-back tearoom. Finally walk down to the **Steekit Yetts**, or Bear Gates, associated with one of the legends of the '45. On his march south, Prince Charles Stuart popped in to visit his old ally at Traquair. As he left, the fifth earl "Vowed [the gates] wad be opened nevermair till a Stuart king was crooned in Lunnon", and the family have kept his promise.

Peebles

Straddling the Tweed, **PEEBLES** has a genteel, relaxing air, its wide High Street bordered by a complementary medley of architectural styles, mostly dating from Victorian times. A stroll around town should include a visit to the **Tweeddale Museum** (April–Sept Mon–Fri 10am–1pm & 2–5pm, Sat & Sun 2–5pm; Oct–March Mon–Fri only; free), housed in the Chambers Institute on High St. William Chambers, a local worthy, presented the building to the town in 1859, complete with an art gallery dedicated to the enlightenment of his neighbours. He stuffed the place with casts of

---

WALKS AROUND PEEBLES

A series of footpaths snake through the hills surrounding Peebles with their rough-edged burns, bare peaks and deep woods. The main local tracks are listed in the *Popular Walks around Peebles* leaflet available from the tourist office. The five-mile-long **Sware Trail** is one of the easiest and most scenic, weaving west along the north bank of the river and looping back to the south. On the way, it passes **Neidpath Castle** (Easter–Sept Mon–Sat 11am–5pm, Sun 1–5pm; £2), a gaunt medieval tower house perched high above the river on a rocky buff. It's a superb setting, but think twice about the entrance fee – the interior, although it does possess a pit prison and an ancient well, is little more than an empty shell. The walk also slips by the splendid skew **rail bridge**, part of the Glasgow line which was finished in 1850. Other, longer footpaths follow the old drove tracks, like the 13-mile haul to St Mary's Loch or the 14-mile route to Selkirk via Traquair House. For either of these, you'll need an Ordnance Survey map, a compass and proper hiking tackle (see "Outdoor Pursuits" in *Basics*). Alternatively, **mountain bikes** can be rented from either *George Pennel Cycles*, 3 High St (☎01721/720844) or *Scottish Border Trails* (☎01721/722934), at the entrance to Glentress forest two miles east of town on the A72. If you need four or more, the latter deliver free within a ten-mile radius.

the world's most famous sculptures, and, although most were lost long ago, today's "Secret Room", once the Museum Room, boasts two handsome friezes: one a copy of the Elgin marbles taken from the Parthenon; the other of the Triumph of Alexander, originally cast in 1812 to honour Napoleon.

Practicalities

Buses to Peebles stop outside the post office, a few doors down from the well-stocked **tourist office**, High St (April & May Mon–Sat 10am–5pm, Sun 10am–2pm; June Mon–Sat 10am–5.30pm, Sun 10am–4pm; July & Aug Mon–Sat 9am–7pm, Sun 10am–6pm; Sept Mon–Sat 10am–5.30pm, Sun 1–4pm; Oct Mon–Sat 10am–4.30pm, Sun 10am–2pm; Nov & Dec Mon–Sat 10am–12.30pm & 1.30–4.30pm; ☎01721/720138). Of the many **B&Bs** dotted around the centre, try the trim and pint-sized *Rowanbrae*, on Northgate, a turning off the east end of High St (☎01721/721630; ③); the *Minniebank Guest House*, Greenside (☎01721/722093; ④), a Victorian villa set beside the river by the main bridge; or *Viewfield*, 1 Rosetta Rd (☎01721/721232; ②), an attractive Victorian house a ten-minute walk west of the bridge – take Old Town (the A72) and follow the road round, turning right up Young St. The best of the more upmarket **hotels** is *The Park Hotel*, just east of the town centre on Innerleithen Rd (☎01721/720451; ⑧). Cheaper alternatives include the mundane *Green Tree Hotel*, 41 Eastgate (☎01721/720582; ⑤), and the relaxing *Kingsmuir Hotel*, south of the river on Springhill Rd (☎01721/720151; ⑦). For **camping**, the *Rosetta Caravan and Camping Park* (April–Oct; ☎01721/720770) is a 15-minute walk north of the High St (directions as for *Viewfield* B&B).

For **food**, the *Olive Tree* delicatessen, High St, serves superb, imaginative sandwiches; the *Crown Hotel*, High St, features good daily specials, and the *Kingsmuir Hotel*, Springhill Rd, has more expensive but excellent bar meals. Other options on High St include the *Prince of India Tandoori Restaurant* and, during the day, the cheap and cheerful *Tatler Café* offers good-value fish and chips. You should also sample the **beers** of the local Broughton brewery – *Old Jock, Greenmantle* and *Broughton Ale*.

Jedburgh

JEDBURGH nestles in the valley of the Jed Water near its confluence with the Teviot out on the edge of the wild Cheviot Hills. During the interminable Anglo-Scottish Wars, it was the quintessential frontier town, a heavily garrisoned royal burgh incorporating a mighty castle and abbey. Though the **Castle** was destroyed by the Scots in 1409, to keep it out of the hands of the English, its memory has been kept alive by local folklore: in 1285, for example, King Alexander III was celebrating his wedding feast in the Great Hall when a ghostly apparition predicted his untimely death and a bloody civil war; sure enough, he died in a hunting accident shortly afterwards and chaos ensued. Today the ruined **Abbey** is the main event, though a stroll round Jedburgh's old town centre is a pleasant way to wile away an hour or two.

The Town

The remains of **Jedburgh Abbey** (April–Sept Mon–Sat 9.30am–6pm, Sun 2–6pm; Oct–March Mon–Sat 9.30am–4pm, Sun 2–4pm; £2.50), right in the centre of town, date from the twelfth century. Benefiting from King David's patronage, the monks developed an extravagant complex on a sloping site next to the Jed Water, the monastic buildings standing beneath a huge red sandstone church. All went well until the late thirteenth century, when the power of the Scots kings waned following the death of Alexander III and the prolonged civil war that ensued. The abbey was subsequently burnt and badly damaged on a number of occasions, the worst being inflicted by the English in 1544.

The canons gamely repaired their buildings, but were unable to resist the Reformation and the monastery closed in 1560. However, the Abbey Church remained a parish kirk for another three centuries and has survived particularly well preserved.

Entry to the site is through the bright **visitor centre** at the bottom of the hill, whose explanation of the abbey's history uses both contemporary quotations and "mood music" – chanting monks and the like. Next to the centre are the scant remains of the cloister buildings; the **Abbey Church**, which lies on an east–west axis, is best entered from the west through a weathered Norman doorway with gables, arcading and ornamented windows. Behind the doorway lies the splendidly proportioned three-storeyed nave, a fine example of the transition from Norman to Gothic design, with pointed window arches surmounted by the round-headed arches of the triforium, which, in turn, support the lancet windows of the clerestory. This delicacy of form is, however, not matched at the east end of the church, where the squat central tower is underpinned by the monumental circular pillars and truncated arches of the earlier, twelfth-century choir.

It's a couple of minutes' walk from the abbey round to the tiny triangular **Market Place**. Up the hill from here, at the top of Castlegate, **Jedburgh Castle Jail and Museum** (closed for refurbishment until late 1996) will exhibit displays on prison life throughout the ages. The prison buildings themselves are, for the period, remarkably comfortable, reflecting the influence of reformer John Howard. Finally, **Mary, Queen of Scots' House** (March to mid-Nov daily 10am–4.30pm; £1.50), situated at the opposite end of the town centre, is something of a misnomer: it's true that Mary stayed here in this bastle house during the assizes of 1566, but she didn't stay long and there's little on show connected with her visit. The attempt to unravel her complex life is cursory, the redeeming features being a copy of Mary's death mask and one of the few surviving portraits of the Earl of Bothwell.

Practicalities

Jedburgh's **bus station**, a few yards from the abbey, is the starting point for a wide range of services around the Borders. Footsteps away on Murray's Green, the **tourist office** (April, May & Oct Mon–Sat 10am–5pm, Sun 12–4pm; June & Sept Mon–Sat 9.30am–6pm, Sun 12–4pm; July & Aug Mon–Fri 9am–8.30pm, Sat 9am–7pm, Sun 10am–7pm; Nov–March Mon–Fri 10am–4.30pm; ☎01835/863435) has a vast array of information and a comprehensive list of local **accommodation**. Try the *Kenmore Bank Guest House*, Oxnam Rd (☎01835/862369; ⑤), a Victorian villa overlooking the Jed Water and five minuites' walk south of the abbey; the *Glenbank Country House Hotel*, Castlegate (☎01835/862258; ⑥); or the *Glenfriars Hotel*, The Friars (☎01835/862000; ⑥), a big old house in its own grounds near the north end of High St. Alternatively, there are several **B&Bs** among the pleasant and antique row houses of Castlegate, notably *Mrs Bathgate*, no. 64 (April–Oct; ☎01835/862466; ②) and *Mrs Poloczek*, no. 48 (☎01835/862504; ④). There's another cluster just west off High St on Friarsgate (also known as The Friars), including the neat and modern bungalow of *Willow Court* (☎01835/863702; ③) and the Victorian *Froylehurst Guest House* (March–Nov; 01835/862477; ③). The *Jedwater Caravan and Camping Park* (April–Oct; ☎01835/840219) occupies a riverside site four miles south of town on the A68, while the *Elliot Park* caravan and **campsite** (March–Sept; ☎01835/863393) is beside the Edinburgh road about a mile north of the centre.

Considering its heavy tourist trade, Jedburgh has surprisingly few **restaurants**. During the day, the *Brown Sugar* coffee bar, by Market Place, serves up good-quality sandwiches, salads and cakes. At night, stick to the *Castlegate Restaurant*, 26 Castlegate. **Jethart Snails**, a local speciality on sale everywhere, are sticky boiled sweets designed to corrupt the firmest of fillings.

Teviotdale, Ewes Water and Liddesdale

If you're heading southwest from Jedburgh, there are two clearly defined routes. The first, along the A698 and then A7, tracks up **Teviotdale** to **Hawick**, before slipping through the dramatic uplands which stretch as far as the English Border. En route you change dales – joining **Ewes Water** at the Dumfries boundary.

The route down Liddesdale, along the B6357, is slower but even more picturesque, on a remote road flanked by dense forests, barren moors and secluded heaths. If you do come this way, stop off at solitary **Hermitage Castle**, a well-preserved fourteenth-century fortress.

The Galashiels to Carlisle **bus** travels the length of Teviotdale and Ewes Water (Mon–Sat 6 daily, Sun 3 daily). Buses from Jedburgh connect with this service at Hawick. There are no buses along the length of Liddesdale – the best you'll do is the occasional, school-term-only service from Langholm to Canonbie and Newcastleton; ring *Telfords Coaches* (☎013873/75677) for details.

Teviotdale and Ewes Water

Fourteen miles from Jedburgh is the unprepossessing mill town of **HAWICK** (pronounced "Hoyk"), its many factory outlets swarming with visitors and bearing witness to its history as centre of the region's knitwear and hosiery industry. To learn about the industry and the town in general, visit the **Hawick Museum and Scott Gallery** (April–Sept Mon–Sat 10am–noon & 1–5pm, Sun 2–5pm; Oct–March Mon–Fri 1–4pm, Sun 2–4pm; £1), near the town centre in Wilton Lodge Park. There's a **youth hostel** (called "Snoot") near here too (April–Sept; ☎01450/880259; Grade 3), in an old church in the remote hamlet of Roberton (6 miles west on the B711). There are wooded walking trails close by and weekend pony-trekking run by the hostel.

Beyond Hawick, the scenery improves as the road twists its way south between the bulging heathery hills that shadow the river. At Teviothead the road leaves the dale to cross over into Dumfries, where the **Ewes Water** strips down to **LANGHOLM**, a stone-built mill town at the confluence of the Esk, Ewes and Wauchope waters. The town, which flourished during the eighteenth-century textile boom, is now a low-key holiday spot. In 1892 this was the birthplace of the poet **Hugh MacDiarmid**, a co-founder of the Scottish National Party and a key player in the literary renaissance that fired the nationalist movement between the two world wars. MacDiarmid, born Christopher Murray Grieve, looked to the Scotland of the eighteenth century, lionizing Walter Scott and Robbie Burns while heaping scorn on the Anglicized gentry. This didn't go down well with the burghers of Langholm, who did their best to ignore the poet altogether. Indeed, when MacDiarmid died in 1978, at the age of 86, some of them even tried to prevent him being buried in the local churchyard.

If you want to **stay**, try the convenient *Eskdale Hotel*, Market Place (☎01387/380357; ⑤)) or *Langholm Guest House*, 81 High St (☎013873/81343; ③).

On from Langholm

Four roads lead out of Langholm, the most enjoyable being the narrow country lane that snakes its way east over the hills to **Newcastleton** in Liddesdale. Otherwise, choose between the rustic 30-mile journey west to **Dumfries** (see p.137); the far slower, and rather dreary trip northwest up **Eskdale** for (ultimately) Selkirk and the Tweed Valley; or the shorter journey south to **Gretna Green** (see opposite).

If you're travelling by **bus** from Langholm, it takes about three hours to get to Dumfries, changing at Lockerbie (4 buses weekly), whilst Gretna Green can be reached via the better-served Carlisle route. There aren't any services to Selkirk, along Eskdale and only an occasional bus to Newcastleton (see p.129).

Liddesdale

Heading south out of Jedburgh on the A68, it's about a mile to the B6357, a narrow byroad that leads over the moors to the hamlet of Bonchester Bridge. From here, the road cuts south through Wauchope Forest and carries on into **Liddesdale**, whose wild beauty is at its most striking between Saughtree and Newcastleton. In between the two, take the turning to **Hermitage Castle** (April–Sept Mon–Sat 9.30am–6pm, Sun 2–6pm; Oct–March Sat 9.30am–4pm, Sun 2–4pm; £1.20), a bleak and forbidding fastness devilled by all sorts of horrifying legends: one owner, William Douglas, starved his prisoners to death; whilst Lord de Soulis, another occupant, engaged the help of demons to fortify the castle in defiance of the king, Robert the Bruce. Not entirely trusting his demonic assistants, Soulis also drilled holes into the shoulders of his vassals, the better to yoke them to sledges of building materials. Bruce became so tired of the complaints that he exclaimed, "Boil him if you please, but let me hear no more of him". Bruce's henchmen took him at his word and ambushed the rebellious baron. Convinced, however, that Soulis had a pact with his demonic familiar, Redcap, that made him difficult to kill ("ropes could not bind him, nor steel weapons touch"), they bound him with ropes of sifted sand, wrapped him in lead and boiled him slowly .

From the outside, the castle remains an imposing structure, its heavy walls topped by stepped gables and a tidy corbelled parapet. However, the apparent homogeneity is deceptive: certain features were invented during a Victorian restoration, a confusing supplement to the ad hoc alterations that had already transformed the fourteenth-century original. The ruinous interior is a bit of a letdown, but look out for the tight Gothic doorways and gruesome dungeon.

It's a short journey on to **NEWCASTLETON**, a classic estate village built for the hand-loom weavers of the third Duke of Buccleuch in 1793. The gridiron streets fall either side of a long main road that connects three geometrically arranged squares – nice enough to while away the odd hour. You can **stay** the night at the *Liddesdale Hotel* (☎013873/75255; ④)) and sample some local trout or pheasant.

The road leaves Liddesdale ten miles southwest of Newcastleton at Canonbie. Around here, sandwiched between the **Esk** and the **Sark**, was what was known as the **"Debateable Land"**, a pocket-sized territory claimed – but not controlled – by both England and Scotland from the fourteenth to the early eighteenth century. In the prevailing chaos, the Border Reivers flourished and famed outlaws like Kinmont Willie, Jock o' the Side and Clym of the Cleugh established fabulous reputations for acts of cruelty and kindness in equal measure. They could certainly die in style too: caught by James V, a chieftain named Johnnie Armstrong offered a colossal bribe and asked for a pardon; when this was refused and the noose was round his neck, he coolly disclaimed: "To seik het water beneath cauld ice, surely it is a great follie – I hae asked grace at a graceless face."

Annandale: Gretna Green to Moffat

Cutting through **Annandale**, the M/A74 connects Carlisle with Glasgow. This is the fastest way to cross Southern Scotland but it's an unpleasantly busy road, jam-packed with trucks and lorries. You could break your journey by stopping off at **Gretna Green**, whose name is synonymous with elopements and quick weddings, before travelling the 30 miles north to the charming market town of **Moffat**, bypassed by the main road, which makes an ideal base for exploring the surrounding uplands. Bus services along Annandale are quick and frequent.

Gretna to Lockerbie

There's not much to the twin villages of **GRETNA GREEN** and **GRETNA** except their curious history, the result of the quirks of the British legal system. Up until 1754 English couples could buy a quick and secret wedding at London's Fleet Prison, bribing imprisoned clerics with small amounts of money. The Hardwicke Marriage Act brought an end to this seedy wheeze, enforcing the requirement of a licence and a church ceremony. However, in Scotland, a marriage declaration made before two witnesses remained legal. The consequences of this difference in the law verged on farce: hundreds of runaway couples dashed north to Scotland, their weddings witnessed by just about anyone who came to hand – ferrymen, farmers, tollgate keepers and even self-styled "priests" who set up their own "marriage houses".

Gretna and Gretna Green, due to their position beside the border on the main turnpike road to Edinburgh, became the most popular destination for the fugitives, but, even in emergency, class distinctions were maintained: the better-off headed for the staging post at Gretna Hall, the rest went elsewhere. The first "priest" was the redoubtable Joseph Paisley, a 25-stone goliath who – in business from 1754 to 1812 – gave a certain style to the ceremony by straightening a horseshoe, a show of strength rather than a symbolic act. His melodramatic action did, however, lead to stories of Gretna weddings being performed over the blacksmith's anvil, and the "priests" were more than happy to act out the rumour. Both villages boomed until the marriage laws were further amended in 1856, but some business continued right down to 1940, when marriage by declaration was made illegal.

Today, Gretna Green's **Old Blacksmith's Shop**, next to the **tourist office** (April, May & Oct daily 10am–5pm; June–Sept daily 9.30am–6pm; Nov–March Mon–Sat 10am–4.30pm & 2–5pm; ☎01461/338500) on the east side of the A74, is a tacky place stuffed with souvenirs and a handful of marital mementoes. On the other side of the road, roughly half a mile away, the rather more genteel Gretna Hall **Blacksmith's Shop and Museum** (April–Oct daily 9am–5pm; 50p) has another modest but more diverting collection of bygones. You can still "get married" over the anvil at Gretna, although the ceremony has no legal force.

There are lots of places to **stay** in and around Gretna and Gretna Green. The tourist office has the full list, but the nicest options are to be found in Gretna: try either of two modernized farmhouses, the *Surrone Guest House*, Annan Rd (☎01461/338341; ⑤), or The Beeches, Loanwath Rd (☎01461/337448; closed Dec; ③), which has just two (non-smoking) rooms.

Ecclefechan and Lockerbie

It's about nine miles from Gretna to the tidy hamlet of **ECCLEFECHAN**, birthplace of the historian and essayist **Thomas Carlyle** (1795–1881). Born into a strongly Calvinist family, Carlyle's highly successful account of the *French Revolution* (1837) set out his theory of history as "Divine Scripture": the French aristocracy had reaped the rewards of their corruption and indulgence. However, with no clearly defined political ideology, his radicalism soon began to wane – reinforced by the failure of contemporary activist movements to live up to his idealistic expectations. Disillusioned, Carlyle was eventually to became the strongest voice for the moral concerns of the Victorian bourgeoisie, and as such a litmus paper of his age. Supposedly an irritable and melancholic character, his marriage was turbulent, but when his wife died in 1866 he never recovered and was a semi-recluse for many years before his death (see p.110). His old home, the whitewashed **Arched House** (May–Sept Mon–Fri & Sun 1.30–5pm; £1.50), is now a tiny museum, featuring among the personal memorabilia a bronze cast of his hands, old smoking caps and his cradle. Perhaps surprisingly, there's little here to indicate either the man's stern demeanour or his Calvinist roots.

The quiet country town of **LOCKERBIE**, eight miles from Ecclefechan, was catapulted into the headlines on Wednesday December 21, 1988, when a *Pan-Am* Jumbo Jet, flying from Frankfurt to New York via Heathrow, was blown up by a terrorist bomb concealed in a transistor radio. All the crew and passengers died and the plane's fragments crashed down on Lockerbie, killing a further eleven. Those who planted the bomb, apparently Arab terrorists now resident in Libya, are still to be brought to book, although Anglo-American efforts to have them extradicted seem to be fizzling out. The local people have set up a Remembrance Garden on the outskirts of town, but this is no place for the casual visitor.

Moffat

Encircled by hills and dales, **MOFFAT** is a good-looking market town, its wide and elegant **High Street** flattered with simple brick cottages and grand Georgian mansions. The latter hark back to the eighteenth century, when Moffat was briefly a modish spa, its sulphur springs attracting the rich and famous. One disappointed customer suggested they smelt of bilge-water – but they were good enough for luminaries Robbie Burns and James Boswell, who came to "wash off the scurvy spots".

Moffat is no longer quite so fashionable, but while you're here take a look at the John Adam-designed **Moffat House Hotel** and the neighbouring **Colvin Fountain**, whose sturdy bronze ram was accidentally cast without any ears. Not far away, the dark shadows of the **Black Bull** pub once quartered John Graham of Claverhouse as he planned his persecution of the Covenanters on behalf of Charles II. For details of the town's history, pop into the **museum** (Easter–Sept Mon, Tues & Thurs–Sat 10.30am–1pm & 2.30–5pm, Sun 2.30–5pm; 50p). The tourist office (see below) has a helpful compendium of local **walks**, one of the best being the short but brisk hike up to the top of Gallow Hill, from where there are great views out over Annandale; allow a couple of hours.

Practicalities

Buses to Moffat drop passengers on High Street near the **tourist office** (April, May Sept & Oct daily 10am–5pm, June–Aug daily 9.30am–6pm; ☎01683/220620). The best **hotel** in town is the opulent *Moffat House Hotel*, High St (☎01683/220039; ⑦). Some alternatives include the palatable *Buccleuch Arms* (☎01683/220003; ⑤) and the no-frills *Star Hotel* (☎01683/220156; ④), both on High St. For **B&Bs** try along Beechgrove, a five-minute walk from the town centre: head north along High St, continue down Academy Rd, turn beside Moffat Academy. Here you'll find *Mrs Murray*, no. 12 (☎01683/220538; March–Sept; ③); *Mrs Pirie*, no. 23 (March–Oct; ☎01683/220550; ③); *Gilbert House* (☎01683/220050; ③); and *Springbank* (March–Nov; ☎01683/20070; ②). The *Hammerland's Farm* **camping** and caravan site (March–Oct; ☎01683/220436) sits beside the Selkirk road, about half a mile east of Moffat.

The *Buccleuch Arms* serves the finest **bar meals** in town, while further up High St, the *Valle Verde Trattoria* (closed Wed) has filling, very cheap pizzas, and *Pacitti's* café serves great coffee and average snacks. You might also want to try the local treat, **Moffat toffee**.

Around Moffat

From Moffat, there are three beautiful routes you can take through the most dramatic parts of the Southern Uplands. Of the three, the finest is the A708 between Moffat and Selkirk (see p.124), via **Moffat Water** and **Yarrow Water**. On the way, the Grey Mare's Tail Waterfall provides the opportunity for an exhilarating ramble and St Mary's Loch gives easy access to an especially stimulating section of the Southern Upland Way. Further west, the second route uses the A701, which climbs over the hills at the head of Annandale, cuts down **Tweeddale**, and joins the Tweed Valley near Peebles (see p.126). The third option begins at Elvanfoot on the M/A74, where the B7040 leaves the main road to cross the **Lowther Hills**. Passing through the former lead mining villages of **Leadhills** and **Wanlockhead**, this road reaches Nithsdale north of Drumlanrig Castle (see p.139).

Travelling these routes by **bus** remains difficult. The only service along the A708 is the *Harrier Scenic Bus Service*, which runs from Moffat to Melrose once weekly between July and late September. The *Harrier* also links Moffat and Peebles via the A701 once weekly during the summer. The only way to reach Leadhills and Wanlockhead is on the once- or twice-daily service from Sanquhar in Nithsdale.

Moffat Water and Yarrow Water

Heading northeast from Moffat, the A708 snakes its way through the forests and hills along the lower stretches of **Moffat Water**. Before long the road climbs to wilder terrain, tracking along the bottom of a gloomy gully surrounded by desolate moorland. Beyond, ten miles from town, the 200ft **Grey Mare's Tail Waterfall** tumbles down a rocky crevasse – one of Dumfries' best-known beauty spots. Maintained by the NTS, the base of the falls is approached by a precipitous footpath along the stream, a ten-minute clamber each way from the road. There's a longer hike too, up the other bank, past the head of the falls, and on to remote **Loch Skeen**.

Back on the road, and crossing over into the Borders, it's a few miles further to the pair of icy lakes that mark the start of **Yarrow Water**. Tiny **Loch of the Lowes** to the south and the larger **St Mary's Loch** to the north are separated by a slender isthmus and magnificently set beneath the surrounding hills. This spot was popular with the nineteenth-century Scottish literati, especially Walter Scott and his friend James Hogg, the "Shepherd poet of Ettrick", who gathered to chew the fat at **Tibbie Shiels Inn** on the isthmus (☎01750/42231; ④). The inn takes its name from Isabella Shiel, a formidable and, by all accounts, amusing woman who ruled the place till her death in 1878 at the age of ninety-six. Today, the inn is a famous watering hole on the Southern Upland Way. For a short and enjoyable walk, follow the footpath from the inn along the east side of St Mary's Loch into **Bowerhope forest**. Alternatively, the Southern Upland Way heads across the moors north to Traquair House and south to the valley of the Ettrick Water, both strenuous hikes that require an Ordnance Survey map, a compass and proper clothing (see "Outdoor Pursuits" in *Basics*).

East of St Mary's Loch, the A708 follows the course of the Yarrow Water down to Selkirk, about 17 miles away. You can stay en route at the roadside Broadmeadows **youth hostel** (April–Sept; ☎01750/76262; Grade 3) in **Yarrowford**, near Bowhill House and Selkirk (see p.124).

Tweeddale

Just north of Moffat, the A701 ascends the west side of **Annandale** to skirt the impressive box canyon at its head. Best viewed from the road about six miles from town, the gorge – the **Devil's Beef Tub** – takes its name from the days when rustling Reivers hid their herds here. Walter Scott described the place aptly: "It looks as if four hills were laying their heads together to shut out daylight from the dark hollow place between them". The gorge was also a suitably secret hideaway for persecuted Covenanters during Charles II's "Killing Times".

Beyond the Tub, the road crosses over into **Tweeddale** and soon reaches tiny **Tweedsmuir**, where you could, as an alternative route, take the right turn over the Tweedsmuir Hills to St Mary's Loch (see above). Keeping to the A701, widening Tweeddale loses some of its scenic appeal long before it reaches the village of **BROUGHTON**. Here, there's a modest **museum** (May to mid-Oct daily 2–5pm; £1) inside the old Free Church in honour of novelist John Buchan, who spent his child-hood holidays in the district.

The Lowther Hills

West of Moffat, sandwiched between the M/A74 and Nithsdale, the **Lowther Hills** offer a wild landscape of tightly clustered peaks, bare until the heather blooms, hiding fast-flowing burns and narrow valleys – a dramatic terrain once known as "God's Treasure House" on account of its gold and silver ores. These mineral deposits were much sought after by the impoverished kings of Scotland, who banned their export and claimed a monopoly – draconian measures that only encouraged smuggling. There was lead here too, mined from Roman times right up to the 1950s, and used in the manufac-ture of pottery and glass.

Leadhills and Wanlockhead

Twenty-one miles north of Moffat, tiny **LEADHILLS** has a disconsolate air born of its wilderness surroundings. The terraced cottages of this classic "company town" were built by the mine owners for their employees, but the boom years ended in the 1830s, since when the village has been left pretty much to itself.

A couple of miles away, remote and windswept **WANLOCKHEAD**, at 1500ft the highest village in Scotland, is even smaller than its neighbour. It shares Leadhills' mining history, but Wanlockhead's attempts to lure the tourists have made the villages very different. The **Scottish Lead Mining Museum** (April–Oct daily 11am–4pm; £2) deserves a good hour or two, beginning with the spruce **visitor centre**, which traces the development of the industry and its workforce. Afterwards, highlights of the open-air site include a guided tour of the underground **Loch Nell Mine** and of a couple of restored miners' cottages. There's also a rare example of a wooden **beam engine** and all sorts of industrial bits and pieces, mostly dating from the late 1950s when govern-ment grants sponsored a brief revival in lead mining; the earlier workings were closed in the 1930s. Sometimes the eighteenth-century **library** is open too (early May–late Sept Wed, Sat & Sun 2–4pm), its books purchased from the voluntary subscriptions of its members: at its height, the library had a stock of 2000 volumes.

Wanlockhead straddles the Southern Upland Way, and is thus blessed with a **youth hostel** (April–Oct; ☎01659/74252; Grade 2), sited in the old mine surgeon's house. The museum's visitor centre has the details of a couple of cheap B&Bs.

Biggar and around

Five miles north of the Leadhills turning on the M/A74, Edinburgh traffic leaves the motorway to head northeast along the A702. Most people shoot straight through to the capital – it's only about 40 miles – but, if you're looking to break your journey, the old market town of **BIGGAR** warrants an hour or two. Start your visit at the **Moat Park**

Heritage Centre (April–Oct Mon–Sat 10am–5pm, Sun 2–5pm; £1.50), which occupies a grand neo-Romanesque church near the foot of Kirkstyle (off High St). Inside, a well-presented exhibition traces the history of Upper Clydesdale, and on the upper floor you can see a display of extraordinary table covers made by local tailor Menzies Moffat (1828–1907). Don't miss the banquet-size Royal Crimean Hero Tablecloth, which sets a cartoon strip of notable figures alongside scenes from Scottish country life. Biggar has three other museums; the nearest, the **Gladstone Court Museum** (April–Oct Mon–Sat 10am–12.30pm & 2–5pm, Sun 2–5pm; £1), across Kirkstyle on North Back Rd, boasts a shop-lined Victorian street illustrating different aspects of nineteenth-century life, from the telephone exchange and classroom to the bank and the cobblers. Returning to Kirkstyle, walk over the hill to the footpath beside Biggar burn. To the right is the **Greenhill Covenanters' Museum** (April to mid-Oct daily 2–5pm; 50p), which attempts to explore the development of the Covenanting movement and the religious conflicts that ensued. To the left along the burn lies **Biggar Gasworks Museum** (June–Sept daily 2–5pm; free). Before North Sea gas was piped across the UK, small coal-based gasworks like this one were common. Most were demolished in the 1970s, but Biggar's has survived and even manages to look quite spick-and-span.

Back up High Street, the **sundial** outside the tourist office is the work of local poet-artist Ian Hamilton **Finlay**, a founder of the "concrete poetry" movement; you can see more of his work in Edinburgh's National Gallery of Modern Art.

Practicalities

Regular **bus** services to Biggar arrive from a wide range of towns including Edinburgh, Peebles, Moffat and Dumfries. They stop on High St, near the **tourist office** (Easter–June & Sept to mid-Oct Mon–Sat 10am–5pm, Sun 11am–5pm; July & Aug Mon–Sat 9am–7pm, Sun 11am–5pm; ☎01899/221066). There's a **B&B**, *"Daleside"*, 165 High St (☎01899/220097; ②), a stone's throw away. For **food**, both the *Elphinstone Hotel* and the *Crown*, on High St, have good daily specials.

Around Biggar

Six miles west of Biggar along the A72/73, near the village of Thankerton, the solitary peak of **Tinto Hill** was the site of Druidic festivals in honour of the sun-god Baal, or Bel. It's relatively easy to walk the footpath up to the 2320ft-high summit, from where the views are splendid – you'll also see a Druidic Circle and a Bronze Age burial cairn. A regular **bus** links Biggar with Thankerton.

Just north of Biggar lie the southern extremities of the **Pentland Hills**, the narrow belt of upland extending into the suburbs of Edinburgh. The hills are best visited from the capital, but the pretty little village of **WEST LINTON**, straddling the Lyne Water 12 miles from Biggar, gives ready access to several rambles across the neighbouring hills. If you decide to **stay**, try the large Victorian country house of *Mrs McCallum*, Carlops Rd (April–Oct; ☎01968/660795; ⑤).

THE SOUTHWEST

Up until the eleventh century the whole of **Southwest Scotland** was known as Galloway, where independent chieftains maintained close contacts with the Vikings rather than the Scots. Gradually, this autonomy was whittled away and by the late thirteenth century the region, which comprises the rough triangle of land between the Solway Firth, the Firth of Clyde and the stretch from Dumfries to Kilmarnock, was integrated into Scotland. Indeed, it was here that both Robert the Bruce and William Wallace launched their wars against the English. Later on, from around the seventeenth century, the ports of the Solway Coast prospered with the expansion of local shipping routes over to Ireland, and, later still, the towns along the Firth of Clyde bene-fited from the industrialization of Glasgow. The region subsequently experienced economic decline as trade routes changed, turning busy ports into sleepy backwaters, and these days Southwest Scotland is agreeably laid-back, not crossed by motorway and – with most travellers skipping past on their way to the Highlands and islands – suffering little of the tourist crush familiar further north.

Robert Burns lived and died in this part of Scotland, a fact much exploited by the tour-ist offices. **The Burns Heritage Trail**, a motorist's route across much of the region, passes every conceivable place with which he had any connection, but frankly, unless you're particularly devoted, stick to the Burns sights in **Dumfries** (also Ayr and Alloway).

Extending southwest of Dumfries, the low-lying **Solway Coast** boasts the delight-fully tranquil township of **Kirkcudbright** and a handful of splendid medieval ruins, principally **Caerlaverock Castle** and **Sweetheart Abbey**. Criss-crossed by walking trails that cater for every level of athleticism and any amount of time, the **Galloway Hills** rise just to the north of the coast, their beautiful moors, mountains, lakes and rivers centred on the 150,000-acre **Galloway Forest Park**. After this come the rolling hills of the **Ayrshire Coast**, whose mostly agricultural landscapes are enlivened by a string of wide, flat sandy beaches and the occasional strip of coastal cliff. Here you'll also find the diverting town of **Ayr**, noteworthy for its Burns attractions and beach, and the district's other main resort, **Largs**, with its agreeable setting between hills and sea.

Travelling the region by **bus** presents few problems and there's a good **train** service from Glasgow along the Ayrshire coast to Stranraer. It's also easy to travel on from Southwest Scotland by **ferry**, from Stranraer to Belfast and Larne, in Northern Ireland, and from the port of Ardrossan, north of Ayr, to the Isle of Arran, where you can hopscotch on up the Western Isles.

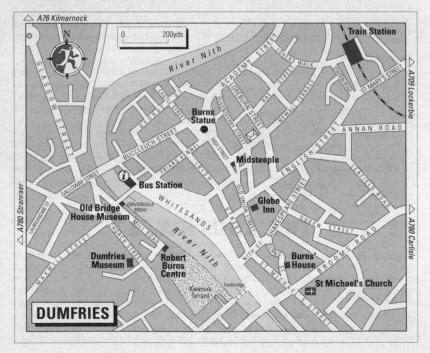

Dumfries and around

With a population of 30,000, bustling **DUMFRIES** crowds the banks of the River Nith a few miles from the Solway Firth. Long known as the "Queen of the South", the town flourished as a medieval seaport and trading centre, its success attracting the attention of many English armies. The invaders managed to polish off most of the early settlement in 1448, 1536 and again in 1570, but Dumfries survived to prosper with its light industries supplying the agricultural hinterland. The town planners of the 1960s badly damaged the town, reducing it to an architectural hotch-potch, with – as the prime example – the graceful fifteenth-century lines of Devorguilla Bridge set against cereal-box apartment blocks. Nevertheless, the town makes a convenient base for exploring the Solway coast, and is at least worth a visit for its associations with Robert Burns, who spent the last five years of his life here.

The Town

Hemmed in by the river to the north and west, the snout-shaped centre of Dumfries radiates out from the pedestrianized **High Street**, which runs roughly parallel to the Nith. At its northern edge is the **Burns Statue**, a fanciful piece of Victorian frippery featuring the great man holding a poesy in one hand, whilst the other clutches at his heart. They haven't forgotten his faithful hound either, who lies curled around his feet.

Heading south down High Street, it's a couple of minutes' walk to **Midsteeple**, the old prison-cum-courthouse, and the narrow alley that leads to the smoky, oak-panelled *Globe Inn*, one of Burns' favourite drinking spots, and still a tavern. Continuing down the street, follow the signs to the **Burns' House** (Easter–Sept Mon–Sat 10am–1pm & 2–5pm, Sun 2–5pm; Oct–Easter Tues–Sat only; 80p), a simple sandstone building where the poet died of rheumatic heart disease in 1796. Inside, there's an incidental collection of Burns' memorabilia – manuscripts, letters and the like – and one of the bedroom windows bears his signature, scratched with his diamond ring.

Burns was buried in a simple grave beside **St Michael's Church**, a monstrous eighteenth-century heap just south of his house. Just 20 years later, though, he was dug up and moved across the graveyard to a purpose-built Neoclassical **Mausoleum**, whose bright white columns hide a statue of Burns being accosted by the Poetic Muse. The subject matter may be mawkish, but the execution is excellent – notice the hang of the bonnet and the twist of the trousers. All around, in contrasting brownstone, stand the tombstones of the town's bourgeoisie, including many of the poet's friends; a plan indicates exactly where each is interred.

From the mausoleum, saunter back along the Nith and cross Devorguilla Bridge to the tiny **Old Bridge House Museum** (April–Sept Mon–Sat 10am–1pm & 2–5pm, Sun 2–5pm; free) of local bric-a-brac – including a teeth-chattering range of Victorian dental gear – and the **Robert Burns Centre** (April–Sept Mon–Sat 10am–8pm, Sun 2–5pm; Oct–March Tues–Sat 10am–1pm & 2–5pm; free but video 80p), sited in an old water mill, which concentrates on the poet's years in Dumfries. On the hill above, occupying an eighteenth-century windmill, the **Dumfries Museum** (April–Sept Mon–Sat 10am–1pm & 2–5pm, Sun 2–5pm; Oct–March Tues–Sat only; free) traces the region's natural and human history and features a camera obscura on its top floor (April–Sept only; 80p).

Practicalities

Dumfries train station, on the east side of town, is a five-minute walk from the centre. The **bus station** stands at the top of Whitesands beside the River Nith on the west edge of the centre, next to the **tourist office** (Nov–March Mon–Sat 10am–4.30pm &

2–5pm; April, May & Oct daily 10am–5pm; June–Sept daily 9.30am–6pm; ☎01387/ 253862) where they will book accommodation for a ten percent refundable deposit.

There are lots of **guest houses** and **B&Bs** in the handsome villas clustered round the train station, including *Morton Villa*, 28 Lovers Walk (☎01387/255825; ②); *Lindean*, 50 Rae St (☎01387/251888; ③); and *Redlands Guest House*, 54 Rae St (☎01387/268382; ③). For a more distinctive setting try along Kenmure Terrace, a short block of attractive old houses overlooking the Nith from beside the footbridge below the Burns Centre. Of the three choices, *The Haven*, no. 1 (☎10387/251281; ③), should be your first port of call. If you're looking for a **hotel**, head for Laurieknowe, a five- to ten-minute walk west from the bus station, where you'll find the *Edenbank Hotel* (☎01387/ 252759; ⑤). *Grierson and Graham*, 10 Academy St (☎01387/259483), offer **bike rental**, useful for reaching the nearby Solway coast.

The cheapest **meals** in town are provided by the popular *YMCA* café *Grapevine*, Castle St (Mon–Fri 10am–3pm, Sat 10am–2.30pm), behind and beyond the Burns Statue. The *Hole in the Wa'* **pub**, down an alley opposite *Woolworth's* on High St, sells reasonable bar food. If you want a pub with more atmosphere, however, you should make your way instead to the earthy *Globe Inn*.

Around Dumfries: the east Solway coast and Nithsdale

The magnificent **Caerlaverock Castle** and the fine early Christian cross at **Ruthwell** are to be found on the shores of the Solway Firth southeast of Dumfries, from where a regular **bus** service runs to both. Alternatively, if you're heading north, the A76 travels the length of **Nithsdale** (there are also regular buses along this route), whose gentle slopes and old forests hide one major attraction, the massive, many turreted seventeenth-century mansion of **Drumlanrig Castle**.

Caerlaverock Castle and Wildlife Centre

The remote and lichen-stained **Caerlaverock Castle**, eight miles from Dumfries (April–Sept Mon–Sat 9.30am–6pm, Sun 2–6pm; Oct–March Mon–Sat 9.30am–4pm, Sun 2–4pm; £2), forms a dramatic triangle with a mighty gatehouse at the apex. It clearly impressed medieval chroniclers. During the siege of 1300, Edward I's balladeer, Walter of Exeter, commented: "In shape it was like a shield, for it had but three sides round it, with a tower at each corner . . . and good ditches filled right up to the brim with water. And I think you will never see a more finely situated castle."

Nowadays, close inspection reveals several phases of construction, which reflect Caerlaverock's turbulent past: time and again, the castle was attacked and slighted, each subsequent rebuilding further modifying the late thirteenth-century original. For instance, the fifteenth-century machicolations of the gatehouse top earlier towers that are themselves studded with wide-mouthed gunports from around 1590. This confusion of styles continues inside, where the gracious Renaissance facade of the **Nithsdale Apartments** was added by the first earl in 1634. Nithsdale didn't get much value for money: just six years later he was forced to surrender his castle to the Covenanters, who proceeded to wreck the place. It was never inhabited again.

From the castle it's about three miles further on to the **Caerlaverock Wildfowl and Wetlands Centre** (daily 10am–5pm; £3), 1400 acres of protected salt marsh and mud flat edging the Solway Firth. A National Nature Reserve and a Wildfowl and Wetlands Trust Refuge, the centre is equipped with screened approaches that link the main observatory to a score of well-situated birdwatchers' hides. It's famous for the 12,000 or so Barnacle Geese which return here in winter. Between May and August, when the geese are away, walkers along a wetlands trail may glimpse the rare natterjack toad. Throughout the year, the wardens run a varied **bird-watching** programme – ring

☎01387/770200 for up-to-date details. Both the castle and the centre are reached along the B725; this is the route the bus takes, mostly terminating at the castle but sometimes continuing to the start of the two-mile lane leading off the B725 to the centre.

The Ruthwell Cross
From the nature reserve it's about seven miles east along the B725 to both the village of **RUTHWELL** and the B724, the minor Dumfries–Annan road which trims its northern edge. Here you should turn down the short, signposted lane to the modest country church. The keys are kept at one of the houses at the foot of the lane; just look for the notice. Inside the church is the **Ruthwell Cross**, an extraordinary early Christian monument dating from the late seventh century when Galloway was ruled by the Northumbrians. The 18ft-high Cross reveals a striking diversity of influences, with Germanic and Roman Catholic decoration and, running round the edge, a poem written in both runic figures and Northumbrian dialect. But it's the Biblical carvings on the main face that really catch the eye, notably Mary Magdalene washing the feet of Jesus.

If you want to **stay**, the comfortable *Kirkland Country House Hotel* (☎01387/870284; ④) is next to the church.

Nithsdale
North of Dumfries the A76 strips along the southern reaches of Nithsdale, a pastoral scene with the Lowther Hills brooding in the distance. After 18 miles, just beyond the antiquated cottages of tiny **Thornhill**, lies **Drumlanrig Castle** (house May to mid-June Mon–Wed & Fri 1–5pm, Sat & Sun 11am–5pm; mid-June to Aug daily except Thurs 11am–5pm; park May to mid-Sept daily 11am–6pm; £4), not in fact a castle at all, but the grandiose stately home of the Duke of Buccleuch and Queensberry. Drumlanrig, which has an imperial, pink-sandstone facade, with cupolas, turrets and towers surrounding an interior courtyard, is graced by a charming horseshoe-shaped stairway – a welcome touch of informality to the stateliness of the structure behind.

Inside, a string of luxurious rooms witness the immense wealth of the family. Among the priceless hoard of antique furnishings and fittings – which include a few mementoes dating to the overnight visit of Bonnie Prince Charlie – are a trio of famous painitings exhibited in the **staircase hall**. These are Rembrandt's *Old Woman Reading*, a sensual composition dappling the shadow of the subject's hood against her white surplice, Holbein's formal portrait of *Sir Nicholas Carew*, and the *Madonna with the Yarnwinder* by Leonardo da Vinci. Other works are by Joost van Cleef, Breughel, Jan Grossaert (otherwise Mabuse) and Van Dyck, and there are endless family portraits by Allan Ramsay and Godfrey Kneller. Also look out for a striking 1950s portrait of the present duchess, all debutante coiffure and high society shoulders, by John Merton, and in the serving room, John Ainslie's *Joseph Florence the Chef*, a sharply observed and dynamic portrait much liked by Walter Scott.

The forested **country park** surrounding the house is criss-crossed by well-maintained footpaths and cycle routes; mountain **bikes** can be rented in the castle precincts. If you're heading here by bus from Dumfries or Ayr, bear in mind it's a one-and-a-half-mile walk from the road to the house.

Leaving Drumlanrig, the A76 slips through the wooded hills of Nithsdale, passing the turning to Wanlockhead (see p.134) en route to **Sanquhar**, a trim market town with an attractive Georgian tolbooth. Pressing on, **Kirkconnel** prefigures the industrial settlements further north, one of them being **Cumnock**, for many years the home of James Keir Hardie, whose bronze bust stands outside the Town Hall. At Cumnock, there's a choice of routes. The A76 ploughs on to Kilmarnock, whilst the A70 crosses the Ayrshire hills to reach the coast of Ayr.

The Solway coast to the Galloway Hills

The creeks, bays and peninsulas of the **Solway coast** string along the Solway Firth, a shallow estuary wedged between Scotland and England. Edged by tidal marsh and mud bank, much of the shoreline is flat and eerily remote, but there are also some fine rocky bays sheltering beneath wooded hills, most notably at Rockcliffe, about 20 miles west of Dumfries. **Kirkcudbright** and **Gatehouse of Fleet** were once bustling ports thronged with sailing ships, but they were bypassed by the Victorian train network and so slipped into economic decline which in effect preserved their handsome eighteenth- and early nineteenth-century town houses and workers' cottages. Both these towns are popular with – but not crowded by – tourists, as are **Sweetheart Abbey**, whose splendid Gothic remains are near Dumfries, and **Threave Castle**, a gaunt tower house perched on an islet just outside Castle Douglas.

Within comfortable striking distance of the coast are the **Galloway Hills**, whose forested knolls and grassy peaks flank lochs and tumbling burns – classic Southern Upland scenery, with scores of trails within **Galloway Forest Park**.

Sweetheart Abbey

NEW ABBEY, a tidy hamlet eight miles south of Dumfries, is home to the red sandstone ruins of **Sweetheart Abbey** (April–Sept Mon–Sat 9.30am–6pm, Sun 2–6pm; Oct–March Mon–Wed 9.30am–4pm, Thurs 9.30am–12.30pm, Sat 9.30am–4pm, Sun 2–4pm; £1.50). Founded by Cistercians in 1273, Sweetheart takes its name from the obsessive behaviour of its patron, Devorguilla de Balliol, who carried her husband's embalmed heart around with her for the last 16 years of her life. The site is dominated by the remains of the Abbey Church, a massive structure that abandons the austere simplicity of earlier Cistercian foundations. The grand, high-pointed window arches of the nave, set beneath the elaborate clerestory, draw the eye to a mighty central tower with a battlemented parapet and flamboyant corbels. The opulent style reflects the monks' wealth, born of their skill in turning the wastes and swamps of Solway into productive farmland.

After the abbey, pop into the **Abbey Cottage** tearooms next door for a great cup of coffee and a piece of homemade cake. **To stay** in the village, try the *Criffel Inn*, 2 The Square (☎01387/850244; ④).

The Colvend coast: Rockcliffe

South of Sweetheart, the A710 cuts across a handsome landscape of rolling farmland on its way to the **Colvend coast**, a six-mile-long, low-key holiday strip extending north from Sandyhills to Dalbeattie. In the middle, nestling round a beautiful cove, is **ROCKCLIFFE**, a beguiling little place from where there are some great walks. At low tide you can waddle out across the mud flats to **Rough Island**, a humpy twenty-acre bird sanctuary owned by the NTS, though it's out of bounds in May and June when the Terns and Oyster Catchers are nesting. Alternatively, you can stroll up the coast along the "Jubilee Path" a mile or so to the **Mote of Mark**, a Celtic hill fort, and continue another couple of miles to the village of **Kippford**, once a ship-repair centre, and now a cosy holiday spot strung out along an estuary. On the way here, you'll walk past the Rough Firth causeway, a more reliable route to Rough Island. Beyond Kippford you can head north to Castle Douglas (see opposite) or continue west along the coast to Kirkcudbright (see p.142). The coastal road drifts across a wide-skied agricultural landscape that's beautifully set against the sea. On the way, a brief signposted detour down a narrow country lane will also take in the evocative remains of **Orchardton Tower** (free), a mid-fifteenth-century fortified tower house, unusual in its circular design.

Rockcliffe has a reasonable range of **accommodation**, but note that reservations are recommended during the summer. There's the attractive *Albany B&B* (☎01556/630355; ③), right on the seafront, and several cottages available for rental by the week:

try *Westlin* (April–Oct; ☎01556/630212), overlooking the bay, which sleeps four for between £140 and £200, or the charming *Port Donnell* cottage rented out by the NTS (details from head office in Edinburgh; ☎0131/226 5922). The only **hotel**, the grand *Barons Craig* (April–Oct; ☎01556/660225; ⑨), occupies a splendid Victorian mansion on the hill above the bay.

Around Castle Douglas

The eighteenth-century streets of **CASTLE DOUGLAS**, 11 miles north of Rockcliffe, were designed by the town's owner, William Douglas, a local lad who made a fortune trading in the West Indies. Douglas had ambitious plans to turn his town into a prosperous industrial and commercial centre, but, like his scheme to create an extensive Galloway canal system, it didn't quite work.

You'll only need to hang around town long enough to get your bearings as the district's two attractions are well outside the centre, but you might consider renting a **bike** here – at *Ace Cycles*, 11 Church St (Mon–Sat 9am–5pm; ☎01556/504542). Beginning from the **bus station**, at the west end of the long main drag, King Street – the **tourist office** (April–Oct daily 9am–5pm; ☎05156/502611) is at the other end – it's about a mile's walk west to **Threave Garden** (daily 9.30am–sunset; £3.50), which can also be reached direct from the A75 – the signposted turning is at the roundabout on the west side of town. The garden features a magnificent spread of flowers and woodland, 60 acres subdivided into over a dozen areas, from the bright, old-fashioned blooms of the Rose Garden to the brilliant banks of rhododendrons in the Woodland Garden and the ranks of primula, astilbe and gentian in the Peat Garden. In springtime thousands turn up for the flowering of over 200 types of daffodil and, from late May onwards, the herbaceous beds are the main attraction, with most of them arranged like islets in a sea of lawn (so that they can be viewed from all sides). The exception is the more formal beds of the Walled Garden, which adjoin the greenhouses and the nursery.

Threave Garden was developed by the NTS as a teaching arena for its School of Horticulture, whose students occupy Threave House, the hulking Victorian mansion that was the residence of the last laird. The **visitor centre** (April to late Oct daily 9.30am–5.30pm) has maps of the garden and the surrounding estate (also NTS property) and provides some background on several botanically minded explorers of yesteryear – though the restaurant's fruit pies are more immediately satisfying.

To reach **Threave Castle** (April–Sept Mon–Sat 9am–6pm & Sun 2–6pm; £1.50), return to the A75 roundabout and cut straight across, down the mile-long country lane which brings you to the start of the footpath to the River Dee. It's a ten-minute walk down to the river where you ring a brass bell for the boat over to the less stern-looking stronghold, stuck on a flat and grassy islet. Built for a Black Douglas, Archibald the Grim, in around 1370, the fortress was among the first of its kind, a sturdy, rectangular structure completed shortly after the War of Independence when clan feuding spurred a frenzy of castle-building. The bleak lines of the original structure are, however, partly obscured by a ricketty, fifteenth-century curtain wall, thrown up as a desperate – and unsuccessful – attempt to defend the castle against James II. Determined to crush the Black Douglases, the king personally murdered the eighth earl after dinner in Stirling and subsequently appropriated his estate. The Covenanters wrecked the place in the 1640s, but enough remains of the interior to make out its general plan, beginning with the storage areas and spitefully gloomy prison in the basement. Up above, the first – and entrance – floor was once reached from the outside by removable timber stairs, while inside a spiral staircase ascended to the upper floors – you can still make out its course. The roof was flat to accommodate stone-throwing machinery with projecting wooden galleries to enable the defenders to drop everything harmful onto the heads of the attackers – from the outside you can still discern the holes where the timber supports were lodged.

Kirkcudbright

KIRKCUDBRIGHT (pronounced "Kirkcoobrie"), hugging the muddy banks of the Dee ten miles southwest of Castle Douglas, has a quaint harbour and most beguiling of town centres, a charming medley of simple brick cottages with medieval pends, Georgian villas and Victorian town houses. This is the setting for **MacLellan's Castle** (April–Sept Mon–Sat 9.30am–6pm, Sun 2–6pm; Oct–March Sat 9.30am–4pm, Sun 2–4pm; £1) a sullen pink-flecked hulk towering above the harbourside. Part fortified tower house and part spacious mansion, the castle dates from the late sixteenth century when a degree of law and order permitted the aristocracy to relax its old defensive preoccupations. As a consequence, chimneys have replaced battlements at the wall-heads and windows begin at the ground floor. Nevertheless, the walls remain impressively thick and there are a handful of wide-mouthed gun loops, though these are haphazard affairs designed to deter intruders rather than beat off an invading army. Inside, it's easy to pick out the vaulted basement – which accommodated the kitchen and storerooms – underpinning three upper storeys, home to a rabbit-warren of well-appointed domestic apartments. Also, keep an eye out for a real curiosity, the laird's lug, or peephole, behind the fireplace of the Great Hall. The castle was built for Sir Thomas MacLellan, who now lies buried in the neighbouring **Greyfrairs Church** (daily 9am–5pm; free), where his tomb is an eccentrically crude attempt at Neoclassicism – it even incorporates parts of someone else's gravestone.

Close by, on the L-shaped High Street, **Broughton House** (April to mid-Oct daily 1–5.30pm; £2) was once the home of Edward Hornel, an important member of the late nineteenth-century Scottish art establishment. Hornel and his buddies – The Glasgow Boys (see p.176) – established a self-regarding artists' colony in Kirkcudbright, and some of their work, impressionistic in style, is on display here. It's all pretty modest stuff, but Hornel's paintings of Japan, a country he often visited, are bright and cheery, and the house itself is a delight. Hornel had the Georgian manison he bought in 1901 modified to include a studio and a mahogany-panelled gallery decked out with a frieze of the Elgin marbles. He also designed the lovely **Japanese garden**.

A couple of minutes's walk away is the church-like **tolbooth**, which once served as court house, prison and town hall. Its clock faces are offset so that they can be viewed down both parts of High Street. Recently the building has been turned into the **Tolbooth Art Centre** (March–May & Oct Mon–Sat 11am–4pm; June–Sept Mon–Sat 11am–5pm & Sun 2–5pm; Nov–Feb Sat 11am–4pm only; £1.50), featuring more examples of the work of Hornel and his associates, whose history is detailed in an explanatory video. The studios on the upper floor are leased to artists and craftworkers, whom you can sometimes watch at work.

Don't miss the **Stewartry Museum** on St Mary St (March, April & Oct daily 11am–4pm; May Mon–Sat 11am–5pm; June–Sept Mon–Sat 11am–5pm, Sun 2–5pm; Nov–Feb Sat only 11am–4pm; £1.50), where, packed into a purpose-built Victorian building, hundreds of local exhibits illuminate the life and times of the Solway Coast. It's an extraordinary collection, cabinets crammed with anything from glass bottles, weaving equipment, pipes, pictures and postcards to stuffed birds, pickled fish and the tri-cornered hats once worn by town officials. There are also examples of book jackets designed by Jessie King and E A Taylor, two of Hornel's coterie.

Practicalities

Buses to Kirkcudbright stop by the harbour, next to the **tourist office** (April–June, Sept & Oct daily 10am–5pm; July & Aug daily 10am–6pm; ☎01557/330494), where you can get help finding accommodation, a service you will probably need in high season. The town has several quality **hotels** – the best among them the *Gladstone House*, a

WALKS AROUND KIRKCUDBRIGHT

Easy and popular walks around Kirkcudbright include the seven-mile round trip up the Dee to **Tongland Power Station** (May–Sept Mon–Sat guided tours 4 times daily; £1; bookings ☎01557/330114), whose turbines and generators are housed in a fine Art Deco building. Another option is the five-mile trek southeast along narrow country roads to **DUNDRENNAN**, an appealing little village hiding the grey-stone ruins of **Dundrennan Abbey** (April–Sept Mon–Sat 9.30am–6pm & Sun 2–6pm; £1). Enough remains of this twelfth-century foundation to be able to appreciate its architectural simplicity, in contrast to the more ornate style adopted by its daughter house, Sweetheart at New Abbey (see p.140). **Bus** service #501 connects Kirkcudbright and Dundrennan (Mon–Fri 4 daily, Sat 2 daily). Further details – including a 30p leaflet, *Walks around Kirkcudbright* – of these and other local walks are available from the Kirkcudbright tourist office.

renovated Georgian town house at 48 High St (☎01557/331734; ⑤), and the *Selkirk Arms*, an attractivly refurbished eighteenth-century hotel just up the road (☎01557/330402; ⑦). For a convenient **B&B**, walk over to Castle St where there's the *Castle Guest House*, no. 16 (Feb–Nov; ☎01557/330204; ③); or stick to High St for both *Mrs Grant*, no. 82 (☎01557/330197; ⑦), and *Mrs Durok*, no. 109A (☎01557/331279; ②). You could also try along Millburn St (follow High St onto St Mary's Place and it's the first turning on the left) at *Millburn House* (☎01577/330926; ④). For **camping**, *Silvercraigs Caravan and Camping Site* (Easter–late Oct; ☎01557/330123) is on a bluff overlooking town at the end of St Mary's Place, five to ten minutes' walk from the centre. **Bikes** can be rented from *Tolbooth Crafts*, St Mary St (no phone).

Kirkcudbright is light on **restaurants**, but the cheap and cheerful *Belfry*, up along St Cuthbert St from the tourist office, serves filling daytime snacks, while the *Selkirk Arms* serves excellent bar meals. The *Auld Alliance*, 5 Castle St (☎01557/330569), is a superior, if pricy, restaurant offering an imaginative mixture of French and Scottish cuisine. For a **drink**, the busy *Masonic Arms*, Castle St, pulls a reasonable pint.

Gatehouse of Fleet

The quiet streets of **GATEHOUSE OF FLEET**, easily reached by bus from Kirkcudbright ten miles to the east, give no clue that for James Murray, the eighteenth-century laird, this spot was to become the "Glasgow" of the Solway Coast – a centre of the cotton industry whose profits had already made him immeasurably rich. Yorkshire mill owners provided the industrial expertise, imported engineers designed aqueducts to improve the water supply, and dispossessed crofters – and their children – yielded the labour. Between 1760 and 1790, Murray achieved much success, but his custom-built town failed to match its better-placed rivals. By 1850 the boom was over, the mills slipped into disrepair, and nowadays tiny Gatehouse is sustained by tourism and forestry.

It's the country setting that appeals rather than any particular sight, but there are some graceful Georgian houses along High Street, which also has an incongruous, granite clock tower and the **Mill on the Fleet Museum** (April–Oct daily 10am–5.30pm; £2.75), gallantly tracing the history of Gatehouse and Galloway from inside an old bobbin mill. The **tourist office** nearby (April–Oct daily 10am–5pm; ☎01557/814212) sells an excellent leaflet on local **walks**. One of them tracks along Old Military Road, passing through deciduous woodland before circling back near the stark remains of **Cardoness Castle** (April–Sept Mon–Sat 9.30am–6pm, Sun 2–6pm; Oct–March Sat 9.30am–4pm, Sun 2–4pm; £1.20). Perched on a hill, this late fifteenth-century stronghold is a classic example of the fortified tower house, with dense walls and tiny windows. It once edged the Water of Fleet river, but this was canalized long ago and today Cardoness overlooks the minor road linking Gatehouse with the A75. Another walk loops southeast from Gatehouse through the forests beside the Water of Fleet river on towards the Solway Firth. En route, you can't miss James Murray's country mansion, converted into the sumptuous *Cally Palace Hotel* (☎01557/814341; ⑨) – though if you stay here, make sure you are in the old house rather than the ugly modern extension. Accommodation in Gatehouse includes the *Murray Arms Hotel* (☎01557/814207; ⑨), a refurbished nineteenth-century mansion close to the clock tower; and some more affordable and convenient **B&Bs**, such as *Mrs Carlisle*, 29 Fleet St (☎01557/814647; ③), and the *Bay Horse B&B*, 9 Ann St (☎01557/814073; ④). The *Angel Hotel* (☎01557/814516), on the main street near the tourist office, provides simple accommodation for ramblers and backpackers from £7.50 per person per night; best to book in advance. You can grab a snack at the museum, and the *Murray Arms* offers delicious **meals**, along with advice on local **fishing**, including permits for guests.

Newton Stewart and Glen Trool

To the west of Gatehouse, the A75 skirts the mud flats of Wigtown Bay before cutting up to **NEWTON STEWART**, an unassuming market town beside the River Cree, famous for its salmon and trout fishing. The excellent **Creebridge House Hotel** (☎01671/402121; ⑦), in an old hunting lodge near the main bridge, arranges fishing permits for around £15 per day, can provide personal gillies (guides) for a further £25 daily, and at a pinch they'll even rent you all the tackle. The season runs from March to mid-October. The hotel serves great **bar food** too – try the fish or the homemade pies.

With its plentiful supply of accommodation (see below) and good bus connections along the A75, Newton Stewart has also become a popular base for **hikers** heading for the nearby **Galloway Hills**, most of which are enclosed within **Galloway Forest Park**. Many hikers aim for the park's **Glen Trool** by following the A714 north for about ten miles to Bargrennan, where a narrow lane twists the five miles over to the glen's **Loch Trool**. From here, there's a choice of magnificent hiking trails, as well as lesser tracks laid out by the forestry commission. Several longer routes curve round the grassy peaks and icy lochs of the Awful Hand and Dungeon ranges, whilst another includes part of the **Southern Upland Way**, which threads through the Minnigaff hills to Clatteringshaws Loch, beside the A712. This is the road that links Newton Stewart with New Galloway.

Practicalities

Reaching Loch Trool by **bus** is a bit of a pain: service #359 makes the 20-minute trip to Glentrool village between three and six times daily, but you have to walk the final four miles. For the more adventurous **trails**, you'll need to be properly equipped; the Newton Stewart **tourist office** (April–Oct daily 10am–5pm; ☎01671/402431), just off the main street opposite the bus station, has bags of helpful literature. If you mean business, be sure to buy the Ordnance Survey maps and *The Galloway Hills: A Walker's Paradise* by George Brittain (£2.50).

The tourist office will provide a full list of local **accommodation** and book a bed on your behalf. In town, the cheapest choice is the convenient Minnigaff **youth hostel** (April–Sept; ☎01671/402211; Grade 2) in an old school house 650 yards from the main street, near the bridge. Alternatively – apart from the *Creebridge House Hotel* – you could try along Corvisel Rd, a quiet residential street of Victorian brownstone houses near the tourist office, where there's *Lynwood* (☎01671/402074; ③) and *Kilwarlin* (April–Oct; ☎01671/403047; ②). On the southeast outskirts of town near the A75/A712 junction, there's also the luxurious *Kirroughtree Hotel* (mid–Feb to Dec; ☎01671/402141; ⑨), a splendid eighteenth-century mansion surrounded by beautiful gardens focused on banks of azaleas and rhododendrons. Nearby are the well-appointed, two-bedroomed log chalets of the *Conifers Leisure Park* (£100–£230 for 4 people depending on season; minimum stay 3 nights; ☎01671/402107). For **camping**, *Caldons Campsite* (April–Oct; ☎01671/402420) is near the car park at the western tip of Loch Trool.

The Queen's Way: New Galloway and The Glenkens

The 20-mile stretch from Newton Stewart to New Galloway, known as the **Queen's Way**, cuts through the southern periphery of **Galloway Forest Park**, a landscape of glassy lochs, wooded hills and bare, rounded peaks. You'll pass all sorts of **hiking trails**, some the gentlest of strolls, others long-distance treks. For a short walk, stop at the **Talnotry Campsite** (April–Oct; ☎01671/402420), about seven miles from Newton Stewart, where the forestry commission has laid out three trails between two and four miles long: each delves into the pine forests beside the road, crossing gorges and burns. The campsite itself occupies an attractive spot among the wooded hills of the park; you can also buy fishing permits here. A few miles further on is **Clatteringshaws Loch**, a reservoir surrounded by pine forest, with a 14-mile footpath running right round. After a few minutes' walk, this runs past **Bruce's Stone**, a huge boulder where Robert the Bruce is supposed to have rested after victory over the English. The trail also connects with the Southern Upland Way as it meanders north towards the **Rhinns of Kells**, the bumpy range marking the park's eastern boundary.

From the lake, it's seven miles further to **NEW GALLOWAY**, nestling in the river valley at the northern tip of Loch Ken. Although little more than one long street lined by neat and attractive stone houses, it provides further easy access to the Southern Upland Way and the Rhinns of Kells, as does the neighbouring village of **DALRY** – which straddles the Southern Upland Way – a couple of miles upstream. New Galloway is in the valley of The Glenkens, which extends south to Castle Douglas via Loch Ken, and north along the river as far as Carsphairn, a desolate hamlet surrounded by wild moors. Carsphairn is well on the way to Ayr – with the A713 continuing to the coast via the attractive Doon Valley. Here, the old ironworks at **WATERSIDE** are being turned into a large-scale, open-air museum.

Practicalities

Connecting with services from Dumfries and Kirkcudbright, the fast and frequent Castle Douglas to Ayr **bus** stops in New Galloway. There's no official tourist office, but **The Smithy Teashop** (March, April & Oct daily 10am–6pm; May–Sept daily 10am–8pm), on High St, provides all the essential information. The village has several **hotels** and **B&Bs** strung along the main drag: try the agreeable *Leamington Hotel* (closed Nov; ☎01644/420327; ④), or *The Smithy* itself (March–Oct; ☎01644/420269; ②), which also serves excellent meals and snacks. If you want to stay in **Dalry**, head for the attractive *Lochinvar Hotel* (☎01644/430210; ④). The nearest **youth hostel** at Kendoon (mid-May to Sept; no phone; Grade 3), is five miles north of Dalry along the B7000, near the Southern Upland Way. It's also about 15 minutes' walk from the A713; if you're travelling there on the Castle Douglas–Ayr bus, ask the driver to tell you when to get off.

The Machars

The Machars, the name given to the peninsula of rolling farmland and open landscapes south of Newton Stewart, is a neglected part of the coastline, with a somewhat disconsolate air. Just six miles off the A75 is **WIGTOWN**, a modest country town whose spacious main street and square occupy a hill above Wigtown Bay. It's a five-minute walk from the square to the tidal flats below, where a simple stone obelisk commemorates two Covenanter martyrs, Margaret McLachlan and Margaret Wilson, who in 1685 were tied to stakes on the flats and drowned by the rising tide.

Whithorn

From Wigtown it's a further 11 miles south to **WHITHORN**, with a sloping, airy high street of pastel-painted cottages. This one-horse town occupies an important place in Scottish history, for it was here in 397 AD that **Saint Ninian** founded the first Christian church north of Hadrian's Wall. Ninian daubed his tiny building in white plaster and called it **Candida Casa**, translated as "Hwiterne" (White House), hence Whithorn, by his Pictish neighbours. Ninian's life is shrouded in mystery, but he does seem to have been raised in Galloway and was a key figure in the Christianization of his country. Indeed, his tomb became a popular place of pilgrimage and, in the twelfth century, a priory was built to service the shrine. For generations the rich and the royal made the trek here, but this ended with the Reformation – and the prohibition of pilgrimages in 1581.

Halfway down the main street, the **Whithorn Dig** (early April to Oct daily 10.30am–5pm; £2.70) exploits these ecclesiastical connections. A video gives background details and a handful of archeological finds serves as an introduction for a stroll round the dig. Be sure to take up the complimentary guide service – you won't make much sense of the complex sequence of ruins without one. Beyond the dig the meagre remains of the priory fail to inspire, unlike the adjacent **Whithorn Museum** (April–Sept Mon–Sat 10.30am–5pm, Sun 2–5pm; £1.20), whose impressive assortment of early Christian memorials includes a series of standing crosses and headstones, the earliest being the Latinus Stone of 450 AD. For **lunch**, the *Diner*, near the Dig, offers basic meals.

The pilgrims who crossed the Solway to visit St Ninian's shrine landed at the **ISLE OF WHITHORN**, four miles south of Whithorn. Not an island at all, it's an antique and tiny seaport hiding the minuscule remains of the thirteenth-century **St Ninian's Chapel**. To **stay**, try the unassuming *Steam Packet Inn* (☎01988/500334; ④), right on the quay. This is also the place to eat and find out details of sea angling trips, which leave the harbour on most days throughout the summer.

Glenluce Abbey and Castle Kennedy Gardens

Heading west from Whithorn, the main road follows the wild and windy shore of Luce Bay on its way back to the A75 near the turning for **Glenluce Abbey** (April–Sept Mon–Sat 9.30am–6pm, Sun 2–6pm; Oct–March Sat 9.30am–4pm, Sun 2–4pm; £1.20; no buses), whose ruins lie in a gentle valley a couple of miles north of the main road. Founded in 1192, Glenluce prospered from the diligence of its Cistercian monks, who drained the surrounding marshes, creating prime farmland. The brothers' fifteenth-century Chapter House has survived pretty much intact, and with its ribbed vault ceiling generates the clearest of acoustics – opera singers practise here. Notice too, the green man motif carved into the corbels and bosses. Popularized in the twelfth century, these grotesques have human or cat-like faces, with large, glaring eyes, frowning foreheads, and prominent teeth or fangs. All (hence the name) have greenery sprouting from their faces, a feature that originated with pagan leaf masks and the Celtic concept of fertility. The thirteenth-century wizard and alchemist **Michael Scot** lived here, supposedly luring the plague into a secret vault where he promptly imprisoned it. Scot, one-time magician to the court of the Emperor Frederick in Sicily, appears in Dante's *Inferno*.

Seven miles from Glenluce and three miles east of Stranraer, **Castle Kennedy Gardens** (April–Sept daily 10am–5pm; £2) flank the shattered, ivy-clad remains of a medieval fortress, situated on a narrow isthmus between two lochs. The gardens are noted for their monkey puzzle trees, magnolias and rhododendrons.

The Rhinns of Galloway

West of the Machars, the **Rhinns of Galloway** is a hilly, hammer-shaped peninsula at the end of the Solway Coast, encompassing two contrasting towns, the grimy port of Stranraer, from where there are regular ferries over to Northern Ireland, and the beguiling resort of **Portpatrick**, the western terminus of the Southern Upland Way. Between the two, a string of tiny farming villages lead down to the **Mull of Galloway**, the windswept headland at the southwest tip of Scotland.

Stranraer

No one could say **STRANRAER** was beautiful. However, if you're heading to (or coming from) Northern Ireland you may well have to pass through, and at least nearly everything's convenient. The **train station** is close to the *Stena Sealink* **ferry terminal** on the Ross Pier, where boats depart for Larne; a couple of minutes' walk away, on Port Rodic, is the town's **bus station**; and nearby, further round the bay, *Seacat* **catamaran** services leave from the West Pier to Belfast. Less handy, however, is the *P&O* ferry to Larne, which leaves from the port of **CAIRNRYAN**, some five miles away.

While you're waiting for a Stranraer ferry, a walk along the dishevelled main street, variously Charlotte, George and High streets, takes in the town's one specific attraction, a medieval tower which is all that remains of the **Castle of St John** (April–Sept Mon–Sat 10am–1pm & 2–5pm; 70p). Inside, an exhibition traces the history of the castle down to its use as a police station and prison in the nineteenth century. The old exercise yard is on the roof.

Stranraer has plenty of basic snack bars, but it's well worth paying a little extra to enjoy a **meal** at the *Apéritif*, just up the hill from the bus station along Bellevilla Road. If you're stranded, the **tourist office** (April–Oct daily 9.30am–5pm) will arrange **accommodation**, or you can try *Fernlea*, Lewis St (✆01776/703037; ③). For **camping**, *Aird Donald Camp & Caravan Park* (✆01776/702025) is ten minutes' walk east of the town centre along London Rd.

Portpatrick and south

Perched on the west shore of the Rhinns, the pastel houses of **PORTPATRICK** spread over the craggy coast above the slender harbour. Until the mid-nineteenth century, when sailing ships were replaced by steamboats, this was the main embarkation point for Northern Ireland, with coal, cotton and British troops heading in one direction, Ulster cattle and linen in the other. Nowadays, Portpatrick is a quiet, comely resort enjoyed for its rugged scenery and coastal hikes, including the 20-minute stroll (take the steep steps near the garages beyond the lighthouse then follow the public footpath) along the sea cliffs to the shattered ruins of **Dunskey Castle**, an L-shaped tower house dating from the early sixteenth century. Portpartick also has a couple of intriguing and competitively priced craft-antique shops – the *Old Lighthouse Pottery* and the *Smugglers Cove* – and there's excellent **sea fishing**; in summer daily trips cost £7 for three hours, £15 for seven.

Portpatrick has several good **hotels** and **guest houses**, the best of which are the *Portpatrick Hotel* (✆01776/810333; ⑧), a grand turreted Edwardian mansion on the hill above the harbour; the comfortable *Carlton Guest House*, beside the harbour on South Crescent (✆01776/810253; ④), and, close by, the bright, white *Knowe Guest House*

(☎01776/810441; ③). For a **meal** and a **drink**, head on down to the *Crown* pub, on the seafront, or the *Auld Acquaintance* coffee shop nearby.

South to the Mull of Galloway

The remoter reaches of the Rhinns of Galloway, extending about 20 miles south from Portpatrick, consist of gorse-covered hills and pastureland crossed by narrow country lanes and dotted with farming hamlets. Of the two shorelines, the west has a sharper, rockier aspect and it's here, near the village of Port Logan, you'll find the **Logan Botanic Garden** (mid-March to Oct daily 10am–6pm; £2), an outpost of Edinburgh's Royal Botanic Garden. There are three main areas: a peat garden, a woodland and a walled garden noted for its tree ferns and cabbage palms (the Gulf Stream keeps the Rhinns almost completely free of frost in a climate that can support subtropical species).

It's a further 12 miles south to the **Mull of Galloway**, a bleak and precipitous headland where wheeling birds – guillemots, razorbills and kittiwakes – and whistling winds circle a bright whitewashed lighthouse. On clear days you can see over to Cumbria and Ireland.

The South Ayrshire coast

Fifty miles from top to bottom, the **South Ayrshire Coast** between Stranraer and Ayr, is easily seen from the A77 coastal road, which leaves Stranraer to trim 30 miles of low, rocky shore before reaching **Girvan**, a low-key seaside resort where boats depart for **Ailsa Craig**, out in the Firth of Clyde. Back on shore, the A77 presses on through the village of **Turnberry**, home to one of the world's most famous golf courses, where the A719 branches off for eighteenth-century **Culzean Castle** (pronounced "Cullane"). From the castle, it's 12 miles further to **Ayr**. Alternatively, if you keep to the main road, you'll pass by the medieval remains of **Crossraguel Abbey** on the way to the old market town of **Maybole**, just nine miles from Ayr. There's a reasonable **bus** service along the coast, a better one between Culzean and Ayr – plus a train line from Stranraer to Girvan, Maybole and Ayr.

Girvan and Ailsa Craig

Set beneath a ridge of grassy hills, **GIRVAN** is at its prettiest round the harbour, a narrow slit beside the mouth of the Girvan Water. Here, overlooked by old stone houses, the fishing fleet sets about its business, and, for a moment, it's possible to ignore the amusement arcades and seaside tat elsewhere in town. From late May to September boats leave the harbour for the ten-mile excursion west to the **Ailsa Craig**, "Fairy Rock" in Gaelic – though the island looks more like an enormous muffin than a place of enchantment. With its jagged cliffs and 1114ft-high summit, Ailsa Craig is a privately owned bird sanctuary that's home to thousands of gannets. The best time to make the trip is at the end of May and in June when the fledglings are trying to fly. Several companies run the **cruise**, but the best are operated by Mark McCrindle (bookings required; ☎01465/713219), whose once or twice daily sailings cost £10 per person for six hours, £7 for four. It takes about an hour to reach the island, so you've a little time to explore the place – weather permitting.

There are regular **bus** services from Stranraer and Ayr to Girvan, which is also on the Glasgow–Stranraer **train** line. The tourist office, on Bridge St, just up from the harbour (Easter–May Mon–Sat 11am–5pm; June Mon–Fri 11am–5pm, Sat & Sun 10am–5pm; Sept daily 11am–5pm; early Oct daily noon–4pm) has a full list of **accommodation**, or among the attractive Victorian villas along the seafront, try the neat and tidy *Thistleneuk Guest House*, 19 Louisa Drive (☎01465/712137; ③).

Culzean Castle

Designed by Robert Adam, **Culzean Castle** (April–late Oct daily 10.30am–5.30pm; £3.50) and the surrounding **country park** (April–late Oct daily 10.30am–5.30pm; Nov–March daily 9am–sunset; £3, combined ticket £5.50) are Ayrshire's premier tourist attractions. The best place to start is at the **visitor centre** in the modernized Home Farm buildings. Here, you can pick up free maps – as well as wildlife leaflets – that help you get your bearings, the layout of the place being rather confusing. From here, it's a few minutes' walk over to the **Castle**, whose towers and turrets rise high above the sea cliffs. Nothing remains of the original fifteenth-century structure, since, in 1777, David Kennedy, the tenth Earl of Cassillis, commissioned Robert Adam to remodel the family home.

The work took 15 years to complete, and, although the exterior, with its arrow slits and battlements, preserves a medieval aspect, the interior exemplifies the harmonious Classical designs Adam loved. On the ground floor, the subtle greens of the old eating room are enlivened by vine-leaf-and-grape plasterwork along the cornice, a motif continued in the adjacent dining room. Nearby, there's the brilliantly conceived oval staircase, where tiers of Corinthian and Ionic columns add height and perspective. All this is a fitting prologue to the impresssive circular saloon, whose symmetrical flourishes deliberately contrast with the natural land and seascapes on view through the windows. Further on, a small exhibition celebrates President Eisenhower's military and civilian career as well as his association with Culzean; Ike stayed here on several occasions and the castle's top floor was given to him by the old owners, the Kennedys, for his lifetime. Nowadays, the top floor accommodates six double bedrooms done out in a comfortably genteel style. Guests eat together in the shared dining room and the chef comes in to do breakfast as well. Although hard to imagine a more distinctive setting, it's at a price: the smallest rooms cost £150 a night, the biggest £300 (reservations on ☎01655/760274).

Leave time for an exploration of the **country park**, whose 565 acres spread out along the sea shore. Criss-crossed by footpaths, the park's densely wooded terrain incorporates cliffs, a beach, a walled garden, where the blooms are at their best in July and August; and the occasional reminder of earlier days – the laird's boat house and gun battery, the old ice and powder houses.

Crossraguel Abbey

Leaving Turnberry on the A77, it's a couple of miles to the hamlet of **KIRKOSWALD** and **Souter Johnnie's Cottage** (mid-April to Sept daily 1.30–5.30pm; early Oct Sat & Sun only 1.30–5.30pm; £1.50), the simple thatched house that was once the home of John Davidson, the boon companion of Robert Burns and original Souter (cobbler) Johnnie of the poet's *Tam o' Shanter*. To the rear of the house, the restored alehouse has life-sized stone figures of Johnnie and other Burnsian characters.

The substantial remains of **Crossraguel Abbey** (April–Sept Mon–Sat 9.30am–6pm; Sun 2–6pm; £1.20), a further three miles along the main road, are mostly overlooked – something of a surprise considering their singularity. Founded as a Cluniac monastery in the thirteenth century, Crossraguel benefited from royal patronage with its abbots holding land "for ever in free regality". The abbots took the temporal side of their work seriously and became powerful local lords. By the early sixteenth century, they had constructed an extensive private compound complete with a massive gatehouse and sturdy tower house. Both still stand – behind what remains of the abbey church – recalling the corruption of the monastic ideal that prodded the Reformation. Behind the gatehouse, you'll also spot the well-preserved dovecot, a funnel-shaped affair that was a crucial part of the abbey's economy; the monks not only ate the doves but also relied on them for eggs.

Ayr and around

With a population of around 50,000, **AYR**, the largest town on the Firth of Clyde coast, was an important seaport and trading centre for many centuries, and rivalled Glasgow in size and significance right up until the late seventeenth century. In recognition, Cromwell made it a centre of his administration and built an enormous fortress here, long since destroyed. With the relative decline of its seaborne trade, Ayr developed as a market town, praised by Robert Burns, who was born in the neighbouring village of **Alloway** (see p.152), for its "honest men and bonny lasses". In the nineteenth century, Ayr became a popular resort for middle-class Victorians, with a new town of wide streets and boulevards built behind the beach immediately southwest of the old town. Nowadays, Ayr is both Ayrshire's commercial centre and a holiday resort, its long sandy beach (and prestigious racecourse) attracting hundreds of Scotland's city dwellers.

The Town

The cramped, sometimes seedy streets and alleys of Ayr's **old town** occupy a wedge of land between Sandgate to Alloway Place in the west, and the south bank of the treacly

River Ayr to the east. Almost all the medieval buildings were knocked down by the Victorians, but the **Auld Brig**, with its cobbles and sturdy breakwaters, has survived from the thirteenth century. The bridge was saved by Robert Burns, or rather his poem *Twa Brigs*, which made it too famous to demolish; an international appeal raised the capital necessary for its refurbishment in 1907.

The bridge connects with High Street where you should turn left and subsequently left again down Kirk Port, a narrow lane leading to the **Auld Kirk** (July & Aug Tues & Thurs only), the church funded by Cromwell as recompense for the one he incorporated into his stronghold. At the lych gate, a plan of the graveyard shows where some of Burns' friends are buried. Notice also the mort-safe (heavy grating) on the wall of the lych gate. Placed over newly dug graves, these mort-safes were a sort of early nineteenth-century corpse security system meant to deter body snatchers at a time when dead bodies – no questions asked – were swiftly bought up by medical schools. The church's dark and gloomy interior retains the original pulpit. Retracing your steps along High Street, take the first left down pedestrianized Newmarket Street, leading onto Sandgate, with the elegant spire of the **Town Buildings**, down towards the New Bridge.

Extending southwest of Sandgate to the Esplanade and the **beach**, the wide, gridiron streets of the Victorian **new town** contrast with the crowded lanes of old Ayr. It was the opening of the Glasgow to Ayr railway line in 1840 that brought the first major influx of holidaymakers and Ayr remains a busy resort today, with many visitors heading for the plethora of trim guest houses concentrated around **Wellington Square**, whose terraces flank the impressive County Buildings dating from 1820. The new town extends north towards the river, with its comfortable villas spreading over what remains of the walls of Cromwell's fort. It's here, off Bruce Crescent, that you'll find St John's Tower, all that's left of the church Cromwell used as his armoury. The northern perimeter of the fortress once overlooked the harbour, which is now the place to go for either a summer **sea angling trip** (reservations on ☎01292/285297) or a **cruise** on the *Waverley*, the last sea-going paddle steamer in the world. There are various excursions out among the islands off the west coast including a once-weekly trip around Alisa Craig for £11 per person; the tourist office has the details.

Practicalities

Ayr **bus station** is at the foot of Sandgate, a ten-minute walk west of both the **train station** and the **tourist office**, on Burns Statue Square (April–June & Sept to early Oct Mon–Sat 9.15am–5pm, Sun 10am–5pm; July & Aug Mon–Sat 9.15am–7pm, Sun 10am–7pm; mid-Oct to March Mon–Sat 9.15am–5pm; ☎01292/288688). They can help with accommodation, a particularly useful service at the height of the season and during important race meetings.

At other times, head straight for the cluster of **hotels** and **guest houses** around Wellington Square, a couple of minutes' walk south of Sandgate along Alloway Place. In particular, try Queen's Terrace where, among others, there's the *Dargil Guest House*, no. 7 (☎01292/261955; ②), *Queens*, no. 10 (☎01292/265618; ③), and the *Daviot*, no. 12 (☎01292/269678; ③). There's another cluster of B&Bs among the attractive Victorian villas of Eglinton Terrace, a short walk north of Wellington Square. These include the *Grasmere Guest House*, no. 2 (March–Oct; ☎01292/611033; ④) and the *Thornton*, no. 9 (☎01292/262948; ④). Ayr **youth hostel**, 5 Craigweil Rd (March–Oct; ☎01292/262322; Grade 1), occupies a grand neo-Gothic mansion behind the beach, a 20-minute walk south of the town centre along Alloway Place (turn right down Blackburn Rd – it's signposted). The *Heads of Ayr Leisure Park* (March–Nov; ☎01292/442269), five miles south of town along the coastal A719, accepts **caravans** and **tents**.

The best **restaurant** in Ayr is *Fouters*, 2a Academy St, in a cellar off Sandgate (☎01292/261391); steaks and seafood are its specialities. Another good choice, using local produce, is the *Boathouse*, 4 South Harbour St, beside the river at the foot of Fort St. For filling and more reasonably priced meals, try *Littlejohn's*, 231 High St. The most enjoyable **pub** in town is the *Tam o' Shanter*, High St, whose ancient walls sport quotes from Robert Burns. There are also several lively bars on and around Burns Statue Square, including *O'Briens*, which frequently showcases Irish folk bands.

Alloway

There's little else but Burnsiana in the small village of **ALLOWAY**, a key stop on the **Burns Heritage Trail** (see p.136) a couple of miles south of Ayr. But you can't make the journey by bus unless you travel on one of the specials heading for *Butlin's*

ROBERT BURNS

The first of seven children, **Robert Burns**, the national poet of Scotland, was born in Alloway on January 25, 1759. His father, William, was employed as a gardener until 1766 when he became a tenant farmer at Mount Oliphant, near Alloway, moving to Lochlie farm, Tarbolton, 11 years later. A series of bad harvests and the demands of the landlord's estate manager bankrupted the family, and William died almost penniless in 1784. These events had a profound effect on Robert, leaving him with an antipathy towards political authority and a hatred of the landowning classes.

With the death of his father, Robert became head of the family and they moved again, this time to a farm at Mossgiel, near Mauchline. Burns had already begun writing poetry and prose at Lochlie, recording incidental thoughts in his *First Commonplace Book*, but it was here at Mossgiel that he began to write in earnest, and his first volume, *Poems Chiefly in the Scottish Dialect*, was published in Kilmarnock in 1786. The book proved immensely popular, celebrated by ordinary Scots and Edinburgh literati alike, with the satirical trilogy *Holy Willie's Prayer*, *The Holy Fair* and *Address to the Deil* attracting particular attention. The object of Burns' poetic scorn was the kirk, whose ministers had obliged him to appear in church to be publicly condemned for fornication – a commonplace punishment in those days.

Burns spent the winter of 1786–87 in the capital, lionized by the literary establishment. Despite his success, however, he felt trapped, unable to make enough money from writing to leave farming. He was also in a political snare, fraternizing with the elite, but with radical views and pseudo-Jacobite nationalism that constantly landed him in trouble. His frequent recourse was to play the part of the unlettered ploughman-poet, the noble savage who might be excused his impetuous outbursts and hectic womanizing.

Burns had, however, made useful contacts in Edinburgh and as a consequence was recruited to collect, write and rearrange two volumes of songs set to traditional Scottish tunes. These volumes, James Johnson's *Scots Musical Museum* and George Thomson's *Select Scottish Airs*, contain the bulk of his songwriting, and it's on them that Burns' international reputation rests with works like *Auld Lang Syne*, *Scots, wha hae*, *Coming through the Rye* and *Green Grow the Rushes, O*. At this time too, though poetry now took second place, he produced two excellent poems; *Tam o' Shanter* and a republican tract, *A Man's a Man for a' that*.

In 1788, Burns married Jean Armour and moved to Ellisland Farm, near Dumfries. The following year, he was appointed excise officer and could at last leave farming, moving to Dumfries in 1791. Burns' years of comfort were short-lived, however. His years of labour on the farm, allied to a rheumatic fever, damaged his heart, and he died in Dumfries on July 21, 1796, aged 37.

Burns' work, inspired by a romantic nationalism and tinged with a wry wit, has made him a potent symbol of "Scottishness". Ignoring the Anglophile preferences of the Edinburgh elite, he wrote in Scots vernacular about the country he loved, an exuberant celebration that filled a need in a nation culturally colonized by England. Today Burns Clubs all over the world mark every anniversary of the poet's birthday with the Burns' Supper, complete with Scottish totems – haggis, piper and whisky bottle.

Wonderwest World theme park (2 hourly) and can get the driver to let you off. The first port of call in Alloway is the whitewashed **Burns Cottage and Museum** (April, May, Sept & Oct Mon–Sat 10am–5pm, Sun 1–5pm; June–Aug Mon–Sat 9am–6pm, Sun 10am–6pm; Nov–March Mon–Sat 10am–4pm; £2.50, includes entry to Burns Monument) for a peep at the poet's birthplace, a dark and dank, long thatched cottage where animals and people lived under the same roof. The two-room museum boasts all sorts of memorabilia – the family Bible, letters and manuscripts – plus a potted history of his life, illuminated by contemporaneous quotes,

The modern, faceless **Tam o' Shanter Experience** (daily 9am–6pm), a few minutes further down the road, is for the most part a souvenir shop selling a good selection of books about, and works of, Burns, though it does show a couple of videos (£2.50), one providing helpful background information on mid-eighteenth-century Ayrshire, the other a dramatic enactment of the poem.

Across the road from here are the plain, roofless ruins of **Alloway Church**, where Robert's father William is buried. Burns set much of *Tam o' Shanter* here. Tam, having got drunk in Ayr, passes "By Alloway's auld haunted kirk" and stumbles across a witches' dance, from which he's forced to flee for his life over the **Brig o' Doon**, a hump-backed bridge. The dance was a riotous affair:

> *But hornpipes, jigs, strathspeys and reels,*
> *Put life and mettle in their heels.*
> *A winnock-bunker in the east,* [window recess]
> *There sat auld Nick, in shape o' beast;*
> *A towzie tyke, black, grim and large,* [shaggy dog]
> *To gie them music was his charge:*
> *He screw'd the pipes and gart them skirl* [made; scream]
> *Till roof and rafters a' did dirl.* [vibrate]

Across the street from the church the thirteenth-century bridge still stands, curving gracefully over the river below the **Burns Monument** (April–Oct only, same hours & ticket as Cottage), a striking Neoclassical temple in a small carefully manicured garden.

The North Ayrshire coast

The **North Ayrshire coast** extends some 30 miles or so from Ayr up to **Largs**, easily the area's most agreeable resort. The busy coastal road (the A78) cuts across this disparate shoreline, where rolling farmland is interrupted by the pockmarks of industrialization. Leaving Ayr, the road trims the outskirts of Prestwick, the site of an international airport, before bypassing **Troon**, an uninspiring resort with a seaside golf course. **IRVINE**, the next settlement along, was once the principal port for Glasgow, its halycon days recalled by the enjoyable **Scottish Maritime Museum** (April–Oct daily 10am–5pm; £2) down at the old harbour, a mile or so southwest of the town centre. The assortment of craft moored to the museum docks includes a dredger, a fishing skiff, a lifeboat, a tug and a "puffer" boat, the last used as an inshore supply vessel along the Clyde and between the islands. The history of the puffers forms part of the museum's well-presented display on Clydeside shipping. Close by, there's the *Magnum Leisure Centre* (daily 9am–10pm), with a swimming pool and other sports facilities, and – at the mouth of the river – a sandy beach. Back on the west edge of the town centre, Irvine's **tourist office** (July & Aug Mon–Sat 9am–6pm, Sun 10am–6pm; Sept–June Mon–Sat 9am–5pm; closed Sun except in April–June 10am–5pm, Sept & Oct noon–4pm; ☎01294/313886) adjoins the train and bus stations as well as the giant shopping centre which leads to High Street. Here a couple of narrow side alleys hint at the town's antiquity – amid the prevailing architectural gloom. One, **Seagate**, boasts ancient cottages and the sturdy remains of Irvine's castle; the other – **Glasgow Vennel** – features the house, no.10, where Burns learnt to dress flax (he didn't enjoy it much), and his lodgings at no.4.

Eight miles inland from Irvine, **KILMARNOCK** is a shabby manufacturing town that's the home of **Johnnie Walker** whisky. There are two-hour guided tours of the bottling plant, on Hill St near the train station, on weekdays from (April–Oct Mon–Fri; ☎01563/23401 for times).

North from Irvine, it's just eight miles to **ARDROSSAN**, where ferries leave for Brodick on the Isle of Arran (see p.288), and another 12 miles to Largs, from where you can catch a ferry across to the nearby island of **Great Cumbrae**, a low-key but popular holiday spot.

Largs and Great Cumbrae

Tucked in between the hills and the sea, **LARGS** remains a traditional family resort, its guest houses and B&Bs spreading out behind an elongated seaside promenade. There's a tiny pier too, set beside an unpretentious town centre that conceals one real surprise: **Skelmorlie Aisle** (June–Aug Mon–Sat 2–5pm; free), a Renaissance gem hidden away beside the old graveyard off Main Street. Once the north transept of a larger church, the aisle was converted into a mausoleum for Sir Robert Montgomerie, a local bigwig, in 1636. Carved by Scottish masons following Italian patterns, the tomb is decorated with Montgomerie's coat of arms as well as symbols of mortality such as the skull, winged hour-glass and inverted torch. Up above, the intricate paintwork of the barrel-vaulted ceiling includes the signs of the zodiac, biblical figures and texts, and – in tiny detail on the painted corbels – the legendary coats of arms of the tribes of Israel.

Back outside on the promenade, it's about a mile south along the shoreline footpath to the **Pencil Monument**, a modern obelisk commemorating the Battle of Largs of 1263. The battle was actually an accident, forced on King Hakon's Vikings when their longships were blown ashore by a gale. The invaders were attacked by the Scots as they struggled through the surf, and, although both sides claimed victory, the Norwegians did retreat north, and abandoned their territorial claims to the Western Isles three years later. The Viking connection is exploited in the new **Vikingar** (daily 9am–6pm; £3.50) exposition, a five-minute walk north of the pier, which traces the history of the Vikings in Scotland with dramatic mood music, dioramas and videos. Alternatively, you can venture out on the Firth of Clyde yourself. *Clyde Marine* of Greenock (☎01475/721281) runs regular cruises out to the islands just off the west coast – principally Bute and Cumbrae – and the old paddle steamer, the *Waverley*, has a comparable itinerary (☎01412/218152). Largs tourist office has all the details.

Great Cumbrae Island

Immediately offshore from Largs lies **Great Cumbrae**, a plump, hilly island roughly four miles long and half as wide. The only settlement of any size is **MILLPORT**, which curves around an attractive hilly bay on the south coast. The town possesses Britain's smallest cathedral, the **Cathedral of The Isles**, which was completed in 1851 to a design by William Butterfield, an enthusiastic member of the high-church Oxford Movement and one of the leading Gothic revival architects of the day. A mile or so away, along the south shore to the east, is the **Marine Life Museum** (Mon–Fri 9.30am–12.15pm & 2–4.45pm, June–Sept also Sat) of the universities of Glasgow and London. The aquarium is excellent, but you're more likely to remember the view of the nuclear power station and iron ore terminal back on the mainland. Get away from this depressing sight by heading inland either on foot or by bike to enjoy the peaceful countryside. **Bike rental** is available in Millport from *Mapes* on Guildford St (☎01475/530444).

It takes 15 minutes for the ferry to cross from Largs to the island's northeast tip, where a connecting **bus** travels on to Millport. The ferries run hourly – more frequently in the summer – so there's no need to overnight on the island, but if you decide to stay in the season, be sure to book a room beforehand at Largs' tourist office. The return ferry fare is £2.65 per person, £11.85 per car (discounts on *Day Saver* returns, Tues–Fri); bikes cost £2 return. Little Cumbrae, the islet opposite Millport, is privately owned.

Largs Practicalities

There are excellent connections to Ayr and Glasgow from Largs' **bus** and adjacent **train station**, on Main St, a short stroll from the pier where **ferries** leave for Great Cumbrae. Beside the pier the **tourist office** (Easter to mid-Oct Mon–Sat 9am–5pm, Sun 10am–5pm, July & Aug closes 6pm; mid-Oct to Easter Mon–Fri 9am–5pm; ☎01475/673765) has heaps of free literature and will help with accommodation. There are lots of **guest houses** and **B&Bs**, including a cluster along Aubery Crescent, a short side street overlooking the coast a few minutes' walk north of the pier. Choose from the *Old Rectory B&B*, no. 2 (☎01475/674405; ③), or the *Ardmore Guest House*, no. 16 (April–Oct; ☎01475/672516; ③). Alternatively, about three miles north of the centre on the A78 is the *Manor House Hotel* (☎01475/520832; ⑨), a grand Victorian pile set in its own grounds and looking out over the seashore. Churchill and Eisenhower met here to plan D-day landings – the decor is a little historic too. *Skelmorlie Mains Campsite* (March–Oct; ☎01475/520794) lies about four miles north of town, also along the A78.

For **food**, the *Green Shutter Tearoom*, along the seafront just south of the pier, serves excellent food and the *Bagel Basket*, Main St, is cheap and simple. *Nardini's*, on the Promenade just north of the pier, sports an unadulterated 1950s decor, but the meals are very disappointing.

travel details

Trains

Ayr to: Glasgow (3 daily; 50min); Stranraer (5 daily; 1hr 20min).

Dumfries to: Carlisle (5–12 daily; 35min); Kilmarnock (2–7 daily, 1hr 5min).

Edinburgh to: Dunbar (4–6 daily; 20min); Musselburgh (hourly; 10min); North **Berwick** (hourly; 30min).

Glasgow to: Ardrossan Harbour (3–5 daily; 50min); Ayr (every 30min; 50min); Carlisle (2–7 daily; 2hr 15min); Dumfries (2–7 daily; 1hr 40min); Kilmarnock (2–7 daily; 35min); Largs (hourly; 1hr); Stranraer (3 daily; 2hr 20min).

Kilmarnock to: Carlisle (2–7 daily; 1hr 40min); Dumfries (2–7 daily; 1hr 5min).

Largs to: Glasgow (hourly; 1hr).

Stranraer to: Ayr (5 daily; 1hr 20min).

Buses

Ayr to: Castle Douglas (Mon–Sat 2 daily; 2hr); Culzean Castle (hourly; 25min); Girvan (hourly; 1hr); Glasgow (1 express daily; 1hr 15min); Largs (hourly; 1hr 10min); New Galloway (Mon–Sat 2 daily; 1hr 20min); Stranraer (3 daily; 2hr).

Dumfries to: Caerlaverock (Mon–Sat 5 daily; 35min); Carlisle (6 daily; 1hr 40min); Castle Douglas (2–4 daily; 45min); Edinburgh (3 weekly; 2hr 20min); Gatehouse of Fleet (2–3 daily; 1hr 30min); Glasgow (express 1–3 daily; 2hr); Gretna (6 daily; 1hr), Kirkcudbright (2–4 daily, 1hr 10min); Lockerbie (hourly; 35min); Newton Stewart (2–3 daily; 2hr); Rockcliffe (2 daily; 1hr 10min); Sanquhar (4 daily; 50min); Stranraer (2–3 daily; 3hr); Thornhill (6 daily; 30min).

Edinburgh to: Aberlady (every 30min; 55min); Berwick-upon-Tweed (3–4 daily; 3hr); Carlisle (3–5 daily; 3hr 25min); Dirleton (every 30min; 1hr 5min); Dunbar (3–6 daily; 1hr 30min); Eyemouth (3–4 daily; 2hr 40min); Galashiels (hourly; 1hr 25min); Haddington (3–6 daily; 1hr 5min); Jedburgh (5 daily; 2hr); Langholm (3–5 daily; 2hr 30min); Melrose (3–9 daily; 1hr 40min); North Berwick (every 30min; 1hr 20min); Peebles (6–8 daily; 1hr).

Galashiels to: Berwick-upon-Tweed (4–7 daily; 1hr 50min); Canonbie (3–5 daily; 1hr 25min); Carlisle (3–5 daily; 2hr); Hawick (6–9 daily; 35min); Langholm (3–5 daily; 1hr 15min); Selkirk (hourly; 15min).

Haddington to: Gifford (4–9 daily; 15min); North Berwick (4–9 daily; 40min).

Jedburgh to: Hawick (3–7 daily; 40min); Kelso (3–6 daily; 30min).

Kelso to: Coldstream (3–4 daily; 20min); Kirk Yetholm (3–6 daily; 20min).

Largs to: Ayr (hourly; 1hr 10min).

Leadhills to: Wanlockhead (2 daily; 5min).

Lockerbie to: Langholm (4 weekly; 35min).

Melrose to: Duns (3–7 daily; 50min); Eyemouth (4–5 daily; 1hr 30min); Galashiels (hourly; 15min); Hawick (Mon–Sat 3 daily; 50min); Jedburgh (hourly; 30min); Kelso (6–8 daily; 35min); Lauder (2–4 daily; 40min); Peebles (hourly; 1hr 10min); Selkirk (Mon–Sat hourly, Sun 3 daily; 20min).

Moffat to: Dumfries (7 daily; 40min); Lockerbie (5 Mon–Sat; 40min).

Newton Stewart to: Ayr (2–5 daily; 2hr 15min); Bargrennan (2–5 daily; 20min); Girvan (2–5 daily;1hr 20min); Glentrool (2–5 daily; 25min); Stranraer (2–9 daily; 40min); Wigtown (Mon–Sat 10 daily, Sun 3 daily; 15min); Whithorn (3–8 daily; 50min); Isle of Whithorn (3–6 daily; 1hr).

Peebles to: Biggar (4–6 daily; 40min).

Selkirk to: Carlisle (every 2hr; 2hr); Hawick (hourly; 20min); Langholm (every 2hr; 1hr).

Stranraer to: Drummore (1–2 daily; 45min); Port Logan (1–2 daily; 35min); Portpatrick (5 daily; 25min).

Ferries

To Arran: Ardrossan–Brodick (up to 5 daily; 55min).

To Great Cumbrae Island: Largs–Millport (summer half-hourly, winter hourly; 15min).

To Larne: Stranraer–Larne (5–10 daily; 2hr 20min); Cairnryan–Larne (3–6 daily; 2hr 15min).

To Belfast: Stranraer–Belfast (hydrofoil 4–5 daily; 1hr 30min).

SCENIC BUS ROUTES

Harrier Scenic Bus Services (with several bus companies involved in running this service, its best to contact tourist offices for details) run round-trip tours from July to September once a week along the following routes:

Moffat–Hawick via Grey Mare's Tail, St Mary's Loch, Bowhill House, Selkirk (2hr each way).
Moffat–Melrose via Grey Mare's Tail, St Mary's Loch, Bowhill House, Selkirk (2hr each way).

Selkirk–Eyemouth via Galashiels, Melrose, Kelso, Coldstream, Berwick-upon-Tweed (2hr 40min each way).
Jedburgh–Eyemouth via Town Yetholm, Berwick-upon-Tweed (1hr 45min each way).

CHAPTER THREE

GLASGOW AND THE CLYDE

R ejuvenated, upbeat **Glasgow**, Scotland's largest city, has not enjoyed the best of reputations. Once an industrial giant set on the banks of the mighty River Clyde, today it can initially seem a grey and depressing place, with the M8 motorway screeching through the centre and crumbling slums on its outskirts. However, in recent years Glasgow has undergone a remarkable overhaul, set in motion in the 1980s by a self-promotion campaign featuring a fat yellow creature called Mr Happy, beaming beatifically that "Glasgow's Miles Better". The city proceeded to generate a brisk tourist trade, reaching a climax after beating Paris, Athens and Amsterdam to the title of European City of Culture in 1990.

The epithet is still apt; Glasgow has some of the best-financed and most imaginative museums and galleries in Britain – among them the showcase **Burrell Collection** of art and antiquities – and nearly all of them are free. There's also a robust social scene and nightlife that is remarkably diverse, though somewhat restricted by the Scottish licensing laws. Its **architecture** is some of the most striking in the nation, from the restored eighteenth-century warehouses of the **Merchant City** to the hulking Victorian prosperity of George Square. Most distinctive of all is the work of local lumi-nary Charles Rennie Mackintosh, whose elegantly streamlined Art-Nouveau designs appear all over the city, reaching their apotheosis in the **School of Art**. It is fitting that a Mackintosh creation, the *Glasgow Herald* building, will be used as the orientation point for the **City of Architecture and Design Festival** in 1999.

Despite all the upbeat hype, however, Glasgow's gentrification has passed by deprived inner-city areas such as the **East End**, home of the **Barras market** and some staunchly change-resistant pubs. This area, along with isolated housing schemes such as Castlemilk and Easterhouse, needs more than a facelift to resolve its complex social and economic problems; and has historically been the breeding ground for the city's much-lauded **socialism**.

Glasgow has also had a long-standing belief in the power of popular culture. Main attractions include the **People's Palace** – one of Britain's most celebrated social history museums – founded in 1898 to extol ordinary lives and achievements, and the **Citizens' Theatre**, formed in 1942 by playwright James Bridie to promote indigenous work for local people, and whose innovative productions still cost next to nothing to see. In addition, Glasgow's **Mayfest**, with its roots in the traditional working-class spring celebrations, has grown to become Britain's second largest arts bash after the Edinburgh festival.

Quite apart from its own attractions, Glasgow also makes an excellent base from which to explore the **Clyde valley and coast**, made easy by the region's reliable rail service. Of the small communities in the Clyde valley, **Lanark** is probably the best-suited for overnight stays, as well as being the home of the remarkable eighteenth-century **New Lanark** mills and workers' village. Beyond that, most of the inland towns (as well as the coastal resorts) are best approached as day trips from Glasgow.

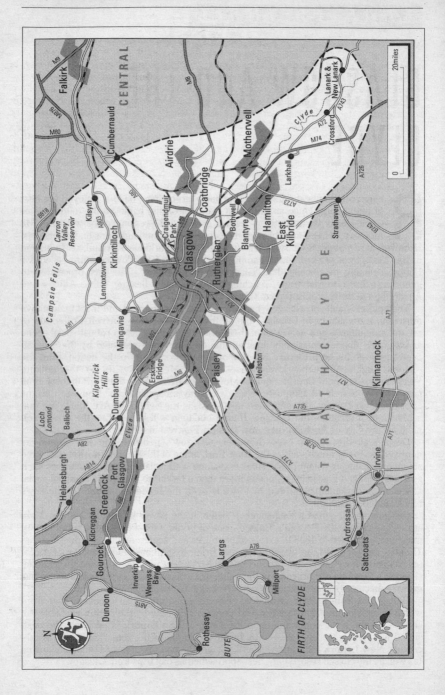

GLASGOW

GLASGOW's earliest **history**, like so much else in this surprisingly romantic city, is obscured in a swirl of myth. The city's name is said to derive from the Celtic *Glas-cu*, which loosely translates as "the dear, green place" – a tag that the tourist board are keen to exploit as an antidote to the sooty images of popular imagination. It is generally agreed that the first settlers arrived in the sixth century to join Christian missionary **Kentigern** – later to become St Mungo – in his newly founded monastery on the banks of the tiny Molendinar Burn.

William the Lionheart gave the town an official charter in 1175, after which it continued to grow in importance, peaking in the mid-fifteenth century when the **university** was founded on Kentigern's site – the second in Scotland after St Andrew's. This led to the establishment of an archbishopric, and hence city status, in 1492, and, due to its situation on a large, navigable river, Glasgow soon expanded into a major **industrial port**. The first cargo of tobacco from Virginia offloaded in Glasgow in 1674, and the 1707 Act of Union between Scotland and England – despite demonstrations against it in Glasgow – led to a boom in trade with the colonies until American independence. Following the **Industrial Revolution** and James Watt's innovations in steam power, coal from the abundant seams of Lanarkshire fuelled the ironworks all around the Clyde, worked by the cheap hands of the Highlanders and, later, those fleeing the Irish potato famine of the 1840s.

The Victorian age transformed Glasgow beyond recognition. The population boomed from 77,000 in 1801 to nearly 800,000 at the end of the century, and new tenement blocks swept into the suburbs in an attempt to cope with the choking influxes of people. Two vast and stately **International Exhibitions** were held in 1888 and 1901 to showcase the city and its industries to the outside world, necessitating the construction of huge civic monoliths such as the Kelvingrove Art Gallery and the Council Chambers in George Square. At this time Glasgow became known as the **"Second City of the Empire"** – a curious epithet for a place that today rarely acknowledges second place in anything.

By the turn of the **twentieth century**, Glasgow's industries had been honed into one massive shipbuilding culture. Everything from tugboats to transatlantic liners were fashioned out of sheet metal in the yards that straddled the Clyde from Gourock to Rutherglen. In the harsh economic climate of the 1930s, however, unemployment spiralled, and Glasgow could do little to counter its popular image as a city dominated by inebriate violence and, having absorbed vast numbers of Irish emigrants, sectarian tensions. The **Gorbals** area in particular became notorious as one of the worst slums in Europe. The city's image has never been helped by the depth of animosity between its two great rival football teams: the Catholic **Celtic** and Protestant **Rangers**, whose warring armies of fans used to clash with monotonous regularity. Nowadays, the "Old Firm" clashes continue with the same passion on the field, but without the subsequent post-match violence.

In the Eighties the promotion campaign began, snowballing towards the 1988 **Garden Festival** and year-long party as **European City of Culture** in 1999. Today, Glasgow is again preparing for another celebration after beating off Edinburgh and Liverpool to become **City of Architecture and Design in 1999**, expected to be the largest celebration of architecture and design ever held. The festival aims to rejuvenate Glasgow's blighted areas, involving schools and local communities in the process. Exhibitions and discussions will focus on the city's architectural heritage alongside visions of the future,

The telephone code for Glasgow and the Clyde is ☎0141.

including the importance of good design in modern everyday living. It proves that Glasgow, despite the many problems still remaining, has successfully broken off the industrial shackles of the past and evolved into a city of stature and confidence.

Orientation

Glasgow is a sprawling place, built upon some punishingly steep hills, and with no really obvious centre. However, as most transport services converge on the area around **Argyle Street** and, 200 yards to the north, **George Square**, this pocket of the city is the most obvious candidate for city-centre status. However, with the renovated upmarket **Merchant City** immediately to the east and the main business and commercial areas to the west, the centre, when the term is used, actually refers to a large swathe from **Charing Cross** train station and the M8 in the west through to **Glasgow Green** in the **East End**. Although run-down, the latter boasts city's social history museum, the People's Palace, and is near its medieval heart at Glasgow Cathedral. Outside the city centre, the **West End** begins just over a mile west of Central station, and covers most of the area west of the M8. In the nineteenth century, as the East End tumbled into poverty, the West End ascended the social scales with great speed, a process crowned by the arrival of the **University**. Today, this is still very much the student quarter of Glasgow, exuding a decorous air, with graceful avenues, parks and cheap, interesting shops and cafés. It's also well connected with the city centre by Underground. The suburbs of Govan and the Gorbals, neither of which hold much for visitors, lie south of the Clyde, as does the area known as **South Side**, a relaxed version of the West End. Here the leafy enclaves of **Queen's Park** are home to the national football stadium, Hampden Park; the main attraction, though, has to be **Pollok Park** and the Burrell Collection. None of the sights here are within walking distance of the city centre, but can easily be reached by train or bus.

Arrival

Glasgow's **airport** (☎887 1111) is out at Abbotsinch, eight miles southwest of the city. To get into town, take *Citylink* bus #500 (£2), which runs to **Buchanan Street** (☎332 7133) bus station, three streets north of George Square, every ten minutes during the day. You could also take *Clydeside 2000* bus #60 or #80 (every 10min during the day) to Paisley Gilmour Street train station, and from there a fast train into **Glasgow Central**, where trains from anywhere south of Glasgow arrive.

Central station sits over Argyle Street, one of the city's main shopping thoroughfares. A **shuttle bus** (free) from the front entrance on Gordon Street travels every ten minutes to **Queen Street station**, at the corner of George Square, for trains to Edinburgh and the north. The walk between the two takes about ten minutes.

All buses arrive at Buchanan Street station, except those run by *Strathclyde Transport* which terminate in depots around the city.

Information

The city's excellent **tourist office**, at 35 St Vincent Place just off George Square (Oct–April Mon–Sat 9am–6pm; rest of the year also Sun; June & Sept closes 7pm; July & August 8pm; ☎204 4400) provides a particularly wide array of maps, leaflets and souvenirs and a free accommodation-booking service. A couple of hundred yards south down Buchanan Street over the St Enoch Underground station sits the neo-Gothic hut of the **Strathclyde Travel Centre** (Mon–Sat 9.30am–5.30pm; ☎226 4826), where you can pick up sheaves of maps, leaflets and timetables. Their comprehensive and colour-coded *Visitors' Transport Guide* is the best free map of the city centre and West End, but if you're staying for longer, or want to explore the tiny streets and alleys that are invariably airbrushed off the tourist maps, it's probably worth investing in a *Bartholomew Glasgow Streetfinder* (£2.99).

City transport

Although it can be tough negotiating the steep hills, **walking** is an ideal way of getting around and exploring any one part of the city. However, as the main sights are scattered – the West End, for example, is a good thirty-minute walk from the centre – you'll need to use the comprehensive **public transport** system.

The best way to get between the city centre, southern suburbs and the West End is to use the city's **Underground**, whose stations are marked with a large U. Affectionately known as the "Clockwork Orange" (there's only one, circular route and the trains are a garish bright orange), the service is extremely easy to use. There's a flat fare of 60p, or you can buy a **day ticket** for £1.80; a **multi-journey ticket** gives ten journeys for £5.40 or twenty for £10.00. Unfortunately, however, the whole system opens late, at 11am, and shuts down at 11.30pm between Monday and Saturday and at 6pm on Sunday.

If you're travelling beyond the city centre or the West End, you may need to use the **bus** and **train** networks. Since deregulation, the city has been besieged with a horde of bus companies in hot competition. The biggest are *Strathclyde Transport*, whose buses can be identified by their orange livery, and *Kelvin Central Buses* in cream and red. If it gets too confusing, pick up the *Visitors' Transport Guide* (see above).

The suburban train network is swift and convenient. Suburbs south of the Clyde are connected to Glasgow Central mainline station, while trains from Queen Street head into the northeast. The grim but functional **cross-city line**, which runs beneath Argyle Street (and includes a low-level stop below Central station), connects northwestern destinations with southeastern districts as far out as Lanark. Trains on both the Queen Street and Central station lines go through **Partick** station, west of the city centre; this is also an Underground stop.

There is no day ticket that combines bus, rail and Underground in Glasgow alone, but if you are in the city for at least a week, it's worth investing in a **Zonecard**, which covers all public transport networks, and is valid for seven days or a month. Costs depend on the number of zones that you want to travel through – a two-zone card, for example, which gets you from Partick in the west to Rutherglen in the east, and as far as the Burrell Collection in the south, will set you back £9.60. This central two-zone core (divided by the Clyde) is ringed with a further six zones around its edge. Ask at the Strathclyde Travel Centre for help to demystify the system. There is also a **Day-Tripper-Ticket**, which covers all the transport networks, going beyond the city zones, and costs £6 for one adult and up to two children, or £11 for two adults and up to four children, although you'd need to spend a very busy day sightseeing to make it worthwhile. Additionally, the **Roundabout Glasgow Ticket** (£3) gives unlimited travel for a day on the underground and rail services from Milngavie in the north to Motherwell in the south. If you want to see the sights, the **Discover Glasgow** tour bus (April–Oct Mon–Sat 9.30am–5pm; £5) starts in George Square and runs a continuous route around all the major attractions in the city centre and West End, allowing you to get on and off as you please.

Should you want to avoid public transport altogether, you can hail black **taxis**, which run all day and night, from the pavement. There are taxi ranks at Central and Queen Street train stations and Buchanan Street bus station. Fare from Central to Pollok Park and the Burrell Collection, a journey of about three miles, costs £5.

As for **driving**, with the M8 motorway running right through the heart of Glasgow, it is one of the country's most car-friendly cities, with plenty of parking meters, and 24-

hour multi-storey car parks at Waterloo Street, Mitchell Street, Oswald Street and Cambridge Street. However, tariffs for the day in the city centre are expensive, and significantly less in the outskirts.

Accommodation

There's a good range of **accommodation** in Glasgow, from an excellent youth hostel in the leafy West End through to some top international hotels in the city centre. Most of the rooms are in the city centre, the West End or down in the southern suburb of Queen's Park. Glasgow's speciality is its profusion of converted Victorian **town houses** in the middle of town, many of which are now privately run B&Bs that offer excellent value for money.

During Mayfest or in summer it's worth **booking ahead** to ensure a good room – at any time of year the **tourist office** will do their utmost to secure you somewhere to stay. They also publish a useful brochure of bargain weekend breaks.

Low-priced **self-catering** rooms and flats are available from the **University of Glasgow** (☎330 5385) from early July to mid-September. The **University of Strathclyde** has various sites, most of which are gathered around the cathedral. Vacation lets (③) and self-catering flats for between four and six people (①; minimum 3 people) can be rented near the main campus in Rottenrow for a minimum of three nights(☎553 4148). For better rooms, available all year (but pricier than many city hotels), call their **Graduate Business School**, Cathedral Street (☎553 6000; ⑦). The **YMCA** at 33 Petershill Drive, Balornock (☎558 6166), three miles northeast of the city centre (10-min walk from Barnhill train station), offers clean, if rather lifeless self-catering flats (③) sleeping between four and six people which are available all year round; there are no dorms.

Glasgow Youth Hostel, 7–8 Park Terrace (☎332 3004), is a Grade 1 hostel nuzzled deep in the splendour of the West End. It's a ten-minute walk south from Kelvinbridge Underground station, or take #11, #44 or #59 *Strathclyde Transport* bus from the city centre, after which it's a short stroll west up Woodlands Road. It's very popular, so book in advance.

The only **campsite** within a decent distance of Glasgow is **Craigendmuir Park**, Campsie View, Stepps (☎779 4159), four miles northeast of the city centre, a 15-minute walk from Stepps train station. It has adequate facilities with showers, a laundry and a shop, but there are only ten pitches.

ACCOMMODATION PRICE CODES

Throughout this book, accommodation **prices** have been graded with the numbers below, according to the cost of the least expensive double room in high season. Although costs will rise slightly overall with the life of this edition, the relative comparisons should remain valid. The bulk of the recommendations will fall in categories ② to ⑥; those in the highest categories are limited to places that are especially attractive. Edinburgh will inevitably be more expensive than equivalent accommodation in the countryside or small towns, and a number of places will have a big mark-up for the three weeks of the Festival. Also bear in mind that many of the swanky hotels often slash their tariffs at the weekend when the business types have gone home, and that many of the cheaper places will also have more expensive rooms. Note that in our accommodation listings price codes are not given for youth hostels and campsites – they all come into the lower end of the ① category.

① under £20	④ £40–50	⑦ £70–80
② £20–30	⑤ £50–60	⑧ £80–100
③ £30–40	⑥ £60–70	⑨ over £100

City centre

Babbity Bowster, 16–18 Blackfriars St (☎552 5055). A traditional and very lively hotel, ... restaurant that makes much of its Scottishness, with haggis and neaps and tatties permanently on the menu. ⑤.

Baird Hall, 460 Sauchiehall St (☎553 4148). Lavish Art Deco building that belies the functional, ex-student rooms, near the School of Art and the upper end of Sauchiehall Street. ③.

Carrick Hotel, 377–383 Argyle St (☎248 2355). One of the cheapest large-chain hotels in the city centre. Dependable rooms, if not very original decor; unexciting bar-meal type menu. ⑤.

Central Hotel, Gordon St (☎221 9680). Imposing, comfortable hotel, with its own leisure centre, in the heart of the action near the stations. ⑦.

Copthorne Hotel, George Square (☎332 6711). Large and impressive eighteenth-century hotel occupying the entire northwestern corner of George Square; rooms are bright and flouncy. Popular bar in the ground floor glass verandah. ⑦.

Enterprize Hotel, 144 Renfrew St (☎332 8095). A small, family town house in a quiet area near Cowcaddens Underground station. "Themed" rooms but not outstanding. ⑤.

Hampton Court Hotel, 230 Renfrew St (☎332 6623 or 5885). Low-key, slightly downbeat and fairly small Victorian house conversion, close to the School of Art and Sauchiehall Street. ③.

Marriott, Argyle St (☎226 5577). Large and luxurious chain hotel with excellent food and popular health centre. Ask for a room out of earshot of the M8. Considerable reductions available at weekends. ⑧.

Rab Ha's, 83 Hutcheson St (☎553 1545). Beautiful and highly individual hotel-cum-restaurant in swish Merchant City. They only have a few rooms, so booking is essential. ⑤.

Town House Hotel, Nelson Mandela Place, 54 W George St (☎332 3320). Sumptuously converted sandstone block with quite a "Scottish" feel. Good reductions during the week. Expensive but original food ⑧.

Victorian House, 212 Renfrew St (☎332 0129). Large and friendly terraced guest house, with some of the cheapest rooms in the city centre. ③.

Willow Hotel, 228 Renfrew St (☎332 2332 or 7075). Well-converted Victorian town house, on the north side of the city centre, offering B&B; clean, spacious rooms. ③.

West End

Alamo Guest House, 46 Gray St (☎339 2395). Good-value, family-run boarding house next to Kelvingrove Park. Small but comfortable rooms. ②.

Ambassador Hotel, 7 Kelvin Drive (☎946 1018). Smallish but comfortable, family-run B&B in lovely surroundings next to the River Kelvin and Botanical Gardens. ④.

Argyll Lodge, 969 Sauchiehall St (☎334 7802). Always busy, this laid-back guest house has only a handful of rooms, on the fringes of the West End. ②.

Hillhead Hotel, 32 Cecil St (☎339 7733). Quiet, welcoming hotel only a couple of minutes' stroll from Hillhead Underground and the excellent local pubs and restaurants. ④.

Hillview Guest House, 18 Hillhead St (☎334 5585). Unassuming and peaceful small B&B near the university and the Byres Road. ③.

Kelvin Park Lorne Hotel, 923 Sauchiehall St (☎334 4891). Well-priced rooms in a dependable, if slightly sterile, international hotel environment with food to match. ⑤.

Kelvin View, 411 N Woodside Rd (☎339 8257). Welcoming B&B, but small rooms, near Kelvin Bridge Underground station. ③.

Lomond Hotel, 6 Buckingham Terrace (☎339 2339). Discreet B&B in beautifully restored Victorian terrace near for Botanic Gardens and Byres Road. ③.

One Devonshire Gardens, 1 Devonshire Gardens, Great Western Rd (☎339 2001). A 10-min walk up the Great Western Road from the Botanical Gardens, this hotel and its expensive gourmet restaurant are among the city's finest. ⑦.

Sandyford Hotel, 904 Sauchiehall St (☎334 0000). A clean, comfortable B&B, good location for Kelvingrove Park and the SECC. ④.

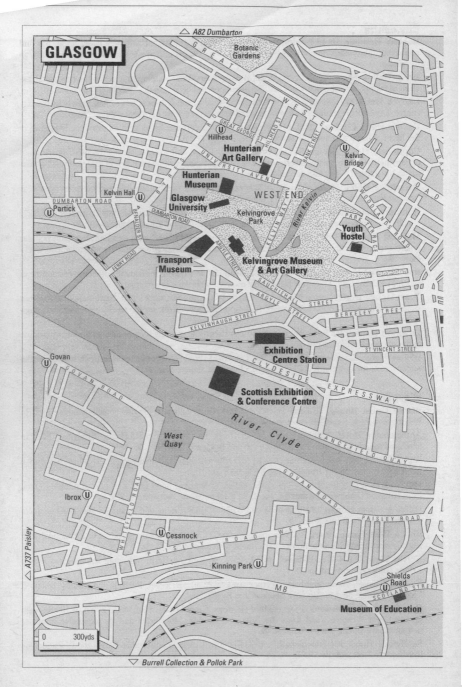

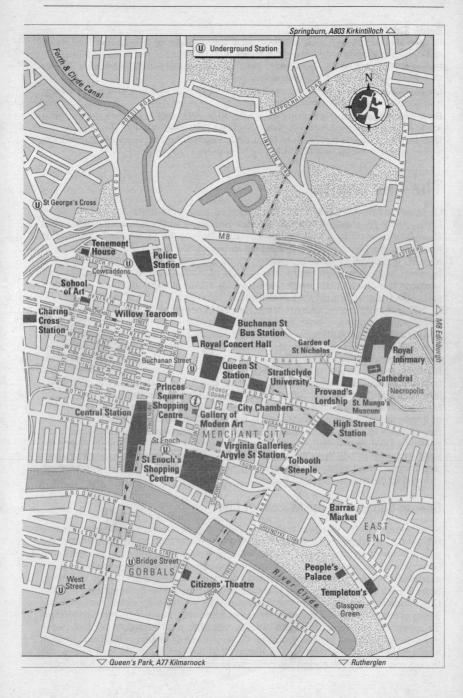

Springburn, A803 Kirkintilloch △

U Underground Station

N

Forth & Clyde Canal

GARSCUBE ROAD

FOSSIL ROAD

KEPPOCHHILL ROAD

PINKSTON ROAD

SPRINGBURN ROAD

M8

U St George's Cross

ROXTON RD

DUCLEUCH ST

Tenement House

Police Station

Cowcaddens

U

CASTLE STREET

School of Art

RENFREW STREET

Charing Cross Station

Willow Tearoom

SAUCHIEHALL STREET

BATH STREET

Buchanan St Bus Station

Royal Concert Hall

Garden of St Nicholas

Royal Infirmary

WEST REGENT STREET

WEST GEORGE STREET

Buchanan Street

CATHEDRAL STREET

Queen St Station

Strathclyde University

Cathedral

ST VINCENT STREET

U

GEORGE STREET

Necropolis

BOTHWELL STREET

Princes Square Shopping Centre

GEORGE SQUARE

Provand's Lordship

St. Mungo's Museum

ARGYLE STREET

i

City Chambers

INGRAM STREET

High Street Station

Central Station

Gallery of Modern Art

MERCHANT CITY

St Enoch

U

Virginia Galleries

Argyle St Station

HIGH STREET

DUKE ST

St Enoch's Shopping Centre

TRONGATE

Tolbooth Steeple

GALLOWGATE

BROOMIELAW

Barras Market

EAST END

NELSON STREET

NORFOLK STREET

GREENDYKE STREET

U Bridge Street

GORBALS

River Clyde

People's Palace

COOK STREET

THE GREEN

U West Street

Citizens' Theatre

CROWN

BALLATER STREET

Templeton's

Glasgow Green

△ M8 Edinburgh

South Side

Boswell Hotel, 27 Mansionhouse Rd (☎632 9812). Informal, relaxing Queen's Park hotel with a superb real-ale bar, and regular folk and jazz nights. ④.

Ewington Hotel, 132 Queen's Drive (☎422 2030). Comfortable and peaceful hotel facing Queen's Park. Excellent, moderately priced subterranean restaurant. ⑦.

Glades Guest House, 142 Albert Rd (☎423 4911). Friendly B&B, with large rooms, in quiet area near Queen's Park and good transport routes. ③.

Reidholme Guest House, 36 Regent Park Square (☎423 1855). Small and friendly guest house in a quiet sidestreet that was designed by Alexander "Greek" Thomson (see p.169). ②.

Queen's Park Hotel, 10 Balvicar Drive (☎423 1123). Faintly shabby, but very welcoming and with a crowd of regular visitors. Good views over the hill of Queen's Park. ④.

The City Centre

Glasgow's enormous **CITY CENTRE** is ranged across the north bank of the River Clyde. At its geographical heart is **George Square**, a nineteenth-century municipal showpiece crowned by the enormous City Chambers at the eastern end. Behind this lies one of the 1980s' greatest marketing successes, the **Merchant City**, an area of massive gentrification partially restored to its nineteenth-century glory. The grand buildings and trendy cafés cling to the borders of the run-down **East End**, a strongly working-class district that chooses to ignore its rather showy neighbour. The oldest part of the Glasgow, around the **Cathedral**, lies immediately north of the East End.

Still in the city centre, Glasgow's commercial core spreads west of George Square, and is mostly built on a large, grid system – possibly inspired by Edinburgh's New Town – with ruler-straight roads soon rising up severe hills to grand, sandblasted buildings. Symbolic of Neoclassical order and mercantile wealth, John Betjeman called this part of Glasgow "the greatest Victorian city in the world". The main shopping areas here are **Argyle Street**, running parallel to the river east–west underneath Central train station, and **Buchanan Street**, which crosses it and leads up to the pedestrianized shopping thoroughfare, **Sauchiehall Street**. Just to the north of here is Rennie Mackintosh's famous **Glasgow School of Art**. Lying between the commercial bustle of Argyle and Sauchiehall streets, and to the immediate west of Buchanan Street, are the contours of an ice-age drumlin (one of three main drumlins in the area), now known as **Blythswood Hill**. The tightly-packed grid of streets piled on its slopes are lined by Georgian buildings filled with offices. In comparison with the bustling shopping parades surrounding it on three sides, this area is remarkably quiet and reserved, crowned by the neat Blythswood Square.

George Square and the Merchant City

Now hemmed in by speeding traffic, the imposing architecture of **George Square** reflects the confidence of Glasgow's Victorian age. Rising high above the centre of the square is an eighty-foot column topped with Sir Walter Scott, although his links with Glasgow were, at best, sketchy. Haphazardly dotted around the great writer's plinth are a number of dignified statues of assorted luminaries, ranging from Queen Victoria to Scots heroes such as James Watt and wee Robbie Burns. The florid splendour of the **City Chambers**, opened by Queen Victoria in 1888, occupies the entire eastern end of the square. Built from wealth gained by colonial trade and heavy industry, it epitomizes the aspirations and optimism of late-Victorian city elders. Its intricately detailed facade includes high-minded friezes typical of the era: the four nations (England, Ireland, Scotland, Wales) of the then United Kingdom at the feet of the throned queen, the British colonies and allegorical figures representing Religion, Virtue and Knowledge.

It's worth taking a free guided tour (Mon–Fri 10.30am & 2.30pm; ☎227 4017) of the labyrinthine interior to get a look at the acres of intricate gold leaf, Italian marble, Wedgwood ceilings and Rococo trimmings.

Equally opulent is the **Merchant's House** opposite Queen Street station (May–Sept Mon–Fri 2–4pm; free), where the grand Banqueting Hall and silk-lined Directors' Room are highlights. Queen Street leads south to the Royal Exchange Square and the graceful Corinthian **Stirling Library**, built for tobacco lord William Cunninghame in 1780 as the most ostentatious of the Glasgow merchants' homes. Since then it has served as the city's Royal Exchange and central library, and refurbishment is currently under way to give it a new lease of life as the city's Museum of Modern Art.

Merchant City

The grid of streets that lies immediately east of the City Chambers is known as the **Merchant City**, an area of eighteenth-century warehouses and homes once bustling with cotton, tobacco and sugar traders, which in the last decade or so has been sand-blasted and swabbed clean with greater enthusiasm and municipal money than any other part of Glasgow in an attempt to bring residents back into the city centre. The cost of living here is prohibitive for most people, however, and many of the gracious warehouses remain smothered with "To let" signs. However, the expensive designer shops with small but immaculate collections sit neatly with bijou bars and cafés to bring some life back into this quiet area. Even though some of the buildings are literally no more than original facades, held in place with vast struts like a film set and nestled next to mock period reconstructions, the area has a simple elegance and upmarket charm. Towards dusk when traffic has died down, floodlights bathe the scrubbed porticos in a range of colours. Look out for the delicate white spire of the National Trust for Scotland's regional headquarters, **Hutcheson's Hall**, at 158 Ingram St (Mon–Fri 9.30am–5pm, Sat 10am–4pm). The NTS have a shop on the ground floor and visitors can see the ornately decorated hall upstairs. Almost opposite, on Glassford Street, the Robert Adam-designed **Trades House** (call ☎552 2418 to arrange a time; free) is easily distinguished by its neat, green copper dome. Built for the purpose in 1794, it still functions as the headquarters of the Glasgow trade guilds. Its history can be traced back to 1605 when fourteen societies of well-to-do city merchants, who were the forerunners of the trade unions, first incorporated. These included a Bakers' Guild, and societies for Hammermen, Gardeners, Bonnet Makers, Wrights and Weavers, although they have since become little more than proto-masonic lodges for men from all sections of Glasgow's business community. The former civic pride and status of the guilds is still evident, however, from the rich assortment of carvings and stained-glass windows, with a lively pictorial representation of the different trades in the silk frieze around the walls of the first-floor banqueting hall.

On Virginia Street, parallel to Glassford Street, the **Virginia Galleries** sit behind the intricately wrought iron gate of no 33. Formerly the city's nineteenth-century tobacco and sugar trading house, the graceful market hall is now a sedate place, filled with a variety of shops selling anything from second-hand clothing to African artefacts.

From Trongate to the East End

Before 1846, **Glasgow Cross** – the junction of **Trongate**, Gallowgate and the High Street – was the city's principal intersection, until the construction of the new train station near George Square shifted the city's emphasis west. The turreted seventeenth-century **Tolbooth Steeple** still stands here, although the rest of the building has long since disappeared, and today the stern tower is little more than a traffic hazard at a busy junction. Further east, down Gallowgate, beyond the train lines, lies the **EAST END**, the district that perhaps most closely corresponds to the old perception of

GLASGOW'S ARCHITECTURE

Glasgow, founded on religion, built on trade and now well established as a cultural centre, is rich in architectural styles: from its medieval cathedral to the modern glass-lined galleries of the Burrell Collection. Most dominant, however, is the legacy of the **Victorian age**, when booming trade and industry allowed merchants to commission the finest architects of the day. As World War II bombing was focused on the shipbuilding centre of Clydebank, most of the city's fine sandstone buildings have survived intact. The celebrated work of Charles Rennie **Mackintosh** (1868–1928) took Glasgow architecture to the forefront of early twentieth-century design, a final flowering of home-spun genius before economic conditions effectively stopped the architectural trade in its tracks.

Glasgow's great expansion was initiated in the eighteenth century by wealthy tobacco merchants who, in an attempt to bask in the reflected glory of Classical times, built the grand edifices of public and municipal importance that still make up much of the **Merchant City**. One of the finest Merchant City views is down Garth Street, where the Venetian windows and Ionic columns of **Trades House**, designed by Robert Adam in 1791, close the vista with a flourish. **Hutcheson Hall**, closing off Hutcheson Street, is another fine monument of civic pride, with a five-bay facade and elegant tower that moves from a square through octagonals to a drum – an early nineteenth-century architectural nod to the Rennaissance by the architect David Hamilton.

Further west, **Royal Exchange Square** is one of the best examples of the typical Glasgow square: treeless, bare and centred around a building of importance. The **Royal Exchange** building of 1829, designed by Hamilton, has a huge corinthian portico which is almost a testimony to pure Classical architecture. The square itself is an excellent example of integrated municipal design, with closely matching Georgian buildings unifying the area into a harmonious whole. Further north, off Queen Street, the open space of **George Square** holds the emphatically Victorian **City Chambers**, its Venetian splendour a testimony to the confidence of the wealthy merchants, built only a couple of years after the crash of the Glasgow bank in 1878.

As workers piled into the centre of Glasgow in the early nineteenth century, filling up the already bursting tenements, wealthy residents began moving west. This expansion was completely uncontrolled and so the gridded streets that line **Blysthwood Hill** (mostly developed after 1820) hold an eclectic range of buildings. However, a harmonious streetscape was created by the predominance of two to three storey terraces, their porches and heavy cornices providing textural relief to the endless sandstone monotony. The dignified proportions and design of **Blysthwood Square** are a highlight of this area; at no. 5 the later Art Nouveau doorway designed by Charles Rennie Mackintosh sits incongrously amongst the Georgian solidity. Above all, the long streets provide a beautiful selection of open ended views, one moment leading into the heart of the city, the next filled with distant hills and sky.

Glasgow. Hemmed in by Glasgow Green to the south, and the old university to the west, this densely packed industrial area essentially created the city's wealth. The Depression caused the closure of many factories, leaving communities stranded in an industrial wasteland. Today isolated pubs, tatty shops and cafés sit amidst this dereliction, in sharp contrast to the gloss of the Merchant City only a few blocks to the west.

Three hundred yards down either London Road or Gallowgate, **The Barras** is Glasgow's largest and most popular weekend market. Red iron gates announce its official entrance, but boundaries are breached as the stalls – selling household goods, bric-a-brac, second-hand clothes and records – spill out into the surrounding cobbled streets. The fast-talking traders are sharp-witted and friendly, and there are plenty of bargains to be had, but you'll be in tenacious competition with locals vying for the goods.

Now desiring to surround themselves with trees and fields, the well-to-do continued their migration west; in the early 1830s, beyond Charing Cross, the Woodlands Hill development was completed – a leafy parkland area in contrast to the treeless town squares of the city centre. Here **Woodside Crescent**, leading into Woodside Terrace, is a severe, fierce line of buildings, with splendid Doric porches and neatly organized gardens. **Park Circus**, on the other hand, is a parade of uninterrupted Georgian magnificence, with delicate detail – such as narrow window slots on either side of the doors – enhancing the dignified crescent. Now predominantly commercial, it is an excellent example of grand planning.

Long since overshadowed by Charles Rennie Mackintosh (see p.172), the design of **Alexander "Greek" Thomson**, in the latter half of the nineteenth century, though well respected in its time, has been much maligned. As his nickname suggests, his work used the essence of Greek architecture and reprocessed it in a highly unique manner. Energetic and talented, he designed buildings from the lowly tenement to grand suburban villas. The St Vincent Street Church (1857), his best work, has a massive simplicity and serenity lightened by the use of exotic Egyptian and Hindu motifs, particularly in the tower with its decorated egg-shaped dome. This fusion of the Classical and the Eastern stands out for its originality at a time when Gothic Revival or Rennaissance work was all the rage. Thomson's buildings have not been given the treatment they deserve, and some were tragically torn down in the municipal clearances of the 1970s.

West from Park Circus lies **Glasgow University** (1866–86), its Gothic Revivalism – the work of Sir George Gilbert Scott – representing everything that Greek Thomson despised; he called it "sixteenth-century Scottish architecture clothed in fourteenth-century French details". Scottish features abound, such as crow-stepped gables, round turrets with conical caps and the top-heavy central tower. Inside, cloisters and quadrants sum up a suitably scholastic severity.

Originally conceived as a convenient way to house the influx of workers in the late 1800s, the Glasgow **tenement** design became more refined as the wealthy middle classes began to realize its potential. Tenements were built by private landlords, the majority constructed in a remarkably short space of time, from around 1860 to 1910. In general these buildings are three to five storeys with two or three apartments per floor. Important rooms are picked out with bay windows, middle stories are emphasized by architraves or decorated panels below sill or above lintel, and street junctions are given importance by swelling bay windows, turrets and domes. West of the university, the streets off **Byres Road** are lined with such grand tenement buildings, in particular the Baronial red sandstone of Great George Street.

World War I put an end to the glorious century of Glasgow building, and the years of depression did little to enhance the city. More recently, glassy office buildings have sprung up, their mirrored walls basking in the reflected glory of the surrounding buildings to disguise their banality of design. More notable modern constructions include the **Burrell Collection** and **St Mungo's Museum**, both successfully designed to suit their surroundings.

Between London Road and the River Clyde are the wide and tree-lined spaces of **Glasgow Green**. Reputedly the oldest public park in Britain, the Green has been common land since at least 1178, when it was first mentioned in records. Glaswegians hold it very dear, considering it to be an immortal link between themselves and their ancestors, for whom a stroll on the Green was a favourite Sunday afternoon jaunt. It has also been the site of many of the city's major political demonstrations – the Chartists in the 1830s and Scottish republican campaigners in the 1920s – and was the traditional culmination of the May Day marches until the 1950s, when the celebrations were moved to Queens Park. Various memorials (some in bad states of disrepair) are dotted around the lawns: the 146-foot **Nelson Monument**; the ornate – but derelict – terracotta **Doulton Fountain**, rising like a wedding cake to the pinnacle where the forlorn Queen Victoria oversees her crumbling Empire; and the stern monument extolling the evils of drink and the glory of God that was erected by the nineteenth-century Temperance movement – today, quite a meeting place for local drunks.

The People's Palace

On the northern end of Glasgow Green, the **People's Palace** (Mon–Sat 10am–5pm, Sun 11am–5pm; free) is a wonderfully haphazard evocation of the city's history. This squat, red-brick Victorian building, with a vast semicircular glasshouse tacked on the back, was purpose-built as a museum back in 1898 – almost a century before the rest of the country caught on to the fashion for social history collections. Although currently undergoing refurbishment – it is due to be completed in 1998, in time for centenary celebrations – viewing is only slightly restricted.

On the ground floor, the medieval city and its first skirmishes with the fiendish English are represented through re-created monastic rooms, pictures and captions, leading into an exhibition of period interiors removed from Stockwell Mansion, the city's last seventeenth-century building, demolished in 1976 after spending its final years as the *Bonny Bingo Hall*. Also on this level is an exhibition about eighteenth-century Glaswegian merchants, complete with smug portraits of tobacco lords and their picture-perfect families. The upper floor is more appealing, a rag-bag collection of nostalgia-soaked ephemera from the lives of ordinary nineteenth- and twentieth-century Glaswegians. There are exhibits on John Maclean, the most notorious of the Red Clydesiders (members of a radical Independent Labour Party formed in the economic slump post-World War I) who became consul to the Bolshevik government in 1918, on trade unions, suffragettes, the City Council and the products that once made Glasgow the "Workshop of the World". On the top floor, the impressive murals by Scottish artist Ken Currie powerfully evoke the spirit of radical Glasgow, starting from the Carlton weavers strike in 1787 up to the Red Clydesiders of the 1920s. The glasshouse at the back of the palace is the **Winter Gardens**, whose café, water garden, twittering birds and assorted tropical plants and shrubs make a pleasant place in which to pass an hour or so.

A hundred yards across the road from the People's Palace you can see the riotously intricate orange and blue Venetian-style facade of **Templeton's Carpet Factory**, built in 1889. William Leiper, Templeton's architect, is said to have modelled his industrial cathedral on the Doge's Palace in Venice; today it houses a centre for small businesses.

Around the Cathedral

Rising north up the hill from the Tolbooth Steeple at Glasgow Cross is Glasgow's **High Street**. In British cities, the name is commonly associated with the busiest central thoroughfare, and it's a surprise to see how forlorn and dilapidated Glasgow's version is, long superseded by the grander thoroughfares further west. The High Street leads up to the **Cathedral**, on the site of Glasgow's original settlement.

Glasgow Cathedral

Built in 1136, destroyed in 1192 and rebuilt soon after, the stumpy-spired **Glasgow Cathedral** (April–Sept Mon–Sat 9.30am–1pm & 2–6pm, Sun 2–5pm; Oct–March closes at 4pm) was not completed until the late fifteenth century, with the final reconstruction of the chapter house and the aisle designed by Robert Blacader, the city's first archbishop. Thanks to the intervention of the city guilds, it is the only Scottish mainland cathedral to have escaped the hands of religious reformers in the sixteenth century. The cathedral is dedicated to the city's patron saint and reputed founder, St Mungo, about whom four popular stories are frequently told – they even make an appearance on the city's coat of arms. These involve a bird that he brought back to life, the bell with which he summoned the faithful to prayer, a tree that he managed to make spontaneously combust and a fish that he caught with a repentant adulterous queen's ring on its tongue.

Because of the sloping ground on which it is built, at its east end the cathedral is effectively on two levels, the crypt actually part of the "lower church". On entering, you arrive in the impressively lofty nave of the upper church, with the lower church entirely hidden from view. Most of this **upper church** was completed under the direction of Bishop William de Bondington (1233–58), although later design elements came from Blacader. Either side of the nave, the narrow **aisles** are illuminated by vivid stained-glass windows, most of which date from this century. Threadbare Union flags and military pennants hang listlessly beneath them, serving as a reminder that the cathedral is very much a part of the Unionist Protestant tradition. Beyond the nave, the **choir** is hidden from view by the curtained stone pulpit, making the interior feel a great deal smaller than might be expected from the outside. In the choir's northeastern corner, a small door leads into the cathedral's gloomy **sacristy**, in which Glasgow University was first founded over 500 years ago. Wooden boards mounted on the walls detail the alternating Roman Catholic and Protestant clergy of the cathedral, testimony to the turbulence and fluctuations of the Church in Scotland.

Two sets of steps from the nave lead down into the **lower church**, where you'll see the dark and musty **chapel** surrounding the tomb of St Mungo. The saint's relics were removed in the late Middle Ages, although the tomb still forms the centrepiece. The chapel itself is one of the most glorious examples of medieval architecture in Scotland, best seen in the delicate fan vaulting rising up from the thicket of cool stone columns. Scots designer Robert Stewart was commissioned in 1979 to produce a tapestry detailing the four myths of St Mungo, which can be illuminated using the button at the bottom of the north-side stairs to reveal its swirl of browns and oranges. Also in the lower church, the spaciously light **Blacader Aisle** was originally built as a two-storey extension; today only this lower section survives, where the bright, and frequently gory, medieval ceiling bosses stand out superbly against the simple white-washed vaulting.

Outside, the atmospheric **Necropolis** rises above the cathedral. Inspired by the Pierre Lachaise cemetery in Paris, developer John Strong created a garden of death in 1833, filled with Doric columns, gloomy catacombs and Neoclassical temples reflecting the vanity of the nineteenth-century industrialists buried here. From the summit, next to the column topped with an indignant John Knox, there are superb views over the cathedral and its surrounding area.

Cathedral Square

Back in Cathedral Square, the **St Mungo Museum of Religious Life and Art** (Mon–Sat 10am–5pm, Sun 11am–5pm; free) focuses on objects, beliefs and art from Christianity, Buddhism, Judaism, Islam, Hinduism and Sikhism. Portrayals of Hindu gods are juxtaposed with the stunning Salvador Dali painting *Christ upon the Cross* – moved here from Kelvingrove Art Gallery – that draws the viewer into its morose depths. In addition to the main exhibition is a small collection of photographs, papers and archive material looking at religion in Glasgow, the power and zealotry of the nineteenth-century Temperance movement, Christian missionaries and local boy, David Livingstone, in particular. Outside is Britain's only permanent "dry stone" Zen Buddhist garden, with slabs of rock, white gravel and moss carefully arranged to suggest the forms of land and sea.

Across the square, the oldest house in the city, the **Provand's Lordship** (Mon–Sat 10am–5pm, Sun 11am–5pm; free) dates from 1471, and has been used, among other things, as an ecclesiastical residence and an inn. Many of the rooms have been kitted out with period furniture, including a re-creation of the fifteenth-century chamber of cathedral clerk Cuthbert Simon, who is seen as a contemplative bewigged wax dummy living in comparative luxury for the age. As a reminder of the manse's earlier history, the upper floor contains cuttings and pictures telling interesting tales of assorted lowlife characters, such as notorious drunkards, match-sellers and prostitutes of eighteenth- and nineteenth-century Glasgow.

Behind this building lies the small **Garden of St Nicholas**; a herb garden contrasting medieval and Renaissnace aesthetics and approaches to medicine; from the muddled clusters of herbs amid stone carvings of the heart and other organs to the controlled arrangement of plants around a small ornate fountain. The garden, bordered by sandstone walkways where you can sit, is an aromatic and peaceful haven away from the High Street.

From Buchanan Street to Sauchiehall Street

The huge grid of streets that runs from Buchanan Street to the M8 a mile to the west, is home to Glasgow's main shopping district as well as its financial and business corporations, piling up the slopes of drumlins shaped by the receding glaciers of the last ice age. The **St Enoch Shopping Centre**, south of George Square, sandwiched between Argyle and Howard streets, is a huge, lofty glass pyramid built around a redundant train station. Among the glossy shops and piped muzak the centre's most unusual feature is its **ice rink** (☎221 5835), complete with cappuccino bar. A short walk north, on Buchanan Street, **Princes Square**, hollowed out of the innards of a soft sandstone building is one of the most stylish and imaginative shopping centres in the country.

CHARLES RENNIE MACKINTOSH

Dark-haired and confident, the figure of **Charles Rennie Mackintosh** (1868–1928) has come to be synonymous with the image of Glasgow. Whether his work was a forerunner of the Modernist movement or merely a sunset of Victorianism, he undoubtedly created buildings of great beauty, idiosyncratically fusing Scots Baronial with Gothic, Art Nouveau and modern design. Though the bulk of his work was conceived at the turn of the century, since the post-war years, Mackintosh's ideas have become particularly fashionable, giving rise to a certain amount of ersatz "Mockintosh" in his home city, with his distinctive lettering and small design features used time and again by shops, pubs and businesses. Fortunately, there are also plenty of examples of the genuine article, making the city something of a pilgrimage centre for art and design students from all over the world.

Although his family did little to encourage his artistic ambitions, as a young child he began to cultivate his interest in drawing from nature during walks in the countryside, taken to improve his health. This talent was to flourish when he joined the **Glasgow School of Art**, in 1884, where the vibrant new director, Francis Newberry, encouraged his pupils to create original and individual work. Here he met Herbert MacNair and the sisters Margaret and Frances MacDonald whose work seemed to be sympathetic with his, fusing the organic forms of nature with a linear, symbolic Art Nouveau style. Nicknamed "The Spook School", the four created a new artistic language, using extended vertical design, stylized abstract organic forms and muted colours, reflecting their interest in Japanese design and the work of Whistler and Beardsley. However, it was architecture that truly challenged Mackintosh, allowing him to use his creative artistic impulse in a three-dimensional and cohesive manner.

His big break came in 1896, when he won the competition to design a new **art school** (see p.174). This is his most famous work, but a number of smaller buildings created during his tenure with the architects Honeyman and Keppie, which began in 1889, document the development of his style. One of his earliest commissions was for a new building to house the **Glasgow Herald headquarters** on Mitchell Street, off Argyle Street. A massive tower rises up from the corner, giving a dynamism to the enclosed space, dispelling the regularity of the horizontal windows; this use of vertical lines was to play a significant part in his later work.

In the 1890s Glasgow went wild for tearooms, where the middle classes could play billiards and chess, read in the library or merely chat over some fine dining. The impos

The interior, all recherché Art Deco and ornate ironwork, has lots of pricy, highly fashionable shops, the whole place set to a soothing background of classical music.

At the northern end of Buchanan Street, where it intersects with the eastern end of Sauchiehall Street, lies the £29 million **Royal Concert Hall**, given a prime city perspective but failing miserably to excite much attention. It looks like a hybrid of a car park and a power station, with three huge flagpoles protruding to proclaim that this is, in fact, a building of note. The showpiece hall plays host to world-class musical events, while the lobbies are used for temporary art exhibitions. These can be seen for free, or you can take a guided tour of the huge hall and its backstage areas (Mon–Fri 2pm; £1.50; ☎332 6633).

Sauchiehall Street runs in a straight line west past some unexciting shopping malls, leading to a few of the city's most interesting sights. Charles Rennie Mackintosh fans should head for the **Willow Tea Rooms**, at 217 Sauchiehall St (above a jewellery shop), a faithful reconstruction (opened in 1980 after over 50 years of closure) on the site of the 1904 original, which was created by the architect for Kate Cranston, one of his few contemporary supporters in the city. Everything from the fixtures and fittings right down to the teaspoons and menu cards were designed by Mackintosh. Taking inspiration from the word Sauchiehall which means avenue of willow, he chose the willow leaf as a theme to unify the whole structure from the tables to the mirrors and the iron work. The motif is most apparent in the stylized

ing Miss Cranston, who dominated the Glasgow tea shop scene, running the most elegant establishments, gave Mackintosh great freedom of design and in 1896 he started to plan the interiors for her growing business. Over the next 20 years he designed articles from teaspoons to furniture and finally, as in the case of the **Willow Tea Rooms**, the structure itself (see above).

Mackintosh designed few **religious builings**; the Queens Cross Church of 1896, still at the junction of Garscube and Maryhill roads in the northwest of the city, is the only completed one standing. Hallmarks include the sturdy box-shaped tower and asymmetrical exterior with complex heart-shaped floral motifs in the large chancel window. To give height to the small and peaceful interior, he used an open arched timber ceiling, enhanced by carved detail and an oak pulpit decorated with tulip form relief. It isn't the most unified of structures, but shows the flexibility of his distinctive style.

The spectre of limited budgets was to haunt Mackintosh throughout his career, and he never had the chance to design and construct with complete freedom. However, these constraints never managed to dull his creativity, as demonstrated by the **Scotland Street School** of 1904 (near the Burrell Collection; see p.182). Here, the two main stairways that frame the entrance are lit by glass-filled bays that protrude from the building. It is his most symmetrical work, with a whimsical nod to history in the Scots Baronial conical tower roofs and sandstone building material.

Mackintosh's forceful personality and originality did not endear him to construction workers; he would frequently change his mind or add details at the last minute, often running a budget overboard. This lost him the support of local builders and architects, despite being admired on the continent, and prompted him to move to Suffolk in 1914, to escape the "philistines" of Glasgow and to re-evaluate his achievements. He now made use of his natural ability to draw flora and fauna, often in botanical detail and coloured with delicate watercolour washes. Whilst living in Port Vendres, on the Mediterranean side of the Franco-Spanish border in 1923–27, he produced a series of still lifes and landscape works which express something of his architectural style. Here, houses and rocks are painted in precise detail with a massive solidity and geometric form, and bold colours unite the patterned texture of the landscape, within an eerie stillness unbroken by human activity. These are a final flowering of his creative talent, a delicate contrast to the massive legacy of stonework left behind in the city that he loved.

linear panels of the bow window which continues into the intimate dining room as if to surround the sitter, like a willow grove, and is echoed in the distinctively high-backed silver-and-purple chairs. These elongated forms were used to enhance the small space and demonstrates Mackintosh's superb talent to fuse function with decoration. Tea is served here from 9.30am until 5pm.

A couple of footsteps west are the **McLellan Galleries,** 270 Sauchiehall St (Mon–Sat 10am–5pm, Sun noon–5pm; charges for some exhibitions), recently restored after a severe fire in 1985. Despite its inauspicious frontage, inside the building is as soothing an example of Classical architecture as anywhere in the city. A grand staircase sweeps you up into the main exhibition space, lit naturally by beautiful pedimented windows. There is no permanent display; the McLellan specializes in imaginative touring and temporary exhibitions, many of which have local themes – in recent years, anything from new Glaswegian art to an eccentric display of the city's rubbish, and in 1996 the biggest ever exhibition of Mackintosh's life and work. For relentlessly avant-garde art and culture, stroll down the same side of Sauchiehall Street to no. 350 and the **Centre for Contemporary Arts** (Mon–Sat 11am–6pm; free), with its eclectically internationalist exhibitions and performances, trendy café and bar that stays open till late (Mon–Wed 11pm, Thurs–Sat midnight).

Glasgow School of Art

Rising above Sauchiehall Street to the north is one of the city centre's steepest hills, where Dalhousie Street and Scott Street veer up to Renfrew Street and, at no. 167, Charles Rennie Mackintosh's **Glasgow School of Art** (guided tours Mon–Fri 11am & 2pm, Sat 10.30am; extra tours April–Sept; £3.50 or £2.00 conc; booking advised; ☎353 4526) – one of the most prestigious in the country, with such notable alumni as artists Robert Colquhoun and Robert Macbryde and, more recently, Steven Campbell, Ken Currie and actor Robbie Coltrane. Widely considered to be the pinnacle of Mackintosh's work, the school is a characteristically angular building of warm sandstone which, due to financial constraints, had to be constructed in two sections (1897–99 and 1907–09). There's a clear change in the architect's style from the earlier severity of the mock-Baronial east wing to the softer lines of the western half.

The only way to see the school is by taking one of the student-led daily guided tours, the extent of which are dependent on curricular activities. You can, however, be sure of seeing at least some of the differences between the two halves and a handful of the most impressive rooms. All over the school, from the roof to the stairwells, Mackintosh's unique touches – light Oriental reliefs, tall-backed chairs and stylized Celtic illuminations – recur like leitmotifs. Even before entering the building up the gently curving stairway, you cannot fail to be struck by the soaring height of the north-facing windows, which light the art studios and were designed, in the architect's inimitable style, to combine aesthetics with practicality.

In the main entrance hall, the school shop sells tour tickets and a good selection of Mackintosh books, posters and cards. Hanging in the hall stairwell is the artist's highly personal wrought-iron version of the "bird, bell, tree, ring and fish" legend of St Mungo. The stairs lead up to the **Director's Room**, where the rounded lines of the central table and arched window contrast with the starkly angular chairs, cupboard and writing desk. You'll see excellent examples of his early furniture in the tranquil **Mackintosh Room**, flooded with soft, natural light, while the **Furniture Gallery**, tucked up in the eaves, shelters an Aladdin's cave of designs that weren't able to be housed elsewhere in the school – numerous tall-backed chairs, a semicircular settle designed for the *Willow Tea Rooms*, domino tables, a chest of drawers with highlighted silver panels and two bedroom suites. Around the room are mounted building designs and a model of the *House for an Art Lover*, which Mackintosh submitted to a German competition in 1901. In recent years, this project – which never saw the light of day in

Mackintosh's lifetime – was resuscitated after Glasgow city council donated a corner of South Side's Bellahouston Park for the house's construction. The building, constructed exactly to Mackintosh's specifications, will house office space for the Glasgow School of Art from spring 1996.

You can peer down from the Furniture Gallery into the school's most spectacular room, the glorious two-storey **Library** below. Here, sombre oak panelling is set against angular lights adorned with primary colours, dangling down in seemingly random clusters. The dark bookcases sit precisely in their fitted alcoves, while of the furniture, the most unusual feature is the central periodical desk, whose oval central strut displays perfect and quite beautiful symmetry.

The Tenement House

Just a few hundred yards northwest of the School of Art – albeit on the other side of the sheer hill that rises and falls down to Buccleuch Street – is the **Tenement House** at no. 145 (March–Oct daily 2–5pm; Nov–Feb by appointment only; NTS; £2.00). This is the perfectly preserved home of the habitually hoarding Agnes Toward, who moved here with her mother in 1911, changing nothing and throwing very little out until she was hospitalized in 1965. On the ground floor, the NTS has constructed a fascinating display on the development of the humble tenement block as the bedrock of urban Scottish housing, with a display of relics – ration books, letters, bills, holiday snaps and so forth – from Miss Toward's life. Upstairs you have to ring the doorbell to enter the living quarters, which give every impression of still being inhabited, with a roaring hearth and range, kitchen utensils, recess beds, framed religious tracts and sewing machine all untouched. The only major change since Miss Toward left has been the reinstallation of the flickering gas lamps she would have used in the early days.

The West End

The urbane veneer of the **WEST END**, an area which contains many of the city's premier museums, seems a galaxy away from Glasgow's industrial image. In the 1800s, the city's focus moved west as wealthy merchants established huge estates away from the soot and grime of city life, and in 1870 the ancient university was moved from its cramped home near the cathedral to a spacious new site overlooking the River Kelvin. Elegant housing swiftly followed, the Kelvingrove Art Gallery was built to house the 1888 International Exhibition, and in 1896 the Glasgow District Subway – today's Underground – started its circuitous shuffle from here to the city centre.

The hub of life in this part of Glasgow is **Byres Road**, running down from the straight Great Western Road past Hillhead Underground station. Shops, restaurants, cafés, some enticing pubs and hordes of roving young people, including thousands of students, give the area a sense of style. Glowing red sandstone tenements and graceful terraces provide a suitably upmarket backdrop to this cosmopolitan district.

Straddling the banks of the cleaned up River Kelvin, the slopes, trees and statues of **Kelvingrove Park** are framed by a backdrop of the Gothic towers and turrets of **Glasgow University** and the **Kelvingrove Museum and Art Gallery**, off Argyle Street in the park.

Kelvingrove Museum and Art Gallery

Founded on donations from the city's chief industrialists, the huge, red-brick fantasy castle of **Kelvingrove Museum and Art Gallery** (Mon–Sat 10am–5pm, Sun 11am–5pm; free) is a brash statement of Glasgow's nineteenth-century self-confidence. On the ground floor, a fairly dusty hall contains the **Scottish Natural History** display,

THE GLASGOW BOYS

The traditional rivalry between Glasgow and Edinburgh was alive and kicking in the late nineteenth century when the Royal Scottish Academy resolutely refused to accept the work of any west coast artist. That was soon to change, however, when in the 1870s a group of painters formed a loose association, centred in Glasgow, that was to invest Scottish painting with a fresh approach inspired by contemporary European trends (in particular the *plein air* painting of the Impressionists). Derisively nicknamed "The Glasgow Boys", only in later years did their work come to be seen as quintessentially Glaswegian and reclaimed with considerable pride. The group was dominated by five men – Guthrie, Lavery, Hornel, Henry and Crawhall – who despite coming from very different backgrounds, all violently rejected eighteenth-century conservatism that spawned little other than sentimental, anecdotal renditions of Scottish history peopled by "poor but happy" families, in a detailed, exacting manner. They called these paintings "gluepots" for their use of megilp, an oily substance that gave the work the brown patina of age, and instead began to experiment with colour, liberally splashing paint across the canvas. The content and concerns of the paintings, often showing peasant life and work, were as offensive as their style to the effete art establishment, as, until then most of Glasgow's public art collections had been accrued by wealthy tobacco lords and merchants.

Sir James Guthrie spent his summers in the countryside, surrounded by like-minded artists, painting in the outdoors and observing everyday life. Instead of happy peasants, his work shows individuals staring out of the canvas, detached and unrepentant, painted with rich tones but without undue attention to detail or the play of light. Typical of his finest work during the 1880s, *A Highland Funeral* (on display in St Mungo's Museum; see p.171) was hugely influential on the rest of the group, who found inspiration in its

where local and global events are marked in the rings of a slice of ancient Douglas Fir. On the opposite side of the main hall sits an unremarkable exhibition of European and Scottish weapons.

However, it's the art collections, the majority of which are upstairs, that are of most interest. The **Scottish Gallery** houses works from the eighteenth and nineteenth centuries, with a glut of Victorian paintings depicting great moments of Scottish history. In this category is James Hamilton's magnificent *Massacre of Glencoe 1692*, portraying a stoic and strong Macdonald clan comforting wailing women as their village is razed to the ground. The gallery also houses late nineteenth-century works by many of the **Glasgow Boys**, among which richly hued works by George Henry and Edward Hornel amply demonstrate their bold experimentation with Japanese art techniques and styles (see above). The **Modern Gallery** begins with the late nineteenth century and a fine collection of Impressionists, from Signac's calming *The Seine at Herblay*, through Renoir, Monet, Sisley and Degas' *Dancers on a Beach*, to Van Gogh's bullish portrait of Glasgow art dealer *Alexander Reid*. Van Gogh and Reid shared rooms together in Paris, during which time Reid bought up works by the burgeoning Impressionists and took them back to Scotland – the collection you see in the Kelvingrove today is largely attributable to him. Twentieth-century paintings in the Modern Gallery include works by Glasgow School of Art graduates Colquhoun and Macbryde, and William Strang's coolly piercing portrait of Vita Sackville-West gazing out from under the rim of an oversized red hat.

The gallery of the **Classical Tradition** takes you from the Florentine and Venetian schools of the fifteenth to the seventeenth century past Sandro Botticelli's delicate *Annunciation* and the rich, vibrant hues of Giorgione's *The Adulteress Brought before Christ*. However, the dark and symbolic portayal of a slaughtered ox, crucified to a stake marks out the work of Rembrandt, next to his quiet portrait *The Man in Armour*. The restrained emotional content, colour and unaffected realism. Seeing it persuaded **Sir John Lavery**, then studying in France, to return to Glasgow. Lavery was eventually to become an internationally popular society portraitist, his subtle use of paint revealing his debt to Whistler, but his earlier work, of the middle class at play, is filled with fresh colour and figures in motion. In 1888 he documented the Glasgow International Exhibition and went on to paint a number of large-scale works, one of which – a massive depiction of Queen Victoria's visit to Glasgow – hangs in the Royal Concert Hall.

Rather than a realistic aesthetic, an interest in colour and decoration united the work of friends **George Henry** and **E A Hornel**. The predominance of colour, pattern and design in Henry's *Galloway Landscape*, for example, is remarkable, while their joint work *The Druids* (both on display in the Kelvingrove), in thickly applied impasto, is full of Celtic symbolism. In 1893 both artists set off for Japan, funded by Alexander Reid and later William Burrell, where their work used vibrant tone and texture for expressive effect and took Scottish painting to the forefront of European trends.

Newcastle-born **Joseph Crawhall** was, by all accounts, a reserved and quiet individual. He combined superb draughtsmanship and simplicity of line with a photographic memory to create watercolours of an outstanding naturalism and freshness. Unlike the forceful Guthrie and Lavery, who craved wealth and success, Crawhall was a shy man who enjoyed hunting and riding in the countryside and was quite happy to paint delicate animal studies throughout his career. William Burrell was an important patron and a good collection of his works resides at the Burrell Collection.

The school reached its height by 1900 and once its members had achieved the artistic respect – and for some the commercial success – they craved, it began to disintegrate and did not outlast World War I. However, the influence of their work cannot be underestimated, shaking the foundations of the artistic elite and inspiring the next generation of Edinburgh painters now known as "Colourists".

Classical tradition is brought up to date by the vigorous bronze sculpture of *Perseus Arming* by the precociously brilliant Victorian Alfred Gilbert, whose most celebrated work is the statue of Eros in London's Piccadilly Circus. The **Realist Tradition** explores the secular aspect of seventeenth- and nineteenth-century art, featuring pastoral landscapes and local figures rather than fallen angels. Look out for Constable's famous depiction of *Hampstead Heath*, and *Modern Italy – The Pifferari*, a glowing portayal of Italian life by Turner that shines out in the gallery like a gem. Boudin, Corot, Millet and Monet are also represented; the presence of these works owes much to the art dealer Alexander Reid, and so it is fitting that his portrait by Van Gogh resides at the end of the gallery, surrounded by the European art that he loved. In contrast, the fantastic view from Loch Lomond is accurately reproduced by the Scots artist John Knox in his *South and North Western View from Ben Lomond* – if you don't have time to climb the mountain this provides a wonderful alternative vistas. The **Victorian Age** contains paintings on popular themes such as lost love, sad partings and tragic unions; like the piteous *The Last Of The Clan* by Thomas Faed, an over-emotional and insensitive depiction of the last departure of a ship, destined for Nova Scotia. In contrast, the gentle and naturalistic *Danai or The Tower of Brass* by Sir Edward Burne-Jones dominates the room in an elaborate altar-like frame and is representative of the pre-Raphaelites, deep interest in ancient legend. The **Modern Period** holds a representative selection of work from Bonnard to Picasso and Matisse. Derain's *Blackfriars*, a depiction of the Thames, shines out in bright and colourful blocks of colour, revealing the basic ground underneath, in an attempt to enhance the unrealistic nature of painting itself. There's some work by **Glasgow Boys**, Henry and Hornel, including Henry's *Japanese Lady with a Fan*, its pattern and decoration inspired by the Far East. Joan Eardley, who spent a long time painting the children and families of the notorious Glasgow Gorbals is representative of the later British tradition along with Stanley Spencer.

The Transport Museum

The twin-towered **Kelvin Hall** is home to the excellent and enormous city **Transport Museum**, a collection of trains, cars, trams, circus caravans and prams, along with an array of old Glaswegian ephemera, whose entrance is in Bunhouse Road (Mon–Sat 10am–5pm, Sun 11am–5pm; free). Near the entrance, "Kelvin Street" is a re-created 1950s cobbled street featuring an old Italian coffee shop, a butcher (complete with plastic meat joints dangling in the window), a bakery (where labels claim that the buns were provided by the university's taxidermy department) and an old-time Underground station. A cinema shows fascinating films – mostly on themes based loosely around transport – of old Glasgow life, with crackly footage of Sauchiehall Street packed solid with trams and shoppers and hordes of pasty-faced Glaswegians setting off for their annual jaunts down the coast. Nearby, the Super X simulator (£1.50) rocks the nauseous viewer around in time with videoed skiing, white-water rafting and other stomach-churning activities. The Clyde Room displays intricate models of ships forged in Glasgow's yards – everything from tiny schooners to ostentatious ocean liners such as the *QE2*.

Glasgow University

Dominating the West End skyline, the gloomy turreted tower of Glasgow's **University**, designed by Sir Gilbert Scott in the mid-nineteenth century, overlooks the glades of the River Kelvin (see "Glasgow Architecture", p.168). Access to the main buildings and museums is from University Avenue, running east from Byres Road. In the dark neo-Gothic pile under the tower you'll find the **University Visitor Centre** (Mon–Sat 9.30am–5pm), which, as well as giving information for potential students, distributes leaflets about the various university buildings and the statues around the campus.

Next door to the University Visitor Centre, the collection of the **Hunterian Museum** (May–Sept Mon–Sat 9.30am–5pm; Oct–April Sat closes 1pm; free), Scotland's oldest public museum dating back to 1807, was donated to the university by ex-student William Hunter, a pathologist and anatomist whose eclectic tastes form the basis of a fairly dry, but frequently diverting zoological and archeological museum. Exhibitions include Scotland's only dinosaur, a look at the Romans in Scotland – the chilly furthest outpost of a massive empire – and a vast coin collection .

On the other side of University Avenue is Hunter's more frequently visited bequest: the **Hunterian Art Gallery** (Mon–Sat 9.30am–5pm; free), best known for its works by James Abbott McNeil Whistler – only Washington DC has a larger collection. Whistler's breathy landscapes are less compelling than his portraits of women, which give his subjects a resolute strength in addition to their fey and occasionally winsome qualities: look out especially for the trio of full-length portraits, *Pink and Silver – the Pretty Scamp*, *Pink and Gold – the Tulip* and *Red and Black – the Fan*.

The gallery's other major collection is of nineteenth- and twentieth-century Scottish art, including the quasi-Impressionist Scottish landscapes of William McTaggart, their bold, broad brush strokes remaining acutely sensitive to delicate patterns of light. McTaggart was a forerunner of the Glasgow Boys movement, represented here by E A Walton – especially in the spirited portrait of his wife – W Y McGregor, Sir David Murray, James Guthrie and Edward Hornel's sweeping, extravagantly colourful canvasses that mix Oriental and Scottish styles with bold panache. A small selection of French Impressionists includes Corot's soothing *Distant View of Corbeil* and works by Boudin and Pissaro.

A side gallery leads to the **Mackintosh House**, a re-creation of the interior of the now-demolished Glasgow home of Margaret and Charles Rennie Mackintosh. An introductory display contains photographs of the original house sliding irrevocably into terminal decay, from where you are lead into an exquisitely cool interior that contains over sixty pieces of Mackintosh furniture on three floors. Among the highlights are the Studio Drawing Room, whose cream and white furnishings are bathed in expansive pools of natural light, and the Japanese-influenced guest bedroom in dazzling, monochrome geometrics.

The Botanic Gardens

At the top of Byres Road, where it meets the Great Western Road, is the main entrance to the **Botanic Gardens** (gardens daily 7am–dusk; Kibble Palace summer daily 10am– 4.45pm; winter closes 4.15pm; Main Range glasshouses summer Mon–Sat 1–4.45pm, Sun noon–4.45pm; winter closes 4.15pm; free). The best-known glasshouse here, the hulking, domed **Kibble Palace** – originally known as the Crystal Palace – was built in 1863 for wealthy landowner John Kibble's estate on the shores of Loch Long, where it stood for ten years, before he decided to transport it into Glasgow, drawing it up the Clyde on a vast raft pulled by a steamer. It remained for over two decades on this spot, used not as a greenhouse but as a Victorian pleasure palace, before the gardens' owners put a stop to the drunken revels that wreaked havoc with the lawns and plant beds. Today the palace is far more sedate, housing a damp, musty collection of swaying palms from around the world. The smell is much sweeter on entering the Main Range glasshouse, home to lurid and blooming flowers and plants – including stunning orchids, cacti, ferns and tropical fruit – luxuriating in the humidity. Quite apart from the main glasshouses, the Botanic Gardens have some beautifully remote paths that weave and dive along the closely wooded banks of the gorged River Kelvin.

Scottish Exhibition and Conference Centre

Down by the riverside, 15 minutes' walk from Kevlingrove Park – and not strictly part of the West End – is the harshly relandscaped **Scottish Exhibition and Conference Centre (SECC)**. It was built in 1985 to kick-start the revival of the Riverbank: two vast adjoining red and grey sheds that make a dutifully utilitarian venue for travelling fairs, mega-concerts and anonymous bars and cafés. The gleaming hotel alongside and the expensive restaurants in the nearby rotunda – one of two access shafts to a long-closed tunnel under the Clyde – have been reasonably successful, but the rotunda's twin on the opposite bank, the **Dome of Discovery**, once a hands-on science museum and showpiece of the 1988 Glasgow Garden Festival site, is an example of what happens when the money runs out – when the festival ended, the gardens rotted and the museum closed. However, plans are being made to turn the area into a science and leisure park with a national science centre, IMAX theatre and maritime heritage centre. Called the "Project for the Millenium", it will hopefully regenerate this forlorn area and bring it back to its former glory.

South of the Clyde

The southern bank of the Clyde, facing the city centre, is home to the notoriously deprived districts of **Govan**, a community yet to find its niche after the shipbuilding slump, and the **Gorbals**, synonymous with the razor gangs of old. On the southern side of Govan the vast bowl of **Ibrox**, home to the rigidly Protestant Rangers football team, proudly displays the Union flag. This Unionist fortress was totally overhauled following the disaster on January 2, 1971, when 66 fans died after a match against bitter arch-rivals Celtic – a stand collapsed as hundreds of early-leavers stampeded back into the stadium after an unlikely last-minute goal.

Inner-city decay fades into altogether gentler and more salubrious suburbs, commonly referred to as **South Side**. These include Queen's Park, a residential area home to Hampden Park football stadium, and the rural landscape of **Pollok Park**, three miles southwest of the city centre, which contains two of Glasgow's major museums: the **Burrell Collection** and **Pollok House**. Buses #34 and #34A from Govan Underground station set down outside the gate nearest to the Burrell. Slightly further to walk is the route from the Pollokshaws West station (don't confuse with Pollokshields West), served by regular trains from Glasgow Central and nearby bus stops on the Pollokshaws Road: *Strathclyde* buses #45, #48 and #57 from Union Street. However, as Pollok Park is only three miles from the city centre, taking a taxi to the Burrell is an inexpensive option.

The Burrell Collection

The lifetime collection of shipping magnate Sir William Burrell (1861–1958), the outstanding **Burrell Collection** (Mon–Sat 10am–5pm, Sun 11am–5pm; free) is, for some, the principal reason for visiting Glasgow. Unlike many other art collectors, Sir William's only real criterion for buying a piece was whether he liked it or not, enabling him to buy many "unfashionable" works, which cost comparatively little, and subsequently proved their worth. He wanted to leave his collection of art, sculpture and antiquities for public display, but stipulated in 1943 that they should be housed "in a rural setting far removed from the atmospheric pollution of urban conurbations, not less than 16 miles from the Royal Exchange". For decades, these conditions proved too difficult to meet, with few open spaces available and a pall of industrial smoke ruling out any city site. However, by the late 1960s, after the nationwide Clean Air Act had reduced pollution, and the vast land of Pollok Park, previously privately owned, had been donated to the city, plans began for a new, purpose-built gallery, which finally opened in 1983. Today the simplicity and clean lines of the Burrell building are its greatest assets, with large picture windows giving sweeping views over woodland and serving as a tranquil backdrop to the objects inside. The sculpture and antiques are on the ground level, arranged in six sections that overlap and occasionally backtrack, while a mezzanine above displays most of the paintings.

On entering the building, the most striking piece, by virtue of sheer size, is the Warwick Vase, a huge bowl containing fragments of a second century AD vase from Hadrian's Villa in Tivoli. Next to it are the first of a series of sinewy and naturalistic bronze casts of Rodin sculptures, among them *The Age of Bronze*, *A Call to Arms* and the infamous *Thinker*. Beyond the entrance hall, on three sides of a courtyard, a trio of dark and sombre panelled rooms have been re-erected in faithful detail from the Burrells' Hutton Castle home, their heavy tapestries, antique furniture and fireplaces displaying the same eclectic taste as the rest of the museum.

From the courtyard, leading up to the picture windows, the **Ancient Civilizations** collection – a catch-all title for Greek, Roman and earlier artefacts – includes an exquisite mosaic Roman cockerel from the first century BC and a 4000-year-old Mesopotamian lion's head. The bulk of it is Egyptian, however, with rows of inscrutable gods and kings. Nearby, also illuminated by the enormous windows, the **Oriental Art** forms nearly one quarter of the complete collection, ranging from Neolithic jades through bronze vessels and Tang funerary horses to cloisonné. The earliest piece, from around the second century BC, is a lovable earthenware watchdog from the Han Dynasty, but most dominant is the serene fifteenth-century *Iohan* (disciple of Buddha), who sits cross-legged and contemplative up against the window and the trees of Pollok Park. Near-Eastern art is also represented, in a dazzling array of turquoise- and cobalt-decorated jugs, and a swathe of intricate carpets.

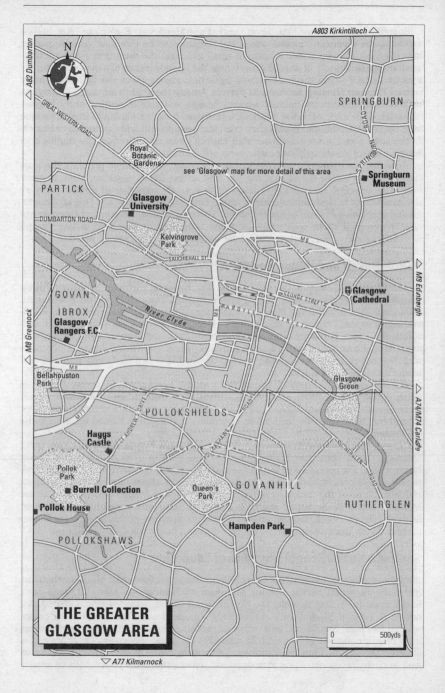

A803 Kirkintilloch △

△ A82 Dumbarton

N

GREAT WESTERN ROAD

SPRINGBURN

SPRINGBURN ROAD

Royal Botanic Gardens

see 'Glasgow' map for more detail of this area

PARTICK

■ **Springburn Museum**

Glasgow University

DUMBARTON ROAD

Kelvingrove Park

SAUCHIEHALL ST

M8

△ M8 Edinburgh

GOVAN

IBROX

Glasgow Rangers F.C.

River Clyde

M8

ARGYLE

GEORGE STREET

STREET

Glasgow Cathedral

△ M8 Greenock

M8

Bellahouston Park

M77

△ A74/M74 Carlisle

Glasgow Green

POLLOKSHIELDS

ST ANDREW'S DRIVE

POLLOKSHAWS ROAD

Haggs Castle

POLLOKSHAWS ROAD

Pollok Park

Burrell Collection

Queen's Park

GOVANHILL

RUTHERGLEN

Pollok House

BUCKLERGLEN ROAD

Hampden Park

POLLOKSHAWS

THE GREATER GLASGOW AREA

0   500yds

▽ A77 Kilmarnock

Burrell considered his **Medieval and Post-Medieval European Art**, which encompasses silverware, glass, textiles and sculpture, to be the most valuable part of his collection. Ranged across a maze of small galleries, the most impressive sections are the sympathetically lit stained glass – note the homely image of a man warming his toes by the fire – and the hundreds of tapestries, among them the fifteenth-century riotous *Peasants Hunting Rabbits with Ferrets*. Among the church art and reliquary are simple thirteenth-century Spanish wooden images and cool fifteenth-century English alabaster, while a trio of period interiors, interrupted by an exhibition of fragile, antique lace, cover the Gothic and Elizabethan eras, and seventeenth and eighteenth centuries. In the latter you can see selections from Burrell's vast art collection, the highlight of which is one of Rembrandt's evocative early self-portraits (1632).

Upstairs, the cramped, and comparatively gloomy mezzanine is probably the least satisfactory section of the gallery, not the best setting for its sparkling array of paintings. The selection incongruously leaps from a small gathering of fifteenth-century religious works to Gericault's darkly dynamic *Prancing Grey Horse* and Degas' thoughtful and perceptive *Portrait of Emile Durant*. Pissarro, Manet, Boudin and Cezanne are also represented along with some exquisite watercolours by Glasgow Boy Joseph Crawhall, revealing his accurate and tender observations of the animal world.

Pollok House and Haggs Castle

A quarter of a mile away down rutted tracks lies the lovely eighteenth-century **Pollok House** (Mon–Sat 10am–5pm, Sun 11am–5pm; free), the manor of the Pollok Park estate and once home of the Maxwell family, local lords and owners of most of southern Glasgow until well into this century. Designed by William Adam in the mid-1700s, the house is typical of its age: graciously light and sturdily built, looking out onto the pristine raked and parterre gardens, whose stylized daintiness contrasts with the heavy Spanish paintings inside, among them two El Greco portraits and works by Murillo and Goya.

The house itself is, however, like so many stately homes, a little sterile, a series of plush period rooms whose ornate furniture you view from behind red sash cordons. Only the servants' quarters downstairs capture the imagination – a virtually untouched labyrinth of tiled Victorian parlours and corridors that includes a good tearoom in the old kitchen.

Close to the eastern entrances to Pollok Park, **Haggs Castle** on St Andrew's Drive (Mon–Sat 10am–5pm, Sun 11am–5pm; free) was built in 1685 as a Maxwell family Baronial hall, the precursor to the far more ornate Pollok House. Today the stark grey turrets and impenetrable stone walls conceal a historical museum aimed squarely at children. Some of the rooms have been decked out with figures and tableaux of the Maxwell family at home, others turned over to interactive exhibitions looking at Scottish history – including an unusually clear explanation of the history and importance of Mary, Queen of Scots.

Scotland Street School Museum of Education

A mile and a half northeast of the Burrell Collection is another great Mackintosh monument, the **Scotland Street School Museum of Education** (Mon–Sat 10am–5pm, Sun 2–5pm; free), slap opposite the Shields Road Underground station. Opened as a school in 1906 to Mackintosh's distinctively angular design, it closed in 1979, since when it has been refurbished as a extremely entertaining education museum, housing a fascinating collection of memorabilia related to life in the classroom. There are reconstructed classrooms from the Victorian, Edwardian, World War II and 1960s eras, as well as changing rooms, a primitive domestic science room and re-creations of a headmaster's office, the school matron's sanitorium and a janitor's lair. If you visit on a week-day during term time, you may stumble on a period lesson going on with local schoolkids struggling to understand their ink blotters, gas masks and archly unsympathetic teachers. Even the faint smell of antiseptic will conjure up memories of scuffed knees and playground tantrums.

The outskirts

Thanks to extensive local government reorganization, most notably in the mid-1970s, Glasgow's boundaries have extended ever outwards to incorporate an increasingly sprawling urban area fringed by vast concrete housing estates – in particular, **Easterhouse** next to the M8 in the east and **Castlemilk** at the foot of the hills in the south – unserviced, largely neglected neighbourhoods that represent the worst horrors of post-war planning.

RUTHERGLEN, four miles southeast of the city centre, is the oldest burgh in Scotland (a full 500 years older than Glasgow), and still harbouring deep resentment about its absorption in 1975 into the anonymous suburbs of its upstart neighbour. Although recent boundary reorganization has restored political independence to this area, it still remains encased within the Glasgow sprawl, defending its proud autonomy in the small town **museum** in King Street (Mon–Fri 10am–5pm, Sun 11am–5pm; free). Here you'll find a good antidote to the rampant Glaswegiania of every other city museum, chronicling the history of the burgh and its constant struggles against Glasgow. The bigger city's desire to annexe Rutherglen had been simmering for centuries – a 1658 document from the town council to the Scots parliament complains that Rutherglen was " . . . in a very mean and low condition these many years bygone by reason of its contiguity with the City of Glasgow, who has all the Commerce and Trading in those parts, so that their Ancient Royal Burgh is likely to decay and ruin". Four trains per hour leave from Glasgow Central low-level station for the ten-minute journey to Rutherglen.

Two miles north of the city centre another museum attempts to tell the story of a similar, once independent community. Trains leave Queen Street station every thirty minutes for **SPRINGBURN** and the tiny **Springburn Museum**, Atlas Square (Mon–Fri 10.30am–5pm, Sat 10am–4.30pm, Sun 2–5pm; free), which aims to recount the life of this seemingly anonymous suburb as the once largest rail engineering yard in Europe. The tight-knit glory days are now long gone, and Springburn's tale makes painfully familiar reading. Pictures recall the community up to the 1950s and its wholesale redevelopment in the 1960s, squeezed into dreadful tower blocks that ended up as student accommodation.

Cafés and restaurants

Glasgow's renaissance has seen an explosion of fine restaurants and European-style bars and cafés, which, in addition to the imput of its diverse and ethnically mixed population, make eating possibilities pretty wide.

The city's **restaurants** cover an impressively international spectrum – incorporating cuisines such as Catalan and Irish along with more familiar dishes from France, Italy, India and China. Traditional **Scottish cuisine** has become very trendy in recent years, with an upsurge in the number of outlets, covering most price ranges, that serve local specialities. There are few exclusively **vegetarian** restaurants, but most places – especially around the Merchant City – have good, imaginative vegetarian choices.

For **budget food**, cafés range from the cheapest, greasiest cholesterol-hole through to bars offering reasonable snacks all day, and frequently into the evening. Unlike in staid Edinburgh, where a lot of places close on Sunday, most of Glasgow's restaurants are open seven days a week.

City centre

The **city centre** boasts the widest range of cuisines in Glasgow, including all its oriental and most of its vegetarian restaurants. The **Merchant City** contains the largest concentration of designer brasseries and some very pricy restaurants, while **Buchanan and Sauchiehall streets** feature the big restaurant and fast-food chains.

Budget food: cafés, diners and pubs

Café Gandolfi, 64 Albion St (☎552 6813). Trendy Merchant City café-bar that attracts hordes of posing beauties, here to enjoy good quality soup, salads and fish dishes.

Delifrance, 119–121 Sauchiehall St. French café with takeaway service, serving cheap and authentic food. Daytime only in winter, open until around 8pm during the summer.

Eat Out, 8–19 W George St. The only gay and lesbian café in Glasgow, this colourful and relaxed establishment, under Queen St train station, is always busy, serving pasta and salads with free coffee refills. Food served daily until 10pm, open until 11pm.

Fratelli Sarti, 133 Wellington St (☎248 2228) & 121 Bath St (☎204 0440). Authentic and popular, the deli (9am–6pm) on Wellington St also serves delicious pizza and pastas in a frantic café open daily until 10pm; the Bath St restaurant (just next door) is larger with the same quality menu and open daily 8pm–10pm.

Granary, 82 Howard St. Well situated near the St Enoch Centre, this affordable café serves quiches, lasagne and other vegetarian favourites complimented by a good variety of salads. Open daily till 5pm.

Junkanoo, 111 Hope St, near Central station (☎248 7102). Boisterous and inexpensive Latin American bar that successfully, and unusually, combines a pleasant drinking atmosphere with some great food, with tapas and chilli looming large. Mon–Thurs open till 11pm, Fri & Sat till midnight, Sun closes at 5pm.

Kings Café, 71 Elmbank St, off Sauciehall St. Good fish-and-chip shop with seating at the back, serving generous helpings of traditional greasy fare and quality pasta to boot.

October Café, top floor, Princes Square Shopping Centre. A variety of different foods, including some vegetarian options, served all day and into the night on the wraparound verandah peering down into the swish designer-shopping paradise. Sun daytime only.

Sloans, Argyll Arcade, off Argyle St. Huge pub-cum-restaurant serving well-cooked food such as pasta and steaks in surroundings that become increasingly like a riotous Victorian gin palace the further up the building you rise.

Tron Theatre, 63 Trongate (☎552 8587). Two atmospheres prevail here. The trendy wrought-iron café-bar caters for the quick lunch and coffee crowd while the old-fashioned Victorian bar is perfect for a laid-back lunch or dinner.

Willow Tea Room, 217 Sauchiehall St. Refined elevenses, lunches and afternoon tea in Mackintosh-designed splendour. Open till 5pm.

Scottish

Babbity Bowster, 16–18 Blackfriars St (☎552 5055). Atmospheric and popular Merchant City bar on the ground level serving excellent Scottish food – anything from hearty broths to haggis, salmon and kippers. The restaurant upstairs is pricier, and more sedate, serving venison, fresh fish and the like. Daily till midnight.

Buttery, 652 Argyle St (☎221 8188). A fine, if slightly snooty, restaurant serving lavish, imaginative and expensive food, with lots of tarted-up traditional Scottish dishes. Open Mon–Sat till 10.30pm.

City Merchant, 97 Candleriggs (☎553 1577). Intimate restaurant in Merchant City that serves good food using Scottish produce from Dingwall haggis to fresh lobster. Open Mon–Sat till 10.30pm.

Crannog, 28 Cheapside St (☎221 1727). Excellent seafood restaurant tucked away underneath the vast motorway bridge. Much of the food, which is very reasonably priced compared with other city seafood joints, is caught by the restaurant and smoked on the premises. Also has a good vegetarian selection. Closed Sun.

Rogano, 11 Exchange Place, near Buchanan St (☎248 4055). Although the food here is not solely Scottish, the Rogano is a Glasgow institution, an absolutely superb but shockingly expensive fish restaurant decked out inside as an authentic replica of the 1930s Cunard liner, the *Queen Mary*. *Café Rogano*, in the basement, is cheaper but not so deliciously ostentatious. Café open till 11.30pm on Sat, both closed Sun.

Latin

Cantina Del Rey, 6 Kings Court (☎552 4044). Behind the St Enoch Centre in a converted railway vault, this spacious restaurant serves authentic Mexican cuisine including fajitas, burritos and frozen margaritas at reasonable prices. Open Sun–Thurs 5–10pm, Fri & Sat till 11pm.

Fire Station, 33 Ingram St (☎552 2929). Merchant City restaurant housed in a huge old fire station, dating from 1900, walled with municipal cast-off marble tiling. The excellent menu, especially the pasta and the indulgent puddings, is moderately priced, and a wide choice of beer and wine is offered.

O'Sole Mio, 32 Bath St. A superb, and easily affordable, city-centre restaurant for unusual pasta dishes, as well as pizzas from their log-fired oven.

Paperino's, 283 Sauchiehall St (☎332 3800). Friendly and comfortable restaurant serving moderately priced pizza and pasta dishes that are popular with students and shoppers alike.

Chinese, Japanese, Southeast Asian and Indian

Blossom, 80 Miller St, Merchant City (☎221 1292). In a city not terribly well blessed with Chinese restaurants, this is undoubtedly one of the best, with a well-priced and wide-ranging menu that includes an unusually good number of vegetarian options.

Ho Wong, 82 York St, just off Argyle St west of Central Station (☎221 3550). Secluded restaurant offering a top-class range of Cantonese and Szehcuan food. Expensive but worth it.

Koh-i-noor, 235 North St, Charing Cross (☎221 1555). Good-value range of diverse Indian dishes, especially notable for its highly reasonable Sunday brunches.

Loon Fung, 417 Sauchiehall St (☎332 1477). Great *dim sum* and inexpensive vegetarian set meals.

Mata Hari, 17 W Princes St, Charing Cross (☎332 9789). Deservedly popular Malaysian restaurant with some unusual – and highly spicy – dishes on the moderately priced menu. Closed Sun.

Moshi Moshi, 7 Buccleuch St (☎353 0777). Slip into this small establishment for a taste of downtown Tokyo where tempting sushi, noodle and tempura dishes are served with Japanese beer or sake.

Vegetarian

Cafe Alba, 61 Otago St (☎337 2282). Situated just off Gibson St, this popular café sells a good selection of vegetarian food. However, it is probably better known for the best home baking in the west.

Granary, 82 Howard St. Well situated near the St Enoch Centre, this affordable café serves quiches, lasagne and other vegetarian favourites complemented by a good variety of salads. Open daily till 5pm.

13th Note, 80 Glassford St (☎553 1638). This Merchant City bar stands out for its all-vegan menu from vegeburgers to chilli with daily specials that tend to have an international theme. Food served daily until early evening only.

Vegville Diner, 93 St Georges Rd (☎331 2220). Good quality and value for money is the name of the game in this colourful diner. The menu consists of innovative and tasty dishes with several Japanese options.

Icelandic

XO, 28–32 Cathedral Square (☎552 3519). Scotland's only Icelandic restaurant, situated upstairs from the Cathedral House café-bar, where you can throw a selection of fish and meat onto a massive slab of oven-heated granite, and watch it fry. Expensive but fun.

West End

Predominantly due to the large local student population, the **West End** is the best area for cheap, stylish restaurants and cafés, and bars serving food, especially around Hillhead Underground station on Byres Road; nearby, the restaurants along **Ashton Lane** dish out unreservedly good meals. On the other side of Byres Road from the station, **Ruthven Lane** is home to some lively restaurants well known for their cheap happy hours.

Budget food: cafés, diners and pubs

Back Alley, 8 Ruthven Lane (☎334 7165). This West End burger joint is Glasgow's best, worlds away from fast-food glop. Enormous burgers, smothered in assorted toppings, to be washed down with good beer and finished off with calorific puddings. Moderately priced, with an early-evening happy hour.

California Gourmet, 291 Byres Rd. Daytime American ice cream and sandwich bar. Full of students enjoying the delicious submarines with up to 13 different fillings.

Chimmy Chungas, 499 Gt Western Rd (☎334 0884). Loud and popular Tex-Mex bar and café that is good for anything from a light snack through to a full blow-out. Sun to Thurs food until 9.30pm, Fri & Sat 10.30pm. Looking down into a large bar, this restaurant is deservedly popular with students taking advantage of lunchtime bargains. Food served daily until 10pm.

Grosvenor Café, 31 Ashton Lane. Small, traditional Italo-Scots café tucked behind Hillhead Underground station with a die-hard clientele, addicted to the no-nonsense food (pizzas, fried food, burgers) served at unbelievably low prices. Slightly more upmarket menu in the evening, although even this is an astonishing bargain. Sun & Mon open till 7pm, Tues–Sat 11pm.

Jinty McGinty's, 21–29 Ashton Lane. Wood-panelled and frosted-glassed Irish pub that, as well as serving excellent stout, maintains a small menu of Irish favourites such as bacon and cabbage, steak and Guinness pie or hearty soups.

Scottish

Ubiquitous Chip, 12 Ashton Lane (☎334 5007). Splendid West End restaurant with a covered patio that resembles an indoor forest. Glasgow's most delicious Scottish food – game, seafood and local cheeses, and occasionally oatmeal ice cream and venison haggis. Expensive. Open daily till 11pm.

Latin

The Big Blue, 445 Gt Western Rd (☎357 1038.) Whitewashed walls and colourful upholstery characterize this low level bar and restaurant that serves simple but tasty pasta dishes. Food served daily until 9pm.

Chimmy Chungas, 499 Gt Western Rd (☎334 0884). Looking down into a large bar, this restaurant is deservedly popular with students taking advantage of lunchtime bargains. Food served daily until 10pm.

Di Maggio's, 61 Ruthven Lane (☎334 8560). Inexpensive, extremely popular West End pizzeria and pasta joint, usually packed solid with bargain-hungry students. Frantic atmosphere with occasional live music.

Joe's Garage, 52 Bank St, next to Glasgow University Union (☎339 5407). Fairly predictable range of pizza and pasta, but the food is good, inexpensive and the imaginative chef's specials are worth a try.

Salsa, 184 Dumbarton Rd (☎337 1416). A smaller version of the *Cantina Del Rey*, this West End branch serves the same good-quality food in a colourful and laid-back atmosphere. Daily noon–11pm.

Indian

Ashoka, 19 Ashton Lane (☎357 5904). Moderately priced West End Dhosa house and Indian restaurant, popular with local students.

Mother India, 28 Westminster Terrace (☎221 1633). Good-quality food at affordable prices in the refreshingly laid-back surroundings of this friendly Indian restaurant. It's unlicensed, so bring your own alcohol; small corkage fee.

Shalimar, 23–25 Gibson St, near Glasgow University (☎339 6453). Mix of students and professionals who appreciate the extensive and good-value menu.

Vegetarian

Bay Tree, 403 Gt Western Rd (☎334 5895). This small co-operative café offers a decent selection of burgers, salads and soups with good daily specials. Try the sugar-free cakes for a guilt-free pudding.

South Side

Although the range isn't as great as elsewhere, **South Side**, a quieter less studenty alternative to the centre or the West End, does offer Glasgow's only Middle Eastern eating place and one of its few Greek restaurants.

Budget food: cafés, diners and pubs

Boswell Hotel, 27 Mansionhouse Rd, Queen's Park (☎632 9812). Unusually cheap and extensive bar-food menu with some offbeat house specialities – a good complement to the wide selection of real ales. Regular live music; food until 9pm.

Jimmy's, 1 Victoria Rd. Splendid fish-and-chip shop serving deliciously fresh battered salmon, haddock, sole, salmon and plaice, seven days a week until 11pm.

Scottish

Ewington, at the *Ewington Hotel*, 132 Queen's Drive (☎423 1152). Facing Queen's Park, this sedate suburban hotel has a cellar restaurant whose very pink and flouncy decor is compensated for by the fine mix of moderately priced traditional Scottish and Continental cuisine. Food daily 6–8.45pm.

Greek and Italian

Di Maggio, 1038 Pollokshaws Rd, Queen's Park (☎632 4194). Less studenty than the West End branch, offering the same selection of gargantuan pizzas and hefty pasta dishes.

Enzo's Trattoria Da Maria, 221 St Andrew's Rd, E Pollokshields (☎429 4604). Cosy, reasonable and traditional trattoria in an unlikely setting, with a few imaginative Italian dishes tucked among the standard pastas and pizzas. Open Mon–Sat till 11pm.

Café Serghei, 67 Bridge St (☎429 1579). One of the few Greek restaurants in Glasgow, serving traditional food in a lively atmosphere.

Middle Eastern

Prince Armany's, 7 Clyde Place (☎420 6660). Tucked under the railway bridge near Bridge St, this restaurant offers Middle Eastern food such as lamb kebabs and delicate vegetable stews served with cous cous or deliciously light Arabian bread. The pre-theatre menu served 5–7pm is an excellent bargain.

Pubs and bars

Not so many years ago, Glasgow's rough image was inextricably associated with its **pubs**, widely thought of as no-go areas for any visitor. Although much of this reputation was exaggerated, there was an element of truth in it. Nowadays, however, you're just as likely to spend an evening in a succession of open and airy café-bars as in a dark, dangerous, nicotine-stained pub. The centre has an admirable range of reliable places to drink; if you tire of the glossy **Merchant City**, head for the **East End**, where a fair number of local spit-and-sawdust establishments make a welcome change. All in all, though, the liveliest area, once again, has to be the **West End**, its good cross section of pubs and bars matching its great restaurants.

City centre

Babbity Bowster, 16–18 Blackfriars St. Lively hang-out at the heart of the Merchant City.

Bay Horse, 19 Bath St. Ordinary Glasgow pub, serving malt whisky, pies and peas.

Bar 91, 91 Candleriggs. Well-designed Merchant City bar, using wrought iron to evoke a stylish atmosphere.

Brahms and Liszt, 71 Renfield St. Candlelit cellar bar that takes great pride in its beer selection, some of which is available by the jug. Great atmosphere, but gets very crowded.

Buzzy Wares, Princes Square Shopping Centre. Glossy bar popular at weekends as a pre-club stop.

Cairns Bar, 5–12 Miller St. Unpretentious, very central pub popular with Glaswegians and serving a wide range of ales and whiskies.

Corn Exchange, 88 Gordon St. Slap opposite Central station, this bar has successfully re-created the feel of a traditional Victorian Glaswegian pub.

The Griffin, 226 Bath St. Friendly, if faintly tacky, three-bar pub with a firm crowd of devotees and regulars – mostly students.

Horseshoe Bar, 17 Drury St. Traditional old pub, reputedly Glasgow's busiest – loud, frantic and great fun, with a very mixed clientele. Karaoke upstairs, with a downstairs bar for quiet conversation.

Maxaluna, 410 Sauchiehall St. Scaling the heights of Glasgow's designer bars, this glass-fronted bar and restaurant serves expensive beer in a busy but remarkably spacious atmosphere. Good for a relaxed coffee during the day.

Nico's, 375–379 Sauchiehall St. Trendy without being painfully so, the ambience in this popular bar strives towards a French flavour – prices, especially for the bottled beer, are steep.

Phileas Fogg, 73 Bath St. Popular with young business people, this stylish bar fills up with a more interesting crowd later in the evening.

R.G's, 73 Queen St. Nostalgia-soaked bar that serves as a focus for Glasgow's rock music heritage – hence the large portraits of local musical luminaries that adorn the walls. A bit cramped, but a fun atmosphere.

Saracen Head, Gallowgate (opposite the Barras market). Unchanged East End pub that offers an enjoyably beery, sawdust-floored wallow. Look out for the tax demand from Robbie Burns displayed on the wall, from the days when he was the local tax officer.

Scotia Bar, 112 Stockwell St. Laid-back bar popular with writers and other tortured souls. Occasional live folk music – Billy Connolly began his career here, telling jokes in between singing folk songs.

Solid Rock Café, 19 Hope St. Glasgow's top rock pub, with heavy rock DJs Thurs–Sun.

Ten, Mitchell Lane. In a tiny street connecting Buchanan and Mitchell streets, *Ten* was designed by the same crew as Manchester's legendary *Hacienda* club. As you'd expect, it's suitably chic, although with a healthy dose of Glaswegian humour to take off the posey edge.

Variety Bar, 401 Sauchiehall St. Crowded bar with faded Art Nouveau appeal and frequented by local art school students.

Victoria Bar, 157–159 Bridgegate. Basic, folksy pub serving a wide selection of real ales.

West End

The Aragon, 131 Byres Rd. Old-fashioned bar with mixed crowd. The main attraction here is the vast beer selection, which includes European fruit beers and weekly guest ales.

Bonham's, 194 Byres Rd. Tall, spacious bar with splendid stained-glass windows. Popular, unpretentious, and serving reasonable daytime food.

Brewery Tap, 1055 Sauchiehall St. Well known for its excellent selection of real ales and imported lager, this pub caters for students and locals alike with seating outside for those long summer evenings.

The Halt, 106 Woodlands Rd. Great beer and a vast selection of whiskies in this relaxed music pub. Regular live jazz.

Living Room, 5–9 Byres Rd. New hotbed for the young and hip, at the southern end of Byres Rd. Wrought iron and candles enhance the pre-club atmosphere. Near *The Volcano* nightclub.

Mitchell's, 157 North St. Next to the domed Mitchell's Library, a comfortable pub with a scholarly atmosphere. Good beer and an excellent refuge.

Partick Tavern, 163–169 Dumbarton Rd. Traditional pub serving good Scottish food in a refreshingly untrendy atmosphere.

Tennent's, 191 Byres Rd. No-nonsense, beery den, a refreshing antidote to all the designer paradises nearby. Large and very popular, especially with real ale aficionados.

Uisge Beatha, 232 Woodlands Rd. The plain frontage broken only by the bar's name in small green neon letters is far from indicative of the eclectic insides, where a trendy and lively crowd relish in the re-created Scottish atmosphere – all kilts, piped music and stripped wood. The name, by the way, is Gaelic for whisky, the "water of life".

The Western Bar, 80 Dumbarton Rd. A world apart from the student haunts nearby, this genuinely friendly working-class stronghold has walls that read like a city social history treatise, with lots of old photographs and faded memorabilia.

Whistler's Mother, 116–122 Byres Rd. Combines a relaxed restaurant with the more basic bar, which is deservedly popular with students and legions of young people. Great decor that doesn't sacrifice comfort for style.

South Side

Athena Taverna, 780 Pollokshaws Rd. Quiet real ale haven near Queen's Park train station, also serving excellent Greek food.

Boswell Hotel, 27 Mansionhouse Rd. Lively Queen's Park pub with great atmosphere and occasional live music. Good selection of real ales, including some unusually potent local brews. Fine bar food (see p.187).

Brazen Head, 1–3 Cathcart Rd. Close to the Citizen's Theatre and decorated by football strips, this Irish-Italian bar is a local haunt and well endowed with Guinness and Gillespies.

Church on the Hill, 16 Algie St. Perched on the hill behind Queen's Par, the wood panelling and brass fittings give an old time atmosphere to the bar and restaurant, which serves American-style food. Seating outside for sunny evenings.

The Granary, 10 Kilmarnock Rd (10-min walk south from Queen's Park). Friendly bar, with busy restaurant that serves a good selection of burgers, steak and Mexican food.

M J Heraghty, 708 Pollokshaws Rd. Tiny pub on the corner of Pollokshaws and Nithsdale roads. Rough working men's pub, particularly crowded when Celtic play. So masculine, they don't even have a women's toilet – you have to go next door.

Samuel Dowes, 69–71 Northside Rd (close to Pollokshields West train station). This South Side favourite offers cheap bar meals and occasionally live music to a welcoming crowd. Ceilidh every Sun and poetry reading on the first Mon of every month.

Satchmo's, 136 Battlefield Rd. Presided over by the watchful eye of Louis Armstrong, this bar, close to the Victoria Infirmary, takes an unpretentious jazz theme and caters for a lively crowd; it's particularly busy on weekends.

Nightlife and entertainment

Glasgow's City of Culture tag resulted in a great liberalization of the city's licensing laws, which transformed the **clubbing** scene almost overnight. Since then, however, many of these laws have been repealed, and a curfew has been passed declaring that no one is to be allowed into a bar or club after 1am (the time has changed twice since being implemented, so check at tourist office first). Considering that many clubs were licensed until 6am during 1990, encouraging club-hopping, the new rules are, in the view of many, absurdly draconian.

Most of Glasgow's nightclubs are in the heart of the main shopping areas off Argyle and Buchanan streets, many of them within walking distance of each other. Establishments are pretty mixed, and although there's still a stack of outdated megadiscos with rigorous dress codes, the last couple of years has seen the arrival of far more stylish haunts. Hours hover from around 9pm to 3am, and cover charges are variable – expect to pay around £3 during the week, rising to around £8 at the weekend. Drinks are usually about thirty percent more expensive than in the pubs.

The city's traditional breadth of art, theatre, film and music is undeniably impressive, especially during **Mayfest**, Glasgow's most concentrated splurge of cultural activity. The majority of the larger **theatres, cinemas** and showpiece **concert halls** are around the shopping streets of the city centre, while the West End is home to student-oriented venues such as the quirky *Grosvenor* cinema. The city's two trendiest theatres, the *Citizens'* and the *Tramway*, are South Side. You can find **details** of the city's events in the *Glasgow Herald* or *Evening Times* newspapers, or the fortnightly listings magazine, *The List* (£1.50), which also covers Edinburgh. To book **tickets** for theatre productions or big concerts, phone the *Ticket Centre* ☎227 5511; or call in at its headquarters at City Hall, Candleriggs, on the Trongate end of Argyle Street (phone bookings Mon–Sat 9am–9pm, Sun noon–5pm; office Mon–Sat 10am–6.30pm, Sun noon–5pm).

Nightclubs

The Arches, Midland St (☎221 9736). Deservedly popular weekend club pounding out predominantly dance and rave-orientated music in converted railway arches, literally under central station, off Jamaica St.

The Cotton Club, 5 Scott St (☎332 0712). Friendly club with a variety of one-nighters including "Club Havana", the last Sun of every month, playing salsa and flamenco and offering free dance lessons. Opposite the art school.

Fury Murray's, 96 Maxwell St, behind the St Enoch Centre (☎221 6511). Student-oriented and lively, with music spanning from the 1960s to rave and techno.

The Garage, 490 Sauchiehall St (☎332 3872). Medium-sized club at the heavier end of the rock spectrum; some dance nights but lacks atmosphere.

Riverside Club, Fox Rd, off Clyde St (☎248 3144). Regular weekend ceilidh that gets absolutely packed out with good-natured, drunken Scottish dancers. Great fun, with a live band and callers involving everyone from seasoned ceilidh dancers to visiting novices. Get there early (8–9pm) to ensure a place.

Sub Club, 22 Jamaica St (☎248 4600). Nightclub aimed squarely at the ravier end of the market. Weekend nights are very trendy.

The Tunnel, 84 Mitchell St (☎204 1000). Stylish club with arty decor – though now a bit faded; the gents' toilet has cascading waterfall walls. Gay night on Mon.

The Volcano, 15 Benalder St (☎337 1100). The major club in the West End, drawing in hordes of students. An eclectic selection of specialist music nights in the week and just a damn good boogie at the weekends.

The Voodoo Room, Cambridge St (☎332 3437). Designer club with bleached wood bar, label-conscious clientele and distinctive music nights from funk to house and garage.

Gay clubs and bars

Austin's, 183 Hope St. Dingy but lively central cellar bar, with a mainly male — and fairly cruisey – crowd of all ages.

Bennett's, 90 Glassford St, Merchant City (☎552 5761). Glasgow's main gay club, predominantly male, fairly old-fashioned but enjoyable nonetheless. Straight nights on Tues.

Club Xchange, Royal Exchange Square, off Queen St (☎204 4599). *Bennett's* biggest rival, this mixed gay club is funkier and more upbeat.

The Court Bar, 69 Hutcheson St. Quiet backstreet pub near George Square, mixed in daytimes and gay in the evenings. Friendlier, and less self-conscious, than most of Glasgow's gay pubs.

Del Monica's, 68 Virginia St. Glasgow's liveliest and most stylish gay bar, very near George Square, with a mixed and hedonistic crowd.

The Waterloo Bar, 306 Argyle St. Very central, garish but enjoyable bar, which gets packed at weekends. Mainly men.

Live music pubs and venues

Barrowlands, 244 Gallowgate (☎226 4679). Legendary East End dance hall, complete with spinning glitterball, that hosts some of the sweatiest, liveliest gigs you will ever encounter. Has a capacity of a couple of thousand, so tends to attract bands that are just breaking into the big time.

Curlers, 256 Byres Rd (☎334 1284). Smooth pub that hosts mid-week jazz and blues.

The Garage, 490 Sauchiehall St (☎332 1120). Good-size venue for bands that are just about to make it big.

King Tut's Wah Wah Hut, 272a St Vincent St (☎221 5279). One of the city's best programmes of bands at this splendid city-centre live music pub. Good bar downstairs if you want to sit out the sweaty gig above.

Nice'n'Sleazy, 421 Sauchiehall St (☎333 9637). Alternative bands most nights in the somewhat cramped downstairs bar.

Scotia Bar, 112 Stockwell St, near the St Enoch Centre (☎552 8681). The folkies' favourite, a mellow musical pub that acts as a magnet for folk players and followers. Regular live gigs and frequent jam sessions.

The 13th Note, 80 Glassford St (☎553 1638). This double level bar in the Merchant City is a good place to sample local music talent with live bands most nights.

Theatre and comedy

The Arches, 30 Midland St (☎221 9736). Trendy base for performances by touring theatre groups.

Blackfriars, 45 Albion Rd (☎552 5924). The city's premier comedy and cabaret venue, renowned for its good-value Sat night line-ups. Also live music, particularly jazz. In the Merchant City.

Centre for Contemporary Arts, 346 Sauchiehall St (☎332 7521). Radical theatre, dance and art.

Citizens' Theatre, 119 Gorbals St (☎429 0022). Glasgow's infamous theatre that grew from working-class roots to become one of the most respected, and adventurous, theatres in Britain. Three stages, with bargain prices for students and the unemployed, together with free preview nights.

King's Theatre, 297 Bath St (☎227 5511). Mainstream shows and comedy, south of Sauchiehall Street.

Mitchell Theatre, 6 Granville St, Charing Cross (☎227 5511). Enjoyable venue for touring groups.

Old Athenaeum, 179 Buchanan St (☎332 2333). A smallish base for the *Scottish Youth Theatre*, as well as for visiting companies and stand-up comedians.

Tramway Theatre, 25 Albert Drive, off Pollokshaws Rd (☎225 5511). Good venue for experimental theatre, dance, music and regular art exhibitions.

Tron Theatre, 63 Trongate (☎552 4267). Varied repertoire of mainstream and experimental productions from visiting companies, together with one of the city's most laid-back bars.

Concert halls

Royal Concert Hall, 2 Sauchiehall St (☎227 5511). Big-name rock and soul stars, orchestras and opera companies.

Scottish Exhibition & Conference Centre, Finnieston Quay (☎248 3000). Soulless and overpriced huge shed with the acoustics and atmosphere of an aircraft hangar, but, unfortunately, the only venue in Glasgow (often the only venue in Scotland) visited by the megastars on their world tours.

Theatre Royal, Hope St (☎332 9000). Opulent home of the Scottish Opera and regular host to visiting classical orchestras, opera companies, theatre blockbusters and occasional comedy.

Cinemas

City Centre Odeon, 56 Renfield St (☎332 3413). Multi-screen cinema with similar programming to the Cannon.

Glasgow Film Theatre, 12 Rose St (☎332 8128). The city's main arthouse and independent cinema.

Grosvenor, Ashton Lane (☎339 4298). Eclectic mix of repertory, mainstream and arthouse movies on two screens in this tiny West End alley. Occasional theme nights and frequent lates for local students.

MGM Filmcentre, 326 Sauchiehall St (☎332 9513). Five-screen mainstream multiplex.

Listings

Airlines *Aer Lingus*, 19 Dixon St (☎0645/737747); *British Airways*, 66 Gordon St (☎0345/ 222111); *Icelandair* (☎0345/81111); *British Airways Express*, Glasgow Airport (☎889 1311); *Lufthansa*, 78 St Vincent St (☎0345/737747); *Northwest*, 38 Renfield St (☎226 4175); *Qantas*, 39 St Vincent Place (☎0345/747767).

Airport enquiries ☎887 1111.

American Express 115 Hope St (☎221 4366). Open Mon–Fri 8.30am–5.30pm, Thurs till 7pm, Sat 9am–noon.

Banks *Bank of Scotland*, 65 Gordon St, 110 St Vincent St, 63 Waterloo St, 235 Sauchiehall St and 55 Bath St; *Clydesdale Bank*, 14 Bothwell St, 7 St Enoch Square, 91 Buchanan St, 344 Argyle St and 120 Bath St; *Royal Bank of Scotland*, 22 St Enoch Square, 76 Gordon St, 140 St Vincent St and 393 Sauchiehall St. English banks in Glasgow include *Barclays*, 90 St Vincent St; *Lloyds*, 12 Bothwell St and *National Westminster*, 14 Blythswood Square.

Books *John Smith's*, 57 St Vincent St; *Waterstone's*, 132 Union St; and *Dillons*, 104–108 Argyle St, all have extensive local studies sections.

Bus enquiries Buchanan Street bus station; for local buses call ☎332 7133, for national ☎0990 505050.

Car rental *Arnold Clark*, 16 Vinnicomb St (☎334 9501); *Avis*, 161 North St (☎221 2827); *Budget*, 101 Waterloo St (☎226 4141); *Hertz*, 106 Waterloo St (☎248 7736). Car-rental firms at the **airport** include *Avis* (☎887 2261); *Budget* (☎887 0501); *Eurodollar* (☎887 7915); *Europcar* (☎887 0414); *Hertz* (☎887 0414).

Consulates *Germany*, 158 W Regent St (☎221 0304); *Italy*, 170 Hope St (☎332 4297); *Norway*, 80 Oswald St (☎204 1353); *Spain,* 389 Argyle St (☎221 6943); *Sweden*, 36 Washington St (☎221 7845).

Exchange Outside banking hours you can change money at *Thomas Cook* in Central station (Mon–Wed, Fri & Sat 8am–7pm, Thurs 8am–8pm, Sun 10am–6pm; ☎204 4496).

Football Of the two big Glasgow teams, you can see *Celtic* at *Celtic Park*, 95 Kerrydale St, off A749 London Rd (☎556 2611), and bitter opponents *Rangers* at the mighty *Ibrox* stadium, Edminston Drive (☎427 8800). Glasgow's other, lesser teams include *Partick Thistle* in *Firhill stadium*, Firhill Rd (☎945 4811) or, on the South Side, lowly *Queen's Park* at the national stadium *Hampden Park*, Mount Florida (☎632 1275). Tickets from £10 depending on the opposing team and match status.

Gay and lesbian contacts *Lesbian and Gay Switchboard* (daily 7–10pm; ☎221 8372), *Lesbian Line* (Wed 7–10pm; ☎552 3355).

Hospital 24hr casualty department at the *Royal Infirmary*, 84 Castle St (☎552 3535).

Left luggage Staffed office available at Buchanan St bus station (daily 6.30am–10.30pm) and 24hr lockers at both Central and Queen St train stations.

Pharmacy *Sinclair's*, 693 Gt Western Rd (daily 9am–9pm; ☎339 0012) and at Central station (Mon–Sat 8am–7pm; ☎248 1002).

Police Cranstonhill Police Station, 945 Argyle St (☎532 3200) and Stewart St station, Cowcaddens (☎532 3000).

Post office George Square (Mon–Fri 8.30am–5.45pm, Sat 9am–7pm; ☎242 4260), with branch offices at 85–89 Bothwell St, 216 Hope St and 533 Sauchiehall St.

Taxis *TOA Taxis* (☎332 7070).

Train enquiries ☎204 2844

Travel agents *Campus Travel*, The Hub, Hillhead St (☎357 0608) and 90 John St (☎552 2867); *Glasgow Flight Centre*, 143 W Regent St (☎221 8989).

THE CLYDE

The temptation to speed through the **Clyde valley** is considerable, especially since the raw beauty of the Highlands, the islands and lakes of Argyll and the urbane sophistication of Edinburgh are all within easy reach of the city. Although many of the towns and villages surrounding Glasgow are decidedly missable, some receive far fewer visitors than they deserve, tarnished with the frequently redundant image of dejected industrial towns clinging to the coat tails of Glasgow.

From the city regular trains dip down the southern bank of the Clyde to **Paisley**, where the distinctive cloth pattern gained its name, before heading up to the Firth of Clyde. Along the northern bank, the train rattles through some of Glasgow's oldest shipbuilding communities before arriving in the ancient Strathclyde capital of **Dumbarton**, whose twin-peaked **castle** dominates the flat estuary for miles around.

Heading southeast out of Glasgow, the river's industrial landscape gives way to a far more attractive scenery of gorges and towering castles. Here you can see the stoic town of **Lanark**, where eighteenth-century philanthropists built their model workers' community around the mills of **New Lanark**, and the spectacular **Falls of Clyde**, a mile upstream.

North of the city lies some wonderful upland countryside. Trains terminate at tiny **Milngavie**, which makes great play of its status as the start of the long-distance walk, the **West Highland Way**. Nearby is the rolling beauty of the **Campsie Fells**, providing excellent walking and stunning views down onto Glasgow and the glinting river that runs through it (see *Central Scotland and Fife* for the full story).

The Firth of Clyde

The shipbuilding industry forged the **Firth of Clyde**. This is still evident today in the numerous yards that pepper the banks as you head west out of the city, especially in the north Clyde communities of **Clydebank**, **Yoker** and **Dalmuir**. The A82 and the rail line run along this northern bank, hemmed in to the shore by the **Kilpatrick Hills** that rise menacingly above.

These days, the two river banks are connected by the concrete parabola of the **Erskine Bridge**, dominating the landscape in a way that even Dumbarton Castle has never managed. The bridge disgorges its traffic onto the M8, which runs straight down south to the textile centre of **Paisley** – billed rather meaninglessly as "Scotland's largest town". In the other direction, the M8/A8 and the main train line cling to the shipyard-lined estuary edge, passing the shipbuilding centre of **Greenock**, the old-fashioned seaside resort of **Gourock**, and **Wemyss Bay**, the ferry port for Argyll and Bute. Of the three, Greenock is by far the most interesting, with an excellent town museum that examines the life and achievements of local boy James Watt.

Paisley

Founded in the twelfth century as a monastic settlement around an abbey, **PAISLEY** expanded rapidly after the eighteenth century as a linen manufacturing town, specializing in the production of highly fashionable imitation Kashmiri shawls. Paisley quickly eclipsed other British centres producing the cloth, eventually lending its name to the swirling pine cone design.

South of the train station, down Gilmour or Smithills streets, lies the bridge over the White Cart Water and the borough's ponderous **Town Hall**, seemingly built back to front as its municipal clock and mismatched double towers loom incongruously over the river instead of facing onto the town. Opposite the town hall, the **Abbey** was built on the site of the town's original settlement but was massively overhauled in the Victorian age. The unattractive, fat grey facade of the church does little justice to the renovated interior, which is tall, spacious and elaborately decorated. The elongated choir, rebuilt extensively throughout the last two centuries, is illuminated by jewel-coloured stained glass from a variety of ages and styles. The abbey's oldest monument is the tenth-century Celtic cross of St Barochan, which lurks like a gnarled old bone at the eastern end of the north aisle.

Paisley's tatty **High Street** leads from the town hall to the west and towards two churches that make far more of an impression on the town's skyline than the modest abbey. The steep cobbles of Church Hill rise away from the High Street up to the grand steps and five-stage spire of the **High Church**, while beyond the civic museum at the bottom of the High Street, the **Thomas Coates Memorial Church** (May–Sept Mon, Wed & Fri 2–4pm) is a Victorian masterpiece of hugely overstated grandeur.

Sitting squat like a giant red predator waiting to pounce, the church is one of the most opulent Baptist centres in Britain, with huge tower-top buttresses and an interior of seemingly endless marble and alabaster.

Between the two churches, Paisley's civic **Museum and Art Gallery** (Mon–Sat 10am–5pm; free) shelters behind pompous Ionic columns that face the grim buildings of Paisley University. The local history section, nearest the entrance, contains an interesting collection of local artefacts from song sheets and spinning threads to the death warrant and executioner's contract for the last public hanging in Paisley in 1858. The most popular part of the museum, which deals with the growth and development of the Paisley pattern and shawls, shows the familiar pine cone (or teardrop) pattern from its simplistic beginnings to elaborate later incarnations. The exhibition also includes an interesting look at the lives of the early weavers and the inhospitable conditions under which they worked.

On Oakshaw Street, which runs along the crest of the hill above the Art Gallery, lies the **Coats Observatory** (Mon, Tues & Thurs 2–8pm, Wed, Fri & Sat 10am–5pm; free). It has recorded astronomical and meteorological information since 1884. Today it houses a ten-inch telescope under its dome, and a couple of small exhibition areas display seismic recorders that documented the horrendous San Francisco earthquake of 1906. The telescopes are used for public viewing on Thursday evenings from the last Thursday in October until the last Thursday in March (7–9pm, weather permitting).

To bring you back down to earth, the harsh reality of eighteenth-century life is recreated in the **Sma' Shot Cottages** (April–Sept only Wed & Sat 1–5pm; free). These old houses can be found in George Place, off New Street. Each with individual themes, they contain perfect re-creations of eighteenth- and nineteenth- century daily life complete with bone cutlery and ancient looms. The nineteenth-century artisan's home is also filled with artefacts from ceramic hot water bottles to period wallpaper and leads you towards the cosy tearoom where you can enjoy some home baking.

Practicalities

Regular **trains** from Glasgow Central connect with Paisley's Gilmour Street station in the centre of town. *Strathclyde Transport* **buses** #39, #53, #54 and #55 stop at Paisley Abbey; however, the train is faster and more convenient. Buses leave Paisley's Gilmour Street forecourt every ten minutes for Glasgow Airport, two miles north of the town. The **tourist office** (April & May Mon–Fri 9am–1pm & 2–5pm, June–Sept Mon–Sat 9am–6pm; ☎889 0711) is in the town hall.

Few people bother to stay in Paisley, except those catching an early flight, and **accommodation** in the town tends to be overpriced. If you do need to stay, the spacious *Rockfield Hotel* at 125 Renfrew Rd (☎889 6182; ⑤) is the nicest alternative. B&Bs include *Ardgowan House*, 92 Renfrew Rd (☎889 4763; ③) and *Greenlaw*, 12 Greenlaw Drive, off the Glasgow road (☎889 5359; ③). Lunchtime and evening bar **meals**, together with reasonably convivial atmospheres, can be found in *Gabriel's Bar* at 33 Gauze St, near the abbey, and the *Bankhouse* on Gilmour St, almost next to the station. *Chez Jules* at 38 New St (☎848 6611) provides more upmarket French cuisine while the *Paisley Arts Centre* across the road has a small bar with seating outside.

From Port Glasgow to Wemyss Bay

PORT GLASGOW is the first of a string of unprepossessing towns that sprawl along the southern coast of the Firth of Clyde. A small fishing village until 1688, when the burghers of Glasgow bought it and developed it as their main harbour, it's a grim place, with nothing to detain you. The train line splits here, one branch heading north along the industrialized coast and the other heading inland before curving round to the ferry port at Wemyss Bay. You can get hourly *City Link* buses to Greenock and Gourock from Buchanan Street bus station.

North of Port Glasgow

GREENOCK was the site of the first dock on the Clyde, founded in 1711, and the community has grown on the back of shipping ever since. Despite its ranks of anonymous tower blocks and sterile shopping centres, the town still retains a few features of interest.

From the Central train station, it's a short walk down the hill to **Cathcart Square**, where an exuberant 245-foot Victorian tower looms high over the Council House, home of the **tourist office** (Mon–Fri 8.45am–4.45pm, Sat 9.30am–12.30pm; ☎01475 724400). On the dockside, reached by crossing the dual carriageway behind the square, the Neoclassical **Custom House** has a lively museum (Mon–Fri 9.30am–12.30pm & 1.30–4pm; free) of the work of the Customs and Excise departments, with a display on illicit whisky distilleries and a computer game in which you search a ship for contraband. From the dock in front, tens of thousands of nineteenth-century emigrants felt their last grain of Scottish soil before departing for the New World.

Greenock's town centre has been disfigured by astonishingly unsympathetic developments. More attractive, and indicative of the town's wealthy past, is the western side of town, with its mock-Baronial houses, graceful churches and quiet, tree-lined avenues. This area can be reached either via Greenock West station, or by taking a ten-minute walk up the High Street from the Council House. One hundred yards from the well-proportioned **George Square**, just behind Greenock West station, the **Mclean Museum and Art Gallery** in Union St (Mon–Sat 10am–noon & 1–5pm; free) contains pictures and contemporary records of the life and achievements of Greenock-born James Watt, prominent eighteenth-century industrialist and pioneer of steam power, as well as featuring exhibits on the local shipbuilding industry and other local trades. The upper gallery houses a curious exhibition that purports to show the district's internationalism through its trading links, with a random selection of oddments from, among others, Japan, Papua New Guinea, India, China and Egypt. The small art gallery on the ground floor contains work by Glasgow Boy Hornel and Colourists Fergusson, Cadell and Peploe.

Accommodation is particularly scarce in Greenock, so it's advisable to book ahead. *The Tontine Hotel* in Ardgowan Square, a few minutes walk west of the Art Gallery, is expensive, but provides a pleasant atmosphere for afternoon tea or an evening meal (☎01475/723316; ⑦). Smaller and more intimate, though the rooms are large, the Classical-style *Lindores Guest House* lies further west, at 61 Newark St (☎01475/783075; ③) *Francs* on West Blackhall St, west of the shopping centre, serves a decent selection of soups, sandwiches and pasta dishes. Alternatively, *La Mortonia*, an Italian **restaurant** on Cathcart Street, and the *Ambassador Indian Restaurant*, 20 Hamilton Gate (facing the supermarket), provide satisfactory evening meals.

On the train line between Greenock and Gourock, **Fort Matilda** station perches below **Lyle Hill**, an invigorating 450-foot climb that is well worth the effort for the astounding views over the purple mountains of Argyll and the creeks and lochs spilling off the Firth of Clyde. West of here lies the dowdy old resort of **GOUROCK**, from where *CalMac* ferries (☎01475/733755) head across to Dunoon and Kilcreggan on the Cowal peninsula (see p.259). Generations of Glaswegians have holidayed here, but today the place is more or less a stop-off point for the ferry terminal. There's an enjoyable seafront swimming pool with a spectacular backdrop of the Argyll mountains, which can be seen in their full glory from Tower Hill, reached from John Street, past the Health Centre. It's a steep climb but the view makes the effort worthwhile. The **tourist office** (Easter–Sept daily 9am–5pm; ☎01475/639467) is in a garish yellow building shaped like a steam kettle (as a reminder of the district's link with James Watt), in the train station car park.

There is little to detain you in Gourock, but if you have to **stay over,** the *Gantock Stakis Hotel*, on the edge of the town, offers access to the leisure centre and dinner all inclusive (☎01475/634671; ⑦). For a **B&B** closer to the pier try the *Clairmont*, run by Mrs Osborne, at 34 Victoria Rd (☎01475/631687; ③). During the day, you can enjoy a decent selection of baked potatoes, sandwiches and other snacks with some great views over the water in the *Café Continental* on Kempock St, or some liquid refreshment in the wood-pannelled *Cleats Bar*.

South of Port Glasgow

The southern branch of the train line from Port Glasgow heads inland, clipping the edge of Greenock before curling around the mountains and moors, playing a flirtatious game of peek-a-boo with the Clyde estuary. The terminus station, at **WEMYSS BAY**, is a startling wrought-iron and glass reminder of the great glory days, when thousands of Glaswegians would alight for their steamer trip "doon the watter". Today, Wemyss Bay station is far quieter, as the ferries chug their way from its exit over to Rothesay, capital of the Island of Bute (see p.261).

Dumbarton

Founded in about the fifth century, today the town of **DUMBARTON** is a brutal concrete sprawl, fulfilling every last cliché about post-war planning and architecture. Avoid the town itself – though *Talking Heads* fans might be interested to know that David Byrne, of big suits fame, was born here – and head one mile southeast to the 2000-year-old **Dumbarton Castle** (April–Sept Mon–Sat 9.30am–6pm, Sun 2–6pm; Oct–March Mon–Wed & Sat 9.30–11.45am & 1.30–4pm, Thurs 9.30–11.45am, Sun 2–4pm; £1.50), sitting almost intact atop a twin plug of volcanic rock overlooking the Clyde. The castle is best reached from Dumbarton East train station, from where you turn right and take the second left, Victoria Street, continuing straight for just over half a mile. As a natural site, Dumbarton Rock could not be bettered – surrounded by water on three sides and with commanding views. First founded as a Roman fort, the structure was expanded in the fifth century by the Damnonii tribe, and remained Strathclyde's capital until its absorption into the greater kingdom of Scotland in 1034. The castle then became a royal seat, from which Mary Queen of Scots sailed for France to marry Henri II's son in 1548, and to which she was attempting to escape when she and her troops were defeated 20 years later at the Battle of Langside. Since the 1600s, the castle has been used as a garrison and artillery fortress to guard the approaches to Glasgow – most of the current buildings date from this period.

The solid eighteenth-century Governor's House lies at the base of the rock, from where you enter the castle complex proper by climbing the steep steps up into the narrow cleft between the two rocks, crowned by the oldest structure in the complex, a fourteenth-century portcullis arch. Vertiginous steps ascend to each peak – to see both you must climb more than 500 steps. The eastern rock is the highest, with a windy summit that affords excellent views over to the lakes, rivers and mountains beyond Dumbarton town.

If you have an interest in shipbuilding, you may want to visit the **Denny Tank** (Mon–Sat 10am–4pm; £1), the world's oldest working ship model experiment tank; at around 110 yards long, it's used to test scale models of ships prior to the expensive business of construction. Explanatory panels cover the whole process from wax modelling to the experiments themselves. It is on Castle Street, three streets west of Victoria Street.

Practicalities

Regular **trains** run from Glasgow's Queen Street station to Dumbarton East and Dumbarton Central stations. Take the first stop for access to the castle and accommodation. The **tourist office** (daily April & May 10am–5pm; June–Sept 9.30am–6pm; Oct–March 10am–4pm; ☎01389/742308)) is situated out of town on the A82 and mainly caters for the vast number of car-bound tourists on the way to the Highlands. Likewise, **accommodation** is clustered around this artery of traffic and the busy Glasgow Road, that leads into Dumbarton proper. The *Dumbuck Hotel*, Glasgow Rd (☎01389 34336; ⑤), offers spacious and comfortable rooms, while *Kilmalid House*, 17 Glenpath, is a quiet **B&B** (☎01389 732030; ③), off Barnhill Rd and opposite the large and eminently avoidable *Hotel Cladhan*. To reach this area from Dumbarton East train station, turn left at the exit and continue until you reach Greenhead Road, which will take you straight up to the A82. There is the usual selection of takeaways focused on the High Street in the centre of town. However, try the *Burgh Bar* for some decent **pub food** during the day.

The Clyde valley

The landscape becomes more rural as the River Clyde heads east out of Glasgow, passing the last of a string of shipbuilding yards in Rutherglen, and criss-crossing the M74 as both river and road head southeast into Lanarkshire. Less than ten miles from central Glasgow, **Bothwell Castle** lies about a mile northeast from the **Blantyre** tenement, in which the explorer David Livingstone was born. Two miles further upstream, the valley's largest settlements, **Motherwell** and **Hamilton**, straddle either side of the river and motorway. Motherwell is a depressed town, hard hit by the closure of its steel works in 1992, and although Hamilton fancies itself as more upscale, there is little for the visitor in either place. Sandwiched between the two, the enormous **Strathclyde Country Park** features a glassy 200-acre man-made loch, the focus of many sports and outdoor pursuits.

From here the river winds through lush market gardens and orchards that bloom far below the austere lines of **Craignethan Castle**, before passing beneath the sturdy little town of **Lanark**, probably the best base from which to explore the valley. **New Lanark**, on the river bank, is a remarkable planned village dreamed up by eighteenth-century industrialists, David Dale and his son-in-law, Robert Owen. Travel around the area is relatively simple, with good train and bus services. Frequent low-level trains leave Central Station for Lanark via Motherwell and Hamilton via Blantyre. At Buchanan Street bus station, *Kelvin Central Buses* operates a regular service to Hamilton, buses #55, #56, #62, #63 or #67; for Blantyre take #62 and #63, and for Bothwell #55 and #56. To Lanark, it's best to take the train, as there's only a very limited commuter bus service.

From Hamilton to Craignethan Castle

Although the town of **Hamilton** itself has little to offer the visitor, it lies under the watchful gaze of the old hunting lodge built in 1732 for the aristocratic Hamilton family. Designed by the Scots architect William Adam, this building is the centrepiece of Chatelherault Park (Hunting Lodge 10.30am–4.45pm; park closes 9pm; free), a pleasant area with walks that follow the Avon water and explore the surrounding countryside, past the ruins of Cadzow Castle and some 600-year-old oaks. To reach the park, take bus #53 or #54 from Hamilton Central train station, both of which stop at the entrance.

BLANTYRE, now a colourless suburb of Hamilton, was a remote Clydeside hamlet when explorer and missionary David Livingstone was born there in 1813. From Blantyre station a right turn brings you to a quiet country lane. The entire tenement block at the bottom of the lane, now painted a brilliant white, has been taken over by the **David Livingstone Centre** (Mon–Sat 10am–6pm, Sun 12.30–6pm; £2.50), showing his life from early years as a mill worker up until his death in 1873 searching for the source of the River Nile. In 1813, the block consisted of 24 one-room tenements, each occupied by an entire family. Today the Livingstone family room shows the claustrophobic conditions under which he was brought up; all the others feature slightly defensive exhibitions on the missionary movement with tableaux of scenes from his life in Africa, including the infamous meeting with Stanley. Unfortunately, due to vandalism, the thatched huts donated by the government of Malawi which housed changing exhibitions on African themes have had to be removed. Smaller exhibitions on Blantyre and the Clyde valley area are now held inside the main "Africa Pavilion" building.

A mile or so from Blantyre, **Bothwell Castle** (April–Sept Mon–Wed & Sat 9.30am–6pm, Thurs 9.30am–1.30pm, Sun 2–6pm; Oct–March Sat–Wed 9.30am–4pm, Thurs 9.30am–12.30pm; £1.50) is one of Scotland's most dramatic citadels, a great red sandstone bulk looming high above a loop in the river. The oldest section is the solid *donjon*, or circular tower, at the western end, built by the Moray family in the late 1200s to protect themselves against the English king Edward I during the Scottish wars of independence. Such was the might of the castle, Edward only finally succeeded in capturing it in September 1301 after ordering the construction and deployment of a massive siege engine, wheeled from Glasgow to Bothwell in order to lob huge stones at the castle walls. Over the next two centuries, the castle changed hands numerous times and was added to by each successive owner, with the last section, the Great Hall, in the grassy inner courtyard. Despite its jigsaw construction, today the overwhelming impression is of the almost impenetrable strength of the castle, its solid red towers – whose walls reach almost 16ft thick in places – standing firm centuries after their construction. **Buses** #55 and #56 from Glasgow to Hamilton will drop you off on the Bothwell Road, near the castle entrance. By car, it is best approached from the B7071 Bothwell–Uddingston road.

The section of the Clyde Valley southeast from Hamilton to Lanark has appropriately become known as "Greenhouse Glen", where the winding road, lined with small stone villages and inordinate numbers of garden centres, gives occasional glimpses of the river through the trees. Buses #17 and #217 from Hamilton and Lanark stop off at **CROSSFORD**, five miles short of Lanark, where the River Nethan forks off from the Clyde. From here you can either climb a difficult mile through the wooded Nethan valley up to the gaunt clifftop ruins of **Craignethan Castle** (April–Sept Mon–Sat 9.30am–6.30pm, Sun 2–6.30pm; March & Oct daily 9.30am–4.30pm; £1.50), or, if driving, take the extremely tortuous three-mile signposted route. The last major castle to be built in Scotland, Craignethan was constructed by Sir James Hamilton of Finnart, Master of Works to James V, in 1530. Hamilton, inspired by new styles of artillery fortification in Italy, built a unique *caponier*, a dank vault wedged into the dry moat between the two sections of the castle. From here, defenders could spray the ditch with small arms fire from behind the safety of walls 5ft thick. It was from Craignethan, owned by loyalist James Hamilton, that Mary, Queen of Scots left on May 13, 1568, ultimately for defeat at Langside, followed by exile and imprisonment in England. The castle, like so many others in Scotland, is said to be inhabited by her ghost, as Craignethan was probably the last time she was ever amongst true friends. Whatever the truth, Craignethan does have a spooky quality about it, its stillness only interrupted by the shriek of circling crows. The most intact parts of the castle are the gloomy *caponier* and the musty cellars underneath the vast main tower, from which gun holders still protrude.

Lanark and New Lanark

The neat little market town of **LANARK** is an old and distinguished burgh, sitting in the purple hills high above the River Clyde, its rooftops and spires visible for miles around. Beyond the world's oldest bell, cast in 1130 and visible in the Georgian Church of St Nicholas, there's little to see in town and most people make their way to **NEW LANARK** (daily 11am–5pm; £2.95), a mile below the main town on Braxfield Road.

Although New Lanark is served by an hourly bus from the train station, it's well worth the steep downhill walk to get there. The first sight of the village, hidden away down in the gorge, is unforgettable: large broken curving walls of honeyed warehouses and tenements, built in Palladian style, lined up along the turbulent river's edge. The community was founded by David Dale and Richard Arkwright in 1785 to harness the power of the Clyde waterfalls in their cotton-spinning industry, but it was Dale's son-in-law, Robert Owen, who revolutionized the social side of the experiment in 1798, creating a "village of unity". Believing the welfare of the workers to be crucial to industrial success, Owen built adult educational facilities, the world's first day nursery and playground, and schools in which dancing and music were obligatory and there was no punishment or reward.

The Neoclassical building at the very heart of the village was opened by Owen in 1816 under the utopian title of **The Institute for the Formation of Character**. With a library, chapel and dance hall, the Institute became the main focus of the community, and today you can see an introductory video about New Lanark and its founders in the spacious congregational hall. Of the three vast old mill buildings open to visitors, one houses the **Annie McLeod Experience**, where a chairlift whisks visitors through a social history of life here from the imaginary perspective of a young mill girl. With a plethora of special effects – low light diffused through aromatic fog, holograms and lasers – the ten-minute journey portrays honest and unsentimental pictures of village life. Other exhibits in the mills include huge spinning wheels and contemporaneous children's games.

The village itself is just as fascinating: everything, from the co-operative store to the workers' tenements and workshops, was built in an attempt to prove that industrialism need not be unaesthetic. Other attractions include **Classic Car Collections** (daily 11am–5pm; £1.95), which houses a selection of cars from the last century to the present; on a similar theme, the **Railway Kingdom** (Mon–Sat 11am–5pm; £1.50) features Scotland's largest model railway on a quarter-mile of track. Situated in the Old Dyeworks, **The Scottish Wildlife Trust Visitor Centre** (April–Sept Mon–Fri 11am–5pm, Sat & Sun 1–5pm; Oct–Dec & Feb–March only Sat & Sun 1–5pm; closed Jan) provides information about the history and wildlife of the area. Friendly rangers give details of the walks around the tree-lined valley; the longest is an eight-mile round trip. Further on, past the visitor centre, a path along the Clyde leads you past the small falls of green water on which the Lanark project was first founded, and the Bonnington hydroelectric station to the major **Falls of The Clyde**, where at the stunning tree-fringed **Cora Linn**, the river plunges 90ft in three tumultuous stages. It is a stunning marker point for the Clyde Walkway, a path that follows the river from Glasgow Green to this valley forest.

Practicalities

By **train**, Lanark is the terminus on the line from Glasgow Central station. The town's **tourist office** (Jan to mid-April Mon–Fri 9am–5pm; mid-April to Oct Mon–Fri 9am–5pm, Sat 10am–5pm, Sun noon–5pm; Nov & Dec Mon–Fri 9am–5pm, Sat 10am–5pm; ☎01555/661661) is housed in a circular building in the Horsemarket, next to Somerfield, 100 yards to the west of the station. **Accommodation** varies from the spectacular wooded surroundings of the *Cartland Bridge Hotel* on the town's edge just off the A73 Glasgow Road (☎01555/664426; ⑦), to faintly seedy town centre pubs such as the *Royal Oak*, opposite the train station at 39 Bannatyne St (☎01555/665895; ②). **B&Bs** include *Mrs Gray's*, 49 West Port, the continuation of High St (☎01555/663663; ②) and *Mrs Gair's*, 10 Park Place (☎01555/664403; ②). The brand new **youth hostel** (☎01555/666710; Grade 1) is beautifully sited amongst the reconstructed buildings of New Lanark itself, and is an excellent spot for enjoying the surrounding countryside in peace once the village closes down at 5pm. It has self-catering and drying facilities, and the occasional musical evening. There are plenty of cheap **cafés** and take-aways on High Street; *The Cross Café* is a popular old-time Italian-run café, with a good atmosphere. There are some more pricy Indian and Italian **restaurants** along Wellgate. The rather posh *Clydesdale Hotel*, at 15 Bloomgate, serves meals in the cellar bar until 9pm, while the far less pretentious *Crown Tavern*, a quiet drinking haunt in Hope Street, serves reasonable food until 9.30pm. Other good local pubs include the *Horse and Jockey* in High Street or the *Wallace Cave* in Bloomgate. Young people congregate in the *Woodpecker Inn*, tucked behind High Street off the tiny Wide Close alley.

travel details

Trains

Glasgow Central to: Ardrossan (every 30min; 45min); Ayr (every 30min; 50min); Birmingham (5 daily; 3hr 50min); Blantyre (every 30min; 20min); Carlisle (hourly; 2hr 25min); Crewe (7 daily; 3hr 35min); East Kilbride (Mon–Sat every 30min; 30min); Gourock (every 30min; 47min); Greenock (every 30min; 40min); Hamilton (every 30min; 25min); Kilmarnock (hourly; 40min); Lanark (Mon–Sat hourly; 50min); Largs (hourly; 1hr); London (8 daily; 5hr 45min); Manchester (2 daily; 3hr 50min); Motherwell (every 20min; 30min); Newcastle-upon-Tyne (7 daily; 2hr 30min); Paisley (every 15min; 10min); Port Glasgow (every 15min; 30min); Queen's Park (every 15min; 6min); Rutherglen (every 20min; 10min); Stranraer (3 daily; 2hr 10min); Wemyss Bay (hourly; 55min); York (7 daily; 3hr 30min).

Glasgow Queen Street to: Aberdeen (hourly; 2hr 35min); Aviemore (3 daily; 2hr 40min); Balloch (Mon–Sat every 30min; 45min); Dumbarton (every 20min; 25min); Dundee (hourly; 1hr 20min); Edinburgh (every 30min; 50min); Fort William (3 daily; 3hr 40min); Helensburgh (every 30min; 45min); Inverness (3 daily; 3hr 25min); Mallaig (3 daily; 5hr 15min); Milngavie (Mon–Sat every 30min; 22min); Oban (3 daily; 3hr); Perth (hourly; 1hr); Springburn (Mon–Sat every 30min; 13min); Stirling (hourly; 30min).

Buses

Glasgow to: Aberdeen (12 daily; 4hr); Aviemore (hourly; 3hr 30min); Campbeltown (3 daily; 4hr 20min); Dundee (hourly; 2hr 15min); Edinburgh (every 20min; 1hr 15min); Fort William (4 daily; 3hr); Glencoe (4 daily; 2hr 30min); Inverness (hourly; 4–5hr); Kyle of Lochalsh (4 daily; 5hr); Lochgilpead (3 daily; 2hr 40min); Loch Lomond (hourly; 45min); London (5 daily; 7hr 30min); Newcastle-upon-Tyne (1 daily; 4hr); Oban (3 daily; 3hr); Perth (hourly; 1hr 35min); Pitlochry (hourly; 2hr 20min); Portree (4 daily; 6hr); Stirling (hourly; 45min); York (1 daily; 6hr 30min).

Flights

Glasgow to: Birmingham (Mon–Fri 9 daily, Sat & Sun 3 daily; 1hr); London (Heathrow Mon–Fri 20 daily, Sat & Sun 8 daily, Stansted Mon–Fri 4 daily, Sat & Sun 1 daily; Gatwick Mon–Fri 7 daily, Sat & Sun 3 daily; 1hr 15min); Manchester (Mon–Fri 8 daily, Sat 1 daily, Sun 3 daily; 50min).

CHAPTER FOUR

CENTRAL SCOTLAND

Within easy reach of Edinburgh and Glasgow, **central Scotland** is a much visited area; not least for its spectacular and varied countryside, ranging from the picture-postcard beauty of the Central Lowlands to the wilder more challenging terrain of the Highlands, which officially begin here. The **Highland Boundary Fault**, the dramatic physical divide running southwest to northeast across the region, has rendered central Scotland – from medieval to modern times – the main stage for some of the most important events in Scottish history. Today the landscape is not only littered with remnants of the past – well-preserved medieval towns and castles, royal residences and battle sites – but also coloured by the many romantic myths and legends that have grown up around it.

At the heart of the **Central Lowlands**, above the industrial belt around Falkirk and Grangemouth, is venerable **Stirling**, its imposing castle perched high above the town. Historically one of the most important bridging points across the River Forth, it was the site of two of the most famous battles fought under Robert the Bruce during the **Wars of Independence** (1296–1328). To the west and north of Stirling the magnificent scenery centres on the fabled mountains, glens, lochs and forests of the **Trossachs**, a unique and beautiful area of high peaks and steep-sided glens that stretches west from **Callander** to the eastern banks of Loch Lomond. The geography and history of the area caught the imagination of **Sir Walter Scott**, who took so much delight in the tales of local clansman **Rob Roy** MacGregor, the notorious seventeenth-century outlaw, that he set them down in his novel of the same name. Visitors flocked to the Trossachs and according to one contemporaneous account, after Scott's *Lady of the Lake* was published in 1810, the number of carriages passing Loch Katrine rose from 50 the previous year to 270. Thanks to Scott and to William and Dorothy Wordsworth's effusive praise, Queen Victoria decided to visit, placing the area firmly on the tourist map. Today however, the trappings of tourism – evident in twee shops and tearooms in every small town – don't impinge too much on the experience.

Lying to the east of the Central Lowlands is **Fife**, the only one of Scotland's seven original Pict kingdoms to survive relatively intact. Neither Norse nor Norman influence found its way to this independent corner, and nine and a half centuries later, when the government at Westminster redrew local boundaries in 1975 and again in 1995, the Fifers stuck to their guns and successfully opposed any changes. Here you'll find coastal fishing villages and sandy beaches and the self-assured town of **St Andrews**, inextricably linked in the public consciousness with **golf**.

North of St Andrews on the west bank of the River Tay is the ancient town of **Perth**, surrounded by beautiful rugged country. At nearby **Scone**, Kenneth Macalpine established the capital of the kingdom of the Scots and the Picts in 846. When this settlement was washed away by floods in 1210, William the Lion founded Perth as a royal burgh and it stood as Scotland's capital until 1452. The four great monasteries of Perth reflected the town's political and religious importance, but were all destroyed during the Reformation after a sermon by John Knox at St John's Church. North of Perth, the Highlands begin in earnest. From **Loch Tay** onwards, beyond the agreeable town of **Aberfeldy**, the countryside becomes more sparsely populated and more spectacular, with the **Grampian Mountains** to the east offering

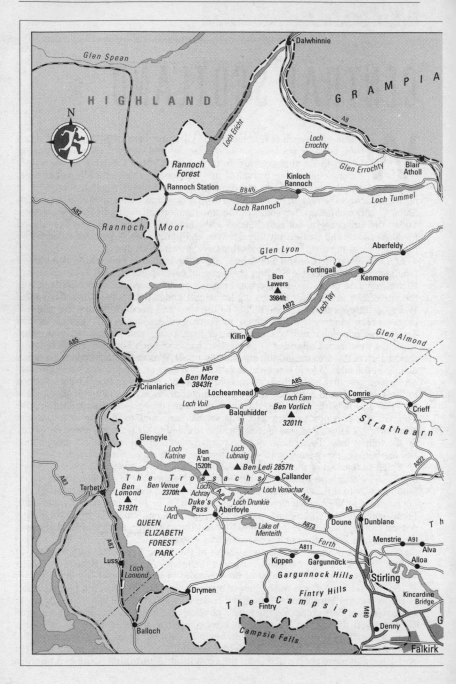

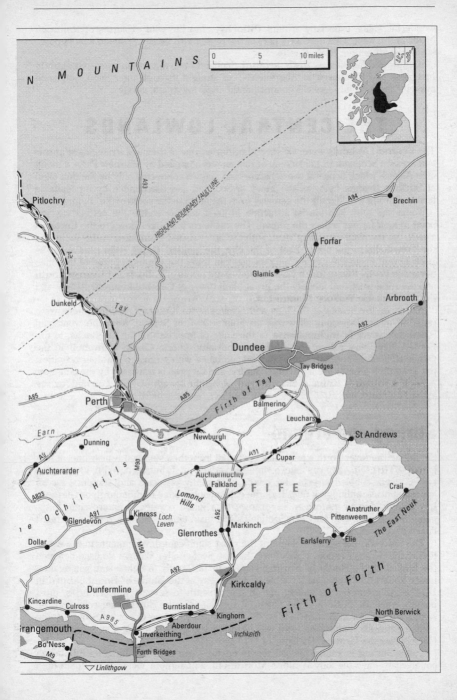

N M O U N T A I N S

0   5   10 miles

A93

HIGHLAND BOUNDARY FAULT LINE

Pitlochry

Brechin

A94

Forfar

Glamis

Dunkeld

Tay

Arbroath

A92

Dundee

Tay Bridges

A85

Perth

Balmerino

A85

Firth of Tay

Leuchars

Earn

Newburgh

St Andrews

Dunning

A9

A31

Cupar

Auchterarder

Auchtermuchty

Falkland

F I F E

Crail

A823

the Ochil Hills

A91

Lomond
Hills

A92

Anstruther
Pittenweem

The East Nouk

Glendevon

Kinross

Loch
Leven

Markinch

Dollar

Glenrothes

Earlsferry

Elie

M90

A92

Firth of Forth

A92

Kirkcaldy

Dunfermline

Kincardine

Culross

A985

Burntisland

North Berwick

Kinghorn

Grangemouth

Aberdour

Inchkeith

Bo'Ness

Inverkeithing

M9

Forth Bridges

▽ Linlithgow

wonderful walks, especially around **Pitlochry**, and the wild expanses of **Rannoch Moor** to the west. This northerly part of the region also boasts Scotland's most popular tourist attraction, **Blair Castle**.

Central Scotland is easy to **get around**. Scotland's two main train lines – Glasgow to Inverness and Edinburgh to Aberdeen – cut straight through the region, and good intercity and local bus services connect all the main towns and villages.

THE CENTRAL LOWLANDS

The **Central Lowlands** were, for several centuries, one of the most strategically important areas in Scotland. In 1250 a map of Britain was compiled by Matthew Paris, a monk of St Albans, which depicted two separate land masses connected only by the thin band of **Stirling Bridge**. Lying at the heart of Scotland and surrounded by inhospitable terrain, Stirling was literally the gateway from the north to the south of the country.

Today the town is a tourist attraction in itself, its fine **castle** the perfect vantage point to look far out across the region. The castle rock plunges down to the **Carse of Forth**, the flat plain extending west, with the little visited **Campsies** to the south and the **Trossachs** to the north. East of the city, the gentler **Ochil Hills** runs as far as Loch Leven. From the castle's heights you can trace the winding course of the once navigable **Forth River**, which links the industrial towns of **Falkirk** and **Grangemouth** and the rural west, and identify the great blunt tower of **Cambuskenneth Abbey** and the unmistakable **Wallace Monument**.

Alongside the beauty of the hills and villages of the Central Lowlands, there are a range of other diversions all within an hour's drive of Stirling: from the wonderful island monastery of **Inchmahome** in the Lake of Menteith in the Trossachs, to the Forth Valley's airy palace of **Linlithgow** and atmospheric **Castle Campbell** in the Ochils Hillfoots. These attractions can be combined with a range of outdoor activities; the Trossachs provide great walking country, and the area is traversed by the **Glasgow – Loch Lomond – Killin cycle way** and, along the length of Loch Lomond, by the **West Highland Way**.

Stirling and around

Straddling the River Forth a few miles upstream from the estuary at Kincardine, at first glance **STIRLING** appears like a smaller version of Edinburgh. With its crag-top castle, steep, cobbled streets and mixed community of locals and students, it's an appealing place, although it does lack the cosmopolitan edge of Edinburgh or Glasgow. It's historic, due to its former importance as a much coveted river crossing, but – geographically trapped between Scotland's two main cities – Stirling remains at heart decidedly provincial.

The town was the scene of some of the most significant developments in the evolution of the Scottish nation. It was here that the Scots under William Wallace defeated the English at the **Battle of Stirling Bridge** in 1297, only to fight – and win again – under Robert the Bruce just a couple of miles away at the **Battle of Bannockburn** in 1314. Stirling enjoyed its golden age in the fifteenth to seventeenth centuries, most notably when its castle was the favoured residence of the Stuart monarchy and the setting for the coronation in 1543 of the young Mary, future Queen of Scots. By the early eighteenth century the town was again besieged, its location of strategic importance during the Jacobite rebellions of 1715 and 1745.

Today Stirling is known instead for its **castle** – just as beautiful as its Edinburgh counterpart – and the lofty **Wallace Monument**, a mammoth Victorian monolith high on Abbey Craig to the northeast. The **University**, also, has helped to maintain the town's profile.

Stirling is at its liveliest during the summer, with buskers and street artists jostling for performing space in the pedestrianized centre. If you get decent weather – which isn't all that uncommon despite the proliferation of surrounding hills – there's very much a holiday air about the place, with kids rushing around the castle ramparts, backpackers struggling up the steep hill to the youth hostel, and students, many of whom choose to stay here over the summer, spilling out of the cafés.

Arrival, information and accommodation

The **train station** (☎01786/464754) is the centre of town on Station Rd; the **bus station** (☎01786/473763) nearby on Goosecroft Rd. To reach the town centre from the train station, walk up Station Road and turn left at the mini-roundabout; from the bus station cut through the Thistle Shopping Centre opposite to reach the main drag, Port Street.

Stirling's **tourist office** is in the heart of the town centre at 41 Dumbarton Rd (June–Sept Mon–Sat 9am–6pm, Sun 10am–4pm; Oct–May Mon–Sat 9am–5pm; ☎01786/475019). This is the main office for Loch Lomond, Stirling and the Trossachs, with a wide range of books, maps and leaflets, and a free accommodation-booking service. Because of Stirling's compact size – barely five miles from the centre to the outermost fringes – sightseeing is best done on foot.

If you're in Stirling between May and October, you'll need to book a room by lunchtime at the latest, or you're likely to be stranded. The tourist office carries details of **accommodation**; most of the **B&Bs** are concentrated in the residential area nearby, and on Causewayhead Road which leads to the university. A good option for accommodation is the **King's Park** area – immediatley south of the tourist office – an opulent Victorian suburb built for Glasgow industrialists and merchants and composed of tree-lined avenues and splendid villas, some wonderfully Italianate with towers and balconies.

Hotels and B&Bs

Park Lodge Hotel, 32 Park Terrace (☎01786/474862). Magnificently sited and luxurious, overlooking the park and castle and with a haute-cuisine restaurant. ⑨.
The Heritage, 16 Allan Park (☎01786/473660). On the northern edge of King's Park, pretty rooms look up at the castle. Good Scottish/French restaurant too. ⑤.

ACCOMMODATION PRICE CODES

Throughout this book, accommodation **prices** have been graded with the numbers below, according to the cost of the least expensive double room in high season. Although costs will rise slightly overall with the life of this edition, the relative comparisons should remain valid. The bulk of the recommendations will fall in categories ② to ⑥; those in the highest categories are limited to places that are especially attractive. Edinburgh will inevitably be more expensive than equivalent accommodation in the countryside or small towns, and a number of places will have a big mark-up for the three weeks of the Festival. Also bear in mind that many of the swanky hotels often slash their tariffs at the weekend when the business types have gone home, and that many of the cheaper places will also have more expensive rooms. Note that in our accommodation listings price codes are not given for youth hostels and campsites – they all come into the lower end of the ① category.

① under £20	④ £40–50	⑦ £70–80
② £20–30	⑤ £50–60	⑧ £80–100
③ £30–40	⑥ £60–70	⑨ over £100

No.10, 10 Gladstone Place (☎01786/472681). Friendly and pleasant B&B. ③.
Whitegables, 112 Causewayhead Rd (☎01786/479838). A friendly B&B with TVs in all the rooms. ③.

Youth hostel, campsite and campus accommodation

At the top of the town (a strenuous trek with a backpack), the cheapest option is the **youth hostel** in a recently converted church on St John St (☎01786/473442; Grade 1). All rooms have showers and toilets en suite, and you get a free continental breakfast.

If you prefer to stay out of town, try the **campus accommodation** at Stirling University (June–Aug; ☎01786/467141; ③), a couple of miles north of the town centre. Regular buses (#53 & #58) leave from Murray Place at the end of the main street (last services around 10.15pm). You can rent Scandinavian-style **chalets** in the University's landscaped grounds (June–August; sleeps 6 for around £300 per week). Also on campus is the new *Stirling Management Centre* (all year; ☎01786/451666; ⑥), as popular with tourists as with the conference guests towards whom it was originally aimed, with luxurious en-suite rooms looking out at the Wallace Monument. There's a **campsite**, the *Witches Craig* at Blairlogie, three miles east of the town off the A91 road to St Andrews (April–Oct; ☎01786/474947).

The Town

Stirling evolved from the top down, starting with its castle and gradually spreading south and east onto the low-lying flood plain. At the centre of the original **Old Town**, Broad Street was the main thoroughfare, with St John Street running more or less parallel, and St Mary's Wynd forming part of the original route to Stirling Bridge below. In the eighteenth and nineteenth centuries, as the threat of attack decreased, the centre of commercial life crept down towards the River Forth, with the modern town – commonly called the **Lower Town** – growing on the edge of the plain over which the castle has traditionally stood guard.

Stirling Castle

Stirling Castle (April–Sept Mon–Sat 9.30am–6pm, Sun 10.30am–4.45pm; Oct–March daily 9.30am–5pm; HS; £3.50; though undergoing major restoration work until 2001, only small areas will be closed at any one time) must have presented would-be invaders with a formidable challenge. Its impregnability is most daunting when you approach the town from the west, from where the sheer, 250ft drop down the side of the crag is most obvious. The rock was first fortified during the Iron Age, though what you see now dates largely from the fifteenth and sixteenth centuries. Presently undergoing a massive restoration scheme (due to be completed in 2001), small parts of the castle may be inaccessible.

The **visitor centre** (same times as castle) on the esplanade shows an introductory film giving a potted history of the castle, but the best place to get an impression of its gradual expansion is in the courtyard known as the **Upper Square**. Here you can see the magnificent **Great Hall** (1501-3), with its lofty dimensions and huge fireplaces perhaps the finest medieval secular building in Scotland. The exterior of the **Palace** (1540–42) is richly decorated with grotesque carved figures and Renaissance sculpture, including, in the left-hand corner, the glaring bearded figure of James V in the dress of a commoner. Inside in the royal apartments are the **Stirling Heads**, 56 elegantly carved oak medallions, which once comprised the ceiling of the Presence Chamber, where visitors were presented to royalty. Otherwise the royal apartments are bare, their emptiness emphasizing the fine dimensions and wonderful views. The **Chapel Royal** (1594) was built by James VI for the baptism of his son, and replaced an earlier chapel, not deemed sufficiently impressive. The interior is lovely, with a seventeenth-century fresco of elaborate scrolls and patterns.

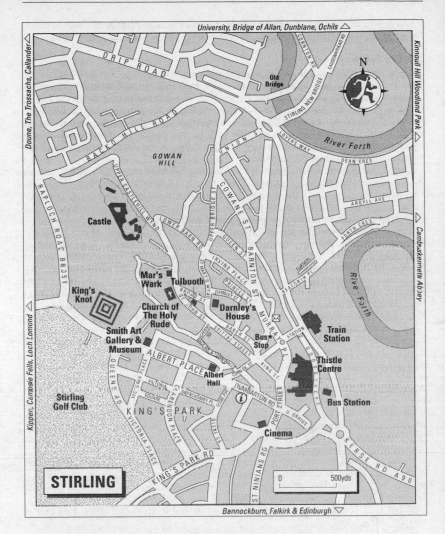

The castle also houses the impressive Argyll and Sutherland Highlanders **museum**, with its collection of well-polished silver and memorabilia, including a seemingly endless display of Victoria Crosses won by the regiment. The setup in the recently restored castle **kitchens** re-creates the preparations for the spectacular Renaissance banquet given by Mary, Queen of Scots for the baptism of the future James VI. As well as an audio-visual display describing how delicacies for the feast were procured and an abundance of stuffed animals, in various stages of preparation (who, we are assured, died natural deaths), the kitchens feature *faux* recipe books with such delights as sugar wine glasses, golden steamed custard and dressed peacock.

From the **Douglas Gardens** you can see the surprisingly small window from which the eighth Earl of Douglas, suspected of treachery, was thrown by James II in 1452. There is a bird's-eye view down to the **King's Knot**, a series of grassed octagonal mounds which in the seventeenth century were planted with box trees and ornamental hedges.

The Old Town

Leaving the castle, head downhill into the old centre of Stirling, fortified behind the massive, whinstone boulders of the **town walls**, built in the mid-sixteenth century and intended to ward off the advances of Henry VIII, who had set his sights on the young Mary as a wife for his son, Edward. The walls now constitute some of the best-preserved town defences in Scotland, and can be traced by following the path known as **Back Walk**. This circular walkway was built in the eighteenth century and in the upper reaches encircles the castle, taut along the edge of the crag, offering panoramic views of the surrounding countryside.

Argyll's Lodging, five minutes walk down the hill from the castle's visitor centre, is a romantic Renaissance mansion built by Sir William Alexander of Menstrie. Currently being converted, the ground and first floors, restored in seventeenth-century town house style, will open to the public in June 1996; the second floor will house the University of Stirling's *Institute for International Scottish Studies*.

The richly decorated facade at the top of Broad Street on Castle Wynd hides the dilapidated **Mar's Wark**, a would-be palace which the first Earl of Mar, Regent of Scotland and hereditary Keeper of Stirling Castle, started in 1570. His dream house was never to be realized, however, for he died two years later and what had been built was left to ruin, its degeneration speeded up by extensive damage during the 1745 Jacobite Rebellion. Behind here is the **Church of the Holy Rude** (May–Sept Mon–Fri 10am–5pm, Sunday service), a fine medieval structure, the oldest parts of which, including the impressive oak hammerbeam roof, date from the early fifteenth century. Go in during the day and imagine the ceremony that was held here in 1567 for the coronation of the infant James VI – later the first monarch of the United Kingdom – and come back in the evening to the atmospheric graveyard, from where you can watch the sun set. Just south of the church on the edge of the crag, the grand E-shaped **Guildhall** was built as a 1649 almshouse for "decayed [unsuccessful] members of the Guild of Merchants". Above the entrance, John Cowane, the wealthy merchant who founded the hospital, is commemorated in a statue which, it is said, comes alive at Hogmanay.

Broad Street was the site of the marketplace and centre of the medieval town. Many of its buildings have been restored in recent years, and preservation work continues. Down here, past the **Mercat Cross** (the unicorn on top is known, inexplicably, as "the puggy"), the **Tolbooth**, sandwiched between Broad and St John streets (with the entrance on Broad St), was built in 1705 by Sir William Bruce, who designed the Palace of Holyrood House in Edinburgh. It was used as both a courthouse and, after 1809, a prison, from where the unfortunate were led to execution in the street outside. **Darnley's House**, at the bottom of Broad Street, was where Mary Queen of Scots' husband is believed to have lodged while she lorded it up in the castle; it is now a touristy coffee shop.

The Lower Town

The further downhill you go in Stirling's Lower Town, the more recent the buildings become. Follow St John Street into Spittal Street, and then on down into King Street, where austere Victorian facades block the sun from the cobbled road. Stirling's main **shopping** area is down here, along Port Street and Murray Place, while the **Smith Art Gallery and Museum** (April–Oct Tues–Sat 10.30am–5pm, Sun 2–5pm; Nov–March Tues–Fri noon–5pm, Sat 10.30am–5pm, Sun 2–5pm) is a short walk west up Dumbarton Road. Founded in 1874 with a legacy from local painter and collector Thomas Stuart Smith, it houses a permanent exhibition relating the history of Stirling, and a range of changing displays of arts and crafts, contemporary art and photography.

The fifteenth-century **Old Bridge** over the Forth lies on the edge of the town centre (a 20-min walk from Murray Place). Although once the most important river crossing in Scotland – the lowest bridging point on the Forth until the new bridge was built in 1831 – it now stands virtually forgotten, an almost incidental reminder of Stirling's former importance. An earlier, wooden **bridge** nearby was the focus of the Battle of Stirling Bridge in 1297, where William Wallace defeated the English.

Eating

At the top of town, *No. 39*, 39 Broad St, next to the Tolbooth Theatre, serves filling pub grub for under a fiver, including a better-than-average selection of vegetarian dishes, in anodyne surroundings. The elegant three-storey *Darnley Coffee House* on Bow St (continuation of Broad St), serves good, reasonably priced lunches and teas, amid an impressive plain barrel-vaulted interior. On Albert Place, the *Café Albert* in Victorian grandeur of *Albert Hall*, is a good, well-priced place to lunch.

More upmarket is *Herman's* at 32 St John St (☎01786/450632), with its handsomely austere interior. The downstairs brasserie is open at lunchtime; the Austrian/Scottish evening main courses start at £7. The quality of the cooking at *Pierre Victoire*, 41 Friars St, just round the corner from the Murray Place bus stop (☎01786/448171), is unpredictable, but the set lunch is a great bargain at around £5 per person for three courses. *Italia Nostra*, close by at 25 Baker St (☎01786/473208) serves good well-priced Italian food and is very lively, especially at weekends. At the *East India Club*, 7 Viewfield Place, a five-minute walk from the centre (☎01786/471330), you can enjoy fabulous Indian food, Postmodern "Raj" decor, and the friendliest service in town. Their buffet (Sun–Wed) costs around £12 per person for three courses and as much as you can eat. Slightly more expensive is the delicious and elegantly served Cantonese food at *The Regent*, 30 Upper Craigs (☎01786/472513).

If you're planning a high-class **picnic** or are self-catering, try *Clive Ramsay Delicatessen and Fine Foods* at 28 Henderson St, Bridge of Allan (buses #51 & #52 from Murray Place).

Nightlife and entertainment

Not known for its club scene, nightlife in Stirling revolves around **pubs** and **bars** and is dominated by the student population. The lively *Barnton Bar and Bistro* on Barnton St, serves a good selection of beers and food in a setting of wrought-iron and marble tables. Try to visit in the morning (from 10.30am) to sample one of their huge breakfasts. Also popular with students is the real ale at the *Settle Inn*, 91 St Mary's Wynd. Stirling's oldest ale house, built in 1733 with a barrel-vaulted roof, it has a patina that testifies to centuries of smoking and drinking. A new pub with a fairly convincing "old world" feel is the *Hog's Head* at the top of Friars St, which has a good range of real ales.

Near the **university**, try *The Meadowpark* pub, on Kenilworth Rd, especially lively during semester. If you want to carry on after the pubs close, you could try *Rainbow Rocks*, a mainstream music **nightclub** off Baker St (see the *Stirling Observer* for weekly details). In July and August there are **ceilidhs** in the wonderful venue of the *Guildhall*, near the castle (usually on Mon at 8pm, but check with the tourist office; £3.50). Although geared to tourists rather than locals, the ceilidhs can be fun; there's often singers and professional dancers too. The larger *Albert Hall* is a good venue for classical and pop/rock **concerts**, and recently summer rock concerts have been held on the castle esplanade. Another very popular Stirling event held on the esplanade is the annual **Beating of the Retreat**, followed by a firework display (usually in mid-July; seated ticket £5).

The main venue for **theatre** and **film** is the excellent *MacRobert Arts Centre* (☎01786/461081) on the university campus (see below), which shows a good selection of drama and mainstream and art-house films.

Around Stirling

North of Stirling, a ten-minute walk from the fine Victorian spa town of **BRIDGE OF ALLAN, Stirling University** was, until 1992 (when all British colleges and polytechnics acquired university status), the youngest university in Scotland, and once one of the most radical. The university exemplifies successful 1960s architecture, and the landscaped grounds are beautiful – resplendent with daffodils in spring, rhododendrons along the sides of the artificial Airthrey Loch in summer, and the rich colours of the Ochil Hills as a backdrop in autumn. Stranded on the northern edge, **Airthrey Castle** is a prepossessing late-eighteenth-century affair built by Robert Adam, now housing CELT, the Centre for English Language Teaching. The Pathfoot building displays in its main corridor a rich collection of portraits and landscapes by J D Fergusson (see p.244), given to the university by his widow. Frequent **buses** run to the university from Murray Place in Stirling.

Overlooking the university from one mile to the southwest is the prominent **Wallace Monument** (daily March–Oct 10am–5pm; July & Aug 9am–6pm; £2.50), built in 1861–9, a rocket-like tribute to Sir William Wallace ("the hammer and scourge of the English"), who has recently been portrayed by Mel Gibson in the film *Braveheart*. It was from the nearby Wallace's Pass that the Scottish hero led his troops down to defeat the English at the Battle of Stirling Bridge in 1297. Exhibits inside the monument include Wallace's long steel sword, swathed in tartan, and the Hall of (Scottish) Heroes, a row of stern white marble busts featuring John Knox and Adam Smith, among many, less significant others. If you can manage the climb – 246 spiral steps up, well worth it on a clear day – there are superb views across to Fife and Ben Lomond from the top of the 220ft tower.

A woodland path weaves its way from the monument to the ruins of **Cambuskenneth Abbey**, about a mile east of Stirling (ruin open all hours April–Sept, grounds all year; HS; free). Founded in 1147 by David I on the site of an Augustinian settlement, the abbey is distinguished by its early-fourteenth-century bell tower, though there's little else to see there now. Its history, however, makes it worth a brief look; the Scots parliament met here in 1326 to pledge allegiance to Robert the Bruce's son David, and James III (1451–88) and his wife, Queen Margaret of Denmark, are both buried in the grounds, their graves marked by a nineteenth-century monument erected at the insistence of Queen Victoria.

Above the university on the edge of the Ochil Hills (see p.222) are the wild moors of **Sheriffmuir**, where the Earl of Mar fought the crown forces in 1715. Access to the area is by car up steep single-track roads, but the splendid hills are worth the effort. In summer you can take "hacks" from the **Drumbrae Farm Riding Centre** (☎01786/832247) whose ponies are plump and reliable. The *Sheriffmuir Inn*, sitting in glorious isolation (follow the signs from Dunblane), serves food and is a popular pub during the summer.

Frequent trains, and buses #58 or #258, make the journey to **DUNBLANE**, four miles north of Stirling. This small, attractive city has been an ecclesiastical centre since the seventh century, when the Celts founded the Church of St Blane here. **Dunblane Cathedral** (April–Sept Mon–Sat 9.30am–12.30pm & 1.30–6pm, Sun 2–6pm; Oct–March Mon–Sat 9.30am–12.30pm & 1.30–4pm, Sun 2–4pm; HS; free) dates mainly from the thirteenth century, and restoration work carried out a century ago has returned the cathedral to its Gothic splendour. Inside, note the delicate blue-purple stained glass, and the exquisitely carved pews, screen and choir stalls, all crafted in the early twentieth century. Also of interest is the little alcove with its thin stained-glass window, thought to be a hermit's cell, a tenth-century Celtic cross and a sadly worn thirteenth-century double effigy of the fifth Earl of Strathearn and his countess. The cathedral, praised in the highest terms by John Ruskin ("I know not anything so perfect in its simplicity, and so beautiful, in all the

Gothic with which I am acquainted"), stands serenely amid a clutch of old-world buildings, among them the seventeenth-century Dean's House, which houses the tiny cathedral **museum** (June–Sept Mon–Sat 10.30am–12.30pm & 1.30–4.30pm; free) with exhibits on local history. On a hill overlooking the city is the luxurious **Dunblane Hydro**, a great Victorian *palazzo* run by the Stakis Hotel group (☎01786/822551; ⑧), which offers tennis and archery lessons and woodland walks.

Five miles northwest of Stirling (Mon–Sat buses #59 & #211), the **Blair Drummond Safari Park** (April–Oct daily 10am–4.30pm; £6), is an attempt to recreate the African bush and Limpopo. The only wildlife park in Scotland, it's good for a family day out, with everything from big cats to sea lions, and a 3-D cinema and performing clown for good measure. The unlikely background to the park is **Blair Drummond Castle**, a Victorian Baronial extravaganza, now a Rudolph Steiner residential home. Just north past the safari park on the right hand side of the road to Doune is a secluded **graveyard**, the final resting place of the Home Drummond family, who owened Blair Drummond Castle, and their servants. One faithful retainer, as a stone records, served the family all his life, and to within an hour of his death.

DOUNE, eight miles northwest of Stirling, is a sleepy village with a violent past. The ruined, fourteenth-century **Castle** (April–Sept Mon–Sat 9.30am–6pm, Sun 2–6pm; Oct–March Mon–Wed & Sat 9am–4pm, Sun 2–4pm; HS; £2) is a marvellous pile standing on a small hill in a bend of the River Teith. Built by Robert, Duke of Albany, it eventually ended up in the hands of the Earls of Moray (whose descendants still own it), following the execution of the Albany family by James I. In the sixteenth century it belonged to the second earl, James Stewart – son of James V and half-brother of Mary, Queen of Scots – murdered in 1592 and immortalized in the ballad the *Bonnie Earl of Moray*. Today the most prominent features of the castle are its mighty 95ft gatehouse, with its spacious vaulted rooms, and the kitchens, complete with medieval rubbish chute.

The present earl has a fabulous collection of flash vintage cars, which are on show one mile northwest of town in the **Doune Motor Museum** (April–Nov daily 10am–4.30pm; £2.75) off the A84. Among the examples of gleaming paintwork and tanned upholstery you can see legendary models of Bentley, Lagonda, Jaguar, Aston Martin and the second oldest Rolls Royce in the world (built in 1905). To get to Doune from Stirling, take bus #59 or #259 which leave hourly, or every two hours on Sunday.

A couple of miles south of Stirling, just north of the village of **BANNOCKBURN**, the **Bannockburn Heritage Centre** (April–Oct daily 10am–5.30pm; NTS; £2) stands close to where Robert the Bruce won his mighty victory over the English at the **Battle of Bannockburn** on June 24, 1314. It was this battle, the climax of the Wars of Independence, which united the Scots under Bruce and led to independence under the Declaration of Arbroath (1320) and the Treaty of Northampton (1328).

Outside, a concrete rotunda encloses a cairn near the spot where Bruce planted his standard after beating Edward II. Of the original bore stone, only a fragment remains, safely on display in the visitor centre. Over-eager visitors used to chip pieces off, and the final straw came when a particularly zealous enthusiast attempted to blast enough of it away to make two curling stones. Pondering the scene is an equestrian statue of Bruce, on the spot from where he is said to have commanded the battle, which was fought on the boggy carse down towards the burn.

The Campsies: hills and villages

Southwest of Stirling, the **Campsies**, an area of gently rolling hills and fertile farmland, include the Gargunnock and Fintry Hills and villages and, further south, the **Campsie Fells**. Although the area is often overlooked in the rush to reach the more spectacular Trossachs, it's worth taking a detour here for the fine walks and fishing on offer and the many quiet and pretty hamlets, most notably Fintry. To the north, the Campsies are bordered by the flat swathe of the **Carse of Forth**, which separates it from the Trossachs. The carse, blocked in the east by the volcanic crag on which Stirling Castle is perched, partly accounts for Stirling's historical importance: for politicians, soldiers and merchants, the treacherous path north, edged by deep marshes and moss, was only accessible from the town. Finally drained in the eighteenth century by local landowners, the carse was transformed into lush and productive farmland, now traversed by the main road west from Stirling to the heart of theTrossachs, the A811. Heading this way, the first you'll see is the long stretch of the Gargunnock Hills to your left, which derive their distinctive stepped look from ancient lava flows. You can also approach and explore the area from the south from Falkirk, or Glasgow along the A803/A891, which winds along the northern edges of Glasgow's commuter belt, where almost every view is spoilt by industrial blight. Beyond **Lennoxtown**, however, the Campsie Fells are interrupted by nothing but sheep and waterfalls, the roads narrow and winding, and there are few signs of habitation. In winter it's an eerie sight, with the mists rolling in from the moors.

Hikers might want to follow the **Campsie Fells Trail** (for information call Stirling ☎01786/475019 or Glasgow ☎0141/204 4400), which links the Campsie villages (these include Fintry, Kippen, Gargannock, Balfron and Lennoxtown), or the **Forth and Clyde Canal** walk which gives access to the second-century **Antonine Wall** (see p.220). The area also encompasses part of the West Highland Way (this starts in Milngavie; see p.193), and there are various options for course and game fishing (you can get details from Stirling's tourist office; see p.205). Plenty of **buses** run through the region from Stirling (#10, #107, #210; 3 or 4 daily, fewer at weekends), and a **postbus** service (Mon–Sat) operates from **Denny**, roughly five miles south of Stirling (reached from Stirling bus station on buses #39, #81 or #81A). The postbus stops at **Fintry**, from where two buses (Mon–Sat) head further west to Balfron, the birthplace of architect Alexander "Greek" Thomson, who designed many of Glasgow's finest Victorian buildings (see p.169).

Gargunnock and Kippen

Six miles west of Stirling just off the A811, **GARGUNNOCK**, although mainly composed of eighteenth-century cottages, has a seventeenth-century grey crow-stepped church at the heart of the village. It is also home to the oldest **agricultural show** in Scotland held here every summer since 1795. The views from the village over the great green of the carse and across to the mountains of the Trossachs are spectacular. To the east of the village in rolling park land is handsome **Gargunnock House**, ancestral home of the Stirlings; Chopin is reputed to have spent two weeks here improving the family's keyboard skills. Recently restored and renovated, the house was begun in 1580, with pediments and a Classical facade added in 1794. It sleeps 16 people, and can be rented from the Landmark Trust (☎01628/825925) for around £1,500 per week, depending on the season. There is one **pub** in the centre of the village, the over-renovated *Gargunnock Inn*, which serves run-of-the-mill food.

More appetizing meals can be had in **KIPPEN**, which can be reached by a lovely unmarked walk. The walk (1hr 30min) leads from the west of Gargunnock – the village is a dead end – through a path of beech trees and into the Leckie Estate, at the heart of which is the privately owned **Leckie Castle**, a sixteenth-century Laird's House where the Lady of Leckie entertained Bonnie Prince Charlie in 1745. Following the farm road to the left as you look down at Leckie Castle, you will eventually come to the Burnton of Boqhuan, a row of eighteenth-century red-stone cottages; take the left hand fork past the Burnton, until the track comes to a steep field. Cross the field to the far gate and continue up the track and you will soon begin the descent into Kippen. You can have a good **lunch** at *The Cross Keys*, an eighteenth-century hotel-pub on the main street (☎01786/870293; ③). There is little to do in Kippen other than enjoy wandering through its pretty cobbled street of eighteenth-century houses and a smithy, beautifully restored by the NTS, and the adjoining ruined church and graveyard. You can get a bus back from here to Stirling.

Fintry

The key settlement in the Campsies is **FINTRY**, a picture-postcard village at the head of Strathendrick valley and at the centre of the Campsie Fells Trail, that is a regular winner of the "Best Kept Small Village in Scotland" award. There are a couple of **places to stay**: if you're feeling flush, try the wonderful *Culcreuch Castle Hotel* (☎01360/860228; ⑨), a fourteenth-century thick-walled and parapeted pile on the northern side of the village. The castle is set in a country park which contains eight small wooden lodges, available for rent for £200–300 per week. The *Clachan Hotel* (☎01360/8602367; ④), a seventeenth-century hostelry next to the kirk at the east end of town, does pub food and B&B.

Drymen

At the western end of the Campsie Fells, all roads meet at the small village of **DRYMEN**, which sits peacefully on the hills overlooking the winding Endrick water as it nears Loch Lomond. Although once you have seen the pretty eighteenth-century Parish Church, there's nothing to actually do in the village, Drymen's reputation as the "gateway to east Loch Lomondside" means it gets extremely busy during the summer. If you want to **rent a bike** to follow the Loch Lomond **cycleway**, try *Lomond Activities*, 64 Main St (☎01360/660066; £10 per day). Ten miles southeast of town in the Blane Valley, Lang Brothers' **Glengoyne Distillery** (April–Nov Mon–Sat 10am–4pm, Sun 12–4pm; £2) offers interesting guided tours – although the snooty staff don't make it worth going out of your way for unless it's the only distillery you're likely to visit. If you want to stay, the no frills *Winnock Hotel* (☎01360/660245; ②) has a restaurant and is prettily sited on the village green.

Loch Lomond

Loch Lomond – the largest stretch of fresh water in Britain – is almost as famous as Loch Ness, thanks to the ballad about its "bonnie, bonnie banks", the Scottish folk song said to be written by a Jacobite prisoner. However, all is not bonnie at the loch nowadays, especially on its overdeveloped west side, fringed by the A82; on the water itself, speedboats tear up and down on summer weekends, destroying the tranquility which so impressed the likes of Queen Victoria, the Wordsworths and Sir Walter Scott.

Nevertheless, the west bank of the loch is an undeniably beautiful stretch of water, and despite the crowds, gives better views than the heavily wooded east side. **LUSS**, the setting for the enormously popular Scottish TV soap *Take the High Road*, is the prettiest village, though its picturesque streets can become unbearably crowded in summer. **BALLOCH**, a brash holiday resort at the loch's southern tip, is the place to head for if you want to take a boat trip; various operators offer cruises around the 33 islands scattered near the shore.

The tranquil east bank is far better for walking than the west, and can only be traversed in its entirety by the West Highland Way footpath, from where you can head on through **Queen Elizabeth Forest Park** (see p.217), or take the stiff but hugely rewarding three-hour hike from **ROWARDENNAN** to the summit of Ben Lomond, the subject of the Scottish proverb "Leave Ben Lomond where it stands" – just let things be.

BEN LOMOND

Ordnance Survey Landranger map No.56

Ben Lomond (3192ft), the most southerly of the "Munros", is one of the most frequently climbed hills in Scotland; its commanding position above Loch Lomond affording amazing views of both the Highlands and Lowlands. You should allow five to six hours for the climb.

The tourist route, a beaten track, starts in Rowardennan at the car park at the rear end of the public road just beyond *Rowardennan Hotel*. The route rises through forest and crosses open moors to gain the southern ridge, which leads to the final pyramid. The path zigzags up, then rims the crags of the northeast corrie to reach the summit.

You can return the same way or start off westwards, then south, to traverse the subsidiary top of Ptarmigan down to the youth hostel in Rowardennan and then along the track to the start.

Practicalities

The West Highland **train** – the line from Glasgow to Mallaig, with a branch line to Oban – joins Loch Lomond 17 miles north of Balloch at **TARBET**, and has one other station further on at **ARDLUI**, at the mountain-framed head of the loch. There are plenty of **buses** along the shore from Balloch.

Loch Lomond's **tourist office** (daily April–June, Sept & Oct 10am–5.30pm; July & Aug 9.30am–7.30pm; ☎01389/753533) is above the marina in Balloch. They'll reserve a room for you without charge at one of the many local **hotels** and **B&Bs**, such as the comfortable *Balloch Hotel*, Balloch Rd (☎01389/752579; ⑥), which also has a decent restaurant, or the friendly *Gowanlea Guest House*, Drymen Rd (☎01389/752456; ③). A couple of miles up the west side of the loch at minuscule **ARDEN** is Scotland's most beautiful **youth hostel**: a turreted building complete with ghost (March–Oct; ☎01389/850226; Grade 1). Caravan parks abound on the west side of the loch; tents are best pitched at the secluded Forestry Commission **campsite** (April–Oct; ☎01360/870234) two miles south of Rowardennan at Cashel on the east bank.

Passenger ferries cross between Inverbeg and Rowardennan, where there is an eponymous **hotel** (☎01360/870251; ③) and a wonderfully situated **youth hostel** (March–Oct & New Year; ☎01360/870259; Grade 1), which also serves as an activity centre for canoeing, archery and orienteering. On the northeast shore of the loch is the *Inversnaid Lodge* (☎01877/386254; ④), once the hunting lodge of the Duke of Montrose, it now has a photography centre with instruction and workshops from guest tutors. There is no road from Rowardennan up the east of the loch to Inversnaid; you have to take the B829 west from Aberfoyle. From Inversnaid you can take the mile-long lochside walk to Rob Roy's cave, a hideout which is said to have given shelter to both Rob Roy and Robert the Bruce.

As for **eating**, on the west side of the loch the *Inverbeg Inn*, signposted off the A82, is the most convenient place to stop, with bar snacks and outdoor seating from which to view the loch. It also has a few comfortable **rooms** (☎01436/860678; ⑥). On the east side, there's little option but to take a picnic.

The Trossachs

Often described as the Highlands in miniature, the **Trossachs** area boasts a magnificent diversity of scenery, with dramatic peaks and mysterious, forest-covered slopes that live up to all the images ever produced of Scotland's wild land. This is Rob Roy country, where every waterfall, hidden cave and barely discernible path was once frequented by the seventeenth-century Scottish outlaw who led the Clan MacGregor. Strictly speaking, the name "The Trossachs", normally translated as either "bristly country" or "crossing place", originally referred only to the wooded glen between **Loch Katrine** and Loch Achray, but today it is usually taken as being the whole area from **Callander** in the east to Queen Elizabeth Forest Park in the west, right up to the eastern banks of Loch Lomond.

This is fabulous walking territory. **Ben Venue** and **Ben A'an**, on the southern shores of Loch Katrine, and **Ben Ledi**, just northwest of Callander, espeically, offer challenging climbs and, on clear days, stunning views. The weather, however, is unpredictable, and every year there are fatalities in the Trossachs Mountains, so be sure to follow the necessary safety precautions (see p.38). Less taxing walks can be made from the **Queen Elizabeth Park Visitor Centre**, on the A821 north of Aberfoyle. It's a good idea to consult the *Bartholomew* guide *Walk Loch Lomond and the Trossachs*, which grades walks according to difficulty. The **Trossachs Trundler** (May–Sept Mon–Fri & Sun; contact any tourist office for details) is a gleaming vintage bus which takes a circular route linking Callander, Loch Katrine and Aberfoyle, stopping at various points en route. The bus is timed to connect with sailings of the SS *Sir Walter Scott* on Loch Katrine. It costs £3.95 for a day pass or £6.20 to include the bus fare from Stirling to Callander.

The Trossachs' high tourist profile was largely attributable in the early days to Sir Walter Scott, whose *The Lady of the Lake* and *Rob Roy* were set in and around the area. Since then, neither the popularity – nor beauty – of the region have waned, and in high season the place is jam-packed. Autumn is a better time to come, when the hills are blanketed in rich, rusty colours and the crowds are thinner. In terms of where to stay, **Aberfoyle** has a slightly dowdy air, even at the height of summer, so it is better to opt for the romantic seclusion of the **Lake of Menteith**, or the handsome country town of **Callander**.

Aberfoyle and Lake of Menteith

Like Brigadoon waking once a year from a mist-shrouded slumber, each summer the sleepy little town of **ABERFOYLE**, 20 miles west of Stirling, dusts itself down each summer for the annual influx of tourists. Its position in the heart of the Trossachs is ideal, with **Loch Ard Forest** and **Queen Elizabeth Forest Park** stretching across to

---

ROB ROY

"Rob Roy, hero or villain?" ponders the tourist literature, in the great spirit of inquiry. Given that Rob Roy's clan, the MacGregors, have the distinction of having invented the term blackmail (from the levying of black meal through protection rackets), and that Rob Roy himself achieved fame through cattle-rustling and thieving, the evidence seems to point to the "villain" thesis. His life, though, dramatizes the clash between the doomed clan culture of the Gaelic-speaking Highlanders, and the organized feudal culture of lowland Scots, which effectively ended with the defeat of the Jacobites at Culloden in 1746.

Rob Roy (meaning "Red Robert" in Gaelic) was born in 1671 in Glengyle just north of Loch Katrine and started life as a cattle farmer, supported by the powerful Duke of Montrose. When the Duke withdrew his support, possibly having been robbed of £1000 by Rob Roy, the latter became a bankrupt and a brigand, plundering the rich carse land and revenging himself on the Duke. He was present at the Battle of Sherrifmuir in 1715, ostensibly as a Jacobite but probably as an opportunist – the chaos would have made cattle raiding easier. Eventually captured and sentenced to transportation, Rob Roy was pardoned and returned to Balquhidder, where he remained until his death in 1734. Rob Roy's life has been much romanticized ever since Sir Walter Scott's 1818 version of the story in his novel *Rob Roy*, a process continued in the recent film starring Liam Neeson.

Ben Lomond and **Loch Lomond** to the west, the long curve of Loch Katrine and **Ben Venue** to the northwest, and **Ben Ledi** to the northeast.

Don't come here for lively nightlife or entertainment, but for a good, healthy blast of the outdoors. The town itself is well equipped to lodge and feed visitors (though booking is recommended), and is an excellent base for walking and pony-trekking, or simply wandering the hills. You might like to wander to Doon Hill to the north of Aberfoyle; cross the bridge over the Forth and follow signs to the **Fairy Knowe** (knoll). A toadstool marker points you through oak and holly trees to the summit of the knowe where there is a pine tree, said to contain the unquiet spirit of the Reverend Robert Kirk, who studied local fairy lore and published his inquiries in *The Secret Commonwealth* (1691). Legend has it that as punishment for disclosing supernatural secrets, Robert Kirk was forcibly removed to fairyland where he has languished ever since, although his mortal remains can be found in the nearby graveyard. This short walk should preferably be made at dusk, when it is at its most atmospheric. About four miles east of Aberfoyle towards Doune, the **Lake of Menteith** is a superb fly-fishing centre and Scotland's only lake (as opposed to loch), so named due to a historic mix-up with the word *laigh*, the Scots for "low-lying ground", which applied to the whole area. To rent a **fishing boat** contact the Lake of Menteith Fisheries (☎01877/385664).

From the northern shore of the lake you can take the little ferry boat (April–Sept Mon–Sat 9.30am–6.30pm, Sun 2–6.30pm, returning 7pm; £2) to the **Island of Inchmahome**, and explore the lovely ruin of the Augustine abbey. **Inchmahome Priory** is perhaps the most beautiful island monastery in Scotland. Founded in 1238, its remains rise tall and graceful above the trees. The masons employed to build the Priory are thought to be those who built Dunblane Cathedral (see p.210); certainly the western entrance there resembles that at Inchmahome. The nave of the church is roofless, but in the choir are preserved the graves of important families from the surrounding area. Most touching is a late-thirteenth-century double effigy depicting Walter, the first Stewart Earl of Menteith, and his Countess Mary who, feet resting on lion-like animals, turn towards each other and embrace. Also buried at Inchmahome is Robert Bontine Cunninghame Graham (1852–1936), the adventurer, scholar, socialist and Scottish nationalist, who was Liberal MP for northwest Lanarkshire for 25 years and the first president of the National Party of Scotland. A pal of Buffalo Bill in Mexico as well as an intimate friend of the novelist Joseph Conrad, Cunninghame Graham had a ranch in Argentina, where he was affectionately known as "Don Roberto".

Five-year-old **Mary, Queen of Scots** was hidden at Inchamahome in 1547 before being taken to France; there's a knot garden in the west of the island known as Queen Mary's bower, where legend has it, the child Queen played. Traces remain of an orchard planted by the monks, but the island is thick now with oak, ash and Spanish chestnut. On an inaccessible close-by island is the ruined castle of **Inchtalla**, the home of the Earls of Menteith in the sixteenth and seventeenth centuries.

Practicalities

Regular **buses** from Stirling to Aberfoyle pull into the car park on Main St. The **tourist office**, directly next door, has full details of local accommodation, sights and outdoor activities (April–Oct daily 9.30am–7pm; ☎01877/382352). Nearby is the **Scottish Wool Centre**, selling all the usual jumpers and woolly toys – a popular stop-off point with tour buses.

For **accommodation** the *Covenanter's Inn* (☎01877/382347; ③) at the northern end of town (turn left across the bridge and it's up behind the trees on the right), is a warren of a place. The bedrooms are different shapes and sizes and public rooms vary from a small, welcoming library to a spacious bar, wood-panelled restaurant and games room – tartan-carpeted throughout. You could also try the *Inverard Hotel*, Loch Ard Rd (☎018772/382229; ④), a large country house with well-furnished rooms and good views over the River Forth and the hills beyond. There are scores of **B&Bs** in the town itself including the comfortable Tudor-style *Craigend*, 1 Craiguchty Terrace (☎01877/382716; ③); and many dotted around the surrounding countryside, among them *Creag-ard House* (☎01877/382297; ④) in the pretty village of Milton, just two miles west of Aberfoyle. It looks out at Ben Lomond and Loch Ard, to which it has fishing and boating rights. More expensive than Aberfoyle, the **Lake of Menteith** is an atmospheric and beautiful place to stay. *The Lake Hotel and Restaurant* (☎01877/385258; ⑦) at Port of Menteith has a lovely lakeside setting next to the Victorian Gothic parish church, and a classy restaurant. Another option is the handsome *Lochend Chalets* (☎01877/385268) on the lake which sleep four to six people, and cost £240–595 per week in summer.

A couple of miles south of Aberfoyle on the edge of Queen Elizabeth Forest Park, *Cobleland Campsite* (☎01877/382392 or 382383) is run by the Forestry Commission: it covers five acres of woodland by the River Forth (little more than a stream here) and has 100 pitches. Further south is the family-run *Trossachs Holiday Park* (☎01877/382614) – twice the size, but with fewer pitches. Both sites are open from April to October, and both offer **bikes** for rent.

Just east of Aberfoyle on the road to Stirling is the *Braeval Old Mill*, (dinner & Sun lunch; ☎01877/382711), one of the best **restaurants** in Scotland. Plain on the outside and pleasingly austere inside, the *Braeval* serves delicious and exquisitely presented gourmet food for around £30 per head. There's a range of decent eating places in the town centre; try the *Country Kitchen* or *The Coach House*, both licensed restaurants on Main St.

Duke's Pass

Even if you have to walk it, don't miss the trip from Aberfoyle to Callander which for part of the way takes you along the **Duke's Pass** (so called because it once belonged to the Duke of Montrose), as it weaves its way through the **Queen Elizabeth Forest Park** to just south of Loch Katrine. A **bus** runs through the pass from Aberfoyle and then on to Callander

The A821 twists up out of Aberfoyle, following the contours of the hills and snaking back on itself in tortuous bends. About halfway up is the park's excellent **visitor centre** (April–Oct daily 10am–6pm; ☎01877/382258), which details the local fauna and flora. From here various marked paths wind through the forests giving splendid views over the lowlands and surrounding hills. About a mile further on, a track to the right

---

QUEEN ELIZABETH FOREST PARK

Covering 75,000 acres on the edge of the Highlands, **Queen Elizabeth Forest Park** is a spectacular tract of wilderness bordering **Loch Lomond**, and incorporating **Loch Ard**, **Loch Achray** and **Loch Lubnaig**, as well as **Ben Venue**, **Ben A'an** and **Ben Ledi**. Managed by the Forestry Commission, it is used partly for leisure and recreation and is criss-crossed by way-marked paths and trails, including part of the **West Highland Way** and, on the western side, access to **Ben Lomond** (3192ft). Among its varied wildlife habitats are the forests north of Balmaha, which are home to red and roe deer, as well as wild goats. The park **visitor centre** is just outside **Aberfoyle** (see above).

Accommodation in the park is available at two **campsites** – one on the banks of Loch Lomond at Cashel (near Rowardennan; see p.214), and the other beside the River Forth at Cobleland, south of Aberfoyle. There are also **log cabins** on the shores of Loch Lubnaig in Strathyre (south of Lochearnhead; see p.219). To book cabins call ☎0131/334 0303; cabins for five cost £299 per week.

Full details about the park are available from the **Forest Enterprise**, Aberfoyle, Stirling FK8 3UX (☎01877/382383) and the **Countryside Ranger Service**, Stirling District Council, Municipal Buildings, Stirling FK8 2HU (☎01786/432363).

marks the start of the **Achray Forest Drive**, a worthwhile excursion by car or foot which leads through the forest and along the western shore of **Loch Drunkie**, before rejoining the main road. After another couple of miles, a road branches off to the left, leading to the southern end of **Loch Katrine** at the foot of **Ben Venue** (2370ft, a strenuous walk), from where the historic steamer, the SS *Sir Walter Scott*, has been plying the waters since 1900, chugging up the loch to Stronachlachar and the wild Rob Roy country of Glengyle where he was born (April–Sept 4 daily, except Sat 2 daily; £3.40). To climb Ben A'an (1520ft), start from the *Trossachs Hotel* on the north bank of Loch Arhray. No longer a hotel, it retains the splendid exterior designed by the outlandishly named Lord Willoughby d'Eresby in 1852.

The final leg of the pass is along the tranquil shores of **Loch Venachar** at the southern foot of Ben Ledi. Look out for the small **Callander Kirk** in a lovely setting at the edge of the loch, where services are still held on the first Sunday of each month at 3pm – presumably because it takes all morning (or month) to get there.

Callander and around

CALLANDER, on the eastern edge of the Trossachs, sits quietly on the banks of the River Teith roughly ten miles north of Doune, at the southern end of the **Pass of Leny**, one of the key routes into the Highlands. Larger than Aberfoyle, it is an even more popular summer holiday base and a convenient springboard for exploring the surrounding area. Its wide main street recalls the influence of the military architects who designed the town after Bonnie Prince Charlie's Jacobite Rebellion of 1745.

Callander first came to fame during the "Scottish Enlightenment" of the eighteenth and nineteenth centuries, when the glowing reports given by Sir Walter Scott and William Wordsworth prompted the first tourists to venture into the wilds by horsedrawn carriage. Development was given a boost when Queen Victoria chose to visit, and then by the arrival of the train line – long since closed – in the 1860s.

The present community has not been slow to capitalize on its appeal, establishing a plethora of restaurants and tearooms, antique shops, second-hand book stores, and shops selling local woollens and crafts. The chief formal attraction is the **Rob Roy and Trossachs Visitor Centre** at Ancaster Square on the main street (Jan & Feb Sat & Sun only 10am–5pm; March–May & Oct–Dec daily 10am–5pm; June & Sept daily 9.30am–6pm; July & Aug daily 9am–7pm; £2), an entertaining and partisan account of the life of the diminutive red-head featuring a talking statue of "Soft Southerner" Daniel Defoe. Defoe was sent to Scotland on a government spying mission in 1705, and became fascinated by Rob Roy's exploits.

Practicalities

Callander's **tourist office** is in the Rob Roy and Trossachs Visitor Centre (same times; ☎01877/330342); it will book accommodation for you if you want to **stay**. Good choices include *Arden Guest House*, Bracklinn Rd (☎01877/330235; ③), a Victorian house in its own gardens with good views down over the countryside; the handsome Victorian *Crook Linn Country House* (☎01877/330103; ③), also set above the town; the *Ben A'an Guest House* (☎01877/330 317; ②) on the main street; and the small and pretty *Highland House Hotel*, South Church St (☎01877/330269; ④). For more luxury, try the *Roman Camp Hotel*, signposted off the main street (☎01877/330003; ⑨), a turreted and romantic seventeenth-century country house in 20-acre gardens on the River Teith. The *Invertrossachs Country House* (☎01877/331126; ⑥) west of Callander on the southern shores of Loch Venachar is a plush Edwardian mansion offering superior B&B. Despite its popularity, there are few **restaurants** worth recommending in Callander. The best place is in the *Roman Camp Hotel*, which serves splendid Scottish produce in refined surroundings. For pub food try the *Murtle Inn* on the eastern edge of Callander or the *Lade Inn* at **KILMAHOG**, a couple of miles west of town, which has appetizing barbecues and grills, along with a good selection of wines, whiskies and beers.

On to Lochearnhead

On each side of Callander, pleasant and less-than-arduous walks wind through a wooded gorge to the **Falls of Leny** to the north and **Bracklinn Falls** to the south – both distances of only a mile or so. Longer **walks** of varying degrees of exertion thread their way through the surrounding countryside, the most challenging being that to the summit of **Ben Ledi** (2857ft), for which you should be well shod and prepared (see p.38).

North of town, you can walk or ride the scenic six-mile **Callander to Strathyre Cycleway**, which forms part of the network of cycleways between the Highlands and Glasgow. The route is based on the old Caledonian train line to Oban, which closed in 1965, and runs along the western side of **Loch Lubnaig**. To rent bikes, try *Wheels Cycles Hire*, Manse Lane, Callander (£10 per day including map and helmet; ☎01877/331100). To the north, Rob Roy is buried in the small yard behind the ruined church at tiny **BALQUHIDDER**, where he died in 1734. Oddly enough, considering the Rob Roy fever that plagues the region, his grave – marked by a rough stone marked with a sword, cross and a man with a dog – is remarkably underplayed. If you want to **stay** in Balquhidder, go to the award winning eighteenth-century farmhouse *Monachyle Mhor* hotel (☎01877/384622; ④), which has a terrific restaurant looking out to Loch Voil.

Watersports are the life force of the village of **LOCHEARNHEAD**, at the western head of Loch Earn, a substantial body of water running east into Perthshire and fed by waters off the slopes of **Ben Vorlich** (3201ft) to the south. A more impressive stretch of water is **Loch Tay**, about 15 miles north of Callander, which points northeastwards like a 14-mile finger towards Aberfeldy (see p.250).

The Forth Valley

The **Forth Valley** stetches some 40 miles southeast of Stirling along the Firth of Forth. The area has long been known for its industry, historically for the famous – but now redundant – Carron Ironworks near **Falkirk**, which was founded in 1759 and manufactured "carronades" (small cannons) for Nelson's fleet, and more recently for BP's petrochemical plant at **Grangemouth**. The lights and fires of the refineries are spectacular at night; inspiring Bertrand Tavernier to make a movie in Scotland, the dour 1979 sci-fi *Death Watch*.

Given the lack of good accommodation in the Forth Valley, the area is best seen as a day trip from either Stirling or Edinburgh. Unless you are particularly interested in steam trains in which case definitely visit **Bo'ness** – the only unmissable outing is to **Linlithgow Palace**.

If you're coming from the east, across the Kincardine Bridge, you may want to pop into the signposted **tourist office** at Pine'N'Oak Layby, Kincardine Bridge (mid-April to May Mon–Sat 11am–5pm, Sun 1–5pm; June–Aug daily 10am–6pm; Sept Mon–Sat 11am–5pm, Sun 1–5pm; ☎01324/831422). The regular train service between Stirling and Edinburgh makes Falkirk and Linlithgow easily accessible; for other destinations you'll have to rely on the comprehensive network of buses.

Falkirk and around

FALKIRK, the Forth Valley's main commercial centre, was the site of two major battles, one in 1298, when William Wallace fell victim to the English under Edward I, and the other in 1746, when Bonnie Prince Charlie, retreating northwards, sent the

Hanoverians packing in one of his last victories over government troops. Traditionally a livestock centre, Falkirk was transformed in the eighteenth century by the construction of first the Forth and Clyde Canal, allowing easy access to Glasgow, and then the Edinburgh and Glasgow Union Canal, which continued the route through to Edinburgh. Just 20 years later, however, the trains arrived, and the canals became obsolete.

The town today is a busy local shopping centre, whose only formal attraction, set in Callendar Park, is **Callendar House** (Mon–Sat 10am–5pm, plus April–Sept Sun 2–5pm; £1.60), which was owned by the staunchly Jacobite Livingston family. The house is being restored, apparently more with conference guests in mind than tourists. The Georgian kitchens though are fabulous, with gleaming utensils, a huge mechanized spit and a costumed kitchen maid who dispenses information about life below stairs whilst chopping apples. In the area surrounding Falkirk, the wide network of old industrial **canals** offers good opportunities for boating, canoeing and strolling.

In **BONNYBRIDGE**, five miles west of Falkirk (take bus #37 from Falkirk), is **Rough Castle**. Built in AD 142, this was one of the forts which were set up, at two-mile intervals, to defend the entire length of the Roman **Antonine Wall**. In the opposite direction, the industrial town of **GRANGEMOUTH** sits at the edge of the Forth, its industrial chimneys spewing out smoke visible for miles around. If industrial heritage is your scene, it's worth a visit to the **museum** on Bo'ness Rd in the Charing Cross area of town (July & Aug Mon–Sat 10am–5pm; free), which tells the history of Grangemouth as one of Scotland's first planned industrial towns.

The Pineapple, north of Falkirk (turn off the A905 onto the B9124; or take bus #75), qualifies as one of Scotland's most exotic and eccentric buildings, a 45ft-high stone pineapple built as a garden folly in the 1770s for the fourth Earl of Dunmore. The folly was an elaborate joke on Lord Dunmore's part; returning from a spell as Governor of Virginia, where sailors would put a pineapple on a gatepost to announce their return, he chose to signal his homecoming on a grand scale. The folly is now owned by the NTS, and the outhouse can be rented for holidays (see below).

Practicalities

Falkirk's centrally located **bus** station is at Callender Riggs. Regular **trains** run from Glasgow Queen Street, Edinburgh and Stirling to Falkirk Grahamston Station (as opposed to Falkirk High Station, which is further from the centre), from where it's a five-minute walk to the **tourist office**, 2–4 Glebe St (April & May daily 9.30am–6pm; June & July Sun–Thurs 9.30am–6pm, Fri & Sat 9am–6pm; Aug daily 9.30am–8pm; Sept & Oct daily 9.30am–6pm; Nov–March Mon–Sat 9.30am–12.30pm & 1.30–5pm; ☎01324/620244). If you want to **stay**, the modern *Stakis Falkirk Park Hotel*, Camelon Rd (☎01324/628331; ⑤), at the west end of town overlooking Dollar Park, is your best bet, with comfortable rooms. The outhouse of The Pineapple folly can be rented through the Landmark Trust (☎01628/825925); it sleeps four, and costs around £550 per week.

You can **eat** Mexican food and hear **live music** at *Behind the Wall*, 14 Melville St, a brasserie-style café with a beer garden. There's a *Pierre Victoire* at 14 Princes St, and a more upmarket French **restaurant**, *Pierre's* (☎01324/635843), near the town centre at 140 Graham's Rd.

Linlithgow

Roughly equidistant (15 miles) from Falkirk and Edinburgh is the ancient royal burgh of **LINLITHGOW**. The town itself has largely kept its medieval layout, but development since the 1960s has sadly stripped it of some fine buildings, notably close to the **Town Hall** and **Cross** – the former marketplace – on the long High Street.

You should head straight for **Linlithgow Palace** (April–Sept Mon–Sat 9.30am–6pm & Sun 2–6pm; Oct–March Mon–Sat 9.30am–12.30pm & 1.30–4pm, Sun 2–4pm; £2), a splendid fifteenth-century ruin romantically set on the edge of Linlithgow Loch and associated with some of Scotland's best-known historical figures – including the ubiquitous Mary, Queen of Scots, who was born here in 1542. A royal manor house is believed to have existed on this site since the time of David I. Fire razed the manor in 1424, after which James I began construction of the present palace, a process that continued through two centuries and the reign of no fewer than eight monarchs. From the top of the northwest tower, Queen Margaret looked out in vain for the return of James IV from the field of Flodden in 1513. The ornate octagonal **fountain** in the inner courtyard, with its wonderfully intricate figures and medallion heads, flowed with wine for the wedding of James V and Mary of Guise. Bonnie Prince Charlie visited during the 45, and one year later the palace was burned, probably accidentally, whilst occupied by General Hawley's troops.

This is a great place to take children; the rooflessness of the castle creates unexpected vistas and the elegant rooms with their intriguing spiral staircases seem labyrinthine. The galleried **Great Hall** is magnificent, as is the adjoining kitchen, which has a truly cavernous fireplace. Don't miss the dank downstairs **brewery**, which produced vast quantities of ale; 24 gallons was apparently a good nightly consumption in the sixteenth century.

St Michael's Church, adjacent to the palace, is one of Scotland's largest pre-Reformation churches, consecrated in the thirteenth century. The present building was completed 300 years later, with the exception of the hugely incongruous aluminium spire, tacked on in 1946. Inside, decorative woodcarving around the pulpit depicts queens Margaret, Mary and Victoria.

Running through Linlithgow is part of the **Union Canal**, the 31-mile artery opened in 1822, which linked Edinburgh with Glasgow via Falkirk. On summer weekends the Linlithgow Union Canal Society runs short trips on the *Victoria*, a diesel-powered replica of a Victorian steam packet boat. The boat departs from the Manse Road canal basin, uphill from the train station at the southern end of town (☎01506/842575; £1). A walk along the canal towpath leads eventually to the centre of Edinburgh, but involves negotiating a path across a section of the Edinburgh ring road.

Practicalities

Frequent **buses** between Stirling and Edinburgh stop at the Cross. The town is also on the main train routes from Edinburgh to both Glasgow Queen Street and Stirling; the **train station** is at the southern end of town. From the station head downhill for High Street, where the **tourist office** is in the Burgh Halls building at the Cross (April–July daily 10am–6pm; Aug daily 10am–8pm; Sept daily 10am–6pm; Oct–March Thurs–Mon 11am–4pm; ☎01506/844600).

For **accommodation** try *The Star and Garter*, 1 High St (☎01506/845485; ④), at the east end of town, a comfortable old coaching inn that also serves inexpensive bar meals. The Victorian *Pardovan House* is an excellent **B&B** (May–Sept; ☎01506/834219; ②) at Philipstoun, a couple of miles west of Linlithgow, or you could try the friendly *Belsyde Farm*, Lanark Rd (☎01506/842098; ③), a late-eighteenth-century house on a sheep and cattle farm beside the Union Canal. There are very few places to **eat** in Linlithgow; however, you might try *The Four Marys*, opposite the Cross on High St, which serves good **pub food**, or, at the opposite end of the street, the smaller *West Port Hotel*, 18–20 West Port (☎01506/847456; ②), is more basic but has a popular **bar** downstairs which also serves food.

The only official **campsite** in the area is at the fully serviced *Beecraigs Caravan Park* (☎01506/844516) about four miles south of town, and part of the larger Beecraigs Country Park. There are only 39 pitches, however, so get there early or telephone first.

Around Linlithgow

The small hillside town of **BO'NESS**, roughly four miles north of Linlithgow – which has traditionally looked down its nose at its pint-sized neighbour – sprawls in a less than genteel fashion down to the Forth, where a riverside path is separated from the road by a strip of scrub. On a clear day there are good views across the Forth to beautiful Culross (see p.226). The **Bo'ness and Kinneil train**, which has its headquarters at the old station at the eastern end of the waterfront road, is Scotland's largest vintage train centre, and in summer (July & Aug daily; April–Oct Sat & Sun; ☎01506/822298) runs lovingly kept steam trains to Birkhill, just over three miles away. There's a small **tourist office** at Hamilton's Cottage (May–Sept daily 11am–5pm; ☎01506/826626), but if you can't find it – even some of the locals don't know it's there – then ask at the post office on the waterfront road. If you want to **stay the night**, the only option is the *Richmond Park Hotel*, 26 Linlithgow Rd (☎01506/823213; ④), which has comfortable rooms and, set in its own grounds, offers good views across the Forth to the Fife hills. The moderately priced **restaurant** serves a fair choice of dishes, including some vegetarian, and the airy conservatory is a popular place to drink.

Further down the coast from Bo'ness and four miles northeast of Linlithgow, boldly positioned on a rocky promontory in the Forth, lies the village of **BLACKNESS**, once Linlithgow's seaport but now known for the fifteenth-century **Blackness Castle** (April–Sept Mon–Sat 9.30am–6pm, Sun 2–6pm; Oct–March Mon–Sat 9.30am–4pm except Thurs 9.30am–noon, Sun 2–4pm; £1.20), which, after the Treaty of Union in 1707, was one of only four in Scotland to be garrisoned. Said to be built in the shape of a galleon, the castle offers grand views of the Forth bridges from the narrow gun slits in its northern tower.

General Tam Dalyell, the seventeenth-century Scottish royalist, spent part of his youth at the **House of the Binns** (May–Sept daily 2–5pm except Fri; NTS; £3), occupying a hilltop site about two miles east of Linlithgow. Inside you can see ornate plaster ceilings, paintings, period furniture and family relics not much changed since Tam's day.

The Ochils

The rugged **Ochil Hills** stretch for roughly 40 miles northeast of Stirling, along the northern side of the Firth of Forth, forming a steep-faced range which drops down to the flood plain of the Forth Valley and is sliced by a series of deep-cut, richly wooded glens. Although they provide a dramatic backdrop for the region's towns, villages and castles, this is gentler country than, say, the Trossachs, with the hills gradually giving way to the pastoral landscape of Fife.

The area has been at the centre of Scotland's wool production for centuries, rivalled only by the Borders. The cottage industry of **Clackmannanshire**, immediately east of Stirling, capitalized on the technological advances of the industrial revolution and by the mid-nineteenth century there were over 30 mills in the space of half as many miles.

Recent times have seen a change in the industry, with the old family firms and handknitters unable to compete with modern technology. Nonetheless, you can still see traditional producers working in shops and private houses, especially on the **Mill Trail** that links the main towns, historic sites and modern mill shops. A glimpse of a different past is offered by various fortified tower houses – Clackmannanshire was a convenient base from which the country's powerful families could keep abreast of developments at the Royal Court at Stirling. None of them are open to the public at present, but substantial remains can still be seen at the Bruce house at Clackmannan and the Erskine's at **Alloa**, which has recently been restored. Above the picturesque town of **Dollar** (once

Dolour) is a wooded glen which you ascend, with the Burn of Sorrow and the Burn of Care rushing by, to reach **Castle Campbell**, once called Castle Gloom. Despite the preponderance of mournful names, the town, the walk (see overleaf) and the castle make for a wonderful outing. Beyond Dollar the road runs south along the Devon Valley to Kinross, on the shores of Loch Leven.

There are no trains to destinations in the Ochils, but there are regular **buses** between Stirling and Yetts o' Muckhart (northeast of Dollar), and from Alloa to Tillicoultry.

The Ochil Hillfoots

Three miles or so northeast of Stirling, the small and very appealing village of **BLAIRLOGIE** sits amidst orchards and gardens below a private castle. **Logie Old Kirk**, a ruined church and graveyard dating from the late seventeenth century, is beautifully sited by Logie Burn. Immediately to the rear looms **Dumyat** (pronounced "Dum-eye-at"), which offers spectacular views from its 1376ft summit.

MENSTRIE, a mile east, is noted for **Menstrie Castle** (May–Sept Sat & Sun; free), a much-restored, sixteenth-century stone-built mansion (on Castle Rd), which is totally at odds with the housing estate that now hems it in. The castle was the birthplace of Sir William Alexander, later first Earl of Stirling, who in 1621 set off to found a Scots colony in Nova Scotia. There's little to actually see now, but an exhibition room displays the coats-of-arms of the 109 subsequent baronets of Nova Scotia.

As well as a strong tradition of weaving, **ALVA**, five miles further on, was also known for its silver mining – an industry long since gone. From here you can follow **Alva Glen**, a hearty mile and a half walk dipping down through the hills, which takes in a number of waterfalls. The **Mill Trail** starts from Glentana Mills, Stirling St, which doubles as a **tourist office** (April–Oct daily 10am–5pm; June–Sept until 6pm; ☎01259/769696).

Dollar

Nestling in a fold of the Ochils on the northern bank of the small River Devon where mountain waters rush off the hills, **DOLLAR** is the most affluent of the hillfoot towns. Its Academy, founded in 1820 with a substantial bequest from local lad John MacNabb, has become one of Scotland's most respected private schools – the pupils and staff of which account for around a third of the town's population. Above the town, the dramatic chasm of **Dollar Glen** is commanded by **Castle Campbell** (April–Sept Mon–Sat 9.30am–6pm, Sun 2–6pm; Oct–March Mon–Wed & Sat 9.30am–4pm, Thurs 9.30am–noon, Sun 2–4pm; NTS & HS; £1.50), formerly, and still unofficially, known as Castle Gloom – a fine and evocative tag but, prosaically, a derivation of an old Gaelic name. A one-mile road leads up from the main street, but it becomes very narrow, very steep, and stops short of the castle, with only limited parking at the top. There is a marked walk through the glen to the castle, past mossy crags and rushing streams (see below).

The castle came into the hands of the Campbells in 1481, who changed its name from Castle Gloom in 1489. John Knox preached here in 1556, although probably from within the castle, rather than from the curious archway in the garden as is traditionally claimed. In 1654 the castle was burned by Cromwell's troops; the remains of a graceful seventeenth-century loggia and a roofless hall bear witness to the destruction. However, the oldest part of the castle, the fine fifteenth-century tower built by Sir Colin Campbell, survived the fire; look out for the claustrophobic pit-prison just off the Great Hall and the latrines with their vertiginous views to the ground. You can also walk round the roof of the tower, where there's a wonderful view of the hills behind the castle, and down the glen to Dollar.

WALKING ABOVE DOLLAR

Ordnance Survey Landranger map no.58

Classical Dollar Academy, dominating the town nestling below, has "house" names Hill, Castle, Glen and Devon and a walk combining three of these is highly recommended. The River Devon rises far in the Ochils but does a huge loop round Glendevon and the crook of Devon before turning to flow along the valley below the Ochil scarp. Allow two hours for the glen and castle, another hour if adding Dollar Hill.

Walk up the Burnside from the town centre (clock tower) and then on by a footpath from the top bridge beside the burn to pass an open area and reach the wooded glen (NTS). At the fork, double back to go along The Long Bridge, which runs tight between the cliffs along the line of the rushing water. Keep an eye on small children as in some places the path is steep and unfenced. Note the cleft at the end – this is not the way up to the castle. Other bridges eventually lead you out near the Castle Campbell, perched between the Burn of Care and the Burn of Sorrow.

You can return to Dollar by the small tarred road, which just stops short of the castle but, if you want to venture furher, Dollar Hill (Bank Hill on the *O S* map) is easily accessible by going up the burn to a bridge over the Sorrow. From here it is a direct descent to Dollar via the golf course. There is also an old drovers' road through to Glendevon, but you'll need to arrange transport back to Dollar from there. Leaving the castle the road dips, then climbs to a cottage (start of the track to Glendevon) and a car park (good view of the keep), before descending steeply to the town below.

You may be tempted to **stay** at Dollar; try the pretty *Burnside House*, 24 West Burnside (☎01259/743192; ②), or the *Castle Campbell Hotel* on Bridge St (☎01259/742519; ⑥). A luxurious alternative is *The Gean House* in nearby Alloa (☎01259/219275; ⑨), an elegant Edwardian mansion house set in 20 acres of parkland; it's also a good option for a special meal in the plush walnut-panelled restaurant, which serves simple high-quality **food**. Another less pricy alternative, offering Scottish food, is the *Harvieston Inn*, just out of Tillicoultry on the main road to Dollar.

The Devon Valley

Beyond Dollar, the A91 leads through the hills to Kinross and runs along the southern edge of the **Devon Valley**, passing through the hamlets of **Pool o' Muckhart** and **Yetts o' Muckhart**.

The scenic A823 cuts up from Yetts o' Muckhart through the valley itself, where there is a large **campsite** with good facilities (all year; ☎01259/781246) just beyond the village of **GLENDEVON**. The road continues from here to **Gleneagles**, with its famous hotel and golf course (see p.248).

In the other direction, south of Yetts o' Muckhart, the same road crosses the River Devon at **Rumbling Bridge** – effectively two bridges; the newer one, built in the early nineteenth century, sweeping over the top of the old one, which dates from 1713. The observation point offers breathtaking views of the magnificent, 120ft-deep **gorge**, and you can follow a shady path along the river, through the lush vegetation flourishing in the damp, limestone walls of the chasm.

Kinross and Loch Leven

Although still by no means a large place, **KINROSS**, on the A977 a mile west of the loch, has been transformed in the last couple of decades by the construction of the nearby M90 Edinburgh–Perth motorway. The old village is still there, at the southern end of the main street, but apart from the views of Loch Leven, its charm has been eroded by amorphous splodges of modern housing, which threaten to nudge it into the loch itself. The best time to visit is on Sunday, when the stalls of a large and lively

covered market spring up on the southern edge of town, pulling in crowds who come to rifle through anything from kitsch ornaments to leather jackets.

During the summer a **ferry** departs regularly to ply the trout-filled waters of **Loch Leven**. In recent years the loch has become a National Nature Reserve and the location of international fishing competitions, and it also features **Castle Island**, where Mary, Queen of Scots, was imprisoned for 11 months in 1567–68. On the island, the ruined fourteenth-century **Douglas Castle** (April–Sept Mon–Sat 9.30am–6.30pm, Sun 2–6.30pm; HS; £2) stands forlorn, little more than a tower. Nevertheless, it's easy to imagine the isolation of the incarcerated Mary, who is believed to have miscarried twins while here. She managed to charm the 18-year-old son of Lady Douglas into helping her escape: he stole the castle keys, secured a boat in which to row ashore, locked the castle gates behind them and threw the keys into the loch – from where they were retrieved three centuries later.

FIFE

The ancient Kingdom of **Fife**, designated as such by the Picts in the fourth century, is a small area (barely 50 miles at its widest points), but one which has a definite identity, inextricably bound with the waters which surround it on three sides – the Tay to the north, the Forth to the south, and the cold North Sea to the east. That the Fifers managed to retain their "Kingdom" when local government was reorganized in 1975 and 1995, is perhaps testimony to their will.

Despite its size, Fife encompasses several different areas, with a marked difference between the semi-industrial south and the rural north. In the **south**, the recent closure of the coal mines has left local communities floundering to regain a foothold, and the squeeze on the fishing industry up the coast may well lead to further decline. In the meantime many of the villages have capitalized on their unpretentious appeal and welcomed tourism in a way that has enhanced rather than degraded their natural assets; the perfectly preserved town of **Culross** is unmissable. East of Culross is Dunfermline, an overdeveloped town with stunning remains of the first Benedictine priory in Scotland.

Central Fife is dominated in the south by **Kirkcaldy**, the region's largest town, and in the north by **Cupar**, Fife's capital. Although only separated by 20 miles, they couldn't be more different: the former is something of an industrial blackspot in an otherwise green area, while the latter is a charming market town set in the rolling scenery for which Central Fife is known.

Tourism and agriculture are the economic mainstays of the **northeast** corner of Fife, where the landscape varies from the gentle hills in the rural hinterland, to the windswept cliffs, rocky bays and sandy beaches on which scenes from the film *Chariots of Fire* were shot. The fishing industry is still prominent, as is evident in the beautiful and ancient villages lining the shore of the East Neuk from Crail on the eastern tip down to Earlsferry. **St Andrews**, Scotland's oldest university town, and the home of the world-famous Royal and Ancient Golf club, is on the northeast coast. Development here has been cautious, and the hills and hamlets of the surrounding area retain an appealing and old-fashioned feel.

The main **transport route** through the region is the M90 from Edinburgh to Perth, which edges Fife's western boundary. The coastal route is more attractive, however, and also affords relatively easy access into the centre of Fife. The train line follows the coast as far north as Kirkcaldy and then cuts inland, towards Dundee, stopping at Cupar and Leuchars (catch a bus from here to St Andrews) on the way. Exploration of the eastern and western fringes by public transport requires some thought as there is no train service and buses are few and far between.

The south coast

Although the **south coast** of Fife is predominantly industrial – with everything from cottage industries to the refitting of nuclear submarines – thankfully only a small part has been blighted by insensitive development. Even in the old coal-mining areas, disused pits and left-over slag heaps have either been well camouflaged through landscaping or put to alternative use as recreation areas. If you're driving, it's tempting once you've crossed the river to beat a path directly north up the M90 motorway; however, if you do decide to stop off, you'll find the area has much to offer.

It was from **Dunfermline** that Queen Margaret ousted the Celtic Church from Scotland in the eleventh century; her son, David I, founded an abbey here in the twelfth century, which acquired vast stretches of land for miles around. Today, even though the lands no longer belong to the town, Dunfermline remains the chief town and the focus of the coast. **Culross** was once a lively port, which enjoyed a thriving trade with Holland; the Dutch influence obvious in the lovely gabled houses. The town fell into decline for around 200 years but has been lovingly restored this century by the NTS.

Fife is linked to Edinburgh by the two **Forth bridges**. You used to be able to take guided walks across the historic rail bridge, whose boldness of concept was all the more remarkable for coming so hard on the heels of the Tay Bridge disaster of 1879 (see p.241); today, however, you'll have to be satisfied with seeing it from a train or a boat (for more on the Forth bridges see p.88). The towns and villages of the south coast are connected by **trains** from Edinburgh via the Forth Rail Bridge, and there is a good local **bus** service.

West of the bridges

Crossing the bridge from the south, with unattractive views of the shipyard at Inverkeithing and the naval dock at Rosyth, the A985 then heads west along the Forth before approaching **CULROSS** (pronounced "Cooros"). Buses from Glasgow via Stirling and Alloa stop at Culross, and there are also services from Dunfermline and Falkirk. One of Scotland's most picturesque settlements, the town's development began in the fifth century with the arrival of St Serf on the northern side of the Forth at "Holly Point", or Culenros, and it is said to be the birthplace of St Mungo, who travelled west and founded Glasgow cathedral. The town today is in excellent condition, thanks to the work of the NTS, which has been restoring its whitewashed, red-tiled buildings since 1932.

Make your first stop the **National Trust Visitor Centre** (Easter–Sept daily 1.30–5pm; combined ticket for Town House, Palace and Study, £3.50), in the **Town House** on the main road in the centre of Culross, for an excellent introduction to the burgh's history. Here some of the 4000 witches executed in Scotland between 1560 and 1707 were tried and held up in the upper floor of the Town House while awaiting execution in Edinburgh. Behind the ticket office is a tiny prison with built-in mannacles, where people were locked up as punishment for minor offences. The focal point of the community is the ochre-coloured **Culross Palace** (Easter–Sept daily 11am–5pm), built by wealthy coal merchant George Bruce in the late sixteenth century; not a palace at all – its name comes from the Latin *palatium*, or "hall" – but a grand and impressive house, with lots of small rooms and connecting passageways. Inside, well-informed staff point out the wonderful painted ceilings, pine panelling, antique furniture and curios; outside, dormer windows and crow-stepped gables dominate the walled court in which the house stands. The garden is planted with grasses, herbs and vegetables of the period, carefully grown from seed. The café serves homemade food, and is open from 10.30am–4.30pm.

A cobbled alleyway known as **Back Causeway**, complete with raised central aisle formerly used by noblemen to separate them from the commoners, leads up behind the Town House to the **Study** (Easter–Sept daily 1.30–5pm), a restored house that takes its name from the small room at the top of the corbelled projecting tower, reached by a turnpike stair. Built in 1610, its oak panelling in Dutch Renaissance style dates from around 20 years later. Further up the hill lie the remains of **Culross Abbey**, founded by Cistercian monks on land given to the Church – in return for a greater chance of salvation – by the Earl of Fife in 1217. The nave of the original building is a ruin, a lawn studded with great stumps of columns. Although it is difficult to get a sense of what the abbey would have looked like, the overall effect is of grace and grandeur. A ladder leads to a vaulted chamber, now exposed to the elements on one side, which feels as if it is suspended in mid-air. This adjoins the fine seventeenth-century **manse**, hung with clematis, and the choir of the abbey, which became the Parish Church in 1633. Inside, wooden panels detail the donations given by eighteenth-century worthies to the parish poor, and a tenth-century Celtic cross in the north transept is a reminder of the origins of the abbey as a religious site – there was a Celtic church here in 450. Alabaster figures of Sir George Bruce, his lady, three sons and five daughters decorate the splendid family tomb, the parents lying in state and the children lined up and kneeling in devotion. A brass plaque tells the story of Edward, Lord Bruce of Kinloss, who was defeated by Sir Edward Sackville in a duel fought in Bergen in Holland in 1613. The luckless lord had been buried in Holland, but a persistent rumour that his heart had been taken back to Scotland was proved true when it was found during building work in the church in 1808, embalmed in a "silver casket of foreign workmanship".

The graveyard of the church is fascinating. Many of the graves are eighteenth century, with symbols depicting the occupation of the person who is buried; the gravestone of a gardener has a crossed spade and rake and an hourglass with the sand run out – the latter a symbol of mortality used on many of the graves. Note the Scottish custom, still continued, of marking women's graves with maiden names, even when they are buried with their husband.

Beyond Culross, the B9037 continues west to **Kincardine**, where the **Kincardine Bridge** provides a second crossing point over the Forth before the Old Bridge at Stirling.

Dunfermline

Scotland's capital until the Union of the Crowns in 1603, **DUNFERMLINE** lies seven miles inland east of Culross, north of the Forth bridges. This "auld, grey toun" is built on a hill, dominated by the abbey and ruined palace at the top. Up until the late nineteenth century, Dunfermline was one of Scotland's foremost linen producers, as well as a major coal-mining centre, and today the town is a busy place, its ever-increasing sprawl attesting to its booming economy. At the heart of the town is the imposing abbey, and the dramatic skeleton of the palace.

In the eleventh century, **Malcolm III** (Canmore) offered refuge here to Edgar Atheling, heir to the English throne, and his family, who while fleeing the Norman Conquest were fortuitously shipwrecked in the Forth. Malcolm married Edgar's sister, the Catholic Margaret, in 1067, and in so doing started a process of reformation that ultimately supplanted the Celtic Church. Margaret, an intensely pious woman who was canonized in 1250, began building a Benedictine priory in 1072, the remains of which can still be seen beneath the nave of the present church; her son, **David I**, raised the priory to the rank of abbey in the following century. In 1303, during the first of the **Wars of Independence** (1296-1328), the English king Edward I occupied the castle, conducting a military campaign which culminated in the siege of Stirling Castle the following year. He had the church roof stripped of lead to provide ammunition for his army's catapults, and also appears to have ordered the destruction of most of the monastery buildings, with the exception of the church and some of the monks' dwellings. **Robert the Bruce** helped rebuild the abbey, and when he died of leprosy was buried here 25 years later, although his body went undiscovered until building began on a new parish church in 1821. His heart, which was first taken on crusade to Spain by Sir James Douglas, now lies in Melrose Abbey in southern Scotland (see p.119).

The Town

Dunfermline's **centre**, at the top of the hill around the abbey and palace, holds an appeal of its own, with its narrow, cobbled streets, pedestrianized shopping areas and gargoyle-adorned buildings. One of the best of these, the **city chambers** on the corner of Bridge and Bruce streets, is a fine example of late-nineteenth-century Gothic Revival style. Among the ornate porticoes and grotesques of dragons and winged serpents which adorn the exterior are the sculpted heads of Robert the Bruce, Malcolm Canmore, Queen Margaret and Queen Elizabeth I.

Dunfermline Abbey (April–Sept Mon–Sat 9.30am–6.30pm, Sun 2–6.30pm; Oct–March Mon–Wed & Sat 9.30am–4.30pm, Thurs 9.30am–12.30pm, Sun 2–4.30pm; £1.50) is comprised of the twelfth-century nave of the medieval monastic church, with an early nineteenth-century parish church spliced on. A plaque beneath the pulpit marks the spot where Robert the Bruce's remains were laid to rest for the second time, while Malcolm and his queen, Margaret, who died of grief three days after her husband in 1093, have a shrine outside. The enormous stonework graffiti, "King Robert the Bruce", at the top of the tower is attributable to an overexcited architect thrilled by the discovery of Bruce's remains. The nearby pink harled **Abbot House**, possibly four-teenth century, is best seen from the outside. The building, variously used as an abbot's house, an iron foundry, an art school and a doctor's surgery, has just emerged from a three-year restoration programme. A bold attempt has been made to address the fact that nothing remains of the original interior, and that there are no interesting artefacts to display. The upstairs rooms consist of "exhibitions": every square inch being painted with scenes of Dunfermline life, medieval and modern, with sinister life-size models of local figures dotted about. You can visit the witches'-coven-style café downstairs first to decide if you are willing to pay the entrance fee to see more.

The guest house of Margaret's Benedictine monastery, south of the abbey, became the **Palace** (same times as abbey) in the sixteenth century under James VI, who gave both it and the abbey to his consort, Queen Anne of Denmark. Charles I, the last monarch to be born in Scotland, came into the world here in 1600. All that is left of it today is a long, sand-stone facade, especially impressive when silhouetted against the evening sky. The four redundant walls next to the palace are those of the refectory, connected via the gatehouse to the kitchen, which was tacked on at the palace's eastern end.

Pittencrieff Park, known to locals as "the Glen", covers a huge area in the centre of town. Bordering the ruined palace, the 76-acre park used to be owned by the Lairds of Pittencrieff, whose 1610 estate house, built of stone pillaged from the palace, still stands within the grounds. In 1902, however, the entire plot was purchased by the local, rags-to-riches industrialist and philanthropist Andrew Carnegie, who donated it to his home town. This was just as much sweet revenge as beneficent public spirited-ness: the young Carnegie, had been banned from the estate according to a former laird's edict that no Morrison would pass through the gates. Since his mother had been a Morrison, Carnegie could do little but gaze through the bars on the one day a year that the estate was open to the rest of the public. Today **Pittencrieff House** (May–Oct daily except Tues 11am–5pm; free) displays exhibits on local history, the glasshouses are filled with exotic blooms, and the Pavilion coffee shop offers refreshment. In the centre of the park are the remains – little more than the foundations – of **Malcolm**

Canmore's Tower, which may be the location of Malcolm's residence, known to have been somewhere to the west of the abbey. Dunfermline – meaning "fort by the crooked pool" – takes its name from the tower's location: "Dun" meaning hill or fort, "Fearum" bent or crooked, and "Lin" (or "Lyne/Line") a pool or running water.

Just beyond the southeast corner of the park, the modest little cottage at the bottom of St Margaret Street is **Andrew Carnegie's Birthplace** (April–Oct Mon–Sat 11am–5pm, Sun 2–5pm; Nov–March daily 2–4pm; £1.50). The son of a weaver, the young Carnegie (1835–1919) lived upstairs with his family, while the room below housed his father's loom shop. Following the family's emigration to America in 1848, he worked on the railroads before becoming involved with the iron and then the steel industries. From 1873 he began his acquisition of steel-production firms, later to be consolidated into the Carnegie Steel Company; when he retired in 1901 to devote himself to philanthropy, Carnegie was a multi-millionaire. His house, an ordinary two-up two-down, has been preserved as it was at the end of the last century, and the adjacent Memorial Hall details his life and work.

Practicalities

Trains from Edinburgh connect with Dunfermline, whose **train station** is southeast of the centre, halfway down the long hill of St Margaret's Drive. You can walk (15min) up the hill from here to the **tourist office**, next to Abbot House, Maygate (April–Sept Mon–Sat 10am–6pm, Sun 11am–3pm; Oct–March Mon–Sat 10am–4pm; ☎01383/720999). There's an hourly bus from Edinburgh and two-hourly services from Glasgow, Perth and Dundee. From the **bus station**, cut through the upstairs floor of the shopping centre and then right along High Street (about a 5-min walk). If you do want to **stay**, options include the comfortable *Davaar House Hotel*, 126 Grieve St (☎01383/721886; ④), in a tastefully furnished Victorian town house. There are some good, well-priced ethnic **restaurants** in Dunfermline. Try *Blossom's*, 6–8 Chalmers St, for Chinese food, or *Khan's*, 33 Carnegie Drive, for Indian cuisine. For cheap and cheerful French cooking, try *Café Rene*, also on Carnegie Drive. *Il Pescatore* on the coast at Limekilns (about 5 miles south of the town on the B9156) is a great traditional Italian place, once patronized by Prince Andrew and his naval chums. If you want a drink in town, try the *Watering Hole*, New Row.

East of the bridges

Fife's **south coast** curves sharply north at the mouth of the River Forth, exposing the towns and villages to an icy east wind that somewhat undermines the sunshine image of their beaches. If you've got the time, though, or fancy an alternative route to St Andrews, after crossing the bridge, cut off to the east along the A921, following the train line as it clings to the northern shore of the mouth of the Forth. Here you'll find a straggle of Fife fishing communities which have depended on the crop of the sea for centuries, and now make popular, although not especially attractive, holiday spots. The **train** line from Inverkeithing and twice hourly **buses** (#7 & #7a) from Dunfermline run along the coast, stopping at all the following towns.

North Queensferry

Cowering beneath the bridges is **NORTH QUEENSFERRY**, a small fishing village, which, until the opening of the road bridge, was the northern landing point of the ferry across the Forth, and a nineteenth-century bathing resort. Built on a rocky outcrop, the place is comparatively well preserved for somewhere which takes such a battering from the elements, and there are good views across the Forth and of the bridges. The massive spans of the rail bridge – inspiration for Iain Bank's postmodern novel, *The Bridge* – loom frighteningly large from such close range. Today, with the bridge beginning to stain and rust, the famous saying about a seemingly endless task "like painting the Forth Rail Bridge" has somewhat lost its impact. Also here is the new **Deep-Sea World** (daily 9.30am–6pm; £5.25), a huge aquarium that boasts the world's largest underwater viewing tunnel, through which you glide on a moving walkway while sharks, conger eels and all manner of creatures from the deep swim nonchalantly past.

Inverkeithing

The North Queensferry peninsula gives way to Inverkeithing Bay and **INVERKEITHING**, a medieval watering place established by David I in the twelfth century and granted a charter by William I around 1165, thanks to its strategic location and safe harbour. Modern Inverkeithing is unprepossessing, with housing estates sprawling around the more attractive old town centre. The **Parish Church of St Peter**, on Church St near the train station, began as a wooden Celtic church before Queen Margaret set to work, and ended up as a Norman stone structure bequeathed to Dunfermline Abbey in 1139. The oldest part of it today is the fifteenth-century tower, the rest having been razed by fire in 1825.

Aberdour

Beyond Inverkeithing, **ABERDOUR** clings tight to the walls of its **Castle** (April–Sept Mon–Wed & Sat 9.30am–6.30pm, Sun 2–6.30pm; Oct–March closes 4.30pm; £1.50) at the southern end of the main street. Once a Douglas stronghold, the castle is on a comparatively modest scale, with gently sloping lawns, a large enclosed seventeenth-century garden and terraces. The fourteenth-century tower is the oldest part of the castle, the other buildings having been added in the sixteenth and seventeenth centuries, including the well-preserved dovecote. Worth more perusal is **St Fillan's Church**, also in the castle grounds, which dates from the twelfth century, with a few sixteenth-century additions, such as the porch restorated from total dereliction earlier this century. There's little else to see here apart from the town's popular **silver sands** beach, which, along with its watersports, golf and sailing, has earned Aberdour the rather optimistic tourist board soubriquet the "Fife Riviera". From Aberdour you can take a ferry to Inchcolm Island to see its ruined medieval Abbey (see p.88).

If you want to **stay** you could try the friendly *Aberdour Hotel* on High St (☎01383/ 860325; ⑤), which also has an inexpensive **restaurant** downstairs. The real gem though is *Hawkcraig House*, Hawkcraig Point (☎01383/860335; ③), a guest house with a good restaurant in an old ferryman's house overlooking the harbour.

Burntisland

From Aberdour it's three miles to the large holiday resort of **BURNTISLAND**, with its fine stretch of sandy beach. The busy High Street runs the length of the waterfront, hemmed in by buildings at the western end, where you'll find the unkempt **train station**. Offices now occupy **Rossend Castle** (beyond the west end of High St), a fifteenth-century tower with sixteenth century additions, sadly not open to the public. Mary, Queen of Scots, stayed in 1563 and Pierre de Chastelard, an eager French poet, was discovered in her bedchamber. Chastelard, having been warned once already about hiding in the young queen's private rooms at Holyrood Palace, was whisked off to St Andrews where, proclaiming "Adieu, thou most beautiful and most cruel Princess in the world", he was executed.

Burntisland's **tourist office** is at 4 Kirkgate (April–Sept Mon–Thurs 9am–5pm, Fri & Sat 9am–4.30pm; Oct–March Mon–Thurs 9am–5pm, Fri 9am–4.30pm; ☎01592/872667). Although almost every house along the Links, just beyond High St, sports a **B&B** sign, the choice of **hotels** is limited to four. The *Inchview Hotel*, 69 Kinghorn Rd (☎01592/ 872239; ⑤), a listed Georgian building looking out across the sea, and *Kingswood Hotel*, Kinghorn Rd (☎01592/872329; ⑥), are the most comfortable. The latter, in a leafy road just north of town, will also organize fishing and shooting trips for guests, and offers good bar meals, high teas and dinners. Other **eating** options include the *Charene Hotel*, 241 High St, for cheap lunches, afternoon teas and dinners, with a limited vegetarian selection. *The Smugglers Inn*, 14 Harbour Place, does snacks and bar meals.

Kinghorn

Shortly before reaching **KINGHORN**, the coastal road from Burntisland passes a **Celtic Cross** commemorating Alexander III, the last of the Celtic kings, who plunged over the cliff near here one night in 1286, when his horse stumbled. Kinghorn, an ancient settlement, today is a popular but not too crowded holiday centre, with few formal attractions but a good beach. The ugly brown pebble-dashed **parish church**, looking over the beach and whipped by wintry winds at the land's edge, dates from 1894, though the site has been used as a church for centuries and the small graveyard – popular with local genealogists – is filled with lichen-covered, semi-legible tombstones from the eighteenth century. At the opposite (southern) end of town, a hill lined with Spanish-style villas leads down to the waterfront and the beach at **Pettycur Bay**, where fishing boats cluster round the small harbour and brightly coloured lobster nets dot the sands.

Regular trains from Edinburgh and Dundee arrive at Kinghorn's **train station**, just off High St. The best **place to stay** is *The Longboat Inn*, 107 Pettycur Rd (☎01592/ 890625; ④), overlooking the River Forth, just above the beach at Pettycur Bay. Ask for a room with a balcony, from where you'll get good views across to Edinburgh and the Lothians. Decent bar meals are available in the wine bar and full meals in the moderately priced **restaurant**. For B&B try the *Coach House*, 9 Rossland Place (☎01592/ 890592; ②) or *Craigo-er*, 45 Pettycur Rd (☎01592/890527; ③).

Kirkcaldy and around

The ancient royal burgh of **KIRKCALDY** (pronounced "Kirkcawdy") is familiarly known as "The Lang Toun" for its four-mile-long esplanade which stretches the length of the waterfront. The esplanade was built in 1922–23 – not just to hold back the sea, but also to alleviate unemployment – and runs parallel for part of the way with the shorter High Street. If you're here in mid-April, you'll see the historic **Links Market**, a week-long funfair that dates back to 1305, and is possibly the largest street fair in Britain.

Incidentally, though there's little to show for it today, architect brothers Robert and James Adam were born in Kirkcaldy, as was the eighteenth-century scholar, philosopher and political economist Adam Smith, whose great work *The Wealth of Nations* (1776), established political economy as a separate science.

The Town

Kirkcaldy doesn't hold a great deal of interest for the visitor, its charms largely obliterated by overdevelopment. However, a stroll along the promenade is pleasant on a sunny day and there's a large range of the major chain stores in the town centre. The town's history is chronicled in its **Museum and Art Gallery** (Mon–Sat 10.30am–5pm, Sun 2–5pm; free) in the colourful War Memorial Gardens between the train and bus stations. The museum covers everything from archeological discoveries to the tradition of the local Wemyss Ware pottery and the evolution of the present town. Established in 1925, in the past 70 years the gallery has built up its collection to around 300 works by some of Scotland's finest painters from the late eighteenth century onwards, including works by the fine portraitist Sir Henry Raeburn, the historical painter Sir David Wilkie, and Scottish "Colourists" S J Peploe and William McTaggart. For a town which is known primarily for linoleum production and whose reputation is firmly rooted in the prosaic, the art gallery is an unexpected boon.

Just beyond the northern end of the waterfront, Ravenscraig Park is the site of the substantial ruin of **Ravenscraig Castle**, a thick-walled, fifteenth-century defence post, which occupies a lovely spot above a beach. The castle looks out over the Forth, and is flanked on either side by a flight of steps – the inspiration, apparently, for the title of John Buchan's novel, *The 39 Steps*. Sir Walter Scott also found this a place worthy of comment, using it as a setting for the story of "lovely Rosabella" in *The Lay of the Last Minstrel*.

Beyond Kirkcaldy lies the old suburb of **Dysart**, where tall ships once arrived bringing cargo from the Netherlands, setting off again with coal, beer, salt and fish. Well restored, and retaining historic street names such as Hot Pot Wynd (after the hot pans used for salt evaporation), it's an atmospheric place of narrow alleyways and picturesque old buildings. In Rectory Lane, the birthplace of John McDouall Stuart (who in 1862 became the first man to cross Australia from the south to the north) now holds the **McDouall Stuart Museum** (June–Aug Mon–Sat 2–5pm; NTS; free), giving an account of his emigration to Australia in 1838 and his subsequent adventures.

Practicalities

Kirkcaldy's **train** and **bus stations** are in the upper part of town – keep heading downhill to get to the centre. For the **tourist office**, 19 Whytecauseway (April–Sept daily 10am–6pm; Oct–March Mon–Thurs 9am–5pm, Fri 9am–4.30pm; ☎01592/267775), follow the road for about ten minutes round to the right from the bus station. If you want to stay in Kirkcaldy, the office's **accommodation** booking service is a life-saver; there are only few places to stay in the centre, and the layout of the rest of the town is not easy to follow because of the way it falls across the hillside. In Kirkcaldy town centre the *Parkway Hotel*, Abbotshall Rd (☎01592/262143; ⑥), offers smart rooms and traditional breakfasts, while the smaller, more refined *Dunnikier House Hotel*, Dunnikier Park, Dunnikier Way (☎01592/268393; ④), serves fine local food and is set in pleasant grounds. The *Strathearn Hotel*, 2 Wishart Place, on Dysart Rd (☎01592/652210; ④), is a welcoming place set in its own gardens, a couple of miles north of the centre of town. You can get cheaper rooms along the road in **Dysart**, at the *Royal Hotel*, Townhead (☎01592/654112; ③), which occupies one of the village's historic buildings.

The *Royal Hotel* is a good place for eating, as is the *Old Rectory Inn*, West Quality St, also in Dysart. In Kirkcaldy, itself, try *Giovanni's*, 66 Dunnikier Rd for traditional Italian **food**, or *Maxin*, 5 High St, for Chinese.

There's a good **arts cinema** with a restaurant and bar, which is housed in the Adam Smith Theatre on Bennochy Rd in the town centre (☎01592/260498)

Around Kirkcaldy

Inland from Kirkcaldy, the old **mining towns** of Cowdenbeath, Kelty, Lochgelly and Cardenden huddle together, their fires virtually extinguished by a blanket of economic depression. These are neglected places, and indeed are rarely even seen by visitors shooting up to St Andrews on the coastal route or zooming along the M90 to Perth. Take the train, however, and you'll weave through this forlorn stretch as the line leaves the coast and heads inland.

Ten miles inland from Kirkcaldy, **GLENROTHES** is a new town in much the same mould as any other. Stark, concrete and utilitarian, it is the European headquarters of the Californian company *Hughes Microelectronics*, who, along with similar operations, have given the town much-needed wealth and self-confidence. Only a short time ago, a sign at Markinch train station to the west (Glenrothes' nearest station) boldly announced,

"Welcome to Glenrothes, the Capital of Fife". So outraged at this audacity were the residents of Cupar, Fife's real capital for centuries, that the sign had to be removed.

If you have even a passing interest in castles and their construction, try to visit **Balgonie Castle**, two miles east of Glenrothes on the B921 off the A911. Set above the River Leven, this splendid castle with its fourteenth-century keep and fine open courtyard has a somewhat unkempt appearance from the outside; only a small plaque stating that it is home to the Laird and Lady of Balgonie suggests it's inhabited. Don't be put off by the huge, but docile, Irish wolfhounds, or by the fact that you may have to wait some time at the door of the keep before anyone hears your knock. Once inside, you are guaranteed a uniquely personal tour from the laird or a member of his family; the castle has the distinction of being open every day of the year (roughly 10am–5pm) except when the fourteenth-century chapel is being used for candlelit weddings. The tour gives in-depth information on the architecture of the castle and its owners and occupiers, including Rob Roy who stayed here with 200 clansmen in 1716. Balgonie was partly restored in 1971 and the present laird, who hails from the West Midlands, but is always attired in a kilt, has continued the process.

The Howe of Fife

Completely different from the industrial landscape of Kirkcaldy and Glenrothes, the **Howe of Fife**, lying north of Glenrothes, is a low-lying stretch of ground ("howe") lying at the foot of the twin peaks of the heather-swathed **Lomond Hills** – West Lomond (1696ft) and East Lomond (1378ft). The area makes an ideal stopping point on the way to St Andrews, with **Falkland Palace** and the handsome market town of **Cupar**. Frequent **buses** run throughout the area, with regular services threading their way towards Dundee from Kirkcaldy. The **train** also comes this way, stopping at Cupar and Leuchars before crossing the Tay Bridge to Dundee.

Falkland

Nestling in the lower slopes of East Lomond, the narrow streets of **FALKLAND** are lined with fine and well-preserved seventeenth- and eighteenth-century buildings. The village grew up around **Falkland Palace** (April–Oct Mon–Sat 11am–5.30pm, Sun 1.30–5.30pm; NTS; £4, gardens only £2), which stands on the site of an earlier castle, home to the Macduffs, the Earls of Fife. James IV began the construction of the present palace in 1500; it was completed and embellished by James V, and became a favoured royal residence. Charles II stayed here in 1650, when he was in Scotland for his coronation, but after the Jacobite rising of 1715 and temporary occupation by Rob Roy, the palace was left to ruin, remaining so until the late nineteenth century when the keepership was acquired by the third Marquess of Bute. He restored the palace entirely, and today it is a stunning example of Early Renaissance architecture, complete with corbelled parapet, mullioned windows, round towers and massive walls. A **guided tour** (40min) takes in a cross section of public and private rooms in the south and east wings. The former is better preserved and includes the stately drawing room, the Chapel Royal (still used for Mass) and the Tapestry Gallery, swathed with splendid seventeenth-century Flemish hangings. Outside, the **gardens** are also worth a look, their well-stocked herbaceous borders lining a pristine lawn, and with the oldest tennis court in Britain – built in 1539 for James V and still used.

When not playing tennis, the royal guests at Falkland would hunt deer and wild boar in the forests which then covered the Howe of Fife, stretching towards Cupar, ten miles northeast. There are still deer here today, at the **Scottish Deer Centre** (April–Oct daily 10am–5pm; July & Aug closes 6pm; £4), three miles west of Cupar on the

A91, which specializes in the rearing of red deer, and is also home to species of sika, fallow and reindeer. It's a good place for children, who can pet the tamer animals, and there are play and picnic areas and guided nature trails.

Falkland is also a good base for **walks**, with several leading from the village; but for the more serious hikes to the summits of East and West Lomond, you have to start from Craigmead car park about two miles west of the village (always follow the usual safety precautions; see p.38).

If you want to **stay** in Falkland, there's a **youth hostel**, Back Wynd (March–Sept; Nov–Feb Sat only; ☎01337/857710; Grade 3). Directly opposite the palace is the *Hunting Lodge Hotel*, High St (☎01337/857226; ⑤), and just up the road, the *Covenanter Hotel* – both are comfortable. For B&B try the attractive *Oakbank Guest House*, The Pleasance (☎01337/857287; ③).

Cupar

Straddling the small River Eden and surrounded by gentle hills, **CUPAR**, the capital of Fife, has retained much of its medieval character – and its self-confident air – from the days when it was a bustling market centre. A livestock auction still takes place here every week. In 1276 Alexander III held an assembly in the town, bringing together the Church, aristocracy and local burgesses in an early form of Scottish parliament. For his troubles he subsequently became the butt of Sir David Lindsay's biting play, *Ane Pleasant Satyre of the Thrie Estaitis* (1535), one of the first great Scottish dramas.

Situated at the centre of Fife's road network, Cupar's main street, part of the main road from Edinburgh to St Andrews, is plagued with thundering traffic. The **Mercat Cross**, stranded in the midst of the lorries and cars which speed through the centre, now consists of salvaged sections of the seventeenth-century original, following its destruction by an errant lorry some years ago.

One of the best reasons for stopping off at Cupar is to visit the **Hill of Tarvit** (Easter to mid-Oct daily 1.30–5.30pm; NTS; £3; gardens open all year daily 10am–sunset; £1), an Edwardian mansion two miles south of town remodelled by Sir Robert Lorimer from a late-seventeenth-century building. The estate, formerly the home of the geographer and cartographer, Sir John Scott, includes the five-storey, late-sixteenth-century **Scotstarvit Tower**, three quarters of a mile west of the present house (keys available from house during season only). Set on a little mound, the tower is a fine example of Scots tower house, providing both fortification and comfort. The entire estate was bequeathed to the NTS in 1949 (part of which they rent out; see below), and the house contains an impressive collection of eighteenth-century Chippendale and French furniture, Dutch paintings, Chinese porcelain, and a restored Edwardian laundry.

Practicalities

Cupar's **tourist office** (May Mon–Sat 9.30am–5pm; June–Sept Mon–Sat 9.30am–5.30pm, Sun 2–5pm; ☎01334/652874) is based in The Granary Business Centre in Coal Rd. The **train station** is immediately south of the centre; **bus** #23 from Stirling to St Andrews stops outside. If you want to **stay**, try the friendly *Eden House Hotel*, 2 Pitscottie Rd (☎01334/652510; ④), which also serves good inexpensive Scottish food. You can rent the small cottage at the foot of the Scotstarvit tower from the NTS for around £200 per week (☎0131/243 9331). There are several good B&Bs in and around Cupar; try the Mill Cottage, Cults Mill just outside town (☎01334/654980; ③). If money is no object, the best hotels are out of the centre: *Balbirnie House Hotel*, Balbirnie Park (☎01592/610066; ⑨), is a magnificent Georgian mansion five miles southwest of town, complete with 416 acres of parkland; and five miles north of Cupar in **LETHAM**, the *Fernie Castle Hotel* (☎01337/810381; ⑥) occupies a real castle and offers bar meals as well as a more expensive à la carte menu. There is no shortage of good **restaurants** in the area; try the excellent *Ostler's Close*, 25 Bonnygate (☎01334/655574), or take the B940 east to the renowned *Peat Inn* (see p.239). For drinks and bar food try *Watts* next to the tourist office.

Ceres and on to St Andrews

Unusually for Scotland, **CERES**, two miles east of the Hill of Tarvit, is set around a village green. Occupying several well-preserved seventeenth-to-nineteenth-century buildings is the **Fife Folk Museum** (April–Oct Sat–Thurs 2.15–5pm; £1.60), which exhibits all manner of historical farming and agricultural paraphernalia. The pillory that used to restrain miscreants on market days still stands at the entrance of the old burgh tollbooth, and at the village crossroads is an unusual seventeenth-century stone carving of a man in a three-cornered hat with a toothy grin and a beer glass on his knee, said to be a depiction of a former provost.

Continuing east on the B939, you will soon come to **Magnus Muir**, halfway between Cupar and St Andrews, site of the murder of the controversial and oppressive Episcopalian Archbishop of St Andrews by a band of Covenanters in 1679; during the stuggle, Archbishop Sharp's daughter, Isabella, was wounded trying to protect him. One of the culprits, Hackston of Rathillet, was captured in Edinburgh and gruesomely executed. His hands were buried in Cupar's graveyard.

St Andrews and around

Confident, poised and well groomed, **ST ANDREWS**, Scotland's oldest university town and a pigrimage centre for golfers from all over the world, is on a wide bay on the northeastern coast of Fife. It's often referred to in tourist literature as "the Oxford or Cambridge of the North", and, like Cambridge, by and large St Andrews *is* its university.

According to legend, the town was founded, pretty much by accident, in the fourth century Saint Rule – or Regulus – a custodian of the bones of Saint Andrew on the Greek island of Patras, had a vision in which an angel ordered him to carry five of the

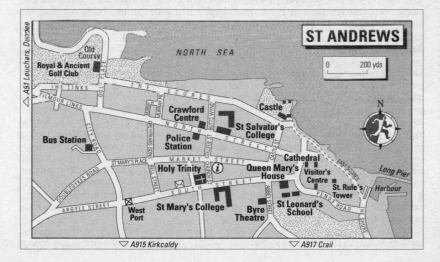

saint's bones to the western edge of the world, where he was to build a city in his honour. The conscientious courier set off, but was shipwrecked on the rocks close to the present harbour. Struggling ashore with his precious burden, he built a shrine to the saint on what subsequently became the site of the cathedral, and Saint Andrew became Scotland's patron saint and the town its ecclesiastical capital.

Local residents are proud of their town, with its refined old-fashioned ambience. Thanks to a strong and well-informed local conservation lobby, many of the original buildings have survived. Almost the entire centre consists of listed buildings, while the ruined castle and cathedral have all but been rebuilt in the efforts to preserve their remains. If you're here in early August, make sure to get to the two-day **Lammas Fair**, Scotland's oldest surviving medieval market, complete with town crier. The other main event in the St Andrews calendar is the **Kate Kennedy Pageant**, usually held on the third Saturday in April, which involves an all-male procession of students taking to the streets dressed as characters associated with the university, from Kate Kennedy herself, niece of one of the university founders, to Mary, Queen of Scots.

There are two main excursion areas from St Andrews. The most popular, with its beaches and little fishing villages is the **East Neuk**, stretching from Fife Ness to Largo Bay; the other is the **Tay coast**, which runs around Fife's northeast headland and along the Tay estuary almost to Perth. **Bus** #95 runs from Leven up the coast to Dundee.

Arrival and information

St Andrews is not on the train line. The nearest **train station** is on the Edinburgh–Dundee–Aberdeen line at **Leuchars**, five miles northwest across the River Eden, from where regular (but not always connecting) buses make the trip into town (15min). The price of the rail ticket to Leuchars does not include the bus trip to St Andrews. Frequent **buses** from Edinburgh and Dundee terminate at the bus station on City Rd at the west end of Market St. The **tourist office**, 70 Market St (Mon–Sat 9.30am–5pm, Sun 2–5pm; ☎01334/472021), holds comprehensive information about St Andrews and northeast Fife.

If you're **driving**, the town's fiendish **parking** system requires vouchers (30p per hour) which you can get from the tourist office and some local shops. Scratch out the month, day, date and hour from the card, display it in your car, and cross your fingers that you've worked it out correctly.

Accommodation

Although rooms in St Andrews cost more than in the surrounding area, they often get booked up in the summer, when reserving ahead is strongly recommended. Most of the **guest houses** are around Murray Place and Murray Park between The Scores and North Street. Good ones include *Aedel House*, 72 Murray Place (☎01334/472315; ②) and *Bell Craig Guest House* at 8 Murray Park (☎01334/472962; ②). On North Street, try *Aslar House* at no. 120 (☎01334/473460; ④) or *Cadzow Guest House* at no. 58 (☎01334/476933; ④). Between June and September, the **university** (☎01334/462000; ④) offers about 200 rooms in various locations, all on a B&B basis with dinner optional. More upmarket are the various **hotels** lining The Scores, beyond the eastern end of the Old (golf) Course, overlooking the bay. The *St Andrews Golf Hotel*, at no. 40 (☎01334/472611; ⑨) occupies a three-storey town house, with chintzy, comfortable bedrooms – those at the front have great views – good food and an extensive wine list.

As you come into town from Leuchars, you'll see the entrance to the swanky *Rusacks Hotel*, 16 Pilmour Links (☎01334/474321; ⑨) on the left. From the airy lobby to its spacious rooms, this is a refined place whose old-fashioned style is in keeping with the town's air of respectability. A little further up the road is the *Tudor Inn*, 129 North St (☎01334/474906; ④) – its uncharacteristic black-and-white Tudor facade more English than Scottish. Although less luxurious than the above hotels, this is good value as long as you're not sleeping above the noisy downstairs bar. A couple of miles west of St Andrews on the B939 to Ceres is *Ruffets* (☎01334/478703; ⑧), an elegant 1920s country house. The garden provides much of the produce for the hotel's restaurant. The *Peat Inn* hotel (☎01334/840206; ⑨), five miles south of town on the A915 and then one mile west on the B940, has plush suites in a modern building tucked behind the old coaching inn; it also houses a wonderful and very popular restaurant (see p.239).

The Town

The centre of St Andrews still follows the medieval layout. Wandering its three main thoroughfares, North Street, South Street and Market Street, which run west to east towards the ruined Gothic cathedral, are several of the original university buildings from the fifteenth century. Narrow alleys connect the cobbled streets, attic windows and gable ends shape the rooftops, and here and there you'll see old wooden doors with heavy knockers and black iron hinges.

The ruin of the great **St Andrews Cathedral** (visitor centre: April–Sept Mon–Sat 9.30am–6pm, Sun 2–6pm; Oct–March Mon–Sat 9.30am–4pm, Sun 2–4pm; £1.50; grounds Sun am only), at the east end of town, gives only an idea of its former importance. The cathedral was founded in 1160, but not finished and consecrated until 1318, in the presence of Robert the Bruce; it was the largest cathedral in Scotland. But on June 5, 1559, the Reformation took its toll, and supporters of John Knox, fresh from a rousing meeting, plundered the cathedral and left it to ruin. Stone was still being taken from the cathedral for various local buildings projects as late as the 1820s.

Standing above the harbour where the land drops to the sea, the cathedral site can be a blustery place, with the wind whistling through the great east window and down the stretch of turf that was once the central aisle. In front of the window a slab is all that remains of the high altar, where the relics of St Andrew were once enshrined. Previously, it is believed that they were kept in **St Rule's Tower**, the austere Romanesque monolith next to the cathedral, which was built as part of an abbey in 1130. From the top of the tower (a climb of 157 steps), there's a good view of the town and surroundings, and of the remains of the monastic buildings which made up the priory. Around the entire complex is a sturdy wall dating from the sixteenth century, over half a mile long and with three gateways.

Southwest of the cathedral enclosure lies **the Pends**, a huge fourteenth-century vaulted gatehouse which marked the main entrance to the priory, and from where the road leads down to the harbour, passing prim **St Leonard's**, one of Scotland's leading private schools for girls. The sixteenth-century, rubble-stonework building on the right as you go through the Pends is **Queen Mary's House**, where she is believed to have stayed in 1563. The house was restored in 1927 and is now used as the school library.

Down at the **harbour**, gulls screech above the fishing boats, keeping an eye on the lobster nets strewn along the quay. If you come here on a Sunday morning, you'll see students parading down the long pier, red gowns billowing in the wind, in a time-honoured after-church walk. The beach, **East Sands**, is a popular stretch, although it's cool in summer, and positively biting in winter. A path leads south from the far end of the beach, climbing up the hill past the caravan site and cutting through the gorse; this makes a pleasant walk on a sunny day, taking in hidden coves and caves.

North of the beach, the rocky coastline curves inland to the ruined **St Andrew's Castle** (April–Sept Mon–Sat 9.30am–6pm, Sun 2–6pm; Oct–March Mon–Sat 9.30am–

4.30pm, Sun 2–4.30pm; £2), with a drop to the sea on three sides and a moat on the fourth. Founded around 1200 and extended over the centuries, it was built as part of the palace of the Bishops and Archbishops of St Andrews and was consequently the scene of some fairly grim incidents at the time of the Reformation. There's not a great deal left of the castle, since it fell into ruin in the seventeenth century, and most of what can be seen dates from the sixteenth century, apart from the fourteenth-century Fore Tower.

The Protestant reformer George Wishart was burned at the stake in front of the castle in 1546, as an incumbent Cardinal Beaton looked on. Wishart had been a friend of John Knox's, and it wasn't long before fellow reformers sought vengeance for his death. Less than three months later, Cardinal Beaton was stabbed to death and his body displayed from the battlements before being dropped into the "bottle dungeon", a 24ft pit hewn out of solid rock which can still be seen in the Sea Tower. The perpetrators then held the castle for over a year, and during that time dug the secret passage which can be entered from the ditch in front. Outside the castle, the initials "GW" are carved in stone.

St Andrews University is the oldest in Scotland, founded in 1410 by Bishop Henry Wardlaw. The nominal founder is James I to whom the Bishop was tutor, and the king was certainly a great benefactor of the university. The first building was on the site of the Old University Library and by the end of the Middle Ages three colleges had been built: St Salvator's (1450), St Leonard's (1512) and St Mary's (1538). At the time of the Reformation, St Mary's became a seminary of Protestant theology, and today it houses the university's Faculty of Divinity. The **quad** here has beautiful gardens and some magnificent old trees, perfect for flopping under on a warm day.

GOLF IN ST ANDREWS

St Andrew's **Royal and Ancient Golf Club** (or "R&A") is the governing body for golf the world over, dating back to a meeting of 22 of the local gentry in 1754, who founded the Society of St Andrews Golfers, being "admirers of the ancient and healthful exercise of golf". It acquired its current title after King William IV agreed to be the society's patron in 1834.

The game itself has been played here since the fifteenth century. Those early days were instrumental in establishing Scotland as the home of golf, for the rules were distinguished from those in the French game by the fact that participants had to manoeuvre the ball into a hole, rather than hit an above-ground target. (Early French versions were, in fact, more like croquet.) The game developed, acquiring popularity along the way – even Mary, Queen of Scots, was known to have the occasional round. It was not without its opponents, however, particularly James II who, in 1457, banned his subjects from playing since it was distracting them from archery practice.

St Andrews' status as a world-renowned **golf** centre is particulary obvious as you enter the town from the west, where the approach road runs adjacent to the famous **Old Course**. At the eastern end of the course lies the strictly private **clubhouse**, a stolid, square building dating from 1854. The first British Open Championship was held here in 1873, having been inaugurated in 1860 at Prestwick in Ayrshire, and since then, the British Open is held here regularly, pulling in enormous crowds. The eighteenth hole of the Old Course is immediately in front of the clubhouse, and has been officially christened the "Tom Morris", after one of the world's most famous golfers. Pictures of Nick Faldo, Jack Nicklaus and other golfing greats, along with clubs and a variety of memorabilia which they donated, are displayed in the admirable **British Golf Museum** on Bruce Embankment, along the waterfront below the clubhouse (April–Oct daily 10am–5.30pm; Nov–March Thurs–Mon 11am–3pm; £3.50). There are also plenty of hands-on exhibits, including computers, video screens and footage of British Open championships, tracing the development of golf through the centuries.

If you've got children in tow you may want to visit the huge **Sea Life Centre** on The Scores, at the west end of town close to the golf museum (daily 10am–6pm; July & Aug closes 9pm; £4.25), which examines marine life of all shapes and sizes with displays, live exhibits, observation pools and underwater walkways. Also good for children is the 50-acre **Craigtoun Country Park** (April–Sept daily 10.30am–6.30pm; £2), a couple of miles southwest of town on the B939. As well as several landscaped gardens there is a miniature train, trampolines, boating, crazy golf and picnic areas, and a country fair each May with craft stalls, wildlife exhibits, and showjumping displays.

Eating and drinking

St Andrews has no shortage of **restaurants** and **cafés**. In town, *Littlejohns*, at the east end of Market St, serves hearty burgers and steaks, while *The Vine Leaf Restaurant*, St Mary's Place (✆01334/477497) is known for its well-priced, quality dishes made from local produce, in particular a good range of seafood.

Both *Brambles*, 5 College St, and *The Merchant's House*, 49 South St, offer inexpensive home baking, while the *Victoria Café*, 1 St Mary's Place, serves baked potatoes and toasted sandwiches. This is a popular student haunt, and a good place in which to have a few drinks in the evening. *Ma Belle's*, 40 The Scores, in the basement of the *St Andrews Golf Hotel*, is a lively pub serving cheap food and catering for locals as much as students. The basement bar underneath the *Rusacks Hotel*, 16 Pilmour Links, also fills up quickly. Here you can collapse in large leather armchairs and sofas, study the book-spines in the shelves painted on the wall, or have a game of snooker.

For truly great food, at a price, head for the *Peat Inn* (✆01334/840206), five miles south of town on the A915 and then one mile west on the B940. This is one of Britain's top restaurants, serving a varied menu of local specialities. The dining area is intimate without being cramped, and a three-course meal – perhaps featuring lobster broth, venison or roast monkfish – will set you back at least £35 per head.

With its big student population, St Andrews has lots of good **pubs**. Locals and tourists mix with the students at the *Tudor*, 129 North St, which has a late night licence on Thursdays and Fridays and live bands from time to time. The *Central* on Market St serves huge pies and a powerful beer brewed by Trappist monks. The *Cellar Bar*, on Bell St, has a good range of real ales and malt whiskies, with live music in the upstairs wine bar.

The East Neuk

South of St Andrews, the **East Neuk** (*Neuk* is Scots for "corner") is a region of quaint fishing villages, all crow-stepped gables and tiled rooves. Perhaps the prettiest of these is **Crail**; with a picturesque pottery near the harbour, but the best beaches are at the resorts of **Elie** and **Earlsferry**, which lie next to each other about 12 miles south of St Andrews. The villages between St Andrews and Elie fall into two distinct types: either scattered higgledy-piggledy up the hillside like **St Monans**, between Pittenweem and Elie, or neatly lined along the harbour like **Anstruther**, between Crail and Pittenweem.

Anstruther
ANSTRUTHER is home to the wonderfully unpretentious **Scottish Fisheries Museum** (May–Sept Mon–Sat 9.30am–5.30pm, Sun 2–5pm; £2.50), quite in keeping with the no-frills integrity of the area in general. Set in a complex of sixteenth- to nineteenth-century buildings on a total of 18 different floors, it chronicles the history of the fishing and whaling industries in ingenious displays. Moored in the harbour outside is the **North Carr Lightship** (Easter–Oct daily 11am–5pm; £1.40), which for almost 45 years served off Fife Ness. Have a look around to get a feeling of life on

---

SCOTLAND'S SECRET BUNKER

Inland between St Andrews and Anstruther on the B940 (bus #61 takes you to within 2 miles of the bunker) is the idiosyncratic **Scotland's Secret Bunker** (April–Oct daily 10am–5pm; Nov–Easter weekends only; £4.75). Opened to the public in 1994, the bunker is just off the secrets list. Entrance is through an innocent-looking farmhouse then you walk down a vast ramp to the bunker, which is 100ft below ground and encased in 15ft of reinforced concrete. In the event of a nuclear war the bunker would have become Scotland's new administrative centre. From here, government and military commanders would have co-ordinated fire-fighting and medical help for Scotland (there are equivalent centres in England and Wales which aren't open to the public) from a switchboard room with 2800 phone lines. The bunker, which could house 300 people, was due to be equipped with air filters, a vast electricity generator and its own water supply; the best of 1950s technology, today it has a rather kitsch James Bond feel about it. The only concession to entertainment was a couple of cinemas, which now show Fifties newsreel giving painfully inadequate instructions to civilians in the event of nuclear war. Appropriately, the bunker has not been spruced up for tourists, and remains uncompromisingly spartan. Part of the complex is still operational, and remains secret.

---

board. A **tourist office** operates from the museum during the summer (May, June & Sept Mon–Sat 9.30am–5.30pm, Sun 11am–5pm; July & Aug Mon–Sat 9.30am–5.30pm; Sun 2–5pm).

The current lighthouse, erected in 1816 by Robert Louis Stevenson's grandfather, is several miles offshore from Anstruther on the rugged **Isle of May**, where you can also see the remains of Scotland's first lighthouse, built in 1636, which burned coals as a beacon. The island is now a nature reserve and bird sanctuary, and can be reached by boat from Anstruther (May–Sept; ☎01333/310103; one sailing per day; £9). Between April and July the dramatic sea cliffs are covered with breeding kittiwakes, razorbills, guillemots and shags, while inland there are thousands of puffins and eider duck. Grey seals also make the occasional appearance. Check up on departure times, as crossings vary according to weather and tide, and allow between four and five hours for a round trip: an hour each way, and a couple of hours there. Take plenty of warm, waterproof clothing.

At the end of a graceful avenue of trees, **Kellie Castle** (April–Oct daily 1.30–5.30pm; £3; garden and grounds all year daily 9.30am–sunset; £1), a couple of miles northeast of Anstruther on the B9171, has an unusual but harmonious mix of twin sixteenth-century towers linked by a seventeenth-century building. Abandoned in the early nineteenth century, the castle was discovered in 1878 by Professor James Lorimer, the distinguished political philosopher, who took on the castle as an "improving tenant". The Professor, his artist wife and their children restored the building and made it their home; the family atmosphere evident in an upstairs nursery crammed with Victorian toys. The wonderful gardens, where space is broken up by arches, alcoves and paths which weave between profuse herbaceous borders, were designed by the Professor's son Robert aged just sixteen. Later Sir Robert Lorimer, he became a well-known architect specializing in restorations and war memorials; among his restoration works is the Hill of Tarvit in Cupar (see p.234).

You may choose to **stay** in Anstruther, a pretty and peaceful base for exploring the surrounding area. There are plenty of good **B&Bs**; try the lovely *Hermitage Guest House* (☎01333/310909; ③) on Ladywalk; the *Beaumont Lodge Guest House* (☎01333/310315; ②) and *The Spindrift* (☎01333/310573), both on Pittenweem Rd; or *The Sheiling* (☎01333/310697; ②) at 32 Glenogil Gardens. There is a **campsite** nearby at Crail, the *Sauchope Links* (☎01337/450460). There is a fine **fish restaurant** in Anstruther, the *Cellar* (☎01333/310378), in one of the village's oldest buildings, once a cooperage and smokehouse.

The Tay coast

Looking across to Dundee and Perthshire, the **Tay coast**, a peaceful wedge of rural hinterland on the edge of the River Tay, offers little in the way of specific attractions, but a lot of undiscovered hideaways. Gentle hills fringe the shore, sheltering the villages – several of which only acquired running water and street lights in the past decade or two – that lie in the dips and hollows along the coast.

LEUCHARS, five miles north of St Andrews, is known for its RAF base, from where low-flying jets screech over the hills, appearing out of nowhere and sending sheep, cows and horses galloping for shelter. There is a beautiful twelfth-century church in the village, with fine Norman stonework. Romantic **Earlshall Castle** (private), just east of Leuchars, is the home of the Baron and Baroness of Earlshall, whose ancestor, Sir William Bruce, built the castle in 1546.

Northeast of Leuchars, **Tentsmuir Forest** occupies the northeasternmost point of the Fife headland, and is also a nature reserve with a good beach and peaceful wood-land walks – so peaceful that you would never guess it's only five miles or so from the **Tay bridges** and Dundee just the other side (80p toll charge on the road bridge). The current Tay **rail bridge** is the second to span the river on this spot, the first having collapsed in a terrifying disaster during a storm on December 28, 1879, which claimed the lives of around 100 people in a train crossing the bridge at the time. The event was recorded by the poet, William McGonagall, who has gone down in history as being responsible for some of the most banal verse ever written, including some memorably trite rhyme about the disaster:

> *So the train mov'd slowly along the Bridge of Tay,*
> *Until it was about midway,*
> *Then the central girders with a crash gave way,*
> *And down went the train and passengers into the Tay!*
> *The storm Fiend did loudly bray,*
> *Because ninety lives had been taken away,*
> *On the last Sabbath day of 1879,*
> *Which will be remember'd for a very long time.*

There's a **camping** and **caravan** site at **TAYPORT**, a popular resort a couple of miles east of the bridge, from where one of Scotland's oldest ferries once ran across the river. Here the "silvery Tay" more than justifies this traditional description, shimmering in the light whatever the season. There are good views across the river from the shingly cove at **BALMERINO**, a quaint hamlet five miles further on, just below the ruin of **Balmerino Abbey** (daily dawn–dusk), surrounded by venerable old trees, including an enormous gnarled Spanish chestnut, which has stood here for four centuries. The Cistercian abbey was founded in 1229 by Alexander II and his mother Ermengarde, who is buried here, and built by monks from the abbey at Melrose in the Borders. Destroyed by the English in 1547, reconstruction work was halted for good by the Reformation. Unfortunately, the only substantial part of the remains is unsafe and inaccessible.

Lindores Abbey, seven miles or so further west along the coast, dates from the century before and was a Benedictine settlement. The west tower still stands, silhouet-ted against the sky, and there are views down to nearby **NEWBURGH**, stunning on a summer evening, with the setting sun lighting up the mud flats below and skimming across the Tay. Newburgh itself is a fairly quiet, slightly rough-edged place. Originally a fishing village, it evolved due to its proximity to the abbey, and is now known for the admirable **Laing Museum** (April–Sept Mon–Fri 11am–6pm, Sat & Sun 2–5pm; Oct–March Wed & Thurs noon–4pm, Sun 2–5pm; free). The collection, donated by the banker and historian Dr Alexander Laing in 1892, includes a fine array of antiques and geological specimens gathered in the area.

PERTH AND THE HIGHLANDS

Genteel **Perthshire**, although now officially part of Perthshire and Kinross, still retains its own identity: an area of scenic valleys and glens, rushing rivers, and peaceful lochs, it's the long-established domain of Scotland's country-club set. First settled over 8000 years ago, it was taken by the Romans and then the Picts, before Celtic missionaries established themselves here, enjoying the amenable climate, fertile soil and ideal defensive and trading location.

The hub of the region is the port of **Perth**, which for centuries has benefited from its inland position on the River Tay. Salmon, wool and, by the sixteenth century, whisky – *Bell's, Dewar's* (which has now moved to Glasgow) and the *Famous Grouse* whiskies all hail from this area – were exported from here, while a major import was Bordeaux claret. Today, perhaps Perth's greatest attraction is the wonderful **Fergusson Gallery**.

A place of magnificent beauty, where the snowcapped peaks of soaring mountains fall away down forested slopes to long, deep lochs on the valley floor, the area is dominated by the western **Grampian Mountains**, a mighty range that controls transport routes, influences the weather and tolerates little development. The **Breadalbane Mountains** run between **Loch Tay** and **Loch Earn**; as well as providing walking and watersports, the area is dotted with fine towns and villages, like **Aberfeldly** at the western tip of Loch Tay and **Dunkeld** with its eighteenth-century whitewashed cottages and elegant ruined cathedral. Among the wealth of historical sites in Perthshire are the splendid Baronial **Blair Castle** north of Pitlochry, and the breathtaking Italianate gardens at **Drummond Castle** near Crieff.

Transport connections in the region are at their best if you head straight north from Perth, along the train line to Inverness, but buses – albeit often infrequent – also trail the more remote areas. Keep asking at bus stations for details of services, as the further you get from the main villages the less definitive timetables become.

Perth

Surrounded by fertile agricultural land and beautiful scenery, **PERTH** was for several centuries Scotland's capital. Viewed from the hills to the south, Perth still justifies Sir Walter Scott's glowing description of it in the opening pages of his novel *The Fair Maid of Perth*. Scott writes of approaching Perth from the south:

> . . . *the town of Perth with its two large measures or inches, its steeples and towers; the hills of Moncreiff and Kinnoul faintly rising into picturesque rocks, partly clothed with woods; the rich margin of the river studded with elegant mansions; and the huge Grampian Mountains, the northern screen of this exquisite landscape.*

During the reign of James I, Parliament met here on several occasions, but its glory was short-lived: the king was murdered in the town's Dominican priory in 1437 by the traitorous Sir Robert Graham, who was captured in the Highlands and tortured to death in Stirling. During the Reformation, on May 11, 1559, John Knox preached a rousing sermon in St John's Church, which led to the destruction of the town's four monasteries (by those Knox later condemned as "the rascal mulititude") and quickened the pace of reform in Scotland. Despite decline in the seventeenth century, the community expanded in the eighteenth and has prospered ever since – today it is a finance centre, and still an important and bustling market town. Its long history in **livestock trading** is continued throughout the year, notably with the Aberdeen Angus shows and sales in February and October, and the Perthshire Agricultural Show; and grain, malt and timber are still shipped out regularly from the harbour at the southern end of town.

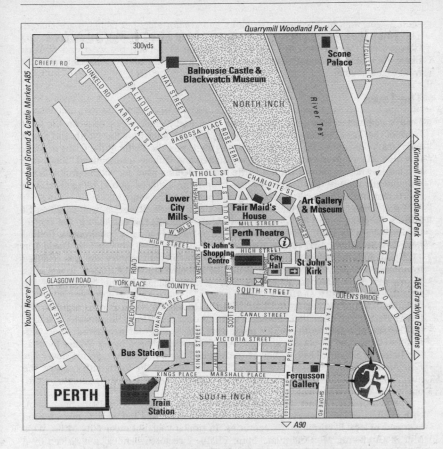

Arrival, information and accommodation

Perth is on the main train lines north from Edinburgh and Glasgow and is well connected by bus; the **bus** and **train stations** are on opposite sides of the road at the west end of town where Kings Place runs into Leonard St. The **tourist office**, 45 High St (Mon–Sat 9am–5pm; ☎01738/638353), is a ten-minute walk away.

Of the numerous **hotels** in Perth's town centre, try the *Station Hotel*, on Leonard St (☎01738/624141; ⑤), right by the station, or *Stakis Perth*, West Mill St (☎01783/628281; ⑥). The *Salutation Hotel*, 34 South St (☎01738/630066; ④), claims – not without some justification – to be one of Scotland's oldest hotels, having been established in 1699. Large-scale refurbishment in 1992 has left the place spick-and-span.

There are **B&Bs** and guest houses all over town, notably on the approach roads from Crieff and Stirling. In the centre, Marshall Place, overlooking the South Inch, is the place to look. Of the many possibilities along here *Kinnaird House*, 5 Marshall Place (☎01738/628021; ③) offers a warm welcome in a lovely town house, with well-equipped en-suite rooms. In an elegant Georgian terrace facing the park is the *Park Lane Guest House*, 17 Marshall Place (☎01738/637218; ③). On the other side of the river, at *Ballabeg*, 14 Keir St (☎01738/620434; ②), you'll feel like one of the family as soon as you walk in. Rooms are spacious and comfortable, but facilities are shared. The **youth hostel** is housed in an impressive old mansion with 64 rooms at 107 Glasgow Rd (March–Oct; ☎01738/623658; Grade 1) beyond the west end of York Place. Its a fair walk from the bus station – if you've got a heavy rucksack you might want to take bus #7.

The Town

Perth's compact **centre** occupies a small area, easily explored on foot, on the west bank of the Tay. Two large areas of green parkland, known as the North and South Inch, flank the centre. The **North Inch** was the site of the Battle of the Clans in 1396, in which 30 men from each of the clans Chattan and Quhele (pronounced "Kay") met in a battle, while the **South Inch** was the public meeting place for witch-burning in the seventeenth century. Both are now used for more civilized public recreation, with sports matches to the north, and boating and putting to the south.

A good variety of shops line **High Street** and **South Street**, as well as filling **St John's** shopping centre on King Edward Street. Opposite the entrance to the centre, the imposing **City Hall**, is used by Scotland's politicians for party conferences. Behind here lies **St John's Kirk** (daily 10am–noon & 2–4pm; free), founded by David I in 1126, although the present building dates from the fifteenth century and was restored to house a war memorial chapel designed by Robert Lorimer in 1923–8. It was in St John's that John Knox preached his fiery sermon calling for the "purging of the churches from idolatry" in 1559.

In the north of the centre, the **Fair Maid's House**, on North Port, is arguably the town's best-known attraction, although you can only see it from the outside. Standing on the site of a thirteenth-century monastery, this cottage of weathered stone with small windows and an outside staircase was the setting chosen by Sir Walter Scott as the house of Simon Glover, father of the virginal Catherine Glover, in his novel *The Fair Maid of Perth*. Set in turbulent times at the close of the fourteenth century, the novel tells a traditional story of love, war and revenge, centring on the attempts by various worthies to win the hand of Catherine.

The nearby **Art Gallery and Museum** on George St (Mon–Sat 10am–5pm; free), with exhibits on local history, art, natural history, archeology and whisky, gives a good overview of local life through the centuries. In similar vein, at **Lower City Mills**, West Mill St (April–Aug Mon–Sat 10am–5pm; £1.50), a restored oatmeal mill driven by a massive waterwheel recalls Victorian Perth. The Round House, a domed circular structure on Marshall Place at the edge of the Tay, used to house the waterworks, and is the unlikely setting for the excellent **Fergusson Gallery**. The gallery holds a collection of the paintings, drawings and sculpture of J D Fergusson, the foremost artist of the Scottish "Colourist" movement. Changing and imaginative exhibitions explore Fergusson's preoccupation with light and the sea, and his relationships with fellow modernists. His lifelong companion was the dancer and painter Margaret Morris; her summer schools, held annually for 40 years, provided Fergusson with models and inspired his monumental paintings of bathers, in pure bright colours.

North of the town centre, and adjacent to the North Inch, the elegantly restored Georgian terraces beyond the Fair Maid's House give way to newer buildings, which have gradually encroached on the former territory of the fifteenth-century **Balhousie Castle**, off Hay St (May–Sept Mon–Sat 10am–4.30pm; Oct–April Mon–Fri 10am–3.30pm; free). The castle sits incongruously in a peaceful residential area and has been restored in Scots Baronial style with turrets and crow-stepped gables. Originally the home of the Earls of Kinnoull, who have lent their name to Kinnoull Hill across the Tay to the east of Perth, it now houses the headquarters and **museum of the Black Watch**. This historic regiment – whose name refers to the dark colour of their tartan –

was formed in 1739, having been built up by General Wade earlier in the century, who employed groups of Highlanders to keep the peace. The museum chronicles its history through a good display of paintings, uniforms, documents, weapons and photographs.

A number of attractions lie around Perth. A mile north of Perth on the A9, in the Inveralmond Industrial Estate, is the **Caithness Glass** factory (April–Oct Mon–Sat 9am–5pm, Sun 11am–5pm; Nov–March Mon–Sat 9am–5pm, Sun noon–5pm; free); there is a viewing area where you can watch glass-blowing (take bus #5, #6 or #10 from Mill St in Perth).

For outdoor distractions, head for **Bell's Cherrybank Gardens** (May–Oct daily 9am–5pm; £1), a mile west of the centre, where you'll find 18 acres of well-kept gardens, including the largest collection of heathers in Britain, interspersed with a waterfall, pools, aviary and children's play area. If it's a fine day, this is a good place to bring the children. On the other side of the Tay, the **Branklyn Gardens**, Dundee Rd (March–Oct daily 9.30am–sunset; NTS; £2), comprise an astonishing collection of Alpine plants and dwarf rhododendrons, spread across a compact two acres of hillside. Looking over the gardens from the north is **Kinnoull Hill**, which also offers splendid views of Perth, the Tay and the surrounding area from its 783ft summit (a 20-min walk from the car park on Braes Rd). Pick up a leaflet from Perth's tourist office for details of the hill's various woodland walks.

Eating and drinking

There's a fair selection of decent **eating places** in Perth: many ethnic restaurants and pubs offer cheap and satisfying food and there are several upmarket options. Within striking distance of the youth hostel is a good basic Indian restaurant, the *Café Kamran*, 13 York Place. The *Good Luck Food Palace*, 181 South St, serves well-priced Chinese cuisine. *Pierre Victoire*, 38 South St (☎01738/444222), has cheap and cheerful French food. The best choice for a classier meal is *Number Thirty Three*, 33 George St (☎01738/633771), a stylish fish restaurant with Art Deco decor; whose oyster bar serves delicious snacks, while the à la carte restaurant has more substantial fish dishes and good puds. *Strangeways*, 24 George St, is a popular bar and bistro. A new Irish **pub** in the town centre, *Mucky Mulligans*, 97 Canal St, claims to be the first "Dublin cottage-style" pub in Scotland and serves specialities like Irish stew all day; every night there's live Irish folk music. Nearby, *Twa Tams*, on Scott St, has inexpensive meals and regular live music. There are numerous little **coffee shops** in town like *Brambles*, 11 Princes St, and *Willows*, 12 St John's Place.

North of Perth

Just a couple of miles north of Perth (along the A93; bus #7 from South St in Perth every 20min, or #26 and #46 every hour) on the eastern side of the Tay, **Scone Palace** (pronounced "Scoon") is worth every penny of the admission charge levied by its owners, the Earl and Countess of Mansfield, whose family has owned it for almost four centuries (mid-April to mid-Oct daily 9.30am–5pm; £4.50). The two-storey building is stately but not overpowering; it is far more a home than an untouchable monument, and the rooms, although full of priceless antiques and lavish furnishings, feel lived in and used.

Restored in the nineteenth century, the palace today consists of a sixteenth-century core surrounded by earlier buildings, most built of red sandstone, complete with battlements and the original gateway. The abbey that stood here in the sixteenth century, and where all Scottish kings until James I were crowned, was one of those destroyed following John Knox's sermon in Perth. In the extensive grounds which surround the palace lies the Moot Hill, which was once the site of the famous Coronation **Stone of Destiny** (see overleaf).

THE STONE OF DESTINY

Legend has it that the Stone of Destiny (also called the Stone of Scone) was "Jacob's Pillow", on which he dreamed of the ladder of angels from earth to heaven. Its real history is obscure, but it is known that it was moved from Ireland to Dunadd by missionaries, and thence to Dunstaffnage, from where Kenneth MacAlpine, king of the Dalriada Scots, brought it to the abbey at Scone in 838. There it remained for almost 500 years, used as a coronation throne on which all Kings of Scotland were crowned.

In 1296, an overeager Edward I stole what he believed to be the Stone and installed it at Westminster Abbey. Apart from a brief interlude in 1950, when Scottish nationalists stole it back again and hid it in Arbroath for several months, it has been there ever since.

Speculation surrounds the authenticity of the Stone at Westminster, for the original is said to have been intricately carved, while the one seen today is a plain block of sandstone. Many believe that the canny monks at Scone palmed this off onto the English king and that the real Stone of Destiny lies hidden in an underground chamber, its whereabouts a mystery to all but a chosen few.

Inside, a good selection of sumptuous rooms are open to visitors, including the library, which has exchanged its books in favour of an outstanding collection of porcelain, one of the foremost in the world, with items by Meissen, Sèvres, Chelsea, Derby and Worcester. Look out too for the beautiful papier-mâché travelling dishes, Marie-Antoinette's writing desk, and John Zoffany's exquisite eighteenth-century portrait of the *Lady Elizabeth Murray* [daughter of the second earl] *with Dido*. You could easily spend at least a morning here, enjoying the gardens with strutting peacocks, a fenced-off area with Highland cattle, picnic spot, donkey park, children's playground and a grand and fragrant pine garden, which was planted in 1848 with exotic conifers.

Huntingtower Castle

Not quite as grand as Scone, but nonetheless worth a visit, is **Huntingtower Castle** (April–Sept Mon–Sat 9.30am–6.30pm, Sun 2–6.30pm; Oct–March Mon–Wed & Sat 9.30am–4.30pm, Sun 2–4.30pm; £1.50), three miles northwest of Perth (on the A85; bus #15 from Scott St in Perth). Two three-storey towers formed the original fifteenth- and sixteenth-century tower house, and these were linked in the seventeenth century by a range to provide more room. Formerly known as Ruthven Castle, it was here that the Raid of Ruthven took place in 1582, when the 16-year-old James VI, at the request of William, fourth Earl of Ruthven, came to the castle only to be held captive by a group of conspirators demanding the dismissal of favoured royal advisers. The plot failed and the young James was released ten months later. Today the castle's chief attractions are its splendid sixteenth-century painted walls and ceilings – you'll see them in the main hall in the east tower.

Dunkeld and Birnam

DUNKELD, 12 miles further on up the A9 (trains from Perth to Inverness stop here; buses #23 & #24, Sun #22 & #34), was proclaimed Scotland's ecclesiastical capital by Kenneth MacAlpine in 850. Its position at the southern boundary of the Grampian Mountains made it a favoured meeting place for Highland and Lowland cultures, but in 1689 it was burned to the ground by the Cameronians – fighting for William of Orange – in an effort to flush out troops of the Stuart monarch, James VII. Subsequent rebuilding, however, has created one of the area's most delightful communities, and it's well worth at least a brief stop to view its whitewashed houses and historic cathedral. The **tourist office** is at The Cross in the town centre (April–June Mon–Sat 9.30am–5.30pm, Sun 11am–4pm; July & Aug Mon–Sat 9am–7.30pm, Sun 11am–7pm; Sept & Oct Mon–Sat 9.30am–5.30pm, Sun 11am–4pm; Nov & Dec Mon–Sat 9.30am–1.30pm; ☎01350/727688).

Dunkeld's partly ruined **cathedral** is on the northern side of town, in an idyllic setting amid lawns and trees on the east bank of the Tay. Construction began in the early twelfth century and continued throughout the next 200 years, but the building was more or less ruined at the time of the Reformation. The present structure, in Gothic and Norman style, consists of the fourteenth-century choir and the fifteenth-century nave. The choir, restored in 1600 (and several times since), now serves as the parish church, while the nave remains roofless apart from the clock tower. Inside, note the leper's peep near the pulpit in the north wall, through which lepers could receive the sacrament without contact with the congregation. Also look out for the great effigy of "The Wolf of Badenoch", Robert II's son born in 1343. The wolf acquired his name and notoriety when, after being excommunicated from the Church for leaving his wife, he took his revenge by burning the towns of Forres and Elgin and sacking Elgin cathedral. He eventually repented, did public penance for his crimes and was absolved by his brother Robert III.

Dunkeld is linked to its sister community, **BIRNAM**, by Thomas Telford's seven-arched bridge of 1809. This little village has a place in history thanks to Shakespeare, for it was on "Dunsinane Hill" to the southeast of the village that Macbeth declared: "I will not be afraid of death and bane/Till Birnam Forest come to Dunsinane", only to be told by a messenger:

> *As I did stand my watch upon the Hill,*
> *I look'd toward Birnam, and anon me thought*
> *The Wood began to move ...*

The **Perthshire Visitor Centre** just south of Birnam, down the A9 at Bankfoot (March–Sept daily 9am–6pm; £2) offers "The Macbeth Experience", which encompasses – on film and through talking dummies – bloodshed, ghosts and an untimely death. Several centuries later another literary personality, Beatrix Potter, drew inspiration from the area, recalling her childhood holidays here when penning the *Peter Rabbit* stories. The new **Beatrix Potter Garden** (open to the public) in Birnam celebrates the connection.

There are plenty of places to stay in Dunkeld, including some large **hotels**: the *Atholl Arms Hotel* (☎01350/727219; ④), the *Royal Dunkeld* (☎01350/727322; ④), and the Victorian Gothic *Birnam Hotel* (☎01350/727462; ⑦), all in the village. Just to the north, the luxurious *Stakis Dunkeld* (☎01350/727771; ⑨) is set at the end of a long drive which winds through the hotel's lush estate, where you can fish, shoot, cycle and stroll. For **B&B**, try the pretty *Birnam Bank Cottage* (☎01350/727201; ②), Birnam Glen, Dunkeld, or *The Top Inn* (☎01350/727699; ②), Birnam. There are a few mediocre **eating places** on Dunkeld's main street; the best food options are lunch at the *Atholl Arms* or a more expensive dinner at the *Stakis Dunkeld*.

Driving north on the A9 to Pitlochry, you can stop off and walk the mile and a half to **The Hermitage** (also buses from Perth to Pitlochry stop near here), set in the wooded gorge of the River Braan. This pretty eighteenth-century folly, also known as Ossian's Hall, was once mirrored to reflect the water, but the mirrors were smashed by Victorian vandals, and the folly more tamely restored. The hall, appealing yet incongruous in its splendid setting, neatly frames a dramatic waterfall.

Strathearn

Strathearn – the valley of the River Earn – stretches west of Perth, across to **Loch Earn** and the watersports centre at **Lochearnhead**. Agricola was here around 2000 years ago, trying to establish a foothold in the Highlands; later the area was frequented by Bonnie Prince Charlie and Rob Roy, both bound up in the north–south struggle between Highlands and Lowlands.

South of Strathearn, the small town of **AUCHTERARDER** sees its fair share of visitors, many of whom come to play golf (for more on the game see p.238) at the swanky **Gleneagles Hotel** nearby (☎01764/662231; ⑨). There is a **tourist office** on High St (April–Oct Mon–Sat 9.30am–5.30pm, Sun 11am–4pm; Nov–March Mon–Fri 9.30am–1.30pm; ☎01764/663450). As well as the local bus service, the **Loch Earn Trundler**, a classic 1950s bus, links Callander, Lochearnhead, Comrie and Crieff, and the **Loch Tay Trundler** runs from Callander to Lochearnhead, Kenmore and Aberfeldy (for details call ☎01786/442707). These are the only buses which connect Loch Earn with the rest of the valley.

Dunning

Just southeast of the valley, it is worth taking a detour from the busy A9 to the quiet village of **DUNNING**, five miles east of Auchterarder on the B8062, which has an impressive history. The village was once the capital of the Picts and was the place where Kenneth I, King of the Picts and Scots, died in 860. Dunning was destroyed by the Jacobites and subsequently rebuilt, which accounts for its homogeneous appearance, the houses all being late eighteenth and early nineteenth century. **St Serf's** survived, a rugged church with a Norman tower and arch. Just west of the village is an extraordinary monument, a pile of stones surmounted by a cross, and scrawled with the words: *Maggie Wall, Burnt here, 1657*. Maggie Wall was burned as a witch, and the rumour is that local women replenish the white writing on the monument every year; you may suspect the local tourist board, but something uncanny and uncompromising about the monument suggests otherwise.

Crieff and around

At the heart of the valley is the old spa town of **CRIEFF**, which lies in a lovely position on a south-facing slope of the Grampian foothills. Cattle traders used to come here in the eighteenth century, since this was a good location – between Highland and Lowland – for buying and selling livestock, but Crieff really came into its own with the arrival of the railway in 1856. Shortly after that, Morrison's Academy, now one of Scotland's most respected schools, took in its first pupils, and in 1868 the grand old *Crieff Hydro* (☎01764/655555; ⑨), then known as the *Strathearn Hydropathic*, opened its doors – still the nicest place to stay in town, despite being dry (of alcohol). Cheaper **B&B** options are *Greenhead House*, 52 Burrell St (☎01764/654603; ②), and the comely *Bank Guest House*, 32 Burrell St (☎01764/653409; ②). There's a pleasing mixture of Edwardian and Victorian houses, with a busy little centre which still retains something of the atmosphere of the former spa town. The **Crieff Visitor Centre** (daily 9.30am–5pm) is a "craftsy" place, crammed with pottery and paperweights. The **tourist office** is in the town hall on High St (Mon–Sat 9.30am–5pm, Sun 11am–4pm; Nov–March Mon–Fri 9.30am–5pm, Sat 9.30am–noon; ☎01764/652578).

From Crieff, it's a short drive or a walk (20min) to the **Glenturret Distillery** (March–Dec Mon–Sat 9.30am–6pm, Sun noon–6pm, last tour 4.30pm; Jan & Feb Mon–Fri 11.30am–4pm, last tour 2.30pm; free), just off the A85 to Comrie. To get there on public transport, catch any bus going to Crieff, Comrie or St Fillans and ask the driver to drop you at the bottom of the Glenturret Distillery road, from where it's a five-minute walk. This is Scotland's oldest distillery, established in 1775, and a good one to visit, if only for its splendid isolation. Four miles southeast of Crieff on the B8062 (Crieff/Auchterarder bus) is the **Innerpeffray Library** (Mon–Sat 10am–12.45pm, 2–4.45pm, Sun 2–6pm; Oct–March closed Thurs; £1.50). Founded in 1691, it is the oldest library in Scotland, and is a must for bibliophiles, with mainly theological and classical books.

If you enjoy ornate gardens, on no account miss the **Drummond Castle Gardens** near Muthill, two miles south of Crieff on the A822 (bus #17 from Crieff towards Muthill, then a mile and a half walk up the castle drive). The approach to the garden is extraordinary, up a dark avenue of trees; crossing the courtyard of the castle to the grand terrace, you can view the garden in all its symmetrical glory. It was laid out by John Drummond, second earl of Perth, in 1630, and shows clear French and Italian influence, although the central structural feature of the parterre is a St Andrews cross. Italian marble statues punctuate the long lines of the cross, and the overall effect is of exceptional harmony and grace. The castle itself (closed to the public) is a wonderful mixture of architectural styles. There is a blunt fifteenth-century keep on a rocky crag, adjoining a much modified Renaissance mansion house.

Comrie

COMRIE, a pretty conservation village another five miles along the River Earn, has the dubious distinction of being the location where more seismic tremors have been recorded than anywhere else in Britain, due to its position on the Highland Boundary Fault. Earthquake readings are still taken at **Earthquake House**, about 600 yards off the A85, on the south side of the river. The building itself is not open to the public, but there are information panels outside, and if you're really keen you can look through the windows at a model of the world's first seismometer, set up here in 1874.

If you've got children with you, an excellent place to take them is the **Auchingarrich Wildlife Centre** (daily 10am–dusk; £3.50), a couple of miles south of Comrie on the B827 (bus #15 from Crieff to Comrie, then a 2-mile walk). Recently established in a blustery hillside location, it covers 100 acres and provides lots of opportunities to pet the farm animals and admire the rare and ornamental birds.

Loch Earn

At the eastern edge of Strathearn is **Loch Earn**, a gently lapping Highland loch dramatically edged by mountains. The A85 runs north along the lochshore from the village of **ST FILLANS**, at the eastern tip, to the main settlement, **LOCHEARNHEAD**, at the western edge of the loch. This wide tranquil expanse of water is ideal for **watersports**, and perfect for beginners. *Lochearnhead Watersports* (☎01567/830330) organizes and teaches a wide variety of activities, including water-skiing, windsurfing, Canadian canoeing, kayaks and jet-biking. You can also rent **mountain bikes** here. Lochearnhead is also a good base for **walking**, and the water-sports centre runs "heritage rambles". For **accommodation** try the *Clachan Cottage Hotel* (☎01567/830247; ⑤), and for B&B *Earnknowe* (☎01567/830238; ③) with a cara-van to let in the grounds for around £120 per week. There are some good **self-catering** options in Lochearnhead: from *Earnknowe* you can rent attractive stone cottages in the village (2–6 people; around £280 per week). There are also Scandinavian-style wooden chalets (☎01567/830211) with very good facilities (sleep 6; around £250 per week). A nice little whitewashed cottage (☎0131/313 0467 or 01764/670004) can be rented in St Fillans for around £220 weekly. Perhaps the best choice for the area as a whole though, is the chalet-like *Four Seasons Hotel* (☎01764/685333; ⑥) in St Fillans with a wonderful lochside location. It's also the best choice for **eating**; there are few other options in the area.

Around Loch Tay

The mountains and valleys of **Glenalmond**, north of Strathearn, give way to the 14-mile-long, freshwater **Loch Tay**, just north of which is moody **Ben Lawers** (3984ft), Perthshire's highest mountain; from the top there are incredible views towards both the Atlantic and the North Sea. The ascent – which should not be tackled without all the right equipment (see p.38) – takes around three hours from the NTS **visitor centre** (mid-April to Sept daily 10am–5pm; £1; ☎01567/820397), which is at 1300ft and reached by a track off the A827 along the northern side of the loch. The centre has an audio-visual show, slides of the mountain flowers – including the rare Alpine flora found here – and a nature trail with accompanying descriptive booklet.

The **mountains of Breadalbane** (pronounced "Bread-*al*bane"), named after the Earls of Breadalbane, loom over the southern end of Loch Tay. Glens Lochay and Dochart curve into the north and south respectively from the small town of **KILLIN**, where the River Dochart comes rushing out of the hills and down the frothy **Falls of Dochart**, before disgorging into Loch Tay. There's little to do in Killin itself, but it does make a convenient base for some of the area's best walks. One of the most appealing places to **stay** is the *Dall Lodge Hotel*, Main St (☎01567/820217; ②), which the owner, who lives in the Far East, has filled with all manner of exotic bits and pieces. The dining room serves fine local produce. There is also a **youth hostel** (April–Oct; ☎01567/820546; Grade 2), in a fine old country house just beyond the northern end of the village, with views out over the loch.

North of the loch

Beyond Breadalbane, the mountains tumble down into **Glen Lyon** – at 34 miles long the longest enclosed glen in Scotland – where, legend has it, the Celtic warrior Fingal built 12 castles. Access to the glen is usually impossible in winter, but the narrow roads are passable in summer. You can either take the road from Killin up to the **Ben Lawers Visitor Centre**, four miles up Loch Tay, and continue going, or take the road from Fortingall, which is a couple of miles north of the loch's northern end. The two roads join up, making a round trip possible, but bear in mind there is no road through the mountains to Loch Rannoch further north. **FORTINGALL** itself is little more than a handful of thatched cottages, although locals make much of their 3000-year-old yew tree – believed (by them at least) to be the oldest living thing in Europe. The village also lays claim to being the birthplace of Pontius Pilate, reputedly the son of a Roman officer stationed here.

On a slight promontory at Loch Tay's northern end and overlooking the River Tay, **KENMORE**'s whitewashed houses and well-tended gardens cluster around the gate to **Taymouth Castle** – built by the Campbells of Glenorchy in the early nineteenth century and now a private golf club. The village's sporting reputation is due partly to various boat rental places around this end of the loch, and also to **Croft-na-Caber** (☎01887/830588), an impressive **outdoor pursuits** complex on the southern bank of the loch, which offers water-skiing, fishing, hill walking, cross-country skiing, sledging and various forms of shooting. The complex also offers comfortable **accommodation** in either its own hotel (☎01887/830236; ⑤) or in well-equipped chalets overlooking the loch. You don't have to stay here to use the facilities, however, and tuition or equipment rental is available by the hour, half-day, full day or longer. As an example of prices, a day's sailing or windsurfing instruction costs around £40. You can also stay at the overwhelmingly Scottish *Kenmore Hotel*, in the village square (☎01887/830205; ⑤), which is the descendant of Scotland's oldest inn, established here in 1572. Even if you don't stay, stop off for a meal or drink.

Aberfeldy

A largely Victorian town six miles or so further on, **ABERFELDY** makes a good base for exploring the area. The **tourist office** at The Square in the town centre (April–June, Sept & Oct Mon–Sat 9.30am–5.30pm, Sun noon–4pm; July & Aug Mon–Sat 9am–7pm, Sun 11am–6pm; Nov–March Mon–Fri 9.30am–5.pm, Sat 9.30am–1pm; ☎01887/

820276) gives details of the so-called Locus Project, a local initiative which has devised a series of looped trails that take in all the main sights.

Aberfeldy sits at the point where the Urlar Burn – lined by the silver birch trees celebrated by Robert Burns in his poem *The Birks of Aberfeldy* – flows into the River Tay. The Tay is spanned by **Wade's Bridge**, built by General Wade in 1733 during his efforts to control the trouble in the Highlands, and, with its humpback and four arches, is regarded as one of the general's finest remaining crossing points. Overlooking the bridge from the south end is the **Black Watch Monument**, a pensive, kilted soldier, erected in 1887 to commemorate the peacekeeping troop of Highlanders gathered together by Wade in 1739.

The small town centre is a busy mixture of craft and tourist shops, its main attraction the superbly restored early-nineteenth-century **Aberfeldy Water Mill** (Easter–Oct Mon–Sat 10am–5.30pm, Sun noon–5.30pm; £1.80), a mill which harnesses the water of the Urlar to turn the wheel that stone-grinds the oatmeal in the traditional Scottish way.

One mile west of Aberfeldy, across Wade's Bridge, **Castle Menzies** (April to mid-Oct Mon–Fri 10.30am–5pm, Sun 2–5pm; £2.50) is an imposing, Z-shaped, sixteenth-century tower house, which until the middle of this century was the chief seat of the Clan Menzies. With the demise of the Menzies line the castle was taken over by the Menzies Clan Society, who since 1971 has been involved in the lengthy process of restoring it. Now the interior, with its wide stone staircase, is refreshingly free of fixtures and fittings, with structural attributes such as the plasterwork ceilings on show.

If you want to **stay** in Aberfeldy, *Moness House Hotel and Country Club*, Crieff Rd (☎01887/820446; ④) occupies a whitewashed country house and offers luxurious **self-catering** cottages, as well as fishing, golf and watersports. *Guinach House*, by the Birks (☎01887/820251; ⑦), in pleasant grounds near the famous silver birches, is a tastefully decorated house converted into a small hotel, with a good dining room. *Farleyer House* (☎01887/820332; ⑦), a mile out of Aberfeldy on the B846, is highly recommended as a hotel and **restaurant**. For B&B, try *Novar*, 2 Home St (☎01887/820779; ②) or *Marvis Bank*, Taybridge Drive (☎01887/820223; ②), both attractive stone cottages.

Pitlochry

Surrounded by hills just north of the confluence of the Tummel and Tay rivers at Ballinluig, **PITLOCHRY** spreads gracefully along the eastern shore of the Tummel, on the lower slopes of Ben Vrackie (see "Walks around Pitlochry" below). Even after General Wade built one of his first roads through here in the early eighteenth century, Pitlochry remained little more than a village. Queen Victoria's visit in 1842 helped to put the area on the map, but it wasn't until the end of the century that Pitlochry established itself as a popular holiday centre.

Today the busy main street is a constant flurry of traffic, locals and tourists. Beyond the train bridge at the southern end of the main street (Atholl Rd leading to Perth Rd) is Bells' **Blair Atholl Distillery**, Perth Rd (Oct–Easter Mon–Fri 9am–5pm; Easter–Sept also Sat 9am–5pm & Sun noon–4pm), where the excellent visitor centre illustrates the process involved in making the Blair Atholl Malt. Whisky has been produced on this site since 1798, in which time production has been stepped up to around two million litres a year, making this only a medium-sized distillery.

A perfect contrast to the Blair Atholl is the **Edradour Distillery** (March–Oct Mon–Sat 9.30am–5pm, Sun 2–5pm; Nov–Feb Mon–Sat 10.30am–4pm), Scotland's smallest, in an idyllic position tucked into the hills a couple of miles east of Pitlochry on the A924. A whistle-stop audio-visual presentation covering more than 250 years of production precedes the tour of the distillery itself.

On the western edge of Pitlochry, just across the river, lies Scotland's renowned "Theatre in the Hills", the **Pitlochry Festival Theatre** (season runs from Easter to early Oct; ☎01796/472680). Set up in 1951, the theatre started in a tent on the site of what is now the town curling rink, before moving to the banks of the river in 1981. Backstage tours, covering all aspects of theatre production (generally Thurs & Fri 2pm; £2.50; booking essential), run through the day, while a variety of productions – both mainstream and offbeat – are staged in the evening.

A short stroll upstream from the theatre is the **Pitlochry Power Station and Dam**, a massive concrete wall which harnesses the water of the man-made Loch Faskally, just north of the town, for hydro-electric power. Although the visitor centre (April–Oct daily 9.40am–5.30pm) explains the ins and outs of it all, the main attraction here, apart from the views up the loch, is the **salmon ladder**, up which the salmon leap on their annual migration – a sight not to be missed.

Practicalities

Access to Pitlochry is easy by public transport, thanks to its position on the main train line to Inverness, and regular buses running from Perth. The **bus** stop and the **train** station are on Station Rd, at the north end of town, ten minutes' walk from the centre and the **tourist office**, 22 Atholl Rd (Mon–Fri 9am–1pm & 2–5pm, Sat 9.30am–1.30pm; ☎01796/472215). The office has details of attractions in the surrounding area, and also offers an **accommodation** booking service.

Birchwood Hotel, E Moulin Rd (☎01796/472477; ⑥), occupies a lovely Victorian country house at the top of town, set in four acres of grounds, and has a particularly good restaurant. Close by, the friendly *Castlebeigh House*, 10 Knockard Rd (☎01796/472925; ④), has good views from the bedrooms. Further along the road, the magnificent and much pricier *Pitlochry Hydro*, Knockard Rd (☎01796/472666; ⑧) looks out over the Tummel Valley. At Tummel Bridge, the *Kynachan Lodge* (☎01882/634214; ⑥) is decorated with oriental *objets d'art* and bonsai trees and is a very good choice for food. In the town centre, there are a number of cheaper hotels along the main street, including the comfortable *McKays Hotel*, 138 Atholl Rd (☎01796/473888; ④), and many

---

WALKS AROUND PITLOCHRY

Ordnance Survey Landranger maps Nos. 43 & 52

Pitlochry is surrounded by good walking country. The biggest lure has to be **Ben Vrackie** (2733ft), which provides a stunning backdrop for the *Festival Theatre* and deserves better than a straight up-and-down walk; however, the climb should only be attempted in settled weather conditions, with the right equipment and following the necessary safety precautions (see p.38). A good "round" goes by quiet Loch Faskally to **Killiecrankie Visitor Centre** (refreshments available) and then heads up the hill by a seldom used route before returning via Moulin. Allow a full day for the complete walk.

Head through Pitlochry northwards and branch off to pass the *Green Hotel* and reach attractive Loch Faskally. Another time perhaps walk right round it; for now follow the shore and take the signs up the River Garry to go through the **Pass of Killiecrankie**. This is in the care of the NTS, which has a visitor centre with interpretive displays, books and souvenirs for sale, and a large-scale map showing some of the features for "next time". If you only want to go this far, allow a couple of hours.

From the NTS centre walk north up the old A9 and branch off on the small tarred road signposted **Old Faskally**; twisting up under the new A9 and past a house and the gates of Old Faskally. Keep on the tarred road till near the farm then turn off right and, shortly after, left over a cattle grid to go up beside a shelter belt of conifers. Starting with the cattle grid there must be half a dozen types of barrier to be faced before the open hillside is reached.

guest houses and **B&Bs**. Try *Craigroyston House*, 2 Lower Oakfield (☎01796/472053; ③), and *Comar House*, Strathview Terrace (☎01796/473531; ③). The **youth hostel** (☎01796/472308; Grade 1) is a fine stone mansion on Knockard Rd at the top of town.

Pitlochry is the domain of the tearoom and pitifully short of **restaurants** and pubs; the best option is the *Killiecrankie Hotel* (☎01796/473220) at Killiecrankie three miles north on the A9. The food is hearty and well priced. In town, try the very popular *Festival Theatre* or the nearby *Porthacraig Inn & Restaurant*, both of which have beautiful riverside locations.

Loch Tummel and Loch Rannoch

Between Pitlochry and Loch Ericht lies a sparsely populated, ever-changing panorama of mountains, moors, lochs and glens. Venturing into the hills is difficult without a car – unless you're walking – but infrequent local buses do run from Pitlochry to the outlying communities in the surrounding area, and the train to Inverness runs parallel to the A9.

West of Pitlochry, the B8019/B846 twists and turns along the Grampian mountainsides, overlooking **Loch Tummel** and then **Loch Rannoch**. These two lochs, celebrated by Harry Lauder in his famous song *The Road to the Isles*, are joined by Dunalastair Water, which narrows to become the River Tummel at the western end of the loch of the same name. This is a spectacular stretch of countryside and one which deserves leisurely exploration. **Queen's View** at the eastern end of Loch Tummel is a fabulous vantage point, looking down the loch across the hills to the misty peak of Schiehallion (3520ft), the "Fairy Mountain", whose mass was used in early experiments to judge the weight of the Earth. The Forestry Commission's **visitor centre** (April–Oct daily 9.30am–5pm; ☎01350/727284) interprets the fauna and flora of the area, and also has a café.

Beyond Loch Tummel, **KINLOCH RANNOCH** marks the eastern end of Loch Rannoch. This small community is popular with backpackers, who stock up at the local store before taking to the hills again; you can also **stay** at *Cuilmuir Cottage* (☎01882/

At the top end of the trees fork right, round the top of the field and through a gate. After about 50 yards, turn up and back, left, onto a lesser track to a gate at the top of the field (the road onwards ends at two small reservoirs). Go through the kissing gate and along to finally leave the cultivated land through the hill dyke.

The track zigzags up heathery pasture to an old wall and a gate in a fence just beyond: go through the gate then bear right across the open hillside, crossing the **Allt Eachainn**, the burn that drains this corrie, dominated by Ben Vrackie's summit cone, before heading up the hill opposite in another series of bends, clearly seen from below. Also visible from below is a footpath bearing off left as the slope steepens, which you should follow through the heather towards the pass. It goes over the saddle of a dark heathery prow and, 220 yards beyond, brings you to the pass looking down on **Loch a' Choire**. The tourist track from Pitlochry/Moulin (our way down) crosses below the dam of the loch and makes up the peak direct. The steep track can be seen from the col; skirt north of the loch to join this.

A summit view indicator helps to work out the confusion of hills in view. If the summit is windy Loch a' Choire may be a better place to picnic; or even to opt out of the last steep ascent. As Ben Vrackie is an isolated summit, weather can change quickly and clouds render route-finding difficult. The descent from Loch a' Choire is clearly pathed and runs across the moors to reach forest level. A stile crosses the fence into the birch and pine that leads down to a small car park. Follow the minor road from it down to the hamlet of **Moulin** and on to Pitlochry.

632218; ③). Part of the building is an eighteenth-century croft; the atmosphere is rustic and the food delicious. The road follows the loch to its end and then heads six miles further into the desolation of **Rannoch Moor**, where **Rannoch Station**, a lonely outpost on the Glasgow to Fort William West Highland train, marks the end of the line. The only way back is by the same road as far as Loch Rannoch, where it's possible – but not always advisable, depending on conditions – to return on a (very) minor road along the south side of the lochs. The round trip is roughly 70 miles.

Blair Atholl to Loch Ericht

Four miles north of Pitlochry, the A9 cuts through the **Pass of Killiecrankie**, a breathtaking wooded gorge which falls away to the River Garry below. This dramatic setting was the site of the **Battle of Killicrankie** in 1689, when the Jacobites quashed the forces of General Mackay. Legend has it that one soldier of the Crown, fleeing for his life, made a miraculous jump across the 18ft **Soldier's Leap**, an impossibly wide chasm halfway up the gorge. Queen Victoria, visiting here 160 years later, contented herself with recording the beauty of the area in her diary. Exhibits at the slick NTS **visitor centre** (April–Oct daily 10am–5.30pm; £1; ☎01796/473233) recall the battle and examine the gorge in detail.

Before leading the Jacobites into battle, Graham of Claverhouse, Viscount ("Bonnie") Dundee, had seized **Blair Castle** (April–Oct daily 10am–6pm; £5), three miles up the road at Blair Atholl. Seat of the Atholl dukedom, this whitewashed, turreted castle, surrounded by parkland and dating from 1269, presents an impressive sight as you approach up the drive. A piper may be playing in front of the castle: he is one of the Atholl Highlanders, a select group retained by the duke as his private army – a privilege afforded to him by Queen Victoria, who stayed here in 1844. Today the duke is the only British subject allowed to maintain his own force.

A total of 32 rooms are open for inspection, and display a selection of paintings, furniture, plasterwork and the like that is sumptous in the extreme, although the vast number of stuffed animals may be to everyone's liking. The Tapestry Room, on the top floor of the original Cumming's Tower, is hung with Brussels tapestries and contains an outrageous four-poster bed, topped with vases of ostrich feathers which originally came from the first duke's suite at Holyrood Palace in Edinburgh. The Ballroom, also, with its timber roof, antlers and melange of portraits, is Baronial Scotland at its best. The castle has a self-service restaurant.

Highland cows graze the ancient landscaped grounds and peacocks strut in front of the castle. There is a **riding stable** from where you can take treks and explore further. Formal woodland walks give artfully contrived vistas; a statue of Diana, half-glimpsed as you approach, stands at a confluence of wooded paths. Walled and neglected, the ruined Japanese water garden is fascinating. There is also a **caravan park** (☎01796/ 481263) in the grounds.

Beyond Blair Atholl, the A9 follows the line of **Glen Garry** and the River Garry through the Grampian Mountains. The road climbs continuously, sweeping past the eastern end of **Glen Errochty**, on towards the barren **Pass of Drummochter** and to the bleak little village of Dalwhinnie at the northern end of **Loch Ericht**. The scenery is marvellous all the way, but there is literally nothing here apart from the mountains and moors.

travel details

Trains

Falkirk Grahamston to: Edinburgh (every 30min; 35min); Glasgow Queen Street (every 30min; 25min); Linlithgow (every 30min; 13min).

Kirkcaldy to: Aberdeen (hourly; 2hr); Dundee (hourly; 40min or 1hr); Edinburgh (23 daily; 40min); Perth (7 daily; 40min); Pitlochry (4 direct daily; 1hr 15min; 4 indirect, change at Perth; 1hr 25min).

Linlithgow to: Edinburgh (hourly; 20min); Falkirk Grahamston (every 30min; 13min); Glasgow Queen Street (hourly; 30min).

Perth to: Aberdeen (hourly; 1hr 40min); Dundee (hourly; 25min); Edinburgh (9 daily; 1hr 25min); Glasgow Queen Street (hourly; 1hr 5min); Kirkcaldy (7 daily; 40min); Pitlochry (8 daily; 30min).

Pitlochry to: Edinburgh (5 daily; 2hr); Glasgow Queen Street (3 daily; 1hr 45min); Kirkcaldy (4 direct daily; 1hr 15min; 1 indirect, change at Perth; 1hr 45min); Perth (8 daily; 30min); Stirling (3 daily; 1hr 10min).

Stirling to: Aberdeen (hourly; 2hr 15min); Dundee (hourly; 1hr); Edinburgh (hourly; 1hr); Falkirk Grahamston (hourly; 28min); Glasgow Queen Street (hourly; 30min); Linlithgow (hourly; 35min); Perth (hourly; 30min); Pitlochry (5 daily; 1hr 15min).

Buses

Bo'ness to: Edinburgh (5 daily; 45min); Stirling (3 daily, 35min).

Dundee to: Glenrothes (7 daily; 1hr 10min); St Andrews (every 30 min; 35min); Kirkcaldy (7 daily; 1hr 35min); Stirling (9 daily; 1hr 30min).

Dunfermline to: Edinburgh (2 daily; 40min); Glenrothes (15 daily; 1hr 5min); Kirkcaldy (every 30min; 1hr); St Andrews (11 daily; 2hr).

Glenrothes to: Dundee (7 daily; 1hr 10min); Dunfermline (12 daily; 1hr 10min); Kirkcaldy (hourly; 20min); St Andrews (7 daily; 40min).

Kirkcaldy to: Dundee (16 daily; 1hr 10min); Dunfermline (hourly; 1hr); Glenrothes (hourly; 20min); St Andrews (16 daily; 50min).

Perth to: Dunblane (every 30 min; 35min); Dunfermline (every 30 min; 50min); Edinburgh (12 daily; 1hr 20min); Glasgow (20 daily; 1hr 35min); Gleneagles (12 daily; 25min); Inverness (3 daily; 2hr 30min); London (4 daily; 9hr); Stirling (18 daily; 50min).

St Andrews to: Dundee (every 30min; 40min); Dunfermline (Mon–Sat 13 daily; 1hr 40min); Edinburgh (12 daily; 2hr); Glasgow (6 daily; 2hr 50min); Glenrothes (hourly; 45min); Kirkcaldy (16 daily; 1hr); Stirling (6 daily; 2hr).

Stirling to: Aberfoyle (4 daily; 45min); Bo'ness (3 daily; 35 min); Callander (11 daily; 45min); Dollar (13 daily; 35min); Doune (14 daily; 30min); Dunblane (20 daily; 1hr 15min); Dundee (9 daily; 1hr 30min); Dunfermline (13 daily; 50min); Edinburgh (hourly; 1hr 35min); Falkirk (every 45min; 30min); Glasgow (34 daily; 1hr 10min); Gleneagles (16 daily; 30min); Inverness (2 daily; 3hr 30min); Killin (2 daily; 2hr); Linlithgow (hourly; 1hr); Lochearnhead (2 daily; 1hr 40min); Perth (15 daily; 50min); Pitlochry (2 daily; 1hr 30min); St Andrews (6 daily; 2hr).

CHAPTER FIVE

ARGYLL

C ut off for centuries from the rest of Scotland by the mountains and sea lochs that characterize the region, **Argyll** remains remote, its scatter of offshore islands forming part of the Inner Hebridean archipelago (the remaining Hebrides are dealt with in *Skye and the Western Isles*). Geographically, as well as culturally, this is a transitional area between Highland and Lowland, boasting a rich variety of scenery, from lush, subtropical gardens warmed by the Gulf Stream to flat and treeless islands far out in the Atlantic. It's in the folds and twists of the countryside and the views out to the islands, that the strengths and beauties of mainland Argyll lie

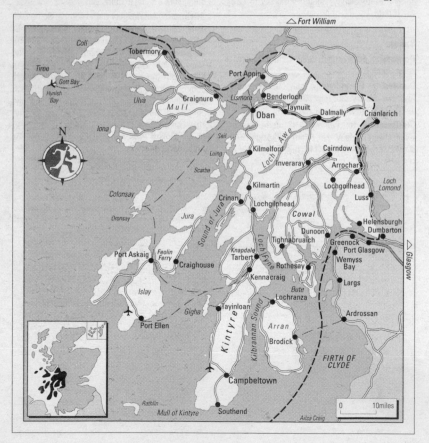

– the one area of man-made sights you shouldn't miss is the cluster of **Celtic and prehistoric sites** near Kilmartin. The overall population is tiny; even **Oban**, Argyll's main administrative centre and chief ferry port, has barely even a thousand inhabitants, while the prettiest, **Inveraray**, boasts a mere four hundred.

The eastern duo of **Bute** and **Arran** – once a separate county in their own right – are the most popular of Scotland's more southerly islands, the latter justifiably so, with spectacular scenery ranging from the granite peaks of the north to the Lowland pasture of the south. Of the Hebridean islands covered in this chapter, mountainous **Mull** is the most visited, though it is large enough to absorb the crowds, many of whom are only passing through en route to the tiny isle of **Iona**, a centre of Christian culture since the sixth century. **Islay**, best known for its distinctive malt whiskies, is fairly quiet even in the height of summer, as is neighbouring **Jura**, which offers excellent walking opportunities. And for those seeking still more solitude, there are the remote islands of **Tiree** and **Coll**, which, although swept with fierce winds, boast more sunny days than anywhere else in Scotland.

The region's name derives from *Aragàidheal*, which translates as "Boundary of the Gaels", the Irish Celts who settled here in the fifth century AD, and whose **kingdom of Dalriada** embraced much of what is now Argyll. Known to the Romans as *Scotti* – hence Scotland – it was the Irish Celts who promoted Celtic Christianity, and whose Gaelic language eventually became the national tongue. After a brief period of Norse invasion and settlement, the islands (and the peninsula of Kintyre) fell to the immensely powerful Somerled, who became King of the Hebrides and Lord of Argyll in the twelfth century. Somerled's successors, the MacDonalds, established Islay as their headquarters in the 1200s, but were in turn dislodged by Robert the Bruce. Of Bruce's allies, it was the **Campbells** who benefited most from the MacDonalds' demise, and eventually, as the dukes of Argyll, gained control of the entire area – even today they remain one of the largest landowners in the region.

In the aftermath of the Jacobite uprisings, the islands of Argyll, like the rest of the Highlands, were devastated by the **Clearances**, with thousands of crofters evicted from their homes in order to make room for profitable sheep-farming – "the white plague" – and cattle-rearing. Today the traditional industries remain under threat, leaving the region ever more dependent on tourism and a steady influx of new settlers to keep things going, while Gaelic, once the language of the majority in Argyll, retains only a tenuous hold on the outlying islands of Islay, Coll and Tiree – all officially part of Scotland's *Gàidhealtachd,* or Gaelic-speaking areas.

It's on Argyll's west coast that the unpredictability of the **weather** can really affect your holiday. If you can, avoid July and August when the crowds on Mull, Iona and

---

ACCOMMODATION PRICE CODES

Throughout this book, accommodation **prices** have been graded with the numbers below, according to the cost of the least expensive double room in high season. Although costs will rise slightly overall with the life of this edition, the relative comparisons should remain valid. The bulk of the recommendations will fall in categories ② to ⑥; those in the highest categories are limited to places that are especially attractive. Edinburgh will inevitably be more expensive than equivalent accommodation in the countryside or small towns, and a number of places will have a big mark-up for the three weeks of the Festival. Also bear in mind that many of the swanky hotels often slash their tariffs at the weekend when the business types have gone home, and that many of the cheaper places will also have more expensive rooms. Note that in our accommodation listings price codes are not given for youth hostels and campsites – they all come into the lower end of the ① category.

① under £20	④ £40–50	⑦ £70–80
② £20–30	⑤ £50–60	⑧ £80–100
③ £30–40	⑥ £60–70	⑨ over £100

Arran are at their densest – there's no guarantee the weather will be any better than during the rest of the year, when you might have more chance of avoiding the persistent Scottish midge (for more on which see p.18). And lastly, a word on **accommodation**: a large proportion of visitors to this part of Scotland come here for a week or two and stay in self-catering cottages. On some islands and in more remote areas, this is often the only accommodation available – in peak season, you should book several months in advance (for more on self-catering see p.28).

Gare Loch and Loch Long

Most people approach Argyll from Glasgow, from where there's a choice of two routes: the most popular is along Loch Lomond (see p.213); a quieter route (and the one which the train takes) is along the shores of **Gare Loch** and **Loch Long** to Arrochar, which marks the beginning of Argyll proper. Apart from Helensburgh, however, there's little to see along the shores of either loch. Both are littered with decaying industrial remains, including the nuclear submarine base at Faslane on Gare Loch and the oil tanks at Finnart on Loch Long. Only occasionally is it possible to glimpse the "unspeakably beautiful" landscape described by eighteenth-century travellers.

Helensburgh

HELENSBURGH, 20 miles or more northwest of Glasgow, is a smart, Georgian grid-plan settlement laid out in an imitation of Edinburgh's New Town. In the eighteenth century it was a well-to-do commuter town for Glasgow and a seaside resort, whose bathing-master, **Henry Bell**, invented one of the first steamboats, the *Comet*, to transport Glaswegians "doon the watter". Today Helensburgh is a stop on the route of the *Waverley*, the last sea-going paddle steamer in the world, which does a zigzag tour of the lochs of Argyll throughout the summer (pick up a timetable from the tourist office).

The inventor of TV, John Logie Baird, was born here, as was Charles Rennie Mackintosh, who in 1902 was commissioned by the Glaswegian publisher Walter Blackie to design **Hill House** (Easter–Dec daily 1.30–5.30pm; NTS; £2.80), on Upper Colquhoun St. Without doubt the best surviving example of Mackintosh's domestic architecture, the house – right down to light fittings – is stamped with his very personal interpretation of Art Nouveau, characterized by his sparing use of colour and stylized floral patterns. The effect is occasionally overwhelming – it's difficult to imagine actually living in such an environment – yet it is precisely Mackintosh's attention to detail that makes the place so special (for more on Mackintosh see p.172). After exploring the house, head for the kitchen quarters, which have been sensitively transformed into a tearoom.

Practicalities

Hill House is a good walk (20min) from Helensburgh Central train station, up Sinclair Street, or just five minutes from Helensburgh Upper train station (where the Oban and Fort William trains stop). The **tourist office** is on the ground floor of the clock tower by Gare Loch (April–Oct Mon–Fri 10am–4.30pm, Sat & Sun 10am–5pm; ☎01436/672642). **Accommodation** options include the luxurious *Commodore*, 112–117 West Clyde St (☎01436/676924; ⑤), or the smaller *Imperial*, at no. 12–14 (☎01436/676924; ③); there are also **B&Bs** such as *Kyra*, at no. 100 (☎01436/675576; ②), and *Ashfield*, 38 William St (☎01436/672259; ②).

Cowal and Bute

West of Helensburgh, the claw-shaped **Cowal peninsula**, formed by Loch Fyne and Loch Long, is the most visited part of Argyll. The landscape here is extremely varied, ranging from the Highland peaks of the Argyll Forest Park in the north, to the gentle low-lying coastline of the southwest, but most visitors confine themselves to the area around **Dunoon** (which has Cowal's only tourist office) in the east, leaving the rest of the countryside relatively undisturbed. The island of **Bute** is in many ways simply an extension of the peninsula, from which it is separated by the merest slither of water; its chief town, **Rothesay**, rivals Dunoon as the major seaside resort on the Clyde.

Argyll Forest Park

The **Argyll Forest Park** stretches from Loch Lomond south as far as Holy Loch, providing the most exhilarating scenery on the peninsula. The park includes the **Arrochar Alps**, north of Glen Croe and Glen Kinglas, whose Munros offer some of the best climbing in Argyll: Ben Ime (3318ft) is the tallest of the range, The Cobbler (2891ft) easily the most distinctive – all are for experienced walkers only. Less threatening are the peaks south of Glen Croe, between Loch Long and Loch Goil (the latter branches off Loch Long), known as **Argyll's Bowling Green** – no ironic nickname but an English corruption of the Gaelic *Baile na Greine* (Sunny Hamlet). At the other end of the scale, there are several gentle forest walks clearly laid out by the Forestry Commission.

Approaching from Glasgow by road (A83), you enter the park from **ARROCHAR**, at the head of Loch Long. The village itself is ordinary enough, but the setting is dramatic, and it makes a convenient base for exploring the northern section of the park. There's a **train station**, a mile or so up the Tarbert road (A83), and numerous **hotels** and **B&Bs** – try the *Lochside Guest House* (☎01301/702467; ②) or the *Mansefield Hotel* (☎01301/702282; ③). Two miles beyond Arrochar at **ARDGARTAN**, there's a lochside Forestry Commission **campsite** (mid-March to Oct; ☎01301/702293), a **youth hostel** (Feb–Dec; ☎01301/702362; Grade 1), and a **tourist office** (April & Oct Mon–Fri 11am–4pm, Sat & Sun 10am–5pm; May–Sept daily 9am–6pm; ☎01301/702432), which can give you lots of information on hiking in the forest park and also organizes less strenuous walking activities.

Loch Goil and Loch Eck

Approaching Cowal from the east, you're forced to climb **Glen Croe**, a strategic hill pass whose saddle is called – for obvious reasons – Rest-and-be-Thankful. Here the road forks, with the single-track B828 heading down to **LOCHGOILHEAD**. The setting is difficult to beat, but the village has been upstaged by the Drimsynie Leisure Centre, a giant holiday complex a mile to the west, notable for its **European Sheep and Wool Centre**; this hosts sheep shearing and sheep dog shows and its own Miss World-style sheep contest. A road tracks the west side of the loch, petering out after five miles at the ruins of **Carrick Castle**, built around 1400 and used as a hunting lodge by James IV.

If you'd rather skip Lochgoilhead, continue along the A83 from the Rest-and-be-Thankful down the grand Highland sweep of **Glen Kinglas** to **CAIRNDOW**, at the head of Loch Fyne. A mile or so around the head of the loch on the A83 is the famous *Loch Fyne Oyster Bar* (☎01499/600264), which sells more oysters than anywhere else in the country, plus lots of other fish and seafood treats. The restaurant is excellent, but you might prefer to get a picnic together and head for the **Ardkinglas Woodland Garden** (daily dawn to dusk; £1) – formerly Strone Garden – on the southern edge of Cairndow, which contains exotic rhododendrons and a superb collection of conifers, including the country's tallest, which rises to over 200ft.

From Cairndow, the A815 heads southwest to Strachur before heading inland to **Loch Eck**, an exceptionally narrow freshwater loch, squeezed between steeply banked woods, and a favourite for trout fishing. Superior bar food or an **overnight stay** can be had at the *Coylet Inn* (☎01369/840426; ③), halfway down the loch's eastern shores. Alternatively, there's a rugged, scenic road that heads east to the pretty village of **ARDENTINNY** on the west side of Loch Long, which boasts the finest sandy beach on Cowal. There's just one **hotel**, the *Ardentinny* (☎01369/810209; ④), plus a smattering of cheaper **B&Bs** and the *Glenfinart* **caravan park** (April–Oct; ☎01369/810256) – though this only has limited space.

At the southern tip of Loch Eck are the **Younger Botanic Gardens** (mid-March to Oct daily 10am–6pm; £1.50), an offshoot of Edinburgh's Royal Botanic Gardens, especially striking for its avenue of Great Redwoods, planted in 1863 and now over 100ft high. You could combine a visit here with one of the most popular of the park's forest **walks**, the rocky ravine of **Puck's Glen**; the walk begins from the car park a mile south of the gardens (1hr 30min round trip).

Dunoon

In the nineteenth century, Cowal's capital, **DUNOON**, grew from a mere village to a major Clyde seaside resort, a favourite holiday spot for Glaswegians. Nowadays, tourists tend to arrive by ferry from Gourock, and though their numbers are smaller, Dunoon remains by far the largest town in all Argyll, with 13,000 inhabitants. The whole area is still suffering, however, from the closure of the US nuclear submarine base on nearby Holy Loch in 1992, which has severely depressed the local economy.

Apart from its practical uses, and its fine pier, there's little to tempt you to linger in Dunoon. The centre of town is dominated by a grassy lump of rock known as **Castle Hill**, crowned by Castle House (which has recently opened as a local museum), built in the 1820s by a wealthy Glaswegian, and subject of a bitter dispute with the local populace over closure of the common land around his house. The people eventually won, and the grounds remain open to the public to this day. Another more violent scene in local history is commemorated by a memorial on a nearby rock: at least 36 men of the Lamont clan were executed by their rivals, the Campbells who hanged them from "a lively, fresh-growing ash tree" in 1646. The tree couldn't take the strain, and had to be cut down two years later – tradition has it that blood gushed from the roots when it was felled. If you've time on your hands, you could pay a visit to the **Cowal Bird Garden** (April–Nov daily 10am–6pm; £2.75), one mile northwest along the A885 to Sandbank, which harbours parrots, macaws, pheasants, peacocks and other fowl, plus a small rare breeds farm. If the weather's fine, the **Ardnadam Heritage Trail**, a little further up the road, will take you to the wonderful Dunan viewpoint looking out to the Firth of Clyde; if the weather's bad, you could head for *Dunoon Ceramics*, on Hamilton St, which produces various styles of high-quality porcelain and bone china, and offers tours around the factory.

Practicalities

It's a good idea to take advantage of Dunoon's **tourist office** (the only one in Cowal) on Alexandra Parade (Easter–Oct Mon–Thurs 9am–5.30pm, Fri 9am–5pm, Sat 10am–5pm, Sun 10am–2pm; Oct–Easter Mon–Fri only; ☎01369/703785). The shorter, more frequent of the two **ferry crossings** across the Clyde from Gourock to Dunoon is the half-hourly *Western Ferries* service to Hunter's Quay, a mile north of the town centre; *CalMac* has the prime position, however, on the main pier. If you need to **stay** the night, look no further than the central *Caledonian* on Argyll St (☎01369/702176; ③); around Hunter's Quay, try *Foxbank* on Marine Parade (☎01369/703858; ②). Plusher accommodation can be had at the *Argyll* on Argyll St (☎01369/702059; ④), or the highly reputable *Ardfillayne*, West Bay (☎01369/702267; ⑥).

The nearest **campsites** are the lochside *Buthkollidar* (April–Oct; ☎01369/830563), south of Dunoon on Bullwood Rd, followed by *Cot House* at Kilmun (April–Oct; ☎01369/840351), on the north side of Holy Loch, or else there's the *Stratheck* site by the Botanical Gardens at Loch Eck (April–Oct; ☎01369/840472). For **bike rental**, head for the *Highland Stores*, Argyll St. *Chatters*, 58 John St, is Dunoon's best **restaurant**, offering delicious Loch Fyne seafood and Scottish beef. The town also boasts a two-screen cinema (a rarity in Argyll) on John St, but by far Dunoon's most famous entertainment is the **Cowal Highland Gathering**, the largest of its kind in the world, held here on the last weekend in August, and culminating in the awesome spectacle of the massed pipes and drums of over 150 bands marching through the streets.

Southwest Cowal

The mellow landscape of **southwest Cowal**, in complete contrast to the bustle of Dunoon or the Highland grandeur of the forest, becomes immediate as soon as you head west to Loch Striven, where, from either side, there are few more beautiful sights than the **Kyles of Bute**, the thin slithers of water that separate the bleak bulk of north Bute from Cowal, and constitute some of the best sailing territory in Scotland.

COLINTRAIVE, on the eastern Kyle, marks the narrowest point in the Kyles – barely more than a couple of hundred yards – and is the place from which the small *CalMac* car ferry to Bute departs. However, the most popular spot from which to appreciate the Kyles is the A8003 as it rises dramatically above the sea lochs before descending to the peaceful, lochside village of **TIGHNABRUAICH** on the western Kyle. The **youth hostel** (April–Sept, ☎01700/811622; Grade 2), situated above the village, is well used thanks to the excellent *Tighnabruaich Sailing School*, which offers week-long courses from beginners to advanced. The *Royal Hotel* (☎01700/811239; ⑤), by the waterside, does exceptionally fine bar meals; the *Burnside* café/bistro is also good. In neighbouring **KAMES**, the *Kames Hotel* (☎01700/811489; ⑤) has wonderful views over the Kyles, as does *Piermount* (☎01700/811218; ②) and *Ferguslie* (April–Sept; ☎01700/811414; ②).

The Kyles can get busy in July and August, but you can escape the crowds by heading for Cowal's deserted west coast, overlooking Loch Fyne. The one brief glimpse of habitation en route is the luxurious, whitewashed *Kilfinan Hotel* (☎01700/821201; ⑦), set back from a sandy bay seven miles along the B8000 from Tighnabruaich. The road rejoins the coast at **OTTER FERRY**, which has a little sandy beach and a wonderful pub and oyster restaurant, *The Oystercatcher*, with tables outside if the weather's good. There was once a ferry link to Lochgilphead from here, though the "otter" part is not derived from the furry beast but from the Gaelic *an oitir* (sandbank), which juts out a mile or so into Loch Fyne. If you're heading for Kintyre, Islay or Jura, you can avoid the long haul around Loch Fyne – some 70 miles or so – by using the **ferry service to Tarbert** (mid April to mid-Oct) from Portavadie, three miles southwest of Kames.

Isle of Bute

Thanks to its consistently mild climate and Rothesay's ferry link with Wemyss Bay (see p.196), the island of **Bute** has been a popular holiday and convalescence spot for Clydesiders – particularly the elderly – for over a century. Even considering the island's small size (15 miles long and up to 5 miles wide) you can escape the crowds; most of its inhabitants are centred around the two wide bays on the east coast of the island.

Bute's one and only town, **ROTHESAY**, is a long-established resort, set in a wide sweeping bay, backed by green hills, with a classic promenade and pagoda-style Winter Gardens. It creates a better general impression than Dunoon, though it, too, has passed its prime. However, even if you're just passing through, you must pay a visit to the ornate **toilets** (daily 8am–9pm; 10p) on the pier, which were built in 1899 and have since been declared a national treasure (gentlemen have the best time as the porcelain urinals steal the show). Rothesay also boasts the militarily useless, but architecturally impressive, moated ruins of **Rothesay Castle** (April–Sept Mon–Sat 9.30am–6pm, Sun 2–6pm; Oct–March closes 4pm; £1.50), hidden amid the town's backstreets but signposted from the pier. Built in the twelfth century, it was twice captured by the Vikings in the 1400s; such vulnerability was the reasoning behind the unusual, almost circular curtain wall, with its four big drum towers, of which only one remains fully intact.

A very good reason for coming to Bute, is to visit **Mount Stuart** (June–Sept Weds & Fri–Mon 11am–5pm; £5), three miles south of Rothesay. Once home of the fantastically wealthy Marquess of Bute, the mansion was opened to the public for the first time in 1995. In deliberate defiance against the popular trend for Scottish Baronial, the third Marquess built (between 1879 and World War II) an incredible High Gothic fancy, drawing architectural inspiration from all over Europe. The sumptuous interior was decked out by craftsmen who worked with William Burges on the Marquess' earlier medieval concoctions at Cardiff Castle. The gardens, established in the eighteenth century by the third Earl of Bute, who had a hand in London's Kew Gardens, are equally lovely.

For the best overall view of the island, take a walk up **Canada Hill** above the freshwater Loch Fad, which all but divides Bute in two. The northern half of the island is hilly, uninhabited and little visited, while the southern half is made up of Lowland-style farmland. The early monastic history of the island is recalled at **St Blane's Chapel**, a twelfth-century ruin beautifully situated in open countryside on the west coast, close to the very southernmost tip. Bute's finest sandy beach is **Scalpsie Bay**, further up the west coast, beyond which lies **St Ninian's Point**, where the ruins of a sixth-century chapel overlook another fine sandy strand and the uninhabited island of **Inchmarnock**.

Practicalities

Rothesay's **tourist office**, 15 Victoria St (April Mon–Fri 9am–5.30pm, Sat 10am–5pm; May also Sun 10am–5pm; June & Sept Mon–Fri 9am–6pm, Sat 10am–6pm, Sun 10am–5pm; July & Aug Mon–Sat till 7pm also Sun 10am–5pm; Oct Mon–Thurs 9am–5.30pm, Fri 9am–5pm, Sat & Sun 10am–5pm; Nov–March Mon–Thurs 9am–5.30pm, Fri 9am–5pm; ☎01700/502151) can help with accommodation, though there's no shortage of B&Bs along the seafront from Rothesay to Port Bannatyne. The grandest **place to stay** is the giant, former spa sanatorium *Glenburn Hotel*, Glenburn Rd (☎01700/502500; ⑤). Others like the *Commodore* at 12 Battery Place (☎01700/502178; ③) or the distinctive *Glendale*, at no. 20 (☎01700/502329; ②), both up East Princes St, are more modest; the *Bute House Hotel* (☎01700/502481; ③), on West Princes St, is vegetarian- and even vegan-friendly. For **bike rental**, try *Calder Bros*, Bridge St, or the *Bute Electrical Centre,* East Princes St.

Apart from the plush *Queen's Restaurant* in the *Victoria Hotel* on Victoria St, **food** options are limited to pasta and steak at *Oliver's*, also on Victoria St, or the simple dishes served at the *Winter Gardens* bistro on the prom. Bute holds its own **Highland Games** on the last weekend in August – Prince Charles as Duke of Rothesay occasionally attends – plus a newly established international **folk festival** on the last weekend in July, and a mainly trad-**jazz festival** during May Bank Holiday.

Inveraray and around

A classic example of an eighteenth-century planned town, **INVERARAY** was built on the site of a ruined fishing village in 1745 by the third Duke of Argyll, head of the powerful Campbell clan, in order to distance his newly rebuilt castle from the hoi polloi in the town and to establish a commercial and legal centre for the region. Today

Inveraray, an absolute set-piece of Scottish Georgian architecture, has a truly memorable setting, the brilliant white arches of Front Street reflected in the still waters of Loch Fyne, which separate it from the Cowal peninsula.

The town

With a population of just 400 and squeezed onto a headland some distance from the duke's new castle, there's not much more to Inveraray's "New Town" than its distinctive **Main Street** (running west from Front St), flanked by whitewashed terraces, whose window casements are picked out in black. At the top of the street, the road divides to circumnavigate the town's Neoclassical church, originally built in two parts: the southern half served the Gaelic-speaking community, while the northern half (still in use) served those who spoke English.

East of the church is **Inveraray Jail** (daily April–Oct 9.30am–6pm; Nov–March 10am–5pm; £2.50), whose attractive Georgian courthouse and grim prison blocks ceased to function in the 1930s. The jail is now an imaginative and thoroughly enjoyable museum, which graphically recounts conditions from medieval times up until the nineteenth century. You can also sit in the beautiful semicircular courthouse and listen to the trial of a farmer accused of fraud.

During the replanning of the town, the **Inveraray Cross** was moved to its present position at the other end of Main Street near the loch (another cross from Tiree was placed in the castle gardens); both date from the fifteenth century and feature intricate figural scenes. Moored at the nearby pier is Inveraray's latest attraction, **Arctic Penguin** (daily April–Oct 9.30am–6pm; Nov–March 10am–5pm; £2.85), a handsome, triple-masted schooner built in Dublin in 1911 – it's full of nautical nick-nacks and displays on the maritime history of the Clyde, but only really worth a wander round in wet weather. For a panoramic view of the town, castle and loch, you can climb the **Bell Tower** (May–Sept Mon–Sat 10am–1pm & 2–5pm, Sun 2–5pm; £1.20) of All Saints' Church, accessible through the screen arches on Front Street. Built, after World War I, as a memorial to the fallen Campbells by the tenth Duke of Argyll, the tower contains a ringing peal of ten bells, which are apparently the second heaviest in the world – it takes four hours to ring a complete peal.

Inveraray Castle

Slightly removed from the New Town, to the north, the neo-Gothic **Inveraray Castle** (April–June, Sept & Oct Mon–Thurs & Sat 10am–1pm & 2–5.30pm, Sun 1–5.30pm; July & Aug Mon–Sat 10am–5.30pm, Sun 1–5.30pm; £3) remains the family home of the Duke of Argyll. Built in 1745 by the third duke, it was given a touch of the Loire with the addition of dormer windows and conical roofs in the nineteenth century. Inside, the most startling feature is the armoury hall, whose displays of weaponry – supplied to the Campbells by the British government to put down the Jacobites – rise through several storeys (look out for Rob Roy's rather sad-looking sporran and dirk handle, the traditional dagger worn in Highland dress). Gracing the castle's extensive grounds is one of three elegant bridges built during the relandscaping of Inveraray (the other two are on the road from Cairndow), while the **Combined Operations Museum** (same times as castle; £1) in the old stables recalls the wartime role of Inveraray as a training centre for the D-Day landings, during which over half a million troops practised secret amphibious manoeuvres around Loch Fyne.

Argyll Wildlife Park, Auchindrain and Crarae

If you've got children in tow, the **Argyll Wildlife Park** (daily 9.30am–6pm; £3), two miles south of Inveraray, along the A83 to Campbeltown, provides some light relief, allowing children to come face to face with Scotland's indigenous fauna, from sika deer

to wildcats. Three miles further on, the **Auchindrain Folk Museum** (April daily
except Sat 10am–5pm; May–Sept daily; £2.20) is in fact an old township of around 20
thatched buildings packed full of domestic memorabilia to give an idea of life here
before the Clearances, and before the planning of towns like neighbouring Inveraray.
Demonstrations illustrate the old "run rig" strip-farming methods used in the eighteenth and nineteenth centuries, and the informative **visitor centre** has a good bookshop and a tearoom. Another four miles down the road is **Crarae Garden** (daily 9am–
6pm/dusk), laid out earlier this century as a "Himalayan ravine" in a deep glen that
tumbles down into Loch Fyne. It is this dramatic setting that sets Crarae apart from the
innumerable other gardens of Argyll, and provides the scenic backdrop for the
garden's rhododendrons, azaleas, and wide variety of eucalyptus and conifers.

Practicalities

Inverary's **tourist office** is on Front St (April–Oct Mon–Fri 10am–4pm, Sat & Sun
noon–4pm; May to mid-June & late Sept Mon–Sat 9am–1pm & 2–5.30pm, Sun 11am–
5pm; mid-June to mid-Sept Mon–Sat 9.30am–6.30pm, Sun 11am–5pm; Nov–March
Mon–Fri 10am–4pm, Sat & Sun noon–4pm; ☎01499/302063), as is the town's chief
hotel, the historic *Great Inn* (April–Oct; ☎01499/302466; ⑤), where Dr Johnson and
Boswell stayed. There's a **B&B** on Main Street South, *Lorona* (☎01499/302258; ②),
and a couple beyond the petrol station on the Campbeltown road (A83): *Arch House*
(☎01499/302289; ②) and *Glen Eynord* (☎01499/302031; ②). The **youth hostel** (mid-
March to Sept ☎01499/302454; Grade 2) is just up the Oban road (A819). The old
Royal Navy base, two miles down the A83, is now the *Argyll Caravan Park* (April–Oct;
☎01499/302285). The **bar** of the *George Hotel* in the middle of town is the liveliest spot,
while for tea and cakes, try *The Grouser*. The best place to sample Loch Fyne's delicious fresh fish is the restaurant of the aforementioned *Loch Fyne Oyster Bar* (see
p.259), six miles back up the A83 towards Glasgow.

Loch Awe

Legend has it that **Loch Awe** – at over 25 miles in length, the longest stretch of fresh
water in the country – was created by a witch and inhabited by a monster even more
gruesome than the one at Loch Ness. The southern shores of the loch are the most
peaceful, with gentle hills and, on the western side, the magnificent **Inverliever
Forest**, where the Forestry Commission have laid out a series of none-too-strenuous
forest walks around Dalavich. The most spectacular of the lot is the hour-long walk
from Inverinan up to the Royal Engineers' wooden footbridge which takes you over a
pretty waterfall.

Dotted around the north of the loch, where it's joined by the A819 from Inveraray to
Oban, are several tiny islands sporting picturesque ruins; on **Inishail** you can see a
crumbling thirteenth-century chapel which once served as a burial ground for the
MacArthur clan; the ruined castle on **Fraoch Eilean** dates from the same period.
Fifteenth-century **Kilchurn Castle**, strategically situated on a rocky spit – once an
island – at the head of the loch and once a Campbell stronghold, has been abandoned
to the elements since being struck by lightning in the 1760s, and is now one of Argyll's
most photogenic lochside ruins.

If you have time to linger, it's worth seeking out two interesting churches in the
area. The first is an unusual octagonal **parish church**, built in the early nineteenth
century and set on high ground above the River Lochy beyond the village of
DALMALLY, two miles east of Kilchurn. The second, **St Conan's Church** in the
village of **LOCHAWE**, a mile or so west of Kilchurn, was designed in the early part of

this century by a Campbell, whose foray into every style from Roman to Norman manages somehow to meld successfully.

Further west, gorged into the giant granite bulk of Ben Cruachan (3695ft), is the underground **Cruachan Power Station** (daily 9am–4.30pm; £2), built in 1965. A mildly interesting half-hour guided tour sets off every hour from the **visitor centre** by the loch, taking you to a viewing platform above the generating room deep inside the mountain. Using the water from an artificial loch high up on Ben Cruachan to drive the turbines, the power station can become fully operational in less than two minutes, supplying electricity during surges on the National Grid. Sadly it takes ten percent more electricity to pump the water back up into the artificial loch, so the station only manages to make a profit by buying cheap off-peak power and selling during daytime peak demand. If you're keen to go, make sure you get there before the queues start to form as they do during summer.

In order to maintain the right level of water in Loch Awe itself, a dam was built at the mouth of the loch, which then had to be fitted with a special lift to transport the salmon – for which the loch is justly famous – upriver to spawn. From the dam, the River Awe squeezes through the mountains via the gloomy rock-walled **Pass of Brander** (which means "ambush" in Gaelic), where Robert the Bruce put to flight the MacDougall clan, cutting them down as they fought with one another to cross the river and escape.

Before you reach **TAYNUILT**, there's a signpost off the A85, which runs through the pass, to **Bonawe Iron Furnace** (April–Sept Mon–Sat 9.30am–12.30pm & 1.30–6pm, Sun 2–6pm; £2), founded by Cumbrian ironworkers in 1753 and now restored as an industrial heritage site. It was clearly cheaper, in those days, to import iron ore from south of the border, rather than transport charcoal to the Lake District, since several iron furnaces were established in the area, of which Bonawe was the most successful. A whole series of buildings in various states of repair are scattered across the factory site, which employed 600 people at its height, and eventually closed down in 1876.

From the pier beyond the iron furnace, twice-daily **boat cruises** explore the otherwise inaccessible reaches of Loch Etive; phone *Loch Etive Cruises* (☎01866/822430) for more details.

Practicalities

The nicest **places to stay** around Loch Awe are on the western shores, beginning with the *Ford Hotel* (☎01546/810273; ④), at the loch's southernmost tip. At Dalavich, there's a *Forest Holidays* campsite (April–Oct; ☎01855/811397) and forest chalets for rent, while at Kilchrenan, further north, there's the *Taychreggan Hotel* (☎01866/833211; ⑦) and the *Thistle-Doo* B&B (☎01866/833339; ③). For luxurious accommodation, there's the *Ardanaiseig Hotel* (☎01866/833333; ⑨), four miles down a dead-end track from Kilchrenan. An even wider choice of B&Bs and guest houses is on offer at Dalmally and Taynuilt. Shortly before you reach Bonawe and Taynuilt, a sign to the right invites you to visit the *Inverawe Fisheries and Smokery*, where you can buy traditionally smoked local fish and mussels, or **picnic** while you admire the view over the loch.

Oban and around

The solidly Victorian resort of **OBAN** enjoys a superb setting – the island of Kerrera providing its bay with a natural shelter – distinguished by a bizarre granite amphitheatre, dramatically lit at night, on the hilltop above the town. Despite a population of just 7000, it's by far the largest port in northwest Scotland, the second-largest town in Argyll, and the main departure point for ferries to the Hebrides. If you arrive late, or are catching an early boat, you may well find yourself staying the night (though there's no real need otherwise); if you're staying elsewhere, it's a useful base for wet-weather activities and shopping, although it does get uncomfortably crowded in the summer.

The Town

The only real sight in Oban is the town's landmark, **McCaig's Folly**, a stiff ten-minute climb from the quayside. An imitation of the Coliseum in Rome, it was the brainchild of a local banker a century ago, who had the twin aims of alleviating off-season unemployment among the local stonemasons and creating a family mausoleum. Work never progressed further than the exterior walls before McCaig died, but the folly provides a wonderful seaward panorama, particularly at sunset. Equally beautiful evening views can be had by walking along the northern shore of the bay, past the modern, Roman Catholic **Cathedral of St Columba** – built by Sir Giles Gilbert Scott, architect of Battersea Power Station – to the rocky ruins of **Dunollie Castle**, a MacDougall stronghold on a very ancient site, successfully defended by the laird's Jacobite wife during the 1715 uprising but abandoned after 1745.

You can pass a few hours admiring the fishing boats in the harbour and looking out for scavanging seals in the bay; or, if the weather's bad, you can shelter in the new, somewhat pretentiously named Oban Experience Centre by the new train station (the old Victorian one was demolished in 1988). You can also take a 45-minute guided tour of the **Oban Distillery** (Mon–Fri 9.30am–4.15pm; Easter–Oct also Sat; £2), in the centre of town off George St, which ends with a dram of whisky. **The World in Miniature** (Easter–Oct Mon–Sat 10am–5pm, Sun 2–5pm; £1.50), on the north pier, contains an assortment of minute "dolls' house" rooms, with even a couple of mini-Charles Rennie Mackintosh interiors to admire.

Practicalities

The *CalMac* **ferry terminal** for the islands is a stone's throw from the **train station**, itself adjacent to the **bus terminus**. A host of private **boat operators** can be found around the harbour, particularly along its northern side: their excursions – direct to the castles of Mull, to Staffa and the Treshnish Islands – are worth considering, particularly if you're pushed for time, or have no transport. Alternatively, you can rent a **bike** from *Oban Cycles*, 9 Craigard Rd (☎01631/566996), or a **boat** from *Borroboats*, on the Gallanach Rd (☎01631/563292).

The **tourist office** (April & Oct Mon–Fri 9am–1pm & 2–5.30pm, Sat & Sun 10am–4pm; May to mid-June & late Sept Mon–Sat 9am–5.30pm, Sun 9am–4pm; late June & early Sept Mon–Sat closes 7pm; July & Aug Mon–Sat closes 9pm & Sun 5pm; Nov–March Mon–Fri 9am–1pm & 2–5.30pm, Sat & Sun noon–4pm; ☎01631/563122) is tucked away on Argyll Square just east of the bus station; a small fee is charged for finding **accommodation**. Should you wish to look for yourself, there's a whole host of grandiose Victorian **hotels** to choose from on the quayside, ranging from the *Columba* (☎01631/562183; ⑥) on the north pier to the *Palace* (☎01631/562294; ④) on George St, plus dozens of **B&Bs** on Dunollie Rd beyond George St – try *Glendale* (☎01631/563877; ②) or *Glengorm* (April–Oct; ☎01631/565361; ②) – and on Ardconnel Rd, just below McCaig's Tower. The official **youth hostel** (March–Sept; ☎01631/562025; Grade 1) is on the Esplanade, just beyond the Catholic cathedral; plus there's an **independent hostel** run by Jeremy Inglis at 21 Airds Crescent (☎01631/565065), and one called the *Backpackers' Lodge*, Breadalbane St (☎01631/562107). The nearest **campsite** is about two miles south of Oban at *Gallanachmore Farm* beside the sea (April to mid-Oct; ☎01631/566624).

Oban's best **restaurant** is *The Gathering* (☎01631/565421), Breadalbane St, which excels in, among other things, fish and seafood; the *Waterfront* (☎01631/563110), between the train station and the quay, does cheaper bar food as well as à la carte meals. The town's **fish-and-chip** shops are also better than average; try *Onorio's* on George St. Oban's one and only half-decent **pub** is the *Oban Inn* opposite the north pier, with a clas-

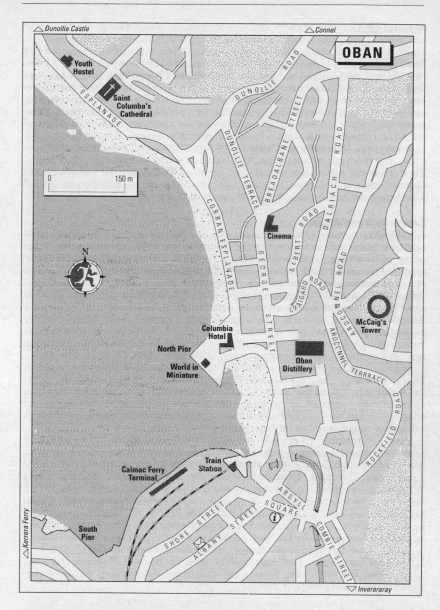

sic dark-wood-and-brass bar downstairs and food in the lounge upstairs. One thing to bear in mind if you're arriving early in the morning on an overnight ferry is that there's nowhere to grab even a bacon sandwich until at least 8am. Oban's nightlife doesn't bear thinking about, but you might want to make use of the town's **cinema**, confusingly known as *The Highland Theatre* (☎01631/562444), at the north end of George St.

Around Oban

There are a few, palpably low-key attractions around Oban – good if it's raining and you have children with you, but if not don't bother going out of your way. A couple of miles east of Oban, up Glencruitten Road, the **Rare Breeds Farm Park** (late March–Oct daily 10am–5.30pm; mid-June to Aug closes 7.30pm; £2.50) displays rare but indigenous species of deer, cattle, sheep and so forth – with a children's corner where they can meet the baby animals. Less compelling for youngsters is the **Salmon Centre**, seven miles south of Oban; for £2 you can view the cages out in the loch. The real reason for coming here, though, is to sample the wonderful seafood in the farm's excellent restaurant. **Dunstaffnage Castle** (April–Sept Mon–Sat 9.30am–6pm, Sun 2–6pm; £1.50), two miles up the coast from Oban, has even less to offer for children or adults. The curtain wall battlements are safe and fun to climb and give out views across to Lismore, Appin and Morvern, but there's not much else to get excited about this old MacDougall fort, which was later handed over to the Campbells.

Benderloch and Appin

At **CONNEL**, five miles up the coast from Oban, you can't fail to admire the majestic steel cantilever bridge built in 1903 to take the old branch line across the sea cataract at the mouth of Loch Etive, north to Ballachulish. The name Connel comes from the Gaelic *conghail* (tumultuous flood), which refers to the rapids, caused by the water at low ebb rushing over a ledge of rock between the two shores of the loch. The A828 crosses Connel Bridge to take you onto the hammerhead peninsula of **Benderloch** (from *beinn eadar dà loch*, "hill between two lochs"), on whose northern shores, overlooking Loch Creran, is **Barcaldine Castle**, an early seventeenth-century Campbell tower house, recently modernized and privately owned but occasionally open to the public – enquire at Oban tourist office. On its own 300-acre island, further north still, is **Eriska House**, a turreted, Scottish Baronial pile, now the exclusive *Isle of Eriska Hotel* (☎01631/720371; ⑨).

Since the weather in this part of Scotland can be bad at almost any time of the year, it's as well to know about the **Sea Life Centre** (Feb–Nov daily 10am–6pm; Dec & Jan Sat & Sun only; £3), further along the shores of Loch Creran on the A828. Here you can see locally caught sea creatures at close quarters – look out for the octopus and stingray – before they are returned to the sea at the end of the season. The centre's self-service *Shoreline* restaurant features a small oyster bar.

Having circumnavigated the loch, you enter the district of **Appin**, setting for Robert Louis Stevenson's *Kidnapped*, a fictionalized account of the "Appin Murder" of 1752, when Colin Campbell was shot in the back, allegedly by one of the disenfranchised Stewart clan. The name Appin derives from the Gaelic *abthaine*, meaning "Lands belonging to the Abbey", in this case the one on Lismore, which is still linked to Port Appin by a passenger ferry. One of Argyll's most romantic ruined castles, **Castle Stalker**, occupies an island just north of Port Appin. Built by the Stewarts, it was taken by the Campbells on two occasions, but is now privately owned and being restored – ask at Oban tourist office for the latest on visiting. If you're looking for something to do in Appin, head for the *Linnhe Marine Water Sports Centre* (☎01631/730227), in Lettershuna (just beyond Port Appin), which rents out boats of all shapes and sizes, offers sailing and windsurfing lessons, not to mention water-skiing, simulated clay-pigeon shooting and even pony trekking.

Isle of Kerrera

Gallanach, two miles down the coast from Oban, is the ferry departure point for the low-lying island of **Kerrera**, which shelters Oban harbour from the worst of the westerly winds. Measuring just five by two miles, it is easily explored on foot, and gives panoramic views from its highest point – 600ft above the sea – over to Mull, the Slate Islands, Lismore, Jura and beyond. The island has a total population of around 50, so unless you're staying at *Glenview House* (☎01631/563335; ③), you should bring your own food and drink. The passenger-only ferry (Mon–Sat) lands at **Port Kerrera**. If the weather's fine and you feel like lazing by the sea, head for the island's finest sandy beach, **Slatrach Bay**, just one mile west of the ferry slip. Otherwise, the most rewarding trail is down to **Gylen Castle**, a clifftop ruin on the south coast, built in 1582 by the MacDougalls and burnt to the ground by the Covenanter General Leslie in the Civil War. You can head to the ferry back via the Drove Road, where cattle from Mull and other islands were once herded to be swum across the sound to the market in Oban.

Isle of Lismore

Legend has it that saints Columba and Moluag both fancied the skinny island of **Lismore** as a missionary base, but as they raced towards it Moluag cut off his finger and threw it ashore ahead of Columba, claiming the land for himself. Lismore, situated in Loch Linnhe to the north of Oban, is undoubtedly one of the most fertile of the Inner Hebrides – its name, coined by Moluag himself, derives from the Gaelic *lios mór*, meaning "great garden" and at one time it supported more than 1000 inhabitants. The population today is less than a sixth of that size.

Of Moluag's sixth-century foundation nothing remains, but in 1236 the island became the seat of the Bishop of Argyll, and shortly afterwards the diminutive **Cathedral of St Moluag** was built at **CLACHAN**, a mile and a half north of Achnacroish, where the car ferry from Oban terminates. The remnants of the cathedral are now incorporated into the parish church, which, though much altered, exhibits elements of the original medieval building. East of the church, **Tirefour Castle**, a circular stone fort over 2000 years old, occupies a commanding position and boasts walls almost 10ft thick in places. West of Clachan are the much more recent ruins of **Castle Coeffin**, an old MacDougall fortress once believed to have been haunted by the ghost of Bhcothail, sister of the Norse prince Caiffen. Two other places worth exploring are **Salen**, an abandoned quarry village on the west coast, and the ruins of **Achadun Castle**, in the southwest, where the bishops are thought to have resided.

Two **ferries** serve Lismore; a *CalMac* car ferry from Oban to Achnacroish (Mon–Sat 2 daily; 50min), and a shorter passenger-only crossing from Port Appin to the island's north point (Mon–Sat every 2hr; 15min). There's a **postbus** round the island (Mon–Sat; check with Oban tourist office for times). **Accommodation** on the island is limited to a trio of B&Bs – try *Achnacroish* (☎01631/760241; ③) or the *Schoolhouse* (☎01631/760262; ②) – all of them unlicensed so bring your own booze.

The Slate Islands and the Garvellachs

Eight miles south of Oban on the A816, a road heads off west to a small group of islands commonly called the **Slate Islands**, which at their peak in the mid-nineteenth century quarried over nine million slates annually. Today they're almost entirely depopulated, and an inevitable air of melancholy hangs over them, but their dramatic setting amid crashing waves makes for a rewarding day trip.

Isle of Seil

The most northerly of the Slate Islands is the **Seil**, separated from the mainland by the thinnest of sea channels and spanned by Thomas Telford's elegant hump-backed **Clachan Bridge**, known as the "only bridge over the Atlantic". The main village on Seil is **ELLANBEICH**, its neat white terrraces of workers' cottages crouching below the black cliffs of Dùn Mór on the westernmost tip of the island. This was once the tiny island of *Eilean a'Beithich*, separated from the mainland by a narrow channel until the intensive slate quarrying succeeded in silting it up. Confusingly, the village is often referred to by the same name as the nearby island of Easdale, since they formed an interdependent community based exclusively around the slate industry.

Isle of Easdale

Easdale remains an island, though the few hundred yards that separate it from Ellanbeich have constantly to be dredged to keep the channel open. On the eve of a great storm of November 23, 1881, Easdale, less than a mile across at any one point, supported 452 inhabitants. That night, waves engulfed the island and flooded the quarries – the island never really recovered, slate quarrying stopped in 1914, and by 1960 the population was reduced to seven. Recently many of the old cottages have been restored, some as holiday homes, others sold to new families (the present population stands at around 30). The **museum** (April–Oct daily 10.30am–4.30pm; £1), near the main square, has a useful historical map of the island, which you can walk round in about half an hour. The **ferry** from Ellanbeich runs on demand (April–Sept Mon–Sat 7.30–8am, 9am–1pm, 2–6pm & 7–9pm, Sun 10.30am–1pm & 3–5pm; Oct–March restricted hours only, check at the Oban tourist office), and there's a nice **tearoom** near the quayside, plus a **B&B** further inland (☎01852/300438; ②).

Isle of Luing

At the southern tip of Seil a year-round car ferry (Mon–Sat 8am–6pm) frequently crosses the narrow, treacherous Cuan Sound to **Luing** (pronounced "Ling"), a long, thin, fertile island which once supported a population of 600 crofting families. During the Clearances the population was drastically reduced to make way for cattle; Luing is still renowned for its beef and has cultivated a successful new crossbreed named after it.

CULLIPOOL, the main village with its post office, general store and tearoom, lies a mile or so southwest; quarrying ceased here in 1965, and the place now relies on tourism and lobster fishing. You can take a boat trip from Cullipool across the treacherous Sound of Luing, to abandoned **Belnahua**, the most northerly of the group of islands offshore to the west. Luing's only other village, **TOBERONOCHY**, lies on the more sheltered east coast, three miles southeast of Cullipool. Its distinctive white cottages, built by the slate company in 1805, nestle below a ruined chapel, which contains a memorial to the 15 Latvian seamen who drowned off Belnahua during a hurricane in 1936. The only **accommodation** available on the island is in self-catering slate cottages – contact *Donra Holidays* (☎01631/564339).

Isle of Scarba and the Garvellachs

Scarba is the largest of the islands around Luing, a brooding 1500ft hulk of slate, inhospitable and wild – the few families who once lived here had all left by the mid-nineteenth century. To the south, the raging **Gulf of Corrievrechan** is the site of one of the world's most spectacular whirlpools, thought to be caused by a rocky pinnacle below the sea. It remains calm only for an hour or two at high and low tide; at flood tide, accompanied by a westerly wind, water shoots deafeningly some 20ft up in the air. Inevitably there are numerous legends about the place, which is known as *Coire Bhreacain* (Speckled Cauldron) in Gaelic, concerning *Cailleach* (Hag), the Celtic storm goddess.

Boat trips, from Oban and Toberonochy and the Cuan Sound on Luing, visit a string of uninhabited islands west of Luing, known collectively as the **Garvellachs**. Their name derives from the largest of the group, **Garbh Eileach** (Rough Rock), which was inhabited as recently as 50 years ago. The most northerly, **Dùn Chonnuill**, contains the remains of an old fort thought to have belonged to Conal of Dalriada, and **Eileach**

an Naoimh (Holy Isle), the most southerly of the group, is where the Celtic missionary Brendan the Navigator founded a community in 542, some 20 years before Columba landed on Iona. Nothing survives from Brendan's day, but there are a few ninth-century remains, among them a double-beehive cell and a grave enclosure. One school of thought has it that the island is Hinba, Columba's legendary secret retreat, where he buried his mother.

Isle of Mull

The second largest of the Inner Hebrides, **MULL** is by far the most accessible – just 40 minutes from Oban by ferry. First impressions largely depend on the weather: without the sun the large tracts of moorland, particularly around the island's highest peak, Ben More (3196ft), can appear bleak and unwelcoming. There are, however, areas of more gentle pastoral scenery around Dervaig in the north and Salen on the east coast, and the indented west coast varies from the sandy beaches around Calgary to the cliffs of Loch na Keal. The most common mistake is to try and "do" the island in a day or two: Mull is a place that will grow on you only if you have the time and patience to explore.

Historically, crofting, whisky distilling and fishing supported the islanders (*Muileachs*), but the population – which peaked at 10,000 – decreased dramatically in the nineteenth century due to the Clearances and the 1846 potato famine. On Mull, it is a trend that has been reversed, mostly due to the large influx of settlers from elsewhere in the country which has brought the current population up to around 2500. One of the main reasons for this resurgence is, of course, tourism – over half a million visitors come here each year – although oddly enough, there are very few large hotels or campsites. Public transport is limited, and the roads are predominantly single-track, which can cause serious congestion in summer.

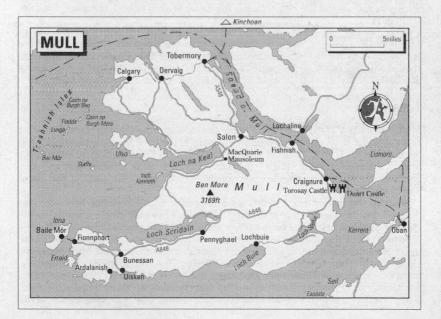

Around Craignure

CRAIGNURE is the main entry point to Mull, linked to Oban by several car ferries daily; a faster, less frequent car ferry service crosses from Lochaline on the Morvern peninsula (see p.420) to Fishnish, six miles northwest of Craignure. Fishnish is just a slipway and Craignure itself is little more than a scattering of cottages, though there is a **tourist office** (mid-April to mid-Oct Mon 7.15am–5.30pm, Tues–Fri 8.15am–7.30pm, Sat 6.15am–5.30pm, Sun 10.30am–5.30pm; mid-Oct to mid-April Mon 9.30am–5.30pm, Tues–Fri 8.30am–5.30pm, Sat 6.30am–5.30pm, Sun 4.30–5.30pm; ☎01680/812377), several **guest houses**, a **campsite** by the sea (☎01680/812496), plus the occasional bus connection with Tobermory; and **bike rental** possibilities too (☎01680/812487).

Two castles lie immediately southeast of Craignure. The first, **Torosay Castle** (mid-April to mid-Oct daily 10.30am–6.30pm; £3.50), a full-blown Scottish Baronial creation, is linked to Craignure by the narrow gauge *Mull Rail* link (mid-April to mid-Oct). The magnificent gardens (daily 9am–7pm; £1.50) with their avenue of eighteenth-century Italianate statues, Japanese section, and views over to neighbouring Duart, are the real highlight. The house itself, in the mid-nineteenth-century style, is stuffed with junk relating to the present owners, the little-known Guthries, all of it amusingly captioned but of no great interest, with the possible exception of the belongings of the late David Guthrie-James, who was something of an adventurer and a POW in Colditz. Also in the grounds are the *Isle of Mull Weavers* (daily 9am–5.30pm; free), who give demonstrations of traditional weaving using old dobby looms.

Lacking the gardens, but on a much more romantic spit of rock, 15 minutes' walk east of Torosay, **Duart Castle** (May–Sept daily 10.30am–6pm; £3) is a restored medieval fortress, the headquarters of the once-powerful MacLean clan until the late seventeenth century when it was left to rot by the Campbells. Only in 1911 did the MacLeans manage to buy it back and restore it – the 27th clan chief now lives there. You can learn more about the MacLean clan (and the world scout movement) inside, peek in the dungeons and ascend the ramparts; but the castle is seen to best advantage from the Oban ferry.

Both Torosay and Duart are inundated with visitors in the high season – not so **LOCHBUIE**, a peaceful, sandy bay ten miles or so southwest of Craignure. The shore is dominated by the fifteenth-century ivy-strewn ruins of **Moy Castle**, an old MacLean stronghold, and north of the castle is one of the few **stone circles** in the west of Scotland; with eight stones all about 6ft high and dating from the second century BC.

Tobermory

Mull's chief town, **TOBERMORY**, is easily the most attractive fishing port on the west coast of Scotland, its clusters of brightly coloured houses and boats sheltering in a bay backed by a steep bluff. Founded in 1788 by the British Fisheries Society – the upper town is a classic grid-plan village – it never really took off as a fishing port and only survived due to the steady influx of crofters evicted from other parts of the island during the Clearances.

If you're staying any length of time on Mull, you're bound to end up here – for one thing, it has the island's sole stationary bank, the *Clydesdale* (there's also a mobile *Bank of Scotland*; ask at the tourist office for details). But practicalities aside, there's little to do other than watch the harbour go about its business, or take a stroll to the upper town to admire the view. You could also pay a visit to the small **Mull Museum** (Mon–Fri 10.30am–4.30pm, Sat 10.30am–1.30pm; 70p), on Main St. Alternatively, there's the minuscule **Tobermory Distillery** (Easter–Sept Mon–Fri 10am–4pm; £2) at the south end of the bay, founded in 1795 but closed down three times since then. Today, it offers a guided tour finishing off with a tasting. One endearing feature of the

THE TOBERMORY TREASURE

The most dramatic event in Tobermory's history was in 1588 when a ship from the Spanish Armada sank in mysterious circumstances while having repairs done to its sails and rigging. The story goes that one of the MacLeans of Duart was taken prisoner, but when the ship weighed anchor, he made his way to the powder magazine and blew it up. However, several versions of the story exist, and even the identity of the ship is in dispute: some say it was the treasure-laden Spanish galleon *Florida*, while others assert that it was the *San Juan de Sicilia*, a troop carrier for the Spanish Armada. Whatever the truth, the possibility of precious sunken booty at the bottom of Tobermory harbour has fired the greed of numerous lairds and kings – in the 1950s Royal Navy divers were engaged by the Duke of Argyll in the seemingly futile activity of diving for treasure, and in 1982, another unsuccessful attempt was made.

town is its diminuitive **Clock Tower**, erected by the author Isabella Bird in 1905 in memory of her sister who died of typhoid on the island in 1880.

Practicalities

The **tourist office** (Feb & March Mon–Fri 10am–4pm; April & Oct Mon–Fri 9am–1pm & 2–5.30pm, Sat & Sun noon–4pm; May to mid-June and late Sept Mon–Sat 9am–1pm & 2pm–5.30pm, Sun 11am–4pm; mid-June to mid-Sept Mon–Sat 9.30am–6.30pm, Sun 10am–1pm & 2–5pm; ☎01688/302182) is in the same building as the *CalMac* ticket office at the northern end of Main St; while you're there, be sure to pick up the free Mull listings broadsheet *Round & About*. If you want to rent a **bike**, head for the youth hostel (see below), or *Tom-a'Mhuillin* (☎01688/302164) on the Salen road.

The tourist office can book you into a **B&B** for a small fee – not a bad idea since many places are a stiff climb from the harbour. There are, however, several on Main St – try the excellent *Fàilte* (☎01688/302495; ④) and the *Tobermory Hotel* (☎01688/302091; ⑤) – though these two tend to fill up early – or the *Mishnish Hotel* (☎01688/302009; ⑤). The island's friendly **youth hostel** is also on Main St (mid-March to Sept ☎01688/302481; Grade 3). The grand Victorian *Western Isles Hotel* (☎01688/302012; ⑦) overlooks the bay, as do several of the cheaper B&Bs on Argyll Terrace such as *Kilmory* (☎01688/302232; ②) or *Ivybank* (☎01688/302250; ②). The nearest **campsite** is *Newdale* (April–Nov; ☎01688/302306), one and a half miles outside Tobermory on the B8073 to Dervaig; facilities here are basic, there's no hot water or showers.

Tobermory's best **restaurant** is the *Strongarbh House* (☎01688/302328) behind the *Western Isles Hotel*. The *Back Brae* (evenings only), on the corner of Back Brae and Main St, also serves good local food, and offers a three-course menu for £11.50; for cheaper, filling dishes, head along Main St to *Gannets*. Top-notch picnic food is available at *Tobermory Fish Farm* shop on Main St, or even, perhaps, the *Chocolate Factory*, up Back Brae. The lively bar of the *Mishnish Hotel*, is the local hangout, and the focus of Mull's annual **Traditional Music Festival**, a feast of Gaelic folk music held on the last weekend in April. Mull's other major musical event is the annual **Mendelssohn on Mull Festival**, held over ten days in early July, which commemorates the composer's visit here in 1829.

Along the west coast

The gently undulating countryside west of Tobermory, beyond the Mishnish lochs, provides some of the most beguiling scenery on the island. Added to this, the road out west, the B8073, is exceptionally dramatic, with fiendish switchbacks much appreciated during the annual Mull Rally, which takes place each October. The only village of any size is **DERVAIG**, which nestles beside a narrow sea loch just eight miles south-west of Tobermory, distinguished by its unusual pencil-shaped church spire and the dinky little cottages on its main street. Dervaig is home to the underfunded *Mull Little Theatre*, one of the smallest professional theatres in the world, which puts on an adventurous season of plays adapted for just two resident actors (May–Sept; booking recommended ☎01688/400245). The theatre lies within the grounds of the *Druimard Country House* (☎01688/400345; ⑥), which offers pricy but excellent pre-theatre dinners. Charles Dickens once stayed at the *Ardbeg House* (☎01688/400254; ④), still one of Dervaig's finest **hotels**; other B&B options include *Antuim Farm* (April–Oct; ☎01688/400230; ③) on the Salen road, *Adrich Farm* (☎01688/400264; ③) on the Calgary road, or vegetarian-friendly *Glenbellart* (☎01688/400282; ③) on the main street. A mile north of the village, you can stay at *Mucmara Lodge* (☎01688/400223; ③), next door to the *Sea Life Surveys* (same phone number) which organizes boat trips to the Treshnish Isles, plus whale-watching and seal trips.

A little beyond Dervaig, the **Old Byre Heritage Centre** (Easter–Oct daily 10.30am–6.30pm; £2.50) is better than many of its kind, with a video on the island's history and a passable tearoom. The road continues cross-country to **CALGARY**, once a thriving crofting community, now an idyllic holiday spot boasting Mull's finest sandy bay, with wonderful views over to Coll and Tiree. There's just one **hotel**, the lovely *Calgary Farmhouse* (☎01688/400256; ⑥), which has an excellent restaurant, *The Dovecote*, in what was once a dovecote; an unofficial **campsite** by the beach; and a splendid wild hillside **garden** at the House of Treshnish (April–Oct only), overlooking the bay.

Salen and the Isle of Ulva

SALEN, on the east coast halfway between Craignure and Tobermory where Mull is at its narrowest, makes a good central base for exploring the island. It has none of Tobermory's charm, but it does have several **B&Bs** – try *Glenmore* (☎01688/300442; ②) on Pier Rd. On the main street, the *Coffee Pot* serves snacks, the *Puffer Aground* more substantial meals, and *On Yer Bike* **rents bikes**. Four miles southwest, back on the west coast, you must pass through the *Gruline Home Farm* (☎01680/300380; ③) in order to reach the **Macquarie Mausoleum**, a simple buttressed tomb, set within a walled clearing surrounded by pine trees and rhododendrons, lovingly maintained by the National Trust of Scotland, on behalf of the National Trust of Australia. Within lies the body of Lachlan Macquarie (1761–1824), the "Father of Australia", who, as the effusive epitaph explains, served as the enlightened governor of New South Wales for 12 years from 1809, when he was appointed by the British to replace William Bligh, formerly of the *Bounty*.

Salen is the closest major town to the island of **Ulva** (from the Norse for "wolf island"), which lies just 100 yards or so off the west coast of Mull. The population peaked at around 600 in the early nineteenth century, when Ulva exported huge quantities of kelp for glass and soap production. That was before the kelp industry collapsed and the 1846 potato famine hit, after which the remaining population was evicted; nowadays barely 20 people live here. A small passenger-only ferry (signposted "Ulva Ferry" from Salen; bicycles also welcome) to Ulva is available on demand (April–Sept Mon–Fri 8am–5pm; June–Aug also Sun; £2 return). On Ulva, *The Boathouse*, the licensed tearoom and **visitor centre** near the ferry slip, sells sandwiches, seaweed dishes and fresh oysters, and features a display on the history of the island. There's no **accommodation**, but with permission from the present owners (☎01688/500226), you can camp rough overnight.

Isle of Staffa and the Treshnish Isles

Five miles southwest of Ulva, **Staffa** is the most romantic and dramatic of Scotland's many uninhabited islands. On its south side, the perpendicular rock face features an imposing series of black basalt columns, known as the Collonade, which have been cut by the sea into cathedralesque caverns, most notably **Fingal's Cave**. The Vikings knew about the island – the name derives from their word for "Island of Pillars" – but it wasn't until 1772 that it was "discovered" by the world. Turner painted it, Wordsworth explored it, but Mendelssohn's *Die Fingalshölle*, inspired by the sounds of the sea-wracked caves he heard on a visit here in 1829, did most to popularize the place – after which Queen Victoria gave her blessing too. The geological explanation for these polygonal basalt organ pipes is that they were created by a massive subterranean explosion some 60 million years ago. A huge mass of molten basalt ejaculated onto land and, as it cooled, solidified into what are, essentially, crystals. Of course, confronted with such artistry, most visitors have found it difficult to believe that their origin is entirely natural – indeed, the various Celtic folk tales, which link the phenomenon with the Giant's Causeway in Ireland, are certainly more appealing. To **get to Staffa**, join one of the many boat trips from Oban, Ulva Ferry, Dervaig and Fionnphort, weather permitting (return trips for around £10–15 per person).

Several boat trips combine a visit to Staffa with a tour of the archipelago of uninhabited volcanic islets that make up the **Treshnish Isles** northwest of Staffa. The most distinctive is **Bac Mór**, shaped like a puritan's hat and popularly dubbed the Dutchman's Cap, while **Lunga**, the largest island, is visited for its wildlife; it is a nesting place for auks and puffins, and an autumn breeding ground for grey seals. The two most northerly islands, **Cairn na Burgh More** and **Cairn na Burgh Beg**, have the remains of ruined castles: the first of which served as a lookout post for the lords of the Isles and was last garrisoned in the Civil War; Cairn na Burgh Beg hasn't been occupied since the 1715 Jacobite uprising.

Ben More and the Ross of Mull

Round the coast from Ulva Ferry, the road (A8073) hugs the shores of Loch na Keal, which almost splits Mull in two. South of the loch rise the terraced slopes of **Ben More** (3169ft), a mighty extinct volcano. Beyond Derryguaig, the road carves through the sheer cliffs before heading south past the Gribun rocks which face the tiny island of **Inch Kenneth**, once owned by the Mitford family. There are great views out to Staffa and the Treshnish Isles as the road climbs over the pass to Loch Scribain, where it joins the equally dramatic Glen More road (A848) from Craignure.

Stretching for 20 miles west of the road junction as far as Iona is the rocky peninsula known as the **Ross of Mull**, which, like much of Scotland, appears blissfully tranquil in good weather, and desolate and bleak in bad. Most visitors simply drive through the Ross en route to Iona, but given that accommodation is severely limited on Iona, it's worth considering staying here. The *Pennyghael Hotel* (Easter–Oct; ☎01681/704205; ⑦), overlooking Loch Scridain, is a luxury option; **BUNESSAN**, roughly two thirds of the way along the Ross, has more choice with the *Assapol Country House* (Easter–Oct; ☎01681/700258; ⑤) and B&Bs such as *Ardtun House* (☎01681/700264; ②). If you have children who need entertaining, be sure to check out the **Angora Rabbit Farm** (daily except Sat 11am–5pm; £1.50), near Bunessan, where children can stroke the comical, long-haired bunnies, and watch their fur being clipped and then spun.

Two miles away on the secluded south coast near **Uisken**, there's a fine sandy beach; so, too, at neighbouring **ARDALANISH** – you can stay at *Ardalanish Farm* (☎01681/700265; ②). **FIONNPHORT**, facing Iona, is the least attractive place to stay; try *Seaview* (☎01681/700235; ②) or *Bruach Mhor* (☎01681/700276; ②), which caters for vegetarians and vegans. The basic *Fidden Farm* **campsite** (☎01681/700427), a mile south along the Knockvologan road by Fidden beach, is the nearest to Iona. Fidden beach looks out to the **Isle of Erraid**, accessible across the sands at low tide. Stevenson is believed to have written *Kidnapped* (its hero, David Balfour, gets shipwrecked here) in one of the island's cottages, overlooking the Torran Rocks, to the south, where his father and uncle built the Dubh Artach lighthouse. The island is now in Dutch ownership, and cared for by the Findhorn Community (for more on which, see p.387).

Isle of Iona

Less than mile off the southwest tip of Mull, **IONA**, although just three miles long and no more than a mile wide, manages to encapsulate all the enchantment and mystique of the Hebrides. It is frequently tagged "the cradle of Christianity": St Columba arrived here from Ireland in 563 and established a monastery which was responsible for the conversion of more or less all of pagan Scotland as well as much of northern England. This history and the island's splendid isolation have lent it a peculiar religiosity; in the words of Dr Johnson, "that man is little to be envied . . . whose piety would not grow warmer among the ruins of Iona". Today, however, the island can barely cope with its thousands of day-trippers, so to appreciate the special atmosphere and to have time to see the whole island, including the often overlooked west coast, you should plan on staying at least one night.

Some history

Legend has it that **St Columba** (Colum), born in Donegal in 521, was a direct descendant of the Irish king, Niall of the Nine Hostages. A scholar and soldier priest, who founded numerous monasteries in Ireland, he became involved in a bloody dispute with the king when he refused to hand over a psalm book copied illegally from the original owned by St Finian of Moville. At the Battle of Cooldrumman, Columba's forces won, though with great loss of life; repenting this bloodshed, he went into exile with 12 other monks, eventually settling on Iona in 563. The Gaelic name for the island is *I-Chaluim-cille* (Island of Columba's Church), often abbreviated simply to *I* (Gaelic for "island"). Columba's miraculous feats included defeating the Loch Ness monster and banishing snakes (and, some say, frogs) from the island.

During his lifetime, Iona enjoyed a great deal of autonomy from Rome, establishing a specifically Celtic Christian tradition. Missionaries were sent out to the rest of Scotland and parts of England, and Iona quickly became a respected seat of learning and artistry; the monks compiled a vast library of intricately illuminated manuscripts – most famously the *Book of Kells* (now on display in Trinity College, Dublin) – while the masons excelled in carving peculiarly intricate crosses. Two factors were instrumental in the demise of the Celtic tradition: relentless pressure from the established Church, and a series of Viking raids which culminated in the massacre of 68 monks on the sands of Martyrs' Bay in 803.

In the eleventh century it was rebuilt as an Augustinian monastery, and by the thirteenth century, Iona had become a more conventional centre for the Benedictine order, its masons enjoying a second flowering of stone carving. By 1500 Iona had achieved cathedral status, but the complex was ransacked during the Reformation as a bastion of the papal Church, during which nearly all the island's 350 crosses were destroyed. Although plans were drawn up at various times to turn the abbey into a Cathedral of the Isles, nothing came of them until its then owner, the Duke of Argyll, donated the abbey buildings to the Church of Scotland, who restored the abbey church for worship by 1910. Iona's modern resurgence began in 1938, when George MacLeod, established a group of ministers, students and artisans to begin rebuilding the remainder of the monastic buildings. What began as a male, Gaelic-speaking, strictly Presbyterian community is today mostly a lay, mixed and ecumenical retreat. The entire abbey complex has been successfully restored and the island, apart from the church land and a few crofts, now belongs to the NTS.

Baile Mór

The frequent passenger ferry from Fionnphort stops at the island's main village, **BAILE MÓR** (literally "large village"), which is in fact little more than a single terrace of cottages facing the red sandstone rocks. Just inland, the ruins of a small **Augustinian nunnery** are built of the same red sandstone. Founded in around 1200, the nunnery fell into disrepair after the Reformation and, if nothing else, gives you an idea of the state of the present-day abbey before it was restored. At a bend in the road just beyond the nunnery stands the fifteenth-century **MacLean's Cross**, a fine example of the distinctive, flowing, three-leaved foliage of the Iona school. To the north the **Iona Heritage Centre** (Mon 10.30am–4.30pm, Tues–Sat 9.30am–4.30pm; £1), in a manse, built, like the nearby parish church, by the ubiquitous Thomas Telford, has displays on the history of the island.

The Abbey

No buildings remain from Columba's time: the present **Abbey** dates from the arrival of the Benedictines in around 1200, was extensively rebuilt in the fifteenth and sixteenth centuries, and restored virtually wholesale in the 1900s. Adjoining the facade is a small steep-roofed chamber, believed to be St Columba's grave, now a small chapel. The three high crosses in front of the abbey date from the eighth to tenth centuries, and are decorated with the Pictish serpent-and-boss and Celtic spirals for which Iona's early Christian masons were renowned. For reasons of sanitation, the cloisters were placed, contrary to the norm, on the north side of the church (where running water was available to flush away the monkish faeces); entirely reconstructed in the late 1950s, they now shelter a useful historical account of the abbey's development.

South of the abbey, Iona's oldest building, **St Oran's Chapel**, has a Norman door dating from the eleventh century. It stands at the centre of the sacred burial ground, **Reilig Odhráin**, which is said to contain the graves of 60 kings of Norway, Ireland and Scotland, including Shakespeare's Duncan and Macbeth. Archeological evidence has failed to back this up; it's about as likely as the legend that the chapel could only be completed through human sacrifice. Oran, one of the older monks in Columba's entourage, apparently volunteered to be buried alive, and was found to have survived the ordeal when the grave was opened a few days later. Declaring that he had seen hell and it wasn't all bad, he was promptly re-interred for blasphemy. The best of the early Christian gravestones and medieval effigies which once lay in the Reilig Odhráin are now the chief exhibits of the **Abbey Museum**, in the old infirmary behind the abbey.

POSSIBLE WALKS ON IONA

In many ways the landscape of Iona – low-lying, treeless with white sandy coves backed by machair – is more reminiscent of the distant islands of Coll and Tiree than it is of neighbouring Mull. Few tourists bother to stray from Baile Mór, yet in high season there is no better way to appreciate Iona's solitary beauty.

Perhaps the easiest jaunt is up **Dùn I**, Iona's only real hill, which rises to the north of the abbey to a height of 300ft – a great place to wander at dawn or dusk. The west coast has some great sandy beaches; the **Camus Cul an Taibh** (Bay at the Back of the Ocean) by the golf course is the longest. More sheltered is the tiny bay on the south coast, Port na Curaich, also known as **Columba's Bay**, thought to be where the saint first landed and dotted with over 50 small cairns. More difficult to reach is the **disused marble quarry** at Rubha na Carraig Géire, on the southeasternmost point of Iona. Quarried intermittently for several centuries, it was finally closed down in 1914; much of the old equipment still visible, rusting away by the shore.

The grave that most visitors now head for, however, is that of the leader of the Labour Party, **John Smith**, who was buried here, with permission from the local council, despite strong opposition from the islanders. The decision to grant a plot in the cemetery to Smith, a frequent visitor to Iona, but a mainlander born in the town Ardrishaig, appears now to have been an unfortunate mistake. The sheer number of political pilgrims has caused the desecration of neighbouring tombstones, and barriers have had to be erected to try to stem the damage. It remains to be seen whether more drastic measures will need to be taken.

Practicalities

There's no **tourist office** on Iona, and as demand far exceeds supply, you should organize **accommodation** in advance. Of the island's two, fairly pricy, hotels, the *Argyll* (April–Oct; ☎01681/700334; ⑥) is the nicer. B&Bs are cheaper but fill quickly: try *Cruachan* (March–Oct; ☎01681/700523; ②), *Finlay Ross* (☎01681/700357; ③) or the vegetarian *Iona Cottage* (☎01681/700579; ③); for longer stays, self-catering is available on Bishop's Walk (☎01681/700329). If you want to stay with the Iona Community, contact the MacLeod Centre (☎01681/700404) – you must be prepared to participate fully in the daily activities, prayers and religious services. **Camping** is possible with the crofter's permission. Visitors are not allowed to bring cars onto the island, but **bikes** can be rented from *Finlay Ross* (see above). The Iona Community also organizes **guided walks** around the island (March–Oct Wed 10.15am).

Food options are limited to hotel restaurants (the *Argyll* is particularly good) or the *Martyrs' Bay* restaurant by the pier. The coffee house (daily 11am–4.30pm) run by the Iona Community just west of the abbey serves homemade soup and delicious cakes.

Coll and Tiree

Coll and **Tiree** are among the most isolated of the Inner Hebrides, and if anything have more in common with the outlying Western Isles than with their closest neighbour, Mull. Each is roughly twelve miles long and three miles wide, both are low-lying, treeless and exceptionally windy, with white sandy beaches and the highest sunshine records in Scotland. Like most of the Hebrides, they were once ruled by Vikings, and didn't pass into Scottish hands until the thirteenth century. Coll's population peaked at 1440, Tiree's at a staggering 4450, but both were badly affected by the Clearances, which virtually halved the populations in a generation. Coll was MacLean country, but is now two thirds owned by a Dutch millionaire; Tiree has been divided into crofts, though it remains a part of the Duke of Argyll's estate. Nominally at least, both islands are part of the *Gàidhealtachd* or Gaelic-speaking area of the Hebrides, but the percentage of English-speaking newcomers is rising steadily.

The *CalMac* ferry from Oban calls at Coll and Tiree every day throughout the year except Thursdays and Sundays – which means you should plan on staying at least one or two nights. Tiree also has an **airport** with daily flights (Mon–Sat) to and from Glasgow. The majority of visitors stay for at least a week in self-catering accommodation (see p.28), though there are B&Bs and hotels on the islands. The only public transport on the islands is the **postbus** on Tiree which calls at all the main settlements.

Isle of Coll

The fish-shaped island of **Coll** (population 150) lies less than seven miles off the coast of Mull. The *CalMac* ferry drops off at Coll's only village, **ARINAGOUR** on the western shore of Loch Eatharna, where half the population now lives. Here, you'll find the island's post office, petrol pump, church, school, two shops, a laundrette and a nine-hole golf course to the northwest.

On the southwest coast there are two edifices – Coll's only formal attractions – both known as **Breachacha Castle**, built by the MacLeans. The oldest, at the head of Loch Breachacha, is a fifteenth-century tower house with an additional curtain wall, recently restored, and a training centre for overseas aid volunteers. The "new castle", to the northwest, made up of a central block built around 1750 and two side pavilions added a century later, has been converted into holiday homes. Among the first visitors were Dr Johnson and Boswell, who stayed here after a storm forced them to take refuge en route to Mull, and who thought the place to be a mere tradesman's box.

There's little else to see, though you could take a walk over the strip of **giant sand dunes** which link Crossapol, the westernmost tip of Coll, with the rest of the island at low tide; wander along to **Ben Hogh** – at 339ft, Coll's highest point – two miles west of Arinagour; or take a look at the **Cairns of Coll**, a series of prehistoric mounds which rise out of the sea off the northern coastline around the almost abandoned hamlets of Bousd and Sorisdale.

In Arinagour, two **hotels** look over the bay: the *Isle of Coll Hotel* (☎01879/230334; ④), and the more modern *Tigh-na-Mara* (Feb–Nov; ☎01879/230354; ③), which also offers **bike rental**. At **ACHA**, two miles west of Arinagour, there's also *Arinagour Farmhouse* (☎01879/230443; ②) and *Achamore* (☎01879/230430; ③). The island's **campsite** (☎01879/230374), which offers basic facilities, is on Breachacha Bay, in the old walled gardens of the castle; you can also stay in the *Garden House* **B&B** (phone as for campsite; ③). The *Isle of Coll Hotel* doubles as the island's social centre, but for a change from hotel food, try the *Coll Bistro* (Easter–Oct) in Arinagour, which serves delicious lobster and Mull salmon, as well as venison and beef.

Isle of Tiree

Tiree, as its Gaelic name *Tir-Iodh* (Land of Corn) suggests, was once known as the breadbasket of the Inner Hebrides, thanks to its acres of rich machair. Nowadays crofting and tourism are the main sources of income for the resident population of more than 800, and every October, the windswept sandy beaches attract large numbers of windsurfers for the International Windsurfers' Championships.

The *CalMac* ferry calls at **SCARINISH**, on a headland to the west of the great sandy beach (*Tràigh Mhór*), of Gott Bay. The village has a post office, general store, pub and bank, and a petrol pump by the pier. The airport is about three miles west of Scarinish. It's just one mile across the island from Gott to Vaul Bay, on the north coast, where the well-preserved remains of a dry-stone broch, **Dun Mor** – dating from the first century BC – lie hidden in the rocks to the west of the bay. From here it's another two miles west along the coast to the *Clach a'Choire* or **Ringing Stone**, a huge glacial boulder decorated with mysterious prehistoric markings, which when struck with a stone gives out a musical sound. The story goes that should the Ringing Stone ever be broken in two, Tiree will sink beneath the waves. A mile further west you come to the lovely **Balephetrish Bay**.

The most intriguing sights lie in the bulging western half of the island, where Tiree's two landmark hills rise up. The highest of the two, **Ben Hynish** (463ft), is unfortunately occupied by a "golf ball" radar station which tracks incoming transatlantic flights; the views from the top, though, are great. Below Ben Hynish, to the east, is the island's largest village **BALEMARTINE**, a mile or so north of the abandoned **Hynish harbour**, designed by Robert Stevenson in the 1830s in order to transport building materials for the 140ft **Skerryvore Lighthouse**, which lies on a sea-swept reef some 12 miles southwest of Tiree. The harbour features an ingenious reservoir to prevent silting, and a tall granite signal tower, by the row of lightkeepers' houses, that has been turned into a **museum** telling the history of the Herculean effort required to erect the lighthouse (automatic since 1954). The best place to get a glimpse of Skerryvore is from the spectacular headland of **Kenavara** (*Ceann a'Mhara*), two miles west of Ben Hynish, across the golden sands of Balephuil Bay. Kenavara's cliffs are home to literally thousands of sea birds, including fulmar, kittiwakes, shags and cormorants; the islands of Barra and South Uist are also visible on the northern horizon.

Practicalities

The only transport around the island is the **postbus** which calls at all the main settlements. Otherwise, you'll need to make use of the **bike rental** facilities at the *Tiree Lodge* on Gott Bay. Of the two **hotels** in and around Scarinish, the *Tiree Lodge* (☎01879/220353; ④), a mile or so along Gott Bay, has the edge over the *Scarinish* (☎01879/220308; ③), overlooking the old harbour. You could also try the *Kirkapol* B&B (☎01879/220729; ③), a converted old kirk by *Tiree Lodge*, or *The Sheiling* (May–Sept; ☎01879/220503; ③), near the airport. Overlooking Balephetrish Bay is the *Balephetrish Guest House* (☎01879/220549; ③) and *Sandy Cove* (April–Oct; ☎01879/220334; ②). There are no official campsites, but **camping** is allowed with the crofter's permission. As for **eating**, just north of Barapol, *The Glassary* (☎01879/220684; ③) serves local lamb, beef and carrageen seaweed pudding, and offers accommodation too.

Isle of Colonsay

Isolated between Mull and Islay, **Colonsay** – eight miles by three at its widest – is nothing like as bleak and windswept as Coll or Tiree. Its craggy hills even support the occasional patch of woodland, plus a bewildering array of plant and birdlife, wild goats and rabbits, and one of the finest quasi-tropical gardens in Scotland. That said, the population is precariously low at around 100, down from a pre-Clearance peak of just under 1000, and the ferry link with Oban infrequent and incovenient (Mon, Wed & Fri only; 2hr 30min). The number of self-catering cottages steadily increases year by year, but, with no camping or caravanning and just one hotel, there's no fear of mass tourism taking over, and Gaelic remains widely spoken.

The *CalMac* ferry terminal is at **SCALASAIG**, on the east coast, where there's a post office, a petrol pump, and a store. Two miles north of Scalasaig, inland, is **Colonsay House**, built in 1722 by Malcolm MacNeil. In 1904, the island and house were bought by the wealthy Lord Strathcona, who made his fortune building the Canadian Pacific Railway. He was also responsible for the house's lovely gardens and woods, which are open to the public, and are slowly being restored to their former glory; the house itself has since been converted into holiday flats. Giant breakers roll in from the Atlantic across **Kiloran Bay**, Colonsay's most impressive white sandy beach to the north of Colonsay House, though the shell beach at Balnahard, two miles northeast along a rough track, is even more deserted and backed by rabbit-infested dunes. The island's west coast forms a sharp escarpment, at its most spectacular just west of Kiloran around **Beinn Bhreac** (456ft).

The island's only **hotel**, in **KILORAN**, the other main settlement, two miles north of Scalasaig, is the *Isle of Colonsay* (March–Oct; ☎01951/200316; ⑨), which does dinner, bed and breakfast. As well as the various self-catering options offered by the MacNeils (March–Nov, Christmas and New Year; ☎01951/200312), there are two **B&Bs**: *Garvard Farmhouse* (☎01951/200343; ④) down by the Strand, and *Seaview* (April–Oct; ☎01951/200315; ④) in Kilchattan. All accommodation for the summer needs to be booked well in advance; self-catering cottages tend to be booked from Wednesday to Wednesday, because of the ferries. The hotel should be able to organize **bike rental**, and there's a **postbus** for those without their own transport.

Isle of Oronsay

Isle of Oronsay (occasionally Oransay), half a mile to the south, is only an island when the tide is in, and, as you can't stay overnight, is basically just a day trip from Colonsay. The two are separated by "The Strand", a mile of tidal mud flats which act as a causeway for two to four hours at low tide; check locally for current timings. Although legends (and etymology) link saints Columba and Oran with both Colonsay and Oronsay, the ruins of the **Oronsay Priory** date back only as far as the fourteenth century. Abandoned since the Reformation, it still has the original church and cloisters, and the Oronsay Cross, a superb example of late medieval artistry from Iona. There are also over 30 grave slabs in the Prior's House, though you'll need a torch to inspect them properly.

Mid-Argyll

Mid-Argyll is a vague term which loosely describes the central wedge of land south of Oban and north of Kintyre, extending west from Loch Fyne to the Atlantic. Lochgilphead, on the shores of Loch Fyne is the chief town in the area, though it has little to offer beyond its practical use – it has a tourist office, a good supermarket and is the regional transport hub (if that's the right word). The highlights of this gently undulating scenery lie along the sharply indented west coast, in particular the rich Celtic remains in the Kilmartin valley, one of the most important prehistoric sites in Scotland. Public transport is thin on the ground, with buses to and from Inveraray and Kilmartin, but little else.

Kilmartin and Dunadd

In the tiny village of **KILMARTIN**, eight miles nouth of Lochgilphead, the nineteenth-century **church** shelters the **Kilmartin Crosses**: one depicts Christ on each side and dates from the tenth century, the other, slightly more recent, is smothered with intricate Celtic knotting. You can also see an interesting collection of medieval grave slabs of the Malcolms of Poltalloch, in a separate enclosure in the graveyard. Kilmartin's castle is ruined beyond recognition; head instead for **Carnasserie Castle**, on a high ridge a mile up the road. Built in the 1560s, it represents the transition between fully fortified castles and later mansion houses, and has several original fireplaces, gunloops and shot-holes.

The **Kilmartin valley**, fanning out south of the village, is one of the most important prehistoric sites in Scotland. The most significant relic is the **linear cemetery**, where several cairns are aligned for more than two miles, beginning just south of Kilmartin. Whether these represent the successive burials of a ruling family or chieftains, nobody can be sure. The best view of the cemetery's configuration is from the Bronze Age Mid-Cairn, but the Neolithic South Cairn, dating from around 3000 BC, is by far the oldest and the most impressive, with its large chambered tomb roofed by giant slabs.

Close to the Mid-Cairn, in a small copse, the **Templewood** stone circles appear to have been the architectural focus of burials in the area from Neolithic times to the Bronze Age. Visible to the south are the impressively cup-marked **Nether Largie standing stones**, the largest of which looms over 10ft high. **Cup- and ring-marked rocks** are a recurrent feature of prehistoric sites in the Kilmartin valley and elsewhere in Argyll. There are many theories as to their origin: some see them as Pictish symbols, others as African death symbols, primitive solar calendars and so on. The most extensive markings are at **Achnabreck**, off the A816 towards Lochgilphead, but there are other well-preserved rocks in **Slockavullin**, a mile or so west of Templewood.

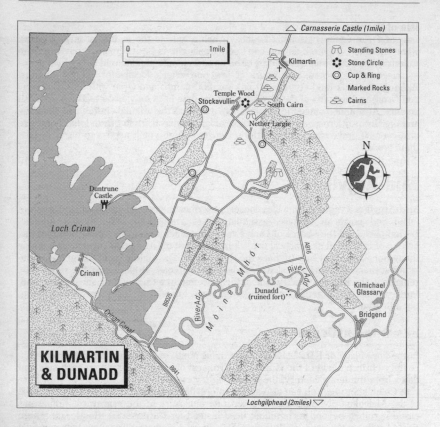

△ Carnasserie Castle (1mile)

KILMARTIN & DUNADD

Standing Stones
Stone Circle
Cup & Ring
Marked Rocks
Cairns

Kilmartin
Temple Wood
Stockavullin
South Cairn
Nether Largie
Duntrune Castle
Loch Crinan
Crinan
Crinan Canal
River Add
Mòine Mhór
Dunadd (ruined fort)
Kilmichael Glassary
Bridgend
B8025
B841

Lochgilphead (2miles) ▽

Dunadd

The peaty plain of Mòine Mhór (Great Moss), which opens up to the south of Kilmartin, is home to the Iron Age fort of **Dunadd**, one of Scotland's most important Celtic sites, occupying a distinctive 176ft-high rocky knoll once surrounded by the sea but currently beside the winding River Add. It was here that Fergus, the first King of Dalriada, established his royal seat, having arrived from Ireland around 500 AD. Its strategic position, the craggy defences and the view from the top are all impressive, but it's the **stone carvings** between the twin summits which make Dunadd so remarkable: several lines of inscription in ogam, (an ancient alphabet of Irish origin), the faint outline of a boar, a hollowed-out footprint and a small basin. The boar and the inscriptions are probably Pictish, since the fort was clearly occupied long before Fergus got there, but the footprint and basin have been interpreted as being part of the royal coronation rituals of the kings of Dalriada. It is thought that the Stone of Destiny was used at Dunadd before being moved to Scone Palace (see p.245) and eventually to Westminster Abbey in London.

Practicalities

If you don't fancy staying in Lochgilphead, there are several options within a mile radius of Kilmartin. The *Kilmartin Hotel* (☎01546/510250; ④) is in the village itself; *Ri-Cruin* (☎01546/510231; ③) and *Tibertich* (☎01546/510281; ②) are local sheep farms offering **B&B**; and there are further possibilities in the nearby village of Kilmichael Glassary. *The Cairn* (☎01546/510254), opposite the church in Kilmartin, is a great place for lunch, afternoon teas or a moderately expensive evening **meal**, featuring superb Scottish and some Mediterranean dishes.

Knapdale

Forested **Knapdale** – from the Gaelic *cnap* (hill) and *dall* (field) – forms a buffer zone between the Kintyre peninsula and the rest of Argyll, bounded to the north by the Crinan Canal, and to the south by West Loch Tarbert.

Crinan Canal

In 1801 the nine-mile-long **Crinan Canal** opened, linking Loch Fyne with the Sound of Jura across the bottom of the Mòine Mhór, thus cutting out the long and treacherous journey around the Mull of Kintyre. John Rennie's original design, although an impressive engineering feat, had numerous faults and by 1816 Thomas Telford had to be called in to take charge of the renovations.

The largest concentration of locks – there are 15 in total – is around Cairnbaan, but the best place to view the canal in action is at **CRINAN**, the picturesque fishing port at the western end of the canal. Crinan's tiny harbour is, for the moment at least, still home to a small fishing fleet, though the majority of the traffic on the canal itself is now made up of pleasure boats. Every room in the *Crinan Hotel* (☎01546/830261; ⑨) looks across Loch Crinan to the Sound of Jura – one of the most beautiful views in Scotland, especially at sunset when the myriad islets and the distinctive Paps of Jura are reflected in the still, golden waters of the loch. If the *Crinan* is beyond your means, there are some cheaper but less well-appointed **B&Bs**. Lunch at the *Crinan* is recommended, but may be beyond the reach of some; the bar meals are not correspondingly good and no bargain. Tea and delicious calorific cakes can be had from *Lock 16* right on the quayside.

Knapdale Forest and Loch Sween

South of the canal, **Knapdale Forest**, planted in the 1930s, stretches virtually uninterrupted from coast to coast, across hills sprinkled with tiny lochs. The Forestry Commission has set out several lovely **walks**, the easiest of which is the circular, mile-long path which takes you deep into the forest just past **Achanamara** (5 miles south of Crinan). The three-mile route around **Loch Coille-Bharr**, which begins from a bend in the B8025, to Tayvallich, is fairly gentle; the other walk, although half a mile shorter, is more strenuous, starting from the B841 (halfway between Crinan and Lochgilphead), which runs along the canal, and ascending the peak of **Dunardry** (702ft).

Six miles south of Achanamara, on the shores of Loch Sween is the "Key of Knapdale", the eleventh-century **Castle Sween**, the earliest stone castle in Scotland, but in ruins since 1647. The tranquility and beauty of the setting is spoiled by the nearby caravan park, an eyesore which makes a visit pretty depressing. You're better off continuing south to the thirteenth-century **Kilmory Chapel**, also ruined but with a new roof protecting the medieval grave slabs and the well-preserved MacMillan's Cross, an 8ft-high fifteenth-century Celtic cross showing the crucifixion on one side, and a hunting scene on the other. If you want to **stay**, try the *Kilberry Inn* (☎01880/770223; ⑤), 20 miles southwest of Lochgilphead on B8024, which guarantees peace and quiet, plus excellent home cooking.

Lochgilphead

The regional hub of Mid-Argyll is **LOCHGILPHEAD**, which as the name suggests lies at the shallow, muddy, head of Loch Gilp. It's a planned town in the same vein as Inveraray, but without the pristine whitewashed terraces or the mountainous backdrop. If you're staying in the area, you're bound to find yourself here at some point, as Lochgilphead is currently Argyll's regional capital, and has the only bank and super-market for miles. The **tourist office**, 27 Lochnell St (April & Oct Mon–Fri 10am–1pm & 2–5pm, Sat & Sun noon–4pm; May to mid-June and late Sept Mon–Sat 10am–1pm & 2–5pm, Sun 11am–4pm; mid-June to mid-Sept Mon–Sat 9.30am–6.30pm, Sun 10am–5pm; ☎01546/602344) will help find you **accommodation**. If you are looking yourself the *Stag*, Argyll St (☎01546/602496; ⑤), is overpriced; others include the *Argyll*, Lochnell St (☎01546/602221; ③), or *Kilmory House*, Paterson St (☎01546/603658; ②). *The Smiddy*, on Smithy Lane, does the best **home cooking** in town. If you're desperate for something to do in wet weather you could pay a visit to *Highbank Pottery*, a short distance up the Oban road (A816), where they make grotesque little ceramic animals, and offer guided tours of the premises (Mon–Fri 10.30am & 2pm; nominal fee). A better idea, in fine weather, is to head for *Castle Riding Centre* (☎01546/603274) at Brenfield Farm, three miles south of Lochgilphead, which runs highly enjoyable riding courses lasting from a day to a week, plus trekking, pub rides, and even **rents out bikes**, golf equipment, the lot.

Kintyre

But for the mile-long isthmus between West and the smaller much East Loch Tarbert, **KINTYRE** (from the Gaelic *ceann tire*, "land's end") would be an island. Indeed, in the eleventh century, when the Scottish king, Malcolm Canmore, told Magnus Barefoot, King of Norway, he could lay claim to any island he could navigate his boat round, Magnus succeeded in dragging his boat across the Tarbert isthmus and added the peninsula to his Hebridean kingdom. After the Wars of the Covenant, when the vast majority of the population and property was wiped out by a combination of the 1646 potato blight coupled with the destructive attentions of the Earl of Argyll, Kintyre became a virtual desert until the earl began his policy of transplanting Gaelic-speaking Lowlanders to the region.

Getting around Kintyre without your own transport is a slow business, though services have improved. There are two or three buses a day from Glasgow to Campbeltown, via Tarbert and the west coast, and even a skeleton service down the east coast. Bear in mind, if you're driving, that the new west coast road is extremely fast, whereas the single-track east coast road takes more than twice as long. Campbeltown has an airport, with regular flights from Glasgow, which is only 40 miles away by air, compared to over 120 miles by road. There are also plans afoot to end Campbeltown's isolation by establishing a ferry link with Barrycastle in Northern Ireland.

Tarbert

A distinctive rocket-like church steeple heralds the fishing village of **TARBERT** (in Gaelic *an tairbeart*, meaning "isthmus"), sheltering an attractive little bay backed by rugged hills. Tarbert's herring industry was mentioned in the Annals of Ulster as far back as 836 AD – though right now the future of the local fishing industry is under threat from EU quotas. Tourism is an increasingly important source of income, as is the money that flows through the town during the last week in May, when the yacht races of the Rover Series take place. Other than shop and watch life go by in the harbour, there's little to do in Tarbert. Of Robert the Bruce's fourteenth-century **castle** above the town, there are now only scant remains, though the view from the over-grown rubble makes a trip up here worthwhile. Only head for the **An Tairbeart Heritage Centre** (Easter–Oct daily 10am–dusk), if you're really desperate for some-thing to do.

The **tourist office** (same times as for Lochgilphead; ☎01880/820429) is on the harbour. If you need to **stay**, there's the *Columba* hotel on the waterfront (☎01880/820808; ③), or *Springside* B&B on Pier Rd (☎01880/820413; ②). If you're just looking for a fill-up, the **bar snacks** at the *Islay Frigate Hotel* on the harbour should suffice, but for the best fish and seafood in the whole of Argyll, head for *The Anchorage* nearby (☎01880/820881), unforgettable not least for its eccentric proprietor. You can **rent bikes** from Mr Leitch (☎01880/820287).

One reason you might find yourself staying in Tarbert is its proximity to no fewer than four **ferry terminals**: the nearest is the new *CalMac* service east to Portavadie on the Cowal peninsula; the busiest terminal is just under eight miles south at **Kennacraig** which runs daily sailings to Islay; further south is the Gigha ferry from Tayinloan, and on the opposite coast the Claonaig ferry to Arran runs from April to October.

Isle of Gigha

Gigha (pronounced "Geeya", with a hard "g") is a low-lying, fertile island, just three miles off the west coast of Kintyre. The island's Ayrshire cattle produce over a quarter of a million gallons of milk a year, despite the fact that Gigha's creamery closed down in the 1980s – some of it goes to produce the distinctive fruit-shaped cheese which is one of the island's main exports. Like many of the smaller Hebrides, the island was sold by its original lairds, the MacNeils, and has been put on the market twice in less than ten years, causing great uncertainty amongst the 120 or so inhabitants, who have to endure these periods of instability as best they can.

The ferry from Tayinloan, 23 miles south of Tarbert, deposits you at the island's only village, **ARDMINISH**, where you'll find the post office and shop. The only sights, as such, are the **Achamore Gardens** (daily 9am–dusk; £2), a mile and a half south of Ardminish. Established by the first post-war owner, Sir James Horlick of hot drink fame, they are best seen in early summer, ablaze with rhododendrons and azaleas.

Gigha is so small – six miles by one – that most visitors come here just for the day. However, it is possible to **stay**, either with the McSporrans, at the *Post Office House* (☎01583/505251; ③), or at the *Gigha Hotel* (March–Oct; ☎01583/505254; ⑥), which also runs self-catering flats dotted over the island. Caravans and camping are not allowed on Gigha. Tea, coffee and cakes are best taken by the shore at the *Boathouse* (May–Sept) which overlooks the ferry pier. For something more substantial, the *Gigha Hotel* does really good bar meals. **Bike rental** is available at the McSporrans'.

The west coast

Kintyre's bleak **west coast** ranks among the most exposed stretches of coastline in Argyll. The Atlantic pounds the monotonous shoreline, while the persistent westerly wind forces the trees against the hillside. That said, there are numerous deserted sandy beaches to enjoy with great views over to Gigha, Islay, Jura and even Ireland – though, as always in Scotland, everything depends upon the weather. Apart from the luxury late-Victorian *Balinakill Country House* at Clachan (☎0188/740206; ⑥), accommodation along the coast is limited to the odd **B&B**, though there are several blustery **campsites**: *Point Sands* (April–Oct; ☎01583/441263) in Rhunahaorine, two miles north of Tayinloan, is near a long stretch of sandy beach, as is *Muasdale Holiday Park,* three miles south of Tayinloan (April–Oct; ☎01583/421207). One of the few **places to eat** along the coast is the *North Beachmore Farm*, signposted off the A83 south of Tayinloan, which gives superb views over the coast, and serves good, low-priced meals, tea and cakes.

The **Killean Church**, three miles south of Tayinloan, is one of the few conventional sights on the entire coast, a ruined twelfth-century edifice whose graveyard contains some unusual, carved, medieval grave slabs. **Glenbarr Abbey** (daily except Tues 10am–5.30pm; £2.50) is an eighteenth-century laird's house filled with tedious memorabilia about the once powerful MacAlister clan, now reduced to augmenting their income by giving personal guided tours of their house to the trickle of tourists that passes this way. Still, there are plenty of musty old sofas to lounge around in, a tearoom, and attractive grounds which provide a brief respite from the Atlantic winds.

The only major development along this coast is at **MACHRIHANISH**, at the southern end of Machrihanish Bay, the longest continuous stretch of sand in Argyll. Once a thriving, salt-producing and coal-mining centre – you can still see the miners' cottages at neighbouring Drumlemble – Machrihanish now survives solely on tourism. The main draw, apart from the beach, is the seabird observatory at Uisaed Point, and the golf course between the village and the combined military and civil Campbeltown airport on the nearby flat and fertile swathe of land known as the Laggan. **Accommodation** options include *The Beachcomber* (☎01586/810355; ③), *Ardell House* (March–Oct; ☎01586/810235; ④), or the **campsite** (March–Sept; ☎01586/810366).

Campbeltown

There's little to recommend **CAMPBELTOWN** beyond its setting, in a deep bay sheltered by Davaar Island and the surrounding hills. However, with a population of 6500, it is one of the largest towns in Argyll, and if you're staying in the southern half of Kintyre, here is by far the best place to stock up on supplies. Originally known as Kinlochkilkerran (*Ceann Loch Cill Chiaran*), the town was renamed in the seventeenth century by the Earl of Argyll – a Campbell – when it became one of the main points for immigration from the Lowlands. As is evident from the architecture, Campbeltown's heyday was the Victorian era, when shipbuilding was going strong, coal was shipped by canal from Drumlemble, the fishing fleet was vast and Campbeltown Loch was said to be made of whisky.

Nineteenth-century visitors to Campbeltown frequently found the place engulfed in a thick fog of pungent peat smoke from the town's 34 **whisky distilleries**. Nowadays, only *Glen Scotia* and *Springbank* are left to maintain this regional sub-group of single malt whiskies which is distinct from Highland, Islay or Lowland varieties (see p.31 in *Basics* for more on whisky). Neither distillery is keen on encouraging visitors, however, though you can buy a guide to Campbeltown's former distilleries from the tourist office. The town's one major sight is the **Campbeltown Cross**, a fourteenth-century blue-green cross with figural scenes and spirals of Celtic knotting, which presides over the main roundabout on the quayside. Until the last war, it used to be rather more impressive in the middle of the main street outside the **Town House**, with its distinctive eighteenth-century octagonal clock tower. Back on the harbour is the **"Wee Picture House"**, a dinky little Art Deco cinema on Hall St, built in 1913 and now doubling as a bingo hall (Tues & Fri) and movie house.

It used to be said that Campbeltown had almost as many churches as it did distilleries, and even today the townscape is dominated by its church spires, in particular, the top-heavy crown spire of **Longrow Church**. On the road to Machrihanish, the church known locally as the "Tartan Kirk", partly due to its Gaelic associations, but mainly for its stripey bell-cote and pinnacles, has now become the **Campbeltown Heritage Centre** (Mon–Fri noon–5pm, Sat 10am–5pm, Sun 2–5pm; £1). A beautiful wooden skiff from 1906 stands where the main altar once was, and there's plenty of stuff on the local whisky industry, and St Kieran, the sixth-century "Apostle of Kintyre", who lived in a cave – which you can get to at low tide – not far from Campbeltown. A dedicated ascetic, he would only eat bread mixed with a third sand and a few herbs; he wore chains, had a stone pillow and slept out in the snow – unsurprisingly, at the age of just 33, he died of jaundice.

Perhaps most rewarding is the trip to **Davaar Island**, linked to the peninsula at low tide by a mile-long bank of shoal, or *dòirlinn* as it's known in Gaelic. You'll need to find out the times of the tides from the tourist office before setting out; you have around six hours in which to make the return journey from Kildalloig Point, two miles or so east of town. Davaar is uninhabited and used for grazing (hence no dogs are allowed); its main attraction, besides the wealth of rock flora, is the cave painting of the crucifixion executed in secret by local artist, Archibald MacKinnon, in 1887, and touched up by the same man after he'd owned up in 1934; a year later aged 85, he died.

Practicalities

Campbeltown's **tourist office** on the Old Quay (Feb, March, Nov & Dec Mon–Fri 9am–5.30pm; April & Oct Mon–Fri 9am–5.30pm, Sat & Sun noon–4pm; May to mid-June and late Sept Mon–Sat 9am–1pm & 2–5.30pm, Sat & Sun 11am–5pm; mid-June to mid-Sept Mon–Sat 9.30am–6.30pm, Sun 10am–6pm; ☎01586/552056) can help with **accommodation**. The *White Hart Hotel* on Main St (☎01586/552440; ④) is the town's chief hotel; otherwise there's *Westbank Guest House*, Dell Rd (☎01586/553660; ③), or cheaper still *Barbreck* (☎01586/552173; ②), Kilkerran Rd. There are few **places to eat**, unless you're prepared to fork out for an expensive meal with all the trimmings in the *White Hart Hotel*, or *Seafield Hotel* (☎01586/554385) on Kilkerran Rd. You can rent bikes at *The Bike Shop*, Longrow (☎01586/554443).

Southend and the Mull of Kintyre

Travelling south from Campbeltown to the bulbous, hilly end of Kintyre takes you through some of the most spectactular scenery on the whole peninsula. Consequently, SOUTHEND itself, one of those bleak, blustery spots beloved of fixed caravan sites, comes as something of a disappointment. It does have a sandy beach, but the nicest spot for swimming is **Macharioch Bay**, three miles east, which looks out to distant Ailsa Craig in the Firth of Clyde.

Out to sea, but closer to Southend, is **Dunaverty Rock**, where a force of 300 Royalists was massacred by the Covenanting army of the Earl of Argyll in 1647 despite having surrendered voluntarily. A couple of miles beyond lies **Sanda Island**, which contains the remains of St Ninian's chapel, plus two ancient crosses and a holy well; it's now a holiday retreat (☎01586/553134). Below the cliffs to the west of Southend, a ruined thirteenth-century chapel marks the alleged arrival point of St Columba prior to his trip to Iona, and on a rocky knoll nearby a pair of footprints carved into the rock are known as "Columba's footprints", though only one is actually of ancient origin.

Most people venture south of Campbeltown to make a pilgrimage to the **Mull of Kintyre** – the nearest Britain gets to Ireland, whose coastline, just 12 miles away, is visible on clear days. Although the Mull was made famous by the mawkish number one hit by one-time local resident, Paul McCartney, with the help of the Campbeltown Pipe Band, there's nothing specifically to see in this godforsaken storm-racked spot but the view. The roads up to the "Gap" (1150ft) – where you must leave your car – and down to the lighthouse, itself 300ft above the ocean waves, are terrifyingly precipitous.

There are few places to **stay** in this remote region. Southend's only hotel is currently closed; try instead *Ormsary Farm* (☎01586/830665; ③), or *Low Cattadale* (☎01586/830665; ③), or the **campsite** at *Machribeg Farm* (Easter–Sept; ☎01586/830249), all in Southend.

The east coast

The **east coast** of Kintyre is gentler than the west, less battered by the Atlantic winds – though you need to have a fair amount of time on your hands if you're driving the 30 or so miles up to Skipness on the slow, winding, single-track B842.

The ruins of **Saddell Abbey**, a Cistercian foundation thought to have been founded by Somerled in 1160, lie ten miles up the coast from Campbeltown, set at the lush, wooded entrance to Saddell Glen. The abbey fell into disrepair in the sixteenth century, and though the remains are not exactly impressive, they do shelter a collection of medieval grave slabs decorated with full-scale relief figures of knights. There's also a splendid memorial to the last Campbell laird to live at Saddell Castle, which he built in 1774, which still stands by the shoreline (privately owned).

A little further north, the fishing village of **CARRADALE** is the only place of any size on the east coast and something of a holiday resort. The village itself is drab, but the tiny, sandy harbour with its small fishing fleet, and the sandy bay to the south, make up for it. There are a couple of **hotels** – the *Ashbank* (☎01583/431650; ③) is the best value, while the bar of the *Carradale Hotel* (mid-Feb to Dec; ☎01583/431223; ④) is the hub of village social life – and several **B&Bs**, including *Mains Farm* (April–Oct; ☎01583/431216; ②) and *Seaview East* (☎01583/431316; ②), plus *Carradale Bay* **campsite** (Easter–Sept; ☎01583/431665) right by the sandy beach. A little further up the road, a wet weather possibility is a visit **to Grogport Tannery** (daily 9am–6pm; free tour), which produces naturally coloured, organically tanned sheepskins.

The B842 ends twelve miles north of Carradale at **CLAONAIG**, little more than a slipway for the summer car ferry to Arran. Beyond here, a dead-end road winds its way along the shore a few miles further north to **SKIPNESS**, where the considerable ruins of an enormous thirteenth-century castle and a chapel look out across the Kilbrannan Sound to Arran. You can sit outside and admire both, whilst enjoying fresh oysters, mussels and the like from the excellent seafood cabin at *Skipness House*, which also offers **accommodation** in a family home (☎01880/760207; ⑦).

Isle of Arran

Shaped like a kidney bean, **Arran** is the most southerly (and therefore the most accessible) of all the Scottish islands. The Highland–Lowland dividing line passes right through its centre – hence the tourist board's aphorism about "Scotland in miniature" – leaving the northern half underpopulated, mountainous and bleak, while the lush southern half enjoys a milder climate. Despite its immense popularity, the tourists, like the population, tend to stick to the southeastern quarter of the island, leaving the west and the north relatively undisturbed.

There are two big crowd pullers on Arran: **geology** and **golf**. The former has fascinated students, since James Hutton came here in the late eighteenth century to confirm his theories of igneous geology. A hundred years later, Sir Archibald Geikie's investigations were a landmark in the study of Arran's geology, and the island remains a popular destination for university and school field trips. As for golf, Arran boasts no fewer than seven courses, including three of the eighteen-hole variety at Brodick, Lamlash and Whiting Bay, and a twelve-hole course at Blackwaterfoot.

Although tourism is now by far its most important industry, at twenty miles in length, Arran is large enough to have a life of its own. While the history of the Clearances on Arran, set in motion by the local lairds, the dukes of Hamilton, is as depressing as elsewhere in the Highlands, in recent years it has not suffered from the depopulation which has plagued other, more remote islands. Once a county in its own right (along with Bute), Arran has been left out of the new Argyll and Bute district in the recent county boundary shake-up, and is now coupled instead with mainland North Ayrshire, with which it enjoys closer transport links, but little else.

Transport is good: daily **buses** circle the island (Brodick tourist office has time-tables) and in summer there are two **ferry services**, one from Ardrossan (all year) in Ayrshire to Brodick, and a smaller ferry from Claonaig on the remote Kintyre peninsula to Lochranza in the north (mid-April to mid-Oct).

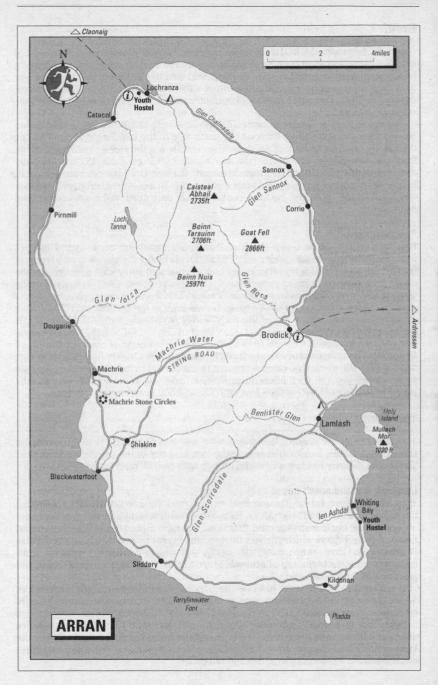

ARRAN

Brodick

Although the resort of **BRODICK** (from the Norse *breidr vik*, "broad bay") is a place of little charm, it does at least have a grand setting in a wide, sandy bay set against a backdrop of granite mountains. Its development as a tourist resort on the Clyde was held back for a long time by its elitist owners, the dukes of Hamilton, though nowadays, as the island's capital and main communication hub, Brodick is by far the busiest town on Arran.

The dukes lived at **Brodick Castle** (Easter–Sept daily 11.30am–5pm; Oct Sat & Sun only; NTS; £3.50), on a steep bank on the north side of the bay. The interior is for the dedicated period furniture buff only; more accessible are the views over Brodick Bay, from the flower-filled walled grounds (all year daily 9.30am–dusk; £2) and the very good tearooms. The **Arran Heritage Museum** (Easter–Oct Mon–Sat 9am–5pm; £1), is a somewhat dry collection of old tools and furniture in a converted crofter's farm halfway between the castle and the town centre – really only worth visiting to escape from bad weather.

Practicalities

Brodick's **tourist office** (April–Oct Mon–Sat 9am–7.30pm, Sun 10am–5pm; Oct–April Mon–Sat 9am–5pm, Fri till 7.30pm; ☎01770/302401) is by the *CalMac* pier, with reams of information on bus and ferry services, accommodation and every kind of activity on the island from pony trekking to paragliding. Unless you've got to catch an early-morning ferry, there's very little reason to stay in Brodick. There are, however, plenty of rooms close to the ferry terminal, in old Victorian **hotels** such as the *Douglas* (☎01770/302155; ③) as well as more modest places like the *Glencloy Farmhouse* (☎01770/302351; ④). Of the many **B&Bs**, try the *Belvedere*, on Alma Rd (☎01770/302397; ②); the nearest **campsite** is *Glenrosa* (April–Oct; ☎01770/302380), a mile or so north of the town centre, off String Rd. The only **restaurant** which really stands out is *Creelers* (mid-March to Oct; ☎01770/302810), a superb seafood restaurant by the Arran Heritage Museum on the road to the castle. You can **rent bikes** from *Brodick Cycles* (☎01770/302460), opposite the village hall, or from *Mini-Golf Cycle Hire* (☎01770/302272) near the pier.

The south

The southern half of Arran is less spectacular, and less forbidding than the north; the land is more fertile, and for that reason the vast majority of the population lives here. The tourist industry has followed them, though with considerably less justification.

Lamlash and the south coast

With its distinctive Edwardian architecture and mild climate **LAMLASH** epitomizes the sedate charm of southeast Arran. Its major drawback is its bay, which is made not of sand but of boulder-strewn mud flats. You can take a boat out to the slug-shaped hump of **Holy Island** which shelters the bay, and is now owned by a group of Tibetan Buddhists who have set up a meditation centre – providing you don't dawdle, it's possible to scramble up to the top of Mullach Mòr (1030ft), the island's highest point, and still catch the last ferry back.

If you want to **stay** in style, head for the *Glenisle Hotel* (April–Oct; ☎01770/600 258; ⑥), or the much smaller *Lilybank Hotel* (☎01770/600230; ③), which does superb homemade food; cheaper B&Bs such as *Douglas Villa* (☎01770/600261; ②) are easy enough to find, and *Middleton's* **campsite** (April to mid-Oct; ☎01770/600255) is just five minutes' walk north of the centre. The best **restaurant** in Lamlash is undoubtedly the *Carraig Mhor* near the pier (☎01770/600453), which offers an exclusive and expensive menu featuring fresh local game, fish and seafood.

Although it has been an established Clydeside resort for over a century now, **WHITING BAY**, four miles south of Lamlash, is actually pretty characterless. However, there are plenty of **places to stay**, among them the *Royal Hotel* (☎01770/700286; ④); *Viewbank* (☎01770/700326; ③), or *Silverhill North* (☎01770/700414; ②), and a **youth hostel** (mid-Feb to Oct; ☎01770/700339; Grade 2); for **bike rental** go to *Whiting Bay Hires* (☎01770/700382) on the jetty. Elsewhere the easiest point of access to the sea is at **KILDONAN**, a small village off the main road, with just one hotel, *Drimla Lodge* (☎01770/820296; ④), the odd B&B like *Dippen House* (☎01770/820223; ②), and a **campsite** (☎01770/820210). There's a nice sandy beach below the village, and, at its east end, a ruined castle looking out to tiny island of Pladda.

Blackwaterfoot and Machrie

BLACKWATERFOOT, on the western end of String Rd that bisects the island, is less a Clyde-style resort than a genuine Hebridean fishing village, and, like Lochranza, a good place to escape the worst of Arran's summer crowds. If you want to **stay**, there's the Victorian *Blackwaterfoot Hotel* (March–Oct; ☎01770/860202; ④) and plenty of cheaper B&Bs: try *Midmar* (☎01770/860413; ③), *Parkhouse* (☎01770/860392; ②), or *Broombrae* (☎01770/860435; ②), a mile or so south of town in Kilpatrick.

North of Blackwaterfoot the wide expanse of **Machrie Moor** boasts a wealth of Bronze Age sites. No fewer than six **stone circles** sit east of the main road; although many of them barely break the peat's surface, the tallest surviving monolith is over 18ft high. The most striking configuration is at Fingal's Cauldron Seat, with two concentric circles of granite boulders; legend has it that Fingal tied his dog to one of them while cooking at his cauldron. Incidentally, **King's Cave**, two miles along the coast north from Blackwaterfoot, is where Robert the Bruce is thought to have encountered the famously patient arachnid, while hiding during his final bid to free Scotland in 1306 .

The north

The desolate north half of Arran – effectively the Highland part – features bare granite peaks, the occasional golden eagle and miles of unspoilt scenery, within reach only to those prepared to do some serious hiking. Arran's most accessible peak is also the island's highest, **Goat Fell** (2866ft) – take your pick from the Gaelic, *goath*, meaning "windy", or the Norse *geit-fjall*, "goat mountain" – which can be ascended in just three hours from Brodick (return journey 5hr), though it's a strenuous hike (for the usual safety precautions see p.38). From Goat Fell, experienced walkers can follow the horeshoe of craggy summits and descend either from the saddle below Beinn Tarsuinn (2706ft) or from Beinn Nuis (2597ft).

Another good base for hiking is the pretty little seaside village of **CORRIE**, six miles north of Brodick, where a procession of pristine cottages line the road to Lochranza. There are numerous self-catering flats, as well as a couple of hotels and B&Bs: try *Blackrock Guest House* (☎01770/810282; ③); **bike rental** is available from *The Spinning Wheel* (☎01770/810640). At Sannox, two miles north, the road leaves the shoreline and climbs steeply, giving breathtaking views over to the scree-strewn slopes around Caisteal Abhail (2735ft). If you make this journey around dusk, be sure to pause in **Glen Chalmadale**, on the other northern side of the pass, to catch a glimpse of the red deer who come down to pasture by the water.

The ruined castle which occupies the mud flats of the bay, and the gloomy north-facing slopes of the mountains which frame it, make for one of the most spectacular settings on the island – yet **LOCHRANZA**, despite being the only place of any size in this sparsely populated area, attracts far fewer visitors than Arran's southern resorts. That may be set to change in the year 2001, when the island's first legal whisky distillery for over 150 years, located in Lochranza, begins to produce its first single malt.

In the meantime, there's a **tourist office** by the *CalMac* pier (mid-May to Sept Mon–Sat 9am–5pm; ☎01770/830320), a **youth hostel** (mid-Feb to Oct; ☎01770/830631; Grade 2) overlooking the castle, and a well-equipped **campsite** (Easter–Oct; ☎01770/830273) by the golf course on the Brodick Rd. Plusher **accommodation** can be had at the *Apple Lodge Hotel* (☎01770/830229; ⑤), the *Lochranza Hotel* (☎01770/830223; ④), or *Belvaren* B&B (☎01770/830647; ②).

An alternative is to continue a mile or so southwest along the coast to **CATACOL**, where the friendly *Catacol Bay Hotel* (☎01770/830231; ③) takes the prize as the island's best pub by far: good, basic pub food (with several veggie options and real chips), great beer on tap, a small adjoining campsite, and seal and shags to view on the nearby shingle. The pub also puts on live music most weeks, and hosts a week-long folk festival in early June.

Isle of Islay

Islay (pronounced "eye-la") is famous for one thing – single malt **whisky**. The smoky, peaty, pungent quality of Islay whisky is unique, recognizable even to the untutored palette, and five of the six distilleries that still function put on free guided tours, ending with the customary complimentary tipple. Yet despite the fame of its whiskies, Islay remains relatively undiscovered, much as Skye and Mull were some 20 years ago. Part of the reason, no doubt, is that it takes a pricy, two-hour ferry journey from Kennacraig on Kintyre to reach the island; and once there, you'll find no luxury hotels or fancy restaurants.

In medieval times, Islay was the political centre of the Hebrides, with Finlagan Castle, near Port Askaig, the seat of the MacDonalds, lords of the Isles. As an official part of the *Gàidhealtachd*, you'll see bi-lingual signs in Bowmore, Port Charlotte and elsewhere. The picturesque, whitewashed villages you see on Islay today, however, date from the planned settlements founded by the Campbells in the late eighteenth and early nineteenth centuries. Apart from whisky and solitude, the other great draw is the **birdlife**, in particular the scores of white-fronted and barnacle geese who winter here. For two weeks in late May/early June, the Islay Festival *Feis Ile* takes place, with whisky tasting, pipe bands, folk dancing and other events celebrating the island's Gaelic culture. There are no public transport services provided on a Sunday, and you'll then have to rely on the **postbus**; check times with the island's tourist office in Bowmore.

Port Ellen and the south

Notwithstanding the ferry from Kennacraig, **PORT ELLEN**, the largest place on **Islay**, is a sleepy little place, laid out as a planned village in 1821 and named after the wife of the founder. The neat terraces along the harbour are pretty enough, but the bay is dominated by the now disused whisky distillery – the smell of malt which wafts across the harbour comes from the modern maltings just off the Bowmore road. For information about the southern half of Islay, check out the ad hoc **tourist office** (open to greet ferry passengers) based in a caravan beside the *White Hart Hotel*. As well as the two hotels, the *Trout Fly* restaurant has **rooms** (☎01496/302204; ③), or you could try any of the B&Bs on Frederick Crescent. There's also an **independent hostel**, *Kintra Bunkbarns* (☎01496/302051; ①), with a B&B at *Kintra Farm* (☎01496/302051; ③) which runs an adjacent **campsite** with good facilities (April–Sept), all in **KINTRA**, three miles northwest of Port Ellen, at the southern tip of Laggan Bay.

From Port Ellen, a dead-end road heads off east along the coastline, passing three functioning distilleries in as many miles. First comes **Laphroaig distillery** (free tours by arrangement only; ☎01496/302418) which produces the most uncompromisingly

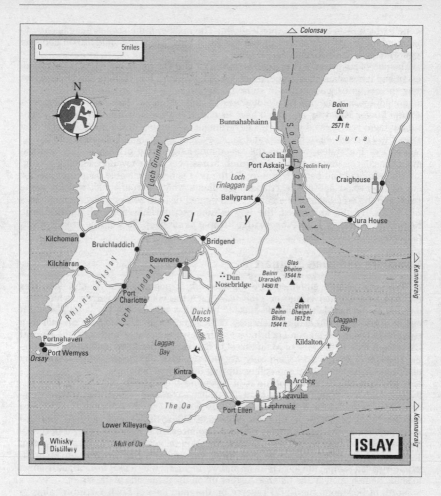

△ Colonsay

0 _____ 5miles

N

Bunnahabhainn

Beinn
Oir
▲
2571 ft

J u r a

Caol Ila
Port Askaig
Feolin Ferry

Craighouse

Loch
Finlaggan

Ballygrant

Jura House

Kilchoman

Bruichladdich

Bridgend

I s l a y

Kilchieran

Bowmore

Glas
Bheinn
1544 ft
▲

Dun
Nosebridge

Beinn
Uraraidh
1490 ft
▲

Port
Charlotte

Duich
Moss

Beinn
Bhán
1544 ft
▲

Beinn
Bheigeir
1612 ft
▲

Claggain
Bay

Portnahaven

Laggan
Bay

Kildalton

Port Wemyss

Orsay

Kintra

Ardbeg
Lagavulin
Laphroaig

The Oa

Port Ellen

Lower Killeyan

Mull of Oa

△ Kennacraig

△ Kennacraig

🥃 Whisky
Distillery

ISLAY

smoky of the Islay whiskies. As every bottle of Laphroaig tells you, translated from the Gaelic the name means "the beautiful hollow by the broad bay", and, true enough, the whitewashed distillery is indeed in a gorgeous setting by the sea. The **Lagavulin distillery** (Mon–Fri by appointment; £2; ☎01496/302400), a mile down the road, produces a superb 16-year-old single malt, while the **Ardbeg distillery**, another mile on, sports the traditional pagoda-style roofs of the malting houses – though sadly it's one of the few not to encourage visitors. Each tour offers a free taster, but a bottle of the stuff is no cheaper at source, so expect to pay at least £20.

Armed with a bottle of your choice, you could do worse than head down to the shoreline just beyond Lagavulin and have a tot or two beside **Dunyvaig Castle** (*Dùn Naomhaig*), a romantic ruin on a promontory looking out to the tiny isle of Texa. There are a handful of B&Bs along the rapidly deteriorating road – try *Tigh-na-Suil* **B&B** (☎01496/302483; ③). A mile beyond this, the simple thirteenth-century **Kildalton Chapel** boasts a wonderful eighth-century Celtic cross made from the local "bluestone", which is, in fact, a rich bottle-green. The quality of the scenes matches any to be found on the crosses carved by the monks in Iona: Mary and child are on one side with what look like elephants on the other.

The nub of land west of Port Ellen is known as **The Oa** (pronounced "o"). This wind-swept and inhospitable landscape, much loved by illicit whisky distillers and smugglers over the centuries, culminates in some pretty awesome cliffs around the Mull of Oa, inhabited by, among others, golden eagles and choughs. The road disintegrates around **Lower Killeyan**, and you'll have to walk the last mile to the cliff's edge, where a monument was erected by the US government in memory of the 266 men who died when the *Tuscania* was torpedoed and sank seven miles offshore in February 1918.

North of Port Ellen, between the seven-mile-long strand of Laggan Bay and the mountains of the southeast, lies the **Duich Moss** peat bog, a favoured feeding ground for white-fronted and barnacle geese. As the peat is also a valuable source of fuel for the islanders and one of the crucial ingredients which flavours malt whisky, some years ago the area became the subject of a heated dispute between environmentalists and locals. To the uninitiated, the bog is nondescript, enlivened only by the large Norse earthworks of **Dun Nosebridge** (Norse *knaus-borg*, "fort on the crag") which rises above the River Laggan.

Bowmore and Loch Gruinart

BOWMORE, Islay's administrative capital with a population of around 900, was founded as a planned village in 1768 to replace the village of Kilarrow, which was deemed by the local laird to be too close to his own residence. It's a striking place, laid out in a grid plan rather like Inveraray, with Main Street climbing up the hill in a straight line from the pier on Loch Indaal to the town's crowning landmark, the **Round Church**. A little to the west of Main Street is **Bowmore distillery** (guided tours Mon–Fri 10.30am & 2pm, Sat 10.30am only; £2; ☎01496/810671), the first of the legal Islay distilleries, founded in 1779 and still occupying its original buildings.

Islay's only official **tourist office** is in Bowmore (Feb, March, Nov & Dec Mon–Sat 9.30am–1pm & 2–5pm; April–Oct Mon–Fri 9.30am–1pm & 2–5.30pm, Sat & Sun noon–4pm; May to mid–June & late Sept Mon–Sat 9.30am–1pm & 2–5.30pm; mid-June to mid-Sept Mon–Sat 9am–5.45pm, Sun 2–5pm; ☎01496/810254), and can help you find accommodation anywhere on Islay or Jura. The nicest of Bowmore's several **hotels** is the *Lochside* on Shore St (☎01496/810244; ④). Alternatively, there's *Lambeth House* on Jamieson St (☎01496/810597; ②). For **food**, head for the *Harbour Inn*, on Main St, where you can sample the local prawns and warm yourself by a peat fire, or settle down to some homely food at *The Cottage*, further up on the same side of the street.

North of Bowmore, the RSPB reserve on the mud flats of **Loch Gruinart** aims to encourage the barnacle geese to winter here rather than on the valuable peat bogs at Duich Moss; in summer this is a good place to spot lapwings, snipes and redshanks. Bird-watchers should hole themselves up in *Loch Gruinart House* (☎01496/850212; ②) by the reserve, or at the rudimentary *Craigens Farm* **campsite** by the loch (April–Oct; ☎01496/850256). Three miles to the west lies the freshwater **Loch Gorm**, occasional winter home of the rare Greenland white-fronted goose.

The Rhinns of Islay

PORT CHARLOTTE, named after the founder's mother, is generally agreed to be Islay's prettiest village, the "Queen of the Rhinns" ("rhinns" is derived from the Gaelic word for promontory), its immaculate cottages hugging the sandy shores of Loch Indaal. East of the village, the imaginative **Museum of Islay Life** (April–Sept Mon–Sat 10am–5pm, Sun 2–5pm; Oct–March Mon–Fri 10am–4.30pm; £1.50), has a children's corner, a good library of books about the island, and tantalizing snippets about eighteenth-century illegal whisky distillers. The **Islay Field Centre** (Mon, Wed, Fri & Sun 2–5pm; £2), housed in the former distillery warehouse, is also worth a visit for anyone interested in the island's fauna and flora. As for **accommodation**, there's the *Lochindaal Hotel* (☎01496/850202; ④), plus scores of B&Bs: the wonderful *Taigh-na-Creag*, 7 Shore St (☎01496/850261; ③) and *Craigfad Guest House*(☎01496/850244; ③) as well as a youth hostel (mid-Feb to Oct; ☎01496/810385; Grade 2), housed in an old bonded warehouse. The *Croft Kitchen*, near the museum, serves hot meals including several vegetarian dishes.

The coastal road culminates seven miles south of Port Charlotte at **PORTNAHAVEN**, a fishing and crofting community since the early nineteenth century. The familiar Hebridean cottages wrap themselves around the steep banks of a deep bay; in the distance, you can see Portnahaven's twin settlement, **PORT WEMYSS**, a mile south. A short way out to sea are two islands, the largest of which, Orsay, sports the **Rhinns of Islay Lighthouse**, built by Robert Louis Stevenson's father in 1825. There are few amenities in this isolated part of Islay, but you'll get **rooms** at *Glenview House* (☎01496/860303; ②) in Portnahaven.

Those in search of still more solitude should head for the isolated **west coast** of the Rhinns, inhabited mostly by sheep, and peppered with sandy beaches. You can stay at *Tormisdale Croft* (☎01496/860239; ②), a B&B which serves organic home cooking and has welcoming peat and driftwood fires; it's situated across the moor on the road to **Kilchiaran**, a couple of miles from Port Charlotte. Alternatively, there are B&Bs such as *Altan* (☎01496/850391; ②) and the wonderful *Kilchoman House* restaurant (☎01496/850382), both in **KILCHOMAN**, further north from Kilchiaran along the coast. Kilchoman's church is in a sorry state of disrepair, but its churchyard contains a fine medieval cross, and several grave slabs; nearby is the burial ground of the American, French and British servicemen drowned when HMS *Otranto* went down in a storm in October 1918.

Port Askaig and around

Islay's other ferry connection with the mainland, and its sole link with Jura, is from **PORT ASKAIG**, a scattering of buildings which tumble down a little cove by the narrowest section of the Sound of Islay. The *Port Askaig Hotel* (☎01496/840245; ⑧) by the pier is the plushest on the island, with views over to the Paps of Jura; there are cheaper B&Bs to choose from, too, such as *Meadowbank* (☎01496/840679; ③). A short walk north along the shore from Port Askaig will bring you to the **Caol Ila distillery** (guided tours Mon–Fri 10.30am & 2pm; ☎01496/840207; £2), named after the Sound of Islay (*Caol Ila*) which it overlooks. **Bunnahabhainn distillery** (Mon–Fri free guided tours by appointment; ☎01496/840646) is a couple of miles further up the coast.

Isle of Jura

The long whale-shaped island of **Jura** – or, to be more accurate the distinctive Paps of Jura (so-called because of their smooth breast-like shape, though confusingly there are three of them), the tallest of which, Beinn Oir, rises to 2571ft – seems to dominate every view off the coast of Argyll. Twenty-eight miles long and eight miles wide, Jura is one of the wildest and most mountainous of the Inner Hebrides, its entire west coast uninhabited and inaccessible except to the dedicated walker. The island's name derives from the Norse *dyr-oe* (deer island); appropriately enough, the current deer population outnumbers the 200 humans by twenty-five to one.

Anything that happens on Jura happens in **CRAIGHOUSE**. *Western Ferries* runs a regular car ferry service all year from Port Askaig to Feolin Ferry, eight miles away.

Craighouse distillery (☎01496/820240), which looks out across Small Isles Bay to the mainland of Knapdale, is the island's only industry besides crofting and tourism, and welcomes visitors. The one hotel, the *Jura Hotel* (☎01496/820243; ⑤), is supplemented by a smattering of B&Bs, such as the *Fish Farm House* (☎01496/820304; ③) or *Mrs Woodhouse*, 7 Woodside (☎01496/820379; ②). At **Jura House**, three miles south of Craighouse, you can visit the organic walled garden (daily dawn–dusk; £2) which specializes in Antipodean plants.

In April 1946 Eric Blair (better known by his pen name of **George Orwell**), suffering badly from TB and intending to give himself "six months' quiet" in which to write his novel, *1984*, moved to a remote farmhouse called Barnhill, on the northern tip of Jura. He lived out a spartan existence there for two years but was forced to return to London shortly before his death. The house, 23 miles north of Craighouse up an increasingly poor road, is as remote today as it was in Orwell's day, and sadly there is no access to the interior.

travel details

Trains

Glasgow (Queen St) to: Arrochar & Tarbert (Mon–Sat 4 daily, Sun 3 daily; 1hr 15min); Dalmally (3 daily; 2hr 15min); Helensburgh Central (every 30min; 45min); Helensburgh Upper (Mon–Sat 4 daily, Sun 3 daily; 45min); Oban (3 daily; 3hr).

Buses (excluding the postbus)

Brodick to: Blackwaterfoot (Mon–Sat 8–9 daily; 25min); Lamlash (Mon–Sat 10 daily; 15min); Lochranza (Mon–Sat 5 daily, Sun 4 daily; 40min).

Campbeltown to: Carradale (Mon–Sat 3–4 daily; 45min).

Colintraive to: Rothesay (Tues–Thurs at least 2 daily; 30min); Tighnabruaich (Tues–Thurs at least 2 daily; 35min).

Craignure to: Fionnphort (Mon–Sat up to 4 daily; 1hr 15min).

Dunoon to: Colintraive (Mon–Sat at least 2 daily; 45min); Inveraray (Mon–Sat at least 2 daily; 1hr 10min); Lochgoilhead (Mon & Fri 2 daily; 1hr 15min); Rothesay (Mon–Sat at least 1 daily; 1hr 30min); Tighnabruaich (at least 2 daily; 1hr 25min)

Glasgow to: Campbeltown (Mon–Sat 3 daily, Sun 2 daily; 4hr 20min); Inveraray (Mon–Sat 6 daily, Sun 4 daily; 1hr 40min); Kennacraig (Mon–Sat 2 daily, Sun 1 daily; 3hr 30min); Lochgilphead (Mon–Sat 3 daily, Sun 2 daily; 2hr 40min); Oban (Mon–Sat 3 daily, Sun 2 daily; 3hr); Tarbert (Mon–Sat 3 daily, Sun 2 daily; 3hr 15min).

Kennacraig to: Claonaig (1 daily except Wed; 15min).

Lochgilphead to: Kilmartin (Mon–Sat 1 daily; 40min).

Oban to: Benderloch (Mon–Sat 6 daily; 25min); Ellanbeich (up to 3 daily; 45min); Kilmartin (Mon–Sat 1 daily; 1hr 5min); Lochgilphead (Mon–Sat 1 daily; 1hr 20min).

Rothesay to: Kilchattan Bay (Mon–Sat 5 daily, Sun 3 daily; 25min); Mount Stuart (Mon–Sat up to 9 daily; Sun 5 daily; 12min).

Tarbert to: Claonaig/Skipness (Mon–Sat 3–4 daily; 30/35min); Kennacraig (Mon–Sat 2–3 daily; 15min).

Tighnabruaich to: Otter Ferry (1 daily; 30min).

Tobermory to: Calgary (Mon–Fri 3 daily, Sat 2 daily; 3hr); Craignure (Mon–Sat 5 daily, Sun 2 daily; 1hr); Dervaig (Mon–Fri 4 daily, Sat 2 daily; 30min); Fishnish (Mon–Sat 5 daily, Sun 2 daily; 50min).

Car ferries (summer timetable)

To Arran: Ardrossan–Brodick (Mon–Sat 5 daily, Sun up to 4 daily; 55min); Claonaig–Lochranza (10 daily; 30min); Rothesay–Brodick (Mon & Thurs 1 daily; 1hr 45min).

To Bute: Brodick–Rothesay (Mon & Thurs 1 daily; 1hr 45min); Colintraive–Rhubodach (frequently; 5min); Wemyss Bay–Rothesay (10 daily; 30min).

To Coll: Oban–Coll (daily except Thurs & Sun; 3hr).

To Colonsay: Kennacraig–Colonsay (Wed 1 daily; 3hr 35min); Oban–Colonsay (Mon, Wed & Fri up to 2 daily; 2hr 10min).

To Dunoon: Gourock (McInroy's Point)–Dunoon (Hunter's Quay) (every 30min; 20min); Gourock–Dunoon (every 1hr; 15min).

To Gigha: Tayinloan–Gigha (hourly; 20min).

To Iona: Fionnphort–Iona (Mon–Sat frequently; Sun hourly; 15min).

To Islay: Kennacraig–Port Askaig (Mon–Sat up to 2 daily; 2hr); Kennacraig–Port Ellen (up to 2 daily; 2hr 10min).

To Kintyre: Portavadie–Tarbert (hourly; 30min)

To Lismore: Oban–Lismore (Mon–Sat up to 3 daily; 50min)

To Luing: Seil (Cuan Ferry)–Luing (every 30min; 5min)

To Mull: Kilchoan–Tobermory (Mon–Sat 6 daily; July & Aug also Sun 5 daily; 35min); Oban–Craignure (Mon–Sat up to 6 daily, Sun up to 5 daily; 40min); Lochaline–Fishnish (Mon–Sat every 40–45min, Sun hourly; 15min); Oban–Tobermory – passengers only (Mon, Wed & Sat; 1hr 45min).

To Tiree: Oban–Tiree (daily except Thurs & Sun; 4hr 15min).

Flights

To Campbeltown: Glasgow (Mon–Fri 2 daily; 35min); Islay (Mon–Fri 1 daily; 20min).

To Islay: Campbeltown (Mon–Fri 1 daily; 20min); Glasgow (Mon–Sat 2 daily; 40min).

To Tiree: Barra (Tues–Thurs 1 daily; 20min); Glasgow (Mon–Sat 1–2 daily; 45min).

CHAPTER SIX

SKYE AND THE WESTERN ISLES

A procession of Hebridean islands, islets and reefs off the northwest shore of Scotland, **Skye and the Western Isles** between them boast some of the country's most alluring scenery. It's here that the turbulent seas of the Atlantic smash up against an extravagant shoreline hundreds of miles long, a geologically complex terrain whose rough rocks and mighty sea cliffs are interrupted by a thousand sheltered bays and, in the far west, a long line of sweeping sandy beaches. The islands' interiors are equally dramatic, a series of formidable mountain ranges soaring high above great chunks of boggy peat moor, a barren wilderness enclosing a host of tin lakes, or lochans.

Skye and the Western Isles were first settled by Neolithic farming peoples in around 4500 BC. They lived along the coast, where they are remembered by scores of incidental remains, from passage graves through to stone circles – most famously at **Calanais** (Callanish) on Lewis. Viking colonization gathered pace from 700 AD onwards – on Lewis four out of every five place names is of Norse origin – and it was only in 1266 that the islands were returned to the Scottish crown. James VI (and I of England), a Stuart and a Scot, though no Gaelic-speaker, was the first to put forward the idea of clearing the Hebrides, though it wasn't until after the Jacobite uprisings, in which many Highland clans disastrously backed the wrong side, that the Clearances began in earnest.

The isolation of the Hebrides exposed them to the whims and fancies of the various merchants and aristocrats who caught "island fever" and bought them up. Time and again, from the mid-eighteenth century onwards, both the land and its people were sold to the highest bidder. Some proprietors were relatively progressive – like **Lord Leverhulme**, who tried to turn Lewis into a centre of the fishing industry in the 1920s – while others were autocratic – **Colonel Gordon of Cluny**, who bought Benbecula, South Uist, Eriskay and Barra, forced the inhabitants onto ships bound for North America at gunpoint – but always the islanders were powerless and almost everywhere they were driven from their ancestral homes, robbing them of their particular sense of place. However, their language survived, ensuring a degree of cultural continuity, especially in the Western Isles, where even today, the mother tongue of the vast majority is **Gaelic**.

Aficionados of this part of Scotland swear that each island has its own distinct character, and that is to some extent true, although you can split the grouping quite neatly into two. **Skye** and the so-called **Small Isles** – the improbably named Canna, Rum, Eigg and Muck – are part of the Inner Hebrides, which also include the islands of Argyll (see the *Argyll* chapter). Beyond Skye, across the unpredictable waters of the Minch, lie the Outer Hebrides or Outer Isles, nowadays known as the **Western Isles**, a 130-mile-long archipelago stretching from **Lewis** and **Harris** in the north to **Barra** in the south.

Although this area is one of the most popular holiday spots in Scotland, the crowds only become oppressive on Skye, and even here, most visitors stick to a well-trodden

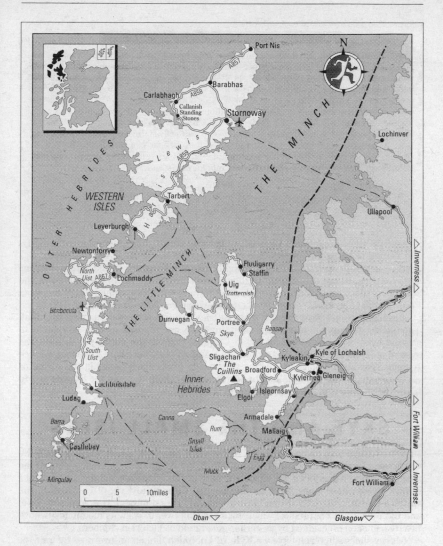

sequence of roadside sights that leaves the rest of the island unaffected. The main attraction, the spectacular scenery, is best explored on **foot**, following the scores of paths that range from the simplest of cross-country strolls to arduous treks. There are four obvious areas of outstanding natural beauty to aim for: on Skye, the harsh peaks of the **Cuillins** and the bizarre rock formations of the **Trotternish peninsula**, both of which attract hundreds of walkers and mountaineers; on the Western Isles, the mountains of **North Harris**, together with the splendid sandy beaches that string along the Atlantic seaboard of **South Harris** and the **Uists**.

The tourist world and that of the islanders tend to be mutually exclusive, especially in the Western Isles. There are, however, ways to meet people – not so much by sitting

---

---

in the pubs (they are few and far between in these parts), than by staying in the B&Bs and getting to know the owners. You could, too, join the locals at church, where visitors are generally welcome. This is a highly **religious region**, dotted with numerous tiny churches, whose denominations differ from island to island. In general terms, the south is predominantly Catholic, while the Calvinist north is a stronghold of the strict Free Church of Scotland – more familiarly known as the "Wee Frees" (see p.318).

Travelling around Skye and the Western Isles requires some degree of forethought. The *CalMac* **ferries** run to a complicated timetable, and the **bus** services are patchy to say the least. Also, in accordance with Calvinist dogma, the entire public transport system of Lewis and Harris closes down on **Sunday**; elsewhere only a skeleton service remains. You should consider visiting the islands (particularly Skye) in the spring or early autumn, rather than the height of the summer, both to avoid the crowds and to elude the attentions of the pesky **midge** (see p.18).

SKYE AND THE SMALL ISLES

Justifiably **Skye** was named after the Norse word for cloud (*skuy*), earning itself the Gaelic moniker, *Eilean a Cheo* (Island of Mist). Yet despite the unpredictability of the weather, tourism has been an important part of the island's economy for almost a hundred years now, since the train line pushed through to Kyle of Lochalsh in the western Highlands in 1897. From here, it was the briefest of boat trips across to Skye, and the Edwardian bourgeoisie was soon swarming over to walk its mountains, whose beauty had been proclaimed by an earlier generation of Victorian climbers.

Most visitors still reach Skye via **Kyle of Lochalsh**, linked to Inverness by train, or by crossing the new Skye Bridge on one of the frequent buses over to **Kyleakin**, on the western tip of the island. However, this part of Skye is pretty dull, and the more scenic approach – and the main way to get to the **Small Isles** – is from the **ferry** port of **Mallaig**, further south (see p.423). Linked by **train** with Glasgow, the Mallaig boat (up to 7 sailings a day) takes 30 minutes to cross to **Armadale**, on the gentle southern slopes of the Sleat peninsula. A third option is the privately operated car **ferry** which leaves the mainland at Glenelg, about 25 miles south from Kyle of Lochalsh, to arrive at **Kylerhea**, from where the road heads inland towards **Portree**.

If you're carrying on to the Western Isles, it's 57 miles from Armadale to the opposite end of Skye, where **ferries** leave **Uig** for Tarbert on Harris and Lochmaddy on

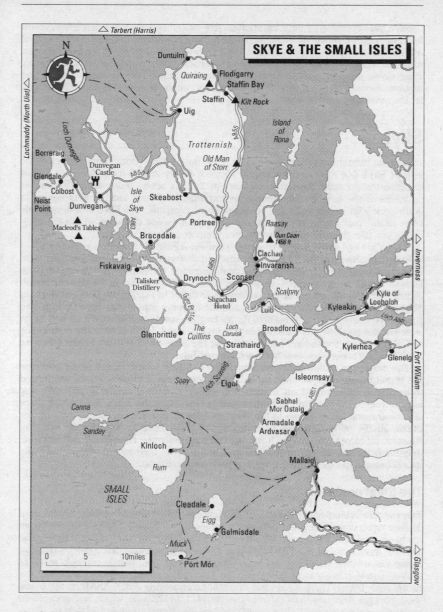

North Uist. From Mallaig, the round-trip passenger **ferry** crossing to the rocky and frugal **Small Isles** takes around seven hours depending on the route, and far longer in rough weather. The boat bypasses at least one of the islands each weekday, but it drops by each of the four – **Canna**, **Rum**, **Eigg**, and **Muck** twice on Saturdays, when the sailing times make a day trip to one of them perfectly feasible.

Skye has several substantial **campsites**, five official and several independent **youth hostels** – all of which recommend advance bookings from mid-July to the end of August – and a string of great **hotels**. Most visitors arrive by car, as the **bus** services, while adequate between the villages, peter out in the more remote areas, and virtually close down on Sundays. Accommodation on the Small Isles is more limited and requires forward planning at all times of the year; public transport is non-existent and, for the most part, unnecessary.

Skye

Jutting out from the mainland like a giant wing, the bare and bony promontories of the **Isle of Skye** (*An t-Eilean Sgiathanach*) fringe a deeply indented coastline that makes the island never more than 25, sometimes as little as seven, miles wide. This causes problems at the height of the tourist season when the main road system begins to bottleneck with coach tours and minibuses and caravans. Yet Skye is a deceptively large island, and you'll get the most out of it – and escape the worst of the crowds – only if you take the time to explore the more remote parts of the island.

You might not guess it from the large number of English settlers who run much of the tourist industry – the B&Bs, museums and so forth – but Skye remains the most important centre for **Gaelic culture** and language outside of the Western Isles. Despite the Clearances, which saw an estimated 30,000 emigrate in the mid-nineteenth century, around 40 percent of the population is fluent in Gaelic, the Gaelic college on Sleat is the most important in Scotland, and the extreme Sabbatarian Free Church (see p.318) maintains a strong presence. As an English-speaking visitor, it's as well to be aware of the tensions that exist within this idyllic island. For a taste of the resurgence of Gaelic culture, try and get here in time for the Skye and Lochalsh Festival, *Feis an Eilean*, which takes place over two weeks in mid-July.

The most popular destination on Skye is the **Cuillins**, whose jagged peaks dominate the island during clear weather, though to explore them at close quarters, you'll need to be a fairly experienced and determined walker. Equally dramatic in their own way are the rock formations of the **Trotternish** peninsula, in the north, from which there are inspirational views across to the Western Isles. If you want to escape the summer crush, shuffle off to **Glendale** and the cliffs of Neist Point or head for the island of **Raasay**, off Skye's east coast. Of the two main settlements, **Broadford** and **Portree**, only the latter has any charm attached to it, though both have tourist offices, and make useful bases, especially for those without their own transport.

The Sleat peninsula

Ferry services (Mon–Sat up to 7 daily; mid-May to mid-Sept also Sun 4 daily; 30min) from Mallaig connect with the **Sleat peninsula** (pronounced "Slate"), Skye's southern tip, an uncharacteristically fertile area that has earned it the sobriquet "the Garden of Skye". The *CalMac* ferry terminal is at **ARMADALE** (*Armadal*), an elongated hamlet stretching along the wooded shoreline. Armadale **youth hostel** (mid-March to Sept; ☎01471/ 844260; Grade 2) is a ten-minute walk up the A851 to Broadford, overlooking the bay; the hostel rents **bikes**. There are several B&Bs in neighbouring **ARDVASAR**, to the south-west, plus the *Ardvasar Hotel* (March–Dec; ☎01471/844223; ⑤), which has an excellent restaurant and a lively bar; a cheaper alternative is the *Bistro* café on Armadale pier.

Just past the youth hostel, you'll find the **Clan Donald Visitor Centre** (April–Oct daily 9.30am–5.30pm; gardens open all year; £3.20), whose handsome 40-acre gardens surround the nineteenth-century remains of Armadale Castle. Part of the castle has been turned into a museum that traces the history of the Gaels, concentrating on medieval times when the Donalds were the Lords of the Isles. It's well done, and the sound effects – savage clanging swords and battle songs – just about compensate for the lack of original artefacts. For more substantial information, you'll have to return to the refurbished stable block beside the entrance, where the bookshop carries a wide range of Scottish history books.

A couple of miles up the road is the **Sabhal Mòr Ostaig**, a modern, independent Gaelic college founded by Sir Iain Noble, an Edinburgh merchant banker, who owns a large chunk of the peninsula. The college runs a variety of extremely popular, short courses in Gaelic language, music and culture, and longer, full-time courses in Gaelic business, computing and media. If you're looking for a book on beginners' Gaelic, the college bookshop has a good selection.

Continuing northeast, it's another six miles to **ISLEORNSAY** (*Eilean Iarmain*), a secluded little village of ancient whitewashed cottages that was once Skye's main fishing port. With the mountains of the mainland on the horizon, the views out across the bay are wonderful, overlooking a necklace of seaweed-encrusted rocks and the tidal **Isle of Ornsay** itself, which sports a trim lighthouse, built by Robert Louis Stevenson's father. You can **stay** at another of Sir Iain Noble's enterprises, the mid-nineteenth-century *Isle Ornsay Hotel* (☎01471/833332; ⑦), a pricy place (also known by its Gaelic name *Hotel Eilean Iarmain*), whose **restaurant** serves great seafood.

Kyleakin and Kylerhea

The aforementioned Sir Iain Noble is also one of the leading advocates of (and investors in) the privately financed **Skye Bridge**, which now links the tidy hamlet of **KYLEAKIN** (*Caol Acain*) with the Kyle of Lochalsh (see p.427), just half a mile away on the mainland. The bridge, initially welcomed by the vast majority of islanders, cost the Anglo-German contractors a cool £30 million, which they are aiming to recoup by charging over £5 each way for cars and more than £30 for lorries and coaches, making it the most expensive toll bridge in Europe, and no cheaper than the ferry it replaces. Some locals are so disenchanted with the new bridge, they are hoping to continue providing a ferry service.

There's nothing much to see or do in Kyleakin – you're well advised to just keep going – but you could have a quick look at the scant remains of **Castle Moil**, a fourteenth-century keep poking out into the straits on top of a diminutive rocky knoll. If you're marooned, the official **youth hostel** (☎01599/534585; Grade 1) is a couple of hundred yards from the ferry dock; close by, there's a *Backpackers' Guesthouse* (☎01599/534510), and a long line of cheap **B&Bs** including *Mrs MacLennan*, 16 Kyleside (☎01599/534468; ⑦). **Bike rental** is available from *Skye Bikes* (☎01599/534795) on the pier.

You can still have the romance of a trip "over the sea to Skye" at the Mallaig-Armadale crossing, or by taking the ferry service (mid-April to mid-Oct frequent; 15min) from Glenelg to **KYLERHEA**, a peaceful little place, some four miles down the coast from Kyleakin. **Seal trips** (£4.50), organized by *Castle Moil Seal Cruises*, also set off from the ferry pier, taking you to view the seal colony on Eilean Mhal (4 daily; £4.50; ☎01599/534641). Alternatively, you can walk half an hour up the coast to the Forestry Commission **Otter Hide**, where if you're lucky, you may be able to spot one of these elusive creatures.

Broadford

Heading west out of Kyleakin or Kylerhea brings you eventually to the island's second-largest village, charmless **BROADFORD** (*An t-Ath Leathann*), whose mile-long main street curves round a wide bay. Despite its rather unlovely appearance, Broadford is a useful base for the southern half of Skye, and something of a wet weather retreat, with the unusual **Skye Serpentarium** (Easter–Oct daily 10am–5pm; £2), full of snakes, lizards and frogs to amuse bored children, and the **International Otter Survival Funds** visitor centre (March–Oct daily 9.30am–5.30pm; £1), where you can watch a video link-up with the centre's otter pen.

More pragmatically, Broadford has a **tourist office** (April, May & mid-Sept to late Oct Mon–Sat 9.30am–5.30pm; June to mid-July & late Aug to mid-Sept Mon–Sat 9.30am–7pm; mid-July to late Aug Mon–Sat 9.30am–9pm, also Sun 12.30–4.30pm; ☎01471/822361), next door to the *Esso* garage on the main road, and a bank and bakery at the west end of the village. The official **youth hostel** is on the west shore of the bay (June–Oct; ☎01471/822442; Grade 1), or there's the much more beautiful and primitive *Fossil Bothy* (☎01471/822297), a small, independent hostel on the east side of the bay. You can **rent bikes** from the official youth hostel or from *Fairwinds Guest House* (April–Oct; ☎01471/822270; ③).

Scalpay, Luib and The Braes

The main road (A850) from Broadford to Portree continues to hug the coast for the next ten miles, giving out views across Loch na Cairidh to the **Isle of Scalpay**, a huge heather-backed lump that looks something like a giant scone, rising to 1298ft at the peak of Mullach na Carn. The island is part deer farm, part forestry plantation, and is currently owned by a merchant banker.

As the road twists round into Loch Ainort, you come to **Luib Folk Museum** (daily 9am–6pm; £1), housed in a restored "black house" (see p.319), and heralded by a rather tacky cardboard cut-out of Bonnie Prince Charlie. More surprising still, the museum has only a tenuous connection with the 1745 uprising, but is, in fact, a fascinating insight into the way of life of the island's crofters around the turn of the century. It's run by local museum magnate and manic restorer, Peter MacAskill, who's also responsible for two other museums in restored black houses on the island.

From the head of Loch Ainort, the main road takes a steep short cut across a pass to Loch Sligachan, while a prettier, minor road meanders round the coast – either way, you'll reach **SCONSER**, departure point for the car ferry to Raasay (see below). On the opposite side of Loch Sligachan are the crofting communities of **The Braes**, who staged a successful rent strike in 1881 against their landlords, the MacDonalds. After eviction summonses were burnt by the crofters, a detachment of 50 Glasgow police were drafted in and took part in a "battle" which aroused a great deal of publicity for the crofters' cause (for more on which, see p.307).

Isle of Raasay

Though it takes only 15 minutes to cross to the island from Sconser (Mon–Sat 9 daily), which offers great walks across its bleak and barren hills, **Raasay**, a nature conservancy area, remains well off the tourist trail. For much of its history, the island was the property of a branch of the Jacobite MacLeods of Lewis, and practically destroyed by government troops in the aftermath of the 1745 uprising. Bonnie Prince Charlie spent a miserable night in a "mean low hut" on Raasay during his flight and swore to replace the burnt turf cottages with proper stone houses. The island's ageing population now numbers just 150, most of them members of the Free Presbyterian Church, a Calvinist offshoot of the already very strict Free Church (see p.318). Strict observance of the Sabbath – no work or play on Sundays – is the most obvious manifestation for visitors, who should respect the islanders' feelings.

The ferry docks at the southern tip of the island, an easy walk (15min) from **INVERARISH**, a tiny village set within thick woods on the island's southwest coast. A further half-mile along the coast, in **CLACHAN**, is the *Raasay Outdoor Centre*, which occupies the grand Georgian mansion built by the MacLeods in the late 1740s – to be all but ruined by government troops a few years later. Today the place is being restored, and offers comfortable **accommodation** in tastefully bohemian rooms (March–Oct; ☎01478/660266; ③). You can also **camp** in the grounds, and, for a daily cost of £30, join in the centre's activity programme – anything from sailing, windsurfing and canoeing, through to climbing and hill walking. Close by, there are comfortable rooms at the likeably old-fashioned *Isle of Raasay Hotel* (☎01478/660222; ⑤), which sits above the seashore looking out over Skye; it also serves delicious traditional Scottish food.

The grounds of the *Outdoor Centre* slope down to Clachan's tiny **harbour**, which is overlooked, from the top of a smal lumpy hill, by two weathered stone mermaids with intimidating biceps. To the north, along the coast, lies the hamlet of **OSKAIG**, from where a rough track cuts up the steep hillside to reach, by turning right at the road, Raasay's isolated put beautifully placed **youth hostel** (mid-May to Sept; ☎01478/660240; Grade 3).

Most of the rest of Raasay is starkly barren, a rugged and rocky terrain of sandstone in the south and gneiss in the north, with the most obvious feature being the curiously truncated basalt cap on top of **Dun Caan** (1456ft), where Boswell "danced a Highland dance" on his visit to the island with Dr Johnson in 1773 – you may feel like doing the same if you're rewarded with a clear view over to the Cuillins and the Outer Hebrides. The trail to the top of the peak is fairly easy to follow, a splendid five-mile trek up through the forest and along the burn behind Inverarish. The quickest return is made down the northwest slope of Dun Caan, but – by going a couple of miles further – you can get back to the ferry along the path by the southeast shore, passing the occasional abandoned crofters' village.

The Cuillins and around

For many people the **Cuillins**, whose sharp snow-capped peaks rise mirage-like from the flatness of the surrounding terrain, are Skye's *raison d'être*. When the clouds finally disperse, they are the dominating feature of the island, visible from every other peninsula on Skye. There are basically three approaches to the Cuillins: from the south, by foot or by boat from Elgol; from the *Sligachan Hotel* to the north; or from Glen Brittle to the west of the mountains. Glen Sligachan is by far the most popular route, dividing as it does the granite of the **Red Cuillins** to the east from the dark, coarse-grained gabbro of the **Black Cuillins**, to the west. With some 20 Munros between them, these are mountains to be taken seriously, and many routes through the Cuillins are for experienced climbers only (for more on safety see p.38).

Elgol and Glen Sligachan

The only reason to visit the desparate-looking village of **ELGOL**, 14 miles west of Broadford, is to take the boat trip, which bobs its way across Loch Scavaig (April–Oct 1–2 daily), past a seal colony, to the tight entrance of **Loch Coruisk** (*coire uish*, cauldron of water). A wild, glacial loch, this needle-like shaft of water, nearly two miles long but only a couple of hundred yards wide, lies in the shadow of the highest peaks of the Black Cuillins, a wonderfully dramatic landscape.

The return trip takes an hour or so and costs around £6 (£5 one-way) – for details of sailing times, ring the skipper, Donald MacKinnon (☎01471/866244). From Loch Coruisk, there are numerous possibilities for walking amidst the Red Cuillins: the most popular route, though, is to head north over the pass into **Glen Sligachan**. Whenever possible, the boat also calls in at the sandy bay of **Camasunary**, to the southeast of Loch Coruisk, from here you can either head north to Glen Sligachan, take the coastal path back to Elgol (4hr and difficult), or climb up to the Am Mam shoulder, for a stunning view of the mountains with the islands of Soay, Rum, Canna and Sanday lying out to sea. From Am Mam the path leads down to the Elgol road, joining it just south of Kirkabost.

At the northern end of Glen Sligachan, just three miles southwest of Sconser, is the *Sligachan Hotel* (April–Nov; ☎01478/650204; ⑦) and its adjacent **campsite**, strategically placed for hikers. Elgol has a couple of **B&Bs**: try *Mrs MacKinnon*, at 4 Drinen (☎01471/866255; ②), or *Strathaird House* (☎01471/866269; ③), above Kilmarie Bay four miles back towards Broadford; there's also an independent hostel, another two miles further back, *Blaven Bunkhouse* (☎01471/822397). The only public transport along the Elgol road is the **postbus**, which leaves Broadford every weekday morning and returns in the afternoon to connect – in theory at least – with the Loch Coruisk boat; check the times and details at Broadford tourist office.

Glen Brittle and the Black Cuillins

Six miles along the Dunvegan road (A863) from the *Sligachan Hotel*, there's a turning which quickly leads to the entrance to stony **Glen Brittle** (with the settlement, Glenbrittle, at its southern end), edging the western peaks of the Black Cuillins. Climbers and serious walkers tend to congregate at the **youth hostel** (mid-March to Sept; ☎01478/640278; Grade 2) or the **campsite** (April–Sept; ☎01478/640404), a mile or so further south behind the wide sandy beach at the foot of the glen. During the summer, there's one **bus** a day from Portree to the hostel and Glen Brittle; both the youth hostel and the campsite have grocery stores, the only ones for miles.

From the valley a score of difficult and strenuous trails lead into the **Black Cuillins**, a rough semicircle of peaks that, rising to about 3000ft, surround Loch Coruisk. One of the easiest walks is the five-mile round trip from the campsite up **Coire Lagan**, to a crystal-cold lochan squeezed in among the sternest of rock faces. Above the lochan is Skye's highest peak and the most difficult of the Munros, Sgurr Alasdair (3257ft), while Sgurr na Banachdich is the only other accessible Munro in the Cuillins (for the usual walking safety precautions see p.38).

If the weather's bad and outdoor activities impossible, you could while away an afternoon at **Talisker whisky distillery** (April–Oct Mon–Fri 9.30am–4.30pm; July & Aug also Sat; Nov–March Mon–Fri 2–4.30pm; by appointment only; ☎01478/640203), which produces a very smoky, peaty single malt. Talisker is the island's only distillery, situated on the shores of Loch Harport at **CARBOST** (and not, confusingly, at the village of Talisker itself).

Dunvegan and the Duirnish peninsula

After the Glen Brittle turning, the A863 slips across bare rounded hills to skirt the bony sea cliffs and stacks of the west coast 20 miles or so north to **DUNVEGAN** (*Dùn Bheagain*), an unappealing place strung out along the east shore of the sea loch of the same name. Just to the north of the village, **Dunvegan Castle** (April–Oct Mon–Sat 10am–5.30pm & Sun 1–5.30pm; £4) perches on top of a rocky outcrop, sandwiched between the sea and several acres of beautifully maintained gardens. It's been the seat of the Clan MacLeod since the thirteenth century, but the present greying, rectangular fortress with its uniform battlements and dummy pepper pot dates from the 1840s. In medieval times, the castle could only be entered from the sea, and the mighty warships of the MacLeods were famous throughout Scotland, but now a bridge spans the old moat, leading to a small, unassuming entrance.

The half-dozen rooms open to the public sport all sorts of clannish trinkets, including a drinking horn, which each new chief was supposed to drain at one draught "without setting down or falling down", and an intriguing display on the remote archipelago of St Kilda (see p.331), long the fiefdom of the MacLeods. There's a lock of hair from the head of Bonnie Prince Charlie (whom the MacLeods, in fact, fought against), but most intriguing of all are the battered remnants of the **Fairy Flag** in the drawing room. This yellow silken flag from the Middle East may have been the battle standard of the

Norwegian king, Harald Hardrada, who had been the commander of the imperial guard in Constantinople. Hardrada died trying to seize the English throne at the Battle of Stamford Bridge in 1066, his flag allegedly carried back to Skye by his Gaelic boatmen. More fancifully, MacLeod family tradition asserts that the flag was the gift of the fairies, blessed with the power to protect the clan in times of danger – and as late as World War II, MacLeod pilots carried pictures of it for luck.

From the jetty outside the castle there are regular seal-spotting **boat trips** out along Loch Dunvegan, as well as longer and less frequent sea cruises. Dunvegan's newest tourist attraction is the **Giant Angus MacAskill Museum** (Mon–Sat 9.30am–6pm, Sun 12.30–5pm; £2), the weakest of Peter MacAskill's three museums on Skye, housed in a restored thatched smithy. The museum's eponymous hero was, in fact, born in the Outer Hebrides in 1825 and emigrated to Nova Scotia when he was just six. He toured with the midget, Tom Thumb, who it is said used to dance on his outstretched hand, but died of a fever at the age of just thirty-eight.

Duirnish and Glendale

The hammerhead **Duirnish peninsula** lies to the west of Dunvegan, much of it inaccessible to all except walkers prepared to scale or skirt the area's twin flat-topped peaks – Healabhal Bheag (1600ft) and Healabhal Mhor (1538ft) – known as **MacLeod's Tables**. The main areas of habitation lie to the north, along the western shores of Loch Dunvegan, and in the broad green sweep of **Glen Dale**, attractively dotted with white farmhouses and dubbed "Little England" by the locals, due to its high percentage of "white settlers", English incomers searching for a better life. Glen Dale's current predicament is doubly ironic given its history, for it was here in 1882 that local crofters, following the example of their brethran in The Braes (see p.304), staged a rent strike against their landlords, the MacLeods. Five locals – who became known as the "Glen Dale Martyrs" – were given two-month prison sentences, and eventually, in 1904, the crofters became (and remain) the only owner-occupiers in the Highlands.

All this, and a great deal more about crofting, is told through contemporary news cuttings at **Colbost Folk Museum** (daily 10am–6pm; £1), the oldest of Peter MacAskill's three Skye museums, situated in a restored black house, four miles up the road from Dunvegan. A guide is usually on hand to answer questions, the peat fire smokes all day, and there's a restored illegal whisky still round the back. A little further up the shores of the loch is the **Borreraig Park Exhibition Croft** (daily 9am–6pm or later; £1.50), run by the eccentric Spike Manwaring-Spencer, a Liverpudlian settler who has amassed a huge open-air museum of traditional horse-drawn farm machinery.

At Borreraig itself, where there was once a famous piping college, is the **MacCrimmon Piping Heritage Centre** (Easter to late May Tues–Sun noon–5.30pm; late May–early Oct 11am–5.30pm; £1.50), on the ancestral holdings of the MacCrimmons, heriditary pipers to the MacLeod chiefs for three centuries, until they were sent packing in the 1770s. The plaintive sounds of the *piobaireachd* of the MacCrimmons, the founding family of Scottish piping, fill this illuminating museum – to hear the real thing, go to the annual recital held in Dunvegan Castle early in August. In the village of Glendale itself, at Holmisdale House, an English settler has gathered together mountains of childhood toys and games from the last hundred years, and opened a **Toy Museum** (Mon–Sat 10am–6pm; £2), which manages to appeal to all ages.

The west coast of Duirnish is mostly uninhabited now, due to the Clearances of the 1830s, when the villagers were given the choice of emigration or prison. For walkers, though, it's a great area to explore, with blustery but easy footpaths leading to the dramatically sited lighthouse on **Neist Point**, Skye's most westerly spot, which features some fearsome sea cliffs, and gives out wonderful views across the sea to the Western Isles – you can even stay at the lighthouse, too, in one of two self-catering cottages (☎01470/511200).

Alternatively, you can head for the sheer 1000ft **Biod an Athair** at the western side of the mouth of Loch Dunvegan; be warned, however, there's no path, so it's a bit of a slog.

Practicalities

It's unlikely you'll want to stay in Dunvegan, but there are several reasonably priced **hotels** and **B&Bs** dotted along the main road, including the family-owned *Tables Hotel* (☎01470/521404; ④), and the vegetarian B&B, *Kensalroag House* (April–Nov; ☎01470/521306; ②). Other possibilities include the luxurious *Harlosh House* (April–Oct; ☎01470/521367; ⑧), four miles south of Dunvegan, or *Janet Kernachan*, 4 Lephin (March–Sept; ☎01470/511376; ②) and *Mrs Hampson* (☎01470/521338; ③), both in Glendale itself. There are two **campsites**, one (April–Sept; ☎01470/220206) about half a mile east of the Dunvegan out towards Portree, and a more basic one a short distance west along the head of the Loch Dunvegan. The culinary highlight in the area is the *Three Chimneys* restaurant (☎01470/511258), located beside Colbost Folk Museum, which serves sublime meals and its famous marmalade pudding.

Portree

PORTREE is the only real town on Skye, and unless you studiously avoid it, you're bound to end up here at some point. Originally known as *Kiltragleann* (the church at the foot of the glen), it takes its current name (*Portrigh*, Port of the King) from the state visit James V made in 1540 to assert his authority over the chieftains of Skye. In actual fact, it's one of the most attractive fishing ports in northwest Scotland, its deep cliff-edged harbour filled with colourful fishing boats and circled by the restaurants and guest houses. The harbour is bordered by **The Lump**, a steep and stumpy peninsula that was once the site of public hangings on the island, attracting crowds of up to 5000, the unfortunates dragged from the neighbouring jail-cum-courthouse that now houses the tourist office. Up above the harbour is the spick-and-span town centre, centred around **Somerled Square** and built in the late eighteenth century, when it became the island's administrative and commercial centre.

The **Royal Hotel** was where Bonnie Prince Charlie took leave of Flora MacDonald (see p.310). A mile or so out of town on the Sligachan road, the **Skye Heritage Centre** (*Dualchas an Eilein*), also known as *Aros* (April–Oct daily 9am–9pm; Nov–March daily 9am–6pm; £3.50), displays a collection of dioramas and videos that trace the troubled history of the island – an enjoyable way to pass a couple of hours if it's raining. For an alternative and more contemporary view of the island's heritage, head for **An Tuireann Arts Centre**, housed in a converted fever hospital on the Struan road (daily 10am–5pm; free), which puts on exhibitions, stages concerts, and has a fine café with a range of hot meals, including several veggie options.

Practicalities

Buses to Portree arrive in Sommerled Square, from where it's a couple of minutes walk along Wentworth and Bank streets to the **tourist office** (Sept–March Mon–Fri 9am–5pm; April & May Mon–Sat 9am–5.30pm; early to mid-June Mon–Sat 9am–7pm; mid-June to mid-July & mid-Aug to end Aug Mon–Sat 9am–8pm; mid-July to mid-Aug 9am–10pm; ☎01478/612137), who will, for a small fee, book accommodation for you – especially useful at the height of the season. They also have bus timetables and a good selection of maps and guides. The tourist office has the details of local **car rental** firms too, among them *Ewen MacRae*, at the *BP* station about a mile out of town on the A850 to Dunvegan (☎01478/612554); for **bike rental**, go to *Island Cycles* (☎01478/613121) on the Green; for horse rental head for *Skye Riding Centre* (☎01470/532233) four miles along the Uig road (A856). **Boat trips** leave the pier for excursions out along the Sound of Raasay three times daily from April to October – the trip takes two hours and costs £6 per person.

Portree has a good range of comfortable and convenient, if rather pricy, **hotels**, including the *Caledonian*, on Wentworth St (☎01478/612641; ⑤); *The Kings Haven*, overlooking the harbour at 11 Bosville Terrace (☎01478/612290; ④); and the converted fishermen's houses of the *Rosedale Hotel*, which has splendid views out to sea from Beaumont Crescent (☎01478/613131; ⑥). There are plenty of **B&Bs**, too, several of which are clustered on and around the harbour: try *The Pink Guest House* (☎01478/612263; ④), or, on Bosville Terrace, *Harbour View* (☎01478/612069; ③) and the *Coolin View Guest House* (☎01478/612300; ④). The *Portree Backpackers* **hostel** (☎01478/613332) is also on the quayside; Torvaig **campsite** (April–Oct; ☎01478/612209) lies a mile and a half north of town on the A855 Staffin road.

The best **food** in town is at the *Ben Tianavaig Bistro*, 5 Bosville Terrace (☎01478/612152), which does vegetarian meals and top-quality fresh seafood. Other good choices are the restaurant in the *Rosedale Hotel*, and, for a budget feast, the excellent fish-and-chip shop out towards the pier on Quay St. *The Café*, an ice-cream parlour below the *Caledonian Hotel* on Wentworth St, serves real capuccino and espresso, plus a selection of cakes.

The Trotternish peninsula

Protruding 20 miles north from Portree, the **Trotternish peninsula** boasts some of the island's most bizarre scenery, particularly on the east coast, where volcanic basalt has pressed down on the softer sandstone and limestone underneath, causing massive landslides. These, in turn, have created sheer cliffs, peppered with outcrops of hard, wizened basalt, which run the full length of the coastline. These pinnacles and pillars are at their most eccentric in the Quiraing, above Staffin Bay. The peninsula is best explored with your own transport, but an occasional bus service along the road encircling the peninsula gives access to almost all the coast (ask for times at the Portree tourist office).

The east coast

The first geological eccentricity on Trotternish, six miles north of Portree along the A855, is the **Old Man of Storr**, a distinctive, pear-shaped column of rock, which along with its neighbours is part of a massive landslip, with huge blocks of stone still occasionally breaking off the cliff face of the Storr Mountain (2358ft) above and sliding downhill. At 165ft, the Old Man is a real challenge for climbers – less difficult is the brief and boggy footpath up to the foot of the column from the car park beside the main road, though it's often closed by the forest rangers when it gets too waterlogged. Eight miles further north, there's another car park for the **Kilt Rock**, whose tube-like, basaltic columns rise precipitously from the sea. A mile or two up the minor road which cuts across the peninsula from Staffin Bay, there's a path up to the savage rock formations of the **Quiraing**. a forest of mighty pinnacles, which include the 120ft Needle, the Prison, and the Table, a great sunken platform where Victorian ramblers picnicked and played cricket.

For **accommodation** between the Old Man and Kilt Rock, head for the *Glenview Inn* (☎01470/562248; ③), with its very good adjoining restaurant. One of the island's best B&Bs is *Quiraing Lodge* (☎01470/562330; ③), set in an acre of well-tended garden a few minutes' walk from the main road. Overlooking Staffin Bay and loomed over by the scowling mass of the Quiraing, the *Lodge* serves delicious vegetarian food and also **rents bikes**. There's a caravan and **campsite** (mid-April to Sept; ☎01470/562213) at the south end of Staffin; for food, head for *The Oystercatcher* tearoom restaurant, which serves up wonderful seafood platters. Another excellent base for exploring the Quiraing is the exquisite *Flodigarry Country House Hotel* (☎01470/552203; ④), with its lovely wrought-iron loggia and partly castellated walls, further up the coast between

BONNIE PRINCE CHARLIE

Prince Charles Edward Stewart – better known as **Bonnie Prince Charlie** or "The Young Pretender " – was born in Rome in 1720, where his father, "The Old Pretender", claimant to the British throne, was living in exile. At the age of 25, having little military experience, no knowledge of Gaelic, an imperfect grasp of English and a strong attachment to the Catholic faith, the Prince set out for Scotland on a French ship, disguised as a seminarist from the Scots College in Paris. He arrived on the Hebridean island of Eriskay in July 1745, and was immediately implored to return to France by the clan chiefs, who were singularly unimpressed by his lack of army. Charles was unmoved and went on to win the battle of Prestonpans, marching on London and reaching Derby before finally calling a retreat. Back in Scotland, he won one last victory at Falkirk, before the final disaster at Culloden in April, 1746.

The prince spent the following five months in hiding, with a price of £30,000 on his head, and literally thousands of government troops searching for him. He certainly endured his fair share of cold and hunger whilst on the run, but the real price was paid by the Highlanders themselves, who risked their lives (and often paid for it with them) by aiding and abetting the Prince. The most famous of these was, of course, 23-year-old **Flora MacDonald**, whom Charles met on South Uist in June 1746. Flora was persuaded – either by his beauty or her relatives, depending on which account you believe – to convey Charles "over the sea to Skye", disguised as an Irish servant girl by the name of Betty Burke. Flora was arrested just seven days after parting with the Prince in Portree, and was held in the Tower of London until her release in July 1747. She went on to marry a local man, had seven children and lived to the age of sixty-eight.

Charles eventually boarded a ship back to France in September 1746, but, despite his promises – "for all that has happened, Madam, I hope we shall meet in St James' yet" – never returned to Scotland, nor did he ever see Flora again. After mistreating a string of mistresses, he eventually got married at the age of 52 to the 19-year-old Princess of Stolberg, in an effort to produce a Stewart heir. They had no children, and she eventually fled from his violent drunkenness; in 1788, a none too "bonnie" Prince Charles died in the arms of his illegitimate daughter in Rome. Bonnie Prince Charlie became a legend in his own lifetime, but it was the Victorians who really milked the myth for all its sentimentality, conveniently overlooking the fact that the real consequence of 1745 was the virtual annihilation of the Highland way of life.

the mountains and a fossil-strewn beach. Behind the hotel is the cottage where local heroine Flora MacDonald and her family lived from 1751 to 1759, though currently it's not open to the public on anything like a regular basis. The hotel restaurant, concentrating on local produce, is superb, if expensive – light lunches and snacks are available at the bar, a favourite haunt of residents from the neat and tidy **independent hostel**, *Dun Flodigarry Backpackers' Hostel* (☎01470/552212), a couple of minutes' walk away.

The west coast

Beyond **Flodigarry**, the road (A855) veers off to the west coast, rounding the tip of the Trotternish ridge before reaching **DUNTULM**, whose heyday as a major MacDonald power base is recalled by the shattered remains of a headland fortress abandoned by the clan in 1732 after a clumsy nurse dropped one of their babies from a window onto the rocks below. The swanky *Duntulm Castle Hotel* (Easter–Oct; ☎01470/552213; ④) is close by, and provides wonderful views across the Minch to the Western Isles. Heading down the west shore of the Trotternish, it's two miles to the cluster of restored thatched houses that make up the **Skye Museum of Island Life** (April–Oct Mon–Sat 9.30am–5.30pm; £1.50), though the emphasis here is strictly on tartan kitsch and the museum shop. Behind the museum up the hill are the graves of **Flora MacDonald** and her husband. Thousands turned out for her funeral in 1790, creating a funeral procession a mile long – her enormous Celtic cross headstone is inscribed with a simple, contemporaneous tribute by Dr Johnson, who visited her in 1773: "Her name will be mentioned in history, if courage and fidelity be virtues, mentioned with honour".

A further four miles south is the ferry port of UIG (*Uige*), which curves its way round a dramatic, horseshoe-shaped bay. Uig **campsite** (April–Oct; ☎01470/542360) is by the shore near the dock, while the **youth hostel** (mid-March to Oct; ☎01470/542211; Grade 2) is high up on the south side of the village, with exhilarating views over the bay. Nearby, at the other end of the accommodation spectrum, the *Uig Hotel* (April–Oct; ☎01470/542205; ⑥) serves up great homemade **food**; cheaper B&Bs include *Braeholm* (☎01470/542396; ③) and *Idrigill House* (☎01470/542316; ②). The *Sgitheanach*, at the pier, offers filling pub meals, and the garage by the ferry terminal does great coffee if you're waiting for the ferry to Tarbet (Harris) or Lochmaddy (North Uist). **Bike rental** is available from *North Skye Bicycle Hire*, **pony-trekking** from the *Uig Hotel*, and **windsurfing and canoeing** is organized by *Whitewave* (☎01470/542414).

The Small Isles

The history of the **Small Isles**, which lie to the south of Skye, is typical of the Hebridean islands: early Christianization, followed by a period of Norwegian rule that ended in 1266 when the islands were handed back into Scottish hands. Their support for the Jacobite cause resulted in hard times after the failed rebellion of 1745, but the biggest problems came with the introduction of the **potato**, in the mid-eighteenth century. The consequences were as dramatic as they were unforeseen: the success of the crop and its nutritional value – when grown in conjunction with traditional cereals – eliminated famine at a stroke, prompting a population explosion. In 1750, there were just 1000 islanders, but by 1800 their numbers had almost doubled.

At first, the problem of overcrowding was camouflaged by the **kelp** boom, in which the islanders were employed, and the islands' owners made a fortune, gathering and burning local seaweed to sell for use in the manufacture of gunpowder, soap and glass. But the economic bubble burst with the end of the Napoleonic Wars and, to maintain their profit margins, the owners resorted to drastic action. The first to sell up was Alexander Maclean who sold Rum as grazing land for **sheep**, got quotations for shipping its people to Nova Scotia, and gave them a year's notice to quit. He also cleared Muck to graze cattle, as did the MacNeills on Canna. Only on Eigg was some compassion shown; the new owner, a certain Hugh MacPherson, who bought the island from the Clanranalds in 1827, actually gave some of his tenants extended leases.

Since the Clearances each of the islands has been bought and sold several times, though only Eigg and Muck are now privately owned: **Muck** is owned by the benevolent laird, Lawrence MacEwan, while **Eigg** changed hands in 1995 for £1.5 million, passing to a flame-throwing holistic artist from Stuttgart. The other islands were bequeathed to national agencies: **Rum**, the largest and most visited of the group, possessing a cluster of formidable volcanic peaks and the architecturally remarkable Kinloch Castle, passed to the Nature Conservancy Council (now known as Scottish Natural Heritage) in 1957; and **Canna**, by far the prettiest of the Small Isles with its high basalt cliffs, went to the NTS in 1981.

Canna

Measuring a mere five miles by one, and with a Catholic and Gaelic-speaking population of just 20, **Canna** is run as a single farm by the NTS. The island enjoys the best harbour in the Small Isles, a horn-shaped haven at its southeastern corner protected by the tidal island of Sanday, now linked to Canna by a footbridge. For visitors, the chief pastime is walking: from the dock it's about a mile across a grassy basalt plateau to the bony sea cliffs of the north shore, and about the same to the top of Compass Hill (458ft) – so called because its high metal content distorts compasses – from where you get great views across to Rum and Skye. From the buffeted western tip of the island, you can spy the **Heiskeir of Canna**, a curious mass of stone columns sticking up 30ft above the water, some seven miles offshore.

With permission, you may **camp rough** on Canna, otherwise the only place is the NTS-owned *Tighard*, half a mile from the jetty, which sleeps a maximum of ten people and costs around £300 per week, rising to £500 in July and August. Booking forms are available from *Holiday Cottages*, NTS, 5 Charlotte Square, Edinburgh (☎0131/226 5922). Remember, however, that there are no shops on Canna (bar the post office), so you must bring your own supplies.

Rum

Like Skye, **Rum** is dominated by its Cuillins, which, though they may only reach a height of 2664ft at the summit of Askival, rise up with comparable drama to the south of the island. The majority of the island's 40 or so inhabitants now live in **KINLOCH**, on the east coast, all but one of them employed by Scottish Natural Heritage. Loch Scresort, the pencil-thin harbour of Rum, is too shallow to take the passenger **ferry** from Mallaig, so incomers have to hop off onto the island tender, which lands them just a few minutes' walk along the shore from Kinloch. The island's best beach is at **KILMORY**, to the north, though it is periodically out of bounds to the public, since this is the part of the island given over to the study of Rum's large red deer population. When the island's human head count peaked at 450 in 1791, the hamlet of **Harris** housed a large crofting community – all that remains now are several ruined black houses and the Bulloughs' extravagant Neoclassical mausoleum.

Rum's chief attraction, though, is **Kinloch Castle**, a reddish sandstone edifice completed in 1901 (and now a hotel), whose elongated arcades and squat turrets dominate the village of Kinloch. It's an odd-looking place, a hesitant attempt at the Gothic style, but the interior, past the main hall draped with animal skins and a forest of antlers, is extraordinary, packed with the knick-knacks collected by a self-made millionaire, one Sir George Bullough, who used the place as a part-time hunting lodge. If you're not staying, ask the manager to show you around; Bullough, keen to impress his guests, not only paid a piper to play at every sunset, but also had an orchestrion, an electrically driven barrel organ crammed in under the stairs to grind out an eccentric mixture of pre-dinner tunes – *The Ride of the Valkyries* and *Ma Blushin Rosie*, among others, are still played. The *pièce de resistance*, though, has to be Bullough's Edwardian **shower**, whose six dials, on the hooded head-piece, fire high-pressure water from every angle imaginable. Outside, but long gone, great glasshouses once sheltered tropical trees, and heated pools were stocked with turtles and alligators, though these were eventually removed at the insistence of the terrified staff. The year before the construction of his house was completed, Bullough had, at his own expense, sent a hospital ship to the Boer War. He was rewarded with a knighthood, but, as the grandson of a Lancashire weaver, was still kept at arm's length by the aristocracy, who mocked both him and the unlettered taste of his castle. Hurt, Sir George began to keep strangers off the island and the house was barely used when he died in 1939.

Practicalities

Since **accommodation** is limited, many people simply come on a day trip – if you plan to stay longer, you should contact the reserve manager at the *White House* (☎01687/462026), and book well in advance. Bear in mind, too, that Rum is the wettest of the generally wet Small Isles, and a haven for midges – come prepared for both. If you can't afford to stay at the *Kinloch Castle Hotel* (☎01687/462037; ⑨), where rates include a superb dinner and breakfast, there's also a 30-bed independent **youth hostel** (number as for the hotel) behind the hotel, in the old servants' quarters. The bistro here dishes up good-value meals, though of course a meal at the castle itself is the ultimate Rum experience. Other accommodation options in Kinloch include several cheap and simple **bothies** rented by the Nature Conservancy Council and **camping** on the foreshore near the jetty (call the *White Horse* to book). The resident reserve manager will advise on local **walks** too, the most dramatic being the trail along the southern shoreline beneath the mountain peaks.

Eigg

Having recently passed into new ownership – that of fire-worshipping German artist, Professor Marlin Eckhard (brush-name Maruma) – **Eigg** is currently facing an uncertain future. Whisky distilling, organic wool production, wave power and the conversion of the island's lodge into a health clinic have all been hinted at, but what exactly Eckhard has in mind remains to be seen. The new owner, though clearly an easy target for ridicule, has been cautiously welcomed so far by the island's population of 76, who were none too impressed with their last laird, former Olympic bobsleigher and gelatine heir Keith Schellenburg.

Eigg's main village, **GALMISDALE**, where the ferry drops anchor (again passengers are transferred to the island by a smaller boat), is in the southeast, overlooked by the island's great landmark, **An Sgurr**, a 290ft basalt stump that rises out of the 1000ft hill. The view from the latter out to Rum is spectacular, and around the summit is a large colony of Manx shearwater. The other special feature of the island – which measures just five miles by three – is the "**Singing Sands**", to the north of the crofting hamlet of **CLEADALE**. Here, the beach is comprised of quartz, which crunches underfoot when dry (hence the name), while above rise the eccentric sandstone clifftops of Camas Sgiotaig. The best of three places to **stay** on Eigg is the refurbished, three-bedroomed croft house, *Lageorna* (☎01687/482405; ②); even cheaper hostel-style accommodation is available at *Laig Farm* (☎01687/482437); and there's a shop and post office at Galmisdale.

Muck

Smallest and most southerly of the Small Isles, **Muck** is low-lying, mostly treeless and extremely fertile, and as such shares more characteristics with the likes of Coll and Tiree than its nearest neighbours. Its name derives from *muc*, the Gaelic for "pig" – or, as some would have it, *muc mara*, "sea pig" or porpoise, which abound in the surrounding water – and has long caused much embarassment to generations of lairds who preferred to call it the "Isle of Monk", because it had briefly belonged to the medieval church. **GALLANACH** is the island village, with a fine beach and plenty of opporunities for observing Muck's rich wildlife; **PORT MOR**, on the southeast corner of the island, is where the ferry drops anchor and discharges its passengers onto a smaller vessel. The MacEwan family, which has owned the island since 1879, runs the island as a single farm, with around 25 inhabitants. To **stay** here, contact the island Estate Office, which takes bookings for a handful of self-catering cottages (☎01687/462365), and gives permission for **rough camping**.

THE WESTERN ISLES

The wild and windy **Western Isles** – also known as the Outer Hebrides – vaunt a strikingly hostile mix of landscapes from windswept golden sands to harsh, heather-backed mountains and peat bogs. An elemental beauty pervades each one of the more than 200 islands that make up the archipelago, only 13 of which are actually inhabited by a total of just over 30,000 people. The influence of the Atlantic Gulf Stream ensures a mild but moist climate, though you can expect the strong Atlantic winds to blow in rain on two out of every three days even in summer. Weather fronts, however, come and go at such dramatic speed in these parts, there's little chance of mist or fog settling and fewer problems with midges.

The most significant difference between Skye and the Western Isles is that here, tourism is much less important to the islands' fragile economy – still mainly concentrated around crofting, fishing and weaving – and the percentage of "white settlers" is a lot lower. The Outer Hebrides remain the heartland of **Gaelic** culture, with the language spoken by the vast majority of islanders, though its everyday usage remains under constant threat from the national dominance of English. Its survival is, in no small part, due to the all-pervading influence of the Free Church, whose strict Calvinism is the creed of the vast majority of the population, with only South Uist, Barra and parts of Benbecula adhering to the relatively more relaxed demands of Catholicism.

The interior of the northernmost island, **Lewis**, is mostly peat moor, a barren and marshy tract that gives way abruptly to the bare peaks of **North Harris**. Across a narrow isthmus lies **South Harris**, presenting some of the finest scenery in Scotland, with wide sandy beaches trimming the Atlantic in full view of the mountains and a rough boulder-strewn interior lying to the east. Further south still, a string of tiny, flatter islets, mainly **North Uist, Benbecula, South Uist** and **Barra**, offer breezy beaches, whose fine sands front a narrow band of boggy farmland, which, in turn, is mostly bordered by a lower range of hills to the east.

In direct contrast to their wonderful landscapes, the Western Isles claim only the scrawniest of villages, unhappy-looking places that straggle out along the elementary road system. Only **Tarbert**, on Harris, and **Lochmaddy**, on North Uist, sustain a modicum of charm; **Stornoway**, Lewis's only town, is eminently unappealing. Many visitors, walkers and nature watchers forsake the settlements altogether and retreat to secluded cottages and B&Bs – though this is difficult without your own transport.

Visiting the Western Isles

British Airways operates fast and frequent **flights** from Glasgow to Stornoway on Lewis, Barra and Benbecula on North Uist. *British Airways Express* (also known as *Loganair*) has small planes flying from Stornoway to Benbecula and Barra. But be warned, the weather conditions on the islands are notoriously changeable, making these flights both prone to delay and sometimes stomach-churningly bumpy. On Barra, the other complication is that you land on the beach, so the timetable is adjusted with the tides. *CalMac* **car ferries** run from Ullapool in the Highlands to Stornoway; from Uig, on Skye, to Tarbert and Lochmaddy; and from Oban to South Uist and Barra. There's also an **inter-island ferry** from Lochmaddy to Tarbert (for more on ferry services see "Travel Details" at the end of the chapter).

Although travelling around the islands is time-consuming, for many people this is part of their charm. A series of inter-island causeways makes it possible to drive from one end of the Western Isles to the other with just two interruptions – the *CalMac* **ferry** trip from Harris to North Uist, and the one from South Uist to Barra. A couple of smaller companies operate additional inter-island routes, some of them connecting with the islands' distinctly low-key **bus** service – though you should certainly not count on an onward bus connection when you arrive. Note, too, that although several local companies – but none of the big multinationals – offer **car rental**, you're not permitted to take their vehicles off the Western Isles.

The islands' six official **youth hostels** – there are also several independents – are geared up for the outdoor life, occupying remote locations on or near the coast. Four of

GAELIC IN THE WESTERN ISLES

Except in Stornoway, and Balivanich on North Uist, **road signs** are now exclusively in **Gaelic**, a difficult language to the English-speaker's eye, with complex pronunciation (see p.552), though as a (very) general rule, the English names can often provide a rough pronunciation guide. Particularly if you're driving, it's essential to buy the bilingual Western Isles map, produced by the local tourist board, *Bord Turasachd nan Eilean*, and available at most tourist offices. To reflect the signposting we've put the Gaelic first in the text, with the English equivalent in brackets. Thereafter we've stuck to the Gaelic names, to try to familiarize readers with their (albeit variable) spellings – the only exceptions are in the names of islands and ferry terminals, where we've stuck to the English names after the first mention, partly to reflect *CalMac*'s own policy.

them are run by the *Gatliff Hebridean Hostels Trust*, who have renovated several isolated crofters' cottages. None of these has phones, you can't book in advance, you really need to bring your own bedding, and, although each has a simple kitchen, you must take your own food. If you're after a little more comfort, then the islands have a generous sprinkling of reasonably priced **B&Bs** and **guest houses** – many of which are a lot more elegant than the hotels.

Leodhas (Lewis)

Shaped rather like the top of an ice-cream cone, **Lewis** is the largest and most populous of the Western Isles and the northernmost island in the Hebridean archipelago. After Viking rule ended in 1266, the island was fought over by the MacLeods and MacKenzies, until eventually being sold by the latter in 1844. The new owner, Sir James Matheson, invested heavily in new industries, as **Lord Leverhulme** did with the fishing industry when he aquired the island (along with Harris) in 1918. Though undoubtedly a benevolent despot, Leverhulme's unpopularity with many on Lewis, and his financial difficulties, forced him to give up his grandiose plans in 1923, when he gifted the island to its inhabitants. His departure, however, left a big gap in the economy, and between the wars thousands more emigrated.

Most of the island's 20,000 inhabitants – two thirds of the Western Isles' total population – now live in the crofting and fishing villages strung out along the northwest coast, between Calanais and Port Nis. On this coast you'll find the islands' best-preserved **prehistoric remains** – at Carlabhagh and Calanais – as well as a smattering of ancient crofters' houses in various stages of abandonment. The landscape is mostly flat peat bog – hence the island's name, derived from the Gaelic *leogach* (marshy) – with a gentle shoreline that only fulfils its dramatic potential around Rubha Robhanais (the Butt of Lewis), a group of rough rocks on the island's northernmost tip, near Port Nis. To the south, where it is physically joined with the Isle of Harris, the land rises to just over 1800ft, providing a more exhilirating backdrop for the excellent beaches, peppered along the isolated coastline to the southwest of Calanais.

Most visitors use Stornoway, on the east coast, as a base for exploring the island, though this presents problems if you're travelling by **bus**. There's a regular service to Port Nis and Tarbert, and although the most obvious excursion – the 45-mile round trip from Stornoway to Calanais, Carlabhagh, Arnol and back – is almost impossible to complete by public transport, the tourist office's minibus tours make the trip on most days from April to October.

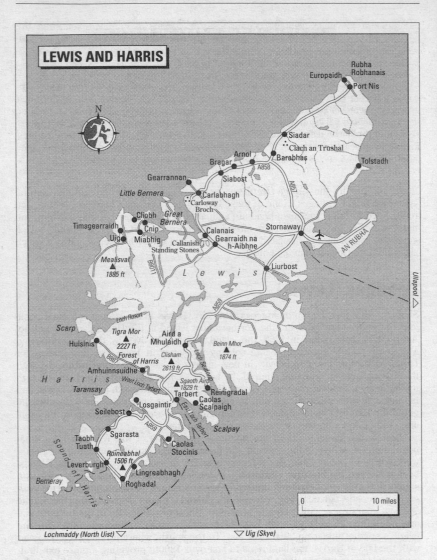

Steornabhagh (Stornoway)

In these parts, **STORNOWAY** is a buzzing metropolis, with some 8000 inhabitants (including a small Gaelic-speaking Pakistani community), a one-way system, pedestrian precinct and all the trappings of a large town. It is a centre for employment, a social hub for the island's youth, and perhaps most importantly of all, home to the **Comhairle nan Eilean** (Western Isles Council), set up in 1974, which has done so much to promote Gaelic language and culture, and try to stem the tide of anglicization. Despite its valiant attempts in that quarter, it is perhaps better known for its supremely incompetent finanicial dealings, which lost the islands £23 million, following the collapse of the *Bank of Credit and Commerce International* (BCCI) in 1991. For the visitor, however, the town is unlikely to win any great praise – aesthetics are not its strongpoint, and the urban pleasures on offer are limited.

For centuries life in Stornoway has focused on its **harbour**, whose deep and sheltered waters were thronged with coastal steamers and fishing boats in their nineteenth-century heyday, when over 1000 boats were based at the port. Today, most of the catch is landed on the mainland, and, despite the daily comings and goings of the *CalMac* ferry from Ullapool, the harbour is a shadow of its former commercial self. The nicest section of the harbour is Cromwell Street Quay, by North Beach, where the remaining fishing fleet ties up for the night, and where the fish market takes place. On the other side of the water to the west are the wooded grounds of **Lews Castle**, a nineteenth-century Gothic pomposity now turned into a further education college, while Stornoway's commercial centre, to the east, is little more than a string of tatty shops and rough-edged bars. There's little to see, though you could drop by the town hall, on the harbour front, which now houses the **An Lanntair Art Gallery** (Mon–Sat 10am–5.30pm; free), featuring the work of local artists.

Practicalities

The best thing about Stornoway is the convenience of its services. The island's **airport** is four miles east of the town centre, a £5 taxi ride away, and the **ferry** terminal only a couple of minutes' walk along the harbour front from the **bus station** on South Beach. You can get the timetables of the area's most useful bus routes from the nearby **tourist office**, 26 Cromwell St (mid-Oct to March Mon–Fri 9am–5pm; April to mid-Oct Mon–Fri 9am–6pm, Sat 9am–5pm; ☎01851/703088), which also sells tickets for the £5-per-person minibus **trips** to Calanais, Carlabhagh and Arnol; failing that, taxis cost around £30 for a maximum of four people. The *Bank of Scotland* has a cashpoint opposite the tourist office, and there are two supermarkets nearby, too.

The tourist office will also, for a small booking fee, fix you up with local **accommodation** (for out-of-town reservations it charges slightly more). If you prefer to look for yourself, try the **B&Bs** along Matheson Rd: *Mrs C Macleod*, at no. 19 (☎01851/704180; ②), and *Mrs A Macleod*, at no. 12 (☎01851/702673; ③), are both good. Other convenient options include *Mrs MacMillan*, 64 Keith St (☎01851/704815; ②), and *Mrs Skinner*, 29 Francis St (☎01851/703482; ③). Stornoway's **independent hostel** is a basic affair about five minutes' walk from the ferry at 47 Keith St (March–Nov; ☎01851/703628). The nearest **campsite**, the *Laxdale Holiday Park* (April–Oct; ☎01851/703234), lies a mile or so along the road to Barabhas, on Laxdale Lane. Two of the more established of Stornoway's several **car rental** firms are *Mackinnon Self-Drive*, 18 Inaclete Rd (☎01851/702984) and *Arnol Motors* (☎01851/710548), Arnol (see p.319); for **bike rental** go to *Alex Dan's Cycle Centre*, 67 Kenneth St (Mon–Sat 9am–6pm; ☎01851/704025 or 702934).

As for **food**, you can get satisfying snacks and lunches from the *An Lanntair Art Gallery*'s coffee shop, while *John MacIver's* fish and chip shop, 6 Church St, is one of several similar places. The *Fisherman Cafeteria* (Mon–Fri 8am–5pm) serves good-value, filling meals in the *National Mission to Deep Sea Fishermen* building on North Beach; the *Crown Hotel*, nearby on Castle St, serves huge main courses as part of its evening menu – the fish, especially, is delicious; the *Park Guest House*, on James St, is another good place to sample the local shellfish; for a more surreal experience, head for *Ali's*, the tandoori place near the bus station on South Beach. The few **pubs** that exist on Lewis are in Stornoway; try either *The Criterion* on Point St, or the *Royal Hotel*, Cromwell St. The most famous watering hole, though, is the bar of the aforementioned *Crown Hotel*, now named after Prince Charles, who drank a cherry brandy here whilst on a school sailing trip (and, more controversially, whilst still under 18).

RELIGION IN THE WESTERN ISLES

Sharply divided – although with little emnity – between the Catholic southern isles of Barra and South Uist, and the Protestant north of North Uist, Harris and Lewis, it is difficult to underestimate the importance of **religion** in the Western Isles. Most conflicts arise from the very considerable power the ministers of the Protestant Church, or Kirk, wield in secular life in the north, where the creed of **Sabbatarianism** is very strong. Here, Sunday is the Lord's Day, and virtually the whole community (irrespective of their degree of piety) stops work – all shops close, all pubs close, all garages close and there's no public transport, but perhaps most famously of all, even the swings in the children's playgrounds are padlocked.

The other main area of division is, paradoxically, within the Protestant Church itself. Scotland is unusual in that the national church, the **Church of Scotland**, is presbyterian (ruled by the ministers and elders of the church) rather than episcopal (ruled by bishops). At the time of the main split in the Presbyterian Church – the so-called **1843 Disruption** – a third of its ministers left the Church of Scotland, protesting at the law which allowed landlords to impose ministers against parishioners' wishes, and formed the breakaway **Free Church**. Since those days there has been a partial reconciliation; although, in 1893, there was another break, when a minority of the Free Church became the Free Presbyterian Church, while still more slowly made their way back to the Church of Scotland. The remaining rump of the Free Church – better known as the "**Wee Frees**" – has its spiritual heartland on Lewis. To confuse matters further, as recently as 1988, the Free Presbyterian Church split over a minister who attended a requiem mass during a Catholic funeral of a friend – he and his supporters have since formed the breakaway Associated Presbyterian Churches.

The various brands and subdivisions of the Presbyterian Church may appear trivial to outsiders, but to the churchgoers of Lewis, Harris and North Uist (as well as much of Skye and Raasay) they are still keenly felt. In part, this is due to social and cultural reasons: Free Church elders helped organize resistance to the Clearances, and the Wee Frees have done the most to help preserve the Gaelic language. A Free Church service is a memorable experience, and in some villages it takes place every evening (and twice on Sundays): there's no set service or prayer book, only Biblical readings, plainchant and a fiery sermon all in Gaelic; the pulpit is the architectural focus of the church, not the altar, and communion is taken only on special occasions. If you want to attend one, the Free Church on Kenneth Street in Stornoway, which attracts 1500 people, has reputedly the largest Sunday evening congregaton in the UK.

Barabhas (Barvas) to Port Nis (Port of Ness)

Northwest of Stornoway, the A857 crosses the vast, barren **peat bog** of the interior, an empty wilderness riddled with stretch marks formed by peat cuttings and pockmarked with freshwater lochans. The whole area was once covered by forests, but these disappeared long ago, leaving a smothering deposit of peat that is, on average, 6ft thick, and is still being formed in certain places. Tourists tend to cross this barren landscape at speed, while ecologists have identified these natural wetlands as important "carbon sinks", whose erosion should be protected. For the people of Lewis, the peat represents a valuable energy resource, with each crofter being assigned a slice of the bog. The islanders spend several very sociable weeks each spring cutting the peat, turning it over and leaving it neatly laid out in the open air to dry, returning in summer to collect the dried sods and stack them outside their houses. Though tempting to take home as souvenirs, these piles are the fruits of hard labour, and remain the island's main source of domestic fuel, its pungent smoke one of the most characteristic smells of the Western Isles.

Twelve miles across the peat bog the road divides, heading southwest towards Calanais (see below), or northeast through **BARABHAS** (Barvas), and a whole string of bleak, fervently Free Church, crofting and weaving villages. Be prepared for the fact that these scattered settlements have none of the photogenic qualities of Skye's white-washed villages. The churches are plain and unadorned, the crofters' houses are fairly modern and smothered in grey, concrete rendering, the stone cottages and enclosures of their forebears often lie half-abandoned in the front garden, while a rusting assort-ment of discarded cars and vans now serves to store peat bags and the like. Three miles north beyond Barabhas, the road passes the 20ft monolith of **Clach an Trushal**, the first of a series of prehistoric sights between the crofting and weaving settlements of **Baile an truiseil** (Ballantrushal) and **Siadar** (Shader).

The main road continues through a string of straggling villages, terminating at the remote village **PORT NIS** (Port of Ness), nestled round its tiny harbour. Each year in September, local hunters set sail from here for the **Isle of Sula Sgeir**, 40 miles to the north, to harvest the young gannet (*guga*) colony that nests high up on the islet's sea cliffs. It's a dangerous activity, but then, for some reason unknown to outsiders, boiled gannet and potato is a favourite Lewis dish.

From Port Nis, a minor road heads two miles north to the hamlet of **EUROPAIDH** (Eoropie) and the **Teampull Mholuaidh** (St Moluag's Church), an austere stone structure dating from the twelfth century. Five centuries later, the traveller Martin Martin noted "[everyone went to church] and then [after] standing silent for a little time, one of them gave a signal . . . and immediately all went into the fields, where they fell a drinking their Ale and spent the remainder of the Night in Dancing and Singing". Unfortunately, services today aren't quite as stimulating as they used to be.

From Europaidh, a narrow road twists north to the bleak and blustery tip of the island, **Rubha Robhanais** – well known to devotees of the BBC shipping forecast as the Butt of Lewis – where a lighthouse sticks up above a series of sheer cliffs and stacks, alive with a cacophony of sea birds, and a great place for seal spotting. The lighthouse is closed to the public and there's nothing in the way of refreshment, so you'd be better off backtracking half a mile or so, where there's a path down to the tiny sandy bay of **Port Sto**, a more sheltered spot for a picnic than the Butt itself.

Several **B&Bs** line the main road between Barabhas and Port Nis: one of the most comfortable is *Harbour View* (☎01851/810735; ③), located in an old boat builder's house overlooking Port Nis harbour, and offering good home-cooked food. Other places to stay include the modern Gaelic croft of *Ms Catriona MacLeod* (☎01851/810240; ③) in Coig Peighinnean (Five Penny Borve), four miles northeast of Barabhas, and *Mrs Alice MacLeod* (May–Oct; ☎01851/810496; ③) in Lional (Lionel). The luxury option is *Galson Farm* (☎01851/850492; ④), an eighteenth-century farmhouse in Gabhsann Bho Dheas (South Galson), halfway between Barabhas and Port Nis.

Arnol to Calanais (Callanish)

Heading southwest from the crossroads near Barabhas brings you to the village of **ARNOL**, which meanders down towards the sea. At the far end of the village is the **Black House Museum** (April–Sept Mon–Sat 9.30am–6.30pm; Oct–March Mon–Sat 9.30am–4pm; £1.50), which dates from the 1870s and was inhabited right up until 1964. Built low against the wind, the house's thick walls are made up of an inner and outer layer of loose stone on either side of a central core of earth, a traditional type of construction which attracted the soubriquet "black house" around 1850, when build-ings with single-thickness walls were introduced to Lewis from the mainland and were commonly called "white houses" (*tigh geal*) by the locals – even though they weren't all white. Thus traditional dwellings came to be called "black houses" (*tigh dubh*).

The Black House Museum is typical of its type, with a chimney-less roof overlaid with grassy sods and oat-straw thatch, lashed down with fishnets and ropes. Beneath, a simple system of wooden tie beams supports the roof, which covers both the living quarters and the attached byre and barn. The post-war wallpaper inside has been removed to reveal the sooty roof rafters above the living room, where, in the centre of the stone and clay floor, the peat fire was the focal point of the house. As one of the children described her house in a school essay of the 1950s: "During winter, many neighbours come in each night. We form a circle round the fire and discuss many subjects . . . . The Blackhouse is definitely the cosiest you can find."

Returning to the main road, it's about a mile or so to **BRAGAR**, where you'll spot a stark arch formed by the jawbone of a blue whale, washed up on the nearby coast in 1920. The spear sticking through the bone is the harpoon, which only went off when the local blacksmith was trying to remove it, badly injuring him. Another two miles on at **SIABOST** (Shawbost), local school children created the appealingly amateurish **Shawbost Folk Museum** (Mon–Sat 9am–6pm; free) in 1970. The converted church contains a real hotch-potch of stuff – most of it donated by locals – including a rare Lewis brick from the short-lived factory set up by Lord Leverhulme, an old hand-driven loom and a reconstructed living room with a traditional box bed. Behind the church is a **campsite** (May–Oct; ☎01851/710504).

Five miles on, there is a sprawling trio of hamlets that all translate as Carloway and confusingly run into each other; first is Mullach Charlabhaigh (Upper Carloway), then Carlabhagh (Carloway) and finally **DUN CHARLABHAIGH** (Doune Carloway). Here **Carloway Broch** perches on top of a conspicuous rocky outcrop overlooking the sea about 400 yards from the road. Scotland's Atlantic coast is strewn with the remains of over 500 brochs, or fortified towers, but this is one of the best preserved, its dry-stone circular walls reaching a height of over 30ft on the seaward side. The broch consists of two concentric walls, the inner one perpendicular, the outer one slanting inwards, the two originally fastened together by roughly hewn flagstones, which also served as look-out galleries reached via a narrow stairwell. The only entrance to the roofless inner yard is through a low doorway set beside a crude and cramped guard cell. As at Calanais (see below), there have been all sorts of theories about the purpose of the brochs, which date from between 100 BC and 100 AD; the most likely explanation is that they were built to provide protection from Roman slave traders.

From Carlabhagh, the middle hamlet, you can turn down the mile-long road to the beautifully remote coastal settlement of **GEARRANNAN** (Garenin), where several of the old thatched crofters' houses have been restored, one of which now serves as a primitive **youth hostel** (no phone; Grade 3). The nearest store is back in Carlabhagh.

Five miles south of Dun Charlabhaigh lies the village of **CALANAIS** (Callanish), site of the islands' most dramatic prehistoric ruins, the **Callanish Standing Stones**, whose monoliths – nearly 50 of them – occupy a dramatic lochside setting. There's been years of heated debate about the origin and function of the stones – slabs of gnarled and finely grained gneiss up to 15ft high – though almost everyone agrees that they were lugged here by Neolithic peoples between 3000 and 1500 BC. It's also obvious that the planning and construction of the site – as well as several other lesser circles nearby – was spread over many generations. Such an endeavour could, it's been argued, only be prompted by the desire to predict the seasonal cycle upon which these early farmers were entirely dependent, and indeed, many of the stones are aligned with the position of the sun and the stars. This rational explanation, based on clear evidence that this part of Lewis was once a fertile farming area, dismisses as coincidence the ground plan of the site, which resembles a colossal Celtic cross, and explains away the central burial chamber as a later addition of no special significance. These two features have, however, fuelled all sorts of theories ranging from alien intervention to human sacrifice.

You can't actually walk between the stones anymore, only by the fence that surrounds them. An adjacent black house has been refurbished as a **tea shop**, but there's an even bigger **visitor centre** now built on the other side of the stones (thankfully out of view). Nearby, beside the village post office, is the **B&B** of *Mrs Cathy Crossley*, 24 Calanais (March–Oct; ☎01851/621236; ②); there's another, just as good, *Mrs Catherine Morrison*, at no. 27 (March–Oct; ☎01851/621392; ③). In neighbouring **BREASCLEIT** (Breasclete), there are two excellent, albeit more expensive, guest houses: *Corran View* (☎01851/621 300; ④) and *Eshcol* (☎01851/621357; ④). Further, smaller stone circles lie in more natural surroundings a mile or two to the southeast of Calanais, around **GEARRAIDH NA H-AIBHNE** (Garynahine).

The Uig peninsula

From Gearraidh na h-Aibhne, the main road leads back to Stornoway, while the dead-end single-track B8011 heads off west towards the remote **Uig peninsula**, in the much hillier, southwest coast of Lewis. After three miles there's another crossroads, with the B8059 heading eventually over a small sea channel to the island of **Bearnaraigh** (Great Bernera), the largest of the 40 or so islands in Loch Roag, whose crofters successfully defied the attempts at eviction by the landlord and took part in the **Bernera Riot** of 1872, during which three locals were arrested and later aquitted. It's a bleak, rocky island, with a few small lobster-fishing settlements, but four miles away on the island's north coast near the abandoned hamlet of **BOSTADH** (Bosta), there's a precious little bay of golden sand, which looks out to the nearby island of Bearnaraigh Beag (Little Bernera). If you want to stay, there are a couple of **B&Bs** on the island, including *Mrs A A MacDonald* (☎01851/612347; ②) in Tobson, a mile south of Bostadh.

There are more superb golden sands on the western shores of West Loch Roag, though it's a long drive back down the B8059 and along the B8011 to reach them – 16 miles along the B8011 from the crossroads to Miabhig (Miavaig), then a further mile off the main road northeast to **CLIOBH** (Cliff). The breakers on the beach below Cliobh make it unsafe for swimmers, who should continue another mile to **CNIP** (Kneep), to the east of which is **Traigh na Berie**, a glorious strand of shell sand, backed by dunes. Two miles southwest of Miabhig are the **Traigh Chapadail** (Uig Sands), the most prized of all the golden beaches in Lewis, overlooked by the lovely lodge and guest house, *Baile na Cille* (☎01851/672241; ④), in **TIMSGEARRAIDH** (Timsgarry). It was in the nearby village of **Eadar dha fhadhail** (Ardroil) in 1831 that a local cow stumbled across the **Lewis Chessmen**, twelfth-century Viking chess pieces carved from walrus ivory that now reside in Edinburgh's Museum of Antiquities (see p.78) and the British Museum in London.

Na Hearadh (Harris)

The "division" between Lewis and **Harris** – they are, in fact, one island – is embedded in a historical split in the MacLeod clan, lost in the mists of time. The border between the two was also a county boundary until 1975, with Harris lying in Inverness-shire, and Lewis belonging to Ross and Cromarty. Nowadays, the dividing line is rarely marked even on maps, though for the record, it comprises Loch Resort in the west, Loch Seaforth in the east, and the six miles in between. Harris itself is more clearly divided by a minuscule isthmus, into the wild, inhospitable mountains of North Harris and the gentler landscape and sandy shores of South Harris.

Along with Lewis, Harris was purchased in 1918 by **Lord Leverhulme**, and after 1923 when he pulled out of Lewis, all his efforts were concentrated here. In contrast to Lewis, though, Leverhulme and his ambitious projects were broadly welcomed by the people of Harris. His most grandiose plans were drawn up for Leverburgh (see p.325), but he also purchased an old Norwegian whaling station in Bun Abhain Eadara in 1922, built a spinning mill at Geocrab and began the construction of four roads. Financial difficulties, a slump in the tweed industry and the lack of market for whale products meant that none of the schemes was a whole-hearted success, and when he died in 1925, the plug was pulled on all of them.

Since the Leverhulme era, unemployment has been a constant problem in Harris. Crofting continues on a small scale, supplemented by the Harris Tweed industry, though the main focus of this has shifted to Lewis. Fishing continues on Scalpay, while the rest of the population gets by on whatever employment is available: road works, crafts and, of course, tourism. There are regular **bus** connection between Stornoway and Tarbert and an occasional service which circumnavigates South Harris (see also "Travel Details" at the end of this chapter).

Tairbeart (Tarbert)

The largest place on Harris is the ferry port of **TARBERT**, sheltered in a green valley on the narrow isthmus that marks the border between North and South Harris. The town's mountainous backdrop is impressive, though there's nothing much to the place – just a few terraces sloping up from the dock. However, it does boast the only **tourist office** (April to mid-Oct Mon–Sat 9am–5pm; summer also Tues, Thurs & Sat 8–9pm; ☎01859/502011) on Harris, close to the ferry terminal. The office can arrange accommodation and has a full set of bus timetables, but its real value is as a source of information on local walks.

If you wish to base yourself in Tarbert, you could do worse than stay at the easygoing, old-fashioned *Harris Hotel* (☎01859/502154; ⑤), five minutes' walk from the ferry back towards Stornoway. Cheaper, equally convenient places to stay include the *Allan Cottage Guest House* (April–Oct; ☎01859/502146; ④), in the old telephone exchange, and a couple of nearby **B&Bs**, *Rockcliffe* (☎01859/502386; ③) and *Dunard* (☎01859/502340; ③). Excellent, reasonably priced **food** is served at both the *Harris Hotel* and the *Allan Cottage*.

Ceann a Tuath na Hearadh (North Harris)

The A859 north to Stornoway takes you over a boulder-strewn saddle between mighty **Sgaoth Aird** (1829ft) and **Clisham** (2619ft), the highest peak in the Western Isles. This bitter terrain offers but the barest of vegetation, with the occasional cluster of crofters' houses sitting in the shadow of a host of pointed peaks, anywhere between 1000ft and 2500ft high. These bulging, pyramidical mountains reach their climax around the dramatic shores of the fjord-like **Loch Seaforth**. If you're planning on walking in North Harris, and can afford it, consider using the spectacular *Ardvourlie Castle* (☎01859/502307; ⑧), ten miles north of Tarbert by the shores of Loch Seaforth, as a launch pad.

A cheaper, but equally idyllic spot is the *Gatliff Trust*'s **youth hostel** (no phone; Grade 3) in the lonely coastal hamlet of **REINIGEADAL** (Rhenigdale), until very recently only accessible by foot or boat. To reach the hostel without your own transport, walk east five miles from Tarbert along the road to **CAOLAS SCALPAIGH** (Kyles Scalpay). After another mile or so, watch for the sign marking the start of the path which threads its way through the peaks of the craggy promontory that lies trapped between Loch Seaforth and East Loch Tarbert. It's a magnificent hike, with superb views out along the coast and over the mountains, but you'll need to be properly equipped (see p.38) and should allow three hours for the one-way trip.

Caolas Scalpaigh looks out across East Loch Tarbert to the island of **Scalpaigh** (Scalpay) – from the Norse *skalp-ray* (the island shaped like a boat) – accessible via the short *CalMac* car ferry crossing from Carnach, a mile on. The island's tightly knit fishing community is surprisingly bouyant, maintaining a relatively large population of 450.

HARRIS TWEED

Far from being a picturesque cottage industry, as it's sometimes presented, the production of **Harris Tweed** is vital to the local economy with a well-organized and unionized workforce. Traditionally the tweed was made by women, from the wool of their own sheep, to provide clothing for their families. Each woman was responsible for the entire process, from the washing and scouring of the wool through to its dyeing, carding, spinning and warping; finally the cloth was dipped in sheep urine and "waulked" by a group of women, who beat the cloth on a table whilst singing Gaelic waulking songs. Harris Tweed was originally made all over the islands, and was known simply as *clò mór* (big cloth).

In the mid-nineteenth century, the Countess of Dunmore, who owned a large part of Harris, started to sell surplus cloth to her aristocratic friends, thus forming the genesis of the modern industry, which now employs about 400 mill workers and a further 650 weavers – though demand, and employment, fluctuates wildly as fashions change. To earn the official Harris Tweed Association trademark of the Orb and the Maltese Cross, the fabric has to be hand-woven on the Outer Hebrides from 100 percent pure new Scottish wool, while the other parts of the manufacturing process must take place only in the local mills.

The main centre of production is now Lewis, where the wool is dyed, carded and spun; you can see all these processes by visiting the **Lewis Loom Centre**, on Point St in Stornoway (Mon–Sat 10am–6pm; £1.50). In recent years, there has been a revival of traditional tweed-making techniques, with several small producers, like *Clo Mór* in Liceasto (☎01859/530364), religiously following old methods. One of the more interesting aspects of the process is the use of indigenous plants and bushes to dye the cloth: yellow comes from rocket and broom, green from heather, grey and black from iris and oak, and, most popular of all, reddish brown from crotal, a flat grey lichen scraped off rocks.

It's a pleasant and fairly easy day's hike from the ferry terminal to the far side of the island – three miles away – where the Stevensons' Eilean Glas lighthouse looks out over the sea to Skye. Apart from self-catering cottages in the lighthouse buildings themselves, you can **stay** on the island at *Suil-Na-Mara* B&B (☎01859/540278; ②).

The only other road on North Harris is the winding, single-track B887, which clings to the northern shores of West Loch Tarbert, and gives easy access to the awesome mountain range of the (treeless) **Forest of Harris** to the north. Not far along the B887, you pass through **Bun Abhainn Eadara** (Bunavoneadar), where some Norwegians established a short-lived whaling station – the slipways and chimney can still be seen. Seven miles further on, the road takes you through the gates of **Amhuinnsuidhe Castle**, and right past the front door, much to the annoyance of the castle's owners, who have tried in vain to have the road re-routed. As it is, you have time to admire the castle grounds, before continuing another five miles to **HUSINIS** (Hushinish), where you are rewarded with a very secluded sandy beach.

A pier to the north of the bay serves the nearby island of **Scarp** (occasional ferries), a hulking mass of rock rising to over 1000ft, abandoned as recently as 1971 and now populated only by holiday cottages. In 1934, the German scientist Gerhardt Zucher conducted an experiment with rocket mail, but the letter-laden missile exploded on impact and the idea was shelved.

Ceann a Deas (South Harris)

The mountains of **South Harris** are less dramatic than in the north, but the scenery is equally breathtaking. There's a choice of routes from Tarbert to the ferry port of Leverburgh, which connects with North Uist (passengers only): the east coast, known as Na Baigh (Bays), is rugged and seemingly inhospitable, while the west coast is endowed with some of the finest stretches of golden sand in the whole of the archipelago, buffeted by the Atlantic winds. A bus sets off from Tarbert, twice weekly, travelling out along the east coast, and returning via all points along the west coast a little under two hours later. Buses do circumnavigate South Harris, but never all in a day, so you'll have to spend a night at some point along the route – for more information see "Travel details" at the end of this chapter or contact Tarbert tourist office.

Na Baigh (Bays)

Paradoxically, most people on South Harris live along the harsh eastern coastline of **Bays** rather than the more fertile west side. But not by choice – they were evicted from their original crofts to make way for sheep-grazing. Despite the uncompromising terrain – mostly bare rock and heather – the crofters managed to establish "lazybeds" (small raised plots between the rocks fertilized by seaweed and peat) which they continue to work even today. The narrow sea lochs provide shelter for fishing boats, while the interior is speckled with freshwater lochans, and the whole coast now served by the meandering Golden Road (so called because of the expense of constructing it).

There are just a few places to stay along the coast, the most obvious being the two hostels south of Tarbert: the official **youth hostel** (late March–Sept; ☎01859/530373; Grade 3) is in a converted school in **CAOLAS STOCINIS** (Kyles Stockinish), six miles to the south; an **independent hostel** (☎01851/511255) lies only three miles to the south in **DRINISIADAR** (Drinishader). Other possibilities include *Mrs Val Ruffles* B&B (☎01859/530244; ③) in **AIRD MHIGHE** (Ardvey), who happily caters for veggies, or the modern bungalow guest house of *Two Waters* (☎01859/530246; ⑤) in **LICEASTO** (Likisto), both of which are on Loch Stockinish.

Six miles beyond Liceasto at **Lingreabhagh** (Lingarabay), the road skirts the foot of **Roineabhal** (1508ft), the southernmost mountain of the island and known as *an aite boidheach* (the beautiful place). The vast majority of the locals are currently fighting to prevent *Redland Aggregates* building one of Europe's largest **superquarrys** here, which would demolish virtually the entire mountain over the next 70 years. Environmentalists charge that local fishing grounds would be badly affected, the devout are up in arms over the possibility of Sunday working, and the initial promise of a hundred much needed new jobs has been reduced on the evidence of a public enquiry to just twenty-five. At the time of writing the Secretary of State for Scotland was due to make the final decision about the moutain's future.

A mile or so from Rubha Reanais (Renish Point), the southern tip of Harris, is the old port of **ROGHADAL** (Rodel), where a smattering of ancient stone houses lies among the hillocks surrounding the dilapidated harbour. On top of one of these grassy humps, with sheep grazing in the graveyard, is the castellated tower and thick-walled nave of **St Clement's Church**, burial place of the MacLeods of Harris and Dunvegan in Skye. Dating from the 1520s, the church's gloomy interior is distinguished by its wall tombs, notably that of the founder, Alasdair Crotach (also known as Alexander MacLeod), whose heavily weathered effigy lies beneath an intriguing cartoon strip of vernacular and religious scenes – elemental representations of, among others, a stag hunt, the Holy Trinity, St Michael, and the Devil weighing the souls of the dead. Look out, too, for the *sheila-na-gig* below a carving of St Clement himself.

The west coast

The main road from Tarbert into South Harris snakes its way west across the lunaresque interior to emerge, after ten miles, at the hamlet of **SEILEBOST**, situated above the first of a chain of sweeping sandy **beaches**, backed by rich machair, that stretches for nine miles along the Atlantic coast. In good weather, the scenery is stunning, foaming breakers rolling along the golden sands set against the rounded peaks of the mountains to the north and the islet-studded turquoise sea to the west. A short distance out to sea is the island of **Tarasigh** (Taransay), an impressive hulk of an island that was abandoned as recently as 1974.

Nobody bothers much if you camp or park down on the dune-edged beach; alternatively, you can find shelter at the **B&Bs** and **guest houses** dotted along the road. Good-value B&Bs include *Moravia* (March–Oct; ☎01859/550262; ③) in **LOSGAINTIR** (Luskentyre), on the north side of the loch; *Mrs Lena MacLennan* (April–Oct; ☎01859/ 550285; ④), and *Mrs Mary MacDonald* (May–Sept; ☎01859/550215; ③), both in **HORGABOST**, a mile or so beyond Seilebost. The swankiest accommodation is three miles further south at *Scarista House* (May–Sept; ☎01859/550238; ⑧), which looks out to sea from above the beach in the village of **SGARASTA** (Scarista). *Mrs Mary Morrison*'s B&B (April–Sept; ☎01859/520228; ③) is the lee of the sharp headland bordering Harris's last tidal beach in the bayside village of **TAOBH TUATH** (Northton).

From here, the road veers to the southeast to trim the island's south shore, eventually reaching the sprawling settlement of **AN T-OB**, better known as Leverburgh, after Lord Leverhulme, who planned to turn the place into the largest fishing port on the west coast of Scotland. From a jetty about a mile south of the main road, a passenger **ferry** leaves for Berneray and North Uist (contact Donald MacAskill on ☎01876/540230), though you need to plan ahead if you're going to the latter as public transport is very limited. There are several **B&Bs** strung out within a two-mile radius of Leverburgh: try *Garryknowe*, Ferry Rd (April–Oct; ☎01859/520246; ③), not too far from the jetty, or *Paula Williams* (☎01859/520319; ③), who specializes in vegetarian and vegan cooking.

Uibhist a Tuath (North Uist)

After the stunning scenery of Harris, the much flatter scenery of **North Uist** – 17 miles long and 13 miles wide – cannot help but be something of an anticlimax. Over half the surface area is covered by water, creating a distinctive lochan-studded landscape reminiscent of north Lewis. The main attractions for visitors are its vast sandy beaches, which extend – almost without interruption – along the north and west coast, and the smattering of prehistoric sites on the island.

There are two main sea approaches to North Uist: the first is the passenger ferry from Leverburgh on South Harris to Port nan Long (Newtonferry), though the only public transport on from here is the **postbus**, so check timings before you set out. Most people take either the Oban or the Tarbert **car ferry**, which docks at the principal village, Lochmaddy, on the east coast. A twice-daily **bus** leaves Lochmaddy for Lochboisdale in South Uist, but to travel the coastal road, again you'll need to consult the timetable of the local postbus.

Loch nam Madadh (Lochmaddy) and around

Despite being situated on the east coast, some distance away from any beach, the ferry port of **LOCHMADDY** is easily the best base for exploring the island. The village itself, occupying a narrow, bumpy promontory, is nothing special, though it does have the added incongruity of 16 brown weatherboarded houses, which arrived from Sweden in 1948. If the weather's bad or you've time to kill, take a look round **Taigh Chearsabhagh** (Mon–Sat 10am–5pm; £1.50), a converted eighteenth-century merchant's house, which now harbours the local museum, arts centre and café.

The **tourist office** (mid-April to mid-Oct Mon–Sat 9am–5pm; ☎01876/500321), near the quayside, has local bus and ferry timetables, and can help with accommodation. Right by the tourist office is the spick-and-span *Lochmaddy Hotel* (☎01876/500331; ⑦), whose restaurant serves outstanding seafood and whose bar is the liveliest place on the whole island. The hotel rents out boats and sells fishing permits for brown trout, sea trout and salmon. There are a couple of nice Victorian **B&Bs** – the *Old Courthouse*

(☎01876/500358; ③), and the *Old Bank House* (☎01876/500275; ③). The **official youth hostel** is *Ostram House* (mid-May to Sept; ☎01876/500368; Grade 2), half a mile from the ferry dock. Not far beyond, the **independent** hostel in the *Uist Outdoor Centre* (☎01876/500480) offers four-person bunk rooms.

The only **bike rental** on the island is at *Morrison Cycle Hire* (☎01876/580211), nine miles away in Cairinis (Carinish), but they will deliver to Lochmaddy if you phone them. A rather more unusual mode of transport is on offer at *Hougharry Horsedrawn Holidays* (☎01876/510223), based in Ceann a Bhaigh (Bayhead), on the west coast. **Horse-drawn Romany caravans** are available for daily rental or for longer overnight trips. The aforementioned *Uist Outdoor Centre* also offers a wide range of outdoor activities from canoeing to rock climbing.

Two prehistoric sights lie within easy cycling distance of Lochmaddy (or even walking distance if you use the postbus for the outward journey). The most significant is the **Barpa Langass**, a large mostly intact chambered cairn seven barren miles to the southwest along the A867; a mile to the southeast is the small stone circle of **Pobull Fhinn**. Three miles northwest of Lochmaddy along the A865 is **Na Fir Bhreige** (The Three False Men), three standing stones which, depending on your legend, mark the graves of three spies buried alive, or three men who deserted their wives and were turned to stone by a neo-feminist witch.

Bearnaraigh (Berneray)

For those in search of still more seclusion, there's the low-lying island of **Berneray** – eight miles in circumference with a population of just over 100 – accessible via a short car ferry journey from Newtonferry, eight miles north of Lochmaddy (or passenger ferry from Leverburgh on South Harris). The island's main claim to fame is as the birthplace of Giant MacAskill (see p.307) and as the favoured holiday hideaway of that other great eccentric, Prince Charles, lover of Gaelic culture and royal potato picker to local crofter, "Splash" MacKillop. Apart from the sheer peace and isolation of the place – though the causeway from North Uist may yet put paid to that – the island's main draw for non-royals is the three-mile long sandy beach on the west coast, two miles across country from the ferry dock. Should you wish to stay, try the **B&Bs** of *Mrs MacLeod* (☎01876/540254; ③) or *Donald MacKillop* (☎01876/540235; ③); or the simple *Gatliff Trust* **youth hostel** (no phone; Grade 3), in a pair of thatched black houses two miles from the dock, on the north side of Bays Loch.

The coastal road

The A865, which skirts the northern and western shoreline of North Uist for more than 30 miles, takes you through the most scenic sections of the island. Once you've left the boggy east coast and passed the road off to Newtonferry, the road slips past a couple of wide and sandy river estuaries before reaching the rolling hills that slope down to the sea in the northwest corner of the island. It's around here, about 17 miles from Lochmaddy, that you'll find **Scolpaig Tower**, a castellated folly on an islet in Loch Scolpaig, erected as a famine relief project in the nineteenth century. A footpath leads down from the road to the tower and beyond, to the rocky shoreline of **Griminish Point**, the closest landfall to St Kilda (see p.331) – which is sometimes visible on the horizon.

Roughly three miles south of Scolpaig Tower, is the **Baranald RSPB Reserve**, one of the last breeding grounds of the corncrake, among Europe's most endangered birds. Sightings are rare even here, and you'll only get to hear it if you stay up half the night. The two-mile walk long the headland of the reserve, however, should give ample opportunity for spotting skuas, gannets and Manx shearwaters out to sea – guided walks take place throughout the summer (for more details, contact the warden, who lives on

South Uist; ☎01878/602188). A good place for "twitchers" (birders) to **stay** is at *Mrs Joan MacDonald* (☎01876/510279; ②) overlooking the beautiful beach at **HOGHA GEARRAIDH** (Hougharry), a mile south of Tigh a Ghearraidh.

Offshore, to the south of the nature reserve, lie two tidal dune islands, the largest of which is **Baile Sear** (Baleshare), with its fantastic three-mile long beach. In Gaelic the island's name means "east village", its twin "west village" having disappeared under the sea during a freak storm. This also isolated the **Monarch Islands**, once connected to North Uist at low tide, now eight miles out to sea. Baile Sear is now connected by a causeway, to the south of Clachan a Luib – the crossroads with the A867 from Lochmaddy. Continuing south, the A865 passes **Teampull na Trionaid** (Trinity Church), a large pre-Reformation church, now in some state of ruin, connected by a barrel-vaulted passage to a rather better-preserved, but equally ancient chapel.

On leaving North Uist the main road squeezes along a series of causeways, built by the military in 1960, that trim the west edge of **Griomasaigh** (Grimsay), a peaceful, little-visited lobster-fishing island, before heading across the tidal sands to Benbecula.

Beinn na Faoghla (Benbecula)

Blink and you could miss the pancake-flat island of **Benbecula** (put the stress on the second syllable), sandwiched between Protestant North Uist and Catholic South Uist. Most visitors simply trundle along the main road that cuts across the middle of the island in less than five miles – not such a bad idea, since nearly half the island's 1200 population are Royal Artillery personnel, working at the missile range on South Uist.

Economically, the area has, of course, benefitted enormously, though the impact on the environment and Gaelic culture (with so many English-speakers around) has been less positive. There is talk of the military pulling out altogether – a devastating prospect for most islanders. Nearly all the military personnel live in the barracks-like housing developments of **BAILE A MHANAICH** (Balivanich), the grim, grey capital of Benbecula in the northwest. The only reason to come here at all is if you happen to be flying into or out of Balivanich airport (direct flights to Glasgow, Barra and Stornoway), or need to stock up on provisions, best done at the NAAFI "family store", the only one in the UK that's open to the public. If you're unfortunate enough to need to stay here, there are a couple of **B&Bs**: *Mrs Margaret MacDonald* (☎01870/602129; ③) or *Culla Bay View* (☎01870/602201; ③), a mile south in **AIRD**. There are also two places where you can grab a bite to eat: the *Low Flyer*, situated in one of the barracks-type buildings opposite the post office, and the airport café. **Car rental** is available from *Ask Car Hire* (☎01870/602818) in neighbouring **Uachdar**.

The nearest **campsite**, *Shell Bay* (April–Oct; ☎01870/602447) is in the south of the island at **LIONACLEIT** (Liniclate), which also boasts the island's most comfortable hotel, *Dark Island Hotel* (☎01870/602414; ⑥) – no charmer from the outside, but with the best restaurant around, featuring local specialities such as peat-smoked salmon and lumpfish caviar.

Uibhist a Deas (South Uist)

To the south of Benbecula, the island of **South Uist** is arguably the most appealing of the southern chain of islands. The west coast boasts some of the region's finest beaches – a necklace of gold and grey sand strung 20 miles from one end to the other – while the east coast features a ridge of high mountains rising to 2034ft at the summit of Beinn Mhor. The only blot on the landscape is the Royal Artillery missile range, which occupies the northwest corner of the island, shattering the peace and quiet every so often.

The Reformation never reached South Uist (or Barra), and the island remains Roman Catholic, as is evident from the slender modern statue of *Our Lady of the Isles* that stands by the main road below the small hill of **Rueval**, known to the locals as "Space City" for its forest of aerials and golf balls, which help track the missiles heading out into the Atlantic. To the south of Rueval is the freshwater **Loch Druidibeg**, a breeding ground for greylag geese (there's a hide along the road to the north) and a favourite spot for mute swans.

A whole series of country lanes lead west from the main road to the old crofters' villages that straggle along the coast, but – although the paths are rarely more than three miles long – it's surprisingly easy to get lost, tramping round in circles before you stumble upon the shore. This is not the case, however, at **TOBHA MOR** (Howmore), with its easy mile-long walk from the main road to the gorgeous beach. The village is the prettiest place for miles, the shattered ruins of its medieval chapel and burial ground standing near a cluster of neat little black houses, one of which the *Gatliff Trust* operates as a **youth hostel** (no phone; ungraded).

Six miles south of Tobha Mor, the main road passes the cairn that sits amongst the ruins of **Flora MacDonald**'s birthplace (also see p.310), before continuing for another seven miles to the ferry terminal of **LOCH BAGHASDAIL** (Lochboisdale). Like Lochmaddy in North Uist, Lochboisdale occupies a narrow, bumpy promontory and is the island's chief settlement, though, if anything, it has less to offer than Lochmaddy, with no youth hostel and just the *Lochboisdale Hotel* (☎01878/700332; ⑤) for somewhere to have a drink and a bite to eat. If you're arriving here late at night on the seven-hour boat trip from Oban (or Castlebay on Barra; 1hr 50min), you should try to book accommodation in advance; otherwise you'll have to get your head down beside the **tourist office** (Easter to mid-Oct Mon–Sat 9am–1pm & 2–5pm; also open to meet the night ferry; ☎01878/700286). There are also several **B&Bs** within comfortable walking distance of the dock: try *Bayview* (March–Oct; ☎01878/700329; ②), or *Lochside Cottage* (☎01878/700472; ②). **Bike rental** is available from *NJ Cycle Hire*.

If you're heading on south to the island of Barra from South Uist, there's an alternative to the *CalMac* ferry from Lochboisdale: the passenger ferry from **Ludag jetty**, ten miles by road from Lochboisdale (buses 2 daily), which lands at Eoligarry on the north coast of Barra.

Eiriosgaigh (Eriskay)

Also from Ludag, a frequent car ferry slips across to Haun jetty on the hilly island of **Eriskay**, famous for its peculiar breed of pony, originally used for carrying peat and seaweed, and its patterned jerseys (on sale at the post office). For a small island, Eriskay has had more than its fair share of historical headlines. It was on the island's main beach on the west coast on July 23, 1745, that Bonnie Prince Charlie landed on Scottish soil – a big pink convolvulus grows there to this day, said to have sprung from the seeds Charles brought with him from France. The Prince, as yet unaccustomed to much hardship, spent his first night in a local black house, and ate a couple of flounders, though he apparently couldn't take the peat smoke and chose to sleep sitting up rather than endure the damp bed.

Eriskay's other claim to fame came in 1941 when the SS *Politician* sank on its way from Liverpool to Jamaica, along with its cargo of bicycle parts, £3 million in Jamaican currency and 243,000 bottles of whisky, inspiring Compton Mackenzie's book – and the Ealing Comedy (filmed here in 1948) – *Whisky Galore!* (released as *Tight Little Island* in the US). The ship's stern can still be seen to the east of the Isle of Calvey at low tide, and one of the original bottles (and lots of other related memorabilia) is on show in the bar of *The Politician* in the main village of **BAILE** (Balla).

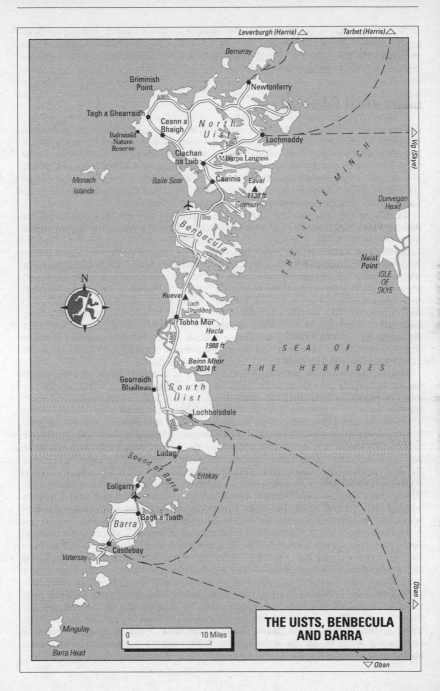

Leverburgh (Harris) △   Tarbet (Harris) △

Berneray

Griminish
Point
A865

Newtonferry

Tagh a Ghearraidh

Ceann a
Bhaigh

*North
Uist*

Balranald
Nature
Reserve

Clachan
na Luib

Lochmaddy

A867

Barpa Langass

△ Vig (Skye)

Monach
Islands

Baile Sear

Cairinis

Eaval
1138 ft

Dunvegan
Head

Grimsay

N

Benbecula

THE LITTLE MINCH

Neist
Point

ISLE
OF
SKYE

Rueval

Loch
Druidibeg

Tobha Mor

Hecla
1988 ft

Beinn Mhor
2034 ft

SEA   OF

THE   HEBRIDES

Gearraidh
Bhailteas

*South
Uist*

Lochboisdale

B888

Ludag

Sound of Barra

Eriskay

Eoligarry

Bagh a Tuath

Barra

Castlebay

Oban △

Vatersay

Mingulay

0   10 Miles

Barra Head

**THE UISTS, BENBECULA
AND BARRA**

▽ Oban

Also worth a look is **St Michael's**, the island's Catholic church which stands on raised ground above the village, built in 1903 in a vaguely Spanish style. As for **accommodation**, there's a self-catering flat (✆01878/720274) but no B&Bs and few amenities – just a shop and a post office.

Barraigh (Barra)

Just four miles wide and eight miles long, **Barra** has a deserved reputation of being the Western Isles in miniature. It has sandy beaches, backed by machair, glacial mountains, prehistoric ruins, Gaelic culture, and a laid-back Catholic population of just under 1500. The only settlement of any size is the old herring port of **BAGH A CHAISTEIL** (Castlebay), which curves around the barren hills of a wide bay on the south side of the island (ferries from Lochboisdale, on South Uist, and Oban stop here). Barra's religious allegiance is immediately apparent thanks to the large Catholic church, Our Lady, Star of the Sea, which overlooks the Castlebay, and the Madonna and Child which stands on the slopes of Heaval (1260ft), the largest peak on Barra, and a fairly easy hike from the bay.

As its name suggests, Castlebay has a castle in its bay, the medieval islet-fortress of **Kisimul Castle** (opening times subject to tides – check at the tourist office), ancestral home of the MacNeil clan. The MacNeils owned Barra from 1427 to 1838, when they sold it to the infamous Colonel Gordon of Cluny, who offered to clear the island and turn it into a state penal colony. The government declined, and in 1937, the 45th chief of the MacNeil clan bought back the castle (and 12,000 acres). It has since been restored to something of its original appearance, making a visit just about worth the effort, though it's best viewed from the ferry. Most people, however, come to Barra for the peace and quiet, walking across the hilly interior or making the 12-mile excursion right round the island by road.

Barra airport, on the north side of the island, is a sight in itself, with the planes having to land and take off from the shell sands of **Tràigh Mhór** (Cockle Strand); the exact timing of the flights depends on the tides, since at high tide the beach (and therefore the runway) is covered in water. Tràigh Mhór is also famous for its cockles and cockleshells, the latter being used to make harling (the rendering used on most Scottish houses). In 1994, mechanical cockle extraction using tractors was introduced, and quickly began to decimate the cockle stocks and threaten the beach's use as an aiport – as a result it has now been banned, in favour of traditional hand-raking.

To the north of the airport, connected by a thin strip of land, is the coastal village of **EOLAIGEARRAIDH** (Eoligarry), with a passenger ferry link to Ludag on South Uist. Above the village is **Cille-Bharra**, burial ground of the MacNeils (and Compton Mackenzie), situated beside the ruins of a medieval church and two chapels, one of which has been re-roofed to provide shelter for several carved grave slabs.

To the south of Barra, the island of **Bhatarsaigh** (Vatersay), shaped rather like an apple core, has recently been linked to the main island by a causeway – a mile or so to the southwest of Castlebay – to try to stem the depopulation which has brought the current head count down to just seventy. If you prefer, you can still catch a passenger ferry direct from Castlebay to Uidh jetty on the northeast tip of the island. The main settlement (also known as Vatersay) is on the south coast, and to get to it you must cross a narrow isthmus, with the golden sands of Vatersay Bay to the east, and the stony beach of Bàgh Siar, a few hundred yards to the west. Above the dunes to the north of the isthmus is the **Annie Jane Monument**, a granite needle erected to commemorate the 450 emigrants who lost their lives when the *Annie Jane* ran aground off Vatersay in 1853.

Practicalities

A **postbus** does the rounds of the island (Mon–Sat); you can get **bike rental** from *MacDougall Cycles*, 29 St Brendan Rd (☎01871/810284). Near the jetty, the **tourist office** (April to mid-Oct Mon–Sat 9am–1pm & 2–5pm; also open for late ferry arrivals; ☎01871/810336) will advise on walking routes; it also has details of accommodation, including several cheap **B&Bs** clustered in and around Castlebay – try *Tigh-na-Mara* (April–Oct; ☎01871/810304; ③), or *Grianamul* (April–Oct; ☎01871/810416; ③) – as well as two **hotels**, the *Craigard* (☎01871/810200; ⑥) and the *Castlebay* (☎01871/810223; ⑤). The *Kisimul Gallery* offers a limited selection of food and a good bakery.

If you're looking for a more isolated spot, the *Isle of Barra Hotel* (April–Oct; ☎01871/810383; ⑥) overlooks the sandy beach of Halaman Bay on the west coast near **TANGASDAL** (Tangasdale). On the other side of the island at **BAGH A TUATH** (Northbay), you've a choice of *Northbay House* (April–Oct; ☎01871/890255; ③) or *Suidheachan* (May–Sept; ☎01871/890243; ③), the former home of Compton Mackenzie.

Mingulay and St Kilda

George MacLeod at the *Isle of Barra Hotel* (☎01871/810383) and Ray Burnett of *Celtic Quests*, The Old Schoolhouse, Torlum, Benbecula (☎01870/602334) organize frequent sea trips to the sea cliffs of **Mingulay**, whose last two inhabitants were evacuated in 1934. Ray also arranges full-scale, but infrequent, expeditions out across the Atlantic to the nature reserves on the NTS-owned **St Kilda** archipelago, roughly 40 miles north west of Barra.

The last 36 Gaelic-speaking inhabitants of **Hirta**, St Kilda's main island, were evacuated at their own request in 1930, ending several hundred years of a peculiarly harsh existence – well recorded in Tom Steel's book *The Life and Death of St Kilda*. Today, presuming you can get permission from the NTS to land – even tour operators have to negotiate long and hard – you can visit their old village, recently restored by volunteers, and struggle up the massive cliffs, where the islanders once caught puffins, young fulmars and gannets.

travel details

Trains

Glasgow (Queen St) to: Mallaig (Mon–Sat 3 daily, Sun 1–2 daily; 5hr 10min); Oban (3 daily; 3hr).

Inverness to: Kyle of Lochalsh (Mon–Sat 3 daily; 2hr 30min)

Buses (excluding the postbus)

Glasgow to: Broadford (2–4 daily; 5hr 30min); Kyleakin (2–4 daily; 5hr 15min); Portree (2–4 daily; 6hr 10min); Sconser (2–4 daily; 5hr 45min); Uig (2–4 daily; 6hr 35min).

Lionacleit to: Lochboisdale (Mon, Thurs, Fri & Sat 1 daily to meet the late ferry; 55min).

Lochboisdale to: Ludag (Mon–Sat 2 daily; 30–45min).

Lochmaddy to: Balivanich (Mon–Sat 1 daily; 1hr); Lochboisdale (Mon–Sat 1 daily; 2hr).

Portree to: Armadale (Mon–Sat 2 daily, 1hr 30min); Broadford (5–15 daily; 45min); Carbost (Mon–Fri 2–3 daily; 35min); Duntulm (Mon–Sat 1–3 daily; 50min); Dunvegan (Mon–Sat 1–2 daily; 50min); Edinburgh (2–3 daily; 6hr 30min); Glen Brittle (Mon–Fri 3 daily; 40min); Inverness (3–4 daily; 3hr 15min); Kyleakin (5–15 daily; 1hr); Sconser (5–15 daily; 20min); Sligachan (5–15 daily; 20min); Staffin (Mon–Sat 1–2 daily; 30min); Uig (Mon–Sat 3 daily; 25min).

Stornoway to: Callanish (Mon–Sat 1 daily; 1hr); Carloway (Mon–Sat 1 daily; 1hr 20min); Port of Ness (1 daily except Wed & Sun; 1hr 20min); Tarbert (Mon–Sat up to 2 daily; 1hr 15min).

Tarbert to: Leverburgh (Mon–Sat 1 daily; 1hr 30min); Rodel (Mon–Sat 2 daily; 1hr 20min); Stockinish (Mon–Sat 1 daily; 30min).

Ferries (summer timetable)

To Barra: Oban–Castlebay (Mon, Wed, Thurs & Sat; 5hr); Lochboisdale–Castlebay (Tues, Thurs, Fri & Sun; 1hr 45min).

To Berneray: Newtonferry–Berneray (car ferry Mon–Sat 6 daily; 10min); Newtonferry–Berneray (passenger ferry Mon–Sat 2 daily; 10min).

To Canna: Mallaig–Canna (Mon, Wed, Fri & Sat; 2hr 30min–4hr 15min); Eigg–Canna (Mon & Sat; 2hr 45min–3hr); Rum–Canna (Mon, Wed & Sat; 1hr–1hr 45min); Muck–Canna (Sun; 2hr 15min).

To Eigg: Mallaig–Eigg (Mon, Tues, Thurs & Sat; 1hr 30–1hr 50min); Muck–Eigg (Tues, Thurs & Sat; 45–50min); Rum–Eigg (Fri & Sat; 1hr 15min–2hr); Canna–Eigg (Fri & Sat; 2hr 15min–3hr).

To Harris: Uig–Tarbert (Mon–Sat 1–2 daily; 1hr 45min); Lochmaddy–Tarbert (Mon–Sat 1–2 daily; 1hr 45min–4hr); Newtonferry–Leverburgh (Mon–Sat 2 daily; 30min).

To Lewis: Ullapool–Stornoway (Mon–Sat up to 3 daily; 3hr 30min).

To Muck: Mallaig–Muck (Tues, Thurs & Sat; 2hr 40min–4hr 45min); Rum–Muck (Sat; 1hr 15min); Eigg–Muck (Tues, Thurs & Sat; 45min); Canna–Muck (Sat; 2hr 15min).

To North Uist: Tarbert–Lochmaddy (Mon–Sat 1–2 daily; 2hr); Uig–Lochmaddy (1–2 daily; 1hr 45min); Leverburgh–Newtonferry (Mon–Sat 2 daily; 30min).

To Raasay: Sconser–Raasay (Mon–Sat 9 daily; 15min).

To Rum: Mallaig–Rum (Mon, Wed, Fri & Sat; 1hr 45min–3hr 30min); Eigg–Rum (Mon & Sat; 1hr 30min–2hr); Muck–Rum (Sat; 1hr 15min); Canna–Rum (Wed, Fri & Sat; 1hr–1hr 15min).

To Scalpay: Kyles Scalpay–Scalpay (Mon–Sat up to 11 daily; 10min).

To Skye: Mallaig–Armadale (up to 7 daily; 30mins); Glenelg–Kylerhea (mid-April to mid-Oct frequent daily service; 15min).

To South Uist: Oban–Lochboisdale (daily except Tues & Sun; 7hr); Castlebay–Lochboisdale (Mon, Wed, Thurs & Sat; 1hr 50min).

Flights

To Barra: Benbecula (Mon–Fri 1 daily; 20min); Glasgow (Mon–Sat 1–2 daily; 1hr 20min); Tiree (Tues–Thurs 1 daily; 20min).

To Benbecula: Barra (Mon–Fri 1 daily; 20min); Glasgow (Mon–Sat 1 daily; 1hr); Stornoway (Mon–Fri 2 daily; 35min).

To Stornoway: Benbecula (Mon–Fri 2 daily; 35min); Glasgow (Mon–Sat 1–2 daily; 1hr); Inverness (Mon–Sat 1–2 daily; 40min).

CHAPTER SEVEN

NORTHEAST SCOTLAND

A large triangle of land thrusting into the North Sea from a line drawn roughly from Perth up to Forres, east of Inverness, the **northeast** of Scotland takes in the county of Angus and the city of Dundee to the south (plus for the purposes of this guide, the part of Perthshire and Kinross around Glen Shee, Meigle and Blairgowrie), and, beyond the **Grampian Mountains**, the counties of Aberdeenshire and Moray and the city of Aberdeen. Geographically diverse, the landscape in the south is made up predominantly of undulating farmland, but, north of the Firth of Tay, this gives way to wooded glens, mountains and increasingly harsh land fringed by a dramatic coast of cliffs and long sandy beaches.

The northeast was the southern kingdom of the **Picts**, reminders of whom are scattered throughout the region in the form of numerous symbolic carved stones found in fields, churchyards, and museums – such as the one at **Meigle**. Remote, self-contained and cut off from the centres of major power in the south, the area never grew particularly prosperous, and a few feuding and intermarrying families, such as the Gordons, the Keiths and the Irvines, grew to wield disproportionate influence, building the region's many **castles** and religious buildings and developing and planning its towns.

Although much of the northeast remains economically deprived, parts have, however, been transformed by the discovery of oil in the North Sea in the 1960s, particularly **Aberdeen**, Scotland's third-largest city. Aberdeen is the region's most stimulating urban centre, a fast, relatively sophisticated city that continues to ride on the crest of the **oil** boom. In stark contrast, **Dundee**, the next largest metropolis in the northeast, is low key and rather depressed; although it does boast a splendid site on the banks of the Tay and makes a useful base for visiting nearby **Glamis Castle**, famous from Shakespeare's *Macbeth*. A little way up the Angus coast lie the historically important towns of **Arbroath**, where Robert the Bruce was declared King of Scotland, and **Montrose**, where Edward I was forced to sign over his kingdom. Inland, the **Angus glens** cut picturesquely through the hills, their villages, such as **Blairgowrie** and **Kirriemuir**, perfect centres for hikers and skiers.

North of the glens, **Deeside** is a wild, unspoilt tract of land made famous by the royal family, who have favoured **Balmoral** as one of their prime residences since Queen Victoria fell in love with it back in the 1840s. Beyond, the **Don Valley** is less visited, although it does generate something of a tourist season in the winter, when keen skiers head for the **Lecht** area; while **Speyside**, a little way west, is more tranquil and best known as Scotland's premier **whisky**-producing region. Despite the blots of **Peterhead** and **Fraserburgh**, the route further north, around the northeast coast, fringed with mighty oil rigs, offers the best of Aberdeenshire and Moray, with rugged cliffs and remote fishing villages, barely sheltered from the ferocious elements.

Northeast Scotland is well served by an extensive road network, with the A92 following the coast from Dundee to Aberdeen and beyond, and the area north and east of Aberdeen dissected by a series of efficient routes. **Trains** from the south stop at Dundee and Aberdeen, and other towns on the coast. Inland, there is one branch line from Aberdeen northwest to Elgin and on to Inverness. A reasonably comprehensive scheduled **bus service** is complemented by a network of **postbuses**. Only in the most remote and mountainous parts does public transport disappear altogether.

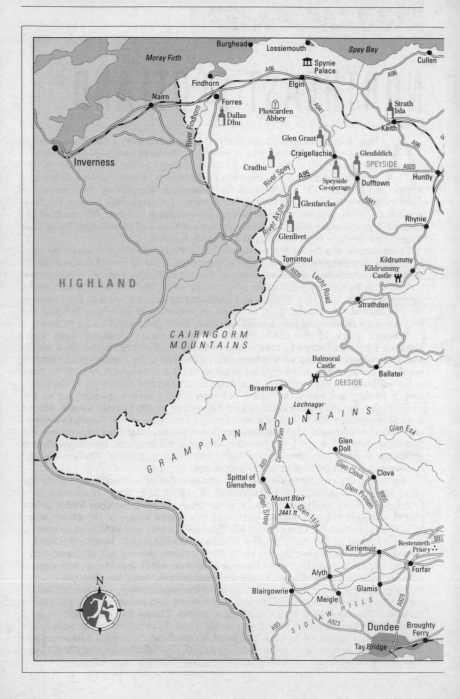

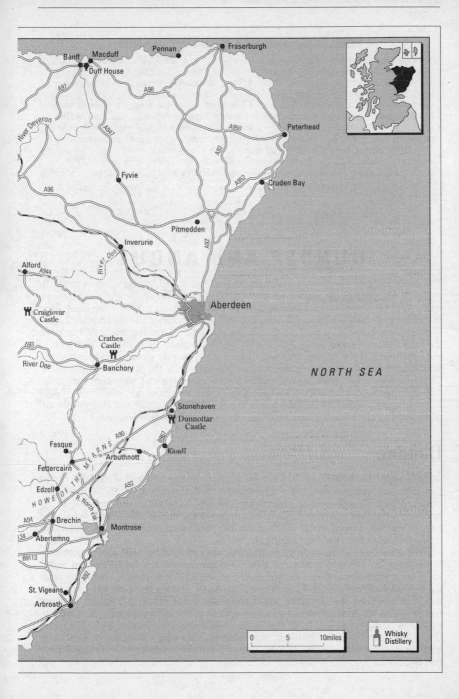

ACCOMMODATION PRICE CODES

Throughout this book, accommodation **prices** have been graded with the numbers below, according to the cost of the least expensive double room in high season. Although costs will rise slightly overall with the life of this edition, the relative comparisons should remain valid. The bulk of the recommendations will fall in categories ② to ⑥; those in the highest categories are limited to places that are especially attractive. Edinburgh will inevitably be more expensive than equivalent accommodation in the countryside or small towns, and a number of places will have a big mark-up for the three weeks of the Festival. Also bear in mind that many of the swanky hotels often slash their tariffs at the weekend when the business types have gone home, and that many of the cheaper places will also have more expensive rooms. Note that in our accommodation listings price codes are not given for youth hostels and campsites – they all come into the lower end of the ① category.

① under £20	④ £40–50	⑦ £70–80
② £20–30	⑤ £50–60	⑧ £80–100
③ £30–40	⑥ £60–70	⑨ over £100

DUNDEE AND ANGUS

The predominantly agricultural county of **Angus**, east of the A9 and north of the Firth of Tay, holds much of the northeast's greatest scenery and is relatively unspoilt by tourist crowds who tend to head further west for the Highlands proper. The coast from Montrose to Arbroath is especially inviting with scarlet cliffs and sweeping bays, then further south towards Dundee gentler dunes and sands. **Dundee** itself, although not the most obvious tourist destination, makes for a less snooty alternative to Aberdeen.

In the north of the county, the long fingers of the **Angus glens** – heather-covered hills tumbling down to rushing rivers – are overlooked by the southern peaks of the Grampian Mountains. Each has its own feel and devotees, Glen Clova being, deservedly, one of the most popular, along with Glen Shee, which attracts large numbers of people to its ski resort. Handsome market towns like Brechin, Kirriemuir and Blairgowrie are good bases for the area. Angus is also liberally dotted with **Pictish remains**.

Dundee

At first sight, **DUNDEE** can seem a grim place. In the nineteenth century it was Britain's main processor of jute – the world's most important vegetable fibre after cotton. Today, though economically depressed and somewhat overshadowed by its northerly neighbour, Aberdeen, it's still a a refreshingly unpretentious and welcoming city, wonderfully placed on the banks of the Tay, with some good museums and useful transport connections throughout Angus.

Even prior to its Victorian heyday, Dundee was a town of considerable importance. It was here in 1309 that Robert the Bruce was proclaimed the lawful King of Scots, and during the Reformation it earned itself a reputation for tolerance, sheltering leading figures such as George Wishart and John Knox. During the Civil War, the town was destroyed by the Royalists and Cromwell's army; later the Stuart Viscount Dundee, who was granted the city for his services to the crown after the Restoration, razed the place to the ground in the Battle of Killiecrankie. Dundee picked itself up in the 1700s, its train and harbour links making it a major centre for shipbuilding, whaling and the manufacture of jute, although little investment was ploughed back into the city.

Despite a burst of prosperity after World War II, there's little left to show today of Dundee's former glory. Furthermore, its self-image hasn't been helped by the imposition of a couple of garish central shopping malls and the seemingly endless spread of 1970s housing estates around the city edges. There's still enough, however, of its Victorian centre, backed by glimpses of the blue Tay, to please.

Many of its populace still depend on D C Thomson, the local publishing giant that produces the timelessly popular *Beano* and *Dandy* comics, as well as the *Sunday Post,* for their dwindling employment prospects. Dundee was also where marmalade was invented in the nineteenth century by a local housewife determined not to let a cargo of Seville oranges go to waste. Hence the saying that Dundee was built on three Js – jam, jute and journalism. In terms of tourist sights, all signs lead to the extravagant development around **RRS Discovery** (Captain Scott's Antarctic explorer ship), although museums like the **McManus Art Galleries** and the hilltop **Mills Observatory**, with breathtaking views over the road and rail bridges on the Tay, are less commercialized and just as interesting.

The telephone code for Dundee is ☎01382.

Arrival, information and city transport

Dundee's **airport** (☎643242) is five minutes' drive west from the city centre. There are no buses but a taxi will only set you back about £2. By **train**, Taybridge Station is on South Union St (☎228046) about 300 yards south of the city centre, near the River Tay. Long-distance **buses** arrive at the Seagate bus station (☎228345), a couple of hundred yards east of the centre.

Dundee's very helpful **tourist office** is right in the centre of things at 4 City Square (May, June & Sept Mon–Sat 8.30am–8pm, Sun 11am–8pm; July & Aug Mon–Sat 8.30am–9pm, Sun 11am–9pm; Jan–April & Oct–Dec Mon–Fri 9am–6pm, Sat 10am–noon & 1–4pm; ☎434664) and sells train and bus tickets as well as booking accommodation. You can also pick up the free monthly *What's On* listings magazine here, detailing local events and exhibitions. The city's two daily newspapers are the morning *Courier & Advertiser* and the *Evening Telegraph & Post*, available at any newsagent.

Dundee's centre is pretty compact, and you won't have much need for **public transport**, unless you're staying out at Broughty Ferry (see below); local **buses** operate from along High Street and around the Albert Square area (more information on ☎201121) – the journey costs 65p. **Taxi** ranks are dotted around City Square or you could call *Taxis City Cabs* (☎566666), *Discovery Taxis* (☎732111) or *Handy Taxis* (☎225825).

Accommodation

In a city that's only just getting used to tourists, **accommodation** isn't plentiful, but is comparitively cheap and there are some excellent guest houses. At present the cheapest beds are available in summer at vacated student residences; however, at the time of writing plans were afoot to build a youth hostel – check with the tourist office or the SYHA office in Dundee (☎322150). Rooms out at Broughty Ferry may prove marginally cheaper if you don't mind a 20-minute bus ride into the city – #8, #10 and #12 leave from outside *Littlewoods* in the centre of town. The **tourist office** charges ten percent of the first night's tariff for booking accommodation, which is then reimbursed by the hotel.

Hotels

Carlton House Hotel, 2 Dalgleish Rd (☎462056). Comfortable rooms in central, nineteenth-century building. Rates include breakfast. ③.

Shaftesbury Hotel, 1 Hyndford St (☎669216). A converted jute merchant's house in a residential area very near town. Has a good and pleasantly informal restaurant. ③.

Strathdon Hotel, 277 Perth Rd (☎665648). Family-run hotel in the west end of Dundee. The rooms are good, and the food is even better – breakfast is included and 3-course dinner without wine costs around £15. ④.

Queens Hotel, 160 Nethergate (☎322515). Friendly, old hotel with grand sweeping staircase, fine views of the Tay and good food. ⑤.

Woodlands Hotel, 13 Panmure Terrace, Broughty Ferry (☎480033). Smart town house in a back street of this Dundee suburb. Substantial bar snacks and full meals available. ④.

Guest houses and B&Bs

Clepington Guest House, 67 Clepington Rd (☎458833). Very welcoming and comfortable guest house near the football ground to the north of the city centre. ③.

Errolbank Guest House, 9 Dalgleish Rd (☎462118). Good views of the Tay. Some rooms with bathrooms. ②.

Fisherman's Tavern, 12 Fort St, Broughty Ferry (☎775941). Rooms above a pub with decent food and over 30 malt whiskies. ②.

Hillside, 43 Constitution St (☎223443). Homely, central B&B with 4 comfortable rooms. ③.

Kemback Guest House, 8 McGill St (☎461273). Right in the middle of town, with TVs in every room. ②.

Campus accommodation

Duncan of Jordanstone College of Art, Perth Rd (☎223261, ext. 353). Flats or shared cottage in leafy campus. Early July to mid-Sept only. ②.

University of Dundee (☎344039). Self-catering flats on and off campus and B&B accommodation in the halls of residence. Open March, April and July–Sept only. Includes use of university swimming pool and sports centre. ②.

The City

The best approach to Dundee is across the mile-and-a-half-long **Tay Road Bridge** from Fife. Offering a spectacular panorama of the city spread over its river bank, the bridge, opened in 1966, has a central walkway for pedestrians. This vast man-made construction is home to around million pairs of starlings – watch them circle at dusk. (For cars, it is free to enter Dundee, but an 80p toll is levvied on departure.) More impressive as an engineering feat is the neighbouring **Tay Rail Bridge**, opened in 1887 to replace the spindly structure destroyed in a storm only 18 months after it was built in May 1878. The crew and 75 passengers on a train passing over the bridge at the time died.

Dundee's city centre is focused on the municipal stronghold of City Square, a couple of hundred yards north of the Tay. The square and its surrounding streets have been much spruced up in recent years, with fountains, benches and trees making it a far more relaxing environment, though the shops remain the mundane mass of chain stores you see all over Britain. The main thoroughfare, which passes by City Square, starts as Nethergate in the west, becomes High Street in the centre then divides into Murraygate and Seagate. Opposite this junction is the mottled spire of **St Paul's Episcopal Cathedral** (Mon–Fri 10am–4pm), a rather gaudy George Gilbert Scott Gothic Revival structure, notable for its vividly sentimental stained glass and the floridly gilded high altar. Fifty yards further down Seagate, the **Seagate Gallery** (Tues–Sat 10am–5pm; free), a centre predominantly for local printmakers, houses travelling exhibitions of all kinds of contemporary art, with the chance to see (and buy) the work of local artists.

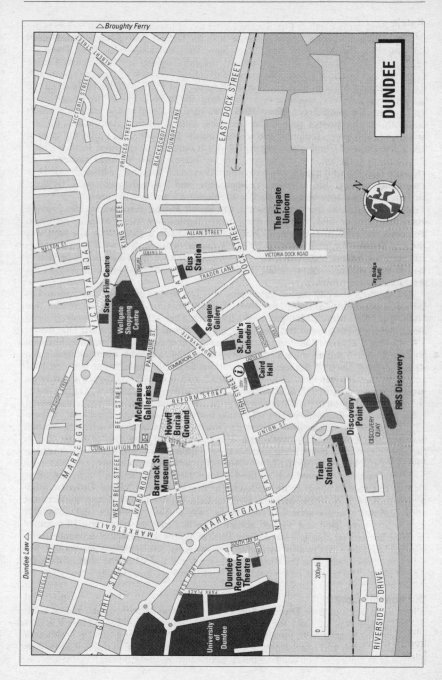

DUNDEE

A hundred yards north of City Square, at the top of handsome Reform Street, is the attractive **Albert Square**, whose centrepiece is the Gilbert Scott-designed **McManus Art Galleries and Museum** (Mon 11am–5pm, Tues–Sat 10am–5pm; free), Dundee's most impressive Victorian structure with its delightful sweep of outside curved stone staircases and Gothic touches. This gives an excellent overview of Dundee's past, with displays ranging from an Iron Age ring ditch house and Pictish stones to those on the city's industrial history, spanning everything from the three Js to the Tay Bridge disaster. Upstairs, the magnificent **Albert Hall** – crowned by a roof of 480 pitch-pine panels in a Gothic arch – houses stained-glass exhibits, antique musical instruments, decorative glass, gold, silver, sculpture and some exquisite furniture. Don't miss the table at which the Duke of Cumberland signed the death warrants of captured Jacobites after the Battle of Culloden. On the same floor, the barrel-roofed **Victoria Gallery**'s red walls are heaving with nineteenth- and twentieth-century paintings. Although some are undeniably syrupy, the notable Pre-Raphaelite and Scottish collections (William McTaggart's seascapes being a particular highlight) are well worth perusal.

Across Ward Road from the museum, the **Howff Burial Ground** on Meadowside (daily 9am–5pm or dusk) has some great carved tombstones dating from the sixteenth to nineteenth centuries. Originally gardens belonging to a monastery, the land was given to Dundee for burials in 1564 by Mary, Queen of Scots. Nearby is the run-of-the-mill **Barrack Street Museum** (Mon–Sat 10am–5pm; free), with a motley collection of stuffed local wildlife – the skeleton of a whale, washed up on a beach nearby, is the most impressive exhibit.

Just south of the city centre, moored by the Tay Bridge and the train station, lies Dundee's great tourism hope, **Discovery Point** (April–Oct Mon–Sat 10am–5pm, Sun 11am–5pm; Nov–March Mon–Sat 10am–4pm, Sun 11am–4pm; £4), a massively overblown development around the hugely impressive **Royal Research Ship Discovery**. The ship itself, a three-mast steam-assisted vessel, was one of the last traditional British-built (in Dundee) sailing ships, berthed here since 1986, and now sitting alongside is a **visitor centre**. Used by Captain Scott in various Antarctic explorations between 1901 and 1929, the ship has been elegantly restored, with polished wood panels and brass trimmings giving scant indication of the privations suffered by the crew. Temperatures on board would plummet to -28° in the Antarctic, and turns at having a bath came round every 47 days. Enthusiastic guides spin some fascinating yarns about the boat's colourful history, and the audio-visual spectacular you experience before boarding is compelling enough, if mercilessly overhyped. The introductory film, *Locked in the Ice*, is certainly impressive, culminating in the screen splitting to release a huge model of the freed ship's bow surging heroically out towards the audience on a carpet of dry ice.

In total contrast, moored behind the Customs House on Victoria Dock (the other side of the road bridge), is the endearingly simple wooden frigate **Unicorn** (mid-March to Sept daily 10am–5pm; £2). Built in 1824, it's the oldest British warship still afloat and was in active service as recently as 1968. During its service years, over 300 men would have lived and worked aboard. The fact that its 46 guns – 18 pounder cannons are still on display – were never fired in aggression probably accounts for its survival. Although the interior is sparse, the cannons, the neck-twisting rooves, the splendid figureheads, and the displays and wonderful model of the ship in its fully-rigged glory (23.5 miles of rope would have been used) are fascinating.

Out from the centre

A mile or so north of town, **Dundee Law** is the plug of an extinct volcano and, at 571ft, the city's highest point. Once the site of a seventh-century defensive hill fort, it is now an impressive lookout, with great views across the whole city and the Tay – although the climb is steep and often windy. It takes 30 minutes to walk to the foot of the law from the city centre, or you can take buses #3 or #4 from Albert Square.

The city's other volcanic plug of rock sits a mile to the west of Dundee Law. **Balgay Hill** is crowned by the wooded **Lochee Park**, at the summit of which sits the **Mills Observatory** (April–Sept Mon–Fri 10am–5pm, Sat 2–5pm; Oct–March Mon–Fri 3–10pm, Sat 2–5pm; free), a unique municipal amenity in Britain. In summer, there's little to be seen through the telescope – winter nights are the best for stellar observation – but well-explained, quirky exhibits and displays chart the history of space exploration and astronomy, and on sunny days, you can play at being a human sundial or a shadow clock and take in the fantastic views over the city through little telescopes. The observatory also has special opening times to coincide with eclipses and other heavenly wonders (details on ☎667138). Buses #2, #36 and #37 drop you in Balgay Road, at the entrance to the park.

Four miles east of Dundee's city centre lies the seaside settlement of **BROUGHTY FERRY**, now engulfed by the city as a reluctant suburb. It's a pleasant enough little resort, and on land at least far more unspoilt than Dundee. The level of pollution on the beach itself, however, is pretty dire – all of the city's sewage seems to end up here. If you can't bear the sight of this, **Broughty Castle and Museum**, right by the seashore (Oct–June Mon–Thurs & Sat 10am–1pm & 2–5pm; July–Sept Mon–Thurs & Sat 10am–1pm & 2–5pm, Sun 2–5pm; free), is worth a look. Built in the fifteenth century to protect the estuary, its four floors now house local history exhibits, covering the story of Broughty Ferry as a fishing village and the history of whaling, as well as details of local geology and wildlife.

Just north of Broughty Ferry, at the junction of the A92 and B978, the chunky bricks of **Claypotts Castle** constitute one of Scotland's most complete Z-shaped tower houses. Built from 1569 to 1588, its two round towers have stepped projections to support extra rooms – a sixteenth-century architectural practice that makes Claypotts look like it's about to topple. On going to print the castle was closed, and not expected to reopen until late 1996 or early 1997; call Historic Scotland to check (☎0131/668 8800).

Eating, drinking and nightlife

The **West End** of Dundee, around the principal University and Perth Road, is the best area for eating and drinking. The city centre, while good for a few pubs, is a bit of a non-starter for decent food. As in any city, be alert in the centre after dark, especially at weekends.

Restaurants

Deep Sea, 81 Nethergate (☎224449). The best of Dundee's fish-and-chip restaurants, excellent for huge and tasty portions.

Dellos, 134a Nethergate (☎226529). Warm, friendly and cheap Italian trattoria opposite the *Deep Sea*, open Mon–Sat daytime and Thurs–Sat evenings. Popular with students.

Gunga Din, 99B–101 Perth Rd (☎665672). Best of the studentland Indian restaurants, deservedly popular for its excellent dishes.

Pancake Place, 24 Reform St (☎223008). Reliable city centre daytime eating place (Wed–Fri closes 8pm), part of a Scottish chain.

Raffles, 18 Perth Rd (☎201139). Gorgeous, fairly pricy, Scottish food in a relaxed environment. Good for vegetarians.

Royal Oak, 167 Brook St (☎229440). Pub food far above the average, served daily until 8.30pm. International menu includes Thai and Spanish.

Pubs

Gauger, Seagate. A lively and predominantly gay bar opposite the *Seagate Gallery*.

Laing's, 8 Roseangle, off Perth Rd. Usually packed due its great-value food and great views over the Tay. The beer garden is heaving on rare warm summer nights.

Lucifer's Mill, Session St. A converted jute mill, with a mainly student clientele. Good for up-and-coming indie/blues bands and a great chill out room.

McGonagall's, 142–146 Perth Rd. A small and cheerful bar (with good light meals) dedicated to the memory of Dundee's uniquely dreadful Victorian poet, William McGonagall. Examples of his excruciating work adorn the walls.

Mercantile, 100 Commercial St. Popular with the grey suit brigade, but worth persevering for the excellent range of beers and quality pub snacks.

O'Neill's, North Lindsay St. Beery Irish bar, with frequent live Celtic music.

Nightlife

When it comes to post-pub nightlife, Dundee's offering is muted, to say the least. The three **nightclubs** are all on top of each other in South Ward Rd, midway between the centre and the University precincts. *Fat Sam's* is the most studenty place, with music tilted towards indie, *De Stihl's* caters for an older, less raucous crowd and the newest – the *Mardi Gras* – offers more mainstream dance and chart sounds.

Aside from the clubs, the prodigious *Dundee Repertory Theatre* (☎223530) on Tay Square, north of Nethergate, is excellent for indigenously produced contemporary **theatre**, as well as being a focus for many of the city's **festivals**, the best of which are the Jazz and Blues Festival in early June and the Folk Festival in early July. In St Mary Place (off Lochee Rd) the *Dundee Arts Centre* (☎201035) is good for community-based theatre, dance and music. The best venue for **classical** music, including visits by the Royal Scottish Orchestra and other bigwigs, is *Caird Hall* (☎223141), whose bulky frontage dominates City Square. For **movies**, the *Cannon* (☎225247) on Seagate or the *Odeon* multiplex (☎400855), in the Stack Leisure Park (off Harefield Rd), are predictably mainstream. For slightly more esoteric viewing, try the *Steps Film Centre* (☎434037) at the back of the *Wellgate* shopping centre, off Victoria Rd.

Listings

Airport Riverside Drive, Dundee (☎ 643242).

Banks *Bank of Scotland*, 11 Reform St (☎229131); *Clydesdale Bank*, 96 High St (☎824404); *Royal Bank of Scotland*, 3 High St (☎228111); *TSB*, Meadowside (☎228801).

Bike rental Nicholson's, 2 Forfar Rd (☎461212).

Books *Blackwell's*, 95 Nethergate; *Waterstone's*, 34 Commercial St.

Car rental *Arnold Clark*, 14–22 Trades Lane (☎225382); *Eurodollar*, 45–53 Gellatly St(☎224073); *Mitchell's*, 90 Marketgait (☎223484).

Bus enquiries *Scottish Citylink* and *National Express* for Perth, Dundee and Tayside (☎01738/626848 or 0141/331 1341); *Strathtay Scottish Omnibuses Ltd* for local buses (☎228345).

Currency exchange *Thomas Cook*, City Square (Mon–Fri 9am–5.30pm, Sat 9am–5pm; ☎200204).

Football Until 1995, Dundee was in the enviable position of being home to two Scottish premiership teams facing each other across Tannadice Street. Sadly, Dundee United, at Tannadice Park, dropped into Division One, leaving Dundee FC ruling the roost at Dens Park. Tickets cost about £10 per match.

Gay, Lesbian and Bisexual Switchboard ☎202620.

Genealogical research *Tay Valley History Society*, 179 Princes St (☎461845).

Golf Public courses at Ashludie, Golf Avenue, Monifieth (☎532967); Caird Park (☎451147); Camperdown Country Park (☎432688).

Hospital Dundee Royal Infirmary (with 24hr accident and emergency), Barrack Rd (☎660111).

Left luggage Tay Bridge Station (☎228046). Small 24hr lockers cost £2.

Pharmacy *Boots*, High St (Mon–Wed, Fri & Sat 8.30am–5.45pm, Thurs 8.30am–7pm); Sunday opening (noon–1pm) is done on a rota basis.

Police Tayside Police HQ, Bell St (☎223200).

Post office *GPO*, 4 Meadowside (Mon–Fri 9am–5.30pm, Sat 9am–7pm; ☎203532).
Rape crisis centre ☎201291.
Travel agents *Campus Travel*, Airlie Place (☎200412); *Ramsay Travel*, Crichton St (☎200394).

Around Dundee

There are a handful of sights in the southern corner of Angus within easy reach from Dundee. North of the city, over the Sidlaw Hills, **Meigle** has one of Scotland's foremost collections of Pictish stones, while the splendid **Glamis Castle** was the setting of Shakespeare's *Macbeth*.

Meigle

Hourly buses run from Dundee to the tiny village of **MEIGLE**, 15 miles northwest in the fertile bed of the Tay Valley. Housed in a modest former school building, the **Meigle Museum** (April–Sept Mon–Sat 9.30am–12.30pm & 1.30–6pm, Sun 2–6pm; £1.20) holds some 30 early Christian and Pictish inscribed stones, dating from the seventh to the tenth centuries, found in and around the nearby churchyard. The majority are either gravestones that would have lain flat or cross slabs, inscribed with the sign of the cross and usually standing. Most impressive is the 7ft-tall great cross slab, said to be Guinevere's gravestone, carved on one side with a portrayal of Daniel surrounded by lions, a beautifully executed equestrian group, and mythological creatures including a dragon and a centaur. On the other side various beasts are surmounted by the "ring of glory" – a wheel containing a cross carved and decorated in high relief. The stone is all the more impressive for its deliberate two-tone effect, the slab of sandstone red at the base and merging into grey at the top. The exact meaning and purpose of the stones and their enigmatic symbols is obscure, and why so many of the stones were found at Meigle is also a mystery. The most likely theory suggests that Meigle was once an important ecclesiastical centre which attracted secular burials of prominent Picts.

Glamis Castle

Regular buses (4 daily; 40min; £2.90) leave Dundee daily for the pink-sandstone **Glamis Castle** (April–Oct daily 10.30am–5.30pm; castle and grounds £4.50, grounds only £2.20), a mile north of the picturesque village of **GLAMIS** (pronounced "Glahms"). A wondrously over-the-top, L-shaped five-storey pile, set in an extensive landscaped park complete with deer and pheasants, this is one of the most famous Scottish castles. Shakespeare chose it as a central location in Macbeth and its royal connections (as the childhood home of the Queen Mother and birthplace of Princess Margaret) make it one of the essential stops on every bus tour of Scotland. It is also thought to be one of the country's most haunted buildings.

Approaching the castle down the long main drive provides an unforgettable view. The mêlée of turrets, towers and conical roofs appear fantastically at the end of the sweeping avenue of trees, framed by the Grampian Mountains. The bulk of the current building dates from the fifteenth century, although many of the later additions (particularly from the seventeenth century) give it its startling Disneyesque appearance. Glamis began as a comparatively humble hunting lodge, used in the eleventh century by the kings of Scotland. In 1372, King Robert II gave the property to his son-in-law, Sir John Lyon, who built the core of the present building. His descendants, the Earls of Kinghorne and Strathmore – the fourteenth of which was the Queen Mother's father – have lived here ever since.

Most of the castle can only be seen on the guided tours; if you have to wait, you can easily kill some time in the park or in the new underground exhibition in the **Coach House**. This covers everything from the castle's supply of water, electricity and gas, to numerous bits of memorabilia relating to the Queen Mother. Family wedding photos and present lists from down the ages demonstrate the shifting status of the aristocracy – an 1890 list bristles with colonial souvenirs, such as an Indian necklace of cheetah claws, clasped with old gold, whereas a 1990 list reels off a familiar litany of toasters, place mats, napkins and an electric blanket.

The guided tour starts upstairs with a whirl around the heavily Victorian **Dining Room**. The garish silver ship that forms the centrepiece of the table display was a golden wedding gift to the 13th earl from his estate workers in 1903. Another present – the grandfather clock in the corner – came from their 27 grandchildren, including a three-year-old Elizabeth Bowes-Lyon, later the Queen and now the Queen Mother. Ceiling bosses (English roses and Scottish thistles) commemorate the union of the two crowns. The atmosphere changes dramatically in the fifteenth-century **Crypt**, more properly the Lower Hall of the original tower house. Ponderous Jacobean furniture, mounted animal heads and armour re-create the room's medieval origins. The crypt's 12ft-thick walls enclose a haunted "lost" room, reputed to be have been sealed with the red-bearded Lord of Glamis and Crawford (also known as Beardie Crawford) inside after he dared to play cards with the Devil one Sabbath. From here, the tour passes up a seventeenth-century staircase, whose hollow central pillar was a primitive system of central heating. Dozen upon dozen of antlers line the stairwell.

Next is the arch-roofed **Drawing Room**, with delightful wedding-cake plasterwork (dated 1621). Classical portraits line the walls, the most notable being the vast Jacob de Wet family grouping of the third earl, who was responsible for many of the castle's seventeenth-century alterations. De Wit painted the earl in Classical armour that, unfortunately, looks like a flimsy negligée. The highlight of the tour is the family **Chapel**, completed in 1688. Jacob de Wit was commissioned to produce the frescoes from the family Bible, although his depictions of Christ wearing a hat and St Peter in a pair of glasses have raised eyebrows ever since. The chapel is said to be haunted by the spectre of a grey lady, the ghost of the sixth Lady Glamis who was burnt as a witch under orders of James V. The **Billiard Room**, complete with full-sized table and a beautiful polished walnut piano that cost £199 when it was commissioned in 1866, was redecorated, and the plasterwork ceiling added, for the 1903 celebrations of the thirteenth earl's golden wedding anniversary. Of the paintings and tapestries lining the walls, the vast and colourful *Fruit Market* by Flemish artist Frans Snyders draws the most attention. **King Malcolm's Room**, so called because it is believed he died nearby in 1034, is most notable for its carved wooden chimneypiece, on which many of its most decorative panels are, in fact, highly polished leather.

From here, the tour passes into the **Royal Apartments**, which are far less grand than might be expected. The Queen Mother's delicate gilt four-poster bed was a wedding present from her mother, who embroidered the names and dates of birth of her ten children into its panels. **Duncan's Hall**, a fifteenth-century guardroom, is the traditional – but inaccurate – setting for Duncan's murder by Macbeth (it actually took place near Elgin). Finally, the tour concludes with a random set of family diplays that include the Queen Mother's old doll's house.

Glamis' grounds are worth a few hours in their own right. Highlights include the lead statues of James VI and Charles I at the top of the main drive, the seventeenth-century Baroque sundial, the formal gardens and the verdant walks out to Earl John's Bridge and through the woodland. In Glamis village the humble **Angus Folk Museum** (Easter–Sept daily 11am–5pm, Oct Sat & Sun 11am–5pm; NTS; £2), housed in six low-slung cottages in Kirk Wynd, has a bewildering array of local ephemera, including bizarrely named agricultural implements, a nineteenth-century horse-drawn hearse and a section on local bothies.

The Angus coast

Two roads link Dundee to Aberdeen and the northeast coast of Scotland. By far the most pleasant option is to take the slightly longer A92 coast road which joins the A94 at Stonehaven, just south of Aberdeen, a route that can also be followed by bus or train. The train line hugging this stretch of coast from Dundee is one of the most picturesque in Scotland, stopping at **Arbroath** and the old seaport of **Montrose**. Trains leave at least hourly, and take around 20 minutes to reach Arbroath and a further 15 minutes to Montrose.

Arbroath

Since it was settled in the twelfth century, local fishermen have been landing their catches at **ARBROATH**, where the Angus coast starts to curve in from the North Sea towards the Firth of Tay. The **Arbroath smokie** – a line-caught haddock, smoke-cured over smouldering oak chips and then poached in milk – is probably one of Scotland's best-known dishes, and is best eaten the original way, with a knob of butter, rather than in the more fancy pâtés and mousses that are now becoming popular. Although it has a great location, with long sandy beaches and stunning sandstone cliffs on either side of town, Arbroath, like Dundee, has suffered from short-sighted development, its historical associations all but consumed by pedestrian walkways, a mess of a one-way system and ugly shopping centres.

Chiefly due to its harbour, Arbroath had, by the late eighteenth century, become a trading and manufacturing centre, famed for sail-making (the *Cutty Sark's* sails were made here) and boot-making. Arbroath's real glory days, however, came much earlier in the thirteenth century with the completion of **Arbroath Abbey** (April–Sept Mon–Sat 9.30am–6pm, Sun 2–6pm; Oct–March Mon–Sat 9.30am–4pm, Sun 2–4pm; £1.20), whose pink-stone ruins, described by Dr Johnson as "fragments of magnificence", stand on Abbey Street, clearly visible from High Street. Founded in 1178 by King William the Lion, and dedicated to his old schoolmate Thomas à Becket, whom he acknowledged as a "sharer of his tribulations" in England, it was completed in 1233, and became an abbey in 1285.

One of the most significant events in Scotland's history occured here, when on April 6, 1320, a group of Scottish barons drew up the **Declaration of Arbroath**, asking the Pope to reverse his excommunication and recognize Robert the Bruce as king, asserting Scotland's independence from the English: "For, so long as one hundred remain alive, we will never in any degree be subject to the dominion of the English." It was duly despatched to Pope John XXII in Avignon, who in 1324 agreed to Robert's claim.

The abbey was dissolved during the Reformation, and by the eighteenth century it was little more than a source of red sandstone for local houses. However, there is still enough left to get a good idea of how vast the place must have been: the semicircular west doorway is more or less intact, complete with medieval mouldings, and the south transept has a beautiful round window, once lit with a beacon to guide ships. The **Abbot's House** has also survived, used as a private dwelling long after the complex was abandoned, and now housing a small museum with exhibits that include an ancient headless statue thought to represent the abbey's founder.

Down by the harbour, the elegant Regency **Signal House Museum** (Mon–Sat 10am–5pm, July & Aug also Sun 2–5pm; free) stands sentinel as it has since 1813. The interior is now given over to some excellent local history displays. A school room, fisherman's cottage and lighthouse kitchen have all been carefully re-created, with the addition of realistic smells.

There's not much else to see in Arbroath besides the abbey, but there are some great **walks** in the vicinity. From the Signal House, you can wander through the huddled cottages of the **Fit o' the toon**, the harbour district where the smell of Arbroath smokies usually hangs heavy in the air. Beyond it, the seafront road heads into Victoria Park; at the far end of the road, a path climbs up over the red sandstone cliffs of **Whiting Ness**, stretching endlessly on to the horizon and eroded into a multitude of inlets, caves and arches that warrants hours of leisurely exploration. *The Arbroath Cliffs Nature Trail Guide*, available free from the tourist office, picks out 20 good viewing points along the first one and a half miles, and also gives details on the local fauna, flora and birds – you may even see puffins. Nearly four miles out of Arbroath, the path comes to the foot of the neat little fishing village of **Auchmithie**; four (very windy) miles further north is the crest of **Lunan Bay**, a classic sweep of glorious sand crowned by the eerie ruins of Red Castle at the mouth of the Lunan Water.

St Vigeans

Although now little more than a northwestern dormitory of Arbroath, the pristine hamlet of **ST VIGEANS** is a fine example of a Pictish site occupied and colonized by the Christians – the church is set arrogantly on the pre-Christian mound at the centre of the village. Many Pictish and earlier remains are housed in the wonderful little **museum** (April–Sept daily 9.30am–6pm; collect the key from cottage no. 7 if closed; free). The stones here show the usual range of Pictish symbols: discs, Z-rods, the mysterious beast often erroneously called an elephant, mirror and elegant line work. The most significant is no.1, the Drosten Stone, presumed to be a memorial – although nothing is known about Drosten's identity. One side depicts a hunt, laced with an abundance of Pictish symbolism; the other side bears a cross, which dates it among later stones, around 850 AD.

On the other side of the rail line, and half a mile up the lane to Newbigging, Nether Newbigging Farmhouse is the home of the **Hopi Gallery** (ring for opening times; ☎01241/873998), a showcase for the considerable talent of local craftmakers and artists.

Practicalities

Arbroath's **tourist office**, at Market Place right in the middle of town (Jan–March & Oct–Dec Mon–Fri 9.30am–5pm, Sat 9.30am–12.30pm; April–June & Sept Mon–Sat 9.30am–5.30pm; July & Aug Mon–Sat 9.30am–6pm, Sun 1–5pm; ☎01241/872609), will recommend local walks and can book accommodation. **Buses** stop at the station on Catherine St (☎01241/870646), about a five-minute walk south of the tourist office, while **trains** arrive at the station just across the road on Keptie St (for enquiries call Dundee ☎01382/228046).

The best part of Arbroath to **stay** in is down by the harbour: try *Harbour House Guest House*, 4 The Shore (☎01241/878047; ②), or the *Sandhutton Guest House*, 16 Addison Place (☎01241/872007; ②). The harbour is also the place for **eating and drinking**: a number of sea-salty pubs along the harbour front offer Arbroath smokies – the *Commercial Bar* on the seafront is a favourite with local fishermen, or check out the *Smugglers Tavern* on The Shore, where you can also try over 180 varieties of rum.

Montrose and around

"Here's the Basin, there's Montrose, shut your een and haud your nose." As the old rhyme indicates, **MONTROSE**, a seaport and market town since the thirteenth century, can sometimes smell a little rich, mostly because of its position on the edge of a virtualy landlocked two-mile-square lagoon of mud known as the Basin. But with the wind in the right direction, Montrose, now an important North Sea oil base, is a great little town to visit, with a pleasant old centre and a good museum. The Basin too is of interest: flooded and emptied twice daily by the tides, it is a rich nature reserve for the host of geese, swans and waders who frequent the ooze to look for food. A **Scott Wildlife Trust** visitor and study centre, half a mile out of town on the A92 Arbroath road, has recently opened alongside the Basin (ask at tourist office for details).

Montrose locals are known as Gable Endies, because of the unusual way in which the town's eighteenth- and nineteenth-century merchants, influenced by architectural styles they had seen on the Continent, built their houses gable end to the street. Most of the gabled houses line the wide **High Street**, which today is split down the middle by banks of flowerbeds and trees. Off either side of the road are numerous tiny alley-ways and quiet courtyards, pleasant to explore for an hour or so. The most obvious landmark is the 220ft **kirk steeple** at the lower end of High Street.

Two blocks behind the steeple, in Panmure Place on the western side of **Mid Links** park, the **Montrose Museum and Art Gallery** (Mon–Sat 10am–5pm; free) is one of Scotland's oldest museums, dating from 1842. For a small town museum, it has some particularly unusual exhibits, among them the so-called Samson Stone, which bears a carving of Samson slaying the Philistines. Dating from around 900 AD, the piece is one of three Pictish stones found about a century ago on a deserted island nearby on the River Esk. On the upper floor, the maritime history exhibits include a cast of Napoleon's death mask and a model of a British man-of-war, sculpted out of bone by Napoleonic prisoners at Portsmouth. Most intriguing, however, is the enigmatic message on a scrap of paper found in a bottle at nearby Ferryden beach in 1857, written by the chief mate of a brigantine 80 years earlier: "Blowing a hurricane lying to with close-reefed main topsails ship waterlogged. Cargo of wood from Quebec. No water on board, provisions all gone. Ate the dog yesterday, three men left alive. Lord have mercy on our souls. Amen".

By the entrance of the museum, a winsome study of a boy by local sculptor William Lamb (1893–1951) is a taster for more of his work, best seen in the **William Lamb Memorial Studio** on Market St (July & Aug Sun 2–5pm, other times by arrangement; free; ☎01674/673232). Here a variety of his works include bronze heads of the Queen, Princess Margaret and the Queen Mother, the earnings from which enabled him to buy the studio in the 1930s. Lamb's striking work is made the more impressive by the fact that he taught himself to sculpt with his left hand, having suffered a war wound in his right.

After the impressive wildlife of Montrose Basin, it's easy to ignore the town's fabulous golden sea shore. The beech road, Marine Avenue, across from the town museum, heads down through sand dunes and golf links to car parks fringing the fine, wide beach overlooked by a slender white lighthouse.

Around Montrose: the House of Dun

Across the Basin, four miles west of Montrose, is the Palladian **House of Dun** (late April–late Oct daily 11am–5pm; NTS; £3, grounds only free), reachable by way of the regular Montrose–Brechin bus – ask the driver to let you off outside; alternatively, Bridge of Dun station, the terminus of the Caledonian steam rail line from Brechin, is a 15-minute, signposted, walk away (see overleaf). Built in 1730 for David Erskine, Laird of Dun, to designs by William Adam, the house was opened to the public in 1989 after extensive restoration, and is crammed full of period furniture and *objets d'art*. Inside, the ornate relief plasterwork is the most impressive feature, extravagantly emblazoned with Jacobite symbolism. You can also see some gorgeous pieces of intricate needle-work, stitched by the illegitimate child of King William IV, Lady Augusta, who married into the Dun family in 1827. The most decorative example is strewn across a huge four-poster given to her as a wedding present by her father.

The buildings in the courtyard – a hen house, gamekeeper's workshop and potting shed – have also been renovated. Modern additions include a tearoom and a weaving shed, and a shop where local weavers give displays of their traditional skills.

Practicalities

The Montrose **tourist office** is in a former public toilet next to the Library, where Bridge St merges into the lower end of High St (April, May & Sept Mon–Sat 10am–5pm; June–Aug Mon–Sat 9.30am–5.30pm; ☎01674/672000). Most **buses** stop in High St, while the **train** station lies a block back on Western Rd (hourly trains from Dundee and Aberdeen). For B&B **accommodation**, try *Oaklands*, over the river bridge at 10 Rossie Island Rd (☎01674/672018; ②), or the friendly *Murray Lodge Hotel*, 2–8 Murray St (☎01674/678880; ③), the northern continuation of High St. **Bike** rental is available from *Plan Green*, 33 Ferry St (☎01674/677199).

For **eating**, *Nelson's*, Wharf St (down by the harbour), is popular with visitors for its seafood; however, the liveliest place to eat in Montrose is unquestionably *Roo's Leap*, a newish café-bar in an old golf club off the northern end of Traill Drive near the beach. The food is an unlikely, but excellent, mix of Scottish, American and Australian. If you want a **drink**, High St has the no-frills *Market Tavern* by the kirk steeple, and, further down, the *Cornerhouse Hotel*, which hosts folk nights on Tuesdays. The *Salutation Inn*, 69–71 Bridge St, serves good, cheap food and has a beer garden.

Brechin

About nine miles inland from Montrose and served by frequent buses, **BRECHIN** is a pretty if soporific town, whose chief attraction is the stumpy **Cathedral** on Chanonry Wynd. There's been a religious building of sorts here since the arrival of evangelizing Irish missionaries in 900 AD, and the red sandstone structure has become something of a hotch-potch of architectural styles – what you see today chiefly dates from an extensive rebuilding in 1900. The oldest surviving part of the cathedral, the 106ft round tower on the southwest corner, was built as protection against Viking raids (the door is built a secure 6ft above the ground). The pointed roof was a later addition, the gentle tapering of the design an impressive engineering feat. Inside you can see various Pictish stones, illuminated by jewel-coloured stained-glass windows. There are good **walks**, with impressive views up to the Cathedral, from the wooded paths below Bridge Street.

To the north of the main streets and the Cathedral, St Ninian Square is home to Brechin's **museum** (Tues & Thurs 9.30am–6pm, Wed 9.30am–8pm, Fri & Sat 9.30am–5pm; free), a one-room jumble of history, civic memorabilia, geology and painting. Across the square is the elegant train station of the **Caledonian Railway** (talking timetable ☎01356/622992, enquiries ☎01674/810318), operating on summer Sundays and bank holidays from Brechin to the Bridge of Dun. Lying adjacent is the **tourist office** (April, May & Sept Mon–Sat 10am–5pm; June–Aug Mon–Sat 9.30am–5.30pm; ☎01356/623050), where they have details of the **postbuses** from Brechin to the Angus glens. For **eating** and **drinking** there are few options; you could try the crusty old-fashioned *Dalhousie Hotel Bar*, on the corner of St David and Market streets.

The Angus glens

Lying on the southernmost edges of the Grampian Mountains' heather-covered lower slopes, the **Angus glens** – or "Braes o' Angus" – are tranquil valleys penetrated by few roads that offer some of the most rugged and majestic landscape of northeast Scotland.

It's a rain-swept, wind-blown, sparsely populated area, whose links with tourism are fairly new. The first snows nearly always see the roads closed, sometimes as early as

October, and in the summer there are ferocious **midges** to contend with. Nevertheless, most of the glens, particularly **Glen Clova**, are now well and truly discovered, and at the height of summer you may find yourself in a traffic jam – unheard of ten years ago. The rolling hills and dales attract hikers, bird-watchers and botanists in the summer, grouse shooters and deer hunters in autumn and a growing number of skiers in winter. The most useful road through the glens is the A93, which cuts through **Glen Shee** to Braemar on Deeside (see p.371). It's pretty dramatic stuff, threading its way over Britain's highest main road pass – the **Cairnwell Pass** at 2199ft. **Buses** ply along the A93 through most of Glen Shee en route to Deeside; for Glen Clova and Prosen, you'll have to use the **postbuses** from Kirriemuir (or Brechin; see above); for the other glens you'll need your own transport.

Glen Shee and Glen Isla

Sprawled over the flanks of four mountains, the **skiing** area at **Glen Shee**, the most visited and best known of the Angus glens, is probably the largest in Scotland. The place comes into its own during the winter season – January to March – when an increasing number of skiers, predominantly from the cities of central Scotland, brave the ridiculously cold temperatures and bitter winds. Ski lifts and tows give access to gentle beginners' slopes; experienced skiers can try the more intimidating Tiger run. In summer it's all a bit sad, with lifeless chair lifts, muddy banks, and expanses of woodland cut back for the pistes. Still, hang-gliders take advantage of the cross winds between the mountains and adventurous walkers enjoy peaceful hikes.

The well-heeled town of **BLAIRGOWRIE** (officially Blairgowrie and Rattray), little more than one main road set among raspberry fields on the glen's southern-most tip, is as good a place as any to base yourself – and is particularly useful in winter if you plan to ski. Right on the river, the town's only claim to fame is that St Ninian once camped at Wellmeadow, a pleasant grassy triangle in the town centre, by an ancient watering hole – a spot now marked by a modern well. The **tourist office** is nearby at 26 Wellmeadow (Easter–June & mid-Sept to Oct Mon–Sat 9.30am–5.30pm, Sun 11am–4pm; July to mid-Aug Mon–Sat 9am–7pm, Sun 11am–6pm; Nov–Easter Mon–Fri 9.30am–5pm, Sat 9.30am–1.30pm; ☎01250/872960). You can **rent bikes** from the year-round *Blairgowrie Caravan Park* (☎01250/872941), on Rattray's Hatton Rd, where you can also **camp**, and, 300 yards from the tourist office, from *Mountains and Glens*, Railway Rd (☎01250/874206).

If you need a place to **stay**, the *Compass Christian Centre*, Glenshee Lodge, 17 miles north of Blairgowrie (☎01250/885209; ①), is a good place to meet other hikers, although it is not, unfortunately, served by public transport. Over the bridge spanning the fast-flowing River Ericht, Blairgowrie melts into its twin community of **Rattray**. On the main street, Boat Brae, is the excellent *Ivy Lodge* B&B (☎01250/873056; ②), offer-ing sweeping views of the river and surrounding hills, as well as free use of a floodlit tennis court. The opulent, ivy-covered *Kinloch House* (☎01250/884237; ⑨), one of the area's most prestigious hotels, is set in its own vast grounds three miles west of town on the A923. There are loads of places to **eat and drink**. Around the main square

---

SKIING IN THE ANGUS GLENS

For **information on skiing** in the Angus glens call the *Glenshee Chairlift Company* (☎013397/41320) or the *Ski Hotline* (☎01891/654656). There are numerous **lift passes**, all of which increase in price in the high season (weekends and Feb to mid-April), when adult passes cost around £12.50 for a day, or £50 for five days. **Ski rental** starts at around £8 a day. If you need tuition, the *Glenshee Ski School* (☎013397/41216) charges £10 for a day's instruction.

make for the *Victoria Hotel* for hearty lunches and dinners and, tucked down towards the river bridge, the *Crown Bar*, complete with 116 different malt whiskies.

Nearly 20 miles north of Blairgowrie, the **SPITTAL OF GLENSHEE**, though ideally situated for skiing, is little more than a tacky service area, only worth stopping at for a quick drink or bite to eat. It is, however, handily close to one of the nicest places to stay in the area, the *Dalmunzie House* (☎01250/885224; ⑥), a gorgeous, turreted, Highland sporting lodge, evoking the peace and tranquility that once pervaded this area – to reach it, take the signposted road from just beyond the *Spittal Hotel*.

Dominated by Mount Blair (2441ft), and with a proliferation of woods, **Glen Isla**, east of Glen Shee, is also known as the Green Glen. A lot less dramatic than its sister glens, it suffers from an excess of angular conifers alongside great bald chunks of hillside waiting to be planted. Along its southern borders on the B954, the River Isla narrows and then plunges some 60ft into a deep gorge to produce the classically pretty waterfall of **Reekie Linn**. It's known as the "smoking fall", either because of the yellow clouds of wild broom that drift overhead in summer, or more probably because of the water mist produced when the fall hits a ledge and bounces a further 20ft into a deep pool known as the Black Dub.

The glen cheers up enormously north of the tiny hamlet of **KIRKTON OF GLENISLA**, straddling the B951. Here, the cosy *Glenisla Hotel* (☎01575/582223; ③) is great for eating and drinking, and a good base for walking or pony trekking (contact the nearby *Trekking Centre*; ☎01575/582333). A couple of miles short of Kirkton, there's an **independent hostel**, the *Highland Adventure* (☎01575/582238) at **KNOCKSHANNOCH**. It offers a pick-up service from **ALYTH**, the gateway to the glen, a planted town so neat and ordered that even its burn has been canalized into something that looks entirely artificial. Alyth, also home to a forgettable folk museum, is on regular bus routes from Dundee and Kirriemuir.

Kirriemuir, Forfar and Glen Prosen, Clova and Doll

The sandstone town of **KIRRIEMUIR**, known locally as Kirrie, is set on a hill with glens Clova and Prosen as its backdrop. Despite the influx of hunters up for the "season", it's still a pretty special place, a haphazard confection of narrow closes, twisting wynds and steep braes. The main cluster of streets have all the appeal of an old film set, with their old-fashioned bars, tiled butcher's shop, tartan outlets and haberdasheries somehow managing to avoid being contrived and quaint – although the rapid re-cobbling of the town centre, around a twee statue of Peter Pan, undermines this somewhat.

In the nineteenth century, as a linen manufacturing centre, it was made famous by a local handloom-weaver's son, J M Barrie, with his series of novels about "Thrums", in particular *A Window in Thrums* and his third novel, *The Little Minister*. The author was to become more famous still as the creator of Peter Pan, the little boy who never grew up, which Barrie penned in 1904 – some say as a response to a strange upbringing dominated by the memory of his older brother, who died as a child. Barrie's **birthplace**, a plain little whitewashed cottage at 9 Brechin Rd (Easter–Sept Mon–Sat 11am–5.30pm, Sun 2–5.30pm; Oct Sat 11am–5.30pm, Sun 1.30–5.30pm; NTS; £1.50), displays his writing desk, photos and newspaper clippings, as well as copies of his works. The washhouse outside – romantically billed as Barrie's first "theatre" – was apparently the model for the house that the Lost Boys built for Wendy in Never-Never Land. Barrie chose to be buried at the nearby St Mary's Espiscopal Church in Kirrie, despite being offered a more prestigious plot at London's Westminster Abbey.

High above the B957 to Brechin, Kirriemuir Hill is crowned by a sporadically opened camera obscura (call Mr Tucker on ☎01575/572081) in the old cricket pavilion. On the other side of the town centre, a couple of hundred yards down the road to

Glamis (A928), is the **Aviation Museum** (April–Sept Mon–Sat 10am–5pm, Sun 11am–
5pm; free), the lifetime collection of Richard Moss, who'll invariably be your guide
through the jumble of military uniforms, photos, World War II memorabilia (including
British and German propaganda leaflets) and *Airfix* models.

Kirrie's helpful **tourist office** (April, May & Sept Mon–Sat 10am-5pm; June–Aug
Mon–Sat 9.30am-5.30pm; (☎01575/574097) is in the tacky new development, behind
Visocchi's in the main square. **Accommodation** can be found at *Crepto*, Kinnordy
Place (☎01575/572746; ②), the *Re-Union* bar in the main square (☎01575/572259; ②)
or the excellent *Thrums Hotel* (☎01575/572758; ③) on Bank St. *Visocchi's* is great for
daytime **food**, the *Thrums Hotel* a good bet in the evening. Of the **pubs**, the *Kilt and
Clogs*, behind the tourist office, is the current favourite, although live music is more
likely at the *Re-Union*, the *Airlie Arms Hotel*, Reform St or, facing out over the newly
cobbled main square, the *Ogilvy Arms*. **Postbuses** into Glen Clova and Prosen leave
from the main post office, Reform St, at 8.30am (Mon–Sat). The Glen Clova bus goes
all the way to Glen Doll, the Prosen bus stops at the village of Glenprosen and
returns to Kirriemuir. A second Glen Clova bus leaves around 1pm but only goes as
far as Clova village before returning to Kirriemuir. Hourly buses connect with Forfar
for onward travel.

Forfar and around

Five miles southeast of Kirrie is Angus' county town and the ancient capital of the
Picts, **FORFAR**. Although hardly the most thrilling town in the district, exuding a solid
conservatism, it warrants an afternoon's exploration. The old Picitsh connections are
still evident in Forfar's strong support for the Scottish National Party (SNP), with a
profusion of Scottish flags and stirring messages on civic buildings. The wide High
Street is framed by some impressive Victorian architecture and small old-fashioned
shops. Midway along, the **Meffen Institute Museum and Art Gallery** (Mon–Sat
10am–5pm; free) exhibits Neolithic, Pictish and Celtic remains and a thoroughly enjoyable collection of re-created historical street scenes. The most disturbing examines the
town's seventeenth-century passion for witch-hunting, with a taped re-creation of locals
baying for blood. They also have a wonderful interactive computer catalogue of all the
Pictish stones in Angus.

A series of glacial lochs peter out in the west of the town at Forfar Loch, now
surrounded by a pleasant country park. Two miles east, high above the wooded Loch
Fithie, are the impressive remains of **Restenneth Priory** (free access), approached
along an easy-to-miss side road off the B9113. Built by King Nechtan of the Picts in
about the eighth century, it was adapted as an Augustinian priory in the twelfth
century. Still something of a Picitsh shrine, it's common to find mementoes and flowers
left by pilgrims. The splayed foot spire, first seen beckoning from the road, was added
in the fifteenth century.

Midway between Forfar and Brechin, straddling the ridge-topping B9134, is the
hamlet of **ABERLEMNO**, whose open-air Pictish stones (Oct–April boxed out of sight
in weatherproofed wood) are amongst the best anywhere. In the churchyard, just off
the main road, an eighth-century cross slab combines a swirling Christian Celtic cross
with Pictish beasts on one side and an elaborate Pictish battle scene on the other,
thought to commemorate victory over the Northumbrians in 685 AD. Three other
stones, bristling with Pictish and early Christain symbols, sit by the main road, overlooking huge sweeps of valley and mountain. Bus #21A, shuttling between Forfar and
Brechin, stops in Aberlemno.

Forfar's **tourist office** (April, May & Sept Mon–Sat 10am–5pm; July & Aug Mon–Sat
9.30am–5.30pm; ☎01307/467876) is tucked in a corner of the *David Wardhaugh* estate
agency, 38–40 East High St, directly in front of the soaring steeple of the parish church.
Numerous shops and bakers stock the famous **Forfar Bridie**, a huge folded pastry

case of mince, onion and seasonings. Some of the best can be found at *Saddlers*, opposite the tourist office. Otherwise, all-day **food** and **drink** can be found at the *Royal Hotel*, Castle St, by the Town Hall.

Dykehead and Glen Prosen

Glen Prosen and Glen Clova divide at the low-key hamlet of **DYKEHEAD**, five miles north of Kirrie. **Accommodation** is available at the *Royal Jubilee Arms Hotel* (☎01575/540381; ③), an old inn scarred by a grim modern conversion that is, nonetheless, excellent for all-day food, drink and Sunday night **ceilidhs**. Good B&B can be found a quarter of a mile up the Glenprosen road at the *Burnside Lodge* (☎01575/540294; ②), the house where Captain Scott and fellow explorer Doctor Wilson planned their ill-fated trip to Antarctica in 1910 and 1911. A mile further on, a roadside **stone cairn** commemorates the expedition. High above the road to the right, in the middle of a vast conifer plantation, towers the **Airlie Memorial**, a favourite vantage point locally, built in memory of the local landowner who was killed in the Boer War.

From here, Glen Prosen proper unfolds before you. Little has changed since Scott was here, and it remains essentially a quiet wooded backwater, with all the wild and rugged splendour of the other glens but without the crowds. To explore the area thoroughly you need to go on foot, but a good road circuit can be made by heading north from Kirriemuir to **PEARSIE** and then on to **GLENPROSEN** village – little more than a kirk and a coffee shop. The two roads that flank this southern section of the glen meet here, and you can return by the less scenic northern road via the Scott memorial. Facilities are scarce in this remote valley; the village coffee shop will help sort out short-term accommodation, or, a mile further beyond, there is an excellent complex of self-catering cottages at **BALNABOTH** (from £150 per week for two; ☎01575/540302).

The best walk in the area is the reasonably easy four-mile **Minister's Path** (so called because the parish priest would walk this way twice every Sunday to conduct services in both glens), connecting Prosen and Clova. Take the footpath between the kirk and the bridge in Glenprosen village, then the right fork where the track splits and continue over the colourful burnt moorland down into Clova. As there is no afternoon return service by postbus from Prosen to Kirriemuir, you either have to stay the night or follow the Path to its end, **Wester Eggie**, and pick up the Clova village postbus (Mon–Sat at 3.30pm).

Glen Clova and Glen Doll

Of all the Angus glens, **Glen Clova** – which in the north becomes Glen Doll – with its stunning cliffs, heather slopes and valley meadows, is the firm favourite of many. Although it can get unpleasantly congested in peak season, the area is still remote enough to be able to leave the crowds with little effort. Wildlife is abundant, with deer on the mountains, wild hares and even grouse and the occasional buzzard. The meadow flowers on the valley floor and arctic plants (including great splashes of white and purple saxifrage) on the rocks also make it something of a botanist's paradise.

The B955 from Dykehead and Kirriemuir divides at the Gella bridge over the swift-coursing River South Esk (unofficially, road traffic is encouraged to use the western branch of the road for travel up the glen, the eastern side down). Six miles north of Gella, the two branches of the road join up once more at the hamlet of **CLOVA**, little more than the hearty *Clova Hotel* (☎01575/550222; ③, or £4 per person per night in the hotel's outside bunkhouse accommodation), a car park and a picnic site. In summer, the hotel is a regular venue for barbeques, ceilidhs and even pleasure flights by helicopter or balloon. An excellent, if fairly strenuous, four-hour walk from behind the old school at the back of the hotel leads up into the mountains and around the lip of **Loch Brandy**, which legend predicts will one day flood and drown the valley below.

WALKS FROM GLEN DOLL

Ordnance Survey Landranger Maps Nos. 43 & 44

Many of the routes mentioned here are well-established old drovers' roads, largely crossing the Royal estate of Balmoral. Prince Charles' favourite mountain – Lochnagar – can be seen from all angles. The walks should always be approached with care; make sure to follow the usual safety precautions (see p.38).

Capel Mounth to Ballater (15 miles, 7 hours). Head across the bridge from the car park, turning right after a mile when the track crosses the Cald Burn. Out of the wood, the path zig-zags its way up fierce slopes before levelling out on the moorland plateau. Soon descending, the path crosses a scree near the eastern end of Loch Muick. With the loch to your left, walk down along the scree till you reach the River Muick, crossing the bridge to take the quiet track along the river's northern shore to Ballater.

Capel Mounth round trip (15 miles, 8 hours). Follow the above to Loch Muick, then follow the path down to loch level and double back on yourself along the loch's southern shore. When the track crosses the Black Burn, either take the steep left fork or continue along the shore for another mile, heading up the dramatic Streak of Lightning path that follows Corrie Chash. Both paths meet at the ruined stables below Sandy Hillock. Just beyond, take the path to the left, descending rapidly to the waterfall by the bridge at Bachnagairn, where a gentle burnside track leads the three miles back to Glen Doll car park.

Jock's Road to Braemar (14 miles, 7 hours). Take the road north from the car park past the youth hostel. After almost a mile, follow the signposted Jock's Road to the right, keeping on the northern bank of the burn. Pass a barn, Davey's Shelter below Cairn Lunkhard and continue on to a wide ridge towards the path's summit at Crow Craigies (3018ft). From here, the path bumps down over scree slopes to the head of Loch Callater. Go either way round the loch, and follow the Callater Burn at the other end, eventually hitting the main A93 two miles short of Braemar.

North from Clova village, the road turns into a rabbit-strewn lane coursing along the riverside for four miles to the car park and informal **camp site** in **Glen Doll**. This is right in the heart of the southern Grampian mountains, as can be seen from the towering humps of Craig Mellon (2841ft) and Cairn Broadlands (2795ft) overlooking the site. It is also a useful starting point for numerous superb **walks** (see above). From the car park, it's only a few hundred yards further to the **youth hostel** (mid-March to Oct, ☎01575/550236; Grade 2), a cheerful restored hunting lodge that incorporates a squash court amongst the usual facilities.

Edzell and Glen Esk

Travelling around Angus, you can hardly fail to notice the difference between organic settlements and planted towns built by paranoid landowners who forcibly rehoused local people in order to keep them under control, especially after the Jacobite risings. One of the better examples of this phenomenon, **EDZELL**, along the B966 five miles north of Brechin (regular buses from Brechin), was cleared and rebuilt with Victorian rectitude a mile to the west of its original site in the 1840s. The long, wide and ruler-straight main street is lined with prim nineteenth-century buildings, now doing a roaring trade as genteel tea shops and antique emporia.

The original village (identifiable from the cemetery and surrounding grassy mounds) lay immediately to the west of the impressive ruins of **Edzell Castle** (April–Sept Mon–Sat 9.30am–6pm, Sun 2–6pm; Oct–March Mon–Sat 9.30am–4pm, Sun 2–4pm; HS; £2), itself a mile west of the planted village. The castle was the seat of the aristocratic Crawford Lindsay family from 1358 until 1715, when the last Lindsay owner, by then a stable hand on the Orkney Islands, had to sell up in dire poverty. The Earl of Panmore bought the much-rebuilt pile, only to have it confiscated from him for his part in the Jacobite rebellion of 1745. Edzell is a good example of a comfortable tower house, whose main priority became luxurious living rather than defence. In the ruined tower house, look out for the intricate decorative corbelling on the roof, the vast fireplace in the first-floor hall and the telltale signs of building from different ages, thrown together in one apparently unified whole.

It is, however, the **pleasance garden** that makes a visit to Edzell essential, especially in late spring and early to mid-summer. The garden was built in 1604, at the height of the optimistic Renaissance by Sir David Lindsay, and its refinement and extravagance are evident. The walls contain sculpted images of erudition: the Planetary Deities on the east side, the Liberal Arts (including a decapitated figure of Music) on the south and, under floods of lobelia, the Cardinal Virtues on the west wall. In the centre of the garden, low-cut box hedges spell out the family mottoes and enclose voluminous beds of roses.

Four miles southwest of Edzell, lying either side of the lane to Bridgend, are the **Catherthuns**, twin Iron Age hill forts that were, however, probably occupied at different times. The surviving ramparts on the White Caterthun (978ft) are the most impressive, easily reached from the small car park below. A huge oval of fallen stones around the summit indicates the greater rampart, as well as giving the hill its "white" epithet (the ramparts of Brown Caterthun, 942ft, by contrast, are of turf and heather). It is believed that White Caterthun was the later fort, occupied by the Picts in the first few centuries AD. Views from both, over the mountains to the north and the plains and foothills to the south, are stunning.

Just north of Edzell, a 15-mile road climbs alongside the River North Esk to form **Glen Esk**, the most easterly of the Angus Glens and, like the others, scarcely populated. Nine miles along the Glen, the excellent **Glenesk Folk Museum** (Easter–May Sat–Mon noon-6pm; June to mid-Oct daily noon–6pm; £1), brings together records, costumes, photographs, maps and tools from the Angus Glens, depicting the often harsh way of life for the inhabitants. The museum is housed in an old shooting lodge and its *Retreat* tearoom is a welcome break for parched walkers.

Accommodation is best in the new Edzell village. For B&B, try *Mrs De Costa*, 24 High St (☎01356/648201; ②). You can **camp** one and a half miles away en route to Glen Esk at the *Glen Esk Caravan Park* (April–Oct; ☎01356/648565).

ABERDEENSHIRE AND MORAY

Aberdeenshire and Moray cover some 3500 square miles of open and varied country dotted with historic and archeological sights, from neat NTS properties and eerie prehistoric rings of standing stones to quiet kirkyards, serene abbeys and a rash of dramatic castles. Geographically, the counties break down into two distinct areas: the **hinterland**, once barren and now a patchwork of farms, with high mountains, sparkling rivers and gentle valleys, and the **coast**, a classic stretch of rocky cliff, remote fishing villages and long, sandy beaches.

For visitors, **Aberdeen** (officially a separate adminstrative area) is the city of most obvious interest in the region, with its well-kept buildings (it's often voted Britain's cleanest city), museums and gorgeous parks. From here, it's a short hop west to **Deeside**, annually visited by the royal family and a popular holiday area. Beyond lies the **Don Valley**, quiet usually but hectic during the ski season, when skiers take to the slopes at the Lecht, and **Speyside**, the centre of a network of more than half of Scotland's malt whisky distilleries. To the north, the **coast** offers some dramatic scenery, punctuated by picturesque villages that haven't changed much in centuries.

Aberdeen has an **airport**, and **trains** run from here north along the coast to Inverness and to major points further south. **Buses** can be few and far between, often running on schooldays only, but the main centres are well served. By car, signposted **trails** set up by the tourist board make following the Speyside whisky trail and visiting the northeast coast and castles a painless experience.

Aberdeen and around

Some 120 miles from Edinburgh, on the banks of the rivers Dee and Don and smack in the middle of the northeast coast, **ABERDEEN** is commonly known as the Granite City. The third-largest city in Scotland, it's a place that people either love or hate. As Lewis Grassic Gibbon, one of the northeast's most eminent novelists, summed it up: "One detests Aberdeen with the detestation of a thwarted lover. It is the one hauntingly and exasperatingly lovable city of Scotland." The beauty of Aberdeen's famous **granite** architecture is definitely in the eye of the beholder. Some extol the many hues and colours of the grandiose designs, while others see only uniform grey and find the city grim, cold and unwelcoming. The weather doesn't help: Aberdeen lies on a latitude north of Moscow and the driving rain (even if it does transform the buildings into sparkling silver) can be tiresome.

Since the 1970s, **oil** has made Aberdeen an almost obscenely wealthy and self-confident place – only four percent of Scotland's population live in the city, yet it has eight percent of the country's spending power. Despite (or perhaps because of) this, it can seem a soulless city; there's a feeling of corporate sterility and sometimes, despite its long history, Aberdeen seems to exist only as a departure point and service station for the transient population of some ten to fifteen thousand who live on the 130 oil platforms out to sea.

That said, Aberdeen's **architecture** is undeniably striking: a granite cityscape created in the nineteenth century by three fine architects: Archibald Simpson and John Smith in the early years of the century, and, subsequently, A Marshall Mackenzie. Classical inspiration and Gothic-revival styles predominate, giving grace to a material once thought of as only good enough for tombs and paving stones. In addition, in the last few years the city's tourist board has tried to restyle Aberdeen's image from Granite City to **Rose City**. Every spare inch of ground has been turned into a flower bed, the parks some of the most beautiful in Britain. This positive floral explosion – Aberdeen has been debarred from *Britain in Bloom* competitions because it kept winning – has certainly cheered up the general greyness, but nonetheless the new image, just like the first, is always at the mercy of the weather.

Staying in such a prosperous place has its advantages. There are plenty of good restaurants and hotels, local transport is efficient and nearly all the sights are free, including Aberdeen's splendid **Art Gallery**. The city boasts a genuinely lively **harbour**, and stays alive at night with a thriving pub culture and a fair number of theatres, both mainstream and innovative. Nearby, down to the southern border of Aberdeenshire, **Dunnottar Castle** is the main draw. Beyond lies **Fasque House** and the neat village of **Fettercairn**, which makes a good day trip from Aberdeen.

Some history

In the twelfth century, Alexander I noted "Aberdon" as one of his principal towns and by the thirteenth century, it had become a centre for **trade and fishing**, a jumble of timber and wattle houses perched on three small hills, with the castle to the east and St Nicholas' kirk outside the gates to the west.

It was here that **Robert the Bruce** sought refuge during the Scottish Wars of Independence, leading to the garrison of the castle by Edward I and Balliol's supporters. During the night in 1306, the townspeople attacked the garrison and killed them all, an event commemorated by the city's motto "Bon Accord", the watchword for the night.

The victory was not to last, however, and in 1337 Edward III stormed the city, forcing its rebuilding on a grander scale. A century later the Bishop Elphinstane founded the Catholic **University** in the area north of town known today as **Old Aberdeen**, while the rest of the city developed as a mercantile centre and important port.

Industrial and economic expansion led to the Aberdeen New Streets Act in 1800, setting off a hectic half-century of development that almost led to financial disaster. Luckily, the city was rescued by a boom in trade: in the **shipyards** the construction of **Aberdeen Clippers** revolutionized sea transport, and gave Britain supremacy in the China tea trade, and in 1882, a group of local businessmen acquired a **steam** tugboat for trawl fishing: sail gave way to steam and fisher families flooded in.

By the mid-twentieth century Aberdeen's traditional industries were in decline, but the discovery of **oil** in the North Sea transformed the place from a depressed port into a boom town. Lean times in the 1980s shook the city's confidence, but Aberdeen remains an extremely prosperous city – though what will happen when the oil runs out is anybody's guess.

The telephone code for Aberdeen is ☎01224.

Arrival, information and city transport

Aberdeen's **airport**, seven miles northwest of town, is served by flights from most parts of the UK and a few European cities. The express airport bus (Mon–Fri; £2) runs to Union St and the bus station; after 6pm and at weekends, you'll have to depend on the #27A (every 90min; 30min). Both the **bus** (☎212266) and **train** (☎594222) stations are on Guild St, in the centre of the city.

Aberdeen is also linked to Lerwick in Shetland, Stromness in Orkney and the Faroe Isles by *P&O* Scottish **ferries**, with regular crossings from Jamieson's Quay in the harbour.

Information
From the stations it's a two-minute walk up the hill to Union Street, Aberdeen's main thoroughfare, and the **tourist office** at St Nicholas House, Broad St, just off the north side of Union St (Oct–May Mon–Sat 9am–5pm, Sun 10am–2pm; June & Sept Mon–Sat 9am–6pm, Sun 10am–4pm; July & Aug Mon–Fri 9am–8pm, Sat 9am–6pm, Sun 10am–6pm; ☎632727). They'll book accommodation for you, charging ten percent of the first night's room rate, redeemable at your hotel. They also run tours of the city, sell theatre, train and bus tickets plus a good selection of pamphlets on the best **walks** in Aberdeen – well worth the small investment of 25p.

You'll find Aberdeen's free monthly **listings magazine**, the snappily titled *City of Aberdeen Arts & Recreation Listings*, a useful guide to current events – it's available in most of the pubs and shops. The tourist board also produces a free monthly *What's On* leaflet and runs the 24-hour *What's On Line* (☎636363). *The Vibe*, available at arts venues and trendier bars, is a bi-monthly freesheet with good details on nightlife. Alternatively, track down a copy of the monthly *57° North* magazine, which combines clubbing news with comedy, features, green issues and a comprehensive round-up of the city's extensive live music scene. The best place for more esoteric information – anything from t'ai chi workshops to festivals and ceilidhs – is the *Lemon Tree Arts Centre*, 5 West North St (☎642230).

City transport
Aberdeen is best explored by foot, but you might need to use **local buses** to reach some of the sights, including Old Aberdeen, in the north of the city. Make sure you

OIL AND ABERDEEN

When **oil** was discovered in BP's Forties Field in 1970, Aberdonians rightly viewed it as a massive financial opportunity, and, despite fierce competition from other east coast British ports and communities in Scandinavia and Germany, the city succeeded in persuading the oil companies to base their headquarters here. Land was made available for housing and industry, millions invested into the harbour and offshore developments, new schools opened and the airport expanded to include a heliport, which has since become the busiest in the world.

The city's **population** swelled by 60,000, and earnings escalated from 15 percent below the national average to a figure well above it. Wealthy oil companies built prestigious offices, swish new restaurants, upmarket bars and shops, but as Aberdeen rode on the crest of this new economic wave its other industries were neglected.

At the peak of production in the **mid-1980s**, 2.6 million barrels a day were being turned out, and the price had reached $80 a barrel – from which it plummeted to $10 during the slump of 1986. The effect was devastating – jobs vanished at the rate of a thousand a month, house prices dropped and Aberdeen soon discovered just how dependent on oil it was. The moment oil prices began to rise again, more bad luck struck with the loss of 167 lives in the **Piper Alpha disaster** and the government implemented an array of much needed but very expensive safety measures.

Plans have been put forward to avoid such a crisis happening again, but have been shelved following the recent upturn in oil prices, and while the rest of Britain suffers its worst-ever recession, Aberdeen has lower than four percent unemployment and millions have been reinvested into the oil fields. However, the city faces a fierce tight to keep ahead of new **foreign competition** for investment and secure employment for future generations of Aberdonians. Signs are, with the oil boom past its peak, that the city may well have to look beyond such a single-issue economy for the future.

carry lots of coins: fares (25p–£1.10) depend on distance travelled. There is no all-inclusive day ticket – the minimum is a bus pass for a week (£9.60). Alternatively, buy a **Farecard** (£2, £5 or £10), which saves worrying about change, from the main **transport office**, 395 King St; the City Council offices next to the tourist office, Broad St; or the permanently busy city-centre kiosk outside *Marks & Spencer*, Union St. For information on this and local bus services generally, call ☎643000. Maps are available from the tourist office, the kiosk and the bus station.

Taxis, which operate from ranks throughout the city centre, are rarely necessary, except late at night. If you don't manage to hail one, call *Mairs Taxis* (☎724040).

Accommodation

As befits a high-flying business city, Aberdeen has a large choice of **accommodation**. Unfortunately, though, as most visitors *are* here on business, much of it is characterless and expensive, although some of the swankier places sometimes offer good-value weekend deals. Predictably, the best budget options are the **B&Bs** and **guest houses**, most of which are strung along Bon Accord St and the Great Western Rd, linked by buses #17, #18 and #19 to town. If you're really strapped for cash, head for the **youth hostel**, or try the **student halls** left vacant for visitors in the summer months. There's also a **campsite** in the suburbs.

Hotels
Albert and Victoria Private Hotel, 1–2 Albert Terrace (☎641717). Listed building at the west end of Union St – convenient for town centre and quiet at night. ②.

Brentwood Hotel, 101 Crown St (☎595440). Spick-and-span refurbished old hotel south of Union St. Often full during the week as it's popular with business people. ③.

Caledonian Thistle Hotel, Union Terrace (☎640233). The best of the posh hotels – an impressive Victorian edifice just off Union St. ⑦.

Cedars Private Hotel, 339 Grt Western Rd (☎583225). Small hotel with friendly atmosphere. ③.

Ferryhill House Hotel, 169 Bon Accord St (☎590867). One of the most historic pubs in Aberdeen with colourful rooms and good food. ③.

Mannofield Hotel, 447 Grt Western Rd (☎315888). Charming old granite building, once a posh private house, a mile west of town. Excellent value 3-course dinners. ③.

Palm Court Hotel, 81 Seafield Rd, (☎310351). Plush West End establishment with popular conservatory bistro-bar. ④.

Queen's Hotel, 51–53 Queen's Rd (☎209999). Cheerful city centre hotel, recently refurbished, with a good culinary reputation. ④.

B&Bs and guest houses

Bracklinn Guest House, 348 Grt Western Rd (☎317060). Welcoming Victorian house with elegant furnishings – one of the city's best B&Bs. ②.

Campbell's Guest House, 444 King St (☎625444). Highly recommended breakfasts. One mile from the city centre and handy for the beach. ②.

Crynoch Guest House, 164 Bon Accord St (☎582743). Convenient location in a street lined with guest houses. ②.

Fourways Guest House, 435 Grt Western Rd (☎310218). A converted manse in the West End of town. ②.

Klibreck, 410 Grt Western Rd (☎316115). Non-smoking stately granite guest house. ②.

Salisbury Guest House, 12 Salisbury Terrace (☎590447). Family-run, comfortable, clean guest house. ②.

Hostels, campsites and campus accommodation

Crombie Johnstone Halls, College Bounds, Old Aberdeen (☎273301). Private rooms in probably the best of the student halls available, in one of the most interesting parts of the city. ①.

Hazelhead (☎321268). Five miles west of centre. Grassy campsite with a swimming pool nearby. Follow signs from ring road or take buses #4 or #14. April–Sept. ①.

King George VI Memorial Hostel, 8 Queen's Rd (☎646988). Grade 1 SYHA youth hostel with rooms for 4–6, but no café. Closed early Jan to early Feb. Bus #14 and #15 from the train station. Curfew is 2am.

The City

Aberdeen divides neatly into five main areas. The **city centre**, roughly bounded by Broad Street, Union Street, Schoolhill and Union Terrace, features the opulent **Marischal College**, the colonnaded **Art Gallery** with its fine collection, and homes that predate Aberdeen's nineteenth-century town planning and have been preserved as **museums**. Union Street continues west to the comparatively cosmopolitan **West End**, where much of the city's decent nightlife, plus a couple of sights, can be found amid its tall grey town houses. To the south, the **harbour** still heaves with boats serving the fish and oil industries, while north of the centre lies twee **Old Aberdeen**, a village neighbourhood presided over by **King's College** and **St Machar's Cathedral** that is a sanctuary from the rush of the city and harbour. The magnificent **beach** marks the city's entire eastern border.

The city centre

Any exploration of the city centre should begin at the east end of the mile-long **Union Street**, whose impressive architecture, rather lost among the shoppers and chain stores, finishes up at **Castlegate**, where Aberdeen's long-gone castle once stood, and which these days holds a somewhat scruffy and uninteresting **market** (Thurs–Sat). The view up gently rising Union Street – a jumble of grey spires, turrets and jostling cream buses – is quintessential Aberdeen. City life used to revolve around the late seventeenth-century **Mercat Cross**, which is now dwarfed by mighty granite buildings such as the Salvation Army Citadel and the Town House (fronted by the *Clydesdale Bank*). It's worth a look, however, carved with a unique portrait gallery of the Stuart sovereigns alongside some fierce gargoyles.

A discreet door on the side of the Town House leads into the **Tolbooth Museum** (April–Sept Tues–Sat 10am–5pm, Thurs 10am–8pm, Sun 2–5pm; free), quarried out of the seventeenth-century prison lurking behind the steely grey nineteenth-century exterior. The museum takes the theme of law and imprisonment throughout; and climbing the claustrophobic staircases and squeezing into tiny, airless cells certainly gives plenty of opportunity to appreciate the harsh realities of incarceration. At the top of the building, a remarkable audio-visual display, featuring a talking model of a Jacobite prisoner, complete with rattling chains, explains the background and atmosphere of the 1745 Jacobite uprising as well as ensuring that the hairs on the back of your neck bristle nervously. Other displays include some fascinating maps and 3D models charting Aberdeen's development from its old town beginnings.

Nearby, on King Street, the sandstone **St Andrew's Episcopal Cathedral**, where Samuel Seabury, America's first bishop, was consecrated in 1784, offers a welcome relief to the uniform granite. Inside its spartan whiteness is broken by impressive and florid gold ceiling bosses of the then 48 states of the USA on one side and, on the other, 48 local families who remained loyal to the Episcopal Church during the eighteenth-century Penal Laws. Even more resplendent is the gilded baldachino canopy over the High Altar. To the right is the Suther Chapel, dominated by the Seabury Centenary window, a light, bright and intensely sentimental splash of primary colours.

West down Union Street brings you to Broad Street, where, cowering behind modern offices, sits Aberdeen's oldest surviving private house, **Provost Skene's House** at 45 Guestrow (Mon–Sat 10am–5pm; free), dating from 1545. In the sixteenth century all the well-to-do houses in the area looked like this, with mellow stone and rounded turrets – only the intervention of the Queen Mother in 1938 saved the house from being demolished like its neighbours. Little has been altered since the Provost of Aberdeen lived here from 1676 to 1685 and the house is now a museum. Its fully restored period rooms with oak panelling, fine plaster and well-preserved furniture offer a pertinent glimpse of how a rich Aberdonian merchant lived in the seventeenth century. Don't miss the Long Gallery, where a series of ornate tempera High Church paintings from 1622 shows a spirited defiance against the Protestant dogma of the time.

Nearby, on Broad Street, stands Aberdeen's most imposing edifice and the world's second largest granite building after the Escorial in Madrid – the exuberant **Marischal College**, whose tall, steely grey pinnacled neo-Gothic facade is in absolute contrast to the eyesore that houses the tourist office opposite. This spectacular architecture with all its soaring, surging lines has been painted and sketched more than any other in Aberdeen, and though not to everyone's taste – it was once described by a minor art historian as "a wedding cake covered in indigestible grey icing" – there's no escaping the fact that it is a most extraordinary feat of sculpture. The college itself was founded in 1593 by the fourth Earl Marischal, and co-existed as a separate Protestant university from Catholic King's, just up the road, for over two centuries. Charles I endeavoured to reconcile the two as a single entity, but they split again during the Reformation and it wasn't until 1860 that they were united as the University of Aberdeen. The facade fronts an earlier quadrangle designed by Archibald Simpson in 1837–41. After the merger, the central tower was more than doubled in height by A Marshall Mackenzie in 1893 and the profusion of spirelets added, though the facade was not totally completed until 1906.

Behind the tower, through the college entrance, the Mitchell Hall's east window illustrates the history of the university in stained glass. The fan-vaulted lobby, once the

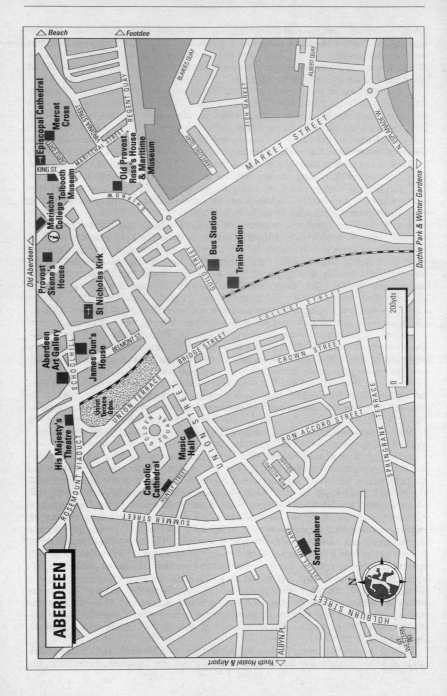

college's old hall, now houses the wonderful **Anthropological Museum** (Mon–Fri 10am–5pm, Sun 2–5pm; free), made up of two large rooms that contain a wealth of weird exhibits, among them a series of Eskimo soapstone carvings, an outrigger canoe carved from a breadfruit tree from Papua New Guinea, a macabre Hawaiian head crafted from basketry and with real dogs' teeth, and a Tibetan prayer wheel. Most bizarre are the high-relief mummy case of an Egyptian five-year-old girl and a stomach-churning foot, unbound and preserved in brine. The "Encyclopaedia of the Northeast" exhibition – running alphabetically from Aberdeen through to Whisky – is well labelled and amazingly varied.

On the corner of Schoolhill and Union Street stands the long **St Nicholas Kirk** (Mon–Fri noon–4pm, Sat 1–3pm; free), actually two churches in one with a solid, central bell tower rising from the middle, from where the 48-bell carillon, the largest in Britain, regularly chimes across the city. There's been a church here since at least 1157, but as the largest kirk in Scotland, it was severely damaged during the Reformation and divided into the West and the East Church, separated today by the transepts and crossing; only the north transept, known as Collinson's aisle, survives from the twelfth century. The Renaissance-style **West Church**, formerly the nave of St Nicholas, was designed in the mid-eighteenth century by James Gibbs, architect of St Martin in the Fields in London's Trafalgar Square. Inside, there's a canopied gallery especially for the city councillors – the most grandiose pew is reserved for the Lord Provost. The **East Church** was rebuilt over the groin-vaulted crypt of the restored fifteenth-century St Mary's Chapel (entered from Correction Wynd), which back in the 1600s was a place to imprison witches – you can still see the iron rings to which they were chained. Take time to explore the large peaceful churchyard, which with its green marble tombs and Baroque monuments seems a million miles from the bustling main street. A little further west up Schoolhill, **James Dun's House** (Mon–Sat 10am–5pm; free) is a smallish, two-storey Georgian house built for the rector of Aberdeen's grammar school in 1769 and now housing contemporary art exhibitions and moderately interesting displays on the city's history.

Opposite, Aberdeen's **Art Gallery** (Mon–Wed, Fri & Sat 10am–5pm, Thurs 10am–8pm, Sun 2–5pm; free) was purpose-built in 1884 to a Neoclassical design by Mackenzie. You enter into the airy **Sculpture Court** around a delicate fountain-like piece by Dame Barbara Hepworth. Another Hepworth sculpture – *Requiem* – in polished walnut sits behind. Some of the more modern pieces (Fred Bushie's glaringly bright steel sculpture in particular) might seem out of place amongst the gilded columns and chequerboard flooring, but the combined effect is successfully pleasing. Contemporary British paintings, many by Scottish artists, line the walls.

The adjoining rooms are filled with more British art, including a characteristically vivid Gilbert and George composition, *Jungled, and Gexhi*, and a remarkable tubular alloy sculpture by Eduardo Paolozzi. At the back, the **Decorative Arts** gallery includes handmade paper, costume, silk banners, batik and appliqué. Local skill can be seen in the ornate Aberdonian silver, talent from far afield in the exquisite eighteenth-century Chinese libation cups, carved from rhino horn. Off this gallery is the **Memorial Court**, a calming, white-walled circular room under a skylit dome that serves as the city's principal war memorial. It also houses the Lord Provost's *Book of Condolence* for the 167 people who died in the 1988 Piper Alpha oil rig disaster in the North Sea.

Upstairs houses the majority of the gallery's painting collection. On the balcony overlooking the central Sculpture Court are works by British impressionists and modernists; don't miss Stanley Spencer's joyful portrait of the British seaside in *Southwold*, and his dramatic *Crucifixion*. Also of note are pieces by Gwen and Augustus John, Robert Brough's half-dazed *View of Elgin* and Duncan Grant's haunting *Self-portrait*.

From here, the two-room **MacDonald collection** of nineteenth-century British art leads off to the left. At first the sheer number of Victorian landscapes crowding the walls may be disconcerting, but closer inspection will prove rewarding. Highlights include John MacWhirter's vast, sun-drenched *Morning – Isle of Arran*, the sheer weariness of Robert McGregor's *Les Moulières* (The Mussel Gatherers), pre-Raphaelite works by Rosetti, Burne-Jones and the other usuals, and paintings by "Boys" from the Glasgow school (see p.176). The second MacDonald room houses 92 paintings of Victorian artists – mostly self-portraits. Local artists on display include John Phillip (1817–67), so heavily influenced by Velázquez and Murillo that he became known as "Spanish Phillip". Another Aberdonian, William Dyce (1806–64), features large, with several examples of his intensely photographic canvasses.

Side rooms off the central balcony house landscapes and portraits from the seventeenth-century onwards. Particularly arresting is Sir Edwin Landseer's 1860 *Flood in the Highlands*, where scenes of tempestuous devastation around the edges – including some grotesquely convulsed animals – seem slightly out of synch with the comparitively calm family group in the centre. The nineteenth-century foreign room is, of course, popular for its impressionist collection (including Boudin, Courbet, Sisley, Monet, Pissaro and a deliciously bright Renoir, *La Roche Guyon*). A fabulous, sinewy cast of a Rodin male figure is the room's sculptural highlight. Off to the side, the dimly lit **Murray Room** contains prints, drawings and watercolours, features from a fifteenth-century Flemish illuminated manuscript and Edward Lear's comically annotated pen ink and wash view of *Boche di Cattaro*. Modern paintings of Aberdeen complete the collection.

West of the gallery, across the rail bridge, the sunken **Union Terrace Gardens**, bordered by the sparkling light-grey granite buildings of Union Terrace, are a welcome relief from the hubbub of heavy traffic on Union Street. Overlooking the scene is a hulking great statue of the "Guardian of Scotland", William Wallace. In summer you'll catch free brass bands and orchestral performances, making it a great place to have a picnic. From here there are views across to the three domes of the Central Library, St Mark's Church and His Majesty's Theatre, traditionally referred to as "Education, Salvation and Damnation".

The West End

Tatty gentility characterizes much of the **West End**, the area around the westernmost part of Union Street, which roughly begins at the great granite columns of the city's **Music Hall**. A block north is **Golden Square**, a misnomer as the trim houses, pubs and restaurants surrounding the statue of the Duke of Gordon are uniformly grey. The city has invested much in gentrifying the area north of Union Street, with the resultant cobbles, old-fashioned lamps and mushrooming designer boutiques. Huntly Street, west of Golden Square, heads off towards the curiously thin spire of **St Mary's Catholic Cathedral** (daily 8am–5pm), a typically foreboding example of Victorian Gothic church architecture.

On the southern side of Union Street, wedged between Bon Accord Street and Bon Accord Terrace, **Bon Accord Square**, is a typical, charming Aberdeen square. In the middle, a grassy centre surrounds a great hulk of granite, commemorating **Alexander Sampson**, architect of much of nineteenth-century Aberdeen. West of Bon Accord Terrace is Justice Mill Lane, home to many of the city's favourite bars and nightclubs, and also to the **Sartrosphere** (school terms Mon & Wed–Fri 10am–4pm, Sat 10am–5pm, Sun 1.30–5pm; school holidays Mon–Sat 10am–5pm, Sun 1.30–5pm; £3), Aberdeen's thoroughly entertaining hands-on science exhibition. The Sartrosphere itself – an ingenious illusion of a vast globe surrounded by numerous images of oneself – is created by walking into a open square of four mirrors with a patterned panel head of you. Other exhibits include a superb 3D map of northeast Scotland, examples of interactive technology and a new biological section in which you can see inside beehives and an anthill.

The harbour

The old cobbled road of Shiprow winds from Castlegate, at the east end of Union Street, down to the north side of the harbour. Just off this steep road, well signposted, is Aberdeen's oldest surviving building, **Old Provost Ross's House** (Mon–Sat 10am–5pm; free), dotted with numerous tiny windows and boasting the original main doorway set into an arched recess. Actually two houses joined together, it was rescued by the NTS in 1954 and became the **Maritime Museum** 30 years later in deference to the eighteenth-century shipping merchant who once lived here. Through the small rooms, low doorways and labyrinthine corridors it tells in detail the many aspects of Aberdeen's nautical history. A wide range of ship models, some used by shipbuilders during construction, others built in painstaking detail by bored sailors, and still more folded into bottles, litter the place, along with numerous paintings and first-hand oral histories. One room focuses on the city's whaling industry between the mid-eighteenth and the mid-nineteenth centuries, while another is devoted to the herring trade. At the top of the house, an exhibition documents Aberdeen's move into the oil industry, with a magnificently detailed scale model of a rig.

At the bottom of Shiprow, the cobbles meet Market Street, which runs the length of the **harbour**. Here brightly painted oil-supply ships, sleek cruise ships and peeling fishing boats jostle for position to an ever-constant clatter and the screech of well-fed seagulls. Follow your nose down the road to the **fish market**, best visited early (7–8am) when the place is in full swing. The current market building dates from 1982, but fish has been traded here for centuries – the earliest record dating back to 1281 when an envoy of Edward I's was charged for 1000 barrels of sturgeon and 5000 salt fish.

Back at the north end of Market Street, Trinity Quay runs to the shipbuilding yards and down York Street to the east corner of the harbour. Here you'll come to Aberdeen's "fitee" or **Footdee** (bus #14 or #15 from Union Street), a nineteenth-century fishermen's village of higgledy-piggledy cottages which back onto the sea, their windows and doors facing inwards to protect from storms but also, so they say, to prevent the Devil from sneaking in the back door. This area, although not dangerous, is now the city's red-light district.

From Market Street it's a 20-minute bus ride (#6 from Market St or #25 from Union St) to **Duthie Park** on Polmuir Road and Riverside Drive (10am–dusk; free), opened as public gardens in the eighteenth century. The rose garden, known as Rose Mountain due to its profusion of blooms, is great in summer, but the real treat is the Winter Gardens – jokingly held to be a favourite haunt with mean Aberdonians saving on their heating bills. To be fair, the place is most stunning in bad weather, offering a steamy jungle paradise of enormous cacti, exotic plants and even tropical birds. From the northwestern corner of Duthie Park, a great cycle and **walkway** – the **Old Deeside Line** – leads out of the city and past numerous old train stations.

Old Aberdeen

An independent burgh until 1891, the tranquil district of **Old Aberdeen**, a 20-minute bus ride north of the city centre, has always maintained a separate village-like identity. Dominated by King's College and St Machar's Cathedral, its medieval cobbled streets, tiny wynds and little lanes are conserved beautifully, with few cars except along St Machar's Drive, and only one bus (#25 from Union St).

The southern half of High Street is overlooked by **King's College Chapel** (Mon–Fri 9am–5pm), the first and finest of the college buildings, completed in 1495 with an imposing Renaissance spire. Named in honour of James IV, the chapel's west door is flanked by his coat of arms and those of his queen. The chapel stands on the quadrangle, whose gracious buildings retain a medieval plan but were built much later; those immediately north were designed by Mackenzie early this century, with the exception of Cromwell Tower at the northeast corner, which was completed in 1658. The first thing you notice inside the chapel is that there is no aisle. Within this unusual plan the screen, the stalls (each unique) and the ribbed arched wooden ceiling are rare and beautiful examples of medieval Scottish wood-carving. The remains of Bishop Elphinstone's tomb and the carved pulpit from nearby St Machars are also here. A spanking new **visitor centre**, in the main college buildings, tells the tempestuous tale of the establishment of the University of Aberdeen, which came about finally in 1860 when Protestant Marischal College and sceptical King's College were merged, well over 200 years after the first attempt. Rivalry between the two establishments (which led to well-charted brawls in the streets) has always been intense. Other studies here include the begrudged arrival of women in the university and some great old archive footage of the opening of the new Marischal College in 1906.

From the college, the cobbled High Street leads a short way north to **St Machars Cathedral** on the leafy Chanonry (daily 9am–5pm; free), overlooking Seaton Park and the River Don. The site was reputedly founded in 580 by Machar, a follower of Columba, when he was sent by the latter to find a grassy platform near the sea, over-looking a river shaped like the crook on a bishop's crozier. This setting fitted the bill perfectly, and the cathedral, a huge fifteenth-century fortified building (only half the length of the original after the collapse of the central tower in 1688), is one of the city's first great granite edifices and a well-known Aberdonian landmark. Inside, the stained-glass windows are a dazzling blaze of colour, and above the nave the heraldic oak ceiling from 1520 is illustrated with nearly 50 different coats of arms from Europe's royal houses and Scotland's bishops and nobles.

Next door to the cathedral, the **Cruickshank Botanic Gardens** (Jan–April & Oct–Dec Mon–Fri 9am–4.30pm; May–Sept Mon–Fri 9am–4.30pm, Sat & Sun 2–5pm; free), laid out in 1898, offer lovely glimpses of the cathedral through the trees. In spring and summer its worth checking out the flowerbeds, but don't bother with the dreary zoological museum.

A wander through Seaton Park will bring you to the thirteenth-century **Brig' o' Balgownie**, which gracefully spans the River Don, nearly a mile north of the cathedral. Still standing (despite Thomas the Rhymer's prediction that it would fall were it ever to be crossed by an only son riding a mare's only foal) the bridge is best visited at sunset – Byron, who spent much of his childhood in Aberdeen, remembered it as one of his favourite places.

The beach

Among large British cities, Aberdeen could surely claim to have the best **beach**. Less than a mile to the east of Union Street is a great two-mile sweep of clean sand, broken by groynes and lined all along with an esplanade. On a sunny day, most of the city seems to be down there. The southern end of the beach is a cosy collection of arcades, a couple of fairly tatty amusement parks, a vast leisure centre, cafés and bars. As you head further north, most of the beach's hinterland is devoted to successive golf links.

Eating, drinking and entertainment

Aberdeen is certainly not short of good places to **eat**, though you will find it more pricy than elsewhere in northeast Scotland. Union Street and the surrounding area has a glut of attractive **restaurants** and **cafés**. As for **nightlife**, like most ports of call Aberdeen caters for a transient population with a lot of disposable income and a desire to get drunk as quickly as possible. Every time a shop closes down in Union Street it seems to reopen as a loud, flashy bar. That said, there are still a number of more traditional old **pubs** which, though usually packed, are well worth digging out.

Restaurants and cafés

Ashvale, 46 Great Western Rd. One of Scotland's finest – and biggest – fish-and-chip shops, with seating for 300. The fish is best, though they also serve inexpensive stovies, meat pies, etc. Open daily until late.

Drummonds, 1 Belmont St (☎624642). Just off Union St, this is a stylish, café and wine bar during the day and a noisy music venue in the evening.

Elronds Café, *Caledonian Thistle Hotel*, 10–14 Union Terrace (☎640233). Surprisingly inexpensive lunch and dinner menu, considering its central location in a marble-floored and exclusive hotel.

The Fortune, 176 Crown St. Frugal-looking place with good, Chinese food.

Invernecky, Beach Esplanade. Best of the beach caffs, great for big breakfasts and ice-cream specials.

La Lombarda, Castlegate (☎640916). Smart upstairs trattoria and livelier basement bistro/café in one of the city's oldest established restaurants.

Lemon Tree, 5 W North St (☎642230). Home-made Scottish food. Very reasonably priced, and a buzzing atmosphere with a theatre upstairs.

Littlejohn's, 46 School Hill. Loud, lively and trendy theme bar-cum-restaurant for steaks, pizza and popular international dishes.

Owlies, Unit C, Littlejohn St (☎649267). Plain French brasserie food, with plenty of vegetarian options.

Poldino's, 7 Little Belmont St (☎647777). Lively, expensive Italian restaurant.

Silver Darling Restaurant, Pocra Quay, N Pier (☎576229). Excellent, if pricy, seafood restaurant in the Footdee. Closed Sat lunch.

Wild Boar, 16 Belmont St (☎625357). Upbeat brasserie with well-priced vegetarian food, soups and pastas. A popular evening venue. Closed Sat lunch.

Pubs and bars

Bex Bar, Justice Mill Lane. Studenty and trendy, the place gets packed at the weekend as a pre-club haunt.

The Blue Lamp, Gallowgate. Friendly pub with a good jukebox.

Carriages, *Brentwood Hotel*, 101 Crown St. Unusually lively hotel cellar bar with the city's largest range of real ales and ciders. Also serves excellent bar food.

Cocky Hunters, 504 Union St. Small live music bar, popular with trendies and students.

Ferryhill House, Bon Accord St. Pub with its own garden and very good food.

Glenlivet Bar, 43 Regent Quay. Cheeriest, most cosmopolitan of the harbourside bars.

Henry J Beans, Windmill Brae. Yuppie-ish, buzzy bar.

Ma Cameron's Inn, Little Belmont St. Aberdeen's oldest pub, though only a section remains of the original. Serves food. Closed Sun.

The Prince of Wales, 7 St Nicholas Lane. Aberdeen's most highly regarded pub, with a long bar and flagstone floor. Very central and renowned for its real ales, it's often crowded.

St Machar Bar, 97 High St, Old Aberdeen. The cathedral quarter's sole pub, an old-fashioned bar inevitably full of King's College students.

Triple Kirks, Belmont St. Imaginative church conversion, now an extremely popular drinking hole, with regular live music. Popular with clubbers and theatregoers.

Clubs and live music venues

Franklyn's, Justice Mill Lane. Part of the same complex as the *Bex Bar* and catering for the same studenty crowd. Chart-oriented dance music is the staple.

Joy, 1 Regent Quay. Trendy dance, acid jazz and groove club.

Lemon Tree, 5 W North St. Arts centre with a great buzz at present. The laid-back café-bar is home to regular live music, comedy and folk.

Ministry of Sin, 16 Dee St. The hottest dance club for miles; Sunday nights are legendary.

O'Henrys, Adelphi Close. Flash studenty club just off Union St.

The Pelican, *Metro Hotel*, Market St. Hot and sweaty club with good bands – mainly indie.

Theatres and concert halls

Aberdeen Arts Centre, 33 King St (☎635208). A variety of theatrical productions alongside a programme of lectures and exhibitions.

Capital Theatre, Union St (☎583141). Visiting mainstream rock and pop acts.

Cowdray Hall, Schoolhill (☎646333). Classical music, often with visiting orchestras.

His Majesty's, Rosemount Viaduct (☎641122). Aberdeen's main theatre, in a beautifully restored Edwardian building, with a programme that ranges from highbrow drama and opera to pantomime.

Lemon Tree, 5 West North St (☎642230). Avant-garde events with off-the-wall comedians and plays – many are a spin-off from Edinburgh's festival.

Music Hall, Union St (☎632080). Big-name comedy and music acts.

Cinemas

Arts Centre, King St (☎635208). Small repertoire of lesser-known and art-house movies.

Cannon, Union St (☎591477). Mainstream general releases.

Lemon Tree, 5 West North St (☎642230). Shows art-house and esoteric films.

Odeon, Justice Mill Lane (☎587160). Much the same line-up as at the *Cannon*.

Listings

Airport (☎722331).

Bike rental *Aberdeen Cycle Centre*, 188 King St (☎644542); *Neil Ross Cycles*, 232 King St (☎626360).

Books *Dillons*, 269–271 Union St (☎210161), has a wide range of arts-oriented books; *Kaos*, 19 Diamond St (☎620212), stocks comics and American crime and sci-fi; and*Waterstones*, 236b Union St (☎571655), boasts a particularly well-stocked Scottish section.

Car rental *Budget* (☎771777) in the airport; *Caledonian Car and Small Van Hire* (☎584751) on Caledonian Rd just off Bon Accord St in town.

Exchange *Thomas Cook*, 335–37 Union St (Mon–Sat 9.30am–5.30pm; ☎212271).

Ferries *P&O* (☎572615).

Hospital *The Royal Infirmary*, on Foresterhill, northeast of the town centre, has a 24hr casualty department (☎681818).

Left luggage Small 24hr lockers at the train station cost £2.

Lesbian and Gay Switchboard (Wed & Fri 7–10pm; ☎633500)

Maps *Aberdeen Map Shop*, 74 Skene St (☎637999).

Pharmacy *Boots*, 161 Union St (Mon–Sat 8am–6pm; ☎211592).

Police The main police station is on Queen St (☎639111).

Post office Aberdeen's central post office is at 33 Castle St (Mon–Fri 9am–5.30pm, Sat 9am–12.30pm; ☎588260).

Public transport Information Line (6am–midnight; ☎633333).

Swimming *Bon Accord Baths and Leisure Centre*, Justice Mill Lane (☎587920).

Travel agents *U Travel*, 110 High St (Mon–Fri 9.30am–4.30pm; ☎273559).

Southern Grampians

South of Aberdeen, the A92 and the main train line follow the coast to **Stonehaven**, a pretty harbour town and base for the nearby **Dunottar Castle**, a surreal ruin right on the cliffs. The area to the south and west is known as the **Mearns**, an agricultural district of scattered population and gathering hills towards the Angus glens. **Fettercairn** is the most obvious base, especially for its proximity to **Fasque**, the old home of prime minister Gladstone.

Stonehaven is easily reached by bus or train from Aberdeen or Montrose, although public transport inland into the Mearns is virtually non-existent.

Stonehaven and around

A busy pebble-dashed town, **STONEHAVEN** attracts hordes of holidaymakers in the summer because of its sheltered Kincardine coastline. The town itself is split into two parts, the picturesque working harbour area being most likely to detain you. At one end of the harbour, Stonehaven's oldest building, the **Tolbooth** (June–Sept Mon & Thurs–Sat 10am–noon & 2–5pm; Wed & Sun 2–5pm; free), built as a storehouse during the construction of Dunnottar Castle (see below) is now a museum of local history and fishing. **Boat trips** can be arranged with the harbour master (☎01569/762741).

The old High Street – lined with some fine town houses and civic buildings – connects the harbour and its surrounding old town with the late eighteenth-century planned centre on the other side of the River Carron. On New Year's Eve, High Street is the location of the ancient ceremony of **Fireballs**, when people get raging drunk and parade its length, swinging metal cages full of burning debris around their heads. This, it is said, wards off evil spirits for the year ahead. The **new town** focuses on the giant market square, overlooked by the dusky pink granite market hall with its impressive steeple and a wonderfully stern notice warning "No Bills. Commit No Nuisance Here". Evan Street heads inland from the market square before swinging right into Arduthie Road, which climbs up to the train station, a good 15-minute walk from the centre.

Practicalities

The **tourist office** is at 66 Allardice St, the main street past the square (April–June, Sept & Oct daily 10am–1.15pm & 2–5pm; July & Aug daily 10am–7.30pm; ☎01569/762806). If you want to **stay**, *Arduthie House*, Ann St, is a good B&B (☎01569/762381; ②), as is the *Braemar*, Evan St (☎01569/764841; ②). Down by the harbour, the *Marine Hotel* (☎01569/762155; ③) is decidedly shabby to stay in, but a great place for eating and drinking. If money is no object, *Muchalls Castle* (☎01569/731170; ⑥), a luxurious seventeenth-century fortified laird's house is four miles north of Stonehaven, just off the A92. For a cheaper near-castle experience on the Dunottar estate, *Dunottar Mains Farm* (☎01569/762621; ②) does B&B (April–Sept). For **food**, the *Tolbooth Fish Restaurant*, on the harbour, is pricy but worth it, while *Robert's Bakery*, next to the tourist office, has good sandwiches and cakes. Try the *Marine Hotel* or the *Ship Inn* on the harbour for drinking or pub food. In the "new" town, there's regular live **music** at the *Belvedere Hotel* on Evan St, a folk club at the *St Leonard's Hotel*, Bath St, and generally a lively time at the *Hook and Eye*, Allardice St. Stonehaven's respected **folk festival** takes place in mid-July.

Dunnottar Castle, Kineff and Arbuthnott

Two miles outside Stonehaven (the tourist office sells a walking guide for the scenic amble), **Dunnottar Castle** (late March–Oct Mon–Sat 9am–6pm, Sun 2–5pm; £2.50) is a huge ninth-century fortress set on a three-sided sheer cliff jutting into the sea – a spot dramatic enough to be chosen as the setting for Zeffirelli's movie version of *Hamlet*. Once the principal fortress of the northeast, much of Dunnottar now stands in ruins, though the scatter of remains is worth a good root around; don't miss the so-called Marischal's Suite, which gives dramatic views out to the crashing sea. Siege and blood-stained drama splatter the castle's past. In 1297 William Wallace burned the whole English Plantaganet garrison alive here, and one of the more gruesome tales from the castle's history tells of the imprisonment and torture of 122 men and 45 women Covenanters in 1685 – an event, as it says on the Covenanters' Stone in the churchyard, "whose dark shadow is for evermore flung athwart the Castled Rock".

Four miles south of Dunnottar Castle, **CATTERLINE** is a clifftop hamlet typical of those along this stretch of coast – worth a visit for the views and the delicious, well-priced **lobster** at the *Creel Inn*, which also offers **B&B** (☎01569/750254; ④).

Tiny **KINEFF**, lying among fields tumbling down to the sea, is four miles further down the coast. The village church is, for the most part, an eighteenth-century successor to the one in which the Scottish Crown Jewels were hidden as Cromwell marched on Scotland in 1651. Popular tradition has it that the wives of the Dunnottar garrison commander and the Kineff parish minister hid the Crown under an apron and carried the state Sceptre, disguised as a distaff, with bundles of flax. The state's most precious assets were successfully hidden here for nine years. Memorials and interpretive boards inside the beautifully light and simple church tell the story.

Some five miles inland, the straggling village of **ARBUTHNOTT** is the centre for fans of prolific local author, **Lewis Grassic Gibbon** (1901–35), whose romanticized realism perfectly encapsulates the spirit of the Mearns. His descriptions were often quite awesome – Glasgow, for example, he neatly penned as "the vomit of a cataleptic commercialism". *Sunset Song*, his most famous work, is an essential read for those travelling in this area. The community-run **Grassic Gibbon Centre** (April–Oct daily 10am–4.30pm; £1.75), on the B967 through the village, is a great introduction to this fascinating and self-assured man who died so young. He is buried (under his real name of James Leslie Mitchell) in the corner of the little village graveyard, overlooking the forested banks of the Bervie Water off the main road. The parish church itself, one of the few surviving intact in Scotland that predate the Reformation, is interesting for its Norman arch, unusual fifteenth-century circular bell tower and glorious thirteenth-century chancel.

Fettercairn and Fasque House

Eight miles southeast of Arbthnott on the tiny B9120 (and served by buses from Montrose), the village of **FETTERCAIRN** is renowned for its handsome arch, erected in 1861 after Queen Victoria stayed at the local pub, the *Ramsay Arms* (☎01561/340334; ④), which is still a good place to stay or to stop for a drink. One mile west, and well signposted, the **Fettercairn distillery** (Mon–Fri 10am–4.30pm; free) is Scotland's second oldest, with free tours and the customary free taster at the end.

A short drive north on the Edzel–Banchory road, the once beautiful but now somewhat neglected **Fasque House** (May–Sept daily except Fri 1.30–5.30pm; £3) – childhood home of four times prime minister William Ewart Gladstone – is set in grounds filled with deer, pheasants and rabbits. Built in 1809 by Sir Alexander Ramsay, a leading Angus farmer, the estate passed into the Gladstone family in 1829 when Sir John Gladstone, William's father and a rich grain broker, bought the land and added various extensions, developing the gardens and building roads and bridges. Today, in all its intriguing decrepitude, Fasque House offers a great insight into how the affluent landowner lived in the Victorian era. Downstairs, domestic implements litter the place in a refreshingly haphazard manner – you can see old coal scuttles and bedpans and, in the kitchen, an array of enormous copper pans. Upstairs gives the impression of being equally untouched, with a library crammed full of the young Gladstone's books, a splendid Victorian bathroom complete with shower, and bedrooms looking much as the nineteenth-century maids would have left them, with bed covers turned back.

Deeside

More commonly known as Royal **Deeside**, the land stretching west of the coast along the River Dee revels in its connections with the royal family, who have regularly holidayed here, at **Balmoral**, since Queen Victoria bought the estate. Eighty thousand Scots turned out to welcome her on her first visit in 1848, but some weren't so charmed – one local journalist remarked that the area was about to be "desolated by cockneys and other horrible reptiles". Today, however, the locals are fiercely protective of their connections, forever retelling stories of their encounters with blue-bloods.

Considering Victoria had her pick of the country in which to establish a holiday home, it comes as quite a surprise that this windswept, rainy spot should have attracted her so much. Her visitors thought the same: Count von Moltke, then aide-de-camp to Prince Frederick William of Prussia, observed, "It is very astonishing that the Royal Power of England should reside amid this lonesome, desolate, cold mountain scenery", while Tsar Nicholas II whined, "The weather is awful, rain and wind every day and on top of it no luck at all – I haven't killed a stag yet". However, the Queen adored the place, and the woods were said to remind Prince Albert of Thuringia, his homeland.

Deeside is undoubtedly beautiful in a fierce, craggy, Scottish way, and the royal presence has certainly put a stop to any unattractive mass development. Villages strung along the A93, the main route through the area, are as picturesque as you'll find anywhere, and the facilities for visitors, who boost the local economy no end, are first class, with a couple of youth hostels, some outstanding hotels and plenty of castles and scenic walks.

Bluebird Northern buses from Aberdeen regularly chug along the A93, serving most of the towns on the way to Braemar, past Balmoral to the west; and from June to September the *Heatherhopper* also runs along the A93 on the way to Pitlochry (see p.251).

From Aberdeen to Banchory

West of Aberdeen is low-lying land of mixed farming, forestry and suburbs. Easily reached from the main road are the castles of **Drum** and **Crathes**, both pleasant stop-overs, while the uneventful town of **Banchory** serves as a convenient base if you intend to spend some time in Deeside.

Drum Castle

Ten miles west of Aberdeen, less than a mile from the A93, **Drum Castle** (Easter–June & Sept daily 1.30–5.30pm; July & Aug daily 11am–5.30pm; Oct Sat & Sun 1.30–5.30pm; NTS; £3.50) stands in a clearing in the ancient **woods of Drum** (daily 9.30am–dusk), made up of the splendid pines and oaks that once covered this whole area before mass forest clearance made way for shipbuilding. The castle itself combines a 1619 Jacobean mansion with Victorian expansions and the original, huge thirteenth-century keep. Built initially as a royal fortress, Robert the Bruce gave Drum Castle to his armour bearer, William de Irvine, in 1323 for services rendered at Bannockburn. From that point on, until the NTS stepped in in 1976 (a full 24 generations), the castle was in Irvine hands. To get a sense of the medieval atmosphere of the place, ascend the Turnpike Stair, above the Laigh Hall where a 700-year-old window seat gives views of the ancient forest. The castle also has a peaceful walled rose garden (April–Oct daily 10am–6pm).

Crathes Castle and Gardens

Three and a half miles east of Banchory on the A93, **Crathes Castle and Gardens** (mid-April to late Oct daily 11am–5.30pm; £4; gardens daily 9.30am–dusk; £1.50) encompass a splendid sixteenth-century granite tower house, which appears to have been more for decoration than defence, adorned with flourishes such as overhanging turrets, gargoyles and conical roofs. Its thick walls, narrow windows and tiny rooms loaded with heavy old furniture make Crathes rather claustrophobic, but it is saved by some wonderfully painted ceilings, either still in their original form or sensitively restored; the earliest dates from 1602. Unfortunately, in each room a tartan-kilted Scottish woman recites a well-rehearsed and detailed historical monologue that's difficult to escape, making it necessary to be selective in your wandering – don't miss the Room of the Nine Nobles, where great heroes of the past, among them Julius Caesar, King David and King Arthur, are skilfully painted on the beams. More intriguing still is the Green Lady's Room, where a mysterious child's skeleton was found beneath the floor and the ghost of a young girl, sometimes carrying a child, is said to have been spotted – most recently in the 1980s. Here on the ceiling you'll see moral commandments written in Latin, and paintings of grotesque faces and strange designs that make a chilling *memento mori*. The Muses Room, with portrayals of the nine muses and seven virtues, is also impressive. Beware the "trip stair", originally designed to foil seventeeth-century burglars.

Banchory

BANCHORY, meaning "fair hollow", is useful as a place to stay. It's easy to laugh at the tourist bumph that claims the "Gateway to Deeside" has an "Alpine feel", but the town does have a certain charm, flanked by hills on one side and the River Dee on the other. It's really just a one-street town, and there's not much to see, though the small local **museum** on Bridge St, behind High St (June–Sept Mon–Wed, Fri & Sat 2–5.15pm; free), might warrant 30 minutes or so – especially if you're a fan of local boy James Scott Skinner, fiddler and composer of such tunes as *The Bonnie Lass o' Bon Accord*. Alternatively, you can watch salmon leap all year round from the little footbridge where the Dee joins the Feugh River to the south of town.

Practicalities

The **tourist office**, in the museum (July & Aug daily 9.30am–7pm; Sept–June Mon–Sat 9.30am–1.15pm & 2–5pm; ☎01330/822000), can provide information on walking and fishing in the area. Opposite, *Parkers Lounge Café*, next to the busy nightclub, sells good basic food.

There are several reasonable **hotels** here and in the surrounding countryside. *Banchory Lodge* (☎01330/822625; ④) is a rambling Georgian house just ten minutes' stroll from Banchory at the confluence of the rivers Dee and Feugh. More cheaply, *Burnett Arms Hotel*, 25 High St (☎01330/824944; ③), is a former coaching inn right in town, and the *Old Police House*, 3 Bridge St (☎01330/824000; ②), is a decent **B&B**. Outside Banchory on the Inchmarlo road, the smart *Tor-Na-Collie Hotel* (☎01330/822242; ④) was once a retreat for Charlie Chaplin and his family, and serves splendid Scottish salmon, venison and malt whisky in its upscale restaurant. For **youth hostelling**, the *Wolf's Hearth Hostel*, ten miles northwest of Banchory, just outside Tornaveen on the B9119 (☎013398/83460), is open all year. On the lower slopes of Corennie Moor, the hostel has magnificent views over Deeside.

Ballater and Balmoral

Passing the workaday town of **ABOYNE**, about ten miles west of Banchory, the A93 arrives after another ten miles at the neat little town of **BALLATER**, hemmed in by fircovered mountains. This unassuming place was dragged from obscurity in the nineteenth century when it was discovered that the local waters were useful in curing scrofula. Scrofula is no longer a problem, but you can still buy Ballater spring water, and the town remains a busy place – these days due to its proximity to Balmoral, which lies eight miles to the west.

It was in Ballater that Queen Victoria first arrived in Deeside by train from Aberdeen back in 1848 – she wouldn't allow a station to be built any closer to Balmoral – Ballater's supremely elegant train station, in the centre of town but still displays its Victorian timetables. The local **shops**, having provided the royals with household basics, also flaunt their connections, sporting oversized crests above their doorways.

Ballater is a good base for local **walks**, including out to the glacial Loch Muick, some eight miles southwest, where the Capel Mounth drovers' route (see p.353) continues over the mountains to Glen Doll. A fairly strenuous all-day trek from the Spittal of Glenmuick car park, at the head of the loch, leads up and around Lochnagar (3789ft), the mountain much painted and written about by the current Prince of Wales.

Ballater practicalities

The **tourist office** is opposite the station in Station Square (mid-April to mid-May & Oct daily 10am–1.15pm & 2–5pm; mid-May to late June and Sept daily 9.30am–1.15pm & 2–6.30pm; late June to Aug daily 9.30am–7pm; ☎013397/55306). There are plenty of reasonable **B&Bs**: *Mrs Cowie*, 3 Braemar Rd (☎013397/55699; ②) is the cheapest. Hotels worth trying include the welcoming *Deeside*, Braemar Rd (☎013397/55420; ③) or the nearby *Auld Kirk* (☎013397/55762; ③), complete with spire and an excellent restaurant. For **camping**, the *Anderson Road Caravan Park* (book through the council on ☎01569/762001) down towards the river, has around 60 tent pitches. There are numerous **places to eat**, from smart hotel restaurants to bakers and coffee shops. For non-touristy drinking, try the back bar (entrance down Golf St) of the *Prince of Wales*, which faces the main square. **Bike rental** (as well as canoeing, off-road driving, fishing and gliding) is available from *Making Treks* on Station Square (☎013397/55865).

Balmoral Castle and Crathie Church

Originally a sixteenth-century tower house built for the powerful Gordon family, **Balmoral Castle** (May–July Mon–Sat 10am–5pm; £2.50) has been a royal residence since 1852, when it was converted to the Scottish Baronial mansion that stands today. The royal family traditionally spend their summer holidays here, but despite its fame, it can be something of a disappointment even for a dedicated royalist. For the three months when the doors are nudged open the general riff-raff are permitted to view only the ballroom and the grounds; for the rest of the year it is not even visible to the paparazzi who converge en masse when the royals are in residence here in August.

Opposite the castle's gates on the main road, the otherwise dull granite church of **CRATHIE**, built in 1895 with the proceeds of a bazaar held at Balmoral, is the royals' local church. Princess Anne chose the place as the venue for her second marriage to her former equerry, Commander Tim Laurence. A small **tourist office** operates in the car park by the church on the main road in Crathie (April–June & Sept daily 10am–1.15pm & 2–5.30pm; July & Aug daily 10am–5.30pm).

Braemar

Continuing for another few miles, the road rises to 1100ft above sea level to the upper part of Deeside and the village of **BRAEMAR**, situated where three passes meet and overlooked by a family unimposing **Castle** (Easter–Oct daily 10am–6pm; £1.90) of the same name. Signs as you enter Braemar boast that it's an "Award Winning Tourist Village", which just about sums it up, as everything seems to have been prettified to within an inch of its life or have a price tag on it. That said, it's an invigorating, outdoor kind of place, well patronized by committed hikers, although probably best known for its Highland Games, the annual **Braemar Gathering** (every first Sat of Sept). Games were first held here in the eleventh century, when Malcolm Canmore set contests for the local clans in order to pick the bravest and strongest for his army. Attracting "Heavies" – famous Scottish clan members – from around the world, it's an overcrowded, notoriously popular event; Braemar's caber, for the tossing event, is particularly famous, a stripped pine measuring nearly 20ft and weighing 132 pounds. Since Queen Victoria's day it has become customary for successive generations of royals to attend and it is now a huge event. You're unlikely to get in if you just turn up. If you're keen enough to plan that far in advance, tickets are available in about February and March from the Bookings Secretary, BRHS, Coilacriech, Ballater, AB35 5UH (☎013397/55377).

MORRONE – BRAEMAR'S BEACON

Ordnance Survey Landranger map No.43.

Late August and through autumn, when the mountain is plush with extravagant colours, is the best time to ascend Morrone. In winter, it can be a spectacular viewpoint but very exposed. Allow four hours for the walk.

Make your way up Chapel Brae at the west end of Braemar, passing a car park and pond, then Mountain Cottage, and swinging left up through fine birch woods (a nature reserve). Keep right of the fences and house. The track bears right (west), and at a fork take the left branch up to the Deeside Field Club view indicator. Skirt the crags above this to the left and the path is obvious thereafter. The summit provides a fantastic and huge view of the Cairngorms. There's a cluster of buildings here and a Braemar Mountain Rescue relay mast – as reception is so good. You can descend by the upward route but an easy continuation is to head down by the rescue post's access path, which twists along and then down into Glen Clunie. Turn left along the minor road back to Braemar; the walk finishes by walking through the local golf course.

If you've come as far as Braemar, it's worth travelling six miles west to the end of the road and the **Linn of Dee**, where the river plummets savagely through a narrow rock gorge. From here there are countless **walks**, for the casual rambler or full-time hiker, into the surrounding countryside.

Practicalities

Braemar's **tourist office** is in the modern building known as the Mews in the middle of the village on Mar Rd (mid-March to mid-May daily 10am–1.15pm; mid-May to June & Sept daily 10am–7pm; July & Aug daily 10am–8pm; Oct & Nov daily 10am–1.15pm & 2–6pm; ☎013397/41600). **Rooms** are scarce in Braemar in the lead up to the gathering, so you'll need to book in advance. *Clunie Lodge Guest House*, Clunie Bank Rd (☎013397/41330; ①) on the edge of town, is a good **B&B** with lovely views up Clunie Glen, and there's a **youth hostel** at Corrie Feragie, 21 Glenshee Rd (Jan–Oct; ☎013397/41659; Grade 3). Alternatively, the cheery *Braemar Bunkhouse*, 15 Mar Rd (☎013397/41517 or 41242; ①) is right in the thick of the village; they also rent **bikes**. The *Invercauld Caravan Club Park* (☎013397/41373), just south of the village off the Glenshee Rd, has 15 **camping** pitches. Standard and fairly pricy hotel **food** can be had from the bars of the *Invercauld* (on the main road from Ballater near the river bridge) or *Moorfield* (overlooking the Games Park) hotels, or for some cheap stodge try the *Braemar Takeaway* by the river bridge. For **drinking**, the *Invercauld Arms* in the middle of town is a youthful hangout with a pool table. The *Moorfield Hotel* has regular live music, as does the surprisingly informal cocktail bar of the grand *Fife Hotel*, where dances and ceilidhs are frequent. Throughout the summer, the village children, together with some local pipers, put on a weekly show of Highland dancing in the Village Hall (Tues).

The Don Valley and the Lecht

The quiet countryside around the **Don Valley**, once renowned for its illegal whisky distilleries and smugglers, used also to be a prosperous agricultural area. As the region industrialized, however, the population drifted towards Dundee and Aberdeen, and nowadays little remains of the old farming communities but the odd deserted crofter's cottage. From Aberdeen, the A944 leads west towards **Alford**, where it meets the River Don; they then continue together past ruined castles into the Upper Don Valley and the heather moorlands of the eastern Highlands. This remote, and under-visited area, is positively littered with ruined castles, Pictish sites, stones and hillforts, of which it is impossible to be exhaustive here. There are some excellent free leaflets in the Grampian Archaeology series (available from all tourist offices), which give far more detail. The Lecht Road, from Corgaff to the hilltop town of **Tomintoul**, rises steeply, making the area around it, simply known as the **Lecht**, an ideal skiing centre. Buses are scarce, many designed for tourists and only running from April to September.

Alford and around

ALFORD, 25 miles west of Aberdeen, only exists at all because it was chosen, in 1859, as the terminus for the Great North Scotland Railway. The town has made a concerted effort to relaunch itself as a major tourist centre, opening up some dubious "family" attractions such as a heritage centre, swanky golf course and a dry ski slope. The best of the sights is the **Grampian Transport Museum** on Main St (April–Oct daily 10am–5pm; £2.50), a large and rather soulless display of transport through the ages. Unusual exhibits include the *Craigevar Express*, a strange, three-wheeled steam-driven vehicle developed by the local postman for his rounds before the invention of the engine; and, incongruously, a beautiful Art Deco Belgian dance organ with over 400 pipes and a full set of drums. You'll also see traction engines, a 1902 dogcart used for transporting gun dogs, a portable steam engine and hundreds of other more familiar vehicles from fire engines to horse-drawn carriages.

Practically next door is the terminus for the **Alford Valley Railway** (April, May & Sept Sat & Sun 11am–5pm; June–Aug daily 11am–5pm; ☎019755/62326), a two-foot narrow-gauge train that runs for about a mile from Alford Station through wooded vales to the wide open space of **Murray Park**; the return journey takes an hour. The station is also home to the **tourist office** (April–June, Sept & Oct daily 10am–5pm; July & Aug daily 10am–6pm; ☎019755/62052).

Craigievar Castle

Six miles south of Alford, **Craigievar Castle** (☎013398/83635) is a fantastic pink confection of turrets, gables, balustrades and cupolas bubbling over from the top three storeys. It was built not with defence in mind, but by a Baltic trader known as Willy the Merchant in 1626, who was evidently allowed to let his whimsy run riot. The castle's massive popularity – it features on everything from shortbread tins to tea towels all over Scotland – has, unfortunately, been its undoing and the owners, the NTS, are planning to undertake extensive and emergency repair work. Consequently, they are asking people to refrain from visiting, a situation likely to last throughout much of the 1990s – for current details on their policy, telephone the castle direct.

Lumsden and Rhynie

The A944 heads west from Alford, meeting the A97 just south of the village of **LUMSDEN**, the surprising centre of Scottish sculpture. A contemporary **Sculpture Walk** – heralded by a fabulous skeletal black horse at its southern end – runs parallel to the main road, coming out near the premises of the **Scottish Sculpture Workshop** (Mon–Fri 10am–4pm; ☎01464/861372), just beyond the *Lumsden Arms* pub.

The village of **RHYNIE**, folded beautifully into the hills three miles further north up the A97, is forever associated with one of the greatest Pictish memorials, the **Rhynie Man**, a remarkable 6ft boulder, discovered in 1978 and depicting a rare whole figure, clad in a tunic and holding what is guessed to be a ceremonial axe. It can be seen in the foyer of the regional council's headquarters at Woodhill House in Aberdeen. Of the Pictish remains that have stayed in Rhynie, the most remarkable is the **Craw Stone**, standing sentinel on a ploughed hill, above an idyllic burnside cemetery, reached by a lane at the south end of the village. The stone is carved with a wonderful example of the long-snouted Pictish beast that has been variously described as an elephant, a dolphin or, most likely, a water kelpie. Aerial photographs have shown the Craw Stone to be surrounded by ditches, indicating the site was probably a Pictish hillfort; and therefore offers one of the few chances to see a carved stone in its original position.

On the other side of Rhynie village – an orderly little place around its grassy central square – is the **Tap O'Noth** Pictish hillfort, most easily reached from the car park a mile or so along the A941 to Dufftown. The second highest hillfort in Scotland, there are substantial remnants of the wall around the lip of the summit, which show evidence of vitrification (fierce burning), probably to fuse the rocks together, not to ward off attackers as was originally thought.

Rhynie is a reasonable – if very quiet – **place to stay**. Cheapest and best is the *Gordon Arms Hotel*, Main St (☎01464/861615; ②).

The Upper Don Valley

Ten miles west of Alford stand the thirteenth-century stone ruins of **Kildrummy Castle** (April–Sept Mon–Sat 9.30am–6.30pm, Sun 2–6.30pm; Oct–March Sat 9.30am–4pm, Sun 2–4pm; £1.50). An impressive set of ruins, Kildrummy has seen some particularly hideous moments of conflict. During the Wars of Independence Robert the Bruce sent his wife and children here for their own protection, but the castle blacksmith, bribed with as much gold as he could carry, set fire to the place and it fell into English hands. Bruce's immediate family survived, though his brother was executed and the entire garrison hung, drawn and quartered. Meanwhile, the duplicitous blacksmith was rewarded for his help by having molten gold poured down his throat. Other sieges took place during the subsequent centuries: Balliol's forces attacked in 1335, Cromwell took over in 1654 and the sixth Earl of Mar used the castle as the headquarters of the ill-fated Jacobite risings in 1715. Following John Erskine's withdrawal Kildrummy became redundant and it was abandoned as a fortress and residence and fell into ruin. Beside the ruins is a Scottish Baronial-style castle built in 1901, now the *Kildrummy Castle Hotel* (☎019755/71288; ⑤), with all the trappings associated with a mansion house – wood-panelled rooms, Victorian furniture and a great garden.

About four miles southwest of Kildrummy along the A97, the ruins of **Glenbuchat Castle** (free access) loom above the road. A tower house built in the 1590s, it was transformed – notice the architectural additions, such as the upstairs partition walls and newer windows – into a residential property before being abandoned in the 1840s. The road (by now the A944) sweeps round into the dissipated parish of **STRATHDON**, little more than a succession of occasional buildings by the roadside. On the parish's eastern fringe, above the main road, the *House of Newe* (☎019756/51247; ③), a large seventeenth-century outhouse of the demolished Castle Newe, is a relaxing place to stay. It also offers residential art courses. Two miles east along the A944, just south of the road, *Bigfoot Adventures* at Heugh Head (☎019756/51312) **rents bikes** and organizes other outdoor pursuits. On the other side of the road from Strathdon's car park sits an enormous rabbit-infested moated mound, all that remains of the area's pre-Kildrummy castle and church, the Doune of Invernochty. A few grassy walls survive on top, including around the hollow of the old Norman church.

The A944 twists and turns its way westwards, past the much photographed road sign to Lost and on to **Corgarff Castle** (April–Sept Mon–Sat 9.30am–7pm, Sun 2–7pm; Oct–March, contact key-keeper for times; HS; £1.50). This is by no means a romantic ruin, instead an ugly white house set within a vaguely interesting star-shaped wall, but it too has an eventful history. Built in 1537 – the wall was added in 1748 – it was first attacked in 1571, during a religious feud between the Forbes, family of the laird of the castle, and the Gordons, who torched the place killing the laird's wife, family and servants. In 1748, in the aftermath of Culloden, the Hanoverian government turned Corgarff into a barracks – note the musket loops in the wall – in order to track down local Jacobite rebels, and finally, in the mid-nineteenth century, the English Redcoats were stationed here with the unpopular task of trying to control whisky smuggling. Today there's little to see inside, but the place has been restored to resemble its days as a barracks, with stark rooms and rows of hard, uncomfortable beds. Just short of the castle by Rowan Tree Cottage, a track bumps south off the main road to *Jenny's Bothy* at **DELLACHUPER** (☎019756/51449; ①), a beautifully remote **hostel** with private rooms and no dorms.

Tomintoul

Just past Corgarff, at Cock Bridge, the road leaps up towards the ski slopes of the Lecht and, four miles further on, **TOMINTOUL** (pronounced "*Tom*-in-towel"), at 1150ft the highest village in the Scottish Highlands. Tomintoul owes its existence to post-1745 landowners' panic when, as in other parts of the north, isolated inhabitants were forcibly moved to new, planted villages, where a firm eye could be kept on everybody. A garrison – one of the fiercest in Scotland – operated here. Consequently, the village atmosphere is decidedly odd (not helped by a recent financial scandal concerning local bigwigs), its long, thin layout reminiscent of a Wild West frontier town. Queen Victoria, passing through, wrote that it was "the most tumble-down, poor looking place I ever saw". That said, it is useful as a starting – or resting – point for walkers, or as a base for skiing in the Lecht area during January and February.

Practicalities

In the central square the **tourist office** (April, May & Oct Mon–Sat 10am–5.45pm, Sun 2–5.45pm; June & Sept Mon–Sat 9.30am–6.15pm, Sun 2–6.15pm; July & Aug Mon–Sat 9.30am–7.15pm, Sun 10am–1pm & 2–7.15pm; ☎01807/580285) also acts as the local **museum**, with mock-ups of an old farm kitchen and a smithie, and some information on local wildlife and geography (same times; free).

Bus connections to Tomintoul are creaky and generally more plentiful from the north; during the summer a thrice-weekly service shuttles along the beautiful long-distance **Speyside Way** footpath (through distillery country and Dufftown) between Tomintoul and Spey Bay on the coast. Details can be obtained from the Grampian public transport unit (☎01224/682222). If you need a place to **stay**, you could try the **youth hostel**, Main St (mid-May to Sept; no phone; Grade 1), or the more luxurious *Glenavon Hotel* on the main square (☎01807/580218; ③), whose bar doubles as the local nightclub. Tomintoul's one B&B is *Conglass Hall*, Main St (☎01807/580291; ②). For **eating**, the *Clockhouse* bistro on Main St serves great food and also rents mountain **bikes** (☎01807/580474).

SKIING THE LECHT

The Lecht offers dry ski slope skiing all year; snow skiing, however, is only possible in January and February. Experienced skiers won't find much to tax them, but for learners the gentle slopes are a good introduction. The Lecht is also Scotland's only area to offer floodlit **night skiing**. Lift passes cost £9.50 a day for adults, £7.50 for a half-day. Ski and boot rental costs £9 a day from the ski school at the base station (☎019756/51440), which also provides tuition for £5 an hour, £12 for four one-hour sessions.

For **information on skiing and road conditions** here call the base station or the *Ski Hotline* (☎01891/654654).

North of the Don

About 13 miles northeast of Tomintoul, **Dufftown** lies at the heart of Speyside, and is a far more amenable base for following the malt whisky trail than nearby **Keith,** a relative ghost town, as is the ancient burgh of **Huntly,** east of Dufftown. **Inverurie,** further towards Aberdeen, is the best centre for walking and exploring castles such as Fyvie to the north. There are good **bus** connections between the main towns, as well as the **rail** line from Inverness to Aberdeen, running through Huntly, Keith and Inverurie.

Dufftown

The cheery community of **DUFFTOWN,** founded in 1817 by James Duff, the fourth Earl of Fife, proudly proclaims itself "Malt Whisky Capital of the World", and indeed it exports more of the stuff than anywhere else in Britain. Dominating the southern approach to the town along the A941 are the gaunt hilltop ruins of **Auchindoun Castle**. Although you can't go inside, it's enjoyable to wander along the track from the main road to this three-storey keep encircled by Pictish earthworks.

Following the A941 through the town brings you past the **Glenfiddich Distillery** (see below) and up to the old Dufftown train station, currently being restored for a steam line through to Keith (they hope to be running diesel trains by summer 1996 and steam by summer 1997). Behind the Distillery, the ruin of the thirteenth-century **Balvenie Castle** (April–Sept daily 9.30am–6.30pm; £1.20) sits on a mound overlooking vast piles of whisky barrels. The castle was a Stewart stronghold, later captured by the Jacobites, and finally abandoned after the 1745 uprising, when it was last used as a government garrison.

Practicalities

The four main streets converge on Main Square, surrounded by craft- and bookshops and cafés. For maps and information on the **whisky trail,** head straight to the **tourist office** inside the rather handsome clock tower at the centre of the square (April, May & Oct Mon–Sat 10am–5.30pm; June & Sept Mon–Sat 9.30am–6pm, Sun 2–5pm; July Mon–Sat 9.30am–6.30pm, Sun 12.30–6pm; Aug Mon–Sat 9.30am–7pm, Sun 12.30–7pm; ☎01340/820501). Also on the square, the *Morven* offers good, cheap B&B **accommodation** (☎01340/820507; ①), while the *Fife Arms Hotel* (☎01340/820220; ③) is a good-value traditional hotel with large rooms. Alternatively, there's the *Davaar* B&B, Church St (☎01340/204640; ②), which also offers excellent, traditional Scottish meals.

For **eating,** try the *Glenfiddich Café* just beyond the tourist office on Church St or, for more substantial meals, the popular *Task of Speyside*, Balverie St, just off the square. Next door, the *Mason Arms* pub has a busy pool room, frequented mainly by a young crowd. The *Grouse Inn* round the corner is quieter, with a good selection of whiskies. **Rent bikes** from *Mini-Cheers* (☎01340/820559), right on the Main Square.

Huntly

Situated on a low plain surrounded by hills, **HUNTLY,** a small town ten miles east of Dufftown and on the main train route from Aberdeen to Inverness, has little going for it today apart from its proximity to the Malt Whisky Trail. There's been a castle here, however, since the twelfth century. It was the power centre of the Gordons, who ruled from **Huntly Castle** (April–Sept Mon–Sat 9.30am–7pm, Sun 2–7pm; Oct–March Mon–Sat 9.30am–4pm, Sun 2–4pm; HS; £1.50), a ten-minute walk from the town centre, down Castle Street and through an elegant arch. Set in a peaceful clearing on the banks of the Deveron river, this is one of the smallest and prettiest castles in the area, despite being rather skeletal. Built over a period of five centuries, it has sheltered the likes of

THE MALT WHISKY TRAIL

Speyside's **Malt Whisky Trail** is a clearly signposted 70-mile meander around the region via eight distilleries. In this so-called Golden Triangle lies the largest concentration of malt-whisky-making equipment in the world. Unless you're seriously interested in whisky, it's best to just pick out a couple that appeal, although the truly unique claims of each malt make it difficult to choose one over another. Hopefully the list below will help.

All the distilleries offer a guided tour (usually free) with a tasting to round it off – if you're driving you will be offered a miniature to take away with you. Indeed, travelling the route by car is probably the best way to do it, but for those without their own transport, the *Speyside Rambler* offers a connecting service to some of the distilleries during the summer; for more information call ☎01343/544222. Alternatively you could rent a mountain bike for around £10 a day from *Mini-Cheers*, 5 Fife St, Dufftown (☎01340/820559).

Cardhu, B9102 at Knockando (May–Sept Mon–Sat 9.30am–4.30pm; Oct–April Mon–Fri only; £2). This distillery was established over a century ago, when the founder's wife, Helen Cumming, was nice enough to raise a red flag to warn local crofters when the authorities were on the lookout for their illegal stills.

Dallas Dhu, Mannachie Rd, Forres (April–Sept Mon–Sat 9.30am–6.30pm, Sun 2–6.30pm; Oct–March Mon Wed & Sat 9.30am–4.30pm, Thurs 9.30am–12.30pm, Sun 2–4.30pm; £2). The last distillery of the nineteenth century, preserved in its Victorian splendour. Easily reached by bus or train.

Glenfarclas, Ballindalloch off the A95, 17 miles southwest of Keith (June–Sept Mon–Fri 9am–4.30pm, Sat 10am–4pm, Sun 1–4pm; Oct–May Mon–Fri only; £2). Includes an exhibition in four languages and a gallery for watching the cask-filling. The whisky here has been described as going down "singing hymns".

Glenfiddich, A941 just north of Dufftown (April to mid-Oct Mon–Sat 9.30am–4.30pm, Sun noon–4.30pm; mid-Oct to March Mon–Fri only; free). Probably the best known of malt whiskies, and the most touristy of the distilleries. Unlike the other distilleries on the trail, Glenfiddich is actually bottled on the premises – prepare yourself for the lethal-smelling bottling plant. The gift shop sells a 50-year-old bottle, a snip at £5000. Right beside the car park you'll see the unspectacular ruins of Balvenie Castle.

Glen Grant, Rothes (May–Sept Mon–Fri 10am–4pm; free). Back in 1840, when it was established, this was Speyside's largest producer, but today this is one of the least interesting stops on the trail. Children under eight not admitted.

Glenlivet, B9008, 10 miles north of Tomintoul (April–Oct Mon–Sat 10am–4pm; free). First licensed distillery in the Highlands, following the 1823 Act of Parliament which aimed to reduce illicit distilling and smuggling. Good display of old whisky tools and artefacts. Children under eight not admitted.

Speyside Cooperage, Craigellachie, 4 miles north of Dufftown (all year Mon–Fri 9.30am–4.30pm, plus Easter–Sept Sat 9.30am–4.30pm; £1.70). After all the distilleries, it's a good idea to see the ancient art of cooperage – the painstaking building of the whisky barrels. Buses to Craigellachie from Elgin.

Strathisla, Keith (mid-May to mid-Sept Mon–Fri 9am–4.30pm; £4). A small old-fashioned distillery claiming to be Scotland's oldest (1786) and situated in a highly evocative highland location on the strath of the Isla river. The malt itself is pretty rare, and used as the heart of the better-known Chivas Regal blend.

Robert the Bruce and James IV (who attended a wedding here), and in 1562 became the headquarters of the Counter-Reformation in Scotland. After the Battle of Corrichie, brought about by the fourth earl's third son's wish to marry Mary, Queen of Scots and which effectively brought the Gordons' 250-year rule to an end, the castle was pillaged and its treasures sent to St Machars Cathedral in Aberdeen. The castle suffered again during the Civil War, when its Irish garrison were starved into submission and the men were then hanged and their officers beheaded. Meanwhile the Earl of Huntly, who had supported Charles I and declared, "you can take my head off my shoulders, but not my heart from my sovereign", was shot against his castle's walls with his escort, after which the place was left to fall into ruin.

Today you can still make out the twelfth-century motte, a grassy mound on the west side of the complex, separated from the outermost wall by a wide ditch within which the foundations of a stone tower house built in 1400 can be traced. The main castle ruin, with its splendid doorway fronted by an elaborate coat of arms, dates from the mid-fifteenth century, though its impressive bay windows are much later additions. In the basement, a narrow passage leads to the prisons, where medieval graffiti of tents, animals and people adorn the walls.

Seven miles south of Huntly and served by the occasional bus, the modest chateau-style **Leith Hall** (May–Sept daily 2–6pm; early to late Oct Sat & Sun 2–6pm; £3) is worth visiting even when closed for a wander around its 286-acre grounds (daily 10am–dusk). Since 1650 home to the Leith and Leith-Hay family, the vast estate of varied farm and woodlands includes ponds, eighteenth-century stables, a bird-observation hide and signposted countryside walks. Inside, you can see personal memorabilia of the successive Leith lairds along with an array of grand furniture and paintings. The sixth, seventh and eighth lairds, were in the armed services overseas, so anyone with military interests or a penchant for British imperial history will have a field day.

Three miles northwest of Huntly, between the A920 to Dufftown and the A96 to Keith (signposted from both), the **North East Falconry Centre** (March–Sept daily 10am–6pm; Oct & Nov daily 10am–4pm; £3.50) is home to some fabulous falcons, owls and eagles, with flying demonstrations four times daily.

Practicalities

Huntly's **tourist office**, 7a The Square (April to late Oct daily 10am–5pm, July & Aug till 6pm; ☎01466/792255), is most useful for finding accommodation – they charge you ten percent, redeemable on the first night's stay.

One of the area's best **B&Bs** is *Faitch Hill Farmhouse* (☎01466/720240; ③), four miles outside town at **GARTLY**, which has won numerous awards for outstanding cooking and hospitality. In Huntly itself, the *Dunedin Guest House*, 17 Bogie St (☎01466/794164; ②), near the train station, is a good bet, or for more luxury, you could try *Huntly Castle Hotel* (☎01466/792696; ④), the former home of the Duke of Gordon, which stands just behind the castle ruins. A couple of miles north of the main road to Keith is the best **pub** in the region: the *Borve Brew House* at Ruthven, where the home-brewed specialist ales draw people from miles. **Bikes** can be rented from the *Nordic Ski Centre* on the Hill of Haugh (☎01466/704428).

Inverurie and around

From Huntly the A96 and the rail line sweep southeast towards the coast, where some 17 miles west of Aberdeen, the granite town of **INVERURIE** makes the most convenient base for visiting a number of relics and castles in the area. The tiny **tourist office** is in the town hall on Market Place (early April to May & Oct daily 10am–1.30pm & 2–5pm; June & Sept daily 10am–5pm; July & Aug daily 10am–6pm; ☎01467/620600), a few yards from the station. Despite its size, it has a large stash of leaflets useful for finding the local sites, which are often badly signposted. Before leaving Inverurie, catch if you can the **Thainstone Mart**, just off the A96 south of town, one of Europe's largest most impressive livestock sales (Mon, Wed, Thurs & Fri). On Sundays, an indoor market and car boot sale take over.

The closest of the ruined castles, within walking distance of the centre, towards the south end of town, is the **Bass**. What appears to be two unimpressive large tufted mounds in the middle of a field, with stairs leading to the 60ft summit, was in fact the first Norman motte and bailey castle in this part of Scotland, built in 1160 by David, the youngest brother of King Malcolm IV.

Bennachie

The granite hill **Bennachie**, two miles west of town, is possibly the site of the Mon Graupius, Scotland's first ever recorded battle in 84 AD when the Romans defeated the Picts. At 1733ft, this is one of the most prominent tors in the region, and is traditionally embarked upon by walkers from near the **Chapel of Garioch** (pronounced "Geery") off the A96 about five miles northwest of town. Allow two hours for the hike up Bennachie, and try to avoid the weekends when it can be busy – from the top you can see every ancient monument in the district and beautiful vistas of Aberdeenshire.

Maiden Stone and Loanhead Stone Circle

Six miles northwest of Inverurie on the B9001, the spooky **Loanhead Stone Circle** has been standing in this beautiful location since 5000 or 4000 BC. Ten upright stones and a recumbant enclose a low ring cairn; the amount of bones buried below – the remains of over 30 people – suggests that the circle was used for rituals around 1500 BC. A couple of miles further northwest, protruding from the edge of a field, the **Maiden Stone** is a 10ft Pictish gravestone, carved from red granite and inscribed with, among other things, dragons, an elephant, a comb and a mirror. No one quite knows who was buried here, but legend has it as the daughter of a laird who died in mysterious circumstances during her elopement.

Fyvie Castle

Some thirteen miles north of Inverurie and on the bus route, stands the huge, ochre mansion of **Fyvie Castle** (May & Sept daily 2–6pm; June–Aug daily 11am–6pm; early Oct Sat & Sun 2–6pm; NTS; £3). Scottish Baronial to the hilt, Fyvie's fascinating roofscape sprouts five curious steeples, one for each of the families who lived here from the thirteenth to the twentieth century. Beginning life as a typical courtyard castle, with a protective wall over 6ft thick, over the ensuing centuries the place met with considerable architectural expansion. The Chancellor of Scotland bought Fyvie in 1596 and was probably responsible for the elaborate south front with its gables and turrets; his grandson sympathized with the Jacobites and, following his exile, the estate was confiscated and handed over to the Gordons. In 1889 the castle was sold to the Forbes-Leith, a local family which had made a fortune in America and which was responsible for the grand Edwardian interior. The exquisite dining room is nowadays rented out for corporate entertaining by oil companies who hob-nob among the Flemish tapestries, Delft tiles and the fine collection of paintings that includes feathery Gainsborough portraits and 12 works by Sir Henry Raeburn.

The coast to Forres

The **coastal region** of northeast Scotland from Aberdeen to Inverness is a rugged, often bleak, landscape which is in parts virtually inaccessible. Still, if the weather is good, it's well worth spending a couple of days meandering through the various little fishing villages and the miles of deserted, unspoilt beaches. Keen walkers have the best run of the area; some of the cliffs are so steep that you have to hike considerable distances to get the best views of the coast.

Most visitors bypass **Peterhead** and **Fraserburgh**, the two largest communities, and head instead to smaller places such as **Cruden Bay** with its good beach, or the idyllic village of **Pennan** and nearby **Cullen**. The other main attractions are the working abbey at **Pluscarden** and the Findhorn Foundation, an infamous spiritual community, near **Forres**.

This area is fairly well served by buses, and trains from Aberdeen and Inverness stop at Elgin, Forres and Nairn. Even so, it's preferable to have your own **transport** for reaching some of the best, far-flung places.

Pitmedden Gardens to Peterhead

Fourteen miles north of Aberdeen, just on the outskirts of Pitmedden village, the **Pitmedden Gardens** (May–Sept daily 10am–5.30pm; £3) are the creation of Alexander Seton – formerly Lord Pitmedden, before James VII removed his title as punishment for opposing his Catholicism. Seton spent his enforced retirement on perfecting an elaborate garden project he had begun in 1675, and today the utterly orderly gardens, 471 feet square, have been restored to their seventeenth-century pattern, comprising an upper and lower enclosure filled with floral designs, neat box hedges, pavilions, fountains and sundials. In the lower garden (best viewed from the terrace), the layout of three of the flowerbeds mimics those of Holyroodhouse in Edinburgh, while the fourth flowerbed, with its crest of arms, and the weather vane, surmounted by soldiers, are tributes to Seton's father who died fighting against the Covenanters in Aberdeen. Entrance to the gardens also takes in the **Museum of Farming Life**, where you'll see old tools and a chilly, dark bothy that was once home to the workers of the 100-acre Pitmedden estate.

Tolquhon Castle
One of the area's most secluded ruins, **Tolquhon Castle** (April–Sept Mon–Sat 9.30am–7pm, Sun 2–7pm; Oct–March Mon–Sat 9.30am–4pm, Sun 2–4pm; £1.50), is tucked away off a dirt track a mile or so northwest of Pitmedden. Of the medieval remains, the gatehouse facade is the most prepossessing; very much intact, it has a handsome arched portal protected by drum towers and enriched with all manner of sculpted figures and coats of arms. You can still make out what each room was used for: the kitchen has two huge ovens gouged out of the wall, and one of the bedrooms is complete with a dungeon with an ominous trapdoor – even in the sixteenth century, responsibility for law and order still fell on the local laird and at any one time there could have been eight or nine prisoners below.

To the right of the castle, along another mud track, a converted farmhouse turned **art gallery** (Mon–Wed, Fri & Sat 11am–5pm, Sun 1–5pm; free) exhibits local art and sells expensive jewellery and crafts.

Haddo House and Gardens
Four miles north of Pitmedden, the huge Palladian mansion of **Haddo House** (Easter–June & Sept daily 1.30–5.30pm; July & Aug daily 11am–5.30pm; Oct Sat & Sun 1.30–5.30pm; NTS; £3.50), completed to a design by William Adam in 1735, is set in 177 acres of woodland, lakes and ponds. Since 1731 Haddo has been the seat of the Gordons and several earls and marquesses of Aberdeen – the grounds, now home to otters, red squirrels, pheasants and deer, were created from a wasteland by the fourth earl in the early years of the last century. The house is now renowned for staging local music, drama and arts: check with the NTS in Aberdeen (☎01224/641122) for details of the high-quality productions.

Cruden Bay and around
When the A952 juts east towards Peterhead and the coast, it passes **CRUDEN BAY**, a pretty village with a sandy beach that makes a good starting point for two excursions along the coast. The first, less than a mile due east, is the huge pink granite ruin of

Slains Castle, whose stark beauty overlooking the sea is said to have inspired Bram Stoker to write *Dracula*. This eerie castle, built in 1597 but remodelled in Gothic style in the nineteenth century, is surprisingly badly signposted; it can be reached in about 15 minutes by walking along Cruden Bay's main Bridge Street and through the car park at the end, from where you should just head for the sea and along the cliffs.

A precarious three-mile walk along the cliff north of Cruden Bay, past the castle, brings you to the **Bullers of Buchan**, a splendid 245ft deep-sea chasm, where the ocean gushes in through a natural archway eroded by the sea. This is some of the finest cliff scenery in the country and attracts a variety of nesting sea birds. Alternatively, there's a car park just off the A975, from where a rough (and not particularly safe) footpath leads past some old cottages to the very edge of the chasm.

Peterhead and around

Unless you have a particular penchant for baked-bean factories and power stations, **PETERHEAD**, the easternmost mainland town in Scotland, is best avoided. It calls itself a spa town, but don't let that fool you into imagining anything picturesque: as the busiest white-fish port in Europe, with annual catches valued at over $75 million, the harbour is a mass of rusted, dented and dripping boats which gently ooze oil into the murky waters. Fishing, along with a high-security jail, used to be Peterhead's sole source of income until the arrival of the oil industry in the 1970s. The town's population increased rapidly from 13,000 to 18,000 and though the community is now one of the richest in Britain, many inhabitants say they regret the passing of the less money-orientated days of the past – a yen for the old days that is also evident in the use of the Scottish dialect, Doric.

The oldest building in Peterhead is the 400-year-old **Ugie Salmon Fish House** on Golf Rd at the mouth of the River Ugie, at the north end of town (Mon–Fri 9am–noon & 2–5pm, Sat 9am–noon; free), where you can watch the traditional (and extremely malodorous) smoking of salmon and trout in what is actually Scotland's oldest fish-smoking house – the finished product is for sale at reasonable prices. Peterhead's only other attraction is the **Arbuthnot Museum** on St Peter St (Mon–Sat 10am–1.30pm & 2.30–5pm, closed Wed pm; free), whose array of coins and Eskimo artefacts was collected by the local trader Adam Arbuthnot, born in 1773. The history of local whaling, weaving, cooperage and granite quarrying is also highlighted.

Peterhead's **tourist office** is on Broad St (April, June, Sept & Oct Mon–Sat 10am 5pm; July & Aug Mon–Sat 10am–6pm, Sun 2–5pm; ☎01779/471904); should you be inclined to **stay**, the most comfortable hotel is the modern *Waterside Inn* (☎01779/ 471121; ④), set on the banks of the River Ugie at the edge of town on the A952 towards Fraserburgh. For **eating**, fish and chips is your best bet: the *Tasty Plaice*, on Station Rd, does great fish suppers.

Aden Country Park

From Peterhead, a direct bus travels the nine miles to the 230-acre **Aden Country Park** (daily 9am–dusk; free), just beyond Mintlaw. Laid out in the grounds of an old aristocratic estate, the park includes woodlands, a lake, a river and a huge variety of plant and animal life, and also boasts the **North East of Scotland Agricultural Heritage Centre** (April & Oct Sat & Sun noon–5pm; May–Sept 11am–5pm; free). The main feature of this living history museum is Home Farm, a unique semicircular farmstead built around the beginning of the nineteenth century. A pastoral atmosphere is generated with sound effects of crowing, clucking, mooing and neighing, along with the occasional song, and in the horseman's cottage you'll see demonstrations of traditional home-baking. There's also a thoughtful exhibition on farming techniques from the early primitive, back-breaking farm clearings to today's high-tech machines.

Fraserburgh and the north coast

Ten miles or so north of Aden Park, **FRASERBURGH** is a large and fairly severe look-ing town in the same vein as Peterhead, though its economy still relies only on fishing. An eighteenth-century lighthouse protrudes, oddly enough, from the top of the little sixteenth-century **Fraserburgh Castle** – beware of the weather here: the highest wind speeds in the country, 140mph, were recorded on this spot in 1989. The building now houses the **Scotland Lighthouse Museum** (April–Sept Mon–Sat 9.30am–6.30pm, Sun 2–6.30pm; Sept–April closes at 4.30pm; £2.50; ☎01346/511022), which exhibits lights from lighthouses all over Scotland, has a display on the Stevensons who designed many of them, and includes a tour round the nearby lighthouse at Kinnairds Head.

Though there's little reason to hang around, you can pick up local information from Fraserbugh's **tourist office** in Saltoun Square (April to mid-Oct Mon–Sat 10am–5pm, Sun 2–5pm; July & Aug Mon–Sat 10am–6pm, Sun 11am–5pm; (☎01346/28315). The *Coffee Shoppe*, 30 Cross St, is a great little place for sandwiches, soup and cakes.

It is best to continue on to the hamlet of Pennan, about 12 miles west of Fraserburgh, along a particularly beautiful stretch of coast road lined with pretty churches and cottages and affording the occasional, startling glimpse of the sea below. On the way, you could pause briefly at **Pitsligo Castle** (free access), a spooky ruin half a mile south of the workaday fishing town of **Rosehearty**. Pitsligo is one of the ances-tral homes of the Forbes family, one of whom – multi-millionaire American publisher, Malcolm Forbes – bought and made safe the castle just a year before his death in 1990. Another diversion is to the ruined church (dating back to pre-Norman times) and cave-backed beach at **OLD ABERDOUR**, overlooked by the clifftop ruins of the sadly inaccesible Dundarg Castle. Four miles west of Old Aberdour, a right turn down a steep and hazardous decline leads to **PENNAN**, which came into the limelight when village scenes from the successful British film *Local Hero* were filmed here in 1982. There's little to do but enjoy the view; if the weather is good you can spot the occa-sional shoal of porpoise.

Pennan's sole place to **stay** is the *Pennan Inn* (☎01346/561201; ④), one in the single row of lovely whitewashed cottages huddled together along the seafront and built right into the cliff face. The inn can arrange fishing and boat trips, and its excellent **restau-rant** serves fantastic mussels along with a wide range of whiskies – you'll need to book in advance.

Macduff and Duff House

Heading west along the coast from Pennan brings you after ten miles to **MACDUFF**, a famous spa town during the nineteenth century and now with a thriving and pleasant harbour. In late July, it holds the annual **Tarlair Music Festival** (phone Banff tourist office for details), around a vast clifftop swimming pool, where sound resonates around the rocks and cliffs, to the east of town. Recent years have seen headline acts such as the folk/rock group *Runrig* and pop band *Wet Wet Wet*. Just over the River Devoron via a beautiful seven-arched bridge is the extravagant **Duff House** by the golf course (April–Sept Wed–Mon 10am–5pm; Oct–March Thurs–Sun 10am–5pm; HS; £2.50), an elegant Georgian Baroque house built to William Adam's design in 1730. Originally intended for one of the northeast's richest men, William Braco, who became Earl of Fife in 1759, the house was clearly built to impress, and could have been even more splendid had Adam been allowed to build curving colonnades either side; Braco's refu-sal to pay for carved Corinthian columns to be shipped in from Queensferry caused such bitter argument that the laird never actually came to live here and even went so far as to pull down his coach curtains whenever he passed by.

The house has been painstakingly restored and reopened as an outpost of the **National Gallery of Scotland**'s extensive collection. To give you an idea of how dilapidated this magnificent house had become, study the photos in the rococo vestibule. The first room to the left off the vestibule is the **Prince of Wales' Bedroom**, so called because it was used by the future Edward VII. His mother, Queen Victoira, can be seen, looking unusually fresh-faced, in the bust under the mirror. Most noticeable, however, is the luxuriant four-poster bed, hung in pink damask. Beyond the back of the vestibule is the dining room, hung with ponderous eighteenth-century portraits, amongst which Allan Ramsay's *Elizabeth, Mrs Daniel Cunyngham* leaps out for its delightfully cool composition. To the left is the **Private Drawing Room**, best for the bust of William Adam and the sweeping canvasses of Welsh landscapist Richard Wilson (1714–82). On the other side of the ground floor, Countess Agnes' Boudoir, formerly Lord Macduff's dressing room, contains a riotous gilded rococo mirror and El Greco's heartfelt *St Jerome in Penitence*, which dominates a wall of mainly religious art. This leads into the **Hunting Room**, mainly filled with treasures from Dunimarle in Fife. Magdalene Erskine, who bought the house in 1835 and bequeathed, on her death, its collection to be used to found an art gallery, can be seen as a little girl, added later to the painting of the family grouping by David Allen in 1788. Note how all the women are shown disproportionately tiny and doll-like next to the men and boys.

Ascending the **Great Staircase**, all eyes are drawn to the enormous copy of Raphael's *Transfiguration* by Inverness' Grigor Urquhart (1797–1846). Most of the accompanying portraits are also Scottish. A couple of rooms straight ahead, given over to the local authority, are filled with interpretive and history boards, as well as a stunning model of the house as originally intended, complete with the never-built collonaded wings.

Upstairs, the **North Drawing Room** contains the only piece of furniture original to the house, in the shape of the 1760s mirror, but more obvious is the bewilderingly bold gold and cherry red ceiling, a not entirely successful Victorian pastiche of Adam's style. In the **Great Drawing Room**, William's son Robert Adam's symmetrical Classicism meets French opulence head on, and, somehow, it works. The best example of this is the 1764 furniture suite of two gilded sofas and two chairs originally designed by the younger Adam and built by Chippendale, combining the Classical reference of lion's paw feet and the Rococo influence of florid gold shells.

Outside the house, there are good walks in the parkland, especially along the River Deveron to the noted local beauty spot, the **Bridge of Alvah**, a couple of miles south.

Banff

Duff House is perched on the edge of **BANFF**, the old lodge house near the main car park by the bridge now housing the **tourist office** (April to mid-Oct daily 10am–5pm, until July & Aug until 6pm; ☎01261/812419). Here, you can pay a £1 deposit for a thoroughly enjoyable **walkman tour** of the town, both the grand Georgian upper town and, down by the harbour, the older, scruffier **Scotstown**. There are lots of good views, interesting buildings and juicy snippets of ancient gossip. For sea swimming, head to the **Links Beach** on the west side of town. The other beach, at the mouth of the Deveron, is susceptible to strong currents and is best avoided.

Taking the A97 Sandyhill Road (signposted Aberchirder) southwest brings you, after a mile, to the excellent **Colleonard Sculpture Park**, otherwise known as the world's only garden of archetypal abstractionism. Sculptor Frank Bruce, usually to be found around the site, began his outdoor collection in 1965. A man of immense talent, he carves figures and scenes of great vitality and intensity from tree trunks, which he then places around the wonderfully peaceful site.

Banff is a pretty good base. **B&Bs** include *Castlehill*, 58 Castle St (an extension of the High St (☎01261/818372; ③)), or, over the river in the heart of Macduff, *Mrs Grieg's*, 11 Gellymill St (☎01261/833314; ②). Four miles south of Macduff, off the A497 Turriff road, the elegant and welcoming Regency *Eden House* (☎01261/821282;

③) is in extensive grounds overlooking the Deveron valley. **Camping** is best near the beach at the *Banff Links Caravan Park* (April–Sept; ☎01261/812228). There are plenty of cafés and pubs for **food and drink**, notably the upstanding *Market Arms*, a sixteenth-century town house on High Shore, or the endearingly tatty *Ship Inn* on Deveronside, by the shore.

Cullen

Twelve miles west of Banff, past the quaint village of **Portsoy**, renowned for its green marble once shipped to Versailles, is **CULLEN**, served by bus from Aberdeen. The town, strikingly situated beneath a superb series of snaking rail viaducts, is made up of two sections – Seatown, by the harbour, and the new town on the hillside. There's a lovely stretch of sand, pleasantly sheltered from the winds by the hills behind Seatown, where the colourful houses huddle end-on to the sea – confusingly numbered according to the order in which they were built.

Cullen's lovely old **kirk**, about a 20-minute walk from the centre, dates back to the 1300s, and is still packed out on a Sunday morning. Inside you'll see an ornate lairds' enclosure for the likes of the Duffs and Ogilvies who worshipped here; Alexander Ogilvie, who expanded the church in 1543, is buried in an ornate tomb, and there are a few lairds' graves in the yard, though the holiday apartments beyond the wall rather ruin the atmosphere.

Most of the **B&Bs** are set back from the sea shore on Seafield Place. They're all much of a muchness, but no. 11 is friendly and comfortable (☎01542/840819; ②). There's little action in the evening; a drink and a fish supper at the local pub is probably your best bet.

Elgin and around

Inland, about 15 miles southwest of Cullen, the lively market town of **ELGIN** grew up in the thirteenth century around the River Lossie. It's an appealing place, still largely sticking to its medieval street plan, with a busy main street opening out onto an old cobbled marketplace and a tangle of wynds and pends.

On North College Street, just round the corner from the tourist office and clearly signposted, is the still lovely ruin of **Elgin Cathedral** (April–Sept Mon–Sat 9.30am–6pm, Sun 2–6pm; Oct–March Mon–Wed & Sat 9.30am–noon; £1.20, or £2 joint ticket with Spynie Palace). Once considered Scotland's most beautiful cathedral, rivalling St Andrews in importance, today it is little more than a shell, though it does retain its original facade. Founded in 1224, the three-towered cathedral was extensively rebuilt after a fire in 1270, and stood as the region's highest religious house until 1390 when the so-called Wolf of Badenoch (Alexander Stewart, Earl of Buchan and illegitimate son of Robert II) burnt the place down, along with the rest of the town, in retaliation for being excommunicated by the Bishop of Moray when he left his wife. The cathedral survived this onslaught, but went on to suffer even more during the post-Reformation, when all its valuables were stripped and the building was reduced to common quarry for the locals. Unusual features include the Pictish cross slab in the middle of the ruins and the cracked gravestones with their *memento mori* of skulls and cross bones.

At the very top of High Street is one of the UK's oldest museums, the **Elgin Museum** (April–Sept Mon–Fri 10am–5pm, Sat 11am–4pm, Sun 2–5pm; £1), housed in this building since 1843. Along with the usual local exhibits, there's a weird anthropological collection including reptilian skulls, a shrunken head from Ecuador, a head-hunter's basket decorated with monkey skulls, and Indian sculptures. Strangest of all is the grinning mummy from Peru, thought to have been a princess. The "Making of Moray" exhibition contains an informative display of Pictish remains, which includes a couple of the Burghead Bull stones and fragments from the assumed Pictish royal court nearby at Kinneddar. A few doors back along High Street is *The Legend*, a shop associated with the Findhorn Foundation (see p.387) and a good source of local alternative information.

The newly pedestrianized and extremely handsome High Street, leading west, widens out on to the market place, the Plainstones, and the impressive Neoclassical parish **church of St Giles** (July & Aug Mon–Fri 2–5pm), built by Archibald Simpson in 1827–8.

Just outside the centre on the A941, a converted mill makes a light and airy venue for the **Moray Motor Museum** (April–Oct daily 11am–5pm; £1.50), a collection of some 25 ancient, fully polished vehicles including a 1929 Rolls Royce Phantom, a 1920 Jaguar, a 1914 Renault, a great old Bentley and a selection of motorbikes with their side cars.

Practicalities

Elgin is well served by public transport, with the Aberdeen–Inverness train stopping here several times a day. The **bus station** is at the opposite end of High St (✆01343/544222), while the **train station** (call Inverness ✆01463/238924 for information) is slightly less convenient on the south side of town on Station Rd (turn right out of the station, left at the island and up Moss St to reach the centre).

The **tourist office**, 17 High St (Jan–March, Nov & Dec Mon–Fri 9.30am–5pm; April, May & Oct Mon–Fri 9.30am–5.45pm, Sat 9.30am–1pm & 2–5.45pm; June & Sept Mon–Sat 9.30am 6.15pm, Sun 2 5.15pm; July & Aug Mon–Sat 9.30am–7.15pm, Sun noon–5.45pm; ✆01343/542666), will book **accommodation**. The quiet *Carronvale*, 18 South Guildry St (✆01343/546864; ②), is one of the nicest **B&Bs** in town; for more luxury, the castle-like *Mansion House Hotel* (✆01343/548811; ⑥), one of the most exclusive in the region, offers Scottish and French dishes. For **food and drink**, *Littlejohn's Brasserie*, 199 High St, is part of a popular Scottish chain of TexMex and Cajun theme restaurants. Otherwise, try *Giles Café-bar*, Batchen St, south off the middle of the High St, or the slightly overdone *Thunderton House* pub, Thunderton Place, off High St, part of which is rebuilt from the seventeenth century old Great Lodge of Scottish kings. Other **pubs** include the *High Spirits* in the Old Kirk on Moss St, the fusty old *Ionic Bar*, 37 High St or, for **live rock** and pop, *The Venue* nearby.

Pluscarden Abbey

About seven miles southwest of Elgin, **Pluscarden Abbey** (daily 5am–10.30pm; free) looms impressively large in a peaceful clearing off an unmarked road. Founded in 1230 for a French order of monks, the abbey remains a working facility, its serene interior wafting with the scent of incense and flooded with red and gold light from stained-glass windows. In 1390 Pluscarden was another of the properties burnt by the Wolf of Badenoch; recovering from this, it became a priory of the Benedictine Abbey of Dunfermline in 1454 and continued as such until monastic life was suppressed in Scotland in 1560. The abbey's revival began in 1897 when the Catholic antiquarian, John, third Marquis of Bute, started to repair the building. His son donated it, in 1948, to a small group of Benedictine monks from Gloucester, who are still in the process of restoring the place, having introduced modern additions such as the splendid stained glass.

Lossiemouth, Spynie Palace and Duffus

Elgin's nearest seaside town, **LOSSIEMOUTH**, five miles north across the the flat land of the Laich of Moray, is generally known as Lossie, a cheery (if fairly golf-oriented) resort, blessed with two sandy beaches. The glorious duney spit of the **East Beach** is reached over a footbridge across the River Lossie from the town park. In the easternmost part of the older harbour's grid of stone streets, Pitgaveny Street has the tiny **Fisheries Museum** (Easter–Sept Mon–Sat 10am–5pm; 50p), which includes some interesting scale models of fishing boats and a re-creation of the study of James Ramsay Macdonald (1866–1937), Britain's first Labour prime minister. On Prospect Terrace, above the harbour district in the airier "new" town, laid out in the nineteenth century, there's an excellent viewpoint to his memory.

Lossiemouth's development as a port came when the nearby waterways of **SPYNIE**, three miles inland, silted up and became useless to the traders of Elgin. Little remains of the settlement, although the hulking shape of **Spynie Palace** (April–Sept Mon–Sat 9.30am–6.30pm, Sun 2–6.30pm; Oct–March Sat & Sun 2–4.30pm; HS; £1.20; joint ticket with Elgin Cathedral £2) indicates its former significance.

Until 1224, Holy Trinity Church, which was part of the palace (there's no evidence of it today), was the cathedral of the Bishopric of Moray, before the honour passed to Elgin. The building remained, however, an integral part of the local ecclesiastical set-up, primarily as the bishop's palace, right through until that office was abolished in the Scottish Church in 1689. The enormous rectangular David's Tower – seen looming for miles around – is the largest tower house in Scotland and was built around a previous cylindrical corner tower during the time of Bishop David Stewart (1461–77). Views from the top, over the Spynie Canal, the much diminished sea loch and the Moray Firth, are stunning. Under the tower is a beautiful fourteenth-century beehive-roofed storage cellar. Next door, a slightly later cellar contains the wide-mouthed gun holes installed by Bishop Patrick Hepburn (1538–73), who, as a Catholic, survived the Reformation at Spynie for a full 13 years. The tower overlooks a wide courtyard, fringed with remains of the palace's domestic buildings.

Straight roads and water ditches criss-cross the flat land west of Spynie. Past the sinister shapes and frequent flights of RAF Lossiemouth is the spreadeagled settlement of **DUFFUS**, five miles west of Lossie. Old Duffus is no more than a farm or two and the motte and bailey **castle** (free access). The weight of this stone and lime edifice, which replaced the original timber fortress in the fourteenth century, has proved too much for the artificial mound on which it sits, and a large section – including a well-marked and still odorous latrine – now leans at a rakish angle. New Duffus, two miles northwest, is best known as the gateway to **Gordonstoun School**, the spartan (but hugely expensive) public school favoured by royalty, although Prince Charles reportedly despised its fresh-air-and-cold-showers puritanism. A quarter of a mile down the lane to Gordonstoun lie the remains of the Duffus old kirk, dating from at least 1226. A fine fourteenth-century parish cross, some beautifully inscribed trades graves and an 1830 watch house against grave-diggers are the highlights. Judging by the number of discarded cigarette packets, you're also likely to see a few Gordonstoun pupils at leisure.

Burghead

Nondescript **BURGHEAD** was, before the imposition of the town in 1805–9 – a tightly-packed grid of streets on the natural promontory – the site of an important Iron Age fort and the ancient Pictish capital of Moray. The **Burghead Bulls** were crafted here – at least 25 unique Pictish carvings, all but six of which were destroyed when the town was built; a couple are in the tiny museum (Tues 2–5pm, Thurs 5–8pm, Fri 2–5pm, Sat 10am–noon; free), adjoining the library on the main Grant Street. Others can be seen in Elgin Museum, the Royal Museum in Edinburgh and the British Museum in London. Peeking up among the streets, a few ditches and earthworks can be made out. A **well**, tucked away down King Street (key available from Mrs Main, 69 King St; if she's out, the key and interpretive boards are left in the porch), is the most remarkable surviving feature. Under a barrel roof, an impressive underground chamber surrounds a tank fed by springs, believed to have been the water supply for the Iron Age and Pictish forts. The headland tip, immediately to the west, is pocked with the scant remains of earlier defences. Two earth ramparts meet on Doorie Hill, off Bath Street, upon which an eerie burned out pillar sits. This is where the **Clavie** – a burning tar barrel still carried around the town on 11 January, to mark the old calendar's new year – ends its annual journey. From the harbour, a wide sweep of sandy beach coasts five miles around Burghead Bay to Findhorn.

If you need to **stay** in Burghead, the *Red Craig* hotel (☎01343/835663; ③), in a glorious site above the headland on the east side of town, does B&B, camping, food, drink and regular music and dances.

The Findhorn Foundation

The **Findhorn Foundation** on the B9011, about ten miles east of Elgin (Mon–Sat 9am–5pm, Sun 2–5pm; free), particularly well known in Germany, Scandinavia and the States, is a magnet for soul-searchers from around the world. Set up in 1962 by Eileen and Peter Caddy (see below), the foundation has blossomed from its early core of three adults and three children into a full-blown community, with classes and facilities for hundreds of people. Bizarrely enough, despite its enormous growth, the foundation is still situated on the town's caravan and camping park (April–Oct; ☎01309/690203), creating an intriguing combination of people on site. Many of the original caravans have metamorphosed into more permanent structures, including some fascinating houses and community spaces employing the latest in ecological methods. It's an amazing place and, however cynical you might be, well worth at least a flying visit. The Findhorners have also built a magnificent arts centre, **Universal Hall**, complete with irridescent glass frontage. **B&B** (details from the visitor centre on ☎01309/690311) is available on site. **FINDHORN** village, to the immediate northwest of the Foundation, has a magnificent beach, a delightful harbour and a couple of good pubs. It is the third village of the name; the other two succumbed to the shifting sands of the Moray Firth.

THE FINDHORN FOUNDATION

Just over 30 years ago, with little money and no employment, Peter and Eileen Caddy, their three children and friend Dorothy Maclean, settled on a caravan site at Findhorn. Dorothy believed she had a special relationship with what she called the "devas", in her own words "the archetypal formative forces of light or energy that underlie all forms in nature – plants, trees, rivers, etc", and from the uncompromising sandy soil they built a garden filled with remarkable plants and vegetables far larger than had ever been seen in the area. Dorothy Maclean has since left the foundation, and the gardens, though beautiful, are not quite as outstanding as they once were.

The Original Caravan – as it is marked on the site's map – still stands, surrounded by a whole host of newer timber buildings and other caravans. The Foundation is now home to a couple of hundred people, with around 8000 visitors every year. The buildings, employing solar power, earth roofs and other green initiatives, are remarkable in themselves and show the commitment of the Findhorners to a sustainable future. Public amenities such as the arts centre, holistic health centre, café and excellent shop demonstrate their considerable effort to bring in the local community, most of whom are either indifferent or quietly accepting. Spiritual therapies are on offer, as are classes in numerous holistic healing arts. The Foundation also owns Cluny Hill College and Newbold House in nearby Forres and a west coast island retreat.

As can be expected, the Foundation is not without its controversy, a local JP declaring that "behind the benign and apparently religious front lies a hard core of New Agers experimenting with hallucinatory techniques marketed as spirituality", a predictable enough charge from local conservative thought. Findhorn, now a public company, is also accused of being overly well heeled; certainly any mention of the activities on offer is quickly followed by talk of the cost. However, most people here, although honest about the downsides of community living, are extremely positive about its benefits.

Forres

FORRES, one of Scotland's oldest agricultural towns, is of little note except for its pretty, flower-filled parks. The 20ft **Sueno Stone**, on the eastern outskirts of town, is one of the most remarkable Pictish stones in Scotland, now housed in a glass case to prevent further erosion. The stone was found buried in 1726 and mistakenly named after Swein Forkbeard, King of Denmark, though it more probably commemorates a battle between the people of Moray and the Norse settlers in Orkney. Carvings on the east face can be read as one of the earliest examples of war reportage, with the story told from the arrival of the leader and his guard at the top to the decapitated corpses of the vanquished at the bottom.

Forres has a small **tourist office** (April, May, Oct & Nov Mon–Sat 10am–5.30pm; June & Sept Mon–Sat 9.30am–6pm, Sun 2–5pm; July & Aug Mon–Sat 9.30am–6.30pm, Sun noon–6pm; ☎01309/672938), tucked away in the town's pitifully dull **Falconer Museum** (May, June, Sept & Oct Mon–Sat 10am–5.30pm; July & Aug Mon–Sat 9.30am–6.30pm, Sun 2–5pm; Nov–April Mon–Sat 10am–4.30pm; free) on Tolbooth St, just off High St. **Buses** stop outside St Leonard's Church on High St. Call *Northern Scottish* in Elgin (☎01343/544222) for details of buses heading east, and *Highland Scottish* in Inverness for details of services to the west. If you want **to stay** in Forres, try the *Tormhor* **B&B**, 11 High St (☎01309/673837; ③), which has large, comfortable rooms in a Victorian house overlooking splendid flower-filled gardens.

Brodie Castle

Eight miles east of Nairn (see p.404), just off the A96, **Brodie Castle** (April–Sept Mon–Sat 11am–5.30pm, Sun 1.30–5.30pm; NTS; £3.50/£1.80), dating from 1567, is a classic Z-shaped Scottish tower house set in lovely grounds (open all year; free) with drifts of daffodils in spring. Although it's now the property of the NTS, the 25th earl of Brodie still lives here, and his presence very much contributes to the albeit slightly stagey country-house atmosphere. The huge, light and airy drawing room with its view of the garden is often used for piano concerts. Inside, there are all the rooms you'd expect: a panelled dining room with fabulous plasterwork, several bedrooms complete with four-posters, and a massive Victorian kitchen and servants quarters, all linked by winding passages. The collections of furniture, porcelain and especially paintings are outstanding, with works by Jacob Cuyp and Edwin Landseer, among others. To end your trip there's a **tearoom**, where the staff dishes out splendid home-baked cakes.

travel details

Trains

Aberdeen to: Arbroath (every 30min; 1hr); Dundee (every 30min; 1hr 15min); Edinburgh (1–2 hourly; 2hr 35min); Elgin (hourly; 1hr 40min); Forres (hourly; 1hr 55min); Glasgow (1–2 hourly; 2hr 35min); Huntly (hourly; 45min); Inverurie (hourly; 20min); Keith (hourly; 1hr); Montrose (every 30min; 45min); Nairn (hourly; 2hr 5min); Stonehaven (every 30min; 15min).

Dundee to: Aberdeen (every 30min; 1hr 15min); Arbroath (hourly; 20min); Montrose (hourly; 15min).

Elgin to: Forres (hourly; 15min); Nairn (hourly; 25min).

Buses

Aberdeen to: Arbroath (hourly; 1hr 20min); Ballater (hourly; 1hr 45min); Banchory (hourly; 55mins); Banff (hourly; 1hr 55min); Braemar (4–6 daily; 2hr 10min); Crathie (for Balmoral) (4–6 daily; 1hr 55min); Cruden Bay (hourly; 50min); Cullen (hourly; 1hr 50min–2hr 30min); Dufftown (2 weekly; 2hr 10min); Dundee (hourly; 2hr); Elgin (hourly; 2hr 35min–3hr 40min); Forfar (2 daily; 1hr 20min); Forres (5 daily; 2hr 35min); Fraserburgh (hourly; 1hr 20min); Fyvie (hourly; 1hr); Huntly (2 daily; 1hr 35min); Inverurie (4 daily; 45min); Macduff (hourly; 1hr 50min); Mintlaw (for Aden Park) (hourly; 50min); Montrose (hourly; 1hr); Nairn (5 daily; 2hr 50min); Peterhead (every 30min; 1hr 15min); Pitmedden (hourly; 50min); Stonehaven (every 30min; 25–45min).

Ballater to: Crathie (June–Sept 3 weekly; 15min); Tomintoul (June–Sept 1 daily; 1hr).

Banchory to: Ballater (June–Sept 2 weekly; 45min); Braemar (June–Sept 2 weekly; 1hr 20min); Crathie (June–Sept 2 weekly; 1hr); Spittal of Glenshee (June–Sept 2 weekly; 2hr).

Dufftown to: Elgin (7 daily; 1hr); Keith (5 weekly; 40min).

Dundee to: Aberdeen (hourly; 2hr); Arbroath (every 15min; 40min–1hr); Blairgowrie (every 30min; 50min–1hr); Forfar (every 30min; 30min); Glamis (2 daily; 40min); Kirremuir (hourly; 1hr 10min); Meigle (hourly; 40min); Montrose (hourly; 1hr 15min).

Elgin to: Aberdeen (hourly; 3hr 15min); Burghead (Mon–Sat hourly; 30min); Duffus (Mon–Sat hourly; 15min); Forres (hourly; 25min); Huntly (3 daily; 50min); Inverurie (3 daily; 1hr 45min); Lossiemouth (every 30min; 20min); Nairn (4–6 daily; 40min); Pluscarden (1 daily; 20min); Tomintoul (June–Sept 1 daily; 1hr 15min).

Forres to: Elgin (hourly; 25min); Findhorn (Mon–Sat 8 daily; 20min).

Fraserburgh to: Banff (2 daily; 55min); Macduff (2 daily; 45min).

Montrose to: Brechin (hourly; 20min).

Peterhead to: Cruden Bay (every 30min; 20min).

Ferries

Aberdeen to: Faroe Islands (1 weekly; 22hr); Lerwick, Shetland (6 weekly; 14hr); Stromness, Orkney (1 weekly; 10hr).

Flights

Aberdeen to: Dundee (1 daily; 35min); Edinburgh (4 daily; 40min); Glasgow (3 daily; 45min); Birmingham (Mon–Fri 2 daily; 1hr 30min); London (Heathrow 8 daily, Manchester (Mon–Fri 6 daily, Sat 2, Sun 1; 1hr 20min); Stansted 3 daily, Gatwick 4 daily; 1hr 30min).

CHAPTER EIGHT

THE HIGHLANDS

Scotland's **Highlands** cover the northern two thirds of the nation and encompass some of its most fabulous scenery: mountains, glens, lochs and rivers contrast with moorland and fertile farms, and the whole sparsely populated area is surrounded by a magnificent coastline. This varied landscape is without doubt the main attraction of the region, but you may be surprised at just how remote much of it is. The vast peat bogs in the bleak north, for example, are among the most extensive and unspoilt wilderness areas in Europe, while a handful of the west coast's isolated crofting villages can still only be reached by boat.

Exposed to slighty different weather, and, to some extent, different historical influences, each of the three coastlines has its own distinct character. Along the fertile **east coast**, green fields and woodland run down to the sweeping sandy beaches of the **Moray, Cromarty,** and **Dornoch Firths**, while further northeast, rolling moors give way to peaty wastes and sheep country. Stretching east–west from **John O'Groats** to the wind-lashed **Cape Wrath**, the **north coast** proper, backed by the vast and ecologically unique bog lands of the **Flow Country**, is wilder and more rugged, with sheer cliffs and sand-filled bays bearing the brunt of frequently fierce Atlantic storms. Visitors with limited time tend to stick to the more scenic **west coast**, whose jagged shoreline of sea lochs, rocky headlands and white-sand coves is set against some of Scotland's most dramatic mountains, looking across to the Hebrides on the horizon.

Cutting diagonally across the heart of the southern Highlands, the **Great Glen** provides an alternative focus for your travel, linking the long thin sliver of **Loch Ness**, in the centre of the region, with the key towns of Inverness on the east cost, and Fort William in the west. From here it's possible to branch out to some fine scenery, most conveniently the great mass of **Glen Coe**, but also the remote and tranquil **Ardnamurchan peninsula** and the lochs and glens that lead up to **Kyle of Lochalsh** – the most direct route to Skye (see p.303). In the opposite direction, south of the Great Glen, the ski resort of **Aviemore** makes a convenient – if not the most appealing – base for exploring the spectacular **Cairngorm Mountains**.

Of the major urban centres of the Highlands, **Inverness** is an obvious springboard for more remote areas, with its good transport links and facilities, while on the western

---

SAFETY IN THE SCOTTISH HIGHLANDS

The **mountains** of the Scottish Highlands, while not as high or as steep as the Alps, are so far north that weather conditions – including blizzards and icy winds of up to 100mph – can be fatal. In 1993, some 54 climbers died, many of them inexperienced walkers who did not realize the levels of danger involved. It's essential to take proper precautions. *Always* put safety first: never underestimate just how fast the weather can change (or how extreme the changes can be); don't venture off-track if you're inexperienced; and be sure to set out properly equipped, with warm, waterproof clothing, decent footwear, a compass, all the maps you might need, and some food in case you get stuck. Make sure, too, that someone knows roughly where you have gone and when you expect to be back (remember to contact them again on your return).

GETTING AROUND THE HIGHLANDS

Unless you're prepared to spend weeks on the road, the Highlands are simply too vast to see in a single trip. Most visitors, therefore, base themselves in one or two areas, exploring the coast on foot, and making longer hops across the empty interior by car, bus or train. **Getting around** the Highlands, particularly the remoter parts, is obviously easiest if you've got your own transport, but with a little forward planning you can see a surprising amount using **buses** and **trains**, especially if you fill in with **postbuses** (timetables are available at most post offices). The infamous A9, a fast but notoriously dangerous road, is a key route into the area, sweeping north from Inverness; in the west, the A82, which follows the line of the Great Glen, and the A835, which leads north across the interior, are the main arteries. However, the most romantic approach to the region has to be via the famous **West Highland Railway**, Scotland's most scenic and brilliantly engineered rail route, which crosses country that can otherwise only be seen from long-distance footpaths. The line has been under threat for the past few years from cut-backs forced by the recent privatization of *British Rail* (now *Scotrail*), but looks safe for the time being. After climbing around Bein Odhar on a unique horseshoe-shaped loop of viaducts, the line traverses desolate Rannoch Moor, where the track had to be laid on a mattress of tree roots, brushwood and thousands of tons of earth and ashes. Skirting Loch Ossian, the train then circumnavigates Ben Nevis to enter Fort William from the northeast, through the dramatic Monessie Gorge and the southernmost reach of the Great Glen.

coast, **Fort William**, backed by Ben Nevis, and the planned eighteenth-century port of **Ullapool** are both well placed for exploring some of the spellbinding countryside. In the northeast, **Thurso** is a solid stone town with a regular ferry service to the Orkneys, and the old port of **Wick** was once the centre of Europe's herring industry – although it's fair to say that neither of these towns are particularly endearing in themselves. Further south lie **Dornoch**, with its sandstone fourteenth-century cathedral, and **Cromarty**, whose vernacular architecture ranks among Scotland's finest.

INVERNESS AND AROUND

Inverness, 105 miles northwest of Aberdeen on the A96, is the largest town in the Highlands – a good base for day trips and a jumping-off point for many of the more remote parts of the region. You could do worse than spend a day here, looking around the shops, museums and the striking sandstone castle that presides imperiously over the town. To some extent, the area around the **Moray Firth** is a commuter belt for Inverness, but it also boasts a lovely coastline and some of the region's best castles and historic sites. The gentle, undulating green landscape is well tended and tranquil; a fertile contrast to the windswept moorland and mountains that virtually surround it.

A string of worthwhile sights punctuates the main coast route to Inverness from Aberdeen. The low-key holiday resort of **Nairn**, with its long white-sand beaches and championship golf course, stands within striking distance of several monuments, including the whimsical **Cawdor Castle**, featured in Shakespeare's *Macbeth*, and **Fort George**, one of several impressive Hanoverian bastions erected in the wake of the Jacobite rebellion. The infamous battle and ensuing massacre that ended Bonnie Prince Charlie's ill-fated uprising took place on the outskirts of Inverness at **Culloden**, where a small visitor centre and memorial stones recall the gruesome events of 1745.

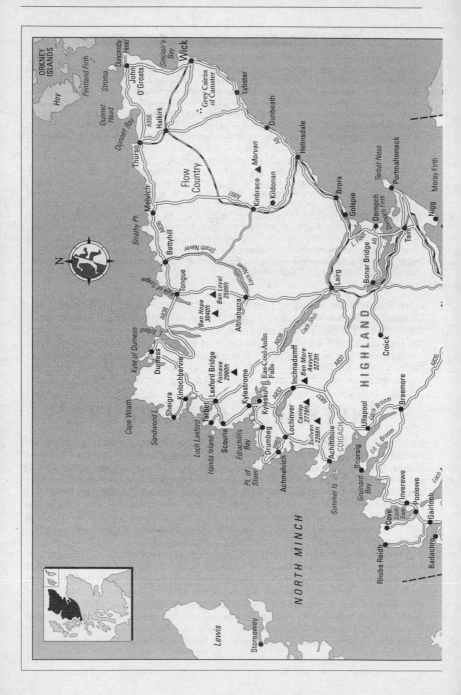

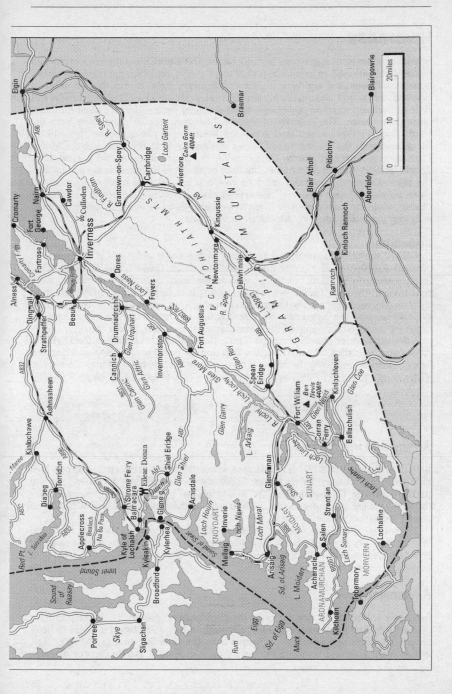

Inverness

Straddling a nexus of major road and rail routes, **INVERNESS** is the prosperous hub of the Highlands, and an inevitable port of call if you're exploring the region by public transport. **Buses** and **trains** leave for communities right across the far north of Scotland, and it isn't uncommon for people from as far afield as Thurso, Durness and Kyle of Lochalsh to travel down for a day's shopping here – Britain's most northerly chain-store centre. The majority of visitors, however, approach the town from the south, dropping down to sea level across the heather-clad plateau of the Monadhliath Mountains, with the snow-streaked slopes of Ben Wyvis to the west and the Moray Firth tapering away northwards. The journey to the centre is less scenic, passing miles of light industry and car showrooms, but once beyond this Inverness is not an unattractive place. Crowned by a pink sandstone **castle**, it has retained much of its medieval street layout (although unsightly concrete blocks overshadow the period buildings in places), while the salmon-packed River Ness, which flows through the centre, is lined with leafy parks and prosperous-looking stone houses.

Some history

Inverness' sheltered harbour and proximity to the open sea made it an important entrepôt and shipbuilding centre during medieval times. David I, who first imposed a feudal system on Scotland, erected a castle on the banks of the Ness to oversee maritime trade in the early twelfth century, promoting it to Royal burgh status soon after. Bolstered by receipts from the lucrative export of leather, salmon and timber, the town grew to become the kingdom's most prosperous northern outpost, and an obvious target for the marauding Highlanders who plagued this remote border area.

A second wave of growth occurred during the eighteenth century as the Highland cattle trade flourished. The arrival of the **Caledonian canal** and rail link with England brought further prosperity, heralding a tourist boom that reached its highpoint in the Victorian era, fostered by the English royal family's enthusiasm for all things Scottish.

> The telephone code for Inverness is ☎01463.

Arrival and information

Inverness **airport** (☎232471) is at Dalcross, seven miles east of the city; an airport bus, #311 (Mon–Fri 11 daily, Sat 7; 10min; £2.30), meets most flights. A **taxi** will set you back around £10. The **bus station** (☎233371) lies just behind Academy St, one of the three city-centre main streets not pedestrianized; the **train station** (☎238924) is nearby on Station Square.

The **tourist office**, five minutes' walk from the station towards the river on Castle Wynd (Mon–Fri 9am–5pm, Sat & Sun 10am–4pm; ☎234353), stocks a wide range of literature on the area, and will book accommodation. The friendly staff also hands out useful free maps of the city and environs.

Accommodation

Inverness is one of the few places in the Highlands where you're unlikely to have problems finding **somewhere to stay**, although in July and August it's wise to book ahead. The main agglomeration of **hotels** is on the riverside south of Ness Bridge, where you'll also find some of the town's most congenial **B&Bs**. Scores of other

TOURS AND CRUISES

Inverness is the departure point for a range of day **tours** and **cruises** to nearby attractions, including Loch Ness and Moray Firth areas, which can be difficult to reach on public transport. Among the most popular is *Guide Friday*'s open-topped double decker tour of **Inverness** (every 40min; £4) which lasts between 30min and 2hr, depending on how many times you get on and off the two buses that run the circular route; and the Culloden tour (every 40min; £6). Tickets can be bought on the buses, which leave from the tourist office or at *Guide Friday*'s booth in the train station; both also act as booking agents for the several bus companies running tours to **Loch Ness**. Prices range between £6 and £10 depending on the duration of the trip and the standard of transport. Among the best deals is the *Forbes* minibus tour (book through the tourist office). Alternatively, take in the Loch **by boat**. *Jacobite Cruises* (☎710188) runs round trips from its mooring on Glenurquart Rd, a mile and a half south of the town centre near Ness Islands (May–Sept 10am & 2pm; £8/£6). Finally, buses leave Inverness every day during the summer for the gruelling whistle-stop bus tour of the **Orkney Islands** (7.30am–9pm; £39). Advance bookings may be made at the tourist office, or on ☎1955/611353). For **Dolphin spotting cruises** see p.402.

small B&B places are scattered along Kenneth St, five minutes' walk west of the river. The town's two budget travellers' **hostels** are more central, a stone's throw up the hill from the castle.

You can pre-book accommodation through the tourist office, or in the train station concourse at the *Thomas Cook* booth, but bear in mind that both places levy a booking fee, and charge the hotel or guest-house owner a hefty commission that is then passed on to you in your room tariff.

Hotels

Brae Ness, Ness Bank (☎712266). A homely Georgian hotel overlooking the river and St Andrew's Cathedral with a non-smoking licensed restaurant for residents. ④.

Columba, Ness Walk (☎231391). Huge, central hotel opposite the castle and just over the bridge from the town centre, whose tariffs, which include breakfast, drop at weekends. Popular with bus parties and business people. ⑤.

Glen Mhor, 9–12 Ness Bank (☎234308). Large, welcoming riverside hotel 5 minutes from the centre, with friendly owners, solidly Scottish ambience, and a popular restaurant. Discounts for stays of 2 days or more; good value at this price. ④.

ACCOMMODATION PRICE CODES

Throughout this book, accommodation **prices** have been graded with the numbers below, according to the cost of the least expensive double room in high season. Although costs will rise slightly overall with the life of this edition, the relative comparisons should remain valid. The bulk of the recommendations will fall in categories ② to ⑥; those in the highest categories are limited to places that are especially attractive. Edinburgh will inevitably be more expensive than equivalent accommodation in the countryside or small towns, and a number of places will have a big mark-up for the three weeks of the Festival. Also bear in mind that many of the swanky hotels often slash their tariffs at the weekend when the business types have gone home, and that many of the cheaper places will also have more expensive rooms. Note that in our accommodation listings price codes are not given for youth hostels and campsites – they all come into the lower end of the ① category.

① under £20	④ £40–50	⑦ £70–80
② £20–30	⑤ £50–60	⑧ £80–100
③ £30–40	⑥ £60–70	⑨ over £100

Glenmoriston, 20 Ness Bank (☎712738). Very classy and comfortable hotel slap on the riverside with well-appointed rooms and a top-notch Italian restaurant. ⑦.

B&Bs

Craigside Lodge, 4 Gordon Terrace (☎231576). Spacious rooms, great views, and close to the centre. Pricier than your average B&B, but worth the extra. ②–③.

Edenview, 26 Ness Bank (☎234397). Very pleasant with a location as good as the expensive hotels, 5 minutes' walk from the centre on the river. Non-smoking. ②.

Heathfield, 2 Kenneth St (☎230547). A very comfy B&B tucked away in a secluded backstreet, with central heating, colour TVs and some en-suite rooms. Plenty of good fall-backs nearby, too. ②.

Kathleen Silver, Old Drummond House, Oak Ave (☎238904). Converted Georgian mansion on the southern outskirts. Great vegetarian breakfasts. ②.

Macrae House, 24 Ness Bank (☎243658). Right on the river, friendly, and with large, comfortable rooms. ②.

Youth Hostels

Inverness Student Hotel, 8 Culduthel Rd (☎236556). A sociable 50-bed independent hostel with laundry, self-catering facilities, breakfasts, fine views and coffee and tea on tap.

SYHA Hostel, Old Edinburgh Rd (☎231771; Grade 1). Big and busy youth hostel in the centre of town, but the management is notoriously misanthropic. Check in early. Closed Jan.

Camping

Bught Caravan and Camping Site, Bught Park (☎236920). Inverness' main campsite, on the west bank of the river near the sports centre. Good facilities, but it can get very crowded at the height of the season.

Bunchrew Caravan and Camping Park, Bunchrew, 3 miles west of Inverness on the A862 (☎237802). Well-equipped site on the shores of the Beauly Firth, with hot water, showers, launderette and a shop. It's very popular with families, so you'll have to contend with hordes of kids as well as the midges.

The Town

The logical place to begin a tour of Inverness is the central **Town House** on Castle Street. Built in 1878, this Gothic-style pile hosted Prime Minister Lloyd George's emergency meeting to discuss the Irish crisis in 1921, and now accommodates the council offices. There's nothing of note inside, but the old **Mercat Cross** next to the main entrance is worth a look. Presiding over the small square where formerly merchants and traders carried out their business, the cross rests on an ancient **Clachnacuddin stone**, or "stone of tubs" – so-called because the washerwomen of Inverness used to rest their buckets on it on their way back from the river. A local superstition holds that as long as the stone remains in place, Inverness will continue to prosper.

Looming directly behind the Town House and dominating the horizon is Inverness **Castle** (mid-May to Sept Mon–Sat 9am–5pm), a predominantly nineteenth-century redsandstone edifice perched above the river. The original castle formed the core of the ancient town, which had rapidly developed as a port trading with Europe after its conversion to Christianity by St Columba in the sixth century. Two famous Scots monarchs were associated with the building: Robert the Bruce wrested it back from the English during the Wars of Independence, destroying it in the process, and Mary, Queen of Scots had the governor of the second castle hanged from its ramparts after he had refused her entry in 1562. This structure was also destined for destruction, held by the Jacobites in both the 1715 and the 1745 rebellions, and blown up by them to prevent it falling into government hands. Today's imposing but hardly inspiring edifice houses the Sheriff Court; you can go in, but there's little to see. Around 7.30pm during the summer, a **lone piper** clad in full Highland garb performs for tourists on the espla-

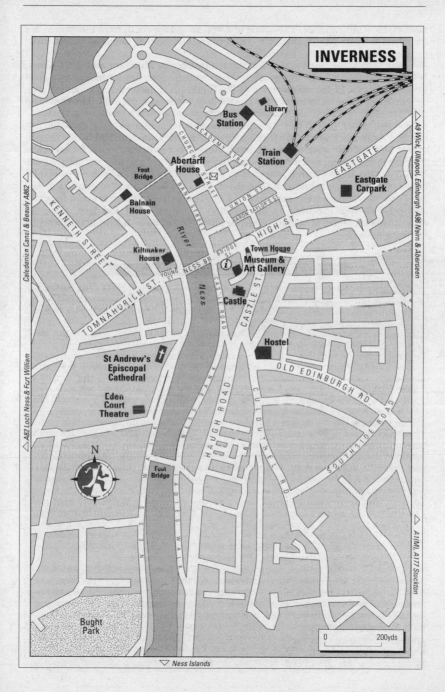

INVERNESS

Library
Bus Station
Train Station
Abertarff House
Foot Bridge
Balnain House
Eastgate Carpark
EASTGATE
ACADEMY STREET
CHURCH STREET
BANK STREET
UNION ST.
BARON TAYLOR'S ST.
HIGH ST.
River Ness
KENNETH STREET
Kiltmaker House
TOMNAHURICH ST.
YOUNG ST.
NESS BR.
BRIDGE ST.
Town House
Museum & Art Gallery
Castle
CASTLE ST.
CASTLE ROAD
Hostel
OLD EDINBURGH RD.
CUDUHEL RD.
SOUTHSIDE ROAD
St Andrew's Episcopal Cathedral
Eden Court Theatre
NESS WALK
NESS BANK
HAUGH ROAD
LADIES WALK
Foot Bridge
N
Bught Park

Caledonian Canal & Beauly A862
A82 Loch Ness & Fort William
A9 Wick, Ullapool, Edinburgh, A96 Nairn & Aberdeen
A1(M), A177 Stockton

0   200yds

▽ *Ness Islands*

nade at the south entrance. The statue of a woman staring south from the terrace is a memorial to Flora MacDonald, the clanswoman who helped Bonnie Prince Charlie escape to Skye in the wake of Culloden.

Before leaving the castle area, check out the **Inverness Museum and Art Gallery**, in the same building as the tourist office (Mon–Sat 9am–5pm; free), which gives a good general overview of the development of the Highlands. Informative sections on geology, geography and history cover the ground floor, while upstairs you'll find a muddled selection of silver, taxidermy, weapons and bagpipes, alongside a mediocre art gallery.

The two other noteworthy historic monuments on this side of town lie five minutes' walk north of the castle down Church Street. Distinguished by its stepped gables and circular stair tower, **Abertaff House** is reputedly the oldest complete building in Inverness, erected in the late sixteenth century and now occupied by the NTS. The **Old High Church,** founded by St Columba in 1171 and rebuilt on several occasions since, stands just along the street, hemmed in by a walled graveyard. Any Jacobites who survived the massacre of Culloden were brought here and incarcerated prior to their execution in the cemetery. Between 12.30 and 1pm, when the church is briefly open to visitors, you'll be shown bullet holes left on gravestones by the firing squads.

THE TRUTH ABOUT TARTAN

Tartan is big business and an essential part of the tourist industry. Every year, hundreds of visitors return home clutching tartan monsters, foreign-made souvenirs tied with foreign-made tartan ribbon, or lengths of cloth inspiringly named Loch This, Ben That or Glen Something-Else, fondly believing that they are bringing authentic history with them. The reality is that tartan is an ancient Highland art form that romantic fiction and commerical interest have enclosed within an almost insurmountable wall of myth.

Real tartan, the kind that long ago was called "Helande", was a fine, hard and almost showerproof cloth spun in Highland villages from the wool of the native sheep, dyed with preparations of local plants, and with patterns woven by artist-weavers. It was worn as a huge single piece of cloth, which was belted around the waist and draped over the upper body, rather like a knee-length toga. The colours of old tartans were clear but soft, and the broken pattern gave superb camouflage; unlike modern versions, whose colours are either so strong that the pattern is swamped or so dull that it has no impact.

Tartan did not become popular in the Lowlands until the beginning of the eighteenth century, when it was adopted as the anti-Union badge of Jacobitism, and it was not until after '45 that the Lowlands took over it completely. The 1747 ban on wearing tartan put an end to the making of tartan in Highland glens; instead, whole villages on the Lowland fringes devoted themselves to supplying the needs of the army and emigrant Highlanders in the colonies and, after the ban was lifted in 1782, those of the home market. The wars abated and the colonies became more self-sufficient, and what had become a major industry faced hard times. At first the remedy was sought in a proliferation of new patterns for, despite the existence of a handful with "clan" names, tartan was, in the main, a small-scale "fashion fabric". Then Sir Walter Scott set to work, glamourizing the clans; George IV visited Edinburgh in 1822 and wore a kilt, and, finally, Queen Victoria set the royal seal of approval on both the Highlands and tartan.

At about this time, the idea that every clan had, from time immemorial, had its distinguishing tartan also become highly fashionable. To have the "right" to wear tartan, one had to belong, be it ever so remotely, to a clan, and so the way was paved for the what's-my-tartan lists that appear in the tartan picture books and the tartan souvenir shops and, even today, make up the foundation of much wishful genealogy. Great feats of genealogical gymnastics were performed in the concoction of these lists but they could not include every name; for others, there were "district", "national" and "political" tartans, which could be worn for what might be called "sentimental" reasons. As more tartans were wanted, more were invented: myth grew upon myth and the art form suffered.

Balnain House

One of Scotland's most novel museums stands over the footbridge that crosses the Ness just below the Old High Church. An immaculately restored, white-painted Georgian mansion, **Balnain House** (Tues–Sat 10am–5pm; £1.50) has a modest performance space and an interactive exhibition that will appeal as much to the casual visitor as folk music aficionados. The exhibition traces the development of Highland music from its prehistoric roots (ringing rocks, cast-bronze battle horns and ancient Gaelic songs) to the modern electric folk-rock. CD listening posts and a short video allow you to sample snatches of numerous other musical styles from the region, including clan-gathering and spell-casting songs, complex Shetland fiddle reels and the haunting choral singing of the Hebrides. There's also a congenial café downstairs where ceilidhs, music sessions and recitals take place throughout the summer, together with a shop selling traditional Highland instruments, CDs and cassettes.

Elsewhere on the west bank

A five-minute walk upstream (south) from Balnain House brings you to the **Kiltmaker Centre** on the corner of Huntly St (mid-May to Sept Mon–Sat 9am–9.30pm, Sun 10am–5pm; Oct to mid-May Mon–Sat 9am–5pm; £2). Entered through the factory shop, a small **visitor centre** sets out everything you ever wanted to know about tartan. The finished products are, of course, on sale in the showroom downstairs, along with all manner of Highland knitwear and woven woollies.

Rising from the west bank directly opposite the castle, **St Andrews Episcopal Cathedral** was intended by its architects to be one of the grandest buildings in Scotland. However, funds ran out before the giant twin spires of the original design could be completed, hence Inverness isn't officially a city, but a town. The interior is pretty ordinary, too, though it does claim an unusual octagonal chapter house.

From the cathedral, you can wander a mile or so upriver to the peaceful **Ness Islands**, an attractive public park reached and linked by Edwardian bridges. Laid out with mature trees and shrubs, the islands are the favourite haunt of local anglers. Further upstream still, the river runs parallel with the **Caledonian Canal**, designed by Thomas Telford in the early nineteenth century as a link between the east and west coasts, joining Loch Ness, Loch Lochy and Loch Linnhe. Today its main use is recreational, and there are **cruises** through part of it to Loch Ness.

Eating and drinking

Inverness isn't famed for its gastronomy, but there is no shortage of passable **places to eat**. The best food is served in the posh riverside hotels, where evening reservations are essential. Otherwise, take your pick from the numerous café-restaurants dotted around town, or, if you're on a tight budget, head across Ness Bridge to the fast-food joints ranged along Young Street, where punters from the nearby pubs tuck into hot pizza or fish and chips after closing time.

Restaurants

Bishop's Table Restaurant, Eden Court Theatre. Upmarket self-service restaurant with a nice bar and views. Imaginative food, with good salads, quiches, soups and a speciality dish daily.

Brahms and Liszt, 75 Castle St. The nearest thing here to a wine bar, serving good-value continental-style snacks and main meals, with occasional live music, late buffets and a well-stocked bar.

Castle Restaurant, 41 Castle St. The locals' choice: an old-established café that does a roaring trade in down-to-earth Scottish food – meat pies and fry-ups with piles of chips. Open at 8am for breakfast; closed Sun.

Dunain Park Hotel Restaurant, Dunain Park (☎224532). Award-winning Scots-French restaurant in a country-house hotel set in lovely gardens on the river just southwest of town. Expensive, but a good choice for a leisurely dinner.

Glen Mhor Hotel Restaurant, 9 Ness Bank (☎234308). Brasserie specializing in classy Scottish cuisine (mainly local salmon, beef and game) for lunch and dinner; particularly generous, moderately priced set Sunday lunches, too.

Hayden's, at *The Islands*, 11 Bank Rd (☎231833). Traditional Scottish dishes with specialities from around the world, including several pasta options. Well placed for pleasant after-dinner strolls beside the Ness.

Lettuce Eat, Drummond St. Seriously filling takeaway sandwiches and soups for under £1.50. Closes at 4pm.

Pizza Gallery, 1 Bridge St. A cheerful, family-run pizza parlour that's actively nice to children.

River café and Restaurant, 10 Bank St, near the Grieg St footbridge (☎714884). Hot and healthy wholefood lunches and evening meals, with a great selection of freshly baked cakes and good coffee.

Rose of Bengal, Ness Bank. This northern outpost of the subcontinent, down on the river bank, provides standard Indian food and tandoori.

Nightlife and entertainment

Nightlife in Inverness revolves around a handful of recently revamped "theme pubs" that host regular live music sessions. You'll have to run the gauntlet of bouncers to get in, and the bands tend to be run-of-the-mill R&B outfits, but drinks are at standard pub prices and the atmosphere easy-going. The ersatz-Irish *Lafferty's*, Academy St, is currently among the most popular of the bunch, along with the *Phoenix* next door and the *Market Bar*, off Church St. *Brahms & Liszt*, a congenial bar-bistro opposite the castle, also lays on bands and complementary buffets most weekends during the summer. However, the town's trendiest **music** and **dance** venue has to be the *Railway Club* on Strother's Lane. In a dowdy working mens' club between the back of the train station and a DIY store, it showcases local **indie bands and DJs** on Fridays and Saturdays.

Finally, the basement café at Balnain House museum, on the east bank of the Ness, opposite Grieg St footbridge, hosts informal **folk sessions** on Thursday nights that sometimes turn into ceilidhs if enough inebriated tourists make up numbers. Entrance is free, and there's a small bar serving malts, bottled beers and filter coffee. In addition, the museum stages regular recitials and workshops by accomplished Highland musicians and touring artists; details are posted in the café and the lobby upstairs.

Cinemas include *La Scala*, Railway Terrace near the bus station (☎233302), which screens the current mainstream movies; while the *Eden Court Theatre* across the river (☎221718) offers popular and art-house alternatives during the summer, together with plays by touring theatre companies.

Listings

Bike rental *Thornton Cycles*, 23 Castle St (☎222810).

Books The *Inverness Bookshop* at Greyfriars' Hall, Church St (☎239947) stocks a vast range of second-hand books, mostly paperbacks and titles relating to the Highlands.

Car rental *Europcar* (☎235337) has an office at the *Highlander Service Station*, Milburn Rd, and a desk at the airport; in town there's a *Hertz* (☎711479) in the train station on Station Square, and a *Budget* (☎235337) around the corner on Railway Terrace; *Sharp's Reliable Wrecks*, the cheapest car rental option, is at the Highland Rail House, Academy St (☎236684).

Exchange The tourist office's small bureau de change (Mon–Sat 9am–noon & 2–8.30pm, Sun 9am–noon & 2–6pm) changes cash and currency for a standard charge of £2.50. *Thomas Cook*, 9–13 Inglis St (Mon–Fri 9am–5pm; ☎711921) is an even cheaper option if you have its travellers' cheques; otherwise, try the *Bank of Scotland*, 9 High St (Mon–Fri 9am–5pm except Wed 10am–5pm; ☎663266), which levies a minimum commission of £5.

Hospital Inverness casualty department (☎704000) is at the Raigmore Hospital, over a mile south-east of the city centre.

Left luggage Train station lockers cost £1 for 24hrs; the left luggage room in the bus station costs around the same but closes at 6pm.

Library Inverness library, housed in the Neoclassical building opposite the bus station, has an excellent **genealogical research** unit (June–Sept 11am–1pm & 2–5pm, Oct–May Mon–Fri 2–5pm) where you can dig up information on your Highland forebears. Consultations with the resident genealogist cost £12 per hour, but are free if shorter than 10 minutes.

Post office 14–16 Queensgate (Mon–Thurs 9am–5.30pm, Fri 9.30am–5.30pm. Sat 9am–12.30pm; ☎234111).

Pharmacy *Boots*, Eastgate Shopping Centre (daily 9am–5.30pm, Thurs till 7pm; ☎225167).

Sports centre The spanking new Inverness sports centre (Mon–Fri 9am–10.30pm, Sat & Sun 9am–5.15pm), over a mile south of the town centre near the river, boasts a large pool, gym and facilities for a wide range of other indoor sports.

Swimming pool The town's main pool (Mon & Tues 8am–7pm, Wed 8am–3pm, Thurs 8am–8pm, Fri 8am–7pm, Sat 9am–9pm, Sun 8–9am & 11am–4pm) is located close to the harbour, half a mile north along the river from the shopping precint

The Moray Firth

East of Inverness lies the fertile, sheltered coastal strip of the **Moray Firth**, its many historic sites and castles accessible as day trips from Inverness, or en route to and from Aberdeen. Both the countryside and the amount of attractions around here make a good contrast to the purely scenic splendours you'll encounter once you head further north into the Highlands. The notoriously dangerous A96 traverses this stretch and is well served by public transport, details of which feature in the accounts below.

Culloden

Overlooked by the bleak and bracken-clad mass of Benn Bhuidhe, the windswept moorland of **CULLODEN** (site open all year, visitor centre Feb–Nov daily 10am–4/5.30pm; NTS; £2), five miles east of Inverness, witnessed the last ever battle on British soil when, on April 16, 1746 the Jacobite cause was finally subdued – a turning point in the history of the Scottish nation.

The second Jacobite rebellion had begun on August 19, 1745, with the raising of the Stuarts' standard at Glenfinnan on the west coast (see p.422). Shortly after, Edinburgh fell into Jacobite hands, and **Bonnie Prince Charlie** began his march on London. The English, however, had appointed the ambitious young **Duke of Cumberland** to command their forces, and this, together with bad weather and lack of funds, eventually forced the Jacobites to retreat north. They ended up at Culloden, where, ill fed and exhausted after a pointless night march, they were hopelessly outnumbered by the English. The open, flat ground of Culloden Moor was also totally unsuitable for the Highlanders' style of courageous but undisciplined fighting, which needed steep hills and lots of cover to provide the element of surprise, and they were routed. After the battle, in which 1500 Highlanders were slaughtered (many of them as they lay wounded on the battlefield), Bonnie Prince Charlie fled west to the hills and islands, where loyal Highlanders sheltered and protected him. He eventually escaped to France, leaving his erstwhile supporters to their fate – and, in effect, the end of the clan system. The clans were disarmed, the wearing of tartan and playing of bagpipes forbidden, and the chiefs became landlords greedy for higher and higher rents. Culloden also unleashed an orgy of violent reprisals on Scotland, as unruly English troops raped

THE DOLPHINS OF MORAY FIRTH

The **Moray Firth**, the great wedge-shaped bay forming the eastern coastline of the Highlands, is one of only three areas in UK waters that supports a resident population of **dolphins**. A little over a hundred of these beautiful, intelligent marine mammals live in the estuary, the most northerly breeding ground for this particular species – the bottle-nosed dolphin (*Tursiops truncatus*) – in Europe, and you stand a good chance of spotting a few, either from the shore, or a boat.

Tursiops truncatus is the largest dolphin in the world, typically growing to a length of around 13ft and weighing between 396 and 660 pounds. The adults sport a tall, sickle-shaped dorsal fin and a distinctive beak-like "nose", and usually live for around 25 years, although a number of 50-year-old animals have been recorded. During the summer, herds of 30 to 40 dolphins have been known to congregate in Moray Firth; no one is exactly sure why, although experts believe the annual gatherings, which take place between late June and August, may be connected to the breeding cycle. Another peculiar trait of the Moray Firth school is its habit of killing porpoises. Several porpoise corpses with serrated tooth marks have been washed ashore in the area, the dolphins tossing dead or dying porpoises around in the waves as if for fun.

Both adults and calves frequently leap out of the water, "bow riding" in front of boats and performing elegant synchronized swimming routines together. This, of course, makes them spectacular animals to watch, and "**dolphin spotting**" has become something of a craze in the Moray Firth area. Arguably the best place in Scotland, if not in Europe, to look for them is **Chanonry Point**, on Black Isle (see p.445) – a spit of sand protruding into a narrow but deep channel, where converging currents bring fish close to the surface, and thus the dolphins close to shore; the hour or so before high tide is the most likely time to see them. **Kessock Bridge**, one mile north of Inverness, is another prime dolphin-spotting location. A team of zoologists from Aberdeen University studying the Moray Firth dolphins has set up a small listening post and **visitor centre** here (daily 10am–5pm; free), where specially installed hydrophones allow you to eavesdrop on the clicks and whistles of underwater conversations.

In addition, several companies run dolphin-spotting **boat trips** around the Moray Firth. However, researchers claim that the increased traffic is causing the dolphins unneccessary stress, particularly during the all-important breeding period, when passing vessels are thought to force calves underwater for uncomfortably long periods. They have therefore devised a "**code of conduct**" for boat operators, based on the experiences of countries where dolphin watching has become highly disruptive. So if you decide to go out on a spotting cruise, make sure the operator is a member of the Dolphin Space Programme's Accreditation Scheme; by the summer of 1995, only four outfits in the Moray Firth had made it on to this list: *Dolphin Ecosee* in **Cromarty** (see p.450), *Seaboard Marine* and *J R Mackenzie* from **Tain** (see p.452), and *Sea Fair Charters* of **Nairn** (see p.404).

and pillaged their way across the region; within a century, the Highland way of life had changed out of all recognition.

Today you can walk freely around the battle site; flags mark the position of the two armies, and **clan graves** are marked by simple headstones. The **Field of the English**, for many years unmarked, is a mass grave for the 50 or so English soldiers who died; and nearby, a stone marks the spot where the Duke of Cumberland is said to have watched the proceedings. Thirty Jacobites were burnt alive outside the old **cottage** next to the visitor centre; inside, it has been restored to its eighteenth-century appearance. The recently inaugurated **visitor centre** itself provides background information through detailed displays and a slide show. In April, on the Saturday closest to the date of the battle, there's a small commemorative **service**. The visitor centre has a reference library, and will check for you if you think you have an ancestor who died here. **Buses** (#12; 15min) leave Inverness eight times daily from the post office to Culloden, the last one returning at 6.30pm from the car park in front of the visitor centre.

The Clava Cairns

If you're visiting Culloden with your own transport, make a short detour to the **CLAVA CAIRNS**, an impressive collection of prehistoric burial chambers grouped around the banks of the Nairn River, a mile southeast of the battlefield. Erected sometime between the fourth and third millennia BC, the three cairns, which are encircled by **standing stones** in a spiny of mature beech trees, are of two different kinds: one with spoke-like stone lines emanating from them, the other with a narrow passageway cut into its middle. Archeological excavations carried out here in the nineteenth century yielded traces of human remains, suggesting that the structures must originally have been tombs, but little else is known about the nomadic herdsmen who are thought to have built them.

Kilravock Castle

Surrounded by lawns and pine trees, **KILRAVOCK** (pronounced Kil*rawk*) **CASTLE** (April–Sept Wed 2–5.30pm, or by prior arrangement ☎01667/493258), five miles north of Culloden, is more like a stately home than a fortress. Dating from the fifteenth century, it is the seat of the Rose family, whose founding father, a Norman, settled here in 1190. The best-known Rose of Kilravock, however, is the one who entertained Bonnie Prince Charlie here on the eve of the battle of Culloden in 1745. Although not a Jacobite himself, the laird felt duty-bound by the traditional code of Highland hospitality to accommodate the rebel prince, even though he feared the consequences. According to one contemporary chronicler, the Duke of Cumberland actually rode out here himself on his 25th birthday to grill Rose over the affair, famously exclaiming, "I hear, sir, you've been entertaining my cousin!". He decided not to punish the Highlander, though, and for some reason left behind his knee-length riding boots, which are displayed in the castle along with the bowl from which Bonnie Prince Charlie is alleged to have been served a glass of punch by his host.

Today, the Rose family maintain Kilravock as a wonderfully old-fashioned **hotel** (same number as above; ③), whose spacious, well-appointed rooms are superb value if you don't mind the ban on alcohol and cigarettes, or grace being said before meals (the establishment is run according to strict Christian principles). In addition, garden enthusiasts should not miss the opportunity to visit the castle **grounds** (Mon–Sat 10am–4pm; free), which harbour a tangle of woodland trails.

Cawdor Castle

The pretty, if slightly self-satisfied village of **CAWDOR**, eight miles east of Culloden, is the site of the **Cawdor Castle** (May–Sept daily 10am–5pm; £4.50), apocryphally known as the setting for Shakespeare's *Macbeth* (the fulfilment of the witches' prediction that Macbeth was to become Thane of Cawdor sets off his tragic desire to be king). Though visitors descend here in their droves each summer because of the site's literary associations, the castle, which dates from the early fourteenth century, could not possibly have witnessed the grizzly historical events on which the Bard's drama was based. However, the immaculately restored monument – a fairy-tale affair of towers, turrets, hidden passageways, dungeons, gargoyles and crenellations whimsically shooting off from the original keep – is still well worth a visit.

The Cawdors have lived here for six centuries, and there are plenty of signs of life as you tour the interior, along with the usual stately-home tapestries, pictures and opulent furniture. As you wander around, look out for the **Thorn Tree Room**, a vaulted chamber complete with the remains of an ancient tree – carbon-dated to 1372 and an ancient pagan fertility symbol believed to ward off fairies and evil spirits. According to Cawdor family legend, the fourteenth-century Thane of Cawdor dreamt he should build on the spot where his donkey lay down to sleep after a day's wandering – the animal chose this tree and building began right away.

A good way to wind up a visit to Cawdor is a stroll around the **grounds**, which feature an attractive walled garden and a topiarian **maze**. **Buses** (#12) run direct to the castle from Inverness post office. The last bus back leaves at 5pm from outside the main gates.

Fort George

Eight miles of undulating coastal farmland and estuarine mud flats separate Cawdor Castle from **Fort George** (April–Sept Mon–Sat 10am–6pm, Sun 2pm–6pm; Oct–March Mon–Fri 10am–4.30pm; £2.50), an old Hanoverian bastion considered by military architectural historians to be one of the finest fortifications in Europe. Crowning a sandy spit that juts into the middle of the Moray Firth, it was built (1747–69) as a base for George II's army, in case the Highlanders should attempt to rekindle the Jacobite cause. By the time of its completion, however, the uprising had been firmly quashed and the fort has been used ever since as a barracks; note the armed sentries at the main entrance and the periodic crack of live gunfire from the nearby firing ranges.

Apart from the sweeping panoramic views across the Firth from its ramparts, the main incentive to visit Fort George is the **Regimental Museum of the Queen's Own Highlanders**. Displayed in polished glass cases is a predictable array of regimental silver, coins, moth-eaten uniforms and medals, along with some macabre war trophies, ranging from blood-stained nineteenth-century Sudanese battle robes to Iraqi gas masks gleaned in the Gulf war. The background blurb detailing the heroic deeds performed by various recipients of Victoria Crosses makes compelling reading. The **chapel** is also worth a look, squat and solid outside and all light and grace within.

Walking on the northern, grass-covered casemates, which look out into the estuary, you may be lucky enough to see the school of bottle-nosed dolphins (see p.402) swimming in with the tide. This is also a good spot for birdwatching: a colony of kittiwakes occupies the fort's slate roof tops, while the white-sand beach and mud flats below teem with waders and seabirds.

The easiest way to get to Fort George by public transport is by **bus** from Inverness (Mon–Sat 7 daily; 20min), or Nairn (3–4 daily; 20min), eight miles east.

Nairn

Apparently one of the driest and sunniest places in the whole of Scotland, **NAIRN**, about six miles north of Cawdor, began its days as a peaceful community of fishermen and farmers. The former spoke Gaelic, the latter English, allowing James VI to boast that a town in his kingdom was so large that people at one end of the main street could not understand those at the other end. Nairn became popular in Victorian times, when the train line offered a convenient link to its revitalizing sea air and mild climate, and today it still relies on tourism: its windy, coastal golf course, the **Links** (venue for the 1999 Walker Cup), is one of the most popular in Scotland – just as well, as the Moray Firth has become a notorious pollution blackspot of late. The town, however, is in top gear for redevelopment: a leisure park, projected marina and yet more golfing amenities are mushrooming at the back of the excellent beach by the harbour. Nearby, amid the huddled streets of old Fishertown (the town centre is known as new Fishertown), is the tiny **Fishertown Museum** (June–Aug Mon–Sat 10am–5pm; free), signposted from the town centre or the harbour. The more interesting exhibits focus on the parsimonious and puritanical life of the fishing families.

Nairn's helpful and well-stocked **tourist office** is at 62 King St (Easter–May, Sept & Oct Mon–Sat 10am–5pm; June–Aug daily 9am–6pm; ☎01667/452753). For **accommodation**, *Greenlawns*, 13 Seafield St (☎01667/452738; ①), is a small **B&B** filled with antiques; although more expensive, the *Golf View Hotel* (☎01667/452301; ④), overlooking the golf course and sea, is also good value. **Bike** rental is available from *Nairn Watersports* (☎01667/455416) down by the harbour.

West of Inverness: the Beauly Firth

West of Inverness, the Moray Firth becomes the **Beauly Firth**, a sheltered sea loch bounded by Black Isle in the north and the wooded hills of The Aird to the south. Since the opening in 1982 of the **Kessock Bridge** across the Moray Forth from Inverness, this whole area has become something of a backwater, although the A862, which skirts the rocky and seaweed-strewn shoreline, affords good views north and west, offering a more scenic alternative to the faster A9 route north.

Beauly

The sleepy stone-built town of **BEAULY**, ten miles west of Inverness, lying at the head of the Firth on the banks of the Beauly River, sits at the mouth of one of Scotland's most renowned salmon-fishing streams. Ranged around a single main street that widens into a spacious market place, the town is of interest only for the skeletal remains of **Beauly Priory** (daily 10am–5pm; free), which lurk at the north end of the square in a quiet graveyard garden. Founded in 1230 by the Bisset family for the Valliscaulian order, it was destroyed during the Reformation and now is in ruins.

The locals will tell you the name Beauly was bestowed on the town by Mary, Queen of Scots, who, on returning from her French chateau, allegedly cried, *"Ah, quelle beau lieu!"* (What a beautiful place!). In fact, it derives from the Lovat family, who came to the region from France with the Normans in the eleventh century. Among the more notorious members of this dynasty was Lord Simon Lovat, whose legendary misadventures included a kidnap attempt on a nine-year-old girl, followed by forced marriage to her mother. He was outlawed for this, but went on to play an active role in the Jacobite uprisings, expediently swapping sides whenever the one he was spying for looked likely to lose. Such chicanery earned him the nickname "The Old Fox of '45", but failed to save him from the chop: Lovat was eventually beheaded in London (ironically enough for backing the wrong side at Culloden). The Victorian monument in the square, opposite the Priory, commemorates the more illustrious career of one of Simon Lovat's descendents, Simon Joseph, the sixteenth Lord Lovat, who founded a fighting unit during the South African Boer War.

Practicalities

Beauly has a surprising number of places to **stay**. The most comfortable, and with a good restaurant, is the modern *Priory Hotel* (☎01463/782309; ⑤) at the top of town, which also has a good restaurant. The *Lovat Arms Hotel* (☎01463/782313; ⑤), at the opposite end of the main street, is a more traditional option, whose conservatory lounge hosts occasional ceilidhs. If you're looking for cheaper accommodation, try the *Heathmount Guest House* (☎01463/782411; ③), one of several pleasant B&Bs in a row of large Victorian houses just south of the *Lovat* on the main road.

Finding **somewhere to eat** in Beauly isn't a problem, either. Both of the town's hotels sport pricy à la carte restaurants, while the *Archdale Hotel*'s cosy café, at the bottom of the square, serves a range of inexpensive snacks and main meals, including several vegetarian specialities. Otherwise, head for the *Beauly Tandoori*, which dishes up moderately priced Indian food to eat in or take away, or the *Genoa Restaurant*, an old-fashioned chippy; both are on the main square.

Muir of Ord

MUIR OF ORD, a desultory little town four miles north of Beauly, is visited in huge numbers for the **Glen Ord Distillery** (July & Aug Mon–Sat 9am–4pm, Sun noon–5pm; Sept–June Mon–Fri 9am–4pm; free), in its northern outskirts overshadowed by brooding Beinn nam Fitheach. Its well-laid-out **visitor centre** explains the mysteries of whisky production with a tour that winds up in the cellars, where you get to sample a selection of the famously peaty Glen Ord malts, most of which find their way into well-known blends on sale in the distillery shop.

Inverness Traction operates two **buses** each day to the distillery (#19 from Inverness bus station at 10am or 2pm); both get you to Glen Ord in time for a tour, leaving around an hour later.

THE GREAT GLEN

The **Great Glen**, a huge rift valley formed 400 million years ago by volcanic upheavals, rips through the southern Highlands from Inverness diagonally across to Fort William. Smoothed by glaciers that only retreated around 8000 BC, it's not particularly spectacular by Scottish standards, but provides an obvious and rewarding route from the east to west coast.

Of the Great Glen's three long, sliver-thin lochs, the most famous is **Loch Ness**, home to the mythical beast and linked to the other two, Loch Lochy and Loch Linnhe, by the **Caledonian Canal**. Surveyed by Thomas Watt in 1773, this famous waterway was completed in the early 1800s by Thomas Telford to enable ships to pass between the North Sea and the Atlantic without having to navigate Scotland's treacherous northern coast. However, only 22 miles of it are bona fide canal; the other 38 exploit the Glen's natural lochs and rivers, flowing west to reach the Atlantic.

The traditional and most rewarding way to travel through the valley is by **boat**. A flotilla of kayaks, small yachts and pleasure vessels take advantage of the canal and its old wooden locks during the summer, among them *Jacobite Cruises* (see p.403 for details). The Forestry Commission has also established an excellent **cycle path** through the Glen, divided into 12 manageable stages that make a tranquil alternative to the hazardous A82. A leaflet outlining the route, through winding timber trails, towpaths and stretches of minor roads, is available at most tourist offices, or direct from Forestry Commission, Strathoich, Fort Augustus PH32 4BT (☎01320/366322). In addition, the Great Glen is well served by **buses**, with four or five daily services between Inverness and Fort William, and a couple of extra buses covering the section between Fort William and Invergarry during school terms.

Loch Ness

Loch Ness' fame has little to do with its appearance. It's long and undeniably scenic, with rugged heather-clad mountains sweeping up from a steep, wooded shoreline, but if it weren't for its legendary inhabitant, **Nessie**, the **Loch Ness Monster**, you'd probably drive past without a second glance – especially as the busy A82, which runs southwest along the north side of the loch to Fort William, gives little opportunity to pull

"NESSIE"

The world-famous Loch Ness monster, affectionately known as **"Nessie"** (and by serious aficionados as *Nessiteras rhombopteryx*), has been around a long time. The first mention of her crops in St Adamnan's seventh-century biography of St Colomba. While on his way to evangelize the pagan inhabitants of Inverness, the saint allegedly calmed the monster after she attacked one of his monks. Present-day interest, however, is probably greater outside Scotland than in, dating from the 1930s when the A82 was built along the loch's western shore. Recent encounters range from glimpses of ripples by anglers, to the famous occasion in 1961 when 30 hotel guests saw a pair of humps break the water's surface and cruise for about half a mile before submerging.

The most convincing sightings, however, have been those backed up by hard photographic evidence. Several seemingly conclusive images are showcased in the two "Monster Exhibitions" at **Drumnadrochit**, but the most impressive of these – including the renowned black-and-white movie footage of Nessie's humps moving across the water, and the photo of her neck and head – have recently been exposed as fakes. Even the respected British naturalist and broadcaster, David Bellamy, once indulged in a "foot print" hoax as a marketing ploy for a brand of monster merchandise he was endorsing at the time.

Hi-tech sonar surveys carried out over the past two decades have failed to come up with conclusive evidence, but it's hard to dismiss Nessie as pure myth. Too many locals have mysterious tales to tell, which they invariably keep to themselves for fear of ridicule by incredulous outsiders. Loch Ness also has an undeniably enigmatic air; even the most hardened cynics rarely resist the temptation to scan the waters for signs of life, just in case . . .

over. Nessie's notoriety, however, ensures a steady flow of visitors through the settlements dotted along the loch, in particular **Drumnadrochit**. Perched atop a rock at the lakeside nearby, **Castle Urquhart**, one of the area's more impressive ruins, also attracts a deluge of bus parties during the summer. Few of these, though, press on as far as **Fort Augustus**, at the more scenic southwest tip of Loch Ness, where you can visit a working Benedictine monastery and watch queues of boats tackling one of the Caledonian Canal's longest flight of locks.

Although the vast majority of visitors travels along the west shore of Loch Ness, on the A82, the opposite, **eastern side** – skirted by the sinuous single-track B862/852 (originally a military road built to link Fort Augustus and Fort George) affords far more spectacular views. However, buses from Inverness only run as far south as **Foyers**, so you'll need your own transport to complete the whole loop around the Loch, taking in the most impressive stretch between Fort Augustus and the high, hidden **Loch Mhor**, where the imposing Monadhliath range looms to the south.

Drumnadrochit

Situated above a verdant, sheltered bay 15 miles from Inverness, **DRUMNADROCHIT**, practically the first chance to draw breath as you head down the A82, is the epicentre of Nessie hype, sporting a rash of tacky souvenir shops and two rival monster exhibitions whose head-to-head scramble for punters occasionally erupts into acrimonious exchanges – detailed with relish by the local press. Of the pair, the **Original Loch Ness Monster Exhibition** (April–June daily 10am–6pm; July & Aug daily 10am–9pm; Sept–Nov daily 10am–6pm; £3.50) is the least worthwhile – basically a gift shop with a shoddy audio-visual show tacked on the side. If you're genuinely interested in "Nessie" lore, the **Official Loch Ness Monster Exhibition** (April–June daily 9.30am–5.30pm, July & Aug daily 9am–8.30pm; Sept & Oct daily 9.30am–6pm; £4.50), though more expensive (and no more "official" than the other), is a much better bet, offering an in-depth rundown of eye-witness accounts through the ages and mock-ups of the various research projects carried out in the loch. **Cruises** of the loch can also be booked here; they leave two or three times daily from **Temple Pier**, and last about an hour (£4.50).

Castle Urquhart

Most photographs allegedly showing the monster have been taken a couple of miles further south, around the fourteenth-century ruined lochside **Castle Urquhart** (July & Aug daily 10am–8pm; Sept–June daily 10am–5pm; £3). Built as a strategic base to guard the Great Glen, the castle played an important role in the Wars of Independence. It was taken by Edward I of England and later held by Robert the Bruce against Edward III, only to be blown up in 1692 to prevent it from falling to the Jacobites. It's pretty dilapidated today, but looks particularly splendid floodlit at night when all the crowds have gone.

Practicalities

By far the nicest **hotel** around Drumnadrochit is the *Lewiston Arms* in the adjoining village of **LEWISTON** (☎01456/450225; ③), an old inn with a big garden and good food – turn right at the *Esso* petrol station. Otherwise there's the family-run *Benleva Hotel* (☎01456/450288; ③) beside the loch. For **B&B**, you could do a lot worse than *Gilliflowers* (☎01456/450641; ②), a seventeenth-century farmhouse tucked away down a country lane in Lewiston, or the modern *Drumbuie* (☎01456/450634; ②), which has great views, en-suite rooms, a guest lounge with a log fire, and a resident herd of Highland cattle. Near the latter and signposted from the main road (take the first turning on the left after the *Esso* station), is the *Loch Ness Backpackers Lodge* at Coiltie Farmhouse (☎01456/450807). They also organize nightly boat trips and have recommended walks outlined on their noticeboards. If you fancy a ride around the Loch on the Forestry Commission's new cycle path, **mountain bikes** may be rented from a stall on Drumnadrochit village green (☎01456/450554); and they provide maps and rain capes on request.

All the hotels in the area serve good **bar food**; in Drumnadrochit the *Glen Restaurant*, and the *Hungry Piper*, 200 yards down the road, cater mainly for bus parties with basic grills, while *Fiddlers Bistro*, next door to the *Glen*, is more upmarket, offering local steaks, salmon and appetizing home-baked pizza.

Glen Urquhart and Glen Affric

You can head west from Drumnadrochit on the A831 through **Glen Urquhart**, a fairly open valley with farmland giving way to scrubby woodland and heather as you near **CANNICH**. The **youth hostel** here (mid-May to Sept; ☎01456/415244; Grade 2) makes a good base for exploring **Glen Affric**, claimed by many to be Scotland's loveliest valley. It's real calendar stuff, with a rushing river and Caledonian pine and birch woods opening out onto an island-studded loch, that was considerably enlarged after the building of the dam, one of many hydroelectric schemes around here. Hemmed in by a string of Munros, the glen is great for picnics and pottering, particularly on a calm and sunny day, when the loch is still, reflecting the islands and surrounding hills.

The area also offers some tremendous **hiking**. Among the most popular routes is the one winding west through Kintail to Shiel bridge, on the west coast near Kyle of Lochalsh (about 25 miles), which takes at least two full days; a remote but recently revamped **youth hostel** (no phone; Grade 2) makes a convenient night stopover halfway into the walk on the banks of the burn above Loch Affric. The trail is easy to follow, but can get horrendously boggy if there's been a lot of rain, so allow plenty of time and take adequate wet weather gear.

Invermoriston and Glen Moriston

Heading south, **INVERMORISTON** is a tiny, attractive village on the shore of Loch Ness, from where you can follow well-marked woodland **trails** past a series of grand waterfalls. Dr Johnson and Boswell spent a couple of nights here planning their journey to the Hebrides; nowadays you could stay at the *Glenmoriston Arms Hotel* (☎01320/351206; ⑤), an old-fashioned inn with more than 100 malt whiskies on offer at the bar.

If you're driving on from Invermoriston to the west coast, roads (A887/87) are good: this is a main commercial (and tourist) route, as there is no access to this stretch of coast from the south. It's a bleak, somewhat awesome stretch through **Glen Moriston** and beside Loch Cluanie, with serious peaks on either side and little sign of human habitation as the road climbs.

Fort Augustus

The south of Loch Ness is far more attractive than its opposite end, and the road skirting the water's edge allows plenty of opportunities to pull over for a little monster watching. **FORT AUGUSTUS**, at the loch's southwestern tip, was named after George II's son, the chubby lad who later became the "Butcher" Duke of Cumberland of Culloden fame; it was built as a barracks after the 1715 Jacobite rebellion. Today, it's a tiny village, dominated by comings and goings along the **Caledonian Canal**, which leaves Loch Ness here, and by its large **Benedictine Abbey**, a campus of grey Victorian buildings founded on the site of the original fort in 1876. The abbey used to house a Catholic boys school, but this was forced to close in 1993 and has now been converted into a go-ahead **heritage centre** (April–Sept daily 9am–5pm; Oct–March daily 10am–4pm; ☎01320/366233; £4), where a walkman tour-cum-sound-and-light-show covers the area's history and sociology.

Traditional Highland culture is also the subject of **The Clansmen Centre's** lively and informative exhibition (Easter to mid Oct daily 10am–8.30pm; £2), on the banks of the canal. Guides sporting sporrans and rough woollen plaids talk you through the daily life of the region's seventeenth-century inhabitants inside a mock-up of a turf-roofed stone croft, followed by demonstrations of weaponry in the back garden, where you're encouraged to try on traditional Highland garb for yourself. Most of the young staff work here for fun, donning their kilts and dowdy women's period costumes on their free weekends to fight mock battles with enthusiasts from other parts of the Highlands, which must be why they are so unnervingly adept at wielding broadswords.

Practicalities

Fort Augustus' small **tourist office** (April–June Mon–Sat 10am–5pm; July & Aug 9am–8pm; Sept & Oct 9am–6pm; ☎01320/366367) hands out useful free maps detailing popular **walks** in the area. They'll also help sort out **fishing permits** if you fancy trying your luck in the loch or nearby river.

The best-value **accommodation** in Fort Augustus has to be the Benedictine Abbey's guest rooms (☎01320/366233; ②), which are clean, spacious and private. The entrepreneurial monks also run a small *Backpackers' Lodge* with self-catering and laundry facilities, and some inexpensive double rooms (②). The *Bothy Bite Bunk House* (☎01320/366700), in the centre of the village by the canal, offers more of the same, but is even cheaper. Otherwise, try the *Old Pier* (☎01320/366418; ③), a great B&B right on the loch where there are log fires in the evenings – often very welcome even in summer – and home-cooked dinners. The small, friendly *Caledonian Hotel* (☎01320/366256; ④) overlooks the Abbey, while the good-value *Brae Hotel* (☎01320/366289; ③), just off the main road as you approach the village from the north, lies in wooded surroundings.

The Benedictine Abbey serves great, cheap **food** that will appeal particulary to vegetarians and health-conscious travellers. For a meatier meal, try the *Bothy Bite*, which does a couple of Scottish specialities with a good range of moderately priced fish, steak and pie dishes. **Nightlife** in Fort Augustus is predictably sedate, except on Saturday nights when the British Legion club (home of the village's only pool table) hosts its rowdy weekly bingo session (non-members welcome); the *Poachers* on the main road is the liveliest pub, drawing a mixed clientele of locals, yachties and backpackers.

North from Fort Augustus: East Loch Ness

The tranquil and scenic **east side of Loch Ness** is skirted by General Wade's old military highway, now converted into the B862/852. From Fort Augustus, this narrow single-track road swings inland through the near deserted Stratherrick valley, dotted with tiny lochans and flocks of scruffy sheep, before dropping down to rejoin the loch at **FOYERS**, where there are numerous marked forest trails and an impressive waterfall.

Three miles further north at **INVERFARIGAIG** stands **Bolestine House**, former residence of the infamous satanist and occult guru, **Alastair Crowley**. The self-styled "Great Beast" of Black Magic lived here between 1900 and 1918, amid rumours of devil worship and human sacrifice. In the 1970s, Led Zepellin's Jimmy Page bought the place, but sold it after the tragic death of his daughter some years later. Set back in its own grounds, the house still has a gloomy air about it, and is not open to the public.

A much warmer welcome awaits visitors at the sleepy village of **DORES**, nestled at the top end of Loch Ness, where the *Dores Inn* makes a pleasant pit stop. Only nine miles from Inverness, the old pub, which serves an excellent pint of 80 shilling and inexpensive bar food, is popular with Invernesians, who trickle out here on summer evenings for a stroll along the grey-pebble beach. Dores is also the headquarters of Loch Ness' last full-time monster spotter, Steve Feltham, who lives in a clapped-out van behind the beach. Making and selling miniature models of Nessie to pay for his diesel, Steve has kept up a constant vigil at the lochside for more than four years, scanning the surface of the water with his video camera for conclusive film footage. He also collects information on the latest sightings, published in a quarterly *Newsletter* on sale in Dores post office, and takes small groups out over the loch on monster-spotting trips.

South from Fort Augustus to Fort William

The fast A82 runs **south from Fort Augustus** along the side of **Loch Lochy** towards Spean Bridge and Fort William, giving fine views across the loch to the steep slopes of **Ben Tee** on its northern side. At Spean Bridge the minor B8004 branches down to **GAIRLOCHY**, lying at the loch's southern tip, where you once more encounter the **Caledonian Canal** – you can walk easily anywhere along this stretch of the canal, although the best access point is where the B8004 crosses it. The countryside along this last section of the Great Glen is gentle, and a little unexciting, with the valley opening out as you approach Loch Linnhe. The canal debouches into the sea via a series of 11 locks, known as **Neptune's Staircase**, which cover a drop of 80ft and presented Telford with quite an engineering challenge. It's worth a detour round the north side of Loch Lochy to lonely **Loch Arkaig**, a 20-minute drive that takes you through a pass, ablaze with rhododendrons in early summer, into country that feels a hundred miles from anywhere.

Meanwhile, the A82 climbs south from Spean Bridge to the famous **Commando Memorial**, erected for the men who trained in the area and later lost their lives during World War II. The group of guano-splashed bronze soldiers, sculpted in 1952 by Scott Sutherland, stands on a raised promontory that overlooks an awesome sweep of moor and mountain, taking in Lochaber and the Ben Nevis massif.

THE NEVIS RANGE SKI STATION

The Nevis Range Ski Range, seven miles northeast of Fort William on the A82, boasts Scotland's only **cable car** system (July & Aug daily 10am–8pm; Sept–Nov daily 10am–5pm; mid-Dec to June daily 10am–5pm; £5.50), in the **AONACH MHOR** ski area – a popular attraction during both winter and the summer off-season period. Built in 1989 with hefty grant aid from the regional council, the one-and-a-half mile gondola ride (15 min) gives an easy approach to some high-level walking, but for most tourists it simply provides an effortless means to rise 2000ft and enjoy the spectacular views from the terrace of the self-service **restaurant** at the top. Return tickets cost £5.50 and can be booked at the Nevis Range gondola station (☎01397/704008).

In July and August, you can also ski on the Nevis Range's 246ft **dry slope** (July & Aug Mon–Thurs 11am–12.30pm & 2–3.30pm; Sept & Oct, ring ☎01397/705825 for times). The ticket price for each 90-minute session (£6) includes ski rental and instruction.

Fort William and around

The area **around Fort William** is a blend of rugged mountain terrain and tranquil sea loch. The gentle and more rounded hills of the southwest give way to altogether more dramatic scenes as you travel north, with **Ben Nevis** – at 4406ft Britain's highest peak – looming over **Loch Linnhe**, a long sea loch at the southern end of the Great Glen from whose rocky western shore rise the wild peaks of the Ardnamurchan peninsula. Fort William, and the surrounding area, has a turbulent and bloody history, founded in 1655 and named in honour of William III, it was successfully held by government troops during both the Jacobite risings; while the country to the southwest is inextricably associated with Bonnie Prince Charlie's fleeings after Culloden. Grandiose **Glen Coe**, half an hour's drive south of Fort William, is another historic site with a violent past, renowned as much for the infamous massacre of 1692 as for its magnificent scenery. Nowadays the whole area is unashamedly given over to tourism, and Fort William itself swamped by bus tours throughout the summer, but, as ever in the Highlands, within a 30-minute drive you can be totally alone.

Fort William

With its stunning position on Loch Linnhe and the snow-streaked bulk of Ben Nevis rising behind, **FORT WILLIAM**, known by the many walkers and climbers that come here as "Fort Bill", should be a gem. Sadly, ribbon bungalow development and an ill-advised dual carriageway have wrecked the shore, out-of-place modern buildings mar the outskirts, and the main street is largely given over to tacky tourist gift shops.

Arrival and information

Fort William is easily reached by **bus** from Inverness, and by **train** (the **stations** are next door to each other at the east end of High St) direct from Glasgow via the famous, scenic West Highland Railway (see p.391). If you're **driving**, parking can be a nightmare: try the big car park down beside the loch, at the west end of town. The **tourist office**, Cameron Square, just off High St (Mon–Fri 9am–5pm, Sat 9am–4pm; ☎01397/703781), hands out free town maps and can help you arrange onward transport to many of the less visited areas of the west coast. **Mountain bikes** are available for rent at *Off Beat Bikes* (☎01397/704008) on Macrae's Lane, behind High St; and they also have a branch at the Nevis Range gondola station – good for easy access to the area's high ridges.

Accommodation

Fort William's plentiful **accommodation** ranges from large luxury hotels to budget hostels and bunkhouses. Numerous B&Bs are also scattered across the town, many of them in the suburb of **Corpach**, one and a half miles north along the Mallaig road. Note that a wide array of places to stay in this area may be reserved through the tourist office for a £1 booking fee, or you can ask for its free *Essential Guide* and telephone around yourself. Glen Nevis's **youth hostel**, (all year except Nov; ☎01397/702336; Grade 1) is large and modern, but you may want to avoid it during mid-summer when it's chok-full of teenagers.

Alexandra Hotel, The Parade (☎01397/702241). Established hotel slap in the town centre, with well-appointed rooms and a restaurant. ⑦.

Beinn Ard, Argyll Rd (☎01397/704760). A very central and comfortable B&B, offering some en-suite rooms and panoramic views of Loch Linnhe. ②.

Ben Nevis Bunkhouse, Achintee Farm, Glen Nevis (open all year; ☎01397/702240). A much more civilized option than the neighbouring *SYHA*, with hot showers, self-catering kitchen and TV room.

Calluna, Heathcroft (☎01397/700451). Central, small family-run budget hostel with standard facilities.

Cuildorag House, Onich (☎01855/821529). A lochside B&B, 8 miles south of Fort William on the A82, renowned for its appetizing and healthy breakfasts. ②.

The Cruachan, Achintore Rd (☎01397/702022). Popular and moderately priced hotel overlooking the loch, 5 minutes' walk from Fort William centre. ③.

Fort William Backpackers, Alma Rd (open all year; ☎01397/700711). A friendly independent hostel 5 minutes' walk from the train station, whose all-in price includes bed linen, use of kitchen, and free tea and coffee.

Glen Nevis Caravan and Camping Park (☎01397/702191); good facilities include hot showers, a shop and restaurant.

The Grange, Grange Rd (☎01397/705516). B&B in an old stone house, with three en-suite doubles and a spacious garden. Vegetarian breakfasts on request. Non-smoking. ②.

Rhu Mhor, Alma Rd (☎01397/702213). Congenial B&B 10 minutes from the town centre, offering better than average breakfasts. Vegetarians/vegans catered for by arrangement. ②.

The Smiddy Lodge, Station Rd (open all year; ☎01397/772467). A cosy 12-bed hostel in the suburb of Corpach, one and a half miles north of town on the Mallaig road; regular buses run here from Fort William station.

The Town

Fort William's downturn started in the nineteenth century, when the original fort, which gave the town its name, was demolished to make way for the train line. Today there's very little to detain you in the town centre, although it's worth taking at least a short look at the **West Highland Museum**, on Cameron Square, just off High St (July & Aug Mon–Sat 9.30am–5.30pm, Sun 2–5pm; Sept–June Mon–Sat 10am–5pm; £1.50). This splendidly old-fashioned and idiosyncratic collection, housed in a crumbling building that is earmarked for refurbishment in early 1996 (it will remain open throughout), covers virtually every aspect of Highland life and makes a refreshing change from state-of-the-art museums. There's a good section on Highland clans and tartans and, among interesting Jacobite relics, a secret portrait of Bonnie Prince Charlie, seemingly just a blur of paint that resolves itself into a portrait when viewed against a brass cylinder. Look out, too, for the long Spanish rifle used in the assassination of a local factor (the landowner's tax-collector-cum-bailiff) – the murder that subsequently inspired Robert Louis Stevenson's novel, *Kidnapped*.

Excursions from town include the popular day trip to Mallaig (see p.423) on the **Jacobite Steam Railway** (June–Sept Tues–Fri & Sun depart 10.30am, return 4.05pm). Heading along the north shore of Loch Eil to the west coast via historic Glenfinnan (see p.422), the journey takes in some of the region's most spectacular scenery. Five **seal cruises** also leave from the town pier every day, offering the chance to spot the marine life of Loch Linnhe, including otters and an array of seabirds.

Glen Nevis

A ten-minute drive out of town, **Glen Nevis** is indisputably among the Highlands' most impressive glens: a classic U-shaped glacial valley hemmed in by steep bracken-covered slopes and swathes of blue-grey scree. Herds of shaggy highland cattle also graze the valley floor, where a sparkling river gushes through glades of trees. With the forbidding mass of Ben Nevis rising steeply to the north, it's not surprising this valley was chosen as the location for several scenes in the movie *Rob Roy*. Apart from its natural beauty, Glen Nevis is also the starting point for the ascent of Scotland's highest peak, and you can **rent mountain equipment** and **mountain bikes** at the trailhead. **Buses** run as far as the youth hostel, departing from Middle St (between High St and the loch in Fort William).

Eating

Most **eating** places in Fort William are pretty basic. The *Good Food Stop* at the *Alexandra Hotel* does inexpensive grills, fish and pasta dishes, and is open all day. *McTavish's Kitchen*, an American-style "Scottish" restaurant on High St, has a predictable menu of moderately priced steaks and seafood, with a couple of vegetarian options; during summer, it also hosts nightly **Scottish entertainment** sessions (8.30–11.30pm)

GLEN NEVIS: WALKS AND HIKES

Harvey's Ben Nevis Walkers Map and Guide

The above **map** is available in the the Fort William tourist office and several shops around town. Anyone keen to do some serious **planned walking** should contact Donald Watt (☎01397/704340), the leader of the Lochaber Mountain Rescue Team, who organizes half- and whole-day walks.

Of all the **walks in and around Glen Nevis**, the ascent of **Ben Nevis**, Britain's highest summit, inevitably attracts the most attention. In high summer, the trail is teeming with hikers, whatever the weather. However, this doesn't mean the mountain should be treated casually. It can snow on top any day of the year and more people perish here annually than on Everest, so take the necessary precautions (see p.350); in winter, of course, the mountain should be left to the experts.

The most obvious route to the summit, a Victorian pony path up the whaleback south side of of the mountain, built to service the observatory that once stood on the top, starts from the Glen Nevis youth hostel, two miles southeast of Fort William (reached by bus #17 from Middle St). This climbs steadily from the trailhead, swinging onto a wide saddle with a small loch before veering right to cross the Red Burn. A series of seemingly endless zig-zags rises from here over boulderfields on to a plateau, which you cross to reach the summit, marked by cairns, a shelter and a trig point. Return via the same route or, if the weather is settled and you're confident enough, make the side trip from the saddle mentioned earlier into the **Allt a'Mhuilinn glen** for spectacular views of the great cliffs on Ben Nevis' north face. The Allt a'Mhuilinn may be followed right down to valley level as an alternative route off the mountain, reaching the distillery on the A82 a mile north of Fort William. Allow a full day for the climb.

If you don't fancy a hike up the mountain, a great **low-level walk** runs from the end of the road at the top of the glen. The good but very rocky path leads through a dramatic gorge with impressive falls and rapids, then opens out into a secret hanging valley, carpeted with wild flowers, with a high waterfall at the far end. It's a pretty place for a picnic and if you're really energetic you can walk on over **Rannoch Moor** to **Corrour Station**, where you can pick up one of four daily trains to take you back to Fort William.

WALKS AROUND GLEN COE

Ordnance Survey Landranger Map No.41.

Flanked by sheer-sided Munros, Glen Coe offers some of the Highlands' most challenging hiking routes, with long steep ascents over rough trails and notoriously unpredictable weather conditions that claim lives every year. The **walks** outlined below number among the glen's less ambitious routes, but still require a map. It's essential that you take the proper precautions (see p.390), and **stick to the paths**, both for your own safety and the sake of the soil, which has become badly eroded in places.

A good introduction to the splendours of Glen Coe is the half-day hike over **the Devil's staircase**, which follows part of the old military road that once ran between Fort William and Stirling. The trail, a good option for families and less experienced hikers, starts at the village of **Kinlochleven**, due north across the mountains from Glen Coe at the far eastern tip of Loch Leven (take the B863): head along the single-track road from the British Aluminium Heritage Centre to a wooden bridge, from where a gradual climb on a dirt jeep track winds up to Penstock Farm. The path, a section of the West Highland Way, is marked from here onwards by thistle signs, and is therefore easy to follow uphill to the 1804ft pass and down the other side into Glen Coe. The Devil's Staircase was named by 400 soldiers who endured severe hardship to build it in the seventeenth century, but in fine settled weather the trail is safe and affords stunning views of Loch Eilde and Buachaille Etive Mor. A more detailed account of this hike features in *Great Walks: Kinlochleven (No.4)* leaflet, on sale at most tourist offices in the area.

Another leaflet in the *Great Walks* series (*No.5: Glen Coe*) gives a good description of the **Allt Coire Gabhail** hike, another old favourite. The trailhead for this half-day route is in Glen Coe itself, at the car park opposite the distinctive Three Sisters massif on the main A82 (look for the giant boulder). From the road, drop down to the floor of the glen and cross the River Coe via the wooden bridge, where you have a choice of two onward paths; the easier route, the less worn one, peels off to the right. Follow this straight up

---

popular with tourists. The pick of the bunch, though, has to be the *Crannog Seafood Restaurant* on the pier, where oysters, langoustines, prawns and salmon are cooked with flair in an elegantly converted fish shop; the wine list is also excellent, although the prices make it best kept for a treat.

Glen Coe

Stern and breathtakingly beautiful, **Glen Coe** (literally "Valley of Weeping"), 16 miles south of Fort William on the A82, is one of the best-known Highland glens: a spectacular mountain valley, bounded on both sides by sheer cliffs and jagged rock summits. In 1692 it was the site of a famous massacre, after Alastair MacDonald, chief of an unruly and cattle-stealing clan, missed the deadline for taking an obligatory oath of allegiance to William III. This gave the authorities the excuse they needed "to root out that damnable sept", and government troops were billetted on the MacDonalds. Entertained by the clan with traditional hospitality – a matter of honour in the Highlands – they waited ten days for orders from Fort William and then turned on their hosts, slaying about 38 and causing more than 300 to flee in a blizzard.

Today, the glen, a honey-pot property of the NTS since the 1930s, is virtually uninhabited, and provides outstanding **climbing** and **walking**. Many famous mountaineers have gained experience on the demanding **Buachaille Etive Mhor** and its neighbouring peaks. A small NTS **visitor centre** (April–Oct 10am–5.30pm; 50p), slap in the middle of the glen by the side of the main road, houses a rudimentary audio-visual show about the massacre, along with a gift shop selling the usual books, postcards and Highland kitsch (including cassettes of some positively surreal easy-listening bagpipe music).

the Allt Coire Gabhail for a couple of miles until you rejoin the other (lower) path, which has ascended the valley beside the burn via a series of rock pools and lively scrambles. Cross the river here via the stepping stones and press on to the false summit directly ahead – actually the rim of the so-called "Lost Valley" which the Clan MacDonald used to flee to and hide their cattle in when attacked. Once in the valley, there are superb views of Bidean, Gearr Aonach and Beinn Fhada, which improve as you continue on to its head, another 20–30 minutes' walk. Unless you're well equipped and experienced, turn around at this point, as the trail climbs to some of the glen's high ridges and peaks.

Undoubtedly one of the finest walks in the Glen Coe area that does not entail the ascent of a Munro is the **Buachaille Etive Beag (BEB) circuit**, for which we recommend you check out the *Ordnance Survey Pathfinder Guide: Fort William and Glen Coe Walks*. Following the text-book glacial valleys of Lairig Eilde and Lairig Gartain, the route entails a 1968ft climb in only nine miles of rough trail, and should only be attempted by relatively fit hikers. Park near the waterfall at The Study – the gorge part of the A82 through Glen Coe – and walk up the road until you see a sign pointing south to "Loch Etiveside". The path angles up from here, criss-crossing the Allt Lairig Eilde before the final pull to the top of the pass, a rise of 787ft from the road. The burn flowing through Glen Etive to Dalness is, confusingly, also called the Allt Lairig Eilde; follow it's west bank path until you reach a fenced-off area, and then cross the stream, using the trail that then ascends Stob Dubh (the "black peat") directly from Glen Etive to gain some height. Next, pick a traverse line across the side of the valley to the col of the Lairig Gartain, and onwards to the top of the pass – a haul of around 984ft that is the last steep ascent of this circuit. The drop down the other side towards the estate lodge of Dalness is easy. When you reach the single-track road, follow the path signposted as the "Lairig Gartain", northeast to a second pass, from where an intermittent trail descends the west (left) side of the River Coupall valley, eventually rejoining the A82. Much the most enjoyable path back northeast down the glen from here is the roughly parallel route of the old military road, which offers a gentler and safer return with superb views of the Three Sisters – finer than those ever seen by any motorist.

Other than a small **youth hostel** (☎01855/811219; Grade 1), **accommodation** in the Glen is limited to the *Clachaig Inn*, on the narrow back road to Glencoe village (☎01855/811252; ③–④), a well-known climbers' haunt with 19 rather stark rooms, most of which have facilities en suite. The restaurant specializes in not too pricy Scottish cooking, but its strict dress code and minimum charge make it a lot less relaxing than the two bars, which are warmed by cosy log fires and serve a good range of real ales and malt whiskies.

STRATHSPEY AND THE CAIRNGORMS

Rising high in the heather-clad hills above Loch Laggan, 40 miles due south of Inverness, the **River Spey**, Scotland's second longest river, drains northeast towards the Moray Firth through one of the Highlands' most spellbinding valleys. Famous for its ski slopes, salmon fishing, and ospreys, **Strathspey** forms a broad cleave between the mighty Monadhliath mountains in the north and the craggy large and grey Cairngorm range to the south. Outdoor enthusiasts flock here year-around to take advantage of the superb hiking, abundant water and winter snows, but the valley is also a major transport artery, funnelling traffic along trans-Grampian road and rail routes between Edinburgh and Inverness.

Of Strathspey's scattered settlements, **Aviemore** absorbs the largest number of visitors, particularly in mid-winter when it metamorphoses into the UK's busiest ski resort.

The village itself isn't up to much, but the 4000ft summit plateau of the Cairngorm is often snow-capped, providing stunning mountain scenery on a grand scale. Sedate **Kingussie**, further up the valley, is an older established holiday centre, popular more with anglers and grouse hunters than canoeists and climbers, while the Georgian town of **Grantown-on-Spey**, jumping-off point for the famous **Loch Garten Nature Reserve**, makes another good base for exploring the area. Most of upper Strathspey is privately owned by the **Glen More Forest Park** and **Rothiemurchus Estate**, who provide between them a plethora of year-round outdoor facilities, with masses of **accommodation** of all types. Both bodies actively encourage the recreational use of their land, which gives you the freedom to go virtually anywhere you want.

Aviemore

AVIEMORE was first developed as a resort in the mid-1960s, as the brutal concrete **Aviemore Centre** bears witness: a shabby assortment of cavernous concrete buildings and incongruous high-rise hotels. The village proper, a sprawling jumble of traditional stone houses and tacky tourist shops, isn't much better, but if you can brave all this, Aviemore does make a good springboard for more scenic parts of the valley.

Winter sports in Aviemore

Scottish skiing on a commercial scale first really took off in Aviemore. By European and North American standards it's all on a tiny scale, but occasionally snow, sun and lack of crowds coincide and you can have a great day. *Highland Guides* in Inverdruie (☎01479/861276) sells equipment and maps; for a rundown of ski schools and rental facilities in the area, check out the tourist office's *Ski Scotland* brochure.

The **Cairngorm Ski Area**, about eight miles southeast of Aviemore, above Loch Morlich in Glen More Forest Park, is well served by **buses** from Aviemore. You can **rent skis** from the *Day Lodge* at the foot of the ski area (☎01479/861261), which also has a shop, a bar and restaurant, and sells tickets for the drag lifts.

WALKS AROUND AVIEMORE

Ordnance Survey Landranger Map No.36.

Walking is an obvious attraction in the Aviemore area. If you want to walk the **high tops**, it makes sense to take the chair lift up from the *Day Lodge* (see previous page). You should always follow the usual safety rules (see p.350).

In addition to the high mountain trails, there are some lovely **low-level** walks around Aviemore. It'll take you about an hour or so to complete the gentle circular walk around pretty **Loch an Eilean**, beginning at the end of the back road that turns east off the B970 two miles south of Aviemore. The visitors centre at the lochside provides more information on the many woodland trails that criss-cross this area. A longer walk starts at the near end of **Loch Morlich**. Cross the river by the bridge and follow the dirt road, turning off after about 20 minutes to follow the signs to Aviemore. The path goes through beautiful pine woods and past tumbling burns, and you can branch off to Coylumbridge and Loch an Eilean. Unless you're prepared for a 25-mile hike, don't take the track to the Lairig Ghru, which eventually brings you out near Braemar. The routes are all well marked and easy to follow and depending on what combination you put together can take anything from two to five hours.

Another good shortish (half-day) walk leads along well-surfaced forestry track from **Glenmore Lodge** up towards the **Ryvoan Pass**, taking in **An Lochan Uaine**, known as the "Green Loch" and living up to its name, with amazing colours that range from turquoise to slate grey depending on the weather. The track narrows once past the loch and leads east towards Deeside, so retrace your steps if you don't want a major trek.

If there's lots of snow, the area around Loch Morlich and into the Rothiemurchus Estate provides enjoyable **cross-country skiing** through lovely woods, beside rushing burns and even over frozen lochs. If you really want to know about survival in a Scottish winter, you could try a week at **Glenmore Lodge** (☎01479/861276) in the heart of the Glen More Forest Park at the east end of Loch Morlich. This superbly equipped and organized centre, run by the Scottish National Sports Council, offers winter courses in hill walking, mountaineering, alpine ski mountaineering, avalanche awareness and much besides.

To add to the winter scene, there's a herd of **reindeer** at Loch Morlich, and the **Siberian Husky Club** holds its races in the area.

Summer activities

In summer, the main activities around Aviemore are **watersports**, and there are two centres that offer sailing, windsurfing and canoeing. The *Loch Morlich Watersports Centre* at Kincraig (☎01479/861221), five miles or so east of Aviemore at the east end of the loch, rents equipment and offers tuition in a lovely setting with a sandy beach, while, up-valley, the *Loch Insh Watersports Centre* (see below) offers the same facilities in more open and less crowded surroundings. It also rents **mountain bikes**, boats for loch fishing, and gives ski instruction on a 164ft dry slope.

Riding and **pony trekking** are on offer up and down the valley; try the *Ballintean Riding Centre* (☎01540/65132) in Kingussie (see overleaf), or the *Carrbridge Trekking Centre*, Station Rd, Carrbridge, a few miles north of Aviemore (☎01479/84602).

Fishing is very much part of the local scene; you can fish for trout and salmon on the River Spey, and the Rothiemurchus Estate has a stocked trout-fishing loch at Inverdruie, where success is virtually guaranteed. Permits cost around £3.50 per day and are sold at *Speyside Sports* in Aviemore, one mile down the road toward the ski grounds from the tourist office, and at *Loch Morlich Watersports* (see above), which also rents rods and tackle.

Practicalities

Aviemore's **train station** is just north of the **tourist office** on the main drag, Grampian Rd (Mon–Sat 9am–5pm; ☎01479/810363). It offers an accommodation-booking service, free maps and endless leaflets on local attractions.

Accommodation is not a problem around here. The *Balavoulin Hotel* (☎01479/810672; ③) and *Ver Mont Guest House* (☎01479/810470; ②), both on Grampian Rd, are good value. There are also plenty of B&Bs: *Mrs Shaw*, 7 Cairngorm Ave (☎01479/811436; ②), near the war memorial, is the cheapest. Also close to the tourist office is a large **youth hostel** (closed mid-Nov to Dec; ☎01479/810345; Grade 1). At **GLENMORE**, in the Glen More Forest Park a few miles east of Aviemore, the well-signposted *Badaguish Centre* (☎01479/ 861285), housed in three log cabins, has dorm beds for 60 people and good facilities for disabled visitors. There are also two more independent youth hostels near the village of **KINCRAIG**, six miles south of Aviemore: the upmarket *Loch Insh Watersports Centre* (☎01540/651272), beautifully sited beside the loch, and *Balaachroick* (☎01540/651323), where the all-in price includes bed linen and as much porridge as you like for breakfast.

All the hotels do run-of-the-mill **bar food**. The *Old Bridge Inn*, down by the river below the bridge on the way to Loch Morlich, has more choice than most, as does the *Gallery Bistro* right in the centre of **INVERDRUIE**, a tiny village a mile southeast of Aviemore on the road to Loch Morlich.

Kingussie

KINGUSSIE (pronounced King*yoo*sie) lies 12 miles south of Aviemore and is far cosier, stacked around a single main street (also the A9). Beyond its usefulness as a place to stay, the chief attraction here is the excellent **Highland Folk Museum**

(April–Oct Mon–Sat 10am–6pm, Sun 2–6pm; Nov–March Mon–Fri 10am–3pm; £2.50). An absorbing collection of buildings, exhibitions and artefacts covering every aspect of Highland life, the complex includes a farming museum, an old smokehouse, a mill, a Hebridean "black house" (see p.319) and a traditional herb and flower garden; most days in summer there's a demonstration of various traditional crafts. East across the river on a hillock stand the ruins of **Ruthven Barracks**, the best preserved of the garrisons built to pacify the Highlands after the 1715 Rebellion and stunningly floodlit at night. Taken by the Jacobites in 1744, it was blown up in the wake of Culloden to prevent it from falling into enemy hands. Ruthven was also the place from where clan leader Lord George Murray dispatched his acrimonious letter to Bonnie Prince Charlie, holding him personally responsible for the string of blunders that had precipitated their defeat.

Kingussie's **tourist office** is on King St, off the High St (May–Sept daily 10am–6pm; ☎01540/661297). If you want to base yourself here, try *The Auld Poor House*, Laggan Cottage (☎01540/661558; ②), a congenial **B&B**, ten minutes' walk northeast of the village on the B9152. As its name implies, this old stone building used to be a charitable home for local destitutes, and its present owner loves to quip that "soups is once again served and de-lousing rules still apply". If it's full, *Theodore Cottage*, Duke St (☎01540/661886; ③), or *Bhuna Monadh* (☎01540/661186; ③), 85 High St, are good fallbacks. The *Cross Restaurant*, in a converted tweed mill nearby on Tweed Mill Brae (March–Nov & Christmas; ☎01540/661166) is one of the best **restaurants** in the region, serving innovative dishes using prime local ingredients – expensive, but worth it. They also keep a couple of luxurious rooms with four-poster beds (⑨).

Cheaper food is available at several cafés and pubs on the High Street. The *Royal Hotel* serves standard bar meals, with some vegetarian options, a good choice of cask ales and some 250 malts. *The Tipsy Laird* nearby serves traditional Scottish high teas and filling grills, while the *Café Volante* is the place to head for a cheap-and-cheeful fish 'n' chips supper. Finally, cosy *Retro Café* specializes in toasties and home-baked cakes, and offers a choice of eleven kinds of coffee prepared in five different ways.

Grantown-On-Spey

Buses run from Aviemore and Inverness to the tiny Georgian town of **GRANTOWN-ON-SPEY**, about 15 miles northwest of Aviemore, which, if you've got your own transport, makes another good base for exploring Strathspey and the Cairngorm area. Activity is concentrated around the attractive central square, where there's a **tourist office** on High St (May–Sept daily 9am–6pm; ☎01479/872773) and plenty of **accommodation**: *Cumbrae*, South St (☎01479/873216; ②), *Mrs Lawson*, 2 Mossie Rd (☎01479/872076; ②), and *Fearna House*, Old Spey Bridge (☎01479/872016; ②), all do comfortable, good-value B&B. If you're after something more upmarket, head for the large seventeenth-century *Garth Hotel*, Castle Rd (☎01479/872836; ④), or the marginally less expensive *Tyree House Hotel* (☎01479/872615; ③) on High St; both are open all year round and have good restaurants that serve Scottish specialities.

Loch Garten Nature Reserve

The **LOCH GARTEN NATURE RESERVE**, eight miles south of Grantown-on-Spey (or seven miles north of Aviemore), is famous as the nesting site of one of Britain's rarest birds. A little over 50 years ago, the **osprey**, known in North America, where they are relatively common, as the "fish hawk", had completely disappeared from the British Isles. Then, in the mid-1950s, a single pair of these exquisite white-and-grey eagles mysteriously reappeared and built a nest in a tree on the loch. Despite the RSPB, which now adminsters the reserve, keeping its exact location a secret, a gang of egg stealers made off with one year's batch. Thereafter, the area became the centre of an effective high-security operation; and now the birds are present in healthy numbers. The **best time to visit** Loch Garten is during the nesting season, between late April and August, when the RSPB opens an observation hide complete with powerful telescopes; you can also rent binoculars for trips elsewhere in the reserve – home to several other species of rare birds and animals, including the crossbill, capercaillie, whooper swan and red squirrel.

Loch Garten can be difficult to reach without your own transport, although the popular **Strathspey Steam Railway**, which runs between Aviemore and nearby **Boat of Garten**, will get you to within a couple of miles of the reserve.

THE WEST COAST

For many people, the Highlands' starkly beautiful **west coast** – stretching from the Morvern peninsula (opposite Mull) in the south, to wind-lashed Cape Wrath in the far north – is the epitome of "Bonnie Scotland". Serrated by long blue sea lochs, deep glens and rugged green mountains that sweep from the shore line, its myriad islets, occasional white-sand beaches and turquoise bays can, on rare sunny days, look like a picture postcard of the Mediterranean. This also is the least populated part of Britain, with just two small towns, and yawning tracts of moorland and desolate peat bog between crofting settlements.

The **Vikings**, who ruled the region in the ninth century, called it the "South Land" – from which the modern district of Sutherland takes its name – and established a firm clan system, with clansmen holding land owned by their chiefs in return for rent or service. After Culloden, the Clearances emptied most of the inland glens of the far north, however, and left the population clinging to the coastline, where a herring-fishing industry developed. Today, tourism, crofting and salmon farming are the mainstay of the local economy, supplemented by EU construction grants and subsidies for the sheep you'll encounter everywhere.

For visitors, **cycling** and **walking** are the obvious ways to make the most of the superb scenery, and countless lochans and crystal clear rivers offer superlative trout and salmon **fishing**. The shattered cliffs of the far northwest are an ornithologist's dream, harbouring some of Europe's largest and most diverse **seabird colonies**, and the area's craggy mountaintops are the haunt of the elusive golden eagle.

The most visited part of the west coast is the stretch between Kyle of Lochalsh and Ullapool. Lying within easy reach of Inverness, this area boasts the region's more obvious highlights: the awesome mountainscape of **Loch Torridon**, **Gairloch**'s sandy beaches, the famous botanic gardens at **Inverewe**, and **Ullapool** itself, a picturesque and workaday fishing town from where ferries leave for the Outer Hebrides. However, press on further north, or south, and you'll get a truer sense of the isolation that makes the west coast so special. Traversed by few roads, the remote northwest corner of Scotland is wild and bleak, receiving the full force of the north Atlantic's frequently ferocious weather. The scattered settlements of the far southwest, meanwhile, tend to be more sheltered, but they are separated by some of the most extensive wilderness areas in Britain – lonely peninsulas with evocative Gaelic names like **Ardnamurchan**, **Knoydart** and **Glenelg**.

Tempered by the Gulf Stream, the west coast's weather ranges from stupendous to diabolical. Never count on a sunny morning meaning a fine day; it can rain here at any time, and go on raining for days. Beware, too, as always in this part of the world, of the dreaded **midge**, which drives even the hardiest of locals to distraction on warm summer evenings.

Without your own vehicle, **getting around the west coast** can be a problem. Buses and trains are frequent between Inverness and Kyle of Lochalsh, Fort William and

Mallaig, and Ullapool is well connected to Inverness by bus. However, services peter out as you venture further afield, and you'll have to rely on **postbuses**, which go just about everywhere, albeit slowly and at odd times of day. **Driving** is a lot less problematic: the roads aren't busy, though frequently single-track and scattered with sheep, requiring constant vigilance; and remember to re-fuel whenever you can, as pumps are few and far between. Finally, **motorcyclists** should avoid breaking down around here at all costs: most recovery policies will only get you as far as the nearest garage, and the only source of spares in the region is Inverness.

Morvern to Morar: the "Rough Bounds"

The remote southwest corner of the Highlands, from the **Morvern peninsula** to the busy fishing and ferry port of **Mallaig**, is a dramatic, lonely region: an inhospitable mix of bog, mountain and moorland cleaved by sea lochs and fringed by stunning white beaches that give wonderful views to the Skye and the Western Isles. Its Gaelic name translates as the "**Rough Bounds**", implying a region geographically and spiritually outside current thought and behaviour, and, mainly due to its geography, among Scotland's most sparsely populated areas. Even if you haven't got a car, you should spend a few days here exploring by foot – there are so few roads that some determined hiking is almost inevitable.

The southwest Highlands' main road is the A830, which winds in tandem with the rail line across the mountains from Fort William to Mallaig. Along the way, the road passes **Glenfinnan**, the much photographed spot at the head of stunning **Loch Shiel** where Bonnie Prince Charlie gathered the clans to start the doomed Jacobite uprising of 1745. Buses and trains along this main drag are frequent; elsewhere, you'll have to rely on daily post- or school buses. If you have your own transport, the five-minute ferry crossing at **Corran Ferry** (every 15min), a nine-mile drive south of Fort William down Loch Linnhe, provides a more direct point of entry for Morvern and the rugged **Ardnamurchan peninsula**.

Morvern

Bounded on three sides by sea lochs and, in the north, by desolate Glen Tarbet, the remote southwest part of the Rough Bounds region, known as **Morvern**, is unremittingly bleak and empty. Most visitors only travel through here to get to **LOCHALINE** (pronounced Loch*aa*lin), a remote community on the **Sound of Mull**, from where a small ferry chugs to **Fishnish** – the shortest crossing from the mainland. The village, little more than a scattering of houses and a diving school around a small pier, is a popular anchorage for yachts cruising the west coast, but holds little else to detain you. However, the easy stroll to the nearby fourteenth-century ruins of **Ardtornish Castle**, reached via a track that turns east off the main road one and a half miles north of Lochaline, makes an enjoyable detour. If you're looking for somewhere good to **eat**, try the tiny *Lochaline Hotel* (☎01967/421657; ③), which serves quality bar food, and has a couple of small but comfortable **rooms**.

Sunart and Ardgour

The predominantly roadless regions of **Sunart** and **Ardgour** make up the country between **Loch Shiel**, **Loch Sunart** and **Loch Linnhe**, north of Morvern: the heart of Jacobite support in the mid-eighteenth century, and a Catholic stronghold to this day. The area's only real village is sleepy **STRONTIAN**, grouped around a green on an inlet of the **Loch Sunart**. In 1722, lead mines here yielded the first ever traces of the element **strontium**, subsequently named after the village. Worked by French POWs, the same mines also furnished shot for the Napoleonic wars. Strontian's other claim to fame is the **"Floating Church"**, which was moored nearby in Loch Sunart in 1843. After being refused permission by the local laird to found their own "kirk", or chapel, on the estate, members of the Free Presbyterian Church (see p.318), bought an old boat on the River Clyde, converted it into a church and then had it towed up the west coast to Loch Sunart.

Travelling by public **transport**, you can get to Strontian on the 8am bus from Kilchoan (see below), and on a bus that leaves Corran Ferry at 10.50am. In term time there's also a direct school bus from Fort William that leaves at 3.45pm. Strontian's **tourist office** (Easter–Oct Mon–Fri 9am–5pm, Sat 10am–4pm, Sun 10am–2pm; ☎01967/402131) will book **accommodation** for a small fee. *Loch View* (☎01967/402465; ②) is excellent value, with large rooms in a fine lochside Victorian house. *Sea View* (☎01967/402060; ②) next door, a small cottage swathed in flowers, is a good fall-back, and welcomes dogs. If you're after something more upmarket, Strontian also has a couple of good hotels. The *Strontian* (☎01967/402029; ③), on the main road, is pretty and comfortable, with an ultra-basic **bothy** for walkers in its back yard; while the posher *Loch Sunart* (☎01967/402471; ⑤) occupies a splendid site right by the water. For a real treat, you could check into the luxurious *Kilcamb Lodge* (☎01967/402257; ⑥), a restored country house set in its own grounds on the lochside, whose restaurant serves top-notch gourmet **food** at very reasonable prices. Otherwise, the best place to eat is the *Strontian Hotel*, which does a run-of-the-mill selection of inexpensive main meals, including some vegetarian choices.

The Ardnamurchan peninsula

A tortuous single-track road (the B8007) winds west from Sunart along the northern shore of Loch Sunart to the wild **Ardnamurchan peninsula**, the most westerly point on the British mainland. Comprising a varied landscape of rocky, heather-clad hills, sea loch, woodland, shell-sand beaches and hidden coves, the peninsula, which lost most of its inhabitants during the infamous Clearances (see p.522), is today virtually deserted apart from the handful of tiny crofting settlements clinging to its jagged coastline. However, Ardnamurchan remains a naturalists' paradise, harbouring a huge variety of birds, animals and wildflowers that are at their best in late May to July, when the machair is carpeted with thrift and wild iris.

Glenmore Natural History Centre
An inspiring introduction to the diverse flora, fauna and geology of the unspoilt Ardnamurchan is the **Glenmore Natural History Centre** (April–Oct 10am–5pm; £2.50), nestled on a seaweed-strewn lochside near the hamlet of **GLENBORRODALE**. Brainchild of local photographer Michael MacGregor (whose stunning work enlivens postcard stands along the west coast), the centre is housed in a sensitively designed timber building, complete with turf roof and wildlife ponds. TV cameras relay live coverage of the comings and goings on feeding tables and underwater pools, and a superb audio-visual show features MacGregor's photographs of the area accompanied by specially composed music. The small café serves good home-baked cakes and snacks.

Kilchoan and around
KILCHOAN, nine miles west of the Glenmore Centre, is Ardnamurchan's main village – a straggling crofting township overlooking the Sound of Mull that still enjoys a marvellous sense of isolation. Between mid-April and mid-October, a **ferry** runs from here to Tobermory (6 daily; 35min) and the **tourist office** (Easter–Oct Mon–Sat 9am–6.45pm, Sun 10.30am–5.15pm; ☎01972/510222) will help with and book accommodation.

Hotels include the *Meall mo Chridhe Hotel* (☎01972/510328; full board ⑦), a converted eighteenth-century *manse*, or minister's house, on the water's edge, or the cheaper *Sonachan Hotel* (☎01972/510211; ④). For **B&B**, try *Doirlinn House* (March–Oct; ☎01972/510209; ③), or *Hillview* (☎01972/510322; ③), just north of the village at Achnaha (you'll need your own transport). Among the best places in Kilchoan to **eat** is the *Meall mlo Chridhe Hotel*, which specializes in west coast seafood and game, served with home-grown vegetables (reservations essential for non-residents; bring your own wine). The *Far View Cottage* (☎01972/510357; ④), a small hotel on the outskirts of the village, also serves good food (daily £15-per-head set menu). For down-to-earth bar meals, head for the local pub, *Kilchoan House Hotel*, on the main road. The only direct **bus** to Kilchoan leaves from Corran Ferry at 10.30am, arriving four hours later.

Beyond Kilchoan the road continues to wild and windy **Ardnamurchan Point**, with its unmanned **lighthouse** and spectacular views west to Coll, Tiree and across to the north of Mull. The shell-strewn sandy beach of **Sanna Bay**, about three miles north of the point, offers truly unforgettable vistas of the Small Isles to the north, circled by gulls, terns and guillemots.

Moidart

North of the Ardnamurchan peninsula, the **Moidart** district's largest settlement is **ACHARACLE**, an ancient crofting village lying at the sea end of **Loch Shiel**. Surrounded by gentle hills, it's an attractive place whose scattered houses form a real community, with several shops, a post office, and plenty of **places to stay**. Try the central *Loch Shiel Hotel* (☎01967/431224; ③), where you can get reasonable **bar food**. *Belmont* (☎01967/431266; ②) is a comfortable central B&B, as is *Mrs Cliff*'s (☎01967/431318), just across the road. Acharacle's village hall is often used for **ceilidhs**: look out for the notices in the shops.

Castle Tioram

A mile north of Acharacle, a side road running north off the A861 winds for three miles or so past a secluded estuary lined with rhododendron thickets and fishing platforms to **Loch Moidart**, a calm and sheltered sea loch. Perched atop a rocky promontory in the middle of the loch is **CASTLE TIORAM**, one of Scotland's most atmospheric historic monuments. Reached via a sandy causeway, the thirteenth-century fortress, whose Gaelic name means "dry land", was the seat of the MacDonalds of Clanranald until destroyed by their chief in 1715 to prevent it from falling into Hanoverian hands while he was away fighting for the Jacobites. Today, the surviving walls and tower enclose an inner courtyard and a couple of empty chambers.

Glenfinnan

Approaching Moidart from the north by train, or via the fast Fort William–Mallaig road (the A830), you pass a historic site with great resonance for Scots. **GLENFINNAN**, 19 miles west of Fort William at the head of Loch Shiel, was where Bonnie Prince Charlie raised his standard to signal the start of the Jacobite uprising of 1745. Surrounded by other loyal clansmen, the young rebel prince waited to see if the Cameron of Loch Shiel would join his army. The drone of this powerful chief's pipers drifting up the glen was eagerly awaited, for without him and the Stuarts' attempt to claim the English throne would have been sheer folly. Despite strong misgivings, however, Cameron did decide to support the uprising, and arrived at Glenfinnan on a sunny August 19 with 700 men, thereby encouraging other less convinced clan leaders to follow suit.

Assured of adequate backing, the prince raised his red-and-white silk colour, proclaimed his father King James III of England, and set off on the long march to

London from which only a handful of the soldiers gathered at Glenfinnan would return. The spot is marked by a column, crowned with a clansman in full battle dress, erected as a tribute by Alexander Macdonald of Glenaladale in 1815. Set against a backdrop of grandiose Highland scenery, this atmospheric place inevitably stirs up nationalistic sentiments among Scots, and a certain sympathy for the Jacobite cause among visitors. The **visitor centre** (April–Oct daily 9.30am–6pm; £1), opposite the monument, gives an account of Prince Charlie's ill-fated odyssey around Britain, finishing with the rout at Culloden (see p.401).

Morar

Once beyond the startling turquoise sea loch of Loch Ailort, in the district of **Morar**, getting around is easier, and there are train and bus links to Fort William along the A830.

ARISAIG, scattered round a sandy bay at the west end of the Morar peninsula, makes a good base for exploring this bit of the coast. There's nothing in the way of specific attractions, but if the weather's fine you can spend hours wandering along the beaches and quiet back roads, and there's a small seal colony at nearby **RHUMACH**, reached via the single-track lane leading west out of the village along the headland. A daily boat also leaves from here during the summer for the Small Isles (see p.311); contact Murdo Grant (☎01687/546224). **Accommodation** in the village is plentiful. *Kinloid Farm House* (☎01687/450691; ②) is one of several pleasant B&Bs with sea views; while the more upmarket *Old Library Lodge* (☎01687/450651; ⑥) has a handful of well-appointed but overpriced rooms, some of them in a 200-year-old converted stable overlooking the waterfront. The restaurant downstairs, serving moderately priced lunches and à la carte dinners (reservations recommended), is renowned for adding an exotic twist to fresh local ingredients – try Mallaig cod with Moroccan marinade.

Stretching for eight miles or so north of Arisaig is a stunning string of white-sand beaches backed by flowery machair, with barren granite hills rising straight up behind. However, the views are somewhat marred by the abandoned cars, decrepit caravans, piles of rusting metal and general rubbish that blight this part of the coast. The next settlement of any significance is **MORAR**, where the famous beach scenes from *Local Hero* were shot. Since the film crew left, however, a bypass has been built around the village, and the white sands, plagued by the rumble of frozen-cod lorries, are no longer the unspoilt idyll Burt Lancaster paddled ecstatically around in the early 1980s.

Loch Morar – rumoured to be the home of Morag, a lesser-known rival to Nessie – runs east of Morar village into the heart of a huge wilderness area, linked to the sea by what must be one of the shortest rivers in Scotland. Hemmed in by heather-decked mountains, it featured in the recent blockbuster movie, *Rob Roy*: the cattle-rustling clansman's cottage was sited on its roadless northern shore.

Mallaig to Loch Duich

A cluttered, noisy port whose pebble-dashed houses struggle for space with great lumps of granite tumbling down to the sea, **MALLAIG**, 47 miles west of Fort William along the A830 (regular buses and trains run this route), is not a pretty town. But as the main ferry stop for Skye and the Small Isles (see p.300), it is always full of visitors. The continuing source of the town's wealth is its thriving fishing industry: on the quayside piles of nets, tackle and ice crates lie scattered around a bustling modern market. When the fleet is in, trawlers encircled by flocks of raucous gulls choke the harbour, and the pubs, among the liveliest on the west coast, host bouts of serious drinking.

If you're waiting for a ferry or train, you could fill in some time at **Mallaig Marine World**, north of the train station near the harbour (daily 9am–7pm; £2.50), where tanks of sea creatures share space with informative exhibits about the port. Two minutes' walk south of the railway bridge, the **Mallaig Heritage Centre** (May–Sept Mon–Sat 9.30am–5pm, Sun 1–5pm; £1.80), displaying old photographs of the town and its environs, is also worth a browse. In addition, there are a couple of enjoyable **walks** around the town. The trail to **Mallaigmore**, a small cove with a white-sand beach and isolated croft, begins at the top of the harbour on East Bay; follow the road north past the tourist office and turn off right when you see the signpost between two houses. The round trip takes about an hour.

The stretch of coast **north of Mallaig** encompasses the lonely **Knoydart** and **Glenelg** peninsulas, two of Britain's last true wilderness areas, as it heads towards **Kyle of Lochalsh**, the main departure point for Skye. This whole region is also popular with Munro baggers, harbouring a string of summits over 3000ft. The famous Five Sisters massif and Kintail Ridge, flanking the A87 a short way south of Kyle, offer some of the Highlands' most challenging **hikes** and are easily accessible by road, but to get to the wild heart of Knoydart or Glenelg, you'll have to trek for a couple of days, hopping between headlands by fishing boat and sleeping rough in old stone bothies (most of which are marked on Ordnance Survey maps).

Practicalities

Mallaig is a compact place, concentrated around the harbour, where you'll find the **tourist office** (Mon–Sat 9am–8pm, Sun 10am–5pm; ☎01687/462170) – which will book accommodation for you – and the **bus** and **train stations**. The *CalMac* ticket office (☎01687/462403), serving passengers for Skye and the Small Isles, is also nearby, and you can arrange transport to Knoydart by telephoning Bruce Watt (☎01687/462320), whose three-weekly boat to Inverie (Mon, Wed & Fri) continues east along Loch Nevis to Tarbet; the loch is sheltered, so crossings are rarely cancelled. Mr Watt also operates cruises across to Loch Coruisk on Skye (see p.305) on Tuesdays.

There are plenty of **places to stay**, with budget travellers making a beeline for *Sheena's Backpackers' Lodge* (☎01687/462764), a refreshingly laid-back independent **hostel** overlooking the harbour, with mixed dorms, self-catering facilities, a sitting room and a cosy en-suite double-bedded room with its own coal fire (②). For **B&B**, head around the harbour to East Bay, where you'll find the immaculate *Western Isles Guest House* (☎01687/562320; ③); *Quarterdeck* (☎01687/462604; ③) and *Springbank* (☎01687/462459; ③), nearby, are good fallbacks. Finally, the *West Highland Hotel* (☎01687/462210; ⑤) is a delightfully old-fashioned place in the centre of town, with splendid views. The only commendable **restaurant** in town is the moderately priced *Cabin*, on the harbour, which specializes in delicious fresh seafood straight off the boat.

The Knoydart peninsula

To get to the **Knoydart peninsula**, you have to catch a fishing boat from Mallaig or Glenelg, or else hike for a day across rugged moorland and mountains (see "Practicalities"). Either way, you'll soon appreciate why many regard this as Britain's most dramatic and unspoilt wilderness area. Flanked by Loch Nevis ("Loch of Heaven") in the south and the fjord-like inlet of Loch Hourn ("Loch of Hell") to the north, Knoydart's nobbly green peaks (four of them Munros) sweep straight out of the sea, shrouded for much of the time in a pall of grey mist. Unsurprisingly, the peninsula tends to attract walkers, lured by the network of well-maintained **trails** that wind east into the wild interior, where Bonnie Prince Charlie is rumoured to have hidden out after Culloden.

A little over a century ago, more than 1500 crofters and fishers eked a living from this inhospitable terrain. Now, Knoydart only supports a population of around 60, most of whom live in the tiny hamlet of **INVERIE**, nestled beside a sheltered bay on the south side of the peninsula, where there's a pint-sized post office, a shop and mainland Britain's most remote pub, *The Old Forge*.

Practicalities

Bruce Watt's *Sea Cruises* boat chugs into Inverie from Mallaig (Mon, Wed & Fri 10.15am & 2.15pm; ☎01687/462320). To arrange for a boat crossing from Arnisdale in Glenelg contact Mr MacTavish (☎01599/522211) or Len Morrison (☎01599/522211) – it costs between £8–25 depending on passenger numbers and where you ask to be dropped off.

There are two main **hiking routes into Knoydart**: the trailhead for the first is **Kinloch Hourn**, a crofting hamlet at the far east end of Loch Hourn which you can get to by road (turn south off the A87 six miles west of Invergarry), from where a well-marked path winds around the coast to Inverie; you can also pick up this trail by taking a boat from Glenelg, on the north shore of Loch Hourn. The second path into Knoydart starts at the west side of **Loch Arkaig**, approaching the peninsula via Glen Dessary. These are both long hard slogs over rough, desolate country, so take wet-weather gear, plenty of food, warm clothes and a good sleeping bag, and leave your name and expected time of arrival with someone when you set off.

Most of Knoydart's **accommodation** is concentrated in and around Inverie. *Torrie Shieling* (☎01687/462669; £13 per night), an upmarket independent hostel located three-quarters of a mile east of the village on the side of the mountain, is popular with hikers and families, offering self-catering facilities, comfy wooden beds in four-person rooms, and superb views across the bay. The Knoydart Estate runs a cheaper and more cramped **bunkhouse** (☎01687/462331), in addition to the very posh *Inverie House* (☎01687/462331; ⑥), where you can sleep in four-posters and dine on gourmet food. In Inverie village itself, *Pier House* (☎01687/462347; ②, full board ③), a pleasant, inexpensive B&B, serves à la carte evening meals to non-residents (3 courses for £15) and also rents out **moutain bikes**. If you want total isolation *and* all the creature comforts, though, book into the beautiful *Doune Stone Lodges* (☎01687/462667; full-board ⑦), on the remote north side of the peninsula. Rebuilt from ruined crofts, this place has pine-fitted en-suite double rooms right on the shore, near the ruins of an ancient Pictish fort. They'll pick you up by boat from Mallaig if you book ahead. Most visitors **eat** at their hotel or guest house while in Knoydart; alternatively try the *Old Forge*'s generous bar meals, served indoors beside an open fire. *Inverie House* also opens its upscale restaurant to non-residents.

The Glenelg peninsula

Further north, the **Glenelg peninsula**, jutting out into the Sound of Sleat, is the isolated and little-known crofting area featured in Gavin Maxwell's otter novel, *Ring of Bright Water*. Maxwell disguised the identity of this pristine stretch of coast by calling it "Camusfearnà", and it has remained a tranquil backwater in spite of the traffic that trickles through during the summer for the Kylerea ferry to Skye. You can also approach the peninsula from the east by turning off the fast A87 at Shiel Bridge on Loch Duich, from where a narrow single-track road climbs a tortuous series of switch-backs to the Mam Ratagan Pass (1115ft), affording spectacular views over the awesome Five Sisters massif. Following the route of an old military highway and drovers' trail, the road, covered each morning by the **postbus** from Kyle (departs 9.45am) drops down the other side through Glen More, with the magnificent **Kintail Ridge** visible to the southeast, towards the peninsula's main settlement, **GLENELG**, strewn along a pebbly bay on the Sound of Sleat. A row of little whitewashed houses surrounded by trees, the village is dominated by the rambling, weed-choked ruins of **Fort Bernera**, an eighteenth-century garrison for English government troops, but now little more than a shell. The *Glenelg Inn* (☎01599/522273; ⑨) has luxurious, cosy **rooms** overlooking the bay and an excellent à la carte restaurant, which also serves cream teas, cakes and quality coffee during the day.

The tiny **Glenelg–Kylerea ferry** (April–Oct frequent; for more details call ☎01599/ 511305) shuttles across the Sound of Sleat from a jetty northwest of the village. In former times, this choppy channel used to be an important drovers' crossing: 8000 cattle each year were herded across from Skye to the mainland, with tails attached to the heads of the beasts behind.

One and a half miles south of Glenelg village, a sign points left off the road to the **Glenelg Brochs**, some of the best-preserved iron-age monuments in the country. Standing in a sheltered stream valley, the circular towers – *Dun Telve* and *Dun Troddan* – are thought to have been erected around 2000 years ago to protect the surrounding settlements from raiders. They're still in wonderful condition, with gently curving dry-stone walls, stone lintels and chimney stacks intact.

A narrow back road snakes its way southwest beyond Glenelg village through a scattering of old crofting hamlets and timber forests. The views across the Sound of Sleat to Knoydart grow more spectacular at each bend, reaching a highpoint at a windy pass that takes in a vast sweep of sea, loch and islands, including, on a clear day, the Outer Hebrides. Crouched around the rocks below the pass is the tiny village of **SANDAIG**, where Gavin Maxwell and his otters lived in the 1950s. Swinging east, the road winds down to the waterside again, following the north shore of Loch Hourn as far as **ARNISDALE**, a single row of old cottages ranged behind a long pebble beach, with a massive scree slope behind. You can get here on the **postbus** from Kyle of Lochalsh (1 daily at 9.45am, arrive 1.25pm), but there's no accommodation (the locals make their money from salmon farming). However, you can catch a boat across the loch to Knoydart (see p.424).

To stay in the area, continue one mile along the road to **CORRAN**, a minuscule whitewashed fishing hamlet at the water's edge. Aside from the arrival of electricity and a red telephone box, the only major addition to this gorgeous village in the last hundred years has been *Mrs Nash*'s homely **B&B** (☎01599/522336; ②) and tea hut, where you can enjoy hot drinks and home-baked cake in a "shell garden", with breathtaking views on all sides. Corran is served by a daily **postbus**, which leaves here at 7am for Kyle of Lochalsh and returns at 9.45am.

Loch Duich

Skirted on its northern shore by the A87, **Loch Duich**, the boot-shaped inlet that forms the northern shoreline of the Glenelg peninsula, features prominently on the tourist trail, with buses from all over Europe thundering down the 16 miles from **SHIEL BRIDGE** to Kyle of Lochalsh on their way to Skye. The most dramatic approach to the loch, however, is from the east through Glen Shiel, where the mountains known as the **Five Sisters of Kintail** surge up to heights of 3000ft – a familiar sight from countless tourist brochures, but an impressive one nonetheless. With steep-sided hills hemming in both sides of the loch, it's sometimes hard to remember that this is, in fact, the sea. There's a congenial **SYHA youth hostel** just outside Shiel Bridge at **RATAGAN** (March–Oct; ☎01599/511243; Grade 2), popular with walkers newly arrived off the Glen Affric trek from Loch Ness (see p.408).

Eilean Donan Castle

After Edinburgh's hilltop fortress, **Eilean Donan Castle** (April–Oct daily 9am–5pm), ten miles north of Shiel Bridge on the A87, has to be Scotland's most photographed

HIKING IN GLEN SHIEL

Ordnance Survey Map No.33.

The mountains of **Glen Shiel**, sweeping southeast from Loch Duich, offer some of the best hiking routes in Scotland. Rising dramatically from sea level to over 3000ft in less than a couple of miles, they are also exposed to the worst of the west coast's notoriously fickle weather. Don't underestimate either of these two routes. Tracing the paths on a map, they can appear deceptively short and easy to follow; however, unwary walkers **die** here every year, often because they failed to allow enough time to get off the mountain by nightfall, or because of a sudden change in the weather. Neither of the routes outlined below should be attempted by inexperienced walkers, nor without a map, a compass and a detailed trekking guide – the SMC's *Hill Walks in Northwest Scotland* is recommended. Also make sure to follow the usual safety precautions outlined on p.390.

Taking in a bumper crop of Munros, the **Five Sisters traverse** is deservedly the most popular trek in the area. Allow a full day to complete the whole route, which begins at the first fire break on the left-hand side as you head southeast down the glen on the A87. Strike straight up from here and follow the ridge north along to Scurr na Moraich (2874ft), dropping down the other side to Morvich on the valley floor.

The distinctive chain of mountains across the glen from the Five Sisters is the **Kintail Ridge**, crossed by another famous hiking route that begins at *The Cluanie Inn* on the A87. From here, follow the well-worn path south around the base of the mountain until it meets up with a stalkers' trail, which winds steeply up Creag a' Mhaim (3108ft) and then west along the ridgeway, with breathtaking views south across Knoydart and the Hebridean Sea.

monument. Presiding over the once strategically important confluence of Lochs Aish, Long and Duich, the forbidding crenellated tower rises from the water's edge, joined to the shore by a narrow stone bridge and with sheer mountains as a backdrop.

The original castle was established in 1230 by Alexander II to protect the area from the Vikings. Later, during the Jacobite era, it was occupied by troops dispatched by the King of Spain to help Bonnie Prince Charlie. However, when King George heard of their whereabouts, frigates were sent to weed the Spaniards out, and the castle was blown up with their stocks of gunpowder. Thereafter, it lay in ruins until restored in the 1930s by the Maclean family, still the local lairds, owners and occupants of the castle during the winter months. Eileen Donan has also been the setting of several major movies, including *Highlander*, starring Christopher Lambert (large numbers of film stills are sold at the ticket office). Only two rooms – a banquet hall and the troops' quarters – are open to the public, with displays of various Jacobite and clan relics whose charm is rather hard to detect amid the attentions of the tour parties that file through here in the summer.

Food and limited **accommodation** are available less than a mile away in the hamlet of **DORNIE**, where the *Castle Inn*, Francis St (☎01599/555205; ④) has a handful of comfortable rooms. For a little more luxury, head north out of the village to the *Loch Duich Hotel* (☎01599/555213; ⑤), which has splendid doubles overlooking the loch and a small restaurant serving upmarket bar snacks and evening meals.

Kyle of Lochalsh to Scoraig Peninsula

KYLE OF LOCHALSH, seven miles northeast of Eileen Donan Castle, is a busy town – a transit point on the route to Skye and an important train terminal. Straggling down the hill towards the pier and train station, it's not particularly attractive – concrete buildings, rail junk and myriad signs of the fishing industry abound – and is ideally somewhere to pass through rather than linger. Since the **Skye road bridge** was opened in 1995, the traffic rumbles freely over the channel a mile north of town, bypassing Kyle completely, leaving its shopkeepers bereft of the passing trade they used to enjoy. The new bridge, built with private sector money, has also sparked controversy over its high tolls (£5.20 for cars); the inhabitants of Skye and Kyle often complain they are being "held to ransom".

Practicalities

Buses stop at the pier. On going to press, timetables were being redrawn because of the new bridge (so check with the companies below), but it seems likely that services will run to Glasgow via Fort William (3 daily; 5hr); and to Inverness via Invermoriston (Mon–Sat 4 daily, Sun 2; 2hr). These routes can become very crowded, so book through *Skye-Ways Express Coach Services*, Ferry Pier (☎01599/534328), or *Scottish Citylink* (☎0990/898989). The train station is about five minutes south of the pier; three or four **trains** run daily to Inverness (2hr 30min). Curving north through Achnasheen and Glen Carron, the train line is a rail enthusiast's dream.

The **tourist office** (April, May & mid-Sept to late Oct Mon–Sat 9.30am–5.30pm; June to mid-July & late Aug to mid-Sept Mon–Sat 9.30am–7pm; mid-July to late Aug Mon–Sat 9.30am–9pm, Sun 12.30–4.30pm; ☎01599/534276), about five minutes' walk up the hill from the train station towards the pier, opposite the monster car park on the headland, will book **accommodation** for you, which is useful as there are surprisingly few places, particularly in high summer. The *Kyle Hotel*, Main St (☎01599/534204; ⑤), is a traditional mid-range hotel, but if you're feeling flush, splash out at the *Lochalsh Hotel* (☎01599/534202; ⑧), a wonderfully situated place looking out at Skye, with fabulous seafood and an air of dated luxury. For **B&B**, try *Mrs Finlayson*, Main St (☎01599/534265; ③), five minutes' walk from the train station; or *Crowlin View* (☎01599/534286; ③), a traditional house with sea views, one and a half miles north of Kyle on the Plockton road. The *Seagreen Restaurant*, also on the Plockton road (but closer to the centre) has good, moderately priced, fresh seafood and vegetarian **meals**.

Plockton

A ten-minute train ride north of Kyle at the sea end of islet-studded **Loch Carron**, lies **PLOCKTON**: a chocolate-box row of neatly painted fishers' houses ranged around the curve of a tiny harbour. Originally known as *Am Ploc*, the settlement was a minuscule crofting hamlet until the end of the eighteenth century, when a local laird transformed it into a prosperous fishery, renaming it "Plocktown". Today, it's self-consciously twee and touristy, full of yachtsmen, second-home owners and craft shops. The unique brilliance of Plockton's light has also made it something of an artists' hang out, and during the summer the picturesque waterfront, with its row of shaggy palm trees, flower gardens and pleasure boats, is invariably punctuated by painters dabbing at their easels.

If you want to **stay**, the friendly, cosy *Haven Hotel* (☎01599/544223; ⑤) near the seafront is renowned for its excellent food; the family-run *Creag-nan-Daroch Hotel*, Innes St (☎01599/544222; ④) makes a comfortable alternative. The *Plockton Hotel*, Harbour St (☎01599/544274; ⑥), also overlooks the quay and serves good seafood. Of the 15 or so **B&Bs**, *The Shieling* (☎01599/544282; ③) on a tiny headland at the top of the harbour, is the most attractively placed, with great views on both sides. Excellent-value farmhouse B&B is available at *The Craig Rare Breeds Farm*, midway between Plockton and Stromeferry (☎01599/544205; ②), which does particularly good breakfasts (vegetarian if preferred); you can also check out the ancient breeds of Scottish farm animals rubbing shoulders with llamas and peacocks. The top place to **eat** is the *Haven*'s restaurant, whose gourmet food is in a league of its own. *The Old Schoolhouse* is the next best option, serving reasonably priced steaks, seafood and vegetarian dishes; the *Buttery*, part of the grocer's, on the corner of Main St by the sea, is also open all day for snacks and inexpensive meals. All the hotels, of course, are happy to feed non-residents.

The Applecross peninsula

The most dramatic approach to the **Applecross peninsula** (the English-sounding name is actually a corruption of the Gaelic *Apor Crosan*, meaning "estuary") is from the south, along the infamous **Bealach na Ba pass** (literally "Cattle Pass"). Crossing the forbidding hills behind **Kishorn** and rising to 2000ft, with a gradient and switchback bends worthy of the Alps, this route, the highest road in Scotland and a popular cycling *piste*, is hair-raising in places, but the panoramic views across the Minch to Raasay and Skye more than compensate. The other way in is from the north: a beautiful coast road that meanders slowly from **Shieldaig** on Loch Torridon, with tantalizing glimpses of the Cullins to the south.

The sheltered, fertile bay of **APPLECROSS** village, where the Irish missionary monk Maelrhuba founded a monastery in 673 AD, comes as a surprise after the bleakness of the moorland approach. It's an idyllic place; you can wander along lanes banked with wild iris and orchids, and explore beaches and rock pools on the shore. It's also quite an adventure to get here by **public transport**. The nearest rail head is 17 miles northeast at Strathcarron Station, near Achnasheen, which you have to reach by 9.45am to catch the **postbus** to Shieldaig, on Loch Torridon. From here, a second postie leaves for Applecross at 11.30am (90min). No buses of any kind run over the Bealach na Ba pass. The old *Applecross Inn* (☎01520/744262; ③), right beside the sea, serves real ales, sandwiches and great seafood suppers. Two even more appealing **B&Bs** lie further down the lane towards **Toscaig**, with its pier and inquisitive seals: *Camustiel* (☎01520/744207; ②), a converted manse on the sea shore, and *John Pearson* (☎01520/744272; ③), whose isolated cottage looks over to Skye. There's also **camping** at the *Flowertunnel Restaurant*, off the road to the pass, which sells cakes and freshly baked bread.

Loch Torridon

Loch Torridon marks the northern boundary of the Applecross peninsula, its awe-inspiring setting backed by the menacing mountains of **Liathach** and **Beinn Eighe**, tipped by streaks of white quartzite. The greater part of this area is composed of the reddish Torridonian sandstone, whose 750-million-year-old beds can be seen on the precipices of Liathach; there are also numerous deeply eroded and ice-smoothed corries. Much of Beinn Eighe is forested with Caledonian pinewood, which once covered the whole of the country, and houses pine marten, wildcat, fox and badger – you may even see buzzards and golden eagles. There's also a wide range of flora, with the higher rocky slopes producing spectacular natural alpine rock gardens.

There's an unsightly modern **youth hostel** in the village of **TORRIDON** (Feb–Oct, Christmas & New Year; ☎01445/791284; Grade 1), as well as a couple of **B&Bs** four miles further up the coast at the tiny hamlet of **Inveralligin**: *Mrs Finan* (☎01445/791325; ③), and *Grianan* (☎01445/791264; ②), which also does evening meals by arrangement. Seven miles west of Torridon, **SHIELDAIG**, an attractive little lochside village below the main road, harbours another batch of B&Bs including *Tigh Fada* (☎01520/755248; ③) and, a little out of the village, *Innis Mhor* (☎01520/755339; ③); both may be booked through the tourist office. For more luxury, the rambling Victorian *Loch Torridon* (☎01445/791242; ⑦), set amid well-tended lochside grounds, is one of the area's top **hotels**.

WALKING AROUND TORRIDON

Ordnance Survey Outdoor Leisure map No.8.

There are difficult and unexpected conditions on virtually all hiking routes around Torridon, and the weather can change very rapidly. If you're relatively inexperienced but want to do the magnificent ridge walk along the **Liathach** (pronounced *Lee*-a-gach, or *Lee*-ach) massif, or the strenuous traverse of **Beinn Eighe** (pronounced Ben *Ay*), join a guided hike: contact the long-time NTS ranger, Seamus MacNally on ☎01445/791221, or Cam MacLeay on ☎01445/791216.

For those confident to go it alone (using the above map), one of many possible routes takes you behind Liathach and down the pass, **Coire Dubh**, to the main road in Glen Torridon. This is a great, straightforward walk if you're properly equipped (see p.390), covering 13 miles and taking in superb landscapes. Allow yourself the **whole day**. Start at the stone bridge on the Diabaig road along the north side of Loch Torridon. Follow the Abhainn Coire Mhic Nobuil burn up to the fork at the wooden bridge and take the track east to the pass (a rather indistinct watershed) between Liathach and Beinn Eighe. The path becomes a little lost in the boggy area studded with lochans at the top of the pass, but the route is clear and, once over the watershed, the path is easy to follow. At this point you can, weather permitting, make the rewarding diversion up to the Coire Mhic Fhearchair, widely regarded as the most spectacular corrie in Scotland; otherwise continue down the Coire Dubh stream, ford the burn and follow its west bank down to the Torridon road, from where it's about four miles back to Loch Torridon.

A rewarding walk even in rough weather is the seven-mile hike up the coast from **Lower Diabeg**, ten miles northwest of Torridon village, to **Redpoint**. On a clear day, the views across to Raasay and Applecross from this gentle undulating path are superlative, but you'll have to return along the same trail, or else make your way back via Loch Maree on the A832. If you're staying in **Shieldaig**, the road that winds up the peninsula running north from the village, covered by the postbus each morning, makes a pleasant 90-minute round walk.

Loch Maree

About eight miles north of Loch Torridon, **Loch Maree** (pronounced Mu*ree*), dotted with Caledonian pine-covered islands, is one of the west coast's scenic highlights, best viewed from the road (A832) that drops down to its southeastern tip through Glen Docherty. It's also surrounded by some of Scotland's finest deer-stalking country: the remote, privately owned *Letterewe Lodge* on the north shore, accessible only by helicopter or boat, lies at the heart of a famous deer forest. Queen Victoria stayed a few days here at the *Loch Maree Hotel* (☎01445; 791288; ⑤), whose respectable air has altered little since.

The A832 skirts the southern shore of Loch Maree, passing the **Beinn Eighe Nature Reserve**, five miles northwest of Kinlochewe, the UK's oldest wildlife sanctuary. Established to preserve the ancient Caledonian oak forest that still survives on Loch Maree's little islets, the reserve also encompasses a large tract of inhospitable mountain and moorland. The **Aultroy Visitor Centre** (May–Oct daily 10am–5pm) on the A832 gives details of the area's rare plant species, many of which have endured here since the last ice age, and sells pamphlets describing two excellent **walks** in the reserve: a woodland trail through lochside forest, and a more strenuous half-day hike around the base of Beinn Eighe. Both start from the car park a mile north of the visitor centre, where you'll find a vending machine that dispenses the route guides.

Gair Loch

Three buses each week run from Inverness (Mon, Wed & Sat) to **GAIRLOCH**, scattered around the sheltered northeastern shore of the loch of the same name. Lying within easy reach of several tempting sandy beaches and some excellent coastal walks, this former crofting township thrives during the summer as a low-key holiday resort. The **Gairloch Heritage Museum** (Easter–Sept daily 10am–5pm; free), has eclectic, appealing displays covering geology, archeology, fishing and farming, that range from a mock-up of a croft house to an early knitting machine. Probably the most interesting section is the archive, an array of photographs, maps, genealogies, lists of place names and taped recollections, mostly in Gaelic, made by elderly locals.

The area's real attraction, however, is its beautiful coastline. To get to one of the most impressive stretches, head around the north side of the bay and follow the single-track B8021 beyond Big Sand (a cleaner and quieter beach than the one in Gairloch) to the tiny crofting hamlet of **Melvaig** (reachable by the 9.05am Gairloch postbus), from where a narrow surfaced track runs out wind-lashed **Rubha Reidh** (pronounced Roo-a *Ree*) **Point**. The converted **lighthouse** here, which looks straight across the Minch to Harris in the Outer Hebrides, serves slap-up afternoon teas and home-baked cakes (Thurs & Sun noon–5pm). You can also **stay** in its comfortable and relaxed bunkhouse, or double rooms (book ahead in high season; ☎01445/771263; ②); you can be driven out here from Gairloch for £4 return. Around the headland from Rubha Reidh lies secluded **Camas Mór** beach, which has to rank among the most picturesque in Scotland. For a great half-day walk, follow the marked footpath inland (southeast) from here along the base of a sheer scarp slope, and past a string of lochans, ruined crofts and a remote wood to **Midtown** on the east side of the peninsula, five miles north of Poolewe on the B8057. However, unless you leave a car at the end of the trail or arrange to be picked up, you'll have to walk or hitch back to Gairloch as the only transport along this road is an early-morning post van.

A more leisurely way to explore the coast is a **wildlife-spotting cruise**: *Sail Gairloch* departs (10am, 2 & 5pm) from the Shieldaig mooring, five miles south of Gairloch, and heads off across the bay in search of dolphins, porpoises, seals and even the odd whale. You can also **rent a boat** for the day through Gairloch's chandlery shop (☎01445/712458) – popular with sea anglers.

Badachro and beyond

Three miles south of Gairloch, a narrow single-track lane (built with the Destitution Funds raised during the nineteenth-century potato famine) peels west off the main A832, past wooded coves and inlets on its way south of the loch to **BADACHRO**, a former fishing village. These days, it's a sleepy place; life revolves around the white-washed *Badachro Inn* (March–late Oct; ☎01445/714255), a characterful pub on the waterfront offering cheap and cheerful **bar food**. The hospitable landlord and his wife have a couple of **B&B rooms** (③).

Beyond Badachro, the road winds for five more miles along the shore to **Redpoint**, a minuscule hamlet that has no accommodation but marks the trailhead for the wonderful coast walk to **Lower Diabeg**, described on p.431. Even if you don't fancy a full-blown hike, follow the path a mile or so to the exquisite beach hidden on the south side of the headland, which you'll probably have all to yourself. Redpoint is served by a Gairloch **postbus** (see below).

Gair Loch practicalities

Without your own transport, you'll have to depend upon **postbuses** to get around Gair Loch. Two services (one for each side of the loch) leave from in front of the post office: one at 9.05am for Melvaig, and the other at 11.20am for Redpoint.

There's a good choice of **accommodation** in Gairloch, most of it mid-range; the central **tourist office** (May–Oct Mon–Sat 9am–7pm, Sun 1–6pm; Nov–April Mon–Sat 9am–5pm; ☎01445/712130) will help if you have problems finding a vacancy. Try the large family-run *Myrtle Bank Hotel* (☎01445/712214; ⑥), on the lochside, which has a decent restaurant, or the *Mountain Lodge*, Strath Square (☎01445/712316; ④), more laid-back, with log fires and a relaxing wood terrace overlooking the loch; its restaurant is a little overpriced. **B&Bs** are scattered all around Gair Loch from Big Sand to Charleston on the other side of the bay. In the village centre near the bus stop, *Burnbridge House*, Shore St (☎01445/712167; ③), a large traditional stone building, has sea views and plenty of parking. Gaelic-speaking Miss Mackenzie, at nearby *Duisary* (☎01445/712252; ②), is another good choice. If you have a car, the best has to be *Little Lodge* (☎01445/712237; ③) at North Erradale, north along the coast towards Rubha Reidh, which has immaculately furnished rooms, a log burning stove, Cashmere goats and dramatic sea views; its meals are excellent and good value. If you're hostelling, there's a particularly pleasant **youth hostel** (mid-May to Sept; ☎01445/712219; Grade 2), two miles up the Rubha Reidh road at **Carn Deag**, which looks over the bay and is only a short walk from Big Sand.

All of Gairloch's hotels open their restaurants to non-residents, and most of the pubs serve bar **food**. In addition, the *Gairloch Sands Pizza Bar* in the *Gairloch Sands Hotel* (5-min walk round the bay from the tourist office), dishes up burgers and full-on American breakfasts with all the trimmings, as well as home-baked pizza. For authentic inexpensive pasta alongside pricier seafood and meat, try *Gino's* in the *Millcroft Hotel*.

Poolewe

It's a 15-minute hop by bus over the headland from Gairloch to the trim little village of **POOLEWE** on the sheltered south side of **Loch Ewe**, at the mouth of the River Ewe as it rushes down from Loch Maree. One of the area's best **walks** begins near here, signposted from the lay-by-cum-viewpoint on the main A832, a mile south of the village. It takes a couple of hours to follow the easy trail across open craggy moorland to the shores of Loch Maree, and thence to the car park at **Slatterdale**, seven miles southeast of Gairloch. If you don't want to cover the same route twice, start from Slatterdale, leaving your car here, and pick up the *Westerbus* at around 7pm when it passes the lay-by mentioned earlier, which will drop you back at Slatterdale. Also worthwhile is the drive along the small side road running northwest of Poolewe along the south of the loch to **COVE**. Here you'll find an atmospheric cave that was used by the "Wee Frees" as a church into this century; it's quite a perilous scramble up, however, and there's little to see once there. The route is also covered by a Poolewe **postbus** (1.40pm). *Mrs MacDonald* (April–Oct; ☎01445/781354; ③) offers upscale **B&B** here, with fine loch views.

Other accommodation in the area includes *Pool House Hotel* (☎01445/781272; ⑦), right by the sea in Poolewe village, but this is a bit overpriced; try the more old-fashioned *Poolewe Hotel* (☎01445/781241; ⑤), on the Cove road. For B&B in Poolewe, *Fasgadh* (☎01445/781352; ②) is basic but cheap; the marginally posher *Bruach Ard* (☎01445/781214; ③), four miles north at Inversdale, has mostly en-suite rooms. There's also an excellent NTS **campsite** between the village and Inverewe Gardens (April–Oct ☎01445/781229). The *Bridge Cottage Café*, at the village crossroads, serves good coffee and home-baked cakes during the summer.

Inverewe Gardens

Half a mile across the bay from Poolewe on the A832, **Inverewe Gardens** (April–Sept daily 9.30am–9pm; Oct–March daily 9am–5pm; NTS; £3.50), a verdant oasis of foliage and riotously colourful flower beds, form a vivid contrast with the austere wildness of the rest of the coast. They were originally the brainchild of the late **Osgood Mackenzie**, who inherited the surrounding 12,000-acre estate from his stepfather, the laird of Gairloch, in 1862. Taking advantage of the area's famously temperate climate (a consequence of the **Gulf Stream**, which draws a warm water current from Mexico to within a stone's throw of these shores), Mackenzie collected plants from all over the world for his walled garden, still the nucleus of the complex. Protected from Loch Ewe's corrosive salt breezes by a dense brake of Scots pine, rowan, oak, beech and birch trees, the fragile plants flourished on rich soil, brought here as ballast on Irish ships to overlay the previously infertile beach gravel and sea grass. By the time Mackenzie died in 1922, his garden sprawled over the whole peninsula, surrounded by 100 acres of woodland. Today the NTS strives to develop the place along the lines envisaged by its founder.

Around 180,000 visitors each year pour through here, but they are easily absorbed. Interconnected by a labyrinthine network of twisting paths and walkways, more than a dozen gardens feature exotic plant collections from as far afield as Chile, China, Tasmania and the Himalayas. Strolling around the lotus ponds, palm trees, and borders ablaze with exotic blooms, it's amazing to think you're at the same latitude as Hudson's Bay and St Petersburg. Mid-May to mid-June is the best time to see the **rhododendrons** and **azaleas**, while the **herbaceous garden** reaches its peak in July and August, as does the wonderful Victorian vegetable and flower garden beside the sea. Look out, too, for the grand old **eucalypts** in the Peace Plot, which are the largest in the northern hemisphere, and the nearby **Ghost Tree** (*Davidia involucrata*), which represents the earliest evolutionary stages of flowering trees. You'll need at least a couple of hours to do the whole lot justice, and leave time for the **visitor centre** (April, May, Sept & Oct Mon–Sat 10am–5pm, Sun 2–5pm; June–Aug Mon–Sat 9.30am–6pm, Sun noon–6pm), which houses an informative display on the history of the garden. **Guided walks** leave from here every weekday at 1.30pm.

Gruinard Bay and the Scoraig Peninsula

Three buses each week (Mon, Wed & Sat) run the 20-mile stretch along the A832 from Poolewe past **Aultbea**, a small NATO naval base, to the head of **Little Loch Broom**, surrounded by a salt marsh that is covered with flowers in early summer. The road, more or less following the coast, offers fabulous views and passes a string of tiny, anachronistic villages. During World War II, **Gruinard Island**, in the bay, was used as a testing ground for biological warfare, and for years was ringed by huge signs warning the public not to land. The anthrax spores released during the testing can live in the soil for up to a thousand years, but in 1987, after much protest, the Ministry of Defence had the island decontaminated and it was finally declared "safe" in 1990.

The road heads inland before joining the A835 at **Braemore Junction** above the head of **Loch Broom** (3 Inverness–Ullapool buses stop here daily). Just nearby is **CORRIESHALLOCH**, site of the spectacular 164ft **Falls of Measach**, which plunge through a mile-long gorge. You can overlook the cascades from a special observation platform, or from the impressive suspension bridge that spans the chasm, whose 197ft vertical sides are draped in a rich array of plant life, with thickets of wych elm, goat willow and bird cherry miraculously thriving on the cliffs. North from the head of Loch Broom to Ullapool is one of the so-called **Destitution Roads**, built to give employment to local people during the nineteenth-century potato famines.

Hotels along here include the bleak, modern *Ocean View Hotel* at **Laide** (☎01445/731385; ③) which looks pretty tacky, but is good value and in a great position; the *Dundonnell Hotel* (☎01854/612366; ⑤), at the head of Little Loch Broom, is more upmarket – you can stop at either for a meal in the bar. By far the best B&B is *The Old Smiddy* (☎01445/731425; ③) on the main road at Laide. Crammed with travel trophies, family memorabilia, books and paintings by local artists (some on sale), this former smithy has fine mountain views to the east, and does outstanding food, including *pukka* Indian dishes. The *Sail Mhor Croft* (☎01854/633224) on the lochside at **Dundonnell** is a small independent youth **hostel**.

The Scoraig peninsula

The bare and rugged **Scoraig peninsula**, dividing Little Loch Broom and Loch Broom, is one of the most remote places on the British mainland, accessible only by boat from **Badluarach**, two miles off the A832 on the south shore of Little Loch Broom, or on foot. Formerly dotted with crofting townships, it is now deserted apart from tiny **SCORAIG** village, crouched at the isolated western tip of the headland, where an "alternative" New Age community has established itself, complete with windmills, organic vegetable gardens and a Lilliputian primary school. Understandably, Scoraig's inhabitants resent being regarded as tourist curiosities, so only venture out here if you're sympathetic to the community and its aims. A post **boat** leaves Badluarach jetty for the village (Mon, Wed & Fri 10am; 5min); the nearest **bus** stop is south from here at **Badcaul**, on the A832, which you can get to by *Westerbus* from Inverness (Mon, Wed & Sat 5pm; 2hr). Alternatively, **walk** to Scoraig from the hamlet of **Badrallach**, towards the southeastern end of the peninsula, which you can drive to or reach on foot by crossing the pass above the *Altnaharrie Hotel* opposite Ullapool (see p.436). Once you've arrived, **accommodation** is limited to the pleasant *Samadhan* guest house (☎01854/633260; ② including breakfast and dinner), which also does inexpensive wholefood packed lunches. It prefers an advance deposit of 25 percent for longer stays. This place tends to be block-booked during the summer with retreats and workshops, so phone ahead.

Ullapool

ULLAPOOL, the northwest's principal town, was founded at the height of the herring boom in 1788 by the British Fishery Society, on a sheltered arm of land jutting into Loch Broom. The grid-plan town is still an important fishing centre, though its ferry link to Stornoway on Lewis (see p.316) means that in high season the town's personality is practically swamped by visitors. Even so, it's still a hugely appealing place and a good base for exploring the northwest Highlands – especially if you are relying on public transport. Regular buses run from here to Inverness (an easier approach if you are driving than via the sinuous north–south coastal route) and along the coast. Accommodation is plentiful; and Ullapool is an obvious hideaway if the weather is bad, with cosy pubs, a new swimming pool, and the nearest thing on the west coast to an arts centre, *The Ceilidh Place*.

Arrival and information

Forming the backbone of its grid plan, Ullapool's two main arteries are the lochside **Shore Street**, and parallel to it, **Argyle Street**, further inland. **Buses** stop at the pier, in the town centre near the ferry dock, from where it's easy to get your bearings. The well-run **tourist office** (Easter–Nov Mon–Fri 9am–6pm, Sat 10am–6pm, Sun 1–6pm; ☎01854/612135), directly opposite the bus stop, offers an accommodation-booking service. If you're heading on to the Outer Hebrides, there are three daily **ferries** (Mon–Sat; 2hr 30min); for precise timings, contact *CalMac* on ☎01584/612358.

ULLAPOOL: WALKS, HIKES AND CYCLE RIDES

Ordnance Survey Maps Nos. 15, 19 & 20.

Ullapool is at the start of several excellent **hiking trails**, ranging from sedate shoreside ambles to long and strenuous ascents of Munros. However, the weather here can change very quickly, so take the necessary precautions (see p.350). More detailed descriptions of the routes outlined below are available from the youth hostel, Shore St (20p each), and are recommended; the hostel also rents out the relevant up-to-date OS **maps** – essential for the hill walks.

An easy half-day ramble begins at the north end of Quay Street: cross the river here and follow its bank left towards the sea until you reach a second river and cross the bridge. A single-track road leads to a hilltop **lighthouse** from where you gain fine views across the sea to the Summer Isles. Return the same way or via the main road (A835).

For a harder half-day hike, head north along Mill Street on the east edge of town to Broom Court retirement home – trailhead for the **Ullapool hill walk** (look for the sign next to the electricity generator). A rocky path zig-zags steeply up from the roadside to the summit of Meall Mor, where there are great views of the area's major peaks. This is also a prime spot for botanists, with a rich array of plants and flowers, including two insect-eating species, sundew and butterwort. The path then drops sharply down the heather-clad north side of Meall Mor into Glen Achall, where you turn left onto the surfaced road running past the limestone quarry; the main road back to Ullapool lies a further half-hour's walk west. A right turn where the path meets the road will take you up to **Loch Achall** and the start of an old drovers' trail across the middle of the Highlands to Croick (see p.454). A well-maintained bothy at **Knockdamph**, 11 miles further on, marks the midway point of this long-distance hike, which should not be undertaken alone or without proper gear.

If you're reasonably experienced and can use a map and compass, a **day walk** well worth tackling is the **rock path to Achinver**. The route, which winds along one of the region's most beautiful and unspoilt stretches of coastline to a small youth hostel (May–Sept; book ahead on ☎01584/622254; Grade 3), is easy to follow in good weather, but gets very boggy and slippery when wet. Solid footwear, a light pack and a route guide are essential. The warden and assistants here can also give advice on more serious **mountain hikes** in the area. Among the most popular is the walk **to Scoraig** (see p.434), following the old coast route over the pass to Badrallach, on the south side of the peninsula, and then northwest to Scoraig village itself, where you can spend the night. The only drawback with this rewarding route is that to start from Scoraig, you have to rely on the *Altnaharrie Hotel*'s pricy and sporadic ferry boat to get you back to Ullapool (to check times call ☎01854/633230); miss the boat and the only accommodation for miles is the ultra-expensive hotel. If you have a **mountain bike**, the return trip to Scoraig via Badrallach can be completed in a single day.

Alternatively, try the **Rhidorroch estate** track, which turns right off the A835 just past the *Mercury Hotel* (2 miles out of Ullapool), and then heads past the limestone quarry mentioned earlier to Loch Achall and beyond. At the *East Rhiddorroch Lodge*, ignore the suspension bridge and strike up the steep hill ahead on to open moorland and secluded Loch Damph, where there's a small bothy. A much easier but no less scenic cycle route is the tour of Loch Broom, taking in the hamlets of **Letters** and **Loggie** on the tranquil western shore, which you can get to via a quiet single-track road (off the A832 once you've cycled south and round the loch from Ullapool). At the end of this, a jeep track heads for the vitrified iron-age fort at **Dun Lagaidh**; you have to return by the same route. Good cycles are available for **rent** at *Ullapool Mountain Bike Hire*, 11 Pulteny St (☎01854/612260), which also does spares and repairs, and provides helpful route guides of less obvious landrover tracks on private estates in the area.

Accommodation

Ullapool, a popular holiday centre in summer, has all kinds of **accommodation**, ranging from one of Scotland's most expensive hotels, the *Altnaharrie*, to innumerable guest houses and B&Bs, plus a well-situated campsite and an excellent **youth hostel**, Shore St (mid-March to Oct; ☎01854/612254; Grade 2).

Altnaharrie Hotel (☎01854/633230). A world-famous, select hotel with a very highly regarded restaurant across the loch from town – you're collected by launch. ⑨.

Arch Inn, 11 W Shore St (☎01854/612454). One of Ullapool's oldest inns, right on the harbour, offering comfortable mid-range rooms. ④.

Ardale, Market St (☎01854/612220). Good-value central B&B in a modern family home. ②.

Brae Guest House, Shore St (☎01854/612421). A great guest house in a beautifully maintained traditional building right on the lochside. ③.

The Ceilidh Place, W Argyle St (☎01854/612103). Tasteful and popular hotel, with the west coast's best bookshop, relaxing first-floor lounge, great bar-restaurant, sea views, and laid-back atmosphere. ⑦.

The Celidh Place Bunkhouse (May–Oct; details as above). A good-value bunkhouse, with generous off-season discounts; £9–12.50 per person for dorms. ②.

Ferry Boat Inn, Shore St (☎01854/612366). Traditional inn right on the waterfront with a friendly atmosphere and good food. ③.

The Kist, Moss Rd (☎01854/612269). One of Ullapool's cheaper B&Bs; bookable through the tourist office. ②.

The Shieling, Garve Rd (☎01854/612947). Outstandingly comfortable guest house with immaculate rooms, spacious sitting room overlooking the loch, and superb breakfasts (try their homemade venison and leek sausages). Rooms 4 & 5 have the best views. ③.

Tigh Na Mara, Ardinrean (☎01854/655282). Twelve miles from Ullapool on the opposite (west) shore of Loch Broom, and one of Scotland's most renowned vegetarian B&Bs, offering wonderful rooms and gourmet veggie/vegan breakfasts. Well out of town, but worth the trip. ③.

The Town

Most of the action in Ullapool centres on the **harbour**, which has an authentic and salty air, especially when the boats are in. During summer, booths advertise **trips** to the Summer Isles – a cluster of uninhabited islets two to three miles offshore – to view seabird colonies, dolphins and porpoises, but if you're lucky you'll spot marine life from the waterfront. Otters occasionally nose around the rocks near the *Ferry Boat Inn*, and on peaceful summer evenings seals swim past begging scraps from the boats moored in the middle of the loch. The majority of these rusting tubs are Russian and Eastern European **factory boats** that come here to buy fish direct from the local trawlers, which they then process and freeze. Their heavily tattooed crews, known as "Klondykers", regularly wander around town weighed down with brand-new audio equipment, crates of fruit and boxes of coffee. You'll even spot Russian notices announcing local events, and the odd sign in Cyrillic script.

The only conventional "sight" in town is the **museum**, W Argyle St (April–Oct Mon–Fri 10am–5pm; free), in the old parish church, whose recently revamped exhibition features displays on crofting, fishing, local religion, and some interesting stuff on emigration. During the Clearances, Ullapool was one of the ports through which evicted crofters left to start new lives in Canada, Australia and New Zealand.

Eating and drinking

Ullapool has a wide array of places to **eat and drink**, ranging from the cheap and cheerful chippies at the harbour front to one of Scotland's most expensive gourmet restaurants. If you're a seafood fan, though, you won't do better than the *Morefield*, which serves up some of the best fish dishes on the west coast.

Altnaharrie Hotel (☎01854/633230). World-class cuisine by the renowned chef Gun Erikson; superb, but steep at around £70 for dinner and hard to get a table if you're a non-resident.

Arch Inn 11 W Shore St. This friendly local pub, home of the Ullapool football team, serves reasonable bar food, but is essentially a watering hole.

The Ceilidh Place, W Argyle St (☎01854/6122886). Filling snacks at the excellent bar, or full meals, including imaginative and healthy seafood and vegetarian dishes, served in the spacious restaurant, with occasional live music. The good coffee shop does great cakes and homemade ice cream.

Ferry Boat Inn, Shore St. Ullapool's best pub, known locally as the "FBI", serves good food at moderate prices, washed down with a pint of real ale at the lochside – midges permitting. Live folk sessions most Wed & Thurs.

John MacLean's, Shore St. A wholefood shop/deli with a small café upstairs that serves blow-out breakfasts, pizzas, pies and grills, with a selection of freshly baked cakes. They even have the most northerly *Gaggia* coffee machine in Britain.

Morefield, Morefield Lane. Huge portions of succulent seafood; easily Ullapool's best-value, although not so great for vegetarians. The bar has good fish at lower prices.

Tigh Na Mara, Ardindream, on Loch Broom's west side (☎01854/655282). Gourmet vegetarian and vegan food with a difference: specialities include wild mushroom vol au vents, almonds in whisky and lime sauce, vegetarian haggis and seaweed roly-poly. Bring your own wine and reserve.

North of Ullapool

North of Ullapool, the mountain peaks become more widely spaced and settlements smaller and fewer, linked by twisting single-track roads and shoreside footpaths that make excellent hiking trails. You can easily side-step the tourist traffic by heading down the peaceful back roads, which, after twisting through idyllic crofts, invariably end up at a deserted beach or windswept headland with superb views west to the Outer Hebrides.

Ten miles north of Ullapool, a precariously narrow and twisting single-track road west off the A835 squeezes between lower slopes of Cul Beag (2523ft) and Stac Pollaidh (2012ft) and the north shore of majestic Loch Lurgainn to reach the **Coigach peninsula**. Dominated by the awesome bulk of Ben More Coigach (2439ft), rising almost vertically up from sea level, this jagged headland is among the most idyllic of Scottish coastal scenery, with a string of sandy beaches and the Summer Isles scattered a couple of miles offshore.

Coigach's main settlement is **ACHILTIBUIE**, an old crofting village strung out above a series of white-sand coves and rocks tapering into the Atlantic, from where a fleet of small fishing boats carries sheep, and tourists, to the island-grazing pastures during the summer. The village also attracts large numbers of gardening enthusiasts, thanks to the space-station-like structure overlooking its main beach. Dubbed "The Garden of the Future", the **Hydroponicum** (Easter early Oct 10am–5pm; 4–7 tours daily) is a kind of glorified greenhouse that maximizes the natural growing power of the feeble Scottish sunshine, while protecting the plants inside from the cold and the acidic soil. The results – tropical plants, fruit, and fragrant flowers and herbs thriving in four separate "climate rooms" – speak for themselves; you can also taste its famous strawberries in the *Lily Pond* café-restaurant, which serves healthy meals, desserts and snacks, in addition to samples of its home-grown produce. Also worth a visit is the **Achiltibuie Smokehouse** (May–Sept Mon–Sat 9.30am–5pm; free), three miles north of the Hydroponicum at **Altandhu**, where you watch meat, fish and game being cured in the traditional way and can buy some afterwards.

If you can afford it, check into the wonderful *Summer Isles Hotel* (April–Oct; ☎01854/622282; ⑥), just up the road from the school, which enjoys a near-perfect setting above a sandy beach with views over the islands, and is virtually self-sufficient.

The hotel buys in Hydroponicum fruit and veg, but has its own dairy, poultry, and even runs a small smokehouse, so the food in its excellent restaurant (open to non-residents) is about as fresh as it comes. Among Achiltibuie's several **B&Bs**, *Dornie House* (☎01854/622271; ②) is the only one you can book through the tourist office, with a couple of en-suite rooms. There's also a beautifully situated small 20-bed **SYHA youth hostel** (mid-May to Sept; ☎01854/622254; Grade 3) three miles down the coast at **Achininver**, which is handy for Coigach's many mountain hikes.

Lochinver

The coast road running **north from Coigach** is narrow and rough in places, but unre-mittingly spectacular, dominated by the forbidding peaks of Cul Beag (2523ft), Cul Mor (2785ft) and the distinctive sugar-loaf Suilven (2398ft), standing like a line of gargantuan sentinels to the east. A scattering of pebble-dashed bungalows on a shel-tered sea loch heralds your arrival at **LOCHINVER**, the last sizeable village before Thurso. Hemmed in by rocky hillocks that block mountain views, it's a grim little place. However, there's a bank with a cashpoint machine at the south end of the loch – a rarity in these parts – and a better-than-average **tourist office** (April–Oct Mon–Fri 10am–5pm, Sun 10am–4pm; ☎01571/844330), whose new **visitor centre** gives an inter-esting run-down of the area's geology, wildlife and history; a national park ranger is also on hand upstairs to advise on walks. The majority of Lochinver's visitors are well-heeled fishing enthusiasts, so **accommodation** tends to be upmarket. However, a good mid-range option is the *Albanach Hotel* (☎01571/844407; ④) at Baddaidarach, an attractive nineteenth-century building set in a walled garden that is renowned for its excellent seafood, caught locally and served in a lovely wood-panelled dining room; its lunches are particularly good value, with homemade oatcakes and a couple of vegetar-ian specialities on offer. Dozens of **B&Bs** advertise through the local tourist office: *Bracklock* (April–Oct; ☎01571/844253; ②) is the cheapest; while *Veyatie* (☎01571/844424; ③), a modern bungalow on the north side of the bay, has marginally more comfortable en-suite rooms, some with sea views. Finally, if you're on a tight budget, the *Seamens' Mission*, down at the new harbour, is the best place to eat filling basic meals (some vegetarian), and it stays open until 10pm.

Anglers should note that Lochinver is *the* place in the area to stock up on **fishing** gear. *The Fish Selling Co*, next to the pier, has the usual range of rods, reels and bait, while the newsagent in the village, though slightly more pricy, is better for those obscure bits and bobs that can make all the difference.

Inverkirkaig Falls

Approaching Lochinver from the south, the road bends sharply through a wooded valley where a signpost for **Inverkirkaig Falls** marks the start of a long but gentle **walk** to the base of Suilven – the most distinctive mountain in Scotland. Serious hikers use the path to approach the mighty peak, but you can follow it for an easy three-to-four-hour ramble, taking in a waterfall and a tour of a secluded loch. If you're travelling by vehicle, use the car park below the excellent *Achins Bookshop* near the trailhead, which is well stocked with titles on Scotland and the Highlands, and has a café serving cream teas, cakes and good coffee.

East of Lochinver

The area to the **east of Lochinver**, traversed by the A837 and bounded by the gnarled peaks of the Ben More Assynt massif, is a wilderness of mountains, bleak moorland, mist and scree. Dotted with lochs and lochans, it's also an anglers' paradise, home to the only non-migratory fish in northern Scotland, the brown trout, and numerous other sought-after species, including the Atlantic salmon, sea trout, Arctic char and a massive prize strain of cannibal ferox. **Fishing** permits for this area are like gold dust during the summer, snapped up months in advance by exclusive hunting-lodge hotels, but you can sometimes obtain last-minute cancellations (try *The Inver Lodge* on ☎01571/ 844496).

Although most of the land here is privately owned, 27,000 acres are managed as the **Inverpolly National Nature Reserve**, whose visitor centre (mid-May to mid-Sept daily 10am–5pm; ☎01854/666234) at **Knockan Cliff**, 12 miles north of Ullapool on the A835, gives a thorough overview of the diverse flora and wildlife in the surrounding habitats. The eminent nineteenth-century geologists Horn and Peach also discovered the theory of "fault thrusting" here, and an interpretative **Geological Trail** shows you how to detect the movement of rock plates in the nearby cliffs.

Further north, on the rocky promontory that juts into eastern Loch Assynt, stand the jagged remants of **Ardveck Castle** (free access), a MacLeod stronghold from 1597 that fell to the Seaforth Mackenzies after a siege in 1691. Previously, the Marquis of Montrose had been imprisoned here after his defeat at Carbisdale in 1650. The rebel duke, whom the local laird had betrayed to the government for £20,000 and 400 bowls of sour meal, was eventually led away to be executed in Edinburgh, lashed back-to-front on his horse.

The *Inchnadamph Hotel* (☎01571/822202; ⑤) on Loch Assynt, is a wonderfully traditional Highland retreat; inside the walls are covered with the stuffed catches of its past guests (worth a look even if you're not planning to stay). The **hotel** offers fine old-fashioned cooking in its moderately priced restaurant and is popular with anglers who get free fishing rights to the Loch Assynt, as well as several hill lochs backing onto Ben More – haunts of the infamous ferox trout.

North from Lochinver: the coast road

Two possible routes lead **north from Lochinver**: the fast A387, along the shore of Loch Assynt, or the narrow coastal road (the B869) that local people love to dub "The Breakdown Zone" because its ups and downs claim so many victims during summer. Hugging the indented shoreline, this route, covered by **postbus** from Lochinver (daily 3.15pm), is the more scenic, offering superb views of the Summer Isles, as well as a number of rewarding side trips to beaches and dramatic cliffs. Unusually, most of the land and lochs around here are owned by local crofters rather than wealthy landlords. Helped by grants and private donations, "**The Assynt Crofters Trust**" made history in 1993 when it pulled off the first ever community buyout of estate land in Scotland. The trust now owns the lucrative **fishing** rights to the area, too, selling permits for a mere £3 per day (£15 per week) through local post offices, or the newsagent and tourist information office in Lochinver.

Heading north, the first village worthy of a detour from the road is **ACHMELVICH**, whose tiny bay cradles the whitest beach and most stunning turquoise water you'll encounter this side of the Seychelles. Unfortunately, there's a noisy campsite behind it, so you have to pick your way across the surrounding headlands for total peace and quiet. Achmelvich's 40-bed **youth hostel** (April–Sept; ☎01571/844480; Grade 3) overlooks the beach – with no shower, you'll have to make do with basin baths.

The side road that branches north off the B869 between Stoer and Clashnessie ends abruptly by the automatic lighthouse at **Raffin** – built in 1870 by the Stevenson brothers (one of whom was the author Robert Louis Steveson's dad) – but you can continue for two miles along a well-worn track to **Stoer Point**, named after the colossal rock pillar that stands offshore known as "**The Old Man of Stoer**". Surrounded by sheer cliffs and splashed with guano from the seabird colonies that nest on its 200ft sides, it was climbed for the first time in 1961.

DRUMBEG, nine miles further on, is a major target for trout anglers, lying within reach of countless lochans linked in a puzzle formation of streams and pools. Permits to fish them are sold at the post office (£3 per day), but you'll need a detailed map and a compass to find your way in and out of this area without getting hopelessly lost. Alternatively, contact Assynt's only qualified fly-fishing guide and instructor, ex-game keeper Callum Miller, on ☎01933/833231, who charges very reasonable hourly rates and can provide all the necessary equipment. *Culkein* (☎01571/833257; ②), an excellent-value **B&B**, is right on the tip of the headland with fabulous views over **Edrachillis Bay**'s dozens of tiny islands. If you turn off the main road at the primary school and follow the signs you'll soon reach *Taigh Druimbeag* (☎01571/833209; ③), an old Edwardian house with period furniture and a large garden which does superb three-course evening meals for residents.

Kylesku to Kinlochbervie

KYLESKU, 33 miles north of Ullapool and around six miles west of Drumbeg, is the site of the award-winning road bridge spanning the mouth of Lochs Glencoul and Glendhu. It's a pleasant place for a short stay, with plenty of good walks and congenial hotels by the water's edge above a small slipway. The family-run *Kylesku Hotel* (April–Oct; ☎01971/502231; ⑤) has en-suite rooms, a welcoming bar popular with locals, and an excellent restaurant serving imaginative fresh seafood, including lobster, crab, muscles and local salmon (you can watch the fish being landed on the pier). *Statesman Cruises* runs **boat trips** (daily 11am & 2pm; round trip 2hr; £7.50; ☎01571/844446) from the jetty below the hotel to the 650ft **Eas-Coul-Aulin**, Britain's highest waterfall, at the head of Loch Glencoul; seals, porpoises and minke whales can occasionally be spotted along the way.

It is also possible to reach Eas-Coul-Aulin on foot: a rough trail (3hr) leaves the A894 three miles south of Kylesku, skirting the south shore of Loch na Gainmhich (known locally as the "sandy loch") to approach the falls from above. Great care should be taken here as the path above the cliffs can get very slippery when wet; the rest of the route is also difficult to follow, particularly in bad weather, and should only be attempted by experienced, properly equipped and compass-literate hikers (see p.350). However, there are several less demanding **walks around Kylesku** if you just fancy a gentle amble: one of the most popular is the half-day low-level route along the north side of Loch Glendhu, beginning at **Kylestrome**, on the opposite side of the bridge from the hotel. Follow the surfaced jeep track east from the trailhead and turn left on to a footpath that leads through the woods. This eventually emerges on to the open mountainside, dropping down to cross a burn from where it then winds to a boarded-up old house called *Glendhu*, where there's a picturesque pebble beach. Several interesting side trips and variations to this walk may be undertaken with the help of the detailed Ordnance Survey Landranger Map No.15 , but you'll need a compass and wet-weather gear in case of bad weather .

Ten miles north of Kylesku, the widely scattered crofting community of **SCOURIE**, on a bluff above the main road, surrounds a beautiful sandy beach whose safe bathing has made it a popular holiday destination for families, walkers and trout anglers. There's plenty of good **accommodation**; the best by far is the charming *Scourie Lodge* (☎01971/502248; ③), an old shooting retreat with a lovely garden; the welcoming owners also do great evening meals. **BADCALL** village, three miles south of Scourie and even more remote, has a couple of B&Bs, including Mrs Mackay's *Stoer View* (☎01971/502411; ②), whose clean and comfortable rooms look over Edrachillis Bay to Stoer Point. For a little more luxury, try the nearby old-established *Edrachillis Hotel* (☎01971/5020080; ⑥), which enjoys a spectacular situation on the bay, and serves reasonable food.

Handa Island

Visible just offshore to the north of Scourie is **Handa Island**, a huge chunk of red Torridon sandstone surrounded by sheer cliffs and carpeted with machair and purple-tinged moorland. Teeming with **seabirds**, it's an internationally important wildlife reserve and a real feast for ornithologists, with vast colonies of razorbills and guille-mots breeding on its guano-splashed cliffs during summer. From late May to mid-July, large numbers of puffins waddle comically over the turf-covered clifftops where they dig their burrows.

Apart from a solitary warden, Handa is deserted. Until midway through the last century, however, it supported a thriving, if somewhat eccentric, community of croft-ers. Surviving on a diet of fish, potatoes and seabirds, the islanders, whose ruined cottages still cling to the slopes by the jetty, devised their own system of government, with a "queen" (Handa's oldest widow) and "parliament" (a council of men who met each morning to discuss the day's business). Uprooted by the 1847 potato famine, most of the villagers eventually emigrated to Canada's Cape Breton; today, Handa is private property, administered as a nature sanctuary by the Scottish Wildife Trust.

You'll need about three hours to follow the footpath around the island – an easy and enjoyable walk taking in the north shore's **Great Stack** rock pillar and some fine views across the Minch: a detailed route guide is featured in the SWT's free leaflet available from the warden's office when you arrive. Weather permitting, **boats** leave for Handa throughout the day (until around 4pm) from the tiny settlement of **TARBET**, three miles northwest of the main road and reachable by **postbus** from Scourie (Mon–Sat 1 daily; 3pm), where there's a small car park and jetty. However, if you're travelling south, you may prefer to pick up the *Laxford Cruises* boat that sails from **FANAGMORE** (Easter–Oct daily 10am, noon & 2pm, July & Aug also 4pm; £7.50), a mile further up the coast (reached by the same postbus as above). Camping is not allowed on the island, but the SWT maintains a **bothy** for birdwatchers (reservations essential, ☎0131/312 7765), while in Tarbet, Rex & Liz Norris run a comfortable little **B&B** (☎01971/502098; ②) overlooking the bay. For **food**, Tarbet's excellent *Seafood Restaurant* serves delicious, moderately priced fish and vegetarian dishes, and a good selection of home-made cakes and desserts in its airy waterfront conservatory.

Kinlochbervie and beyond

Beyond Scourie, the road sweeps inland through the starkest part of the Highlands; rocks piled on rocks, bog and water create an almost alien landscape, and the stony coastline looks increasingly inhospitable – there's no public transport at all on the 20-mile stretch from here to Durness.

Eight miles or so north of Scourie, at **Rhiconich**, you can branch off the main road to **KINLOCHBERVIE**, a major fishing port crouching among the rocks in a daunt-ingly hostile setting. Trucks from all over Europe pick up cod and shellfish from the trawlers here, crewed mainly by eastcoast fishermen. The *Old Schoolhouse Restaurant and Guest House* (☎01971/521383; ⑤) provides comfortable **accommodation** and home-cooked meals, while the more upmarket *Kinlochbervie Hotel* (☎01971/521275; ⑧) is well known for its excellent food.

Beyond Kinlochbervie, a single-track road takes you through isolated **Oldmoreshore**, a working crofters' village scattered above a stunning white-sand beach, to **BLAIRMORE**. The road ends a couple of miles further west at **Sheigra**, where you can park for the four-mile walk across peaty moorland to deserted **Sandwood Bay**. Few visitors make this half-day detour north, but the beach at the end of the rough track is possibly the most beautiful in Scotland. Flanked by rolling dunes and lashed by fierce gales for much of the year, the shell-white sands are said to be haunted by a bearded mariner – one of many sailors to have perished on this notori-ously dangerous stretch of coast since the Vikings first navigated it over a millennium ago. Around the turn of the last century, the beach, whose treacherous **undercurrents** make it unsuitable for swimming, also witnessed Britian's most recent recorded sighting of a mermaid. Plans are afoot to bulldoze a motorable road up here, so enjoy the tranquility while you can. Cape Wrath, the most northwesterly point in mainland Britain, lies a day's hike north. However, most people approach the headland from Durness on the north coast (see below).

THE NORTH COAST

Convoys of frozen-fish trucks rumble year-round to within a stone's throw of Cape Wrath, and a constant stream of sponsored walkers, caravans and tour groups makes it to John O'Groats, but surprisingly few visitors travel the whole length of the Highlands' wild **North Coast**. Those that do, however, rarely return disappointed. Pounded by one of the world's most ferocious seaways, Scotland's rugged northern shore is backed by barren mountains in the west, and in the east by lochs and open rolling grasslands. Between its far ends, mile apon mile of crumbling cliffs and sheer rocky headlands shelter bays whose perfect white beaches are nearly always deserted, even in the height of summer. This is a great area for **birdwatching**, too, with huge seabird colonies clustered in clefts and on remote stacks at regular intervals along the coast; seals also bob around in the surf offshore, and in winter, whales put in the odd appearence in the more sheltered estuaries of the northwest.

Getting around this stretch of coast without your own transport can be a slow and frustrating business: **John O'Groats** and **Thurso**, the area's main town and springboard for the Orkneys, are well connected by **bus** with Inverness, but further west, after the main A836 peters into a single-track road, bus services dry up altogether. The only public transport between Thurso and **Durness**, in the far northwest, is a convoluted series of **postbus** connections via Lairg (see p.454). You can, however, travel direct to Durness on a daily bus from Inverness, calling at the remote and beautiful villages of **Bettyhill** and **Tongue** en route.

Durness and around

Scattered around a string of sheltered coves and grassy clifftops, **DURNESS**, the most northwesterly village on the British mainland, straddles the turning point on the main road as it swings east from the inland peat bogs of the interior to the north coast's fertile strip of limestone machair. First settled by the Picts around 400 BC, the area has been farmed ever since; its crofters being among the few not cleared off estate land during the nineteenth century. Today, Durness is the centre of several crofting communities and a good base for a couple of days, with plenty of accommodation, a couple of decent pubs, and rewarding coast walks. Even if only passing through, it's worth pausing here to see the **Smoo Cave**, a gaping hole in a sheer limestone crag, and to visit beautiful **Balnakiel beach**, to the west. In addition, Durness is the jumping-off point for roadless and rugged **Cape Wrath**, the windswept promontory at the Scotland's northwest tip, which has retained an end-of-the-world mystique lost long ago by John O'Groats.

The Smoo Cave

A short walk south of Durness village centre lies the 200ft-long **Smoo Cave**, a natural wonder, formed partly by the action of the sea, and partly by the small burn that flows through it. Tucked away at the end of a narrow sheer-sided sea cove, guides will show you the illuminated interior, although the much-hyped rock formations are less memorable than the short rubber-dinghy trip you have to make to get to them. In winter to late spring, this is made even more fun by the waterfall that crashes through the middle of the cavern. However, for a really novel view of the cave, try **abseiling** down its gigantic entrance. Instruction and equipment rental costs £5–10, depending on whether you attempt the 30ft or 100ft cliff. Alternatively, hop in the boat that leaves from Smoo Cave for a **wildlife tour** of the coast around Durness. Taking in stretches of the shoreline only accessible by sea, the trip (May–Sep daily, times depending on weather and tide; 90min; £6) takes in seabird colonies at close hand, and sightings of seals, puffins and porpoises are also common.

Balnakiel

A narrow road winds northwest of Durness to the tiny **BALNAKIEL**, whose name derives from the Gaelic *Baile ne Cille* (Village of the Church). The ruined chapel that today overlooks this remote hamlet was built in the seventeenth century, but a church has stood here for at least 1200 years. A skull-and-crossbones stone set in the south wall marks the grave of **Donald MacMurchow**, a seventeenth-century highwayman and contract killer who murdered 18 people for his clan chief (allegedly by throwing them from the top of the Smoo Cave). The "half-in, half-out" position of his grave was apparently a compromise between his grateful employer and the local clergy, who initially refused to allow such an evil man to be buried on church ground. Balnakiel is also known for its **golf course**, whose ninth and final hole involves a 155-yard drive over the Atlantic; you can rent equipment from the clubhouse. The **Balnakiel Craft Village** (daily 10am–6pm; free), back towards Durness, is worth a visit. Housed in an imaginatively converted 1950s military base, the campus consists of a dozen or so workhops where you can watch painters, potters, leather workers, candle makers, patchwork quilters, horn carvers, soft-toy makers and weavers in action. However, as most of the craftspeople are English or "incomers", you won't see many Scottish crafts here.

The white-sand **beach** on the east side of Balnakiel Bay is a stunning sight in any weather, but most spectacular on sunny days when the water turns to brilliant turquoise. For the best views, head along the path that winds north through the dunes behind it; this eventually leads to **Faraid Head** – from the Gaelic *Fear Ard* (High Fellow) – where you stand a good chance of spotting puffins from late May until mid-July. The fine views over the mouth of Loch Eriboll and west to Cape Wrath make this round **walk** (3–4hr) the best in the Durness area.

Cape Wrath

An excellent day trip from Durness begins three miles south of the village at **Keoldale**, where a foot-passenger ferry (May–Aug hourly 9.30am–4.30pm; Sept 4 daily; no motorcycles; ☎01971/511376) crosses the Kyle of Durness estuary to link up with the minibus (May–Sept; ☎01971/511287) that runs out to **Cape Wrath**, 11 miles further along a dirt track. The UK mainland's most northwesterly point, the headland takes its name not from the stormy seas that crash against it for most of the year, but from the Norse word *parph*, meaning "turning place" – a throwback to the days when Viking war ships used it as a navigation point during raids on the Scottish coast. These days, a lighthouse (another of those built by Robert Louis Stevenson's father) warns ships away from the treacherous rocks. Looking east to the Orkneys and west to the Outer Hebrides, it stands above the famous **Clo Mor cliffs**, the highest sea cliffs in Britain and a prime breeding site for **seabirds**. You can **walk** from here to remote Sandwood Bay (see p.441), visible to the south; although the route, which cuts inland across lochan-dotted moorland, is hard to follow in places. Hikers generally continue south from Sandwood to the trail end at Blairmore, six miles west of Kinlochbervie, and hitch from there back to the main road where you can catch buses north to Durness. Don't attempt this route south–north: if the weather closes in, the Cape Wrath minibus stops running.

As an alternative to the Cape Wrath minibus, you can rent a **mountain bike** from the Durness youth hostel. However, much of the land bordering the headland is a **military firing range**, so check the firing times with the tourist office before you set off.

Durness Practicalities

Durness is connected by regular **bus** services to Inverness, Lochinver and Ullapool, but getting here by public transport from anywhere else on the north coast is very difficult. Amazingly, there are no longer any direct buses between here and Thurso, which you can only reach by postbus – a five-hour journey involving two changes (at Tongue and Bettyhill). Precise timings of these, and other, **postbus** services are displayed in the village shop and at the youth hostel.

Durness has an enthusiastic **tourist office** (March–Oct Mon–Sat 9am–6pm; ☎01971/511259), in the village centre, which can help with accommodation; its small visitor centre also houses some excellent interpetative panels detailing the area's history, geology, flora and fauna. Of the several **hotels** clustered together nearby, the *Parkhill* (☎01971/511209; ③) is best value, while *Rowan House* (☎01971/511252; ③), near the charmless *Smoo Cave Hotel*, is a cosy and immaculately clean B&B overlooking the sea. If neither has any vacancies, try *Puffin Cottage* (☎01971/511208; ③). There's also a friendly **youth hostel** (mid-May to Sept; ☎01971/511244; Grade 3), a mile and a half east of town, and **camping** at *Sango Sands Caravan and Camping Site*, Harbour Rd (☎01971/511262), which has the added advantage of a good **bar** and **restaurant**. The *Cape Wrath Hotel* (☎01971/511212; ⑥), right by the ferry point, is a solidly traditional place popular with anglers; overlooking the estuary, it's the best hotel within easy reach of the village, although the rooms are a little pricy. **Eating** options in Durness are largely confined to bar food: the *Smoo Cave Hotel* is fine for something cheap and cheerful, but for a classier gourmet meal, reserve a table at the *Cape Wrath Hotel*'s restaurant, whose set menus cost around £15 per head.

Loch Eriboll

Ringed by ghost-like limestone mountains, deep and sheltered **Loch Eriboll**, six miles east of Durness, is the north coast's most spectacular sea loch. Servicemen stationed here during World War II to protect passing Russian convoys nicknamed it "Loch 'Orrible", but if you're looking for somewhere wild and unspoilt, you'll find this a perfect spot. Porpoises and otters are a common sight along the rocky shore, and minke whales occasionally swim in from the open sea.

Overlooking its own landing stage at the water's edge, *Port-Na-Con* (mid-March to Oct; ☎01971/511367; ③), seven miles from Durness on the west side of the loch, is a wonderful **B&B**, popular with anglers and divers (it'll refill air tanks for £2.50). Top-notch food is served in its small **restaurant** (open all year, including Christmas), with a choice of vegetarian haggis, local kippers, fruit compôte and homemade croissant for breakfast, and adventurous three-course evening meals for around £10; the menu always includes a gourmet vegetarian dish. Non-residents are welcome, although you'll need to book. If *Port-Na-Con* is full, a good fallback is the nearby *Choraidh Croft* (Easter–Nov; ☎01971/511235; ②), a modern lochside B&B on a working croft. This also does good-value lunches and evening meals, and offers plenty of choice for vegetarians/vegans.

Tongue

It's a long slog around Loch Eriboll and east over the top of A Mhòine moor to the pretty crofting township of **TONGUE**. Dominated by the ruins of **Varick Castle**, the village, an eleventh-century Norse stronghold, is strewn over the east shore of the **Kyle** of **Tongue**, which you can either cross via a new causeway, or by following the longer and more scenic single-track road around its southern side. When the tide recedes, this shallow estuary becomes a mass of golden sand flats, superb on sunny days with the sharp profiles of Ben Hope (3040ft) and Ben Loyal (2509ft) looming to the south.

In 1746, the Kyle of Tongue was the scene of a naval engagement that sealed the fate of Bonnie Prince Charlie's Jacobite rebellion. In response to a plea for help from the Prince, the King of France dispatched a sloop and £13,600 in gold coins to Scotland. However, the Jacobite ship, the *Prince Charles*, was spotted by the English frigate, *Sheerness*, and fled into the Kyle, hoping that the larger enemy vessel would not be able to follow. It did, though, and soon forced the *Prince Charles* aground. Pounded by English cannon fire, its Jacobite crew slipped ashore under cover of darkness in an attempt to smuggle the treasure to Inverness, but they were followed by scouts of the local Mackay clan, who were not "out" in '45. The next morning, a larger platoon of Mackays waylayed the rebels, who, hopelessly outnumbered and out-gunned, began throwing the gold into the nearest lochan (most of it was recovered later). The Prince, meanwhile, had sent 1500 of his men north to rescue the treasure, but these too were defeated en route; historians have wondered ever since whether the missing men might have altered the outcome of the battle of Culloden.

If you want to stay in Tongue, *Rhian Cottage* (☎01847/611257; ②), a pretty white-washed house with an attractive garden, and *Woodend* (☎01847/611332; ②), at the top of the village down a side road, with panoramic views of the estuary, are both pleasant and comfortable **B&Bs**. The *Ben Loyal Hotel* (☎01847/611216; ⑤) and *Tongue Hotel* (☎01847/611206; ③) are more luxurious; both do **bar food**. There's also a beautifully situated and friendly SYHA **youth hostel** (mid-March to Sept; ☎01847/55301; Grade 2), a mile north of the village centre on the east shore of the kyle.

South from Tongue: the Flow Country

From Tongue, you can head 40 miles or so **south** towards Lairg (see p.454) on the A836, skirting the edges of the **Flow Country**. This huge expanse of bog land came into the news a few years ago when ecology experts, responding to plans to transform the area into forest, drew media attention to the threat to this fragile landscape, described by one contemporary commentator as of "unique and global importance, equivalent to the African Serengeti or Brazil's rainforest". Some forest was planted, but the environmentalists eventually won and the forestry syndicates have had to pull out.

Bettyhill to Dounreay

BETTYHILL, a major crofting village, straggles along the side of a narrow tidal estuary, and down the coast to two splendid beaches. Forming an unbroken arc of pure white sand between the Naver and Borgie Rivers, **Torrisdale beach** is the more impressive of the pair, ending in a smooth white spit that forms part of the **Invernaver Nature Reserve**. During summer, arctic terns nest here on the river banks, dotted with clumps of rare Scottish primroses, and you stand a good chance of spotting an otter or two. In the village, the mildly interesting **Strathnaver Museum** (Easter–Sept Mon–Sat 10am–1pm & 2–5pm; £1.50), housed in the old church, is full of locally donated bits and pieces, including a room dealing with the Clearances. You can also see some Pictish stones and a 3800-year-old early Bronze Age beaker. This and other artefacts were found around Strathnaver, the river valley south of the village, whose numerous prehistoric sites are mapped on an excellent pamphlet sold at the entrance desk .

Bettyhill's small **tourist office** (March–Sept Mon–Sat 9am–5pm; ☎016412/521342) can book **accommodation** for you. The central *Bettyhill Hotel* (☎016412/521352; ③) is pretty basic; half a mile away, near the windswept beach, the friendly *Farr Bay Inn*

(☎016412/521230; ④) has a lot more character, and does excellent **bar food**. There are also several good-value **B&Bs**, including *Shenley* (☎016412/521421; ②), a grand detached house on the hillside with four comfortable rooms, and *Hadenrigg* (☎01641/521240; ②), just off the road above the estuary (a mile north of the bridge across the kyle), which has just one double-bedded room and offers wholefood breakfasts with fresh homemade yoghurt.

As you move west from Bettyhill, the north coast changes dramatically; the single-track road widens and sprouts white lines, and the hills on the horizon recede to be replaced by fields fringed with traditional flagstone hedges. At the hamlet of **MELVICH**, 12 miles from Bettyhill, the A897 cuts south through the open valleys of Strath Halladale and the Strath of Kilodonan, both of which offer excellent salmon fishing, to **Helmsdale** on the east coast (see p.457).

Five miles further east, **DOUNREAY** Nuclear Power Station, a surreal collection of stark domes and chimney stacks marooned in the middle of nowhere, is still a fairly major local employer, in spite of the fact its three fast breeder reactors were decommissioned in April 1994. A permanent exhibition details the processes (and, unsurprisingly, the benefits) of nuclear power, and you can take a tour (Easter–Sept daily 10am–5pm; free). Don't, however, expect to hear much about the area's "leukaemia cluster", nor the worryingly high levels of radiation reported over the years on the nearby beaches.

Thurso

Approached from the isolation of the west, **THURSO** looks like a major metropolis. In fact, it's simply a small service town, grey and tidy, with well-planned streets and the higgledy-piggledy remnants of the fishing port it once was strung around a broad bay. The town's name derives from the Norse word *Thorsa*, literally "River of the God Thor", and in Viking times this was a major gateway to the mainland. Later, ships set sail from here for the Baltic and Scandinavian ports loaded with meal, beef, hides and fish. The nearby Dounreay Nuclear Power Station ensured continuing prosperity after World War II; workers from the plant (dubbed "Atomics" by the locals) settled in Thurso in large numbers, and their disappearence following its 1994 closure has hit the local economy hard.

Traill Street is the main drag, turning into the pedestrianized High Street precint at its northern end. Apart from a handful of mediocre shops, there's not much to see; most visitors who linger are on their way to the Orkney ferry, which leaves from nearby **Scrabster**. If you've got time to fill, however, check out the ruined twelfth- to sixteenth-century **Old St Peter's Kirk**, in the old part of town near the harbour on the way to the **beach** (turn right when you get to the end of High St). You could also visit the average display at the **Thurso Heritage Museum**, High St (Mon–Sat 10am–5pm; 50p), which houses a reconstructed croft house and the prehistoric Pictish "Ulbster Stone", intricately carved with enigmatic symbols.

Practicalities

It's a ten-minute walk from the **train station**, down Princes St and Sir George St, to the **tourist office**, Riverside Rd (April–Oct Mon–Sat 9am–6pm, July & Aug also Sun 10am–6pm; ☎01847/892371). The **bus station**, close by, runs regular buses to John O'Groats, Wick and Inverness. However, there's no public transport west along the north coast from Thurso; you'll have to travel via Lairg, or else catch an early-morning **postbus** to Bettyhill, from where a second postbus leaves later in the day for Durness. **Ferries** operate daily from adjoining Scrabster to Orkney. You can book ahead through *P&O Scottish Ferries*, Aberdeen (☎01224/572615) or through any local tourist office. If you just fancy a day trip to Orkney see "John O'Groats" opposite.

Thurso is wellstocked with good-value **accommodation**: the tourist office has a full list. On Traill St, both the *Central Hotel* (☎01847/893100; ③) and the *Royal Hotel* (☎01847/893191; ③) are good value. Of the **B&Bs**, *Mrs Oag*, 9 Couper St (☎01847/894529; ②), east of High St near the town hall, is the cheapest, a welcoming place that serves huge breakfasts. Also worth a try are *Mrs Budge* (☎01847/893205; ③), 6 Pentland Crescent next to the beach front, and *Mrs Faulkner*, 1 Campbell St (☎01847/895759; ③) – both central and clean. **Food**, though not adventurous, is always fresh and great value. Most of the restaurants are in the hotels; *Johnston's Café*, Traill St, is good for quick snacks, and the *Pentland Hotel* does upmarket bar meals. For inexpensive and good Chinese, Indian and seafood dishes, try the *Fountain Restaurant*, Sinclair St; and if you're looking for an enjoyably rowdy local **pub**, check out the *Central*, Traill St. Finally, the *Upper Deck*, right by the harbour at Scrabster, does copious, well-prepared and moderately priced steaks and wicked puddings. **Nightlife** is as limited as you'd expect, but the *Pentland Hotel*, Princes St, hosts a Highland Night once a week, and there are occasional concerts and ceilidhs at the town hall, High St. Ask at the tourist office for a copy of the monthly, *What's On in Caithness*.

Dunnet Head to Duncansby Head

Despite the plaudits that John O' Groats customarily receives, Britain's northernmost mainland point is in fact **Dunnet Head** – at the far side of Dunnet Bay, an impressive sweep of sandy beach backed by dunes about six miles east of Thurso. The bay is becoming well known by **surfers**, and even in the winter you can usually spot intrepid figures far out in the Atlantic surf.

For Dunnet Head, turn off at **DUNNET**, at the east end of the bay, onto the B855, which runs for four miles over windy heather and bog to the tip of the headland, crowned with a 350ft Victorian lighthouse. The red cliffs below it are startling, with weirdly eroded rock stacks and a huge variety of seabirds; on a clear day you can see the whole northern coastline from Cape Wrath to Duncansby Head, and across Pentland Firth to the Orkneys. The *Northern Sands Hotel* (☎01847/851270; ⑥), in Dunnet village, is worth a stop, if only to eat in the restaurant; its Italian owner produces homemade pasta, very popular with the locals.

John O'Groats

Familiar from endless postcards, **JOHN O' GROATS** comes as something of an anti climax. The views north across the churning waters to the Orkneys are fine enough, but the village itself – neither the most northerly, nor most westerly point in Britain – turns out to be little more than a windswept grassy slope leading down to the sea, dominated by an enormous car park that is jammed throughout the summer with enormous tour buses. Collectors of kitsch seaside souvenirs, however, will have a field day in the many gift shops here. The village gets its name from the Dutchman, Jan de Groot, who obtained the ferry contract for the crossing to the Orkneys in 1496. The eight-sided house he built for his eight quarrelling sons (so that each one could enter by his own door) is echoed in the octagonal tower of the much photographed *John O' Groats Hotel* (☎01955/611203; ③), good as a stop-off for a quick drink and an inexpensive place to spend the night.

John O'Groats is connected by regular **buses** to Wick (6–7 daily; 55min) and Thurso (Mon–Fri 4 daily, Sat 2 daily; 40min). *Thomas & Bews* (☎01955/611353) runs a daily passenger ferry across to Burwick in the Orkney Islands (May–Sept 4 daily; 45min; £22 return), the last one at 6pm; officially this is a foot-passenger service, but it will take bicycles and motorbikes if it isn't too busy. The **tourist office** (April–Oct Mon–Sat 9am–5pm; ☎01955/611373) by the car park will help you sort out **accommodation**. The *Caber-feidh Guest House* (☎01955/611219; ③), at the junction of the Wick and

Thurso roads, has a handful of comfortable en-suite rooms and a bar, while *Heaven Gore* (☎01955/611314; ②) is a large and good-value B&B a mile west along the Thurso road. If you're on a tight budget, head for the small **youth hostel** (April–Oct; ☎01955/611424; Grade 2) at Canisbay, one and a half miles west of John O'Groats.

Duncansby Head

If you're disappointed by John O' Groats, press on a couple of miles further east to **Duncansby Head**, which, with its lighthouse, dramatic cliffs and well-worn coastal path, has a lot more to offer. The **birdlife** here is prolific, and south of the headland lie some spectacular 200ft cliffs, cut by sheer-sided clefts known locally as *geos*. This is also a good place from which to view the Orkneys. Dividing the islands from the mainland is the infamous **Pentland Firth**, one of the world's most treacherous waterways. Only seven miles across, it forms a narrow channel between the Atlantic Ocean and North Sea, and for 14 hours each day the tide rips through here from west to east at a rate of ten knots or more, flooding back in the opposite direction for the remaining ten hours. Combined with the rocky sea bed and a high wind, this can cause deep whirlpools and terrifying 30 to 40ft towers of water to form when the ebbing tide crashes across the reefs offshore. The latter, known as the "**Bores of Duncansby**", are the subject of many old mariners' myths from the time of the Vikings onwards.

THE EAST COAST

The **east coast** of the Highlands, between Inverness and Wick, is nowhere near as spectacular as the west, with gentle undulating moors, grassland, and low cliffs where you might expect to find sea lochs and mountains. Washed by the cold waters of the North Sea, it's markedly cooler, too, although less prone to spells of perma-drizzle. The fast A9 is the region's main transport artery; winding in tandem with the Inverness–Thurso train line, it never strays far from the coast, which veers sharply northeast exactly parallel with the Great Glen, formed by the same geological fault.

From around the ninth century AD onwards, the **Norse** influence was more keenly felt here than any other part of mainland Britain, and dozens of Scandinavian-sounding names recall the era when this was a Viking kingdom. The clan system the Norsemen left behind, however, did not take root as firmly as it did elsewhere in Scotland. Instead, the northeast evolved more or less separately, avoiding the bloody tribal feuds that wrought such havoc further south and west. Nevertheless, the ninetheenth-century **Clearances** hit the region hard, as countless ruined cottages and the empty moorland wastes show. Hundreds of thousands of crofters were evicted, and forced to emigrate to New Zealand, Canada and Australia, or else take up fishing in one of the numerous herring ports established on the coast. The recent oil boom has brought a transient prosperity to many of these over the past two decades, but the area remains one of the country's poorest, reliant on sheep farming, fishing and tourism.

The one stretch of the east coast that's always been relatively rich is the **Black Isle**, whose main town, **Cromarty**, is the region's undisputed highlight, with a crop of elegant eighteenth-century houses looking north across the Dornoch Firth. In late-medieval times, pilgrims poured through here en route to the red-sandstone town of **Tain** to worship at the shrine of St Duthac, where the former sacred enclave has now been converted into one of the many "heritage centres" that punctuate the route north. Beyond **Dornoch**, a famous golfing resort renowned for its salubrious climate and sweeping beach, the ersatz-Loire chateau, **Dunrobin Castle**, is the main tourist attraction, a monument as much to the iniquities of Clearances as to the eccentricity of Victorian taste. The award-winning Timespan Heritage Centre further north at **Helmsdale** recounts the human cost of the landlords' greed, while the area around the port of **Lybster** is littered with the remains of more ancient civilizations. An obvious destination if you're heading north is **Wick**. However, the east coast's largest town, huddled around a small bay and fishing harbour, turns out to be a lot less appealing than the countryside around it: a treeless, windswept tract of open farmland and bog, dotted peat-black lochans and divided by endless stone walls that converge on white-washed crofts.

The Black Isle and around

Sandwiched between the Cromarty and Beauly Firths, the **Black Isle** is not an island at all, but a fertile peninsula whose rolling hills, prosperous farms, and stands of decid-uous woodland make it more reminiscent of Dorset or Sussex than the Highlands. It probably gained its name because of its mild climate: there's rarely frost, which leaves the fields "black" all winter; another explanation is that the name derives from the Gaelic word for black, *dubh* – a possible corruption of St Duthus (see p.452).

Black Isle is littered with dozens of prehistoric sites, but the main incentive to make the detour east from the A9 is to visit the picturesque eighteenth-century town of Cromarty, huddled at the northeast tip of the peninsula. A string of villages along the south coast is also worth stopping off in en route, while **Chanonry Point** is among the best **dolphin-spotting** sites in Europe.

Avoch, Fortrose and Rosemarkie

The most rewarding approach to Cromarty is along the south side of Black Isle, via the A832 from Kessock Bridge. Hugging the shore, a narrow side road branches off this to the attractive little harbourside fishing village of **AVOCH** (pronounced *Auch*). **FORTROSE**, a few miles further east, is a lacklustre resort dominated by the ruins of a twelfth-century **cathedral**. Founded by King David I, it now languishes on a lovely yew-studded green, hemmed in by red-sandstone and colour-washed houses, where a horde of gold coins dating from the time of Robert III was unearthed in 1880. There's also a memorial to the Seaforth family, whose demise the Brahan Seer famously predicted (see below).

There's a memorial plaque to the seer at nearby **CHANONRY POINT**, reached by a back road from Fortrose; the thirteenth hole of the golf course here marks the spot where he met his death. Jutting into a narrow but deep channel in the Moray Firth (gouged to allow war ships into the estuary during the last war), the point, fringed on one side by a wonderful white-sand **beach**, is also an excellent place to look for **dolphins** (see p.402). Come here around high tide, and you stand a good chance of spotting a couple leaping through the surf in search of fish brought to the surface by converging currents.

ROSEMARKIE, a one-street village north of Fortrose at the opposite (northeast) end of the beach, is thought to have been evangelized by St Boniface in the early eighth century; indeed, local legend has it that the carved Pictish stone in the church-yard marks his grave. A collection of even better-preserved Pictish artefacts is on display at Rosemarkie's **Groam House Museum** (May–Oct Mon–Sat 10am–5pm, Sun 2–4.30pm; Nov–April Sat–Sun 2–4pm; £1.50), at the bottom of the village. In addition to a bumper crop of intricately carved standing stones (among them the famous Rosemarkie Cross Slab), the museum shows films on local topics such as the Picts and Brahan Seer. A lovely mile-and-a-half woodland **walk** along the banks of a sparkling burn to **Fairy Glen**, begins at the car park just beyond the village on the road to Cromarty. Inexpensive bar **food** is also available at the wonderfully old-fashioned *Plough Inn*, down the lane from the museum.

Cromarty

An ancient legend recalls that the twin headlands flanking the entrance to the Cromarty Firth, known as The Sutor Rocks (from the Gaelic word for shoemaker), were once a pair of giant cobblers who used to protect Black Isle from pirates. Nowadays, however, the only giants in the area are Nigg and Invergordon's colossal oil rigs, marooned in the estuary like metal monsters marching out to sea. Built and serviced here for the Forties North Sea oil field, they form a surreal counterpoint to the cobbled streets and choco-late-box workers' cottages of **CROMARTY**, the Black Isle's main settlement. Sheltered by the Sutors at the northeast corner of the peninsula, the town, an ancient ferry cross-ing point on the pilgrimage trail to St Duthac's shrine in **Tain**, is a perfect example of an eighteenth-century Scottish seaport forced out of business by the arrival of the train line. It was a Royal Burgh five centuries before the advent of train travel, but only became a prominent port in 1772 after the entrepreneurial local landlord, George Ross, founded a hemp mill here. Imported Baltic cannabis was spun into cloth and rope in the mill, fuel-ling a period of prosperity during which Cromarty acquired some of Scotland's finest Georgian houses; these, together with the terraced fishers' cottages of the nineteenth-century herring boom have earned for the town the somewhat corny epithet "the jewel in the crown of Scottish vernacular architecture".

To get a sense of Cromarty head straight for the award-winning museum house in the old **Courthouse**, Church St (daily Easter–Oct 10am–6pm; Nov–Easter noon–4pm; £2), which tells the history of the town using audio-visuals and animated figures (not as dreadful as they sound, and children love them). You are also issued with a personal stereo, a tape and a map for a walking tour around the town. **Hugh Miller**, the nine-teenth-century stonemason turned author, geologist, folklorist and Free Church campaigner, was born in Cromarty, and his **birthplace**, a narrow, cramped thatched cottage nearby on Church St (May–Sept Mon–Sat 10am–1pm & 2–5.30pm, Sun 2–5.30pm; NTS; £1.50), has been restored to look as it did when he lived there, with a small collection of his personal belongings. Once you've seen that you've really seen Cromarty, although there's an excellent **walk** out to the south Sutor stacks. You can pick up the path by leaving town on Miller Road, and turning right when the lane becomes "The Causeway"; follow this through the woods and past eighteenth-century Cromarty House until you reach the junction at Mains Farm; a left turn here takes you across open fields and through woods to the top of the headland, from where there are superb views across the Moray Firth.

Before you move on, bear in mind, too, that Bill Fraser will take you out in his boat to see seals, porpoises and bottle-nosed **dolphins** just off the coast (June–Sept daily every 90min), or killer whales (orcas) on longer cruises during the winter (4hr); if you're interested, contact him on ☎013817/600323. The tiny two-car Nigg–Cromarty **ferry** (April–Oct 9am–6pm), the smallest in Scotland, also doubles up as a cruiser on summer evenings; you can catch it from the jetty near the lighthouse.

Practicalities

Four **buses** each day run to Cromarty from Inverness (45min), returning from the stop near the playing fields on the western outskirts of town. During summer, **accommodation** is in short supply, so book ahead. Most upmarket is the traditional *Royal Hotel* (☎01381/600217; ⑥), down at the harbour, which has rather small but richly furnished rooms overlooking the Firth, and an excellent bar-restaurant. For **B&B**, try *The Cobbles*, Church St (☎01381/600374; ②), a cosy and immaculate place run by Scotland's most avid dolphin spotters, or *The Old Commercial*, Bank St (☎01381/600540; ②), whose affable Canadian expat owners serve delicious corn-meal muffins for breakfast. The *Retreat* (☎01381/600400; ②), and *Mrs Robertson* (☎01381/600488; ②), both on Church St, are two more very good-value B&Bs in attractive old houses.

The most down-to-earth place in Cromarty to **eat** is the *Cromarty Arms*, which serves basic, inexpensive bar meals, and a good selection of real ales and malts. They also host a lively karaoke night and occasional C & W bands on Fridays. If you're after something a little more sophisticated, head for the *Thistle Restaurant*, Church St, whose quality cuisine has a distinctly Scottish flavour, with several seafood and vegetarian specialities; dinner isn't cheap, but its gourmet lunches only cost around £5. The *Royal Hotel* also has a top-notch restaurant that serves wonderful, though pricy, Scots dishes; you can order cheaper meals in the cosy public bar, warmed by an open fire and with great views out over the Firth.

Strathpeffer

STRATHPEFFER, a Victorian spa town surrounded by hills and trees, is a congenial place to stop over. During its heyday, this was a renowned European health resort complete with a **Pump Room**, where visitors could chat while they sipped the water. Today, sadly, several of its fine buildings are in a sorry state, although two or three mammoth faded hotels remain. Activity is concentrated around the main square, where you can sample sulphur-laden water at the **Water Sampling Pavilion**.

Within striking distance of the bleak Benn Wyvis massif, Strathpeffer is also a popular base for walkers. One of the best full-day **hikes** in the area begins from the SYHA youth hostel, at the west end of the village, from where a forestry track leads through dense woodland to the top of the Peffer *strath*, or stream valley. Three quarters of a mile further on, you can make a short side trip up to **Knock Farrill**, a vitrified knoll 100ft above the path that affords fine panoramic views up the Cromarty Firth and over the surrounding mountains. To extend this walk, drop down the south side of the knoll to the surfaced road and carry on until you get to a "T" junction, where you should turn left for Dingwall; the route is marked, and there's plenty of transport back to Strathpeffer.

Practicalities

Buses run regularly between Dingwall and Strathpeffer (Mon–Sat), dropping passengers in the square, where you'll find a small **tourist office** (Easter–Nov Mon–Sat 10am–5pm; ☎01997/421415) with information on points west as well as local areas. The **hotels** in the village are very popular with bus tours, but often have room: the vast *Ben Wyvis* (☎01997/421323; ④) is adequate, in nice grounds east of the main square on the Dingwall road; while north of the main square, a converted Victorian villa, complete with turrets, houses the *Holly Lodge Hotel* (☎01997/421254; ⑤). Nearby, the *Inver Lodge* (☎01997/421392; ②) and *Francisville* (☎01997/421345; ②), both west of the main square, offer good **B&B**, although *Scoraig*, 8 Kenneth St (☎01997/421847; ②) is cheaper. If you don't mind dorms, head for the rambling 70-bed **youth hostel** (mid-March to Sept; ☎01997/421532; Grade 2), a mile southwest of the main square up the hill towards Jameston.

Dingwall and the Cromarty Firth

Most traffic nowadays takes the upgraded A9 north from Inverness, bypassing the small provincial town of **DINGWALL** (from the Norse *thing*, "parliament", and *volle*, "place"), a former port that was left high and dry when the river receded during the last century. Today, it's a tidy but dull service and market town with one long main street that's bustling all day and moribund by dinner time. Dingwall's only real claim to fame is that it was the birthplace of Macbeth, whose family occupied the now ruined castle on Castle Street.

If you need to **stay**, *Victoria Lodge*, Mill St (☎01349/862494; ②), and *Kirklee* (☎01349/863439; ②) are standard B&Bs, while the posh *Tulloch Castle Hotel*, Castle Drive (☎01349/861325; ⑥), a former Highland clan headquarters, and the two-star *Royal Hotel*, High St (☎01349/862130; ④), are both comfortable upmarket options with most mod cons.

Northeast of Dingwall, the **Cromarty Firth** has always been recognized as a perfect natural harbour. During World War I it was a major **naval base**, and today its sheltered waters are used as a centre for rig repair for the North Sea oil fields. The 15-mile stretch of the fast A9 from **Alness** to Tain passes several villages which have boomed with the expansion of the oil industry, notably **Invergordon**, on the coast just west of Nigg Bay. The extraordinary edifice on the hill behind **EVANTON**, ten minutes west along the A9 from Alness, is the **Fyrish Monument**, built by a certain Sir Hector Munro partly to give employment to the area, and partly to commemorate his own capture of the Indian town of Seringapatam in 1781 – hence the design, resembling an Indian gateway. If you want to get a close-up look, it's a tough 2-hour walk through pinewoods to the top.

Around the Tain peninsula

Bounded in the south by the Cromarty Firth, and in the north by the Dornoch Firths, the hammer-shaped **Tain peninsula** tapers into the gaping Moray Firth at Nigg, one of the main ferry crossings on the old coast route north. Its largest settlement is the little red-sandstone town of **TAIN**, tucked into a hillside overlooking the sea. This was the birthplace of **Saint Duthus**, a missionary who inspired great devotion in the Middle Ages: his miracle-working relics were enshrined in a sanctuary here in the eleventh century, and in 1360 **St Duthus Collegiate Church** was built, visited annually by James IV, who usually arrived here fresh from the arms of his mistress, Janet Kennedy, whom he had conveniently installed in nearby Moray. A good place to get to grips with the peninsula's past is the recently opened **Tain Through Time** exhibition (April–Oct daily 9.30am–5.30pm; Nov–March Thurs–Mon noon–4pm; £2.75), which uses sound-and-light shows and gregarious guides in period costumes to flesh out the historical facts. The ticket price also includes a tour of the church and neighbouring **museum** on Castle Brae (just off High St), housing medicore archeological finds and clan memorabilia. There's not a great deal more to see in Tain, but check out High Street's castellated sixteenth-century **Tolbooth**, with its stone turrets and old curfew bell.

The *Mansfield House Hotel* (☎01862/892052; ⑥), a modernized mansion-hotel in the Scottish-Baronial mould, is also renowned for its cooking, while the more modest *Golf*

View Guest House (☎01862/892856; ③), three minutes' drive from the town centre Knockbreck Rd, offers comfortable B&B. For inexpensive typically Scottish-style hot **meals**, try *Strachan's Restaurant*, High St (open all day).

Portmahomack

Although few people bother to explore the Tain area as far east as **Tarbat Ness** on the tip of the peninsula, if you're driving it's well worth setting aside a couple of hours to make the detour. The village of **PORTMAHOMACK** is a green, windswept place, sprawling down the hill and round a sheltered bay full of sailing boats – check out the whitewashed **Tarbat Old Church**, with its odd tower and balustraded entrance at the back. There's also a lighthouse at the point (one of the highest in Britain), reached along narrow roads running through fertile farmland, with sweeping views of the gorse-covered sandstone cliffs. A good seven-mile **walk** starts here (2–3hr round trip): head south from Tarbet Ness jetty for three miles, following the narrow passage between the foot of the cliffs and the foreshore, until you get to the hamlet of Rockfield. A path leads past a row of fishers' cottages from here to Potmahomack, then joins the tarmac road running northeast back to the lighthouse.

If you do make it to Portmahomack, you could have **lunch** at the *Oystercatcher*, Main St, which serves lobster, homemade soups and salads; they also have a few very-good-value **rooms** (☎01862/871560; ②). Otherwise, if you want to stay, you could try the *Caledonian Hotel* (☎01862/871345; ③) further along Main St, which looks over across the beach to the Dornoch Firth.

Bonar Bridge and around

Before the causeway was built across the Dornoch Firth, traffic heading along the coast used to skirt around the estuary, crossing the Kyle of Sutherland at **BONAR BRIDGE**. In the fourteenth and fifteenth centuries, the village harboured a large iron foundry. Ore was brought across the peat moors of the central Highlands from the west coast on sledges, and fuel for smelting came from the oak forest draped over the northern shores of the nearby kyle. However, James IV, passing through here once on his way to Tain, was shocked to find the forest virtually clear-felled and ordered that oak saplings be planted in the gaps. Although now hemmed in by spruce plantations, the beautiful ancient woodland east of Bonar Bridge dates from this era.

Carbisdale Castle

Towering high above the rocky and salmon-packed River Shin, three miles north-west of Bonar Bridge, the daunting neo-Gothic profile of **Carbisdale Castle** (not open to the public) overlooks the Kyle of Sutherland, as will as the battlefield where the gallant Marquis of Montrose was defeated in 1650, finally forcing Charles II – if he wanted to be received as king (see p.518) – to accede to the Scots demand for presbyterianism. It was erected between 1906 and 1917 for the dowager Duchess of Sutherland, following a protracted family feud. After the death of her husband, the late Duke of Sutherland, the will leaving her the lion's share of the vast estate, was contested by his stepchildren from his first marriage. In the course of the ensuing legal battle, the Duchess was found in contempt of court for destroying important documents pertinent to the case, and locked up in Holloway prison for six weeks. However, the Sutherlands eventually recanted (although there was no personal reconciliation) and, by way of compensation, built their stepmother a castle worthy of her rank. Designed in three distinct styles (to give the impression it was added to over a long period of time), Carbisdale was eventually acquired by a Norwegian shipping magnate in 1933, and finally gifted, along with its entire contents and estate, to the SYHA, which has turned it into what must be one of the most opulent

youth hostels in the world (March–Sept except May 8–18; ☎0159/421232; Grade 1). Sadly, the interior has been ruined in the process; gutted of its former splendours, it's now overrun by large school parties, who swarm past fake-marble statues and along corridors lined with tacky art prints.

The best way to get here by public transport is to take a **train** to nearby **Culrain** station, which lies within easy walking distance of the castle. **Buses** from Inverness (3 daily; 1hr 30min) and Tain (4 daily; 25min) only run as far as **Ardgay**, three miles south.

Croick Church

A mile or so southwest of Bonar Bridge, the scattered village of **ARDGAY** stands at the mouth of Strath Carron, a wooded river valley winding west into the heart of the Highlands. It's worth heading ten miles up the strath to **Croick Church**, which harbours one of Scotland's most poignant and emotive reminders of the Clearances. Huddled behind a brake of wind-bent trees, the graveyard surrounding the tiny grey chapel sheltered 18 families (92 individuals) evicted from nearby Glen Calvie during the spring of 1845 to make way for flocks of Cheviot sheep, introduced by the Duke of Sutherland as a quick money earner (see p.456). A reporter from *The Times* described the "wretched spectacle" as the villagers filed out of the glen " . . . in a body, two or three carts filled with children, many of them infants". An even more evocative written record of the event is preserved on the diamond-shaped panes of the chapel windows, where the villagers scratched graffiti memorials still legible today: "Glen Calvie people was in the churchyard May 24th 1845", "Glen Calvie people the wicked generation", and "This place needs cleaning".

Lairg

Eleven miles north of Bonar Bridge, the A836 cuts across **Strath Fleet**, with its attractive river, woodlands and farms, to **LAIRG**, a bleak and scattered town at the eastern end of lonely **Loch Shin**. On fine days, the vast wastes of heather and deer grass surrounding the town can be beautiful, but in the rain it can be a deeply depressing landscape. Lairg is predominantly a **transport hub**, and there's nothing to see in town. However, a mile southeast on the A839, there are many signs of early settlement at nearby **Ord Hill**, where archeological digs have recently yielded traces of human habitation dating back to Neolithic times. The **tourist centre** (Mon–Sat 9am–5pm, Sun 1–5pm; ☎01549/402160) hands out leaflets detailing the locations of hut circles and other sites. Every year Lairg hosts an August **lamb sale**, the biggest one-day livestock market in Europe, when sheep from all over the north of Scotland are bought and sold.

Practicalities

Lairg, at the centre of the region's **road system**, is distinctly hard to avoid: the A838, traversing some of the loneliest country in the Highlands, is the quickest route for Cape Wrath; the A836 heads up to Tongue on the north coast; and a few miles south of Lairg, the A837 pushes west through lovely Strath Oykel, to Lochinver on the west coast. For non-drivers, Lairg is on the main **train** line and the nexus of several **postbus** routes around the northwest Highlands. A daily bus from Inverness also passes through en route to Durness. Trains arrive north of the main road along the loch; buses stop right on the loch.

There's no tourist office in Lairg. Should you need to **stay**, try *Ben Avon*, Station Rd (April–Oct; ☎01549/402428; ②), *Old Coach House* (May–Oct; ☎01549/402378; ②) at Achany, or *Carnbren*, 300 yards across the bridge (all year; ☎01549/412259; ②).

Dornoch

DORNOCH, eight miles north of Tain, lies on a flattish headland overlooking the Dornoch Firth. Surrounded by sand dunes and blessed with an exceptionally sunny climate by Scottish standards, it's something of a middle-class holiday resort, with solid Edwardian hotels, trees and flowers in profusion, and miles of **sandy beaches** giving good views across the estuary to the Tain peninsula. The town is also renowned for its championship **golf course**, ranked eleventh in the world and the most northerly first-class course in the world.

Dating from the twelfth century, Dornoch became a Royal Burgh in 1628. Among its oldest buildings, which are all grouped round the spacious **Square**, the tiny **Cathedral** was founded in 1224 and built of local sandstone. The original building was horribly damaged by marauding Mackays in 1570, and much of what you see today was restored by the Countess of Sutherland in 1835, though her worst Victorian excesses were removed this century, when the interior stonework was returned to its original state. A later addition were the stained-glass windows in the north wall, which were endowed by the expat American-based Andrew Carnegie (see p.229). You can climb the tower (July & Aug Mon–Fri 7.30–8pm). Opposite, the fortified sixteenth-century **Bishop's Palace**, a fine example of vernacular architecture, with stepped gables and towers, has been refurbished as an upmarket hotel (see below). Next door, the **Old Town Jail** (Mon–Sat 10am–5pm; free) has a mock-up of a nineteenth-century cell and a bookshop.

In 1722, Dornoch saw the last burning of a witch in Scotland. The unfortunate old woman, accused of turning her daughter into a pony and riding her around town, ruined her chances of acquittal by misquoting the Gaelic version of the Lord's Prayer during the trial, and was sentenced to burn alive in a barrel of boiling tar – an event commemorated by the **Witch's Stone**, just south of the Square on Carnaig Street.

Practicalities

Buses from Tain and Inverness stop in the Square, where you'll also find a **tourist office** (Mon–Sat 9am–1pm & 2–5pm; ☎01862/810400). There's no shortage of **accommodation**. Near the golf course on the northeast edge of town, the *Trentham Hotel* (☎01862/810391; ③) is friendly and comfortable if a bit staid. The characterful *Dornoch Castle Hotel* (☎01862/810216; ⑥), in the Bishop's Palace on the Square, has been tastefully converted, with a cosy old style bar and relaxing tea garden. Of the B&Bs, there are two offering good-value: *Fiona MacLean*, 11 Gilchrist Square (☎01862/811024; ②), and *Trevose* (☎01862/810269; ②), on the Square and swathed in roses. For **food**, the stultifyingly floral restaurant in the *Mallin House Hotel*, Church St, north of the Square (☎01862/812335), is terrific, and the *Cathedral Café* serves delicious soup and baked goodies.

Golspie to Wick

Ten miles north of Dornoch on the A9 lies the straggling grey town of **GOLSPIE**, whose status as an administrative centre does little to relieve its dullness. It does, however, boast an 18-hole golf course and a lovely sandy beach, while half a mile further up the coast, the Big Burn has several rapids and waterfalls that can be seen from an attractive woodland trail (beginning at the *Sutherland Arms Hotel*).

Dunrobin Castle

The main reason to stop in Golspie, though, is to look around **Dunrobin Castle** (May–Oct Mon–Sat 10.30am–4.30pm, Sun 1–4.30pm; June–Sept Sun until 5.30pm;

£3.70), overlooking the sea a mile north of town. Approached via a long tree-lined drive, this fairy-tale confection of turrets and pointed roofs – modelled by the architect Sir Charles Berry (designer of the Houses of Parliament) on a Loire Chateau – is the seat of the infamous Sutherland family, at one time Europe's biggest landowners and the principal driving force behind the Clearances in this area. Staring up at the pile from the midst of its elaborate formal gardens, it's worth remembering such extravagance was paid for by uprooting literally thousands of crofters from the surrounding glens. Much of the extra income generated by the evictions was squandered on the castle's opulent interior, which is crammed full of fine furniture, paintings (including two Canalettos), tapestries and *objets d'art* displayed in a mausoleum-like gloom.

Set aside at least an hour for Dunrobin's amazing **museum**, housed in an eighteenth-century building at the edge of the garden. Inside, hundreds of disembodied animals' heads and horns peer down from the walls, alongside other more macabre appendages, from elephants' toes to rhinos' tails. Bagged by the fifth Duke and Duchess of Sutherland, the trophies vie for space with other fascinating family memorabilia, including one of John O'Groat's bones, Chinese opium pipes, and such curiosities as a "picnic gong from the South Pacific". There's also an impressive collection of ethnographic artefacts acquired by the Sutherlands on their frequent hunting jaunts, ranging from an Egyptian sarcophagus to some more locally found, finely carved Pictish stones.

The Sutherland Monument

You can't miss the 100ft **Monument** to the first Duke of Sutherland, which peers proprietarily down from the summit of the 1293ft **Beinn a'Bhragaidh**, a mile north-west of Golspie. An inscription cut into its base recalls that the statue was erected in 1834 by ". . . a mourning and grateful tenantry" to " . . . a judicious, kind and liberal landlord . . . (who would) open his hands to the distress of the widow, the sick and the traveller". Unsurprisingly, there's no reference to the fact that the Duke, widely regarded as Scotland's own Josef Stalin, forcibly evicted 15,000 crofters from his one-million-acre estate – a fact which, in the words of one local historian, makes the monument ". . . a grotesque representation of the many forces that destroyed the Highlands". Campaigners are lobbying to have it broken into pieces and scattered over the hillside, so that visitors can walk over the remains to a new, more appropriate memorial; there have even been several attempts to blow the statue up. However, the Sutherland estate and local council have continually resisted moves to replace it.

It's worth the wet, rocky **climb** (round trip 90min) to the top of the hill for the wonderful views south along the coast past Dornoch to the Moray Firth and west towards Lairg and Loch Shin. It's a steep and strenuous walk, however, and there's no view until you're out of the trees, about ten minutes from the top. Take the road opposite *Munro's TV Rentals* in Golspie's main street, which leads up the hill and past the fountain to a farm; from here, follow the Beinn a'Bhragaidh footpath (BBFP) signs along the path into the woods.

Brora

BRORA, on the coast six miles north of Golspie, once boasted the only bridge in the region – whence its name, which means "River of the Bridge" in Norse. These days, however, the small grey town harbours little of interest, although it's accessible by **bus** and **train** and does have *Capaldi's* on High St, which sells brilliant homemade Italian ice cream. A mile or so north of town, the **Clynelish Distillery** (Mon–Fri 9.30am–4.30pm; free) will give you a guided tour and a free dram. The best **B&B** in the area is *Clynelish Farm*: turn left after the *BP* garage (℡01408/621265; ③), a working Victorian stone farmhouse with en-suite rooms, built to provide employment for dispossessed crofters after the Clearances. The rooms here are spacious, with views over the fields to the Moray Firth (evening meals by arrangement).

Helmsdale

Eleven miles up the A9 from Golspie, **HELMSDALE** is an old herring port, founded in the nineteenth century to house the evicted inhabitants of **Strath Kildonan**, which lies behind it. Today, the sleepy-looking grey village attracts thousands of tourists, most of them to see the **Timespan Heritage Centre**, beside the river (Easter–Oct Mon–Sat 10am–5pm, Sun 2–5pm; £2.75). It's a remarkable venture for a place of this size, telling the local story from prehistoric times to the present through hi-tech displays, sound effects and an audio-visual programme. For a spot of light relief after the exhibition, head across the road to the sugary pink and frilly **Mirage Restaurant**. The proprietress has become something of a Scottish celebrity, modelling herself on the romantic novelist Barbara Cartland, who has a shooting lodge nearby. Photographs proudly displayed on the walls show the paroxide-blond restauranteuse posing with her heroine, while the fittings and furnishings reflect her predeliction for all things pink and kitsch, with fish tanks, fake-straw parasols, and plastic seagulls set off to a tee by the C & W soundtrack. She also dishes up great fish 'n' chips, grills and puddings.

Helmsdale's **tourist office** (April–Sept Mon–Sat 10am–5pm; ☎01431/821640) will book accommodation for you. Most of the **B&Bs** are on the outskirts of town; *Broomhill House*, Navidale Rd (☎01431/821259; ③), is the best of the bunch, with bedrooms in a turret added to the former croft by a miner who struck it lucky in the Kildonan gold rush (see below). If full, try *Torbuie*, in Navidale, on the A9 less than a mile from the village (☎01431/821424; ②), or *Hazelbank*, in Westhelmsdale, half a mile up the river from the tourist office (☎01431/821427; ②), which both offer comfortable rooms. There's also a **youth hostel** (mid-May to Sept; ☎01431/821577; Grade 3), about half a mile north of the harbour.

Baile an Or

From Helmsdale the single-track A897 runs up the Strath Kildonan to the north coast, following the path of the Helmsdale river, a strictly controlled and extremely exclusive salmon river frequented by the royals. Some eight miles up the Strath at **BAILE AN OR** (Gaelic for "goldfield"), gold was discovered in the bed of the Kildonan Burn in 1869; a gold rush ensued, hardly on the scale of the Yukon, but quite bizarre in the Scottish Highlands. A tiny amount of gold is still found every year; if you fancy **gold-panning** yourself, pick up a free licence and the relevant equipment from Helmsdale's gift and fishing-tackle shop, *Strath Ullie*, opposite the Timespan Heritage Centre.

From Helmsdale to Wick

Just north of Helmsdale, the A9 begins its long haul up the **Ord of Caithness**. This steep hill used to form a pretty impregnable obstacle, and even now the desolate road gets blocked during winter snowstorms. Once over the narrow pass, the landscape changes dramatically as heather-clad moors give way to miles of treeless green grazing lands, peppered with derelict crofts and latticed by long drystone walls. This whole area was devasted during the Clearances; the ruined village of **BADBEA**, reached via a footpath running east off the main road a short way after the pass, is a poignant monument to this cruel era. Built by tenants evicted from nearby Ousdale, the settlement now lies deserted, although its ruined hovels show what hardship the crofters had to endure: the cottages stood so near the windy cliff edge that children had to be tethered to prevent them from being blown into the sea.

DUNBEATH, hidden at the mouth of a small strath, 12 miles north of Ord of Caithness, was another village founded to provide work in the wake of the Clearances. The local landlord built a harbour here in 1800, at the start of the herring boom, and the settlement flourished briefly. Today, it's a sleepy place, with lobster pots stacked at the quayside and views of windswept **Dunbeath Castle** (closed to the public) on the opposite side of the bay. The novelist **Neill Gunn** was also born here, in one of the terraced houses under the flyover that now swoops above the village; you can find out more about him at the **Dunbeath Heritage Centre** (Easter–Oct Mon–Sat 10am–5pm; £2.25), signposted from the road. The best of the handful of modest **B&Bs** here is *Tormore Farm* (☎01593/731240; ②), a large farmhouse with four comfortable rooms, half a mile north of the harbour on the A9.

The final stretch of road before Wick winds gently along the coast, with great views over the cliffs and out to sea to the oil rigs perched on the horizon. The planned village of **LYBSTER**, established at the height of the nineteenth-century herring boom, once had 200-odd boats working out of its harbour. Today, although still a busy fishing port, it's a grim collection of grey pebble-dashed bungalows centred on a broad main street. Most visitors head straight for the nearby **Grey Cairns of Camster**, seven miles due north and one of the most memorable sights on the northeast coast. Surrounded by bleak moorland, these two enormous prehistoric burial chambers, constructed around 4000–5000 years ago, were immacualtely designed, with corbelled drystone roofs in their hidden chambers, which you can crawl into through narrow passageways. More extraordinary ancient remains lie at **East Clyth**, two miles north of Lybster on the A9, where a path leads to the "Hill o' Many Stanes". Some 200 boulders stand in the ground here, forming in 22 parallel rows that run north to south; no one has yet worked out what they were used for, although archeological studies have shown there were once 600 stones in place.

Wick

Originally a Viking settlement called *Vik*, after the bay on which it stands, **WICK** has been a Royal Burgh since 1140. It's actually two towns: Wick proper, and **Pultneytown**, immediately south across the river, a messy, rather run-down community planned by Thomas Telford in 1806 for the British Fisheries Society to encourage evicted crofters to take up fishing.

Wick's heyday was in the mid-nineteenth century, when it was the busiest herring port in Europe, exporting tons of fish to Russia, Scandinavia and the West Indian slave plantations. Robert Louis Stevenson described it as " . . . the meanest of man's towns, situated on the baldest of God's bays", and it's still a pretty grim place, in spite of a bustling shopping centre, and some solid Victorian civic architecture. Pultneytown, lined with rows of fishermen's cottages, is the area most worth a wander, not least for the **Wick Heritage Centre**, in Bank Row near the harbour (June–Sept Mon–Sat 10am–5pm; £1). Housed in a row of old fishery buildings, this little museum is crammed with lots of good stuff on the herring industry, and a huge photographic collection covering the town's history from the 1880s.

Rising steeply from a needle-thin promontory three miles north of Wick are the dramatic fifteenth- to seventeenth-century ruins of **Sinclair** and **Girnigoe castles**, which functioned as a single stronghold for the Earls of Caithness. In 1570 the fourth earl, suspecting his son of trying to murder him, imprisoned him in the dungeon here until he died of starvation.

Practicalities

The **train** station and **bus** stops are next to each other behind the hospital. Frequent **local buses** run to Thurso and up the coast to John O' Groats. Wick also has an

airport (☎01955/602294), a couple of miles north of the town, with direct flights from Edinburgh, Aberdeen and Orkney and connections further south.

From the train station head across the river down Bridge St to the **tourist office**, just off High St (Mon–Fri 9am–5pm, Sat 9am–1pm; ☎01955/602596), which gives out a full **accommodation** list. Next door, the *Wellington Guest House*, 41–43 High St (☎01955/603287; ③), is reasonable value, as is the modern *County Guest House*, 101 High St (☎01955/602911; ③). The *Harbour Guest House*, 6 Rose St (☎01955/603276; ②), in a tiny terrace off the Inner Harbour in Pultneytown, offers comfortable rooms in a lovely old building. The best-value **B&B** in Wick is *Leask's* (☎01955/606512; ②), at Holy Terrace on the north side of the harbour, which has a handful of small but inexpensive rooms (with shared bathroom) looking over the rooftops to the port.

As for **eating**, the *Lamplighter Restaurant*, High St, serves enormous helpings of imaginative food; in the same building, *Houston's* cheerfully churns out good burgers. The *Lorne Restaurant* (open evenings only), near the Heritage Centre, is moderately priced and produces more than adequate servings of meat and two veg. *Gravelli's*, at either end of the High St, is a real find, trapped in a time warp, while both the cafés serve piles of fish 'n' chips, along with authentic pizza. Of the **pubs**, the *Camps*, at the east end of High St, is among the liveliest in the evenings, with occasional **live music**.

travel details

Trains

Aviemore to: Edinburgh (7 daily; 2hr 55min); Inverness (Mon–Sat 8 daily, Sun 4; 40min); Newtownmore (Mon–Sat 8 daily, Sun 4; 20min).

Dingwall to: Helmsdale (Mon–Sat 3 daily; 2hr); Inverness (Mon–Sat 3 daily; 25min); Kyle of Lochalsh (Mon–Sat 3 daily; 1hr 55min); Lairg (Mon–Sat 3 daily; 1hr 10min); Thurso (Mon–Sat 3 daily, 3hr 20min); Wick (Mon–Sat 3 daily; 3hr 20min).

Fort William to: Arisaig (4 daily; 1hr 10min); Crianlarich (3 daily; 1hr 40min); Glasgow (2–3 daily; 4hr); Glenfinnan (4 daily; 55min); London (1 daily; 11hr 40min), Mallaig (4 daily; 1hr 25min).

Inverness to: Aviemore (Mon–Sat 9 daily, Sun 4; 40min); Dingwall (Mon–Sat 3 daily; 25min); Edinburgh (Mon–Sat 7 daily, Sun 2; 3hr 30min); Helmsdale (2–3 daily; 2hr 20min); Kyle of Lochalsh (Mon–Sat 3 daily; 2hr 40min); Lairg (Mon–Sat 3 daily; 1hr 40min); London (Mon–Sat 5 daily, Sun 2; 8hr 35min); Plockton (2–3 daily; 2hr 15min); Thurso (Mon–Sat 3 daily; 3hr 45min); Wick (Mon–Sat 3 daily; 3hr 45min).

Kyle of Lochalsh to: Dingwall (Mon–Sat 3 daily; 1hr 55 min); Inverness (Mon–Sat 3 daily; 2hr 30min); Plockton (Mon–Sat 2–3 daily; 20min).

Lairg to: Dingwall (Mon–Sat 3 daily; 1hr 10min); Inverness (Mon–Sat 3 daily; 1hr 40min); Thurso (Mon–Sat 3 daily; 2hr 5min); Wick (Mon–Sat 3 daily; 2hr 5min).

Mallaig to: Arisaig (4 daily; 15min); Edinburgh (2–3 daily; 8hr 20min); Glasgow (2–3 daily; 5hr 20min); Fort William (4 daily; 1hr 25 min); Glenfinnan (4 daily; 35 min).

Newtownmore to: Aviemore (Mon–Sat 9 daily, Sun 4; 20min); Inverness (Mon–Sat 9 daily, Sun 4; 55min).

Thurso to: Dingwall (Mon–Sat 3 daily; 3hr 20min); Inverness (Mon–Sat 3 daily; 3hr 45min); Lairg (Mon–Sat 3 daily; 2hr 5min).

Wick to: Dingwall (Mon–Sat 3 daily; 3hr 20min); Inverness (Mon–Sat 3 daily; 3hr 45min); Lairg (Mon–Sat 3 daily; 2hr 5min).

Buses

Aviemore to: Grantown-on-Spey (5 daily; 40min); Inverness (10 daily; 40 min); Newtownmore (10 daily; 20min).

Dornoch to: Inverness (3 daily; 1hr 10min); Thurso with connections for Wick (3 daily; 2hr 20min).

Fort William to: Aracharachle (Mon–Sat 2–3 daily; 1hr 45min); Drumnadrochit (8 daily; 1hr 30min); Fort Augustus (8 daily; 1hr); Inverness (8 daily; 2hr); Mallaig (1 daily; 1 hr 50min).

Gair Loch to: Dingwall (3 weekly; 2hr); Inverness (3 weekly; 2hr 20min); Redpoint (1 daily; 1hr 35min).

Inverness to: Aberdeen (hourly; 3hr 30min); Aviemore (Mon–Sat 7 daily, Sun 12; 40min); Cromarty (4 daily; 45min); Drumnadrochit (4–5 daily; 25min); Durness (June–Sept 1 daily; 4hr

30min); Fort Augustus (4–5 daily; 1hr); Fort William (4 daily; 2hr); Gairloch (1 daily; 2hr 20min); Glasgow (14 daily; 3hr 35min–4hr 25min); John O'Groats (April–Sept 2 daily; 3hr 40min); Kirkwall (April–Sept 2 daily; 5hr 20min); Kyle of Lochalsh (3–4 daily; 2hr); Lairg (June–Sept Mon–Sat 1 daily; 2hr 10min); Lochinver (1 weekly; 2hr 30min); Nairn (Mon–Sat hourly; 50min); Newtownmore (8 daily; 1hr 10min); Oban (Mon–Sat 1 daily; 4hr 15min); Perth (10 daily; 2hr 35min); Tain (hourly; 1 hr 15min); Thurso (Mon–Sat 3 daily, Sun 1; 3hr 30 min); Ullapool (2–4 daily; 1hr 25min); Wick (Mon–Sat 3 daily; 1hr 55min).

Kyle of Lochalsh to: Inverness (Mon–Sat 2 daily, Sun 1; 2hr); Fort William (3 daily; 1hr 50min); Glasgow (3 daily; 5hr).

Lochinver to: Inverness (1 weekly; 2hr 15min).

Mallaig to: Aracharachle (1 daily; 1hr 45min); Fort William (1 daily; 2hr).

Thurso to: Bettyhill (1 weekly; 1hr 20min); Inverness (Mon–Sat 2 daily, Sun 1; 2hr 30min); Wick (Mon–Sat 2 daily, Sun 1; 35min).

Wick to: Inverness (Mon–Sat 2 daily, Sun 1; 2hr 55min); Thurso (Mon–Sat 2 daily, Sun 1; 35min).

Ferries

To Lewis: Ullapool–Stornoway, see p.332.

To Mull: Kilchoan–Tobermory, see p.297.

To Orkney: Scrabster–Stromness, see p.509.

To Skye: Mallaig–Armadale; Glenelg–Kylerhea, see p.332.

To the Small Isles: Mallaig–Eigg, Rhum, Muck, and Canna, see p.332.

Flights

Inverness to: Glasgow (Mon–Fri 2 daily; 50min); London (up to 7 daily; 1hr 25min).

CHAPTER NINE

ORKNEY AND SHETLAND

Arching out into the North Sea, in the face of furious tides and bitter winds, the Orkney and Shetland islands gather neatly into two distinct and very different clusters. Often referring to themselves first as Orcadians or Shetlanders, and with unofficial, but widely-displayed, flags, their inhabitants regard Scotland as a separate entity. This feeling of detachment arises from their distinctive geography, history and culture, in which they differ not only from Scotland but also from each other.

To the south, just a short step from the Scottish mainland, are the 70 or so **Orkney Islands**. With the major exception of Hoy, which is high and rugged, these islands are low-lying, gently sloping and fertile, and for centuries have provided a reasonably secure living from farming, with some fishing. In spring and summer the days are long, the skies enormous and the meadows thick with wild flowers. There is a peaceful continuity to Orcadian life reflected not only in the well-preserved treasury of **Stone Age settlements**, such as Skara Brae, and **standing stones**, most notably the Stones of Stenness, but also in the rather conservative nature of society here today.

Another 60 miles north, the **Shetland Islands** are in nearly all respects a complete contrast. Higher and more dramatic, here the steep cliffs, teeming with thousands of seabirds, rise straight out of the water to form barren heather-coated hills, while ice-

---

ISLAND WILDLIFE

Orkney and Shetland support huge numbers of **seabirds**, particularly during the breeding season, from April to July, when cliffs and coastal banks are alive with thousands of guillemots, razorbills, puffins, fulmars and, particularly in Shetland, gannets. Terns are often to be found on small offshore islets or gravelly spits. On coastal heathland or moorland you should see arctic skuas, great skuas, curlews and occasionally whimbrel or golden plover. Many kinds of wild duck are present, especially in winter, but eiders are particularly common. In autumn and spring, large numbers of migrants drop in on their way north or south and very rare specimens may turn up at any time of year. Fair Isle, in particular, has a long list of rarities; and Shetland's isolation has produced its own distinctive sub-species of wren. Some of the best or most accessible bird sites have been noted in the text.

The separation of the islands from the mainland has also meant that some species of **land mammal** are absent and others have developed sub-species. For instance, Shetland has no voles but Orkney its own distinctive type. However, both groups have considerable populations of seals and otters. Further offshore you may well see porpoises, dolphins and several species of whale including pilot, sperm and killer.

Neither of the island groups support many **trees** and very few of those that are here are native. However, the clifftops, moorlands and meadows of both Orkney and Shetland are rich with beautiful **wild flowers**, including pink thrift, the pale pink heather-spotted orchid, red campion and, in wetter areas, golden marsh marigolds, yellow iris and insect-eating sundew. Notable **smaller plants** include the purple scottish primrose, which grows only in Orkney and the far north of Scotland, and the Shetland (or Edmondston's) mouse-eared chickweed with its delicate white flower streaked with yellow, which grows only on the island of Unst.

scuplted sea inlets cut deep into the land, offering memorable coastal walks in Shetland's endless summer evenings. With a scarcity of fertile ground, Shetlanders have traditionally been crofters rather than farmers, often looking to the sea for an uncertain living in fishing or the naval and merchant services. Perhaps because life has been so hard, islanders have tended to enthusiastically seize new opportunities such as fish farming and computing – Shetland now boasts its own Internet hub. Nevertheless, the past is seldom forgotten; the Norse heritage is clear in every road sign and in the rich archeological sites of **Jarlshof** and the **Broch of Mousa**.

Since people first began to explore the North Atlantic, Orkney and Shetland have been stepping stones on routes between Britain, Ireland and Scandinavia; and both groups have a long history of **settlement**, certainly from around 3500–4000 BC. The **Norse** settlers, who began to arrive from about 800 AD, with substantial migration from around 900 AD, left the islands with a unique cultural character. Orkney was a powerful Norse earldom, and Shetland (at first part of the same earldom) was ruled directly from Norway for nearly 300 years after 1195. The Norse influence is clearly evident today in dialects, accents and place names; and with neither group ever part

DIALECT AND PLACE NAMES

Between the tenth and seventeenth centuries the language of Orkney and Shetland was **Norn**, a Scandinavian tongue not dissimilar to modern Faroese and Icelandic. After the end of Norse rule and with the transformation of the church, the law, commerce and education, Norn gradually lost out to Scots and English. Today, Orkney and Shetland have their own dialects and individual islands and communities within each group have local variations. The **dialects** have a Scots base, with some Old Norse words; however, they don't sound strongly Scottish, with the Orkney accent – which has been likened to the Welsh one – especially distinctive. Listed below are some of the words you're most likely to hear, including some birds' names and common elements in place names. In most cases, the Shetland form is given; the Orkney terms are very similar if not identical.

alan	storm petrel	*neesick*	porpoise
ayre	beach	*norie*	(or *tammie-norie*) puffin
bonxie	great skua	*noup*	steep headland
böd	fisherman's store	*noost*	hollow place where a boat
bruck	rubbish		is drawn up
burra	heath rush	*peerie*	in Orkney, sometimes
corbie	raven		(*peedie*) small
crö	sheepfold	*plantiecrub*	small drystone enclosure
du	familiar form of "you"	or *plantiecrö*	for growing cabbages
dunter	eider duck	*quoy*	enclosed, cultivated
eela	rod-fishing from small boats		common land
ferrylouper	incomer (Orkney)	*reestit*	cured (as in reestit mutton)
fourareen	four-oared boat	*roost*	tide race
foy	party or festival	*scattald*	common grazing land
haa	laird's house	*scord*	gap or pass in a ridge of
hap	hand-knitted shawl		hills
kame	ridge of hills	*scootie alan*	arctic skua
kishie	basket	*shaela*	dark grey
maa	seagull	*shalder*	oystercatcher
mallie	(Shetland)	*simmer dim*	summer twilight
or *mallimak*	(Orkney) fulmar petrel	*sixern*	six-oared boat
mool	headland	*solan*	gannet
moorit	brown	*soothmoother*	incomer (Shetland)
mootie	tiny	*tystie*	black guillemot
muckle	large	*voe*	sea inlet

of the Gaelic-speaking culture of Highland Scotland, the Scottish influence is essentially a Lowland one.

From October to April the **weather** can bring real drama; in late spring and summer, there are often long dry spells with lots of sunshine, but you need to come prepared for wind, rain and, most frustrating of all, the occasional sea fog.

ORKNEY

Just a short step from John O' Groats, the **Orkney Islands** are a unique and fiercely independent grouping. In spring and summer the meadows and clifftops are a brilliant green, shining with wild flowers, while long days pour light onto the land and sea – a sharp contrast to the bleak enormity of the rugged western Highlands. For an Orcadian the "**Mainland**" invariably means the largest island in Orkney, rather than the rest of Scotland, and throughout their history they've been linked to lands much further afield, principally Scandinavia. In the words of Orcadian poet George Mackay Brown:

> *Orkney lay athwart a great sea-way*
> *from Viking times onwards, and its lore*
> *is crowded with sailors, merchants, adventurers,*
> *pilgrims, smugglers, storms and sea changes.*
> *The shores are strewn with wrack, jetsam,*
> *occasional treasure.*

Small communities began to settle in the islands around 4000 BC, and the village at **Skara Brae** on the Mainland is one of the best-preserved Stone Age settlements in Europe. This and many of the other older archeological sites, including the **Stones of Stenness** and **Maes Howe**, are concentrated in the central and eastern parts of the Mainland. Elsewhere the islands are scattered with chambered tombs and stone circles, a tribute to the sophisticated religious and ceremonial practices taking place here from around 2000 BC. More sophisticated **Iron Age** inhabitants built fortified villages incorporating stone towers known as **brochs**, protected by walls and ramparts, many of which are still in place. Later Pictish culture spread to Orkney and the remains of several of their early Christian settlements can still be seen, the best at the **Brough**

GETTING TO ORKNEY

Orkney is connected to the mainland by four **ferry** routes. *P&O Scottish Ferries* (☎01856/850655) runs car ferries once a week (June–Aug 2 weekly) from **Aberdeen** (8hr) and daily services on the much shorter crossing (1hr 45min) from **Scrabster**, about two miles northwest of Thurso on the north coast; both arrive at Stromness. *Orcargo* (☎01856/873838) has a service from **Invergordon** (10hr) to Kirkwall. The other mainland connection is a passenger ferry between **John O'Groats** and **Burwick** on South Ronaldsay (May to mid-Sept; 45min); the *Orkney Bus* service from Inverness connects directly with this ferry. A **day trip** is also offered from Inverness or John O'Groats, with a tour of some of the major sights on the Mainland; details of both ferry and bus are available from *John O'Groats Ferries* (☎01955/611353). There's also a weekly or, from June to August, twice-weekly *P&O* service from Stromness and to **Lerwick** in Shetland.

There are direct flights to Orkney from **Wick, Inverness, Aberdeen, Edinburgh** or **Glasgow**, with good connections from **Birmingham, London and Manchester**. There are also flights between Orkney and **Shetland**. All of these services are operated into Kirkwall Airport by *British Airways* (☎01856/872233) or its franchised subsidiary *British Airways Express*, locally still often known by its old name, *Loganair* (☎0345/222111 or ☎01856/872494).

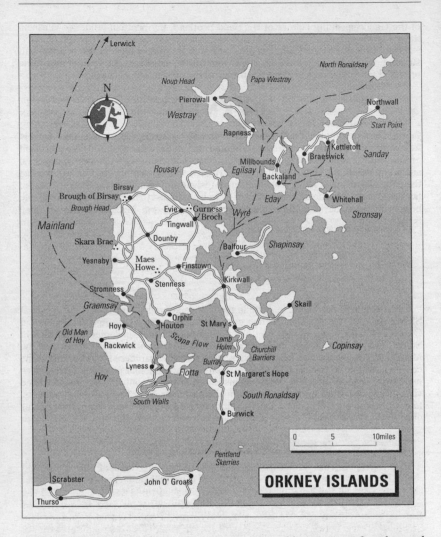

ORKNEY ISLANDS

of Birsay in the West Mainland, where a group of small houses are gathered around the remains of an early church. Later, around the ninth century, **Norse** settlers from Scandinavia arrived, and the islands became Norse earldoms, forming an outpost of this powerful and expansive culture that was gradually forcing its way south. The last of the Norse earls was killed in 1231, but they had a lasting impact on the islands, leaving behind not only their language but also the great **St Magnus Cathedral** in Kirkwall, one of Scotland's most outstanding pieces of medieval architecture.

After the end of Norse rule, the islands became the preserve of **Scottish earls,** who exploited and abused the islanders, although a steady increase in sea trade did offer some chance of escape. French and Spanish ships sheltered here in the sixteenth century, and the ships of the **Hudson Bay Company** recruited hundreds of Orcadians to work in the Canadian fur trade. The islands were also an important staging post in the **whaling industry** and the **herring boom**, which brought great numbers of small Dutch, French and Scottish boats. More recently, the naval importance of **Scapa Flow** brought plenty of money and activity during both world wars, and left the seabed scattered with **wrecks**, making for wonderful **diving** opportunities, and the clifftops dotted with gun emplacements. Since the war, things have quietened down somewhat, although in the last two decades the **oil industry**, which now has a large terminal on the island of **Flotta**, and **European Community** funding have brought surprise windfalls, stemming the exodus of young people. Meanwhile, many disenchanted southerners have become "incomers" moving north in search of the peace and simplicity of island life.

The Mainland is joined by causeways to the southern island of **South Ronaldsay**, and centres on the capital of **Kirkwall**; although you'll most likely arrive at the port of **Stromness**, an old fishing town and main ferry terminal on the far western shore. Dividing into fairly distinct western and eastern sections, the Mainland is relatively heavily populated and intensely farmed throughout. Further afield, the **smaller islands** (linked to the Mainland by regular ferries) are bleaker and wilder: the southern island of **Hoy**, the second largest in the archipelago, presents a superbly dramatic landscape, with some of the highest seacliffs in the country; more exposed still are the ten **northern isles** – low, elemental outcrops, sprawled out into the ocean.

Rolling out of the sea "like the backs of sleeping whales" (Mackay Brown), the Orkney Isles offer excellent **walking**, with beautiful arching white-sand beaches. There is also some good **fishing** to be had in both salt and fresh water, with the rivers and lochs providing some of the best trout and sea-trout fishing in Britain.

Getting Around

On the Orkney Mainland, **scheduled buses** connect Kirkwall to Stromness, Dounby, Houton, Tingwall, Evie, Rendall, Deerness, Burray, South Ronaldsay and, less frequently, Birsay. However, services aren't frequent and many of the most interesting areas are some way from the bus routes. **Cycling** is cheap and effective as there are few steep hills, distances are not too long and in summer, at least, the weather is usually not prohibitive. **Bikes** can be rented in Kirkwall, Stromness and on some of the smaller islands. Bringing a **car** to Orkney is straightforward, if not exactly cheap; alternatively, you can rent one in Kirkwall, Stromness or on several of the islands. Especially if time is limited, it may be worth considering one of the guided **tours** available by bus or minibus operated by *Go-Orkney* or *Wildabout* among others; details are available from the tourist offices.

Getting to the other islands from the Mainland isn't difficult; *Orkney Islands Shipping Company* (☎01856/872044) operates several sailings daily to Hoy, Shapinsay and Rousay and between one and three, depending on route and season, to all the others except **North Ronaldsay**, which has a weekly boat on Fridays. *British Airways Express* flies to **Eday**, **North Ronaldsay**, **Westray**, **Papa Westray**, **Sanday** and **Stronsay**. Travel between individual islands by sea or air isn't so straightforward, but careful study of timetables can reduce the need to come all the way back to Kirkwall.

Kirkwall

Sheltered at the south end of its wide bay, the old heart of Orkney's capital, **KIRKWALL** huddles around the base of the St Magnus Cathedral. The town has two principal focal points: the **harbour**, which bustles with ferries, cargo ships, yachts and fishing boats, and the main shopping street, **Albert Street**, which twists back towards the cathedral through a tight knot of paved streets, old stone houses and narrow alleys.

By Orkney standards, Kirkwall is a bustling metropolis; a busy market town and home to the island's most important businesses, its more exotic restaurants and better-stocked shops, as well as two distilleries. It hosts several lively **festivals** including the Orkney Folk Festival in May, a celebration of St Magnus in June and of science in September. An interesting place to spend some time, with unusual, quietly impressive architecture and a gentle, unhurried atmosphere, Kirkwall also makes an ideal base from which to explore the Mainland or make day trips to the northern isles.

The telephone code for Kirkwall is ☎01856.

Arrival, information and accommodation

Most visitors come to Orkney **by sea** (from either Scrabster or Aberdeen), and arrive at the ferry terminal in Stromness, in the southwest corner of the Mainland. Ferries are met by buses to Kirkwall (40min). Arriving **by plane**, the airport is about three miles southeast of Kirkwall on the A960. It's not served by buses, but a taxi into town should only set you back about £6.

Kirkwall itself is an easy place in which to orientate yourself as there's really only one main street – **Albert Street** – and the prominent spire of the St Magnus Cathedral clearly marks the town centre. The **tourist office**, on Broad St, beside the cathedral graveyard (daily 8am–8pm; ☎872856), books accommodation and gives out an excellent free leaflet, the *Kirkwall Heritage Guide*, which takes you through all the buildings of interest. Most events are advertised in the *Orcadian* (Thurs) and there's a "What's On Diary" on *BBC Radio Orkney* (Mon–Fri 7.30–8am, 93.7MHz FM).

There's an excellent range of **accommodation** in Kirkwall. If you want a basic room, the SYHA **youth hostel** (☎872243) on the road to Orphir, about half a mile southeast of the town centre, isn't beautiful on the outside but is very well looked after and comfortable. The helpful tourist office has details of **B&Bs** and can book you in for a ten percent fee which is deducted from the money the owner receives. Alternatively, an easy place to start looking is on the Cromwell Road, on the waterfront just east of the harbour. There are several reasonable B&Bs here, including *Craigwood* (☎872006; ②). Other good, central B&Bs include *Mrs Bain*, 6 Fraser's Close (☎872862; ②); *Briar Lea*, 10 Dundas Crescent (☎872747; ③); *Mrs Parkins*, 7 Matches Square (☎872440; ②); and *Mrs Forsyth*, 21 Willowburn Rd (☎874020; ②). **Camping** is available at *Pickaquoy* (mid-May to mid-Sept; ☎873535), on the west side of town; it's well equipped with clothes, washing and drying facilities.

ACCOMMODATION PRICE CODES

Throughout this book, accommodation **prices** have been graded with the numbers below, according to the cost of the least expensive double room in high season. Although costs will rise slightly overall with the life of this edition, the relative comparisons should remain valid. The bulk of the recommendations will fall in categories ② to ⑤; those in the highest categories are limited to places that are especially attractive. Edinburgh will inevitably be more expensive than equivalent accommodation in the countryside or small towns, and a number of places will have a big mark-up for the three weeks of the Festival. Bear in mind that many of the swanky hotels often slash their tariffs at the weekend when the business types have gone home, and that many of the cheaper places will also have more expensive rooms. Note that in our accommodation listings price codes are not given for youth hostels and campsites – they all come into the lower end of the ① category.

① under £20	④ £40–50	⑦ £70–80
② £20–30	⑤ £50–60	⑧ £80–100
③ £30–40	⑥ £60–70	⑨ over £100

Hotels and Guest Houses

Albert, Mounthoolie Lane (☎876000). Completely refurbished and right in the heart of the town. ⑤.

Ayre, Ayre Rd (☎873001) Smart and friendly; on the waterfront. ⑦.

Foveran, 2 miles out on the A964 to Orphir (☎872389). Modern but homely buildings set among fields. Very well equipped and comfortable, with a good restaurant. ⑥.

Kirkwall, Harbour St (☎872232). Well-maintained and quite imposing Victorian pile on the waterfront. ⑥.

Queen's Hotel, Shore St (☎872200). Comfortable and convenient for the centre. ④.

Sanderlay Guest House, 2 Viewfield Drive (☎872343). A family welcome; well-equipped rooms. ②.

West End Hotel, 14 Main St (☎872368). Recent refurbishment has left character and slight shabbiness intact; comfortable and welcoming, with huge breakfasts. ④.

The Town

Towering above the town, the **St Magnus Cathedral** (daily 9am–1pm & 2–5pm) is the very heart of Kirkwall, and its most intriguing conventional sight, a unique building that employs traditional architectural techniques but gives them a distinctive Orkney twist. The building was begun in 1137 by the Orkney Earl Kol of Agdir, who decided to make full use of a growing cult surrounding the figure of his uncle Magnus Erlendson. Magnus had shared the earldom of Orkney with his cousin Hakon Paulson from 1103, but Hakon grew jealous of his cousin's popularity and had him killed in 1115. When Magnus's body was buried in Birsay a heavenly light was said to have shone overhead, and his grave soon became a place of pilgrimage attributed with miraculous powers and attracting pilgrims from as far afield as Shetland. When Kol of Agdir finally took over the earldom he built the cathedral in his uncle's honour, moving the centre of religious and secular power from Birsay to Kirkwall.

The first version of the cathedral, which was built using yellow stone from Eday and red stone from the Mainland, was somewhat smaller than today's structure, which has been added to over the centuries, with a new east window in the thirteenth century, the extension of the nave in the fifteenth century and a new west window to mark the building's 850th anniversary in 1987. Today the soft sandstone is badly eroded, particularly around the doorways, but it's still an immensely impressive building, its shape and style echoing the great cathedrals of Europe. Inside, the atmosphere is surprisingly intimate, the pink sandstone columns drawing you up to the exposed brickwork arches, while around the walls a series of gravestones and monuments include the bones of Magnus himself, a monument to the dead of HMS *Royal Oak* (which was torpedoed in Scapa Flow in 1939 with the loss of 833 men; see p.474) and the tomb of the arctic explorer John Rae, who was born in Stromness. There's also a collection of gravestones from the sixteenth and seventeenth centuries, carved with chilling inscriptions calling on the reader to "remember death waits us all, the hour none knows".

Alongside the church are the ruined remains of the **Bishop's Palace** (April–Sept Mon–Sat 9.30am–6pm, Sun 2–6pm; £1.20). Built in the twelfth century for Bishop William of Old, the palace consisted of a main hall for ceremonial occasions and a tower which probably served as the bishop's private residence. The palace was rebuilt in the late fifteenth century and restored in the sixteenth, by Bishop Robert Reid, the founder of Edinburgh University. Today the walls and tower still stand, and a narrow spiral staircase takes you to the top for a good view of the cathedral and across Kirkwall's rooftops.

The neighbouring **Earl's Palace**, which dates from 1600, is rather better preserved; it's reckoned to be one of the finest examples of Renaissance architecture in Scotland. With its dank dungeons, massive fireplaces and magnificent central hall, it is a much grander building than the Bishop's Palace and has an confident solidity. Inside, a series of excellent displays analyzes the uses of the various rooms, and it's easy enough to imagine the way in which the earl lived here and conducted his ruthless business. The roof is missing, but many domestic details remain, including a set of toilets and the stone shelves used by the clerk to do his filing.

The turreted towers of the Earl's Palace are echoed by those of the Victorian **Town Hall**, opposite the cathedral. Nearby, **Tankerness House** (Mon–Sat 10.30am–12.30pm & 1.30–5pm; May–Sept also Sun 2–5pm; April–Sept £1, otherwise free), a former home for the clergy that has been renovated countless times over the years, first in 1574 and most recently in the 1960s, houses a simple but informative **museum** that takes you through Orkney history from the very beginning – well worth a look before you visit the main archeological sites. Among its collection, there are some unusual artefacts, including a collection of *ba* balls (used in a traditional Orkney street game, played every year at Christmas and New Year), Pictish board games, an Iron Age bone shovel and early bowls made from whales' vertebrae. In addition, there are a couple of rooms which have been restored as they would have been in 1820, when the building was a private home, together with a space for temporary exhibitions. On a warm summer afternoon, the **gardens** (which can be entered either from the house itself or from a gate on Tankerness Lane) are thick with the buzz of bees and brilliant blooms.

Further afield (a mile or so south of the town centre on the Holm road), is the **Highland Park** distillery, billed as "the most northerly legal distillery in Scotland". The distillery has been in operation for more than 200 years, although it was closed during World War II, when it was used as a military food store and the huge vats served as communal baths. You can decide for yourself whether the taste still lingers by partaking of the regular guided tours of its beautiful old buildings and the customary free dram afterwards (Easter–Oct Mon–Fri 10am–4pm; June–Aug also Sat 10am–4pm; Nov–March Mon–Fri tours at 2 & 3.30pm only; £2).

Eating and drinking

Kirkwall offers a good selection of **cafés** and **restaurants**. The range and quality of food has steadily improved in recent years, with local fish and shellfish increasingly in evidence.

Some **pubs** to try include the *Bothy Bar* in the *Albert Hotel*, which sometimes has live music and is attached to *Matchmakers* disco (open as a disco on Thurs, Fri & Sat nights; but selling bar meals at other times), the public bar in the *Kirkwall* and the cosy lounge bar in the *Queen's* hotel. Two miles beyond Kirkwall Airport on the A960, there's usually a good atmosphere, sometimes with live music, at the *Quoyburray Inn*.

Albert Hotel, Mounthoolie Lane (☎876000). Good meals in the bar and restaurant with use of local produce.

A La Olla, in The Shore, Anchor Building, 8 Bridge St (☎875019). Mexican café/restaurant doing fairly inexpensive snacks at lunchtime and meals at night.

Buster's Diner, Mounthoolie Place. Reasonable burgers, pizza, pancake and ice cream; friendly and inexpensive.

Foveran Hotel, 2 miles out on the A964 to Orphir (☎872389). One of the best eating places in Orkney; a relatively long menu includes some good vegetarian choices. Strong on local produce.

Golden Dragon Chinese Restaurant, up the back steps at 25a Bridge St (☎872933). Probably the better of Kirkwall's two Chinese restaurants, but still a little bland.

Kirkwall Hotel, Harbour St (☎872232). French-tinged menu, with imaginative use of local seafood and beef, in a relatively grand setting.

Mumataz Indian Restaurant, 7 Bridge St (☎873537). Good food, friendly service and moderate prices. Small range of European dishes.

Pomona Café, Albert St. Something of a local institution, with simple food: teas. coffees, cakes, pies, sandwiches and toasties.

Queen's Hotel, Shore St (☎872200). Some quite ambitious bar meals here and the integral *Buckingham Restaurant* is also good.

St Magnus Café, opposite the cathedral on Broad St. Teas, sandwiches, soup in basic surroundings. Closes around 4pm, but is open again Mon & Thurs 7–10pm.

Trenabies, 16 Albert St. Easy-going restaurant serving a good breakfast, sandwiches, baked potatoes, pasta, pizza and other inexpensive meals.

West End Hotel, Main St (☎872368). Excellent and good-value bar meals – chicken, scampi, steak and so on.

Listings

Airport ☎872421.

Banks There are branches of all the big Scottish banks on the main street.

Bike rental *Paterson's* Tankerness Lane (☎873097).

Bookshops *Leonard's* or *Stevenson* at the corner of Bridge St and Albert St, *Spence* at 42 Broad St or second-hand from *M E McCarty* at 54 Junction Rd.

Bus companies *Birsay Bus Service* (Birsay–Kirkwall; ☎721312); *Causeway Coaches* (Kirkwall to St Margaret's Hope, Burwick ferry terminal; ☎831444); *Deerness Bus Service* (Deerness–Kirkwall; ☎741215); *James D Peace* (Kirkwall to Stromness; ☎872866); *Rosie Coaches* (Kirkwall to Tingwall and Evie; ☎751227); *Shalder Coaches* (Stromness Kirkwall to connect with mainland ferry; ☎850809).

Car rental *J&W Tait*, Sparrowhawk Rd (☎872490); *Peace's*, Junction Rd (☎872866); *W R Tullock*, Castle St (☎871168).

Consulates *Denmark* and *Germany*: J Robertson, Shore St (☎872961); *Netherlands* and *Norway*: J Spence (☎872268).

Exchange In addition to the banks, the tourist office in Broad St runs an exchange service (daily 8am–8pm in summer).

Fishing tackle and diving equipment *Eric Kemp*, 31–33 Bridge St (☎872137).

Golf The Orkney Golf Club, an exposed course west of the town with good views, welcomes visitors (☎872457).

Laundry *Launderama*, Albert St (Mon–Fri 8.30am–5.30pm, Sat 9am–5.30pm).

Medical care Balfour Hospital, Kirkwall Health Centre and Dental Clinic, New Scapa Rd (☎872763).

Post office Junction Rd (Mon–Fri 9am–5pm, Sat 9.30am–12.30pm).

Travel agents *Going Places*, 15 Broad St (☎873734); *Ridgway Travel*, 67 Albert St (☎873359).

The West Mainland

The great bulk of the **West Mainland** is Orkney's most fertile, productive ground, fringed by some spectacular coastline and littered with impressive historical sites, ranging from the prehistoric village of **Skara Brae** to the battered concrete huts that mark the remains of Twatt military airfield, a large World War II RAF base.

Today this part of the island is still heavily farmed, and there are few real villages. There are still some areas, however, which are too barren to cultivate, and the high ground and wild coastline are protected by several interesting **wildlife reserves**, while a handful of small lochs offers superb **trout fishing**.

Evie and the Broch of Gurness

Overshadowed by the great wind turbines on Burgar Hill, the little village of **EVIE**, on the north coast, looks out across the turbulent waters of **Eynhallow Sound** towards the island of Rousay. At the western end of the white sands of Evie, the **Broch of**

Gurness (April–Sept Mon–Sat 9.30am–6.30pm, Sun 2–6.30pm; £2) is the best preserved of more than 500 pre-Christian-era villages dotted across the islands – like the others built to a simple pattern, with a compact group of homes clustered around a central tower. The walls and partitions of the houses have survived amazingly well, so has the main tower, which was probably retreated to in times of attack, with its thick, fortified walls and independent water supply.

To the south of Evie, a small road climbs high over the shoulder of **Burgar Hill**, skirting along the side of the huge **RSPB Birsay Moors Reserve**, which embraces most of Burgar Hill and reaches down to the marshland and the shores of Lowrie's Water. The high heather-coated ground provides good hunting for kestrels, merlins and hen harriers, while the loch is used as a nesting site by red-throated divers. The moor is also a source of traditional fuel, and you can make out the areas in which peat is cut, with small stacks often drying on the hillside. Just north of Evie, a road leads up to the **aerogenerator** established here in 1983. Harnessing Orkney's wind, it supplies electricity to the national grid; and research done here has paved the way for wind-power developments elsewhere in Britain. Information about the project and the RSPB reserve is available at the **visitor centre** below the huge towers.

Birsay: the Earl's Palace, Brough of Birsay and Kirbuster

Northwest from Evie, the parish of **BIRSAY** was the centre of Norse power in Orkney for several centuries, until the earls moved to Kirkwall following the construction of the cathedral. Today a tiny cluster of homes is gathered around the ruins of the **Earl's Palace** at Birsay, which was built in 1574 at the back of a beautiful little bay. The crumbling walls and turrets retain plenty of their grandeur, although there is little remaining evidence of domestic detail. When it was occupied, the palace was surrounded by flower and herb gardens, a bowling green and archery butts. By comparison, the Earl's Palace in Kirkwall seems fairly humble.

Just over half a mile northwest of the palace is the **Brough of Birsay**, a small Pictish settlement on a tidal island that can be reached during the two hours each side of high tide. Don't get stranded, unless you plan to camp, in which case make sure you're well provided for. The focus of the village was the twelfth-century **St Peter's Church**, the shape of which is mapped out by the remains of its walls. Southwest, on the other side of Birsay Bay, is **Marwick Head**. On it stands the memorial to Lord Kitchener and the crew of the HMS *Hampshire* who died near here when the ship struck a mine in June 1916. Marwick Head is an **RSPB reserve**.

Two miles east of Birsay, at **KIRBUSTER** (between the Loch of Hundland and the Loch of Bardhouse), the **Kirbuster Farm Museum** (March–Oct Mon–Sat 10.30am–1pm & 2–5pm, Sun 2–5pm) is worth a short detour, offering an interesting insight into the hardships of life on an Orkney croft in the last century, when open peat fires filled the rooms with smoke and roofs were protected with heather thatch. Housed in a traditional structure, with cold stone floors, blackened cooking pots over the fire and fish fillets drying in the smoke, the display is arranged to show the dramatic improvements in croft life which took place last century; one room has bare stone walls and a fire in the centre of the room, while the other has wallpaper and a fireplace. Most remarkable of all is that the house was inhabited in very much the same way until 1961.

Skara Brae

About five miles south of Birsay, the beautiful white curve of the **Bay of Skaill** is home to **Skara Brae** (April–Sept Mon–Sat 9.30am–6.30pm, Sun 11.30am–6.30pm; Oct–May Mon–Sat 9.30am–4.30pm, Sun 2–4.30pm; £2), the remains of a small fishing and farming village that was inhabited between 3000 and 2500 BC and rediscovered in 1850 after a fierce storm by the laird of Skaill (whose massive seventeenth-century home, now converted into self-catering flats, is set a little way behind the bay).

The village is very well preserved, its houses, many of which still stand, huddled together and connected by narrow passages which would have been covered over with turf. For centuries it was buried in the dunes, which protected a vast array of domestic detail, including dressers, fireplaces, beds and boxes, all carefully put together from slabs of stone. Archeologists have discovered two distinct types of house: an earlier, smaller structure, built around a central hearth, with beds built into the wall; and larger, later homes that have the beds in the main living area with cupboards behind them. Other evidence shows that the inhabitants were settled farmers eating sheep, cattle and grain, as well as fish and shellfish, and using lamps fuelled by the oil from whales, seals and seabirds.

Maes Howe, the Stones of Stenness and the Ring of Brodgar

The main road leads back towards Kirkwall via the village of **DOUNBY**, a quiet, former market town, and skirts the shores of Loch Harray (Orkney's most famous trout loch), to reach the great Neolithic burial chamber of **Maes Howe** (April–Sept Mon–Sat 9.30am–6pm, Sun 2–6pm; Oct–May Mon–Sat 9.30am–4pm, Sun 2–4pm; £2). The chamber occupies a central position on the Mainland and is proof positive of the ingenuity of prehistoric communities in Orkney. Dating from 2750 BC, its incredible state of preservation is partly due to the massive slabs of sandstone it was constructed from, the largest of which weighs over three tons. The central chamber is reached down a long stone passage and contains three cells built into the walls, each of which was plugged with an enormous stone. When the tomb was opened in 1861, it was found to be virtually empty, thanks to the work of generations of grave-robbers, who had only left behind a handful of human bones. It is known for certain that the Vikings broke in here in the twelfth century, probably on their way to the crusades, because they left behind large amounts of graffiti. These runic inscriptions, cut into the walls of the main chamber and still clearly visible today, include phrases such as: "Many a beautiful woman has stooped in here, however pompous she might be" and "These runes were carved by the man most skilled in runes in the entire western ocean".

The area surrounding Maes Howe was a religious centre for Orkney's Stone Age inhabitants; of the many remains dating back to that era, the closest are the **Stones of Stenness**, just over a mile to the west – a circle of 12 rock slabs, the tallest of which is over 16ft high. Less than half a mile from these, the **Ring of Brodgar** is a nearly complete ring of 27 stones, beautifully sited on a narrow spit of land between two lochs.

West Mainland practicalities

You can easily base yourself in Kirkwall or Stromness, but many good **places to stay** are scattered throughout the West Mainland. There are welcoming **B&Bs** such as *Asgard,* Germiston Rd, Orphir (☎01856/811300; ②) or *Linnadale*, Heddle Rd, Finstown (☎01856/761300; ③). Moving northwards *Mrs Kirkpatrick* (☎01856/841656; ③) offers very comfortable rooms on the loch shore at Sandwick. Other friendly places include: *Woodwick House* (☎01856/751330; ④) at Evie; *Dounby House* (☎01856/771535; ②) in Dounby; *Primrose Cottage* (☎01856/721384; ②) at Marwick; *Fiddlers' Green* (formerly *Linkshouse*; ☎01856/721221; ③) in Birsay. The *Smithfield Hotel* (☎01856/771215; ⑤) in the middle of Dounby is a pleasant village inn with good food. Other **hotels** include the *Barony Hotel* (☎01856/721327; ④) on the north shore of the Loch of Boardhouse and the *Merkister Hotel* (☎01856/771515; ⑥) at the north end of the Loch of Harray. Both make a comfortable base and specialize in fishing holidays; the *Merkister* also boasts a bird hide. **Camping** is available at the *Eviedale Centre* (April–Oct; ☎01856/751270).

For **eating**, all the hotels do lunches or bar meals; other places for a snack or something more filling include the *Dale Kitchen* at Evie, the *Northdyke* a mile or so north of Skara Brae and the top-floor restaurant at *Tormiston Mill*.

Stromness

The Orkney I was born into was a place
Where there was no great distinction between
the ordinary and the fabulous; the lives of
living men turned into legend.

                    Edwin Muir

Orkney's great harbour town, **STROMNESS** is perhaps more than anywhere else the historical heart of the islands. It was here, in the shelter of Hamnavoe, or Haven Bay, on the edge of the great natural harbour of Scapa Flow, that ships from all around the world came and went, sweeping the town into a series of booms, unloading a cargo of sea tales and embarking hundreds of Orcadians on weird and wonderful expeditions.

French and Spanish ships sheltered in Hamnavoe as early as the sixteenth century, and for a long time European conflicts made it safer for ships heading across the Atlantic to travel around the top of Scotland rather than through the English Channel, many of whom called in to Stromness to take on food, water and crew. Crews from Stromness were also hired for herring and whaling expeditions for which the town was an important centre. By 1842, the town was a tough and busy harbour, with some 40 or so pubs and reports of "outrageous and turbulent proceedings of seamen and others who frequent the harbour". The herring boom brought large numbers of small boats to the town, along with thousands of young women who gutted and pickled the fish before they were packed in barrels. Today Stromness is still an important harbour town, serving as Orkney's main ferry terminal and as the headquarters of the Northern Lighthouse Board.

Arrival, information and accommodation

However you **arrive**, you'll have no trouble finding your way around as there's really only one street, although it does change its name several times, starting in the north as John Street, and finishing up as South End in the south, with several variations in between, notably Victoria Street. The **tourist office** (Mon–Fri & Sat 8am–8pm, Thurs 8am–6pm, Sun 9am–4pm; ☎01856/850716) is in the ferry terminal building opposite the pier.

The smartest **hotel** in the area is the *Standing Stones* (☎01856/850449; ⑦), four miles away on the southern shore of Loch Stenness. In Stromness itself, the *Stromness Hotel* (☎01856/850610; ⑤) was the town's first; it's showing its age a bit, but the welcome's warm. The *Braes Hotel* (☎01856/850495; ④), on the hill above the south end of the town has the best views. There are several good and friendly **B&Bs**. Very close to the ferry terminal are the excellent *Ferry Inn* (☎01856/850280; ③) and *Mrs Hourston* (☎01856/850642; ②), just behind it. At the southern end of town, on the Ness Rd, *Stenigar* (☎01856/850438; ③) has lots of character. Further out, at Kirbister, *Brettobreck Farm* (☎01856/850373; ②) is a traditional and very homely Orcadian farmhouse. Stromness has a well-equipped **camping** site (☎01856/873535) in a superb setting at Point of Ness, with views out to Hoy; to reach it, keep going southwards along the main street and follow the shore road (South End) for about half a mile.

Stromness also has an official **youth hostel**, on Helly Hole Rd (March–Oct; ☎01856/850589; Grade 2), signposted from the car park outside the *Stromness Hotel*, but it's fairly strictly run, with a curfew and single-sex dorms. Alternatively there's *Brown's Hostel*, 45–47 Victoria St (☎01856/850661), an independent youth hostel with bunk beds in shared rooms and kitchen facilities; it's open all day, and there's no curfew.

The Town

Clustered along the shoreline, Stromness is a tight network of alleyways and slate roofs, crowded onto the lower slopes of **Brinkie's Brae**, which looms up from the harbour front. The single main street, paved with great flagstones and called various names (see above), winds along behind the waterfront, with narrow alleys meandering off up the hill. Originally all of the waterfront houses had their own piers, from which merchants would trade with passing ships; the **cannon** at the southern end of town (on South End) was fired to announce the arrival of a ship from the *Hudson's Bay Company*. Today the trade in American rice and Canadian fur has moved on, but the site of the cannon still gives magnificent views of the harbour, and there are a number of reminders of the town's trading heyday. The **Warehouse**, now home to the *P&O* and tourist offices, was originally built in the 1760s to store American rice. At the southern end of town, on the Ness road, **The Doubles** is a large pair of houses on a raised platform that were built as a home by Mrs Christian Robertson with the proceeds of her shipping agency, which sent as many as 800 men on whaling expeditions in one year.

The **Stromness Museum**, off the southern end of main street (Mon–Sat 10.30am–12.30pm & 1.30–5pm; 80p), houses a collection of salty artefacts gathered from shipwrecks and arctic expeditions, including crockery from the German fleet, beaver fur hats, Cree Indian cloth and part of the torpedo that sunk the HMS *Royal Oak*. The **Pier Arts Centre**, right on the waterfront (Tues–Sun 10.30am–12.30pm & 1.30–5pm), gives a more contemporary account of Orkney life, restored to become an important focus of artistic life in the islands. It has regular exhibitions, often featuring painting and sculpture by local artists.

Eating and drinking

Like any harbour town, Stromness is a good place to eat with plenty of options scattered around the small town centre. The *Ferry Inn* on John St, beside the tourist office, is a small but popular restaurant, serving good, inexpensive meals of fish, steak and scampi. *The Coffee Shop*, on the north side of the car park, behind the *Ferry Inn*, is a friendly little café which offers enormous breakfasts, lunches, sandwiches, vegetarian dishes, afternoon tea, cakes and pies – though it closes at 5pm, as does the *Peedie Coffee Shop* on Victoria St, the town's oldest establishment. For **picnics**, nearby *Argo's Bakery*, has a wide range of the basics and their own excellent bread and biscuits, while *Foodoodles*, also on Victoria St, is a delicatessen offering cheeses, salamis and made-to-order sandwiches.

More expensively, the *Hamnavoe Restaurant* at 35 Graham Place (☎01856/850606) is perhaps Stromness' smartest, making full use of local produce including shellfish, fish and beef, and some delicious vegetarian dishes, all served up at very moderate prices. *The Cafe*, on Victoria St in front of the *Stromness Hotel* on the south side of the car park, with a good harbourside location, is a less pricy option for dinner, serving simple, inexpensive meals of burgers, pizza, pasta and sandwiches. The *Valhala Restaurant*, in the bar of the *Stromness Hotel*, serves a solid but uninspiring menu, including steak, spaghetti and haddock.

Listings

Banks There are branches of the *Bank of Scotland* and *Royal Bank of Scotland* on the main street.

Bike rental *Brown's Hostel*, 45 Victoria St (☎01856/850661); *Orkney Cycle Hire*, 54 Dundas St (☎01856/850255).

Bookshops *J L Broom*, *John Rae*, or *Scapa* second-hand bookshop, are all on the main street.

Car rental *Brass's Self Drive*, Pierhead Office, John St (☎01856/850750).

Fishing tackle *W S Sinclair*, just above the car park on John St.

Laundry Behind the *Ferry Inn*, next to the coffee shop on the north side of the car park (Mon–Sat 9am–5pm).

The East Mainland and South Ronaldsay

Southeast from Kirkwall, the narrow spur of the **East Mainland** juts out into the North Sea and is joined, thanks to the remarkable Churchill barriers, to the smaller islands of Burray and South Ronaldsay. The land here is densely populated and heavily farmed, but there are several interesting fishing villages and a scattering of unusual historical relics.

The East Mainland

The northern side of the East Mainland consists of a series of exposed peninsulas, the first of which, **Rerwick Head**, is marked by the remains of World War II gun emplacements. **Mull Head** – the furthest east – is an **RSPB reserve** with a large colony of seabirds, including arctic terns, that swoop on unwanted visitors, screeching threateningly. The reserve is open to visitors at all times (although without your own transport it is hard to reach). There is a car park at the end of the road (a continuation of the B9050), which is about half a mile from the cliffs. A mile and a half south of the reserve, and a short walk from the car park, is **The Gloup**, an impressive collapsed sea cave; the tide still flows in and out through a natural arch making strange gurgling noises. The name stems from the Old Norse *gluppa*, "a chasm". About two miles north of Deerness, the **Covenanters' Memorial** commemorates the death of around 200 people who were shipwrecked en route to a life of slavery in the West Indies – their offence had been to object to the new English Common Prayer Book.

On the south coast, just east of the village of **ST MARY'S**, is the **Norwood Museum** (May–Sept Tues–Thurs & Sun 2–5pm & 6–8pm; other times by arrangement ☎01856/781217; £2), a display of antiques that is the life's work of Norrie Wood, a local stonemason who started collecting at the age of thirteen. Only about half of the collection is on display, but it's a fascinating and eccentric selection of bits and pieces from around the world, including pottery, painting, medals, furniture, cutlery, clocks, even a narwhale's tusk, all housed in a grand Orkney home. If you want to stay, there's **hotel** accommodation at the *Commodore Motel* at St Mary's, which also seves satisfying bar meals.

The Churchill barriers

The presence of the huge naval base in **Scapa Flow** during both world wars presented a very tempting target to the Germans, and protecting the fleet was always a nagging problem for the Allies. During World War I, blockships were sunk to guard the eastern approaches, but in October 1939, just weeks after the outbreak of World War II, a German U-boat managed to manoeuvre past the blockships and torpedo the battleship

HMS *Royal Oak*, which sank with the loss of 833 lives. The U-boat captain claimed to have acquired local knowledge while fishing in the islands before the war.

Today the wreck of the *Royal Oak*, marked by an orange buoy off the **Gaitnip Cliffs** (on the west coast of the West Mainland, just off the A961 between Kirkwall and St Mary's), is an official war grave. Its sinking convinced the First Lord of the Admiralty, Winston Churchill, that Scapa Flow needed better protection, and in 1940 work began on a series of **barriers** to seal the waters between the Mainland and the string of islands to the south: the tiny uninhabited **Lamb Holm** and **Glimpse Holm**, and the larger **Burray** and **South Ronaldsay**. Special camps were built to accommodate the 1700 men involved in the project; their numbers were boosted by the surrender of Italy in 1942, when Italian prisoners of war were sent to work here. Besides the barriers, which are an astonishing feat of engineering when you bear in mind the strength of Orkney tides, the Italians also left behind the beautiful **Italian Chapel** on Lamb Holm. This, the so-called "miracle of Camp 60", must be one of the greatest adaptations ever, made from two Nissen huts, concrete, barbed wire and parts of a rusting blockship. The chapel deteriorated after the departure of the Italians, but its principal architect, Domenico Chiocchetti, returned in 1960 to restore the building. Today it is beautifully preserved and Mass is said regularly.

South Ronaldsay

At the southern end of the series of four barriers is the low-lying **South Ronaldsay**. The island has a number of old fishing villages, of which the first, **ST MARGARET'S HOPE**, takes its name either from Margaret, the maid of Norway, who died here in November 1290 while on her way to marry Edward II (then Prince Edward) or less romantically from an ancient chapel in the area. Margaret had already been proclaimed the queen of Scotland, and the marriage was intended to unify the two countries. Today St Margaret's Hope is a lovely little gathering of houses at the back of a sheltered bay, and it makes an excellent base from which to explore the area. The **Wireless Museum**, on the entrance road (June–Sept check days and times with the tourist office; £1), a small private collection of communications equipment from the war, has some fairly obscure exhibits including a picture of naval women dancing in costumes made from balloon fabric. The village **Smithy** has also been turned into a museum (check opening times locally), with a few exhibits relating to this now defunct business.

Despite the fact that it is heavily cultivated, South Ronaldsay also offers some excellent walking, particularly out on the **Howe of Hoxa**, where there is a small broch and a beach at the **Sands O'Right** – the scene of an annual ploughing match in August, in which local boys compete with miniature hand-held ploughs. Further south, seals and their pups can be seen in the autumn in **Wind Wick Bay**, and there is an ancient chambered burial cairn, known as the **Tomb of the Eagles**, at the southeastern corner of the island, where human remains were found alongside eagles' bones. The monument is privately operated and as well as a tour there's hands-on contact with the exhibits (daily 10am–8pm or dusk; £2). Finally you reach **BURWICK**, where a passenger ferry connects South Ronaldsay with the Scottish mainland at John O' Groats.

South Ronaldsay Practicalities

Getting to and from South Ronaldsay is relatively easy. There are four daily **buses** (40min) between Kirkwall and St Margaret's Hope, and all ferries arriving at Burwick are met by buses from Kirkwall. However, off the main road you'll have to rely on walking and hitching.

The best place to **stay** is without doubt St Margaret's Hope, The *Creel Restaurant and Rooms* (☎01856/831311; ⑤) on Front Rd has won all sorts of awards for its superb food, making brilliant use of local produce. That, plus friendly service and a genuinely relaxed atmosphere, make this probably the most enjoyable place to eat in Orkney.

The rooms are comfortable too. Other good accommodation in St Margaret's Hope includes the *Murray Arms Hotel* (☎01856/831205; ④), with its popular bar serving appetizing meals, and *The Anchorage* (☎01856/831456; ③), on the seafront; friendly and well equipped, its *Galley Dining Room* offers teas, coffees, lunches, high teas and dinner all year round. Comfortable **B&Bs** include *Blanster House* (☎01856/831549; ②), *Windbreck* (☎01856/831370; ③) and *Bellevue Guest House* (☎01856/831294; ②). For basic rooms, head for *Wheems Bothy*, about a mile and a half from the War Memorial on the side road leading east (☎01856/831537; £5 per person). Mattresses are set in partitioned sleeping areas, ingredients for a wholesome breakfast are provided and organic produce from the croft can be bought. There's a good **café**, the *Coach House*, in St Margaret's Hope, next to the *Murray Arms*.

Hoy

Hoy, Orkney's second largest island, rises sharply out of the sea to the southwest of the Mainland – perhaps the least typical of the islands but certainly the most dramatic, its north and west sides made up of great glacial valleys and mountainous moorland rising to the 1500ft-high mass of Ward Hill and the enormous sea cliffs of St John's Head. This part of the island, though a huge expanse, is virtually uninhabited, with the cluster of houses at Rackwick nestling dramatically in a bay between the cliffs; most of Hoy's 400 or so residents live on the fertile land in the southeast that is home to the villages of Lyness and Longhope.

Around the island

Much of Hoy's magnificent landscape is embraced by the **RSPB North Hoy Reserve** (which covers most of the northwest end of the island), in which the rough grasses and heather harbour a cluster of arctic plants and a healthy population of mountain hares, as well as merlins, kestrels and peregrine falcons, while the more sheltered valleys are nesting sites for snipe and arctic skua. The best access to the reserve is from the single-track road which follows the **White Glen** across the island to Rackwick. Along the way, the road passes the **Dwarfie Stane**, an unusual solid-stone tomb which dates from 3000 to 2000 BC. A couple of miles further on, the road passes the end of a large open valley which cuts away to the north and along which a footpath runs to the village of **HOY** at the island's northwest tip. On the western side of this valley is the narrow gulley of **Berriedale**, which supports Britain's most northerly native woodland, a huddle of birch, hazel and honeysuckle.

RACKWICK, on the west coast of the island, is a spread of crofts which boldly face the Atlantic weather, flanked by towering sandstone cliffs. Rackwick's crofting community went into a steady decline in the middle of this century: its school closed in 1954 and the last fishing boat put to sea in 1963, after which three of the four-man crew were too old to take on the Atlantic surf. These days many of the houses have been renovated as holiday homes and the savage exposure of the place has provided inspiration to a number of artists and writers, including Orkney's George Mackay Brown, who wrote that "when Rackwick weeps, its grief is long and forlorn and utterly desolate". A small **museum** (open all times), beside the walkers' hostel, tells a little of Rackwick's rough history, and the croft of **Burnmouth Cottage**, just behind the beach, which has been traditionally restored to provide accommodation for walkers (see "Practicalities" opposite), gives a good idea of how things used to be.

The cliffs at Hoy's northwestern corner are some of the highest in the country, and provide ideal rocky ledges for the nests of thousands of seabirds, including guillemots, kittiwakes, razorbills, puffins and shags. Standing just offshore is the **Old Man of**

Hoy, reachable by footpath (4 miles) from Rackwick, a great sandstone column some 450ft high, perched on an old lava flow which protects it from the erosive power of the sea. The Old Man is a popular challenge for rock climbers, and a 1966 ascent was the first televised climb in Britain.

On the opposite side of Hoy, along the sheltered **eastern shore**, the high moorland gives way to a gentler environment, similar to that of the other islands. Hoy marks the western boundary of **Scapa Flow** and during both world wars it played an important role in its defence, with several substantial gun emplacements along its eastern shore. At **LYNESS**, which was the main naval base, the naval cemetery is surrounded by the scattered **remains** of hundreds of concrete structures, which served as hangars and storehouses during the war, and some of which are now used as barns and cowsheds. Among these are the remains of what was – incredibly – the largest cinema in Europe. Perhaps the most unusual of the remaining buildings is the black-and-white concrete facade of the old *Garrison Theatre*, on the main road to the south of Lyness; formerly the grand front end of a huge Nissen hut, which disappeared long ago – it's now a private home. The old pump station, which now stands beside the new Lyness ferry terminal, has been turned into the **Scapa Flow Visitor Centre** (Mon–Fri 9am–4pm, Sat & Sun 10.30am–3.30pm; £1), a local museum displaying an interesting collection of pictures and photographs showing how busy the area was during the wars. Wartime bits and pieces include torpedoes, flags, guns, propellers and a paratrooper's folding bicycle.

Further south still, the secure waters of **North Bay** cut a deep inlet, a narrow spit of sand connecting north Hoy with **South Walls**, a fertile peninsula which is more densely populated. The bay itself is ringed with farms and homes and on its south side is the quiet little village of **LONGHOPE**. There is also evidence of early conflict here, with two **Martello towers** that mark the island's southeastern outcrops of Hackness and Crockness, as well as the **Hackness battery**, built between 1813 and 1815 to guard against American and French privateers during the Napoleonic wars. If you want to see inside the restored Hackness tower, a sign indicates the nearby house where you can get the key. The eastern tip of the island looks out over treacherous waters and is marked by the **Cantick Head Lighthouse**, while the churchyard at **OSMUNDWALL** contains a monument to the crew of the Longhope lifeboat who died in 1969 when their boat overturned in strong gales on its way to the aid of a Liberian freighter. The entire eight-man crew was killed, leaving seven widows and ten orphans.

Practicalities

Two **ferry** services run to Hoy: a passenger service from **Stromness** to the village of Hoy on the northwest edge of the island, which also serves the small island of **Graemsay**; sailings are more frequent in summer than winter (check with the tourist office for current times). The roll-on, roll-off car ferry sails from **Houton** on the Mainland to **Lyness** and **Longhope** (6 daily).

If you have time, it's worth staying on Hoy; there are very good, friendly **B&Bs** at *Stonequoy Farm*, Lyness (☎01856/791234; ②), *Burnhouse Farm*, Longhope (☎01856/701263; ③) and the *Old Custom House*, Longhope (☎01856/701358; ②). There are also three hostels providing **basic rooms**, the first two of which can be booked either through the Council's Education Department (☎01856/873535) or direct with the wardens; they are the comfortable *Hoy Outdoor Centre* (☎01856/791261), just up from the pier in Hoy village, and the SYHA-affiliated *Rackwick Outdoor Centre* (mid–March to early Aug; ☎01856/791298; bunk beds with blankets but no sheets). The third, the basic *Burnmouth Cottage* (☎01856/791316; no bedding) lies in a beautiful setting right at the top of the beach.

For **food**, there's not a lot of choice, though as in other islands, B&Bs will often provide an ample and delicious evening meal. The *Hoy Inn* in Hoy village, down beyond the post office, offers appetizing seafood bar meals and snacks. In Lyness the

Anchor Bar, more prosaic than the name suggests, does typical pub food, with steaks and local fish available in the dining room. A good place for a snack or soup is the *Lyness Visitor Centre* café.

The North Isles

Scattered loosely off the northwestern side of the Mainland, Orkney's **North Isles** are swept by strong tides and winter storms. Their spidery jigsaw-piece form is a product of this battering, and their stark beauty is based on a simple combination of mostly fertile soils, rock and sand. All the islands, except North Ronaldsay, can be visited as day trips from Kirkwall, using the excellent ferry service. Each of the islands has its own character and the larger ones offer great walks and some outstanding archeological sites.

Shapinsay

Just a few miles northwest of Kirkwall, **Shapinsay** is the most accessible of the northern isles. The Balfour family, who had made a small fortune in India, constructed their castle in Baronial style here from 1847 by extending an eighteenth-century farmhouse. They also reformed the island's agricultural system and built **BALFOUR** village, a neat and disciplined cottage development, to house estate workers. **Balfour Castle** is a mile or so from the centre of the village and is hidden from it by trees, though its towers and turrets are clearly visible from the ferry on the way in. Guided tours of the building are organized on Wednesday and Sunday afternoons and must be booked in advance through the Kirkwall tourist office (see p.466). It's also possible to stay in the castle; details are given below.

The Balfour's grandiose efforts in estate management have left some appealingly eccentric relics. Melodramatic fortifications around the harbour include the huge and ornate, if not exactly beautiful, **gatehouse**, now a pub. There's a stone **gasometer** which once supplied castle and village and, southwest of the pier, the castellated **Dishan Tower**, built as a dovecot but allegedly adapted as a cold-water shower. Elsewhere, the island is heavily cultivated, but within little more than a couple of miles from the ferry terminal there are nice **walks** by the shore to stretches of sand at the **Bay of Furrowend** in the west, with good birdwatching at **Vasa Loch**, and around the sweeping curve of **Veantro Bay** in the north. At the **East Lairo goat farm** (daily except Thurs 12.15–3pm; £2.50; ☎01856/711341; call to arrange transport from ferry) you can meet a herd of prizewinning goats and sample excellent milk, cheese and yoghurt.

Practicalities

Less than 30 minutes from Kirkwall by **ferry**, Shapinsay is an easy day trip, but there's good accommodation on the island if you want to stay. **B&B** is available at comfortable *Girnigoe* (☎01856/711256; ②, full board ③–④), close to the north shore of Veantro Bay. It is also possible to stay in distinguished and opulent accommodation in *Balfour Castle* (☎01856/711282; full board ⑨), where the owners welcome house guests and can offer them visits by boat to nearby uninhabited islands as well as the use of their library and other beautiful rooms. If you're just here for the day, teas and sandwiches from the *Smithy Café* (May–Sept) are your only choice for lunch.

Rousay, Egilsay and Wyre

Just over half a mile away from the Mainland's northern shore, the island of **Rousay** is dominated by high, heather-covered moorland. It's one of the most interesting of the smaller isles, home to a number of intriguing archeological sites, as well as being one of the more accessible. The group of a dozen or so houses above the ferry terminal is the only settlement of any size, but a single road runs around the edge of the island, connecting a string of small farms and providing an excellent circuit by car, an energetic one by bicycle. In any case it's easy enough to reach the main points of interest on foot from the ferry terminal in the southeast corner of the island.

Only the coastal fringes of the island are cultivated, and the central section is dominated by a cluster of rolling hills, the highest of which is the 750ft-high **Blotchnie Fiold**. This high ground offers good hill walking, with superb panoramic views of the islands, as well as excellent birdwatching: a sizeable section of moorland at the southern end of the island (a short walk from the ferry terminal) is a protected area in the **RSPB Trumland Reserve**. Here you may well catch a glimpse of merlins, hen harriers, peregrine falcons and red-throated divers, although the latter are more widespread just outside the reserve on one of the island's three lochs, which also offer good trout fishing. The north and western sides of Rousay are guarded by two sets of steep cliffs, separated by the rocky shores of **Saviskaill Bay**, and again provide spectacular walks and good birdwatching, with puffins, gulls, kittiwakes and arctic terns all nesting here in the summer.

The southwestern side of Rousay is home to the bulk of the island's archeological remains, strung out along the shores of the tide races of **Eynhallow Sound**, which run between the island and the Mainland. Most are on the Westness Walk, a mile-long heritage trail linking Westness Farm, about four miles northwest of the ferry terminal, with **Midhowe Cairn** about a mile further on. Known as "the great ship of death", this well-preserved communal burial chamber dates from about 3500 BC and measures more than 98ft in length. The central chamber, which is like a stone corridor, is partitioned with slabs of rock, with 12 compartments on each side. Archeologists discovered the remains of 25 people inside the tomb, generally in a crouched position with their backs to the wall. This form of burial in stalled tombs dates from the earliest period in the use of chambered burial cairns in Orkney.

A couple of hundred yards south of the Midhowe Cairn is the **Midhowe Broch**, the remains of a fortified Iron Age village which date from the first century AD, and the best preserved of the six brochs that have been found along this shore. It's also thought to be one of the earliest brochs in the Orkneys, with a compact layout that suggests it was a fortified family house rather than a village.

There is evidence of more recent occupation at the **Knowe of Swandro** (on the shore about a mile south of Midhowe), where archeologists have unearthed the remains of a Norse farmstead of the eleventh or twelfth century. Although there isn't much to see today, a variety of artefacts have been found here, including bone remains from which scientists were able to roughly determine the diet of the average person at the time – a rather unhealthy, vegetable-free mixture of seal, grouse, seabirds, whales, otters and deer. Nearby lie **The Wirk**, the remains of a grand ceremonial hall from the thirteenth or fourteenth century, and the abandoned **St Mary's Church**, on the coast a mile south of Midhowe, which dates from the sixteenth century but was abandoned in 1820, when the island was suffering rapid depopulation. Nearer the ferry terminal are **Blackhammar Cairn**, a stalled tomb of similar form and date to Midhowe, though smaller **Taversoe Tuick**, a near neighbour to the east, is a chambered tomb, unusual in that it exploits its sloping site by having two storeys, one entered from the upper side and one from the lower.

Despite its long history of settlement, Rousay is today home to little more than 200 people, as this was one of the few parts of Orkney to suffer Highland-style clearances, initially by George William Traill at **Quandale** in the northwest. His successor, General Traill Burroughs, built the unlovely **Trumland House** (in the trees, near the ferry terminal) in 1873. Continuing to substitute sheep for people, he built a wall to force crofters onto a narrow coastal strip and eventually provoked so much distress and anger that a gunboat had to be sent to restore order.

Egilsay and Wyre

Sheltering close to the eastern shore of Rousay, the two low-lying smaller islands of Egilsay and Wyre each contain some interesting historical remains. Both are visited by the Rousay ferry as it passes (but only by arrangement; see below). The larger of the pair, **Egilsay**, is dominated by the ruins of the **St Magnus Church**, built on a prominent position in the middle of the island in the twelfth century, probably on the site of a much earlier version. The church, now missing its roof, is the only surviving example of the traditional round-towered churches of Orkney and Shetland and was built as a shrine to the saint who was murdered here in 1115 – a **cenotaph** marks the spot, about a quarter of a mile southwest of the church. Over on **Wyre** are the remains of **Cubbie Roo's Castle**, a twelfth-century Viking stronghold, and the neighbouring **St Mary's Chapel**, a ruined twelfth-century church, of which only a single wall remains.

Rousay Practicalities

Rousay makes a good day trip from the Mainland with regular **ferry sailings** (from Tingwall) and **bus connections** to and from Kirkwall. Some ferries call in at Egilsay and Wyre, but in most cases only if someone specifically asks – to arrange this, and to make sure that they come back for you later, call the ferry terminal in Tingwall (☎01856/751360). *Rousay Traveller* (☎01856/821234) runs flexible and very informative minibus tours (late May–early Sept Mon–Fri; other months/days for groups by arrangement). Tours connect with ferries and last between two and five hours, the longer ones allowing extended walks. You can rent **bikes** from *Helga's*, behind the *Pier Restaurant* at the ferry terminal (☎01856/821293). Next to the pier is the Trumland Orientation Centre, which is packed with information on every aspect of Rousay past and present.

B&B is available at *Maybank,* three miles west of the ferry terminal (☎01856/821225; ②); while *Trumland Farm* (☎01856/821252), a mile or so west of the terminal, has a recently built hostel and a three-bed self-catering cottage sleeping four (£100 per week; shorter lets may be available). The only **hotel** on the island is the *Taversoe*, a couple of miles west of the terminal at Frotoft (☎01856/821325; ④), a modern building added onto an old croft. The hotel has a **restaurant** with excellent home cooking featuring local produce, especially seafood, and vegetarian options; a bar and beer garden overlook the sea. The *Pier Restaurant* (☎01856/821391) right beside the terminal, serves bar-style meals; if you phone in advance, they will pack you a delicious picnic of crab, cheese, fruit and bannock bread. In the evenings, the restaurant functions as a pub.

Eday

Similar in many ways to Rousay and Hoy, the smaller island of **Eday** is dominated by a great block of heather-covered upland, with farmland confined to a narrow strip of coastal ground. Oddly enough, the island is a net exporter of raw materials: peat cut on the high ground is sent to the other northern isles for fuel, and yellow sandstone quarried from the island was used to build the St Magnus Cathedral in Kirkwall.

The island is very sparsely inhabited, and the nearest approximation to a village is the small gathering of houses at **CALFSOUND** in the north, which has the island's only pub. Unless you arrive by plane and touch down at London Airport (right in the middle of the island), you'll probably come ashore at the ferry terminal in **BACKALAND**, at the island's southern tip. The southern end of the island offers some great walking, both on the high ground of **Ward Hill** and **Flaughton Hill** and along the jagged western shoreline to the sheltered curve of the **Sands of Mussetter**. However, the most dramatic cliffs are to be found in the far north (6 miles from the ferry terminal) at **Red Head**, which also gives great views of the other islands and of the uninhabited **Calf of Eday** – itself home to some massive bird colonies.

The northern end of the island is also the focus of Eday's archeological heritage. The best way to explore this part of the island is to follow the signposted **Eday Heritage Walk**, which starts at the **Eday Community Enterprise Shop** on the main road in **MILLBOUNDS**, where there's also a display explaining the island's history. The walk, covering around five miles and taking about three hours, follows the road north past the bird hide at **Mill Loch** to the **Stone of Setter**. Centre stage in the landscape, visible from other prehistoric sites and around 15ft high, this eroded, cracked and still enormous standing stone is Orkney's most spectacular. From here, you can climb the Vinquoy Hill to reach the finest of Eday's chambered cairns, the **Vinquoy Chambered Cairn**, which has been partially restored and has a similar structure to that of the Maes Howe tomb on the Mainland, with large blocks of stone supporting the inside walls and four tomb chambers set into them. Then you can either head back to the shop or continue north to the dramatic cliffs of **Red Head** and walk around the coast to **Carrick House**, the grandest home on Eday, which although private is open to visitors (June to mid-Sept Sun afternoons, Wed groups by appointment; for times call ☎01857/622260). Built originally by the laird of Eday in 1633, it was extended in the original style by successive owners and is an excellent example of an island laird's house. It was once the prison of the pirate John Gow – on whom Sir Walter Scott's novel *The Pirate* is based – whose ship *The Revenge* ran aground here.

Practicalities

Eday's **ferry** terminal is at **Backaland** pier in the south, not ideal for visiting the more interesting northern section of the island, although if you haven't got your own transport you should find it fairly easy to get a lift with someone on the ferry. It's also possible to catch the *British Airways Express* plane from Kirkwall to Eday's London Airport on Wednesdays; for times and fares contact them on ☎01856/873457. You can rent **bikes** from *Millbank* (☎01857/622205) near the post office.

B&B **accommodation** is available at *Skaill Farm*, a traditional farmhouse just south of the airport (closed May; ☎01857/6222271; including dinner ⑤); *Greentoft*, on the eastern side of Ward Hill in the south (☎01857/622269, ②), and *Blett* in the north of the island (☎01857/622248; ③), where there's also a self-catering cottage and a small art gallery. Or you could try **self-catering** at *Carpaquoy* (☎01857/622262; £100 per week), a bungalow sleeping four. The SYHA-affiliated **hostel** just north of the airport is run by *Eday Community Enterprises* (April–Sept; ☎01857/622248; Grade 3). There's a pub, *The Pirate Gow*, overlooking Calf Sound in the north of the island which does **bar meals** on Friday, Saturday and Sunday evenings, specializing in seafood, vegetarian and vegan dishes.

Stronsay

A three-pronged shape to the southeast of Eday, **Stronsay** is a beautiful, low-lying island that for a long time lived off its herring and kelp industries; indeed, at the end of the eighteenth century, the kelp business employed some 3000 people on the island, and during the 1880s Whitehall harbour was one of the main Scottish centres for the curing of herring caught by French, Dutch and Scottish boats, with three hundred boats working out of the port. By the 1930s, however, the herring stocks had been severely depleted and the industry began a long decline.

Today Stronsay supports a sizeable population of farmers, and boasts some interesting bird and plant life and a scattering of vague archeological remains. The only village is **WHITEHALL**, made up of a couple of rows of small fishermen's cottages, and blessed with a hotel and pub. Unless you arrive by plane (at the airstrip at the northern end of the island), it's from here that you'll set out to explore. Stronsay has few real sights, but like all of these northern isles it offers some fantastic walking. The low-lying central land is almost entirely given over to farming and it's on the coast that you'll see the island at its best, with cliffs home to several seabird colonies and seals basking on exposed rocks at low tide. On the island's western arm there are two broad, arching beaches, the **Bay of Holland** and **St Catherine's Bay**, while over in the east there's a small bird reserve on the shores of **Mill Bay**, just south of Whitehall. Birdwatching is at its best here in September and October, when easterly winds bring migrants such as thrushes, warblers, flycatchers and wrynecks.

Practicalities

Stronsay is served by a twice-daily **ferry** service to Whitehall. The island has one very welcoming **hotel**, *The Stronsay* (☎01857/616213; ②), on the quayside in Whitehall; the bar here serves simple meals. For ornithologists, the *Stronsay Bird Reserve* (☎01857/ 616363) offers full board (③), bed and breakfast (②) or camping on the shores of Mill Bay. **B&B** is also available at *Airy* (☎01857/616231; ②). You can **rent cars** (from *D S Peace*; ☎01857/616335) or **boats** (from *J Stevenson*; ☎01857/616341).

Sanday

As its name suggests, **Sanday** is the most insubstantial of the North Isles, a great drifting dune strung out between several rocky points. The island's bays and clean white sands are the finest in Orkney, and in dry, clear weather it's a superb place to spend a day or two.

The island has a long history as a shipping hazard, with many wrecks smashed against its shores, although the construction of the **Start Point Lighthouse** in 1802–6, on the island's exposed eastern tip, reduced the risk for seafarers. Today the islanders survive largely from farming and fishing, supplemented by a small knitting business, based at Wool Hall in Lady Village and a rabbit farm at Breckan, which specializes in the production of Angora wool.

The shoreline supports a healthy seal and otter population, and behind the beaches are stretches of beautiful open grassland, thick with wild flowers during the spring and summer. The entire coastline presents the opportunity for superb walks, with splendid sandy bays protected by jaggy outcrops of rock. Sanday is particularly rich in archeology, with hundreds of sites including cairns, brochs and burnt mounds. The most impressive is the chambered cairn at **Quoyness** (on the peninsula about a mile east of the ferry terminal), which dates from the third millennium BC. The main chamber is 13ft long and holds six small cells, which contained bones and skulls.

Practicalities

Ferries to Sanday arrive in **KETTLETOFT**, a little gathering of houses which is the nearest thing to a village; the **airfield** is just north of here. For **accommodation**, *The Belsair Hotel* (☎01857/600206; ③) in the village is comfortable and does delicious packed lunches as well as offering a varied menu in the restaurant. Car, caravan and trout-fishing boat **rental** is available from Mrs Muir (☎01857/600331).

Westray and Papa Westray

A pair of exposed islands on the western side of the group, **Westray** and **Papa Westray** – or **Papey** as Orcadians call it – bear the full brunt of the Atlantic weather. The southern end of **Westray**, where ferries put in, is relatively gentle, while at the northern end the island rises more sharply, forming dramatic cliffs. The cliffs of **Noup Head**, packed with nesting seabirds during the summer months, are very spectacular, particularly when a good westerly swell is up. The open ground above the cliffs, which is grazed by sheep, is superb maritime heath and grassland, carpeted with yellow, white and purple flowers. Further south, there's an interesting walk from **Tuquoy** to **Langskaill** taking in the **Cross Kirk** which, although ruined, is still one of the most complete medieval churches in Orkney. Along the shore nearby are the eroding remains of a **Norse settlement**; on the east side, the ruined walls on the sea stack known as the **Castle of Burrian** reveal the presence of an early Christian settlement. The stack is an excellent place to see puffins in the nesting season.

Westray has a fairly stable population of 700 or so, producing superb beef, scallops, shellfish and a large catch of whitefish, with its own small fish-processing factory. The main village is **PIEROWALL** in the north, where a handful of impressive ruins includes the seventeenth-century **Notland Castle**, which stands just inland of the village, and the medieval parish church of **St Mary's** (on the northern side of the village), both of which can be visited at all times.

Across the short Papa Sound, the neighbouring island and former medieval pilgrimage centre of **Papa Westray** is connected to Westray by the world's shortest scheduled flight – two minutes in duration, less with a following wind. Try and stroll out to the **Knap of Howar**, on the western shore, a Neolithic farm building from around 3500 BC that makes a fair claim to being the oldest standing house in Europe, and the remains of **St Boniface's Church**, dating from the twelfth century. On the northern tip of the island there's yet another **RSPB reserve** which plays host to one of the largest arctic tern colonies in Europe, as well as arctic skuas, razor bills and guillemots.

Practicalities

Westray is served by roll-on, roll-off car **ferry** from Kirkwall operated by the *Orkney Islands Shipping Company* (June to mid-Sept 2–3 daily; fewer at other times of the year; 1hr 25min; ☎01856/872044). There's also a lift-on, lift-off ferry service from Kirkwall to Papa Westray (Tues & Thurs); otherwise you can catch the passenger-only ferry from Westray to Papa Westray (3–6 daily), which connects with the Westray service from Kirkwall. It's also possible to **fly** to both islands on *British Airways Express* from Kirkwall to Papa Westray (Mon–Sat 2 daily) and to Westray (Mon–Thurs 2 daily, Fri & Sat 1 daily).

There are two **hotels** on Westray. The *Pierowall* (☎01857/677208; ②) is a typical North Isle hotel, simple but welcoming with a popular bar and a reputation for fish and chips. Rather more luxurious is the *Cleaton House* (☎01857/677508; ④) about three miles south of Pierowall; with excellent bar and restaurant meals at good prices, it is one of the best eating places in Orkney. **B&B** accommodation is available at *Sand O' Gill* (☎01857/677374; ②); you can also rent **bicycles** from them. If you'd like to play the somewhat eccentric **golf course** on the links north of Notland Castle, clubs can be rented from *Tulloch's* (☎01857/677373) shop.

On **Papa Westray**, the island's *Community Co-operative* (☎01857/644267) runs a hotel (④), restaurant and SYHA-affiliated hostel at Beltane House; it can also fix up **B&B** (③) and **self-catering** accommodation in a cottage sleeping up to seven (Jun–Aug £190 per week plus fuel).

North Ronaldsay

Isolated by the treacherous waters of the North Ronaldsay Firth, **North Ronaldsay**, Orkney's most northerly island, has a unique outpost atmosphere, brought about by its extreme isolation. Measuring just three miles by one and rising just 66ft above sea level, the island is almost overwhelmed by the enormity of the sky, the strength of wind, and, of course, the ferocity of the sea – so much so that its very existence seems an act of tenacious defiance.

Despite these adverse conditions, North Ronaldsay has been inhabited for centuries. Today the population is mostly over 60, but the island is still heavily farmed, the land dotted with old-style crofts, their roofs made from huge flagstones. With no natural harbours and precious little farmland, the islanders have been forced to make the most of what they have and seaweed has played an important role in the local economy. During the eighteenth century kelp was gathered here, burnt in pits and sent south for use in the chemicals industry. The island's sheep, which are a unique breed, tough and goat-like, feed mostly on seaweed, giving their flesh a dark tone and a rich, gamey taste. A drystone **dyke** running around the edge of the island keeps them off the farmland. During the clipping and dipping season the islanders herd the sheep into stone "punds" in what is one of the last acts of communal farming practised in Orkney. The largest buildings on the island are **Holland House**, which was built by the Traill family who bought the island in 1727, and the **lighthouse**, which towers over 125ft in height, and is the only feature to interrupt the horizon.

Grey and common **seals** are prevalent on the island, and it serves as an important stopping-off point for **migratory birds** passing through on their way to and from breeding grounds in Iceland, Greenland and Scandinavia. The peak times of year for migrants are from late March to early June and from mid-August to early November, although there are also many breeding species which spend the spring and summer here, including gulls, terns, waders and cormorants.

Practicalities

There's a once-weekly ferry to North Ronaldsay, usually on Fridays, but sailing may vary depending on the weather so check with the *Orkney Islands Shipping Company* a day before you hope to travel. A more flexible, if more costly option, is to catch a *British Airways Express* plane from Kirkwall (Mon–Sat 2 daily).

The *North Ronaldsay Bird Observatory*, at Twingness Croft on the southwest tip of the island (☎01857/633200; ③), was established in 1987 by adapting a croft to wind and solar power; it also offers full board **accommodation** (④, dorms £15 per person). **B&B** is available at *Garso*, in the northeast (☎01857/633244; ③), or at *Rinarsay Guest House* (☎01857/633221; ③), both of which have self-catering cottages. *Garso* also operates a car rental and taxi service. **Camping** is possible, but you must ask the permission of landowners. You can rent **bicycles** from *Airfield Goods and Services* (☎01857/633220), by the airfield in the west of the island.

SHETLAND

Many maps place the **Shetland Islands** in a box somewhere off Aberdeen, but in fact Bergen in Norway is a lot closer than Edinburgh and the Arctic Circle nearer than Manchester. The Shetland **landscape** is a product of the struggle between rock and the forces of water and ice that have, over millennia, tried to break it to pieces. Smoothed by the last glaciation, the surviving land has been exposed to the most violent **weather** experienced in the British Isles; it isn't for nothing that Shetlanders call the place "the Old Rock", and the coastline, a crust of cliffs with caves, blowholes and stacks, testifies to the continuing battle. Inland (a relative term, since you're never more than three miles from the sea) the terrain is a gentler mix of moorland, often studded with peaty lochs of a brilliant blue, and green farmland. In winter, gales are routine and Shetlanders take even the occasional hurricane in their stride, marking a calm fine day as "a day atween weathers". There are some good spells of dry, sunny weather from June to September, but it's the "simmer dim", the twilight which replaces darkness at this latitude, which makes Shetland summers so memorable; in June especially, the northern sky is an unfinished sunset of blue and burnished copper.

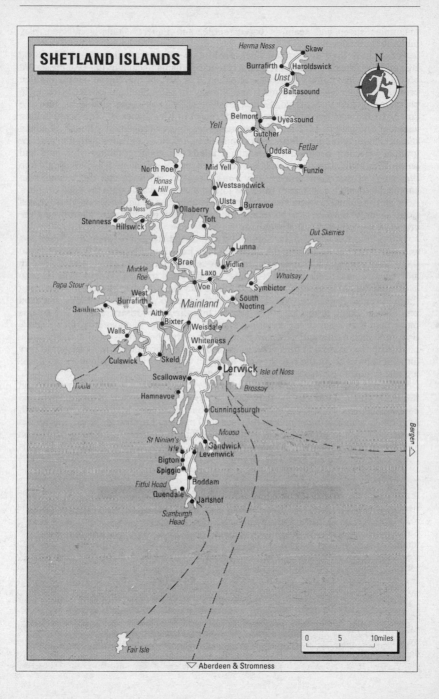

SHETLAND ISLANDS

N

Herma Ness • Skaw
Burrafirth • • Haroldswick
Unst
• Baltasound

Belmont • • Uyeasound
Yell Gutcher •
• Oddsta *Fetlar*

North Roe • Mid Yell •
Ronas Hill ▲ • Funzie
Esha Ness Westsandwick •
Stenness • Ollaberry • Ulsta • Burravoe
Hillswick • Toft

Out Skerries

• Lunna
Brae • Vidlin •
Muckle Roe Laxo • *Whalsay*
Papa Stour Voe • Symbister •
West • South *Brossay*
Sandness • Burrafirth Nooting
Mainland Aithe •
Walls • Bixter • Weisdale •
Whiteness •
Culswick • Skeld •
Foula Scalloway • **Lerwick** *Isle of Noss*
Hamnavoe • *Brossay*

• Cunningsburgh

Mousa
St Ninian's • Sandwick
Isle • Levenwick
Bigton •
Spiggie •
Fitful Head • Boddam
Quendale • • Jarlshof
Sumburgh Head

Bergen △

0   5   10 miles

Fair Isle

▽ Aberdeen & Stromness

Insomniac sheep and seabirds barely settle, and golfers, similarly afflicted, play midnight tournaments.

People have lived in Shetland since **prehistoric times**, certainly from about 3500 BC, and the islands display several spectacular remains, including the best-preserved broch anywhere. For six centuries Shetland was part of the **Norse empire** which brought together Sweden, Denmark and Norway. In 1469, Shetland followed Orkney in being mortgaged to Scotland, King Christian of Norway being unable to raise the dowry for the marriage of his daughter Margaret to King James III. The Scottish king annexed Shetland in 1472 and the mortgage was never redeemed. Though Shetland retained links with other North Sea communities, religious and administrative practice gradually become Scottish; and mainland **lairds** set about grabbing what land and power they could. Later, especially in rural Shetland, the economy fell increasingly into the hands of **merchant lairds**; they controlled the fish trade and the tenants who supplied it through a system of truck, or forced barter. It wasn't until the 1886 Crofters' Acts and the simultaneous rise of herring fishing that ordinary Shetlanders gained some security; however, the boom and the prosperity it brought were short-lived – the economy soon slipped into depression.

During the two world wars, Shetland's role as gatekeeper between the North Sea and North Atlantic meant that the defence of the islands and control of the seas around them were critical; thousands of naval, army and air force personnel were drafted in and some notable relics, such as huge coastal guns, remain. **World War II** also cemented the old links with Norway, Shetland playing a remarkable role in supporting the Norwegian resistance. With a rebirth of the local economy in the 1960s, Shetland was able to claim, in the following decade, that the **oil industry** needed the islands more than they needed it. Careful negotiation, backed up by pioneering local legislation, produced a substantial income from oil which has been reinvested in the community. Now that income is diminishing, local politicians are having to make some very difficult choices about the way they are to spend what's left and the islanders are thinking afresh how to carve out a living in a new century.

Whatever else you do in Shetland you're sure to be based, at least for a day or two, in the lively port of **Lerwick**, the only town of any size and the hub of all transport and communications. Many parts of Shetland can be reached from here in a day trip. **South of Lerwick**, a narrow finger of land runs some 20 miles to **Sumburgh Head**; this area is particularly rich in **archeological remains** including the Iron Age **Broch of Mousa** and the ancient settlement of **Jarlshof**. Twenty-five miles south of Sumburgh Head is the remote but thriving **Fair Isle**, synonymous with knitwear and exceptional birdlife.

GETTING TO SHETLAND

There are three **car ferry** routes to Shetland. From **Aberdeen**, *P&O Scottish Ferries* (☎01224/572615 or 01595/694848) operates a direct overnight service four times a week (5 times in winter) to **Lerwick** (14hr). There's also a twice-weekly afternoon/overnight indirect service (once weekly in winter) which calls at Stromness in Orkney (8hr to Stromness, 8hr on to Lerwick). For a very brief taste of Shetland, *P&O* offers short, ship-based mini-cruises to Shetland, some of which take in Orkney.

The main air operators run their services into **Sumburgh Airport**, 25 miles south of Lerwick; there are connecting bus services. *British Airways* (☎0345/222111 or 01950/ 460345), including its subsidiary, *British Airways Express* (☎01595/840246) – still often called *Loganair* – fly from Aberdeen, Edinburgh, Glasgow, Kirkwall and Wick non-stop and also from Birmingham, Inverness, London and Manchester. *Business Air* (☎0500/ 340146) flies from Aberdeen non-stop and from East Midlands, Edinburgh, Glasgow and Manchester. *Business Air* is usually less expensive, but *BA* has special offers from time to time.

To the **north** and **west**, the Mainland is bleaker and more sparsely inhabited, although the landscape, particularly to the north opens out in scale and grandeur as it comes face to face with the Atlantic. Off the west coast, **Papa Stour** lies just a mile from Sandness and boasts some spectacular caves and stacks; much further out are the distinctive peaks and precipitous cliffs of the **Isle of Foula**. To the **northeast**, Shetland ends with the North Isles of **Yell**, **Unst** and **Fetlar**, reaching far up into the North Sea.

Supporting an impressive array of birds and wildlife, the islands offer excellent **birdwatching** and **walking**. The **fishing** is good, too, with lochs well stocked with brown trout, sea trout in the voes and the chance to go sea angling for ling, mackerel or even shark and halibut. If you are taking a tent with you, **wild camping** isn't usually discouraged in Shetland if done considerately and the landowner asked first.

Getting Around

On the mainland, there are **buses** from Lerwick to Sumburgh, Sandwick, Scalloway, Hamnavoe, Reawick, Skeld, Walls, Sandness, Brae, Hillswick, Laxo (for the Whalsay ferry), and Vidlin. A service involving two ferry crossings also runs from Lerwick to Yell and Unst. Various **tours** by bus, minibus or private car are available; operators include *Leask's* (☎01595/693162) or the more specialist *Shetland Wildlife Tours* (☎01950/ 460254). *Shetland Field Studies Trust* organizes **nature walks**; book through the tourist office. If you want to **rent a car** once on the islands there are several firms to choose from (see "Listings" on p.491). **Hitching** is viable and pretty safe, and **cycling** is a reasonable choice in summer, though some long hills make it fairly energetic.

It's easy to **travel between the islands**; the larger ones have frequent services throughout the day, journey times are mostly less than 25 minutes, and, although fares have risen recently, they're much cheaper than those in Orkney or the Western Isles. Adults are charged around £1 return on most routes (£3.50 or so to Foula, Fair Isle, Papa Stour and Skerries) and a car and driver cross for around £5 return. There are also **air services** linking the Shetland Mainland to **Unst** and **Fair Isle** and sometimes to Whalsay, Out Skerries, Papa Stour and Foula, all operated by *British Airways Express*, nearly always from **Tingwall Airport** five miles west of Lerwick. It's also possible to take other **boat trips** just for pleasure, or for birdwatching or seal-spotting. Operators from Lerwick include *Bressaboats* (☎01595/820205) and *Shetland Sea Charters* (☎01595/692577) and in Sandwick *Tom Jamieson* (☎01950/431367). Specialist services for **diving** or **sea angling** can be tracked down through the Lerwick tourist office (see below for details).

Lerwick and around

For Shetlanders, there's only one place to stop, meet and do business and that's "da toon", **LERWICK**. Very much the focus of Shetland's commercial life, Lerwick is home to about 7500 people, roughly a third of the islands' population. All year, its sheltered harbour at the heart of the town is busy with ferries, fishing boats, oil rig supply vessels and a variety of more specialized craft including seismic survey and naval vessels from all round the North Sea. In autumn and winter particularly, the harbour hosts 60 or more "**klondykers**" – fish factory ships – from eastern Europe and the town is thronged with their crews, who stock up on everything from cabbages to old washing machines and ancient Lada cars. In summer, the quaysides in the centre of town come alive with local pleasure craft, visiting yachts, cruise liners, historic vessels such as the restored "*Swan*" and the occasional tall sailing ship. Behind the old harbour is the compact town centre, solidly stone built with Commercial Street, the main shopping area, at its heart; from here narrow **lanes** rise westwards climbing the hill to the late-Victorian "**new town**".

Lerwick began life as a **temporary settlement**, catering to the Dutch herring fleet in the seventeenth century, which brought as many as 20,000 men. During the nineteenth century, with the presence of ever larger Scottish, English and Scandinavian boats, it became a major fishing centre, and whalers called to pick up crews on their way to their northern hunting grounds. In 1839, the visiting Danish governor of Faroe declared that "everything made me feel that I had come to the land of opulence". Business was conducted largely from buildings known as **lodberries**, each typically having a store, a house and small yard on a private jetty. **Smuggling** was part of the daily routine and there are reputed to be secret tunnels connecting the lodberries to illicit stores. During the late nineteenth century, the construction of the Esplanade along the shore isolated several lodberries from the sea; but further south beyond the *Queen's Hotel* are some that still show their original form. Lerwick expanded considerably at this time and the large houses and grand public buildings established then still dominate, notably the impressive **Town Hall**. Another period of rapid growth began in the 1970s, with the farmland to the southwest disappearing under a suburban sprawl, the town's northern approaches becoming an industrial estate and some shopping and office development moving to new and more car-friendly sites.

The phone code for Lerwick is ☎01595.

Arrival, information and accommodation

Arriving in Lerwick is straightforward; the town is small and everything is within walking distance. Arriving by **ferry** you'll come ashore at the *P&O* terminal in the north harbour, about a mile from the town centre. If you arrive by **plane**, almost certainly at **Sumburgh Airport** at the southern tip of the Mainland, there are regular buses to Lerwick; taxis (around £25) and car rental are also available. **Buses** stop on the Esplanade, very close to the old harbour and Market Cross, or at the **bus station** on Commercial Rd about a quarter of a mile to the north.

The **tourist office** at the Market Cross on Commercial St (Mon–Sat 8am–6pm; ☎693434) is a good source of information and runs an accommodation-booking service (see below). For more details of what's on listen in to "Good Evening Shetland" (*BBC Radio Shetland*, 92.7MHz FM, Mon–Fri 5.30pm) or buy the *Shetland Times* (Fri). Some events are also advertised on Shetland's independent radio station, *SIBC* (96.2MHz FM, 24 hours).

For £1, the tourist office will book your **accommodation**, which in summer can be in short supply; in July, August and over the Folk Festival weekend in April, it's best to book in advance.

Lerwick has lots of good **B&Bs**: *Mrs Irving*, The Old Manse, 9 Commercial St (☎696301; ③); *Mrs Clark*, 9 Knab Rd (☎693101; ③); *Woosung*, 43 St Olaf St (☎693687; ②); or *Miss Goudie*, 78 King Harald St (☎692384; ③). The Lerwick **youth hostel** (mid-April to October; ☎692114; Grade 1) at Islesburgh House on King Harald St offers unusually comfortable surroundings in a building recently refurbished and extended. **Campers** should head for the *Clickimin Caravan and Camp Site*, Lochside (late-April to Sept; ☎694555), a newish site next to a leisure centre with plenty of facilities, including good hot showers.

As befits a town catering extensively to the oil business, Lerwick has a generous supply of **hotel rooms**, well equipped if often rather bland. You're likely to get closer to Shetland life in the older or smaller places. Most accommodation is either close to the old harbour or in the Victorian "new town".

Hotels and guest houses

Carradale Guest House, 36 King Harald St (☎695411). Large, comfortable family home; another upper-range guest house. ③.

Glen Orchy House, 20 Knab Rd (☎692031). A guest house that's almost a hotel, licensed and with good home cooking. ⑤.

Grand Hotel, middle of Commercial St (☎692826). A towering Victorian building in the centre of town, recently modernized. Not as grand as the name implies, it has a nightclub, *Posers*. ⑥.

Knysna Guest House, 6 Burgh Rd (☎694865). Comfortable, well located and with a residents' kitchen. ②.

Kvelsdro House Hotel, Greenfield Place (☎692195). Not large, but quite luxurious with immaculate bedrooms. Pleasant bar and competent restaurant. Hard to find, but locals are used to being asked the way. ⑨.

Lerwick Hotel, 15 South Rd (692166). Modern hotel, with some good sea views and a reliable restaurant, particularly favoured by business travellers. ⑦.

Queen's Hotel, Commercial St (☎692826). Right on the waterfront by the old harbour; a beautiful old building with comfortable accommodation. ⑧.

Shetland Hotel, Holmsgarth Rd (☎695515). An ugly monster behind the ferry terminal, popular with business people and package holiday operators. Its rooms and public areas are well equipped and more appealing than the exterior. ⑧.

The Town

Commercial Street, universally known to locals as "**da Street**", is still very much the core of Lerwick. Its narrow, winding form provides shelter from the elements even on the worst days, and is where locals meet, shop, exchange news and gossip and bring in the New Year to the sound of a harbourful of ships' sirens. The Street's northern end is marked by the towering walls of **Fort Charlotte**; originally built, directly above the beach, for Charles II in 1665–67, during the war with the Dutch, it was attacked and burnt down by them in August 1673. In 1782 it was rebuilt and given its name in honour of George III's queen. Except on rare occasions when it's in active use by the Territorial Army, the fort affords good views from its solid battlements (daily June–Sept 9am–10pm; Oct–May 9am–4pm; free). A walk along Commercial Street reveals an interesting mixture of architectural styles from the powerful Baroque of the **Bank of Scotland** at no. 117 to the plainer houses and lodberries at the south end, beyond the *Queen's Hotel*. One of the plainest, but for its glassy Victorian porch, is the **Old Manse** at no. 9, Lerwick's oldest house, dating from 1685. Further along are the **Anderson Homes** and, still further, the **Anderson High School**, its ornate, Franco-Spanish towers and dormers now unfortunately rather lost among later, less appealing additions. Both were the gift of **Arthur Anderson** (1792–1868), co-founder of the *Peninsular and Oriental Steam Navigation Company (P&O)*.

Now a desirable place to live in, it's not so long ago that the narrow **lanes** that connect the Street to the **Hillhead** were regarded as slumlike dens of iniquity, from which the better-off escaped to the Victorian gridiron "new town" laid out to the west. The stone-flagged lanes run uphill, lined by tall houses with trees, fuschia, flowering currant and honeysuckle pouring over the garden walls. Hillhead is dominated by the splendid **Town Hall** (Mon–Fri 10am–noon & 2–3.30pm; free), a Gothic castle with the stern reverence of a church. Built by public subscription, the many carved stone panels, coats of arms and stained-glass windows celebrate Shetland's history and, in particular, the islands' commercial and cultural links with other parts of Britain and Europe.

On Lower Hillhead, southwest of the Town Hall, the **Shetland Museum** (Mon, Thurs & Fri 10am–7pm, Tues, Wed & Sat 10am–5pm; free) houses an interesting range of Shetland artefacts relating to the islands' history and prehistory. More unusual exhibits include a stone carving by Adam Christie (1869–1950), a Shetlander

UP HELLY-AA

On the last Tuesday in January, whatever the weather, the Victorian "new town" of Lerwick is the setting for the most spectacular part of the **Lerwick Up Helly-Aa**, a huge, fire festival, the largest of several held in Shetland in January and February. Around 900 torch-bearing participants, all male and all in extraordinary costumes, march in procession behind a grand Viking longship. The annually appointed Guizer Jarl and his "squad" appear as Vikings and brandish shields and silver axes; each of the 40 or so other squads is dressed for their part in the subsequent entertainment, perhaps as giant insects, space invaders or ballet dancers. Their circuitous route leads to the King George V Playing Field at which, after due ceremony, all the torches are thrown into the longship, creating an enormous bonfire. A fireworks display follows, then the participants, known as "guizers", set off in their squads to do the rounds of more than a dozen "halls" (which usually includes at least one hotel, the ferry terminal and the Town Hall) from around 8.30pm in the evening until 8am the next morning, performing some kind of act – often a comedy routine – at each.

Up Helly-Aa itself is not that ancient, dating only from Victorian times; but it replaced an older Christmas tradition of burning tar barrels and other sorts of mischief. Around 1870, perhaps as a result of frustration at the controls increasingly imposed by the Town Council, the tar barrellers moved their activities into January, coined the name Up-Helly-Aa and introduced both a torchlight procession and an element of disguise; it was some years, though, before the festival took on its Viking associations. Although this is essentially a community event with entry to halls by invitation only, visitors are welcome at the Town Hall, for which tickets are sold in early January; contact the tourist office well in advance. To catch some of the atmosphere of the event check out the **Up Helly-Aa exhibition** (mid-May to Sept Tues & Sat 2–4pm, Thurs & Fri 7–9pm; £1) in the gallery shed on St Sunniva St, where you can see a full-size longship, costumes, shields and photographs.

who is perhaps best known for his application to patent a submarine invisible to enemies because it would be made of glass.

Eating

On the whole, Lerwick specializes in good plain cooking, filling snacks and fish and chips. The fresh local seafood is used less imaginatively than it could be and price isn't always a reliable guide to culinary skill. The town also has three ethnic restaurants, not to mention a pleasant Norwegian café.

The Candlestick Maker, 33 Commercial Rd (☎696066). Tiny bistro that has been a butchers and bakers, with simple lunches and a fuller evening menu with vegetarian options.

Central Bakery, 124 Commercial St. Small café in a baker's shop, serving soup, sandwiches, pies and cakes. Good for lunch – it closes at 4pm.

The Golden Bengal, 33 North Rd (☎692299). Slightly austere but smart and welcoming Indian restaurant with some interesting vegetarian dishes and occasional buffets.

The Golden Coach, 17 Hillhead (☎693848). Originally specializing in Cantonese and Pekinese food, the cuisine now takes in most of the far east. Erratic, but at its best very good indeed, with comfortable surroundings. Cheaper lunch menu Mon–Fri.

Havly Centre, 9 Charlotte St. A Norwegian Christian centre catering for the spiritual needs of visiting fishermen but much frequented by locals and tourists. A relaxed, friendly atmosphere, with excellent snacks including delicious Norwegian open sandwiches.

Kvelsdro House Hotel, Greenfield Place (☎692195). Good, not too expensive, dinner menu, with local fresh produce including seafood cooked with great care, though few vegetarians options. Bar meals comparatively expensive, but of a high standard.

Lerwick Hotel, 15 South Rd. Wide choice of reasonable bar meals, with a restaurant overlooking the sea serving quite ambitious, well-presented meals.

The New Harbour Café, behind the *Thule Bar* on the Esplanade. Basic, but bright place, doing a range of simple snacks, soups and burgers. Gets very busy at lunchtime.

Queen's Hotel, Commercial St (☎692826). Fair bar meals and a pleasant restaurant serving local seafood, meat and vegetarian dishes.

Raba Indian Restaurant, 26 Commercial Rd (☎695585). Recently expanded, with usually excellent food and friendly service. Good prices.

Solotti's, Commercial St. Something of an institution; a café serving filled rolls, cakes, teas, coffees and great ice cream. No smoking.

Drinking, nightlife and entertainment

At weekends or when the fishing fleet is confined to harbour, Lerwick's **pubs** are great social centres, packed full and brimming with atmosphere; try the downstairs bar in the *Thule* on the Esplanade, an archetypal seaport pub and very much part of Lerwick life; or up Mounthooly St, the upstairs bar in the *Lounge*. Local musicians usually play Saturday lunchtime and some evenings. Afterwards, the crowd move on to *Posers* in the *Grand Hotel* on Commerical St; the town's longest established dance venue.

Music features very strongly in Shetland life and every style has an enthusiastic following. The emphasis in traditional music is firmly instrumental, not vocal; substantial numbers of young people learn the fiddle. In April, musicians from all over the world converge on Shetland for the excellent **Folk Festival**, which embraces a wider range of musical styles than the title might suggest; there are concerts and dances in every corner of the islands. For details telephone the Folk Festival office (☎694757) or write to them at 5 Burns Lane, Lerwick. In October, there's an **Accordion and Fiddle Festival**: similar format, same mailing address but a different musical focus and separately organized. Throughout the year, there are **traditional dances** in local halls all over Shetland; the whole community turns up and you can watch, or join in with, dances like the Boston Two-Step, Quadrilles or the Foula Reel. There are also gigs featuring local groups; rock-tinged folk styles are particularly strong. Names to catch live or recorded include *Dongshung*, *Rock*, *Salt and Nails*, *Hom Bru* and *Fiddlers' Bid*. Legendary local fiddler Aly Bain (see p.540) is usually elsewhere, but you might be lucky. The occasional major concert by visiting bands or orchestras is almost always staged in the **Clickimin Leisure Centre** beside Clickimin Loch on the west side of the town, although smaller ensembles such as string quartets appear in the Town Hall.

Listings

Airports Tingwall Aiport ☎840306; Sumburgh Airport ☎01950/460654.

Banks *Clydesdale, Bank of Scotland* and *Royal Bank of Scotland* are all on Commercial St; the *Trustee Savings Bank* is the gleaming and locally controversial new structure on the Esplanade.

Bike rental *Puffins Pedals*, Mounthooly St (Mon–Sat 9am–4.45pm; ☎695065); and *Eric Brown*, Grantfield Garage, Commercial Rd (Mon, Tues & Thurs–Sat 9am–5pm; ☎01595 693733).

Bookshops *Shetland Times Bookshop*, 73–79 Commercial St (Mon–Sat 9am–5pm, June–Aug also Sun 11am–4pm; ☎695531).

Bus companies *Leasks* (Sumburgh Airport; Vidlin and Laxo for Whalsay; Yell, Unst and Fetlar; ☎01856/693162); *Shalder Coaches,* Sandwick; Walls and Sandness; Brae and Hillswick; Scalloway; ☎880217); *White's Coaches* (Walls and Sandness; ☎809443).

Car rental *Bolts Car Hire*, 26 North Rd (☎693636); *John Leask & Sons*, Esplanade (☎693162); *Star Rent–a–Car*, 22 Commercial Rd (☎692075). All of these have offices at Sumburgh Airport.

Consulates *Denmark, Iceland, Netherlands* and *Sweden* at *Hay and Company,* 66 Commercial Rd (☎692533); *Finland, France, Norway* and *Germany* at *Shearer Shipping Services*, Garthspool (☎692556).

Dentist *Alan Owen*, 90 St Olaf St (☎695769); *Reform Lane Dental Practice*, 7 Reform Lane (☎694486).

Fishing tackle *Rod and Line*, 91 Harbour St.

Laundry *Lerwick Laundry*, 36 Market St (☎693043).

Medical care The Gilbert Bain Hospital (☎74300) and the Lerwick Health Centre (☎693201) are opposite each other on Scalloway Rd. There's a *Complementary Health Clinic* at 47 North Rd (☎692924).

Post office Commercial St (Mon–Fri 9am–5pm, Sat 9am–noon); there's a sub-office in the Toll Clock Shopping Centre, 26 North Rd.

Sports There is a large, modern sports centre incorporating a superb leisure pool at the *Clickimin Leisure Centre*, Lochside, on the west side of town by Clickimin Loch (☎694555). There's also a café and bar.

Travel agents *John Leask & Son*, Esplanade (☎693162); *Shetland Travelscope*, Toll Clock Shopping Centre, 26 North Rd (☎696644).

Around Lerwick

A mile or so southwest from the town centre on the road leading to Sumburgh, **Clickimin Broch** stands on what was once a small island in Clickimin Loch. The settlement here began as a small farmstead around 700 BC and was later enclosed by a defensive wall. The main tower served as a castle and probably rose to around 40ft, though the remains are now not much more than 10ft high. There are two small entrances, one at ground level and the other on the first floor, which are carefully protected by outer defences and smaller walls. Despite the modern housing in the middle distance, it's not hard to imagine the original setting and sense the magical atmosphere of the place. Excavation of the site has unearthed an array of domestic goods that suggest international trade, including a Roman glass bowl thought to have been made in Alexandria around 100 AD.

In earlier times the seasonal nature of the Shetland fishing industry led to the establishment of small stores, often incorporating sleeping accommodation, beside the beaches where fish were landed and dried. These were known as **böds**, although the word was also applied to trading posts established by merchants of the Hanseatic League. About a mile and a half north of the town centre, right off the A970, stands the **Böd of Gremista** (June–Aug Wed–Sun 10am–1pm & 2pm–5pm; £1), the birthplace of Arthur Anderson. Though almost lost among the surrounding industry, the building has been beautifully restored and the displays explore Anderson's life as beachboy – helping to cure and dry fish – naval seaman, businessman, philanthropist, Shetland's first native MP and founder of Shetland's first newspaper. Built later than most (at the end of the eighteenth century) for Anderson's father, the ground floor was originally used as an office and fish-curing station; while, usually, the trader and his family had permanent residence upstairs.

Bressay and Noss

Shielding Lerwick from the full force of the North Sea is the island of **Bressay**, dominated at its southern end by the conical Ward Hill and accessible on an hourly car and passenger ferry from Lerwick. At the end of the nineteenth century, Bressay had a population of more than 1000, due mostly to the prosperity brought by the **Dutch herring fleet**; now about 320 people live here. The island provides interesting cliff and coastal walks, notably to the lighthouse and huge World War I guns at northern and southern ends of the island. In the past, Sir Walter Scott and royal visitors have stayed in the laird's **Gardie House**, one of the largest and, in its Classical detail, finest of Shetland laird houses. If you want to stay on Bressay, the *Maryfield House Hotel* (☎01595/820207; ④) by the ferry terminal is friendly and serves good-value meals in the restaurant and cosy bar. Many visitors, though, are heading straight for Noss, the smaller but spectacular island to the east.

Just off Bressay's western shore **Noss**, which means "a point of rock", was inhabited until World War II but is now given over to sheep-farming and is also a **National Nature Reserve** managed by Scottish Natural Heritage. They operate an inflatable as a ferry (late May–Aug; on demand except Mon, Thurs and when a red flag is flown on Noss; £2.50 return; 2min). You should wait at the landing stage below the car park at the east side of Bressay; if the weather is abnormally windy, check with the Lerwick tourist office to see that the service is operating before setting off. On the island, the old farmhouse of **Gungstie** contains a small **visitor centre** (open whenever the ferry is operating) where you can find out about the island's amazing birdlife and its human history. The adjacent **Pony Pund**, a square stone enclosure, was built for the breeding of **Shetland ponies**. A stud was established here in the latter years of the nineteenth century, when the Marquis of Londonderry needed ponies to replace the women and children who had been displaced by new laws from his coal mines in County Durham. The animals were specially bred to produce "as much weight as possible and as near the ground as it can be got". The stud only lasted for about 20 years and was closed in 1899; studs in England having been established by then to supply demand at lower cost. There are no ponies on Noss today, but it's said that the infuence of the breeding programme can still be seen in those roaming other parts of Sheltand. The most memorable feature of Noss is its cliffed coastline rising to a peak at the massive 500ft **Noup**, from which can be seen vast colonies of cliff-nesting gannets, puffins, guillemots, shags, razorbills and fulmars; a truly wonderful sight and one of the highlights of Shetland. A route around the island is indicated on a map in the visitor centre and marked along the way. If you stray off it, the great skuas (locally called bonxies) and arctic skuas (alans) will do their best to intimidate with dive–bombing raids that may hit you hard. One of the features on the walk is the **Holm of Noss**; until 1864, it was connected to the main island by an extraordinary device called a cradle, a sort of basket suspended on ropes which was intended to allow access for the grazing of sheep. The Foula man who allegedly installed it in the seventeenth century is said to have died when, preferring to climb back down the cliffs, he fell.

The South Mainland

Shetland's South Mainland is a long, thin finger of land, only three or four miles wide, ending in the cliffs of **Sumburgh Head** and **Fitful Head**. The main road hugs the eastern side of the **Clift Hills** which form the peninsula's backbone; on the west side, there's no road between Scalloway and Maywick except for a short spur from Easter to Wester Quarff. It's a beautiful area with wild landscapes but also rich farmland, and has yielded some of Shetland's most impressive archeological treasures.

Cunningsburgh and Catpund

The view opens up to the south soon after leaving Lerwick, at the shoulder of Shurton Hill above **Gulberwick.** To appreciate the coastal scenery here, it's best to leave the main road at **Fladdabister**, a favourite haunt of local artists who come to sketch and paint among the ruins of the old crofts and where, in summer, the meadows are a mass of wild flowers. In **CUNNINGSBURGH**, the first large settlement, the best views are again from the back roads to the east through the hamlets and hay meadows of **Aith** and **Voxter**. At the south end of Cunningsburgh is the Mail Kirkyard, where a remarkable stone carved with an image of a **dog-headed person** with an axe was found in 1992. The illustration is unusual as apparently secular rather than religious; archeologists believe that this indicates a relatively early date.

Half a mile or so south of the Mail junction, the main road crosses the **Catpund Burn**. From the westward loop of the old road at this point, it's possible to scramble up the valley for about 300 yards to a remarkable prehistoric industrial site, the **Catpund Quarries**. In Norse times, this area was the biggest soapstone (steatite) quarry in Britain, if not the world. Products would have included various types of bowl, weights for fishing nets or for looms and possibly items of jewellery. It's not difficult to see where vessels were carved directly from the rock. Goods from here almost certainly found their way to Norse communities in Britain, Ireland, Iceland, Faroe or mainland Europe. The small area revealed by the 1988 excavation of the site is fenced off and a board gives more information, but there's similar evidence over much of the valley floor.

Sandwick to Boddam

Sandwick is a series of settlements about two miles south of Cunningsburgh. From one of these, **LEEBITTON**, in the northeast of the district, you can take a summer ferry to the small island of **Mousa** on which stands the best-preserved broch anywhere. *Tom Jamieson* (☎01950/431367) runs the ferry from the jetty near the impressive laird's house, **Sand Lodge**.

Mousa Broch features in both *Egil's Saga* and the *Orkneyinga Saga*, contemporary chronicles of Norse exploration and settlement. In the former, a couple eloping from Norway to Iceland take refuge after being shipwrecked in 900 AD, while in the latter, the broch is besieged by an Earl Harald Maddadson when his mother is abducted and brought here from Orkney by Erlend the Young, who wanted to marry her. Rising to more than 40ft and with its curving stonework intact, it has a remarkable presence. The low entrance passage leads through two concentric walls to a central courtyard. Between the walls, there are cells and galleries in which **storm petrels** breed and a rough staircase leads to the top (a torch is useful). Elsewhere on Mousa, there are remains of several buildings, some of which housed the 11 families who lived here in the eighteenth century. Seals can often be seen at the bay on the east side.

To the southwest of Sandwick, is **HOSWICK**, where **Da Warp and Weft Visitor Centre** offers teas and snacks as well as an introduction to the history of **Shetland knitwear** (May–Sept Mon–Fri 10am–5pm, Sat 10.30am–4.30pm, Sun 2–5pm; free; ☎01950/431533)

At **Channerwick** on the main road south, it's possible to cross to the west side of the Mainland for St Ninian's Isle (see p.495). Staying on the east side, the next settlement is **LEVENWICK**, where there's a lovely beach of white sand and another broch site.

The signposted side road through **BODDAM** winds around the shore to the **Shetland Crofthouse Museum** (May–Sept daily 10am–1pm & 2–5pm; £1.50), which portrays nineteenth-century crofting life with traditional furniture and fittings including spinning wheels, high-backed Shetland chairs and baskets woven from heather fibres.

To Jarlshof and Sumburgh Head

From Boddam southwards, the landscape changes to a rolling agricultural one often compared with that of Orkney, but is still dominated by the great brooding mass of **Fitful Head** from the west. The main road leads to **Sumburgh Airport**, busy with helicopters and aircraft shuttling to and from the North Sea oil fields, and Shetland's main airport for external passenger services. For those keen on birdwatching, **The Pool of Virkie**, just to the north, is a good place to see a variety of wading birds. Visible in the road cutting, at the south of the west end of the east-west runway, are the excavated outer and inner walls of what may soon prove to be a relatively complete **broch**. Just above this site is **Betty Mouat's cottage**, recently reconstructed to provide basic accommodation. In January 1886, Betty, then 60 years old, set off for

Lerwick in the smack *Columbine* crewed by three local men. A storm swept the skipper overboard and the other two jumped in to try to rescue him; they failed, the skipper drowned and the two men, though they survived lost contact with the smack. Betty and her boat were battered by the storm for nine days and nights, finally running ashore north of Aalesund in Norway. Astonishingly, she survived this experience, existing on some milk which she had with her. She returned to Shetland to became a celebrity, living into her nineties.

Of all the archeological sites in Shetland, **Jarlshof** (April–Sept daily 9.30am–6.30pm, £2; Oct–March the grounds are open at all times; free) is the largest and most complex. There's evidence of more than 4000 years of continuous occupation, with buildings dating from the Stone Age to the early seventeenth century. The guide book, available from the small **visitor centre** where you buy tickets, is almost essential in understanding the many layers of human activity laid out before you. As well as Neolithic and medieval buildings these include a **broch, interconnected wheelhouses** and **Norse longhouses**. Sir Walter Scott, rather than any Viking, was responsible for the name; while visiting Shetland in 1814 he decided to use part of the ruins, the Old House of Sumburgh, in his novel *The Pirate* (see p.481). The **Old House** (only the walls remain) dates from the late sixteenth century, when it was home first to **Robert Stewart**, Lord of the Northern Isles and later to **William Bruce**, first representative in Shetland of another immigrant Scottish family whose land-holdings were to become substantial.

The Mainland comes to a dramatic end at **Sumburgh Head**, about two miles from Jarlshof. The **lighthouse**, designed by Robert Stevenson, was built in 1821; although not open to the public its grounds offer great views to Noss in the north and Fair Isle to the south. This is also the easiest place in Shetland to get close to **puffins**. During the nesting season, you simply need to look over the western wall by the lighthouse gate to see them arriving at their burrows with beakfuls of fish or giving flying lessons to their offspring; on no account should you try to climb over the wall.

North to St Ninian's Isle

Moving north again from Jarlshof, there's much to see on the west of the South Mainland. The road to **QUENDALE** leaves the main road at Boddam and leads to **Quendale Mill** (May–Sept Tues–Sun 10am–1pm & 2–5pm; £1), a beautifully-restored full-size overshot watermill – although rarely operated, there are information panels and a video. Not far from here, near the head of a rocky inlet on the other side of Garths Ness, lies a rusting ship's bow, all that remains of the *Braer*, a Liberian-registered, American-owned oil tanker that ran onto the rocks here at 11.13am on January 5, 1993, a wild Tuesday morning etched in the memory of every Shetlander. The thousands of tonnes of spilt **oil** were churned and ultimately cleansed by huge waves built by hurricane-force winds which, unusually even for Shetland, blew for most of January spreading a mist of oil over the South Mainland, Burra and Tondra.

North of Quendale, the **Loch of Spiggie** is an **RSPB reserve** known particularly for large autumn flocks of almost 400 **whooper swans**, but several types of **duck** as well as greylag geese and waders can be seen, depending on the time of year. **Otters** also live here. There's information about the reserve at the hide on the northern shore. On the other side of the road, the district of **Spiggie** also boasts a long but reasonably sheltered **sandy beach**. The journey north from here is one of the most spectacular in Shetland. Cliffs alternate with beaches and the vivid greens and yellows of the farmland contrast with the black rocks and a sea which may be grey, deep blue or turquoise.

At **BIGTON** village, a signposted track leads down to the tombolo at **St Ninian's Isle**. The **tombolo** – a strip of land with curving shorelines linking it to the Mainland – is the best example of its kind in Britain. It's usually exposed and you can walk over to the island, where there are the ruins of a **church** probably dating from the twelfth century but on the site of an earlier, Pictish, one. The site was excavated in 1958 and treasure, a hoard of 27 objects of **Pictish silver**, was found hidden in a larch box beneath a slab in the earlier building's floor; the larch probably came from the European mainland as it didn't grow in Britain at that time. The treasure included bowls, a spoon and brooches and probably dates from around 800 AD; it may have been hastily hidden during a Norse raid. Replicas are in the Shetland Museum in Lerwick and the originals can be seen in the Museum of Antiquities in Edinburgh.

South Mainland Practicalities

Public transport to the South Mainland is relatively straightforward: there are between three and four **buses** a day between Lerwick and Sumburgh Airport (45min) and between four and six buses daily to Sandwick (35min). Bigton, Spiggie and Quendale are served by two buses on weekdays, one on Sundays.

   Hotels are in very short supply; however, the *Sumburgh Hotel* (☎01950/460201; ⑤), next to Jarlshof, is convenient for the airport, and good for bar meals and occasional live music. **B&Bs in Sandwick** include: *Mrs M. Leask* at 3 Swinister (☎01950/431302; ②), the non-smoking *Marelda* (☎01950/431379; ②) and *Solbrekke* (☎01950/431410; ②). Further south, on the side road to the Croft House Museum and identified by a railway signal, is *Columbine* (☎01950/460582; ②). At **Scousburgh**, overlooking Spiggie, there's *Colsa* (☎01950/460503; ②). **Simple accommodation** is available at the *Cunningsburgh Community Club* (☎01950/431321 or 431241), which has dorm beds, good showers and a well-equipped kitchen; or those with camping gear minus a tent can try the reconstructed *Betty Mouat's* cottage (no phone; book through the tourist office in Lerwick), immediately southwest of Sumburgh Airport. There's tented **camping** at *Levenwick Campsite* (May–Sept; ☎01950/422207), which has adequate facilities and a superb view over the east coast.

Fair Isle

Halfway between Shetland and Orkney and very different from both, **Fair Isle** supports a vibrant community of around 70 people. The north end of the island rises like a wall; the **Sheep Rock**, a sculpted stack of rock and grass on the east side, is one of the island's most dramatic features. The croft land and the settlement, consisting of scattered houses, are concentrated in the east and south.

   At one time the population was not far short of 400, but clearances forced emigration from the middle of the nineteenth century. By the 1950s, the population had shrunk to just 44, a point at which evacuation and abandonment of the island was seriously considered. **George Waterston**, who'd bought the island and set up a **bird observatory** in 1948, passed it into the care of the NTS in 1954 and rejuvenation began. Since then, islanders, the Trust and the Shetland Islands Council have invested in many improvements to housing, the harbour and basic services, including an advanced **electricity system** integrating wind and diesel generation; and crafts including boatbuilding, the making of fiddles, felt and stained glass have been developed. The social and natural history of the island is compellingly told in the **George Waterston Memorial Centre** (opening times vary and are advertised locally; free; ☎01595/760244). Particularly memorable are stories of shipwrecks; *El Gran Grifon*, part of the retreating Spanish Armada, was lost here in 1588 and in 1868 the islanders undertook a heroic rescue of all 465 German emigrants aboard the *Lessing*.

   The present **Bird Observatory** dates from 1969, just above the North Haven where the **ferry** from Grutness in Shetland arrives, and is one of the major European centres for ornithology, and its work in watching, trapping, recording and ringing birds goes on all year. Fair Isle is a landfall for a huge number and range of migrant birds during the spring and autumn passages. Migration routes converge here and more than 340 species, including many rarities, have been noted.

Fair Isle is even better known for its **knitting** patterns, still produced with as much skill as ever by the local knitwear co-operative, though not in the quantities which you might imagine from a walk around city department stores; there are demonstrations at the Hall from time to time, and the George Waterson Memorial Centre fills in the history. The idea that the islanders borrowed all their patterns from the 300 shipwrecked Spanish seamen is nowadays regarded as a somewhat patronizing myth.

Practicalities
The **ferry** connects Fair Isle with either Lerwick (on alternate Thurs; 4hr 30min) or Sumburgh (Tues, Sat & alternate Thurs; 4hr); for bookings contact *J W Stout* (☎01595/ 760222) in advance. You can also fly from the airport at **Tingwall**, six miles northwest of Lerwick (Mon, Wed, Fri & Sat; a day trip is possible on Wed & Fri).

If you want to **stay**, the *Fair Isle Lodge and Bird Observatory* (April–Oct; ☎01595/ 760258; ⑤, dorms with full board £20 per person) offers good home cooking and perhaps the opportunity to lend a hand with the observatory's research programme. For good **B&B** accommodation, there's the beautifully restored eighteenth-century *Auld Haa* (☎01595/760264; ③, full board ⑤), where Sir Walter Scott was once entertained; *Schoolton* (☎01595/760250, ④); or *Barkland* (☎01595/760247; ④), all in the south end of the island.

Scalloway and around

The village of **SCALLOWAY** was once the capital of Shetland, but its importance waned through the eighteenth century as Lerwick, just six miles to the east, grew in trading success and status. Scalloway's prosperity, always closely linked to the fluctuations of the **fishing** industry, has recently been given a boost with investment in new fish-processing factories, and in the impressive North Atlantic Fisheries College on the west side of the harbour.

The best way to approach Scalloway is on the main road from Lerwick; as it crosses the shoulder of the **scord**, the view over the village and the islands to the south and west opens up dramatically. In spite of modern developments nearby, the scene is dominated by the imposing shell of **Scalloway Castle**, built in 1600 for **Earl Patrick Stewart** using forced labour and thus seen as a powerful symbol of oppression. Stewart, who'd succeeded his father Robert to the Earldom of Orkney and Lordship of Shetland in 1593, held court in the castle and gained a reputation for enhancing his own power and wealth through the calculated use of harsh justice, frequently including confiscation of assets. Eventually, he upset influential people and was arrested in 1609; his son attempted an insurrection and both were executed in Edinburgh in 1615. The castle was used for a time by **Cromwell's army**, but eventually fell into ruin and is nowadays carefully maintained in that state by HS. If the door is locked, the key can be borrowed from the knitwear shop immediately to the north, attached to a factory which also has a small pottery; both welcome visitors.

On Main Street, a small **museum** (May–Sept Tues–Thurs 2–5pm, Sat 10am–1pm, 2–5pm; free) run by volunteers is crammed with local relics. It explains the importance of fishing and tells the story of the **Shetland Bus**. West of Scalloway, there's a pleasant if energetic **walk** up **Gallows Hill** (allow 2–3hr), where alleged witches were put to death; and then on to the hamlet of Burwick, a former fishing settlement.

THE SHETLAND BUS

The story of the **Shetland Bus**, the link between Shetland and Norway which helped to sustain the Norwegian resistance through the years of Nazi occupation, is quite extraordinary. Constantly under threat from attack by enemy aircraft or naval action, small Norwegian fishing boats were used to run arms and resistance workers into lonely fjords. The trip took 24 hours and on the return journey brought out Norwegians in danger of arrest by the Gestapo, or those who wanted to join Norwegian forces fighting with the allies. For three years, through careful planning, the operation was remarkably successful; instructions to boats were passed in cryptic messages in BBC news broadcasts. Although local people knew what was going on, the secret was generally well kept. Eventually, 350 refugees were evacuated, and more than 400 tons of arms, large amounts of explosives and 60 radio transmitters were landed in Norway.

Originally established at **Lunna** in the northeast of the Mainland, the service moved to **Scalloway** in 1942, partly because the village could offer good marine engineering facilities at *Moore's Shipyard* at the west end of Main St, where a plaque records the morale-boosting visit of the Norwegian Crown Prince Olav. Many buildings in Scalloway were pressed into use to support the work; explosives and weapons were stored in the Castle. **Kergord House** in Weisdale was used as a safe house and training centre for intelligence personnel and saboteurs. The hazards, tragedies and elations of the exercise are brilliantly described in David Howarth's book, *The Shetland Bus*; their legacy today is a closer, more heartfelt relationship between Shetland and Norway.

Scalloway Practicalities

Transport in the area is provided by a **bus service** from Lerwick (from the bus stop at the *Thule Bar* on the Esplanade) which runs eight times daily to Scalloway and twice a day to Hamnavoe.

Accommodation in Scalloway includes *Brylyn Guest House*, Port Arthur (☎01595/880407; ③), and in Upper Scalloway *Broch Guest House* (☎01595/880767; ③) and *Hildasay Guest House* (☎01595/880822; ③) the latter, which specializes in angling holidays. In Hamnavoe there's a friendly **B&B** run by *Mrs J Marsden*, Setter (☎01595/859688; ②), offering diving and handspinning/dyeing tuition. There aren't many **places to eat**, but the *Castle Café* in Scalloway has an excellent reputation for fish and chips, and the *Kiln Bar* does bar food. The *North Atlantic Fisheries College* has a very pleasant restaurant doing teas and snacks as well as meals, with wonderful harbour views.

Trondra and Burra

South of Scalloway – and connected to the Mainland by bridges – are the islands of **Trondra** and, further south and west, **West** and **East Burra**, which have some beautiful **beaches** with excellent coastal **walks**. **Trondra** is a small island whose main point of interest is at **Burland**, just west of the main road, where there's a **Croft Trail** (May–Sept Mon–Sat 10am–6pm; free) which provides an insight into life on a working croft; there are also some rare native breeds of livestock to be seen.

The next bridge leads west to **West Burra** and almost immediately to **HAMNAVOE**, a planned **fishing** settlement unlike any other in Shetland, established mainly in the early 1900s and still very much a working, sea-going community. The road south from Hamnavoe winds past the white sandy beach at **Meal**, deservedly popular on warm summer days. The road south through **East Burra** ends at the hamlet of **Houss**, distinguished by the tall, ruined laird's house or **haa**. You can walk on southwards across the beach on the track leading to the deserted settlement of **Symbister**; inhabited until the 1940s, it is the site of ancient field boundaries and a burnt mound (Neolithic cooking stones dumped when no longer usable). Half a mile further south, the island ends in cliffs, caves and wheeling fulmars. From there, the island of **South Havra**, topped by the ruins of Shetland's only windmill, is just to the southwest. Once supporting a small fishing community, the island was abandoned, except for the grazing of sheep, in 1923; it was such a perilous existence that children as well as animals had to be tethered to prevent them falling over the cliffs.

The Central Mainland

The districts of Tingwall and Weisdale in the **Central Mainland** are a captivating mix of farms, moors, lochs and Shetland's only significant woodland; the scale of the scenery ranges from the intimate to the vast, with particularly dramatic views from high points above Whiteness and Weisdale. The area also holds strong historical associations, with the **Norse parliament** at Lawting Holm and unhappy memories of nineteenth-century **clearances** at Weisdale.

Tingwall and the Lawting

The green farmland of the Tingwall Valley, containing the two lochs, **Tingwall** and **Asta**, both of which are good for fishing, stretches north from Scalloway. At the northern end of Tingwall Loch is the **Lawting Holm**, a small peninsula once an island and linked to the shore by a causeway. This was the site of the Lawting, "thing" being old Norse for "**parliament**", where local people and officials gathered from time to time to make or amend laws and discuss evidence. From the late thirteenth century, Shetland's laws were based on those of Norwegian King Magnus the Lawmender. It seem that meetings to deal with these matters took place here up to the sixteenth century, after which judicial affairs were dealt with in Patrick Stewart's new castle at Scalloway. Although structures on the holm have long since vanished there's an information board which helps in visualizing the scene. A little further south, a 7ft **stone** by the roadside is said to mark the spot where, in 1389, after a dispute at the Lawting in 1389, **Earl Henry Sinclair** killed his cousin and rival **Marise Sperra** together with seven of his followers.

Just north of the loch is **Tingwall Kirk** and in the burial ground a dank vault from a thirteenth-century church that was demolished in 1788. Inside the vault are several very old tombstones, including one to a local official called a *Foud* – a representative of the king – who died in 1603. It's an eerie place and a torch is useful, a grounding in Latin and Scots even more so.

This relatively fertile part of Shetland seems as appropriate a place as any for the **Agricultural Museum** (July–Sept daily 2–5pm; £1), about 200 yards from the crossroads at Tingwall. The enthusiastic owner has amassed a remarkable treasure trove of equipment from Shetland's crofts and farms and has an intimate knowledge of all of it. Further west, on the main road, is **Tingwall Airstrip**, departure point for flights in a *British Airways Express* eight-seater to Fair Isle, Foula, Papa Stour, Whalsay, Out Skerries and Unst. Westwards again, the road crosses the ridge at Wormdale, giving excellent views, then curves northwards through **WHITENESS**, where the *Hjaltasteyn* workshop (April–Sept Mon 9.30am–noon, Wed 2–4.30pm & Thurs 9.30am–4.30pm; free) produces attractive jewellery, in polished stone, silver and gold. A little further north, by the shore of Weisdale Voe, another jewellery workshop, *Shetland Silvercraft* (Mon–Fri 9am–1pm & 2–5pm; free) also welcomes visitors.

Weisdale

Weisdale is an evocative name in Shetland; in this valley some of the cruellest **clearances** of people in favour of sheep took place in the middle of the nineteenth century. The perpetrator was **David Dakers Black**, a farmer from the county of Angus who began buying land in 1843. Hundreds of tenants were dispossessed and in 1850 the large house of **Kergord**, then called Flemington, was built towards the northern end of the valley from the stones of some of the older houses. The ruined shells of some of the rest still stand on the valley sides; local writers, particularly John J Graham, have recounted the period in novels (notably his *Shadowed Valley*) and drama.

Around Kergord House and on the upper valley sides there are several **tree planta-tions** dating mainly from around 1920 but with a later experimental addition by the Forestry Commission. An amazing range of species is present, from the sycamores and willows which thrive in many Shetland gardens to examples of chestnut, copper beech, monkey puzzle and much else besides. Along with the trees comes a woodland ecosys-tem, with plants like **foxglove**, Britain's most northerly **rookery** and a reliable **cuckoo**. During the war, Kergord House played a role in the Shetland Bus operation; the sabo-teurs who trained here are said to have amused visitors by demonstrating booby-traps and incendiary devices in the garden. Half a mile south of Kergord House is **Weisdale Mill**, built for grain milling and dating from 1855. It is now an arts centre, housing the small, beautifully designed **Bonhoga Gallery** (Wed–Sat 10.30am–4.30pm, Sun noon–4.30pm; free) in which touring or local exhibitions of painting, sculpture and other media are shown. There's a pleasant **café** overlooking the stream.

South of the mill at the head of Weisdale Voe, it's also possible to turn southwards along the west shore where, among trees near the voe's narrowest point, is the ruined house once occupied by **John Cluness Ross** (1786–1853). He settled in the **Cocos Islands** in the Indian Ocean, went into coconut farming and appointed himself king, the first of three in a family dynasty which ruled, some would say oppressed, the island-ers unchallenged for decades.

Central Mainland Practicalities

Transport to the Central Mainland from Lerwick is provided by **buses** heading for Walls or Skeld, all of which run through Tingwall, Whiteness and Weisdale. Buses heading to Brae, Mossbank and the North Isles also pass through Tingwall, as does one service per day from Scalloway via Lerwick to the Sullom Voe Terminal.

The only **hotels** in the area are the *Herrislea House* (☎01595/840208; ④) close to the crossroads at Tingwall and the *Westings* at Wormadale, Whiteness (☎01595/840242; ⑤) boasting a wonderful view over Whiteness Voe and the islands. Friendly **B&Bs** include *Mrs Blance* (☎01595/840315; ②) at North Califf, northeast of Strand Loch in Tingwall or *Dr J L Watt* (☎01595/840518; ③) at Hallibrig in South Whiteness. For **basic accommodation**, the tiny *Böd of Nesbister*, an original fishermens' böd on the beach at Whiteness, can be booked through the tourist office in Lerwick.

For **meals**, there are bar lunches or more substantial evening fare at *Herrislea House* or the *Westings Hotel*. The café in Weisdale Mill is particularly good for snacks in a very pleasant setting.

The Westside and Papa Stour

The **Westside** of Shetland stretches west from Weisdale and Voe to Sandness and Papa Stour. Although there are some important archeological remains and wildlife in the area, the Westside's greatest appeal lies in its scenery and outstanding **walking** opportunities. At its heart, Westside's rolling brown and purple moorland is scattered with dozens of small picturesque lochs gleaming blue or silver and patches of bright green, where cultivation and reseeding have taken place. On the west coast the rounded form of Sandess Hill (750ft) fall steeply away into the Atlantic. The **coastal scenery**, cut by several deep voes, is very varied; aside from dramatic cliffs, there are intimate coves and some fine beaches. The crossroads for the area is effectively **Bixter**, from where you can travel north towards **Aith** and **Voe**, south to **Skeld** and **Reawick** and west to **Walls**, **West Burrafirth** and **Sandness**.

A road winds northwest from **BIXTER** towards Aith and Voe; almost immediatley there's a branch road to **Clousta** and **Noonsbrough**, hamlets by an intimate voe, and, like much of the rest of the Westside, dotted with archeological remains, including a ruined **broch** at Noonsbrough and a number of cairns, prehistoric houses and field systems. **AITH** is the main centre for the area, but there isn't a lot here except a shop and school, and the base for the west of Shetland lifeboat; you can buy sheepskins from an outlet on the south side of village. Just north, **Vementry** (also the name of a Mainland farm) is an island off the coast that boasts the best-preserved **heel-shaped cairn** in Shetland, right on top of the hill. To get there, make arrangements through the tourist office in Lerwick to rent a boat from Vementry Farm. Particularly towards Voe, the landscape is spectacular, with the road climbing high above the shores of the voes past tiny peaty lochs.

Southwest of Bixter, there's excellent walking along the coast between Silwick, Westerwick and **Culswick** (just six houses), with **cliffs**, **caves** and **stacks**. About a mile west of Culswick is one of the better preserved **brochs**. Five miles north, at **Staneydale**, a remarkably large **Neolithic structure** measures more than 40ft by 20ft internally with immensely thick walls, still around 4ft high, whose roof would have been supported by spruce posts. Called a temple by the archeologist who excavated it because it resembled one on Malta, this building, whatever its function, was twice as large as similarly shaped houses and was certainly of great importance, perhaps as some kind of community centre. At nearby **SKELD**, you can visit the *Shetland Smokehouse*, which smokes salmon and other local produce.

Once an important fishing port, **WALLS** (pronounced W*aa*s), appealingly set round its harbour, is now a quiet place. There's a **swimming pool** and a **small museum** (mainly on knitwear; open by special arrangement and only for groups and tours; free; ☎01595/809366). To the south lies the island of **Vaila**, from where in 1837 Lerwick philanthropist Arthur Anderson operated a fishing station in an unsuccessful attempt to break down the system of **fishing tenures** under which tenants were forced to fish for the landlords under pain of eviction. The **haa**, dating from 1696 and greatly extended between 1895 and 1900 by Yorkshire mill-owner **Herbert Anderton**, who had bought the island, is a private home and not open to visitors. Near Bridge of Walls, where the Wall and Sandness roads divide, there's a notable prehistoric site at **Scord of Brouster**. A helpful information board provides an explanation of the layout of various ruined houses and field boundaries, making it easier to imagine what life might have been like for the people who lived on this hillside between 3000 and 1500BC.

The scattered crofting settlement of **SANDNESS** (pronounced *Saa*ness), which you can reach by road or by walking the coast from Walls past the dramatic **Deepdale** and across **Sandness Hill**, is an attractive spot; its fertile fields and wide beach come as a contrast to the peat moorland around. The town's modern **spinning mill** (Mon–Fri 8am–5pm; free) produces pure Shetland wool and welcomes visitors; you can watch how they manage to spin the exceptionally fine Shetland wool into yarn.

Papa Stour

A mile offshore from Sandness and reached by a foot passenger **ferry** from **West Burrafirth** is the quintessentially peaceful island of **Papa Stour** ("big island of the priests"); apart from early Christian connections, it was home, in the eighteenth century, to people who were mistakenly believed to have been lepers (also see p.503). The sea has eroded its volcanic rocks to produce some of the most impressive coastal scenery in Shetland, with **stacks, caves** and **natural arches**. The east side is the most fecund area, partly because much of the soil from the western side was painstakingly transported here. In the nineteenth century, Papa Stour supported around 300 inhabitants, but by the early 1970s there was a population crisis: the island's school had closed, the remaining 16 inhabitants were all past childbearing age and worse still it looked like the post office would close and the mailboat be withdrawn. The islanders made appeals for new blood to revive the fragile economy and managed to stage a dramatic recovery, releasing croft land to young settlers from Britain and overseas. Papa Stour was briefly dubbed "the hippy isle" but in fact it wasn't long before some newcomers moved on, to other parts of Shetland or elsewhere, making a further appeal necessary. Today the island supports a community of 30 or so.

A trail leaflet is available from the tourist office in Lerwick; as well as prehistoric houses and burial cairns. At the **Biggings**, a hamlet halfway along the island's road, are the recently excavated remains of a thirteenth-century **Norse house**, which may have been a royal seat.

Westside Practicalities

Transport to the Westside from Lerwick is provided by **buses** to Walls (3 or 4 most days; 50min) and Skeld (2–3 most days). Minibus feeder services connect with these routes to Aith (1–2 daily), Sandness (1–2 daily) and Dale of Wall (1 daily). In summer, the **ferry** runs from West Burrafirth to Papa Stour (Mon, Wed, Fri & Sat mornings, also on Fri, Sat & Sun evenings); always book in advance and reconfirm 24 hours before departure (☎01595/873227).

The only **hotel** in the area is the beautifully situated *Burrastow House* (☎01595/809307; ⑨), about three miles west of Walls and dating from 1759 but recently extended. There are quite a few B&Bs; in the remoter areas some will provide an evening meal. Friendly places include *Effirth*, just south of Bixter (☎01595/810204; ②); *Reawick House* (☎01595/860273; ③); *Hogan*, Bridge of Walls (☎01595/809375; ②); and *Trouligarth*, west of Walls (☎01595/809373; ②). There's homely accommodation on **Papa Stour** at *North House* (☎01595/873238; ②). For **basic** accommodation, the *Aith Public Hall* is usually available (☎01595/810327). *Burrastow House* is probably the best **place to eat** in Shetland, with excellent and imaginative use of local produce in an informal, intimate setting. Booking is strongly advised for lunch, essential for dinner.

Foula

Southwest of Walls, at "the edge of the world", the island of **Foula** is separated from the nearest point on Mainland Shetland by about 14 miles of ocean. Seen from the Mainland, its distinctive form changes subtly, depending upon the vantage point, but the outline is unforgettable. Its western **cliffs**, the second highest in Britain after those of St Kilda, rise at the **Kame** to some 1241ft above sea level; from its highest point at the **Sneug** (1370ft) a clear day offers a magnificent panorama stretching from Unst to Fair Isle and occasionally even the northern isles of Orkney. On a bad day, the exposure is complete and the cliffs generate turbulent blasts of wind known locally as "flans" which tear down the hills with tremendous force. The cliffs and moorland provide a home for a quarter of a million **birds** – the name of the island is based on the Old Norse for "bird island" – and host the largest colony of great skuas in Britain, with around 2500 pairs. Foula's human population peaked at around 200 at the end of the nineteenth century, but has fluctuated wildly over the years, dropping to three in 1720 following an epidemic of "muckle fever". Today, the gentler eastern slopes provide crofting land which, with sheep grazing, helps to support a community numbering about forty.

Inhabited since prehistoric times, the people here take pride in their separateness from Shetland, cherishing local traditions such as the observance of the **Julian calendar**, officially dropped in Britain in 1752 , where Old Yule is celebrated on January 6 and the New Year arrives on January 13. The island's isolation also meant that more of the **Shetland dialect** survived here than elsewhere; and in the late nineteenth century, Foula's people provided an enormous amount of information on the dialect and its roots in the Norn language for a study undertaken by the Faroese philologist Jakob Jakobsen. The island has a few visible prehistoric remains, but the peat probably covers many more.

Practicalities

A day trip by ferry isn't possible. The summer passenger service to Foula runs from Walls on Tuesdays, Saturdays and alternate Thursdays, with a sailing from Scalloway on remaining Thursdays; it's essential to book and reconfirm (☎01595/753232). There are infrequent **charter flights** to Foula and Papa Stour; check availability with *British Airways Express* at Tingwall Airport (☎01595/840246), five miles or so west of Lerwick.

Choices of **places to stay** on Foula are inevitably limited, and all are on the east side of the island. There's a **B&B** at *Leraback* (☎01595/753226; includes dinner; ④), and the *Ristie Hostel* (☎01595/753233). Self-catering is also possible at *Burns* (☎01595/753232), but remember to take enough **food** for your stay as there's no shop.

The North Mainland, Whalsay and Out Skerries

Heading up the east side of the **North Mainland**, the districts of **Nesting** and **Lunnasting**, jutting out into the North Sea, have few scenic highlights but do offer some gentle walks, with numerous, if uninspiring, archeological remains. To the north, beyond the village of Vidlin, **Lunna House**, and the sheltered harbour below it, was the first base from which the **Shetland Bus** operation was conducted; dating in part from 1660, it is now a small hotel. Down the hill lies the little whitewashed **Lunna Kirk**, built in 1753, with a beautiful interior including a carved central pulpit. Among its features is a "**lepers' squint**" on the outside wall, through which those believed to have the disease could participate in the service without risk of infecting the congregation; there was, however, no leprosy here, the outcasts in fact suffering from a hereditary, non-infectious skin condition.

Whalsay and Out Skerries

The island of **Whalsay**, reached by ferry from Laxo (or in some weather conditions, Vidlin), is a thriving community devoted almost entirely to **fishing**. The islands' crews operate a fleet of large trawlers and have coped with the change and uncertainty that characterize the industry by adapting to new opportunities, investing huge sums in fishing further afield and catching a wider range of species, and have thus sustained a remarkable level of prosperity. The tiny **Pier House**, across **SYMBISTER** harbour from the ferry berth, is one of the two adjacent booths built for the **Hanseatic traders**, and contains a good display on how the Germans traded salt, tobacco, spirits and cloth for Whalsay's salted, dried fish.

At the hamlet of **Sodom**, about half a mile east, is the once home of celebrated Scots poet, writer and republican **Hugh MacDiarmid**, born Christopher Grieve in the Borders town of Langholm (1892–1978). He stayed here from 1933 until 1942, writing about half of his output, including much of his best work – lonely, comtemplative poems about honouring fishing and fishermen, with whom he sometimes went out to sea. Estranged from his first wife and family and with a drink problem, MacDiarmid, practically broken, had sought temporary relief in Shetland. At first, he seems to have fallen in love with the islands, but poor physical and mental health, exacerbated if not caused by chronic poverty, dogged him. Eventually, unwillingly conscripted to work in a Glasgow munitions factory, he left with his new wife and young son, never to return. The cottage has recently been restored to provide basic accommodation for visitors (see p.506).

Of the several **prehistoric remains** on Whalsay, the most notable are houses at **Yoxie** and island fort in the **Loch of Huxter**, both on the southeastern side of the island. The island also has an 18-hole **golf course** in the northeast and a leisure centre with an excellent **swimming pool** close to the school in Symbister.

The **Out Skerries** (reached by ferry from Vildin or Lerwick) consists of three tiny islands, Grunay, Bruray and Housay – the latter two linked by a bridge. That people live here at all is remarkable; that it is one of Shetland's most dynamic communities is astonishing, its affluence based on fishing from a superb, small natural harbour sheltered by all three islands, and on salmon farming in a nearby inlet. There are good, if short, walks, with a few prehistoric remains and an ingenious collection system for rainwater which involves a spiral channel around the island's main hill on Bruray.

Voe, Brae and Sullom Voe

The tight huddle of homes around the pier in the old, southern part of the village at **VOE**, has a strongly Scandinavian appearance and is dominated by the **Sail Loft**. Painted in a rich, deep red, the building was originally used by fisherman and whalers but later for the manufacture of knitwear. Woollen jumpers were knitted here for the 1953 expedition to Mount Everest, and Edmund Hillary wore one on his way to the summit. Today, the building provides simple visitor accommodation. From Voe the main road divides; the northern leg leads to the **Booth of Toft**, the ferry terminal for the island of Yell (see p.506), while the other branch cuts northwest to Brae.

BRAE, a sprawling settlement that still has the feel of a frontier town, was one of four expanded in some haste in the 1970s to accommodate the workforce for the huge **Sullom Voe Oil Terminal**, just to the north. The longest in Shetland, Sullom Voe has always attracted the interest of outsiders in search of a deepwater harbour. During World War II it was home to the Norwegian Air Force and a base for RAF seaplanes. Although the terminal, built between 1975 and 1982, has passed its production peak, it is still the largest of its kind in Europe. Its size, however, isn't obvious from beyond the site boundary and few clues remain to the extraordinary scale of the construction effort, which for several years involved a workforce of 6000 accommodated in two large "construction villages" and two ships. It has, barring one early incident, a good environmental record. Whether it can compete on cost with offshore loading of oil remains to be seen.

Past Brae, a branch off the main road to Mavis Grind, leads over a bridge to the island of **Muckle Roe**. Its eastern side has relatively fertile croft land; the western coastline is wilder and provides excellent walking country.

Northmaven

Mavis Grind, a narrow ithsmus at which it's said you can throw a stone from the Atlantic to the North Sea, or at least to Sullom Voe, marks the start of **Northmaven**, on the west of the North Mainland, unquestionably one of the most picturesque areas of Shetland with its often rugged scenery, magnificent coastline and wide open spaces. Three miles north of the ithsmus, it's worth abandoning the main road to explore the remoter corners; the twisting side road west to **Gunnister** and **Nibon** travels through a wonderful tumbled landscape of pink and grey rock where abandoned fields and broken shells of croft houses provide abundant evidence of past human struggles to make a living. When the road ends, at Nibon, you can view a jigsaw of islands and rocky headlands which, even on a relatively calm day, smash the Atlantic into streams of white foam.

HILLSWICK, the main settlement in the area, was once served by the *North of Scotland, Orkney and Shetland Shipping Company* steamer and in the early 1900s the firm also built a hotel, importing it in the form of a timber kit from Norway; it still stands albeit somewhat altered. Nearer the shore is the much older **Hillswick House** and, attached to it, **Da Böd**, the oldest pub in Shetland, said to have been founded by a German merchant in 1684.

Just outside Hillswick, a side road leads west to **Eshaness** (*Ay*shaness), celebrated for its splendid coastline views. Spectacular **cliffs** and **stacks** are spread out before you as the road climbs away from Hillswick, with stacks called the **Drongs** in the foreground and distant views to the Westside and Papa Stour. About three miles west of Hillswick, a turning northwards off the main road leads to the hamlet of **Hamnavoe**, birthplace of **Johnnie "Notions" Williamson** (1740–1803). A man of many talents, including blacksmithing and weaving, his fame rests on his work in protecting several thousand of the population against **smallpox** using a serum and a method of inoculation he'd invented himself, to the amazement of the medical profession. He used a scalpel to lift a flap of skin without drawing blood, then placed the serum he'd prepared underneath, dressing it with a cabbage leaf and a bandage.

Just before **Stenness** the main road divides, the southern branch leading to a hamlet, which was once one of the most important **deep-sea fishing** stations in Shetland. The remains of a few of the **böds** used by the fishermen are still visible along the sloping pebbly beach where they would dry their catch; from here you can see an impressive natural arch, the **Dore Holm**. At the peak of operations in the early nineteenth century, as many as 18 trips a year were made in up to 70 open six-oared boats, or "sixareens", to the fishing grounds 30 or 40 miles to the west. A mile or so back along the main road a south turning leads to **Tangwick Haa Museum** (May–Sept Mon–Fri 1–5pm, Sat & Sun 11am–7pm; free), which through photographs, old documents and fishing gear, tells the often moving story of this remote corner of Shetland and its role in this dangerous trade. The northern branch of the road ends at the **Eshaness Lighthouse**, a great place to view the cliffs, stacks and, in rough weather, blowholes of this stretch of coast. A useful information board at the lighthouse details the dramatic features here, including a partially collapsed cave and a substantial broch, none of which are difficult to reach on foot and make for a good three-hour walk.

North of **Ronas Voe**, by the shores of Colla Firth, an unmarked road leads up **Collafirth Hill**. At the top, there are the crumbling remains of a NATO radio station, but the natural landscape is much more impressive, with tremendous views on a clear day and a foreground of large, scattered stones and hardly any vegetation. Though the walk isn't quite as straightforward as it looks, scale and distance being hard to judge in this setting, Collafirth Hill is the easiest place from which to approach the rounded contours of **Ronas Hill**, Shetland's highest point (1516ft). The climb, with no obvious path, is exhausting but rewarding (allow 2hr each way; also see the safety precautions on p.38): from the top you can look west to one of the most beautifully sculptured parts of the Shetland coast, as the steep slope of the hill drops down to the arching sand and shingle beach called the **Lang Ayre**, south and east over all of the Mainland, north along the coast of Yell, or out into the daunting expanse of the Atlantic. Also at the summit, among subarctic vegetation and stone patterns formed by freezing and thawing of the thin soil, is a Neolithic or Bronze Age **chambered tomb**, one of the best preserved in Shetland and useful as a shelter from the wind.

North Mainland Practicalities

Transport to the North Mainland is available by two or three daily **buses** from Lerwick to the Laxo ferry terminal (for Whalsay) and to nearby Vidlin; there are also between three and seven buses each day to Brae, one or two in the late afternoon to Hillswick and minibus connections once a day to Eshaness, Ollaberry and North Roe. **Ferries** to and from Whalsay (30min) run about every 45min from early morning until late evening; if you have a car, it's best to book on ☎01806/566259. In bad weather, especially southeasterly gales, the service operates from Vidlin. There are ferries to and from Skerries from Vidlin (Mon 1, Fri–Sun 3 daily; 1hr), and a single trip from Lerwick (Tues & Thurs; 2hr).

Just west of Brae is one of the best **hotels** in Shetland, *Busta House* (☎01806/522506; ⑥), which offers comfortable accommodation in historic surroundings. There's also the interesting but somewhat less luxurious timber-clad *St Magnus Bay Hotel* ((☎01806/ 503371; ⑥) at Hillswick. **Guest houses** include the friendly *Greystones* (☎01806/522322; ③) on the shore at Brae, or the modern *Valleyfield* (☎01806/522450; ③), just to the south, which also has a small **campsite**. North of Vidlin, you can stay in the historic *Lunna House* (☎01806/577237; ③), and on Whalsay at the *Lingaveg Guest House* (☎01806/566489; ③). **B&Bs** include *Mrs Jenner* (☎01595/890204; ②), *Mrs Williamson* (☎01595/890297; ②) and *Mrs Blance* (☎01595/890206; ②), all in South Nesting. Northeast of Vidlin you could try *Mrs Ford* (☎01806/577302; ②) at Lunning. Options in the Brae area include *Mrs Manson* (☎01806/522362; ②) or *Mrs Brown* (☎01806/522407; ②). On Skerries, *Mrs Johnson* (☎01806/515228; ②, with dinner ④) has a friendly B&B at Rocklea. For basic accommodation, if you have an airbed or sleeping mat, try the **camping** böds at the *Sail Loft* in Voe, *The Grieve House* (Hugh MacDiarmid's) on Whalsay or *Johnnie Notions* at Hamnavoe in Eshaness; book all these through the tourist office in Lerwick.

For a **bar meal or a drink**, good pubs and bars to try include *Brae Inn*, in the centre of the village, or *Busta House*, and the *St Magnus Bay Hotel* or *Booth* (more of a bistro) in Hillswick.

The North Isles: Yell, Fetlar and Unst

Stepping out into the wilds of the North Sea, Shetland's three **North Isles** are all predictably windswept and exposed – north from Unst there's no land until eastern Siberia, beyond the North Pole. Boasting landscapes and seascapes rich in elemental beauty and with a strong sense of defiance, weathered by centuries of fierce storms, the islands offer good walks, much birdlife and archeological sites. They're not difficult to reach either; and at less windy times of year, they make good cycling country, with not too many steep hills. Accommodation in the northern isles isn't abundant, so book ahead especially in summer.

To get to the North Isles, a direct **bus** service to Yell, Unst and Fetlar leaves Lerwick every morning except Sunday, taking around two and a half hours to reach Belmont in Unst or Oddsta in Feltar; there's an afternoon service but the Unst connections only operate on Thursdays and, between April and September, on Saturdays. There are also bus **tours** from Lerwick. Get details of all these services from *Leasks* (☎01595/693162). Taking a car is easy, using the inexpensive and frequent **ferry services** and well-timed ferry connections operated by *Shetland Islands Council*: (Lerwick to Baltasound; 2hr). The Mainland ferry terminal for Yell is at Toft; from there, ferries run to Ulsta about every 30 minutes from early morning to late evening (20min). Ferries leave from Gutcher in north Yell for Belmont on Unst (every 15–30min; 10min) or Oddsta on Fetlar (6 daily; 25min).

Yell

Historically, **Yell**, the largest of the North Isles, hasn't had good write-ups. The writer, Eric Linklater, described it as "dull and dark", while the Scottish historian Buchanan claimed it was "so uncouth a place that no creature can live therein, except such are born there". Certainly, if you keep to the fast main road via Westsandwick, which links the ferry terminal at **ULSTA** to the Fetlar and Unst one at **GUTCHER**, you'll pass a lot of uninspiring peat moorland, but the landscape is relieved by **Whale Firth, Mid Yell**

Voe and **Basta Voe**, which cut deeply into it, providing superb natural harbours – and used as undetectable hiding places by German submarines during World War II. Near Whale Firth, at Lumbister, the **RSPB reserve** is scattered in summer with wild flowers and home to merlins and skuas; and in the narrow gorge known as **Daal of Lumbister**, there's a lush growth of honeysuckle, wild thyme and moss campion.

A building dating from 1672 houses the **Old Haa Museum** and café at **BURRAVOE** (late April–Sept Tues–Thurs, Sat 10am–4pm, Sun 2–5pm; free), offering an ideal introduction to life on Yell past and present, with historical material, a small **art gallery** and the work of projects on local music and oral history. Just up the road, **St Colman's Church** (1900) is an isolated but delightful example of Arts and Crafts architecture, built in three Gothic-windowed bays with a curved end, surmounted by a tiny, ornate spire.

The island's largest village, **MID YELL** has a couple of shops, a pub and a **leisure centre** with a good swimming pool. The road south along the east coast from the village gives access to the ruined broch at **Gossabrough**, to the "**White Lady**" – known locally as the "Widden Wife", a ship's figurehead from the *Bohus* wrecked nearby in 1924 – and to some attractive eastern sections of the coast. Just west of Mid Yell, **Windhouse**, dating in part from the early eighteenth century, is said to be haunted by many ghosts – skeletons were found under the floor and in its walls. Its lodge is now basic visitor accommodation; nearby are the remains of a **broch** and a **heel-shaped cairn**. In the north of Yell, the area around **CULLIVOE** has relatively gentle, but attractive, coastal scenery. To the west is **Gloup**, with its secretive, narrow sandy voe. In the nineteenth century, this was one of the largest fishing stations in Shetland; a memorial commemorates the 58 men who were lost when a **great storm** overwhelmed six of their boats in July 1881. This area provides some excellent walking, as does the Atlantic coast further west, where there's an iron age fort and field system at **Burgi Geos**.

Practicalities

If you want to **stay** on Yell, there's the modern *Pinewood Guest House* (☎01957/702427; ③) at Aywick. **B&Bs** include *Mrs Johnson* (☎01957/702153; ②) in Mid Yell; *Westerhouse* (☎01957/744203; ②) and *Bayanne House* (☎01957/744219; ②) at Sellafirth; and *Mrs Tulloch* (☎01957/744201; ②) at Gutcher's post office. For more **basic accommodation**, if you've an airbed or mat, you can stay in *Windhouse Lodge*, on the main road near Mid Yell; book through the tourist office in Lerwick. There isn't a great range of **eating places** on the island but the non-smoking tearoom in the *Old Haa Museum* at Burravoe has soup, snacks and delicious homebakes. There's a simple but friendly restaurant and pub in the tiny hamlet of Westsandwick, and the *Hilltop Bar* in Mid Yell offers lunches and suppers. At the Gutcher ferry terminal, the *Seaview Café* has filled rolls, snacks, soup, teas and coffees.

Fetlar

Known as "the garden of Shetland", **Fetlar** is the most fertile of the North Isles; much of it lush and green, with masses of summer flowers, though the bulk is covered in heather and grass moorland. Around 900 people once lived here; there might well be more than 100 now were it not for the activities of **Sir Arthur Nicolson**, who in the early nineteenth century cleared many of the people at 40 days' notice to make room for sheep. Unlike some other local tyrants, Nicolson's architectural sensibilities were poorly developed; his rotting but still astonishing **Brough Lodge**, a sort of stone ranch built in 1820 at the southwest corner of the island, owes something – most likely an apology – to Gothic, Classical and maybe even Tudor styles.

Today Fetlar's population live on the southern and eastern sides of the island, where the main settlement, **HOUBIE**, has a rather less adventurously styled **laird's house**.

Nearby is a small but welcoming **interpretive centre** (May–Oct Wed–Sun noon–5pm; free) throwing light on local history and selling crafts and knitwear. The island has several notable archeological remains, including the **Funzie Girt**, a Neolithic dyke which divides the island into two, a monastic site at Strandibrough, a ring of stones at Haltadans, brochs, soapstone workings, cairns and a Norse grave. The first three of these are within the **RSPB North Fetlar Reserve**, and it's essential to contact the warden at **Baelans** (☎01957/733246) to find out if a visit is possible. The same applies if you want to seek out the birdlife, which has included regular visits by one or more **snowy owls**. In 1967 they bred here for the first time in Britain, on the southern limit of their range. Breeding continued for several years and around 20 chicks were raised, but recently only females have been present. Fetlar is also one of very few places you'll see the rare, graceful **red-necked phalarope**; a hide has been provided at the east end of the island near **Funzie** (which incidentally is pronounced *Finn*ie).

Elsewhere on Fetlar, particularly on the remoter north coast and on Lambhoga, the higher moorland peninsula to the southwest, there is excellent walking. At Trest, on the south coast, is a beautiful **sandy beach** and the loch behind it, Papil Water, is good for **fishing**.

Practicalities

Accommodation and places to eat on the island are limited to the friendly **B&B** at *Gord* (☎01957/733227; ②), where you can get an evening meal, and **camping** at the *Garths Campsite* (May–Sept; ☎01957/733269), which is well equipped with toilets, showers and drying facilities. There's a **café** at the *Fetlar Shop* (Tues, Wed, Fri & Sat 10am–5pm; Thurs & Sun 10am–1pm).

Unst

Unst has a population of around 1000, of whom 300 or 400 are connected to the **RAF radar base** at Saxa Vord, listening out for any uninvited intruders. The predominantly green landscape features on the eastern side of the strikingly coloured **serpentine rock**; though mainly greyish green, this weathers to rusty orange, and in some stone walls there are pieces which are of an extraordinary deep turquoise hue. The serpentine soil also produces unusual vegetation; grass has a bluish-grey cast, and at the **Keen of Hamar National Nature Reserve**, north of Baltasound, numerous rare plants include the unique mouse-eared chickweed.

In the southeast of the island, not far from the ferry terminal, is **UYEASOUND** with nearby **Muness Castle**, built in 1598 by **Laurence Bruce**, half-brother of Robert Stewart and probably designed by Andrew Crawford who shortly afterwards built Scalloway Castle for Robert's son Patrick; there's a café just nearby. A little to the north is a vast sandy beach, backed by the deserted crofting settlement of Sandwick. Northwest of Uyeasound, along the Westing road, is Shetland's largest **standing stone** near the Loch of Bordastubble; and further on, at Underhoull, are the ramparts of a ruined **broch** next to an iron age **earth house**.

The island's main settlement is at **BALTASOUND**, where old jetties around the bay testify to a bygone herring industry; there's a hotel with a pub, shop, post office and a leisure centre with a pool. Britain's most northerly post office is over the hill to the north, at **HAROLDSWICK**. Here, down near the shore, is the **Unst Boat Haven** (May–Sept daily 2–5pm, otherwise a key is available from the adjacent shop; free), an outstanding and beautifully presented display of historic boats with many tools of the trade and information on fishing; most of the boats are from Shetland, with one from Norway. The fact that the museum exists at all is a testament to the determination of the founder of the collection; the previous building was flattened, and several boats wrecked, in a hurricane in 1992. A little to the north, off the main road, is the **Unst**

Heritage Centre (May–Sept daily 2–5pm, free) where you can find out about other aspects of Unst life such as crofting and its unique geology. The road ends at **Skaw**, with a beautiful beach and the very last house in Britain.

West of Haroldswick is **Burrafirth**, a north-facing inlet surrounded by cliffs and guarded by the hills of **Saxa Vord** and **Hermaness**. Behind the beach and the links is the **Loch of Cliff**, which is good for fishing. **Hermaness National Nature Reserve** is home to more than 100,000 seabirds, the best known of which has been **"Albert Ross"**, a disorientated black-browed albatross from the South Atlantic. Albert's return to the same ledge year after year, ever hopeful that a mate might turn up, soon became celebrated as a harbinger of spring. A **visitor centre** is located in the former lighthouse keepers' houses; and a marked route into the reserve allows you to look down over the jagged rocks of **Muckle Flugga** and the most northerly bit of Britain, **Out Stack**. There are few more dramatic settings for a lighthouse, and few sites could ever have presented as great a challenge to the builders. The views from here are inevitably marvellous and the walk down the west side of Unst towards Westing is one of the finest in Shetland.

Practicalities

The island's **guest houses** and **hotel** are all in Baltasound; there's historic *Buness House* (☎01957/711315; ④), *Clingera Guest House* (☎01957/711579; ②) and Britain's most northerly **hotel**, the *Baltasound Hotel* (☎01957/711334; ⑤), which provides lunches and dinners to non-residents. **B&Bs** include *Barns* (☎01957/755249; ②) at Westing, *Mrs Ritch* (☎01957/711323; ②) at Haroldswick, *Mrs Nicolson* (☎01957/711503; ②) at Baltasound and *Mrs Firmin* (☎01957/775234; ③) at Uyeasound. For more **basic** accommodation, the Independent **youth hostel** at Uyeasound is well equipped (☎01957/755298 or 755311). **Snacks** and teas can be had at the *Nornova Tearoom* just north of Muness Castle or, often on a help-yourself basis, at the *Haroldswick Shop*.

travel details

ORKNEY

Buses

Kirkwall to: Houton (5–6 daily; 30min); St Margaret's Hope (4 daily; 40 min); Stromness (hourly; 40min); Tingwall (3 daily; 25min).

Ferries

Burwick to: John O' Groats (passengers only; 2–4 daily; 45min).

Houton to: Hoy (Lyness) and Flotta (11 daily; 45min).

Kirkwall to: Eday, Stronsay, Sanday, Westray and Papa Westray (1–3 daily; 1–2hr); Invergordon (6 weekly; 10hr); North Ronaldsay (1 weekly); Shapinsay (4–6 daily; 45min).

Stromness to: Aberdeen (1weekly in winter, 2 weekly in summer; 10hr/8hr); Hoy (passengers only; 2–3 daily in summer; 30min); Lerwick (1 weekly in winter, 2 weekly in summer; 8hr); Scrabster/Thurso (1–3 daily except Sun in winter; 1hr 45 min).

Tingwall to: Egilsay, Rousay and Wyre (7 daily; 30min).

Flights

Kirkwall to: Aberdeen (3 daily; 45min); Eday (Wed 2 daily; 12min); Edinburgh (daily; 1hr 20min); Glasgow (4 daily; 2hr 30min); Inverness (2 daily; 50min); North Ronaldsay (Mon–Sat 1–3 daily; 15min); Papa Westray (Mon–Sat 1–2 daily; 12min); Sanday (Mon–Sat 1–3 daily; 20min); Stronsay (Mon–Fri 1–2 daily; 25min); Westray (Mon–Sat 1–2 daily; 12min).

SHETLAND

Buses

Cullivoe to: Ulsta (2 daily; 1hr 15min).

Lerwick to: Brae (2–5 daily; 35min); Hamnavoe (Mon–Sat 2 daily; 30min); Hillswick (1–2 daily; 1hr 15min); Laxo (2–3 daily; 30min); Sandwick (Mon–Sat 4–6 daily, Sun 3–4; 35min);

Scalloway (Mon–Sat 8 daily; 15min); Sumburgh (4–6 daily; 45min); Unst (Mon–Sat 1–2 daily; 2hr 45min); Vidlin (Mon–Sat 2–3 daily; 40min); Walls and Sandness (3–4 daily, 50min); Culswick (daily; 1hr 20min); Yell (Mon–Sat 3 daily, Sun 1; 1hr 20min).

Unst, Yell and Fetlar: Mon–Sat 1 daily; 2hr 30min to Unst and Fetlar.

Ferries

Mainland

Grutness to: Fair Isle (5 fortnightly May–Sept; 2hr 40min).

Laxo to: Whalsay (16–18 daily; 30min).

Lerwick to: Aberdeen (6 weekly; direct sailings 14hr overnight, via Orkney 20hr afternoon/ overnight); Bressay (21 daily; 5min); Fair Isle (fortnightly; 4hr 30min); Out Skerries (2 weekly, 2hr 20min).

Scalloway to: Foula (1 fortnightly May–Sept; 3hr).

Toft to: Yell (22–27 daily; 20min).

Vidlin to: Out Skerries (1 Mon; Fri, Sat & Sun 3); Whalsay, when bad weather prevents sailings from Laxo.

Walls to: Foula (May–Sept 5 fortnightly, otherwise 1 weekly; 2hr 30min).

West Burrafirth to: Papa Stour (Wed–Mon 1–2 daily; 35min).

Other islands

Unst (Belmont) to: Fetlar (direct service; 1–2 daily; 25min).

Yell (Gutcher) to: Fetlar (4–7 daily; 25min); Unst (29 daily; 10min).

Flights

Kirkwall to: Aberdeen (Mon–Fri 3 daily; 45min); Eday (Wed 2; 8min); Glasgow (Mon–Fri 2 daily; 2– 2hr 30min); North Ronaldsay (Mon–Fri 2 daily; 15min); Papa Westray (Mon–Fri 2 daily; 12min); Sanday (Mon–Fri 2 daily; 10min); Stronsay (Mon– Fri 2 daily; 8min); Westray (Mon–Sat 2 daily; 12min); Wick (Mon, Wed, Fri & Sat 1; 15min).

Sumburgh to: Aberdeen (Mon–Fri 7 daily, Sat & Sun 5; 1hr); Fair Isle (1 weekly; 15min); Glasgow (Mon–Fri 3 daily, Sat & Sun 1; 2hr 25min); Kirkwall (2–3 daily; 35min); Unst (Mon–Fri 1 daily; 35min); Wick (Mon–Sat 1 daily; 50min).

Tingwall to: Fair Isle (Mon, Wed, Fri & Sat 1–2; 25min); Unst (Mon–Fri 1 daily; 25min). Also to Foula, Out Skerries, Papa Stour (charter services, seats limited and days and times vary; check with *British Airways Express*).

GETTING TO NORWAY

Thanks to the historical ties and the attraction of a short hop to continental Europe, Norway is a popular destination for Shetlanders and Orcadians. Norwegians often think of Shetland and Orkney as their western isles and, particularly in west Norway, wartime bonds with Shetland are strong. Norwegian yachts and sail training vessels are frequent visitors to Lerwick from Kirkwall.

There are weekly **flights** between June and September from Kirkwall, Orkney (1hr 45min) and twice weekly from Sumburgh, Shetland (1hr) to Bergen and from June to August a weekly **ferry** service from Lerwick (13hr). Short inclusive breaks are available by air from Shetland.

PART THREE

THE
CONTEXTS

Scottish Primrose
(Primula Scotica)

THE HISTORICAL FRAMEWORK

PREHISTORIC SCOTLAND

Scotland, like the rest of prehistoric Britain, was settled by successive waves of peoples arriving from the east. These first inhabitants were **hunter-gatherers**, whose heaps of animal bones and shells have been excavated, amongst other places, in the caves along the coast near East Wemyss, in Fife. Around 4500 BC, **Neolithic farming peoples** from the European mainland began moving into Scotland. To provide themselves with land for their cereal crops and grazing for their livestock, they cleared large areas of upland forest, usually by fire, and, in the process, created the characteristic moorland landscapes of much of modern Scotland. These early farmers established permanent settlements, some of which – like the well-preserved village of **Skara Brae** on Orkney – were near the sea, enabling them to supplement their diet by fishing and to develop their skills as boat builders. The Neolithic settlements were not as isolated as was once imagined: geological evidence has, for instance, revealed that the stone used to make axe-heads found in the Hebrides was quarried in Northern Ireland.

Settlement spurred the development of more complex forms of religious belief. The Neolithic peoples built large chambered burial mounds or

cairns, such as those at **Maes Howe** on Orkney. This reverence for human remains suggests a belief in some form of afterlife, a concept that the next wave of settlers, the **Beaker people**, certainly believed in. They placed pottery beakers filled with drink in the tombs of their dead to assist the passage of the deceased on their journey to, or their stay in, the next world. The Beaker people also built the mysterious **stone circles**, 30 of which have been discovered in Scotland. Such monuments were a massive commitment in terms of time and energy, with many of the stones carried from many miles away – just as they were at Stonehenge in England, the most famous stone circle of all. One of the best known Scottish circles is that of **Callanish** on the Isle of Lewis, where a dramatic series of monoliths (single standing stones) form avenues leading towards a circle made up of 13 standing stones. The exact function of the circles is still unknown, but many of the stones are aligned with the position of the sun at certain points in its annual cycle, suggesting that the monuments are related to the changing of the seasons.

The Beaker people also brought the **Bronze Age** to Scotland. Bronze, an alloy of copper and tin, was stronger and more flexible than its predecessor flint, which had long been used for axe-heads and knives. New materials led directly to the development of more effective weapons, and the sword and the shield made their first appearance around 1000 BC. Agricultural needs plus new weaponry added up to a state of endemic warfare as villagers raided their neighbours to steal livestock and grain. The Bronze Age peoples responded to the danger by developing a range of defences, among them the spectacular **hill forts**, great earthwork defences, many of which are thought to have been occupied from around 1000 BC and remained in use throughout the Iron Age, sometimes far longer. Less spectacular but equally practical were the **crannogs**, smaller settlements built on artificial islands constructed of logs, earth, stones and brush, such as Cherry Island in Loch Ness.

Conflict in Scotland intensified in the first millennium BC as successive waves of **Celtic** settlers, arriving from the south, increased competition for land. Around 400 BC the Celts brought the technology of **iron** with them and, as Winston Churchill put it, "Men armed with iron entered Britain and killed the men of bronze". These fractious times witnessed the construction of hundreds of **brochs** or fortified towers. Concentrated along the Atlantic coast and in the northern and western isles, the brochs were drystone fortifications (built without mortar or cement) often over 40ft in height. Some historians claim they provided protection for small coastal settlements from the attentions of Roman slave traders. Much the best preserved broch is on the Shetland island of Mousa; its double walls rise to about 40ft, only a little short of their original height. The Celts continued to migrate north almost up until Julius Caesar's first incursion into Britain in 55 BC.

At the end of the prehistoric period, immediately prior to the arrival of the Romans, Scotland was divided among a number of warring Iron Age tribes, who, apart from the raiding, were preoccupied with wresting a living from the land, growing barley and oats, rearing sheep, hunting deer and fishing for salmon. The Romans were to write these people into history under the collective name Picti, or **Picts**, meaning painted people – after their body tattoos.

THE ROMANS

The Roman conquest of Britain began in 43 AD, almost a century after Caesar's first invasion. By 80 AD the Roman governor, Agricola, felt secure enough in the south of Britain to begin an invasion of the north, building a string of forts across the Clyde–Forth line and defeating a large force of Scottish tribes at Mons Graupius. The long-term effect of his campaign, however, was slight. Work on a major fort – to be the base for 5000 – at Inchtuthill, on the Tay, was abandoned before it was finished, and the legions withdrew south. In 123 AD the **Emperor Hadrian** decided to seal the frontier against the northern tribes and built **Hadrian's Wall**, which stretched from the Solway Firth to the Tyne and was the first formal division of the island of Britain. Twenty years later, the Romans again ventured north and built the **Antonine Wall** between the Clyde and the Forth. This was occupied for about 40 years, but thereafter the Romans, frustrated by the inhospitable terrain of the Highlands, largely gave up their attempt to subjugate the north, and instead adopted a policy of containment.

It was the Romans who produced the first written accounts of the peoples of Scotland. In the second century AD, the Greco-Egyptian geographer Ptolemy drew up the first known map of Scotland, which identified 17 tribal territories. Other descriptions were less scientific, compounding the mixture of fear and contempt with which the Romans regarded their Pictish neighbours. Dio Cassius, a Roman commentator writing in 197 AD, informed his readers that:

They live in huts, go naked and unshod. They mostly have a democratic government, and are much addicted to robbery. They can bear hunger and cold and all manner of hardship; they will retire into their marshes and hold out for days with only their heads above water, and in the forest they will subsist on barks and roots.

THE DARK AGES

In the years following the departure of the Romans, traditionally put at 450 AD, the population of Scotland changed considerably. By 500 AD the **Picts** occupied the northern isles, and the north and the east as far south as Fife. Today their settlements can be generally determined by place names with a "Pit" prefix, such as Pitlochry, and by the existence of carved symbol stones, like those found at Aberlemno in Angus. To the west, between Dumbarton and Carlisle, was a population of **Britons**. Many of the Briton leaders had Roman names, which suggests that they were a Romanized Celtic people, possibly a combination of tribes maintained by the Romans as a buffer between the Wall and the northern tribes, and peoples pushed west by the Anglo-Saxon invaders landing on the east coast. Both the Britons and the Picts spoke variations of P-Celtic, from which Welsh, Cornish and Breton developed.

On the west coast, to the north and west of the Britons, lived the **Scotti**, Irish-Celtic invaders who would eventually give their name to the whole country. The first Scotti arrived in the Western Isles from Ireland in the fourth century AD, and about a century later their great king, Fergus Mor, moved his base from Antrim to Dunadd, near Lochgilphead, where he founded the kingdom of Dalriada. The Scotti spoke Q-Celtic, the precursor of modern Gaelic. On the east coast, the Germanic **Angles** had sailed north along the coast to carve out an enclave around Dunbar in East Lothian. The

THE NORTHERN ISLES

With their sophisticated ships and navigational skills, the **Vikings**, who began their expansion in the eighth century, soon gained supremacy over the Pictish peoples in Shetland, Orkney, the extreme northeast corner of the mainland and the Western Isles. In 872, the King of Norway set up an earldom in **Orkney** from which **Shetland** was also governed: for the next six centuries the northern isles took a path distinct from the rest of what is now called Scotland, becoming a base for raiding and colonization in much of the rest of Britain and Ireland, and a link in the chain that connected Faroe, Iceland, Greenland and, more tenuously, North America. Norse culture flourished, and buildings such as St Magnus Cathedral in Kirkwall, Orkney, begun in 1137, give some idea of its energy

(see p.467). However, there were bouts of unrest, and finally Shetland was brought under direct rule from Norway at the end of the twelfth century.

When Norway united with Sweden under the Danish crown in the fourteenth century, Norse power began to wane and Scottish influence to increase. In 1469, a marriage was arranged between Margaret, daughter of the Danish King Christian I, and the future King James III of Scotland. Short of cash for her dowry, Christian mortgaged Orkney to Scotland in 1468, followed by Shetland in 1469; neither pledge was ever successfully redeemed. The laws, religion and administration of the northern isles became Scottish, though their Norse heritage is still very evident in place names, dialect and culture.

---

final addition to the ethnic mix was also non Celtic; from around 800 AD, **Norse** invaders began to arrive, settling mainly in the northern isles (see above) and the northeast of the mainland.

The next few centuries saw almost constant warfare among the different groups. The main issue was land, but this was frequently complicated by the need of the warrior castes, who dominated all of these cultures, to exhibit martial prowess. Military conquests did play their part in bringing the peoples of Scotland together, but the most persuasive force was **Christianity**. Many of the Britons had been Christians since Roman times and it had been a Briton, St Ninian, who conducted the first missionary work among the Picts at the end of the fourth century. Attempts to convert the Picts were resumed in the sixth century by St Columba, who, as a Gaelic-speaking Scotti, demonstrated that Christianity could provide a bridge between the different tribes.

Christianity proved attractive to pagan kings because it seemed to offer them extra supernatural powers. As St Columba declared, when he inaugurated his cousin Aidan as king of Dalriada in 574, "Believe firmly, O Aidan, that none of your enemies will be able to resist you unless you first deal falsely against me and my successors". This combination of spiritual and political power, when taken with Columba's establishment of the island of **Iona** as a centre of Christian culture, opened the way for many peaceable contacts between the Picts and

Scotti. Intermarriage became commonplace, and the Scotti king Kenneth MacAlpine, who united Dalriada and Pictland in 843, was the son of a Pictish princess – the Picts traced succession through the female line. Similarly, MacAlpine's creation of the united kingdom of **Alba**, later known as **Scotia**, was part of a process of integration rather than outright conquest. Kenneth and his successors gradually extended the frontiers of their kingdom by marriage and force of arms until, by 1034, almost all of what we now call Scotland was under their rule.

THE MIDDLE AGES

By the time of his death in 1034, **Malcolm II** was recognized as the king of Scotia. He was not, though, a national king in the sense that we understand the term, as under the Gaelic system, kings were elected from the *derbfine*, a group made up of those whose great-grandfathers had been kings. The chosen successor, supposedly the fittest to rule, was known as the *tanist*. By the eleventh century, however, Scottish kings had become familiar with the principle of heredity, and were often tempted to bend the rules of *tanistry*. Thus, the childless Malcolm secured the succession of his grandson **Duncan** by murdering a potential rival *tanist*. Duncan, in turn, was killed by **Macbeth** in 1040. Macbeth was not, therefore, the villain of Shakespeare's imagination, but simply an ambitious Scot of royal blood acting in a relatively conventional way.

The victory of **Malcolm III**, known as Canmore ("bighead"), over Macbeth in 1057 marked the beginning of a period of fundamental change in Scottish society. Having avenged his father Duncan, Malcolm III, who had spent the previous 17 years at the English court, sought to apply to Scotland a range of ideas he had brought back with him. He and his heirs established a secure dynasty based on succession through the male line and introduced **feudalism** into Scotland, a system that was diametrically opposed to the Gaelic system, which rested on blood ties: the followers of a Gaelic king were his kindred, whereas the followers of a feudal king were vassals bought with land. The Canmores successfully feudalized much of southern and eastern Scotland by making grants to their Norman, Breton and Flemish followers, but beyond that, traditional clan-based forms of social relations persisted.

The Canmores, independent of the local nobility, who remained a military threat, also began to reform the **Church**. This development started with the efforts of Margaret, Malcolm III's English wife, who brought Scottish religious practices into line with those of the rest of Europe and was eventually canonized. **David I** (1124–53) continued the process by importing monks to found a series of monasteries, principally along the border at Kelso, Melrose, Jedburgh and Dryburgh. By 1200 the entire country was covered by a network of 11 bishoprics, although church organization remained weak within the Highlands. Similarly, the dynasty founded a series of **royal burghs**, towns such as Edinburgh, Stirling and Berwick, and bestowed upon them charters recognizing them as centres of trade. The charters usually granted a measure of self-government, vested in the town corporation or guild, and the monarchy hoped this liberality would both encourage loyalty and increase the prosperity of the kingdom. Scotland's Gaelic-speaking clans had little influence within the burghs, and by 1550 Scots – a northern version of Anglo-Saxon – had become the main language throughout the Lowlands.

The policies of the Canmores laid the basis for a cultural rift in Scotland between the Highland and Lowland communities. Before that became an issue, however, the Scots had to face a major threat from the south. In 1286 **Alexander III** died, and a hotly disputed succession gave Edward I, the king of England, an opportunity to subjugate Scotland. In 1291 Edward presided over a conference where the rival claimants to the Scottish throne presented their cases. Edward chose John Balliol, in preference to Robert the Bruce, his main rival, and obliged John to pay him homage, thus turning Scotland into a vassal kingdom. Bruce refused to accept the decision, thereby continuing the conflict, and in 1295 Balliol renounced his allegiance to Edward and formed an alliance with France – the beginning of what is known as the "Auld Alliance". In the conflict that followed, the Bruce family sided with the English, Balliol was defeated and imprisoned, and Edward seized control of almost all of Scotland.

Edward had shown little mercy during his conquest of Scotland – he had, for example, had most of the population of Berwick massacred – and his cruelty seems to have provoked a truly national resistance. This focused on **William Wallace**, a man of relatively lowly origins who forged an army of peasants, lesser knights and townsmen that was fundamentally different to the armies raised by the nobility. Figures like Balliol, holding lands in England, France and Scotland, were part of an international aristocracy for whom warfare was merely the means by which they struggled for power. Wallace, by contrast, led proto-nationalist forces determined to expel the English from their country. Probably for that very reason Wallace never received the support of the nobility, and, after a bitter ten-year campaign, he was betrayed and executed in London in 1305.

With Wallace out of the way, feudal intrigue resumed. In 1306 **Robert the Bruce**, the erstwhile ally of the English, defied Edward and had himself crowned king of Scotland. Edward died the following year, but the unrest dragged on until 1314, when Bruce decisively defeated a huge English army under Edward II at the battle of **Bannockburn**. At last Bruce was firmly in control of his kingdom, and in 1320 the Scots asserted their right to independence in a successful petition to the pope, now known as the **Arbroath Declaration**.

In the years following Bruce's death in 1329, the Scottish monarchy gradually declined in influence. The last of the Bruce dynasty died in 1371, to be succeeded by the "Stewards", hence **Stewarts**, but thereafter a succession of Scottish rulers, culminating with James VI in 1567, came to the throne when still children. The power vacuum was filled by the nobility, whose key members exercised control as Scotland's regents while carving out territories where they ruled with the power, if not the title, of kings. At the close of the fifteenth century, the Douglas family alone controlled Galloway, Lothian, Stirlingshire, Clydesdale and Annandale. The more vigorous monarchs of the period, notably **James I** (1406–37), did their best to curb the power of such dynasties, but their efforts were usually nullified at the next regency. **James IV** (1488–1513), the most talented of the early Stewarts, might have restored the authority of the crown, but his invasion of England ended in a terrible defeat for the Scots — and his own death — at the battle of Flodden Field.

The reign of **Mary, Queen of Scots** (1542–67) typified the problems of the Scottish monarchy. Mary came to the throne when just one week old, and immediately caught the attention of the English king, Henry VIII, who sought, first by persuasion and then by military might, to secure her hand in marriage for his five-year-old son, Edward. Beginning in 1544, the English launched a series of devastating attacks on Scotland, an episode Sir Walter Scott later called the "Rough Wooing", until, in the face of another English invasion in 1548, the Scots — or at least those not supporting Henry — turned to the "Auld Alliance". The French king proposed marriage between Mary and the Dauphin Francis, promising in return military assistance against the English. The six-year-old queen sailed for France in 1548, leaving her loyal nobles and their French allies in control, and her husband succeeded to the French throne in 1559. When she returned 13 years later, following the death of Francis, she had to pick her way through the rival ambitions of her nobility and deal with something entirely new — the religious Reformation.

THE REFORMATION

The **Reformation** in Scotland was a complex social process, whose threads are often hard to unravel. Nevertheless, it is quite clear that, by the end of the sixteenth century, the established Church was held in general contempt. Many members of the higher clergy regarded their relationship with the Church purely in economic terms, and 40 percent of known illegitimate births (ie those subsequently legitimized) were the product of the "celibate" clergy's liaisons.

Another spur to the Scottish Reformation was the identification of Protestantism with anti-French feeling. In 1554 Mary of Guise, the French mother of the absent Queen Mary, had become regent, and her habit of appointing Frenchmen to high office was seen as part of an attempt to subordinate Scotland's interests to those of France. There was considerable resentment, and in 1557 a group of nobles banded together to form the **Lords of the Congregation**, whose dual purpose was to oppose French influence and promote the reformed religion. With English military backing, the Protestant lords succeeded in deposing the French regent in 1560, and, when the Scottish Parliament assembled shortly afterwards, it asserted the primacy of Protestantism by forbidding the Mass and abolishing the authority of the pope. The nobility proceeded to confiscate two-thirds of Church lands, a huge prize that did much to bolster their new beliefs.

Even without the economic incentives, Protestantism was a highly charged political doctrine. Luther had argued that each individual's conscience was capable of discerning God's will. This meant that a hierarchical priesthood, existing to interpret God's will, was unnecessary and that the people themselves might conclude their rulers were breaking God's laws, in which case the monarch should be opposed or even deposed. This point was made very clearly to Queen Mary by the Protestant reformer **John Knox** at their first meeting in 1561. Subjects, he told her, were not bound to obey an ungodly monarch.

Knox, a Protestant exile who had returned to Scotland in 1559, was a follower of the Genevan reformer Calvin, who combined Luther's views on individual conscience with a belief in predestination. He argued that an omnipotent God must know everything, including the destinies of every human being. Consequently, it was determined before birth who was to be part of the Elect, bound for heavenly glory, and who was not, a doctrine that placed enormous pressure on its adherents to demonstrate by their godly behaviour that they were of the Elect. This was the doctrine that Knox brought back to Scotland and laid out in his Articles of Confession of Faith, better known as the **Scot's Confession**, which was to form the basis of the reformed faith for over 70 years.

Mary ducked and weaved, trying to avoid an open breach with her Protestant subjects. The fires of popular displeasure were kept well-stoked by Knox, however, who declared "one Mass was more fearful than if ten thousand enemies were landed in any part of the realm, of purpose to suppress the whole religion". At the same time, Mary was engaged in a balancing act between the factions of the Scottish nobility. Her difficulties were exacerbated by her disastrous second marriage to **Lord Darnley**, a cruel and politically inept character, whose jealousy led to his involvement in the murder of Mary's favourite, David Rizzio, who was dragged from the queen's supper room at Holyrood and stabbed 56 times. The incident caused the Scottish Protestants more than a little unease, but they were entirely scandalized in 1567, when Darnley himself was murdered and Mary promptly married the **Earl of Bothwell**, widely believed to be the murderer. This was too much to bear, and the Scots rose in rebellion, driving Mary into exile in England at the age of just 25. The queen's illegitimate half-brother, the Earl of Moray, became regent and her son, the infant James, was left behind to be raised a Protestant prince. Mary, meanwhile, became perceived as such a threat to the English throne that Queen Elizabeth I had her executed in 1587.

Knox could now concentrate on the organization of the reformed Church, or **Kirk**, which he envisaged as a body empowered to intervene in the daily lives of the people. **Andrew Melville**, another leading reformer, wished to push this theocratic vision further. He proposed the abolition of all traces of Episcopacy – the rule of the bishops in the Church – and that the Kirk should adopt a **presbyterian** structure, administered by a hierarchy of assemblies, part-elected and part-appointed. At the bottom of the chain, beneath the General Assembly, Synod and Presbytery, would be the Kirk session, responsible for church affairs, the performance of the minister and the morals of the parish. In 1592, the Melvillian party achieved a measure of success when presbyteries and synods were accepted as legal church courts and the office of bishop was suspended.

James VI (1567–1625) disliked presbyterianism because its quasi-democratic structure – particularly the lack of royally appointed bishops – appeared to threaten his authority. He was, however, unable to resist the reformers until 1610, when, strengthened by his installation as James I of England after Elizabeth's death in 1603, he restored the Scottish bishops. The argument about the nature of Kirk organization would lead to bloody conflict in the years after James' death.

THE RELIGIOUS WARS

Raised in Episcopalian England, **Charles I** (1625–49) had little understanding of Scottish reformism. He believed in the Divine Right of Kings, an authoritarian creed that claimed the monarch was God's representative on earth and, therefore, his authority had divine sanction, a concept entirely counter to Protestant thought. In 1637, Charles attempted to impose a new prayer book on the Kirk, laying down forms of worship in line with those favoured by the High Anglican Church. The reformers denounced these changes as "Popery" and organized the **National Covenant**, a religious pledge that committed the signatories to "Labour by all means lawful to recover the purity and liberty of the Gospel as it was established and professed".

Charles declared all the "Covenanters" to be rebels, a proclamation endorsed by his Scottish bishops. Consequently, when the king backed down from military action and called a General Assembly of the Kirk, the assembly promptly abolished the Episcopacy. Charles pronounced the proceedings illegal, but lack of finance stopped him from mounting an effective military campaign – whereas the Covenanters, well-financed by the Kirk, assembled a proficient army under Alexander Leslie. In desperation, Charles summoned the English Parliament, the first for eleven years, hoping it would pay for an army. But, like the calling of the General Assembly, the decision was a disaster and Parliament was much keener to criticize his policies than to raise taxes. In response Charles declared war on Parliament in 1642.

Until 1650 Scotland was ruled by the Covenanters and the power of the Presbyterian Kirk grew considerably. Laws were passed establishing schools in every parish and, less usefully, banning trade with Catholic countries. The only effective opposition to the theocratic state came from the **Marquis of Montrose**, who had initially supported the Covenant but lined up with the king when war broke out. His army was drawn from the Highlands and islands, where the Kirk's influence was weakest. Montrose was a gifted campaigner who won several notable victories against the Covenanters, but the reluctance of his troops to stay south of the Highland Line made it impossible for him to capitalize on his successes, and he was eventually captured and executed in 1650.

Largely confined to the peripheries of Scotland, Montrose's campaigns were a sideshow to the **Civil War** being waged further south. Here, the Covenanters and the English Parliamentarians faced the same royal enemy and in 1643 formed an alliance. Indeed, it was the Scots army that captured Charles at Newark in Nottinghamshire, in 1646. There was, however, friction between the allies. Many of the Parliamentarians, including Cromwell, were **Independents**, who favoured a looser form of doctrinal control within the state Church than did the Presbyterians, and were inclined towards religious toleration for the law-abiding sects outside the state Church. In addition, the Scots believed the English were tainted with **Erastianism** – a belief in placing the secular authority of Parliament over the spiritual authority of the Church.

The Parliamentarians in turn suspected the Scots of hankering for the return of the monarchy, a suspicion confirmed when, at the invitation of the Earl of Argyll, the future Charles II came back to Scotland in 1650. To regain his Scottish kingdom, Charles was obliged to renounce his father and sign the Covenant, two bitter pills taken to impress the population. In the event, the "presbyterian restoration" was short-lived. Cromwell invaded, defeated the Scots at Dunbar and forced Charles into exile. Until the restoration of 1660, Scotland was united with England and governed by seven commissioners.

Although the restoration of **Charles II** (1660–85) brought bishops back to the Kirk, they were integrated into an essentially presbyterian structure of Kirk sessions and presbyteries, and the General Assembly, which had been abolished by Cromwell, was not re-established. Over 300 clergymen, a third of the Scottish

ministry, refused to accept the reinstatement of the bishops and were edged out of the Church, forced to hold open-air services, called **Conventicles**, which Charles did his best to suppress. Religious opposition inspired military resistance and the Lowlands witnessed scenes of brutal repression as the king's forces struggled to keep control in what was known as "The Killing Time". In the southwest, a particular stronghold of the Covenanters, the government imported Highlanders, the so-called "Highland Host", to root out the opposition, which they did with great barbarity.

Charles II was succeeded by his brother **James VII** (James II of England), whose ardent Catholicism caused a Protestant backlash in England. In 1689, he was forced into exile in France and the throne passed to **Mary**, his Protestant daughter, and her Dutch husband, **William of Orange**. In Scotland, William and Mary restored the full presbyterian structure and abolished bishops, though they chose not to restore the political and legal functions of the Kirk, which remained subject to parliamentary control. This settlement ended Scotland's religious wars and completed its reformation.

THE UNION

Although the question of Kirk organization was settled in 1690, the political issue of the relationship between the Crown and the Scottish Parliament was not. From 1689 to 1697, William was at war with France, partly financed by Scottish taxes and partly fought by Scottish soldiers. Yet many Scots, mindful of the Auld Alliance, disapproved of the war and others suffered financially from the disruption to trade with France. There were other economic irritants too, principally the legally sanctioned monopoly that English merchants had over trade with the English colonies. This monopoly inspired the **Darien Scheme**, a plan to establish a Scottish colony in Panama. The colonists set off in 1698, but, thwarted by the opposition of both William and the English merchants, the scheme proved a miserable failure. The colony collapsed with the loss of £200,000 – an amount equal to half the value of the entire coinage in Scotland – and an angry Scottish Parliament threatened to refuse the king taxes as rioting broke out in the cities.

Meanwhile, in the north, the Highlanders blamed William for the massacre of the

MacDonalds of Glencoe. In 1691, William had offered pardons to those Highland chiefs who had opposed his accession, on condition that they took an oath of allegiance by New Year's Day, 1692. Alasdair MacDonald of Glencoe had turned up at the last minute, but his efforts to take the oath were frustrated by the king's officials, who were determined to see his clan, well known for their support of the Stewarts, destroyed. In February 1692, Captain Robert Campbell quartered his men in Glencoe and, two weeks later, in the middle of the night, his troops acted on their secret orders and slaughtered as many MacDonalds as they could. Thirty-eight died, and the massacre caused a national scandal, especially among the clans, where "Murder under Trust" – killing those offering you shelter – was considered a particularly heinous crime.

The situation in Scotland was further complicated by the question of the succession. Mary died without leaving an heir and, on William's death in 1702, the crown passed to her sister **Anne**, who was also childless. In response, the English Parliament secured the Protestant succession by passing the Act of Settlement, which named the Electress Sophia of Hanover as the next in line to the throne. The Act did not, however, apply in Scotland, and the English feared that the Scots would invite James Edward Stewart back from France to be their king. Consequently, Parliament appointed commissioners charged with the consideration of "proper methods towards attaining a union with Scotland". The project seemed doomed to failure when the Scottish Parliament passed the **Act of Security**, in 1703, stating that Scotland would not accept a Hanoverian

THE HIGHLANDS

The country that was united with England in 1707 contained three distinct cultures: in south and east Scotland, they spoke Scots; in Shetland, Orkney and much of the northeast the local dialect, though Scots-based, contained elements of Old Norn; in the rest of north and west Scotland, including the Western Isles, Gaelic was spoken. These linguistic differences were paralleled by different forms of social organization and customs. The people of north and west Scotland were mostly pastoralists, moving their sheep and cattle to highland pastures in the summer, and returning to the glens in the winter. They lived in single-room dwellings, heated by a central peat fire and sometimes shared with livestock, and in hard times they would subsist on cakes made from the blood of their live cattle mixed with oatmeal. Highlanders supplemented their meagre income by raiding their clan neighbours and the prosperous Lowlands, whose inhabitants regarded their northern compatriots with a mixture of fear and contempt. In the early seventeenth century, Montgomerie, a Lowland poet, suggested that God had created the first Highlander out of horseshit. When God asked his creation what he would do, the reply was "I will doun to the Lowland, Lord, and thair steill a kow".

It would be a mistake, however, to infer from the primitive nature of Highland life that the institutions of this society had existed from time immemorial. This is especially true of the **"clan"**, a term that only appears in its modern usage in the sixteenth century. In theory, the clan bound together blood relatives

who shared a common ancestor, a concept clearly derived from the ancient Gaelic notion of kinship. But in practice many of the clans were of non-Gaelic origin – such as the Frasers, Sinclairs and Stewarts, all of Anglo-Norman descent – and it was the mythology of a common ancestor, rather than the actuality, that cemented the clans together. Furthermore, clans were often made up of people with a variety of surnames, and there are documented cases of individuals changing their names when they swapped allegiances.

At the upper end of Highland society was the **clan chief** (who might have been a minor figure, like MacDonald of Glencoe, or a great lord, like the Duke of Argyll, head of the Campbells), who provided protection for his followers: they would, in turn, fight for him when called upon to do so. Below the clan chief were the **chieftains of the septs**, or sub-units of the clan, and then came the **tacksmen**, major tenants of the chief to whom they were frequently related. The tacksmen sublet their land to **tenants**, who were at the bottom of the social scale. The Highlanders wore a simple belted plaid wrapped around the body – rather than the kilt – and not until the late seventeenth century were certain **tartans** roughly associated with particular clans. The detailed codification of the tartan was produced by the Victorians, whose romantic vision of Highland life originated with George IV's visit to Scotland in 1822, when he appeared in an elaborate version of Highland dress, complete with flesh-coloured tights (for more on tartan see p.398).

monarch unless they had first received guarantees protecting their religion and their trade.

Nevertheless, despite the strength of anti-English feeling, the Scottish Parliament passed the **Act of Union** by 110 votes to 69 in January 1707. Some historians have explained the vote in terms of bribery and corruption. This certainly played a part (the Duke of Hamilton, for example, switched sides at a key moment and was subsequently rewarded with an English dukedom), but there were other factors. Scottish politicians were divided between the Cavaliers – Jacobites (supporters of the Stewarts) and Episcopalians – and the Country party, whose presbyterian members dreaded the return of the Stewarts more than they disliked the Hanoverians. There were commercial considerations too. In 1705, the English Parliament had passed the Alien Act, which threatened to impose severe penalties on cross-border trade, whereas the Union gave merchants of both countries free access to each other's markets. The Act of Union also guaranteed the Scottish legal system and the Presbyterian Kirk, and offered compensation to those who had lost money in the Darien Scheme.

Under the terms of the Act, both parliaments were to be replaced by a new British Parliament based in London, with the Scots apportioned 45 MPs and 16 peers. There were riots when the terms became known, but no sustained opposition.

THE JACOBITE RISINGS

When James VII/II was deposed he had fled to France, where he planned the reconquest of his kingdom with the support of the French king. In 1702, James' successor, William, died and the hopes of the Stewarts passed to his cousin James, the "Old Pretender" (Pretender in the sense of having pretensions to the throne, Old to distinguish him from his son Charles, the "Young Pretender"). The Crown passed to Anne, however, and after her death and the accession of the Hanoverian George I, the first major **Jacobite uprising** occurred in 1715. Its timing appeared perfect. Scottish opinion was moving against the Union, which had failed to bring Scotland any tangible economic benefits. The English had also been accused of bad faith when, contrary to their pledges, they attempted to impose their legal practices on the Scots.

Neither were Jacobite sentiments confined to Scotland. There were many in England who toasted the "King across the water" and showed no enthusiasm for the new German ruler. In September 1715, the fiercely Jacobite John Erskine, Earl of Mar, raised the Stewart standard at Braemar Castle. Just eight days later, he captured Perth, where he gathered an army of over 10,000 men, drawn mostly from the Episcopalians of northeast Scotland and from the Highlands. Mar's rebellion took the government by surprise. They had only 4000 soldiers in Scotland, under the command of the Duke of Argyll, but Mar dithered until he lost the military advantage. There was an indecisive battle at Sheriffmuir in November, but by the time the Old Pretender arrived the following month, 6000 veteran Dutch troops had reinforced Argyll. The rebellion disintegrated rapidly and James slunk back to exile in France in February 1716.

The **Jacobite uprising of 1745**, led by James' dashing son, Charles Edward Stewart (Bonnie Prince Charlie), had little chance of success. The Hanoverians had consolidated their hold on the English throne, Lowland society was uniformly loyalist, and even among the Highlanders Charles only attracted just over a half of the 20,000 clansmen who could have marched with him. Nevertheless, after a decisive victory over government forces at Prestonpans, Charles made a spectacular advance into England, getting as far as Derby. London was in a state of panic: its shops were closed and the Bank of England, fearing a run on sterling, slowed withdrawals by paying out in sixpences. But Derby was as far south as Charles got. On December 6, threatened by superior forces, the Jacobites decided to retreat to Scotland. The Duke of Cumberland was sent in pursuit and the two armies met on **Culloden Moor**, near Inverness, in April 1746. Outnumbered and out-gunned, the Jacobites were swept from the field, losing over 1200 men compared to Cumberland's 300 plus. After the battle, many of the wounded Jacobites were slaughtered, an atrocity that earnt Cumberland the nickname "Butcher". Jacobite hopes died at Culloden and the prince lived out the rest of his life in drunken exile.

In the aftermath of the uprising, the wearing of tartan, the bearing of arms and the playing of bagpipes were all banned. Rebel chiefs lost their land and the Highlands were placed under military occupation. Most significantly, the government prohibited the private armies of the chiefs, thereby effectively destroying the clan system.

THE HIGHLAND CLEARANCES

Once the clan chief was forbidden his own army, he had no need of the large tenantry that had previously been a vital military asset. Conversely, the second half of the eighteenth century saw the Highland population increase dramatically after the introduction of the easy-to-grow and nutritious potato. Between 1745 and 1811, the population of the Outer Hebrides, for example, rose from 13,000 to 24,500. The clan chiefs adopted different policies to deal with the new situation. Some encouraged emigration, and as many as 6000 Highlanders left for the Americas between 1800 and 1803 alone. Other landowners developed alternative forms of employment for their tenantry, mainly fishing and kelping. **Kelp** (brown seaweed) was gathered and burnt to produce soda ash, which was used in the manufacture of soap, glass and explosives. There was a rising market for soda ash until the 1810s, with the price increasing from £2 a ton in 1760 to £20 in 1808, making a fortune for some landowners and providing thousands of Highlanders with temporary employment. Other landowners developed **sheep runs** on the Highland pastures, introducing hardy breeds like the black-faced Linton and the Cheviot. But extensive sheep farming proved incompatible with a high peasant population, and many landowners decided to clear their estates of tenants, some of whom were forcibly moved to tiny plots of marginal land, where they were to farm as **crofters**.

The pace of the **Highland Clearances** accelerated after the end of the Napoleonic Wars in 1815, when the market price for kelp, fish and cattle declined, leaving sheep as the only profitable Highland product. The most notorious Clearances took place on the estates of the Countess of Sutherland, who owned a million acres in northern Scotland. Between 1807 and 1821, around 15,000 people were thrown off her land, evictions carried out by Patrick Sellar, the estate factor, with considerable brutality. Those who failed to leave by the appointed time had their homes burnt in front of them and one elderly woman, who failed to get out of her home after it was torched, subsequently died from burns. The local sheriff charged Sellar with her death, but a jury of landowners acquitted him — and the sheriff was sacked. As the dispossessed Highlanders scratched a living from the acid soils of some tiny croft, they learnt through bitter experience the limitations of the clan. Famine followed, forcing large-scale emigration to America and Canada and leaving the huge uninhabited areas found in the region today.

The crofters eked out a precarious existence, but they hung on throughout the nineteenth century, often by taking seasonal employment away from home. In the 1880s, however, a sharp downturn in agricultural prices made it difficult for many crofters to pay their rent. This time, inspired by the example of the Irish Land League, they resisted eviction, forming the **Highland Land Reform Association** and the **Crofters' Party**. In 1886, in response to the social unrest, Gladstone's Liberal government passed the **Crofters' Holdings Act**, which conceded three of the crofters' demands: security of tenure, fair rents to be decided independently, and the right to pass on crofts by inheritance. But Gladstone did not attempt to increase the amount of land available for crofting and shortage of land remained a major problem until the **Land Settlement Act** of 1919 made provision for the creation of new crofts. Nevertheless, the population of the Highlands has continued to decline during the twentieth century, with many of the region's young people finding city life more appealing.

INDUSTRIALIZATION

Glasgow was the powerhouse of Scotland's **Industrial Revolution**. The passage from Glasgow to the Americas was much shorter than that from rival English ports and a lucrative transatlantic trade in tobacco had developed as early as the seventeenth century. This in turn stimulated Scottish manufacturing since, under the terms of the Navigation Acts, the Americans were not allowed to trade manufactured goods. Scottish-produced linen, paper and wrought iron were exchanged for Virginia tobacco, and when the American Revolution disrupted the trade in the 1770s and 1780s, the Scots successfully turned to trade with the West Indies and, most important of all, to the production of cotton textiles.

Glasgow's west coast location gave it ready access to the sources of raw cotton in the Americas, while the rapid growth of the British Empire provided an expanding market for its finished cloth. Initially, the city's **cotton industry**, like the earlier linen industry, was organized domestically, with spinners and weavers working in their homes, but increased demand required mass production and a need for factories. In 1787, Scotland had only 19 mills; by 1840 there were nearly two hundred.

The growth of the textile industry spurred the development of other industries. In the mid-eighteenth century, the **Carron Ironworks** was founded near Falkirk, specializing in the production of military munitions. Here, the capital and expertise were English, but the location was determined by Scottish coal reserves, and by 1800 it was the largest ironworks in Europe. The basis of Scotland's **shipbuilding** industry was laid as early as 1802, when the steam vessel *Charlotte Dundas* was launched on the Forth–Clyde canal. Within 30 years, 95 steam vessels had been built in Scotland, most of them on Clydeside. The growth of the iron and shipbuilding industries, plus the extensive use of steam power, created a massive demand for **coal** and pit shafts were sunk across the coal fields of southern Scotland.

Industrialization led to a concentration of Scotland's **population** in the central Lowlands. In 1840, one third of the country's industrial workers lived in Lanarkshire alone, and Glasgow's population grew from 17,000 in the 1740s to over 200,000 a century later. Such sudden growth created urban overcrowding on a massive scale, and as late as 1861, 64 percent of the entire Scottish population lived in one- or two-room houses. For most Clydesiders, "house" meant a couple of small rooms in a grim tenement building, where many of the poorest families were displaced Highlanders and Irish immigrants, with the Irish arriving in Glasgow at the rate of one thousand a week during the potato famine of the 1840s.

By the late nineteenth century a measure of prosperity had emerged from industrialization, and the well-paid Clydeside engineers went to their forges wearing bowler hats and starched collars. They were confident of the future, but their optimism was misplaced. Scotland's industries were very much geared to the export market, and after **World War I** they found conditions much changed. During the war years, when exports had been curtailed by a combination of U-boat activity and war production, new industries had developed in India and Japan, and the eastern market for Scottish goods never recovered. The post-war world also witnessed a contraction of world trade, which hit the shipbuilding industry very hard and, in turn, damaged the steel and coal industries. By 1931, for instance, pig iron production was at less than 25 percent of its 1920 output.

These difficulties were compounded by the financial collapse of the early 1930s, and by 1932 28 percent of the Scottish workforce was unemployed. Four hundred thousand Scots emigrated between 1921 and 1931, and those who stayed endured some of the worst social conditions in the British Isles. By the late 1930s, Scotland had the highest infant mortality rate in Europe, while some 30 percent of homes had no toilet or bath. There was a partial economic recovery in the mid-1930s, but high unemployment remained until the start of **World War II**.

THE LABOUR MOVEMENT

In the late eighteenth century, conditions for the labouring population varied enormously. At one extreme, the handloom weavers, working from home, were well-paid and much in demand, whereas the coal miners remained serfs, bought and sold with the pits they worked in, until 1799. During this period, the working class gave some support to the **radical movement**, those loosely connected groups of reformers, led by the lower middle class, who took their inspiration from the French Revolution. One of these groups, "The Friends of the People", campaigned for the extension of the right to vote, and such apparently innocuous activities earnt one member, Thomas Muir, a sentence of 14 years transportation to Australia.

In 1820, the radicals called for a national strike and an insurrection to "show the world that we are . . . determined to be free". At least 60,000 workers downed tools for a week, and one group set off for the Carron Ironworks to seize arms. The government was, however, well prepared. It slammed radical leaders into prison and a heavy military presence kept control of the streets. The strike fizzled out and three leading radicals, all weavers, were later executed.

The 1832 Scottish Reform Act extended the franchise to include a large proportion of the middle class and thereafter political radicalism assumed a more distinctive working-class character, though its ideals still harked back to the American and French revolutions. In the 1840s, the **Chartists** led the campaign for working-class political rights by sending massive petitions to Parliament and organizing huge demonstrations. When Parliament rejected the petitions, the more determined Chartists – the "physical-force men" – urged insurrection. This call to arms was not taken up by the Scottish working class, however, and support for the Chartists fell away. The insurrectionary phase of Scottish labour was over.

During the next 30 years, as Scotland's economy prospered, skilled workers organized themselves into craft **unions**, such as the Amalgamated Society of Engineers, dedicated to negotiating improvements for their members within the status quo. Politically, the trade unions gave their allegiance to the Liberal Party, but the first major crack in the Liberal–Union alliance came in 1888, when **Keir Hardie** left the Liberals to form the Scottish Socialist Party, which was later merged with the Independent Labour Party, founded in Bradford in 1893. Scottish socialism as represented by the ILP was ethical rather than Marxist in orientation, owing a great deal to the Kirk background of many of its members. But electoral progress was slow, partly because the Roman Catholic priesthood consistently preached against socialism.

In the early years of the twentieth century, two small Marxist groups established themselves on Clydeside: the **Socialist Labour Party**, which concentrated on workplace militancy, and the party-political **British Socialist Party**, whose most famous member was the Marxist lecturer John MacLean. During World War I, the local organizers of the SLP gained considerable influence by playing on the fears of the skilled workers, who felt their status was being undermined by the employment of unskilled workers. After the war, the influence of the shop stewards culminated in a massive campaign for the 40-hour working week. The strikes and demonstrations of the campaign,

including one of 100,000 people in St George's Square in Glasgow, panicked the government into sending in the troops. But this was no Bolshevik Revolution – as Emmanuel Shinwell, the seamen's leader and future Labour Party politician, observed, "[the troops] had nothing much to do but chat to the local people and drink their cups of tea". The rank-and-file may have had little interest in revolution, but many of the activists did go on to become leaders within the newly formed Communist Party of Great Britain.

The ILP, now an affiliated part of the socialist **Labour Party**, made its electoral breakthrough in 1922, when it sent 29 Scottish MPs to Westminster. They set out with high hopes of social progress and reform, aspirations that were dashed, like trade union militancy, by the 1930s Depression. At the 1945 general election, Labour won 40 seats in Scotland and, in more recent times, the party has dominated Scottish politics with its gradual eclipse of the Scottish Conservatives: in 1955 the Conservatives held 36 Scottish seats, while in 1995 they had just ten.

Labour's position in Scotland is not, however, completely secure. The ILP MPs of the 1920s combined their socialism with a brand of Scottish nationalism. In 1924, for instance, the MP James Maxton had declared his intentions to "make English-ridden, capitalist-ridden Scotland into the Scottish socialist Commonwealth". The Labour Party maintained an official policy of self-government for Scotland, endorsing home rule in 1945 and 1947, but these endorsements were made with less and less enthusiasm. In 1958, Labour abandoned the commitment altogether and adopted a unionist vision of Scotland, much to the chagrin of many Scottish activists.

In 1971, **Upper Clyde Shipbuilders** stood on the brink of closure, its demise symbolizing the failure of traditional Labour politicians to revive Scotland's industrial base, which had resumed its decline after the end of World War II. In the event, UCS was partly saved by the work-in organized by two Communist shop stewards, Jimmy Reid and Jimmy Airlie. After 14 months, the work-in finally succeeded in winning government support to keep part of the shipyard open, and Scots saw the broadly based campaign waged on its behalf as a national issue – Scottish industries set against an indifferent London government. Many socialist Scots, like James Jack, General Secretary of the Scottish TUC, moved towards some form of nationalism. Twenty-one years later the closure of the steelworks at Ravenscraig, Motherwell, revived many of the same emotions.

THE NATIONALISTS

The **National Party of Scotland** was formed in 1928, its membership averaging about 7000 people, mostly drawn from the non-industrial parts of the country. Very much a mixture of practical politicians and left-leaning eccentrics, such as the poet Hugh MacDiarmid, in 1934 it merged with the right-wing Scottish Party to create the **Scottish National Party**. The SNP, after years in the political wilderness, achieved its electoral breakthrough in 1967 when Winnie Ewing won Hamilton from Labour in a by-election. The following year the SNP won 34 percent of the vote in local government elections and gained control of Cumbernauld, successes that had repercussions within both the Labour and Conservative parties. Both began to work on schemes to give Scotland a measure of self-government, and the term **"Devolution"** was coined. The objective in both cases was to head off the nationalists.

When the Conservatives came to power in 1970, Edward Heath, the prime minister, shelved plans for devolution because the SNP had only secured a 12 percent share of the Scottish vote. The situation changed dramatically in 1974, when Labour were returned to power with a wafer-thin majority. The SNP held seven seats, which gave them considerable political leverage. Devolution was back on the agenda. The SNP had also run an excellent election campaign, concentrating on North Sea oil, which was now being piped ashore in significant quantities. Their two most popular slogans, "England expects . . . Scotland's oil" and "Rich Scots or Poor Britons?", seemed to have caught the mood of Scotland.

The Labour government put its devolution proposals before the Scottish people in a **referendum** on March 1, 1979. The "yes" vote gained 33 percent, the "no" vote 31 percent; although a majority in favour, it was not by the required 40 percent. Not for the first time, Scottish opinion had shifted away from home rule; the reluctance to embrace it was based on uncertainty about what might follow, a concern about too many layers of government and, in some areas, a fear that the resulting assembly might be dominated by the Clydeside conurbation. The incoming Conservative government of Margaret Thatcher set its face against any form of devolution. They argued that the majority of Scots had voted for parties committed to the Union – namely Labour, the Liberal Democrats and themselves – and that only a minority supported the separation advocated by the SNP. At the same time, they asserted that any form of devolution must lead inevitably to the break-up of the United Kingdom and, therefore, that the devolution solutions put forward by other parties could not be what the Scottish people wanted, because the inescapable result would be separation.

To judge by the evidence of opinion polls and central and local government elections, few Scottish voters accepted either this reasoning or the implication that Scots did not know what was good for them. The Conservatives' support in Scotland was further eroded by their introduction of the deeply unpopular **Community Charge** – universally nicknamed the Poll Tax – a form of local taxation that was charged essentially on a per capita basis and took little account of income. The fact that it had been imposed in Scotland a year earlier than in England and Wales was the source of further resentment. In 1992, having largely rejected Conservative ideology and all but a few of the party's candidates, Scots found themselves once again under the Tory government of John Major. Though some Scottish Conservatives quietly supported devolution, their limited influence in the party as a whole was evident in the appointment of Michael Forsyth, one of the most articulate advocates of Thatcherite policy, as Secretary of State for Scotland in the 1995 Cabinet reshuffle.

Throughout the 1980s and 90s, the case for devolution has been made consistently by both Labour and the Liberal Democrats. In 1989, they, together with a cross-section of Scottish organizations, including local government, churches and trade unions, co-operated in the establishment of the **Scottish Constitutional Convention**, a standing conference that has developed detailed proposals for the introduction of a devolved Scottish Assembly. At the time, the SNP saw the Convention as a diversion from their aim of an independent Scotland firmly attached to the European Union and did not join. Since then, however, nationalists have begun to argue that devolution might after all offer a stepping-stone to independence; and not surprisingly, the Conservatives have seized on this as confirmation of their view.

Although the case for devolution has been widely accepted within Scotland, there remain questions about its consequences for the British parliament and constitution. Indeed, the outspoken Member of Parliament for West Lothian, Labour's Tam Dalyell, has criticized his own party for its alleged failure to answer what has become known as the West Lothian Question. Simply put, should Scottish MPs continue to have the same amount of influence over the affairs of the rest of Britain once a Scottish parliament has been established? This is an awkward issue for the Labour Party, because any numerical reduction in Scottish representation at Westminster would threaten its ability to form a British government. There has been no enthusiasm in England, and less than might perhaps have been expected in Wales, for the devolved English and Welsh parliaments that would be needed to create directly equivalent structures in those countries.

THE FUTURE

If the political outlook is uncertain, the same is true of **the economy**. In central Scotland, the decline of the heavy industries, including deep coal-mining, steelmaking, shipbuilding and engineering, has been all but complete. Unemployment has produced profound social problems in parts of Glasgow, Edinburgh and smaller towns. However, there has been a notable growth in service industries; for example, financial services and insurance have had a substantial impact in Edinburgh, Glasgow and some smaller centres such as Perth and Dunfermline. In northeast Scotland, particularly around Aberdeen, the oil industry — although past its boom — continues to underpin an econ-

omy which might otherwise have struggled to cope with the uncertainties of agriculture and, especially, fishing.

Though there have been encouraging signs of recent progress, the Highlands and islands remain an economically fragile area that needs special measures — distance from markets being an obvious and fundamental problem. Prosperity of a temporary sort has been provided in some areas by oil, but the best options for the future are likely to lie in selective, high-quality development in fishing, fish farming and other food-based industries, activities based on the telecommunications network, primary industries such as forestry and quarrying and, last but certainly not least, tourism. Increasingly, the local environment is seen as a major asset for the attraction and success of most kinds of employment. One of the keys to Highland development, some would say the most important of all, is the ownership and control of land. Some of the largest Highland estates continue to be owned and managed from afar, with little regard to local needs or priorities; the recent success of a group of crofters in buying an estate in Assynt may point the way ahead for other communities.

Unquestionably the most striking change in Scotland in the last decade has been a **cultural renaissance**. Especially notable has been the revival of Gaelic, supported by large investments in broadcasting and publishing and demonstrated by the huge popularity among young audiences — few of them Gaels — of bands like Runrig and Capercaillie. But the transformation goes beyond that: old inhibitions about writing in Scots or in Shetland dialect have been laid to rest too, and much of Glasgow's recent success is attributed to the city's focus on the arts. In the light of this cultural confidence, many regard the resolution of present political uncertainties as the key to the release of the country's potential in a new century. It remains to be seen whether such a resolution will be forthcoming, what form it will take and what its effects will be.

THE
WILDLIFE OF
SCOTLAND

A comprehensive account of Scotland's wildlife would take a whole book to cover; what follows is a general overview of the effects of climate and human activity on the country's flora and fauna.

CLIMATE

Scotland's mountains are high enough to impose harsh conditions, especially in the Highlands, and the **Cairngorm plateau** (the largest area of high ground in the whole of Britain) is almost arctic even in summer. Despite this, however, since the easing of the Ice Age about 10,000 years ago, Scotland has developed a rather complex climate, and some areas of the country are quite mild.

The Atlantic tempers conditions on the west coast, and in winter the warmish water of the Gulf Stream swings north, so that at **Inverewe**, for example, you'll find incongruously lush gardens blooming with subtropical plants. Inland, the weather becomes more extreme, but what restricts plant life on many Scottish hills is not the cold so much as the stress of wind and gloomy cloud cover. **Ben Nevis**, for example, is clouded and whipped by 50mph gales for more than two-thirds of the year, and as a result, the tree line – the height to which trees grow up the slopes – may be only 150ft above sea level near the west coast,

but up to over 2000ft on some of the sheltered hillsides inland.

A BRIEF HISTORY

After the Ice Age, "arctic" and "alpine" plants abounded, eventually giving way to woody shrubs and trees, notably the Scots pine. Oak and other hardwood trees followed in some places, but the **Scots pine** remained the distinctive tree, spreading expansively to form the great **Caledonian Forest**. Parts of this ancient forest still remain, miraculously surviving centuries of attack, but it is only comparatively recently that attempts at positive conservation have been made.

Early **settlement**, from the Picts to the Norsemen, led to clearance of large areas of forest, and huge areas were burnt during the clan wars. When centuries of unrest ended with the Jacobite defeat at Culloden in 1745, the glens were ransacked for timber, which was floated downriver to fuel iron smelting and other industries. The clansmen had had a free-booting cattle economy, but during the infamous **Clearances**, both the cattle and the defeated Highlanders were replaced by the more profitable sheep of the new landlords. As also happened on the English downland and moorland, intensive sheep grazing kept the land open, eventually destroying much woodland by preventing natural regeneration.

In Victorian times **red deer** herds, which also graze heavily, provided stalking, and when rapid firing breech-loading guns came into general use around the 1860s, **grouse** shooting became a passion. It's strange to think of birds changing the scenery, but grouse graze heather and thus large areas are burnt to encourage fresh green growth. No tree saplings survive and the open moorland is maintained.

The flatter **lowlands** are now dominated by mechanized farming; barley, beef, turnips and potatoes conspire against wildlife, and pollution and development are as damaging here as elsewhere. Even the so-called **"wilderness"** is under threat. Its own popularity obviously holds dangers, and the unique flora of the Cairngorm peaks, for example, is in danger of being stamped out under the feet of the summer visitors using the ski lifts. But even more damaging than tourism is **conifer planting**. In recent decades, boosted (if not caused) by generous grant aid and tax dodges, large areas of open moorland have been planted with tightly packed monocultural ranks of foreign conifers, forbidding to much wildlife. Coniferization is particularly threatening to large areas of bogland in the "Flow Country" of Caithness and elsewhere, areas that are as unique a natural environment as the tropical rainforests. For these and other similar habitats, registration as an **SSSI** – a Site of Special Scientific Interest – has proved barely adequate, and the only real safeguard is for such areas to be owned or managed by organizations such as **Scottish Nature** (the national agency) or the **Scottish Wildlife Trust**, the **Royal Society for the Protection of Birds** and similar voluntary groups.

WILD FLOWERS

Relic patches of the Scots pine Caledonian Forest, such as the Black Wood of Rannoch and Rothiemurchus Forest below the Cairngorms, are often more open than an oak wood, the pines, interspersed with birch and juniper, spaced out in hilly heather. These woods feature some wonderful wild flowers, such as the **wintergreens** which justify their name, unobtrusive **orchids** in the shape of creeping lady's tresses and lesser twayblade, and, in parts of the northeast especially, the rare beauty of the **twinflower**, holding its paired heads over the summer **needle litter**.

You'll also find old oak woods in some places, especially in the lower coastward lengths of the southern glens. Here the Atlantic influence encourages masses of English bluebell, **wood anemone** and other spring flowers. (In Scotland the English bluebell is known as the **wild hyacinth**, the Scots keeping the name "bluebell" for the summer-flowering English harebell that grows on more open ground.) Scotland, or at least lowland Scotland, has many flowers found further south in Britain – **maiden pink**, orchids, **cowslip** and others in grassy areas. Roadside flowers, such as **meadowsweet** and **meadow buttercup**, **dog rose**, **primrose** and **red campion**, extend widely up through Scotland, but others, such as the **white field rose** and **mistletoe**, **red valerian**, **small scabious**, **cuckoo pint** and **travellers joy** (and the elm tree), reach the end of their range in the Scottish central lowlands.

Scotland's mountains, especially where the rock is limey or basic in character, as on Ben Lawers, for example, are dotted with arctic–alpine plants, such as mountain **avens**, with their white flowers and glossy oak-like leaves, and handsome **purple saxifrage**, both of which favour a soil rich in calcium. Here as elsewhere, the flowers are to be found on ledges and rock faces out of reach of the sheep and deer. Other classic mountain plants are **alpine lady's mantle** and **moss campion**, which grows in a tight cushion, set with single pink flowers.

Higher up on the bleak wind-battered mountain tops, there may be nothing much more than a low "heath" of mosses and maybe some tough low grasses or rushes between the scatterings of rubble. Because this environment encourages few insects, such plants are generally self-fertilizing and some even produce small plants or "bulbils" in their flower heads instead of seed.

A variety of ferns shelter in the slopes amid the tumbled rock screes or in cracks in the rock alongside streams. In Scotland's damp climate, you'll also see many ferns on lower ground, but some, the **holly fern** for one, are true mountain species. **Lichens**, too, are common on exposed rocks, and in the woods bushy and bearded lichens can coat the branches and trunks.

Bogs are a natural feature of much of the flatter ground in the Highlands, often extending for miles. Scottish bogland comprises an intricate mosaic of domes of living bog moss (sometimes bright green or a striking orange or yellow), domes of drier, heathery peat, and pools dotted in between. The wettest areas give rise to specialized plants such as **cranberry**, **bearberry** and also the **sundews**, which gain nutrients in these poor surroundings by trapping and absorbing midges with the sticky hairs on their flat leaves.

At sea level, the rivers spawn estuaries; these and some sea lochs are edged with **salt-marshes**, which in time dry out into "meadows" colourful with **sea aster** and other flowers. The west coast, especially the cliffs of Galloway, shimmers blue with **spring squill** as soon as the winter eases, while the Galloway shore marks the southernmost limit of **Scots lovage**, a celery-scented member of the cow parsley family. A relic of arctic times, the **oysterplant**, with blue-grey leaves and pink bell flowers, also grows here, as it does on the shores of Iceland and Scandinavia.

Scotland has some wonderful **sand dune** systems, which on the back shores harden into grassy patches often grazed by rabbits to create a fine turf.

BIRDLIFE

It might seem unexpected to find birds nesting at over 3000ft, but in Scotland the wind is strong enough to blow patches of icy ground clear of snow, enabling birds to make their homes on the mountains. The **dotterel**, a small wader with a chestnut stomach, is a rare summer visitor to the Cairngorms and other heights – in the Arctic it nests down to sea level. Even rarer is the **snow bunting**, the male black and white, the female brownish – perhaps only ten pairs nest on Scotland's mountains, although they are seen much more widely around the coasts in winter, when the male also becomes brown. The **snowy owl**, at the southern limit of its range, is a regular visitor to Shetland.

More common on the heights is the **ptarmigan**, shy and almost invisible in its summer coat, as it plays hide and seek amongst the lichen-patched boulders – you're most likely to see it on the Cairngorms, as it ventures out for the sandwich crusts left by the summer visitors using the ski lifts. It is resident up here, and moults from mottled in summer to pure white in winter.

The ptarmigan's camouflage helps protect it from the **golden eagle**. This magnificent bird ranges across many Highland areas – there are perhaps three hundred nesting pairs on Skye, the Outer Hebrides, above Aviemore and Deeside, and in the northwest Highlands, each needing a territory of thousands of acres over which to hunt hares, grouse and ptarmigan. The **raven** also has strong links with the mountains, tumbling in crazy acrobatics past the rock faces.

Where the slopes lessen to moorland, the domain of the **red grouse** begins. This game bird not only affects the landscape but also, via the persecution of gamekeepers, threatens eagles and other birds of prey, although they are all theoretically protected. The **cuckoo** might be heard as far north as Shetland – one of its favourite dupes, the **meadow pipit**, is

fairly widespread on any rough ground up to 3000ft. **Dunlin** and other waders nest on the wet moorlands and boglands, where the soft land allows them to use their delicate bills to probe for insects and other food.

You'll come across many notable birds where pine woods encroach onto open moor. One such is the **black grouse**, with its bizarre courtship rituals, when both sexes come together for aggressive, ritualistic display in a small gathering area known as a "lek". The **capercaillie**, found deeper in the forest and perhaps floundering amongst the branches, is an unexpectedly large, turkey-like bird, about three feet from bill to end of tail, which also has a flamboyant courting display. A game bird, it was shot to extinction but reintroduced into Scotland from Europe in 1837. Other birds that favour the pine woods are the **long-eared owl**, many of the **tit** family (including the crested tit in the Spey valley), the **siskin** and the **goldcrest**. The Speyside woods, especially, are a stronghold of the **crossbill**, which uses its overlapping bill to prise open the pine cones.

Scottish **lochs** are as rich in birdlife as the moorlands that embrace them. After fifty years of absence, the **osprey** returned and is now breeding and fishing the waters of Loch Garten and elsewhere. In addition to common species such as **mallard** and **tufted duck**, you might also see **goosander**, **red-breasted merganser** and other wildfowl. The superbly streamlined fish-eating **red-** and **black-throated divers** nest in the northwest, while the **great northern diver**, with its shivery wailing call, is largely a winter visitor on the coasts, though one or two pairs may occasionally nest.

Scotland is also strong on **coastal birds**. **Eider duck** gather in their thousands at the mouth of the Tay, and the estuaries are also a magnet for **waders** and **wild geese** in winter: the total population of barnacle geese from the Arctic island of Spitsbergen winters in the Solway estuary and on the farmland alongside. Other areas to head for if you're interested in seabirds are remote cliffs such as St Abb's Head in the Borders, and the many offshore **"bird islands"**, which, although often little more than bare rock, attract vast colonies that fish the sea around them. Some have their own speciality – **Manx shearwaters** have vast colonies on Rhum for example, while the Shetland isle of Foula has about a third (three thousand pairs) of all the **great skuas** breeding in the northern hemisphere. Remote St Kilda is also stunning, with snowstorms of **gannets**, **puffins**, **guillemots**, **petrels** and **shearwaters**.

In addition to Scotland's resident bird population, and the winter and spring migrants, the western coasts and islands often see transatlantic "accidentals" blown far off course, which give rise to inbred **subspecies**. St Kilda is of particular interest to specialists, not only for its sheer numbers of resident birds but also for the **St Kilda wren**, a distinct subspecies. In northern and parts of eastern Scotland the English all-black carrion crow is replaced by the **"hoodie"** or hooded crow, also found around the Mediterranean, with its distinctive grey back and underparts. Where the ranges of carrion crow and hoodie overlap, they interbreed, producing offspring with some grey patches of plumage.

MAMMALS

By the mid-eighteenth century, much of Scotland's wild animal life – including the Scottish **wolf**, **beaver**, **wild boar** and **elk** – had already disappeared. Although the indigenous **reindeer** was wiped out in the twelfth century, more recently a semi-wild herd of Swedish stock was reintroduced to the slopes of the Cairngorms above Aviemore. Of two other semi-wild species – **Highland cattle** and **Shetland ponies** – the first is a classic case of breeding fitting conditions (they can survive in snowy conditions for fifty days a year), while the second, the smallest British native pony, probably arrived in the later stages of the Ice Age when the ice was retreating but still gave a bridge across the salt water. There are feral **goats** in some places, but probably the most interesting of such animals is the **Soay sheep** of St Kilda. This, Britain's only truly wild sheep, notable for its soft brown fleece, can be seen as a farm pet and in wildlife parks – and is even used to graze some nature reserves in the south of Britain.

Although there are **sika** and **fallow deer** in places, and **roe deer** are widespread, Scotland is the stronghold of **wild red deer** herds, which, despite culling, stalking for sport and harsh winters, still number more than quarter

of a million head. By origin a woodland animal, they might graze open ground – of necessity when the forest has been cleared – but they also move up to high ground in summer to avoid the biting flies and the tourists, and to graze on heather and lichens.

The **fox** is widespread, as are the **mole** and **hedgehog**, but the **badger** is rather more rare. The **wild cat** and **pine marten** live in remote areas, hiding away in the moors and forests. The former, despite its initial resemblance to the family pet, is actually quite different – larger, with longer, striped fur, and a blunt-ended bushy tail that is also striped. The agile cat-sized pine marten, although hunted by gamekeepers, is maintaining reduced numbers, preying on squirrels and other small animals.

Native red **squirrels** are predominantly found in the Highlands, where they are still largely free from competition from the grey, which began to establish themselves about a century ago and now have a strong presence in many lowland areas. **Rabbit** and **brown hare** are widespread, as are the **blue** or **mountain hare** in the Highlands, usually adopting a white or patchy white coat in winter. The north Scottish **stoat** also dons a white winter coat, its tail tipped with black, when it is known as ermine. Although Scotland is too far north for the dormouse and the harvest mouse, **shrews**, **voles** and **field mice** abound, and though there are few bats, the related **pipistrelle** is quite widely seen.

You may also be lucky enough to encounter the **otter**, endangered in the rest of Britain. In Scotland, the otter is found not only in the rushing becks but more often along the western coast and islands, where it hunts the seashore for crabs and inshore fish. The otter is not to be confused with the feral **mink**, escaped from fur farms to take up life in the wild; these mink are a scourge in some areas, destroying birds.

Whales and their kin are frequent visitors to coastal waters and **seals**, including the shy grey seal, are quite common. However, in the hitherto virgin sea lochs of the west coast, both the seals and the coastal otters are under threat from the spread of **fish farms** (for salmon and sea trout). Not only are they poisoned by the chemicals used to keep the trapped fish vermin-free, but they also face the threat of being shot by the fish farm owners when they raid what is to them simply a natural larder.

FISH, REPTILES & INSECTS

Quite apart from the Loch Ness monster, Scotland has a rich water life. The Dee and other rivers are famous **salmon rivers**, fished when the salmon swim upstream to breed in their ancestral gravel headwaters. The fish leap waterfalls on the way, and many rivers which have been dammed or barricaded have "salmon ladders" to help them – these make great tourist attractions. The **sea trout** is also strongly migratory, the **brown or mountain trout** less so, although river or stream dwellers do move upstream and lake dwellers up the incoming rivers to spawn. Related to these game fish is the **powan or freshwater herring**, found only in the poorer northern basins of Loch Lomond, and possibly a relic from Ice Age arctic conditions. The richer southern waters of Loch Lomond and similar lakes contain **roach**, **perch** and other "coarse" fish.

Although the **adder** is common, the **grass snake** is not found in Scotland. Both **lizards** and the snake-like **slowworm** (in fact a legless lizard) are widespread, as are the **frog** and **toad**; the natterjack toad, however, is rarely seen this far north.

Scottish boglands are notable for their **dragon flies**, which prefer acid water, and **hawkers**, **darters** and **damselflies** feature in the south. One Scottish particular is the **blue hawker**, common in parts of the western Highlands. As for **butterflies**, some of the familiar types from further south – common blue, hairstreaks and others – are scattered in areas where conditions are not too harsh. One species with a liking for the heights is the **mountain ringlet**, only seen elsewhere in the Lake District and in the Alps, which flies above 1500ft in the Grampians. Adapted to quite harsh conditions, it is clearly a relic of early post-glacial times. Another mountain butterfly, the **Scotch argus**, no longer found in England or Wales, is widespread in Scotland, and the **elephant hawk moth** can be seen in the Insh marshes below the Cairngorms.

THE ARCHITECTURE OF SCOTLAND

From crofts to castles, the Victorian grand residence to the "new towns", Scotland has a rich legacy of strong, unique buildings. Stonework predominates, from the long houses of the Western Isles to the soft red sandstone that fills the streets of Glasgow. Surrounding countries have also had a substantial influence: the settlements in Orkney and Shetland are linked with the Norse kingdoms, while the ruined church architecture of the central belt is testimony to a long history of battles with the marauding English.

PREHISTORIC TIMES TO THE THIRTEENTH CENTURY

One morning in 1850, after a ferocious storm, the villagers of Orkney woke to find **Skara Brae** (see p.470) – one of the earliest prehistoric sites in Scotland – revealed beneath the beautiful white sands. Situated 19 miles northwest of Kirkwall, this **Neolithic** stone village is so well preserved that you can still see domestic details, typical of the age, such as flagstone box beds, built due to the lack of timber on the islands. Small passages unite what must have been quite a large and intricate settlement of stock farmers, who originally came to Scotland from mainland Europe; a turf roof provided insulation from wind and cold. The chambered

tombs at **Maes Howe** (Orkney; see p.471) are another great architectural achievement, dating from 2750 BC and complete with Viking graffiti from later raids on the islands. These tombs are remarkably well constructed, incorporating monoliths into the fine masonry that supports the narrow passages and small tomb cells. A fairly large community also existed at the **Jarlshof** prehistoric and Norse settlement on Shetland (see p.495), where small stone cells grouped around a central hearth provided the main accommodation, with now ruined outhouses used for bronze work and sheltering cattle. The survival of a number of ritual sites, including many **stone circles**, suggests some form of religious activity in Scotland at this time. One of the most beautiful and well preserved stands at **Callanish** (Lewis; see p.320), where a circle of megaliths rise majestically from the ground with radiating lines of stone in a mysteriously symbolic form. The central stone is nearly 16ft high and sits next to a small chambered cairn, which may have once contained human remains.

Thick-walled stone settlements, such as Skara Brae, were forerunners of the **long house**. Low and narrow single-storey buildings with small windows, a central hearth and turf roof, long houses provided excellent protection from the rough winter winds and were, consequently, still being built up until the end of the nineteenth century. Today they can be seen all over the Western Isles, painted white, often with modern corrugated iron roofs and commonly used for storage.

During the **Bronze Age**, from around 1000 BC, the two predominant types of defensive settlements, made from earth and timber, were spectacular **hill forts**, and artificial islands built in the middle of lochs, called **crannogs**; little now remains of either of these. It wasn't until the **Iron Age** (from around 400 BC) that the next significant architectural development was to occur. For residents of the northwest mainland and the northern islands the need for protection from attack or invasion and from the harshness of the weather was particularly extreme, and so it's here that most of Scotland's 400 or so **brochs**, the majority in ruins, can be found. Circular, windowless and tall – some over 40ft high – these drystone buildings were sturdily built to protect the inhabitants who lived inside, sheltered underneath wooden constructions. Broad at the bottom and narrow at the top, the unusual shape was due to the necessity for a thick base to support the high walls and provide storage and guard rooms. Brochs also had two walls and a spiral staircase leading up to a timber roof – a very useful vantage point. Some were inhabited for several centuries; the finest example is the **Broch of Mousa** from c.100 BC in Shetland (see p.494), which is remarkably well preserved due to its isolated position on a small island, free from the stone stealing that plagued subsequent settlements.

While the north of Scotland generally suffered attack from the Vikings, it was the **Romans** who threatened the Scottish border in 83 AD. Their success was limited, however, and the civilizing influence of Rome was to have barely any effect on the life and tribes of Scotland, who continued to live in brochs and crannogs, or erect primitive buildings of timber, wattle and clay regardless. Of the Roman structures that have survived, the most impressive are the remnants of the **Antonine Wall**, a 36-mile-long construction that stretched from Kilpatrick to Bo'ness. Less substantial than the great Hadrian's Wall, it was originally built as a temporary measure to aid the overthrow of the fierce Pictish tribes, but was soon abandoned.

The subsequent introduction of **Christianity** left a much greater architectural legacy in Scotland. The primitive church of 397 AD at **Whithorn** of (see p.146 marks one of the earliest Christian sites in Scotland, and with the arrival of St Columba at Iona in 563, the Celtic Christian community really came to dominate the country's religious matters. Evidence of this can be seen in the characteristic **round towers** at **Brechin** (Angus; see p.384) and **Egilsay** (Orkney; see p.480). Places of refuge for the monastic fellowship during times of attack, these were well defended with a raised entrance and few windows. The simple and basic structures of the Irish Celtic church conveyed their ascetic religious beliefs, while artistic and creative energies were poured into the making of sculpted crosses and illuminated manuscripts. Fine carving survives at the monastic foundation at **Iona** (see p.276), a religious community that still thrives today. Few other such buildings remain, indicating that they were constructed from materials like timber, clay and turf.

The marriage of Malcolm III to the Saxon princess Margaret, in 1070, signified a dramatic upsurge in Scottish architecture. Malcolm created a feudal society based on agriculture and, more importantly, his wife orchestrated the re-introduction of Latin Christianity to the central areas of Scotland, founding many ecclesiastical buildings and finally bringing a European influence to this region – while the Highlands and islands continued to build in the vernacular tradition. The **Romanesque** (or Norman) style can be seen at its best in **Dalmeny Church** (see p.87). This simple, thick-walled three-cell church has narrow window openings and a round arched doorway crowned by typically Romanesque wall arcading. The Anglo-Norman influence also created larger buildings, cruciform in plan with aisled naves and three storey elevations; these were not actual physical levels but would consist of arches, a middle storey, usually formed by blind arches or decorative wall hangings but sometimes an actual gallery for the local notables, and at the top, stained-glass windows. The thick piers and semicircular arches of **Dunfermline Abbey** (Fife; see p.228) are typically Norman. However, it was the Cistercians who brought the significant pointed arch and lancet window to Scotland and introduced the **Gothic** style to the country's craftsmen. As buildings were either reconstructed or modified in future centuries, the church at **Dunstaffnage** (Argyll; see p.268), with its simple rectangular plan and lancet windows, is a rare example of Early Gothic design. The twelfth-century abbey at **Jedburgh** in the Borders (see p.127) was just one of the abbeys that housed the religious communities being imported from England and France to southern and central parts of the country. Now in ruins, this church is very much in the transitional style between Romanesque and Gothic, as the west front contains a Romanesque round-arched doorway with a thirteenth-century rose window in the main gable. One of the most complete of the ruined Border Abbeys, **Dryburgh Abbey** (see p.121), in beautiful red sandstone, has an unusual vertical emphasis in the main arcade. **Melrose Abbey** (see p.119) contains examples of High Gothic detail, such as delicate tracery and flying buttresses, while **Kelso Abbey** (see p.117) stands out for its simplicity and massive proportions. These great Scottish

Abbeys, with the exception of the austere Cistercian communities, would have been richly decorated with tapestries, murals and carved furnishings. Unfortunately, their position in the southeast of Scotland left them vulnerable to attack from the English and they suffered badly as a result.

In the thirteenth century, the Norman kings brought a more settled period, establishing their authority through a network of loyal nobles who controlled parts of the country but recognized the king as overall ruler. This allowed for the building of great cathedrals, notably those of Glasgow and Elgin. **Glasgow Cathedral** (see p.170) is Scotland's only complete medieval cathedral to survive the Reformation, the verticality of the interior and elegance of the clustered piers monuments to the power of the Gothic tradition. The building itself is an amalgam of influences, from the Early Pointed style of the east end of the choir to the magnificent Late Gothic vaulting of the lower church, and is a poignant reminder of the wealth of architecture that has been lost to the nation over the years. **Elgin Cathedral** (see p.384), once "the ornament of the realm", with its unusual double aisles and rich furnishings, was an extravagant Anglo-Saxon statement of refinement and power, built to impress the Highland clans. It is now in ruins after it was destroyed in 1390 by an earl angry at being excommunicated for leaving his wife.

The popular image of the great Scottish **castle**, the stuff of myth and legend, perched on a rocky crag and often surrounded by woodlands, heather and deer, is remarkably different from the cold reality of daily castle living. Rising in stone above the small peasant dwellings of turf and timber, the castle was a centre of administrative and judicial control, as well as a secure place in times of conflict. **Castle Sween** on Loch Sween (see p.283) is the earliest stone castle in Scotland, built in the eleventh century with a Norman-style round arched doorway leading into the centre of the quadrangular building, once roofed with timber. With its origins in the twelfth century, **Edinburgh Castle** (see p.58) stands out as the archetypal royal Scottish castle. Built on an extinct volcano, it commanded a strong strategic position and served throughout much of its history as a resonant symbol of power and protection. The epitome of the romantic Highland castle,

on the other hand, is the beautifully picturesque **Eilean Donan** on Loch Duich (see p.426), ten miles south of the Kyle of Lochalsh. Originally a small thirteenth-century castle of enclosure, it was used to garrison Spanish troops as part of the Jacobite Rising, and was destroyed by English warships in 1719. The present building is predominantly a reconstruction, initiated at the beginning of the century, an immaculate three-storey keep perched on a rocky outcrop with a dramatic arched bridge.

Developments in warfare and architecture marched hand in hand, and thirteenth-century castles employed a number of defensive techniques: the use of catapults and assault towers, the strengthening of outer walls, and construction of round towers to allow for a better view of the base. Two miles north of Oban, the tall, thick walls of **Dunstaffnage** (see p.268) are topped with a crenellated wall walk and contain few windows but many well-placed firing slits; an outer defence like the moat at **Rothesay** (Isle of Bute; see p.261), which was established c.1204, was also common. Natural defences such as rocky outcrops were particularly impenetrable; **Dirleton Castle** (near North Berwick; see p.111) uses one to great advantage, its weaker side protected by three towers forcing outwards in an aggressive manner, and **Stirling Castle** is similarly well defended (see p.206). Situated on a grassy hilltop, the reinforced tower at **Bothwell Castle** (near Blantyre; see p.198) provided an effective last refuge in an attack.

THE FOURTEENTH AND FIFTEENTH CENTURIES

With the power of the monarch declining and the nobility fighting for territory and power, the **fourteenth century** was a time of great strife and warfare in Scotland; consequently, law and order were overthrown and few buildings constructed. The destruction predominantly affected the Lowlands; the Highlanders being a law unto themselves within their own social system, strategically using the mountains to defend their proud autonomy. Castles continued to be strengthened, often growing in size to accommodate larger buildings. The impressive fourteenth-century castles of **Tantallon** (near North Berwick; see p.112) and **Doune** (Perthshire; see p.211) both contain a massive gatehouse employed to protect the entrance, and provide the lord with accommodation. This gave him full control of the castle's defences, necessary at a time when hired mercenaries were commonly used in private armies. For lesser nobles, the **tower house** was the perfect solution to the conflicting problems of comfort and defence. The tower house became a popular high security residence, being smaller and cheaper than a great castle. Tall and narrow with smooth walls and few windows, these buildings featured a raised entrance and crenellated parapet as the main elements of passive defence – relying on thick walls and great height for effect. Being of a simple yet flexible design, the majority were expanded and decorated in later centuries, and none exist in their original form (see "Sixteenth and Seventeenth Centuries" for examples).

The **fifteenth century**, fluctuating between periods of war and peace, allowed tower houses to retain their popularity among the lesser nobles, being secure, yet comfortable enough for everyday living. High Gothic principles became established in ecclesiastical buildings, and the construction of the great royal residences introduced the spirit of the **Early Renaissance** to Scotland. In the 1420s, James I began to rebuild **Linlithgow Palace** (see p.220) and by 1500 it had become a large and symmetrical structure, in contrast to the random organization of medieval castles. Designed as a quadrangle with an open central court, it was primarily a domestic royal residence with a system of corridors and stairwells and large, regularly placed windows. This hint of Renaissance order and elegance was markedly different from the usual defensive principles of high walls and small window openings. Once considered the finest in the realm, the central chambers would have been luxuriously decorated with painted plaster and wall hangings.

The Gothic style was still favoured in ecclesiastical architecture, most apparent in **Melrose Abbey** (see p.119). Twice destroyed in the fourteenth century, the rebuilding left excellent examples of High Gothic, the east window being the work of the York school of masons, and the richly carved south transept by a French master mason, which accounts for the lavish use of decoration. The flying buttresses are of particular note, being structural not merely decorative. Due to an increase in trade with other countries, wealthy landowners could afford to construct small churches, staffed by secular clergy to pray for the soul of the benefactor. Many small collegiate buildings were built at this time, predominantly with a Late Gothic flavour; the most unusual and extreme is the mid-century **Rosslyn Chapel** (Edinburgh; see p.189), with its elaborate carving and decorative flying buttresses. Also around this time, the castellated features of castles and towers began to creep into church architecture, seen in the use of crow-stepped gables at **St Michael's Church** (Linlithgow; see p.220), or the crenellated parapet at **King's College Chapel** (Aberdeen; see p.363).

THE SIXTEENTH AND SEVENTEENTH CENTURIES

The massacre of the Scots at Flodden in 1513 set the tone for unrest in the early part of the sixteenth century, leaving little opportunity for new buildings or styles. However, the Stewart dynasty continued to breathe the Renaissance spirit into their opulent palaces. A royal holiday home for the Stewart monarchs, **Falkland Palace** (Fife; see p.233), with its reconstructed south range, is an excellent example of **French Renaissance** design, the solid buttresses transformed into Classical columns. This courtly look is also apparent at **Stirling Castle** (see p.206), a true amalgam of styles, perched high up on a rocky outcrop. Here, the Renaissance facade of the Royal Palace, completed in 1540, is merely tacked onto the Gothic structure, with a line of restless statues perched on elegant wall shafts. Ultimately, this fashion did not catch on, as nobles preferred security and comfort over superficial elegance.

The Reformation of 1560 released a tragic wave of wholesale destruction of sculptural and other decorative items in church buildings. The tower house, however, resumed popularity, as a considerable amount of church land had been sold off to nobles, who then wanted to create a mini castle as an emblem of power and prestige. These buildings developed right through to the seventeenth century, often changing dramatically in plan, for example at **Drum Castle** (Aberdeen; see p.369). Originally built in the late thirteenth century, the dignified tower was extended to its full Jacobean glory in the seventeenth century, when the desire for greater comfort and space called for a larger building. The **Scottish Baronial** style, characterized by crow-stepped gables and conical roofs, lightened the austerity of the original tower form and took these buildings to their peak. Excellent examples include **Claypotts Castle** (near Dundee; see p.341), where defensive features have been subsumed to the need for extra accommodation, which is corbelled out at the top of the Z-plan towers. Other castles of note are **Crathes** (Deeside; see p.369), **Fyvie** (near Inverurie; see p.379) and **Glamis Castle** (north of Dundee; see p.343), which was constructed in the early seventeenth century. A later, even more decorative approach can be found at the absurdly pink-hued **Craigievar Castle**, 26 miles west of Aberdeen (see p.373). Built in 1626 and hailed as the finest tower house in Scotland, the crenellation serves to enhance the top-heavy accommodation area, but the beautifully preserved interior contains excellent stucco work. In all of these examples, useful defensive elements have been manipulated for effective decorative purposes.

The religious Wars of the Covenant (1639–44) and invasion of Cromwell (1650) initially discouraged contemporary building in the **seventeenth century**. However, it did see the final development of the **Early Scottish Renaissance**, marked by regular, symmetrical plans, the use of pediments and other decorative details of Classical origin, and an ordered dignified facade. Initiated in 1628, the elaborate **George Heriot's Hospital** in Edinburgh, which is now a school, is an excellent example. Here, Renaissance ideas are not merely decorative items tacked onto the front but incorporated by the architect, **William Wallace**, into the overall design. The quadrangular plan with a tower at each corner is a feast of turrets, chimneys and cupolas that top the symmetrical facade. As the century progressed, the landed classes, having travelled and become more aware of the cultural conditions in England and Europe, began to take a serious interest in the design of their mansions, led by the influential figure of Sir William Bruce, who essentially founded the **Classical** school in Scotland. He undertook the major reconstruction of **the Palace of Holyrood** (Edinburgh; see p.68) in 1671–9, creating a delicate and restrained courtyard frontage of fine proportion and exacting detail. **Drumlanrig Castle** (Dumfries; see p.139), built between 1679 and 1690, is an extravagant mansion, more obviously Classical with a balanced plan and a sweeping double staircase at the entrance.

THE EIGHTEENTH CENTURY

In the early years after the Act of Union (1707), the Scottish economy was at a low ebb. Gradually conditions began to improve as trade, encouraged by the union, began to take off, further enhanced by the agricultural revolution. By mid-century, the industrial age had ignited an architectural explosion. The towns of Edinburgh and Glasgow were to receive the best in **Neoclassical** architecture, as steadily increasing industrial production called for more housing, warehouses and municipal buildings. In line with the rationality and order of the Enlightenment, symmetry and proportion in design came into stride with the English Classicism of Sir Christopher Wren and Inigo Jones. Edinburgh's **New Town**, designed by **James Craig** in 1767, is characterized by symmetrical wide streets and large tree-filled squares, with service lanes that follow the main axis of the roads. Amongst this sandstone glory lies **Charlotte Square** (see p.78), the north side of which was designed by the renowned Classicist **Robert Adam** in 1791. The Venetian windows and restrained use of decoration create a unified facade, the main rooms clearly defined by angular stonework in comparison to the smooth sandstone of the other storeys. Compared with the medieval High Street that descends from the Castle, and the narrow lanes that run from it, these formal squares reflect a new approach to civilized urban living, allowing the upper classes to dwell in their own spacious areas away from the huddle of the Old Town. Adam was the shining light in a talented family of architects, who modified the elegant **Hopetoun House** (Edinburgh; see p.88) in c.1721–60. Set in an excellent position overlooking the Forth, this delicate and symmetrically designed building makes full use of triangular pediments and round-headed windows to recall the noble spirit of Classical times.

Concurrently, an interest in medieval architecture, encouraged by romantic fiction and the cult of the picturesque, led to **Gothic Revivalism**. Here, the pointed arch took over from the geometric rigours of Classicism. **Inveraray Castle** (Argyll; see p.263), built between 1745 and 1761, is one of the first Georgian castles to recreate itself in this neo-Gothic style. Although the interior is inspired by Classicism, the exterior makes use of pointed arches and crenellated parapets, the conical roofs being a later addition. Another neo-Gothic building is **Culzean Castle** (1771–92), attractively situated on a clifftop south of Ayr (see p.149) and extensively remodelled by Robert Adam in the latter part of the century. He designed every detail, from the fine interior plasterwork, complete with swags and urns, to the castellated exterior with mock arrow slits, to give a romantically medieval touch to the dramatic setting.

THE NINETEENTH CENTURY

By the turn of the century, Scotland had changed dramatically, climbing from a poor backwater to become one of the Empire's leading industrial centres. Furthermore, after Queen Victoria "discovered" Scotland in 1842, it became highly fashionable, fuelled by the image of wild clans and rugged, lonely landscapes – a far cry from the bitter reality of life within the rapidly industrializing central belt, populated increasingly by families left homeless by the Highland Clearances. The major cities of Glasgow, Edinburgh and Dundee were expanding at great speed, filling up with warehouses, municipal buildings and workers' accommodation. This ushered in the **Victorian Age** of architecture. Marked by a continuation of the Romantic and Classical idioms established in the eighteenth century, grand buildings celebrated the pride and self-confidence of the industrial giants. A fusion of historical styles became common, and architects increasingly looked for novel ways to decorate their buildings. For instance, the Tudor-Gothic **Donaldson's Hospital** in Edinburgh, designed by **William Playfair** in 1851, fuses a symmetrical plan with elaborate turrets and a central decorated tower. Playfair was also responsible for creating the rich facade at **Floors Castle** (near Kelso; see p.118), in 1838, cloaking the building in a new fashionable guise without changing the basic structural design.

Inspired by simple proportion and logical harmony, the followers of the **Greek Revival** created buildings of massive serenity, using little decoration. In Glasgow, **Alexander "Greek" Thomson** brought a unique interpretation to this style. He created buildings from warehouses to tenements and churches, such as Glasgow's impressive **St Vincent Street Church** (see p.169), an imposing construction that mixes the massive solidity of Greek design with exotic motifs and decoration. In Edinburgh, it was **William Playfair** who created the city's icons of Greek Revivalism: the **Royal Scottish Academy** of 1836 (see p.74) and the **National Gallery of Scotland** of 1857 (see p.75), are both well proportioned with precise detail, the former making more use of scrolls and wreaths, the latter slightly less ponderous and more elegant. With the Gothic style no longer restricted to ecclesiastical architecture, the majestic **Glasgow University** building of 1870, designed by George Gilbert Scott, dominates the skyline of the West End in pseudo-medieval splendour. Similarly in Edinburgh, **The Scottish National Portrait Gallery** of 1885–90, designed by Sir R Rowand Anderson, is richly detailed with pointed arches and turrets.

New materials of the industrial age, such as cast iron, were being used to great effect, in such as buildings as **Kibble Palace** in the Botanic Gardens (Glasgow; see p.179) and the interior of the **Royal Museum of Scotland** (Edinburgh; see p.72), which was based on London's Crystal Palace. The industrial age also gave birth to such great figures of **engineering** as **William Telford**, **Sir Benjamin Baker** and **Sir John Fowler**, who constructed roads and bridges throughout Scotland. Baker and Fowler were responsible for the pinnacle of Scottish engineering that straddles the Firth of Forth in cantilevered steel glory – in total, the **Forth Railway Bridge** spans four and a half miles, took seven years to build and employed more than 5000 men at a time, rivalling the Eiffel Tower in its complexity.

THE TWENTIETH CENTURY

At the turn of the century, Scotland was riding on the crest of a wave, with a healthy economy and solid industrial base; soon, however, a long period of post-war depression was to destroy this security. In any case, while the Victorian well-to-do had been luxuriating in their fine buildings, the workers had lived in slums, a situation that was to result in mass demolition later in the century.

Despite many financial difficulties, Glasgow's **Charles Rennie Mackintosh** began to design exciting new buildings, motivated by the desire for complete organic unity of structure and decoration. Associated with the Art Nouveau school and their push for change after the conservatism of the previous century, he produced some buildings of excellent quality and form. The **Glasgow School of Art** (see p.174) is the archetypal Mackintosh work, fusing the curvilinear shapes of Art Nouveau with the crow-stepped gables and conical roofs of the Scots Baronial tradition. The interior effectively combines practicality with decorative beauty; and the library, in particular, promotes his forward thinking style as it makes use of a strong vertical motif for its columns, lighting and furnishing (for more on Mackintosh, see p.172). Outside of the bustling city at **Hill House** in Helensburgh, Mackintosh, created a domestic building in 1902 that unites the turrets and chimney stack of the Baronial tradition with a modern interior. In the drawing room he creates two "zones", the wide bay window overlooking the Firth, for summer, and a cosy fireplace with a bookcase as a backdrop for winter evenings.

World War I brought a dramatic shift in scientific and artistic sensibilities; with the old ways undermined, people looked more and more to the future. This new atmosphere was represented in the **Art Deco** style, celebrating speed and technology. Typical features include modern, flat roofs, soaring geometric motifs and the use of reinforced concrete, which allowed semicircular glazed bays to project out from the building. However, due to financial constraints, few buildings were actually being erected; some gems that were include Glasgow's **Baird Hall of Residence** in Sauchiehall Street, built in 1938. The architect W Beresford Inglis used two soaring projecting towers with bay windows to give a dynamic prominence to the general bulk of the building. In contrast, the large, brick-covered planes of the **Glasgow Film Theatre** (see p.191), constructed one year later and designed by James McKissack, enhance the squat flat-roofed building. **The Maybury**, on the outskirts of Edinburgh, is a typical "roadhouse" built to cater for the new car-bound tourist, who could gaze up into the regularly spaced windows of the tower, designed to emulate the radiator of a huge limousine.

Despite the innovative ideas for town planning after World War I and the great re-housing plans set in motion after World War II, few public or private buildings of note were produced. Instead vast **suburban sprawls** were constructed in the most economical manner, resulting in their bland architectural character. More recently, the development of housing associations has allowed residents to have some influence over their living space, and tower blocks have been replaced with small, brick buildings laid out in crescents and tree-lined streets. In the public realm, the possibilities of modern technology continued to be explored, for example at the **Exhibition Plant Houses** at Edinburgh's Royal Botanic Garden (see p.82). Built in 1967, the glass skin is held in place by an outside structure of steel and iron to provide the maximum use of space inside. The manipulation of glass to enhance space is also apparent at the **Burrell Collection** (Pollok Park, Glasgow; see p.180), built in 1983 to house the great collection of Sir William Burrell. The architect Barry Gasson effectively fused nature and art, employing large panes of glass to take advantage of the surrounding woodland light, while the geometric use of red sandstone contrasts well with the roughness of the park land.

The current trend for **conservation and renovation** has produced some fine work: the glass-fronted **Festival Theatre** in Edinburgh is a successful and dynamic conversion of an older building, while the massive bulk that is the **Royal Concert Hall** in Glasgow (see p.173) is still waiting for its union with a proposed shopping centre. However, this bias has restricted the possibility for any really distinguished modern buildings or radical flights of fancy to be constructed in Scotland. With few patrons willing or able to push the boundaries towards the twenty-first century, despite the enthusiasm of young Scottish architects, the nation's architecture is in danger of becoming frozen in time and trapped by historicism, a sad irony after the far sighted construction of the Victorian era.

THE MUSIC OF SCOTLAND

Scottish music has entered the 1990s in remarkably fine health, with a bedrock of Celtic groups – led by the Boys of the Lough, Silly Wizard, The Tannahill Weavers and Runrig – storming through traditional material in a blaze of bagpipes and flying fiddles. The current strength and diversity of Scottish music has finally dispelled the once widely held belief that there was no more north of the border thean Andy Stewart and the Bay City Rollers.

There used to be a British television show – still fondly remembered by people who buy Max Bygraves and Val Doonican records – called "The White Heather Show". This, the British public were gleefully informed each week, was the sound of Scotland, all men in kilts, led by the likes of Andy Stewart and Jimmy Shand, with their accordions and sentimental songs of the highlands. The show ran for many years, and – let's not be mean – probably gave an awful lot of people an awful lot of pleasure. It also damned Scottish music with an image of banal glibness from which it looked like never recovering.

While Jimmy Shand's gung-ho accordion playing became an institution and the nation hooted along with Andy Stewart's "Scottish Soldier" and "Donald Where's Your Troosers" (a British number one in the 1960s and the 90s), Scots musicians were donated a legacy that was to dog them for the next two decades.

To make any credible headway beyond the shackles of an image decimated by kilts and highland flings, they were forced to deny the very thing that provided their one claim to be unique in the first place – their Scottishness.

For two decades even the best exponents of a purely Scots music had teetered on the edge of ridicule. The excellent **Ian Campbell Folk Group** (who included future Fairport Daves, Swarbrick and Pegg, while Ian's sons, Aly and Robin, went on to form UB40) had flirted with commercialism and pop sensibilities – as virtually every folk group of the era was compelled to do – and was too often unfairly bracketed with England's derided Spinners as a result. A similar cross was borne by others of the period, particularly **Robin Hall and Jimmie MacGregor** (remembered in Britain for the awful "Football Crazy" novelty hit) and **The Corries**, both of whom were too closely associated with the curse of the White Heather Club. Yet The Corries, especially, laced their blandness with bold enterprise, inventing their own instrumentation and writing the new unofficial national anthem, "Flower of Scotland".

Pop and rock, of course, always had a thriving tradition of Scots bands but mostly their origins were incidental, or laid on as thick as the tartan on the Bay City Rollers' trousers. It was to be the late 1970s before Scots musicians investigated their own musical history with any real sense of purpose. **The Boys of the Lough** led the way, initially driven on by the instinctive brilliance of their Shetland fiddler Aly Bain (see box overleaf), and they were followed by **The Battlefield Band**, who consciously attempted to hack away the old Scots clichés.

Then **Alba** did the unthinkable and introduced bagpipes to a contemporary rock line-up, paving the way for a rush of groups like **Silly Wizard** and **The Tannahill Weavers** to sweep Scots music into the 1980s with pride. Scots bands could at last draw on their evocative national fund of music, free of self-consciousness, and the results were encouraging. In the 1990s, the Scots variant of Celtic music has found contemporary-sounding champions in bands like **Runrig** and **Capercaillie**, who have blended mass rock appeal and techniques with ancient inspirations, while even out-and-out rock bands like **Deacon Blue** and **Simple Minds** have drawn liberally on tradi-

SHETLAND MAGIC: ALY BAIN

Aly Bain has been a minor deity among Scottish musicians for three decades. A fiddle player of exquisite technique and individuality, he has been the driving force of one of Scotland's all-time great bands, **Boys of the Lough**, throughout that time, while latterly diversifying into the roles of TV presenter and author. In these guises, he has been instrumental in spreading the wings of Scottish music to an even greater extent. First and foremost, though, Bain is a Shetlander and his greatest legacy is the inspiration he has provided for a thriving revival of fortunes for Shetland's own characteristic tradition.

Aly was brought up in the capital of Shetland, Lerwick, and was enthused to play the fiddle by **Bob Duncan** – who endlessly played him records by the strathspey king **Scott Skinner** – and later the old maestro **Tom Anderson**. Duncan and Anderson were the last of an apparently dying breed, and the youthful Aly was an odd sight dragging his fiddle along to join in with the old guys at the Shetland Fiddlers Society. Players like Willie Hunter Jnr and Snr, Willie Pottinger and Alex Hughson were legends locally, but they belonged to another age and the magic of Shetland fiddle playing – one inflected with the eccentricity of the isolated environment and the influence of nearby Scandinavia.

By the time the teenage Aly was persuaded to leave for the mainland, Shetland was changing by the minute, and the discovery of North Sea oil altered it beyond redemption, as the new indus-trial riches trampled its unique community spirit and sense of tradition. The old fiddlers gradually faded and died, and Shetland music seemed destined to disappear too.

That it didn't was largely down to Aly. After a spell with Billy Connolly (then a folk artist, before finding comedy success as a professional Glaswegian) on the Scottish folk circuit, Aly found himself working with blues iconoclast Mike Whellans, and then the two of them tumbled into a link-up with two Irishmen, Robin Morton and Cathal McConnell, in a group they called Boys of the Lough. The last thing Aly Bain imagined was that he'd spend the next quarter of a century answering to this name. But he did, and his joyful artistry, unwavering integrity and unquenchable appetite for and commitment to the music of his upbringing kept Shetland music alive in a manner he could never have imagined. Even more importantly, it stung the imagination of the generation that followed.

These days, Shetland music is buzzing again, with its own annual festival a treat of music-making and drinking that belies the impersonal industrialization of Shetland. There are young musicians pouring out of the place, among whom **Catriona MacDonald** – who was also taught by Tom Anderson, in his last days – is the current cream of the crop. She is adept at classical music, and is fast becoming an accomplished master of Norwegian music, and her mum went to school with Aly Bain – which in Shetland these days counts for an awful lot.

tional Scottish modes of melody and instrumentation.

"The White Heather Club" is now well and truly buried, and at last some of the traditions are also being aired in their older forms. The dance music of **Bob Smith's Ideal Band** has had a couple of albums devoted to it, and the extraordinary *strathspey* rhythms of legendary fiddle player **Scott Skinner** have had belated exposure, too. Also getting a fresh listening – especially with the CD releases of the Scottish Tradition Series – are the repertoires of **traditional Gaelic songs**, like those of the wonderful **Cathie-Ann McPhee**, still current in the Scottish rural outposts, and those of the old **travelling singers** – people like the **Stewarts** of Blairgowrie, **Isla Cameron**, **Lizzie Higgins** and, the greatest of them all, Lizzie's mother, **Jeannie Robertson**.

THE PIPES OF WRATH

Bagpipes are synonymous with Scotland yet they are not, oddly enough, a specifically Scottish instrument. The pipes were once to be found right across Europe, and pockets remain, across the English border in Northumbria, all over Ireland, in Spain and Italy, and notably in eastern European countries like Romania and the Czech and Slovak republics, where bagpipe festivals are still held in rural areas. In Scotland, bagpipes seem to have made their appearance around the fifteenth century, and over the next hundred years or so they took on several forms, including quieter varieties, both bellows and mouth blown, which allowed a diversity of playing styles.

The highland bagpipe form known as **pibroch** (*piobaireachd* in Gaelic) evolved around this time, created by clan pipers for military, gathering, lamenting and marching purposes. Legend among the clan pipers of this era were the MacCrimmons (they of the famous "MacCrimmon's Lament", composed during the Jacobite rebellion), although they were but one of several important piping clans, among which were the MacArthurs, Mackays, MacDonalds and others. In the seventeenth and eighteenth centuries, through the influence of the British army, reels and *strathspeys* joined the repertoire, and in the early nineteenth century a tradition of military pipe bands had emerged, and with it a network of piping competitions.

The bagpipe tradition has continued uninterrupted to the present, although for much of this century under the domination of the military and the folklorist Piobaireachd Society. Recently, however, a number of Scottish musicians have revived the pipes in new and innovative forms. **Alan McLeod** succeeded in knitting the pipes into a framework of instruments, playing as a teenager with the band **Alba**, and his lead has been consolidated by the **Battlefield Band**, whose arrangements involve the beautifully measured piping of **Duncan McGillivray**, and **Iain MacDonald**, who had previously piped along with rock instruments in the band **Ossian**.

Alongside all this came a revived interest in traditional piping, and in particular the *strathspeys*, slow airs and reels, which had tended to get submerged beneath the familiar military territory of marches and laments. The century's great modern-day bagpipe players, notably **John Burgess**, received a belated wider exposure. His legacy includes a masterful album and a renowned teaching career to ensure that the old piping tradition marches proudly into the next century.

FOLK AND CELTIC REVIVALS

The Scots' first forays into a new "traditional music" grew out of the folk and acoustic scene in mid-1960s Glasgow and Edinburgh. It was at Clive's Incredible Folk Club, in Glasgow, that **The Incredible String Band** made their debut, led by Mike Heron and Robin Williamson. The Incredibles took an unfashionable glance back into their own past on the one hand, while plunging headlong into psychedelia

and other uncharted areas on the other. Their success broke down significant barriers for them and others, both in and out of Scotland, and a quarter of a century on Robin Williamson is still tinkering around with his Celtic roots, with perhaps less gusto but just as much guile.

In their wake came a succession of Scottish folk-rock crossover musicians. Glasgow-born **Bert Jansch** launched "folk super-group" **Pentangle** with Jacqui McShee, John Renbourn and Danny Thompson, and the flute-playing Ian Anderson found rock success with **Jethro Tull**. Meanwhile, the folk clubs in Glasgow and Edinburgh gave rise to an interesting mix of traditional and pop artists. Among the latter, Barbara Dickson, Gallagher & Lyle, Rab Noakes and Gerry Rafferty went on to mainstream success, while a more traditional Scottish sound was promoted by the likes of **Archie, Ray and Cilla Fisher**, who sang new and traditional ballads, individually and together, the **McCalmans**, who employed bodhráns, mandolins and traditional material, and, perhaps most crucially, **Dick Gaughan**.

Gaughan's passionate artistry towers like a colossus above three decades. He started out in the Edinburgh folk club scene with an impenetrable accent, a deep belief in the socialist commitment of traditional song, and a guitar technique that had old masters of the art hanging on to the edge of their seats. For a couple of years in the early 1970s, he played along with Aly Bain (see opposite) in **The Boys of the Lough**, an Irish-Scottish band that was knocking out fiery versions of trad Celtic material. Gaughan became frustrated, however, by the limitations of a primarily instrumental (and fiddle-dominated) group and subsequently formed **Five Hand Reel**. Again playing Scots-Irish traditional material, they might have been the greatest folk-rock band of them all if they hadn't marginally missed the Fairport/Steeleye Span boat.

Leaving to pursue an independent career, Gaughan became a fixture on the folk circuit and made a series of albums exploring Scots and Irish traditional music and re-interpreting the material for guitar. His "Handful of Earth" (1981) was perhaps the single best solo folk album of the decade, a record of stunning intensity with enough contemporary relevance and historical belief to grip all generations of

EWAN MACCOLL: THE MAN FROM AUCHTERARDER

The single most gifted, influential and inspirational figure in modern British folk song was a man from Auchterarder, Perthshire, called **Ewan MacColl**. He was enthused with the unique spirit and dignity of Scottish music by his parents, both lowlanders, and became a superb ballad singer, devoting himself to the music with such zeal and political sense of purpose that it still colours people's thinking years later.

He is perhaps best remembered now as a gloriously evocative songwriter – with the ability to switch from tender love songs to crushing political venom without apparent change in demeanour. But it was his revolutionary championing of indigenous folk song that caused such a furore, and played such a fierce role in the preservation of folk song, wherever it came from. Singers and musicians, decreed MacColl, should only play music of their own country: a rule he gained much notoriety for imposing at his own folk clubs. It seems a ludicrous notion in hindsight but with American music sweeping the world in the late 1950s and early 60s it may well have saved large swathes of traditional British folk music.

Initially MacColl made his mark in the theatre, and later moved to the BBC, where he allied his theatrical leanings with his love of folk music in a series of documentary dramas in which the lives of people in different industries were illustrated by the shrewd interspersal of his own songs, written in a folk idiom for the series. These eight "radio ballads" were major breakthroughs for folk music, and from that point on MacColl was a central figure in the evolution of British roots music. He continued to perform with his American wife Peggy Seeger almost to his death in 1989, his hatred of the Thatcher government inspiring him to ever greater heights of savagery in his songwriting.

Elvis Costello made his public debut down the bill at a Ewan MacColl gig. Shane MacGowan of The Pogues says the only time he ever set foot in a folk club was when MacColl was appearing. And Elvis Presley recorded one of his songs – the Grammy Award winning "First Time Ever I Saw Your Face". They should be thinking about building some kind of statue up there in Auchterarder.

music fans. And though sparing in his output, and modest about his value in the genre, he's also become one of the best songwriters of his generation too. An amazing man.

GAELIC ROCKING

Scottish music took an unexpected twist in 1978 with the low-key release of an album called "Play Gaelic". It was made by a little-known group called **Runrig**, who took their name from the old Scottish oil field system of agriculture, and worked primarily in the backwaters of the highlands and islands. The thing, though, that stopped people in their tracks was the fact that they were writing original material in Gaelic. This was the first time any serious Scottish working band had achieved any sort of attention with Gaelic material, although Ossian were touching on it around a similar time, as were Nah-Oganaich.

Runrig have since marched on to unprecedented heights. They slowly chipped away at prejudices, conducting their own musical experiments, adopting accordions and bagpipes, sharper arrangements, electric instruments, full-blown rock styles, surviving the inevitable

personnel changes and the continuous carping of critics accusing them of selling out with every new market conquered. They even made one epic concept album, "Recovery", which effectively related the history of the Gael in one collection, provoking unprecedented interest in the Gaelic language after years of it being regarded in Scotland as moribund and defunct.

Runrig are now a long way from the gentle little ceilidh group that started out playing to tiny audiences in the highlands, appearing in front of rock audiences at concert halls around the world where only a partial proportion of the audience are jocks in exile. Their own Gaelic input is marginal these days, but they started a whole new ball rolling.

Although few made the connection, because of their geographical remoteness and isolation from the rest of the scene, Runrig were basically making a logical step on from the work of those classic Edinburgh/Glasgow bands whose names roll off with such ease you imagine there's an umbilical link binding them together: **The Corries** and the **McCalmans**; the **Whistlebinkies** and the **JSD Band**; Silly

Wizard and **The Tannahill Weavers**; **Alba** and the **Battlefield Band**; **Ossian** and **The Boys of the Lough**; **Mouth Music** and **Capercaillie**. Not all of these, by any means, sung in Gaelic, but in each the Gaelic element was strong within the music, in the use either of traditional material or instruments.

Among the ranks of these bands, each with their own agenda and style, are some of Scotland's most important and influential contemporary musicians. **Silly Wizard**, especially, featured a singer of cutting quality in **Andy M Stewart** (and did he need that M), while **Phil and Johnny Cunningham** have subsequently gone on to display a pioneering zeal in their efforts to use their skills on accordion and fiddle to knit Scottish traditional music with other cultures. **Mouth Music**, too, were innovative: a Scots-origin duo of Martin Swan and Talitha MacKenzie, who mixed Gaelic vocals (including the traditional "mouth music" techniques of sung rhythms) with African percussion and dance sounds. The band has recently crossed further over into the dance world, with a new vocalist, while **Talitha MacKenzie** has gone solo, radically transforming traditional Scottish songs, which she clears from the dust of folklore with wonderful multitracked vocals and Mouth Music's characteristic African rhythms.

On a more roots front, **The Whistlebinkies** were notable for employing only traditional instruments, including fine *clarsach* (Celtic harp) played by Judith Peacock.

These bands' collective success has paved the way for more tolerance and encouragement for the "purer" Scots musicians and singers: *clarsach* player **Alison Kinnaird**; singers **Savourna Stevenson**, **Christine Primrose**, **Arthur Cormack** and **Heather Heywood**; and the amazing **Wrigley sisters** from Orkney – teenage girls playing Scottish traditional music in the 1990s with unlimited technical accomplishment and attitude with a capital A.

Above all, though, the Runrig baton has been grabbed by the excellent **Capercaillie**, who themselves have risen from Argyll pub sessions to flirt with mass commercial appeal, reworking Gaelic and traditional songs from the West Highlands. As yet, they don't appear to have compromised their ideals one iota on the way, and don't look as if they intend to, either. Not while the fulcrum of the band revolves around the arrangements of Manus Lunny and the gorgeous singing of Karen Mattheson. It'll be a long time before Scots Gaels are forgotten again with people like them around.

Colin Irwin

(Taken from the *Rough Guide to World Music*.)

BOOKS

Wherever a book is in print, the UK publisher is given first in each listing, separated, where applicable, from the US publisher by an oblique slash. Where books are published in only one of these countries we have specified which one; when the same company publishes the book in both, its name appears just once. Out of print titles are indicated as o/p – these should be easy to track down in second-hand bookshops.

ART, ARCHITECTURE AND HISTORIC SITES

Kitty Cruft and Andrew Fraser, eds. *James Craig 1744–95* (UK Mercat Press). Distinguished authors offer reassessments of Craig's achievement in designing Edinburgh's New Town.

Exploring Scotland's Heritage Series (UK HMSO o/p). Detailed, beautifully illustrated series with the emphasis on historic buildings and archeological sites. Titles include Orkney and Shetland, the Highlands, Grampian, Fife and Tayside, and Lothian and the Borders.

Bill Hare *Contemporary Painting in Scotland* (UK Craftsman House). Features the work of 48 contemporary artists – including John Bellany, Bruce McLean and Elizabeth Blackadder – and gives special attention to the "New Painting" that emerged in the 1980s and developed into a distinctive Scottish style. Expensive and serious.

David King *Complete Works of Robert and James Adam* (Butterworth-Heinemann; UK o/p). Comprehensive and scholarly look at the work of the Adam brothers.

Charles McKean, David Walker and Frank Walker *Central Glasgow* (Rutland Press/State Mutual Book Company). An architectural romp through the city centre and West End, with plenty of photographs and informed comment, *Central Glasgow* is part of the Rutland Press series of 20 illustrated guides to Scottish architecture (they aim to have covered the country by the year 2000). Whilst authoritative, they are not at all stuffy and are conveniently pocket-sized. In addition, the Press has produced studies of such notable figures as James Miller, Basil Spence and Peter Womersley.

Duncan MacMillan *Scottish Art 1460–1990* (Mainstream/Trafalgar). Lavish overview of Scottish painting with good sections on landscape, portraiture and the Glasgow Boys.

Colin McWilliam, ed. *The Buildings of Scotland* (UK Penguin o/p). There are volumes on Fife, Edinburgh and Lothian, all of which provide comprehensive and scholarly coverage of every building of importance. Though easy to understand, they would best suit visitors intending to spend more than a couple of weeks in Scotland.

Alistair Moffat and Colin Baxter *Remembering Charles Rennie Mackintosh* (UK Colin Baxter Photography Ltd). Illustrated biography of Scotland's most celebrated early twentieth-century architect, artist and designer.

Alastair Smart *Allan Ramsay 1713–1784* (UK Scottish National Portrait Gallery). Good study of one of Scotland's most representative eighteenth-century artists, written by a leading Ramsay scholar.

Andrew Gibbon Williams and Andrew Brown *The Bigger Picture: A History of Scottish Art* (UK BBC Books). Originally published to accompany a TV series, this is a richly illustrated survey of Scottish art from 1603 to the present day. Suitable for the lay reader.

HISTORY, POLITICS AND CULTURE

Ian Adams and Meredith Somerville *Cargoes of Despair and Hope* (UK John Donald Publishing). Riveting mixture of contemporary documents and letters telling the story of Scottish emigration to North America from 1603 to 1803.

Ian Bell *Dreams of Exile* (Mainstream/Holt). Admirable biography of Robert Louis Stevenson that seeks to explain his work in terms of Scottish emigration, exile and escape. Does a good job of balancing the real man against his over-romanticized image.

John Buchan *Montrose* (UK Greenwood). Classic account of Montrose's astonishing military campaigns for the Royalist cause in seventeenth-century Scotland. Clan jealousies, religious discord and personal heroism: compelling fact is delivered with a novelist's flair for storytelling.

David Daiches, ed. *A Companion to Scottish Culture* (Polygon/Holmes & Meier). More than 300 articles interpreting Scottish culture in its widest sense, from eating to marriage customs, the Scottish Enlightenment to children's street games.

George MacDonald Fraser *The Steel Bonnets* (HarperCollins). Immensely enjoyable and erudite account of cattle rustling, feud, blackmail, murder and mayhem on the Anglo Scottish border of the sixteenth century.

Rosemary Goring *Chambers Scottish Biographical Dictionary* (UK Chambers). More than 2000 mini biographies of important Scots, both well-known and utterly obscure, in fields such as law, medicine, education, the Church, music and the stage.

Forsyth Hardy *Scotland in Film* (Edinburgh University Press/Colorado University Press). A chronological account of 60 years of Scotland on screen (up to 1989), by a highly influential writer and producer. Hardy is particularly concerned with the accurate expression and depiction of a small nation, and writes persuasively from his own experience in the industry. The book is generously illustrated and includes a filmography of 150 landmark productions.

Magnus Linklater and Robin Denniston *Anatomy of Scotland* (UK Chambers). Social history essays on the workings of Scotland over the past 45 years, covering everything from the law to pop music.

William Laughton Lorimer *The New Testament* (UK Penguin). Magnificent translation into the Scots tongue. Interestingly, only the Devil's words are rendered in English.

Michael Lynch *Scotland: A New History* (UK Pimlico). Probably the best available overview of Scottish history, going up to 1991 and the bid for a national parliament.

James MacKay *Burns: A Biography of Robert Burns* (UK Mainstream). Recent attempt to clear the myths surrounding Scotland's most famous poet, including those created by the man himself.

R F Mackenzie *A Search for Scotland* (UK Fontana o/p). Combining travelogue, autobiography and polemic, Mackenzie presents a highly personal account of the contradictions of Scottish culture and character. Inquisitive and incisive, the book is full of fierce but not uncritical affection for his homeland.

Charles McKean *Edinburgh* (Rutland Press/ State Mutual Book Co). Lively, lyrical account of the development of Scotland's capital right up to the present.

John McLeod *No Great Mischief If You Fall* (Mainstream/Trafalgar) Gloom and doom on the rape of the Highlands; an enraging, bleak but stimulating book debunking some of the myths upheld by the Highland industry.

Frank McLynn *Bonnie Prince Charlie* (UK Oxford University Press o/p). Huge, very readable and more or less definitive biography.

Ann McSween and Mick Sharp *Prehistoric Scotland* (Batsford/New Amsterdam Books). Thematic introductory guide to many of Scotland's prehistoric sites, with atmospheric black-and-white photographs and imaginative illustrations.

Andrew Marr *The Battle for Scotland* (UK Penguin). An intelligent and readable account of Scottish political history from the nineteenth century to 1992. Marr examines the struggle to identify, preserve and perhaps expand the status of a nation "in bed with an elephant".

David Moody *Scottish Family History* (UK Genealogical Publications). Though aimed primarily at amateur genealogists, this book contains a wealth of detail on the nuts and bolts of domestic life in Scotland. Moody's suggestions for understanding the past are consistently practical, encouraging and informative.

John Prebble *Glen Coe* (Penguin o/p/Secker & Warburg o/p), *Culloden* (Penguin/Athenium o/p) and *The Highland Clearances* (Penguin/ Secker & Warburg o/p). Emotive and subjective accounts of key events in Highland history. Essential reading for Jacobite sympathizers.

John Purser *Scotland's Music* (Mainstream/ Trafalgar). Comprehensive overview of traditional and classical music in Scotland – thorough and scholarly but readable.

James D Scarlett *Tartan: The Highland Textile* (Shepheard-Welwyn/Paul & Co Publishing). Detailed and authoritative, Scarlett's up-to-date and near definitive work debunks the myths surrounding tartan and analyzes 500 patterns.

T C Smout *A History of the Scottish People 1560–1830* (Fontana/Scribner o/p) and *A Century of the Scottish People 1830–1950* (Fontana/Yale University Press o/p). Widely acclaimed volumes, brimful of interest for those keen on social history. Smout combines enormous learning with a clear and entertaining style.

Tom Steel *Scotland's Story* (UK Fontana). Good people-based introduction written to accompany a popular British television series.

GUIDES AND PICTURE BOOKS

Colin Baxter and Jim Crumley *Scottish Landscapes*, *Portrait of Edinburgh* (UK Lomond o/p), **Baxter and Jack McLean** *The City of Glasgow* (UK Lomond o/p). Best known for his ubiquitous postcards, Baxter's photographs succeed in capturing the grandeur of Scotland's countryside and cityscapes.

Collins Gem Dictionary (UK HarperCollins o/p). Handy, pocket-sized guide to the mysteries of Scottish vocabulary and idiom.

Joe Fisher *The Glasgow Encyclopedia* (Mainstream/Trafalgar). The essential Glasgow reference book, covering nearly every facet of this complex urban society.

Magnus Magnusson and Graham White, eds. *The Nature of Scotland – Landscape, Wildlife and People* (UK Canongate). Glossy picture-based book on Scotland's natural heritage, from geology to farming and conservation. Good section on crofting.

Oscar Marzaroli *Glasgow's People: 1956–1988* (Mainstream/Trafalgar). Wonderful collection by Glasgow's most sympathetic photographer.

Richard Muir *The Coastlines of Britain* (UK Macmillan o/p). An exploration of all aspects of Scotland's varied coast with chapters on cliffs, beach, dunes, flora and fauna.

Anne Shade *Scotland for Kids* (Mainstream/ Trafalgar). Indispensable advice on where to go

and what to do with children in Scotland, written by a mother of two.

Cecil Sinclair *Tracing your Scottish Ancestors* (UK HMSO o/p). Probably the best guide to ancestry research in the Scottish Record Office; definitely worth reading before visiting General Register House.

FOLKLORE AND LEGEND

Margaret Bennett *Scottish Customs from the Cradle to the Grave* (UK Polygon). Fascinating and sympathetic extensive oral history.

Michael Brander *Tales of the Borders* (UK Mainstream). Part social history and part guide book, a collection of romantic nineteenth-century Border tales retold and put into historical context.

Alan J Bruford and Donald Archie McDonald, eds. *Scottish Traditional Tales* (UK Polygon). A huge collection of folk stories from all over Scotland, taken from tape archives.

Anne Ross *Folklore of the Southern Highlands* (UK Barnes and Noble). A comprehensive collection, with sections on clan lore, witchcraft, spells and taboos, festivals and scores of obscure customs.

Jennifer Westwood *Albion: A Guide to Legendary Britain* (Grafton/Salem House). Highly readable volume on the development of myth in literature, with a section on Scottish legends.

MEMOIRS AND TRAVELOGUES

James Boswell *The Journal of a Tour to the Hebrides* (Penguin/McGraw Hill). Lively diary account of a journey around the islands taken with Samuel Johnson, written by his biographer and friend.

Derek Cooper *Hebridean Connection* (UK Fontana o/p). Written in the 1970s at a time of economic crisis, this is an unsentimental impression of contemporary island life.

David Craig *On the Crofter's Trail* (UK Jonathan Cape). Using anecdotes and interviews with descendants, Craig conveys the hardship and tragedy of the Highland Clearances without being mawkish.

James Hunter *Scottish Highlanders* (Mainstream/Trafalgar). Attempts to explain the strong sense of blood-ties held by people of

Scottish descent all over the world; lots of history and good photographs.

Tom Morton *Spirit of Adventure: A Journey Beyond the Whisky Trails* (Mainstream/ Trafalgar). Offbeat and funny view of Scotland's whisky industry as seen from the back of a motorcycle in appalling weather.

Robert Louis Stevenson *Edinburgh: Picturesque Notes* (UK Barnes and Noble). Charming evocation of Stevenson's birthplace – its moods, curiosities and influences on his work.

Douglas Sutherland *Born Yesterday: Memories of a Scottish Childhood* (Canongate/ Transaction). Childhood memories of growing up in the 1920s and 30s in Orkney, Aberdeenshire and the Moray Firth.

FOOD AND DRINK

Michael Brander *Essential Guide to Scots Whisky* (UK Canongate o/p). A history of whisky from the days of the illicit distillers to the present day, along with a directory of malt.

Catherine Brown *Scottish Cookery* (UK Chambers). Practical, easy-to-follow recipes with interesting background notes on the history of Scottish food and ingredients.

Annette Hope *A Caledonian Feast* (UK Mainstream). Authoritative and entertaining history of Scottish food and social life from the ninth to the twentieth century. Lots of recipes.

Charles McLean *The Pocket Whisky Book* (UK Mitchell Beazley o/p). A tiny, thorough, fact-filled book covering malt, grain and blended whiskies, plus whisky-based liqueurs.

F Marian McNeill *The Scots Kitchen* (UK Mercat Press o/p) and *The Scots Cellar* (UK Lochar o/p). The first is a definitive, learned and entertaining guide to the history of Scots cooking, the second a history on the consumption and appreciation of whisky, ale and wine, with some good, alcoholic recipes.

FICTION

Iain Banks *The Bridge* (UK Sphere) and *The Crow Road* (UK Abacus). Banks' work can be funny, pacy, though-provoking, imaginative and downright disgusting. It is never dull.

D K Broster *The Jacobite Trilogy* (UK Mandarin). Tear-jerking trilogy centred round the tribulations of the Jacobite supporters.

George Mackay Brown *Beside the Ocean of Time* (John Murray). A child's journey through the history of an Orkney island, and an adult's effort to make sense of the place's secrets in the late twentieth century.

John Buchan *The Complete Richard Hannay* (UK Penguin/Godine). This one volume includes *The 39 Steps, Greenmantle, Mr Standfast, The Three Hostages* and *The Island of Sheep*. Good gung-ho stories with a great feel for Scottish landscape. In the US, both Oxford University Press and Godine publish various editions of the Hannay stories. Less well known but better are Buchan's historical romances, for example *The Free Fishers* (UK B&W Publishing), *John Burnet of Barnes* (UK B&W o/p) and *Witchwood* (Canongate/Caroll & Graf).

Moira Burgess and Hamish Whyte, eds. *Streets of Stone* (Mainstream/Salamander). Anthology of contemporary Glaswegian short stories.

George MacDonald Fraser *The General Danced at Dawn* (UK Fontana o/p), *McAuslin in the Rough* and *The Sheikh and the Dustbin* (UK Fontana). Touching and very funny collections of short stories detailing life in a Highland regiment after World War II.

Lewis Grassic Gibbon *A Scots Quair* (Penguin/Schocken o/p). A landmark trilogy, set in northeast Scotland during and after World War I, the events are seen through the eyes of Chris Guthrie, "torn between her love for the land and her desire to escape a peasant culture". Strong, seminal work.

Alasdair Gray *Lanark* (Canongate/Braziller o/p). A postmodern blend of social realism and labyrinthine fantasy: Gray's extraordinary debut as a novelist, with his own allegorical illustrations, takes invention and comprehension to their limits.

Neil M Gunn *The Silver Darlings* (UK Faber & Faber). Probably Gunn's most representative and best-known book, evocatively set on the northeast coast and telling the story of the herring fishermen during the great years of the industry. Other examples of his romantic, symbolic works include *The Lost Glen, The Silver Bough* and *Wild Geese Overhead* (UK Chambers).

James Hogg *The Private Memoirs and Confessions of a Justified Sinner* (Penguin).

Complex, powerful mid-nineteenth-century novel dealing with possession, myth and folklore, as it looks at the confession of an Edinburgh murderer from three different points of view.

James Kelman *The Busconductor Hines* (UK Phoenix). The wildly funny story of a young Glasgow busconductor with an intensely boring job and a limitless imagination. *How Late It Was, How Late* (Secker & Warburg/Norton) is Kelman's award-winning and controversial look at life as seen through the eyes of a blind Glaswegian drunk. A disturbing study of personal and political violence, with language to match.

A L Kennedy *Looking for the Possible Dance* (UK Minerva). Young Scottish writer dissects the difficulties of human relationships on a personal and wider social level.

Alexander MacArthur and Kingsley Long *No Mean City* (UK Corgi). Classic story of razor gangs in 1935 Glasgow.

William McIlvanney *A Gift from Nessus* (UK Mainstream). Moral tale set in 1960s Glasgow that counterposes the outward trappings of materialism with the emptiness of our inner life.

Compton Mackenzie *Whisky Galore* (UK Penguin). Comic novel based on a true story of the wartime wreck of a cargo of whisky on a Hebridean island. Full of predictable stereotypes but still funny.

Naomi Mitchison *The Bull Calves* (UK R Drew). Moving story of a family facing personal and political realities after the failed Jacobite Rebellion of 1745. A generous, humane and thoroughly engrossing read.

Neil Munro *The Complete Edition of the Para Handy Tales* (UK Birlinn o/p). Engaging and witty, the stories relate the adventures of a Clyde puffer captain as he more or less legally steers his grubby ship up and down the West Coast. Despite a fond – if slightly patronizing – view of the Gaelic mind, they are enormous fun.

Colin Nicolson, ed. *Iain Crichton Smith: Critical Essays* (Edinburgh University Press o/p/ Colorado Univeristy Press). A good introduction to the life and works of one of Scotland's leading contemporary writers, who writes poetry and novels in Gaelic and English.

Sir Walter Scott *The Waverley Novels* (Penguin). The books that did much to create the romanticized version of Scottish life and history. Recently the first titles in a new series of critical editions have been published by Edinburgh University Press: *Kenilworth, Tale of Old Mortality, Black Dwarf, St Ronan's Well* and *The Antiquary.* For more on Scott, see p.123.

Muriel Spark *The Prime of Miss Jean Brodie* (Penguin/NAL Dutton). Wonderful evocation of middle-class Edinburgh life and aspirations, still apparent in that city today.

R L Stevenson *Dr Jekyll and Mr Hyde* (Penguin/ Vintage), *Kidnapped* (Penguin/Signet), *The Master of Ballantrae* (Penguin/Oxford University Press) and *Weir of Hermiston* (UK Penguin). Nineteenth-century tales of intrigue and adventure. For more on Stevenson, see p.86.

Nigel Tranter *The Bruce Trilogy* (Hodder & Stoughton/Trafalgar). Massive tome by prolific and hugely popular author on Scottish themes.

Jeff Torrington *Swing Hammer Swing* (UK Minerva). Gripping contemporary account of working-class Glasgow, centred around a week in the life of Tam Clay. Winner of the 1993 Whitbread prize for fiction.

Irvine Welsh *Trainspotting, The Acid House* (UK Minerva) and *Marabou Stork Nightmares* (UK Jonathan Cape). Depending on the strength of your stomach, these trawls through the horrors of drug addiction, sexual fantasy, urban decay and hopeless youth will either make you rejoice at an authentic and unapologetic new voice for the dispossessed, or throw up. Thankfully, Welsh's unflinching attention is not without humour.

POETRY

J K Annaud *Dod and Davie* (UK Canongate). Translation into Scots of Wilhelm Busch's tongue-in-cheek morality tale. Robust and wickedly funny, the book appeals to badly-behaved children of all ages.

George Mackay Brown *Selected Poems 1954–1983* (UK John Murray). Brown's work is as haunting, beautiful and gritty as the Orkney islands which inspire it.

Robert Burns *The Complete Illustrated Poems, Songs and Ballads* (UK Lomond Books o/p). Facsimile edition of the works of Scotland's most famous bard. Oxford University Press publish much of Burns' work in the US.

Douglas Dunn, ed. *The Faber Book of Twentieth-Century Scottish Poetry* (Faber & Faber). All the big names and some lesser known works.

Douglas Dunn, ed *Scotland: An Anthology* (UK Fontana o/p). Wide-ranging anthology featuring both Scottish writers and outsiders that attempts to provide a background to past and present notions of Scottish nationality.

Liz Lochhead *Bagpipe Muzak* (UK Penguin). A great collection of monologues and poems examining contemporary everyday life from a deceptively simple angle.

Norman MacCaig *Collected Poems* (Chatto & Windus/Trafalgar). Justly celebrated for its keen observation of the natural world, MacCaig's work remains intellectually challenging without being arid. His poetry, rooted in the Highlands, uses detail to explore a universal landscape.

Hugh MacDiarmid *Complete Poems* (edited by Michael Grieve & W R Aitken; Carcarnet/Penguin o/p). Complete works of Scotland's finest modern poet.

William MacGonagall *Poetic Gems* (UK Duckworth). Compulsive selection of works by Scotland's much-loved worst poet.

McCaig, Morgan, Lochhead *Three Scottish Poets* (UK Canongate). A representative selection from the work of three well-known poets. Contrasting perspectives – natural, metaphysical, urban, political and feminist – reflect the complexity of the modern Scottish experience.

John McQueen and Tom Scott, eds. *The Oxford Book of Scottish Verse* (UK Oxford University Press). Claims to be the most comprehensive anthology of Scottish poetry ever published.

Tom Scott, ed. *The Penguin Book of Scottish Verse* (UK Penguin). Good general selection.

Roderick Watson, ed. *The Poetry of Scotland* (UK Edinburgh University Press). An accessible anthology of poems in English, Scots and Gaelic (with notes and translations) from the fourteenth century to the present day.

OUTDOOR PURSUITS

Bartholomew Walks Series (UK Bartholomew). The series covers different areas of Scotland including Perthshire, the Borders and Fife, Loch Lomond and the Trossachs, Oban, Mull and Lochaber, and Skye and Wester Ross. Each booklet has a range of walks of varying lengths with clear maps and descriptions.

Andrew Barbour *Atlantic Salmon* (UK Canongate o/p). Complete and easy-to-read rundown on all aspects of the life-cycle of this fascinating fish and its place in the Scottish economy.

Donald Bennet *The Munros*; **Scott Johnstone et al.** *The Corbetts* (UK Scottish Mountaineering Trust). Authoritative and attractively illustrated hillwalkers' guides to the Scottish peaks. SMT also publishes guides to districts and specific climbs.

Hamish Brown *Hamish's Mountain Walk* and *Climbing the Corbetts* (Gollancz o/p). The first is now the classic book on the Munros, done in a single walk, the second its companion volume. *Scotland Coast-to-Coast* (UK Patrick Stephen o/p), *The Fife Coast* (UK Mainstream) and *From Pennines to the Highlands* (UK Lochar) are all guides to suit more experienced walkers and richly painted background sources.

Andrew Dempster *Classic Mountain Scrambles in Scotland* (UK Mainstream). Guide to hill walks in Scotland that combine straightforward walking with some rock-climbing.

Richard Gilbert *Exploring the Far North West of Scotland* (UK Cordee). Comprehensive guide to the wilds of the Highlands.

Michael Madders and Julia Welstead *Where to Watch Birds in Scotland* (UK Christopher Helm). Region-by-region guide with maps, details on access and habitat and notes on what to see when.

Hamish McInnes *West Highland Walks vols 1–4* (UK Hodder & Stoughton). Good walks and accompanying maps, with a text that incorporates history and legend.

Oleg Polunin *Collins Photoguide to the Wild Flowers of Britain and Northern Europe* (UK Collins o/p). An excellent, easy to use field guide.

Ordnance Survey Pathfinder Series (Jarrold Publishing/Seven Hills Book Distribution). Top-quality maps, colour pictures and clear text. Titles include: *Loch Lomond and the Trossachs*, *Fort William and Glen Coe* and *Perthshire*.

Pastime Publications *Scotland for Game, Sea and Coarse Fishing* (UK Pastime

Publications). General guide on what to fish, where and for how much, along with notes on records, regulations and convenient accommodation. Published in association with the Scottish Tourist Board.

Robert Price *Scotland's Golf Courses* (Mercat Press o/p/Macmillan). A thorough lowdown on Scottish courses for serious golfers, with good photographs.

Roger Smith *The West Highland Way, The Southern Upland Way* (HMSO o/p).

Comprehensive guides to long-distance paths across spectacular scenery, containing information on sights, history, nature and help on planning your trek, as well as specially orientated maps. HMSO also publishes an extremely useful series called *Twenty-Five Walks*; each volume, tailored to a particular region of Scotland, has walks of all types, colour pictures and excellent maps.

Brendan Walsh *Scottish Cycling Guide* (UK Mainstream). Selection of cycling tours covering the northwest and the islands.

LANGUAGE

Although Gaelic remains a living language, even in the *Gàidhealtachd* or Gaelic-speaking areas of the Western Isles, parts of Skye and a few scattered islands of Argyll, every encounter you are likely to have with locals will be conducted in Scots, a form of "English" whose peculiar accent, vocabulary and grammar have led many to declare it, too, to be a separate language. In Orkney and Shetland, with their long history of Norse settlement, the dialects spoken today are based on Norn rather than Gaelic; for more on this and a list of place-name terms and other words you are most likely to hear, see p.462.

Scottish **Gaelic** (*Gàidhlig*, pronounced "Gallic") is one of only four Celtic languages to survive into the modern age (Welsh, Breton and Irish Gaelic are the other three). Manx, the old language of the Isle of Man, died out earlier this century, while Cornish was finished as a community language way back in the eighteenth century. Scottish Gaelic is most closely related to Irish Gaelic and Manx – hardly surprising given that it was introduced to Scotland from Ireland around the third century BC. From the fifth to the twelfth centuries, Gaelic enjoyed an expansionist phase, gradually becoming the national language, thanks partly to the backing of the Celtic church in Iona. At the end of this period, Gaelic was spoken throughout what is now Scotland, but from that point onwards it began a steady decline.

Over the next few centuries, even before union with England, power, religious ideology and wealth gradually passed into non-Gaelic hands. The royal court was transferred to

Edinburgh and an Anglo-Norman legal system was put in place. The Celtic church was Romanized by the introduction of foreign clergy, and, most importantly of all, English and Flemish merchants colonized the new trading towns of the east coast. In addition, the pro-English attitudes held by the Covenanters led to strong anti-Gaelic feeling within the Church of Scotland from its inception.

The two abortive Jacobite rebellions of 1715 and 1745 furthered the language's decline, as did the Clearances that took place in the Gaelic-speaking Highlands from the 1770s to the 1820s, which forced thousands to migrate to central Scotland's new industrial belt or emigrate to North America. Although efforts were made to halt the decline in the first half of the nineteenth century, the 1872 Education Act gave no official recognition to Gaelic, and children were severely punished if they were caught speaking the language in school.

Current estimates put the number of Gaelic speakers at 80,000 (just below two percent of the population), the majority of whom live in the *Gàidhealtachd*, with an extended Gaelic community of perhaps 250,000 who have some understanding of the language. In the last decade or so the language has stabilized, thanks to the introduction of bilingual primary and nursery schools, and a huge increase in the amount of broadcasting time given to Gaelic-language programmes. The success of rock bands such as Runrig has shown that it is possible to combine traditional Gaelic culture with popular entertainment and reach a mass audience.

While Gaelic has undergone something of a renaissance, **Scots**, or "Lallans", as spoken by the "English-speaking" majority of Scottish people, is still struggling for recognition. Scots is, of course, closely related to the English spoken south of the border, since it began life as a northern branch of Anglo-Saxon. In the early fifteenth century, it replaced Latin as the country's main literary and documentary language, but has since been drawn closer to southern varieties of English. Many people reject the view that it is a separate language at all, considering it to be, at best, an artificial amalgamation of local dialects. Robbie Burns is the most obvious literary exponent of the Scots language, but there has been a revival this century led by poets such as Hugh MacDiarmid. (For examples of the works of both writers, see "Books".)

GAELIC GRAMMAR AND PRONUNCIATION

Gaelic is a highly complex tongue, with a fiendish, antiquated grammar and, with only eighteen letters, an intimidating system of spelling. Pronunciation is actually easier than it appears at first glance – one general rule to remember is that the **stress** always falls on the first syllable of a word. The general rule of syntax is that the verb starts the sentence whether it's a question or not, followed by the subject and then the object; adjectives generally follow the word they are describing.

SHORT AND LONG VOWELS

Gaelic has both short and long vowels, the latter being denoted by an acute or grave accent.

a as in c**a**t; before nn and ll, like the *ow* in b**ow** (of a boat)

à as in b**a**r

e as in p**e**t

é like the *ai* in r**ai**n

i like the *ee* in str**ee**t, but shorter

í like the *ee* in fr**ee**

o as in p**o**t

ò like the *a* in enth**ra**l

ó like the *ow* in b**ow** (of a boat)

u like the *oo* in sc**oo**t

ù like the *oo* in l**oo**

VOWEL COMBINATIONS

Gaelic is littered with diphthongs, which, rather like in English, can be pronounced in several different ways depending on the individual word.

ai like the *a* in c**a**t, or the *e* in p**e**t; before dh or gh, like the *ee* in str**ee**t

ao like the *ur* in s**ur**ly

ei like the *a* in m**a**te

ea like the *e* in p**e**t, or the *a* in c**a**t, and sometimes like the *a* in m**a**te; before ll or nn like the *ow* in b**ow** (of a boat)

èa as in h**ear**

eu like the *ai* in tr**ai**n, or the *ea* in f**ear**

ia like the *ea* in f**ear**

io like the *ea* in f**ear**, or the *ee* in str**ee**t, but shorter

ua like the *ooe* in w**ooe**r

CONSONANTS

The consonants listed below are those that differ substantially from the English.

b at the beginning of a word as in **b**ig; in the middle or at the end of a word like the *p* in **p**air

bh at the beginning of a word like the *v* in **v**an; elsewhere it is silent

c as in **c**at; after a vowel it has aspiration *before* it

ch always as in lo**ch**, never as in **ch**urch

cn like the *cr* in **cr**owd

d like the *d* in **d**og, but with the tongue pressed against the back of the upper teeth; at the beginning of a word before e or i, like the *j* in **j**am; in the middle or at the end of a word like the *t* in ca**t**; after i like the *ch* in **ch**urch

dh before and after a, o or u an aspirated *g*, rather like someone gargling; before e or i like the *y* in **y**es; elsewhere silent

fh usually silent; somtimes like the *h* in **h**ouse

g at the beginning of a word as in **g**et; before e like the *y* in **y**es; in the middle or end of a word like the *ck* in so**ck**; after i like the *ch* in lo**ch**

gh at the beginning of a word as in **g**et; before or after a, o or u rather like someone gargling; after i sometimes like the *y* in ga**y**, but often silent

l after i and sometimes before e like the *l* in **l**ot; elsewhere a peculiarly Gaelic sound produced by flattening the front of the tongue against the palate

mh like the *v* in **v**an

p at the beginning of a word as in **p**et; elsewhere it has aspiration *before* it

rt pronounced as **sht**

s before e or i like the *sh* in **sh**ip; otherwise as in English

sh before a, o or u like the *h* in **h**ouse; before e like the *ch* in lo**ch**

t before e or i like the *ch* in **ch**urch; in the middle or at the end of a word it has aspiration *before* it; otherwise as in English

th at the beginning of a word, like the *h* in **h**ouse; elsewhere, and in the word *thu*, silent

GAELIC PHRASES AND VOCABULARY

The choice is limited when it comes to **teach-yourself Gaelic** courses, but the BBC *Can Seo* cassette and book is perfect for starting you off. Drier and more academic is *Teach Yourself Gaelic* (Hodder & Stoughton), which is aimed at bringing beginners to Scottish "O" grade standard. *Everyday Gaelic* by Morag MacNeill (Gairm) is the best phrasebook around.

BASIC WORDS AND GREETINGS

yes	tha	night	oidhche	music	ceòl
no	chan eil	here	an seo	book	leabhar
hello	hallo	there	an sin	tired	sgìth
how are you?	ciamar a tha thu?	this way	mar seo	food	lòn
OK	tha gu math	that way	mar sin	bread	aran
thank you	tapadh leat	pound/s	not/aichean	water	uisge
welcome	fàilte	tomorrow	a-màireach	milk	bainne
come in	thig a-staigh	tonight	a-nochd	beer	leann
goodbye	mar sin leat	cheers	slàinte	wine	fion
goodnight	oidhche mhath	yesterday	an-dé	whisky	uisge beatha
who?	cò?	today	an diugh	post office	post oifis
where is...?	càit a bheil...?	tomorrow	maireach	Edinburgh	Dun Eideann
when?	cuine?	now	a-nise	Glasgow	Glaschu
what is it?	Dé tha ann?	hotel	taigh-òsda	America	Ameireaga
morning	madainn	house	taigh	Ireland	Eire
evening	feasgar	story	sgeul	England	Sasainn
day	là	song	òran	London	Lunnain

SOME USEFUL PHRASES

It's a nice day	tha latha math ann	Do you speak Gaelic?	a bheil Gàidhlig agad?
How much is that?	dè tha e 'cosg?	What is the Gaelic for?	Dé a' Ghàidhlig a tha air?
What's your name?	dè 'n t-ainm a th'ort?	I don't understand	chan eil mi 'tuigsinn
Excuse me	gabh mo leisgeul	I don't know	chan eil fhios agam
What time is it?	dé am uair a tha e?	That's good	's math sin
I'm thirsty	tha am pathadh orm	It doesn't matter	's coma
I'd like a double room	'se rùm dùbailte tha mi 'g iarraidh	I'm sorry	Tha mi duilich

NUMBERS AND DAYS

1	aon	11	aon deug	Monday	Diluain
2	dà/dhà	20	fichead	Tuesday	Dimàirt
3	trì	21	aon ar fhichead	Wednesday	Diciadain
4	ceithir	30	deug ar fhichead	Thursday	Diardaoin
5	còig	40	dà fhichead	Friday	Dihaoine
6	sia	50	lethcheud	Saturday	Disathurna
7	seachd	60	trì fichead	Sunday	Didòmhnaich/La na Sàbaid
8	ochd	100	ceud		
9	naoi	1000	mìle		
10	deich				

SURNAMES

The prefix **Mac** or **Mc** in Scottish surnames derives from the Gaelic, meaning "son of". In Scots Mac is used for both sexes, but in Gaelic women are referred to as Nic, for example:

Donnchadh Mac Aodh   Duncan MacKay   Iseabail Nic Aodh   Isabel MacKay

GEOGRAPHICAL AND PLACE-NAME TERMS

The purpose of the list below is to help with place-name derivations and with more detailed map reading.

ach or **auch**, from **achadh**	field
ail, **aileach**	rock
Alba	Scotland
ault, from **allt**	stream
ardan or **arden**, from **àird**	a point of land or height
bal or **bally**, from **baile**	town, village
balloch, from **bealach**	mountain pass
bad	clump of trees
bagh	bay
bàrr	summit
beg, from **beag**	small
ben, from **beinn**	mountain
blair, from **blàr**	field or battlefield
cairn, from **càrn**	pile of stones
craig, from **creag**	rock
cnoc	hill
coll or **colly**, from **coille**	wood
corrie, from **coire**	round hollow in mountainside, whirlpool
cruach	bold hill
dubh	black
dun or **dum**, from **dùn**	fort
drum, from **druim**	ridge
ess, from **eas**	waterfall

eilean	island
fin, from **fionn**	white
gair or **gare**, from **geàrr**	short
garv, from **garbh**	rough
glen, from **gleann**	valley
gower or **gour**, from **gabhar**	goat
inch, from **innis**	meadow or island
inver, from **inbhir**	rivermouth
ken or **kin**, from **ceann**	head
knock, from **cnoc**	hill
kyle, from **caolas**	narrow strait
lag	hollow
loch	lake
meall	round hill
mon, from **monadh**	hill
more, from **mór**	large, great
rannoch, from **raineach**	bracken
ross, from **ros**	promontory
rubha	promontory
sgeir	sea rock
strath, from **srath**	broad valley
tarbet, from **tairbeart**	isthmus
tir or **tyre**, from **tìr**	land
torr	hill, castle
traigh	shore

A SCOTTISH GLOSSARY

AULD Old.

AYE Yes.

BAIRN Baby.

BEN Mountain peak.

BLACK HOUSE Thick-walled traditional dwelling.

BONNIE Pretty.

BOTHY Primitive cottage or hut; farmworker's or shepherd's mountain shelter.

BRAE Slope; hill.

BRIG Bridge.

BROCH Circular prehistoric stone fort.

BURN Small stream or brook.

BYRE Shelter for cattle; cottage.

CAIRN Mound of stones.

CARSE Riverside area of flat alluvium.

CEILIDH Social gathering involving dancing, drinking, singing and storytelling.

CLAN Extended family.

COVENANTERS Supporter of the Presbyterian Church in the seventeenth century.

CORBETT Mountain between 2500 and 3000ft high.

CORBIE-STEPPED Architectural term; any set of steps on a gable.

CORRIE Circular hollow on a hillside.

CRAIG Steep peak or crag.

CRANNOG Celtic lake or bog dwelling.

CROFT Small plot of farmland with house, common in the Highlands.

CROW-STEPPED Same as *corbie-stepped*.

DOLMEN Grave chamber.

DRAM Literally, one-sixteenth of an ounce. Usually refers to a small measure of whisky.

DRUM Narrow ridge.

DUN Fortified mound.

FIRST-FOOT The first person to enter a household on *Hogmanay* (see below).

FIRTH Narrow inlet.

GILLIE Personal guide used on hunting or fishing trips.

GLEN Deep, narrow mountain valley.

HARLING Limestone and gravel mix used to cover buildings.

HOGMANAY New Year's Eve.

HOWE Valley.

HOWFF Meeting place; pub.

INCH Small island.

KEN Knowledge; understanding.

KILT Knee-length tartan skirt worn by Highland men.

KIRK Church.

KYLE Narrow strait or channel.

LAIRD Landowner; aristocrat.

LAW Rounded hill.

LINKS Grassy coastal land; coastal golf course.

LOCHAN Little loch or lake.

MACHAIR Sandy, grassy, lime-rich coastal land, generally used for grazing.

MANSE Official home of a Presbyterian minister.

MUNRO Mountain over 3000ft high.

MUNRO-BAGGING Sport of trying to climb as many Munros as possible.

PEEL Fortified tower, built to withstand Border raids.

PEND Archway or vaulted passage.

PRESBYTERIAN The official (Protestant) Church of Scotland, established by John Knox during the Reformation.

SASSENACH English.

SHINTY Simple form of hockey.

SNP Scottish National Party.

SPORRAN Leather purse worn in front of a kilt.

STRATH Broad flat river valley.

TARTAN Check-patterned woollen cloth, particular patterns being associated with particular clans.

THANE A landowner of high rank; the chief of a clan.

TREWS Tartan trousers.

WEE Small.

WYND Narrow lane.

YETT Gate or door.

INDEX

A

Abbotsford House 122
ABERDEEN 355–366
Accommodation 357
Anthropological Museum 361
Art Gallery 361
Beach 364
Brig' o' Balgownie 364
Cruickshank Botanic Gardens 364
Duthie Park 363
Entertainment 366
Footdee 363
Harbour 363
History 355
Information 356
James Dun's House 361
King's College Chapel 363
Listings 366
Marischal College 359
Maritime Museum 363
Nightlife 365
Oil 357
Old Aberdeen 363
Old Provost Ross's House 363
Provost Skene's House 359
Pubs 365
Restaurants 365
St Machars Cathedral 364
St Nicholas Kirk 361
Tolbooth Museum 359
Tourist office 356
Transport 356
Union Terrace Gardens 362
West End 362
Aberdour 230
Aberfeldy 250
Aberfoyle 215–217
Aberlady 111
Aberlemno 351
Aboyne 370
Accommodation 26–29
Acha 279
Acharacle 422
Achiltibuie 437
Achmelvich 439
Aden Country Park 381
Admission charges 34
Aikwood Tower 124
Ailsa Craig 148
Airports in Scotland 25
Aith 501
Alford 373

Alloway 152
Alva 223
Alyth 350
Annandale 131
Anstruther 239
Applecross 429
Arbroath 345
Arbuthnott 368
Architecture 532–538
Arden 214
Ardentinny 260
Ardgartan 259
Ardgay 454
Ardlui 214
Ardminish 285
Ardnamurchan peninsula 421
Ardrossan 154
Argyll Forest Park 259
Arinagour 278
Arisaig 423
Arnisdale 426
Arran 288–292
Blackwaterfoot 291
Brodick 290
Corrie 291
Holy Island 290
Kildonan 291
Lamlash 290
Lochranza 291
Machrie 291
Whiting Bay 291
Arrochar 259
Auchmithie 346
Auchterarder 248
Aviemore 416
Avoch 449
Ayr 150–152

B

Backaland 480
Badachro 431
Badbea 457
Badcall 440
Bagh a Chaisteil (Castlebay) 330
Baile a Mhanaich (Balivanich) 327
Baile an Or 457
Baile Mór 277
Balemartine 279
Balfour 478
Balivanich (Baile a Mhanaich) 327
Ballater 370
Balloch 213
Balmerino 241
Balmoral 371

Balnaboth 352
Balnakiel 443
Balquhidder 219
Baltasound 508
Banchory 370
Banff 383
Banks 15
Barra (Barraigh) 330
Bass Rock 112
Beaches 40
Bearnaraigh (Berneray) 326
Beauly 405
Beinn na Faoghla (Benbecula) 327
Ben Lomond 214
Ben Nevis 413
Benbecula (Beinn na Faoghla) 327
Bennachie 379
Berneray (Bearnaraigh) 326
Bettyhill 445
Biggar 134
Bigton 495
Birnam 247
Birsay 470
Bixter 501
Black Isle 449
Blackness 222
Blair Castle 254
Blairgowrie 349
Blairlogie 223
Blairmore 441
Blantyre 197
Bo'ness 222
Böd of Grimista 492
Boddam 494
Bonar Bridge 453
Bonnie Prince Charlie 310, 401, 422, 521
Bonnybridge 220
Books 544–550
Bothwell Castle 198
Bowhill House 124
Brae 504
Braemar 371
Breadalbane mountains 250
Brechin 348
Brehan Seer 449
Bressay 492
Broch of Gurness 469
Brodie Castle 388
Brora 456
Broughton 134
Bullers of Buchan 381
Burghead 386
Burns, Robert 152

Burntisland 230
Burra 498
Burraboe 507
Burwick 475
Buses
  from England 6
  in Scotland 20, 156
Bute 261

C

Caerlaverock Castle 138
Caerlaverock Wildlife Centre
  138
Cairndow 259
Cairnryan 147
Calfsound 480
Callander 218
Campbeltown 286
Camping 28
Campsie Fells 211
Canna 311
Cannich 408
Cape Wrath 443
Car rental 24
Carbisdale Castle 453
Carradale 288
Carse of Forth 212
Castle Campbell 223
Castle Douglas 141
Castle Kennedy Gardens 146
Castle Menzies 251
Castle Stalker 268
Castle Tioram 422
Castle Urquhart 408
Castlebay (Bagh a Chaisteil)
  330
Catpund 494
Catterline 367
Cawdor Castle 403
Ceres 235
Chanonry Point 449
Churchill Barriers 474
Claonaig 288
Clava Cairns 403
Clickimin Broch 492
Climbing 38
Clova 352
Coldstream 116
Colintraive 261
Coll 278
Colonsay 280
Comrie 249
Corgarff Castle 374
Corran 426
Corrieshalloch 433
Costs 16

Cove 432
Craighouse 295
Craigievar Castle 373
Craignethan Castle 198
Crathes Castle and Gardens
  369
Crathie 371
Crieff 248
Crinan 283
Crinan Canal 283
Croick Church 454
Cromarty 450
Cromarty Firth 452
Crossford 198
Crossraguel Abbey 149
Cruachan Power Station 265
Cruden Bay 380
Cullen 384
Cullipool 270
Cullivoe 507
Culloden 401
Culross 226
Culzean Castle 149
Cunningsburgh 493
Cupar 234
Currency exchange 15
Customs regulations 14
Cycling 39, 435

D

Dalry 145
Devon Valley 224
Dingwall 452
Dirleton 111
Disabled travellers 41
Dollar 223
Dolphins 402
Dores 410
Dornie 427
Dornoch 455
Dounby 471
Dounreay 446
Drink 30–32, 377
Driving 23
Drum Castle 369
Drumbeg 440
Drumlanrig Castle 139
Drumnadrochit 407
Dryburgh Abbey 121
Drymen 213
Duff House 382
Dufftown 376
Duffus 386
Duke's Pass 217
Dumbarton 196
Dumfries 137

Dunadd 281
Dunbar 113
Dunbeath 458
Duncansby Head 448
DUNDEE 336–343
  Accommodation 337
  Barrack Street Museum 340
  Broughty Ferry 341
  Claypotts Castle 341
  Dundee Law 340
  McManus Art Galleries and
    Museum 340
  Mills Observatory 341
  Nightlife 341
  Restaurants 341
  Royal Research Ship Discovery
    340
  Tourist office 337
  Unicorn 340
Dundrennan Abbey 143
Dunfermline 227
Dunkeld 246
Dunnet 447
Dunning 248
Dunnottar Castle 367
Dunoon 260
Dunrobin Castle 455
Duns 114
Dunstaffnage Castle 268
Durness 442–444
Dykehead 352

E

Earlsferry 239
Easdale 270
East Lothian 109
Ecclefechan 131
Eday 480
EDINBURGH 47–106
  Accommodation 51–57
  Airport 52
  Arthur's Seat 70
  Calton 79
  Cannongate 67
  Castle 58
  Castlehill 61
  Cowgate 70
  Craigmillar Castle 83
  Cramond 87
  Dalkeith 89
  Dalmeny 87
  Dean Village 81
  Entertainment 103–104
  Festival 90
  George Street 77
  Grassmarket 71
  Greyfriars 71
  High Kirk of St Giles 63

High Street 66
History 48
Holyrood 68–70
Hopetoun House 88
Inchcolm 88
Information 52
Lauriston Castle 86
Lawnmarket 62
Leith 84
Listings 105
Midlothian 88
Morningside 83
National Gallery of Scotland 75–77
Newtongrange 89
Nightlife 101–103
Parliament Square 65
Pentland Hills 84
Portobello 84
Princes Street 73
Pubs 98–101
Queen Street 78
Restaurants 90–98
Roslin 89
Royal Botanic Garden 82
Royal Mile 61
Royal Museum of Scotland 72
Royal Observatory 83
Royal Scottish Academy 74
Scott Monument 74
Scottish National Gallery of Modern Art 81
Scottish National Portrait Gallery and Museum of Antiquities 78
Shopping 104
South Queensferry 87
South Side 83
Stockbridge 81
Swanston 84
Tourist office 52
Transport 52
University of Edinburgh 72
Zoo 85
Edzell 353
Egilsay 480
Eigg 313
Eildon Hills 120
Eileen Donan Castle 426
Eiriosgaigh (Eriskay) 328
Elgin 384
Elie 239
Ellanbeich 269
Embassies, British 14
Emergencies 18
Eriskay (Eiriosgaigh) 328
Eshaness 505
Evanton 452
Evie 469

Ewes Water 129
Eyemouth 114

F
Fair Isle 496
Falkirk 219
Falkland 233
Fanagmore 441
Fasque House 368
Ferries
  from Europe 6
  from Ireland 7
  in Scotland 24
Festivals 36–38
Fetlar 507
Fettercairn 368
Findhorn Foundation 387
Fintry 213
Flights
  from Australia and New Zealand 11–13
  from England 3
  from Europe 4
  from the USA and Canada 7–10
  in Scotland 25
Floors Castle 118
Food 29
Forfar 351
Forres 388
Fort Augustus 409
Fort George 404
Fort William 411–414
Fortingall 250
Fortrose 449
Foula 502
Foyers 410
Fraserburgh 382
Fyvie Castle 379

G
Gaelic 42, 315
Gair Loch 431
Gairloch 431
Gairlochy 410
Galashiels 125
Galmisdale 313
Gare Loch 258
Gargunnock 212
Gartly 378
Garvellachs 270
Gatehouse of Fleet 143
Gifford 111
Gigha 285
Girvan 148

Glamis Castle 343
GLASGOW 157–192
  Accommodation 162–166
  Airport 160
  Architecture 168
  Barras 168
  Botanic Gardens 179
  Burrell Collection 180
  Cathedral 170
  Entertainment 191
  George Square 166
  Glasgow Boys 176
  Glasgow Green 169
  Haggs Castle 182
  History 159
  Ibrox 179
  Kelvingrove Museum and Art Gallery 175–177
  Listings 191
  Mackintosh, Charles Rennie 168, 172–173, 174, 182
  McLellan Galleries 174
  Merchant City 167
  Nightlife 189–189
  People's Palace 170
  Pollok House 182
  Provand's Lordship 171
  Pubs 187–189
  Restaurants 183–187
  Rutherglen 183
  School of Art 174
  Scotland Street School Museum of Education 182
  Scottish Exhibition and Conference Centre 179
  Springburn 183
  St Mungo Museum of Religious Life and Art 171
  Tenement House 175
  Tourist office 160
  Transport 161
  Transport Museum 178
  University 178
  Willow Tearoom 173
Glasgow Boys 176
Glenfinnan 422
Glen Affric 408
Glen Clova 352
Glen Coe 414
Glen Doll 353
Glen Esk 353
Glen Isla 350
Glen Nevis 413
Glen Prosen 352
Glen Shee 349
Glen Shiel 427
Glen Trool 144
Glen Urquhart 408
Glenborrodale 421

Glenbuchat Castle 374
Glendevon 224
Glenelg 425
Glenelg peninsula 425
Glenluce Abbey 146
Glenmore 417
Glenmore Natural History
  Centre 421
Glenrothes 232
Golf 40, 238
Golspie 455
Grangemouth 220
Grantown-on-Spey 418
Great Cumbrae Island 154
Great Glen 406
Greenock 195
Gretna 131
Gretna Green 131
Grey Cairns of Camster 458
Gruinard Island 433
Gullane 111
Gutcher 506

H
Haddington 109
Haddo House and Gardens 380
Hamavoe 498
Hamilton 197
Handa Island 441
Haroldswick 508
Harris (Na Hearadh) 321–325
  An T-ob (Leverburgh) 325
  Caolas Stocinis (Kyles
    Stockinish) 324
  Harris Tweed 323
  Horgabost 325
  Liceasto (Likisto) 324
  Reinigeadal (Rhenigidale) 322
  Roghadal (Rodel) 324
  Selibost 324
  Sgarasta (Scarista) 325
  Taobh Tuath (Northton) 325
  Tarbert 322
Harris Tweed 323
Hawick 129
Health 17
Helensburgh 258
Helmsdale 457
Hermitage Castle 130
Hillswick 504
Hirta 331
History 513–526
Hitching 23
Hoswick 494
Hotels 26
Houbie 507
House of Dun 347

Howmore (Tobha Mor) 328
Hoy 476–478
Huntingtower Castle 246
Huntly 376

I
Insurance 16
Inveraray 262–264
Inverdruie 417
Inverewe Gardens 432
Inverfarigaig 410
Inverie 425
Inverkeithing 230
Inverkirkaig Falls 438
Invermoriston 409
INVERNESS 391–401
  Accommodation 394–396
  Balnain House 399
  Caledonian Canal 399
  Castle 398
  History 394
  Kiltmaker Centre 399
  Listings 400
  Museum and Art Gallery 398
  Nightlife and entertainment
    400
  Restaurants 399
  St Andrews Episcopal Church
    399
  Tourist office 394
  Tours and cruises 395
Inverurie 378
Iona 276–278
Irvine 153
Islay 292–295
  Bowmore 294
  Port Askaig 295
  Port Charlotte 294
  Port Ellen 292
  Port Wemyss 295
  Portnahaven 295
Isle of May 240
Isle of Whithorn 146

J
Jarlshof 495
Jedburgh 127–129
John O'Groats 447
Jura 295

K
Kames 261
Kelso 117
Kenmore 250
Kerrera 268
Kettletoft 482

Kilchoan 421
Kildrummy Castle 374
Killin 250
Kilmahog 219
Kilmarnock 154
Kilmartin 281
Kiloran 280
Kilvarock Castle 403
Kincraig 417
Kineff 368
Kinghorn 231
Kingussie 417
Kinloch 312
Kinloch Rannoch 253
Kinlochbervie 441
Kinross 224
Kintyre 284–288
Kippen 212
Kirbuster 470
Kirkcaldy 231–233
Kirkcudbright 142
Kirkoswald 149
Kirkton of Glenisla 350
KIRKWALL 465–469
  Accommodation 466
  Bishop's Palace 467
  Earl's Palace 467
  Highland Park 468
  Listings 469
  Museum 468
  Pubs a 468
  Restaurants 488
  St Magnus Cathedral 467
  Tourist office 466
Kirriemuir 350
Knapdale Forest 283
Knockshannock 350
Knox, John 64, 109
Knoydart peninsula 424
Kyle of Lochalsh 427
Kylesku 440

L
Lairg 454
Lake of Monteith 216
Lammermuir Hills 115
Lanark 198
Langholm 129
Language 551–555
Largs 154
Lauder 115
Leadhills 134
Lecht 375
Leebitton 494
Lennoxlove House 110
Leodhas (Lewis) 315–321
Lerwick 487–492

Accommodation 488
Arthur Anderson School 489
Entertainment 491
Listings 491
Museum 489
Pubs 491
Restaurants 490
Tourist office 488
Town Hall 489
Up Helly-Aa 490
Leuchars 241
Leverburgh 325
Levenwick 494
Lewis (Leodhas) 315–321
Arnol 319
Barabhas (Barvas) 318
Bragar 320
Calanais (Callanish) 319
Callanish Standing Stones 320
Carloway Broch 320
Charlabhaigh (Carloway) 320
Doune Carloway (Dun
Charlabhaigh) 320
Europaidh (Eoropie) 319
Gearrannan (Garenin) 320
Port Nis (Port of Ness) 319
Rubha Robhanais (Butt of
Lewis) 319
Stornoway 316
Uig peninsula 321
Lewiston 408
Liddesdale 130
Linlithgow 220
Lismore 269
Loanhead Stone Circle 379
Loch Awe 264
Loch Baghasdail
(Lochboisdale) 328
Loch Coille-Bharr 283
Loch Duich 426
Loch Eck 260
Loch Eriboll 444
Loch Ericht 254
Loch Garten Nature Reserve
418
Loch Leven 224
Loch Lochy 410
Loch Lomond 213
Loch Long 258
Loch Maree 430
Loch nam Madadh
(Lochmaddy) 325
Loch Ness 406
Loch Ness Monster 407
Loch Rannoch 253
Loch Sween 283
Loch Tay 249
Loch Torridon 429

Loch Tummel 253
Lochaline 420
Lochawe 264
Lochboisdale (Loch Baghasdail)
328
Lochearnhead 219
Lochgilphead 283
Lochgoilhead 259
Lochinver 438
Lochmaddy (Loch nam Madadh)
325
Lockerbie 132
Lossiemouth 385
Lowther Hills 134
Luing 270
Lumsden 373
Luss 213
Lybster 458
Lyness 477

M

Macduff 382
Machars, The 145
Machrihanish 286
Mackintosh, Charles Rennie
168, 172–173, 174, 182
Maes Howe 471
Maiden Stone 379
Mallaig 423
Manderston House 115
Maps 20
Meigle 343
Mellerstain House
Melrose 119–121
Melvich 446
Menstrie 223
Mid Yell 507
Midges 18
Millbounds 481
Millport 154
Mingulay 331
Moffat 132
Moffat Water 133
Moidart 422
Money 15
Montrose 346
Morar 423
Morvern 420
Motorbike rental 24
Mousa Broch 494
Muck 313
Muir of Ord 406
Mull 271–276
Ben More 275
Bunessan 275
Calgary 274

Craignure 272
Dervaig 274
Fionnphort 275
Lochbuie 272
Ross of Mull 275
Staffa 274
Tobermory 272
Treshnish Isles 275
Ulva 274
Mull of Kintyre 287
Music 539–543

N

Na Hearadh (Harris) 321–325
Nairn 404
Nevis Range Ski Station 411
New Galloway 145
New Lanark 198–200
Newburgh 241
Newcastleton 130
Newspapers 35
Newton Stewart 144
Nithsdale 139
Norse dialect 462
North Berwick 111
North Berwick Law 112
North Queensferry 229
North Ronaldsay 483
North Uist (Uibhist a Tuath)
325–327
Northmaven 504
Noss 493

O

Oban 265–267
Oil 357
Old Aberdour 382
Opening hours 33
Orkney 463–484
Oronsay 281
Osmundwall 477
Otter Ferry 261
Out Skerries 504

P

Paisley 193
Papa Stour 501
Papa Westray 482
Pass of Brander 265
Paxton House 116
Pearsie 352
Peebles 126
Pennan 382
Perth 242–245
Accommodation 243
Balhousie Castle 244

Fair Maid's House 244
Fergusson Gallery 244
  Restaurants 245
  Tourist office 243
Peterhead 381
Pierowall 483
Pitlochry 251–253
Pitmedden Gardens 380
Plockton 428
Pluscarden Abbey 385
Police 18
Poolewe 432
Port Glasgow 194
Porthmahomack 453
Portpatrick 147
Post offices 32
Public holidays 33

Q
Queen Elizabeth Forest Park
  217
Quendale 495

R
Rackwick 476
Radio 35
Ravenscraig Castle 232
Rhum 312
Rhumach 423
Rhynie 373
Ring of Brodgar 471
Rob Roy 215
Rockcliffe 140
Rosemarkie 450
Rothesay 261
Rousay 478
Rowardennan 213
Ruthwell Cross 139

S
Sandaig 426
Sanday 482
Sandness 501
Sandwick 496
Scalasaig 280
Scalloway 497
Scapa Flow 474
Scarba 270
Scarinish 279
Scone Palace 245
Scoraig 434
Scoraig Peninsula 434
Scott, Walter 123
Scourie 440
Seil 269
Self-catering 28

Selkirk 124
Shapinsay 478
Shetland 484–509
Shetland Bus 498
Shiel Bridge 426
Shieldaig 429
Skara Brae 470
Skiing 375, 411, 416
Skipness 288
Skye 300–311
  Armadale 302
  Bonnie Prince Charlie 310
  Broadford 303
  Clachan 304
  Cuillins 305
  Duirnish 307
  Duntulm 310
  Dunvegan 306
  Elgol 305
  Flodigarry 310
  Glen Brittle 306
  Inverarish 304
  Isleornsay 303
  Kylcakin 303
  Loch Coruisk 305
  Old Man of Storr 309
  Oskaig 305
  Portree 308
  Raasay 304
  Sconser 304
  Trotternish peninsula 309
Slains Castle 380
Smailholm Tower 122
Smoo Cave 442
South Ronaldsay 475
South Uist (Uibhist a Deas)
  327–330
Southend 287
Spittal of Glenshee 350
Spynie 386
ST ANDREWS 235–239
  Accommodation 236
  British Golf Museum 238
  Castle 237
  Cathedral 237
  Craigtoun County Park 239
  Old Course 238
  Restaurants 239
  Sea Life Centre 239
  St Rule's Tower 237
  Tourist office 236
  University 238
St Abb's Head 113
St Kilda 331
St Margaret's Hope 475
St Mary's 474
St Monans 239
St Ninian's Isle 495

St Vigeans 346
Stevenson, Robert Louis 86
STIRLING 204–211
  Accommodation 205
  Airthrey Castle 210
  Bannockburn 211
  Blair Drummond Safari Park 211
  Bridge of Allan 210
  Cambuskenneth Abbey 210
  Castle 206
  Church of the Holy Rude 208
  Doune 211
  Dumblane 210
  Mar's Wark 208
  Nightlife 209
  Old Bridge 209
  Restaurants 209
  Sheriffmuir 211
  Smith Art Gallery and Museum
    208
  Tourist office 205
  University 210
  Wallace Monument 210
Stoer Point 439
Stonehaven 367
Stones of Stenness 471
Stranraer 147
Strathdon 374
Strathpeffer 451
Stromness 472–474
Stronsay 481
Strontian 420
Student discounts 16
Sumburgh Head 495
Sunart and Ardgour 420
Sutherland Monument 456
Sweetheart Abbey 140
Symbister 503

T
Tain 452
Tantallon Castle 112
Tarbert 284
Tarbet (Central Scotland) 214
Tarbet (Highlands) 441
Tartan 398
Tax regulations 14
Tay bridges 241
Tayport 241
Telephones 32
Television 35
Tentsmuir Forest 241
Teviotdale 129
Thirlestane Castle 115
Threave Castle 141
Thurso 446
Tighinbruaich 261

Tingwall 499
Tipping 43
Tiree 279
Toberonochy 270
Tobha Mor (Howmore) 328
Tolquhon Castle 380
Tomintoul 375
Tongue 444
Torridon 429
Tourist boards 19
Trains
  Eurail passes for North
    Americans 10
  from England 3–5
  from Europe 3–5
  in Scotland 5,
  InterRail passes 5, 10, 13
Traquair House 125
Trondra 498
Trossachs 214
Tweeddale 133

U
Uibhist a Deas (South Uist)
  327–330
Uibhist a Tuath (North Uist)
  325–327

Ullapool 434–437
Ulsta 506
Unst 508
Uyeasound 508

V
Visas 14
Voe 504

W
Walkerburn 125
Walking 38, 390
Walks
  Arbroath 346
  Aviemore 416
  Ben Lomond 214
  Braemar's Beacon 372
  Dollar 224
  Eildon Hills 120
  Glen Coe 414
  Glen Doll 353
  Glen Nevis 413
  Glen Shiel 427
  Iona 277
  Kirkcudbright 143
  Peebles 126
  Pentland Hills 84

Pitlochry 252
Torridon 430
Ullapool 435
Walls 501
Wanlockhead 134
Waterside 145
Wee Frees 318
Weisdale 499
Wemyss Bay 196
West Highland Railway 391
West Linton 135
Westray 482
Whalsay 503
Whisky 377
Whitehall 481
Whiteness 499
Whithorn 146
Wick 458
Wigtown 146
Wildlife 461, 527–531
Wyre 480

Y
Yarrow Water 133
Yell 506
Youth hostels 27

You are A STUDENT

You travel THE WORLD

You want TO SAVE MONEY

Here's how

The International Student Identity Card

Available at Student Travel Offices Worldwide.

Entitles you to discounts and special services worldwide.

ROUGH GUIDE TO SCOTTISH MUSIC
ON CD AND CASSETTE!

Planning a trip to the Highlands or just come back from the Islands? The music of Scotland is one of the strongest living musical traditions in Europe so whatever your travel plans why not check out the Rough Guide to Scottish Music?

Compiled by the World Music Network from top Scottish record labels and featuring leading artists in a striking mix of musical styles from modern Gaelic dance through to traditional vocal music of the Outer Hebrides, the Rough Guide to Scottish Music is a musical journey to the heart of Scotland.

And it's over 60 minutes long and mid-price!

ALSO AVAILABLE:
ROUGH GUIDE TO WORLD MUSIC CD & CASSETTE
contains over 70 minutes of the music from around the world, culled from the top world music labels
ROUGH GUIDE TO WEST AFRICAN MUSIC CD & CASSETTE
is the ideal introduction to the music of West Africa, a region which few areas of the world can match for the range of rhythms, melodies and musical textures found

ABOUT THE WORLD MUSIC NETWORK

The world Music Network is an international information and direct sales network linking all those working in world music with you, the audience. It is free to join and you will be sent information on new and classic releases, live shows and details of special offers and competitions.
To join please fill in the form below, ticking the relevant box

Please send me:
- ☐ copy(ies) of the Rough Guide To Scottish Music   ☐ CD (£8.99 each)   ☐ Cassette (£6.99 each)
- ☐ copy(ies) of the Rough Guide To West African Music   ☐ CD (£8.99 each)   ☐ Cassette (£6.99 each)
- ☐ copy(ies) of the Rough Guide To World Music   ☐ CD (£8.99 each)   ☐ Cassette (£6.99 each)

Prices include UK postage and packing. Overseas customers add £1.00 per CD or Cassette.

☐ Please debit my Visa/Access card number

Signature: .... expiry date: ....
alternatively, Credit Card phone and fax sales available via: (0)171 262 7668 (UK)
or
I enclose payment for £..........
☐ UK cheque or postal order made payable to World Music Network
☐ International Money Order drawn in sterling (£) on a British Bank; payable to World Music Network

☐ I would like to join the World Music Network. Please send me future catalogues and live/media information, without obligation to purchase.

Name..

Address..

....

Country.. Postal Code.......................

Please send your completed form to: **World Music Network, PO Box 3633, London NW1 6HQ**

PHOTOCOPY THIS PAGE IF YOU DO NOT WISH TO DAMAGE YOUR BOOK!